Mexico Handbook

**Richard Arghiris,
Anna Maria Espsäter
& Geoff Groesbeck**

Footprint story

It was 1921

Ireland had just been partitioned, the British miners were striking for more pay and the federation of British industry had an idea. Exports were booming in South America – how about a handbook for businessmen trading in that far away continent? The Anglo-South American Handbook was born that year, written by W Koebel, the most prolific writer on Latin America of his day.

1924

Two editions later the book was 'privatized' and in 1924, in the hands of Royal Mail, the steamship company for South America, it became The South American Handbook, subtitled 'South America in a nutshell'. This annual publication became the 'bible' for generations of travellers to South America and remains so to this day. In the early days travel was by sea and the Handbook gave all the details needed for the long voyage from Europe. What to wear for dinner; how to arrange a cricket match with the Cable & Wireless staff on the Cape Verde Islands and a full account of the journey from Liverpool up the Amazon to Manaus: 5898 miles without changing cabin!

1939

As the continent opened up, The South American Handbook reported the new Pan Am flying boat services, and the fortnightly airship service from Rio to Europe on the Graf Zeppelin. For reasons still unclear but with extraordinary determination, the annual editions continued through the Second World War.

1970s

Many more people discovered South America and the backpacking trail started to develop. All the while the Handbook was gathering fans, including literary vagabonds such as Paul Theroux and Graham Greene (who once sent some updates addressed to "The publishers of the best travel guide in the world, Bath, England").

1990s

During the 1990s the company set about developing a new travel guide series using this legendary title as the flagship. By 1997 there were over a dozen guides in the series and the Footprint imprint was launched.

2000s

The series grew quickly and there were soon Footprint travel guides covering more than 150 countries. In 2004, Footprint launched its first thematic guide: *Surfing Europe*, packed with colour photographs, maps and charts. This was followed by further thematic guides such as *Diving the World*, *Snowboarding the World*, *Body and Soul escapes*, *Travel with Kids* and *European City Breaks*.

2010

Today we continue the traditions of the last 89 years that have served legions of travellers so well. We believe that these help to make Footprint guides different. Our policy is to use authors who are genuine experts who write for independent travellers; people possessing a spirit of adventure, looking to get off the beaten track.

Title page: The archaeological site of Tulum is in a superb location overlooking the Caribbean.
Above: A colourful wall in Oaxaca city.

Mexico is a land of unbridled energy and bravado. Conquest, colonialism and revolutionary upheavals have all stamped their mark on national character, but above all, the Mexican psyche is tied to the land, in all its diversity. The deserts, mountains, jungles and miles of lavish coastline were all regarded as sacred by the builders of Mexico's ancient pyramids.

Mexico is a dazzling celebration of ethnic diversity. Sierras conceal pockets of indigenous tradition where the gods of maize, earth and sky are still revered. Elsewhere, native and European bloodlines have fused in to a uniquely expressive *mestizo* culture with world class literature, art, films, and sizzling culinary creations among its output. Throughout Mexico, the national obsession with death is tempered by an irrepressible love of life, family and a roaring good fiesta. Such occasions are invariably marked by raucous good humour, feisty music, blazing colours, passion and dance. Viva Mexico!

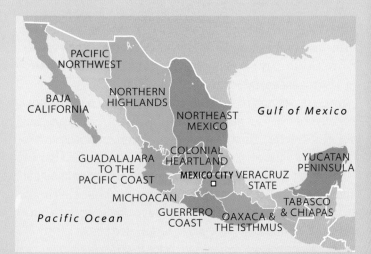

Contents

Planning your trip

MARKUS SEVCIK/SHUTTERSTOCK

A view over the colonial city of
Guanajuato.

Where to go

Mexico's astounding array of options can excite, entice, or even overwhelm many first-time visitors. There's untold scope for adventure activities in the forests and mountains, but you should make time for culture too. Grand colonial cities, small indigenous villages, thriving urban metropolises and the crumbling ruins of ancient civilizations all feature heavily in Mexico's multi-faceted cultural life.

Mexico City is one of the world's great capital cities and with a staggering 22 million inhabitants, it's one of the largest too. A riotous celebration of chaos, culture and style, attractions run the gamut from gritty urban cityscapes to indolent Aztec canals. Beyond the city limits there are the graceful colonial cities of Taxco, Puebla and Cuernavaca, as well as stunning archaeological sites like Teotihuacán and Tula.

A classic destination for RV campers and US expats, Baja California continues to draw crowds with its well-established resorts, isolated beaches and hauntingly desolate landscapes. In recent years, eco and adventure tourism have flourished, especially in the south, with ample opportunities for whale watching, diving, desert hiking and sea kayaking.

The north is a vast and daunting land of deserts, mountains and endless lonely highways. Don't miss the Copper Canyon that competes with Arizona's Grand Canyon for sheer jaw-dropping grandeur. Hikers and climbers will also want to check out the Parque Nacional Cumbres de Monterrey, home to several challenging peaks and over 120 species of birds.

A network of immensely beautiful colonial cities grace the interior of Mexico, including Guanajuato, Zacatecas and

Opposite page: Distinctive red and gold taxis in Mexico City.
Above: A doorway to a temple at the Chicanná Mayan ruins in southern Mexico.

Querétaro. Built on the prodigious wealth of silver mining, many of them and their buildings have been declared World Heritage Sites by UNESCO.

Western Mexico is a bastion of national traditions, such as tequila, mariachis and the Mexican hat dance. The best place to enjoy all of them is Guadalajara, Mexico's second city. But indigenous culture is richly represented in the west too, with scores of evocative Purépecha villages perched upon the shores of Lake Pátzcuaro.

The Pacific coast is a truly vast and legendary stretch of shore with everything from glitzy high-rise resorts to chilled-out bastions of hippy culture. Ramshackle fishing communities, quiet enclaves and blissfully isolated beaches are plentiful, perfect for slinging a hammock and soaking up the sunset.

As the heart of Mexico's oil industry, the Gulf coast may not be as beautiful or popular as the Pacific, but it is wonderfully verdant and free from tourists. Don't miss the steamy, hedonistic port of Veracruz, the archaeological wonder of El Tajín and the urbane university city of Xalapa. For intrepid adventurers there are also plentiful jungle-swathed stretches, untouched beaches, whitewater rapids, beautiful lagoons and mangrove swamps.

Southern Mexico is the country's most popular tourist destination and it's not hard to see why. Mayan ruins, dense jungle, white sand beaches, islands, coral reefs, indigenous villages and colonial cities – the south has it all. Be sure to check out the fine towns of Oaxaca, San Cristóbal de las Casas, Campeche and Mérida, as well as the ruins of Palenque, Uxmal and Chichén Itza. If you want beach time, Tulum is southern Mexico's most hip destination, but there are also plenty of mega-resorts nearby, including the infamous Cancún.

Itineraries

One week

Sadly, one week is barely enough for a teasing taste of Mexico. In such cases, to avoid spending your time on buses, you are strongly advised to limit your trip to a single city or town and its environs. Mexico City is particularly good for this, as are Oaxaca, San Cristóbal de las Casas and Mérida. The colonial splendour of central Mexico can be enjoyed on a relatively compact route from the capital. Commence your journey in Mexico City and head to the historic city of Querétaro. Continue northwest to the fabled town of San Miguel de Allende, now inundated with gringos but still a handsome place. Guanajuato is the next major stop, a UNESECO World Heritage Site replete with stunning architecture. Next head to the fantastic silver mining city of Zacatecas,

BRUCE RAYNOR/SHUTTERSTOCK

Above: The Chihuahua al Pacífico train on its dramatic journey through the Copper Canyon.
Opposite page: The impressive colonial cathedral in Campeche, in the Yucatán Peninsula.

stopping en route at San Luis Potosí if you have time. From Zacatecas you have the option to continue to Durango and the northern highlands, some five hours away.

Two weeks

If you have a yearning for wide open spaces and rugged topography, head north. Commence your trip in Durango and visit some Wild West film sets to get in the spirit. Then continue to the old mining town Hidalgo de Parral and honour the fallen bandit-hero of the Mexican revolution, Pancho Villa. From Parral head to Chihuahua, stock up on some leather boots and catch the bus or train to Creel – the heart of the Copper Canyon. You could easily spend a week exploring the endlessly dramatic countryside before taking the memorable Chihuahua al Pacífico railway to Los Mochis. From there, you can connect with Baja California or the Pacific Coast.

Alternatively, after a few days' exploring Mexico City, head south to the beaches of Oaxaca, before making your way east to San Cristóbal and the Maya ruins of Palenque. Near here is the remote Selva Lacandón, Bonampak and Yaxchilán. From here continue south to Guatemala or out to the Yucatán Peninsula for the beautiful beaches and more Maya ruins of Chichén Itza and Tulum.

Three weeks/a month

You may require three to six months for a really thorough (although by no means complete) exploration of Mexico. A single month, however, should provide a solid sense of any given region. This is also long enough to follow the fabled travellers' route from Mexico City to Tulum. If you're happy to keep on the move, plenty of ground can still be covered in just two weeks, thanks to a fairly efficient bus system.

ALEX ROBINSON

You can cross the US-Mexico border at several points. From Laredo, the route heads south through Monterrey and the port of Tampico before veering inland through the silver mining centre of Pachuca and on to Mexico City.

From Ciudad Juárez on the border, it's a short trip to Chihuahua, the vast Copper Canyon and the glorious railroad down to the Pacific Ocean. The famous train journey is one of several options for leaving Chihuahua on a route heading south that takes in the old silver towns of the colonial heartland of Zacatecas and San Luis Potosí.

On the west coast, Tijuana offers the simplest route to the rugged desert beauty of the Baja California Peninsula, popular for beaches and whale watching. This is also an alternative (and longer) route to the Copper Canyon via Los Mochis. After the Pacific Costa Alegre, head inland for Guadalajara and then Mexico City. Continue southeast from the Mexican Central Highlands to Guatemala and follow the route south, or take in Belize after travelling through the Yucatán Peninsula.

Mexico highlights

See colour maps at end of book

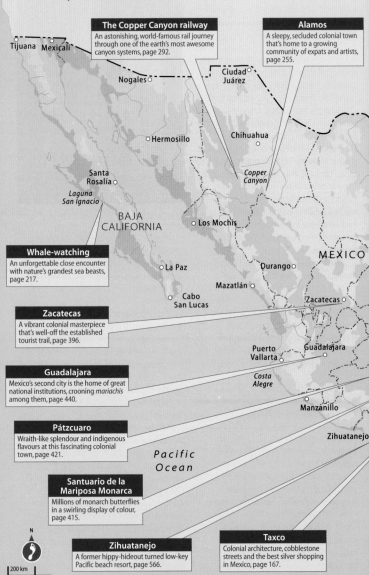

The Copper Canyon railway
An astonishing, world-famous rail journey through one of the earth's most awesome canyon systems, page 292.

Alamos
A sleepy, secluded colonial town that's home to a growing community of expats and artists, page 255.

Tijuana Mexicali

Nogales

Ciudad Juárez

Chihuahua

Hermosillo

Copper Canyon

Santa Rosalía

Laguna San Ignacio

BAJA CALIFORNIA

Los Mochis

MEXICO

Whale-watching
An unforgettable close encounter with nature's grandest sea beasts, page 217.

La Paz

Durango

Mazatlán

Cabo San Lucas

Zacatecas

Zacatecas
A vibrant colonial masterpiece that's well-off the established tourist trail, page 396.

Puerto Vallarta

Guadalajara

Guadalajara
Mexico's second city is the home of great national institutions, crooning *mariachis* among them, page 440.

Costa Alegre

Manzanillo

Pátzcuaro
Wraith-like splendour and indigenous flavours at this fascinating colonial town, page 421.

Zihuatanejo

Pacific Ocean

Santuario de la Mariposa Monarca
Millions of monarch butterflies in a swirling display of colour, page 415.

N

200 km
200 miles

Zihuatanejo
A former hippy-hideout turned low-key Pacific beach resort, page 566.

Taxco
Colonial architecture, cobblestone streets and the best silver shopping in Mexico, page 167.

UNITED STATES

Real de Catorce
A remote and lightly crumbling mining town that almost slipped into oblivion, page 384.

Parque Nacional Cumbres de Monterrey
Rugged beauty and endless hiking opportunities in this soaring national park, page 331.

Teotihuacán
A truly monumental site featuring the world's third largest pyramid, page 146.

Museo Nacional de Antropología
The world's finest anthropology museum with staggering displays on ancient Mexican culture, page 98.

Chichén Itza
Quintessential Mayan ruin featuring grand pyramids, ball courts and astronomically aligned temples, page 700.

Mérida
The sunny capital of Yucatán state, full of grand colonial buildings and plenty of local flavour, page 693.

Veracruz
Exuberant hedonism at one of Mexico's most fabled port and party towns, page 519.

Gulf of Mexico

Nuevo Laredo

Matamoros

Monterrey

Tampico

San Luis Potosí

Querétaro

Teotihuacán

MEXICO CITY

Popocatépetl

Taxco

Puebla

Veracruz

Villahermosa

Palenque

San Cristóbal de las Casas

Mérida

Cancún

Uxmal

Chichén Itza

Tulum

Campeche

Chetumal

Tikal

BELIZE

Monte Albán

Oaxaca

Acapulco

Puerto Escondido

Tapachula

GUATEMALA

HONDURAS

EL SALVADOR

Puerto Escondido
This classic Pacific beach town hosts great parties and world-class surfing waves, pages 602.

Oaxaca City
A bastion of contemporary art, culture and colonial grandeur, page 577.

San Cristóbal de las Casas
The capital of Mexico's Mayan highlands and a fascinating stronghold of indigenous culture, page 637.

Palenque
Eerily atmospheric Mayan ruins with a misty rainforest backdrop, page 654.

Mysterious places

Teotihuacán

The ancient city of Teotihuacán, 49 km north of Mexico City, was revered by the Aztecs as the mythical birthplace of their gods. Rising before the rugged Sierra Madre mountains with dark, imposing pyramids, it flourished between 300 BC and 600 AD, after which it was mysteriously abandoned. Known to have influenced civilizations as far away as Central America, Teotihuacán is replete with all the monumental structures befitting a formidable regional power. Ornate palaces hint at the opulence of its former rulers; temple complexes illustrate the rich intricacies of its religious life; and vast rows of ceremonial platforms reveal a penchant for planning, symmetry and foreboding architectural style. Don't miss the gigantic pyramid of the sun – the third largest pyramid in the world – it supplies unrivalled views of the metropolis and its main thoroughfare, the Avenue of the Dead.

Cenotes of Yucatán

Scientists have yet to fully map the scintillating underground world of the Yucatán – former heartland of Mayan civilization – punctuated by an immense network of subterranean rivers, caverns, caves and natural wells called *cenotes*. In ancient times, *cenotes* were regarded as sacred openings to the underworld. Today you can explore their eerie grandeur by donning some scuba gear and diving into their spooky chambers and passages. Your torch light will reveal a procession of gnarled stalactites, limestone columns and endlessly weird structures that may belong, as the ancient Mayans hinted, to a completely different world.

San Juan Chamula

Nestled in the highlands of Chiapas, southern Mexico, the fiercely resistent Mayan community of San Juan Chamula is a guardian of pre-Hispanic mysteries. Here, the old gods are alive and well, clothed in the robes of saints,

Above: On the top of the Pyramid of the Sun at Teotihuacán.
Opposite page: Buried deep in the jungle are the Maya ruins of Palenque.

URO5R/SHUTTERSTOCK

or else dwelling in their traditional abodes of sacred mountains, caves and springs. In Chamula, the ancient art of shamanism is widely practised, albeit intriguingly fused with Spanish Catholicism. Visit the village church and you're likely to see the faithful masses are immersed in a fog of copal incense, singing, praying, or consuming voracious quantities of locally produced moonshine. Festival time is a particularly evocative occasion when you'll encounter the full force of Chamulan religious life. Archaic rituals, riotous feasts and otherworldly dances upon burning embers – all supply a link to the shadowy world of Mexico's ancient past.

Palenque

Enveloped in thick canopies of foliage, the ruined metropolis of Palenque is one of Mexico's most striking and enigmatic archaeological sites. Built at the zenith of Mayan civilization, the city's richly sculpted facades, elegant statuary and vast hieroglyphic tablets proclaim its status as one of the region's most prosperous and powerful polities. Wander into the surrounding jungle and you'll find yet more ancient structures nestled between the twisted roots, vines and vegetation. Palenque's lush rainforest setting – as much as its cultural and artistic achievements – conspire to make it one of Mexico's most vivid destinations.

The Lacandón Forest

The Lacandón forest, eastern Chiapas state, is home to the last surviving Lacandón Mayans, a jungle-dwelling people known in their own language as Hach Winik (Real People). Once upon a time, the Hach Winik hunted with bows and arrows, practised polygamy and enjoyed an intimate relationship with the gods. Life may now be rapidly changing, but the forest beyond their communities still conceals sacred places like waterfalls, lakes and mysterious ruined cities, where until the last years of the 20th century, the Hach Winik ritually conversed with their ancestors. Among such sites are the ruins of Bonampak, with its intriguing murals

depicting Mayan warfare, and more remotely, perched on the banks of the Usumacinta river, the city of Yaxchilán, home to vociferous howler monkeys and exquisite temple architecture.

Huautla de Jiménez

Nestled high above the clouds, the almost mythical Mazatec town of Huautla de Jiménez lies in the remote sierras of northwestern Oaxaca state. Pockets of outstanding natural beauty lie scattered in its surroundings, including waterfalls, cloud forests, mountain peaks and some of the world's deepest caves. But above all, Huautla is renowned for its mystical traditions, which have drawn intrepid seekers since the 1960s. The Beatles, Timothy Leary and Bob Dylan are reportedly among the pilgrims to have consumed the local hallucinogenic mushrooms, which grow freely in the misty environs and are a major part of Mazatec spiritual life. For some travellers, a visit to Huautla can become a journey of the most profound and mysterious nature – a blazing, visionary trip through the landscapes of the human soul.

Cultural highlights

Guadalajara

While Mexico's second largest city may have lost some of its shine in recent years, it still is the birthplace and arbiter of much that is *puro mexicano*. All *apatios* (natives of Guadalajara) will tell you this area gave birth not just to tequila and mariachi, but also that most Mexican of all pastimes, the *charrera*. The arts scene is second only to that found in the capital, with more than 40 museums and galleries. Its restored centre offers superb colonial architecture, the hippest stores, and chic eateries at every turn. Nearby Zapopan boasts the Basílica of Nuestra Señora de Zapopan and houses the famous image by the same name, reputed to have worked many miracles throughout Guadalajara's long history. The adjacent cities of Tlaquepaque and Tonalá are famous for their glass, ceramics and pottery.

Guanajuato

Many towns have a building or section listed as a World Heritage Site. In Guanajuato's case, the entire city is one. If you had to choose just one place in Mexico to spend a single day capturing the essence of its history and tradition, it would be here. While Oaxaca and Puebla are better known, any Mexican will tell you that the best *artesanías* (handicraft stores), historic neighbourhoods and the country's finest literary extravaganza (the annual International Cervantes Festival) are here. A classical colonial town (founded on silver and boasting an enormous number of baroque churches), Guanajuato is also the site of the shrine of Christ the King, the macabre Mummy Museum, and fittingly, was the birthplace of Diego Rivera, Mexico's second-most famous painter (after his wife, Frida Kahlo). Along with Zacatecas, it still observes many otherwise-extinct traditions during Holy Week, as well as offering *callejoneadas*, nightly group serenades (accompanied by a *burro*) in its downtown.

Metepec

Metepec is a cultural rarity. Almost the entire town is involved in one way or another with the crafting of its famous *árboles de la vida* (trees of life), intricately designed, hand-painted ceramic figurines depicting a wide range of activities and cultural icons. These are now amongst the best-known artistic output of Mexico, making this *pueblo* famous the world over. Centuries ago, it was customary for many Mexican towns to be known for a particular speciality. Nowadays very few villages retain their unique cultural identity, but Metepec is one that does in spades.

Spanish Missions Trail

Three religious orders. Thirty separate missions. One hundred and fifty years. What may sound like a mass of dry statistics in fact constitutes one of the most epic journeys on the continent. From the Franciscan-founded Mission El Descanso in the far north to the Jesuit-built Mission San José del Cabo at the extreme southern tip of the peninsula, these

ALFREDO SCHAUFELBERGER/SHUTTERSTOCK

Opposite page: Mexico's ceramic traditions date back to pre-Classic times .
Above: Panoramic view of Santa Prisca church, with its tiled octagonal dome, Taxco.

outposts occupy some of the most beautiful terrain in Mexico. None of the missions have survived as religious centres but many are now being restored. What makes them so fascinating is the trail that links them together. You'll see everything from chic tropical venues to fishing villages as you travel along the Pacific coast to the arid scrublands of the interior. Apart from its famous resorts, the Baja is still relatively untouched.

Taxco

This old mining town, founded in 1524 and just two hours' drive southwest from Mexico City, shares with Zacatecas a reputation for the finest silver in Mexico (that brought it so much wealth in colonial days), some of the most jaw-dropping architecture and a cable car to mountain top. Its setting – built into the side of a mountain – kept Taxco out of sight for centuries, but it's now one of Mexico's most favoured spots for culture mavens. Santa Prisca church, Casa de Humboldt and the Museum of Viceregal Art are just three unmissable

sights. Taxco was home to the US expat designer William Spratling, who put this picturesque town on the map. It's also allegedly where the margarita cocktail was invented (although at least five other towns claim this honour).

Zacatecas

If you have only a few days to see Mexico and want to squeeze in as much culture as possible, head for this small city that those in the know call *el paraíso escondido* (the hidden paradise). Its historic centre is considered one of the best preserved colonial-era locations on the continent and is a World Heritage Site. The annual Zacatecas cultural, folklore and national fairs are among the largest in the country and almost every week there is an event in town, ranging from hot-air balloon rides to street theatre. There are 13 museums (three of them world class), and more antique, crafts and book stores, as well as galleries, per capita than almost any other city in the country.

six of the best Markets

Mexico has an abundance of markets, from daily bustling big city ones, to weekly affairs in the smaller villages. They often sell everything under the sun from kitchen utensils, to *rebozos* (shawls) and watermelons, with vendors enticing you to step on up, sample their goods, browse, barter, poke and prod – this is Mexico in all its glory and even a humble market in a tiny hamlet can be an excellent place to get to know the country and what it's all about just a little bit better. Remember, bartering and bargaining are the rule of the day here for all goods.

Toclua's Mercado Juárez

Toluca's Mercado Juárez is actually a daily market, but it's often known as the Friday market, since Friday is the day to visit. The market, behind Toluca's bus station, meanders and sprawls at the best of times, but on Fridays it simply swells to gigantic proportions – some say it's the largest in all the country – since people from the outlying villages bring their goods to market to sell. Mercado Juárez sells everything you could possibly need, with a firm emphasis on the utilitarian and this is what makes it so interesting – there's nothing touristy about this market. It's where ordinary Toluqueños shop and although there are some arts and crafts, these are quite rare. Instead you'll get a flavour of Mexican life and a great selection of goods from clothes to fruit and vegetables.

Oaxaca City's markets

It's impossible to choose just the one out of Oaxaca's many colourful markets – they're all worth a wander. The state and the city itself are famed for its arts and crafts and

ALEX ROBINSON

Brightly embroidered huipiles (blouses) in Oaxaca.

several of the central markets, including Mercado de Artesanías in JP García and Zaragoza and Mercado Juárez in 20 de Noviembre, sell excellent handicrafts from the nearby villages or made in workshops in the city itself. Oaxacan markets are also great for cheap and tasty food, such as the oversized tortillas known as *tlayudas* with all manner of fillings, and they are a good place to pick up Oaxacan specialities – such as coffee, chocolate, mole sauce and mescal.

San Cristóbal de las Casas
Santo Domingo Church craft market
Chiapas, like Oaxaca, is famed for its skilled artisans and this small market just north of the town centre has a variety of crafts from leather goods and woollen blankets to textiles (local and Guatemalan) and jewellery.

Chiapas village markets
Many of the small, indigenous villages around San Cristóbal de las Casas have their own weekly markets – colourful, bustling days of frenzied activity. For the best experience go with a local guide. San Juan Chamula's market is on a Sunday, as is San Lorenzo Zinacantán's. Nearby Ocosingo has a smaller daily market of women traders only. All sell a wide variety of local crafts, as well as many other goods.

Mexico City markets
Mexico City has its fair share of markets, always good for last-minute shopping if you're flying back from the capital. This can be particularly good if you didn't make it to some of the states known for their arts and crafts, as pretty much everything can be found in the Mexico City markets, albeit for a higher price. One market that lends itself to quiet browsing, without the vendors hassling, is La Ciudadela craft market near Balderas metro. Prices tend to be good from the start, although bartering is possible and encouraged.

Browse markets in Chiapas, southern Mexico, for Mayan textiles.

Decent crafts from all over the country can be found here.

Mercado de Sonora
The Mercado de Sonora is one of the most unusual markets in the country, specializing in herbal medicines and plants with curative powers. Situated in Avenida Fray Servando Teresa de Mier, this is where local healers, so-called *curanderos/as*, shop. This is where you'll find stalls selling amulets, candles and masks, as well as all sorts of herbs and potions, birds and animals. It's an interesting place for a browse and to gain an insight into the country's witchier heritage.

When to go

The best time to visit Mexico is between October and April, although there are slight regional variations. The rainy season works its way up from the south beginning in May and running through until August, September and even October. This is also hurricane season along the Caribbean. Despite the high profile storm of Hurricane Wilma and a few lesser-known local hurricanes and tropical storms, landfall is relatively rare. If a hurricane does arrive while you're in the area you can get details at www.nhc.noaa.gov. But don't be put off by the term 'rainy season' – in most places and in most years, heavy rain falls for an hour or two a day.

If the time and mood is right, there is little to beat a Mexican **festival**. Fine costumes, loud music, the sounds of firecrackers tipped off with the gentle wafting of specially prepared foods all (normally) with a drink or two. Whether you're seeking the carnival or happen to stumble across a celebration, the events – big or small – are memorable.

Carnival is normally the week before the start of Lent, when you can see some colourful processions. Semana Santa (Easter Week) is an understandably more spiritual affair. On 2 November is Día de los Muertos (Day of the Dead), a famous celebration in Mexico when families visit cemeteries to honour the dead. Christmas and New Year

result in celebrations of some kind, but not always public.

Public holidays throughout the region lead to a complete shutdown in services. No banks, government offices, usually no shops and often far fewer restaurants and bars are open. It is worth keeping an eye on the calendar to avoid changing money or trying to make travel arrangements on public holidays.

DAVID M SCHRADER/SHUTTERSTOCK

Above: Desert landscape in northern Mexico.
Opposite page: Troncones beach in Guerrero.

Mexico

Activity	J	F	M	A	M	J	J	A	S	O	N	D
Whale watching in Baja California, Mexico	★	★	★	★						★	★	★
Monarch butterfly migration						★	★	★	★	★	★	★
Birdwatching	★	★	★								★	★
Whitewater rafting and surfing	★	★	★	★	★	★	★	★	★	★	★	★
Major festivals	★	★	★	★						★	★	★

Rainfall and climate charts

Mexico City

Month	Average temperature in °C	Average rainfall in days
Jan	13.2	02
Feb	13.5	01
Mar	16.6	01
Apr	17.1	03
May	21.7	06
Jun	20.1	13
Jul	17.8	18
Aug	16.4	13
Sep	16.8	13
Oct	15.1	06
Nov	14.0	01
Dec	12.3	01

Ensenada

Month	Average temperature in °C	Average rainfall in days
Jan	13.1	05
Feb	13.7	04
Mar	14.8	06
Apr	15.9	03
May	19.2	01
Jun	20.8	01
Jul	21.7	00
Aug	22.5	00
Sep	21.2	01
Oct	18.6	01
Nov	15.4	04
Dec	12.8	05

Monterrey

Month	Average temperature in °C	Average rainfall in days
Jan	14.2	03
Feb	15.8	03
Mar	20.7	02
Apr	24.0	05
May	28.2	06
Jun	29.9	05
Jul	29.2	05
Aug	28.5	07
Sep	25.6	09
Oct	22.1	06
Nov	17.1	03
Dec	15.0	03

Zacatecas

Month	Average temperature in °C	Average rainfall in days
Jan	10.6	03
Feb	11.8	02
Mar	15.3	01
Apr	17.7	01
May	20.4	03
Jun	21.2	08
Jul	18.4	10
Aug	17.7	10
Sep	16.8	08
Oct	15.6	04
Nov	13.3	01
Dec	11.3	02

Guadalajara

Month	Average temperature in °C	Average rainfall in days
Jan	16.5	02
Feb	18.0	01
Mar	21.5	01
Apr	23.3	01
May	27.2	03
Jun	26.1	14
Jul	23.1	20
Aug	22.4	18
Sep	22.0	14
Oct	21.0	05
Nov	18.8	02
Dec	16.8	02

Puerto Vallarta

Month	Average temperature in °C	Average rainfall in days
Jan	21.6	02
Feb	21.7	01
Mar	22.2	00
Apr	23.9	00
May	27.8	01
Jun	27.9	10
Jul	28.3	15
Aug	28.9	15
Sep	28.7	14
Oct	27.8	05
Nov	25.0	01
Dec	22.8	02

Veracruz

Month	Average temperature in °C	Average rainfall in days
Jan	22.5	05
Feb	23.4	04
Mar	25.7	03
Apr	27.6	03
May	29.0	05
Jun	28.5	15
Jul	28.0	21
Aug	28.0	19
Sep	27.8	18
Oct	27.4	11
Nov	25.6	08
Dec	23.6	06

Oaxaca

Month	Average temperature in °C	Average rainfall in days
Jan	16.7	02
Feb	18.3	02
Mar	20.6	02
Apr	22.2	04
May	22.8	07
Jun	21.7	12
Jul	21.8	08
Aug	21.8	09
Sep	20.5	09
Oct	19.4	04
Nov	18.3	02
Dec	16.7	02

Cancún

Month	Average temperature in °C	Average rainfall in days
Jan	23.3	05
Feb	23.9	04
Mar	25.6	03
Apr	26.7	02
May	27.8	04
Jun	28.9	06
Jul	28.9	04
Aug	28.9	04
Sep	28.3	07
Oct	27.2	08
Nov	25.6	05
Dec	24.4	06

Sport and activities

Canyoning and caving

ⓘ See under **Expediciones Umarike**, page 504.

In the Cumbres de Monterrey national park you'll find the Recorrido de Matacanes circuit, based on the Cascada Lagunillas, and another circuit spilling out from the Cascada El Chiptín, known locally as Recorrido Hidrofobia. In Veracruz is the Cañadas de Cotlamani near Jalcomulco. In Chihuahua, a few operators organize trips to the Copper Canyon near Creel.

In Mexico, caving, or *espeleología*, can be closely related to canyoning as there are some excellent underground river scrambles, the best being the 8km-long Chontalcuatlán, part of the Cacahuamilpa caves near Taxco. There is an underground lagoon here in Zacatecolotla cave. Beside the Matacanes river circuit in Nuevo León there are some large caves.

For purist potholers there are many vertical caves or *sótanos* (cellars) in the Sierra Gorda de Querétaro, as well as La Purificación near Ciudad Victoria. The biggest cave

systems are in Chiapas, especially around Tuxtla Gutiérrez. One of the best elsewhere is the Sótano de las Golondrinas on Santa María river, San Luis Potosí (see Whitewater rafting, page 27), but the most challenging is Pozo Verde, 1070 m deep, near Ocotempa, Puebla.

Cenote diving

ⓘ **Mike Madden's CEDAM Dive Centres**, PO Box 1, Puerto Aventuras, T/F873-5129; **Aquatech**, Villas de Rosa, PO Box 25, Aventuras Akumal No 35, Tulum, T875-9020, www.cenotes.com; **Aktun Dive Centre**, PO Box 119, Tulum, T871-2311, www.aktun dive.com; **Cenote Dive Center**, Tulum, T871-2232, www.cenotedive.com.

There are more than 50 *cenotes* in the Yucatán peninsula – accessible from Ruta 307 and often well signposted – and cave diving has become very popular. But it is a specialized sport and, unless you have a cave diving qualification, you must be accompanied by a

UROSR/SHUTTERSTOCK

qualified dive master. A cave diving course involves over 12 hours of lectures and a minimum of 14 cave dives using double tanks, costing around US$600. Accompanied dives start at around US$60. Some of the best *cenotes* are Carwash, on the Cobá road, good even for beginners, with excellent visibility and Dos Ojos, just off Ruta 307 south of Aventuras. The latter is the second largest underground cave system in the world and has a possible link to the Nohoch Nah Chich, the most famous cenote and part of a subterranean system recorded as the world's largest, with over 50 km of surveyed passageways connected to the sea. A word of warning: *cenote* diving has a higher level of risk than open-water diving – do not take risks and make sure you only dive with recognized operators.

Climbing

ⓘ Details of the operators are listed in the relevant chapters.

The big glaciated volcanoes are within easy reach of Mexico City. Although there are few technical routes, you will require crampons, ice-axe and occasionally rope for safe ascents.

Popocatépetl (5452 m) and Colima Volcano (3842 m) are sporadically erupting, so Pico de Orizaba (Citlatépetl, Mexico's highest volcano at 5760 m) and Iztaccíhuatl (5286 m) are the two main high-altitude challenges. Two good acclimatization climbs are Cofre de Perote (Nouhcampatépetl, 4282 m) and Nevado de Toluca (Xinantécatl, 4558 m). Near Tapachula, Chiapas, Tacaná Volcano (4150 m) is a worthwhile but little-climbed mountain.

Rock climbing is an increasingly popular sport, requiring specialist knowledge and thorough safety systems, so use a reputable operator. On the outskirts of the capital there are two natural high-rises above the smog: the cliffs at Magdalena Contreras to the southwest and at Naucalpan to the northwest. There are numerous small canyons for weekend-long excursions beyond the borders of the Valley of Mexico: Calixtlahuaca, northwest of Toluca, has

MARC PAGANI PHOTOGRAPHY/SHUTTERSTOCK

Opposite page: An underground *cenote* at Dzitnup near Valladolid in southern Mexico. **Above:** Climber on the huge limestone cliffs in Portrero Chico, northeast Mexico.

easy to moderate routes; Piedra Parada near Ixtapan de la Sal has more difficult walls as there are few fissures in the rock; another route is Cerro Catedral, 30 km north of Toluca. North of the city, 70 km east of Querétaro, is the Peñón de Bernal, the world's largest monolith after Ayer's rock. El Chico national park near Pachuca also has excellent climbing, as does the Cañón de Zimapán, both in Hidalgo.

Monterrey has Mexico's best rock. Near Hidalgo is the Potrero Chico big wall, 650 m of limestone nirvana. Also near Monterrey are the Cañón de la Huasteca, Independencia and the Cuerno de Toro. There is a top-grade 600 m cliff at El Trono de Angel in northern Baja California as well as excellent sea-cliff climbing around the peninsula. Finally, there are yet more opportunities in Humira outside Creel.

Diving

ⓘ Details of the operators are listed in the relevant chapters.

Two regions, Quintana Roo and Baja California, are particularly noteworthy. The first offers warm water reefs close to the shore with visibility of over 30 m. Southern Baja has adventurous diving in deep waters.

Cozumel in Quintana Roo has some of the best diving in the world and there are marine parks at Chankanaab and at Palancar Reef with numerous caves, gullies and a horseshoe-shaped diving arena. Also excellent, on the west side of the island, are Santa Rosa and sites off San Fransisco beach. To the southwest are good sites off Laguna Colombia, whilst off Punta Sur there is excellent deep diving. There is concern, however, over damage to the reef by cruise ships. At Isla Mujeres, also in Quintana Roo, the most dived sites include Los Manchones, La Bandera, and a shallow dive south of the island, El Frío, a deep wreck.

Also along this Caribbean coast, Punta Nizuc is accessible from Cancún, while Akumal is famous for wrecks like the Spanish galleon El Matancero. Immediately east of the resort are the Grouper Canyons. Banco Chinchorro is a magnificent biosphere reserve accessible from Majahual and Xcalak. It's a day's boat ride from Progreso, Yucatán, to Arrecife Alacrán.

Southern Baja is warmer than the north, but it is still best to wear a wetsuit, not least to protect from skin-irritating hydroza organisms. There are marine forests and a reef at Cabo Pulmo. The rock formations off Pichilingue are worth seeing and there is a wreck off Isla Espíritu Santo. A fine underwater cavern lies off Isla Cerralvo and the Islas Gaviotas are also dived. If you are experienced enough to brave currents off Cabo San Lucas then there are impressive submarine sandfalls to a depth of 65 m.

Other diving centres include Puerto Vallarta with the good dive training site of Bahía Banderas. Nearby are the Islas Marietas and the reef of the Los Arcos marine park. Puerto Escondido and the Bays of Huatulco offer clear waters, unlike the Gulf of Mexico, although it too has its attractions, such as a reef off Veracruz. Best dive sites are at La Blanquilla, Antón Lizardo and Isla Verde with its wreck.

Protect the reef

Mexico offers some of the finest marine environments in the Caribbean Basin, but the major challenge is to keep it that way. It's important that if you dive or snorkel you take responsibility for your own actions, and that your trip contributes to the preservation rather than the destruction of the reef. Here are a few ways to help:

1 Don't touch the reef! Even a gentle brush can remove the protective covering of mucus from a coral colony and cause the death of an animal community that has taken hundreds of years to develop.
2 Don't remove anything from the reef.
3 Be aware of your fins and where they go! It's very easy to lose track of that

deadly (for the coral) 50 cm on the end of your foot.
4 If you want to snorkel but haven't tried it before, practise your technique before you get close to a coral reef. A shallow bottom of a sandy beach or a pool is perfect.
5 When diving, stop your initial descent before you go straight into the reef below.
6 Lend a hand! Collect any rubbish you find and make sure it's correctly disposed of. Lost fishing nets can be a huge problem for marine life, killing fish, turtles, even dolphins for years afterwards.
7 Support an organization working to protect coral reefs, locally or worldwide. There are many excellent grassroots organizations which deserve your support.

Death and the maiden

Mexico's attitude to death extends well beyond grim fascination. As an intimate part of Mexican identity, death is nothing less than a cherished national obsession. From the conquest to the Independence movement, the Revolution and beyond, Mexico's history – and its heroes – are steeped in blood and transience. Today, untold works of art and literature, festivals, political institutions and traditions serve as vehicles for the nation's complex feelings towards the grim reaper.

On one hand, death is a dreaded and ever-present spectre. Head to a newsstand and you'll discover violent images splashed on the front pages of publications devoted to real-life murders, car crashes or other gruesome incidents. On the other hand, death is to be mocked and reviled.

On 1-2 November, Mexico celebrates Día de los Muertos (Day of the Dead), the quintessential and wholly unique Mexican festival of death. It's a time when families gather in cemeteries to quietly remember departed loved ones ... or otherwise throw a wild fiesta in their honour.

In Mexico City, the occasion is marked by a fantastic competition to build the most impressive *ofrenda* (Day of the Dead altar). Death invades the Zócalo with irrepressible style, hordes of skeletons grinning and dancing, or otherwise engaging in endless contemptuous diversions.

The stars of the show – El Catrín and La Catrina (The Dandy and the Female Dandy) – are ever-present in their sumptuous garb. These two iconic figures were the creation of 19th-century satirist José Guadalupe Posada, who made his name mocking Mexico's upper classes. His sketches of feisty cadavers perfectly capture Mexico's attitude to the hereafter: Death is coming, let's laugh at him.

But the roots of Mexico's death obsession reach deep into the ancestral past, when the

A skeleton at a Day of the Dead celebration.

Otherworld played a more prominent role in the day-to-day affairs of the living.

In Aztec society, the gods demanded continual tributes of blood and flesh to ensure that the sun survived its daily trip through the underworld. Ultimately, the Aztec universe was a dual universe. Life and death were in a constant, dizzying dance, each replenishing the other. Life sprung from Death. Death devoured Life. This may be part of the reason why death in Mexico – in contrast to sombre European renditions – is always portrayed in such resplendent colours. It is as if death itself is a force for life.

In more recent years, a new religious cult has arisen with death as its figurehead. Santa Muerta, the dark sister of the Virgin of Guadalupe, has inspired followers from the urban poor and criminal fraternity. She's a tough and merciless character, loyal to those with tough and difficult lives. But this is merely the latest twist in Mexico's long-running and complicated love affair with death. For whilst society changes, facts of life do not. Perhaps we could all learn something from Mexico's blackly humorous attitude, and in the process, become just a bit more at ease with our ultimate fate.

Death and the maiden ● 25

Fishing

ⓘ Details of the operators are listed in the relevant chapters.

There are resort-based sports fishing fleets along much of Mexico's Pacific coast, from Bahía Kino to Acapulco. At the former there is a fishing tournament in late June/early July and at Manzanillo there is one in February.

Some of the best fishing is in the Sea of Cortés, especially off La Paz, around Islas Espiritú Santo and Cerralvo, and around Loreto. Here, the high season for species like marlin, swordfish, sailfish, roosterfish, dorado, cabrilla and wahoo is May to September. For sierra it is November to January, and yellowtail from March to May. International competitions are in July and August. Tampico, in the Gulf of Mexico, has competitions for robalo (April), marlin (June) and sábalo (July and August).

Hiking

ⓘ Details of the trails are listed in the relevant chapters. See page 46 for information on maps.

The Copper Canyon is a vast wilderness for hiking. Creel is the obvious base but a great

CASSIEDE ALAIN/SHUTTERSTOCK

trek runs from Batópilas to Urique. The best trekking within easy reach of a major city is from Monterrey, particularly in the Cumbres de Monterrey national park.

One of the main attractions of more remote trekking, such as in Oaxaca state and Nayarit, is visiting indigenous communities such as Cora and Huichol villages. However, one should be sensitive to local reactions to tourist intrusion. Baja California's petroglyph cave sites can often only be visited on foot, but here too remember that most sites are sacred and you are legally required to obtain ANAM permission before visiting. Seek advice before trekking in Chiapas and Guerrero, both hideouts for rebel groups.

Kayaking

ⓘ Details of the operators are listed in the relevant chapters.

The warm waters of the Sea of Cortés off Baja California Sur are kayak heaven. Isla Espiritú Santo and Isla Partida are easily accessible from La Paz and you can see stingrays, sea lions, dolphins, porpoises and occasionally grey whales and hammerheads. Further up the coast, Loreto is a good base for hiring gear. At Bahía Coyote, near Santispac, there are many small islands to explore in a day on calm waters.

Another good spot for kayaking is the Bahía de Sayulita, north of Puerto Vallarta, and around the nearby Islas Marietas. In Veracruz State a popular place is Isla de los Sacrificios.

Surfing

ⓘ Details of the best surf spots are listed in the relevant chapters.

Some of the world's most exhilarating surfing is along Mexico's Pacific coast. Highlights are the huge Hawaiian-sized surf that pounds the Baja shoreline and the renowned Mexican Pipeline at Puerto Escondido.

Isla de Todos Santos in front of Ensenada has big swells. It is much frequented by US surfers and is best in winter. There are 20 good beaches around Playa San Miguel. Punta Mirador beside San José and the beach nearby, Km 28, receive some massive waves.

Mazatlán is the point on the mainland where currents escape the shielding effects of the Peninsula and surfing is possible. In front of the town, Isla de Piedra is good, as is Playa Cerritos, just north of the town, along with El Caimanero, near Teacapan, 100 km south.

San Blas is an excellent learning centre. The waves are usually not too big and there are few rocks or dangerous currents. South of San Blas, still in Nayarit, are Playa San Fransisco and Playa Sayulita and the Punta de Mita.

The Colima coast offers good surfing at Boca de Pascuales near Tecomán and at Río Ticla. Before Zihuatanejo are Río Nexpa and Petacalco and, just outside Acapulco, Playa Revolcadero is battered by surf to match its name. Puerto Escondido is, perhaps, the mecca of Mexican surfing. Surfers come here to Playa Zicatela to attempt the pipeline and are duly washed up on the shore.

Whitewater rafting

ⓘ Details of the operators are listed in the relevant chapters.

The most popular run is the Río Antigua/Pescados in Veracruz. The upper stretch, the Antigua, has some good learning rapids (grade 2) running into grade 3, but if you have more than a day, the Pescados (the lower Antigua), near to Jalcomulco, can give a bigger adrenalin rush with some grade 4 whitewater. Also in Veracruz state, 50 km to the north, is the Río Actopan with grade 3 rapids. The biggest rush in Mexico, however, is on the Barranca Grande at Cañon Azul with excellent grade 5 waters. The Filobobos has the Alto Filo (grades 4 and 5) and 25 km from Tlapacoyan to Palmilla.

In San Luis Potosí state there is the turquoise Santa María, accessible beneath the 105 m-high Cascadas de Tamul and running past several ruins, grades 3 and 4, through dramatic countryside known as the Huasteca

Opposite page: Riding the wave in Puerto Escondido, on the Oaxacan coast.
Above: A coloured crested caracara hawk.

Potosina. The Amacuzac, 1½ hours from Mexico City in Morelos state, near Taxco, entered as Dos Bocas, is grades 3 and 4.

Chiapas offers sedate drifting on rivers such as the Lacanjá through the Lacandón jungle to class 4 and 5 rapids on the Río Jalaté.

An adventurous trip is on the Río Grande from near the border between Chihuahua and Coahuila, opposite Big Bend National Park, through the canyons of Santa Elena, Bacuillas and Mariscal.

Wildlife and birdwatching

ⓘ See page 809 for an introduction to the region's wildlife.

Mexico has spectacular and abundant wildlife-watching opportunities, including whale watching off the coast of Baja California mid-December to mid-March. The sheer number of bird species mean ornithologists get positively overexcited, with wetland lagoons and rainforest sites providing some of the most colourful activity. The resplendent quetzal, with its beautifully flamboyant tail feather, would be a lucky sighting, as it is very rare (and possibly non existent) Mexico.

Family travel

Mexico is as adventurous as you want it to be. You can play it safe at mega-resorts like Acapulco, Cancún or Puerto Vallarta, or you can play at being Indiana Jones by exploring the jungles and Maya ruins of the Yucatán Peninsula, the legendary ghost towns of Real de Catorce, or the parks and reserves of Chiapas. Mexico City can be overwhelming, but its nearby archaeological ruins and well-preserved towns like Cuernavaca, Taxco and Xochimilco are well worth visiting. Further north, the Copper Canyon is the setting for a dramatic rail journey, while Baja California – Mexico's desert peninsula – is a prime spot for whale watching and sea kayaking.

City highlights

Built on the site of the Aztec capital of Tenochtlán, metropolitan Mexico City is a somewhat manic metropolis now home to more than 20 million people. Best to take a deep breath, keeps your wits and wallet about you and just focus on one or two highlights.

Plaza de la Constitución, also known as the Zócalo, is Mexico City's historic main square. It is dominated by the cathedral, a baroque giant that took 250 years to complete. For a quick visual guide to Mexico's history, take a look inside the Palacio Nacional, where Diego Rivera's murals recount scenes ranging from the Aztec empire to the revolutionary hero Francisco 'Pancho' Villa. On most days, indigenous dancers dressed in flamboyant costumes and feathered headdresses re-enact Aztec ceremonies, while a short walk away you can see the excavated ruins of Templo Mayor, the Great Temple that was once the sacred centre of the Aztec universe.

The Grander Canyon

Experience one of the world's great train rides with the children. Take the ferry from La Paz to Topolobampo and on to Los Mochis, from where the Chihuahua-Al Pacífico railway rattles inland for 655 km, stopping at several points in the Copper Canyon – an enormous axe-stroke through the Sierra Madre. It's a straight-through 14-hour ride to Chihuahua, but spread this journey over three or four days to take advantage of its hiking, biking and horse riding opportunities.

Row of boats in Xochimilco, Mexico City.

Museums

The Museo Nacional de Antropología houses an enormous collection of pre-Hispanic artefacts, showcasing the best excavated from the Aztec, Maya, Olmec, Toltec and Zapotec civilizations. Look for the Aztec calendar, the Maya Chacmool from Chichén Itzá, and the jade mask from Palenque. Another museum worth visiting is the Papalote Museo del Niño, a children's museum with hands-on science and cultural exhibits and an IMAX cinema.

City getaways

Take a day trip to Venice-like Xochimilco, silver-rich Taxco or mysterious Teotihuacán. In this once great city, children will be eager to climb all 248 steps to the top of the Pyramid of the Sun – the third largest in the world. You can reach Oaxaca by luxury inter-city coach or a short flight. This handsome colonial city has a tree-shaded central plaza surrounded by cafés and a cathedral. Peruse the local market for colourful textiles and handicrafts, sample the traditional mole dishes and visit the ancient Zapotec capital of Monte Albán. Older children may prefer Puebla with its museums (including those dedicated to wildlife, trains, and interactive imagination), parks, and of course, the Africam Safari.

My oh Maya!

In the Yucatán you're never far from an idyllic Caribbean beach, so there's no excuse for not making a hot and sweaty archaeological jaunt into the interior.

Chichén Itzá

This magnificent Mayan site is a must-see. The imposing El Castillo pyramid is always a magnet for children, but once they tire of counting the 91 steps in its four stairways and romping across the ruined city's wide-open plazas they'll discover some fascinating, often gory, clues to its past. The Juego de Pelota, for example, was where the Maya played a killer ballgame – literally - in which contestants sometimes received a fate far worse than a red card. In the Temple of the Skulls,

Wild encounters

Baja California

➔ Boat trips to see whales in Baja's lagoons (Dec-Apr) operate from Guerrero Negro and López Mateos. The whales most commonly seen are the blue, grey, and humpback.

➔ Sea-kayaking trips range from week-long wilderness expeditions suitable for families with adventurous teenagers to shorter excursions based at Espíritu Santo island in the Sea of Cortéz for children as young as 6 (sharing a double kayak with a parent).

Spouts in Baja

Blue whale (max length: 34 m) Produces a tall column of spray rising to 9 m or more.
Grey whale (max length: 15 m) Blow is often heart shaped, reaching a height of 4.5 m.
Humpback whale (maximum length: 19 m) A dense and bushy blow that can rise to 3 m.

youngsters will go pop-eyed over scenes of eagles ripping hearts from human victims.

Tulum

Within a day's range of Cancún and perched on the edge of the ocean, the clifftop ruins of Tulum are best visited in the early morning when sunlight rakes the walls of this coastal Mayan city. Tulum is smaller than Chichén Itzá and the carvings aren't as gruesome, making it a better bet for younger children.

Xel-Ha

Just 13 km from Tulum, Xel-Ha is a Mayan-themed water park. Based around natural creeks, lagoons, caves and forests, it offers everything from swimming with dolphins and snorkelling to jungle walks and a 5-m cliff jump.

Chiapas

If you want jungle and living colour, head for Chiapas, Mexico's most indigenous state, one whose folklore and traditions will dazzle children of all ages while parents marvel at its crafts on display in almost every village.

How big is your footprint?

The travel industry is growing rapidly, and increasingly the impact is becoming apparent. It may seem minor to someone on a trip or holiday but it is anything but that. Air travel has been implicated in global warming and damage to the ozone layer, while resort development can destroy natural habitats and restrict traditional rights and activities. Individual choice and awareness can and does make a difference in many instances; collectively, travellers can have a significant impact in helping shape more responsible travel and hospitality industries.

Travel can have beneficial impacts to which every traveller can contribute, and there has been a phenomenal growth in tourism that promotes and supports the conservation of natural environments, and which is also fair and equitable to local communities. This 'eco-tourism' segment now provides a growing range of destinations and activities in Mexico.

There is much the individual can do to support to Mexico's gradual turn towards more eco-friendly travel. One obvious approach is simply to patronize the growing number of agencies, hotels and tour guides that are eco-conscious themselves (the majority are still found along the coasts, but their numbers are increasing elsewhere in Mexico as well). Apart from this, most businesses are eager to attract more visitors from abroad, and many will welcome a suggestion (if easily implemented) that would make their hotel, shop or site more environmentally conscious, especially if it is underscored that making the switch will attract those visitors looking especially for specifically eco-friendly venues.

RICHARD ARGHIRIS

A traditional dance from the Isthmus of Tehuantepec, Oaxaca, where folkloric customs remain robust.

Responsible travel

Perfect ecotourism would ensure a good living for local inhabitants, while not detracting from their traditional lifestyles, encroaching on their customs, or spoiling their environment. Perfect ecotourism may not exist yet, but everyone can play their part. Here are a few points worth bearing in mind:

▸▸Choose a destination, tour operator or hotel with a proven ethical and environmental commitment.

▸▸Spend money on locally produced goods and services and use common sense if bargaining: your few dollars saved may be a week's salary to others.

▸▸Use water and electricity carefully: travellers may receive preferential supply while the needs of local communities are overlooked.

▸▸Consider staying in local accommodation rather than foreign-owned hotels: the economic benefits for host communities are far greater, and there are greater opportunities to learn about local culture.

▸▸Protect wildlife and other natural resources; don't buy souvenirs or goods unless they are made from materials that are clearly sustainably produced and are not protected under CITES legislation..

▸▸Learn about local etiquette and culture; consider local norms and behaviour and dress appropriately for local cultures and situations.

▸▸Always ask before taking photographs or videos of people.

▸▸Make a voluntary contribution to counter the pollution caused by international air travel. Climate Concern calculates the amount of carbon dioxide you generate, and then offsets it by funding projects that reduce it; visit www.co2.org. Alternatively, you can offset CO2 emissions from air travel through Climate Care's CO2 reduction projects, www.climatecare.org.

Grey whales at Guerrero Negro, Baja California.

Mexico on page and screen

Books to read

Poems by **Sor Juana Inés de la Cruz**, a 17th-century nun and scholar, make for a beautiful read. For a good insight into the Mexican Revolution try *Los de abajo* (*The Underdogs*) by **Mariano Azuela** and the fascinating novel *Hasta no verte, Jesús mío* (*Here's to You, Jesus*) by **Elena Poniatowska**, based on her interviews with an elderly eccentric woman who took part in the fighting in her youth. Two of **Graham Greene**'s books, *The Lawless Road* and *The Power and the Glory* also depict Mexico shortly after the Revolution and during the Cristeros Rebellion. A later book using the Revolution as a dramatic backdrop, is **Laura Esquivel**'s *Like Water for Chocolate*. Published in 1989, this is a love story with a culinary bent, depicting traditional Mexican life from a time gone by. **Juan Rulfo** captures the Mexican landscape in his classic novel *Pedro Páramo*, considered an early magical realist work. Contemporaries **Octavio Paz** and **Carlos Fuentes** have both written extensively about *mexicanidad,* or what it means to be Mexican. The topic of the murky workings of Mexican politics are often touched upon by male writers, but **Angeles Mastretta** bravely ventures where few Mexican women writers have gone before in *Arráncame la vida* (*Tear this Heart Out*). **Malcolm Lowry**'s superb contribution to Mexico-inspired literature, *Under the Volcano*, tells the tragic story of an expat drinking himself to death on Day of the Dead. For insightful and original reading on Mayan history and culture, check out the excellent works of **Linda Schele**.

Films to watch

To find out more about Mexico's Golden Age of Cinema from the 1940s and 50s, take a look at any of the films with Mario Moreno as *Cantinflas*, a comic Chaplinesque character. From the same era are the films by Spanish director Luis Buñuel who spent a number of years in Mexico, making some 20 films during his stay. Particularly compelling viewing is his 1950 feature film *Los Olvidados*, about Mexico City street children. María Novaro's two films, **Lola** (1989) and **Danzón** (1991) show sides of Mexico otherwise little explored in film. Many films from the 1990s have made it internationally, particularly **Como agua para chocolate** (**Like Water for Chocolate**) (1992). It explores the relationship between love, food and duty amongst women in the Mexican Revolution. **El callejón de los milagros** and **Cronos** are two other successful films from the early 90s. Other more recent quality Mexican films include **Amores perros**, **Y tu mamá también** and more recently, **Frida**. In 2009, **Sin nombre** (Without a Name) was released to critical acclaim for its depiction of the challenges facing those who try to cross illegally into the United States. Many great Westerns have also been shot in Mexico, with Sam Peckinpah's **The Wild Bunch** winning on style and power. Perhaps the best way to get to grips with Mexico and the Mexicans on screen is to watch any of the many *telenovelas*, Mexican soap operas.

Contents

Essentials

Getting there

All visitors to Mexico are officially required to have an onward or return ticket. Although rarely enforced, this regulation can create problems. An onward ticket out of any Latin American country may suffice, or proof that you have sufficient funds to buy a ticket (eg a credit card) will often be accepted. International air tickets are expensive if purchased in Latin America.

Air

Buying a ticket

The most expensive fares from Europe and North America correspond to the northern hemisphere holiday season. Peak seasons are 7 December to 15 January and July to mid-September. If you intend travelling during those times, book as far ahead as possible. Check with an agency for the best deal.

The market is highly competitive, with a wide range of offers. Check with discount flight agents and ticket agents listed on page 36, as well as checking the airline websites. Many airlines share passengers across different routes, so you may find that you fly the transatlantic leg with one airline before changing to a different airline for the final leg.

Long-term trips Given the choice, those travelling for several months prefer to leave the return leg of a ticket open in terms of date and departing airport, because they do not know where they will end up. In reality this is not a good idea. Two one-way tickets are more expensive than a return and purchasing a ticket within Mexico is almost always more expensive than it would be from your home country. If you have a return ticket you can normally change the date and often the airport at local travel agents (at a charge).

Discounted fares Most airlines offer discounted fares on scheduled flights, available only through specialist agencies. As a rough guide, a three-month London–Mexico return in August costs approximately £640. In November the same flight falls to £495. Prices from mainland Europe are similar or cheaper, if using a low-cost airline such as **Martinair** or **Iberia**. Flying into one place and out of another can be very useful (eg arriving in Mexico City and leaving from Cancún) but usually costs extra. Deals from Australia and New Zealand have improved in recent years, with special offers occasionally down to AUS$1900 for direct flights to Mexico City, but usually averaging around AUS$3200.

If you buy discounted air tickets always confirm the reservation direct with the airline to make sure the flight still exists. Remember that airlines' schedules change in March and October each year, so double check your return flight. It is also vital to check in advance whether you are entitled to any refund or re-issued ticket if your discounted air ticket is lost or stolen.

Excursion fares These have a restricted validity of either seven to 90 days, or seven to 180 days, depending on the airline. They are fixed-date tickets where the dates of travel cannot be changed after issue without incurring a penalty.

Yearly fares These may be bought on a one-way or return basis, and usually the returns can be issued with the return date left open. You must, however, fix the route.

Packing for Mexico

Take as little as possible. Clothes that are quick and easy to wash and dry are a good idea. Loose-fitting clothes are better in hot climates. Sarongs are versatile: they can be used as a towel, beach mat, skirt, sheet, or scarf, to name but a few. Four musts are good walking shoes, a sun hat, sunglasses and flip-flops or sandals.

In the highlands it can be cold at night, especially in winter, and most hotels do not have heating. Cheaper hotels often provide only one blanket and, while they will provide a second if available, a light sleeping bag that packs up small can be useful. This applies in popular tourist centres such as San Cristóbal de las Casas and Pátzcuaro. If travelling on air-conditioned buses keep warm clothes and a blanket with you, especially if travelling overnight.

Don't load yourself down with toiletries. They're heavy and can be found cheaply and easily. Items like contact lens solutions and tampons may be harder to find outside of major cities.

Probably the most useful single item is a Swiss Army knife (with corkscrew), followed by a money belt, a headtorch/flashlight (many Mexican streets and stairways are poorly lit), a small alarm clock and a basic medical kit.

Take photocopies of essential documents like passport, visas and traveller's cheque receipts. A small padlock is useful for locking up your bag, and the doors of some of the more basic hotels. A karabiner can be handy for clipping your bag on to something.

Those with digital cameras will want to find a way of clearing the camera memory eg by burning to CD or downloading to a website. You'll also need to take recharging gear and related adaptors.

Student (or under-26) fares One way and returns are available, or 'open jaws' (see below). There is also a wider range of cheap one-way student fares originating in Latin America than can be bought outside the continent. There is less availability in the busy seasons and some airlines are flexible on the age limit, others are strict.

Open-jaw fares For people intending to travel a linear route and return from a different point from that which they entered, there are 'open-jaw' or multi-stop flights, which are available on student, yearly, or excursion fares.

E-tickets These are increasingly common. If you are unsure about the use of an e-ticket, telephone the company concerned. If you can't locate a telephone number to call, it's probably best not to book with the company; if you find yourself stuck somewhere, you'll want to talk to a person – not a machine.

Flights from Europe

Fares to Mexico City between February and June can be very low. Most European airlines have a regular weekly service to the capital throughout the year so it is worth considering the capital as an entry/exit point. If you do not stop over in Mexico City, low-cost add-ons are available to Mexican domestic destinations through links with the main airlines.

With the promotion of Cancún as a gateway from Europe, there has been an increase in the number of scheduled flights (**Iberia** flies daily from Madrid and Barcelona to Cancún via Miami; **Air France/American Airlines** flies daily from Paris to Cancún; **Condor Flugdienst** flies from Frankfurt once a week to Cancún, **British Airways** operates a daily flight from London Gatwick to Cancún via Dallas Fort Worth). If starting in the USA and crossing Mexico's northern border, flights can be surprisingly cheap if you get a special offer linking with one of the US international carriers.

Flights from North America

As you might expect, there is a huge range of flights from the USA, with connections to almost 30 Mexican cities. The main carriers (**American Airlines**, **Continental** and **United**) offer daily flights to Mexico City, Guadalajara, Cancún, Monterrey and Puerto Vallarta, as well as less regular flights to other Mexican cities. Direct flights to Mexico are available from Miami, Dallas/Fort Worth, Los Angeles and San Francisco, as well as a number of other US cities.

From Canada the options are less varied, but there are direct flights from Montreal and Toronto, as well as regular flights from other main cities. Keep an eye out for special offers, which can be extremely good value (often at very short notice).

Flights from Latin America

Flight connections from Latin America have improved in recent years. Central America is covered by the **TACA** network, connecting the capitals of each country to Mexico City and some of the smaller regional cities. In South America, connections are to capitals and major cities. If planning a trip to Cuba there are flights from Cancún, Mérida and Mexico City with **Mexicana** and **Cubana**.

Flights from Australia and New Zealand

Flights to Mexico and Central America from Australia and New Zealand are with **United Airlines** and generally connect through Los Angeles.

Ticket agents and airlines

Airline websites are useful for information but are unlikely to offer the best price.

Airlines → *For a full list of airline websites visit www.evasions.com/airlines1.htm.*
AeroMéxico, www.aeromexico.com.
Air France, www.airfrance.com.
Alaska Airlines, www.alaskaairlines.com.
Alitalia, www.alitalia.com.
American Airlines, www.aa.com.
Avianca, www.avianca.com.
British Airways, www.britishairways.com.
Condor, www.condor.de.
Continental, www.continental.com.
Copa, www.copaair.com.
Cubana, www.cubana.cu.
Delta, www.delta.com.
Iberia, www.iberia.com.
Japan Airlines, www.jal.com.
KLM, www.klm.com.
LanChile, www.lanchile.com.

Lufthansa, www.lufthansa.com.
Martinair, www.martinair.com.
Mexicana, www.mexicana.com.
Northwest, www.nwa.com.
Qantas, www.qantas.com.au.
Taca, www.taca.com.
United, www.united.com.
Varig, www.varig.com.

Mexican low-cost airlines
Interjet, www.interjet.com.mx.
MexicanaClick, www.clickmexicana.com.
Mexicanalink, www.mexicana.com.
VivaAerobus, www.vivaaerobus.com.
Volaris, www.volaris.com.mx.

Web resources
www.expedia.com
www.lastminute.com
www.opodo.com
www.orbitz.com
www.priceline.com
www.travelocity.com

Discount flight agents
In the UK
Journey Latin America, 12-13 Heathfield Terrace, London, W4 4JE, T020-8747 8315, www.journeylatinamerica.co.uk.

South American Experience, Welby House, 96 Wilton Rd, Victoria, London, SW1V 1DW, T0845-277 3366, www.southamerican experience.co.uk.

STA Travel, T0871-230 0040, www.statravel. co.uk. 45 branches in the UK. Low-cost student/ youth flights and tours, student ID cards.

Trailfinders, 194 Kensington High St, London, W8 7RG, T020-7938 3939, www.trailfinders.com.

Rest of Europe
Die Reisegalerie, Grüneburgweg 84, 60323 Frankfurt, Germany, T069-9720 6000, www.reisegalerie.com.

Images du Monde, 14 rue Lahire, 75013 Paris, France, T033-1-4424-8788, www.imagenes-tropicales.com. Also has an office in Costa Rica.

Thika Travel, Kerkplein 6, 3628 AE, Kockengen (gem Breukelen), Holland, T0346-242526, www.thika.nl.

North America
Air Brokers International, 685 Market St, Suite 400, San Francisco, CA 94102, T01-800-883 3273, www.airbrokers.com.

Discount Airfares Databases Online, www.etn.nl/discount.htm. Discount agent links.

Exito Latin American Travel Specialists, 108 Rutgers Av, Fort Collins, CO 80525, T1-800-655 4053, www.exito-travel.com.

STA Travel, T1-800-781 4040, www.statravel. com. Branches throughout USA and Canada.

Travel CUTS, 187 College St, Toronto, ON, M5T 1P7, T1-888-359 2887, www.travelcuts. com. Student discount fares.

Australia and New Zealand
Flight Centres, 82 Elizabeth St, Sydney 2000, T133-133, www.flightcentre.com.au; Unit 3, 239 Queen St, Auckland, T0800-243544, www.flight centre.co.nz. Also in other towns and cities.

STA Travel, 841 George St, Sydney, T02-9212 1255, www.statravel.com.au; 267 Queen St, Auckland, T0800-474-400. Also in major towns and university campuses.

Trailfinders, 8 Spring St, Sydney, NSW 2000, www.trailfinders.com.au, T1300-780-212.

Travel.com.au, 76-80 Clarence St, Sydney, T1300-130483, www.travel.com.au.

Airport information
There are several international airports; the busiest are **Mexico City** (see page 70) and **Cancún** (see page 718). **Puerto Vallarta** (see page 494) and **San José del Cabo** (see page 237) are increasingly popular. Air passes are often bought in conjunction with international flights so ask when booking if planning internal flights, see page 40. Make sure you fill in the immigration document before joining the queue to have your passport checked.

As a general rule, try to avoid arriving at night. If that's not possible, book a hotel for the first night and take a taxi or shuttle bus direct to your hotel. It may not be the cheapest way out of the airport, but it is the simplest and safest. Both Cancún and Mexico City airports have tourist information offices, car hire facilities, bus connections, taxis and, in the case of the capital, metro links. For more information see the Ins and outs section of individual chapters. Smaller international airports, which tend to serve a handful of US destinations only, may have fewer facilities, but you should at least be able to flag a taxi to the nearest city centre.

Departure tax This is currently US$40 on international flights (dollars or pesos accepted); always check when purchasing if departure tax is included in ticket price. A sales tax of 15% is payable on domestic plane tickets bought in Mexico.

Main border crossings

To USA
San Diego, **Otay Mesa**, **Tecate**, **Calexico**, **Andrade** in California for Baja California, page 200.
San Luis, **Lukeville**, **El Sásabe**, **Nogales** and **Douglas** in Arizona, see page 243, for northwest Mexico.
El Paso and **Presidio** in Texas and **Columbus** in New Mexico, see page 279, for the northern highlands.
Eagles Pass, **Laredo** and **Brownsville** in Texas, see page 319, for northeast Mexico.

To Guatemala
La Mesilla, **Tecún Umán** and **Talismán**, see page 670.

To Belize
Chetumal, see page 732.

Weight allowances

If flying direct from Europe, the allowance is generally 22 kg for economy and business class or 30 kg for first class. From the USA, the allowance is two bags of up to 32 kg each. Certain carriers (for example **Iberia**, **Air France**) also offer this two-piece allowance out of the UK. Weight limits for internal flights are often lower, so it's best to enquire beforehand.

Boat

Travelling by boat to the region is really only worth considering if you are shipping a vehicle from Europe or the USA. In the UK, **Strand Voyages** has information on occasional one-way services to the Gulf of Mexico from Europe. Cruise ships also ply the waters with major ports on both the Pacific and Atlantic coasts. But given the transitory nature of cruises, you will rarely disembark for more than a day or so.

In Europe
The Cruise People, 88 York St, London, W1H 1QT, T020-772 -2450, www.cruisepeople. co.uk. Also at 1252 Lawrence Av East, Suite 210, Toronto, Canada M3A 1C3, T416-444 2410.
SGV Reisenzentrum Weggis, Globoship, Rütligasse 3, CH-6000 Luzern 7, Switzerland, T+41-248 0048, www.frachtschiffreisen.ch.
Strand Voyages, 357 Strand, London, WC2R OHS, T020-7010 7990, www.strandtravel.co.uk.

In the USA
Freighter World Cruises, 180 South Lake Av, Suite 340, Pasadena, CA 91101-2655, T1-800-531 7774, www.freighterworld.com.
Travltips Cruise and Freighter Travel Association, PO Box 580188, Flushing, New York 11358, T1-800-872 8584, www.travltips.com.

Road

From the USA

There are a multitude of entry points from the USA, the main ones being **Tijuana**, **Nogales**, **Ciudad Juárez**, **Piedras Negras**, **Nuevo Laredo** and **Matamoros**. Details are provided in the relevant chapters. Where you cross may depend on where you wish to end up, as each entry point offers highway access to different parts of the country.

Crossing the border is simple and hassle-free for foot passengers and reasonably straightforward for people travelling with their own vehicle. All border towns have bus terminals with long-distance services. **Greyhound**, www.greyhound.com, runs services from border towns or from towns within the USA, such as Los Angeles or even Chicago.

If you are thinking of travelling from your own country via the USA, or of visiting the USA after Latin America, you are strongly advised to find out about any requirements from a US consulate in your own country before travelling. Although visa requirements for air travellers with round-trip tickets to the USA have been relaxed, it is advisable to have a visa to allow entry by land, or on airlines from South and Central America which are not participating carriers on the 'visa waiver' scheme. Since January 2009, new regulations also require you to register for your visa waiver in advance of travel. Consult the US Department of Homeland Security's online **Electronic System for Travel Authorization (ESTA)**, http://cbp.gov/xp/cgov/travel/id_visa/esta.

From Central America

Guatemala The main border town is **Tapachula**, with a crossing over the Talismán Bridge or at Ciudad Hidalgo. A more interesting route is via **Ciudad Cuauhtémoc** or heading northwest from Santa Elena/Flores towards **Tenosique**. There are also options for road and river travel.

Belize The border crossing at Santa Elena is near **Chetumal**, where public transport can be arranged. A very quiet and more challenging crossing is at **Blue Creek**. Be aware that Central American border towns can be considerably more feisty than their North American counterparts – take care, especially with money changers, who tend to inundate anyone who crosses their path. In addition to exit fees, unofficial 'taxes' may also be levied against you by border officials, but are rarely very high.

Getting around

It may sound obvious but Mexico is larger than many people realize. Be realistic about distances. Travelling from Tijuana to Cancún non-stop by bus takes at least three days and costs US$280-350. If time is short, an internal flight might not work out much more expensive once factors such as food and recovery time have been taken into account.

That said, bus travel remains the most popular style of transport for independent travellers in Mexico. An excellent network criss-crosses the region varying in quality from luxurious intercity cruisers with air conditioning, videos and fully reclining seats, to beaten-up US-style school buses or 'chicken buses'. Travelling under your own steam is very common too. Driving your own vehicle – car, camper van, motorbike and bicycle – offers wonderful freedom and may not be as expensive or as bureaucratic as you think.

Generally, getting around in Mexico is rarely a problem whatever your chosen mode of transport. There is just one caveat that stands good across all situations: be patient when asking directions. Often Mexicans will give you the wrong answer rather than admit they do not know. Distances are notoriously inaccurate so ask a few people.

Air

Most medium-sized towns have an airport and Mexico has an extensive domestic flight service. Prices vary but it is worth considering an aerial 'hop' if it covers a long distance and you get the bonus of a good view. If you know the outline of your itinerary, it is often cheaper to book internal flights before you arrive in the country.

Air passes

If you're looking to cover a great distance in a short time air passes can offer good value. The **Mexipass**, offerered by **Mexicana**, covers much of the country and is valid for three to 90 days. It is available only to those arriving on transatlantic flights and must be purchased before arrival in Mexico. Fares range from US$50-400 per coupon; extra coupons may be bought and reservations may be changed. Several other airlines offer internal routes (a few with international flights as well), including **Aeromar**, **Aeroméxico Connect**, **Taesa**, and **Aviacsa**. You could also consider the **All-America Airpass**, with 27 participating airlines from the USA, the Caribbean, Central and South America. These passes must be purchased in conjunction with an international air ticket.

Low-cost airlines

Toluca's **Adolfo López Mateos International Airport** (see page 155), 64 km west of Mexico City, is the central hub for the low-cost airlines. You get the bargain if you can book ahead, travel at inconvenient times or if there is a special offer. Airlines providing services to different parts of Mexico include: **Interjet** (www.interjet.com.mx), Mexicana Airline's **Mexicana Click** (www.clickmexicana.com), **VivaAerobus** (www.vivaaerobus.com) and **Volaris** (www.volaris.com.mx).

Road

Bus → *Buses are often called camiones, hence 'Central Camionero' for bus station.*

The Mexican bus system is good, but at times complicated and confusing. When buying tickets you may be confronted with a daunting range of options, sometimes leaving from different terminals. There is normally a bus going from where you are to where you want to go. The problem is trying to locate where that bus leaves from. In some cities there is a central bus terminal (in Mexico City there are four – one at each point of the compass broadly serving their respective areas), in others there are separate bus terminals for first and second class. Many first-class bus stations (but not all) are located on the outskirts of town; local buses often depart from markets. A third variation is division by companies.

Bus travel can use up a lot of your budget because the distances covered are great. As a very rough calculation bus travel works out at around US$4.80 per hour spent travelling, depending on the level of competition on the route.

Bus services are generally organized, clean and prompt. Services range from luxury to first and second class. However, travellers should not be beguiled into thinking that it is necessary to purchase an expensive ticket in order to travel comfortably. The service varies greatly between routes. A journey between two cities will almost certainly have a luxury service; a short trip between villages may be on a battered old bus.

The superior classes, **Primera Plus** and **Ejecutiva**, may offer extra services such as reclining seats, toilets, drinks, videos, etc. **ETN** has exceptional buses with very comfortable extra- wide seats but prices are 35-40% more than regular first class. The superior classes are probably best for journeys of more than six hours. **First-class** buses are also comfortable and have reclining seats, toilets and videos. **Second-class** buses may not be available for long-distance routes; they are often antiques (interesting, but frustrating when they break down) and call at towns and villages and go up side roads that the first-class route passes.

In general, it is a good idea to take food and drink with you on a long bus ride, as stops may depend on the driver. When a bus stops for refreshment, remember who your driver is and stay nearby; in busy terminals memorize your bus number so you don't miss it when it leaves. On daytime journeys consider whether you want to see the scenery or a video. If going on an overnight bus, book seats at the front as toilets can get smelly by morning. Also make sure you have a jacket, jumper or blanket to hand as the air conditioning can be very cold at night.

Buses to the Yucatán Peninsula are best booked in advance, especially around Christmas. Bus seats throughout the country are particularly hard to get during school holidays, August and the 15 days up to New Year when many public servants take holidays; transport from Mexico City is booked up early, as are hotels. On intercity services luggage is checked into the hold of the bus and you are provided with a receipt, which offers a degree of security. Always check that your bags are on the right bus.

Inside the bus, lock or clip your luggage to the rack with a cycle lock and chain. Luggage racks on both classes of long-distance bus are spacious and will take a rucksack with a little persuasion.

Fares First-class fares are usually 10% more expensive than second-class ones and the superior classes are even more. On a long journey you can save the price of a hotel room by travelling overnight, but this can sometimes carry risks – check locally on the safety situation before setting out. Look out for special offers, including discounts at some hotel chains. If you do decide to travel at night it may be best to avoid luxury tourist buses that make you a target for thieves, or second-class buses that forgo toll highways and wind through the countryside.

Useful bus links
Information and some bus tickets are available from **Ticketbus**, T01-800-702 8000, www.ticketbus.com.mx.
ADO GL, T01-800-702 8000, www.adogl. com.mx. The Yucatán, southeast, Gulf and northeast Mexico.
Cristóbal Colón, T01-800-702 8000. South of Mexico City. Details on the Ticketbus system.
ETN, www.etn.com.mx, T01-800-8000-386.
Estrella de Oro, T01-800-900 0105, www.estrelladeoro.com.mx. Southwest of Mexico City.

Green Tortoise, www.greentortoise.com. Trips throughout Mexico. Particularly useful if travelling from north of the border.
Grupo Estrella, T01-800-507 5500, www.estrellablanca.com.mx. Covers most of Mexico using several companies.
Omnibus, T01-800-965 6636, www.odm.com.mx. North of Mexico City.
Primera Plus, T01- 800-375 7587, www.primeraplus.com.mx . Mid-central to southern Mexico.
UNO, T01-800-702 8000, www.uno.com.mx. North of Mexico City.

Car
Permits Vehicles may be brought into Mexico on a **Tourist Permit** for 180 days each year. The necessary documents are: passport, birth certificate or naturalization papers;

tourist card; vehicle registration (if you do not own the car, a notarized letter from the vehicle's owner or the hire company is necessary); and a valid international or national driving licence. The original and two photocopies are required for each document. It takes 10 days to extend a permit, so ask for more time than you need. Don't overstay; driving without an extension incurs a US$50 fine for the first five days, rising to half the value of the car. A permit costs US$16.50, payable only by credit card (Visa, MasterCard, American Express or Diners Club), not debit card, in the name of the car owner, as recorded on the vehicle registration. The **American Automobile Association (AAA)** issues Tourist Permits for 'credit card' entry (free to members, US$18 non-members); in California this service is available only to members. If you do not have a credit card, you have to buy a bond in cash to the value of the vehicle according to its age (a set scale exists), which is repaid on leaving Mexico. The bond is divided into two parts, the bond itself and administration; the latter, accounting for about 43% of the total cost, is retained by the authorities; the bond is refunded. The bond is issued by **Afianzadora Mexicana** at US/Mexican border crossings, or by **Sanborn's** (see Insurance, below). It may be waived if you are only going to the State of Sonora.

English versions of leaflets explaining the rules on temporary importation of vehicles state that you must leave at the same crossing by which you entered. The Spanish versions do not say this and in practice it is not important. The temporary importation permit is multiple entry for 180 days; within that period you can enter and leave by any crossing, and as often as you like. However, you must have a new tourist card or visa for each new entry. The Sanborn's website (www.sanbornsinsurance.com) is an excellent source of information.

On entry, go to **Migración** for your tourist card, on which you must state your means of transport. This is the only record of how you entered the country. At the **Banjército** desk sign an *Importación Temporal de Vehículos/Promesa de retornar vehículo*, which bears all vehicle and credit card details so that if you sell your car illegally your credit card account can be debited for the import duty. Next you purchase the *Solicitud de importación temporal*, which costs US$12; it bears a hologram that matches the dated sticker, which must be displayed on the windscreen or, on a motorcycle, on some safe surface. Then go to *Copias* to photocopy all necessary documents and papers issued. The sticker and other entry documents must be surrendered on departure. They can only be surrendered at a Mexican border crossing, with date stickers cancelled by **Banjército** at Immigration. If you neglect to do this, and re-enter Mexico with an expired uncancelled sticker on your car, you will be fined heavily for each 15-day period that has elapsed since the date of expiry. If you intend to return to Mexico within the 180-day period, having surrendered your sticker and documents, keep safe the *Importación Temporal de Vehículos* form and stamped *Cancelado*. If entry papers are lost there can be much delay and expense (including enforcement of the bond) in order to leave the country. **Banjército** offices at borders are open daily, some for 24 hours. Each vehicle must have a different licensed driver (ie you cannot tow another vehicle into Mexico unless it has a separate driver).

On arrival, you have to find the place where car permits are issued; this may not be at the border.

Insurance Foreign insurance will not be honoured in Mexico; you must double check that the company you insure with will settle accident claims inside Mexico. According to the latest official documents, insurance for foreign cars entering Mexico is not mandatory, but it is highly recommended. Arranging insurance when crossing from the USA is very easy as there are many offices at the border. Policy prices vary enormously between companies, according to age and type of vehicle. **Sanborn's Mexican Insurance Service** ① *head office: 2009 S 10th St, McAllen, TX 78505-0310, T956-686 0711, toll free T1-800-222 0158, www.sanbornsinsurance. com*, provides comprehensive full-year cover within Mexico and other parts of Latin America, and provides free 'travelogs' for Mexico and Central America with useful tips. It has offices in every US border town, and many more throughout the country. **Tepeyac** ① *information in Spanish at www.mapfretepeyac.com or through English-speaking agents T1-800-485 4075, www.mexadventure.com*, has offices in most Mexican cities, as well as at border towns and in the USA (eg San Diego).

Entering Mexico from Guatemala presents few local insurance problems thse days. **Tepeyac** (see above), has an office in Tapachula; or contact **Seguros La Provincial** ① *Av General Utrillo 10A, upstairs, San Cristóbal de las Casas; also at Av Cuauhtémoc 1217 ground floor, Sr García Figueroa, Cuauhtémoc, T5-604-0500*. Otherwise, try **Segumex** in Tuxtla Gutiérrez. In Mexico City, **Grupo Nacional Provincial** ① *Río de la Plata 48, T528-67732, www.gnp.com.mx*, has offices in many towns.

Petrol/diesel All *gasolina* is now unleaded. All petrol stations in Mexico are franchised by Petróleos Mexicanos (PEMEX) and fuel costs the same throughout the country (approximately US$0.65 a litre) except near the US border, where it may be a bit cheaper. Unleaded petrol is classified either as *magna*, from the green pumps, or the more expensive *premium*, from the red ones. Diesel is also available. Petrol stations are not self-service. Make sure the pump is set at zero before your tank is filled and that your filler cap is put back on before you drive off. Specify how much you want either in litres or in money; it is normal to give the attendant a small tip.

Assistance The free assistance service of the Mexican tourist department's green jeeps (**Angeles Verdes**) patrol many of Mexico's main roads. Call them toll-free on T01-800-903 9200; every state also has an Angeles Verdes hotline. The drivers speak English, are trained to give first aid, make minor auto repairs and deal with flat tyres. They carry spare fuel and have radio connection. All help is completely free, and you pay cost price for fuel and parts. Although the idea is great, few Mexicans rely on the service in outlying areas and your best bet is to keep your vehicle in good condition and carry out the usual regular checks. More information is available through angelesverdes@sectur.gob.mx.

Road tolls A toll is called a *cuota*, as opposed to a non-toll road, which is a *vía libre*. There are many toll charges and the cost works out at around one peso per kilometre. Check out your route, and toll prices, on the **Traza Tu Ruta** section of www.sct.gob.mx. Some new freeways bypassing city centres charge US$4-12, or more. Because of the high cost of toll roads, they are often quite empty, which means that good progress can be made. Some tolls can be avoided if you seek local or motoring club advice on detours around toll gates (or follow a truck). This may involve unpaved roads, which should not be attempted in the wet. However, the *carreteras libres* are normally perfectly acceptable and more interesting as they often travel through small towns and sometimes beautiful countryside.

In case of accident Do not abandon your vehicle. Call your insurance company immediately to inform it of the accident. Do not leave Mexico without first filing a claim in Mexico. Do not sign any contract or agreement without a representative of the insurance company being present. **Asemex** recommends that you should always carry the policy identification card and the names of the company's adjusters in the car. If anyone is injured or the drivers involved cannot agree who is at fault, the vehicles may be impounded. Drivers will be required to stay in the vicinity in cases of serious accidents, the insured being confined to a hotel (or hospital) until the claim is settled. A helpline for road accidents is available by phoning T02 and asking the operator to connect you to T55-5684 9715 or T55-5684 9761.

Warnings On all roads, when two vehicles converge from opposite directions, or when a vehicle is behind a slow cart, bicycle, etc, the driver who first flashes his lights has the right of way. This also applies when a bus or truck wishes to turn left across the opposing traffic: if the driver flashes his lights he is claiming right of way and the oncoming traffic must give way. At *Alto* (Halt) signs, all traffic must come to a complete stop. Avoid driving at night. Night-time robberies on vehicles are on the increase especially in Guerrero and Oaxaca states. 'Sleeping policemen' or road bumps can be hazardous in towns and villages as there are often no warning signs; they are sometimes marked *zona de topes*, or incorrectly marked as *vibradores*. In most instances, their distinguishing paint has worn away. Roadworks are usually well marked. If your vehicle breaks down on the highway and you do not have a warning triangle or a piece of red cloth to act as a warning, cut branches from the roadside and lay them in the road some distance in front of and behind your vehicle (remember to remove them when you move on).

If you are stopped by police in town for an offence you have not committed and you know you are in the right, do not pay the 'fine' on the spot. Take the policeman's identity number, show him that you have his number and insist on going to the tourist police headquarters to speak to the *jefe* (chief). It is also advisable to go to the precinct station whenever a fine is involved, to make sure it is genuine. If stopped in a remote area, it is not advisable to get into a dispute with a policeman; drugs may be planted in your vehicle or problems may occur. It may be best to pay the bribe, feign stupidity and act as friendly as possible. See also section on police, page 61.

Further information A useful source of advice (whose help we acknowledge here) is the **Recreation Vehicle Owner's Association of British Columbia (RVOABC)** ① *PO Box 73046, Evergreen RPO Surrey, BC, V3R 0J2,* T604-596 9788, *www.rvoabc.org*. Membership costs US$35 a year and members receive a copy of the *RV Times*; Mexican insurance can be arranged. There's a vast amount of information on the web, try www.rvbasics.com for starters. *RVing in Mexico, Central America and Panamá*, by John and Liz Plaxton (ITMB Publishing, Canada, 1996), has been recommended as full of useful information, although it can be difficult to get hold of.

Car hire Car rental is very expensive in Mexico, from US$35-45 a day for a basic model plus 15% sales tax. Rates will vary from city to city. At some tourist resorts, such as Cancún, you can pick up a VW Beetle convertible for US$25 per day. Make sure you have unlimited mileage. Age limit is normally at least 25 and you'll need to place a deposit, normally against a credit card, for damage. Renting a vehicle is nearly impossible without a credit card. It can be cheaper to arrange hire in the USA or Europe. Proceed with caution. It is twice as expensive to leave a car at a different point from the starting point than it is to make a round trip.

Bicycle

Mexico offers plenty of enjoyable places for cycling. The main problems facing cyclists are the heavy traffic that will be encountered on main roads, the poor condition of these roads and the lack of specialized spare parts, particularly for mountain bikes. It is possible to find most bike spares in the big cities, but outside these places it is only possible to find the basics: spokes, tyres, tubes, etc.

Traffic is particularly bad around Mexico City, although there are now plans to lay down dedicated cycle lanes. Consult the tourist office for information on routes. The easiest region for cycling is the Gulf of Mexico coast; many of the roads are dead flat, however they are straight and generally boring. The mountains may appear intimidating, but the road gradients are not too steep as the clapped-out buses and trucks have to be able to climb them. Consequently, much of the best riding is in the sierra. If cycling in Baja, avoid mid-summer; even during October temperatures can reach 45°C and water is always very scarce.

Toll roads are generally preferable to the ordinary highways for cyclists; there is less traffic, more lanes and a wide paved shoulder. Some toll roads have 'no cyclists' signs but the police tend to pay little attention. If you walk your bicycle on the pavement through the toll station you don't have to pay. If using the toll roads, take lots of water as there are few facilities. Cycling on some main roads can be very dangerous; it is useful to fit a rear-view mirror.

Richard's New Bicycle Book (Pan) makes useful reading for even the most mechanically minded. Also recommended is *Latin America by Bike – A Complete Touring Guide* by Walter Sienko (The Mountaineers, 1993). For a first-hand account of travelling through the entire region by bike, read *The Road That Has No End*, by Tim Travis (www.downtheroad.org). Tim and Cindie set out on a round world trip in 2002 and are still going; this book covers the stretch from Mexico to Panama.

The **Expedition Advisory Centre** ① *Royal Geographical Society, 1 Kensington Gore, London, SW7 2AR, T020-7591 3030, www.rgs.org*, publishes a booklet on planning a long-distance bike trip titled *Bicycle Expeditions*, by Paul Vickers (March 1990, available as a PDF from the website or £5 for a photocopy). In the UK, the **Cyclists' Touring Club (CTC)** ① *Parklands, Railton Rd, Guildford, Surrey, GU2 9JX, T0844-736 8450, www.ctc.org.uk*, has information on touring, technical information and discusses the merits of different types of bikes.

Motorcycle

Motorcycling is good in Mexico as most main roads are in decent condition and hotels are usually willing to allow the bike to be parked in a courtyard or patio. In major tourist centres, such as Acapulco, Puerto Vallarta or Cancún, motorbike parts are readily available as there are Honda dealers for bike and jet-ski rentals.

People are generally friendly to motorcyclists and you can make many friends. Buying a bike in the USA and driving down works out cheaper than buying one in Europe. When choosing a bike, make comfort a priority. The motorcycle should be off-road capable without necessarily being an off-road bike. A passport, international driving licence and bike registration document are required.

Security is not a problem in most countries. Try not to leave a fully laden bike on its own. A D-lock or chain will keep the bike secure. An alarm gives you peace of mind if you leave the bike outside a hotel at night. Look for hotels that have a courtyard or more secure parking and never leave luggage on the bike overnight or whilst unattended. Also take a cover for the bike.

Hitchhiking

Hitchhiking is usually easier for single hikers than for couples. It is generally quick, but not universally safe (seek local advice). Do not, for example, try to hitch in parts of Guerrero and Oaxaca states where even driving alone is not recommended. Yet in Baja California in some ways it is the best way to travel. In more out-of-the-way parts, short rides from village to village are usually the rule, so progress can be slow. Getting out of big cities is best done by taking a local bus out of town in the direction of the road you intend to take. Ask for the bus to take the *salida* (exit) to the next city on that road. It is very easy to hitch short distances, such as the last few kilometres to an archaeological site off the main road; offer to pay about US$0.50. Lone women (or even pairs of women) should not hitch under any circumstances. Also avoid hitching close to the US border.

Taxi

To avoid overcharging, the government has taken control of taxi services from airports to cities. Only those with government licences are allowed to carry passengers from the airport and you can usually buy a ticket with a set price to your destination from a booth at the terminal. No tipping is required for airport taxis, except when the driver handles heavy luggage or provides some extra service for you. The same system has been applied at bus stations but it is possible to pay the driver direct. Avoid flagging down taxis in the street at night in Mexico City. It is safer to phone for a *sitio* taxi from your hotel.

Sea

Sailing your own vessel

An increasing number of people are choosing to take advantage of the good-weather sailing and explore the Mexican coast by boat. There are dozens of marinas between Baja California, the Pacific Coast, the Gulf Coast and the Yucatán. A recommended guide to sailing in the region is *Mexico Boating Guide* by Captain Pat Rains (Point Loma Publishing, San Diego). The website www.centralamericanboating.com is also useful.

Train

The only official passenger services are the **Chihuahua-al-Pacífico**, between Los Mochis, Creel and Chihuahua, considered one of the world's greatest rail routes (see page 292), and the **Tequila Express**, a rather cutesy way of moving people from Guadalajara to Tequila so they can drink and not drive. However, some freight trains have passenger wagons – they just don't publish the schedules. If you have a great deal of time and patience and are train mad then you probably can travel through Mexico on trains. Services are said to be ridiculously cheap and stupidly slow – walking may be quicker. Reaching your destination is also likely to be more through luck and persistence than planning.

Maps

ITM, www.itmb.com, produces several maps including one covering all Mexico, Mexico City, Baja California, Mexico North West, Mexico South East, Yucatán Peninsula and a growing selection of regional road maps. The *Mexican Government Tourist Highway* map is free at tourist offices (when in stock). If driving from the USA you get a free map if you buy your insurance at **Sanborn's** in the border cities.

Guía Roji, www.guiaroji.com.mx, publishes a wide range of regional maps, city plans and gazettes, available at most bookshops and news-stands. The website has street, town, city and state search facilities for the entire country.

The **Dirección General de Oceanografía** ① *Calle Medellín 10, near Insurgentes metro station, Mexico City*, sells excellent maps of Mexico's coastline. Detailed state maps and country maps are available from **Dirección General de Geografía y Meteorología** ⓘ *Av Observatorio 192, México 18 DF, T55-5515 1527; Observatorio metro station, go up Calle Sur 114, turn right a short distance down Av Observatorio.* Maps are also available from **Instituto Nacional de Estadística, Geografía e Informática (INEGI)**, which has branches in Mexico City (see page 71) and in state capitals (US$3 per sheet). The **Pemex** road atlas, *Atlas de Carreteras y Ciudades Turísticas*, US$5 in bookshops, has 20 pages of city maps including contour lines, points of interest and service stations. It is rarely on sale in Pemex stations but recommended.

In the UK, an excellent source of maps is **Stanfords** ⓘ *12-14 Long Acre, Covent Garden, London, WC2E 9LP, T020-7836 1321, www.stanfords.co.uk, also in Bristol and Manchester.* Maps can be ordered online and an international delivery service is available.

Sleeping

Hotels and hospedajes

Hotel prices in the lower and middle categories are still very reasonable by US and European standards. Prices of top and luxury hotels have risen more steeply as tourism has increased. English is spoken at the best hotels and is increasingly common throughout Mexico. There is a hotel tax of 1-4%, according to the state, although it is generally levied only when a formal bill is issued.

During peak season (November to April) it may be hard to find a room. The week after Easter is normally a holiday, so resorts remain high, but resorts are not as crowded as the previous week. Discounts on hotel prices can often be arranged in the low season (May to October), but this is more difficult in the Yucatán and Baja California. For hotels in high price brackets it's worth checking their websites for any promotional deals or packages.

Rooms are normally charged at a flat rate, or if there are single rooms they are around 80% the price of a double. Couples should ask for a room with *cama matrimonial* (double bed), which is normally cheaper than a room with two beds. Costs tend to reduce with the number of people sharing a room, making Mexico an economical destination for groups. Always check the room and water supplies before paying in advance. Check-out time is commonly 1100 but bag storage is commonplace. Note that throughout this guide, the term 'with bath' usually means 'with shower and toilet', not 'with bath tub'.

A cheap but reasonable hotel might cost US$15 a night upwards in southern Mexico (away from the coast), US$20-25 in the north. In many of the popular destinations, there is often an established preferred choice budget option. The quality of these fluctuates. The good ones stay on top of the game, the mediocre ones fade and bloom with the fashions.

For those on a really tight budget, ask for a *casa de huéspedes* (boarding house); they are normally to be found in abundance near bus and railway stations and markets. The very cheapest hotels may not have 24-hour water supplies so wash when the water is available. They may be quite dirty too, so pack your own sheet if you intend to stay in a lot of these places (a duvet cover serves as a very good lightweight sleeping bag). Fleas, bedbugs, cockroaches and chirping geckos can all add to the experience!

Motels and auto-hotels, especially in central and south Mexico, are not usually places where guests stay the whole night (you can recognize them by curtains over the garage and red and green lights above the door to show if the room is free). If driving, and wishing to avoid a night on the road, they can be quite acceptable (clean, some have hot

Sleeping price codes

LL over US$200	**L** US$151-200	**AL** US$101-150
A US$66-100	**B** US$46-65	**C** US$31-45
D US$21-30	**E** US$12-20	**F** US$7-11
G under US$7		

Prices refer to the cost of a double room in high season.

water, air conditioning or even a jacuzzi), and they tend to be cheaper than other, 'more respectable' establishments. Beware of 'helpers' who try to find you a hotel, as prices quoted at the hotel desk rise to give them commission.

HostelTrail Latin America ① www.hosteltrail.com, is an online network of hostels and tour companies in Latin America providing up-to-date information for backpackers and independent travellers who pay particular attention to locally run businesses.

Youth hostels

Hostels in Mexico are very much on the increase covering private hostels and International Youth Hostel endorsed accommodation. *Albergues* exist in Mexico, mostly in small towns; they are usually good value and clean, although not necessarily cheaper than hotels, especially for couples. While the hostels take YHA members and non-members, members pay a slightly reduced rate; if staying more than four nights, it normally works out cheaper to become a member. Services vary from place to place. Hostels often have lockers for valuables. For information contact **Hostelling International Mexico** ① *Guatemala 4, Col Centro, Mexico City, T55-5518 1726, www.hostellingmexico.com.*

Many towns have a *Villa Deportiva Juvenil*. While these are essentially the Mexican equivalent of a youth hostel their main market is for groups of Mexican students who may, for example, be taking part in a regional event. It's worth looking out for the option as they are normally very cheap. But while some cater very well for the international traveller, others are barely interested.

Camping

Most sites are called trailer parks, but tents are usually allowed. However, due to their primary role as trailer parks they're often in locations more suited for people with their own transport than people using public transport. *Playas públicas*, with a blue-and-white sign of a palm tree, are beaches where camping is allowed. They are usually cheap, sometimes free and some have shelters and basic amenities. You can often camp in or near national parks, although you must speak first with the guards, and usually pay a small fee.

Paraffin oil (kerosene) for stoves is called *petróleo para lámparas* in Mexico. It is available from an *expendio* (general store), or *despacho de petróleo*, or from a *tlapalería* (hardware store), but not from petrol stations. Methylated spirits is called *alcohol desnaturalizado* or *alcohol del 96* and is available from chemists. Calor gas is widely available. *Gasolina blanca* (white gas) may be bought in *ferreterías* (ironmongers) or paint shops; prices vary widely, also ask for Coleman fuel. Alcohol for heating the burner can be obtained from supermarkets.

Eating and drinking

Food

Eating is a great pastime in Mexico and food is an integral part of the national identity: it's how people socialize, celebrate and do business.

Of all the Mexican staples, corn, or maize, is the most common and has been cultivated over millennia, probably originating in the Valley of Mexico. There are hundreds of dishes or snacks containing corn – *tortillas* being the most obvious. Tortillas are used as the base for myriad dishes; *tacos*, *burritos*, *enchiladas*, *tostadas*, *sopes* and *quesadillas* – anything can be neatly stuffed into the bread and eaten any time of day.

No tortilla is complete without a *salsa* (sauce); Most restaurants have at least two small bowls of salsa on every table. Most establishments and homes make their own salsas, so they are rarely found ready-bottled. *Salsa roja* is based on red tomatoes (*jitomates*) and *salsa verde* on green tomatoes (*tomates*). A basic salsa only contains four to five ingredients, but few taste the same. The secret is in the use of chillies, another Mexican staple that we've come to firmly associate with the nation's cuisine with hot and spicy dishes. This isn't strictly true, since there are some 300 different types of chillies and by no means all of them are hot.

Chillies can be used fresh, as well as dried, smoked, roasted or pickled to achieve different flavours. Some dishes, such as *mole* (see box, page 593), contain various types of chillies to get the balance of flavouring right, including *serrano*, *ancho* and *pasilla*. The best-known chilli internationally is the *jalapeño*, popular in pickled form.

Other staples include avocado-based *guacamole*, often served alongside salsas. *Frijoles*, the ubiquitous beans, usually refried, also accompany most meals any time of day. Rice dishes are often referred to as *sopa seca* (dry soup) along with any other dish that has been boiled in water or broth, such as pastas and risotto.

Mexicans like eating well and often; breakfast can be anything from coffee and a roll, to a full-blown meal of *huevos rancheros* (eggs with red chilli sauce), *chilaquiles* (day-old tortilla wedges smothered in red chilli sauce), *carne asada* (roasted meat) and of course tortillas and *frijoles*. Business breakfast meetings remain ever popular in Mexico and chain restaurants such as **Sanborns** and **Vips** do a brisk morning trade in the cities.

Then *almuerzo* (brunch or lunch) is a quick snack to keep you going until the main meal of the day: *la comida*. Traditionally *la comida* is a two-hour sit-down meal, eaten at home between 1400-1600. It involves three to four courses: the meal starts with a liquid soup, followed by a 'dry soup' of rice or pasta, the main dish (usually meat or fish) and finally a *postre* (dessert). In rural Mexico most people still return home for *la comida*, but in the cities where people often work far away from their abode, this is no longer possible. Many restaurants offer excellent value lunchtime specials: the *comida corrida* ('meal on the run').

La comida ought to set you up nicely for the rest of the day, but there is also a chance to have the *merienda*, in the late afternoon – a snack to fill the gap until *la cena* (supper) in the evening. This is usually a lighter meal than *la comida*, often just *recalentados* (leftovers) from the main meal of the day. Alternatively *antojitos* (snacks) – anything from a tiny taco, to a large *torta* – can be eaten anywhere, at anytime.

Up north you'll find Tex-Mex style cooking, such as *fajitas* and *nachos* and the tortillas tend to be wheat, rather than corn. Along the coasts there is excellent fish and seafood is abundant; hearty, warming stews and broths characterize the Central Highlands; and Yucatán has the hottest chillies (*habaneros*) and the best pork.

Eating price codes

🍴🍴🍴 over US$15   🍴🍴 US$8-15   🍴 under US$8

Prices refer to the cost of a two-course meal for one person, excluding drinks or service charge

Mexico can be rather heavy on the meat, so vegetarians fare less well, but it's still possible to get a good meal and vegetarianism is becoming better known, particularly in places on the tourist trail, such as the coasts, Oaxaca and San Cristóbal.

Modest establishments charge US$1.50-2.50 for breakfast, US$2.50-3.50 for set lunch (US$3-5 for a special *comida corrida*) and US$5-10 for dinner (generally no set menu). A la carte meals at modest establishments cost about US$5; a very good meal can be had for US$10 at a middle-level establishment. Much higher prices are charged by the classiest restaurants in Mexico City and some resorts. Some restaurants give foreigners the menu without the *comida corrida* (set meals), forcing them to order à la carte, often double the price. Street stalls and markets are by far the cheapest – although not always the safest – option and the best chance of trying local food. The best value is undoubtedly in small, family-run places. In resort areas hotels often include breakfast and dinner.

Drink

Mexican **beer** is well-known internationally and there are a number of brands that can easily be found in bars from Helsinki to Hong Kong, notably **Sol** and **Corona**. Other beers worth sampling include **Dos Equis-XX, Montejo, Bohemia, Superior** and **Tecate**. These are mostly light lagers, but there are also some dark beers, such as **Negra Modelo, Indio** and **Dos Equis Obscura**, although the latter can be harder to find. Beer is ever popular, easy to buy and usually relatively cheap. Some beer is drunk with lime juice and a salt-rimmed glass, or as a *michelada*, served with ice, lime, salt and chilli sauce.

Mexican **wine** is cheap and steadily improving in quality; try **Domecq, Casa Madero** or **Santo Tomás. LA Cetto's** wines have been recommended, including their Cabernet Sauvignon, Petite Sirah and Fumé. Some of the best wines produced in Mexico are those from Monte Xanic, produced near Ensenada, Baja California, but these can be expensive.

Although Mexicans love their beer, the nation is best known for its **spirits**. By far the best known, tequila, is made from the fermented juice of the blue agave in the state of Jalisco – originally in a village called Tequila, but now made across the state and in some neighbouring states. Tequila has become increasingly popular internationally, slowly shedding its image as a 'rough spirit', to be drunk for the sake of getting drunk. Instead more refined and aged (*añejo*) tequilas are reaching the market. It's possible to visit some of the distilleries on day trips from Guadalajara: **Sauza, Herradura** and **José Cuervo** are all open to the public.

Lagging behind somewhat in terms of worldwide popularity, mescal is a forerunner to tequila and also made from the agave plant, although not the blue agave. Chiefly produced in Oaxaca (see box, page 595), mescal has yet to be taken over by large-scale production and remains more low-key, although it is starting to attract international attention. In Oaxaca many bars and restaurants have their own brands sourced by local producers. Some of the younger mescals are an acquired taste. It's often these rougher

Chocolate

There is something very seductive about chocolate, whether as a hot drink, a simple bar or a scrumptious cake and all these tasty pleasures we have to thank the ancient Olmecs for. They lived in the area of present day Veracruz from 1500 BC to 400 BC and used the cacao bean in liquid form for hundreds of years. It is thought that chocolate was drunk for several millennia before anyone ever had the idea to try and munch some. The 'beans' are in fact the fleshy seed pods of the temperamental cacao tree, prevalent only in tropical zones, and it was these seed pods that the Olmecs fermented, dried, roasted and removed the skins from, in order to grind them and produce what we today know as cacao or cacao powder. The history of chocolate, stemming from the Nahuatl word *xocolatl*, is long and illustrious – after the Olmec civilization began to decline the habit of chocolate drinking was taken up by the Maya and subsequently by the Aztecs, who really took to the drink in an unprecedented manner. It was through the Aztecs that the conquering Spaniards were introduced to chocolate, but its bitterness was not to their taste and they started adding cane sugar and milk to sweeten it.

Although chocolate in Europe and many other parts of the world has become synonymous with something to eat, in Mexico it's still mostly considered something to drink. Oaxaca is famous for its chocolate drinks and in Chiapas the chocolate is flavoured with toasted corn and *achiote* (a paste made from annatto seeds, spices and chilli), to make *tescalate*, a popular beverage.

mescals that have the (in)famous *gusanito* (worm) added – originally a marketing ploy that worked a little too well, making the worm image somewhat hard to shed.

Pulque is another native brew made from the agave plant, well worth a try. The Aztecs were already making it when the Spaniards arrived and it's pretty potent, so go easy. Rum and brandy are cheap and plentiful, as is the distilled sugarcane spirit, *puro de caña*. The latter is known as *posh* in the southern state of Chiapas where it comes in various flavours (cinnamon and hibiscus flower are delicious). Most of these 'homebrew-style' spirits are drunk in *cantinas* – still firmly a male domain, particularly in rural Mexico. Although women often have a tipple at home during festivities and celebrations, it's mostly in the bigger cities and resorts that women are seen drinking in bars.

Among the **non-alcoholic drinks** (*refrescos*) are a number of international brand soft drinks as well as local ones. It often costs more to buy the bottle with the soft drink, so to safe money ask for a *bolsa con popote* (a plastic bag with a straw). Even more popular are the *aguas frescas* (fresh fruit juices), made with all sorts of fruits, such as mango, lime or watermelon. These are usually sold at street stalls or markets. Mineral water tends to be used, so they are mostly safe to drink, but take care and check the stalls for hygiene. *Licuados* (fruit juices mixed with milk, rather like a milkshake) are usually safe to drink.

Mexico is a great coffee-producing nation and particularly in the states of Oaxaca, Chiapas and Veracruz, excellent locally grown coffee can be had. *Chocolate*, another local product, drunk by the Aztecs with water and spices, is still the drink of choice for many, particularly in the highlands in winter. Other non-alcoholic beverages include *atole* (a corn-based hot drink) and *champurrado* (a chocolate *atole*). If there is a weak spot in Mexico's delicious selection of drinks, it's their tea and those who enjoy a nice cuppa would do well to bring their own tea bags, since good quality black tea can be hard to find. Herbal teas, such as chamomile and mint, on the other hand, are very good and readily available.

Festivals and events

The Mexican calendar is full of festivities – not only are there numerous national holidays, there are also all the local saints and heroes to be celebrated and there's hardly a month of the year that doesn't provide at least a couple of reasons for a full-scale, blow-out party of some sort. And that's not counting all the family festivities, weddings, baptisms, birthdays, first communion, saint's days, a girl's 15th birthday (traditionally celebrated as her coming of age) and many other occasions.

1 Jan A day of rest to recover from the excesses of the night before.

6 Jan Day of the Three Kings, commemorating the arrival of the Three Wise Men. This is traditionally when children get presents and also the day of the breaking of the qRosca cake, a sweet, plaited bread, containing a small doll depicting baby Jesus. The person who gets the doll in their piece of bread has to throw a party before 2 Feb, the next festive day.

2 Feb Día de la Candelaria, commemorates the presentation of Jesus in the temple 40 days after his birth. This is usually celebrated with processions and visits to church, more so in villages than in the bigger cities.

5 Feb Constitution Day is a more sombre and official affair.

14 Feb Valentine's Day, known as the 'Day of Love and Friendship', takes kitsch to new heights. Mexican love songs are crooned and any *zócalo* in any town is packed with couples holding hands.

End Feb/early Mar Carnival takes over Mexico, with a frenzied wild abandon. Parades, loud music, dancing and drinking until all hours takes place all over the country with Veracruz one of the best places to catch the action (see page 529).

21 Mar The nation celebrates the birthday of one of its most famous presidents, Benito Juárez. Some of the best commemorations are held in his state of birth, Oaxaca.

Mar/Apr Semana Santa, or Holy/Easter Week, is the biggest religious celebration after Christmas – a time for family get-togethers and feasting, but also of solemn contemplation, frequent visits to church, processions and ceremonies. Some of the best processions can be seen in Taxco (see page 167).

1 May Labour Day, celebrated across Mexico with workers' processions taking to the street.

5 May Cinco de Mayo, a very important day in the Mexican calendar, is the day the Mexican army defeated the French at the Battle of Puebla in 1862. This is a day to dress up in traditional costume and listen to Mariachi bands. There are even bullfights, now more popular in Mexico than in Spain, and an abundance of tasty food.

15-16 Sep El Día del Grito (The Day of the Cry) and **Independence Day**, respectively. The former refers to the cry of independence uttered by Miguel Hidalgo de Costilla on the eve of 15 Sep 1810. Right across Mexico people gather in town and village squares to shout "viva" for the heroes of the Independence at the top of their voices. The following day sees processions and parades, flag-waving, speech-giving and singing of patriotic songs in even the tiniest hamlet. It's the day to be proud to be Mexican and people come out in all their finery to take part in the festivities.

12 Oct Día de la Raza, or Columbus Day has traditionally been celebrated throughout Mexico, with schools commemorating Columbus and the discovery of America, but in later years indigenous groups have been protesting against this tradition, particularly since the 500th anniversary of the discovery, highlighting the plight of indigenous people across the Americas.

1-2 Nov All Saints' Day and Day of the Dead, belong to Mexico's most loved and well-known traditions. On the night between 1-2 Nov, families visit cemeteries to have a vigil at the graves of their ancestors. This is a night to commemorate those who have passed on, but also to feast with them on the one night of the year that they return to earth to be with their loved ones. It's a night of solemn ritual, where candles are lit at the graveyards, and flowers, food and drink are brought to the graves. There is a more light-hearted side to the festivity as well and as Nov approaches, all manner of skulls and skeletons start to appear in shops and markets; they're made of paper, clay or wood, but also of sugar, candy or chocolate. Traditionally, friends exchange skulls before the Day of the Dead.

20 Nov Revolution Day, commemorates the Mexican Revolution.

12 Dec Day of the Virgin of Guadalupe, Mexico's patron saint. This is best experienced in villages named after Guadalupe herself, where they really go to town on her day, or at the Basílica of Guadalupe in Mexico City, which can get extremely crowded. Processions with effigies of the Virgin take place through towns and villages and special masses are held. The celebrations culminate on 12 Dec, but in parts an entire week is dedicated to the Virgin and by the time the festivities are over people are well and getting into the spirit of Christmas.

16-24 Dec This time is taken up with the evening *posadas*, 9 nights of merry-making, re-enacting Joseph and Mary's search for shelter on the way Bethlehem. There are candlelit processions, where people go from house to house asking for shelter through songs, until they're eventually let in and much eating and drinking ensues. On the night of the last *posada*, **Christmas Eve**, people usually attend late Mass, before returning home for a lavish dinner and the opening of presents, leaving **Christmas Day** as a day of rest.

31 Dec **New Year's Eve**, is often a family occasion, with dinner at home. Traditionally you must eat one grape per bell chime at midnight, making a wish for each grape.

Shopping

Wandering around the colourful markets and *artesanía* shops is one of the highlights of any visit to Mexico. And the variety of wonderful folk art on offer is mind-boggling. A useful website promoting fair trade and sustainable production is www.bioplaneta.com.

Artesanía in Mexico is an amalgam of ancient and modern design. The stronger influence, however, is undoubtedly the traditional popular art forms of indigenous communities the length and breadth of the country, which pour into colonial towns such as Oaxaca, San Cristóbal, Pátzcuaro, and Uruapan. These are convenient market centres for seeing the superb range of products from functional pots to scary masks hanging over delicately embroidered robes and gleaming lacquered chests.

Almost everything can be found in Mexico City and most regional capitals have a *Casa de las Artesanías* with exhibitions, and sometimes sales, of local craftwork. But it is almost invariably cheaper to buy crafts away from the capital or major tourist centres, perhaps from the *artesanos* themselves. Bargaining is usually acceptable but don't push it for what, to you, is only a small amount of money. It is often rewarding to take the time to visit the villages where the designs were originally conceived and where the *artesanía* is still made. Here are some of the products on offer and their sites of making.

Ceramics

Ceramics are crafted out of baked clay or plaster and are polished or glazed or polychrome. Pot-making is usually done by women, although in some parts, such as Michoacán, men paint the pieces. Some of the best pots have a brilliant glaze such as the Patambán pottery found in Michoacán and on sale in Uruapan. The green finish comes from the oxidization of copper whilst its fragility comes from 'eggshell' thin clay working. Also outstanding is the *bandera* pottery of Tonalá (Jalisco) decorated in the Mexican national colours.

Another type of ceramic deals with daily events such as the fishermens' life in Tzintzuntzan near Pátzcuaro, whilst in Ocotlán de Morelos (Oaxaca) the brilliant colouring is linked to the Day of the Dead celebrations.

There are many unusual forms such as the pineapple-shaped Patambán pieces and the *árboles de vida* (trees of life) of Metepec (Estado de México). Cats are a speciality of Tonalá (Jalisco) whilst Ocumicho in Michoacán produces a range of fantastical animals. Ceramic dolls are made on the Isthmus of Tehuantepec.

Items such as candlesticks are sold in Izúcar de Matamoros and Puebla which also produces decorative ceramic tiles. Large porcelain vases are found in Tlaquepaque (Jalisco) and huge earthenware jars all over Guerrero and in Acatlán de Osorio (Puebla).

The finest china in Mexico, the Maiollica design or Talavera, imported from the Mediterranean, is made in Puebla and Guanajuato and a more practical black pottery is the speciality of San Bartolo Coyotepec (Oaxaca) and Dolores Hidalgo.

Lacquerware

Lacquerware, known as *maque* or *laca* is a more regionalized craft found in Chiapas, Guerrero and Michoacán. Prior to the Conquest its colouring was derived from naturally occurring pigments but since the Spanish arrived the decoration has been more artificial although more brightly coloured. Some pieces are even inlaid with gold.

In Chiapas the main centre of production is Chiapa de Corzo, where the speciality is a large cup made from the wood of the calabash tree and stippled with paint applied by fingertip. There is a lacquer museum in the town.

Olinalá is the focus of inspiration for *laca* in Guerrero and its influence spreads to other towns such as Temalacacingo, 20 km away, whilst the Sunday market in Chilapa is a good shopping opportunity. Specialities include large chests, boxes, furniture, toys and gourds shaped into fruit and animal figures. Michoacán has the most elaborate lacquer-work. Pátzcuaro craftsmen inlay gold to wardrobes, screens, trays and plates. Uruapan is also a good town for purchasing lacquer products.

Masks

Textile art is heavily influenced by religious ritual, particularly dances to master natural forces, but as well as being impressively robed, priests, witches and shamans are often masked in the guise of animals such as eagles, jaguars, goats, monkeys, and coyotes, particularly in the states of Guerrero (for example in Chilapa), Sinaloa, Sonora and Nayarit.

Such masks are made from cardboard, wire, wood, hide, tinfoil and other simple materials and decorated with thread, gems, mirrors and crystals. Besides animal spirit invocation, they could be related to fiestas such as the Day of the Dead (where the mask might be a cardboard skull or made of sugar), or burlesque, as at the carnival of Huejotzingo (Puebla) satirizing historical and political events specific to a region like the repulsion of the French invasion. At Tepoztlán, (Morelos), where a small pink mask with distorted features is surmounted by a huge hat, again the target is French intervention, this time under Maximilian.

Masks are also made in Paracho (Michoacán) and Tlaxcala state where the dancer is masked in the appearance of an old man. In Tlaxcala the mask is wooden, the face white and the moustache tiny. Crystal eyes peer out from behind huge eyelashes. At Papantla (Veracruz) black wooden masks stir up African spirits in magic ritual. Devil and clown masks are also commonly found. San Luis Potosí has the Museo Nacional de la Máscara (National Mask Museum), see page 384, and Morelia's Casa de la Cultura (see page 413) also has a collection.

Paper

The art of paper cutting and pasting, *papel picado*, flourishes seasonally around the time of the Day of the Dead celebrations, particularly profiles of dancing *calaveras* (skeletons). Papier mâché *calaveras* also spring up at this time. In pre-Hispanic times, paper was sacred as the material on which to record histories, cosmologies and social mores. Paper banners were used during religious festivals, and some sacrificial victims carried items of paper as they approached the sacrificial stone.

Silver and gold

Silver- and gold-work, known as *orfebrería*, can be found in Taxco and the markets in Mexico City. Jade jewellery is made in Michoacán while semi-precious stones such as onyx, obsidian, amethyst and turquoise are found in Oaxaca, Puebla, Guerrero, Zacatecas and Querétaro.

Textiles

Weaving and textile design has a long and varied lineage. The blouse, of pre-Hispanic origin, for instance, may be found in almost as many different cuts and colours as there are towns in Mexico. The comfortable loose shirt and poncho are ideally suited for hot days and coolish nights, but variations on this practical item of clothing have produced some classic, related, garment types, generally spun in cotton or wool on the traditional *telar de cintura*, a waist-high loom, or *telar de pie*, a pedal operated loom introduced by the Spanish.

The *huipil* is a blouse without sleeves, of varying length, depending upon the area. The best places to buy them are San Cristóbal and Tuxtla Gutiérrez (a white cloth). They are most famous in the towns of Tehuantepec (due to Frida Kahlo's paintings) where they are often a cherry red or black, decorated with large flowers or ribbons.

The *quechquémetl* is a diamond-shaped shirt worn by women that covers just the torso and is woven by indigenous groups in the mountains of Estado de México, Estado de Puebla (where the brocade is elaborately embroidered) and San Luis Potosí.

Ponchos come in two distinctive types: the *sarape*, which is a long garment, and the *jorongo*, which is shorter. They are found all over Mexico but the former is worn especially in the Valle de Oaxaca, where it is made in Santa Ana del Valle and Teotitlán del Valle (an elaborate cloak with Grecian designs, butterflies, suns, etc), and in San Luis Potosí. *Jorongos* from Tuxtla Gutiérrez are made from black wool.

The birthplace of the classic *rebozo*, a dress drawn at the waist and tassled at the hem, is Santa María del Río, south of San Luis Potosí, where it is a delicate silk garment often bought and stored in a small inlaid chest. A *rebozo* of very fine cotton is made in Tenancingo, 50 km south of Toluca, and in Teotitlán del Valle.

Old Spanish-style dresses are made in Chiapa de Corzo whilst various embroidered textiles, including belts and sashes, are elaborated in Cuetzalan (Puebla) and the famous *guayabera* shirt is sold in Mérida. Other specialist Yucateca products such as hammocks and *henequen* bags are covered in the relevant chapters.

There are many other woven items on sale in markets. Quite universal is the *morral*, or shoulder bag. Carpets, rugs and bedspreads are found around Oaxaca state.

Toys

Toy-making is an art in itself in Mexico and the toys aren't just playthings for children, but also small collectables enjoyed by adults. All sorts of materials are used – wood, paper, clay, tin – and many different types of toys are made. Among the most popular are puppets, dolls and pottery animals, as well as musical toys.

Essentials A-Z

Children

Travel with children can bring you into closer contact with Mexican families and generally presents no special problems. Always carry a copy of your child's birth certificate and passport photos. For an overview of travelling with children, visit www.babygoes2.com.

Customs and duty free

Adults entering Mexico are allowed to bring in up to 6 litres of wine, beer or spirits; 20 packs of cigarettes, or 25 cigars, or 200 g of tobacco and medicines for personal use. Goods imported into Mexico with a value of more than US$1000 (except computer equipment, where the limit is US$4000) have to be handled by an officially appointed agent. If you are carrying more than US$10,000 in cash you should declare it. There is no penalty but registration is required. Full details and latest updates are available at www.aduanas.sat.gob.mx.

Disabled travellers

Facilities for disabled travellers are severely lacking in Mexico. Most airports, hotels and restaurants in major resorts have wheelchair ramps and adapted toilets, but pavements can be in a poor state of repair and buses badly equipped. That said, most Mexicans are helpful and will be glad to lend a hand if they can.

Some companies specialize in holidays tailor-made for individuals depending on their level of disability. See the **Global Access-Disabled Travel Network Site**, www.globalaccessnews.com and read *Nothing Ventured*, edited by Alison Walsh (Harper Collins), with personal accounts of worldwide journeys by disabled travellers, plus advice and listings.

Dress

Casual clothing is adequate for most occasions although men may need a jacket and tie in some restaurants. Topless sunbathing is increasingly acceptable in parts of Baja California, but take guidance from others. Dress conservatively when visiting indigenous communities or churches.

Drugs

Users of drugs, even of soft ones, without medical prescription should be particularly careful, as heavy penalties (up to 10 years' imprisonment) are possible even for possession. The planting of drugs on travellers, by traffickers or the police, is not unknown. If offered drugs on the street, make no response at all and keep walking. Note that people who roll their own cigarettes are often suspected of carrying drugs and are subjected to close searches. If you are taking illegal drugs – even ones that are widely and publically used – be aware that authorities do set traps from time to time. Should you get into trouble, your embassy is unlikely to be very sympathetic.

Electricity

127 volts/60 Hz, US-style 2-pin plug.

Embassies and consulates

See www.sre.gob.mx (with English section) for contact details for other embassies.
Australia, 14 Perth Av, Yarralumia, 2600 ACT, Canberra, T00612-6273 3963, www.mexico.org.au.
Belize, 3 North Ring Rd, Belmopan, T00501-822 0406.

Canada, 45 O'Connor St, Suite 1000, Ottawa, Ont, K1P 1A4, T+1-613 233 8988, www.sre.gob.mx/canada.

Denmark, Bredgade 65, 1st floor 1260, Copenhagen, T+45-3961 0500, www.sre.gob.mx/dinamarca.

France, 9 rue de Longchamp, 75116 Paris, T+331-5370 2770, www.sre.gob.mx/francia.

Germany, Klingelhöferstrasse 3, 10785 Berlin, T+4930-269 3230, www.sre.gob.mx/ alemania.

Israel, 25 Hamared St, Trade Tower 5th floor, Tel Aviv 68125, T+97203-516 3938, www.sre.gob.mx/israel.

Netherlands, Nassauplein 28, 2585 EC, The Hague, T+3170-360 2900, www.embamex-nl.com.

New Zealand, 185-187 Featherston St, level 2 (AMP Chambers), Wellington, T+6404-472 5555, www.sre.gob.mx/nuevazelandia.

Switzerland, Welpoststrasse 20, 5th floor, CH-3015, Berne, T+4131-357 4747, www.sre.gob.mx/suiza.

UK, 16 St George St, London, W1S 1FD, T020-7499 8586, www.sre.gob.mx/reinounido.

USA, 1911 Pennsylvania Av, NW, 20006 Washington DC, T+1202-728 1600, www.sre.gob.mx/eua.

Gay and lesbian travellers

Latin America is hardly well-known for its pro-gay stance and Mexico was, until fairly recently, no exception. However, in the last decade things have been steadily improving for the country's gay and lesbian population and hence also for foreign visitors. Although there is a definite divide between urban and rural areas in terms of attitudes towards homosexuality, most major cities now have at least a modest gay scene, gay and lesbian organizations and an annual gay pride march. This is also true for the larger resorts, such as Cancún and Acapulco. These days Mexico City's Zona Rosa, one of the more upmarket shopping and eating areas in the capital, has turned into something of a gay village,

complete with bars, clubs and shops – a good place to pick up one of the free magazines with good listings (in Spanish only). The gay scene here is refreshingly mixed with a good selection of venues for women, whereas in the rest of Mexico places for women are a bit thin on the ground and the prevailing macho culture can make life more difficult for lesbians. Helpful websites include: www.gayscape.com, www.gaytravelnet.com and www.iglta.org.

Health

See your GP or travel clinic at least 6 weeks before departure for general advice on travel risks and vaccinations. Try a specialist travel clinic if your own GP is unfamiliar with health conditions in Mexico. Make sure you have sufficient medical travel insurance, get a dental check, know your own blood group and if you suffer a long-term condition such as diabetes or epilepsy, obtain a Medic Alert bracelet/ necklace (www.medicalert.co.uk). If you wear glasses, take a copy of your prescription.

Vaccinations

It is advisable to vaccinate against polio, tetanus, typhoid, hepatitis A, and rabies if going to more remote areas. Malaria is a danger in the Mexico. Specialist advice should be taken on the best anti-malarials to use.

Health risks

The most common cause of travellers' **diarrhoea** is from eating food contaminated food. In Mexico, drinking water is rarely the culprit, although it's best to be cautious (see below). Swimming in sea or river water that has been contaminated by sewage can also be a cause; ask locally if it is safe. Diarrhoea may be also caused by viruses, bacteria (such as E-coli), protozoal (such as giardia), salmonella and cholera. It may be accompanied by vomiting or by severe abdominal pain. Any kind of diarrhoea responds well to the replacement of water and salts. Sachets of rehydration salts can be bought in most chemists and can be dissolved in boiled water. If symptoms persist, consult a doctor. Tap water in the major cities is safe to drink but it may be advisable to err on the side of caution and drink only bottled or boiled water. Avoid ice in drinks unless you trust that it is from a reliable source.

Travelling in high altitudes can bring on **altitude sickness**. On reaching heights above 3000 m, the heart may start pounding and the traveller may experience shortness of breath. Smokers and those with underlying heart or lung disease are often hardest hit. Take it easy for the first few days, rest and drink plenty of water, you will feel better soon. It is essential to get acclimatized before undertaking long treks or arduous activities.

Mosquitoes are more of a nuisance than a serious hazard but some, of course, are carriers of serious diseases such as **malaria**, so it is sensible to avoid being bitten as much as possible. Sleep off the ground and use a mosquito net and some kind of insecticide. Mosquito coils release insecticide as they burn and are available in many shops, as are tablets of insecticide, which are placed on a heated mat plugged into a wall socket.

If you get sick

Contact your embassy or consulate for a list of doctors and dentists who speak your language, or at least some English. Doctors and health facilities in major cities are also listed in the Directory sections of this book. Good-quality healthcare is available in the larger centres of Mexico but it can be expensive, especially hospitalization. Make sure you have adequate insurance (see below).

Useful websites
www.btha.org British Travel Health Association.
www.cdc.gov US government site that gives excellent advice on travel health and details of disease outbreaks.
www.fco.gov.uk British Foreign and Commonwealth Office travel site has useful

information on each country, people, climate and a list of UK embassies/consulates.
www.fitfortravel.scot.nhs.uk A-Z of vaccine/health advice for each country.
www.numberonehealth.co.uk Travel screening services, vaccine and travel health advice, email/SMS text vaccine reminders and screens returned travellers for tropical diseases.

Identification

ID is increasingly required when visiting offices or tourist sites within government buildings. It's handy to have some form of identification (*identificación* or *credencial*); a photocopied passport will usually do. You are legally required to carry your FMT, or *Forma Migratoria de Turista* (Mexican tourist card, issued on entry), or visa at all times.

Insurance

Insurance is strongly recommended. If you have financial restraints the most important aspect of any insurance policy is medical care and repatriation. You may want cover for personal items too. Read the small print *before* heading off. Coverage for adventure sports, including diving, costs extra but is worth it.

Internet

A list of useful websites is given on page 65. Every major town and most small villages now has at least one internet café. The better ones can often cater for a wide range of internet services, including photo transfer, CD-burning and Skype. Prices vary from place to place but are normally around US$1. Many mid-range and high end hotels have Wi-Fi so you can log-on if you have your own laptop. We list cybercafés in the text. See www.world66.com for information on cybercafés.

Language

The official language of Mexico is Spanish. Outside of the main tourist centres, travelling without some knowledge of Spanish is a major hindrance. There are also some 62 indigenous languages spoken, the most common of which are Nahuatl, Maya, Zapotec and Mixtec.

Some areas (eg Cuernavaca), have become popular places to take Spanish courses. Such centres normally include a range of cultural activities and provide options for homestay. A less well-known centre is likely to have fewer English speakers around. See Language schools under Directory of individual towns.

Language tuition

Arranging language tuition internationally is increasingly popular.

AmeriSpan, 1334 Walnut St (PO Box 58129), 6th floor, Philadelphia, PA 19107, T1-215- 751 1100, T1-800-879 6640, www.amerispan.com (also with offices in Antigua, Guatemala). One of the most comprehensive options, offering Spanish immersion programmes, educational tours, volunteer and internship positions throughout Latin America.

Cactus Language, 4 Clarence House, 30-31 North St, Brighton, East Sussex, BN11EB, T0845-130 4775, www.cactuslanguage training.com. Spanish language courses from 1 week in Mexico, with pre-trip classes in the UK. Also has additional options for volunteer work, diving and staying with host families.

Institute for Spanish Language Studies, T1-800-765 0025 (USA), www.isls.com. Has schools in Mexico offering innovative and flexible programmes.

Spanish Abroad, 5112 N 40th St, Suite 101, Phoenix, AZ 85018, USA, T1-602-778 7623 (USA and Canada), T1-602-778 6791 (worldwide), www.spanishabroad.com. Intensive Spanish immersion programmes.

Media

Newspapers

The influential daily newspapers are: *Excelsior*, *Novedades*, *El Día*, *Uno Más Uno*, *El Universal*, *El Heraldo*, *La Jornada* (www.jornada.unam.mx, more to the left), *Tiempo Libre* (listing cultural activities in Mexico City), *La Prensa* (a popular tabloid, with the largest circulation), *El Nacional* (mouthpiece of the government). In Guadalajara, *El Occidental*, *El Informador* (www.informador.com.mx) and *Siglo 21*. There are influential weekly magazines *Proceso*, *Siempre*, *Epoca* and *Quehacer Político*. The political satirical weekly is *Los Agachados*.

The New York edition of the *Financial Times* and other British and European papers are available at Mexico City Airport and from the **Casa del Libro** in Calle Florencia 37 (Zona Rosa); Hamburgo 141 (Zona Rosa); and Calle Homero (Polanco), all in Mexico City. *The Miami Herald* is stocked by most newsstands.

Radio

World Band Radio Latin America has more local and community radio stations than practically anywhere else in the world; a shortwave (world band) radio offers a practical means to brush up on the language, sample popular culture and absorb some of the richly varied regional music.

International broadcasters also transmit across Mexico in both English and Spanish, including: *BBC World Service*, www.bbc.co.uk/worldservice/index.shtml, for schedules and frequencies; *Voice of America*, www.voa.gov; and Boston-based *Monitor Radio International*, operated by Christian Science Monitor, www.csmonitor.com. *Putumayo World Music*, www.putumayo.com, specializes in the exotic sounds of Mexican music.

Money → *US$1=$13.27 pesos (Nov 2009)*

The monetary unit is the Mexican peso, represented by '$' – the dollar sign – providing great potential for confusion, especially in popular tourist places where prices are higher and often quoted in US dollars (US$). The 3 main ways of keeping in funds while travelling are with US dollars cash, US dollar TCs or credit cards. It is recommended that you take all three.

Cash
The chief benefit of taking US dollars is that they can be exchanged almost everywhere and are often accepted as payment along the US border and in good resorts. Generally, however, it is wise to carry pesos as your main currency. Keep small denominations when making trips away from the major towns and resorts as shopkeepers may struggle to change anything larger than 50 pesos.

Also keep several low-value US dollar bills (US$5 or US$10) which can be carried for changing into local currency when banks or *casas de cambio* are closed, and for use in out-of-the-way places when you may run out of local currency. They are also very useful for shopping: shopkeepers and *casas de cambio* tend to give better exchange rates than hotels or banks (but see below).

If your budget is tight it is essential to avoid situations where you are forced to change money regardless of the rate; watch weekends and public holidays carefully and never run out of local currency.

Exchange
US dollars cash can be easily changed in all cities and towns at banks and *casas de cambio*, and in the more popular places can sometimes be used if you're running short of pesos. When changing money, ask for a mixture of large and small denominations or go to a bank and ask them to change large notes for you. While it is possible to change the euro, sterling and other currencies, not all banks or *casas de cambio* will take them.

Traveller's cheques
Traveller's cheques (TCs) from any well-known bank can be cashed in most towns if drawn in US dollars; TCs from other currencies are harder to cash, and certainly not worth

trying to change outside the largest of cities. If you are stuck, branches of HSBC have been known to change other currencies. *Casas de cambio* are generally quicker than banks for exchange transactions and stay open later; fees are not charged but their rates may not be as good. You may be asked to show your passport, another form of ID or even proof of purchase (but keep it separate from your TCs). Denominations of US$50 and US$100 are preferable, though you will need a few of US$20. Amex and Visa US dollar TCs are recommended as the easiest to change.

Transfer
If you need to make a transfer ask your bank if they can transfer direct to a Mexican bank without using an intermediary, which usually results in greater delays. Beware of short-changing at all times. **Western Union**, www.westernunion.com, has outlets throughout Mexico but the service is more expensive than a traditional bank wire.

Credit and debit cards
Credit and debit cards are ideal for travelling providing ready access to funds without carrying large amounts of cash on your person. In an ideal world taking a couple of cards (one Visa and one MasterCard) will make sure you are covered in most options. It is straightforward to obtain a cash advance against a credit card and even easier to withdraw cash from ATMs. (Remove your credit card from the machine immediately after the transaction to avoid it being retained – getting it back can be difficult.)

ATMs are widespread in Mexican towns and villages. There are 2 systems: **Plus** and **Cirrus**. You may have to experiment to see what combination of options you require. Fortunately, most ATMs give you a language option after you enter your card. The rates of exchange on ATM withdrawals are the best available for currency exchange but your bank or credit card company imposes a handling charge. With a credit card, obtain a credit limit sufficient for your needs, or pay money to put the account in credit. If travelling for a long time, consider a direct debit to clear your account regularly. If you lose a card, immediately contact the 24-hr helpline of the issuer in your home country (find out the numbers to call before travelling and keep them in a safe place). Most card issuers provide a telephone number that allows you to call collect from anywhere in the world in case of card loss or theft; be sure to request it before travelling.

For purchases, credit cards of the Visa and MasterCard groups, American Express (Amex), Carte Blanche and Diners Club can be used. Make sure you know the correct procedure if they are lost or stolen. Credit card transactions are normally at an officially recognized rate of exchange; they are often subject to sales tax. In addition, many establishments in Mexico charge a fee of about 6% on credit card transactions; although forbidden by credit card company rules there is not a lot you can do about this, except get the charge itemized on the receipt and complain to the card company. For credit card security, insist that imprints are made in your presence. Any imprints incorrectly completed should be torn into tiny pieces. Also destroy the carbon papers after the form is completed (signatures can be copied from them).

For lost or stolen cards call:
MasterCard, T1-800-307 7309;
Visa T1-800-847 2911.

Cost of living and travelling

A basic room is likely to set you back about US$15, with occasional cheaper prices available. Comfortable rooms will start at around US$20. Some hotels offer no single rooms, or they may charge 80% of the price of a double. If you are travelling alone this should be built into your budget. Meals start from US$10 a day for those on tight budgets. Activities will tend to be in the region of US$30 and upwards a day. Travel eats up most of your budget, partly because of the vast distances covered. As an average, travel by bus costs around US$4.80 per hr. See Getting around, page 39. Budget travellers should note that there is a definite tourist economy in resort areas, with high prices and, on occasion, unhelpful service. This can be avoided by seeking out those places used by locals; an understanding of Spanish is useful. A very tight daily budget without much travelling or activities would be US$30 per day. US$50-60 per day is a more realistic one.

Opening hours

Banks Mon-Fri 0900-1330 (some stay open later), Sat 0900-1230.
Businesses 0900/1000-1300/1400, then 1400/1500-1900 or later. Business hours vary considerably according to the climate and local custom.

Photography

The use of video cameras is US$3-5 at historical sites. For professional camera equipment, including a tripod, the fee is much higher.

Police

Probably the best advice with regards the police in Mexico is to have as little to do with them as possible. An exception to this rule are the **tourist police**, who operate in some of the big cities and resorts, and provide assistance.

You may be asked for ID at any time (see page 58). If you cannot produce it, you may be jailed. If a visitor is jailed, his or her friends should provide food every day. This is especially important for people on a special diet, such as diabetics. Contact your embassy or consulate and take advice. In the event of a vehicle accident in which anyone is injured, all drivers involved are automatically detained until blame has been established, and this does not usually take less than 2 weeks.

The giving and receiving of **bribes** is not recommended. However, the following advice may prove useful for people travelling in Mexico. Never offer a bribe unless you are fully conversant with the customs of the country. Wait until the official makes the suggestion, or offer money in some form which is not obviously a bribe. Do not assume that officials who accept a bribe are prepared to do anything else that is illegal. You bribe them to persuade them to do their job, or to persuade them not to do it, or to do it more quickly, or more slowly. You do not bribe them to do something which is against the law. The mere suggestion would make them very upset. If an official suggests that a bribe must be paid before you can proceed on your way, be patient and he may relent. Bear in mind that by bribing you are participating in a system that may cause you immense frustration.

Post

Rates are raised in line with the peso's devaluation against the dollar. International service has improved and bright red mail boxes, found in many parts of the city, are reliable for letters. Although it's hard to give reliable delivery times, generally letters to the UK, Australia and Europe take around 2 weeks and to the USA, around 1 week. Parcel counters often close earlier than other sections of the post office in Mexico. Not all these services are obtainable outside Mexico City; delivery times to/from elsewhere in the country may well be longer than those from Mexico City.

Poste restante (*lista de correos* in Mexico) functions reliably, but you may have to ask under each of your names; mail is sent back after 10 days (for an extension write to the Jefe de la Administración of the post office holding your mail, any post office will help you do this). Address the envelope: '*Favor de retener hasta llegada*'. In Mexico, tourists can call T01-800-446 3942 to clarify problems.

Costs
To North America, Central America and the Caribbean: under 20 g = 10.50 pesos; 20-50 g = 17.50 pesos; 500 g-1 kg = 108.50

pesos. To South America and Europe: under 20 g = 13 pesos; 20-50 g = 20.50 pesos; 500 g-1 kg = 275 pesos. To Asia, Africa and Oceania: under 20 g = 14.50 pesos; 20-50 g = 24.50 pesos; 500 g-1 kg = 357.50 pesos.

Punctuality

Punctuality is more of a concept than a reality in Mexico. The *mañana* culture reigns supreme and any arrangement to meet at, say 1900, will normally rendezvous somewhere between 2000 and 2100. However, the one time you are late to catch a bus, boat or plane, it will leave on time – the rule is to arrive early and be prepared to wait.

Safety

Generally speaking, most places in Mexico are no more dangerous than any major city in Europe or North America and the people, if anything, are friendlier and more open. In provincial towns, main places of interest, on daytime buses and in ordinary restaurants the visitor should be quite safe. Nevertheless, in large cities (particularly in crowded places such as markets and bus stations) crime exists, mostly of the opportunistic kind. If you are aware of the dangers, act confidently and use your common sense.

The following tips, endorsed by travellers, are meant to forewarn, not alarm: keep all documents secure; hide your main cash supply in different places or under your clothes. Extra pockets sewn inside shirts and trousers, pockets closed with a zip or safety pin, moneybelts, neck or leg pouches, and elasticated support bandages for keeping money and cheques above the elbow or below the knee have been repeatedly recommended. Pouches worn outside the clothes are not safe. Keep cameras in bags (preferably with a chain or wire in the strap to defeat the slasher) and don't wear fancy wrist-watches or jewellery. Carry your small day pack in front of you.

Safety on public transport

When you have all your luggage with you at a bus or railway station, be especially careful: don't get into arguments with any locals if you can help it and clip, tie or lock all the items together with a chain or cable if you are waiting for some time, or simply sit on top of your backpack. Take a taxi between airport/bus station/railway station and hotel, if you can afford it. Keep your bags with you in the taxi and pay only when you and your luggage are safely out of the vehicle. Avoid night buses unless essential or until you are comfortable travelling in the area; avoid arriving at night whenever possible; and watch your belongings whether they are stowed inside or outside the cabin (rooftop luggage racks create extra problems, which are sometimes unavoidable – many bus drivers cover rooftop luggage with plastic sheeting, but a waterproof bag or outer sack can be invaluable for protecting your luggage and for stopping someone rummaging through the top of your bag). Major bus lines often issue a luggage ticket when bags are stored in the hold; this is generally a safe system. When getting on a bus, keep your ticket handy as you may have to show it at some point. Finally, be wary of accepting food, drink, sweets or cigarettes from unknown fellow travellers on buses or trains; although extremely rare, they may be drugged, and you could wake up hours later without your belongings. So never accept a bar drink from an opened bottle (unless you can see that the bottle is in general use); always have it uncapped in front of you.

Scams

A number of distraction techniques such as mustard smearers and paint or shampoo sprayers and strangers' remarks like "what's that on your shoulder?" or "have you seen that dirt on your shoe?" are designed to distract you for a few critical moments in which time your bag may be grabbed. Furthermore, supposedly friendly assistance asking if you have dropped money or other items in the street, work on the same premise. If someone follows you when you're in the street, let him catch up with you and 'give him the eye'. While you should take local advice about being out at night, do not assume that daytime is any safer. If walking after dark on quiet streets, walk in the road, not on the pavement.

Be wary of 'plain-clothes policemen'; insist on seeing identification and on going to the police station by main roads. Do not hand over your identification (or money – which he should not need to see anyway) until you are at the station. On no account take them directly back to your lodgings. Be even more suspicious if he seeks confirmation of his status from a passer-by. If someone implies they are asking for a bribe, insist on a receipt. If attacked, remember your assailants may well be armed, and try not to resist.

It is best, if you can trust your hotel, to leave any valuables you don't need in a safe-deposit. Always keep an inventory of what you have deposited. If you don't trust the hotel, lock everything in your pack and secure that in your room. If you do lose valuables, you will need to report the incident to the police for insurance purposes.

Student travellers

If you are in full-time education you will be entitled to an **International Student Identity Card (ISIC)**, www.isic.org, which is distributed by student travel offices and travel agencies in over 100 countries. ISIC gives you special prices on all forms of transport (air, sea, rail, etc), and other concessions and services. The ISIC website has a list of card-issuing offices around the world. Student cards must have a photo for discounts in Mexico.

Tax

Don't forget you'll have to pay departure tax if it isn't already included in your ticket.

Telephone → *Country code T+52. IDD T00; operator T020; international operator T090; directory enquiries T040.*

Many of the telecommunications networks have been privatized and prices have fallen considerably and in some areas services have even improved. Consequently, keeping in touch by phone is no longer prohibitive.

Calls made to Mexican numbers are local, regional or international. Most destinations have a 7-digit number (except Mexico DF, Guadalajara and Monterrey which have 8-digit numbers). Most regions have a 3-digit code (except Mexico DF, Guadalajara and Monterrey which have 2-digit codes). The format of a number, depending on the type of call, should be as follows: **local** 7- or 8-digit phone number; **regional** long-distance access code (01) + regional code (2- or 3-digit code) + 7- or 8-digit number; **international** international direct-dialling code (IDD) + country code + regional code + 7- or 8-digit number.

Most **public phones** only accept phone cards (Ladatel); these cost 30 or 50 pesos and available from shops and news kiosks everywhere. AT&T has a US Direct service; for information in Mexico dial T412-553- 7458, ext 359. From LADA phones (see below), dial **01, similar for AT&T credit cards. To use calling cards to Canada T95-800-010 1990. Commercially run *casetas*, or booths (for example **Computel**), where you pay after phoning, are up to twice as expensive as private phones; charges vary from place to place. Computel has offices countrywide with long opening hours. It is better to call collect from private phones, but better still to use the LADA system. Reverse-charge (collect) calls on LADA can be made from any blue public phone, say you want to *llamar por cobrar*; silver phones are for local and direct long- distance calls, some take coins. Others take foreign credit cards (Visa, MasterCard, not Amex; not all phones that say they take cards accept them).

Pre-paid phone cards (eg Ladatel) are available, but expensive for international calls. Of other pre-paid cards, the best value are

those issued by **Ekofon**, www.ekofon.com, available at various airport and other outlets, and through a pre-chargeable account service, which can he set up online.

Internet calls through the Hotmail system or Skype may be possible in internet cafés.

Using a **mobile** in most of Mexico is very expensive. In addition to the hassle of having to recharge your telephone, research carefully whether it is worth your while. Mobile phone calls will be cheaper if you buy a SIM card for the local network; in-country calls are likely to be considerably cheaper than using your home-based account. The initial cost of the SIM card is getting more affordable, but check the cost of calls. Also bear in mind your personal mobile number will not work.

Time

Mexico City is 6 hrs behind GMT. Daylight Saving Time runs from the first Sun in Apr to the last Sun in Oct (when it is 5 hrs behind GMT).

Sonora, Sinaloa, Nayarit and Baja California Sur are 7 hrs behind GMT; Baja California Norte (above 28th Parallel) is 8 hrs behind GMT (but 7 hrs behind GMT during Daylight Saving Time).

Tipping

Normally 10-15%; the equivalent of US$0.25 per bag for porters, the equivalent of US$0.20 for bell boys, and nothing for a taxi driver unless for some kind of exceptional service.

Tour operators

In the UK
Condor Journeys and Adventures, 2 Ferry Bank, Colintraive, Argyll, PA22 3AR, T01700-841318, www.condorjourneys-adventures.com; also has offices in France.
Explore Worldwide, 55 Victoria Rd, Farnborough, Hants, GU14 7PA, T0870-333 4001, www.explore.co.uk.

Galapagos Classic Cruises, 6 Keyes Rd, London, NW2 3XA, T020-8933 0613, www.galapagoscruises.co.uk.
Journey Latin America, 12-13 Heathfield Terrace, London, W4 4JE, T020-8747 8315, www.journeylatinamerica.co.uk.
Last Frontiers, Fleet Marston Farm, Aylesbury, Buckinghamshire, HP18 OQT, T01296-653000, www.lastfrontiers.com.
Select Latin America, 3.51 Canterbury Court, 1-3 Brixton Rd, Kennington Park, London, SW9 6DE, T020-7407 1478, www.select latinamerica.com.
South American Experience, Welby House, 96 Wilton Rd, London, SW1V 1DW, T0845-277 3366, www.southamerican experience.co.uk.
Trips Worldwide, 14 Frederick Place, Clifton, Bristol, BS8 1AS, T0800-840 0850, www.tripsworldwide.co.uk.
Tucan Travel, 316 Uxbridge Rd, London W3 9QP, T020-8896 1600, www.tucantravel.com.
Veloso Tours, 34 Warple Way, London W3 0RG, T020-8762 0616, www.veloso.com.

In North America
Exito Travel, 108 Rutgers St, Fort Collins, CO 80525, T970-482 3019, www.exito-travel.com.
GAP Adventures, 19 Charlotte St, Toronto, Ontario, M5V 2H5, T1-800-708 7761, www.gapadventures.com.
Mila Tours, 100 S Greenleaf Av, Gurnee, Il 60031, T1-800-367 7378, www.milatours.com.
S and S Tours, 4250 S Hohokam Dr, Sierra Vista, AZ 85650, T866-780 2813, www.ss-tours.com.

International
The following have operations in the US, Canada, Europe, Australia and New Zealand.
Dragoman, T01728-861133, www.dragoman.co.uk.
Exodus Travels, T020-8675 5550, www.exodus.co.uk.
LADATCO tours, 2200 S Dixie Highway, Suite 704, Coconut Grove, FL 33133, T1-800-327 6162, www.ladatco.com.

Tourist information

Tourist offices are listed throughout the text. In Europe, information is available in several different languages by calling T00-800-1111 2266. In North America call T1-800-446 3942.

Useful websites
Mexico's web presence is phenomenal, some of the reliable, informative and useful websites that have been round for a while include:
www.latinnews.com Up-to-date site with political comment.
www.mexconnect.com General information.
www.mexicoreporter.com Great website featuring up-to-date reports and articles from the capital and beyond. Cutting-edge web journalism at its liveliest.
www.mexperience.com Well-constructed site updated daily, with current affairs, feature articles and advice on travel in Mexico. Look out for the forum where comments from fellow travellers are exchanged.
www.planeta.com A phenomenal resource which is staggering for its detail on everything from ecotourism and language schools to cybercafés.
www.sectur.gob.mx Tourism Secretariat's site; less glossy links but good information.
www.visitmexico.com Mexico Tourist Board site, a comprehensive multilingual site with information on the entire country.
A couple of general travel websites that are worth a look are **www.bootsnall.com** – see the Mexico and the Central America sections – and **www.tripadvisor.com**.

Visas and immigration

All visitors require a passport to enter Mexico plus a Mexican tourist card (see below) or a visa. See the **National Institute of Migration** (Instituto Nacional de Migración, INM) website, www.inami.gob.mx, for a list of countries whose citizens need visas. Click 'English', then 'I want to travel to Mexico as a tourist'.

If you do not need a visa, you can obtain a **Mexican Tourist Card** (FMT) at the point of entry or in advance at a consulate or embassy. The tourist card, which should be carried at all times, is issued for up to 180 days and should be returned to immigration officials when departing. Although you're only supposed to stay 180 days a year on a tourist card, one correspondent lived in Mexico for 5 years on a tourist card, making visits to the USA 3-4 times a year, with no problems. Tourist cards are not required for cities close to the US border.

Renewal of entry cards or visas can be done at any INM office. In Mexico City the office is at 862 Ejército Nacional, Col Polanco, Mexico City DF, (Mon-Fri 0900-1300). You can find details of offices throughout the country on the INM website, see above. Only 60 days are given, and you can expect to wait up to 10 days for a replacement tourist card. To renew a tourist card by leaving the country, you must stay outside Mexico for at least 72 hrs. Take Tcs or a credit card as proof of finance.

At border crossings with Guatemala and Belize, you may be refused entry into Mexico if you have less than US$200 (or US$350 for each month of intended stay, up to 180 days). Likewise, if you are carrying more than US$10,000 in cash or TCs, you must declare it.

If a person **under 18** is travelling alone or with one parent, both parents' consent is required, certified by a notary or authorized by a consulate. A divorced parent must be able to show custody of a child. (These requirements are not always checked by immigration authorities and do not apply to all nationalities.) Details are available from any Mexican consulate (see page 56).

Weights and measures

The metric system is used.

Women travellers

Some women experience problems, whether accompanied or not; others encounter no difficulties at all. Unaccompanied Western women will at times be subject to close scrutiny and exceptional curiosity. Don't be unduly scared – or flattered. When you set out, err on the side of caution until your instincts have adjusted to the new culture. Women travelling alone could consider taking a wedding ring (a fake one if necessary) to prevent being hassled. To help minimize unwanted attention, do not wear suggestive clothing. Do not feel bad about showing offence. When accepting an invitation, make sure that someone else knows the address you are going to and the time you left. Ask if you can bring a friend (even if you do not intend to do so). Always act with confidence, as though you know where you are going, even if you do not, so you don't attract unwanted attention. Do not tell strangers where you are staying.

Working and volunteering

Two main areas provide opportunities for unskilled volunteers: childcare (often at orphanages or schools) and nature projects. Be warned, spontaneous volunteering is becoming more difficult. Organizations that use volunteers now plan their personnel needs in advance so you may need to make contact before you visit. Many organizations now charge volunteers for board and lodging and projects are often for a minimum of 4 weeks.

Many developed countries have organizations that run volunteer projects. The US Peace Corps, Paul D Coverdell Peace Corps Headquarters, 1111 20th St NW, Washington, DC 20526, T1-800-424 8580, www.peace corps.gov, is the most prominent in the region, working on development projects with 2-year assignments for US citizens in Mexico.

Experiment in International Living, T01684-562577, www.eiluk.org, is the UK element of a US international homestay programme that arranges stays with families in Mexico with social projects based on the ethos that if you want to live together you need to work together. It's an excellent way to meet people and learn the language.

Contents

Mexico City

At a glance

⊖ **Getting around** Metro, buses
and *peseros*.

◉ **Time required** 1-2 weeks to
sample the major attractions.

☼ **Weather** Temperatures are
reasonably moderate throughout
the year. Apr-Oct are warmer,
wetter months; Nov-Mar are cool
and dry.

✕ **When not to go** Good at any
time, but the dry season, Nov-Mar,
can experience worse air pollution.

To Route 57/45 & Querétaro
To Tenayuca & Tlalnepantla
To Route 45/85, Teotihuacán, Pachua & Tampico

Los Indios Verdes
Basílica de Guadalupe

Terminal del Norte

GUSTAVO A MADERO

Av Insurgentes Norte
Carranza

Paseo Jacarandas
Calz México Tacuba
Calz Legaria

Plaza de las Tres Culturas
Av Río Consulado

To Route 134, Toluca & Miguel Hidalgo

Hipódromo de las Américas

CENTRO HISTÓRICO
Av Argentina

Terminal del Oriente (TAPO)
Via Tapo

Pres Masaryk
Paseo de la Reforma
Alameda
Zócalo

POLANCO
ZONA ROSA
Chapultepec

Bosque de Chapultepec

Calz I Zaragoza
Av Río de la Loza

To Route 150/190, Puebla & Veracruz
Blvd Puerto Aéreo

Eje 2 Sur

Av Constituyentes

Terminal del Poniente

Poliforum Cultural Siqueiros

Viaducto
CARRANZA
Eje 4 Sur
IZTACALCO

Av Cuauhtémoc
Eje Central Lázaro Cárdenas
Av Revolución
Anillo Periférico

Plaza México Bullring

Eje 2 Pte
Av Insurgentes Sur
Eje de Tlalpan
Eje 1 Ote
Av Plutarco Elías Calles
Av de la Viga
Eje 5 Sur
Circuito Interior

IZTAPALAPA

To Route 15, Toluca & Guadalajara

Teatro de los Insurgentes

BENITO JUAREZ

Calz Ermita Iztapalapa

Frida Kahlo Museum
Av Río Churubusco
Museo de las Intervenciones
CHURUBUSCO

SAN ANGEL
Av MA de Quevedo
Terminal del Sur
COYOACAN

Av San Jerónimo
Ciudad Universitaria

Olympic Stadium

Anahuacalli/ Diego Rivera Museum

To Desierto de los Leones

Anillo Periférico Sur

Estadio Azteca

Calz de Tlalpan

To Route 95 & Cuernavaca
To Xochimilco

Mexico City is a formidable beast – a sprawling chaos of humanity where life and death are played out in a shifting mosaic of some 22 million lives. Its streets, thronging with noise and movement, are coloured by an endless parade of extraordinary scenes. Aztec dancers stamp out crazed retinues with shimmering, resplendent headdresses. Crowds of protestors run wild at the latest government scandal. Volkswagen Beetles roar wildly through four lanes of traffic. And vociferous street vendors inundate the metro with loud speakers strapped to their backs. A universe unto itself, it would take several lifetimes to explore the multitude of settings and characters harboured by this behemoth destination. Inspirational, alluring, startling and grotesque, it's no wonder Mexico City has inspired generations of writers and artists.

Among its attractions are a wealth of architectural wonders, world-class museums, cultural centres, art galleries, scintillating night clubs and fantastic restaurants. From the grand opulence of shaded colonial plazas to the shivering sprawl of ramshackle shanty towns, this is a city of teeming, insatiable energy.

It is also a city of death and transformation, continually reborn from the ashes of conquest, revolution and natural disasters. Its incarnations – and its scars – are many: Aztec city of Tenochtitlán, colonial heart of New Spain, and federal capital of an independent, post-revolutionary Mexico.

Today, Mexico City, also known as Distrito Federal, or DF, is a vast 21st-century megapolis sprawling up the mountain sides, and sinking, slowly, inexorably, under the weight of its own enormity. Throughout its diverse and rambling neighbourhoods hangs a strangely poetic stench of toil and dirt, sweat and industry, bustle, smog, madness and murder. Like all great imperial capitals, Mexico City possesses style and intrigue in abundance. Expect the unexpected.

Getting there

Benito Juárez International Airport ① *13 km east of the city centre, www.aicm.com.mx,* has two terminals and modern facilities. For airport information, see page 133. It has domestic connections with all major towns in Mexico. For international flights, see Getting there, page 34. Fixed-price taxis to the centre cost US$9-11 with **Sitio 300**, T55-5571 9344; tickets are available from kiosks outside Sala A, where the taxis depart. Do not use unauthorized taxis; scams and rip-offs abound. Metro stop Aérea connects the airport to the city, but this should be avoided if you're carrying heavy luggage or travelling at rush hour.

There are four long-distance bus terminals: Norte (North), Sur (South), Oriente (East) and Poniente (West), divided, more or less, according to the regions they serve. All have good facilities and metro connections. Buses to some locations around Mexico City – Puebla, Cuernavaca, Pachuca and Toluca included – depart directly from the airport. ▶▶ *See Transport, page 133.*

Getting around

Mexico City's metro system is straightforward, cheap and the most convenient form of public transport. Although crowded, it is certainly no more hectic than London's Underground system. It is also less polluting than the alternatives, buses and taxis, which are frequently stuck in congested traffic. One exception is the handy metrobús, which traverses an exclusive bus lane the length of Insurgentes, a major north–south artery (see orientation, below). The Centro Histórico is best explored on foot and, if this is your first visit to Mexico City, it is recommended you get a hotel in this area. You'll be at the heart of the action and a short walk from all the major sights.

Orientation

A relentless and continually expanding urban sprawl of nearly 2000 neighbourhoods, Mexico City's scope is bewildering. It would take many months to explore it entirely, but most visitors will not need to venture beyond a few main areas. The **Centro Histórico** is where all the major sights are concentrated; the **Zócalo** is a good place to start. Several blocks west lies the **Alameda**, a tree-lined park and important landmark. Further west still lies the **Plaza de la República** and the Monumento a la Revolución, a useful orientation point. Southwest of here lies the **Zona Rosa**, Mexico City's once glorious entertainment district, now increasingly tacky. South of the Zona Rosa are the twin hip districts of **Roma**

and **Condesa**, quiet and residential, but also home to burgeoning restaurant and party scenes. West of the Zona Rosa, the verdant **Bosque de Chapultepec** is home to the world-class Museo Nacional de Antropología. To the north is the upmarket **Polanco** district. On the southern fringes of the city lie the moneyed neighbourhoods of **San Angel** and **Coyoacán**, the **University City** and the old Aztec canals of **Xochimilco**. To the north, **Basílica de Guadalupe** is the country's most important religious shrine.

You will find, as you explore the city, that you use two thoroughfares more than any others. The most famous is **Paseo de la Reforma**, a wide, shaded boulevard that runs south from the Basílica de Guadalupe, past the Centro Histórico, through the Zona Rosa and on towards the Bosque de Chapultepec. The other thoroughfare is **Avenida Insurgentes**, a diagonal north–south artery about 35 km long. It passes straight through the Zona Rosa and into neighbouring districts Roma and Condesa. Reforma and Insurgentes bisect at a *glorieta* (roundabout) with a statue of Cuauhtémoc, the last of the Aztec emperors. Other important thoroughfares are: the **Eje Central** (**Lázaro Cárdenas**), which runs south–north via the Alameda, Bellas Artes and Torre Latinoamericana, through Tlatelolco and past the Terminal del Norte (North Bus Terminal); the **Calzada de Tlalpan**, which runs north–south from near the centre, past the Terminal del Sur (South Bus Terminal) and out of the city towards Cuernavaca; the **Circuito Interior**, which encircles the city about 5 km from the centre; the **Periférico** which does the same thing further out; and the **Viaducto Miguel Alemán** crossing from the east, near the airport, and joining the Periférico in the west.

Maps The best maps of the city are from **Guía Roji**, www.guiaroji.com.mx, which produces an excellent A to Z (US$14). A very good pocket map is available free from tourist information booths (see below). Metro stations have useful large-scale wall maps of the immediate area. **Código** publishes some interesting maps of city neighbourhoods and seems to sell advertising space to only the trendiest establishments; they can be picked up free from tourist information booths. Specialized maps for the whole of Mexico can be bought from the **Instituto Nacional de Estadística Geografía e Informática** (INEGI) ① *Balderas 71, T55-5512 1873, www.inegi.gob.mx, Metro Juárez; other branches at the airport and Patriotismo 711, Metro Mixcoac.*

Best time to visit
Spring is the hottest time of year, but the high altitude means the climate is generally mild, except for a few days in mid-winter when it can get quite cold. Even in summer the temperature at night is rarely above 13°C and in winter there can be frosts. The average annual rainfall is 660 mm and most of it falls May-October, usually in the late afternoon.

Tourist information
Dotted around town are **tourist information booths**, operated by the Mexico City Government, which have good maps and can provide general information. Most are open daily 0900-1800. You'll find them at: the airport, domestic arrivals; Museo de Antropologia, Paseo de la Reforma; Basílica, Atrium of Basílica de Guadalupe; Bellas Artes, Juárez, between the Palacio de Bellas Artes and the Alameda Central; Catedral, Plaza del Empedradillo, western side of the cathedral; Cien Metros, at the main entrance of the northern bus terminal; Del Angel, Paseo de la Reforma, in front of the Monumento a la Independencia; Observatorio, at the main entrance of the western bus terminal; TAPO, eastern bus terminal; Tasqueña, southern bus terminal, door 3; Templo Mayor, Plaza del Seminario, on the eastern side of the cathedral; Coyoacán, Jardín Hidalgo 1; and Xochimilco, Pino 36.

There's also an inconveniently located **main office** ① *Nuevo León 56, 9th floor, T55-5553 1260, www.mexicocity.gob.mx*, with a very comprehensive website. **Tourist assistance** ① *toll-free T01800-008 9090*, provides information by telephone. The **Secretaría de Turismo** ① *Masaryk 172, 5th floor, between Hegel and Emerson, Colonia Polanco, Metro Polanco (or bus No 32)*, has information on national attractions, but is inconvenient to get to. Any complaints should be referred to tourist information centres or **tourist police**, in blue uniforms.

For up-to-date cultural listings, track down the Spanish-language *Tiempo Libre*, www.tiempolibre.com.mx, on sale all over the city every Thursday. The **Secretaría de Cultura**, www.cultura.df.gob.mx, has good details on city culture. *Explore Mexico* is a monthly tourist publication with an English-language overview of the city, available in big hotels and some tourist booths. There are various other English-language tourist magazines doing the rounds, most are transient and uninteresting.

Students

The Mexican Students' Union, **SETEJ** ① *Hamburgo 305, Col Juárez, Metro Sevilla, T55-5211 0743, www.setej.org, Mon-Fri 0900-1800, Sat 0900-1400*, issues student cards and deals with insurance. Most museums are free to students and teachers with ID.

Safety and pollution

As with any large city there are grounds for caution at times. Take care in Bosque de Chapultepec, Mercado Merced, the Zona Rosa and major touristy areas, where robberies have occurred. Take care in the centre at night, and at quiet times, when you are advised to travel by taxi. As ever, crowded buses and metro trains are a favourite haunt of pickpockets. The heinous taxi murders of the 1990s are less of an issue these days, but it's still safest to use registered *sitio* taxis (see Transport, page 139). The vast majority of visitors to Mexico City have a trouble-free experience, so don't believe the bad hype. Most violent crime is confined to impoverished neighbourhoods that you'll never see.

Pollution, however, is an issue. The city lies in the Valley of Mexico, a huge basin roughly 110 km long by 30 km wide. Encircling this valley is a chain of mountains that trap the air within the basin. About one in five of Mexico's population share this enclosed area with half the country's manufacturing employment breathing in much of the nation's industrial smog (worst from December to February). Common ailments that creep up over hours or days are a burning sensation in the eyes (contact lens wearers take note) and nose, and a sore throat. Local authorities advise citizens not to smoke or take outdoor exercise. Newspapers provide information on air quality, with warnings and advice.

Background

Tenochtitlán

Mexico City's humble origins can be found in the murky mud and reeds of Lake Texcoco, where the Aztecs, also known as the Mexica, wandered some 400 years before settling in 1325. Little more than *chichimec* (barbarian) hunters, these early Aztecs were regarded with disdain by neighbouring tribes. But in less than 200 years, the Aztecs would have forged one of the most formidable empires in Mesoamerica – a vast military enterprise overseen by their resplendent capital, Tenochtitlán.

But neither the Aztecs nor their Nauahtl-speaking neighbours were the first to settle on the lake; simple hunter-gatherers arrived and evolved here from around 30,000 BC. The first great regional city, Teotihuacán, did not arise for many millennia later, around

The Aztec art of human sacrifice

"Life is because of the gods; with their sacrifice they gave us life…" was the Aztec retort to horrified Catholic missionaries. The Aztec practice of human sacrifice – typically achieved by stretching a victim over a sacrificial stone, slicing open his abdomen with a flint knife, cutting through his diaphragm and tearing his still beating heart from his flesh – is neither unique nor barbarous when seen its proper context.

Historically, human sacrifice was widely practised all over the world, from Rome to Pagan England. Today, many cultures continue to ritually slaughter animals, whilst the Western practice of sacrificing young men in ideologically motivated wars is considered nothing out of the ordinary. Understandably, the first European travellers to Mexico were mortified at the gaily attended spectacles of ritual decapitation, burning, drowning and gruesome dismemberment. But to the Aztecs – inheritors of a millennia-old Mesoamerican tradition – these were customary acts.

What is unique to the Mesoamericans, and the Aztecs in particular, is the centrality of sacrifice in their daily life. In the Aztec myth of creation, the gods sacrificed themselves to create the sun and set it in motion across the sky. From their own dismembered 'flesh' all things were created. Humanity was therefore indebted to the gods and duty-bound to serve them with endless tributes of treasures, animals and human beings – the highest offering of all. Without regular sacrifices, the sun's procession would cease and all life would terminate in an unearthly cataclysm.

To that end, each god had its own preferred sacrificial victim. Huitzilopochtli, the tribal god of warfare and the sun at its zenith, had an appetite for captured warriors. Huehueteotl, the god of fire, demanded victims be roasted alive. Tlaloc, the god of rain, required young children for his work, who were first encouraged to cry and then drowned in water. Whilst women, whose heads were made to fall like ears of harvested maize, were the preferred victims of the earth goddesses.

For the inhabitants of Aztec Tenochtitlán, it was considered a high honour to be selected for such a role. Even captured warriors accepted their fate with a kind of mystical serenity. Perhaps no 'victim' was more honoured than he selected for Tezcatlipoca, the dark god of fate and sorcery. During the 20-day month of Toxcatl, the chosen one became an embodiment of the god himself, publicly worshipped and bestowed with four beautiful women. Later, he gave up his life in a grand and joyous festival of music and dancing, well-attended by adoring crowds.

Whilst such customs clearly do not belong in the 21st century, they should not necessarily be judged from the context of our own morality. The Spaniards, after dismantling the 'satanic' idols of the Aztec faith, went on to murder, torture and enslave Mexico's indigenous peoples with a thoroughly clear conscience.

AD 100, and it would dominate the valley of Mexico until its fall in the eighth century, when the militaristic Toltecs rose to the fore. The Toltecs constructed the city of Tula some 60 km north of present-day Mexico City, but after centuries of dominance they too fell into ruin around AD 1200. Fortunately, the concept of the city-state lived on. Waves of migrants poured into the area and constructed urban centres on the lake shores. The Aztecs were some of the last to arrive on the scene.

The Aztecs traced their lineage to Aztlán, a small island on a lake that some reckon to be present-day Mexcaltitlán in Nayarit state. Spurred by their gods, the war-like Huitzilopochtli chief among them, they departed the homeland in the ninth century. For years they drifted, first through Michoacán, then into the Valley of Mexico, where they soon fell into conflict with local groups. Briefly, they acted as hired warriors for the Culhuacán, but then alienated themselves with their bloodthirsty practices. For centuries more they wandered around the shores of Lake Texcoco, settling here and there, then moving on. Finally, their gods delivered them to the chosen place, as prophesied, where they would behold an eagle perched upon a cactus and devouring a snake. This was to be their new home, the birthplace of Tenochtitlán and, later, Mexico City.

Piece by piece they built their empire, reclaiming fertile mud from the lake bed, constructing floating gardens, cultivating crops, hunting local game and trading resources for bricks and stones. The first temples were built, which would later evolve into great sacred precincts. The population boomed and culture flourished. Meanwhile, god Huitzopochtli's insatiable thirst for human blood led the Aztecs to conquer tribe after neighbouring tribe. Then, after a formidable alliance was struck with neighbouring Texcoco and Tlacopan, forging the so-called 'triple alliance', Tenochtitlán became the most powerful political force in Central Mexico. By the time of the arrival of the Spaniards in 1519, the Aztec capital was vast, occupying a jewel-like island on lake Texcoco and supporting a population of 250,000 inhabitants. It shone with temples and towers, grand markets, schools, libraries and palaces. No longer the simple Chichimec warriors, the Aztecs had evolved into a complex and cultured society where war, poetry and religion were central. But soon, all this would be reduced to dust, as Cortés and his army laid siege to the burgeoning civilization. For details of the Spanish Conquest, see Background, page 763.

Capital of New Spain

After Cortés razed Tenochtitlán, he set about building the capital of New Spain – an administrative centre from which the crown's newly acquired New World territories could be governed. Basing himself in Coyoacán, his first steps were to fortify important buildings and strategic thoroughfares. Subsequently he laid the major roads and plazas in a grid pattern that closely matched the design scheme of the original Aztec city. The vast majority of indigenous inhabitants had been killed by disease, but survivors were quickly enlisted as slave labour. Temples were demolished and their bricks utilized to build new religious structures, often directly on top, thus preserving their symbolic power. He constructed palaces for himself and his fellow conquistadors and, initially, the city centre was the sole preserve of the Spaniards.

Like most colonial enterprises, the early days of the capital were rife with corruption and intrigue. Cortés was soon edged out of power and replaced by an exceptionally brutal *audiencia*, headed by Guzmán, who was specifically appointed by Emperor Carlos V of Spain. After two years of plunder, he was replaced with a new council in 1530, and then, in 1535, by the first viceroy of New Spain, Antonio de Mendoza. In the subsequent decades a silver boom propelled new wealth into the city and Mendoza was able to initiate many grandiose building schemes and renovations. By the end of the century some 250 European mansions had been constructed, which would later earn the capital the nickname 'City of Palaces'. Throughout the 17th century, the construction continued unabated until engineers suddenly realized the city was sinking into the lake bed. Floods inundated the capital, most notably in 1629, when it was submerged for five whole years and business was conducted in boats and canoes. Subsequently the lake area was drained but, even today, many historic buildings suffer dangerous levels of subsidence.

Throughout the colonial era, Mexico City was a multi-cultural and highly racist milieu of indigenous, black, Spanish and *mestizo* peoples. Everyone co-existed in strict hierarchy with *gachupínes* (Spanish-born officials) occupying the social pinnacle. Directly beneath them were the *criollos* (Mexican-born peoples of Spanish descent). Many *criollo* families bought up aristocratic titles when the Bourbon monarchs of Spain sold them in the 18th century, and thus came to participate in the political institutions that were fashioning the city. However, the reality for many *criollos* and the remaining population was one of great poverty and struggle. By the turn of the 18th century, *criollos* and *mestizos* (those born of indigenous and Spanish lineage), vastly underprivileged and vastly outnumbering the *gapuchíne* elite, would demand nothing short of independence from Spain.

From Independence to Revolution

Throughout Mexico's struggle for independence, Mexico City remained a bastion of royalist support. It did not succumb to Hidalgo's famous *grito* (see Background, page 768) or to his attack on the city in 1810, which he inexplicably halted with victory in sight. In 1819, rebellions broke out across Latin America and Mexico City's *gapuchínes* grew increasingly uncomfortable. They sought a modicum of stability in Colonial Agustín de Irtubide, son of a *gapuchíne* father and *crillo* mother. However, Irtubide became sympathetic to the Independence movement after meeting with rebel leader Vicente Guerrero. After cutting a deal, he marched on Mexico City in 1821 and was crowned emperor of the newly independent state in 1822. Two years later, a junta deposed Irtubide, executed him and established a federal republic – the United States of Mexico – with Mexico City as its capital.

In 1829, the last Spanish troops were expelled from the newly independent country. However, peace did not ensue. Instead, several decades of confused instability reigned whilst various conservative and liberal factions struggled for power. Through all this, General Santa Ana was a constant, if capricious and ultimately derisory, force. His 11 years dabbling in politics eventually concluded with the US-Mexican war, in which he shamefully ceded half of Mexico's territory. Zapotec liberal Benito Juárez (see box, page 767) took power from Santa Ana in 1855. In a move that enraged Mexico's conservatives, he instituted a set of reform laws that limited the power of a hideously bloated Catholic church, restricted its finances and confiscated its properties. Several notable convents and monasteries in Mexico City's downtown area were fully or partially demolished, or otherwise put to better use as factories or warehouses. Meanwhile, various groups squabbled for control of the city, until 1861, when Juárez was formally granted presidency.

In 1863, the French called on Mexico to repay its debts and, at the request of Mexican conservatives, installed the Austro-Hungarian archduke Maximilian as emperor. Inspired by the palaces of his European homeland, Maximilian settled into Chapultepec castle and made several regal additions to the city including the Paseo de la Reforma. His reign was short-lived, however, and after he lost support from the conservatives he was soon usurped by Beinto Juárez, who had him duly executed. Juárez reigned until 1872, when he died, and Porfirio Díaz took control.

Under the brutally capable regime of Porfirio Díaz, Mexico City experienced an unprecedented construction boom. The city limits, formerly defined by the *centro histórico*, were extended considerably. Swanky new neighbourhoods rose up in the areas west of Alameda, replete with French-style mansions, swathes of monuments and regal edifices. Inspired by European models of city-building, the dictator poured a fortune into the capital, invited scores of foreign investors and developed the infrastructure too, constructing plentiful new roads, schools, railroads and police stations. His dream was to present a progressive face to the world, but sadly, the capital's modernization was unmatched in the surrounding countryside, which continued to dwindle in poverty and oppression. Civil war erupted in 1911 and through 10 years of violence and bloodshed, Mexico City remained largely true to its conservative roots, despite changing hands several times.

In the aftermath of civil war, a nation searched for its identity. Great muralists like Rivera, Orozco and Siquieros (see box, page 89) were invited to adorn the city's buildings with their visions of the future. These works, imbued with the energy and inspirations of the newly forged society, are some of the capital's most endearing attractions. Meanwhile, resources were poured into education and infrastructure, and the city's population soon exceeded one million. In 1928, former president Alvaro Obregón was assassinated in a restaurant in San Angel and fears about the long-term success of the revolution led to the formation of the Partido Nacional Revolucionario (PNR), or National Revolutionary Party, in 1929. The PNR, after changing its name twice, became the Partido Revolucionario Institucional (PRI), or Institutional Revolutionary Party, and governed the country unchallenged for some 70 years. Meanwhile, during the 1930s, the capital's cultural fluorescence continued when President Lázaro Cárdenas invited political exiles from Europe, many of them artists and intellectuals, with León Trotsky among them.

To the 21st century
By 1940, the country had emerged from the post-revolutionary era and its capital, Mexico City, sustained a population of some 1½ million inhabitants – a number that would swell by over five times during the next 30 years. Miguel Alemán served as president between 1946 and 1952, when the city's character changed dramatically. A host of new roads were constructed, bringing traffic and congestion. The first apartment blocks and skyscrapers were built, including the Torre Latinoamericana. The equally iconic University City was built in the south, relocating intellectuals and students from the city centre. The wealthy moved out of the Centro Histórico and into the swanky areas of Chapultepec, San Angel and Coyoacán, all served by an exclusive new golf club. However, as power and industry grew in Mexico City, the government remained corrupt, and increasingly, centralized and bureaucratic.

During the 1950s and 1960s, Mexico City struggled to accommodate its burgeoning population, much of which now struggled in poverty and deprivation. As ever, the city's student body was a voice of dissent. In October 1968, many months of protests culminated in the massacre of some 300 students in the Plaza de las Culturas, just days before the city was due to host the Olympic games. The government was shamed before the international community and the incident graphically illustrated how far Mexico's human rights needed to go. On a more positive note, the 1960s ended with the inauguration of the metro system, which would once again transform how business was conducted in the capital.

During the 1970s, the city's population rose to an astonishing 14 million and its borders started sprawling into neighbouring states. Real ecological problems made themselves felt, including smog and pollution, which still ravage the city today. Then, on 19th September 1985, a massive earthquake tore the Centro Histórico asunder, demolishing swathes of sub-standard housing and killing some 30,000 inhabitants. Government response to the disaster was slow and hampered by bureaucratic incompetence, disinformation and dishonesty. In reaction, citizens formed support groups to help each other through the crisis – a phenomenon which gave birth to countless pressure groups and political organizations, many of which can be seen making protests in the streets today. One such organization was the Partido de la Revolución Democrática (PRD), or Party of the Democratic Revolution, the first viable alternative to the long-reigning PRI. In 1997 their mayoral candidate, Cuautémoc Cárdenas, was elected to power, breaking PRI hegemony for the first time.

By the turn of the 21st century, Mexico City's population had swollen to 20 million and the Centro Histórico was in a state of decline and general disrepair, visibly impoverished and crumbling in neglect. In response, the government poured 500 million pesos into an ambitious revitalization project which has restored colonial buildings, repaved streets, improved water supplies, created new museums and improved the infrastructure. The PRD continues to govern the city, with former police chief Marcelo Ebrard elected in 2006. In recent years, the capital has enjoyed a tourism boom, although this is increasingly overshadowed by the violence of the drug war raging in its more deprived suburbs and shanty towns.

In April 2009, a notorious outbreak of swine flu caused the entire city to be shut down for several days. Its streets fell eerily silent as the World Health Organization and international media waited to see if the disease would go global. Inevitably, it did. But in Mexico City, where air pollution and respiratory problems are rife, the actual deaths due to the disease (at the time of research) were negligible given its vast population. Unfortunately, the damage to the capital's economy and reputation was already done.

Sights

You will need stamina and perseverance to conquer Mexico City. The best place to start is the Centro Histórico, the city's historic downtown area, easily explored on foot and home to the city's most sumptuous architecture. The Zócalo, or Plaza de la Constitución, lies at its heart, surrounded by important colonial buildings like the Palacio Nacional and Cathedral, as well as the excavated remains of the Aztec Templo Mayor. The surrounding streets conceal fascinating plazas and museums and superb public buildings, like the Antiguo Secretaria de Educación, adorned with scintillating post-revolutionary murals that should not be missed.

A short walk southeast of the Zócalo lies La Merced, home to the largest market in the Americas, whilst west of the Zócalo is the shaded Alameda park and the Palacio de Bellas Artes, a must-see art deco wonder. Yet more great buildings and museums lie in the vicinity, including the national art gallery, the post office, and the Torre Latinoamericana, with its unsurpassed views of the sprawl. The irresistible Plaza Garibaldi, populated by crooning Mariachis, is a short walk away too.

The areas immediately west of the Centro Histórico, including the streets around the Plaza de la República, are less rich in attractions. Come here to find cheap lodgings or experience the working heart of the city. Nearby, the Parisian-style Paseo de la Reforma runs southwest into the once great entertainment district of the Zona Rosa. Today, better entertainment lies south, in the districts of Roma and Condesa, hotbeds of bohemian creativity and culinary talent. A visit to Bosque de Chapultepec, or Chapultepec park, west of the Zona Rosa, is obligatory. It's home to some good museums, including the fantastic Museo de Antropología, and makes a refreshing break from the madness of downtown.

If you have any energy left, there are some notable suburbs that make a good half- or full-day excursion. San Angel and Coyoacán are both pockets of handsome colonial splendour, a world away from modern Mexico City, and also home to diverting museums that honour national icons Frida Kahlo and Diego Rivera. The Ciudad Universitaria, or University City, has intriguing murals, whilst the Aztec settlement of Xochimilco, with its peaceful canals, is definitely worth exploring, preferably on a colourful punted boat. Finally, if you can make a pilgrimage to the shrine of the city's patron saint at Guadalupe.

1 Mexico City centre

➡ Mexico City maps
1 City centre, page 78
2 Centro Histórico: Zócalo & Alameda, page 82
3 Reforma & Zona Rosa, page 96
4 Bosque de Chapultepec & Polanco, page 98
5 Coyoacán, page 107
6 Metro, page 138

To Alameda de Santa María &
Museo del Instituto Geológico

SANTA MARÍA
LA RIBERA

ANAHUAC

Juana Inés de la Cruz

Normal

Laguna de
San Cristóbal

Xólotl
Nopaltzin

TLAXPANA

Netzahualpilli

Laguna de
Mayrán

Tízoc

Av Marina Nacional

HUASTECA

Av Ejército Nacional

VERONICA
ANZURES

Gutemberg

Copérnico

ANZURES

Milton

Descartes

Leibnitz

Museo
de Arte
Moderno

Monumento a
los Niños Héroes

Chapultepec

CONDESA

Casa de los
Mascarones

San
Cosme

Ribera de San Cosme

G Icazbalceta

A Herrera

G Prieto

SAN RAFAEL

Covarrubias

Maestro Antonio Caso

James Sullivan

Villalongin

COLONIA
CUAUHTEMOC

Jardín
del Arte

Museo
Carranza

Monumento
a la Madre

Monumento
a Cuauhtémoc

UK
Embassy

Paseo de la Reforma

French Embassy

US
Embassy

Monumento
Angel de la
Independencia

Japanese
Embassy

ZONA ROSA

Instituto
Mexicano
del Seguro
Social (iMSS)

Mercado
Insurgentes

Insurgentes

JUAREZ

Glorieta de
Insurgentes

Sevilla

Chapultepec

Puebla

Sinaloa

Durango

Sonora

Veracruz

Parque
España

Amsterdam

Plaza
Madrid

Colima

Popocatépetl

Celaya

Parque
México

ROMA

Tabasco

Av Alvaro Obregón

Guanajuato

Querétaro (Eje 2 Sur)

San Luis Potosí (Eje 2a Sur)

Plaza
Cabrera

Biblioteca
Benjamín
Franklin

Museo
de Ce

300 metres

300 yards

To Juanacatlán
Metro Station

N

Sleeping
Benidorm **2**
Carlton **5**
Casa de la Condesa **3**
Casa de los Amigos **4**
Hostel Home **1**
La Casona **8**
Marbella **13**
Mayaland **19**
Milán **6**
Monarca **7**
Palace **9**
Roosevelt **10**

Stanza **11**
Texas **12**

Eating
Bisquet Obregón **2**
Bistrot Mosaico **18**
El Tigre **3**
Flor de Lis **4**
Hip Kitchen **5**
Ixchel **6**
La Bodega **7**
La Parilla Argentina **9**
Lamm **8**

Mama Rosa's **17**
Orígenes Orgánicos **10**
Rojo Bistrot **11**
Tacos Hola **12**
Tierra de Vinos **13**

Bars & clubs
El Mitote **14**
La Bodeguita del Medio **1**
Malafama **19**
Mamá Rumba **15**
Pata Negra **16**
Rexo **20**

Zócalo and around

Zócalo

The Zócalo, also known as Plaza Mayor or Plaza de la Constitución, is Mexico City's spiritual centre, towards which all life gravitates. A vast open space in an otherwise vastly overcrowded metropolis, it has a capacity for 100,000 people, measures 240 m by 220 m, and is the second largest public square in the world after Moscow's Red Square. It is also the site of some major political and religious institutions, including the cathedral on the northern edge and the Palacio Nacional on the eastern edge. The excavated remains of the Templo Mayor, Tenochtitlán's most sacred temple, stand just northeast of the square.

In Aztec times, the Zócalo was a central meeting point for the causeways that connected the island city to the mainland. It also served as a vital public space and was home to a thriving market. This function continued throughout the colonial era, after Cortés levelled the temples and commenced work on the regal structures that flank it today. After Independence, Santa Ana demolished the markets and commissioned a large commemorative column, which was started but never completed. Only its base remains (its *zócalo*) from which the square, and most other important public squares in Mexico, derive their name. In the 19th century, the Zócalo flourished as a beautified garden replete with wrought-iron benches, footpaths, flowers, shady trees and a Parisian-style kiosk. But by the early 20th century, market traders had once again inundated the area and despite several renovations, the Zócalo had fallen into almost total disrepair by the 1970s. It was then levelled and completely paved over. In the 1990s, funds were poured into the area in an attempt to revive it from its increasingly slummy appearance.

Today, the Zócalo is the site of endless frenetic activity. True to its mercantile roots, illegal hawkers peddle their wares, crowds pour in and out, beggars scrounge change, and groups of musicians busk for tourist dollars. In the southwest corner, out-of-work tradesmen can been found with large signs declaring their business hopefully: 'electrician', 'mechanic' or 'painter'. But more than a teeming public square, the Zócalo is a vast stage where important festivals, artistic performances, military parades, gatherings and political rallies take place. In 2006, it was completely taken over by protestors furious at the election results, where they remained for several months. The large flag in the centre of the square, a symbol of Mexico City's ultimate political authority, is ceremonially raised at 0600 (0500 in winter), and lowered, with great pomp and ceremony, at 1800 (1700 in winter).

Cathedral

ⓘ *Daily 0800-2000, free, with a US$1 donation to visit the sacristy. Dress appropriately and be discreet during Mass.*

Mexico City's Metropolitan Cathedral, formally known as the Catedral Metropolitana de la Asunción de María, is the largest and oldest cathedral in Latin America. First built in the aftermath of the Conquest (1525), it was soon deemed too modest for its role as New Spain's principal house of worship. In fact, it was widely regarded as a shocking embarrassment. Rebuilding began in 1573 under the direction of Spanish architect Claudio de Arciniega, who drew inspiration from the great cathedrals of the homeland. It was consecrated in 1667, but work did not finish until 1813, some 240 years after it began. Stylistically, the cathedral combines elements of Gothic, baroque, Churrigueresque, neo-classic and Herrerian. It is singularly harmonious considering the many architects employed to build it. They include Manuel Tolsá, who added the great dome and clock tower. The cathedral is built directly over the ruins of Tenochtitlán's holiest precinct, where the soft soil has been causing the structure to sink, somewhat unevenly, for centuries. There have been many ingenious plans to halt its collapse and recently the rate of subsidence has slowed.

Rather than a typical east-facing configuration, the cathedral's principal facade faces south towards the Zócalo. It is comprised of three rising portals, all surrounded by columns. The main portal features statues of St Peter and St Paul flanking the cathedral's entrance. Directly above, St Andrew and St James guard the second portal, which contains a relief of the Assumption of the Virgin, to whom the cathedral is dedicated. The third portal features an eagle devouring a snake, Mexico's national emblem. Tolsá's bell tower, adorned with representations of Faith, Hope and Charity, rises just behind the facade. The eastern and western facades feature reliefs of the four apostles, whilst the northern facade is the oldest part of the cathedral, built in the Renaissance Herrera style. The cathedral's interior comprises five naves, a central choir and a sacristy. The side naves contain seven chapels each dating from the 17th century, and contain the remains of Agustín de Irtubide. The gleaming and sumptuously gilded Altar of Forgiveness can be admired at the front of the main nave, whilst nearby, the ornate Altar of Kings is richly decorated with images of saints, kings and queens. The cathedral is also home to the highly revered Señor del Veneo, or Lord of Poison, who turned black when he extracted a deadly poison from a devotee who kissed his feet. It is possible to ascend the bell towers, which provide spectacular views of the Zócalo. Ask inside – trips leave when there are enough people, US$1.

Next to the cathedral is the **Sagrario Metropolitano** (1769) with a fine Churrigueresque facade. Unlike the cathedral, it was built on the remains of an Aztec pyramid and, whilst sinking, is more stable than the former.

Palacio Nacional

ⓘ *Daily 0800-1800. Free, but bring ID to enter. Knowledgeable English-speaking guides available. Postcards of the murals are for sale, but much better reproductions of the same works are available in most museums in the city.*

The national palace takes up the eastern side of the Zócalo. Built on the site of the Palace of Moctezuma, the building originally served as a residence for Mexico's first colonial master, Cortés. Initially, it was a fortress-like structure with heavy armaments and fortified towers, which soon became the Vicreregal Palace when it was sold to the crown in 1562. It was subsequently destroyed by angry mobs and rebuilt in colonial baroque in 1692. It has a facade of red volcanic stone called *tezontle* and the top floor was added by President Calles in the 1920s. The Palacio Nacional houses various government departments including the treasury. Over the central door hangs the Liberty Bell, rung every year at 2300 on 15 September by the president, who commemorates independence from Spain and gives **El Grito**: '¡Viva México!' The act declaring Mexican Independence was signed in the Salon of Agreements and Benito Juárez lived in the palace during his tenure as president, with his death mask and some personal effects retained for posterity.

On the first and second floors of the Palacio Nacional, on the left as one enters the great courtyard, an area formerly occupied by government offices has been transformed into elegant galleries. But the real attractions here are the superb frescoes by Diego Rivera that flank the staircase and two walls of the first floor. The right-hand panel by the staircase (1929) depicts pre-Hispanic Mexico. The large central panel (275 sq m, started 1929, finished 1935) shows the history of Mexico from 1521 to 1930, and the panel on the left is known as *El mundo de hoy y de mañana* (The World Today and Tomorrow, 1934). The first fresco (4.92 m by 9.71 m) on the first floor is known variously as *La gran Tenochtitlán* and *El mercado de tlatelolco* (1945), and shows the market of Tlatelolco against a background of the ancient city of

② Centro Histórico: Zócalo & Alameda

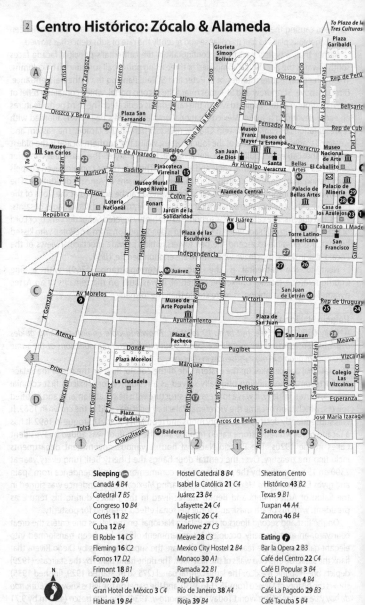

Map labels (streets, plazas & sights):

To Plaza de las Tres Culturas
Plaza Garibaldi
Glorieta Simón Bolívar
Aldama · Arista · Ignacio Zaragoza · Guerrero · Heroes · Soto · Mina · V Trujano
Obispo · R Palacio · Rep de Perú
Belisaric
Rep de Cub
Orozco y Berra · Plaza San Fernando · Zarco · Paseo de la Reforma · Mina · Av del
Pensador Mex · Sta Veracruz · Del 57
Museo San Carlos · Emparán · J Terán · Mariscal · Rosales · Badillo · Hidalgo · G Mora · San Juan de Dios · Av Hidalgo · Santa Veracruz · Museo Nacional de Arte · El Caballito
Museo Franz Mayer · Museo de la Estampa
Puente de Alvarado · Pinacoteca Virreinal · Museo Mural Diego Rivera · Colón · Jardín de la Solidaridad
Alameda Central
Palacio de Bellas Artes · Palacio de Minería · Casa de los Azulejos
Edison · República · Lotería Nacional · Fonart
To 9
Museo San Carlos
Av Juárez · Francisco I Madero
Plaza de las Esculturas · Dolores · Torre Latinoamericana · San Francisco · Gante
A González · C · Turbide · Humboldt · Balderas · Independencia · Revillagigedo · Luis Moya
Av Morelos · D Guerra · Juárez · Artículo 123 · Victoria · San Juan de Letrán · Rep de Uruguay
Atenas · Dondé · Museo de Arte Popular · Ayuntamiento · Plaza de San Juan · San Juan · Meave
Plaza C Pacheco · Márquez · Pugibet · Vizcaína
Plaza Morelos · La Ciudadela · Delicitas · Buentono · Aranda · López · Colegio Las Vizcaínas · Hidalgo · Esperanza
Prim · Bucareli · Tres Guerras · E Martínez · Revillagigedo · Luis Moya · Andrade · José María Izazaga
Plaza Ciudadela · Tolsá · Chapultepec · Arcos de Belén · Salto de Agua
Balderas

N
200 metres
200 yards

Sleeping
Canadá **4** B4
Catedral **7** B5
Congreso **10** B4
Cortés **11** B2
Cuba **12** B4
El Roble **14** C5
Fleming **16** C2
Fornos **17** D2
Frimont **18** B1
Gillow **20** B4
Gran Hotel de México **3** C4
Habana **19** B4
Hostal Amigo **15** C4
Hostal Moneda **31** B5
Hostel Catedral **8** B4
Isabel la Católica **21** C4
Juárez **23** B4
Lafayette **24** C4
Majestic **26** C4
Marlowe **27** C3
Meave **28** C3
Mexico City Hostel **2** B4
Monaco **30** A1
Ramada **22** B1
República **37** B4
Río de Janeiro **38** A4
Rioja **39** B4
San Antonio **41** B4
San Francisco **42** C2

Sheraton Centro
Histórico **43** B2
Texas **9** B1
Tuxpan **44** A4
Zamora **46** B4

Eating
Bar la Opera **2** B3
Café del Centro **22** C4
Café El Popular **3** B4
Café La Blanca **4** B4
Café La Pagoda **29** B3
Café Tacuba **5** B4
Comida Económica
Verónica **34** B4

To Dirección General de Aduanas

➡ **Mexico City maps**
1 City centre, page 78
2 **Centro Histórico: Zócalo
   & Alameda, page 82**
3 Reforma & Zona Rosa,
   page 96
4 Bosque de Chapultepec
   & Polanco, page 98
5 Coyoacán, page 107
6 Metro, page 138

Tenochtitlán. There follow representations of various indigenous cultures – Purépecha, Mixteca-Zapoteca, Totonaca and Huasteca (the last showing the cultivation and worship of maize) – culminating in the final fresco, which shows in narrative form the arrival of Hernán Cortés in Veracruz. These murals were completed between 1942 and 1951.

Templo Mayor
① *Seminario 4 y Guatemala, entrance in the northeast corner of the Zócalo, T55-5542 4784, www.templomayor.inah.gob.mx. Tue-Sun 0900-1700, last tickets 1630. Museum and temple US$4. Guided tours in Spanish, audio guides in English and other languages. There is a café, bookshop and left-luggage office.*

The Templo Mayor, located at the heart of Tenochtitlán's sacred precinct, was the spiritual, social and political centre of the Aztec universe, where the earth, sky and underworld met. On a mundane level, it marked the axis about which the four major quarters of the city were orientated, north, south, east and west. Partly, the temple is believed to be a symbolic representation of the sacred hill, Coatepec, and was the site of important religious ceremonies, which were the mainstay of daily Aztec life. Construction of the temple began in 1325 on the supposed spot where the legendary omen of an eagle perched on a cactus and devouring a snake was beheld, indicating to the wandering tribe where they should settle and build their empire. First as a simple shrine and later, with six subsequent builds, as a grand pyramid, the temple was dedicated to two principal gods: Huitzilopochtli, the beloved god of war and tribute; and Tlaloc, god of rain and agriculture.

In 1519 Cortés and his band of conquistadors arrived in the city. While much impressed by the size and construction of the Templo Mayor, he was disconcerted with the idols it housed, and more so by the acts of ritual sacrifice that took place in their honour. After installing a Christian crucifix in the pyramid, relations between the Aztecs and Spaniards soon worsened, culminating in the conquest and total destruction of the city in 1521. The temple, along with the other sacred structures of Tenochtitlán's holiest quarter, were dismantled and covered with earth.

The temple lay hidden for hundreds of years until the late 19th century, when archaeologists began uncovering a handful of structures and artefacts, most of minor importance. It was not until 1978 that the first big find was struck and electrical workers uncovered a great stone monolith depicting the dismembered moon goddess, Coyolxauqui. For the next four years, a team of archaeologists, headed by Eduardo Matos Moctezuma, initiated the Templo Mayor project and conducted a thorough excavation of the area. Levelling four city blocks and some 13 historic buildings, they resurrected the temple and uncovered over 7000 artefacts, now housed in the superb Templo Mayor museum, which should not be missed. Excavation continues today, with recent finds including an intriguing monolith of the earth goddess Tlaltechutli, uncovered in October 2006. In 2007, a new phase of investigation was initiated, which includes drawing detailed 3D maps of the area.

The site itself can be explored along various outdoor walkways, where the different phases of the temple's development can be seen in excavated sections of walls. Each Aztec ruler was responsible for expanding the complex, which was achieved by adding new layers on top of old ones. The first temple was built by Two-Rabbit around AD 1325, but has not been uncovered by archaeologists. Thought to have been forged from earth and wood, it's doubtful it would have survived the passage of time. The second temple was built around AD 1400 by various rulers, and the few uncovered remnants include two shrines, a *chac-mool* and a sacrificial stone. The most notable contribution of Itzcoatl, builder of the third temple, are eight stone standard bearers thought to have guarded access to the upper shrines.

By the fourth stage of development, the Templo Mayor began to acquire the grandiose characteristics befitting a burgeoning empire capital. Between 1440-1481, Moctezuma I and Axayacatl added fine decorations and sculptures, stone serpent staircases, rich braziers and sumptuous offerings. The more modest fifth stage, initiated by Tizoc around 1486, consisted of a new stucco layer and ceremonial plaza. The sixth temple was vividly inaugurated by Emperor Ahuizotl in 1487. Now walled-off and richly decorated with serpents heads, he ordered the ritual sacrifice of some 1000 prisoners of war, every day for 20 days, as part of the celebrations. Predictably, the streets ran with blood. The seventh and final layer, like the first, has been lost. Destroyed by the Spaniards, we have only historical sources to verify its appearance, which was immense, magnificent and lavishly decorated by most accounts.

Around the Zócalo

The **Suprema Corte de Justicia de la Nación** ⓘ *directly south of the Palacio Nacional on the southeast corner of the Zócalo, Mon-Fri 0900-1700, free, but bring ID*, has frescoes by Orozco including *National Riches* and *Proletarian Struggle*. Other contemporary murals by Cauduro can be seen over the southwest stairwell. The ornate building in the southwest corner of the Zócalo, the **Antiguo Ayuntamiento** (old city hall), is now used for ceremonial purposes and is where visiting dignitaries are granted the Keys to the City. Nearby is the **Gran Hotel**, 16 de Septiembre 82, worth a look for its sumptuous interior.

On the west side of the Zócalo are the **Portales de los Mercaderes** (arcades of the merchants), which have been very busy since they were built in 1524. North of them, opposite the cathedral, is the **Monte de Piedad** (national pawnshop) ⓘ *Mon-Fri 0830-1800, Sat 0830-1300*, established in the 18th century and housed in a 16th-century building that's built over the palace where Cortés and his soldiers stayed before they laid siege to Tenochtitlán. Inside, prices are government controlled and bargains can often be found. Auctions are held each Friday at 1000 (first, second and third Friday for jewellery and watches, fourth for everything else). US dollars are accepted.

On the north side of the Zócalo, behind the cathedral, you'll find the **Centro Cultural de España** ⓘ *Guatemala 18, www.ccemx.org, Tue-Wed 1000-2000, Thu-Sat 1000-2300, Sun 1000-1600, free*, with contemporary exhibitions and occasional parties on the rooftop terrace. The building is historic and well restored. Almost next door is the relatively new **Museo Archivo de la Fotografía** ⓘ *Guatemala 34, www.maf.df.gob.mx, Tue-Sun 1000-1800, free*, housing a wealth of historic Mexico City photographs.

Plaza Santo Domingo

Plaza Santo Domingo, four blocks north of the Zócalo's northwest corner, is an intimate little plaza surrounded by fine colonial buildings. There is the **Antigua Aduana** (former customs house) ⓘ *daily 1000-1730, US$2, Sun US$1.30*, on the east side, and the **Portales de Santo Domingo** on the west side, where public scribes and owners of antiquated hand-operated printing presses are still in business. The church of **Santo Domingo** (1737), in Mexican baroque, is on the north side (note the carving on the doors and facade), whilst the old **Edificio de la Inquisición**, where the torturous tribunals of the Inquisition were held, is at the northeast corner. By standing on tiptoe in the men's room you may be able to see through the window into the prison cells of the Inquisition, not yet open to the public. After being the Escuela Nacional de la Medicina it is now the **Museo de la Medicina Mexicana** ⓘ *Brasil 33, daily 0900-1800, free*, with dusty displays on indigenous and Western medicine.

Antiguo Secretaría de Educación

① *Argentina 28, 3 blocks north of the Zócalo's northeast corner (1 block east of Plaza Santo Domingo). Mon-Fri 0900-1800. Free.*

The **Secretaría de Educación Pública** was built in 1922. For lovers of Mexican murals there are more than 200 to view by a number of different painters, including some of Diego Rivera's masterpieces. Painted between 1923 and 1928, they illustrate the lives and sufferings of the common people, as well as satirizing the rich. Look out for *Día de Muertos* (Day of the Dead) on the ground floor (far left in second courtyard) and, on the first floor, *El pan nuestro* (Our Daily Bread) showing the poor at supper, the wonderfully satirical *El banquete de Wall Street* (The Wall Street Banquet), and the splendidly restored *La cena del capitalista* (The Capitalist's Supper). A long passageway connecting the Secretaría with the older **Antigua Aduana de Santo Domingo** displays the dynamic Siqueiros mural, *Patriots and Parricides*.

Antiguo Colegio de San Ildefonso

① *Justo Sierra 16, 2 blocks north and ½ block east of the Zócalo's northeast corner (1 block south and ½ block east of the Secretaría de Educación), www.sanildefonso.org.mx. Tue-Sun 1000-1700. US$4, free Tue.*

The former **Colegio de San Ildefonso** was built in splendid baroque style in 1749 as a Jesuit school, but later became the Escuela Nacional Preparatoria. There are important frescoes by Orozco (including *Revolutionary Trinity* and *The Trench*) and, in the Anfiteatro Bolívar, by Diego Rivera (*Creation*) and Fernando Leal, all in excellent condition. There is another Leal mural, *Lord of Chalma*, in the stairwell separating the two floors of Orozco works, as well as Jean Charlot's *Massacre in the Templo Mayor*. In a stairwell of the Colegio Chico there are experimental murals by Siqueiros. The whole interior has been magnificently restored. There are occasional important temporary exhibitions. More Orozco frescoes can be seen at the **Biblioteca Iberoamericana** ① *Cuba, between República de Brasil and Argentina*. For more information on the muralists and their work, see boxes page 89 and page 92.

Nearby, also on Calle Justo Sierra, is the **Mexican Geographical Society**; in the courtyard is a bust of Humboldt and a statue of Benito Juárez, plus a display of documents and maps (ask at the door to be shown in). Opposite are the **Anfiteatro Simón Bolívar**, with murals of his life in the lobby, and an attractive theatre, entered through the former **Colegio de San Ildefonso**. Just along the road is the **Museo de la Caricatura** ① *Donceles 99, 2 blocks north of the Zócalo (1 block west of the Colegio de San Ildefonso), Tue-Sun 1000-1800, US$2*. Housed in the former Convento de Cristo, this collection includes works by contemporary cartoonists as well as the influential artist José Guadalupe Posada, famous for his skeletal images that moved well beyond Day of the Dead references. Spanish only.

Plaza Loreto and around

Some two blocks north and two blocks east of the Zócalo's northeast corner (or, if visiting in sequence, two and a half blocks east of the Museo de Caricatura) is the elegant Plaza Loreto, surrounded by a wealth of handsome colonial buildings. Its northern edge is flanked by the church of **Loreto**, built 1816 and now tilting badly. The facade is a remarkable example of 'primitive' or 'radical' neoclassicism. Just north of the church there is a covered market concealing some striking1930s murals. One block west of the market you'll find the church and convent of **San Pedro y San Pablo** (1603), both massive structures now turned over to secular use, one of them housing the **Museo de la Luz** ① *Mon-Fri 0900-1600 and Sat-Sun 1000-1700, US$2*, with exhibitions on light and optics.

Calle Moneda

Calle Moneda runs east–west from the Zócalo's northeast corner, but if walking from the church and convent of San Pedro y San Pablo, it can be reached by heading three blocks south. It is the site of some grand historic buildings, some of which date back to the earliest days of the Spanish colony.

The **Antiguo Palacio del Arzobispado** (old archbishop's palace) is the legendary place where Juan Diego first revealed, to the cunning delight of ecclesiastical authorities, the image of the Virgin of Guadalupe imprinted on his peasant cloak. It now houses the **Museo de la Secretaría de Hacienda y Crédito Público** ① *Moneda 4, Tue-Sun, US$1, free Sun*, with a fine national and international art collection and the archaeological remains of the pyramid of Tezcatlipoca. Nearby is the **Museo Nacional de Culturas** ① *Moneda 13, Tue-Sun 0930-1745, free*, housed by the old city mint, built in 1567, from which the road derives its name (*moneda* means 'currency', or more colloquially, 'change'). It is superbly restored with diverting exhibits on world culture set around a pleasant central patio.

One block east and half a block north is the **Museo José Luis Cuevas** ① *Academia 13, Tue-Sun 1000-1700, US$1.50*, a large colonial building that was formerly the convent of Santa Ines. It houses a permanent collection of paintings, drawings and sculptures by the controversial and contemporary artist José Luis Cuevas. One is two storeys high, *La Giganta*, an impressive woman of bronze. There are also international works and temporary exhibitions. The nearby church of **Santa Ines** has an interesting dome of gold and blue.

Back on Moneda, two blocks further east, the road changes its name to Zapata. Here, **La Santísima Trinidad** (1677, remodelled 1755) should be seen for its fine towers and the rich carvings on its facade. The neighbourhood becomes increasingly shabby beyond this point.

Zócalo to La Merced

It's an interesting walk to La Merced, southeast of the centre, but the surroundings can be sketchy, so take care (or take the metro if you feel uncomfortable). Three blocks south of the Zócalo, the oldest hospital in continental America, **Jesús Nazareno**, is at 20 de Noviembre 82. It was founded in 1526 by Cortés, close to the spot where he and Moctezuma first met. It was remodelled in 1928, save for the patio and staircase. Since 1974 Cortés' bones have been kept in the adjoining church, on the corner of Pino Suárez and República de El Salvador. His memory is not honoured or celebrated.

Diagonally opposite the church, the **Museo de la Ciudad** ① *Pino Suárez 30 y República de El Salvador, Tue-Wed 1000-1800, US$1.50, free Wed, bring photo ID*, shows the geology of the city with life-size figures in period costumes depicting the history of different peoples before Cortés. The permanent exhibition is sometimes inaccessible during temporary shows. In the attic above the museum is the studio of Joaquín Clausell, with walls covered with Impressionist miniatures.

Two blocks south of the museum at Mesones 139 is the Anglican (Episcopal) cathedral, called the **Catedral de San José de Gracia**. Built in 1642 as a Roman Catholic church, it was given by the Benito Juárez government to the Episcopal Mission in Mexico. Juárez himself often attended services here. Continue east and the road changes its name to Corona. After several blocks you will arrive at La Merced market.

Mercado Merced → *Metro Merced*

The gargantuan **Mercado Merced**, said to be the largest market in all the Americas, dates back over 400 years. Its activities are spread over several blocks and it is well worth a visit.

Take care, as robberies have been reported, and it's probably not a good place to flash a camera. In the northern quarter of this market are the ruins of La Merced monastery. The fine 18th-century patio is almost all that survives; the courtyard, on Avenida Uruguay, between Calle Talavera and Calle Jesús María, opposite No 171, is nearly restored. While you're in the area, also be sure to check out the **Mercado Sonora**, opposite La Merced on Avenida Fray Servando Teresa de Mier. This is a **witches' market**, where you'll find all manner of curious trinkets from love potions to giant toads embalmed in glass jars. The old women, beseeching you through the candlelight and snaking incense smoke, only add to the creepy atmosphere.

Zócalo to La Alameda

Avenida Madero

On Avenida Madero, a grandiose avenue that leads west from the Zócalo towards the Alameda, is the late 16th-century **La Profesa church** with a fine high altar and a leaning tower. Occupied by the Jesuits, who first professed their faith there, a large amount of religious art can be admired inside. Opposite stands the **Museo del Estanquillo** ① *Isabel La Católica 26, www.museodelestanquillo.com.mx, Wed-Mon 1000-1800, free*, with a collection of art that's mainly pop-culture.

Around 2½ blocks west, the 18th-century **Palacio de Iturbide** ① *Av Madero 17, Tue-Sun 1000-1700, free*, once the home of Emperor Agustín (1821-1823), has been restored and has a clear plastic roof. Wander around and admire the interior of Tuscan-style columns, hard wood doors, art and carvings. It is now the head office of a bank.

Also on Avenida Madero, near the Alameda, is the 16th-century **Casa de los Azulejos** (House of Tiles). It is brilliantly faced with blue and white 18th-century Puebla tiles. Occupied by the Zapatista army during the Revolution, it is now home to **Sanborn's** restaurant. The staircase walls are covered with an Orozco fresco *Omniscience* (1925). Opposite is the church of **San Francisco**, founded in 1525 by the 'Apostles of Mexico', the first 12 Franciscans to reach the country. It was by far the most important church in colonial days, attended by the Viceroys themselves. Cortés' body rested here for some time, as did the body of Emperor Iturbide.

At the end of Madero, at the corner of Eje Central Lázaro Cárdenas, is the **Torre Latinoamericana** ① *www.torrelatino.com, daily 0900-2200, US$4.50*, which has a viewing platform with telescopes on the 42nd floor, some 139 m up. Although smog often obscures the views, it is nonetheless a thrilling experience to gaze upon the sprawling mosaic-like expanse of Mexico City from such a height. If the air is particularly bad, dusk provides an alternative to take in a brightly twinkling vista. The tower was remodelled in 2006 to celebrate the tower's 50th anniversary.

Calle Tacuba and Plaza Tolsá

Calle Tacuba runs parallel to Madero, reaching westwards from the northwest corner of the cathedral. In Aztec times, this was one of the causeways that connected the island capital to the mainland where Cortés and his soldiers fled during the infamous massacre on the *Noche Triste*. Tacuba concludes near the Alameda, at **Plaza Tolsá**, named after the architect who designed large sections of the Catedral Metropolitana. Here, the bronze **statue of King Carlos IV** known as 'El Caballito', also designed by Tolsá, was the subject of controversy after Independence from Spain, when locals wanted to melt it down to make 'something more useful'. Eventually, however, they could not deny its aesthetic qualities,

Los Tres Grandes

The story of muralism in Mexico has largely been that of 'Los Tres Grandes', Diego Rivera, José Clemente Orozco and David Alfaro Siqueiros, although there were many other artists involved from the start. In 1914 Orozco and Siqueiros were to be found in the Carranza stronghold of Orizaba fomenting social and artistic revolution through the mouthpiece of the pamphlet *La Vanguardia*. Seven years later, out of the turmoil and divisiveness of the Revolution, emerged a need for a visual expression of *mexicanidad* (Mexican identity) and unity, and in 1921 Orozco and Siqueiros answered the call of the Minister of Education, José Vasconcelos, to provide a visual analogue to a rapidly changing Mexico. Rivera was brought onto the team that in buildings like the National Preparatory School and the Ministry of Education, attempted to produce a distinctly Mexican form of modernism, on a monumental scale, accessible to the people. These were ideas forged in Orizaba and later clarified in Europe (where Rivera and Siqueiros saw Italian frescoes) but which derived their popular form from paintings on the walls of *pulquerías* (*pulque* bars) and in the satirical broadsheet engravings of José Guadalupe Posada. Themes were to include pre-Columbian society, modern agriculture and medicine and a didactic Mexican history pointing to a mechanized future for the benefit of all. Siqueiros in particular was keen to transform the working practice of artists who would henceforth work as members of cooperatives.

The 'movement' fell apart almost from its inception. There were riots objecting to the communist content of murals and the beginnings of a long ideological and artistic disagreement between Siqueiros and Rivera, which would culminate on 28 August 1935 at the Palacio de Bellas Artes with Rivera, brandishing a pistol, storming into a Siqueiros lecture and demanding a debate on what the Mexican Mural Renaissance had all been about! The debate ensued over several days before they agreed to disagree.

Despite the failings of the movement many outstanding murals were painted over a long period. With Siqueiros frequently off the scene, in jail or in exile, Los Tres Grandes became the big two; Rivera carving up much of Mexico City as his territory and Orozco taking on Guadalajara. However, Siqueiros outlasted both of them and carried the torch of Muralism and Revolution into the early 1970s. For mural sites, see box, page 92.

and after stints on the Paseo de Reforma and other locations, the 'little horse' settled here. A small museum dedicated to the architect can be found inside the **Palacio de Minería** ⓘ *Tacuba 5, on the plaza, Wed-Sun 1000-1800, US$1*. Just off the southwest corner of the plaza is the magnificent **Correo Central** (central post office) ⓘ *corner of Tacuba y Eje Central Lázaro Cárdenas, Mon-Fri 0900-1800, Sat 1000-1400, free*. Commissioned in 1902 and completed in 1907, this Florentine-style palace was commissioned by Porfirio Díaz as part of his works programme commemorating 100 years of Independence. It is certainly worth a look. Plaza Tolsá is also the site of the national museum of art (see below).

Museo Nacional de Arte
ⓘ *Tacuba 8, opposite Palacio de Minería, Plaza Tolsá, www.munal.com.mx. Tue-Sun 1030-1730, US$2.50.*

The museum was built in 1904 and designed by the Italian architect Silvio Contri as the Palacio de Comunicaciones. The building has magnificent staircases made by the Florentine firm Pignone. It houses a large collection of Mexican paintings, drawings, sculptures and ceramics dating from the 16th century to 1950. It has the largest number of paintings (more than 100) by José María Velasco in Mexico City, as well as works by Miguel Cabrera, Gerardo Murillo, Rivera, Orozco, Siqueiros, Tamayo and Anguiano. The building has been completely restored and modernized. It is considered by many as one of the best museums in the country.

La Alameda and around

The gardens of the **Alameda Central** were once the Aztec market and later the place of execution for the Spanish Inquisition. Beneath the broken shade of eucalyptus, cypress and ragged palms, wide paths link fountains and heroic statues. The Alameda became a popular area for all social classes to stroll casually in the 19th century. It is now much more a common thoroughfare, with many temporary stalls at certain festive times of year. The park is illuminated at night.

Along the south side of the Alameda runs Avenida Juárez, a broad street with a mixture of old and new buildings. Opposite the Palacio de Bellas Artes is a building known as **La Nacional**, which was Mexico City's first skyscraper in the 1930s. Look carefully at its perpendicularity, a result of the 1985 earthquake.

Also on the south side of the Alameda is the **Hemiciclo a Juárez statue** (now on the 20-peso note), designed by Guillermo de Heredia in white marble and inaugurated in 1910 to mark the centenary of Independence. Opposite, the colonial church of **Corpus Christi** is used to display and sell folk arts and crafts. Further west a sunken section of the pavement shelters the **Plaza de las Esculturas** (1998), with elegant 19th-century sculptures.

A stroll down Calle Dolores, a busy and fascinating street, leads to the **Mercado de San Juan**. Three blocks west, on Plaza Ciudadela, is the lively **Mercado de la Ciudadela**, which sells crafts from all over Mexico, and the **Centro de la Imagen** ① *Tue-Sun 1100-1800, free*, with documentary photography and art exhibitions. Meanwhile, the new **Museo de Arte Popular** ① *Revillagigedo 11, a block south of the Alameda, Tue-Sun 1000-1700, free*, exhibits *artesanías* from all the country and is great introduction to Mexican craft traditions, particularly if you're hoping to explore some of the interesting markets outside of the capital. It is housed in an art deco building that once served as the headquarters of the fire department.

Palacio de Bellas Artes

① *Eastern side of the Alameda, T55-5529 9320, www.balletamalia.com. Tue-Sun 1000-1800. US$3. Performances by the Ballet Folklórico de México, Sun 0930 and 2030, Wed 2030; tickets US$37-65.*

A large, showy building, interesting for art deco lovers (see the fabulous stained-glass skylight in the roof), it houses a museum, theatre, a *cafetería* at mezzanine level (serving average continental food at moderate prices) and an excellent bookshop on the arts. The museum has old and contemporary paintings, prints, sculptures and handicrafts. There are spirited Riveras in the room of oils and watercolours. The fresco by Rivera is a copy of the one rubbed out in disapproval at Radio City, New York. Other frescoes are by Orozco, Tamayo and Siqueiros. There are also prestigious temporary fine art exhibitions (no extra charge). On the top floor is a museum of architecture, which holds temporary exhibitions and shows the building's history. The most remarkable thing about the theatre is its glass curtain designed by Tiffany. It is solemnly raised and lowered before each performance of the Ballet Folklórico de México. Operas are also performed here and there are frequent orchestral concerts. The palace was refurbished, inside and out, in 1994 to celebrate its diamond jubilee; the garden in front of the marble apron has been laid out as originally designed. But the palace is listing badly and has sunk 4 m since it was built.

Museo Franz Mayer
① *Northern side of the Alameda, T55-5518 2265. Tue-Sun 1000-1700. US$2.*

The Museo Franz Mayer is housed in the former Hospital de San Juan de Dios, built in the 17th century. Recently rebuilt and exquisitely restored, it houses a library and an important decorative arts collection of ceramics, glass, silver, timepieces, furniture and textiles, as well as Mexican and European paintings from the 16th to the 20th centuries. Its cloister is an oasis of peace in the heart of the city. Nearby is the Jardín Morelos, flanked by two old churches: **Santa Veracruz** to the right and **San Juan de Dios** to the left. The latter has a richly carved baroque exterior; its image of San Antonio de Padua is visited by those who are broken-hearted from love.

Museo Mural Diego Rivera
① *Balderas y Colón, north side of the Jardín de la Solidaridad, at the west end of the Alameda Central. Tue-Sun 1000-1800. US$1.50.*

Diego Rivera's huge (15 m by 4.8 m) and fascinating mural, the *Sueño de una Tarde Dominical en la Alameda Central*, was removed from the earthquake-damaged **Hotel del Prado** on Avenida Juárez in 1985 and now occupies its own purpose-built museum, the Museo Mural Diego Rivera. One of Rivera's finest works, it presents a pageant of Mexican history from the Conquest up to the 1940s with vivid portraits of national and foreign figures, heroes and villains as well as his wife, Frida Kahlo (see box, page 109) and characters from everyday life. It is highly recommended. Next door you'll find the **Laboratorio de Arte Alameda** ① *Dr Mora 7, www.artealameda.inba.gob.mx, Tue-Sun 0900-1700, US$1, free Sun*, located inside the former Convento de Diego and hosting technologically inspired art installations.

Plaza Garibaldi
About four blocks north of Bellas Artes off Eje Central Lázaro Cárdenas is Plaza Garibaldi, an absolute must one evening, ideally on a Friday or Saturday (it tends to be quiet on Mondays) when up to 200 Mariachis in their traditional costume of huge sombrero, tight silver-embroidered trousers, pistol and *sarape*, will play your favourite Mexican serenade for between US$5 (for a bad one) and US$10 (for a good one). If you arrive by taxi you will be besieged. The whole square throbs with life and the packed bars are cheerful. On one side of the plaza is a gigantic and very entertaining eating hall where different stalls sell different courses. The **Lagunilla** market is held about four blocks northeast of the plaza, a hive of activity particularly on Sundays.

Plaza de la República and around

Plaza de la República lies west of the Alameda on Avenida Juárez, a major landmark dominated by the **Monumento a la Revolución**. This enormous and unforgettable Soviet-style structure has a large copper dome and supporting columns set on the largest triumphal arches in the world. It was originally commissioned by Porfirio Díaz as a legislative chamber, but ended up as a kind of mausoleum for heroes of the revolution, with the remains of Madero, Villa, Carranza, Calles and Cardenas contained inside. Beneath the monument

Mural sites

In addition to the centres of mural painting listed in the main text (Palacio Nacional, Suprema Corte de Justicia, Palacio de Bellas Artes, Museo Mural Diego Rivera, Escuela Nacional Preparatoria-San Ildefonso, Secretaría de Educación, Castillo de Chapultepec and below Polyforum Cultural Siqueiros), there are other sites well worth visiting that all lie within walking distance or short metro ride from the centre. Some of these are functioning workplaces, so tact should be shown when visiting: ask permission before heading off into labyrinthine buildings and always check about photo restrictions (invariably flash is prohibited).

Mercado Abelardo Rodríguez
① *Venezuela, 4 blocks northeast of the Zócalo, main entrance on Rodríguez Puebla*, is fascinating as one of the only examples of a concerted attempt by a cooperative of artists of varying abilities, under the direction of Diego Rivera, to teach and record the workers' revolution in an actual workers' environment. Today the work of this food market goes on, but the murals, at all the entrances, are largely ignored by traders and tourists alike. Perhaps the most emblematic is *The Markets* by Miguel Tzab on the ceiling above the stairs at the northwest entrance, while Ramón Alva Guadarrama's *The Labours of the Field*,

at the southeast corner, reflects the market's agricultural base. Most elaborate are the murals of the American Greenwood sisters, Marion and Grace, showing *Industrialization of the Countryside* and *The Mine*, on the stairs either side of the main entrance. Opposite, upstairs, is a relief mural by Isamu Noguchi. For permission to take photos go to the market office behind the restaurant at the southwest entrance.

A location plan of the murals is available at the tourist agency on Venezuela 72, beside the **Teatro del Pueblo** attached to the market. In the theatre foyer is Antonio Pujol's *Problems of the Worker*, much praised at the time of its completion in 1936. In the cloisters of the confusingly named **Patio Diego Rivera** ① *behind the ticket office*, is Pablo O'Higgins's tirade against international fascism, *The Fight of the Workers Against the Monopolies*.

Next to the Museo Nacional de Arte is the **Cámara de Senadores** ① *Hipoteca Beride between Donceles and Tacuba, Metro Allende or Bellas Artes*, which has a violent mural (1957) by Jorge González Camarena on the history of Mexico, starting with the pre-Cortesian battles between eagle and jaguar warriors.

The **Sindicato Mexicano de Electricistas** ① *Antonio Caso 45 (west of Cristóbal Colón monument on Reforma), T55-5535 0386*, has one of Siqueiros' most

you'll find the **Museo Nacional de la Revolución** ① *Tue-Sun 0900-1700*, with lots of exhibits, photographs and videos extolling the virtuous feats of these legendary characters.

The neighbourhoods around the plaza, including **Tabacalera**, are quiet, leafy and residential, if sometimes slightly seamy, as there is a small but mostly innocuous red light district on **Mariscal**. The high concentration of cheap hotels makes this area a long-time favourite of budget travellers, and there are plenty of good street food stalls too, with sizzling offerings that draw droves of office workers at lunch time.

Three blocks north of the plaza, Puente de Alvarado runs east towards Alameda Central, soon changing its name to Hidalgo. It is the site of many bustling market stalls and the Revolución metro stop. Nearby, the **Museo de San Carlos** ① *Puente de Alvarado* important murals, *Portrait of the Bourgeoisie* (1939-1940), located up the second floor stairwell to the left of the entrance. It depicts the revolutionary struggle against international fascism and is considered a seminal work for its use of cinematic montage techniques and viewing points. Before taking photos ask permission in the *secretaría* office on the right at the end of the corridor on the second floor.

A 15-minute walk away is the **Teatro Jorge Negrete** ① *Altamirano 118, Colonia San Rafael, T55-5535 2246, Metro San Cosme*, in the foyer of which is a later Siqueiros mural, *Theatrical Art in the Social Life of Mexico* (1957), precursor in its expression of movement to his mural in Chapultepec Castle. Ask permission to see it in the office at No 128. No photos.

At the **Hospital de La Raza** in what was once an outer entrance hall (but is now at the centre of the building) is Rivera's *History of Medicine* (1953), and to the left of the main entrance, in a naturally lit theatre foyer (usually locked but you can see it through the large frontal windows if there is nobody about with keys), is Siqueiros' *For the Complete Safety of All Mexicans at Work* (1952-1954). Ask a security guard or at main reception for directions to the murals. Take Metro La Raza and from the station head south along the right side of Insurgentes Norte, cross the railway, go straight ahead and

then cross the freeway by the footbridge to the hospital. For permission to take photos here and at other medical centres you must ask at the **Sede IMSS** ① *Hidalgo 230, Metro Bellas Artes*.

Another hospital with a relevant themed mural is the **Centro Médico Nacional** ① *Av Cuauhtémoc*, where Siqueiros' *Apology for the Future Victory of Medicine over Cancer* (1958) has been restored following damage in the 1985 earthquake. Since 1996 it has been on display in the waiting area of the oncology building beyond the main entrance building on the right. At the entrance, as you come up the stairs from the metro station Centro Médico, is a mural by Chávez Morado commemorating the rebuilding of the hospital in which many died during the earthquake.

Before or after visiting the mural sites we recommend reading one or more of the following: *The Murals of Diego Rivera*, by Desmond Rochfort, London, 1987; *Mexican Muralists*, same author, New York, 1984. *Dreaming with his Eyes Open*, by Patrick Marnham, New York and London, 1998, is an immensely readable though not entirely scholastic biography of Diego Rivera, which deals with Orozco, Siqueiros and the other muralists as well as Rivera. See also box, page 89.

50, Metro Revolución, www.mnsancarlos.com, Wed-Mon 1000- 1800, US$2, is in a 19th-century palace, with fine Mexican colonial paintings and a first-class collection of European paintings. It was the home of Señora Calderón de la Barca who wrote *Life in Mexico* while living there.

Santa María la Ribera and San Cosme

These two areas, north of Metro San Cosme, became fashionable residential quarters in the late 19th century. Reach them by walking west along Puente de Alvarado, which changes its name to Avenida Ribera de San Cosme. In these neighbourhoods, many elegant, if neglected, facades can still be seen. On the corner of Ribera de San Cosme and Naranjo next to Metro San Cosme note the **Casa de los Mascarones**. Built in 1766, this was the country house of the Conde del Valle de Orizaba, later the Escuela Nacional de Música. Recently restored, it now houses a university computer centre. The **Museo Universitario del Chopo** ① *Enrique González Martínez 10, between Metro San Cosme and Av Insurgentes Norte, Wed- Sun 1000-1400, 1600-1900,* holds contemporary international photography and art exhibitions in a church-like building designed by Eiffel. In the pleasant **Alameda de Santa María**, between Pino and Torres Bodet, stands an extraordinary Moorish pavilion designed by Mexicans for the Paris Exhibition in 1889. On its return to Mexico, the *kiosko* was placed in the Alameda Central before being transferred to its present site in 1910. On the west side of this square, on Torres Bodet, is the **Museo del Instituto Geológico** ① *Tue-Sun 1000-1700, free.* In addition to its collection of fossils and minerals (and magnificent early 20th-century showcases), the building itself (1904) is worth a visit for its swirling wrought-iron staircases and unusual stained-glass windows of mining scenes by Zettler (Munich and Mexico).

Paseo de la Reforma and Zona Rosa

Paseo de la Reforma is Mexico City's most elegant thoroughfare. Named after Benito Juárez's reform laws of 1861, it was previously known as Carlotta's promenade, after Empress Carlotta, who designed it during the reign of her husband Emperor Maximilian. It was originally intended as a European-style boulevard connecting the Centro Histórico with their castle residence in Chapultepec, then woefully divorced from the centre by tracts of agricultural land. After the execution of Maximilian in 1867, the road acquired its present name.

During the late 19th century Reforma flourished as a kind of bourgeois enclave, where well-heeled and prominent families would take Sunday strolls with their parasols. Like Maximilian, Porfirio Díaz was inspired by the European models of city-building, and commissioned several elegant statues to adorn the road, then at the heart of his vision for a modernized Mexico City. But over the decades, the wealthy sought refuge in quieter places, and after the 1957 earthquake, moved out completely. The corporations moved in, bulldozed the mansions and constructed the high-rise towers of glass that line it today. Since its conception, Reforma has been extended considerably, making it one of Mexico City's principal arteries.

You can walk Reforma from the centre to Chapultepec and admire the buildings and various monuments stationed at the *glorietas* (roundabouts). Allow 1-2 hours and don't expect much respite from the traffic. Commencing at the intersection with Paseo de Bucareli and Juárez, about halfway between Plaza de la República and Alameda Central, you'll find a large yellow sculpture called **El Caballito** (the Little Horse). It represents an abstracted version of the bronze statue of King Carlos IV which once stood there, but has since been relocated to the less prominent Plaza de Tolsá. This junction is also the site of the 1930s lottery building.

The next *glorieta* is home to a statue commemorating the 'discoverer' of the Americas, **Cristóbal Colón** (Christopher Columbus), and is the first of the host commissioned by Díaz. A few luxury hotels and car rental offices occupy surroundings, indicating the shape of things to come for Reforma. Just north lies the Plaza de la República.

At the intersection with Insurgentes stands the proud **Monumento a Cuauhtémoc**, exalting the last Aztec emperor, who clutches his spear in defiance. Díaz commissioned the statue as a symbol of resistance against foreign aggressors, rather than a celebration of native culture. There are a plethora of banks and financial buildings in the surroundings, including Mexico's stock exchange, the Centro Bursátil, slightly further west at the junction with Niza and Río Rhin. Just north of this section is the **Museo Carranza** ⓘ *Lerma y Amazonas*, a museum with items linked to the life of Venustiano Carranza, the famous revolutionary and constitutionalist, and to the Revolution itself.

The next monument, at the junction of Río Tiber and Florencia, is the **Monumento a la Independencia**, also known as 'El Angel'. This golden angel, grasping the wreath of victory in one hand and the chains of tyranny in the other, is the most important and elegant work on Reforma, a symbol of Mexico City itself – or of its soaring spirit, at least. It was commissioned by Díaz to commemorate the centenary of Independence, which coincided with his birthday. It was designed by Antonio Rivas Mercado and built in France. It contains the remains of several heroes from the Independence struggle including Hidalgo and Morelos. The angel is actually a remake of the original 1910 version, which was toppled by the 1957 earthquake. The sight of its broken wings, scattered wildly across the Paseo, unsettled many observers at the time.

The final statue on Refoma before it enters Chapultepec, designed by Juan Olaguibel and added in 1942, is **La Diana Cazadora** (Diana Huntress), which celebrates the female form. For many years its naked body was considered too raunchy for public viewing and covered with a loin cloth. Further west, at the gates Chapultepec itself, stands the **Torre Mayor**. Added in 2003, this green glass tower is 225 m high, earthquake resistant and the tallest skyscraper in Latin America.

Zona Rosa

The famous Zona Rosa (pink zone) lies to the south of Reforma, contained approximately by Reforma, Sevilla, Avenida Chapultepec and Insurgentes Sur. This was formerly the setting for Mexico City's most fashionable stores, restaurants and nightclubs, with roads bearing the names of European cities – perhaps in an attempt to foster an international atmosphere. It suffered considerable damage in the 1985 earthquake and subsequently lost ground to Polanco (see below). In recent times it has seen a revival and is once again a very pleasant area in which to stroll, shop (or window-shop) and dine, with many open-air restaurants. Don't expect too much authenticity, as the majority of the Zona Rosa's establishments cater to tourist clientele, and others are outright tacky. Perhaps the most interesting options are a host of new Korean restaurants established by the area's immigrant population. The Zona Rosa is also increasingly popular with Mexico City's gay and lesbian crowd.

Bosque de Chapultepec and Polanco

Bosque de Chapultepec (meaning 'Hill of Crickets' in Náhuatl), is Mexico City's most verdant park space, replete with winding pathways and exuberant vegetation. It's particularly popular on Sunday, when throngs of families descend to partake in picnics, stroll around, or otherwise enjoy the refreshing shade of the thousands of ahuehuete trees, so sacred to the Aztecs. In the 12th century, the Toltecs revered this space for its fine defensive position and its abundance of natural springs. The Aztecs, too, briefly settled on the hill before being ousted by rival tribes. After the establishment of Tenochtitlán, they returned to claim it, siphoning off the spring water through aqueducts. The poet-king Nezahualcóyotl constructed a palace on the hill, and the whole area became a private resort and hunting grounds to be enjoyed by subsequent generations of Aztec emperors. Each carved their image in a rock near the base of the hill, but sadly, these carvings were destroyed by the Spaniards. Chapultepec was also the residence of the ill-fated Emperor Maximilian, who used to host cricket matches in his idyllic grounds, apparently well-attended by the Cornish miners of Pachuca. The park is divided into three sections. The first and easternmost is the oldest part and the site of the most interesting attractions. Note that Sunday is the best day to enjoy the colourful family atmosphere, but a bad day to see the museums, which are free on Sundays but invariably crowded.

Primera Sección

The first section contains a maze of pathways and is home to Los Pinos, the official residence of the president and most definitely out of bounds. There is a large lake originally built for the pleasure of Emperor Maximilian, but now enjoyed by peddle-boaters. You can rent a vessel yourself (US$5 per hour) if you fancy a cruise. Nearby, there is a smaller lake with an outdoor theatre used for performances of *Swan Lake* and similar renditions. The **zoo** ① *Tue-Sun, 0900-1630, free*, is home to giant pandas and other animals from around the world; it is well laid out, the cages are spacious and most animals seem content. Also close to the lake is the **botanical garden** ① *1000-1600, free*, with specimens from various climatic zones. Along a section of the Paseo Reforma, between the zoo and the Rufino

③ Reforma & Zona Rosa

		Eating ⑦	Les Moustaches 7
NH México 5		Arles 1	Quebracho 8
Prim 7		Beatricita 2	Sushi Itto 9
Royal Zona Rosa 2		Bella Luna 3	Yug 10
Suites Amberes 5		Chalet Suizo 4	
Sleeping ⊜	Suites Havre 9	Fonda del Refugio 5	**Bars & clubs** ⑦
Casa González 1	Uxmal 10	La Puerta del Angel 6	Milán 11
María Cristina 4	Viena 11		

Tamayo museum, you'll find an open-air photo gallery that's worth a perusal. At the western end of Reforma lies the Auditorio Nacional, an important venue for theatrical and musical performances. Chapultepec's first section is also the site of some excellent museums, including the world-class Museo Nacional de Antropología, Museo de Arte Moderno, Museo Rufino Tamayo and the Castillo de Chapultepec, among others. There are shaded spots throughout, and stalls selling snacks of all kinds, especially at weekends.

Castillo de Chapultepec and around

The imposing Castillo de Chapultepec, commissioned in 1785, was preceded by another fortress that served as a weapons arsenal, but was tragically destroyed in a gunpowder explosion. The present structure took several years to complete and was left empty until 1841 when it found its purpose as a military academy. It was here that the famous *niños* heroes – the brave child cadets, now immortalized in a white marble monument at the base of the hill – staved off an attack by US marines in 1847. Rather than surrender to the gringos, the last survivors committed suicide by jumping to their deaths, Juan Escutia among them, who reportedly wrapped himself in the Mexican flag as he plunged. In 1864, Emperor Maximilian and his wife, Empress Carlotta, converted the castle into their personal residence, sculpting the park to their tastes and importing all manner of sumptuous furnishings. Their dream was to recreate their cherished Miramare Castle in Italy.

Today, the **Museo Nacional de Historia** ① *inside the castle, Tue-Sun 0900-1700, US$4*, contains the personal effects of the doomed couple, including luxurious carriages and lavish salons. There are also equally opulent quarters formerly occupied by Porfirio Díaz and exhibitions chronicling Mexican history. There is an impressive mural by Siqueiros, *From the Dictatorship of Porfirio Díaz to the Revolution* (in Sala XIII, near the entrance), and a mural by O'Gorman on the theme of Independence, as well as several others by Camarena. Free classical music concerts are given on Sunday at 1200 by the Bellas Artes Chamber Orchestra (arrive early for a seat), with a view over the Valley of Mexico from the castle's beautiful balconies. A train runs up the hill, US$1 return, or expect a long climb on foot.

Just below the castle are the remains of the **Arbol de Moctezuma**, known as *El Sargento*. This immense tree, which has a circumference of 14 m, was about 60 m high before it was cut down to 10 m. Heading downhill, you'll soon pass the

Museo de Caracol ① *Tue-Sun, 0900-1600, US$4*, designed by Pedro Ramírez Vázquez. This interesting building is shaped like a conch shell, which are revered by the indigenous *conchero* dancers who perform at the city's principal tourist haunts. The museum commemorates the 'struggle of the Mexican people for liberty', with audio explanations of Mexican history and photos of the 1910 revolution. At the base of the hill lies the **Audiorama**, a small garden with benches.

Museo Nacional de Antropología
① *www.mna.inah.gob.mx. Tue-Sun 0900-1900. US$4, Free on Sun. Nearest metro Auditorio or Chapultepec, or take a colectivo down Reforma marked 'Auditorio'. Written explanations*

④ Bosque de Chapultepec & Polanco

Sleeping 🛏	Presidente	Eating 🍴
Casa Vieja 2	Intercontinental 1	Café del Bosque 1
Habita & El Area Bar 3		Cambalache 2

in Spanish and English, audio guide in English, US$4, describes 130 of the exhibits. Guided tours in English or Spanish free with a minimum of 5 people. If you want to see everything in detail, you need at least 2 days. Permission to photograph (no tripod or flash allowed) US$1, US$5 for video camera. On sale are English and Spanish guide books plus a few in French and German, and guides to Mexican ruins including maps. The cafeteria on site is good, recommended, but pricey. Added attractions outside include *voladores spiralling downwards off high poles and musicians.*

The crowning glory of Chapultepec park was built by architect Pedro Ramírez Vásquez to house a vast collection illustrating pre-Conquest Mexican culture. It has a 350-m facade and an immense patio shaded by a gigantic concrete mushroom measuring 4200 sq m,

> ➡ **Mexico City maps**

Embers **3**	Mulége **6**	Bars & clubs 🎧
Fisher's **4**	Pámpano **7**	Barfly **9**
Hacienda de los Morales **5**	Tandoor **8**	

the world's largest concrete and steel expanse supported by a single pillar. The largest exhibit (8½ m high, weighing 167 tonnes) is the image of Tlaloc, the rain god, removed (accompanied by protesting cloudbursts) from near the town of Texcoco to the museum. Inside, the museum is very well organized; each major culture that contributed to the evolution of Mesoamerican civilization is well represented in its own room or *sala*: pre-Classic, Teotihuacán, Toltec, Aztec, Oaxaca, Gulf Coast, Maya, Northern and Western Mexico. Two areas are often missed by visitors: the Torres Bodet Auditorium, where visiting archaeologists, art historians, anthropologists etc give seminars, often in English and usually free; and the Temporary Exhibitions Hall, which is also worth checking out.

Introduction to Anthropology and Mesoamerica The museum's two orientation rooms seek to explore the major concepts, techniques and fields of research that are the foundation of our existing knowledge of ancient Mexico. Introduction to Anthropology examines the four main pillars of anthropological inquiry: physical anthropology, archaeology, linguistics and ethnography. The next room explores the concept of Mesoamerica itself. Much more than a geographic region, Mesoamerica is defined as a uniquely evolved complex of civilizations that flourished from Mexico's Central Plateau as far as Costa Rica in the south. Principally, this room seeks to illustrate the universal characteristics of these cultures.

Origins Today, Mexico is one of the most multi-cultural and ethnically diverse countries in the Americas, but all its ancient peoples arrived by the same passage: the Bering Straight. The origins room focuses on these early hunter gatherers by following their first migratory waves from Asia, 80,000 years ago, to the early farming cultures which flourished after the thaw of the ice age. Particularly interesting are the remains of a mammoth found in Santa Isabel Ixtapan in 1954, which concealed remnants of prehistoric weapons. The room also contains the most ancient skulls in the Americas and has displays on the domestication of maize – a major cultural and evolutionary milestone.

Pre-Classic The artefacts exhibited in the pre-Classic room, dating from 2500-100 BC, illustrate the early practices and concepts that would soon define Mesoamerican culture in its entirety. Rudimentary civic-religious structures emerged that would later flourish into the grand sacred quarters found at the heart of all Mesoamerica's great conurbations. The practice of burying the dead beneath houses began at this time, as a recreated burial chamber from Tlatilco shows. Vital to the success of these early agricultural people was fertility, a major preoccupancy that is reflected by an abundance of 'pretty lady' sculptures, complete with large hips and thighs. The concept of duality is also central to the pre-Hispanic thought and here it is vividly illustrated by two-headed clay statues and masks. Finally, there are statuary representations of Tlaloc, the god of rain, and Huehuetéotl, the old god fire, now well-established gods in the burgeoning Mesoamerican pantheon.

Teotihuacán Teotihuacán, Mesoamerica's first great city, rose to dominance during the Classic era, 100 BC-AD 750. In this room, the exhibited artefacts demonstrate a new mastery of artistic form, with a well-developed pantheon of gods depicted variously, from simple clay statues to exuberant carved reliefs to monumental sculptures fashioned from boulders of volcanic rock. Intricate clay braziers and tripod vessels reveal the rich ceremonial aspect to their society, but it is the abundance of striking masks for which this city's artisans are particularly famous. One of them is exquisitely adorned with a turquoise mosaic, and others, intended for funerary purposes, feature idealized and youthful faces. The room also contains a scale model of the pyramid of Quetzalcoatl, with rows of rain gods and garish feathered serpents painted in their original colour scheme of red and green. A scale model of the city indicates prominent astronomical alignments between the temples and stars.

Toltec The Toltecs of central Mexico (AD 700-1300), were largely concerned with military supremacy, evidenced by a range of artefacts from Cacaxtla, Xochitécal, Xochicalco and, in the later part of this period, Tula. Particularly noteworthy are the large columns representing upright warriors. These warriors supported the roofs of important buildings and can be interpreted, quite literally, as the pillars of Toltec civilization. More humble exhibits include an abundance of metallic plumbate pottery. Carved stone glyphs show the Toltec had developed a writing system, which was later appropriated by the Aztecs, who believed no civilized people should be without written words. Other finds at Toltec sites include Zapotec braziers from Oaxaca, proving the Toltecs had extensive trade networks with other cultures.

The Mexica The room devoted to the Aztecs, or Mexica, is the most dramatic room in the museum. Filled with dark slumbering idols, sensitive types may detect an assuredly weird (and slightly electric) edge to the atmosphere. The most fabulous display is the mighty sun stone, or Aztec calendar, discovered in the Zócalo in 1790. It represents a complete depiction of the Aztec cosmos with primary gods, astrological symbols and numerous feathered serpents. Elsewhere, there are various statues relating to the earth and death, including many rattlesnakes and several unsettling renditions of Mictlantecuhtli (Lord of the Underworld). Other noteworthy gods include the gruesome earth goddess, Coatlicue ('she of the serpent skirt') with her twin snake heads and profusion of sacrificial emblems. Much more joyous is Xochipilli (the god of 'flower and song'), seated on a throne of flowers and butterflies. Interestingly, the stone sculptures depicting Aztec warriors were designed to be as realistic as possible, with pieces of obsidian and shell highlighting eyes and teeth. The room's most valuable item is an obsidian vessel in the shape of a monkey, symbolizing the god of wind.

Oaxaca Cultures The Oaxaca room follows the development of the region's major cultures, the Zapotecs and Mixtecs, from the pre-Classic era through to the Conquest. There is particular emphasis on Monte Albán and Mitla, the region's main conurbations and power centres. Particularly interesting are the various funerary relics, uncovered at places such as Monte Alban's tomb 104, reproduced here with colourful murals and offerings. Clay was utilized widely with productions including magnificent urns, usually depicting gods, often very naturalistic and adorned with complex headdresses. The peoples of Oaxaca were also very adept at crafting precious materials – gold, silver, jade and turquoise among them – exhibited by a wealth of intricate jewellery. Elsewhere, carved stone stele depict sacrificial dancers, ritual mutilation or the politically inspired victories of Monte Albán over its enemies. Note the geometric stepped fret mosaics found adorning the temples at Mitla which are said to represent the shifting movement of a snake.

Gulf Coast Cultures The Olmec, Huastec and central Veracruz civilizations are the focus of the Gulf Coast room. Giant stone heads, uncovered at pre-Classic sites throughout southern Veracruz and Tabasco, are the most impressive display in the Olmec section. Also noteworthy are the chubby childlike 'baby face' figurines, a wealth of ritual masks and a fragment of stela C from Tres Zapotes. Many Olmec designs feature a mysterious hybrid of human and animal characteristics, whilst the elongated foreheads in other productions probably relate to the practice of cranial deformation. El Tajín is the most famous of the Central Veracruz sites and an idealized reproduction of the pyramid of the niches is presented here. The ritual ball game was vigorously practised by these cultures, evidenced by a wealth of carved yokes, palms and axes. Smiling figurines are also peculiar to these peoples, thought to be associated with a rite involving psychotropic drugs. Fertility was a major preoccupation of the Huastec peoples, exemplified by an elegant statue *The Adolescent*, skilfully adorned in stylized patterns of maize. Later pieces of this era display a strong Mexica influence.

The Maya The vast and inspirational Maya collection was drawn from two main areas: the lowlands, including the Yucatán Peninsula and rainforests of present-day Chiapas, and the highlands. It charts the epic development of these enigmatic peoples from the pre-Classic to the post-Classic. Many of these artefacts are the most skilfully designed of all pre-Columbian art. Those belonging to the Classic Maya, particularly, are the epitome of elegance, often adorned with sumptuous hieroglyphics. Spirituality and religion are central concerns of many pieces, such as the stelae from Yaxchilán, which show ritual scenes of blood-letting. Elsewhere, tablets from the temple of the Cross at Palenque depict Chan Balam receiving cosmic and political kingship from his deceased father, the great King Pakal, whose tomb is also reproduced complete with stunning turquoise death mask. Outside there are reproductions of the blood-thirsty Bonampak murals and the elaborate facades from the temple of Hochoob, featuring stylistically distinct Chac masks. Elsewhere there are sculptures of jade and clay, and an incredible array of sacred braziers. Figurines and pottery from Jaina, an island off the coast of Campeche, are particularly interesting and realistic figurines. Note the very distinct change in artistic style as the Maya ushered in the post-Classic era and militaristic Toltec influences came to the fore.

Northern cultures The Northern cultures are distinct from Mesoamerica, lacking the grand institutions or social structures that define those peoples to the south. They comprise three broad groups. The first room is dedicated to Arid American cultures, who were hunters and gatherers that forged an existence from the desert. Items, largely uncovered from the La Candelaria cave in Coahuila, include funerary objects, ornaments, weapons, jewellery and textiles with geometric designs. The second room focuses on Marginal Mesoamerica, which shared features of its developed neighbours to the south and was based on a mixed, but most agricultural economy. Pieces include traditional pottery that evidence contact with the Toltec, Gulf coast and Teotihuacán cultures. Marginal Mesoamericans also traded Cinnabar and had a reverence for the ball game cult. The third room deals with Oasis America, an extension of the southwest cultures of the United States. Finds at the adobe-walled city of Paquimé include distinctive geometric pottery coloured red, black and cream, as well as copper ornaments and pendants.

Western cultures West Mexico is a vast and culturally complex area that includes the present-day states of Guanajuato, Michoacán, and the Pacific coast from Sinaloa to Guerrero. Principal among these cultures are the Tarascans, or Purépechas, a warrior tribe whose relics include weapons, tools, precious jewellery and a wealth of innovate and rather strange pottery, some with unique globular feet. They often sculpted geometric structures into human or animal form, evidenced by a throne in the shape of a coyote. Elsewhere, excavations of tombs have divulged highly stylised clay figurines. The pottery from the Tiro tombs is especially elegant. Note the interesting 'clown' statues, and a dog figurine wearing a human mask (dogs guide deceased souls through the underworld). Some Nayarit pottery from this area apparently served a satirical function, demonstrated by an emaciated old woman with a harelip.

Ethnography The ethnography rooms on the first floor are less dramatic than the archaeological rooms, but fascinating nonetheless, and obligatory if you wish to explore indigenous communities beyond the capital. Various rooms supply an overview of languages, settlement patterns, economy and culture, before exploring Mexico's major indigenous groups in turn, including the Huicholes and Coras, Purépechas, Otomi-Pame, Sierra de Puebla peoples, Oaxaca peoples, Maya, Northwest cultures and Nahuas. It is fascinating to see the cultural threads that connect these people to their ancestors. There are great displays of ritual costumes, pottery, textiles, handicrafts and reproductions of typical living quarters. The documentary videos are particularly enlightening. For more information on Mexico's indigenous peoples, see Background, page 786.

Museo de Arte Moderno
① Tue-Sun 1000-1800. US$1.50, free with ISIC card.

Mexico City's modern art museum, located just off Reforma and close to the eastern entrance to the park, has a superb permanent collection of Mexican art. Memorable works include Orozco's *El Prometo*, several oil paintings by Rivera and O'Gorman, and Siqueros' legendary *Nuestra Imagen*. The real jewel in the crown is Frida Kahlo's *Las Dos Fridas*, but the entire exhibition is a venerable tour de force and an impressive, sweeping portfolio of Mexico's masters. The building itself consists of two circular structures pleasantly set among trees with sculptures in the grounds. Temporary exhibitions are usually held in the smaller of the two buildings; entrance through the larger one. The delightfully light architecture of the larger building is balanced by a heavy, marble staircase, with a curious acoustic effect on the central landing under a translucent dome. There is a good bookshop, gift shop and an open-air cafetería behind the first building.

Museo Rufino Tamayo
① Just off Reforma, cross near the Museo de Arte Moderno, www.museotamayo.org. Tue-Sun 1000-1800. US$1.70, free with ISIC card.

This museum has a fine collection of works by Oaxacan artist Rufino Tamayo and shows contemporary Mexican and international painters. The building of glass and concrete was designed by González de León and Zabludovsky and won the National Architecture award. The interior space is unusual in that it is difficult to know which floor you are on. There is a very pleasant restaurant.

Segunda and Tercera Secciónes
The **second section**, west of Bulevar Manuel Avila Camacho, was added in 1964. It has a large amusement park or **fería** ① Wed and Fri-Sun 1030-2000, US$4, with a wonderful section for children and another for adults. The **Montaña Rusa** ① Sat and Sun only, US$1, is one of the world's largest roller coasters. Nearby, the **Papalote Museo del Niño** ① Mon-Wed 0900-1800, Thu 0900-2300, Sat-Sun 1000-1900, US$7, is a children's museum with lots of interactive displays and a 3D IMAX cinema. Diego Rivera's famous fountain, the **Fuente de Tlaloc**, is near the children's amusement park. Close by are the **Fuentes de las Serpientes** (snake fountains). There are also restaurants overlooking the Lago Mayor and Lago Menor. Buses to the second section depart from Paradero exit at Metro Chapultepec.

The **third section**, which was added in 1974, stretches a long way beyond the **Panteón Civil de Dolores** (cemetery) and has little to interest the tourist save **Atlantis** ① Sat and Sun 1030-1800, US$5, a marine amusement park with performing dolphins. Safety can be an issue in this area.

Polanco

① *To get to Polanco, take a colectivo marked 'Horacio' from Metro Chapultepec or Metro Polanco. To get to Lomas de Chapultepec, take a bus marked 'Km 15' or 'Cuajimalpa' from Antropología or the bus station by Metro Chapultepec. To get to Las Palmas, take a colectivo or bus marked 'Las Palmas' from Antropología or from the bus station by Metro Chapultepec. To get to Santa Fe, take a colectivo marked 'Centro Comercial Santa Fe' from Antropología or a bus from Metro Chapultepec.*

Directly northwest of the Museo de Antropología, lies the luxury residential area known as Polanco, with many interesting art galleries and shops. It does not suffer from the tourists that crowd the Zona Rosa and other so-called chic areas. Many of the old houses have carved stone facades, tiled roofs and gardens, especially on **Calle Horacio**, a pretty street lined with trees and parks. Polanco also contains some of the most modern (and conspicuous) hotels in the city, such as the **Nikko**, **Presidente**, **Camino Real**, and **W**, which are at least worth a walk-in visit. Also here are exclusive private residences, commercial art galleries, fashion stores, expensive restaurants and various other establishments that are collectively a monument to the consumer society; one glaring example of this is the huge **Palacio de Hierro** department store and offices along Av Masaryk. There are also a couple of fairly unremarkable modern churches and, in fact, little of cultural value, with the exception of the **Sala de Arte Siqueiros** ① *Tres Picos 29, www.siqueiros.inba.gob.mx, Tue-Sun 1000-1800, US$1.50*, with contemporary art and striking murals by David Alfaro Siqueiros, the former owner of the building. Traffic is frequently congested; avoid taking a taxi if possible.

Beyond the Auditorio Nacional, Reforma continues west towards the area known as **Lomas de Chapultepec** (or simply 'Las Lomas'), which gradually rises through broad tree-lined avenues to an altitude that leaves most of the pollution behind. It is mostly residential, including many embassies and ambassadorial residences.

To the north, taking a right at the Fuente de Petróleos (Petróleos bridge) up Bulevar Manuel Avila Camacho, you come to the modern office and commercial area of **Las Palmas**, while straight ahead, some 8 km further, beyond Lomas de Chapultepec and on the way out towards Toluca, lies the district of **Santa Fe**, perched on some of the highest ground and therefore in one of the least polluted areas in the city, with some extraordinary, futuristic architecture.

Insurgentes Sur: Roma and Condesa

Roma and Condesa are Mexico City's most hip eating-out quarters. Both flank Insurgentes Sur as it reaches southwards from the Zona Rosa. A favourite haunt of Mexico City's Intelligentsia, Roma and Condesa were first developed as swanky residential districts during the early 20th century, quickly attracting scores of artists, writers, film stars, Jewish immigrants and moneyed types. However, when the 1985 earthquake levelled much of the area, the wealthier citizens left. It was not until the 1990s that new waves of artists and intellectuals began settling into the cheap, neglected, but architecturally stunning housing. Inevitably, a new phase of gentrification followed. Today, Roma and Condesa are quiet, middle-class suburbs filled with bohemian loft spaces, minimalist apartments, leafy parks, galleries, bookshops and restaurants. They are becoming increasingly upmarket. Roma, subdivided into Roma and Roma Norte, can be easily reached on foot from the Zona Rosa. As Insurgentes heads south, it crosses Avenida Chapultepec at a large roundabout, where you'll find the remains of an old aqueduct built in 1779 and located just west, between Calle Praga and Calle Varsovia. Continue south on Insurgentes and the road changes its name to Insurgentes Sur. At this point, it enters Roma Norte.

Roma

Roma is the less gentrified and more urban of the two. Avenida Obregón is its principal boulevard, crossing Insurgentes Sur east to west. It's flanked by trees and restaurants and is the site of a small market on Saturday. At the intersection with Orizaba you'll find the wonderfully restored **Casa Lamm** ① *Obregón 99, www.lamm.com.mx*, a historic mansion built in 1910 by Lewis Lamm, a key figure in Roma's development. It houses an interesting cultural centre with galleries, library, bookshop and a fine restaurant. A few blocks north on Orizaba lies **Plaza de Río de Janerio**, one of the district's oldest public squares and home to some interesting architecture.

Condesa

Neighbouring Condesa, south and west of Roma, comprises Condesa, Hipódromo de la Condesa and Hipódromo. **Hipódromo**, which derives its name from the race track on which it was built, is the site of **Parque Mexico**, a verdant expanse of shady trees, fountains and flowers. Two concentric roads encircle the park, including Amsterdam, which actually follows the path the old race track. This is a great spot for a stroll. Throughout Condesa, you'll find some of the city's finest buildings, including a wealth of sumptuous art deco architecture that harks back to the district's golden age. Perhaps the most famous is **Edificio Basturto** ① *México 187*, a streamlined masterpiece built by Fransisco Serrano in 1938. Also worth a look is the new **Centro Cultural Bella Época** ① *Tamaulipas 202, www.fondodeculturaeconomica.com/bellaepoca/bellaepoca.asp*, a cultural centre housed in an old art deco cinema, with a good bookshop, galleries, art house cinema and coffee shop. Condesa is the heart of a thriving eating out scene. Most of its restaurants are concentrated around the junction of Michoacán, Atlixo and Suárez, but you'll find modest cafés scattered throughout the district.

South on Insurgentes

Heading out of the city centre along Insurgentes towards the delightful *colonias* (suburbs) of San Angel and Coyoacán, there are several sites that should not be missed. Next to the towering World Trade Center, the **Polyforum Cultural Siqueiros** ① *Insurgentes Sur 701, US$0.40, daily 1000-1900, closed for lunch*, includes a 500-seat theatre, art gallery and art museum, with huge frescoes by Siqueiros (including one of the largest in the world), inside the ovoid dome. A little further south is the **Plaza México**, the largest bullring in the world, with capacity for some 55,000 spectators. It is situated in the **Ciudad de los Deportes** ① *just off Insurgentes Sur, Metro San Antonio, or take a colectivo to junction of Insurgentes Sur with Eje 5, T55-5563 1659, tickets US$1-18, cheaper in the sol (sun) than the sombra (shade); up to US$35 in the barreras (front seats)*. It's best to buy tickets, especially for important fights, early on Saturday morning from the *taquillas* at the plaza. The 'México' is one of the world's three most important bullfighting venues and, as virtually every great matador comes to fight in Mexico in the winter months, the chances of seeing an important event are high.

Further south still, is a remarkable building by Alejandro Prieto: the **Teatro de Los Insurgentes** ① *Insurgentes Sur 1587, on the corner of Mercaderes*, a theatre and opera house seating 1300 people. The main frontage consists of a high curved wall covered with mosaic decoration, the work of Diego Rivera.

San Angel

The well-heeled suburb of San Angel lies 13 km southwest of the centre, offering calm respite from the chaos of downtown DF. Replete with narrow cobble-stone streets, opulent old mansions, huge trees and exuberant flowers, it exudes the charm of an era now largely past. San Angel derives its name from a 17th-century Carmelite convent, the Convento de San Angelo Mártir, but owes its most distinguished architecture to the wealthy *chilangos* (inhabitants of Mexico City) who built summer residences here in the 19th century, when San Angel was still a separate town. Despite being swallowed by the capital's urban sprawl, it has managed to retain its tranquil atmosphere and exclusivity with a wealth of upmarket designer stores skirting the streets. To get here, take the metrobús to La Bombilla and walk 300 m west on La Paz. Alternatively, take a bus from Chapultepec park or metro Line 3 to Miguel Angel de Quevado.

Many residents and tourists come to San Angel on a Saturday to visit the **Bazar del Sábado** ① *0900-1400*, a splendid folk art and curiosity market that takes place on its main square, Plaza San Jacinto. This is also the site of one of the oldest mansions in the area, the beautifully furnished and preserved 18th-century **Casa del Risco** ① *Callejón de la Amargura, Tue-Sun 1000-1700, free; library Mon-Fri 0900-2000, Sat 1000-1400, photo ID required*. It contains a collection of Mexican and European paintings from the 15th to the 20th centuries, as well as a library devoted to international law and the Mexican Revolution. Also worth a visit is the church of **San Jacinto**, once belonging to a Dominican convent (1566), located just west of the plaza.

Nearby, the **Centro Cultural San Angel** ① *Av Revolución, opposite Museo del Carmen*, stages exhibitions, concerts, lectures and cultural events. Further north on Revolución, the **Museo de Arte Carrillo Gil** ① *Av Revolución 1608, US$3.35*, has good changing exhibits and a permanent collection including paintings by Orozco and Siqueiros, as well as several of Diego Rivera's Cubist works. There is a good bookshop and cafeteria. Between San Angel and Coyoacán, at the intersection of Insurgentes Sur and La Paz, is the shady **Jardín de la Bombilla**, where you'll find a **monument to Alvaro Obregón**, built on the spot where the former president was assassinated in 1928.

Museo Colonial del Carmen
① *Revolución y La Paz. Daily 1000-1700. US$3, free Sun.*
The former Convento de San Angelo Mártir now houses the Museo Colonial del Carmen, with numerous atmospheric courtyards, old monastic quarters, 17th- and 18th-century furniture, and a large collection of colonial art, including several oil paintings by Cristóbal de Vallalpando. In the crypt are some mummified bodies discovered by marauding soldiers during the Revolution; they're thought to be the early monks and nuns who founded the convent. The **Iglesia del Carmen** is also in the grounds with its distinctive triple domes, strikingly adorned in coloured tiles.

Museo Casa Estudio Diego Rivera
① *Av Altavista y Calle Diego Rivera. Tue-Sun 1000-1800. US$1, free Sun.*
The Museo Casa Estudio Diego Rivera is where Diego and his wife, Frida Kahlo, lived and worked between 1934 and 1940, and was undoubtedly witness to some interesting domestic scenes. The building was designed by their friend Juan O'Gorman and comprises two separate buildings, one for each artist. Rivera's building contains several of his works, reproductions, memorabilia and belongings, including the bed where he died

in 1957. Frida's house hosts temporary and changing exhibits. Opposite the museum is the **Antigua Hacienda de Goicoechea** – now the **San Angel Inn**. Built in the 18th century, the hacienda was the home of the Marquis de Selva Nevada y Conde de Pinillos and has served as an upmarket restaurant since the early 20th century.

Coyoacán

The oldest part of Mexico City, 3 km east of San Angel, Coyoacán is the place from which Cortés launched his attack on the Aztec capital of Tenochtitlán (the name means 'place of the coyotes' in Nahuatl). It is one of the most beautiful and best-preserved parts of the city, with elegant tree-lined avenues, hundreds of fine buildings from the 16th to 19th centuries and carefully tended parks – a world away from the hustle and grind of the centre. Culturally, Coyoacán is one of the liveliest parts of Mexico City, particularly at weekends, and is home to attractive cafés and good shops. The area is best explored on foot, which will take most of a day, although it's often combined with a visit to San Angel.

Ins and outs

To get here from the city centre, it is easiest to take the metro to Coyoacán, Viveros, Miguel Angel de Quevedo or General Anaya and walk the remaining 2-3 km. The *colectivo* from Metro

5 Coyoacán

➡ **Mexico City maps**
1 City centre, page 78
2 Centro Histórico: Zócalo & Alameda, page 82
3 Reforma & Zona Rosa, page 96
4 Bosque de Chapultepec & Polanco, page 98
5 Coyoacán, page 107
6 Metro, page 138

Sleeping
Suites Coyoacán 1

Eating
Churros Rellenos Jordan 1
El Jarocho 5
El Jardín del Pulpo 2
El Caracol de Oro 3
Fabio's 7
El Globo 8
El Morral 9
Hacienda de Cortés 10
La Guadalupana 4
Los Danzantes 11
Mastropiero Café 12
Mesón Antiguo Santa Catarina 6
Moheli 13

Bars & clubs
El Hijo del Cuervo 14

General Anaya to the centre of Coyoacán is marked 'Santo Domingo', get off at Abasolo or at the Jardín Centenario. From San Angel, you can get to Coyoacán via a delightful walk through Chimalistac, across Avenida Universidad and down Avenida Francisco Sosa; or you can take a bus or *pesero* marked 'Taxqueña' as far as Calle Caballocalco.

To reach the centre of Coyoacán from Metro General Anaya, there is a pleasant walk along Héroes del 47 (one block along on the left is the 16th-century church of **San Lucas**), across División del Norte and down Hidalgo (one block along on the left, and two blocks down San Lucas is the 18th-century church of **San Mateo**. If coming from Metro Viveros, two other interesting walks present themselves. One passes through the Viveros de Coyoacán, a large, leafy park that is home to the city's nursery, the other traverses the length of **Francisco Sosa**, said to be the first urban street laid in Spanish America and definitely worth a look.

Fransisco Sosa

At the beginning of this elegant avenue is the 17th-century church of **San Antonio Panzacola**, by the banks of the Río Churubusco. Nearby, on Universidad, is the remarkable, beautiful (and modern) chapel of **Nuestra Señora de la Soledad**, built in the grounds of the 19th-century ex-hacienda El Altillo. A slight detour down Novo leads to the National Watercolour Museum, or **Museo Nacional de la Acuarela** ① *Salvador Novo, Tue-Sun 1000-1800, free*, founded in 1967 and something of a pioneer. The terracotta- fronted residence at **Francisco Sosa 383** ① *Tue-Sun, free; courtyard and garden Mon-Fri 0900-1600*, is said to have been built by Alvarado. Many fine houses follow, mostly built in the 19th century, with large doors and brightly coloured, fortress-like walls. The church of **Santa Catarina**, in the square of the same name, is a fine 18th-century construction painted in mustard tones; on Sunday, at about one o'clock, people assemble under the trees to tell stories, and all are welcome to attend or participate. In the same square, the **Casa de la Cultura Jesús Reyes Heroles** should not be missed, with its galleries and delightful leafy gardens. Just before arriving at the centre you'll see the 18th-century **Casa de Diego Ordaz**.

Plaza Central and around

At the centre of Coyoacán is the Plaza Central, comprising two adjacent squares, the **Jardín Centenario** and **Plaza Hidalgo**. The Jardín Centenario is home to a beautiful statue of two coyotes and was once the atrium of the 16th-century Franciscan monastery, San Juan Bautista. The monastery's church, situated on the east side of Plaza Hidalgo, has a magnificent interior and was added to over the centuries, as evidenced by discernible baroque features. On the north side of Plaza Hidalgo lies the **Casa de Cortés**, in fact built 244 years after the Conquest, on the site of Cortés' house, where the conquistador plotted his attack on Tenochtitlán and planned the building of New Spain. It now houses the tourist office and Palacio Municipal, and contains murals of the torture of the Aztec emperor, Cuauhtémoc, which also took place in Cortés' former home. Nearby, the **Museo Nacional de Culturas Populares** ① *Av Hidalgo, just off Plaza Hidalgo, Tue-Sun 1000-1600, free*, houses permanent and temporary exhibitions on popular Mexican culture. At weekends there are many open-air events on the Plaza Central, especially in the **artesanía market**, just off Plaza Hidalgo, which is well worth a visit.

Plaza de la Conchita and around

Southeast of the centre on Higuera lies the beautiful 18th-century church of **La Conchita** ① *Fri evenings and Sun mornings*, in a pretty square of the same name. The interior, especially the altarpiece, is magnificent. On the corner of Higuera and Vallarta is what is

Frida Kahlo

Frida Kahlo was one of the most significant Mexican painters of the 20th century. She painted using vibrant colours in a style that was influenced by the indigenous cultures of Mexico as well as by European movements such as Symbolism, Realism and Surrealism. Her life was not a happy one; she questioned her European and Mexican roots, very much like the artists of an earlier era who took ideas and subjects originating in the Old World, which they attempted to express in New World terms.

Frida suffered greatly because her treatment after an accident when she was young went terribly wrong, added to which she and her spouse, Diego Rivera, were not a compatible couple. Her anguish is expressed in her paintings on display at the Museo Frida Kahlo, in Coyoacán. Many of her works are self portraits.

Frida's life was the subject of the film *Frida*, filmed on location in San Luis Potosí with Salma Hayek in the title role and Alfredo Molina as Diego Rivera.

reputed to be the **Casa de La Malinche**, Cortés' indigenous mistress and interpreter. Also known as Doña Marina, La Malinche (literally 'the traitor'), was a key historical figure in the Conquest, enabling Cortés to communicate with local tribes and swiftly acquire territory. Although now widely reviled, she is something of a symbolic archetype ('the whore') in Mexico's complex and often contradictory psychology. In fairness, it should be noted that Doña Marina was a slave as much as a mistress, and helped avert many massacres through negotiation. She also bore Cortés a son, the first *mestizo* child in what was to become a nation of *mestizos*. Further south on Higueras, in the **Jardín Cultural Frida Kahlo**, near Plaza de La Conchita, there is a striking bronze statue of Frida Kahlo by the contemporary Mexican sculptor Gabriel Ponzanelli.

Museo Frida Kahlo
ⓘ *Allende y Londres 247. Tue-Sun 1000-1800. US$4, no photographs.*
Admirers of Frida Kahlo will want to visit the Museo Frida Kahlo, or **Casa Azul**, where the legendary artist lived, worked and died – as her art attests – in the considerable suffering of her broken body. The collections are not particularly vast, but the museum offers an interesting glimpse into the daily life of the national heroine. Two rooms are preserved as lived in by Frida and her husband Diego Rivera, and the rest contain drawings and paintings by both, including interesting sketches of archaeological sites. Frida was very interested in folk art, illustrated by the small collection of regional costumes on display. There also numerous cuttings attesting the couples devotion to socialist causes. The outside patio is shady and pleasant, with bubbling fountains and video footage of the couple. The photo of Rivera petting a hairless Aztec dog is particularly charming. The film *Frida* was partly shot here.

La Casa de Trotsky
ⓘ *Río Churubusco 410, between Gómez Farías and Morelos. Tue-Sun 1000-1700. US$2, half price with ISIC card.*
La Casa de Trotsky is where the Russian revolutionary lived before he was murdered by the Stalinist agent Ramón Mercader in 1940. It is a curious place in that it exalts an historical figure generally disapproved of by western societies. In places, the exhibits verge on hero worship, with flattering photos, portraits and a bronze bust. More interesting are the photos depicting Trotsky and Frida Kahlo, with whom he had an affair,

attending picnics or outdoor strolls and often accompanied by Kahlo's husband, Rivera. Other striking documentary exhibits recall the Soviet years when Trotsky was a military commander in the Red Army, as well as Stalin's rather savage campaign to eliminate him, his entire family and any other perceived enemies. Trotsky's actual house is rather dark and sombre, and includes the study where – in the colourful manner of Russian assassinations – he was bludgeoned to death with an ice pick. Outside there is a tomb where his ashes were laid and a red flag keeps the faith.

Museo de las Intervenciones

ⓘ *General Anaya y 20 de Agosto. Tue-Sun 0900-1800. US$3. To get there from Plaza Hidalgo, walk 2 blocks north and then head east on Xicoténcatl. Alternatively, catch a 'General Anaya' bus or walk from Metro General Anaya, 500 m from the museum.*

Situated 2 km northeast of Coyoacán's Plaza Central is the picturesque and partly ruined 18th-century **convent of Churubusco**, now the Museo Nacional de las Intervenciones. The museum's 17 rooms are filled with mementoes, documents, proclamations and pictures recounting foreign invasions, incursions and occupations since Independence. It also holds temporary exhibitions. The site of the museum was chosen because it was the scene of a battle when the US army marched into Mexico City in 1847. This was where the San Patricios, the famous Saint Patrick's Brigade who fought as volunteers on the Mexican side, were captured by the US army. Next door is the 16th-century church of **San Diego**, with 17th- and 18th-century additions. Near the church, on the other side of Calzada General Anaya, is the delightful **Parque de Churubusco**. One block from Tlalpan along Héroes del 47, to the left, is the 18th-century church of **San Mateo**.

Anahuacalli

ⓘ *4 km south of Coyoacán, Museo 150, off División del Norte, T55-5617 4310, www.anahua calliwmuseo.org. Tue-Sun 1000-1800, closed Holy Week. US$4. To get there, go to Metro Tasqueña and take the Tren Ligero to Xotepingo, some 5-10 mins from the museum. Alternatively, take the bus marked División del Norte from outside Metro Salto del Agua.*

The **Museo Diego Rivera Anahuacalli**, usually shortened to just Anahuacalli, houses Diego Rivera's superb collection of pre-Hispanic artefacts. Rivera, who actually designed the somewhat imposing and archaeologically inspired building, never saw its completion. Finished by architect Juan O'Gorman, it did not open until 1963, and today presents a fine collection of pre-Columbian sculptures from the Valley of Mexico and beyond. Much of it is effectively displayed in a pseudo-Mayan tomb and there is a big display here for the Day of the Dead at the beginning of November. There are also limited works by Rivera himself, including sketches for some of his most famous murals.

Ciudad Universitaria

The world-famous University City, 3 km south of San Angel and 18 km from the centre, was founded in 1551, but previously located in the heart of the Centro Histórico. The modern era construction was built from 1949 to 1952 by Juan Alemán, and in 2007, the ensemble was declared a World Heritage Site. It is Latin America's largest university with nearly 300,000 students and no less than five former presidents among its past attendees. Perhaps the most notable building here is the 10-storey **biblioteca** (library), by Juan O'Gorman, its outside walls iridescent with mosaics telling the story of scientific knowledge, from Aztec astronomy to molecular theory. Nearby, other murals by

Siqueiros adorn administrative buildings, whilst the Facultad de Medicina features work by Eppens. South of the Rectoría, the **Museo Universitario de Ciencias y Arte** ⓘ *www.muca.unam.mx, Tue-Sun 1000-1800, free, bring ID*, contains cultural and scientific exhibits. To get to Ciudad Universitaria, take the metrobús south on Insurgentes as far as the terminus, then catch a 'Villa Coapa' bus. Alternatively, take metro Line 3 to Copilco and walk 20 minutes, or catch a bus marked 'CU', along Eje Lázaro Cárdenas. Free buses ferry passengers to different areas of the campus.

Around Ciudad Universitaria

Across the highway is the **Estadio Olímpico**, with seats for 80,000 and a sculpture-painting by Diego Rivera telling the story of Mexican sport. In shape, colour and situation, a world's wonder, but now closed and run down. Beyond the Olympic stadium is the **Jardín Botánico Exterior** ⓘ *daily 0700-1630, 30-min walk, ask directions*, which displays all the cactus species in Mexico. South beyond the Ciudad Universitaria, but still a part of the university, is a cultural complex which includes the **Museo Universitario Contemporáneo de Arte**, art-house cinemas, theatres, and the extraordinary **Espacio Escultórico** – a large circular area of volcanic rock within a circle of cement monoliths. On the opposite side of the road is a large area with huge sculptures; stick to the path as it is easy to get lost in the vegetation.

Tlalpan

Some 4 km south of the Ciudad Universitaria is the bohemian suburb of Tlalpan, replete with colonial houses and gardens. Near the Plaza de la Constitución, the early 16th-century church of **San Agustín** has a fine altar and paintings by Cabrera. It can be reached by taking the metrobús to its southern most terminal and then catching a 'Villa Coapa' bus. The suburb of **Peña Pobre** is 2½ km west, near which, just to the northeast, is the **Pyramid of Cuicuilco** ⓘ *Insurgentes Sur Km 16 y Periférico, Tue-Sun 0800-1800*, believed to be the oldest pyramid in Mexico. It circular in form, dates from the fifth or sixth century BC, and is over 100 m in diameter, but only 25 m high. There is an archaeological museum on site.

Xochimilco

Around 20 km to the southeast of the city centre, Xochimilco has many attractions, not least the fact that it lies in an unpolluted area. Meaning 'the place where flowers grow', Xochimilco was an advanced settlement long before the arrival of the Spaniards. Built on a lake, it developed a form of agriculture using *chinampas* ('floating gardens') where mud was dredged from the lake bed and onto floating rafts. The *chimpanas* soon evolved into highly fertile canal banks and the area is still a major supplier of fruit and vegetables to the city. After the Conquest, the Spaniards recognized the importance of the region and the need to convert the indigenous population, evidenced by a considerable number of 16th- and 17th-century religious buildings in Xochimilco and the other 13 *pueblos* that make up the present-day *delegación*, or municipality. Easiest access is by bus, *colectivo* or metro to Metro Taxqueña, then *tren ligero* (about 20 minutes). Get off at the last stop.

Canals

Xochimilco's peaceful canals are the town's principal attraction, traversed by colourful *trajineras* (punt-like boats), which bear girls' names. There are seven *embarcaderos* (landing stages), the largest of which are **Fernando Celada** and **Nuevo Nativitas** (the latter is a large craft market where most coach-loads of tourists are set down). All are busy at weekends, especially Sunday afternoon, when a feisty carnival atmosphere predominates. Official tariffs operate, although prices are sometimes negotiable. Private boats cost around US$10 per hour (a trip of at least 1½ hours is desirable); floating Mariachi bands will charge US$3.50 per song, marimba groups US$1.50. It should be mentioned that besides the expensive *trajineras* there are *colectivo*-boats operating for US$1-2 for a trip around the canals starting from *embarcadero* **San Cristóbal**. There are reasonably priced tourist menus (lunch US$2) from passing boats or, even better, stock up with a picnic and beers before setting off.

Churches

The indisputable architectural jewel of Xochimilco's modest town centre is the church of **San Bernardino de Siena** and its neighbouring convent, begun in 1535, completed 1595, and housing a magnificent Renaissance-style altarpiece. Nearby, the oldest Spanish-built religious edifice is the tiny **Capilla de San Pedro** (1530). Also worthy of mention are **Nuestra Señora de los Dolores de Xaltocán** with a 17th-century facade and 18th-century retable, **Santa Crucita Analco** and **San Juan Tlaltentli**. All are within walking distance of the centre of Xochimilco. For those interested in church architecture, the villages to the west, south and east of Xochimilco are worth visiting, all reachable by *colectivo* or bus from the centre of Xochimilco. In nearby **Míxquic**, famous for its **Día de los Muertos** (Day of the Dead) celebrations, the church of **San Andrés** was built on the site of an earlier temple using some of the original blocks, with traces of pre-Hispanic designs.

Museo Dolores Olmedo Patiño

ⓘ *Av México 5843 and Antiguo Camino a Xochimilco, 1 block southwest from La Noria tren ligero station, T55-5555 1016, www.mdop.org.mx. Tue-Sun 1000-1800. US$3.50, students US$1.50, free Tue.*

Rare Mexican hairless dogs and peacocks parade through the grounds of this highly recommended museum. It is superbly set in 3 ha of beautiful garden and grassland, on the site of an old 17th-century estate donated by Rivera's friend and patron, Dolores Olmedo. The museum houses a formidable collection of 137 works by Diego Rivera, 25 by Frida Kahlo, and an important collection of drawings by Angelina Beloff. There are also pre-Hispanic artefacts, 19th-century antiques and Mexican folk art. There is a very pleasant open and covered café and a **tourist office** ⓘ *Pino 36, daily 0800-2100.*

North to Guadalupe

Another worthwhile escape from the city centre heads north of the capital, where you can visit the eclectic Plaza de las Tres Culturas, explore outlying archaeological sites, or make your own pilgrimage to Mexico's most important shrine at the Basílica de Guadalupe. The site celebrates two apparitions of the Virgin back in 1531 and draws large numbers throughout the year, and especially on 12 December, her feast day. A trip to the Basílica is easily combined with a visit to the pyramids at Teotihuacán (see page 146).

Plaza de las Tres Culturas

From Plaza Garibaldi near the Alameda, Lázaro Cárdenas leads to Santa María la Redonda, at the end of which is **Plaza Santiago de Tlatelolco** (Metro Line 3 to Tlatelolco), the city's oldest plaza after the Zócalo. The main market of the Aztecs was here, and on it, in 1524, the Franciscans built a huge church and convent. It is now known as the Plaza de las Tres

Culturas since it shows elements of Aztec, colonial and modern architecture. The Aztec ruins have been restored and the magnificent Franciscan church of **Santiago Tlatelolco**, completed in 1609, is now the focus of the massive, multi-storey Nonoalco-Tlatelolco housing scheme (heavily damaged in the 1985 earthquake), a garden city within a city, with pedestrian and wheeled traffic entirely separate. In October 1968, the Plaza de las Tres Culturas was the scene of serious disturbances between the authorities and students, in which a large number of students were killed.

Basílica de Guadalupe

ⓘ *US$3, buses marked 'La Villa' go close to the site, or go by metro to La Villa (Line 6).*

The Basílica de Guadalupe is the most venerated shrine in the whole of Mexico. Hundreds of thousands of people come from all over the country to celebrate the feast of La Virgen de Guadalupe, on 12 December. It was here, in 1531, that the Virgin appeared three times in the guise of an indigenous princess to local *campesino* Juan Diego and imprinted her portrait on his cloak. The cloak is preserved, set in gold, but was moved into the new basilica next door as a massive crack had appeared down the side of the old building. The huge, modern basilica, completed in 1976, was designed by architect Pedro Ramírez Vázquez (who was also responsible for the Museo Nacional de Antropología). It's an impressive building and holds over 20,000 people (very crowded on Sunday) and an estimated 20 million pilgrims visit the shrine every year. The original basilica has been converted into a **museum**. It still houses the original magnificent altar, but otherwise mostly representations of the image on the cloak, plus interesting painted tin plates offering votive thanks for cures, etc from about 1860. A chapel stands over the well that gushed at the spot where the Virgin appeared. Indigenous dance groups provide entertainment in front of the basilica. There are, in fact, about seven churches in the immediate neighbourhood, including one on the hill above, the **Iglesia del Cerrito** (which has excellent views over the city); most of them are at crazy angles to each other and to the ground, because of subsidence. The **Templo de los Capuchinos** has been the subject of a remarkable feat of engineering in which one end has been raised 3.4 m so that the building is now horizontal.

◉ Mexico City listings

Hotel and guesthouse prices

LL over US$200	**L** US$151-200	**AL** US$101-150
A US$66-100	**B** US$46-65	**C** US$31-45
D US$21-30	**E** US$12-20	**F** US$7-11
G under US$7		

Restaurant prices

₩₩₩ over US$15	₩₩ US$8-15	₩ under US$8

See pages 47-51 for further information.

◉ Sleeping

Prices of the more expensive hotels do not normally include 15% tax; service is sometimes included but it's always safest to check in advance. Discounts are often available, especially in low season or at weekends. Breakfast is rarely included in the room price unless otherwise stated. There are hotel reservation services at the airport and bus stations. Tourist information offices can also help you with reservations.

Zócalo and around *p80, map p82*

LL-AL Gran Hotel de México, 16 de Septiembre 82, Metro Zócalo, T55-1083 7700, www.granhotelciudaddemexico.com. One of the city's most elegant hotels with an incredible 1930s-style foyer, superb wrought-iron furnishings and an antique elevator. The 4th-floor restaurant and balcony are superb for people-watching on the Zócalo, especially on Sun morning (breakfast buffet US$10).

AL Majestic (Best Western), Madero 73, Metro Zócalo, T55-5521 8600, www.majestic.com.mx. A beautiful historic building on the Zócalo with a stunning interior of Puebla tiles, antique furnishings and carved wooden beams. Rooms are quiet, interesting and comfortable, with large beds and views of a courtyard. Some of them overlook the Zócalo, as does the magnificent 7th-floor restaurant.

B Catedral, Donceles 95, Metro Zócalo, T55-5518 5232, www.hotelcatedral.com. A good, professional hotel with a high standard of service and amenities including restaurant, bar, taxi, laundry and internet. Rooms are clean, carpeted and spacious with telephone and cable TV. Suites have jacuzzis. Recommended.

B Gillow, Isabel la Católica 17 y 5 de Mayo, Metro Allende, T55-5510 8585, www.hotelgillow.com. A large, elegant hotel in a central location. Rooms are not quite as plush as the lobby, but comfortable and attractive all the same. The best are on 6th floor. Lots of services, hospitable and good value, but the restaurant is mediocre.

C Canadá, 5 de Mayo 47, Metro Allende, T55-5518 2106, www.hotelcanada.com.mx. Smart, modern place with lots of rooms (slightly overpriced) with bath, hot water, telephone, TV and safe. Services include laundry, money exchange and Wi-Fi. Good buffet breakfast. Friendly and helpful.

C-E Hostal Amigo, Isabel la Católica 61, Metro Isabel la Católica, T55-5512 3464, www.hostalamigo.com. Same ownership as **Hostal Moneda** (see below), identical rates and services but fewer rooms, no private bath. Popular central hostel; fun, funky and youthful place, with a crazy barman. Restored in 2005.

C-E Hostel Catedral, Guatemala 4, Metro Zócalo, T55-5518 1726, www.hostelcatedral.com. A thriving hostel in an attractive location just behind the cathedral. 204 beds in a mixture of private rooms (**C**) and dorms (**E**). A wealth of amenities include restaurant, kitchen, bar, laundry, internet, secure storage, travel agency and roof terrace. The bar is popular Tue-Fri with live music or dance classes. Open 24 hrs and there's a wealth of information and tours. Cheaper for YHI members or when booked online.

C-E Hostal Moneda, Moneda 8, 1 block east of the cathedral, Metro Zócalo, T55-5522 5803 (or T01800-221 7265, free in DF), www.hostalmoneda.com.mx. Clean, friendly and safe hostel in a great location. Dorms have 3-6 beds (**E**) and private rooms have bath (**C**). Great rooftop restaurant, for inclusive breakfasts and dinners, with a beautiful view of the cathedral. Free internet and wide range of tours including free city centre walking tour. Part of the **Amigo Hostel Group**, T55-5512 3496, www.amigohostelgroup.com, with hostels in Oaxaca, Campeche, Cancún and Tulum. Book online for up to 15% discount. Recommended.

D El Roble, Uruguay 109, Metro Zócalo, T55-5522 7830, www.hotelroble.com. Popular hotel with clean, modern rooms, all equipped with bath, TV, telephone, safe and Wi-Fi. Good restaurant, although it closes early. Recommended.

D-E Isabel la Católica, Isabel la Católica 63, Metro Isabel la Católica, T55-5518 1213, www.hotel-isabel.com.mx. This old colonial building has large shabby rooms with bath and hot water. Pleasant, popular, clean, helpful and safe (taxi drivers must register at desk before taking passengers). There's a roof terrace and decent restaurant. Rooms on top floor with shared bathroom are cheaper (**E**). Central and a bit noisy but recommended.

D-E Mexico City Hostel, República de Brasil 8, Metro Zócalo, T55-5512 3666, www.mexicocityhostel.com. Neat, tidy and one of the newer hostels in town. Housed in a beautiful colonial building and quieter than **Hostel Catedral** or **Hostel Moneda** (see above). Interesting tours include a visit to a *lucha libre* wrestling match and a crawl around the local nightclubs. Private rooms (**D**) have no bath but are large; dorms have 8, 10 or 12 beds (**E**). Breakfast and Wi-Fi included.

D-E San Antonio, 2nd Callejón, 5 de Mayo 29, Metro Allende, T55-5512 1625. Clean, pleasant, popular, friendly, TV in room. Recommended but get a receipt if staying for several days and paying in advance.

E Congreso, Allende 18, Metro Allende, T55-5510 4446. 80 comfortable rooms with bath, TV and telephone. Good value and clean. Parking available.

E Cuba, Cuba 69, Metro Allende, T55-5518 1380, www.hotelcuba.com.mx. Good-value rooms with wooden floors, big beds, writing desks, telephone and cable TV. The suite has a jacuzzi.

E Habana, República de Cuba 77, Metro Allende, T55-5518 1589. Spacious, clean carpeted rooms with huge beds, writing desks, cable TV and telephone. Staff are friendly and helpful. Can be noisy, but a good location if you're looking to avoid the crowds. Excellent value and highly recommended.

E Juárez, up a quiet alley off 5 de Mayo 17, Metro Allende, T55-5512 6929, hoteljuarez@prodigy.net.mx. Great location near the Zócalo. Rooms are clean and comfortable with marble bathrooms, phone, radio and TV. Book in advance as often full; ask for room with window. A very good budget choice – friendly, helpful and highly recommended.

E Lafayette, Motolinia 40 and 16 de Septiembre, Metro Allende, T55-5521 9640. Simple rooms with bath, TV, hot water and telephone. Clean and quiet (pedestrian area), but check rooms as they vary in size.

E Rioja, 5 de Mayo 45, next door to Canadá, Metro Allende, T55-5521 8333. Rooms are set around a central courtyard with high ceiling. They have shared or private baths, reliable hot water, telephone. Clean, popular and well placed. Normally recommended, but we have received a report of theft from rooms in the hotel – watch your gear just to be safe.

E-F Zamora, 5 de Mayo 50, Metro Allende, T55-5512 1832. Slightly gloomy but generally OK and friendly. Some big rooms work out very economical with more than 2 people. Cheaper rooms without bath available (**F**).

F República, Cuba 57, Metro Allende, T55-5512 9517. Wonderful colonial building with very cheap, if tired, rooms. Charming but run-down – being renovated at the time of research. Rooms have bath and hot water

and are cheaper without TV. Upstairs is quieter. Recommended for budget travellers.

F Río de Janeiro, Brasil 45l, near Colombia close to Plaza Santo Domingo, Metro Allende, T55-5526 2905. Grubby and extremely basic lodgings, head up the stairs and through the metal door. OK if money is really tight. Ultra-cheap without bath.

F Tuxpan, Colombia 11, near Brasil, Metro Allende, T55-5526 1118. Lively location in the heart of a street market. The interior is darkened with rooms set around a central courtyard. Rooms are clean with double beds, TV, hot showers and mirrors on the ceiling. Classy, and economical too.

La Alameda and around *p90, map p82*

LL-AL Sheraton Centro Histórico, Juárez 70, Metro Hidalgo, T55-5130 5300, www.sheraton mexico.com. A very well-appointed hotel with a great location overlooking the Alameda Central. Built on the site of the former **Hotel del Prado**, which collapsed in the 1985 earthquake. It boasts a wealth of amenities and an interesting collage of Diego Rivera murals.

AL de Cortés, Av Hidalgo 85, T55-5518 2181, Metro Hidalgo, www.hoteldecortes.com.mx. The only baroque style hotel in Mexico City and a former pilgrim's guesthouse. Tasteful and attractive rooms, with lots of extras including safes, computer ports and satellite TV. There's a restaurant and a pleasant patio, but no pool.

B San Francisco, Luis Moya 11, T55-5521 8960, Metro Juárez, www.delangel.com.mx. Friendly, good-value hotel with excellent views and comfortable rooms. Credit cards accepted. Good set meals.

C Fleming, Revillagigedo 35, T55-5510 4530, Metro Juárez, www.hotelfleming.com.mx. Comfortable mid-range lodgings with a host of pleasant if unremarkable rooms. Bar, restaurant, Wi-Fi in reception and internet terminals. Suites have jacuzzis. Reliable.

C Marlowe, Independencia 17, T55-5521 9540, Metro San Juan de Letrán, www.hotel marlowe.com.mx. A clean, modern hotel, finished to a high standard. Secure parking and

a good restaurant, but the service is slow. **Concordia**, around the corner, is cheaper.

E Fornos, Revillagigedo 92, Metro Balderas, 5 mins' walk to Alameda, T55-5521 9594. This hotel is extremely clean, but the rooms are slightly small. Each is equipped with carpets, TV, radio and writing desk. There's also parking space and a double with a jacuzzi (**B**). Staff are friendly and the Spanish owner speaks Dutch. Recommended.

Plaza de la República and around
p91, maps p78 and p82

A fairly run-down part of town, but close to the working heart of the city.

A Ramada, Jesús Terán 12, Metro Hidalgo, T55-5566 0277, www.ramada international.com. Formerly **Hotel Jena**, this hotel is clean, professional and well appointed, boasting all the amenities you'd expect from a modern, upmarket hotel. Rooms are large and comfortable. The lobby is airy and attractive.

C Mayaland, Maestro Antonio Caso 23, Metro Juárez, T55-5566 6066, hotelmayalan@ hotmail.com. A large, modern and professional hotel with 100 clean, comfortable, if slightly generic, rooms. There's a convention centre, restaurant, computing hall and travel agency too. Recommended.

C Monaco, Guerrero 12, Metro Hidalgo, T55-5566 8333, www.hotel-monaco.com.mx. Professional, modern hotel with a marble interior. Rooms are large, clean and carpeted with amenities including cable TV, a/c and safe. Buffet breakfast US$5.

D Palace, Ignacio Ramírez 7, Metro Revolución, T55-5566 2400. Clean, comfortable, carpeted rooms with striking blue walls, cable TV, Wi-Fi and phone. Helpful reception has a taxi service and there's a travel agency in the building.

D-F Casa de los Amigos, Ignacio Mariscal 132, Metro Revolución, T55-5705 0521, www.casadelosamigos.org. Single sex dorms and doubles, pay 2 nights in advance, use of kitchen, maximum 15-day stay, run by Quakers for Quakers, or development-work-related travellers; other travellers taken only if space is available. Good information on volunteer work, travel and language schools, breakfast and laundry on roof, safe luggage store, English library. Advance booking advisable. Recommended.

E Carlton, Ignacio Mariscal 32-bis, Metro Revolución, T55-5566 2911. A bit dusty and run down, verging on shabby, but generally OK. Basic furniture and worn-out carpets. Small rooms, but some have fine views (rooms at the front are noisy). Good restaurant.

E Frimont, Jesús Terán 35, Metro Revolución, T55-5705 4169. Corridors are slightly musty, but the rooms aren't bad. They're smallish but comfortable, clean and equipped with desk, telephone and TV. Good views from the 5th floor and decent cheap restaurant.

E Texas, Ignacio Mariscal 129, Metro Revolución, T55-5705 6496, www.granhotel texas.com. Reasonably comfortable, carpeted rooms have bath, cable TV, hot water, dresser and Wi-Fi. Sofas and snacks in reception. Parking.

Paseo de la Reforma and Zona Rosa
p94, map p96

L-AL NH México, Liverpool 155, Metro Insurgentes, T55-5228 9928, www.nh-hotels.com. A reputable chain of hotels with professional service, lots of amenities and predictably high standards. Recommended.

L-AL Royal Zona Rosa (Best Western), Amberes 78, Metro Insurgentes, T55-9149 3000, www.hotel royalzr.com. A tower of glass and steel, this modern hotel has fine rooms and suites ideal for business travellers or holiday-makers.

B María Cristina, Lerma 31, Metro Insurgentes, T55-5566 9688, www.hotelmariacristina.com.mx. Handsome colonial-style hotel with 150 comfortable rooms, helpful staff, secure parking, bookstore and restaurant. Recommended.

B Prim, Versalles 46, Metro Cuauhtemoc, T55-5592 4600, www.hotelprim.com.mx. Clean and comfortable hotel with lots of rooms and staff, including a doorman. Bar, restaurant, laundry, parking and Wi-Fi. Recommended.

B Viena, Marsella 28, Metro Cuauhtémoc, T55-5566 0700, www.posadavienahotel.com.

An attractive, colourful hotel with Mexican art, stained glass windows and impressive craft pieces adorning the corridors. Rooms are comfortable and equipped with telephone, hot water, shaving mirrors and Wi-Fi. There's a good café and restaurant on site. Friendly, helpful and recommended.

B-C Casa González, Lerma y Sena 69, Metro Insurgentes, T55-5514 3302, casa.gonzalez@prodigy.net.mx. A very quiet and secluded hotel with peaceful, flower-filled inner courtyards. Breakfast and other meals available in the 24-hr café. Laundry, Wi-Fi and TV. Interior rooms are more attractive and expensive (**B**). Very helpful and friendly. Highly recommended.

D Uxmal, Madrid 13, quite close to Zona Rosa, Metrobús Reforma. Clean rooms, same owner as the more expensive **Madrid** next door (**AL**), with access to their better facilities. Recommended.

Apartments

Suites Amberes, Amberes 64, Metro Insurgentes, T55-5533 1306, www.suites amberes.com.mx. Attractive and comfortable suites with a wealth of amenities including gym, room service and cable TV.

Suites Havre, Havre 74, Metro Insurgentes, T55-5533 5670, near Zona Rosa. This place has 56 suites with kitchen, phone and service for around US$150 per week or US$515 per month. Recommended for longer stays.

Bosque de Chapultepec and Polanco
p95, map p98

LL Casa Vieja, Eugenio Sue 45, Metro Polanco, T55-5282 0067, www.casavieja.com. Beautiful boutique hotel in a converted mansion. Lodgings include 6 junior suites, 3 master suites and 1 presidential suite. Each is equipped with bar, kitchen, jacuzzi and steam sauna.

LL Habita, Presidente Masaryk 201, Metro Polanco, T55-5282 3100, www.hotel habita.com. This bastion of minimalist beauty boasts superb design and excellent facilities, including spa, gym, rooftop pool, solarium and jacuzzi. Crisp and hip.

LL The Four Seasons, Paseo de la Reforma 500, Metro Sevilla, T55-5230-1818, www.fourseasons.com/mexico. A very elegant and exclusive 8-storey hotel with sumptuous furnishings, stunning grounds and spa facilities. A favourite among high-powered business people, honeymooners and the terminally wealthy.

LL-AL Camino Real, Escobedo 700, Metro Chapultepec, T55-5263 8888, www.camino real.com. This somewhat gargantuan hotel designed by Ricardo Legorreta has some interesting architectural features and all the amenities you'd associate with a business hotel of this category. Comfortable.

LL-AL Presidente Intercontinental, Campos Elíseos 218, overlooking Chapultepec park, Metro Auditorio, T55-5327 7700, www.inter conti.com. Typical Intercontinental quality with great service, comfort and amenities. The ideal hotel for business and pleasure.

Insurgentes Sur: Roma and Condesa
p104, map 78

LL-L Condesa DF, Veracruz 102, Col Condesa, Metro Chapultepec, www.condesa df.com. Chic 1920s building converted into a stylish hotel. Attractive, popular with celebrities.

LL-AL La Casona, Durango 280, Col Roma, Metro Sevilla, T55-5286 3001, www.hotel lacasona.com.mx. This elegant, converted early 20th-century mansion has spacious, attractive rooms and plenty of amenities, including gym, Wi-Fi, spa and valet parking.

A Benidorm, Frontera 217, Col Roma, Metro Hospital General, T55-5265 0800, www.benidorm.com.mx. A very large 5-star hotel on a busy road with predictably comfortable rooms and lots of amenities including events room, parking, gym, gift shop, lobby bar and laundry. More modern than the Hotel Marbella next door.

B Marbella, Frontera 205, Col Roma, Metro Hospital General, T55-5264 7620. Stepping into Marbella's interesting lobby is like stepping into a 1970s time warp. The effect isn't altogether unattractive, though. Furnishings are slightly dated, but 5th-floor rooms are recently renovated and have all the usual amenities. Traffic noise can be a problem.

B Stanza, Obregón 13, corner of Morelia, Col Roma, Metro Cuauhtémoc, T01800-908 9600, www.stanzahotel.com. Professionally run and appointed, the Stanza has an elegant marble lobby and a wealth of amenities including restaurant, gym, bar and Wi-Fi. Rooms are clean and modern with coffee-makers, mini-bars, telephones, safes and spotless bathrooms. Recommended.

C Milán, Obregón 94, Col Roma, T55-5584 0222, Metro Insurgentes, www.hotel milan.com.mx. A good, clean, efficient hotel with lots of staff. Rooms are modern and fresh with marble sinks, fan, telephone and cable TV. Some have good views of the street below.

C Roosevelt, Insurgentes Sur 287, Col Hipódromo Condesa, Metrobús Alvaro Obregón, T55-5208 6813, www.roosevelt. com.mx. Rooms are clean and modern, equipped with cable TV, telephone, safe, writing desk, carpets and Wi-Fi. Some are bigger than others, so ask to see a few. The restaurant downstairs serves tasty Mexican food. Very friendly and helpful.

E Hostel Home, Tabasco 303, Col Roma, Metrobús Alvaro Obregón, T55-5511 1683, www.hostelhome.com.mx. Great little hostel with good clean dorms, kitchen and friendly staff. In a quiet part of town so not as crowded as the hostels in the Centro Histórico, and with a more relaxed atmosphere.

E Monarca, Obregón 32B, Col Roma, Metrobús Alvaro Obregón, T55-5584 0461. Rooms are on the small side, but very clean and comfortable with cable TV, telephone and bath. Mirrors on the ceiling.

Apartments

Casa de la Condesa, Plaza Luis Cabrera 16, Col Roma Sur, Metro Insurgentes, T55-5574 3186, www.extendedstaymexico.com. Very comfortable and attractive suites. Some have great views overlooking the plaza. The same family owns and rents slightly cheaper apartments on Calle Madrid and Calle Paris, very close to Insurgentes and the Zona Rosa.

Hotel Suites del Parque, Dakota 155, Col Nápoles, T55-5536 1450, hotelsuites delparque@prodigy.net.mx. Extremely spacious suites with the usual amenities, the price is good if sharing with up to 4 people, very convenient for the World Trade Center (across the street), good restaurant. No minimum or maximum stay.

Coyoacán *p107, map 107*
AL Suites Coyoacán, Av Coyoacán 1909, Col del Valle T55-5534 8353, www.suites coyoacan.com. One of the few hotels in the area with restaurant, catering facilities and gym.

Apartments
Suites Quinta Palo Verde, Cerro del Otate 20, Col Romero de Terreros, México 21 DF, T55-5554 3575. Pleasant, diplomatic residence-turned-guesthouse, near the university; run by a veterinary surgeon, who is very friendly and speaks English and German. The dogs are sometimes noisy.

North to Guadalupe *p112, map p68*
B Brasilia, near Terminal del Norte bus station, on Av Cien Metros 48-25, T55-5587 8577. Excellent modern hotel with king-size beds and TV. There's a 24-hr traffic jam out the front.
C La Villa de los Quijotes, Moctezuma 20, near Basílica de Guadalupe, Metro La Villa, T55-5577 1088, www.hotelvillaquijotes.com. Modern, quiet, clean rooms, pricey restaurant.

Elsewhere *map p68*
AL JR Plaza, Blv Puerto Aéreo 390, T55-5785 5200. Free airport transport, expensive restaurant, quiet, good rooms with solid furniture, close to the metro.

Youth hostels and campsites
For the nearest camping, see Tepoztlán, page 153, and the road to Toluca, page 160.
See SETEJ, page 72, for information on hotels and other establishments offering lodging for students.

Asociación Mexicana de Albergues de la Juventud, Madero 6, Oficina 314, México 1, DF. Contact by post for information.
Comisión Nacional del Deporte (Condep), runs the Villas Deportivas Juveniles (see below); information office at Glorieta del Metro Insurgentes, Local C-11, T55-5525 2916. Condep will make reservations for groups of 10 or more; to qualify you must be aged 8-65 and have a *Tarjeta Plan Verde* membership card (US$6, valid for 2 years, obtainable within 24 hrs from office at Tlalpan 583, esq Soria, Metro Xola), or a IYHF card.

🍴 Eating

All the best hotels have good restaurants. The number and variety of eating places is vast; this is only a small selection.

Zócalo and around *p80, map p82*
Bar La Opera, 5 de Mayo, Metro Allende, T55-5512 8959. Mon-Sat 1300-2400, Sun 1300-1800. One of the city's most elegant watering holes, open since 1870. Relaxing atmosphere, Mexican appetizers and entrées, and an expensive drinks list. The bullet hole in the ceiling was allegedly left by Mexican revolutionary Pancho Villa.
Café Tacuba, Tacuba 28, Metro Allende. A very old restaurant with stunning tile decor, not touristy and specializing in Mexican food. Very good *enchiladas*, excellent meat dishes, *tamales* and fruit desserts although portions are a little small and service a bit slow. Live music and Mariachis, very popular with local business people. Renowned Mexican politician, Danilo Fabio Altamirano, was assassinated here in 1936. Expensive but recommended.
El Cardenal, Palma 23, Metro Allende. Excellent Mexican food impeccably served in an elegant mansion. Interesting seasonal specialities include *gusanos de maguey* (maguey worms) *flores de maguey* (maguey flowers) and *chiles en nogada*. Breakfasts are tasty with a traditional feast of hot chocolate and sweet rolls.

¶¶¶ Hostería Santo Domingo, 70 and 72 Belisario Domínguez, 2 blocks west of Plaza Santo Domingo, Metro Allende, T55-5510 1612. The oldest restaurant in town with former diners creating a who's who of Mexican history. Good food and service. Excellent live music.

¶¶¶ La Casa de las Sirenas, Tacuba y Seminario, Metro Zócalo, behind the cathedral. This lovely old colonial building houses a classic Mexican restaurant with a fantastic selection of tequilas. Excellent food and service with great views from the rooftop terrace. Recommended.

¶¶¶ Mercaderes, 5 de Mayo 57, Metro Allende. Supposedly located where the Aztec emperor's former palace once stood, this elegant old restaurant serves a range of international dishes and a handful of obscure Mexican specialities too.

¶¶¶ Sanborn's Casa de los Azulejos, Av Madero 17, Metro Bellas Artes. Known as the foreigner's home-from-home, Sanborn's has 36 locations in Mexico, with soda fountain, pharmacy, restaurant, English, German and Spanish magazines, handicrafts, chocolates, etc. This, the most famous branch, is in the 16th-century the 'house of tiles'. Service can be poor, but there are many delicious local dishes in beautiful high-ceilinged room, with an Orozco mural on the staircase. Also has handicraft shops.

¶¶¶-¶¶ Danubio, Uruguay 3, Metro San Juan de Letrán. Founded over 60 years ago by 2 chefs from Spain's Basque region, this well-regarded restaurant is most famous for its seafood – perhaps the best in the city. Some 110 dishes grace the menu, many prepared on the traditional coal and wood stove that's been burning since 1936.

¶¶ El Andalus, Mesones 171, Metro Pino Suarez. The best Lebanese food in the city, served in a secluded old colonial building that's mercifully free of tourists. Fare includes kebabs, houmous, shwarma, falafel and sweet baklava pastries.

¶¶ Los Girasoles, corner of Tacuba and Gante, Metro Allende. Long-standing and popular restaurant serving Mexican cuisine in a big, airy old colonial building that's painted bright yellow to match the flowers. Reasonable food and a few interesting dishes, such as *chapulines* (roasted crickets) and *escamoles* (ant larvae). Pleasant outdoor seating on the plaza.

¶¶ Sushi Roll, 5 de Mayo y Filomeno Mata, about 5 blocks west of the Zócalo, Metro Allende. This Japanese eatery has a clean and pleasant interior. As the name suggests, it serves a large selection of sushi. Very good.

¶¶-¶ Café El Popular, 5 de Mayo 52, on corner of alley to **Hotel Juárez**, Metro Allende. 24 hrs, cheap, busy and popular with Mexicans. The choice includes a plethora of breakfasts and Mexican staples, Oaxacan omelettes, tacos, enchiladas and freshly baked pastries.

¶¶-¶ Café La Blanca, 5 de Mayo 40, Metro Allende. Popular and busy atmosphere at this unpretentious eatery with a large menu of breakfasts, Mexcian staples, and the usual meat, chicken and fish dishes. Recommended.

¶¶-¶ Café La Pagoda, 5 de Mayo and Filomeno Mata, behind **Bar La Opera**, Metro Bellas Artes. Unassuming diner with cosy booth seating and friendly waitresses in 1950s American-style uniforms. Breakfasts, Mexican staples and economical *menú del día*. Clean.

¶¶-¶ Gran Café del Centro, 5 de Mayo 10, Metro Bellas Artes. Smart little café with a chequered floor, reminiscent of a European coffee house. Sweet pastries, set breakfasts, *comida corrida*, fresh coffee, the usual Mexican staples and bar service.

¶ Comida Económica Verónica, República de Cuba, 2 doors from **Hotel Habana** (No 77), Metro Allende. For tasty breakfasts, set *comida corrida* and very hot *chilaquiles*. Good value and delightful staff. Recommended.

¶ Costillitas el Sitio, Uruguay 84, Metro Isabel la Católica. Popular lunchtime taco joint that has been feeding the locals since 1970.

¶ Gili's Pollo, 5 de Mayo, opposite **Hotel Rioja**, Metro Allende. Excellent chicken, eat in or takeaway, cheap, filling and friendly.

¶ Los Vegetarianos, Filomeno Mata 13, Metro Allende. Open 0800-2000. Relaxed outdoor seating and good, cheap vegetarian fare including salads, soups, juices, breakfasts and *menú del día*.

¶ **Maple**, Uruguay 109, next to **Hotel Roble**, Metro San Juan de Letrán. Clean, pleasant restaurant that's recommended for its economical *comida*.

¶ **Mariscos**, República de Uruguay 29a, Metro San Juan de Letrán. Bustling lunch stop and hole-in-the-wall serving good seafood including ceviche, conch, prawn cocktails, fillets and fish soup.

¶ **Rex**, 5 de Febrero 40, Metro Isabel la Católica. Unpretentious grub including rotisserie chickens, *tortas*, ultra-economical *comida corrida* and other wholesome fare.

Cafés, bakeries and sweet shops

Café del Centro, Bolivar 26, Metro Allende. Interesting little café. Dark, intimate and open-front, with great views of the street and the passing people.

Dulcería de Celaya, 5 de Mayo 39, Metro Allende. Famous traditional (and expensive), handmade candy store in lovely old premises.

Panadería La Vasconia, Tacuba 73, Metro Allende. Good bread, also sells cheap chicken and fries.

Pastelería Ideal, Uruguay 74, Metro San Juan de Letrán. Large, popular bakery with a huge array of cakes, breads, sweet rolls and pastries.

Pastelería Madrid, 5 de Febrero 25, 1 block from **Hotel Isabel la Católica**, Metro Pino Suárez. Good pastries and breakfasts.

Super Soya, Bolivar 29, Metro Allende. Health food shop serving a selection of good juices and fruit salads.

La Alameda and around *p90, map p82*

¶¶ **Hong Kong**, Dolores 25a, Metro San Juan de Letrán. One of several Chinese joints in the area, if you've had your fill of Mexican food and need new flavours.

¶¶ **Trevi**, Dr Mora y Colón, Metro Hidalgo. Mediocre diner-style place serving Italian, US and Mexican grub at reasonable prices. Still, an Alameda institution.

¶¶-¶ **Salon Sol**, Juárez 52, Metro Bellas Artes. Economical breakfasts and Mexican staples with plastic chairs and booth seating. Overlooks the Alameda.

¶ **Fonda Santa Rita**, Independencia 10, Metro San Juan de Letrán. Bustling locals' haunt serving *mole poblano*, *quesadillas*, soups, *tortas* and tacos.

Plaza de la República and around
p91, maps p78 and p82

You'll find lots of good street stalls in the residential roads west of La Alameda. They're often busy with hungry lunch crowds.

¶¶¶-¶¶ **La Parilla Argentina**, Lafragua 4, corner of Revolution Monument, Metro Revolución. Tasty Argentine steaks and other meat dishes.

¶¶ **La Habana**, Bucareli y Morelos, Metro Juárez. Not cheap but good, and famed for its excellent coffee and *banderilla* pastries. A great place for breakfast.

¶ **El Tigre**, Iglesias and Mariscal, Metro Revolución. Popular *torta* stand that also serves refreshing fruit *licuados*.

Paseo de la Reforma and Zona Rosa
p94, map p96

¶¶¶ **Chalet Suizo**, Niza 37, Metro Insurgentes. Swiss fondues, shredded veal fillet and German-style beef pot roast are some of the wholesome offerings at this popular Swiss restaurant, established by a celebrity chef. Several European languages spoken.

¶¶¶ **Les Moustaches**, Río Sena 88, Metro Insurgentes. Mon-Sat, 1300-2330. This award-winning French restaurant is one of Mexico City's finest. Classic French dishes like foie gras, onion soup and Gruyère prawns complement more exotic fare like crocodile with kiwi and walnuts. The epitome of elegance and suitably pricey.

¶¶¶-¶¶ **Quebracho**, Río Lerma 175, Metro Insurgentes. Succulent Argentine steaks for all your carnivorous needs. Popular with middle class Mexicans.

¶¶ **Fonda del Refugio**, Liverpool 166, Metro Insurgentes. Founded by writer Judit Van Beuren in the 1950s, this popular Mexican restaurant serves classic national dishes in a colonial setting. Loved by tourists.

Sushi Itto, Hamburgo 141, Metro Insurgentes. Fresh, reliable Japanese fare from this famous chain. Clean and tasty, if somewhat generic.

Bella Luna, Río Lerma and Río Sena, Metro Insurgentes. Tasty, affordable and authentic Oaxacan specialities at this modest little restaurant, including dishes featuring the famous *moles* (chocolate-based sauces).

Yug, Varsovia 3, Metro Insurgentes. This large vegetarian restaurant has an extensive menu of juices, fruits, yoghurt, salads and soups. The breakfast options are especially impressive and there's Mexican fare too – *sin carne*, of course.

Arles, Río Sena 30, Metro Insurgentes. Clean, busy eatery that serves buffet breakfasts, *comida del día* and other unpretentious fare. Popular with the locals.

Beatricita, Londres 188, Metro Insurgentes. Busy locals' haunt that's been serving up economical Mexican food since 1910. Tacos, breakfasts, national dishes and good-value *comida corrida* are on the menu.

La Puerta del Angel, Varsovia y Londres, Metro Insurgentes. Large, slightly faded local eatery where good-value food and spirited Latin music come in equally hearty measures.

Bosque de Chapultepec and Polanco
p95, map p98

Mexico City's very finest restaurants are concentrated in Polanco and Chapultepec. Prices are steep, reflecting the high quality.

Cambalache, Arquimedes north of Presidente Masaryk, Metro Polanco. This Argentine steakhouse serves some excellent cuts and stocks a wide selection of wines. Cosy atmosphere.

Fisher's, Taine 311, Metro Polanco. Superb seafood, and not expensive considering the quality and presentation. No reservations.

Hacienda de los Morales, Vásquez de Mella 525, Metro Polanco (but many blocks west of the station, consider a taxi), T55-5281 4703. Housed in a 16th-century hacienda,

this famous restaurant has lots of style and atmosphere. Serves Mexican specialities such as *chiles en nogada* and roasted goat. Wear a tie and jacket in the evening.

Café del Bosque, inside Chapultepec park, Lago Menor 2da, Metro Constituyentes, T55-5515 4652, www.cafedelbosque.com.mx. This smart little restaurant overlooks a lake. It's a popular spot for breakfast and serves international fare the rest of the time.

Mulegé, Taine 324, Metro Polanco, T55-5203 4988. Trendy, ambient oyster bar. The place to sip martinis and be seen.

Pámpano, Moliere 42, Metro Polanco, T55-5281 2010. Fine cuisine from Mexican chef Richard Sandoval. Contemporary and interesting.

Embers, Séneca y Ejército Nacional, Metro Polanco. Once past the gaudy Disney World exterior, this young, popular restaurant serves 43 types of excellent hamburger and good French fries. Recommended.

Tandoor, Copernico 156, Metro Polanco, T55-5203 0045, www.tandoor.com.mx. Reportedly the best Indian and Pakistani food in the city – and possibly the country. A good range of vindaloos and other delicious, spicy fare.

Insurgentes Sur: Roma and Condesa
p104, map 78

Roma and Condesa are DF's trendiest eating-out districts and a great place to sample the city's culinary talents.

Bistrot Mosaico, Michoacán 10, Condesa, Metrobús Campeche, T55-5584 2932. Closed Mon. Elegant French restaurant serving pricey but authentic cuisine. Lots of ambience and dusty wine bottles on display.

Hip Kitchen, Hippodrome Hotel, Mexico 188, Condesa, Metrobús Alvaro Obregón, T55-5212 2110. Closed Sun. A very fine and popular restaurant serving top-notch Asian-Mexican cuisine.

Lamm, Casa Lamm Cultural Centre, Alvaro Obregón 99, Roma, Metrobús Alvaro Obregón, T55-5514 8501. Closed Mon. Widely revered fine-dining establishment serving excellent Mexican and international cuisine.

₮₮₮-₮₮ El Chisme, Mexico 111, Condesa, Metrobús Campeche, T55-5584 0032, www.elchisme.com.mx. Open for breakfast, closed Fri. Occasional live events at this popular restaurant, including dance and comedy. Well-presented international fare includes pasta, pizzas, crêpes and fondue.

₮₮₮-₮₮ Ixchel, Medellin 65, Roma, Metrobús Durango, T55-3096 5010, www.ixchel.com.mx. Clean, crisp interior at this night-club turned trendy restaurant. Specialities include squash flowers stuffed with Oaxacan cheese and ravioli filled with spinach and goat's cheese. There's also steaks and fish, all well prepared.

₮₮₮-₮₮ La Bodega, Popocatépetl 25, Condesa, Metrobús Alvaro Obregón, T55-5511 7390, www.labodega.com.mx. Closed Sun. Founded in 1973, this famous, bohemian restaurant is housed in an atmospheric colonial building. Mexican specialities include *mole poblano* and *nopal* soup. The wine list is reasonably extensive. Occasional live music.

₮₮₮-₮₮ Lion Wok, Tamaulipas 136, Condesa, Metro Patriotismo, T55-5256 1579. A trendy, young restaurant with a modern interior, serving sushi and wok-fried treats.

₮₮₮-₮₮ Litoral, Tamaulipas 55, Condesa, Metrobús Sonora, T55-5286 2015, www.restaurant elitoral.com. Smart, popular restaurant with crisp white table clothes and wooden floors. Well-presented contemporary dishes include seafood, red meat, chicken, soup and pasta.

₮₮₮-₮₮ Mama Rosa's, Atlixco 105, Condesa, Metro Patriotismo, T55-5211 1640, www.mamarosas.com.mx. Italian-Mexican fusion and international fare at this highly popular and often buzzing eatery on the corner. Dishes include 'rock burgers', filete Sauvignon, stone-baked pizzas and pastas.

₮₮₮-₮₮ Rojo Bistrot, corner of Parras and Amsterdam, Condesa, Metrobús Sonora, T55-5211 3705. Closed Sun. European-style café with dimmed lighting, tasteful decor and French cuisine.

₮₮₮-₮₮ Tierra de Vinos, Durango 197, Roma, Metrobús Durango, T55-5208 5133, www.tierradevinos.com. Closed Sun. Spanish and Mediterranean cuisine. As the name suggests, there is a sensational wine cellar with bottles from around the world.

₮₮ Agapi Mu, Alfonso Reyes 96, Condesa, Metro Patriotismo, T55-5286 1384. Closed Mon. Intimate and hospitable Greek restaurant serving classic dishes like tsatsiki, moussaka and sweet baklava. It can get spirited in the evenings when the ouzo flows liberally.

₮₮ El Japonez, Suarez 42a, Condesa, Metro Patriotismo, T55-5286 0712. Daily 1300-2300. This Japanese restaurant has a crisp, attractive interior and pavement tables outside. Great sushi and spicy rolls.

₮₮ El Ocho, Ozuluama 14, Condesa, Metro Patriotismo. This fun, bright 'creative café' serves burgers, baguettes, bagels, other light meals and international fare. Lots of board games to keep you entertained.

₮₮ Flor de Lis, Huichapan 21, Condesa, Metrobús Sonora, T55-5211 3040, www.flordelis.com.mx. Open for breakfast. Well-established haunt serving lovingly prepared and presented Mexican cuisine, including delicious *chiles en nogada* and *tamales de chicharrón*.

₮₮ Origienes Organicos, Mexico y Cacahuamilpa, Condesa, Metrobús Sonora. This small, busy café-restaurant and health food store, overlooking Plaza Popacatapetl, serves wholesome organic meals including soups, salads and snacks. Some tables outside and free Wi-Fi for clients.

₮₮-₮ Bisquet Obregón, Alvaro Obregón y Mérida, Roma, Metrobús Alvaro Obregón. A hugely popular spot for breakfast and lunch with queues of Mexican families at the weekend. This well-established city-wide chain serves economical national staples.

₮ Amore Pizza, Michoacán 78, Condesa, Metro Patriotismo. Hole-in-the-wall selling pizza by the slice. Quick food on the go.

₮ El Tizoncito, Tamaulipas y Campeche, Condesa, Metro Patriotismo; also at Campeche y Cholula. This well-established and popular eatery serves tacos and other wholesome fast food, all cooked on the grills in front of you and filling the air with delicious smells.

♥ **Tacos Hola**, Amsterdam 135, corner of Michoacán, Condesa, Metrobús Campeche. There's often a small crowd gathered around this little taco joint. Popular and tasty.

Cafés

Café Malafama, Michoacán 78, Condesa, Metrobús Campeche. Large, slick pool hall with a plethora of trendy black and white photos. Coffee by day, beer by night.

Café Maria, Mexico y Iztaccihuatl, Condesa, Metrobús Campeche. This popular café has tables on the pavement so you can sip your frappuccino and watch the world go by. Close to the park and relaxing.

El Péndulo, Nuevo León 115, Condesa, Metrobús Campeche. Great little coffee shop inside a bookstore, for those who are (or wish to appear) intellectual. Light snacks available.

San Angel p106

♥♥♥ **San Angel Inn**, Diego Rivera 50, Metrobús La Bombilla (around 1 km from the stop) T55-5616 2222, www.sanangelinn.com. Mon-Sat 1230- 0030, Sun 1300-2130. Top-quality dining in the former Carmelite monastery. If you can't afford a meal, it's worth going for a drink.

Coyoacán p107, map 107

There are several pleasant *cafeterías* in the Jardín Centenario, some of which serve light snacks and *antojitos*. At the market, between Malintzin and Xicoténcatl, opposite Jardín del Carmen, Metro Viveros, there are exquisite *quesadillas* at Local 31; outside the market try the seafood at **El Jardín del Pulpo**, if you can get a seat. Fruit and vegetable sellers are ready to explain the names and uses of their goods; frequent musical entertainment particularly at lunchtime and on weekends.

♥♥♥ **Los Danzantes**, south side of Jardín del Centenario, Metro Viveros. Highly regarded as a bastion of culinary creativity. Serves mescal from its own distillery and Mexican fusion from the European-trained chef.

♥♥♥-♥♥ **Hacienda de Cortés**, Fernández Leal 74, behind Plaza de la Conchita, Metro Viveros, T55-5659 3741, www.haciendade cortes.com.mx. Exceptionally pleasant surroundings with a large shaded, outdoor dining area. Excellent breakfast and good-value *comida corrida* (US$5); try the *sábana de res con chilaquiles verdes*. Best at the weekend (book in advance) to experience the heart of Mexican family life.

♥♥ **El Caracol de Oro**, Higuera 22, Metro Viveros. Photos, artwork and beautifully painted furniture create a relaxed and bohemian atmosphere at this youthful café-restaurant, imaginatively named 'The Golden Snail'. Menu includes juices, energy drinks, pastas and Mexican dishes.

♥♥ **Mesón Antiguo Santa Catarina**, Plaza Santa Catarina, Metro Viveros. This delightfully situated restaurant in the square of the same name serves good Mexican cuisine at reasonable prices. There's a splendid atmosphere, especially for breakfast or supper, and the interior is adorned with Mexican art and wooden beams. Upstairs there's a terrace overlooking the plaza.

♥♥ **Moheli**, Sosa and Tres Cruces, west side of the Jardín Centenario, Metro Viveros. This popular café-delicatessen serves bagels, baguettes and pastas and has pleasant outdoor seating along the pavement. A great breakfast spot.

♥♥-♥ **El Morral**, Allende 2, Metro Viveros. A good Mexican restaurant with an attractive tiled interior, an array of interesting old photos and other memorabilia. The bathrooms are palatial. Prices double at weekends, no credit cards. Highly recommended.

♥♥-♥ **Fabio's**, overlooking Plaza Hidalgo and the Delegación, Metro Viveros. Chequered table clothes and hanging baskets adorn this Mediterranean restaurant with views. Good *comida corrida*, credit cards accepted.

♥♥-♥ **La Guadalupana**, Higuera y Caballocalco, a few steps behind the church of San Juan Bautista in the centre of Coyoacán, Metro Viveros, T55-5554 6253. Mon-Sat 0900-2300. One of the best-known *cantinas* in Mexico, dating from 1932, fantastic food and a great atmosphere and no apologies for the passionate interest in bull fighting.

¶ **Churros Rellenos 'Jordan'**, Aguayo and Cuatémoc, Metro Viveros. Wholesome home-cooked *comida corrida*, tacos and other fast food. Just one of several economical places in this area.

Cafés and bakeries

El Globo, Caballocalco y Hidalgo, east side of Plaza Hidalgo, Metro Viveros. A stunning bakery with a wide selection of cakes, pastries and breads. Check out the wedding cakes in the windows.

El Jarocho, Allende y Cuatémoc, Metro Viveros. Buzzing little coffee shop with locals queuing up in the street. The interior is filled with coffee sacks and processing paraphernalia. Snacks and pastries on offer too.

Mastropiero Café, Higuera 31, next to the post office, Metro Viveros. A new café that serves as a cultural space with books, dance classes and music. Specialities include *tamales*, chocolate truffles and pizza with white chocolate. Young, friendly owners.

Xochimilco *p111*

¶ **Beto's**, opposite Fernando Celada, Metro Xochimilco. Good, clean and cheap restaurant, US$2 for lunch.

¶ **del Botas**, Pino, to the left of the cathedral, Metro Xochimilco. Serves a first-rate cheap lunch (US$2).

🕭 Bars and clubs

Nightlife in Mexico City is as lively and varied as everything else the city has to offer. From gentle supper clubs with floor shows to loud, brash nightclubs, and from piano bars to *antros* (or disco-bars) and traditional Mexican music – all tastes are catered for. The most popular districts are Condesa, Roma, Zona Rosa, Polanco, San Angel and Coyoacán. You can go for a drink at any time, clubbing starts late with most just getting going by

2400. Prices of drinks and admission vary enormously depending on the area. Remember that, because of the high altitude, one alcoholic drink in Mexico City can have the effect of two at lower altitudes. Many bars and nightclubs are closed on Sun.

Zócalo and around *p80, map p82*
Casa de las Sirenas, Guatemala 32, Metro Zócalo, www.lacasadelassirenas.com. Home to an astonishing stock of more than 250 tequilas, this is the place to develop your knowledge and appreciation of Mexico's proud alcoholic heritage. Great views too.
El Nivel, Moneda 2, Metro Zócalo. Colourful and boozy little *cantina* that's been around for centuries. 100% local, with the odd tourist popping in.

Zócalo to La Merced *p87, map p82*
Pervert Lounge, Uruguay 70, Metro Isabel la Católica. Thu-Sat 2230-0500. Cover charge US$10. Famous dance venue attracting world-class DJs and crowds of revellers. Techno, house and trance plays.

Zócalo to La Alameda *p88, map p82*
Bar La Opera, 5 de Mayo 10, Metro Allende. Fantastic old bar-restaurant with a range of national drinks and a bullet hole in the ceiling left by Pancho Villa. Dark, cosy and possessing great ambience.
Bar Mata, Filomeno Mata 11, Alameda Central, Metro Bellas Artes, T55-5518 0237, Thu-Sat. On the 4th and 5th floors of a colonial building near Palacio de Bellas Artes. Atmosphere conducive to dancing and mingling, especially in the rooftop (5th floor) bar, with great views of the city at night.
La Perla, República de Cuba 44, Metro Allende. Thu-Sat 2000-0400. US$4 cover charge. Seedy but popular little club in the centre. Everything from dance to freaky cabaret has been reported.
Salón Corona, Bolívar 24, betwen Madero and 16 de Septiembre, Metro Allende. Closes around 2400. Big, basic bar full of locals. Good atmosphere.

Zinco Jazz Club, Motolinia 20, Metro Allende, www.zincojazz.com. Wed-Sat 2100-0330. Atmospheric jazz hall located in the basement of an art deco building. Great ambience and captivating live performances. Popular, so book ahead.

La Alameda and around *p90, map p82*

Plaza Garibaldi, Eje Central Lázaro Cárdenas, 5 blocks north of Bellas Artes, Metro Bellas Artes. The place to experience live and spirited Mariachi performances, most vociferous on Fri and Sat nights. Take a taxi and watch out for thieves.

Paseo de la Reforma and Zona Rosa *p94, map p96*

Bar Milán, Milán 18, Metro Cuauhtémoc. Tue-Sat from 2100. Intimate little drinking hole that attracts a bright, young international crowd. Uses a ticket system to dispense drinks at the bar. Eclectic music.
Casa Rasta, Insurgentes 149, Metro Insurgentes, T55-5705 0086. Thu-Sat from 2200. US$20 for men, US$5 for women, but free bar. For reggae lovers, as the name suggests.
El Colmillo, Versailles 52, Metro Cuauhtémoc, T55-5553 0262. Thu-Sat 2200-0400. Attracts a young, chic crowd with techno music downstairs and an exclusive jazz bar upstairs.
El Taller, Florencia y Reforma. Tue-Sun from 2200. Underground gay bar, one of the first in Mexico City.
Yuppie's Sports Café, Génova 34, Metro Insurgentes, T55-5208 2267. Daily 1300-0100. Good Tex-Mex and American-style fare in a pub with every corner adorned with sports memorabilia, TVs broadcast games from Mexico and around the world.

Bosque de Chapultepec and Polanco *p95, map p98*

Barfly, Plaza Mazarik Mall, Metro Polanco, T55-5282 2906. Tue-Sat from 2000. Cosy bar with small dance floor and Cuban dance bands from 2300.
El Area, Habita Hotel, Masaryk 201, Metro Polanco, www.hotelhabita.com. Mon-Sat, from 1900. Swanky roof-top bar where hipsters and jet-setters congregate for evening cocktails.
Mezzanote, Masaryk 407, Metro Polanco, T55-5282 0130. Daily from 1400. Art nouveau decor, ideal for drinking, dining or dancing, especially later in the night. Franchise from the original in Miami, frequented by 30-somethings.

Insurgentes Sur: Roma and Condesa *p104, map 78*

El Mitote, Amsterdam 33, Condesa, Metrobús Sonora, www.elmitote.com. Tue-Sat, from 2000. Popular with locals, a pleasant watering hole set in a charming old building.
Hookah Lounge, Campeche 284, Condesa, Metro Chilpancingo. Mon-Sat from 1300. Styled on an Arabic smoking den with water pipes and molasses tobacco. DJs spin electronic tunes in the evenings.
La Bodeguita del Medio, Cozumel 37, Roma, Metro Sevilla, T55-5553 0246. Extremely popular Cuban bar-restaurant where drinks like *mojitos* became famous, and graffiti is an art form.
Malafama, Michoacán 78, Condesa, Metro Patriotismo. Busy billiards hall with bottled coronas and an array of stylish black and white photography.
Mamá Rumba, Querétaro 230 y Medellín, Roma, Metrobús Sonora, T55-5564 6920. Live music Thu-Sat from 2300. US$6 cover charge. One of the first places in Mexico City with Cuban rhythms, famous for its *rumba*, now with a couple of floors. Also a new branch opened in San Angel (T55-5550 8099) with live music Wed-Sat from 2100. Get there early, it gets packed.
Pata Negra, Tamaulipas 30, Condesa, Metro Patriotismo. Daily 1330-0200. 2 floors of popular bar space that attracts moneyed Mexicans and crowds of international hipsters. Tapas available.
Rexo, Saltillo 1 y Nuevo León, Condesa, Metro Patriotismo, T55-5553 5337. Daily from 1330. Restaurant-bar with Mediterranean food, one of the area's most popular places.

Coyoacán *p107*, map *p107*
El Hijo del Cuervo, Jardín Centenario 17, Metro Viveros, T55-5658 5306. Daily 1300-2400. Small cover charge (up to US$7) depending on show. Attracts students and hip intellectuals of all ages for an interesting mix of rock and *nueva canción*, and the occasional theatre show.
La Guadalupana, Higuera y Caballocalco, Metro Viveros. Atmospheric Coyoacán institution. See Eating, page 124.

⊕ Entertainment

Mexico City *p77*
Listings for all cultural events can be found in the publication *Tiempo Libre*, available every Thu from newsstands (US$1). Monthly programmes are available from the bookshop at the **Palacio de Bellas Artes** (see page 90).

Cinema
A number of cinemas show non-Hollywood films in the original language (Spanish subtitles); check *Tiempo Libre* magazine for details. Most cinemas, except Cineteca Nacional, offer reduced prices on Wed.
Cine Diana, Av Reforma, at the end where Parque Chapultepec starts, Metro Sevilla, T55-5511 3236.
Cinemex Palacio Chino, Iturbide 21, in the Chinese *barrio* south of Av Juárez (also an interesting area for restaurants), Metro Juárez, T55-5512 0348, www.cinemex.com.
Cinemex Plaza Insurgentes, San Luis Potosi 214, Metro Insurgentes, T55-5257 6969, www.cinemex.com.
Cinemex Real, Colón 17, Metro Hidalgo, T55-5257 6969, www.cinemex.com.
Lumiere Reforma, Río Guadalquivir 104, Metro Sevilla, T55-5514 0000.

Art house For arthouse films, courses in film appreciation or an otherwise more involved look at the cinematic form, try:

Cinematógrafo del Chopo, Dr Atl 37, Metro San Cosme, T55-5702 3494. Screens non-commercial films daily.
Cinemex Casa de Arte, France 120, Metro Polanco, T55-5280 9156, www.cinemex.com. Alternative, independent and art-house films.
Cineteca Nacional, México-Coyoacán 389, Metro Coyoacán, T55-1253 9390, www.cinetecanacional.net. Excellent bookshop on cinema and related topics. Hosts the city's international film festival every Nov.
Ciudad Universitaria, Insurgentes Sur 3000, T55-5665 0709, www.filmoteca.unam.mx. The university's cultural centre has 2 good cinemas that regularly screen art-house films.

Theatre
Tickets for many shows can be acquired online from **Ticket Master**, www.ticket master.com.mx, while **Mejor Teatro**, www.mejorteatro.com.mx, has information on current Spanish-language performances.
Auditorio Nacional, Paseo de la Reforma 50, Metro Auditorio, www.auditorio.com.mx. Major concerts and spectaculars (eg presidential inaugurations) are staged here. There are a couple of theatres behind the *auditorio* (ask the tourist office for details).
Centro Cultural Helénico, Revolución 1500, Metrobús Altavista, T55-4155 0919, www.helenico.gob.mx. 450 seats. Occasional major Spanish-language productions.
Palacio de Bellas Artes, Hidalgo 1, Metro Bellas Artes, T55-5512 2593, www.bellas artes.gob.mx. For Ballet Folklórico, opera and classical concerts. (See also page 90.)
Teatro de la Ciudad, Donceles 36, Metro Allende, T55-5510 2197. Hosts the Ballet Folklórico Nacional Aztlán. Tickets US$3-15; very good shows Sun morning and Wed.
Teatro de los Insurgentes, Av Insurgentes Sur 1587, T55-5611 5047, south of the centre. Mostly Spanish-language shows.
Teatro la Blanquita, Lázaro Cárdenas Sur near Plaza Garibaldi, Metro Bellas Artes, T55-5512 8264. Variety show nightly with singers, dancers, comedians, magicians and ventriloquists, very popular with locals.

Teatro Universitario, at UNAM's Centro Cultural, Insurgentes Sur 3000, T55-5665 0709, www.difusion.cultural.unam.mx. 5 theatres for music, dance and drama (see page 110).

On the edge of the Delegación Coyoacán, at the southeast corner of Churubusco and Tlalpan (Metro General Anaya) is the **Central Nacional de las Artes**, T55-4155 0000, www.cenart.gob.mx, a huge complex of futuristic buildings dedicated to the training and display of the performing and visual arts. It has a good bookshop, library and *cafeterías*.

Coyoacán has several small and medium-sized theatres, for example: **Teatro Coyoacán** and **Teatro Usigli**, Eleuterio Méndez, 5 blocks from Metro General Anaya; **Foro Cultural de Coyoacán**, Allende (most events free of charge); Museo Nacional de Culturas Populares, Hidalgo; **Foro Cultural Ana María Hernández**, Pacífico 181; **Teatro Santa Catarina**, Plaza Santa Catarina; the **Teatro Rafael Solana**, Miguel Angel de Quevedo (nearly opposite Caballocalco; **Casa del Teatro**, Vallarta 31; and **Foro de la Conchita**, Vallarta 33.

Also note **El Hábito**, Madrid, and **El Hijo del Cuervo**, Jardín Centenario, for avant-garde drama and cabaret; **Los Talleres de Coyoacán**, Francisco Sosa, dance and ballet; **CADAC**, Centenario, traditional and experimental drama.

⊛ Festivals and events

Mexico City *p77*
17 Mar Día de San José. Several districts celebrate with music and processions.
Mar/Apr Festival del Centro Histórico, www.fchmexico.com. The Centro Histórico becomes a stage for vibrant international performances, concerts and gastronomic gatherings during this anticipated festival.
Mar/Apr Semana Santa. A joyous occasion across the country, but the Passion Play in Ixtapalapa district is particularly memorable, where the crucifixion is vividly re-enacted.
Mar/Apr Feria de la Flor Más Bella del Ejido. Xochimilco's annual festival of flowers sees a wealth of events including a beauty contest.

5 May Cinco de Mayo, National celebration commemorating the failed French invasion. Ixtapala is reported to be the most festive.
25 Jul Día de Santiago. In commemoration of St James, with a slew of folkloric performances at the Plaza de las Tres Culturas.
13 Aug The Fall of Tenochtitlán. In honour of Emperor Cuauhtémoc and the fallen Aztec Empire, troupes of conchero dancers convene on the Plaza de las Tres Culturas.
15 Sep Independence; the largest celebration in the capital when the president gives El Grito: '*Viva México*' from the Palacio Nacional on the Zócalo at 2300, and rings the Liberty Bell (now, sadly, electronic). This is followed by fireworks. Just as much fun, and probably safer, is the *Grito* that takes place at the same time in the plaza in Coyoacán.
16 Sep Military and traditional regional Independence parades in the Zócalo area, 0900-1400, great atmosphere.
1-2 Nov Día de los Muertos. Mexico's national celebration of the dead is a memorable and spirited affair in the capital. Locals compete for the most beautiful and artistic *ofrendas* (altars) with impressive public displays in the Zócalo and across the city. Night-time vigils take place in various locations including the Panteón Civil, Bosque de Chapultepec 2a Sección, San Andres Mixquic, San Lucas Xochimanca, Santa Cecilia Tepetlapa and San Antonio Tecómitl.
22 Nov Fiesta de Santa Cecilia. In honour of the patron saint of musicians, with lots of crooning at Plaza Garibaldi and around.
12 Dec Guadalupana at the Basílica de Guadalupe, is definitely worth a visit if you're in town (see page 113). The heavily attended festival honours the patron saint of Mexico with millions of pilgrims descending upon the sacred site.

○ Shopping

Mexico City *p77*
Art and handicrafts
Fondo Nacional para el Fomento de las Artesanías (**FONART**), Av Patriotismo 691,

Metro Mixcoac, T55-5598 1666; branches at Av Juárez 89, Metro Hidalgo, and Paseo de Reforma 116, Metro Cuauhtémoc. A state organization founded in 1974 in order to rescue, promote and diffuse the traditional crafts of Mexico. Competitive prices and superb quality.

Mercado de Artesanías Finas Indios Verdes, Galería Reforma Norte SA, González Bocanegra 44 (corner of Reforma Norte, near statue of Cuitláhuac, Tlatelolco). Good prices and quality but no bargaining.

Uriarte, Emilio Castelar 95-E, Polanco, T55-5282 2699, and Pabellón Altavista, Calzada Desierto de los Leones 52 D-6, San Angel, T55-5616 3119, www.uriartetalavera.com.mx. Talavera pottery from Puebla.

There are many gift shops in **Coyoacán**: **Mayolih**, Aldama with Berlín, 2 blocks from Museo Frida Kahlo; and **La Casita** on Higuera.

Bicycle shops

Benolto, near Metro Polanco. Stocks almost all cycle spares.

Escuela Médico Militar, near Metro Pino Suárez. Very good shop, stocking all the best-known international makes for spare parts.

Hambling González Muller, Ezequiel Ordóñez 46-1, Col Copilco el Alto, Coyoacán, Metro Viveros, T55-5658 5591. The best place for bicycle repairs in Mexico City. Builds wheels and frames for Mexican racers, reasonable prices, highly recommended.

Tecno-Bici, Av Manuel Acuña 27, Metro Camarones, Line 7. Stocks almost all cycle spares, parts. Highly recommended.

Books, posters and music

American Bookstore, Bolivar 23, Metro San Juan de Letran. Large stocks of Penguin and Pelican books, low mark up.

Casa Libros, Monte Athos 355, Lomas. Large stock of 2nd-hand English books, staffed by volunteers, donated books welcome, all proceeds to the American Benevolent Society.

El Parnaso, Jardín Centenario, Coyoacán, Metro Viveros. One of the most famous book-shops in Mexico City (coffee recommended).

Fondo de Cultura Económico, Miguel Angel de Quevedo. Inexpensive editions in Spanish.

Gandhi, large branches on MA de Quevedo, another opposite Palacio de Bellas Artes. Several shops with a large selection and keen prices. Good range of music, excellent prices.

John Gibbs Publications, T55-5658 5376, www.johngibbs.com. Supplies fine art posters, including images by Diego Rivera and Frida Kahlo, to the city's principal museums and bookshops.

La Torre de Papel, Filomeno Mata 6-A, Club de Periodistas. Sells newspapers from all over Mexico and the USA.

Librería del Sótano, several branches: Av Juárez, Antonio Caso, MA de Quevedo. Inexpensive editions in Spanish.

Librería Madero, Madero 12, Centro. Good, stocks antiquarian books.

Libros y Arte is a chain of literary and art bookshops with branches in the Palacio de Bellas Artes, the airport (area D), the Centro Nacional de Las Artes, the Cineteca Nacional, Coyoacán (Av Hidalgo), Museo del Carmen (San Angel) and the Museo Nacional de las Culturas (Moneda 13, Centro).

Museo Nacional de Antropología, see page 98. Its bookshop sells anthropological books and guides to national archaeological sites.

Palacio de Bellas Artes, see page 90. Good bookshop for the arts and culture.

Sanborn's, branches throughout city, including one in a historic building at Tacuba 2 (see page 120). Also at the airport, Antonio Caso 52, esq Calle Paris (near Plaza República), Isabel Católica 35, Insurgentes 1605. Chain has Mexico's largest selection of English-language magazines and stocks bestselling paperbacks in English.

Second-hand book market, Independencia just past junction with Eje Lázaro Cárdenas. Some English books; also Puente de Alvarado, 100 m from Metro Hidalgo, and Dr Bernard 42, Metro Niños Héroes. Second-hand Spanish and antiquarian booksellers can be found on Donceles between Palma and República de Brasil, about 1½ blocks from the Zócalo.

UNAM, Ciudad Universitaria. The university bookshop has a comprehensive range of books in Spanish.

Clothing and accessories

Mexican jewellery and handmade silver can be bought everywhere. Among the good silver shops are **Sanborn's, Calpini, Prieto,** and **Vendome.**

Joyería Sobre Diseño, Local 159, at the Ciudadela market, is helpful and will produce personalized jewellery cheaply. There are also good buys in perfumes, quality leather and suede articles.

Many small tailors are found in and around República de Brasil, offering suits made to measure in a week or less at a fraction of the price in Europe. Also many off-the-peg tailors, eg **Beleshini**, Juárez 12, opposite the Palacio de Bellas Artes.

At Metro Pino Suárez are several shops selling *charro* clothing and equipment (leggings, boots, spurs, bags, saddles, etc), eg **Casa Iturriaga**. Recommended.

Markets

Bazar del Sábado, San Angel (page 106), Metrobús La Bombilla. Sat from 1100. Expensive but many with many exclusive items; good leather belts, crafts and silver.
Buena Vista craft market, Aldama 187 y Degollado, Metro Guerrero. Mon-Sat 0900-1800, Sun 0900-1400. Excellent quality.
La Ciudadela, Mercado Central de Artesanías, beside Balderas 95, between Ayuntamiento y Plaza Morelos, Metro Balderas, Mon-Sat 1100-1800, Sun 1100- 1400. Government-sponsored market with fixed prices and good selection. Reasonable and uncrowded, and generally cheaper than San Juan, but not for leather. Craftworkers from all Mexico have set up workshops here (best for papier mâché, lacquer, pottery and Guatemalan goods), but prices are still cheaper in places of origin.
Mercado Insurgentes, Londres, Metro Insurgentes. Good for silver, but other items are expensive. The stallholders pester visitors – the only place where they do so.

Mercado Jamaica, Metro Jamaica, Line 4. Has a huge variety of fruits and vegetables, also flowers, pottery, canaries, parrots, geese, and ducks, indoor and outdoor halls.
Mercado La Lagunilla, near Glorieta Cuitláhuac, take a *colectivo* from Metro Hidalgo. Daily, but best on Sun. A flea market covering several blocks where antique and collectable bargains are sometimes to be found, also a lot of rubbish. Good atmosphere but watch your bag.
Mercado Merced (page 87), Metro Merced. Vast general market that covers several city blocks and sells everything. Beware of thieves.
Mercado San Juan, Ayuntamiento y Arandas, Metro Salto del Agua. Mon-Sat 0900-1900, Sun 0900-1600 (don't go before 1000). Good prices for handicrafts, especially leather goods and silver; also cheap fruit and health food.
Mercado Sonora, Metro Merced. Sells secret potions, spells and remedies, animals and birds as well as *artesanías*. Resist the wizened old ladies beseeching you in the darkness.
Tianguis del Chopo, Aldama 211, between Sol and Luna, Metro Buenavista. Sat 1000-1600. Clothes, records, etc, frequented by hippies, punks, rockers and police.

Photography

Foto Regis, Balderas 32, 4th floor, T55-5521 5010, www.fotoregis.com. Mon-Fri 0900-1800, Sat 0900-1400. Good service on a range of makes including Canon, Minolta, Pentax, Hasselblad, Konica and Leica. Reasonably priced as well. Good-quality, reliable development at their shop on Juárez 80, T55-5521 0346.

▲▲ Activities and tours

Mexico City *p77*
Adventure tourism and ecotourism
Al Aire Libre, Centro Comercial Interlomas, Local 2122, Lomas Anáhuac Huixquilucan, T55-5291 9217. Rafting (Ríos Pescados-Antigua, Santa María, Amacuzac), climbing,

caving (Chontalcuatlán, Zacatecoltla, La Joya), ballooning, parapenting.

Asociación Mexicana de Turismo de Aventura y Ecoturismo (AMTAVE), Río y Montaña, Prado Norte 450-T, Lomas de Chapultepec, T55-5520 2041, www.amtave. org. Regulates and promotes many of the agencies listed. Not all areas of adventure sport come under their umbrella, for instance specialist diving agencies remain unattached to any Mexico-based organization, as diving is a mainly regional activity. But a very good wide ranging list of members.

Bullfights

Monumental Plaza México, Rodin 241, Napoles, T55-5563 3961. One of the world's largest bullrings with a near 50,000 capacity. Professional fights run Nov-Mar every Sun. Aspiring professionals practise Jun-Oct. The cheapest seats are in the sunny section; tickets cost around US$20.

Football

Estadio Azteca, south of the city. Sun 1200. To get to the Aztec Stadium take the metro to Taxqueña terminus, then take a tram heading in the direction of Xochimilco as far as Estadio station (about 75 mins from the Zócalo). To find out what's on visit www.esmas.com/ estadioazteca (Spanish only).

Hiking

Club Alpino Mexicano, Coahuila 40 esq Córdoba, Roma, T55-5574 9683, www.club alpinomexicano.com.mx. Small shop (if club door is closed ask here for access). Runs free mountain hiking trips at weekends and runs ice climbing courses. Helpful.

Club de Exploraciones de México, Juan A Mateos 146, Col Obrero, Metro Chabacano, T55-5740 8032, www.cemac.org.mx. Meetings Wed and Fri 1930-2200. Organizes walks in and around the city on Sat and Sun, cheap equipment hire.

For equipment, supplies and repairs: **Coleman Camping Gear**, Vicente Guerrero No 3, local 3, near the corner of Gustavo Baz

Col El Mirador, T55-2628 0622. Coleman camping supplies.

Deportes Rubens, Venustiano Carranza 17, T55-5518 5636, www.dscorp.com.mx/rubens. Good selection of outdoor and climbing gear. **Vertimania**, Federico T de la Chica 12, Plaza Versailles, Local 11-B, Col Satélite, T55-5393 5287. Equipment.

Horse races

Hipódromo de las Américas, west of Blv Avila Camacho, off Av Conscriptos, www.hipodromo.com.mx. Beautiful track with infield lagoons and flamingos, and plenty of atmosphere. Incorporates exhibition and convention centre.

Language schools

UNAM (see page 110) has excellent classes of Spanish language and Mexican culture: **Centro de Enseñanza para Extranjeros**, Av Universidad 3002, T55-5622 2470, www.cepe.unam.mx, US$340 for 6 weeks, 5 different programmes, free additional courses in culture, free use of medical service, swimming pool, library, a student card from here allows free entry to all national monuments and museums and half price on many bus lines (eg **ADO** during summer vacations). See also Language tuition, page 59, and Cultural centres, page 141.

Lucha libre

There are 2 main arenas where you can catch a theatrical *lucha libre* wrestling performance (see box, page 132): **Arena de México**, Dr Lavista 197, Col Doctores, Metro Cuauhtémoc, T55-5588 0508, www.arena mexico.com.mx, Fri from 2030; and **Arena Coliseo**, Perú 77, Metro Lagunilla, T55-5526 1687, Tue and Sun from 1700.

Tour operators

Shop around as prices vary considerably. If possible, use a travel agent that has been recommended to you, as not all are efficient or reliable. Hotels and hostels are often able to book excursions and in some cases flights. This is often more convenient.

The good fight: lucha libre and the legend of El Santo

The phenomenon of two hulking Herculean males – flamboyantly adorned in brightly coloured lycra shorts, gaudy masks and flowing capes – tussling each other to submission is one of the most revered spectacles in Mexico. *Lucha libre*, or 'free fighting', is the second most popular national 'sport' after soccer.

Some 10 stadiums across the capital regularly host fights between *luchadores* (wrestlers), who fall into one of two broad camps. *Rudos*, literally 'rude ones', are the bad guys, who often bend or break the rules and comport themselves in a brusque, impolite and brawling fashion. *Técnicos*, literally 'technicians', are the good guys, gladiatorial-style fighters who follow good conduct. Like all wrestlers around the world, *rudos* and *técinos* are engaged in the age-old battle between good and evil.

Lucha libre was introduced to Mexico in 1933 by retired army colonel Salvador Lutteroth, after he witnessed a wrestling match in the United States. It was an instant hit, especially in the capital, where thousands of young migrants from the countryside had settled in search of work, housing and wholesome entertainment. Over time many unique conventions arose to distinguish Mexican wrestling from other forms, not least the use of masks to conceal the identity the *luchadores*.

Today, important matches often require the loser to forfeit his mask, and therefore his anonymity, in so-called *luchas de apuestas* (matches with wagers).

Losing a mask often signifies the end of a wrestler's career, or at the very least, a descent into shame and obscurity. Wrestlers without masks will sometimes bet their hair instead.

The convention of using masks was popularized by Rodolfo Guzmán, also known as El Santo, 'The Saint', who concealed his identity for some 40 years. Fighting the good fight from 1942 to 1980, he inspired generations of wrestlers with his silver mask and costume, unrivalled *técnico* fighting skills. He bravely won titles through famous signature moves that included the arm camel clutch.

El Santo's sphere of influence extended well beyond the ring with notable charity and film work, including roles in a string of B movies such as *Brain of Evil*, *Santo against the Zombies*, and, arguably his most glorious cinematic moment, *Santo against the Women Vampires*. Nothing short of a national hero, he even had his own comic book series. He quit the ring in 1980 after collapsing into unconsciousness for some three minutes. Four years later, in January 1984, he removed his mask during a TV documentary and revealed his identity for the first time. He died of a heart attack just days later.

Today, *lucha libre* is experiencing continued popularity with princely fighters such as Místico and Superbarrio, who can be seen performing in the Arena Coliseo and other major venues. For more information, see page 131.

American Express, Reforma 350, T55-5207 7282. Mon-Fri 0900-1800, Sat 0900-1300. Helpful.
Corresponsales de Hoteles, Pilares 231, Local 6 Del Valle, T55-5575 5500, www.corresponsales. com.mx. Upmarket hotel reservations.
Grey Line Tours, Londres 166, T55-5208 1163, www.mexitours.com.mx. Reasonably

priced tours, car hire, produces *This is Mexico* book (free).
Hivisa Viajes, Paseo de la Reforma 505 PB Loc 7 Col Cuauhtémoc, T55-5212 0812, www.hivisaviajes.com.mx. One of the most reliable. Good for flights to Europe, Central and South America, and for changing flight dates, English spoken, ask for Icarus Monk.

Mundo Joven Travel Shop, Guatemala 4, Col Centro, T55-5518 1755, www.mundo joven.com. Issues ISIC cards, agents for International Youth Hostel Federation.

Protures Viajes, Av Baja California 46, Col Roma Sur, T55-5482 8282. Recommended agency for flights to Central and South America and Cuba.

Túribus, www.turibus.com.mx. 0900-2100. This open-top double-decker tour bus departs every 30 mins from near the Zócalo and trawls the major sights, including Paseo de la Reforma. Tickets are sold as 1-, 2- or 3-day passes and allow users to get on and off at will. A complete circuit takes around 3 hrs.

Viajes Tirol, José Ma Rico 212, Depto 503, T55-5534 5582. English and German spoken. Recommended.

● Transport

Mexico City *p77*

Air
Airport information

The well-equipped and expanding **Benito Juárez International Airport**, T55-5571 3214, www.aicm.com.mx, with 2 terminals, is divided into sections, each designated by a letter. A row of shops and offices outside each section provides exchange, ATMs and shops. Comprehensive information is available at:

Sala A Domestic Arrivals AeroMéxico, post office, tourist office, exit to taxis and metro, INAH shop, telecommunications office.

Sala A-B AeroMéxico, Bancomer ATM.

Sala B Aerocalifornia, Click Mexicana, Aeromar, Mexicana airline offices.

Sala B-C Entrance to **Continental Plaza** hotel, *casa de cambio*.

Sala C Aviacsa airline office, map shop.

Sala C and D Ladatel telephones just after C. **Exposición Diego Rivera** exhibition hall. Other national airline offices, bookshop.

Sala D National and International Departures, *cambio* opposite, more national airline desks, long-distance telephones, bar

and restaurant. From Sala D you have to leave the building to get to:

Sala F1-3 International check-in, banks. **Sala G International departures**.

Hotel bookings

There are airport information kiosks at Salas A and E1 (international arrivals). There is a hotel desk before passing through customs. The tourist office at A has phones for calling hotels, no charge, helpful, but Spanish only. The travel agency at east exit will book hotels or reconfirm flights.

Money exchange

Pesos may be bought at any of the banks liberally spread throughout the airport. Most foreign currencies or TCs are accepted, as are most credit cards.

Telephone

Many telephones at the airport; keep looking until you find one that works. Look for the **Lada** *multi-tarjeta* phones. There is a telephone office at the far end of Section F, which accepts Amex and, in theory, Visa, MasterCard and other cards.

Transport to/from the airport

Taxi Fixed-price 'Transporte Terrestre' taxis by zone, buy tickets from booths at exits by sections A, E and F; you can buy tickets before passing customs but they are cheaper outside the duty-free area; rates vary, around US$15 to the **Centre/Zócalo**, according to distance (per vehicle, not per person), drivers may not know or may be unwilling to go to cheaper hotels. For losses or complaints about airport taxis, T55-5571 3600 ext 2299; for reservations T55-5571 9344, daily 0800-0200. The fixed-price taxi system is efficient and safe. A cheaper alternative (about 50%) if you don't have too much luggage is to cross the Blv Puerto Aéreo by the Metro Terminal Aérea and flag down an ordinary taxi outside the **Ramada** hotel.

Bus There are regular buses from the city centre to the airport (eg No 20, along north side of the Alameda), but the drawback is that you have to take one to Calzada Ignacio Zaragoza and transfer to a trolley bus at the Blv Puerto Aéreo (ie at Metro Terminal Aérea). Buses to the airport may be caught every 45 mins until 0100 from outside **Hotel de Carlo**, Plaza de la República 35. It takes 1 hr from downtown (and, in the rush hour, most of the day, it is jam-packed), but you can take baggage if you can squeeze it in.

Long distance bus Frequent long-distance buses to **Cuernavaca**, **Puebla**, **Querétaro**, **Toluca**, **Pachuca** and **Cordoba** direct from the airport. See map, page 68, for location of terminals.

Metro To get to the airport cheaply, take the metro to Terminal Aérea and walk, or take metro to Blv Puerto Aéreo and then a *pesero* marked 'Oceanía', which will leave you at the Terminal metro station.

Airline offices

See page 36 for web addresses. Many airline offices on Paseo de la Reforma or Hamburgo. **Aero California**, Reforma 332, Metro Insurgentes, T55-5207 1392. **Aeromar**, Reforma 505, Torre Mayor, Metro Chapultepec, T55-5133 1111. **AeroMéxico**, Reforma 445, Metro Sevilla, T55-5133 4010. **Air Canada**, Blv Avila Camacho 1, 8th floor, T55-9138 0280. **Air France**, Jaime Balmes 8, Metro Polanco, T55-5571 6150. **Alitalia**, Río Tiber 103, 6th floor, Metro Insurgentes, T55-5533 1240. **American Airlines**, Reforma 300, Metro Insurgentes, T55-5209 1400. **Aviacsa**, Benito Juárez Airport, T55-5716 9006. **Avianca**, Reforma 195, Metro Insurgentes, T01-800 123 3120. **British Airways**, Jaime Balmes 8, Los Morales, Metro Polanco, T55-5387 0300. **Continental**, Andrés Bello 45, Metro Auditorio, T55-5283 5500. **Cubana**, Viajes Sol y Son, Homero 613, Metro Polanco, T55-5250 6355. **Delta**, Reforma 381, Metro Sevilla, T55-5279 0909. **Iberia**, Av Ejército Nacional 436, 9th floor, Metro Polanco, T55-1101 1515. **Interjet**, Centro Comercial Antara, Ejército Nacional 843B,

T55-1102 5555. **Japan Airlines**, Reforma 505, Torre Mayor, 13th floor, Metro Chapultepec, T55-5242 0150. **KLM/Northwest**, Andrés Bello 45, Metro Auditorio, T55-5279 5390. **Lufthansa**, Paseo de las Palmas 239, T55-5230 0000. **Magnicharters**, Donato Guerra 9, Metro Juárez, T55-5679 1212. **Mexicana**, Juárez 82, Metro Juárez, T55-5448 0990. **Taca**, Reforma 505, Metro Sevilla, T55-1102 0430. **United Airlines**, Hamburgo 213, local 23-24, Metro Sevilla, T55-5627 0222.

Bus
Local

An efficient new bus service, **Metrobús**, runs the length of Insurgentes from Metro Indios Verdes to San Angel. Plans are underway to extend it further south. The metrobús runs 0430-2400 and is particularly useful for getting to and from the restaurants in Roma and Condesa, as well as the Ciudad Universitaria. You'll need to buy a rechargeable **smartcard** at one of the stops, US$1, and 'touch in' at the barriers. Fares are US$0.50 per journey – top up using the automated machines.

The city's other buses have been coordinated into a single system: odd numbers run north–south, evens east–west. Fares on large buses, which display routes on the windscreen, are US$0.20, exact fare only. There are 60 direct routes and 48 feeder (SARO) routes. Thieves and pickpockets haunt the buses along Reforma and Juárez. A useful route for tourists (and well known to thieves) is No 76, which runs from Uruguay (about the level of the Juárez Monument at Parque Alameda) along Paseo de la Reforma, beside Chapultepec park. A **Peribus** service goes round the entire Anillo Periférico. Most buses run 0500-2000; some routes on Reforma run 24 hrs.

Long distance

This is how Mexico travels. All bus stations have many counters for bus companies, not all are manned and it is essential to ask which is selling tickets for the destination you want (don't take notice boards at face value).

On the whole, the bus stations are clean and well organized. Book ahead where possible. **Terminal del Norte**, Av Cien Metros 4907, T55-5587 1552, www.centraldelnorte.com.mx, for destinations in north Mexico, including US borders. There is a *casa de cambio*, 24-hr cafés, left luggage, pharmacy, bakery and phone offices for long-distance calls (often closed and poorly informed, very high charges). The bus station is at Metro Autobuses del Norte, Line 5. City buses marked 'Cien Metros' or 'Central del Norte' go directly there.

Terminal del Sur, corner of Tlalpan 2205, across from Metro Taxqueña, Line 2, serves **Cuernavaca**, **Acapulco**, **Oaxaca** and **Zihuatanejo** areas. There are direct buses to the centre (Donceles) from Terminal del Sur, and an express bus connects the Sur and Norte terminals. It can be difficult to get tickets to the south; book as far in advance as possible; the terminal can be chaotic.

Terminal Poniente is opposite the Metro Observatorio, Line 1 of the metro, and serves the west of Mexico. You can go to the centre by bus from the *urbano* outside the bus station, Terminal Poniente (US$0.10).

Terminal Oriente (TAPO), Calzada Ignacio Zaragoza, Metro San Lázaro, Line 1 for buses to **Veracruz**, **Yucatán** and southeast, including **Oaxaca** and **Puebla** (2 hrs). It has a tourist information office open from 0900; luggage lockers, US$2.65 per day, key is left with guard; post office, *farmacia* changes TCs.

To **Guatemala**, from TAPO, take a bus to Tapachula, Comitán or Ciudad Cuauhtémoc, only pesos accepted.

Mexico City airport Buses depart from the airport (outside Sala D) to **Córdoba**, **Cuernavaca**, **Pachuca**, **Puebla**, **Querétaro** and **Toluca**, very convenient if you don't want to head into town.

Schedules and fares

Bus frequencies, prices, terminals of departure and journey times are given below. Note that schedules are subject to seasonal changes, as are prices, which are also vary with the vagaries of exchange rates and oil prices. As a general rule, you should expect to pay US$3.50-4.50 per hr of 1st-class travel (50-60 pesos). Luxury services are around 30% more expensive than 1st class; 2nd-class buses are around a third cheaper than 1st class. Services from the airport to Cuernavaca, Puebla, Querétero, Pachuca and Toluca are around US$5 more expensive than standard services from the city.

To **Acapulco** (Sur/Norte) every 30-60 mins, 5 hrs, US$22.50. To **Aguascalientes** (Norte), every 1-2 hrs, 6 hrs, US$27. To **Bahías de Huatulco** (Sur/Norte/TAPO), 1-2 daily from each terminal, 15 hrs, US$52.50. To **Campeche** (TAPO), 5 daily, 17 hrs, US$76.50. To **Cancún** (TAPO), 5 daily, 24 hrs, US$108. To **Chetumal** (TAPO), 4 daily, 19 hrs, US$95. To **Chihuahua** (Norte), 10 daily, 20 hrs, US$90. To **Ciudad Juárez** (Norte), 10 daily, 24 hrs, US$108. To **Cuernavaca** (Sur/Airport), every ½ hr, 1½ hrs, US$7. To **Durango** (Norte), 10 daily, 12hrs, US$54. To **Guadalajara** (Norte/Poniente), hourly, 7 hrs, US$31.50. To **Guanajuato** (Norte), 11 daily, 5 hrs, US$25. To **Guaymas** (Norte), 12 daily, 30 hrs, US$135. To **León** (Norte), hourly, 5 hrs, US$22.50. To **Malinalco** (Norte), 3 daily, 2 hrs, US$9. To **Manzanillo** (Norte), 3 daily, 12 hrs, US$54. To **Matamoros** (Norte), 10 daily, 14 hrs, US$63. To **Matehuala** (Norte), 10 daily, 8 hrs, US$36. To **Mazatlán** (Norte), hourly, 16 hrs, US$72. To **Mérida** (TAPO), 5 daily, 20 hrs, US$90. To **Mexicalli** (Norte), hourly, 48 hrs, US$216. To **Monterrey** (Norte), hourly, 12 hrs, US$54. To **Morelia** (Poniente/Norte), every ½ hr, 5 hrs, US$22.50. To **Nuevo Laredo** (Norte), hourly, 16 hrs, US$72. To **Oaxaca** (TAPO), hourly, 6 hrs, US$27. To **Orizaba** (TAPO), hourly, 5 hrs, US$22.50. To **Pachuca** (Norte), every 15 mins, 1½ hrs, US$6.75. To **Palenque** (TAPO), 2 daily, 14 hrs, US$63. To **Papantla** (Norte), 4 daily, 5 hrs, US$22.50. To **Pátzcuaro** (Poniente), every 1-2 hrs with some from Norte also, 5 hrs, US$22.50. To **Puebla** (TAPO/Norte/Airport), every 15 mins, 2 hrs, US$9. To **Puerto Escondido** (Sur/TAPO), 3-4 daily, 14 hrs, US$63. To **Puerto Vallarta** (Norte) 4 daily, 13 hrs, US$58.50. To **Querétaro** (Norte/Airport), every 30 mins, 3 hrs, US$13.50. To **Saltillo** (Norte), 12 daily, 10 hrs, US$45. To **San Cristóbal de las Casas** (TAPO), 4 daily, 13 hrs, US$58.50. To **San Luis Potosí** (Norte), hourly, 5 hrs, US$22.50. To **San Miguel de Allende** (Norte), hourly, 4 hrs, US$18. To **Tapachula** (TAPO), 6 daily, 18 hrs, US$81. To **Taxco** (Sur), hourly, 2½ hrs, US$11.25. To **Tehuantepec** (TAPO), 2 daily, 11 hrs, US$49.50. To **Teotihuacán** (Norte), every 15 mins, 1 hr, US$4.50. To **Tepic** (Norte), hourly, 10 hrs, US$45. To **Tepoztlán** (Sur), every ½ hr, 1½ hrs, US$6.75. To **Tijuana** (Norte), hourly, 41 hrs, US$184.50. To **Tlaxcala** (TAPO), every ½ hr, 2 hrs, US$9. To **Toluca** (Poniente/ Airport), every 15 mins, 1 hr, US$4.50. To **Tula** (Norte), every ½ hr, 1½hrs, US$6.75. To **Tuxpan** (Norte), hourly, 5 hrs, US$22.50. To **Tuxtla Gutiérrez** (TAPO), 10 daily, 12 hrs, US$54. To **Uruapan** (Poniente/Norte), every 1-2 hrs, 6 hrs, US$27. To **Valle de Bravo** (Poniente), every ½ hr, 3hrs, US$13.50. To **Veracruz** (TAPO), hourly, 5-6 hrs, US$22.50. To **Villahermosa** (TAPO), 12 daily, 11 hrs, US$49.50. To **Xalapa** (TAPO), hourly, 5 hrs, US$22.50. To **Zacatecas** (Norte), hourly, 8 hrs, US$36. To **Zihuatanejo** (Sur), 6 daily, 9 hrs, US$40.50.

Booking

Advance booking is recommended for all trips over 6 hrs. You can book tickets for some destinations through Ticket Bus, www.ticketbus.com.mx, either online or through one of their many offices. Otherwise you must go and queue at the bus stations. This is usually painless, but can occasionally involve a long wait during peak periods. It is essential to book very early if travelling to fiestas during Holy Week or other important celebrations, including all regional festivals. Expect crowds and chaos during such times. At Christmas, many Central American students return home via Tapachula, and buses to/from Mexico City are booked solid for 2 weeks beforehand (except for those lines that do not make reservations). Note that many bus companies require luggage to be checked in 30 mins before departure.

Transport from terminals

All bus terminals operate taxis with voucher systems and there are long queues (check change carefully at the taxi office). It is much easier to pay the driver, although beware of extra charges. The terminals are connected by metro, but this is not a good option at rush hour, or if carrying too much luggage.

Bus companies

Mexico's long-distance bus network is privately owned by a plethora of competing companies, including a staggering array of 2nd-class and 1st-class subsidiaries. As such, the system is complex and initially baffling. In practice though, shopping around for 1st-class fares (where available) does not yield significant differences in cost or service. The most expensive luxury lines are comfortably kitted out with reclining seats and ice-cold a/c (not so comfortable).
Grupo ADO, T55-5133 2424, www.ado.com.mx, is a major player with several 1-class and luxury lines: ADO, ADO GL, UNO, OCC and AU. It serves eastern and southern Mexico, including the states of Puebla, Veracruz, Oaxaca, Chiapas, Tabasco and the Yucatán Peninsula.
Grupo Estrella Blanca, T55-5729 0807, www.estrellablanca.com.mx, is also a formidable empire: Estrella Blanca, Futura Primera, Futura Plus, Transportes Chihuahuenses, Elite, Oriente, Autobuses Americanos, Transportes Frontera, Pacífico and Norte de Sonora are among their lines. The network covers wide areas of central, western and northern Mexico, with some limited services to Oaxaca and Guerrero too.
Estrella de Oro, T55-5649 8520, www.auto bus.com.mx, runs to Guerrero state and coast, Cuernavaca, Puebla and Veracruz.
Estrella Roja, T55-5130 1800, www.estrella roja.com.mx, operates services between Puebla State and the capital.
ETN, T55-5089 9200, www.etn.com.mx, is a reputable operator and runs to major destinations in western, central and northeast Mexico.

Omnibus de México, T800-765 6636, www.odm.com.mx, is also a big name and runs extensive services throughout western, central and northern Mexico.
Primera Plus and **Flecha Amarilla**, T55-5567 7887, www.flecha-amarilla.com.mx, operate throughout central and western Mexico.
Pullman de Morelos, www.pullman.com.mx, is a minor company that serves Cuernavaca and other Morelos destinations.

Car
If you have a car in the city, find a cheap hotel where you can park and explore the city by bus, metro or on foot. If you are planning to hire a car, it is generally cheaper to organize it from the USA or Europe. To reduce pollution, cars are required to stay off the road for 1 working day a week. When driving in the capital you must check which '*hoy no circula*' applies to your vehicle's number plate; if your car is being driven when its number is prohibited, you could be fined US$80. This should not apply to foreign-licensed cars. The regulation covers the State of Mexico as well as the Distrito Federal. The ban applies to the last digit of your number plate: **Mon** 5 & 6; **Tue** 7 & 8; **Wed** 3 & 4; **Thu** 1 & 2; **Fri** 9 & 0. Occasionally, when contamination levels are even worse than usual, the programme runs at weekends too: **Sat**, all even numbers and 0; **Sun**, all odd numbers. Normally, you can drive freely in 'greater' Mexico City weekdays 2200-0500 and on weekends.

Car hire companies
Most care hire firms are concentrated in the Zona Rosa, particularly along Reforma. Local companies tend to be cheaper.
Avis, Reforma 308 (across from US embassy), T55-5511 2228. **Budget**, Atenas 40, T55-5566 8815. **Hertz**, Versalles 6, T55-5128 1699. **National**, Reforma 107, T55-5703 2222.

Cycling
Cycling in the capital is not especially recommended due to the chaotic state of the roads. However, the Mexican government has recently unveiled plans for 'greening' DF which include laying down hundreds of kilometres of dedicated bike lanes. Until then, Bosque de Chapultepec remains a popular area for casual peddling, while the more sedate stretches of Roma and Condesa may be suitable for cyclists too. The *ciclovía* is a classic route that follows the old Cuernavaca railroad – ask the tourist office for a map. Hire bikes from the Paseo de la Reforma, outside the Museo de Antropología, at around US$10 per day, and from enterprising stands around Condesa.

Metro
An efficient, modern system and the best method of getting around the city, especially when the pollution is bad. Trains are fast, frequent, clean and quiet, although over-crowded during rush hours (0730-1000 and 1500-2000). Look out for the colourful *vendedores* with loud speakers strapped to their backs. Between 1800 and 2100 men are separated from women and children at Pino Suárez and certain other central stations. 2 pieces of medium-sized luggage are permitted.

Beware of pickpocketing on the metro. It's not especially dangerous, more a natural aspect of large numbers of people. Pino Suárez, Hidalgo and Autobuses del Norte are particularly infamous for thieves.

Tickets and times
Tickets cost 2 pesos, and it's best to buy several to avoid queuing every time you take a trip. Check train direction before entering the turnstile or you may have to pay again.

The service operates Mon-Fri 0500-2400, Sat 0600-2400, Sun and holidays 0700-2400.

Metro information
Maps of the metro are included in the city maps distributed by the City Tourist Information booths. There is also a metro information service at Insurgentes station on the Pink Line 1, which dispenses maps, and most interchange stations have information kiosks. All the stations have a symbol, eg the grasshopper signifying Chapultepec, and there

6 Mexico City metro

➡ Mexico City maps

1 City centre, page 78
2 Centro Histórico: Zócalo & Alameda, page 82
3 Reforma & Zona Rosa, page 96
4 Bosque de Chapultepec & Polanco, page 98
5 Coyoacán, page 107
6 Metro, page 138

Line	
1	
2	
3	
4	
5	
6	
7	
8	
9	
A	Metro Férreo
B	Tren Ligero

N

Not to scale

is a detailed *plano de barrio* (local street map) of the immediate vicinity at every station. There are 9 lines in service.

Line 1 (pink) from **Observatorio** (by Chapultepec park) to **Pantitlán** in the eastern suburbs. It goes under Av Chapultepec and not far from the lower half of Paseo de la Reforma, the Mercado Merced, and 3 km from the airport.

Line 2 (blue) from **Cuatro Caminos** in the northwest to the **Zócalo** and then south above ground to **Taxqueña**.

Line 3 (olive) from **Indios Verdes** south to the **Ciudad Universitaria** (free bus service to Insurgentes).

Line 4 (turquoise) from **Santa Anita** on the southeast side to **Martín Carrera** in the northeast.

Line 5 (yellow) from **Pantitlán**, via Terminal Aérea (which is within walking distance of gate A of the airport, but some distance from the international gates – opens 0600), up to **Politécnico** (if using La Raza metro stop to connect with Line 3, note that there is a long walk between Lines 5 and 3, through the Tunnel of Knowledge).

Line 6 (red) from **El Rosario** in the northwest to **Martín Carrera** in the northeast.

Line 7 (orange) from **El Rosario** in the northwest to **Barranca del Muerto** in the southwest.

Line 8 (green) from **Garibaldi** (north of Bellas Artes, Line 2), through Chabacano (Line 9) and Santa Anita (Line 4), to **Constitución de 1917** in the southeast.

Line 9 (brown) parallel to Line 1 to the south, running from **Tacubaya** in the west (where there are interesting paintings in the station) to **Pantitlán** in the east.

In addition to the numbered lines:

Line A (Metro Férreo) southeast from Pantitlán as far as **La Paz** (10 stations in all).

Line B, from Buenavista to Ciudad Azteca in **Ecatepec**, north of the city.

Tren ligero From Taxqueña to **Xochimilco**, a very convenient route.

Art in the metro

At the **Zócalo** metro station there is an interesting permanent exhibit about the city. At **Pino Suárez**, the station has been built around a small, restored Aztec temple. Other places of interest in the network include: Line 1, Pino Suárez and Tacubaya; Line 2, Bellas Artes and Panteones; Line 3, La Raza, scientific display in the Tunnel of Knowledge, and south of Coyoacán; Line 4, Santa Anita; Line 5, Terminal Aérea; Line 6, all stations, Line 7, Barranca del Muerto; Line 9, Mixuca.

Taxi

Turismo taxis Operate from 1st-class hotels, the Museo Nacional de Antropología, etc, and are the most expensive.

Sitio taxis (fixed ranks) Operate from bus terminals, railway station and other locations; no meters. About double the normal price but safer. You pay in advance at a booth (check your change); they charge on a zone basis, US$4.60 for up to 4 km, rising to US$22 for up to 22 km (the same system applies at the airport – see above). You can also phone for a *sitio* taxi: **Radiotaxi**, T55-5566 077, **Servitaxis**, T55-5271 2560, **Taximex**, T55-5519 7690, **Transportación Terrestre al Aeropuerto**, for trips to and from the airport, T55-5571 3600.

Taxis on unfixed routes (green or white with a broad red horizontal band; yellow ones should be avoided as they are supposed to have been phased out). These can be flagged down anywhere; tariffs US$0.35 plus 5 cents for each 250 m or 45 seconds; between 2200 and 0600 they charge 20% extra. They have meters (check they are working properly and set at zero); if you do not bargain before getting in, or if the driver does not know the route well, the meter will be switched on, which usually works out cheaper than negotiating a price. Some drivers refuse to use their meter after 1800.

Drivers may not know where the street you want is because the city's numbering is erratic. Try to give the name of the intersection between 2 streets rather than a number.

Warning Lone travellers, especially female, are advised to take only official *sitio* taxis (not VW ones) from hotels or ordered by phone, particularly at night. Tourist police advise that you make a note of registration and taxi numbers before getting in.

Tips and complaints

A tip is not normally expected, except when special help has been given. For information, or complaints, T55-5605 5520; if complaining, make sure you take the taxi's ID number.

Bicitaxi

Another type of taxi travel, the tricycle, is now being encouraged to counter exhaust pollution, and is a good way to see the architecture of the city centre. There are many outside the Palacio Nacional.

Colectivos

Colectivos (often called *peseros* – they used to cost 1 peso) run on fixed routes, often between metro stations and other known landmarks; destination and route displayed on the windscreen. Fares are US$0.20 up to 5 km, US$0.25 up to 10 km and US$0.35 beyond. If a bus runs on the same route, it may be preferable as it has fixed stops.

⦿ Directory

Mexico City *p77*

Banks and currency exchange

Banks Opening hours are generally Mon-Fri 0930-1700, Sat 0900-1300. **Banamex's** offices at Av Isabel la Católica 44, are in a converted baroque palace, ask the porter for a quick look into the magnificent patio. Another worthwhile building is the bank's branch in the Casa Iturbide, Madero 17 and Gante, where Agustín de Iturbide lived as emperor. **Bancomer**, head office at Av Universidad 1200, also Venustiano Carranza y Bolívar, good quick *cambio*, same rate for cash and TCs. **Banca Serfín**, corner of 16 de Septiembre

y Bolívar, or Madero 32, near Bolívar. **Citibank**, Paseo de la Reforma 390, for Citicorp TCs, also gives cash advances against credit cards with no commission. **HSBC** recommended, deals with MasterCard (Carnet) and Visa (usually quicker than Bancomer or Banamex for cash advances against credit card). **American Express** emergency number, T55-5326 2626; office at Reforma 350 esq Lancaster, T55-5207 7049, will change cheques on Sat 0930-1330, also Mon-Fri until 1800 (there are 10 other Amex offices in Mexico City, including at the Hotel Nikko at Campos Elíseos 204, Local 5, T55-5283 1900, and Centro Comercial Perisur, Periferico Surrey 4690, T55-5606 9621). For more details on Visa and MasterCard, see Credit cards, page 60.

Casas de cambio There are many *casas de cambio*, especially on Reforma, Madero and throughout the city centre. Their hours may be more convenient, but their rates can be poor. **Central de Cambios** (Suiza), Madero 58, west of Zócalo, and **Casa de Cambio Plus**, Av Juárez, have been recommended for rates. The **Perisur** shopping centre, Insurgentes and Periférico Sur, has a *casa de cambio*, T55-5606 3698, which is usually open until 1900, with a better exchange rate in the morning. Exchange services also available at the airport.

Currency exchange Always see if there is a special counter for currency transactions to avoid standing in long queues. Branches of all major Mexican banks proliferate in most parts of the city. Cash advances on credit cards are easy with good rates. TCs in most major currencies can be cashed at any branch of **Bancomer** or **Banca Serfín** without undue delay. Banks do not charge commission for changing TCs. The exchange of foreign currency notes, other than dollars, can be difficult apart from at the airport and main bank branches in the city centre. Before buying or selling currency, check the day's exchange rate from a newspaper and then shop around. There is often a great disparity between different banks and *casas de cambio*, particularly in times of volatile currency markets. Hotels usually offer very poor rates.

Cultural centres and libraries

Amistad Británico-Mexicana, Montes Escandinavos 405, Lomas de Chapultepec, T55-2623 0603, www.amistadbm.org.mx. **Anglo-Mexican Cultural Institute**, Maestro Antonio Caso 127, T55-5566 6144. **Biblioteca Benjamín Franklin**, Liverpool 31, T55-5080 2733, Mon-Fri 1000-1900, has books and English-language papers. ID required. **British Council**, Lope de Vega 316, Polanco, T55-5263 1900, www.britishcouncil.org.mx. **Goethe-Institut**, Liverpool 89, T55-5207 0487, www.goethe.de/mexiko, for German books and papers. **Instituto Francés de América Latina**, Campos Elíseos 339, free films Thu at 2030, T55-9171 9703, www.paginas culturales.org.mx. **Instituto Italiano**, Francisco Sosa 77, Coyoacán, T55-5554 0044, www.iicmessico.esteri.it, has 3-week intensive yet painless courses in Spanish, 3 hrs a day.

Embassies and consulates

For up-to-date information check www.sre.gob.mx/acreditadas. **Australia**, Rubén Darío 55, Polanco, T55-1101 2200, www.mexico.embassy.gov.au. **Belize**, Bernardo de Gálvez 215, Lomas Chapultepec, T55-5520 1346, Mon-Fri 0900-1330. **Canada**, Schiller 529, near Anthropology Museum, T55-5724 7900, www.canada.org.mx. **France**, Campos Elíseos 339, T55-9171 9700, www.ambafrance-mx.org. **Germany**, Horacio 1506, T55-5283 2200, www.mexiko.diplo.de, Mon-Thu, 0730-1530, Fri 0730-1500. **Guatemala**, Explanada 1025, Lomas de Chapultepec, T55-5540 7520, Mon-Fri 0900-1300. **Ireland**, Ciudada Blv Manuel Avila Camacho 76, 3rd floor, T55-5520 5803, Mon-Fri 0900-1700. **Italy**, Paseo de las Palmas 1994, T55-5596 3655. **Japan**, Paseo de la Reforma 395, T55-5211 0028. **Netherlands**, Vasco de Quiroga No 3000, piso 7, Edificio Calakmul, T55-5258 9921, www.paises bajos.com.mx. **New Zealand**, Jaime Balmer 8, 4th floor, Edificio Corporativo, T55-5283 9460. **Sweden**, Paseo de las Palmas 1375, T55-9178 5010, www.suecia.com.mx. **UK**, Río Lerma 71, T55-5242 8500, www.embajadabritanica.

com.mx, Mon-Thu 0800-1600, Fri 0800-1330. **USA**, Paseo de la Reforma 305, T55-5080 2000, www.usembassy-mexico.gov, Mon-Fri 0830-1730. If requiring a visa for the USA, it is best to get it in your home country.

Immigration

The **Instituto Nacional de Migración**, of the Secretaría de Gobernación, is at Ejército Nacional 862, Polanco, T55-2581 0100 (with some pages in English). Nearest metro is Polanco, then taxi. Mon-Fri 0900-1330. Get there early, usually long queues, little English spoken. Here you can extend tourist cards for stays over 90 days or replace lost cards; new cards can take just a couple of hours, but charges are as high as US$40; you may be given 10 days to leave the country.

This is also where you have to come to exchange a tourist card for a student visa and for any other immigration matter concerning foreigners. It is essential to be armed with a lot of patience, and to attend with a Spanish speaker if you don't speak the language. The normal procedure is to fill out a form indicating which service you need; you are then given a receipt with a number. See page 65 for more information on visas.

Internet

Rates US$1-3 per hr with many to choose from; ask your hotel for the nearest.

Laundry

Laundrette, Río Danubio, between Lerma and Pánuco and at Chapultepec y Toledo, near Metro Sevilla, expensive. **Lavandería** at Chapultepec y Toledo. **Lavandería Automática Edison**, Edison 91 (Metro Revolución), between José María Iglesias y Ponciano Arriaga, Col Tabacalera (centre). Mon-Fri 0900-1900, Sat 0900-1800. Has automatic machines, US$1.50 per 3 kg, US$1.50 drying. **Lavandería** at Parque España 14 and Antonio Caso 82, near British Council, US$4 for 3 kg, quick service.

Medical services

Doctors Dr César Calva Pellicer (who speaks English, French and German), Copenhague 24, 3rd floor, T55-5514 2529. **Dr Goldberg**, Av de Las Palmas 745, ground floor, pb, Col Lomas de Chapultepec, T55-5540 7300, emergencies T55-5727 7979. **Dr Smythe**, Campos Elíseos 81, T55-5545 7861, recommended by US and Canadian embassies.

Hospitals and clinics Most embassies have a list of recommended doctors and dentists who speak languages other than Spanish. Try the US embassy website for a complete list of hospitals, www.usembassy-mexico.gov/medical_lists.html. **American British Cowdray Hospital** (also known as El Hospital Inglés, or ABC), on Observatorio past Calle Sur 136, T55-5230 8161, also at Santa Fe; very helpful. **Hospital de Jesús Nazareno**, 20 de Noviembre 82, Spanish-speaking, friendly, drugs prescribed cheaply. It is a historical monument (see page 87).

Pharmacies Farmacia Homeopática, Mesones 111-B. **Farmacia Nosarco**, corner of 5 de Febrero and República de El Salvador, stocks a wide range of drugs for stomach bugs and tropical diseases, may give 21% discount. **Sanborn's** chain and **El Fénix** discount pharmacies are the largest chains with the most complete selection. Many supermarkets have good pharmacies.

Vaccination centres Vaccination centre, Benjamín Hill 14, near Metro Juanacatlán (Line 1), Mon-Fri 0830- 1430, 1530-2030, avoid last 30 mins, Sat 0830-1430. Typhoid (free throughout Mexico), cholera and yellow fever (US$2), Tue and Fri only; will give a prescription for gamma globulin. For hepatitis shots you have to buy gamma globulin in a pharmacy (make sure it's been refrigerated) and then an injection there, at a doctor's surgery or the ABC Hospital (see above).

Post office

Correo Central Tacuba y Lázaro Cárdenas, opposite Palacio de Bellas Artes, open for **letters** Mon-Fri 0800-2400, Sat 0800-2000, Sun 0900-1600. For **parcels** Mon-Fri 0800-1800, Sat 0800-1600. Parcels up to 2 kg (5 kg for books) may be sent. It is an interesting historic building with a stunning interior, worth a visit.

EMS Mexpost, accelerated national and international postage, is available at the Central Post Office, the airport, Zona Rosa, Coyoacán and 13 other post offices in the city; payable by weight.

Other post offices (Mon-Fri 0800-1900, Sat 0800-1300) that travellers may find useful: **Centre**, Nezahualcóyotl 184 y Academia 4; **P Arriaga** y Ignacio Mariscal, 2 blocks north of Monumento a la Revolución; **Zona Rosa**, Londres 208; **Tlatelolco**, Flores Magón 90; **San Rafael**, Schultz 102; **Lomas de Chapultepec**, Prado Norte 525; **Buenavista**, Aldama 216; **San Angel**, Dr Gálvez 16; **Coyoacán**, Higuera 23; **Iztapalapa**, Calzada Ermita Iztapalapa 1033; **Xochimilco**, Prolongación Pino 10; also at the **airport** and bus terminals. In all there are 155 branches in the federal capital, so there is no need to go to the Correo Central.

Telephone

See Essentials, page 64, for details of Mexico's telephone system. Finding a public phone that works can be a problem. Most now take phone cards (Ladatel, provided by Telmex), costing 30, 50 and 100 pesos, from shops and news kiosks everywhere. Calls abroad can be made from phone booths with credit cards (via **LADA** system), but this is very expensive. International calls can be made easily from the phone offices in bus terminals. There are several places, including some shops, all officially listed, with long-distance phones. One of the best options for international calls is an **Ekofon** card or account. Also look out for internet cafés that are set up to handle internet calls (eg Skype).

Contents

Footprint features

Around Mexico City

At a glance

◉ **Getting around** Buses, combis, taxis and *colectivos*.

◉ **Time required** 1-2 weeks to visit the main sights; 1 month or more for a thorough exploration.

◐ **Weather** Temperatures are reasonably moderate throughout the year. Apr-Oct are warmer, wetter months; Nov-Mar are cool and dry. Volcanic peaks may receive snow during the winter months.

✖ **When not to go** Good at any time, but evenings can be chilly in the winter months.

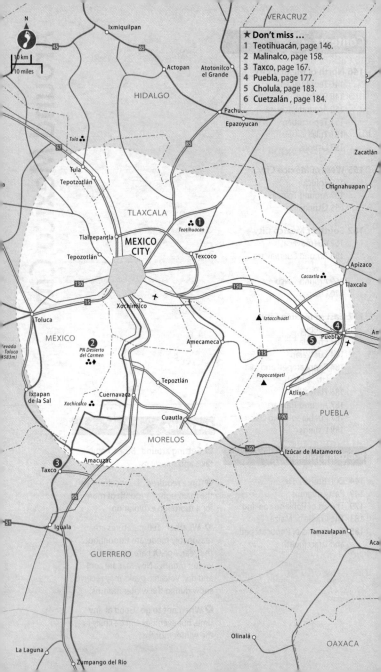

Nourished by the fertile Valley of Mexico, the provinces surrounding the capital have long drawn settlers and travellers – not least the Spaniards, who were keen to exploit the local mineral wealth. Throughout the region, Mexico's colonial past is exalted by an abundance of handsome cities including Cuernavaca, Taxco and Puebla, where time has failed to erode traditional Spanish ideals of beauty – or a long-held reverence for the baroque. Ostentatious mansions, exuberant church facades, splendid palatial gardens and dazzling grand plazas reveal a taste for opulence, drama and the outright grandiose.

But the Spaniards were not the first to lay roots in these lands, where remnants of lost cultures pepper the valley. The vast pyramids of Teotihuacán, more than 2000 years old, hint at civilizations as grand as they were complex, but about which very little is known. Like scattered fragments of a puzzle, the ruined cityscapes, mountain-top altars, mysterious shrines and crumbling old palaces are as entrancing as they are enigmatic.

Fortunately, the living descendants of these city-states offer tentative glimpses of an ancestral past. Hidden away from time and progress, indigenous villages such as Cuetzalán and Tepoztlán are bastions of ancient lore and heritage. Here, the old gods are alive and well, venerated as much as the saints, while the crafts and farming techniques that sustain their communities have changed little since the Spanish Conquest. Dance, traditional dress and archaic languages supply a vivid living link to the saga of ancient Nahua history. What's more, the land – as dramatic and inspirational as the stories it recalls – is a burgeoning draw for outdoors enthusiasts. Challenging volcanoes like Nevado de Toluca and Iztaccíhuatl provide further motivation to explore the rich world surrounding Mexico City.

North of Mexico City

The setting of extraordinary and mysterious panoramas, the lands north of Mexico City have always featured heavily in the life, wars and dramas of the ancient Mesoamerican polities. Mighty Teotihuacán, whose influence reached well into the Mayan heartland, was once central Mexico's most formidable city-state, is as impressive today as it was 1000 years ago. Its vast pyramids, palaces and ornamented temples are a tribute to the grand vision and planning of its creators, whilst its successor, Toltec Tula, was home to militaristic traditions that would inspire generations of cities to come. Perhaps none were more awestruck by these twin civilizations than the Aztecs, who claimed lineage from the Toltecs, and believed, quite understandably, that Teotihuacán had once been inhabited by gods. Back in the realm of mortals, the town of Tepotzotlán, 43 km north of the capital, conceals a treasure of colonial history in the country's finest vice-regal museum. Baroque details, exuberant craftwork and dazzling gold leaf abound. But if you're looking to get off the beaten track, head to the bustling city of Pachuca, where you'll find a robust and slightly surreal tradition of Cornish pasty making. The real attractions here are the surrounding villages, punctuated by the remnants of mining communities, colonial haciendas and crumbling old convents. For outdoor enthusiasts, the nearby Parque Nacional el Chico has refreshing pine forests and hiking trails. ▸▸ *For listings, see pages 152-154.*

Teotihuacán ☺️🚻⛺️🏨 ▸▸ *pp152-154. Colour map 2, B4.*

ⓘ *49 km north of Mexico City. Daily 0800-1700. US$3.50 (extra charge for video camera, tripods not permitted). Son et lumière display, US$4 per person, 45 mins, 1900 in Spanish, 2015 in English (Oct-Jun only); take a blanket or rent one. Arrive early before the vast numbers of ambulantes (wandering vendors) and the tour groups at 1100. Allow 2-3 hrs, longer if you're really keen. There is a perimeter road with a number of places to park a car. The simplest way to visit Teotihuacán is on an organized tour although you can catch an ordinary bus from Terminal del Norte or Indios Verdes. See Transport, page 154.*

Teotihuacán ('place of the gods') has some of the most remarkable relics of an ancient civilization in the world. Thought to date from 300 BC-AD 600, the site's builders remain a mystery. Where they came from and why the civilization disappeared is pure conjecture. It seems that the city may have housed 250,000 people who were peace-loving but whose influence spread as far as Guatemala. However, the 'peace-loving' theory is constantly being challenged. There are definite indications that human sacrifice was being practised at Teotihuacán long before the arrival of the Aztecs to the Valley of Mexico. Recent research indicates that an individual from Teotihuacán arrived at Copán in Honduras and usurped the power of the rightful ruler, thus continuing to spread the influence of Teotihuacán throughout the Maya region. Teotihuacán was not just a ceremonial centre; vast areas of enclaves have been excavated showing that, apart from those zones designated as sacred, there were also areas occupied by artisans, labourers, merchants and representatives of those crafts and professions that contribute to a functioning city. One zone housed merchants from the Maya area, another was occupied by representatives from Monte Albán in Oaxaca. At some point in the seventh century, Teotihuacán was ravaged by fire and may have been looted, causing an exodus of its inhabitants. So completely was it abandoned that it was left to the Aztecs to give names to its most important features. There are many questions still to be answered about Teotihuacán culture and new discoveries are being made all the time.

Sights

There are three main areas: the **Ciudadela**, the **Pyramid of the Sun** and the **Pyramid of the Moon**. The whole is connected by the Avenue of the Dead, which runs almost due north for nearly 4 km. To the west lie the sites of Tetitla, Atetelco, Zacuala and Yayahuala

Teotihuacán

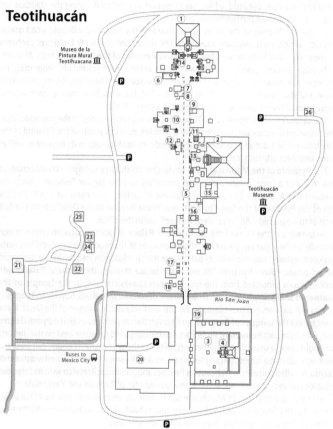

Museo de la Pintura Mural Teotihuacana

Teotihuacán Museum

Río San Juan

Buses to Mexico City

200 metres
200 yards

Pyramid of the Moon **1**
Pyramid of the Sun **2**
Ciudadela **3**

Temple of Quetzalcoatl **4**
Avenue of the Dead **5**
Palace of Quetzalpapalotl,
Jaguars' Palace & Temple
of the Feathered Shells **6**
Temple of Agriculture **7**
Mural of the Mythological
Animals **8**
Jaguar Temple & Mural **9**
Plaza of the Columns **10**
Palace of the Sun **11**

Patio of the Four Little
Temples **12**
Plaza of the Sun **13**
Plaza of the Moon **14**
House of the Priest **15**
Viking Group **16**
Avenue of the Dead
complex with
'Superimposed Buildings'
group **17**
Northwest Cluster **18**

Plaza Two **19**
Great Compound **20**
Palace of Atetelco **21**
Palace of Tetitla **22**
Palace of Zacuala **23**
Patio of Zacuala **24**
Palace of Yayahuala **25**
Palace of Tepantitla **26**

(see below). To the northeast lies Tepantitla, with fine frescoes. The old city is traceable over an area of 3½ km by 6½ km. Capable of holding 60,000 people, the citadel's main feature is the **Temple of Quetzalcoatl** ('the Plumed Serpent', 'Lord of Air and Wind'). Go to the east side of the 1-km square. Behind the largest of the temples (take the right-hand path) lies an earlier pyramid, which has been partially restored. Lining the staircase are huge carved heads of the feathered serpents.

Follow the Avenue of the Dead to the **Plaza of the Sun**. You will pass small grassy mounds, which are unexcavated temples. The plaza contains many buildings, probably for the priests, but is dominated by the massive **Pyramid of the Sun** (64 m high, 213 sq m at the base) and covering almost the same space as the Great Pyramid of Cheops in Egypt. The sides are terraced, and wide stairs lead to the summit. The original 4-m covering of stone and stucco was removed by mistake in 1910. The view from the top gives a good impression of the whole site. But beware, it is a steep climb.

The car park to the north leads to Tepantitla. The murals here depict the rain god Tlaloc. The **museum** ① *admission included in price of ticket*, now lies south of the Pyramid of the Sun. It is well laid out and contains a large model of Teotihuacán in its heyday as well as many beautiful artefacts; recommended.

The **Pyramid of the Moon** is about 1 km further north. On your right a tin roof covers a wall mural of a large, brightly coloured jaguar/puma ('the **Jaguar Temple**'). The plaza contains the 'A' altars – 11 in a peculiar geometric pattern. The pyramid is only half the size of the Pyramid of the Sun. The best view of the Avenue of the Dead is from the first level of this pyramid – 48 steep steps but well worth the climb.

To the west of the Plaza of the Moon lies the **Palace of Quetzalpapalotl** ('the Precious Butterfly'), where the priests serving the sanctuaries of the moon used to live. The palace has been restored together with its patio. Note the obsidian inlet into the highly decorated carved pillars. Follow the path left under the palace through the **Jaguars' Palace**, with catlike murals protected from the sun by green canvas curtains, to the **Temple of the Feathered Shells**. The base of the simple altar is decorated with shells, flowers and eagles.

You will pass several more temples on the west side of the Avenue of the Dead. If you want to visit the **temples of Atetelco**, go through the car park opposite the Pyramid of the Sun, turn right past **Restaurant Pirámides Charlies** (reputed to be the best on the site) and turn right along a small track. Alternatively, to get to them from the museum, exit west and walk right up to main road, turning left after crossing the stream. They are well worth a visit: **Tetitla**, a walled complex with beautiful frescoes and paintings; **Atetelco** with its three tiny temples and excellent murals; and the abandoned sites of **Zacuala** and **Yayahuala**.

At the spring equinox, 21 March, the sun is perfectly aligned with the west face of the Pyramid of the Sun; many ad hoc sun worshippers hold unofficial ceremonies to mark the occasion. This is also Benito Juárez's birthday so entry is free.

At the exit to the rear of the Jaguars' Palace (which is the usual way out), and across the road, is the delightful **Museo de Pintura Mural Teotihuacana** ① *daily 1000-1700, free*, which contains collections and explanations of ancient wall painting.

Pachuca ⬤🅵🅸🅾 ➻ pp152-154. Colour map 2, B4.

→ *Phone code: 771. Altitude: 2445 m.*

Capital of Hidalgo state, Pachuca, 94 km northeast of Mexico City, is also one of the oldest silver mining centres in Mexico. The Aztecs, Spaniards, and more recently the English, all mined here, leaving the hills honeycombed with old workings and terraced with tailings.

Pasty pilgrims

The sight of Cornish pasty shops inundating downtown Pachuca might bemuse some British travellers, who will be used to finding such tasty delicacies in the pubs and chippies of their homeland. It is widely known that Cornish miners brought the humble pasty to this obscure corner of the world. What is less widely known is the deadly journey it involved.

It all began nearly 100 years ago, in the aftermath of Mexico's War of Independence, when the once lucrative mines of the region had fallen into disrepair. Sensing an opportunity to revitalize the industry, foreign investors and entrepreneurs focused their attention on the derelict mines of Pachuca. Under the direction of engineer John Taylor, the British Real del Monte Company was formed, and the finest miners of the age were enlisted as its workforce – the Cornish miners of Great Britain.

But the task of introducing 19th-century mining technology to the backwaters of central Mexico was no easy one. After some preliminary surveys, the company's transport party arrived in Veracruz on 28 May 1825. It would take them nearly an entire year to haul their 50 wagons of equipment and 100 tons of machinery to their intended destination, Real del Monte.

As they trudged arduously through the rainforests of Veracruz, beset by mosquitoes and swarms of carnivorous insects, nearly half of the workforce died from yellow fever. Then, as the survivors escaped the lowlands, wagons in tow, they suffered more disasters on the miles of mountainous mule-tracks that wound erratically into Mexico's interior. Equipment was lost or destroyed, workers died in atrocious accidents, mules buckled under the intense burden of their load. And finally, as the party emerged onto the last leg of their journey, the rains set in unseasonably early, causing the wagons to sink hopelessly into the mire.

But eventually, on 1 May 1826, the miners arrived victorious to much fanfare and jubilation. They brought with them the skills, technology and experience to rebuild the mines, and the humble pasty, of course, staple-diet of every self-respecting miner. But they brought with them something more profound too. Something that would ignite the national spirit and engage the hearts of Mexicans for generations to come: Football. Now all Pachuca needs is a good British pub.

The English also left a small culinary legacy with a Mexicanized version of a Cornish pasty, available all over town in cafés and fast food joints (see box above). Pachuca is home to a handful of mildly diverting attractions and makes a good base for exploring the surrounding countryside. Otherwise there's little reason to linger long in this provincial capital, pleasant enough though it is.

Sights

The city centre is partly pedestrianized and revolves around the Zócalo or Plaza de Independencia, where a large clock tower, designed by the makers of London's Big Ben, houses the city **tourist office** ⓘ *T771-715 1411, www.turismo.hidalgo.gob.mx, 1000-1800*. They are helpful and have a selection of some maps and flyers. Although the centre is largely modern, there are a number of colonial buildings among its narrow, steep and crooked streets. These include the treasury for the royal tribute, **Las Cajas Reales** (1670), Venustiano Carranza 106, now used as offices; **Las Casas Coloradas** (1785), on Plaza Pedro

María Anaya, now the Tribunal Superior de Justicia; and the former **Convento de San Francisco** (1596) on Arista and Hidalgo next to Parque Hidalgo, now home to a good cultural centre (see below). Modern buildings include a **theatre**, the **Palacio de Gobierno** (which has a mural depicting ex-President Echeverría's dream of becoming Secretary-General of the UN), and the **Banco de Hidalgo**. If Pachuca's mining history interests you, the **Museo de la Minería** ① *Mina 110, Wed-Sun 1000-1400, 1500-1800, US$1,* has excellent displays and photographic material. Note that an industrial heritage programme is under way to restore some of the old mining settlements; up-to-date information is available in the museum. For aerial views of the town, there is a mirador which can be reached by catching a 'mirador' bus from the Plaza de la Constitución. A steep 30-minute walk from there you'll arrive at the Monumento a Cristo Rey, a statue of Christ overseeing the city with outstretched arms. If you're in the market for crafts, head to the Casa de las Artesanías, at the junction of Revolución and Juárez.

Centro Cultural de Hidalgo

① *Ex-Convento de San Fransisco, Hidalgo y Arista. Tue-Sun 1000-1800. Free.*

Hidalgo's state's premier cultural centre is worth checking out for its fine museums, archives, galleries and libraries. Located in the former Convento de San Fransisco, the 400-year-old colonial architecture is an attraction in itself. The outstanding **photographic museum** is in the large cloister on the far side of the convent; it has international and historical images from renowned photojournalists. Nearby is the **Fototeca**, with an archive of over one million images that you can search and print for a small fee. Also in the cultural centre is the **Museo Regional de Historia**, which displays chronological exhibits of the state's history. In this complex there is also a library, exhibition hall and souvenir shop, with reproductions of ceramic and metal anthropological items and recordings of indigenous music.

Around Pachuca ● ▶ *pp152-154*

Real del Monte

Real del Monte, a very interesting and attractive small town, is one of a number of mining centres in the area, most of which are no longer operative. Cornish miners came here from England in large numbers in the second quarter of the 19th century. Traces of their presence can still be seen in blue-eyed inhabitants, surnames and, of course, the *pastes* (pasties). Most of the buildings have *techos de dos aguas* (sloping roofs) and are carefully preserved. The **Panteón Inglés** (English cemetery) is on a wooded hill opposite the town; the caretaker will recite stories about families buried there. No lodging is available at present; take a *colectivo* from Pachuca, 10 minutes' drive.

Parque Nacional El Chico

A very popular excursion from Pachuca is to the Parque Nacional el Chico, just west of Real del Monte. A national park since the 19th century, its mountainous pine-forested slopes are a haven for hikers, bikers, and rock-climbers particularly, with well-scaled towers like La Ventana, the highest point in the reserve. Elsewhere you'll find impressive waterfalls and fishing holes that are often frequented by Mexico City weekenders. At the heart of the park is the pleasant mining village of **Mineral del Chico**, with plentiful hotels and bike rental. Be warned, the high altitude brings cold air in the evenings. *Colectivos* to Mineral del Chico depart from Pachuca's Mercado Juárez, Calle Hidalgo, every 30 minutes, US$0.70.

Tepotzotlán ⊙⊙⊙⊙ ⤻ pp152-154. Colour map 2, B4.

→ Phone code: 55.

The charming town of Tepotzotlán is about 43 km northwest of Mexico City, just off the road to Querétaro. It is not to be confused with Tepoztlán, to the south of Mexico City near Cuernavaca. The town centre is quaint and cobblestoned, with a central plaza surrounded by *portales* (arches), restaurants and shops. There is a big market on Wednesday and Sunday when the streets get very congested; on such days you'll find a good selection of handicrafts and jewellery, as well as meat, cheese and other foods. In the third week of December, *pastorelas* (plays based on the temptation and salvation of Mexican pilgrims voyaging to Bethlehem) are held. Tickets can be bought through **Ticket Master**, www.ticketmaster.com.mx. Outside of town, the three-tiered **Arcos del Sitio** is an impressive 440-m-long aqueduct built in the 18th century. It's contained by the 54-ha Parque Sierra de Tepotzotlán, which has good opportunities for hiking.

Iglesia de San Fransisco Javier
ⓘ *Plaza Hidalgo. Daily 0900-1800, Mass on Sun.*
Built in the late 17th century, the Iglesia de San Fransisco Javier is a fine example of baroque design, resplendent with soaring features and a wealth of exuberant detail. The facade facing Plaza Hidalgo is an 18th-century addition and even more ostentatious, belonging to the Churrigueresque tradition that took baroque flamboyance to its limit. The interior is impressive too, with a main altar that's lavishly decorated in gold leaf. Elsewhere are stunningly adorned ceilings, carved wooden pillars, colonial art and endless showy renditions of angels and saints. Adjoining the church is a former Jesuit monastery, now home to the country's best viceregal museum (see below).

Museo Nacional de Virreinato
ⓘ *Plaza Hidalgo, www.munavi.inah.gob.mx. Tue-Sun 0900-1800. US$3.*
The handsome viceregal museum is a comprehensive and well-displayed collection covering all aspects of life under Spanish rule. Formerly a Jesuit monastery, convent and language college, this intriguing complex of cloisters, passages, chapels and gardens took over 150 years to build after the first bricks were laid in 1606. The Jesuits were expelled from New Spain in 1767, and the building did not find its purpose as a museum until 1964, when it was extensively restored and opened to the public. A superb collection of colonial art can be seen here, some of it originally belonging to Mexico City's cathedral. There's also antique furniture, weaponry, statues, textiles, gold and silverware, all fairly sumptuous and impressive. Like the adjoining church, much of the interior is lavishly adorned with sculpted facades overlaid with gold leaf. Other areas recall the quiet solitude of the building's early use as a place of religious meditation and monastic study.

Tula ⊙⊙⊙⊙ ⤻ pp152-154. Colour map 2, B4.

→ Phone code: 773.
ⓘ *65 km north of Mexico City. 0900-1700. Site and museum, US$3. The small restaurant is not always open. Guidebooks in many languages are available at the entrance, fizzy drinks on sale.*
Tula, thought to be the most important Toltec site in Mexico, can be visited as a half-day excursion from Mexico City. In all, two ball courts, pyramids, a frieze in colour, and remarkable sculptures over 6 m high have been uncovered. There are four huge warriors

in black basalt on a pyramid, these are the great Atlantes anthropomorphic pillars. One is a reproduction; the original is on display at the Museo Nacional de Antropología in Mexico City (see page 98). The platform on which the four warriors stand is encircled by a low relief frieze depicting jaguars and coyotes, and Tlaloc masks adorn the walls. Note the butterfly emblem on the chests of the warriors and the *atlatl* (spear-thrower) held by their sides. The butterfly – such an important element in Toltec iconography – was once more to become associated with the warrior class during the Aztec period, when dead warriors became butterflies who escorted the sun to midday. The museum is well worth visiting and there is a massive fortress-style church, dating from 1553, near the market.

The town of Tula itself is pleasant, clean and friendly. If driving from Mexico City, take the turn for Actopan before entering Tula, then look for the Parque Nacional sign (and the great statues) on your left.

◉ North of Mexico City listings

For Sleeping and Eating price codes and other relevant information, see Essentials pages 47-51.

⬤ Sleeping

Teotihuacán *p146, map p147*
A Villas Arqueológicas, San Juan Teotihuacán, T594-956 0909, www.teotihuacaninfo.com. 40 attractive rooms with arched enclaves, whitewashed walls and wooden furniture. Restaurant, bar, pool and Sky TV. Good location close to the pyramids.
B Quinto Sol, Hidalgo 26, San Juan Teotihuacán, T594-956 1881, www.hotel quintosol.com.mx. Comfortable, carpeted rooms with rather garish details like bright red writing desks and purple headboards. Cable TV, Wi-Fi, pool, restaurant and terraces.
C Posada Sol y Luna, Cantu 13, San Juan Teotihuacán, T594-956 2368, www.posada solyluna.com. Sixteen straightforward rooms with TV, private bath and hot water. Restaurant and parking. Comfortable but unexciting.

Pachuca *p148*
B Emily, Plaza Independencia, T771-715 0828, www.hotelemily.com.mx. A smart, tidy hotel with comfortable rooms and marbled floors. Wi-Fi, cable TV, restaurant, gym and parking. Weekend deals sometimes available.
C Gran Hotel Independencia, Plaza Independencia 116, T771-715 0515, www.granhotelindependencia.com. This

historic building, formerly Hotel Grenfell, has clean, pleasant, carpeted rooms with large colonial-style windows, cable TV and tasteful furnishings. Parking and Wi-Fi available.
D Juárez, Barreda 107, just before Real del Monte. Set in superb wooded surroundings. Rooms have bath, some are without windows.
D Los Baños, Matamoros 205, T771-713 0700. The rooms aren't as attractive as the tiled lobby might suggest, but this is not a bad hotel. Rooms have TV, phone and bath, and there's a restaurant too.
D Noriega, Matamoros 305, T771-715 0150. Fantastic building with curved staircases, arched corridors and exuberant foliage spilling over the railings. Rooms are tired though, with basic furniture and ancient TV sets. Restaurant attached.
D San Antonio, 6 km from Pachuca on the road to Mexico City (ask for directions), T771-711 0599. Spacious rooms, good value, clean and quiet. Restaurant.
E America, 3ra de Victoria 203, T771-715 0055. A bright orange building with economical rooms around a courtyard. All have bath, hot water and cable TV.

Around Pachuca *p150*
B Mi Ranchito, Xicotepec de Juárez, T771-764 0212, www.hotelmiranchito.com.mx. A very pleasant, hospitable little hotel with a family atmosphere. Services include pool, tennis court, playground and games room.

Tepotzotlán *p151*

A Tepotzotlán, Inés de la Cruz, T55-5876 0340. Good views. Restaurant, swimming pool and secure parking. Recommended.
D Posada San José, Plaza Virreinal 13, T55-5876 0520. An old colonial building with pleasant rooms and a good atmosphere, if sometimes lacking authenticity.

Camping

Pepe's, Eva Sámano de López, Mateos 62, T55-5876 0515/0616. US$12 a night. The nearest trailer park to the capital. Canadian-run with 55 pads and full hook-ups. Very friendly and clean, hot showers. The owner has a hotel in Mexico City so you can leave your trailer here and stay in the capital. Recommended.

Tula *p151*

A-B Real Catedral, Zaragoza 106, T773-732 0813, www.hotelrealcatedral.com. Attractive colonial building with a renovated modern interior, lots of ambient lighting and a wide range of rooms and suites. Gym, valet parking, Wi-Fi, tour guides and transport.
B Best Western Tula, Zaragoza s/n, T773-732 4575, www.bestwesterntula.com. Clean, tidy rooms at this 'executive class' hotel. A little generic, but services include dry cleaning, valet parking, mini-bar and data ports. Discounts may be available at weekends.
B Sharon, Blv Tula-Iturbe 1, T773-732 0976, www.hotelsharon.com.mx. Business hotel with Large clean rooms, secure parking and restaurant. A little sterile, but recommended.
C Lizbeth, Ocampo 200, T773-732 0045, hotellizbeth@prodigy.net.mx. Close to the bus station, this motel-style place has parking, restaurant and Wi-Fi. Rooms are clean, comfortable and tidy, with phone, cable TV and hot water. Nice and cool. Friendly.
D Casa Blanca, Pasaje Hidalgo 11, T773-732 1186, www.casablancatula.com. Clean motel- style lodgings set around a central courtyard. Pleasant, plant-filled and popular with Mexicans. Wi-Fi, laundry and parking.

🍴 Eating

Teotihuacán *p146, map p147*
Restaurants around the ruins tend to be poor value and unfulfilling.
Los Pinos, Guadalupe Victoria, San Juan Teotihuacán. One of a few decent options. The village makes an interesting detour.

Pachuca *p148*
Reforma, Matamoros 111. This old restaurant has a wood-panelled interior and serves breakfasts and Mexican fare.
La Blanca, Plaza de la Independencia. Atmospheric restaurant with lots of old photos and an interesting interior. Breakfasts, Mexican specialities and the ubiquitous pasty.
Pastes Grenfell, Plaza Independencia. One of the city's better pasty shops, with great value, Cornish-style pasties filled with meat or vegetables – good for a quick bite or food on the go. Recommended.

Tepotzotlán *p151*
Hostería del Monasterio, Plaza Virreinal 1. This atmospheric old restaurant serves good Mexican food and has live music on Sun; try their *café de olla* (sweet coffee with cinnamon).
Artesanías, opposite church. Cheap, economical grub. Recommended.

Tula *p151*
Casa Blanca, Hidalgo 114. Always busy and popular, this large dining hall has lots of character and serves tasty Mexican fare.
Los Negritos, Heroes de Chapultepec y Moctezuma. Good, clean, popular and often recommended for its Mexican food. Pleasant outdoor seating with a courtyard and arches.
Cocina Las Cazuelas, Pasaje Hidalgo 3. Wholesome home-cooked fare prepared on grills in front of you. Good -value *comida corrida*. Recommended.
Azcatimolli Tortas, Rojo del Río 24. Tasty *tortas*, fast food and Aztec grubs.

▲ Activities and tours

Teotihuacán *p146, map p147*
Tour operators
Mexbus, T594-5514 2233 or T01800-523 9412. Day trips from Mexico City, including a stop at the Basílica de Guadalupe, pick-up and return from central hotels, English-speaking guide and lunch for US$30.
Mundo Joven Adventures, Guatemala 4, at Hostal Catedral behind the cathedral, Mexico City, T594-5518 1726, www.mundo joven adventures.com. Daily trips to Teotihuacán with a Guadalupe stop-off.

⊖ Transport

Teotihuacán *p146, map p147*
When using public transport, the site is known as 'Las Pirámides'. 'Teotihuacán' usually refers to the nearby village of the same name.
Bus Autobuses Mexico-San Juan Teotihuacán leave from Terminal del Norte, Mexico City, to Las Pirámides every 15-30 mins, 0700-1800, US$3 one-way. You can also take the metro to Indios Verdes (last stop on Line 3), then a public bus (US$3) to the pyramids. Bus returns from Door 1 (some others from 2 and 3) at the site, supposedly every 30 mins. Some return buses to the capital terminate in the outskirts in rush hour without warning. You can also ride back with one of the tourist buses for about US$5.
Taxi To reach the ruins from the village of San Juan Teotihuacán, *combis*, US$0.60, and taxis, US$1.50, depart regularly from the plaza.

Pachuca *p148*
Bus There are frequent departures from Terminal del Norte in Mexico City, US$5, 1½ hrs. In Pachuca the bus terminal is out of town; take any *colectivo* marked 'Centro', 20 mins, US$0.40, and exit at the main plaza. To **Tula**, hourly from the main bus station in Pachuca, US$5, 2 hrs, and an interesting backdoor route. A 4-lane highway now runs from Mexico City to Pachuca via Venta de Carpio, Km 27, from which a road runs east to Acolman, 12 km, and Teotihuacán, another 10 km.

Tepotzotlán *p151*
Bus From near Metro El Rosario, Mexico City, take a *colectivo*, US$1.50, 1-hr ride. Many Querétaro or Guanajuato buses from Terminal del Norte pass the turn-off at 'Caseta Tepotzotlán' from where you can take a local bus, US$0.40, or walk (30 mins) to the town.

Tula *p151*
Bus First-class buses from Terminal del Norte in Mexico City run to Tula bus terminal every 40 mins 0600-2100, 1½ hrs. US$5.
  Tula bus terminal is 3 km from the archaeological site, take a 'Chapantago' bus (every 20 mins) to the entrance, 5 mins (ask where to get off), or a taxi, US$3. It's also possible to walk, turning right out of the bus station. At the main road, cut diagonally left across road and take first right, which will take you to a bridge over an evil-smelling river. Carry on to the main highway, then turn left.
  Tula–**Pachuca** US$5, 2 hrs; safe to leave belongings at bus station. Also services to **Queretaro** (2¼ hrs), **Guanajuato** and **León**.

West of Mexico City

On the mountainous fringes of the Central Valley lies Toluca, 64 km west of Mexico city, the lesser-visited provincial capital of Mexico state. Home to a sprawling Friday market that draws shoppers and boisterous merchants from afar, the city serves as a convenient jumping-off point for a range of excursions. Climbers should head for the snowcapped volcano of Nevado de Toluca, the fourth highest peak in Mexico, with awesome views and deep blue crater lakes. Nearby, the attractive colonial town of Valle de Bravo is a centre for outdoor activities; there's watersports on its man-made lake, hiking in nearby canyons and, for the more adventurous, hang-gliding from the hills. If all that sounds too exhausting, you can rest up in Ixtapan de la Sal, a spa town and resort that's popular with Mexicans and weekend capitalinos in need of a pamper. Cultural attractions are no less prominent in the hills around Toluca with network of indigenous villages, communities of potters and artisans, ancient monasteries, shrines and diminutive churches. Don't miss the pueblo mágico of Malinalco, a tranquil retreat with its colourful houses and disarming views of the dark, rolling hills. ▶▶ *For listings, see pages 159-161.*

Toluca ●●●● ▶▶ *pp159-161. Colour map 2, B3.*

→ *Phone code: 722. Altitude: 2639 m.*

At 2680 m, Toluca – 64 km west of Mexico City by dual carriageway – is the highest city in Mexico and capital of the state of the same name. It's a friendly, busy place but with few tourist attractions. Famed for confectionery and the local *chorizo* sausage, Toluca is best known for its huge **Friday market**, close to the bus station on Paseo Tollocán and Idisro Fabela. Spreading out across several blocks, modern manufactured goods are sold alongside traditional woven baskets, *sarapes*, *rebozos*, pottery and embroidered goods. Look out for an orange liqueur known as *moscos*, a local speciality. Close to the market, the **Casa de las Artesanías (Casart)** ① *Paseo Tollocán 700*, has an excellent range of local products for sale.

Ins and outs

Getting there **Toluca's International Airport** ① *off Highway 15, T722-273 1544, www.am-ait.com*, is an increasingly popular hub for budget flights. The airport is conveniently located on the edge of the city, just off Highway 15, around 40 km from the capital. Regular buses run to Toluca city centre. A bus from downtown Toluca costs around US$0.25; a taxi costs US$2.

Toluca is easily visited as a day trip starting early from Mexico City (regular buses from Terminal Poniente, one hour). The bus station is away from the centre and confusing. Buses marked 'Centro' run to the centre, US$0.50.

If driving from Mexico City, you can head towards **Parque Nacional Miguel Hidalgo**, or **La Marquesa**, with lakes suitable for watersports and other activities such as hiking and camping in nearby hills. Turning south off Route 15 leads to Chalma and Santiago Tianguistenco with incredible panoramic views of the city and the Valley of Mexico, smog permitting. Entering the Basin of Toluca, the ice-capped Toluca volcano (see page 157) dominates the landscape. ▶▶ *See Transport, page 161.*

Tourist information The **municipal tourist office** ① *Palacio Municipal, Plaza de los Mártires, www.edomexico.gob.mx*, has a free *Atlas Turístico* of the State of México, including street maps of towns of interest. Outside the city centre is the **state tourist office** ① *Urawa y Tollocan, T722-212 5998*, also with good information.

Plaza de los Mártires and around

At the heart of the city is the **Plaza de los Mártires** ('Plaza of the Martyrs'), a large, open public square that's named after the insurgents who were executed there during the War of Independence. Today, it's flanked by some handsome historical buildings. On its south side is the **cathedral**, one of the largest in the country, begun in 1870 but not completed until 1978. Incorporated into its interior is the baroque facade of the 18th-century church of the **Tercera Orden**. Also on the south side is the **Palacio Municipal**, site of the tourist office, and next door, the church of **Veracruz**, housing a Black Christ and a very attractive interior.

Flanking these three structures to the south, west and east are **Los Portales** – a parade of arcaded shops and restaurants where you can buy colourful sugar skulls during **Day of the Dead** festivities. **Portal Madero**, which runs east to west along Hidalgo, is the longest of the three arcades, with some 44 arches. On the west side of the plaza stands the **Palacio de Justicia**, around which are clustered a few minor attractions, including the architecturally interesting **Teatro Morelos** and three art galleries, each dedicated to a Mexican artist. They include the **Museo Felipe Santiago Guttiérez** ① *Bravo Nte 403, Tue-Sun 1000-1800, US$0.30*; the **Museo José María Velasco** ① *Lerdo de Tejada 400, Tue-Sat 1000-1800, Sun 1000-1300, US$0.70*; and the **Museo Taller Nishizawa** ① *Bravo Nte 303, Tue-Sat 1000-1800, Sun 1000-1500, US$0.70*. On the east side of the plaza stands the **Palacio de Poder Ejecutivo**. On the north side lies the stately **Palacio de Gobierno**, with a small park to the east, **Plaza Angel María Garibay**, complete with trees and fountains.

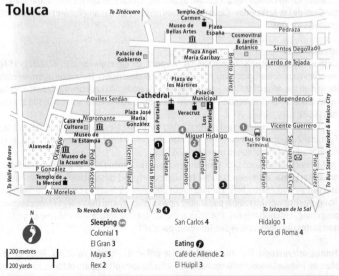

Toluca

Sleeping 🛌
Colonial 1
El Gran 3
Maya 5
Rex 2

San Carlos 4

Eating 🍴
Café de Allende 2
El Huipil 3

Hidalgo 1
Porta di Roma 4

Plaza Angel María Garibay and around

Just north of Plaza Garibay is the **Museo de Bellas Artes** ① *Tue-Sat 1000-1800, Sun 1000-1500, US$0.70, concessions half price, booklet US$1.35,* formerly the Convento del Carmen. It houses seven halls of paintings, from 18th-century colonial baroque to the 20th century, as well as temporary exhibitions. A tunnel is said to run from the former convent to all the central churches. Next door is the **Templo del Carmen**, a neoclassical church with a gold and white interior, and next to that is **Plaza España**. At the eastern end of Plaza Garibay is the **Cosmovitral** and **Jardín Botánico** ① *Tue-Sun 1000-1800, US$0.70.* From 1933 to 1975 the building was the 16 de Septiembre market; it was reopened in 1980 as a formal garden in honour of the Japanese Eizi Matuda, who set up the herbarium of the Estado de Mexico, with fountains and exhibitions, all bathed in the blues, oranges and reds of the vast stained-glass work of Leopoldo Flores Valdéz.

Alameda and around

Four blocks west of Los Portales, the **Alameda** is a large park with a statue of Cuauhtémoc and many tall trees. On Sunday morning it is popular with families strolling among the many stalls. The entrance is at the junction of Hidalgo and Ocampo. Attractions include the **Museo de la Acuarela** ① *east side of Alameda, Ocampo 105,* containing watercolours by Mexican artists, and the **Museo de la Estampa** ① *south side of Alameada, González 305,* with works by Posada, Cuevas and Coronel. The latter has an engraving workshop and holds regular classes.

Centro Cultural Mexiquense

① *4½ km west of the centre, Blv Jesús Reyes Heroles 302, San Buenaventura, T722-274 1200. Tue-Sat 1000-1800, Sun 1000-1500. US$0.70. To get there, take a 'Centro Cultural' bus from Mercado Juárez and exit at the large roundabout by the university, 20 mins.*

The Centro Cultural Mexiquense is one of the most interesting attractions in Toluca. This large, modern cultural centre, built on the site of the Hacienda de la Pila, houses a historical archive, the public library and three cultural museums. The **Museo de Antropología y Historia** is the best of the three, home to some 7000 archaeological artefacts from the state of Mexico. Displayed across five archaeology halls, seven ethnography halls and one history hall, the exhibitions trace the social and historical development of local Pre-Hispanic groups. The **Museo de Culturas Populares** explores local crafts, folklore and lifestyles and contains an abundance of *artesanías*, including a spectacular *árbol de vida* (tree of life), as well as a fine collection charro memorabilia. The **Museo de Arte Moderno** has a small collection of Mexican art.

Around Toluca ⊜🖉🖈 ➤ pp159-161.

Nevado de Toluca

A road branches off the Toluca to Valle de Bravo road at Km 75 to the **Toluca volcano**, (known as Nevado de Toluca or Xinantécatl). At 4583 m Toluca volcano, also known as Nevado de Toluca or Xinantécatl, is the fourth highest mountain in Mexico. There are vast and inspirational views from its two craters, home to the deep blue lakes of the Sun and Moon. During winter it is possible to ski on the slopes and there has been talk about building a ski resort there for years. The volcano is very popular at weekends and you'll find basic lodgings at its *albergue* (**G**).

To get there from Toluca head west on Highway 134 and turn south onto Highway 3 at Km 19. Continue some 7 km south to the village of Raices, just beyond which you'll find a dirt road that snakes up to the mountain to the crater rim.

If you don't have your own transport, the trip can still be done in one day from Toluca. Take the first bus to Sultepec from Toluca at about 0700 (every 2 hours thereafter) and get out just after Raices village. From there you need to hitch a ride 20 km to the crater. This is best accomplished on weekends when more traffic plies the road, but if you don't fancy hitching you can always take a taxi all the way from Toluca, around US$40 return.

Whatever your chosen form of transport, aim to get there by midday before clouds set in. Visitors must leave by 1700. If walking, remember the entrance to the crater, as you face it, is on the far left side of the volcano.

Tenancingo → *Phone code: 714. Altitude: 1830 m.*

West of Mexico City, 48 km south of Toluca, the road descends abruptly through gorges to the busy town of Tenancingo, which has a warm climate year round. The famous Thursday market is two blocks from the bus terminal (continue one block, turn left for two further blocks to the main square) with excellent local cheeses and handcrafted wicker baskets. Increasingly, the townspeople are turning their hands to floriculture, and there are numerous colourful winter gardens dotted about town. They also weave fine *rebozos* (shawls) and make delicious fruit wine.

Overlooking the town is a statue of Christ on a hill, while 30 minutes by bus to the south (unpaved road) is the magnificent 18th-century Carmelite convent of **El Santo Desierto**.

Malinalco → *Phone code: 714.*

About 11 km east of Tenancingo, Malinalco is a friendly, colourful little town that's becoming increasingly popular with weekenders. For now, this *pueblo mágico* remains a sleepy, lesser-visited retreat, nestled in dramatic mountain scenery and slightly tricky to reach. Malinalco is home to some interesting colonial architecture, including the Augustinian **Templo y Ex-convento del Divino Salvador** (1552), in the centre of town. Its nave has a patterned ceiling, whilst the two-storey cloisters are painted with elaborate, early frescoes. Just below the convent, in the main square, a market is held on Wednesdays, while the **tourist office** ① *Palacio Municipal, www.malinalco.net, Mon-Sat 0900-1700*, is just uphill from the plaza. Malinalco's gastronomic specialities include fresh trout, iguana and rabbit soup, and locally produced *pulque* and mescal. There is a *fiesta* on 6 August.

From the edge of town, a path winds up 1 km (20 minutes), to the partly excavated **Malinalco ruins** ① *Tue-Sun 1000-1800, US$2.60*, dating from 1188, and one of the most remarkable pre-Hispanic ruins in Mexico. A fantastic temple, 430 steps up, cut into the side of a mountain, conceals in its interior eagle and jaguar effigies. Apparently, you can feel movement in the rock if you lie on it. The site, which shows Matlatzinca culture with Aztec additions, is very small, but in a commanding position overlooking the valley. Close to the entrance is a small **museum**, US$0.70, with recreated murals and temple chambers.

The site is visible from the town as a ledge on the hillside; the walk up passes a tiny, blue **colonial chapel**. For a better view of the ruins carry straight on where the path leading to the ruins branches off right. This old road is cobbled in places and rises up the mountainside pretty steeply, arriving at a small **shrine** with two crosses (1½ hours' walk). It is possible to camp here but there is no water. Breathtaking views can be seen off both sides of the ridge. The trail carries on down the other side, past avocado trees, for 20 minutes, to the paved road to Tenancingo, almost opposite a brick house with arches. From here, it is possible to catch a bus back over the mountains to Malinalco. An easier, mostly downhill, option would be catch the bus up (ask for the old road) and do the whole hike in reverse.

To get to Malinalco by public transport, most people travel via Tenancingo, but you can also get there from **Chalma**. This is a popular pilgrimage spot and one of Mexico's most famous shrines. From the bus stop, walk uphill past the market to the crossroads where blue *colectivos* run until 2000 (10 km, 20 minutes, US$1). *See Transport, page 161.*

Ixtapan de la Sal → *Colour map 2, B3. Phone code: 721.*

On Route 55, 23 km from Tenancingo, Ixtapan de la Sal is a pleasant leisure resort with medicinal hot springs surrounded by forest. In the centre of this quiet whitewashed town is the **municipal spa** ① *daily 0700-1800, US$3.* At the edge of town is the privately run **Spa y Parque Acuático** ① *0900-1800, US$11*, which has a train running around it and numerous picnic spots. For the hedonist there are 'Roman' baths; for the stiff-limbed, a hot-water pool; for the vain, mud baths. Several other luxury spa facilities are dotted around town. There's also an Olympic pool and rowing boats. Market day is Sunday; a **fiesta** is held on the second Friday in Lent.

Valle de Bravo → *Colour map 2, B3. Phone code: 726.*

The mountain resort of Valle de Bravo, on a branch road of Route 134, is a charming old town located on the edge of an attractive artificial lake. Formed by the construction of a hydroelectric dam, various sporting activities can be pursued on the water, including boating, kayaking, fishing and waterskiing. The surrounding forests are good for hiking, cycling and horse riding, while the nearby **Barranca del Diablo** (Devil's Canyon), in the municipality of Santo Tomás, offers dramatic mountain scenery and rock paintings dating from AD 800. Braver souls might want to try paragliding or hang-gliding off the hills. The town's main **fiesta** runs 26 February to 14 March, whilst the **Festival de las Almas**, late October to early November, brings international music and dance. Valle de Bravo has always been popular with wealthy *chilangos*, so expect large crowds and a feisty atmosphere at weekends and holiday periods. The **tourist office** ① *Díaz y Zaragoza, T726-262 1678, www.valledebravo.com.mx, 0900-1900*, has plentiful information on sports operators and other local attractions.

Some 20 km from town, near the village of Los Saucos, is an important **Monarch butterfly** wintering site (November to March). Guides can be found through the tourist office or near the reserve entrance.

◉ West of Mexico City listings

For Sleeping and Eating price codes and other relevant information, see Essentials pages 47-51.

● Sleeping

Toluca *p155, map p156*
A Del Rey Inn, Km 63 Mexico City–Toluca highway, T722-212 2122. Motel-style accommodation with resort facilities.
B El Gran Hotel, Allende 124, T722-213 9888. A decent, professionally run hotel with clean,

carpeted rooms, wooden furniture, cable TV, heating, a/c and a bar-restaurant. The lobby is glass fronted and strewn with antiques.
C Colonial, Hidalgo Ote 103, T722-215 9700, bus 'Terminal de Autobuses–Centro' passes in front. This big, airy colonial building has an attractive exterior with carved stone details. The interior is dominated by a courtyard and balconies, while rooms are comfortable and tidy with clean bathrooms, TV, telephone, hot water. Coffee available in the morning.

C San Carlos, Portal Madero 210, T722-214 9419, www.hotelsancarlos.com. Nice big rooms with carpets, drinking water, cable TV and hot water. Friendly and recommended.
D Rex, Matamoros Sur 101, T722-215 9300, hotelrex@prodigy.net.mx. Basic rooms have TV, hot water and bath. Ask to see a few, as some are reported to be shabby. Refreshments sold in the lobby.
E Maya, Hidalgo Pte 413, T722-214 4800. Cosy budget lodgings at this little blue house. Rooms are small, but comfortable enough, some cheaper ones have shared bath. Some doors don't have locks. Simple and family-run.
Camping Campo Escuela Nacional de Tantoco, Km 29.5 on Mexico City–Toluca road, T722-5512 2279. Cabins and campsite.

Tenancingo p158
D Lazo, Guadalupe Victoria 100 (1½ blocks from market), T714-402 0083. Clean rooms with shower, leafy courtyard, restaurant.
E Don Ale, corner of Insurgentes y Netzahualcóyotl, T714-402 0516. Good value, with clean rooms, nice balcony and garden and no bugs. Loud TV may annoy some.

Malinalco p158
LL-L Casa Limón, Río Lerma 103, T714-147 0256, www.casalimon.com. Tasteful suites and rooms, exceedingly comfortable, and all with a crisp minimalist style. There's a pool, restaurant and bar. One of Malinalco's finest.
LL-A Las Cúpulas, Ctra Malinalco– Chalma, corner of Camino Real to Tenempa, T714-147 0644, www.lascupulas.com.mx. Manicured gardens, pool, restaurant, temescal and massage are offered at this luxury hotel with 11 rooms. Suites are comfortable and elegant. Rates drop considerably during the week.
C Santa Mónica, Hidalgo 109, T714-147 0031. A lovely little hotel with a peaceful courtyard. Close to the steps for the ruins. Rooms have bath, TV, hot water. Parking facility.
D Asoleandro, Aldama y Comercio, T714-147 0184. A blue, motel-style place with big rooms, a great little pool and a garden with sublime mountain views.

D Villa Hotel, Guerrero 101, T714-147 0001. A good spot on the plaza with brightly coloured, simple rooms. Private bath, hot water, cable TV. Potted plants and views of the mountains.

Ixtapan de la Sal p159
AL Ixtapan Spa, Blv Arturo San Román, T721-143 2440, www.spamexico.com. Gargantuan hotel and golf resort with 220 comfortable rooms, 3 restaurants, pools, gym, tennis courts and spa facilities. Discounts available for longer stays, check the website.
B Vista Hermosa, next to Ixtapan, T721-143 0092, www.hotel-vistahermosa.com.mx. This small, pleasant hotel has 16 comfortable rooms, a restaurant, green spaces and pool. Rates include 3 meals. Good and friendly.
D Casa de Huéspedes Margarita, Juárez. Clean and simple. Recommended.
D Casa Guille, José María Morelos 12, T721-143 0220. Clean, simple rooms with bath.

Valle de Bravo p159
Cheap *posadas familiares* by the plaza.
AL Los Arcos, Bocanegra 310, T726-262 0042. Some rooms with excellent view, swimming pool, restaurant at weekends, unhelpful staff.
D Blanquita's, opposite the church off main plaza. Basic, fairly clean, OK.
Camping Trailer park, Av del Carmen 26, T726-262 1972. Recommended.

🍴 Eating

Toluca p155, map p156
🍴 **El Huipil**, Morelos 102. Good, traditional Mexican cuisine prepared before you at this atmospheric restaurant. Very affordable. Good breakfasts too.
🍴 **Porta di Roma**, Nicolás Bravo Sur 540A. Pasta, pizza, antipasto and other Italian fare.
🍴-🍴 **Hidalgo**, Hidalgo 229. A good spot for breakfast. Also serves steak, hamburgers and Mexican food.
🍴 **Café de Allende**, Allende 102. A bright little locals' café serving coffee, sweet rolls and Mexican staples.

Malinalco p158

¶¶¶-¶¶ Koi, Hidalgo y Morelos. An interesting contemporary space with Japanese and Far Eastern undertones. The eclectic menu includes Cantonese duck, Greek salad, hamburger with Oaxacan cheese, mescal, tequila, sake and Spanish wines. Pleasant outdoor seating.

¶¶ Ehécatl, Hidalgo 110. Pleasant, fountain-filled restaurant with a good atmosphere. Specialities include affordable T-bone and fillet steaks, several types of trout, soups, seafood, burgers and Mexican snacks. The house speciality is trout served in white sauce.

¶¶ Los Pilares, Plaza Principal. An elegant old building filled with pillars and murals. Serves cordon bleu chicken, shrimp cocktails and *trucha navara* (trout stuffed with ham). The drinks menu has lots of wine and tequila, and breakfasts include eggs and *chilaquiles*.

¶¶ Los Placeres, Plaza Principal. A Bohemian space with interesting artwork and a pleasant garden with potted cacti, shade and stunning mountain views. *Chiles en nogada*, meat and the ubiquitous trout are on the menu.

Cafés

Mazinqui Café, Hidalgo, between Progreso and Comercio. Chilled out coffeeshop serving caffeinated beverages, baguettes and snacks.

Valle de Bravo p159

Restaurants on the pier are expensive.

¶¶ Los Pericos, Embarcadero Municipal, T726-262 0558, daily 0900-2000. International menu, specializes in fish dishes.

¶ Alma Edith, Zócalo, breakfast from 0900. Very good, but slow service, *comida corrida*.

¶ El Monarca, Juárez 203. Tasty *comida corrida*.

¶ Mercado. Good, cheap food. The *cecina* (salted beef) in this region is magnificent.

⊖ Transport

Toluca p155, map p156
Air

Toluca's international airport is served by many airlines, including **Continental Airlines**, Volaris and Interjet, with flights to **Baja California**, **Monterrey**, **Chihuahua**, **Houston**, **Acapulco** and **Cancún**, among others. From the airport there are direct buses to/from **Mexico City** (2 hrs).

Bus

To get to the bus station from the centre, take a yellow or orange bus marked 'Terminal' from Ignacio Rayón Norte y Hidalgo Ote. To **Mexico City** (Terminal Poniente, near Metro Observatorio), every 10 mins, 1 hr, US$4. To **Pátzcuaro**, several daily, 6 hrs, US$28. To **Taxco**, hourly, 3 hrs, US$8, a spectacular journey. To **Morelia**, several buses daily, 4 hrs, US$13. Many 2nd-class buses to **Tenango de Arista** (30 mins, US$1.50, 1½-2 hrs) and **Tenancingo**. Also regular buses to **Calixtlahuaca**, 1 hr, US$3.50 from platform 7.

Malinalco p158

To reach Malinalco, travel to **Tenango** or **Tenancingo** (see Toluca transport, above). From there, catch a local *colectivo* to Malinalco, US$1.50, 1-1½ hrs. Alternatively, there a handful of daily departures to Tenancingo from Mexico City's Terminal Poniente, as well as a few direct services to Malinalco from **Toluca**, Sat and Sun only.

Ixtapan de la Sal p159

Bus To **Mexico City** (Terminal Ponient) every 30 mins, 3 hrs, US$11. To **Toluca** every 30 mins, 2 hrs, US$7. Also to **Taxco**, **Coatepec**, **Cuernavaca**.

Car 2 hrs from Mexico City: turn off Route 15 (Toluca highway) at La Marquesa, go through Santiago Tianguis Tenco and join Route 55 at Tenango. The road goes on to the **Grutas de Cacahuamilpa** (see page 169), from where you can continue to Cuernavaca or Taxco.

Valle de Bravo p159

Bus To **Mexico City** (Terminal Poniente) hourly, 3 hrs, US$10; to **Toluca**, hourly, 2 hrs, US$5. There are 2 direct buses a day to **Zitácuaro**, 1½ hrs, US$5.

South of Mexico City

The regions south of Mexico City have always played host to forces of colonial wealth and power. The city of Cuernavaca, home to the fortress-like palace of Cortés, was a favourite retreat of Aztec nobility long before Spain's aristocracy moved in. Punctuated by palatial gardens and grandiose mansions, this 'city of eternal spring' is today a haven for intellectuals, artists, expats and the wealthy classes. It's also a popular spot for learning Spanish, with a wealth of language schools that cater to crowds of foreign students. Further south lies the city of Taxco, reminiscent of the Mediterranean with its haphazard cobblestone streets, flower-swathed houses and superlative mountains views. Built from the wealth of prodigious silver mines, the city remains a bastion of fine metalcraft with superb jewellery on sale in its many shops and markets. But the provinces south of the capital are a stronghold of indigenous heritage, too. The town of Tepoztlán is home to a thriving culture that has inspired generations of anthropologists. At the village of Ixcateopan lie the remains of the last Aztec emperor, Cuauhtémoc, venerated as a holy relic. Whilst at the ruins of Xochicalco, where an ancient solar observatory drew calendar-makers from all over Mesoamerica, the lingering spectre of ancient Nahua history pervades the stunning mountaintops. ▸▸ *For listings, see pages 170-177.*

Cuernavaca ⬤⬤⬤▲⬤⬤ ▸▸ *pp170-177. Colour map 2, B4.*

→ *Phone code: 777. Altitude: 1542 m.*

Cuernavaca lies just outside the Valley of Mexico and is more than 700 m lower than Mexico City. Its agreeable spring-like climate has always made it a popular escape from the smog and grind of the capital. Its Nahuatl name, Cuauhnáhuac, means 'adjacent to the trees' and the area was once a great producer of bark paper and corn. It later flourished into an important religious centre, as seen at the interesting structures at Xochicalco, 40 km away. After the Conquest, the settlement was renamed Cuernavaca and became part of Cortés' sizeable estate. Throughout history, wealthy hacienda owners, politicians and other prominent *capitalinos* have built homes here – most are now stealthily secluded behind high walls. The city was the setting for Malcolm Lowry's infamous 1947 novel *Under the Volcano*, in which the British consul drank himself to death on Día de los Muertos. Cuernavaca gets busy on weekends, and while pleasant enough, is no longer the clean, idyllic retreat it once was. However, many foreign visitors are drawn to the city's famous Spanish schools, which are plentiful and offer competitive rates, see page 174.

Ins and outs

Getting there Buses leave Mexico City from the Terminal del Sur to one of Cuernavaca's four bus stations, each serving a different bus company. The journey takes 1½ hours and costs around US$7. To drive the 89 km from the capital to Cuernavaca, follow Insurgentes Sur all the way south beyond Ciudad Universitaria and then take either the fast *cuota* (toll road), or the picturesque *libre*. Beyond Cuernavaca, Routes 95 and 95D continue south towards Taxco and Acapulco, or you can head east to Tepoztlán, Cuautla and on to the State of Puebla. There is a small airport at Cuernavaca with some domestic flights. ▸▸ *See Transport, page 175.*

Getting around Most of the sights in Cuernavaca are near the centre of town, within easy walking distance of each other. Local buses can be confusing as they take long, round-about routes through the *colonias*. Buses marked 'Centro' or 'Buena Vista' all go to the cathedral. Taxis are plentiful and easy to flag down; agree the price before travelling.

Tourist information There is a **state tourist office** ⓘ *Av Morelos Sur 187, T/F777-314 3872, www.morelostravel.com, Mon-Fri 0800-1700, Sat 1000-1300*, and a **municipal tourist office** ⓘ *Morelos 278, T777-318 7561, http://mac.cuernavaca.gob.mx/turismo, 0900-1700*. There are also kiosks around town, including at the cathedral. For cultural activities, the best place for information is the university building behind the cathedral on Morelos Sur.

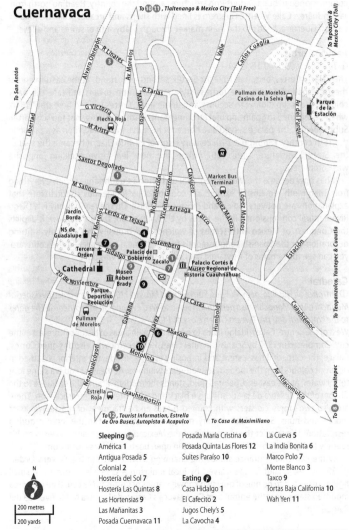

Cuernavaca

Sleeping 🛏	Posada María Cristina 6	La Cueva 5
América 1	Posada Quinta Las Flores 12	La India Bonita 6
Antigua Posada 5	Suites Paraíso 10	Marco Polo 7
Colonial 2		Monte Blanco 3
Hostería del Sol 7	Eating 🍴	Taxco 9
Hostería Las Quintas 8	Casa Hidalgo 1	Tortas Baja California 10
Las Hortensias 9	El Cafecito 2	Wah Yen 11
Las Mañanitas 3	Jugos Chely's 5	
Posada Cuernavaca 11	La Cavocha 4	

Sights

The city has two adjacent squares at its centre, the **Zócalo** and the smaller **Jardín Juárez**. Both are flanked by restaurants, and in the evenings, inundated with roaming Mariachis as well as the usual army of colourful street vendors. At the western end of the Zócalo is the **Palacio de Gobierno**. In the Jardín Juárez is a gazebo by Gustav Eiffel, who was, in accordance with Porfirio Díaz's lust for Parisian-style architecture, commissioned to build various iron structures around the country. Heading north from Jardín Juárez, Calle Vicente Guerrero is lined with shops and arcades. Calle Degollado, east off Guerrero, heads to the main market through a labyrinth of stores and alleys.

Palacio Cortés
① *Tue-Sun 1000-1700. US$2.70*

The Palacio Cortés, begun in 1522 for Cortés' second wife, stands at the eastern end of the tree-shaded Zócalo. The fortress-style ramparts and towers indicate the early colonial preoccupation with security and dominance. Cortés resided here until 1540, when he returned to Spain and met an unpleasant death by pleurisy not too soon after. Subsequently, the palace served as a home for his surviving family, then as a prison in the 18th century. During the 19th century reign of Porfirio Díaz, it became the seat of the State Legislature, until 1967, when the new legislative building opposite was completed.

It has now become the **Museo Regional de Historia Cuauhnáhuac**, with everything from mammoth remains to exhibits on contemporary indigenous culture. Note that explanations are not very logical and mostly in Spanish. On the rear balcony is a Diego Rivera mural commissioned in the 1920s by US Ambassador Dwight Morrow. It depicts the Conquest of Mexico with scenes of violence and brutality that are only a fitting decoration for the Spanish conquistador's former home. Downstairs, in the courtyard, you can see the remains of a pyramid over which the palace was built.

Catedral
① *Entrance on Hidalgo, near Morelos, Sun morning Mass at 1100 is accompanied by a special Mariachi band; Mariachis also perform on Sun and Wed evenings in the cathedral. The gates to the cathedral and the Tercera Orden close at 1400.*

West of the centre, Calle Hidalgo leads to one of the main areas of historical interest in the city. Completed in 1552 by Spanish architect Fransisco Becerra, who also designed Cortés' palace, the cathedral has a stern and imposing exterior. Inside, the interior is bathed in different colours from the modern stained-glass windows. At the west end is a stone font full of water; at the east end, painted gold, stands the modern altar. In the entrance to the Chapel of the Reserva de la Eucarista is a black and white fresco of the crucifixion. There are also two-storey cloisters with painted friezes and a fragment of massed ranks of monks and nuns. Some 17th-century murals were discovered in the interior during restoration. They depict the martyrdom of the Mexican saint San Felipe de Jesús on his journey to Japan, with renditions of monks in open boats and mass crucifixions.

By the cathedral entrance stands the charming small church of the **Tercera Orden** (1529), whose quaint facade, carved by local indigenous craftsmen, contains a small figure suspected to be one of only two known statues of Cortés in Mexico. (The other is a mounted statue near the entrance of Cuernavaca's **Casino de la Selva** hotel, Avenida del Parque s/n).

Museo Robert Brady

ⓘ *Calle Nezahualcoyotl 4, www.bradymuseum.org. Tue-Sun 1000-1800. US$2, café and shop.*
Next to the cathedral, in the Casa de la Torre, the Museo Robert Brady houses an extensive collection of works and artefacts belonging to the American artist. Brady travelled the world in search of artistic acquisitions and the contents of this museum took a whole life-time to amass. His collection of 1300 pieces contains paintings by, among others, Diego Rivera, Frida Kahlo, Paul Klee and Francisco Toledo. There is also colonial furniture, textiles, pre-Hispanic objects, African art and ceramics. It is well worth a visit. Descriptions are in English and Spanish.

Jardín Borda

ⓘ *Calle Morelos. Tue-Sun 1000-1730. US$10.*
The 18th-century Jardín Borda was a favourite resort of Maximilian and Carlota, who had a penchant for European-style gardens and verdant palatial spaces. Inspired by the opulent Palace of Versailles, the residence was originally built for local silver magnate Manuel de la Borda in 1783. It has now been restored and is in fine condition, replete with attractive courtyards, terraces and lush gardens that make a refreshing escape from the daytime heat. There are also interesting exhibition rooms containing romantic art, a café, good bookshop and museum. The gardens hold open-air concerts and boats can be rented on the small lake (US$2-3, depending on duration). Next to the Jardín Borda is the neoclassical church of **Nuestra Señora de Guadalupe**.

Beyond the city centre

Casa de Maximiliano, once the weekend retreat of the ill-fated imperial couple Emperor Maximilian and Empress Charlotte, in the pleasant district of Acapatzingo, is now the **Herbolario y Jardín Botánico** ⓘ *Matamoros 200, Col Acapatzingo, daily 0900-1700, free*, with a peaceful and interesting museum. To get there take a bus from the centre to Acapatzingo and ask the driver for the Museo del Herbolario, or take a taxi (US$1.75).

The house of David Alfaro Siqueiros, the painter, is now a museum, **Taller Siqueiros** ⓘ *Calle Venus 7, daily 1000-1630, US$1.50*, a long way east of the centre. It contains lithographs and personal photographs.

The unusual **Teopanzolco pyramid** ⓘ *Río Balsas y Ixcateopan, 0900-1730, US$2*, is just east of the railway station. The remains of a temple can be seen at the summit of the pyramid. Also in the complex are various structures including a circular building, probably dedicated to Quetzalcoatl.

Around Cuernavaca ⊖⊙▲⊙ ⇒ *pp170-177. Colour map 2, C4.*

In the vicinity of Cuernavaca are many **spas**, such as Xochitepec, Atotonilco, Oaxtepec, Temixco, Las Huertas and Los Manantiales at Xicatlocatla.

Tepoztlán

Tepoztlán, meaning 'where copper abounds', is 24 km northeast of Cuernavaca, with steep cobbled streets, bustling markets and interesting historical architecture. As a bastion of Nahua traditions, this was the village studied by anthropologist Robert Redfield and later by Oscar Lewis, who wrote the classic *Life in a Mexican Village*. Increasingly, it is has become yuppified to cater to wealthy weekenders and tourists. There's a growing hippie contingent too, perhaps drawn by the mystical energies of the surrounding hills and the fact that Tepoztlán was the mythical birthplace of Quetzalcoatl, the feathered serpent. If you're in the area on 7 September there's a raucous festival in honour of Náhua Pulque gods, whilst in the first week of November there is an arts festival with films and concerts held outdoors and in the main church's cloister.

The town is home to a remarkable 16th-century church and convent, **María de la Natividad**. Here, the Virgin and Child stand upon a crescent moon above an elaborate plateresque portal. A mural by Juan Ortega (1887) covers the eastern end of the church. Behind the church there is a small **archaeological museum** ① *Tue-Sun 1000-1800, US$0.75*, with objects from all over Mexico that were collected and donated by Tabascan poet Carlos Pellicer Cámara. There is an **arts and crafts market** on the plaza at the weekend with a good but expensive selection of handicrafts from Mexico, Guatemala and East Asia.

Tepoztlán lies at the foot of the spectacular **Parque Nacional El Tepozteco**, with the small **Tepozteco pyramid** ① *0900-1730, US$2.70, free on Sun*, high up in the mountains. The only way into the park is on foot. It takes 40-60 minutes to climb from the car park at the end of Avenida de Tepozteco. Be warned, the 2-km ascent is quite strenuous, so go before the sun is too high. Signs remind you on the way that you must pay at the top. Five minutes before the entrance, a steel ladder has to be scaled. Ultimately the effort is well worth it, as the altitude at the top is 2100 m and the view of the valley quite expansive. The pyramid here was dedicated to the *pulque* deity, Tepoztecatl.

Cuautla → *Colour map 2, C4. Phone code: 735.*

Take Route 160 from Cuernavaca via Yautepec to the semi-tropical town of Cuautla, meaning 'where trees abound'. This crowded weekend resort for the capital is a popular sulphur spring, known as *aguas hediondas* or stinking waters. The tourists' Cuautla is divided from the locals' Cuautla by a wide river and the locals have the best deal; it is worth crossing the stream. The plaza is pleasant, traffic free and well maintained. There is a market in the streets around 5 de Mayo. The **tourist office** ① *Av Obregón*, is opposite Hotel Cuautla. The **Casa de la Cultura** ① *3 blocks north of the Zócalo*, has information and maps. There is a **museum** and ex-convent next door.

Xochicalco → *Colour map 2, B4.*
① *Daily 0900-1800, US$4, tickets must be bought at the museum.*

The ruined ceremonial centre of Xochicalco lies 36 km southwest of Cuernavaca and is a UNSECO World Heritage Site. It is one of the oldest known fortresses in Mesoamerica and was an important trading point as well as religious centre. The name means 'place of the flower house' although the hilltops are now barren. The site is topped by a pyramid on the peak of a rocky hill, dedicated to the Plumed Serpent, whose coils enfold the whole building and enclose fine carvings which represent priests. Xochicalco was at its height AD 650-900. It was the meeting place of northern and southern cultures and it is believed that both calendar systems were correlated here. The sides of the pyramid are faced with andesite slabs, fitted invisibly without mortar. After the building was finished, reliefs up to 10 cm deep were carved into the stone as a frieze. There are some interesting **underground tunnels** ① *daily 1100-1400*. One of them served as a **solar observatory** where, as the sun nears the tropic of cancer on May 14/15 and July 28/29, a hexagonally shaped chimney casts a shaft of light directly over an image of the sun. There are also ball courts, the remains of 20 large circular altars, a palace and dwellings.

Xochicalco is well worth the 4-km walk from the bus stop; take a torch for the underground part. There is a **museum** about 500 m from ruins, incorporating many ecological principles and housing magnificent items from the ruins; descriptions in Spanish only.

Surrounded by steep slopes and awesome mountain views, Taxco is a popular colonial town with twisting, cobbled streets and many handsome buildings. It's now almost wholly dedicated to tourism. The first silver shipped to Spain came from the mines of Taxco. José de la Borda made his fortune here in the 18th century; he founded the present town and built the magnificent twin-towered rose-coloured parish church of **Santa Prisca**, which soars above everything but the mountains. The picturesque town is now a national monument and all modern building is forbidden.

Ins and outs
Getting there Buses to Taxco leave from Mexico City's Terminal del Sur and arrive at terminals on the edge of town. You should book onward or return bus tickets to Mexico City on arrival. Some buses en route to Mexico City drop passengers on the main highway, some way from the centre. Taxco is connected to Mexico City and Acapulco via Route 95 and the fast *supercarretera* Route 95D. ➤➤ *See Transport, page 175.*

Getting around Taxco is a fairly small town and, although hilly and cobbled, is best experienced on foot. *Combis* (around $0.50) or taxis (around US$2) will take you up the hill from the bus terminals.

Tourist information City tours run from the **tourist office** ① *Av de los Plateros 1, T762-622 2274, daily 0900-1400, 1600-2000,* inconveniently located on the north side of town.

Sights
The central area of Taxco is quite hectic. Roaring taxis, vociferous silver merchants, crowds of shoppers and gawping tourists all contribute to the sense of chaos. The district between the four-storey Mercado and the Carretera Nacional is much quieter, as are those parts up from the main streets where taxis can't go.

There are silver markets all over town that hawkers will try to rope you into visiting, including a large one next to the bus station where pieces can cost 50% less than shops in town (the quality tends to be inferior though). Make sure the silver you buy is authentic and has the '925' stamp (see Shopping, page 174). Alpaca, or nickel silver, contains no silver at all. If you're particularly interested in precious metals, consider visiting the **Museo de la Platería** ① *Plaza Borda 1, US$1.50,* devoted to modern silver-working; and the **Platería La Mina** ① *Av de los Plateros,* where you can see mining techniques.

You can get superb views of the city's haphazard streets from a range of restaurant roof-top terraces, but the best of all are had from the **Teleférico to Monte Taxco** ① *US$3 return.* This precarious cable car is reached by microbus along the main street from Santa Prisca. There is much festivity in Taxco during **Semana Santa** (Holy Week). At this time the price of accommodation rises steeply; book a room in advance.

Plaza Borda
The central Plaza Borda is the bustling heart of the city and an important orientation point. Various overpriced restaurants can be found here, as well as a plethora of expensive silver shops. That said, some of their designs are top-notch and worth the extra cost (see Shopping, page 174). Dominating the plaza is the rose-coloured churrigueresque **Iglesia de Santa Prisca**, designed by Spanish architects Juan Caballero and Diego Durán.

Taxco

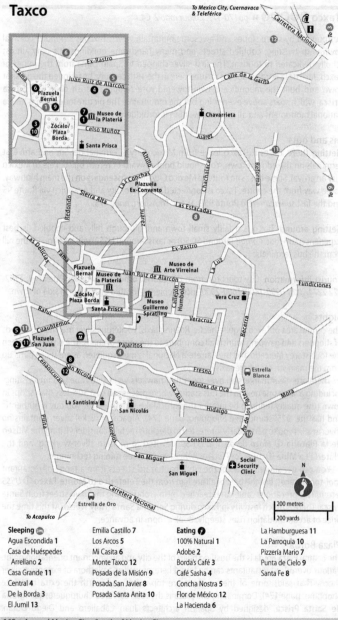

To Mexico City, Cuernavaca & Teleférico

To Acapulco

200 metres
200 yards

N

Sleeping
Agua Escondida **1**
Casa de Huéspedes
  Arrellano **2**
Casa Grande **11**
Central **4**
De la Borda **3**
El Jumil **13**
Emilia Castillo **7**
Los Arcos **5**
Mi Casita **6**
Monte Taxco **12**
Posada de la Misión **9**
Posada San Javier **8**
Posada Santa Anita **10**

Eating
100% Natural **1**
Adobe **2**
Borda's Café **3**
Café Sasha **4**
Concha Nostra **5**
Flor de México **12**
La Hacienda **6**
La Hamburguesa **11**
La Parroquia **10**
Pizzería Mario **7**
Punta de Cielo **9**
Santa Fe **8**

Constructed between 1751 and 1758, its tiled octagonal dome is magnificent. The gilded interior is dazzling too, and there is a fine carved pulpit and paintings by 18th-century artist, Miguel Cabrera. Also on the plaza is the **Casa Borda cultural centre**, with an excellent bookshop. You'll find an economical **craft market** behind the church.

Museo de Arte Virreinal
① *J Ruiz de Alarcón 12. Tue-Sat 1000-1700, Sun 0900-1500. US$1.50.*
Formerly Casa Humboldt, the museum is in the house where German explorer Baron von Humboldt once stayed. Beautiful religious paintings, expositions on colonial trade and objects pertaining to local figures like José de la Borda are among the museum's exhibits. Perhaps most interesting are a host of artefacts recovered from Santa Prisca, including ornate altar pieces, tapestries and textiles. The building itself is a handsome feat of colonial architecture. Labels are in Spanish and English.

Museo Guillermo Spratling
① *Delgado 1, behind Santa Prisca. Tue-Sat 0900-1800, Sun 0900-1500. US$2.*
This museum houses pre-Hispanic artefacts bought by William Spratling, a North American architect who came to Taxco in the 1920s. His designs in silver helped bring the city to world recognition and revived a dwindling industry. On his deathbed Spratling donated his small but diverting archaeological collection to the state. Labels in Spanish only.

Around Taxco ☻ ▸▸ pp170-177. Colour map 2, C4.

Ixcateopan de Cuauhtémoc
Ixcateopan de Cuauhtémoc, Cuauhtémoc's birthplace, is a beautiful and peaceful village where most of the buildings, and even the cobblestones, are made of marble. A statue honouring Cuauhtémoc, the last Aztec emperor, stands at the entrance to town. The old church has been converted into a museum where Cuauhtémoc's skeleton is said to rest in the glass-covered altar-like tomb. The anniversary of Cuauhtémoc's execution by Cortés (22-23 February) is called **Día de la Mexicanidad**. In remembrance, runners come from Mexico City to Ixcateopan via Taxco, carrying a torch representing the identity of the Mexican people. Meanwhile, Aztec dancers, in traditional dress and colourful plumed headdresses, arrive from all over to dance all night and most of the following day. To get here, take a *pesero* from the road out of Taxco towards Acapulco, one hour's drive west through beautiful mountain scenery.

Cacahuamilpa
① *www.cachuamilpa.conanp.gob.mx. Daily 1000-1700. US$2.50, children US$4, including 2-hr tour, Spanish only, every hour on the hour up to 1600 (crowded after 1100 and at weekends), take a torch.*
The Cacahuamilpa caverns, known locally as 'Las Grutas', are some of the largest caves in North America and are well worth a visit. They have enormous chambers, as well as some strange and rather stunning stalactites and stalagmites. Steps lead down from the near the entrance to the caverns and onto the double opening in the mountainside far below, from which an underground river emerges. Guided tours take you 2 km inside; some excursions have gone 6 km. Some visitors have reported underwhelming experiences with these guides, who generally do not speak English. Don't miss the descent to the river exits at the base of the cliff, called Dos Bocas, which is tranquil and less frequently visited.

Warning The disease histoblastose is present in the bat droppings in the cave (if you breath in the tiny fungus it can cause lung tumours); to avoid it you can buy a dentist's face mask (*cubre boca/protección de dentista*) from a pharmacy.

⊙ South of Mexico City listings

For Sleeping and Eating price codes and other relevant information, see Essentials pages 47-51.

⊜ Sleeping

Cuernavaca *p162, map p163*
Hotels tend to be poor value in Cuernavaca, but if you're looking for something upscale then there's plenty of choice. Budget lodgings are clustered along Aragón y León.
LL Hacienda de Cortés, Plaza Kennedy 90, T777-315 8844, www.hotelhaciendade cortes.com. An historic 16th-century sugar hacienda with magnificent colonial architecture, atmospheric gardens, pool and an excellent restaurant. Access by car.
LL Las Mañanitas, Ricardo Linares 107, T777-362 0000, www.lasmananitas.com.mx. This is one of the best hotels in Mexico, sumptuously decorated and built in colonial style, with many birds in the lovely gardens, elegant suites, excellent food and spa facilities. Reservation necessary.
AL Hostería Las Quintas, Av Díaz Ordáz 9, Col Cantarranas, T777-362 3949, www.hosteria lasquintas.com.mx. Built in traditional Mexican style with a magnificent setting and beautiful bougainvillea embracing the exterior. Facilities include restaurant, 2 pools, spa and outdoor jacuzzi. The owner also has a splendid collection of bonsai trees. Fine reputation.
AL Posada María Cristina, Juárez 300, corner of Abasolo, T777-318 5767, www.maria-cristina.com.mx. Tastefully decorated rooms and suites, large grounds, pristine lawns, fountains, arches and colonial-style corridors at this popular hotel. Services include pool, restaurant and secure parking.
AL Posada Quinta Las Flores, Tlaquepaque 210, Col Las Palmas, 30 mins' walk from centre, T777-314 1244, www.quintalas flores.com. You'll find comfortable, tasteful

rooms and a splendid, flower-filled garden at this pleasant hotel. Services include pool, restaurant and parking. Rates include breakfast. Helpful and highly recommended.
A Antigua Posada, Galeana 69, T777-310 2179, www.hotelantiguaposada.com. This mid-range hotel looks much better on the inside than the outside. Each room has its own terrace where breakfast is served in the morning. Services include pool, Wi-Fi, phone, taxi service and tourist information. Clean, comfortable and helpful. There's a 10% discount during the week.
A Posada Cuernavaca, Paseo del Conquistador, T777-313 0800, www.hotel posadacuernavaca.com. Motel-style place with restaurant, pool and pleasant grounds.
A Suites Paraíso, Av Domingo Díaz 1100, T777-313 2444, www.suitesparaiso.com.mx. Modern hotel with pool, restaurant and pleasant patio. Rooms are comfortable and carpeted, if fairly unremarkable. Some have reported poor service.
C Hostería del Sol, Fray Bartolomé de las Casas 5, close to the Palacio de Cortés, T777-312 6892. Loaded with charm and authentically Mexican, this friendly and secluded hotel has lots of tiles, courtyards, patios and flowers. They have just 6 rooms, including a suite (**A**). An events room is also available. Friendly and recommended.
D América, Aragón y León 14, T777-318 6127, www.tourbymexico.com/hotelamerica. In the words of the owners, "bueno, bonito, barato." Simple, clean rooms surround a central court-yard, equipped with basic furniture, fan, hot water and bath, and some cheaper beds have shared bath. Friendly and comfortable enough.
D Colonial, Aragón y León 19, T777-318 6414, hotelcolonialcortes@hotmail.com. Clean, simple rooms overlooking a quiet courtyard filled with plants. Rooms have TV, fan and bath.

D Las Hortensias, Hidalgo 13, T777-318 5265, www.hotelhortensias.com. A simple and slightly grubby hotel with carpeted rooms and cable TV. Centrally located and has a pretty courtyard. Visa accepted.

Tepoztlán p165

Accommodation can be hard to find at weekends; advance booking is recommended. Rates can drop considerably during the week.

LL Posada del Tepozteco, T739-395 0010, www.posadadeltepozteco.com. A very good historic inn, quiet and old fashioned, with an excellent atmosphere and superlative views. Rooms are very comfortable and tasteful, services include pool and terraced restaurant. Popular with celebrities. Highly recommended.

L Posada del Valle, Camino a Meztitla 5, T739-395 0521, www.posadadelvalle.com.mx. A very pleasant, romantic retreat with attractive stonework, great views, colourful gardens and tastefully presented rooms. Services include restaurant, pool and spa facilities for those needing a pamper.

B Casa Iccemanyan, Familia Berlanga, Calle del Olvido 26, T739-395 0096. 4 *cabañas* located in beautiful gardens. Rates include 3 meals (**C** without meals), monthly rates also available. Services include swimming pool, laundry facilities, use of kitchen, restaurant. English, French and German spoken.

B Posada Ali, Nezahualcóyotl 2 C, off Av del Tepozteco, T739-395 1971. A comfortable choice with good value and attractive rooms, pool, suites, views and courtyard.

Cuautla p166

C Jardín de Cuautla, 2 de Mayo 94, opposite Colón bus station, T735-352 0088. Modern and clean, with a pool, but subject to bad traffic noise.

E Casa de Huéspedes Aragón, Guerrero 72. A basic, friendly hotel, good value, where clean rooms have hot water. Recommended.

E Colón, main square. Good, clean and basic budget lodging.

E España, 2 de Mayo 22, 3 blocks from bus station, T735-352 2186. Very good and clean with 30 comfortable rooms. Recommended.

Taxco p167, map p168

Hotels are not great value in tourist-saturated Taxco, but good deals can be found, particularly during the week.

L Monte Taxco, on right entering Taxco, T762-622 1300, www.montetaxco.com.mx. This hotel has a spectacular hilltop setting, pool and golf course. However, some might say the rooms are fading and overpriced. Some mosquitoes.

L Posada de la Misión, Cerro de la Misión 32, T762-622 0063, www.posadamision.com. A very attractive, secluded hotel with elegant finishes, good atmosphere and astounding hill-top views. Services include restaurant, Wi-Fi, pool, jacuzzi and parking.

A de la Borda, on left as you enter Taxco, T762-622 0225, www.hotelborda.com. An elegant, attractive hotel with atmospheric colonial architecture, great views and over 100 comfortable rooms. Services include restaurant, pool and 4 events rooms.

A-C Agua Escondida, Plaza Borda 4, T762-622 1166, www.aguaescondida.com. Great terraces, arches and corridors at this centrally located lodging. There's Wi-Fi, a good pool, restaurant, café, and bar with great views of the plaza. Rooms are plain and comfortable, cheaper downstairs without TV (**B-C**). Prices rise at weekends. Professional and helpful.

C Casa Grande, Plazuela San Juan 7, T762-622 0969, sergio_astudillo@hotmail.com. Pleasant and well furnished, but a bit ramshackle, with windowless rooms and plants around a grand central corridor. Rooms at the top are better, takes credit cards, good value. Wi-Fi available.

C Emilia Castillo, Alarcón 7, T762-622 1396, www.hotelemiliacastillo.com. A charming, colonial-style hotel, just off the main square. Services include bar, massage and silver shop. Very friendly and good value. Book ahead if possible.

C Los Arcos, Juan Ruiz de Alarcón 4, T762- 622 1836, www.hotellosarcos.net. A beautifully reconstructed 17th-century ex-convent with a tree growing out of the central courtyard. Very tastefully decorated with fountains, wooden furniture and Mexican *artesanías*. The best rooms for views are 18 and 19; those rooms overlooking the street are noisy. Lots of character and highly recommended.

C Mi Casita, Altos de Redondo 1, T762-627 1777, www.hotelmicasita.com. This hospitable and historic colonial townhouse has very 12 pleasant rooms, all complemented by tiled bathrooms, attractive wooden furniture and other tasteful details. Comfortable and charming.

C Posada San Javier, Estacadas 32, T762-622 3177, posadasanjavier@hotmail.com. Lots of cooling, plant-filled patios, secluded little bungalows and a pool. Centrally located with Wi-Fi.

C-D Posada Santa Anita, Av de los Plateros 320, T762-622 0752, hpsta54@hotmail.com. Set on a busy main road, rooms are smallish and straightforward, slightly overpriced, but comfortable enough. Cheaper without TV (**D**), parking and sun terrace available. Friendly.

D Casa de Huéspedes Arrellano, Pajaritos 23, below Santa Prisca and Plaza Borda, inside the *artesanía* market, T762-622 0215. Basic, friendly hotel with patios and nice little budget rooms, with or without bath and hot water.

E Central, Pajaritos 27, around the left-hand corner of Casa de Huéspedes Arrellano, T762-622 0365. Reasonable budget lodgings, but most suitable for thrifty backpackers. Rooms come with or without bath, those upstairs are better, and some have little balconies. A room for 7 persons works out very economically (**F**). Hot water 24 hrs. Friendly.

E El Jumil, Reforma 6. Ultra-basic place that's popular with budget-conscious Mexicans. Towels are slung over the walls and a fading mural features a cheery cockroach. Friendly, but can be noisy. For the gritty, impoverished traveller.

● Eating

Cuernavaca *p162, map p163*
Fruit juices are sold from stalls beneath the bandstand on the Zócalo.

₸₸₸ Casa Hidalgo, Hidalgo 6, opposite the Palacio de Cortés, www.casahidalgo.com. A smart, attractive restaurant, popular with moneyed Mexicans. The menu is interesting and international, with strong Mexican and Italian influences, among others.

₸₸₸ Gaia, Juárez 102, www.gaiarest.com.mx. This stylish and romantic restaurant serves an interesting fusion of Mediterranean and Mexican cuisine, creatively prepared by chef Andrea Blanco. The candle-lit garden setting is magical.

₸₸₸ Las Mañanitas, see Sleeping, above. This beautiful and highly reputable restaurant serves imaginatively prepared, delicious Mexican food. Smart, romantic and excellent, but expensive. Amex accepted. A pleasant garden setting replete with exotic birds.

₸₸₸-₸₸ Marco Polo, opposite the cathedral. A good Italian restaurant serving fine pizzas. Also a popular meeting place with great views from the upper-floor balconies. Recommended.

₸₸ La India Bonita, Morrow 20. Fine Mexican food served in a lush colonial garden complete with trees, plants and bubbling fountain. Breakfasts are excellent, with a buffet on Sun 0900-1300. Recommended.

₸₸ Wah Yen, Juárez 306. Tasty Cantonese food, including set menus, fish, vegetable and chicken dishes.

₸₸-₸ Monte Blanco, corner of Motolinía and Galeana. Authentic, home-cooked Mexican food, *menú del día*, tacos, *tortas* and *comida corrida*. A clean interior.

₸₸-₸ Taxco, Galeana 12. Bustling little locals' restaurant with colourful chairs and tablecloths. They serve enchiladas, *mole poblano*, *chiles en nogada*, *quesadillas* and other classic Mexican fare.

₸ La Cavocha, Rayon 2. Unpretentious and ultra-cheap. *Comida corrida*, plastic chairs and *telenovelas* blasting from the TV.

¶ **La Cueva**, Galeana. Locals' haunt under the arches. The usual cheap, high-carb fare.
¶ **Tortas Baja California**, corner of Motolinía and Juárez. Small and bustling fast food joint with lots of locals. *Tortas*, burritos and fish-filled tacos are on the menu.

Cafés and juice bars

El Cafecito, Hidalgo, opposite the cathedral. Cappuccinos and coffee in a pleasant setting.
Jugos Chely's, Galeana, between Abasalo and Hidalgo.

Tepoztlán *p165*

¶¶¶-¶ **El Ciruelo**, Zaragoza 17. A quiet restaurant with pleasant decor and mountain views. Popular with wealthy Mexicans.
¶ **La Costa de San Juan**, by plaza on opposite side of street. Mostly meat and seafood.
¶ **Los Colorines**, Av del Tepozteco 13-B. Good Mexican and vegetarian food in brightly painted, cheery surroundings.
¶ **Tapatía**, Av Revolución 1910 (just across street from church wall). Good food and a pleasant view from the 1st floor.
¶-¶ **Axitla**, at beginning of path up to Tepozteco. Open Fri-Sun and holidays. Mexican and international food in atmospheric, natural surroundings.

Taxco *p167, map p168*

If you hang around Plaza Borda, restaurant touts will approach you with their menus. This is a hit and miss affair (usually miss). If you're on a budget, you'll find lots of cheap taco joints by the Estrella Blanca bus station.
¶¶¶-¶ **100% Natural**, Plaza Borda. This famous franchise, found throughout Mexico, specializes in wholesome, healthy food, all prepared with love. Their fruit smoothies are particularly delicious and almost a meal in themselves. Recommended.
¶¶¶-¶ **La Ventana**, in La Hacienda del Solar, T762-622 0587. Wonderful views of the city and an Italian-Mexican menu. Not as good as it once was, reportedly.
¶ **Adobe**, Plazuela de San Juan. A Mexican restaurant with good decor and atmosphere,

if a bit touristy. Dishes include Oaxacan enchiladas, garlic soup and shrimp specials, and Guerrero-style chicken cooked with paprika, onions and miniature potatoes. Excellent *chilaquiles* and other breakfasts.
¶¶ **La Hacienda**, Plaza Borda 4 (entrance is off the square). A fabulous interior with chic decor and a good atmosphere. Excellent Mexican food and wine at reasonable prices. Also accessible from Hotel Agua Escondido.
¶¶ **La Parroquia**, Plaza Borda. One of a few restaurants on the Zócalo boasting roof-top views. The menu includes red snapper, steak, peppered tenderloin and sangria. OK, but not as good as it likes to think.
¶¶ **Pizzería Mario**, Plaza Borda. Opened 30 years ago, Mario's was the first pizzeria in town, with beautiful view over city, excellent pizzas and pleasant service. Not to be confused with **Café Mario** or **Restaurant Mario**. Highly recommended
¶¶-¶ **Café Sasha**, Alcarón 1. A bohemian café adorned with swirling fractals and other trippy artwork. Serve baguettes, burgers, breakfasts, coffee and beer. The house speciality is vegetable crêpes in coconut curry sauce.
¶¶-¶ **Concha Nostra**, Plazuela San Juan (above Hotel Casa Grande). Pizzas, lasagne, burgers and live rock on Sat. Good views of the plaza, but some have reported that the food is mediocre and the service poor. Cheap for breakfasts, other meals are pricey.
¶¶-¶ **Santa Fe**, Hidalgo 2, opposite **Hotel Santa Prisca**, T762-622 1170. Excellent *comida corrida* (US$6) but disappointing *enchiladas*. Frequented by the locals.
¶ **Borda's Café**, Plaza Borda 6a. A friendly little café adorned with black and white film memorabilia. They serve snacks and light meals, including pork chops, tacos, enchiladas and salads. Lots of good coffee too, including drowsy alcoholic brews laced with kahlua. English speaking.
¶ **La Hamburguesa**, off Plaza San Juan. Excellent and economical home-cooked *comida corrida*, despite the name.
¶ **Mercado**. Cheap *comida corrida* in the market and cheap restaurants on San Nicolás.

Cafés and ice cream parlours
Flor de México, Hidalgo 3. For fresh, sweet ice creams.

Punta de Cielo, Plaza Borda. A swish corporate coffee shop on the plaza. Diverse menu of hot and cold caffeinated drinks.

O Shopping

Cuernavaca *p162, map p163*
Bookshops The bookshop in the **Palacio de Cortés**, to the left of the main entrance, is particularly good on art and history; also at **Jardín Borda** in Morelos. Another good bookshop, **Gandhi Colorines**, Av Teopanzolco 401, not far from the archaeological site of the same name. Second-hand English books at **Guild House**, Tuxtla Gutiérrez, Col Chipitlán, T777-312 5197.
Handicrafts The market behind Palacio de Cortés has moderately priced and interesting silver, textiles and souvenirs.

Taxco *p167, map p168*
Silver There is no shortage of silver shops in Taxco and every other window seems to display bright, shiny trinkets. Some of the most reputable shops are on the Plaza Borda, particularly in the Patio de Artesanías, where you can be assured of original work, high quality and equally high prices. **Alejandro Viveros** and **Pineda's**, especially, are good names here. The Plazuela San Juan is also home to several important shops.

But wander around and touts will quickly approach you, espousing the wares of some nearby co-op or market. **Silver markets**, like silver shops, are ubiquitous. The items for sale tend to be simpler and cheaper, with a poorer quality of craftsmanship. You'll find several bustling markets on the main road close to the Estrella Blanca bus station, as well as on side streets around town. These are the places to stock up on lots of small pieces. If you're looking for something special, you may be better off browsing the big-name shops.

Always look for the .925 mark, which confirms that the silver is of sterling quality (92½% pure). Silver that's 100% pure is only half as strong as sterling silver and unsuitable for most jewellery pieces. Beware of cheap alloys, particularly those containing nickel, which can arouse allergic skin reactions in some people.

▲ Activities and tours

Cuernavaca *p162, map p163*
Language schools
Spanish courses from US$180-300 per week for 5-6 hrs a day. Homestays with local families arranged for US$25-40 a day including meals; prices may differ for each school even if you stay with the same family. Peak time for tuition is summer. At other times (Mar, Apr and Sep-Nov) it may be possible to arrive and negotiate a discount of up to 25%. Choosing a school is best done on personal recommendation. Total up the costs and see what is included; some schools may have a cheaper weekly rate, but higher registration and coursework fees.
Cemanahuac, San Juan 4, Col Las Palmas, CP 62051, T777-318 6407, www.cemana huac.com. Claims high academic standards, field study, also weaving classes.
Centro de Artes y Lenguas, Nueva Tabachín 22-A, T777-317 3126, scale@infosel.net.mx. 1 week minimum, accommodation with families arranged.
Centro de Lengua, Arte e Historia para Extranjeros, Universidad Autónoma del Estado de Morelos, Río Pánuco 20, Col Lomas del Mirador, T777-316 1626. Accommodation with families arranged.
Cetlalic, Madero 721, Col Miraval, CP 62270, T777-313 5450, www.cetlalic.org.mx. Themed courses, plus Mexican and Central American history and culture. Non-profit making. Various levels. Small groups (rnaximum 5 people). Stay with families. Recommended.
Cuauhnáhuac, Morelos Sur 123, Col Chipitlán, CP 62070, T777-312 3673, www.cuauhnahuac. edu.mx. A cooperative language centre

offering standard and intensive Spanish options, and private classes; efficient, helpful.

Cuernavaca Language School, Azalea 3, Jardines de Reforma, CP 62269, T777-311 8956, www.cls.com.mx, or PO Box 4133, Windham, New Hampshire, USA.

Encuentros, Morelos 36, Col Acapantzingo, CP 62440, T777-312 5088, www.learn spanishinmexico.com. A fun, functional approach to acquiring Spanish including twice-weekly visits to places in Cuernavaca

Experiencia, Leyva 200, Col Las Palmas, CP 62050, T777-312 6579, www.experiencia spanish.com. One-to-one, class and hourly sessions. Free *intercambios* (Spanish-English practice) Tue and Wed afternoon, open 5 days a week.

Fenix Language Institute, Nueva Francia 8, Col Recursos, T/F777-313 3285, www.fenixmex.com.

Ideal Latinoamerica, Privada Narciso Mendoza 107, Col La Pradera, CP62170, T777-311 7551, www.ideal-school.com. Various courses, including a professional vocabulary program; family homestay is an option.

Idel, Apdo 1271-1, Calz de los Actores 112, Col Atzingo, T777-313 0157, www.del-site. Tripod.com/idel.html, 5 levels of course.

IMEC, Col Ahumada 19, T777-312 1448, www.imeccuernavaca.com.mx. Various packages and homestay arranged.

Instituto Chac-Mool, Privada de la Pradera 108, Col Pradera, T777-317 1163, www.chac-mool.com. Family homestay arranged.

KUKULCAN, Manuel Mazarí 208, Col Miraval, CP62270, T777-312 5279, www.kukulcan.com.mx.

Spanish Language Institute (SLI), La Pradera 208, Col La Pradera, CP 62170, T777-311 0063, www.asli.com.mx. Minimum 6 hrs per day, classes start every Mon.

Universal, JH Preciado 171, Col San Antón, CP 62020, T777-312 4902, www.universal-spanish.com, 3 levels of language course, tutorials and mini courses on culture.

Universidad Internacional, San Jerónimo 304, Cuernavaca, Apdo Postal 1520, T777-317 1087, www.spanishschool.

uninter.edu.mx. Various courses, including one for healthcare professionals, and free cultural activities such as salsa, folk dancing and cooking.

Tepoztlán *p165*
Language schools

Tepoztlán is becoming a popular alternative to Cuernavaca.

Spanish Communications Institute, Cuauhtemotzín, T739-315 1709, USA T956-994-9977.

⊖ Transport

Cuernavaca *p162, map p163*
Bus

Each bus company has its own terminal: **Estrella de Oro**, Morelos Sur 900, Col Las Palmas, T777-312 3055; **Pullman de Morelos**, Abasolo 106 y Netzahualcóyotl in the centre, T777-318 0907, with a second terminal at Casino de la Selva, Plan de Ayala 102, opposite Parque de la Estación, T777- 318 9205; **Estrella Blanca** on Morelos Norte 503 y Arista, T777-312 5797, also with Futura and Flecha Roja departures; and **Estrella Roja**, Galeana y Cuauhtemotzín, south of the centre. Many minibuses and 2nd-class buses leave from a terminal by the market.

To **Acapulco**, every 2 hrs, Futura, US$25, 4 hrs, or **Estrella de Oro**, every 2 hrs, book well in advance. To **Cuautla**, every 15 mins, Estrella Roja, 0600-2200, US$4, 1½ hrs, or take a minibus from the market terminal, 1 hr via Yautepec, interesting trip. To **Guadalajara**, 5 daily, Estrella Blanca, US$38. To **Mexico City**, every 10 mins, Pullman (Casino de la Selva), US$7, 1½hrs; to **Mexico City Airport**, 10 daily, Pullman (Casino de la Selva), US$12, 2 hrs. To **Puebla**, hourly, Estrella Roja, 0510-1910, US$12, 3 hrs, or Estrella de Oro, hourly. To **Queretero**, 5 daily, Estrella Blanca, US$15. To **San Luis Potosí**, 4 daily, Estrella Blanca, US$32. To **Taxco**, hourly, Estrella de Oro, 1st class, US$6, 1½hrs, or **Estrella Blanca**, hourly,

2nd class (not recommended). To **Tepoztlán**, every 30 mins, **Estrella Roja**, US$2, 30 mins.

Tepoztlán p165

Pullman de Morelos operates services between **Mexico City** (Terminal Sur) and Tepoztlán, every 30 mins, US$5, 1½hrs. More frequent buses pass the toll-booth just outside downtown Tepoztlán, including rapid services to Mexico City and **Cuautla**. Regular 2nd-class services to **Cuernavaca** depart from downtown.

Cuautla p166

Cuautla has 4 bus terminals serving various companies: OCC, Sur y Volcanes, 2 de Mayo y Bravo; **Pullman de Morelos**, also on 2 de Mayo y Bravo; **Estrella de Oro**, 2 de Mayo y Mongoy; **Estrella Roja**, Costena y 2 de Mayo.

To **Cuernavaca**, every 20 mins, **Estrella Roja**, US$4, 1½ hrs. To **Mexico City**, every 20 mins, Estrella Roja, US$7, 2½hrs, or OCC. To **Puebla**, hourly, Estrella de Oro, US$10, 2½ hrs, or **Estrella Roja**. To **Tepoztlán**, every 15 mins, **Pullman**, US$2, 15 mins.

Xochicalco p166

Bus Second-class 'Cuautepec' buses depart from **Cuernavaca** market and go directly to the site entrance. Alternatively, take a Pullman de Morelos bus from Cuernavaca en route to El Rodeo (every 30 mins), Coatlán or Las Grutas; get off at the turn-off 4 km from the site, then take a *colectivo*, US$0.35-1.20 per person, or walk up the hill. From **Taxco**, take bus to Alpuyeca (US$1.60, 1 hr 40 mins) and pick up the bus from Cuernavaca to the turn-off, or taxi from the junction at Alpuyeca directly to ruins (12 km, US$2.50).

Taxco p167, map p168

Air For international flights, Mexico City or Acapulco airports are the closest. Some domestic routes are served by Cuernavaca airport (see page 162).

Bus

Combis take you up the hill from the bus terminal, US$0.35, same fare across town.

There are 2 bus stations: Estrella Blanca, Av de los Plateros, serving Estrella Blanca, Futura and Costa lines; and Estrella de Oro, Ctra Nacional, further south on the edge of town.

To **Acapulco**, 4 daily, Estrella Blanca, US$16, 5 hrs, or with Costa, 4 daily, or Estrella de Oro, 7 daily. To **Chilpancingo**, 7 daily, Estrella de Oro, US$11, 3 hrs. To **Cuernavaca**, 5 daily, Estrella de Oro, US$5, 1½ hrs. To **Mexico City**, 4 daily, Estrella Blanca, US$10, 2½ hrs, or with Costa, 6 daily, or Estrella de Oro, 5 luxury services daily, US$12. Spectacular journey to **Toluca**, avoiding Mexico City, 2nd-class buses only, 3 hrs, US$8. Change at Toluca for **Morelia**.

Cacahuamilpa p169

Estrella Blanca buses from **Taxco** to the caves run 6 times daily. Alternatively, catch a **Toluca** or **Ixtapan**-bound service (Estrella Blanca terminal), US$2, 45 mins; ask the driver for 'las grutas' and walk 400 m downhill from the crossroads. Or, catch an hourly *colectivo* from outside the terminal, US$1.50.

There are direct **Pullman de Morelos** buses from **Cuernavaca**, 1 hr, US$2; or **Flecha Roja**, usually overcrowded at weekends.

⊙ Directory

Cuernavaca p162, map p163

Banks Cambio Gesta, Morrow 9, T777-318 3750, daily 0900-1800. Divisas de Cuernavaca, Morrow 12; many banks in the vicinity of the Zócalo. **Internet** Axon Cyber Café, Av Cuauhtémoc 129-B. California Cybercafé, Lerdo de Tejada 10b, Mon-Sat 0800-2000, Sun 0900-1400. **Laundry** On Galeana, 1½ blocks from the Zócalo. **Post office** On Hidalgo, just off the Alameda. **Telephone** Telmex on Hidalgo, just off the Alameda, LADA phones are outside, almost opposite junction of Nezahualcoyotl.

Taxco *p167, map p168*
Banks Good rates at Cambio de Divisar Argentu on Plazuela San Juan 5. Bancomer, between Plazuela San Juan and Plaza Principal, is OK. **Internet** Azul Cybercafé, Hidalgo, near Plaza San Juan, Mon-Sat 0900-2200. **Laundry** Lavandería La Cascada, Delicias 4. **Post office** On Ctra Nacional about 100 m east of Estrella de Oro bus terminal.

East of Mexico City

East of the capital, the horizon is dominated by the ghostly spectre of two immense volcanoes: ill-tempered Popacatéptl and his sedate mistress, Iztaccíhuatl. Haunting glacial landscapes await those intrepid travellers who conquer the jagged rock faces. For those in search of cultural adventures, the stunning city of Puebla offers a sublime encounter with colonial grandeur. Its streets celebrate the wealth and conservatism of an age now lost, with exuberant baroque churches, crumbling ex-convents, leafy patios, courtyards, plazas, and facades adorned in superb Puebla tiles. The area boasts more ancient history, too: the pre-Hispanic city of Cholula, furiously levelled by Cortés as he marched across the land in search of gold and glory, is home to one of the world's largest pyramids, restored and rising like an aspiring mountain. The modern-day city of Tlaxcala lacks the ancient structures of its neighbours but, like Puebla, has a pleasing abundance of colonial structures, including the Santuario de Ocotlán. For those willing to venture north into Puebla state, the mist-swathed indigenous village of Cuetzalan makes a fascinating and refreshing break from the usual tourist haunts. The highway south, to Oaxaca state, passes notable settlements, including the village of Huautla de Jiménez, where magic mushrooms are consumed like a sacred Eucharist. ▸▸ *For listings, see pages 188-194.*

Puebla ●❷❶⊗●❶❻ ▸▸ *pp188-194. Colour map 2, B4.*

→ *Phone code: 222. Population: 1,346,176. Altitude: 2060 m.*
'City of the Angels', Puebla de los Angeles is one of Mexico's oldest and most famous cities and the capital of Puebla state. It was founded in 1531 by Fray Julián Garcés who saw angels in a dream indicating where the city should be built, hence its name. It is also one explanation of why Puebla wasn't built over pre-Hispanic ruins like many other colonial cities. Talavera tiles are an outstanding feature of Puebla's architecture and their extensive use on colonial buildings distinguishes Puebla from other colonial cities. Puebla is a charming, pleasant and friendly city, always popular with travellers.

Ins and outs
Getting there **Aeropuerto Hermanos Serdán (PBC)** ① *22 km northwest of the city at Km 91.5 of the Ctra Federal México–Puebla, T222-774 2804, www.aeropuertopuebla.com*, receives mostly domestic flights. Taxis from the airport to the city centre leave from outside the departure terminal, US$3.60 with a pre-paid voucher. 'Centro' buses pass on the other side of Bulevar Norte. Puebla is on the main Highway 150 from Mexico City to the Gulf Coast, the same *supercarretera* that branches south, beyond Puebla, to Oaxaca.

The CAPU bus station, Bulevar Norte 4222, is 4 km to the north. To the centre from the terminal take *combi* No 14, US$0.30, which stops at 11 Norte and Reforma at Paseo de Bravo (make sure it's a No 14 'directo', as there is a No 14 that goes to the suburbs). The arrivals terminal has some shops including small grocery, free toilets, long-distance pay phones and taxi ticket booth (but you have to take ramp to the departure terminal to get the taxi).

An important commercial centre, Puebla is also the hub of other lesser routes to towns and villages in the surrounding area. Buses to Cholula depart from the corner of 6 Pte and 13 Nte; transport to Cacaxtla leaves from 10 Pte, between 13 Nte and 11 Nte.

▶ See Transport, page 192.

Getting around Although Puebla is a big city, most of the major sites are around the centre, within easy walking distance of each other. City buses, *colectivos* or taxis will take you to any of the more distant sites.

Orientation Puebla was laid down according to a grid plan and is very logical to navigate provided you remember a few simple rules. The northwest corner of the Zócalo, or Plaza de Armas, marks the intersection of four major arteries: **Reforma** to the west; **Palafox y Mendoza** to the east; **5 de Mayo** to the north; and **16 de Septiembre** to the south. Around this central axes, roads are assigned their appropriate suffix. For example, those running north of the Reforma/Palafox y Mendoza axis terminate **Nte**; those running south of it terminate **Sur**. Conversely, the 5 de Mayo/16 de Septiembre axis marks the change from **Pte** to **Ote**. Note also that roads running east–west are avenidas, while roads running north–south are calles. Simple!

Tourist information The **state tourist office** ① *Calle 5 Ote 3, Av Juárez, T222-777 1519, www.puebla.gob.mx, Mon-Fri 0900- 2000, Sat-Sun 0900-1500*, is behind the cathedral, next to the post office. They are helpful and friendly. The **municipal tourist office** ① *Portal Hidalgo 14, Mon-Fri 0900- 2000, Sat-Sun 0900-1500*, is in the Palacio Municipal on the Zócalo.

Best time to visit The best time to climb the volcano is late October to early March when skies are clear; from May to October the weather is good before noon only.

Zócalo and around

Puebla's Zócalo, or Plaza de Armas, marks the historic centre of the city. A thronging market place until the 19th century, this large, shady plaza still attracts crowds of tourists and city inhabitants, *Poblanos*, with its leafy trees, street performers, arcaded shops, terraced restaurants and architecturally worthy buildings – some dating from the early colonial period. The **Palacio Municipal** is on the north side, to the right of which is the entrance to the **Biblioteca del Palacio** (1996), with some tourist information and books on the city. To the left is the **Teatro de la Ciudad** (1995), where music and drama are performed. There is also an art gallery in the building. The tiled facade of the **Casa de los**

1 Puebla

➡ Puebla maps
1 Puebla, page 178
2 Puebla centre, page 181

The art of Poblano cooking

Step into a typical kitchen in Puebla and you'll know that magic takes place there. Invariably beautified with blue and white *talavera* tiles, great clay pots, stacks of fresh produce and a stunning array of cooking implements, there is little doubt that *Poblanos* are lovers of good food and masters of gastronomy.

A staggering range of ingredients are used in their work, as a visit to a *tianguis* (outdoor market), will quickly reveal. Fresh and dried chillies, mountains of herbs and spices, untold meat, gleaming fruit and a cosmos of multi-coloured vegetables all add to a distinct culinary heritage that includes everything from fruit wines to crystalized candies, meat-filled *mixiotes* to mole-drenched poultry.

Like so many great Mexican achievements, Poblano cuisine resulted from the intriguing fusion of two disparate cultures. In this case, those of the indigenous populations, whose body of knowledge included the cooking and preparation of maize and other local products; and those of the Spanish nuns, who toiled religiously in the steamy kitchens of the city convents, bringing new innovations to existing recipes.

To the nuns of Puebla we owe the city's most famous dishes, widely revered and served in homes and restaurants today. Among these is *chiles en Nogada*. This well-known dish should not be missed and consists of Poblano chillies stuffed with seasoned ground meat, fruit and nuts, then fried in batter and topped with a creamy walnut and pomegranate seed sauce.

Also check out the classic *mole Poblano*: a poultry dish topped with a complex sauce that uses four different kinds of chilli, various aromatic spices, onions, garlic, tomato and dark, bitter chocolate. Traditionally, *mole Poblano* is prepared at weddings with a live turkey that's been passed around the partygoers. The next day the turkey is slaughtered, cooked and served to the wedding couple, who ingest the good feelings of the guests. In Puebla, cooking isn't just sustenance – it's alchemy.

Muñecos, on the northeast corner of the square, is famous for its caricatures in tiles of the enemies of the 18th-century builder. Inside, the **Museo Universitario** ① *2 Norte 1, Tue-Sun 1000-1700, US$1*, contains old physics instruments, seismographs, cameras and telescopes, another has stuffed animals, but most contain religious paintings from the 17th and 18th centuries. Puebla's fine cathedral is on the south side of the Zócalo (see below), whilst 1½ blocks west, the **Museo Bello** ① *Av 3 Pte 302, Tue-Sun, US$2, free Tue, guided tours,* is the house of the collector and connoisseur Bello who died in 1938. It has good displays of Chinese porcelain and Talavera pottery and is beautifully furnished.

Cathedral and around
① *Av 3 Ote y 16 de Septiembre. Daily 0700-12.30 and 1615-1930.*
Puebla's majestic cathedral is one of Mexico's most beautiful religious structures. Construction began in 1575 under the direction of architect Fransisco Becerra, but most work was accomplished some 65 years later, by Bishop Juan de Palafox. The finished building exhibits a range of architectural styles including early baroque and Renaissance. The interior is particularly notable for its marble floors, onyx and marble statuary and gold-leaf decoration. There are statues flanking the altar, designed by Tolsá, which are said to be of an English king and a Scottish queen. The bell tower, the tallest in Mexico, gives a grand view of the city and snowcapped volcanoes, although recently it has been closed to visitors.

Opposite the cathedral and also worth visiting is the library of Bishop Palafox, **Biblioteca Palafoxiana** ① *Av 5 Ote 5, inside the Casa de la Cultura, www.bpm.gob.mx, 1000-1600, US$0.70*, one of the oldest libraries in the Americas with 46,000 antique volumes. The colonial building next to it has a large courtyard, also home to paintings and art exhibitions. Next door, at 5 Ote 9, is the **Tribunal Superior de Justicia**, built in 1762; the courtyard is open to visitors. The **Congreso del Estado** ① *Av 5 Poniente 128*, formerly the Consejo de Justicia, near the post office, is a converted 19th-century Moorish-style town house. The tiled entrance and courtyard are very attractive and it had a theatre inside, shown to visitors on request. It is now the seat of the state government.

Casa del Dean
① *16 de Septiembre y 7 Poniente. US$2.20 plus tip for the guide if wanted.*
The modest but interesting Casa del Dean was built in 1580. The walls of the two remaining rooms are covered with 400-year-old murals in vegetable and mineral dyes, which were discovered in 1953 under layers of wallpaper and paint. In 1984, the house, previously used as a cinema, was taken over by the government and opened to the public. The murals were inspired by the poems of the Italian poet and humanist, Petrarch, and are believed to have been painted by indigenous craftsmen under the direction of the Dean, Don Tomás de la Plaza, whose house it was. The murals contain a mixture of classical Greek, pagan (indigenous) and Christian themes. About 40% have been restored.

Patio de los Azulejos
① *3 Sur between 9 and 11 Poniente 110.*
The Patio de los Azulejos should be visited for its fabulous tiled facades on the former almshouses for old retired priests of the order of San Felipe Neri. The colours and designs are beautiful. The tiny entrance on 16 de Septiembre is hard to find; ring the bell on the top right and you may get a guided tour.

Museo Amparo
① *2 Sur 708, esq 9 Ote, www.museoamparo.com. Wed-Mon 1000-1730. US$3, students half price, free Mon. Audioguides US$0.70, English-language tours on request, US$13.*
Housed by handsome 16th- and 17th-century buildings, the museum has an excellent anthropological exhibition spanning some eight rooms. Punctuated by relaxing colonial courtyards, this is one of the best pre-Hispanic collections in Mexico and particularly aesthetic. There is a strong Olmec contingent, but artefacts from all the country are displayed too. Audiovisual explanations are available in Spanish, English, French and Japanese. Sombre colonial art and furniture are on show upstairs and worth a look. The Museo Amparo is privately owned and run, the legacy of local philanthropist Manuel Espinosa Iglesias. Recommended.

El Parián and around
At the heart of Puebla's most bohemian neighbourhood is the **Plaza y Mercado El Parián**, between Avenida 2 y 4 Oriente and Avenida 6 y 8 Norte, where there are many small shops selling paintings, *artesanías* and onyx souvenirs. Note that onyx figures and chess sets are more attractive and cheaper than elsewhere in Mexico, but the *poblanos* are hard bargainers. In the adjoining **Barrio del Artistas** are artists' studios. Live music and refreshments can be enjoyed at various bars and cafés nearby.

Just north of the Barrio del Artistas, the **Teatro Principal** (1550) ① *Av 8 Ote y Calle 6 Norte*, is possibly the oldest in the Americas, although it was badly damaged by fire in 1902 and had to be rebuilt. West of the *barrio*, the fragile-looking and extravagantly ornamented Sugar Candy House, **Casa del Alfeñique** ① *Av 4 Ote 418, Tue-Sun 1000- 1700, US$1.50*, now the Museo Regional del Estado, is worth seeing.

A couple of blocks of west of the Teatro Principal is the house of Aquiles Serdán, a liberal activist who opposed the dictatorship of Porfirio Díaz. A conflict that took place in this house – in which he and about 17 others were killed – is said to have sparked the 1910 Revolution. It is now full of memorabilia and houses the **Museo de la Revolución Mexicana** ① *6 Oriente 206, Tue-Sun 1000-1630, US$1*.

Two blocks west of El Parián is the **Museo Poblano de Arte Virreinal** ① *Calle 4 Nte 203, Tue-Sun 1000-1700, US$1, free Tue*, with a fine collection of viceregal art. It is housed in the Hospital de San Pedro, dating from the 16th century.

Ex-Convento de Santa Rosa
① *Several blocks north of the Zócalo, 5 Norte 1203. Tue-Sun 1000-1630. US$1.50.*
The former convent now houses the **Museo de Artesanías del Estado** and is well worth a visit for its good display of the many crafts produced in the state of Puebla. However, the

② Puebla centre

➡ Puebla maps
1 Puebla, page 178
2 Puebla centre, page 181

200 metres
200 yards

Sleeping 🛏
Camino Real **12**
Casona de la China
  Poblana **14**
Colonial **2**
El Sueño **15**
Imperial **10**
Palace **11**
Provincia Express **1**
Puebla Plaza **5**
Ritz **9**
Royalty **4**
Teresita **6**
Victoria **7**
Virrey de Mendoza **8**

Eating 🍴
Colonial **5**
El Mural de
  los Poblanos **9**
Fonda Santa Clara **1**
La China Poblana **8**
La Gardenia **2**
La Princesa **7**
La Zanahoria **4**
Mesón Sacristía de
  la Compañía **3**
Vittorio's **6**

Bars & clubs 🍸
La Boveda **10**
Librería Cafetería
  Teorema **11**

real highlight is a priceless collection of 16th-century Talavera tiles on the walls and ceilings of its extraordinary vaulted kitchen. It was here that the nuns are said to have invented the famous *mole poblano*.

Ex-Convento de Santa Mónica
① *Av 18 Pte 103, on the corner of 5 de Mayo. Tue-Sun 1000-1800. US$2.50.*
The **Museo de Santa Mónica** is housed in a former convent where generations of nuns hid after the reform laws of 1857 made the convent illegal. An underground network of secret tunnels and hidden corridors concealed them for more than 60 years while they continued to practise their faith. Furthering the fine accomplishments of *poblano* cuisine, the nuns invented the local speciality and national dish *chiles en nogada* (stuffed poblano chillies). The nuns were 'discovered' in 1935 (it's likely, however, that they were already well known) and the building was subsequently converted into a religious museum.

Iglesia de Santo Domingo
① *5 de Mayo 407. Daily 0700-1230 and 1615-1930. Free.*
One of the most stunning sights in Puebla is the **Capilla del Rosario** of the church of Santo Domingo (1596-1659). The baroque architecture displays a beauty and prodigality of form that served as example and inspiration for all later baroque in Mexico. Inside, the chapel is a riot of detailed gold leaf. The altar of the main church is also decorated with gold leaf, with four levels from floor to ceiling of life-size statues of religious figures.

There is a strong indigenous flavour to Puebla's baroque; this can also be seen in the churches of Tonantzintla and Acatepec; it is evident to a lesser extent in the opulent decorative work in the cathedral. Beyond the church, up towards the Fuerte Loreto (see below), there is a spectacular view of the volcanoes.

Centro Cívico Cinco de Mayo
In the suburbs of Puebla the **Cinco de Mayo Civic Centre**, with a stark statue of Benito Juárez, is, among other things, a regional centre of arts, crafts and folklore. It is near the **Museo Regional de Puebla** ① *daily 1000-1700, US$3*, which has magnificent collections but little information. Also nearby is the **Museo de Historia Natural**, auditorium, planetarium, fairgrounds and an open-air theatre. In the same area, the forts of Guadalupe and Loreto were the scene of the **Battle of Puebla**, in which 2000 Mexican troops defeated Maximilian's 6000 European troops on 5 May 1862 (although the French returned victorious 10 days later). This is why 5 May is a holiday in Mexico. Inside the **Fuerte Loreto**, which has views of the city (and of its pollution), is a small museum, **Museo de la No Intervención** ① *Tue-Sun 1000-1700, US$3*, depicting the battle of 1862.

Africam Safari
① *8 km south of Puebla, Km 16.5, Blv Cap Carlos Camacho, T222-281 7000, www.africam safari.com.mx. Open 1000-1700, US$11.50, children, US$10.70. To get there, take a bus from the CAPU terminal.*
The Africam Safari offers safari-style encounters with diverse wildlife including tigers, giraffes, antelopes and rhinos. These can be admired from the safety of your own vehicle or on a tour bus, which leave regularly. Some areas of the zoo can be explored on foot and there are llama rides for children. Africam Safari is home to over 3000 animals in all.

The Cradle of Maize

No event was more critical in the emergence of Mesoamerican civilization than the domestication of plants, especially maize, which afforded Mexico's tribes a sedentary lifestyle based on agriculture, rather than hunting. The earliest remains of domesticated maize (dating to 5000 BC) were discovered in the Tehuacán Valley in a region of Puebla state known as the Cuna del Maiz (Cradle of Maize). These maize plants had already been subjected to thousands of years of genetic engineering and barely resembled

their wild ancestor, *teosinte* – a tiny plant with miniscule edible fruits. By selectively breeding plants to produce ever greater yields, the ancient Mesoamericans were eventually able to engineer the full-bodied cobs we all recognize today. Maize quickly became the staple diet of the Americas, for when fashioned into tortillas and served with beans, it provides all the protein and nutrition necessary for survival. Even now, many indigenous people regard maize as sacred, believing that the gods fashioned the first man from it.

Cholula ●⊖❂⊙ ⇒ *pp188-194*.

The small, somnolent town of Cholula, home to the Universidad de las Américas, was once as influential as Teotihuacán. When Cortés arrived, it was a holy centre with some 100,000 inhabitants and 400 *teocallis* (shrines), grouped round the great pyramid of Quetzalcoatl. After the Cholulans tried (and failed) to ambush Cortés, he slaughtered the population and razed their shrines, vowing to build a chapel for each one destroyed; in fact, there are 'only' about 70 churches. Now a virtual suburb of Puebla, the town has quite a lively nightlife thanks to the local student population.

Zócalo and around

At the centre of town lies the Zócalo, with the Franciscan fortress church of **San Gabriel** (1552) ① *Mon-Sat 0600-1200, 1600-1900, Sun 0600-1900*, built over the pyramid of Quetzalcoatl and housing an interesting library of antique books. Next to it is the **Capilla Real** ① *Mon-Sat 1000-1200, 1530-1800, Sun 0900-1800*, a Moorish-style construction with 49 domes. The **Museo de la Ciudad de Cholula** ① *5 de Mayo y Calle 4 Pte, Thu-Tue 0900-1500*, has archaeological artefacts recovered from the pre-Hispanic settlement, as well as colonial art dating from its evangelization.

Zona Arqueológica

① *0900-1800, US$2.70, guides US$6.50. From the Zócalo follow Av Morelos and cross the railway.* Cholula's archaeological zone is home to the gargantuan **Pirámide Tepanapa**, resembling a small naturally formed mountain. Its base measures 350 m by 350 m, making it the world's largest pyramid, but at 66 m high, it is not the tallest. Eight kilometres of tunnels have been dug into the structure to explore its architecture. Some of them are open to the public, giving a clearer idea of the layers that were superimposed through its various phases of construction. Near the tunnel entrance is a the **Patio de los Altares**, with sacrificial altars and large stone carvings reminiscent of Gulf Coast cultures. There is also a **museum** with scale models of the site and reproduction frescoes. The 16th-century chapel of **Los Remedios**, on top of the pyramid, gives a fine view of the town, valleys and mountains.

Cuetzalan ◉◐◐◉ ▸▸ pp188-194. Colour map 2, B5.

→ *Phone code: 233.*
An interesting day trip from Puebla is to Cuetzalan market (via Tetela-Huahuaxtla), which is held on Sunday in the Zócalo (three hours' walk up). In the first week of October each year dancers from local villages gather and *voladores* 'fly' from the top of their pole. The Nahua sell *huacales* (cradles) for children, machetes and embroidered garments. Women decorate their hair with skeins of wool. The **Día de los Muertos** (2 November) is interesting here. Big clay dogs are made locally: unusual stoves that hold large flat clay plates on which *tortillas* are baked and stews are cooked in pots; these are also available in nearby Huitzilán. You can also go via Zaragoza, Zacapoaxtla and Apulco, where you can walk along a path, left of the road, to the fine 35-m waterfall of **La Gloria**. The **tourist office** ① *Calle Hidalgo y Bravo*, is helpful and can provide a good map.

Around Cuetzalan
From Cuetzalan it is a 1½-hour walk to the well-preserved pyramids of **Yohualichan** ① *Wed-Sun, US$3*, from the Totonac culture. There are five excavated pyramids, two of them equivalent to that at El Tajín (see page 532), and three still uncovered. There has been earthquake damage, though. Take a bus from Calle Miguel Alvarado Avila y Calle Abosolo, more frequent in morning and market days, to San Antonio and get off at the sign Pirámides Yohualichan (30 minutes, bad road), then walk 2 km to the site. In the Cuetzalan area are 32 km of caverns with lakes, rivers and wonderful waterfalls. These include **Tzicuilan** (follow Calle Emiliano Zapata, east of town) and **Atepolihuit** (follow Carretera Antigua up to the Campo Deportivo, west of town). Children offer to guide visitors to the ruins and caves.

Popocatépetl and Iztaccíhuatl ◉◐◐◉ ▸▸ pp188-194.

Snowcapped Popocatépetl, the smoking-mountain warrior, and his princess Iztaccíhuatl, rise majestically to the east of the capital en route to Puebla. In December 2000, **Popocatépetl** (5452 m), known familiarly as Don Goyo, had its largest eruption for 500 years. The crater lid, which was in part blown sky high, had increased, according to experts, to 14 million cubic metres; not only did smoke and ash rise to a height of more than 10 km, but the volcano also threw out incandescent rocks for a radius of up to 2 km. There was a similar eruption less than a month later, and since then, it has suffered a string of mostly moderate eruptions. Its last strong explosion was in January 2008, when an 8-km-high ash plume was thrown into the sky. For the foreseeable future it will not be possible to climb, or get close to, Popocatépetl. The volcano has been closed to climbers since 1994; access is restricted in a radius of 12 km from the crater. Furthermore, outsiders should exercise discretion about visiting villages in the danger area out of respect for the inhabitants. Ask locally for up-to-date information and advice. Fortunately, nearby **Iztaccíhuatl** (5286 m) has remained reassuringly dormant and still makes for a reasonably challenging climb. See also box, page 808.

The road to Amecameca and beyond → *Colour map 2, B4. Phone code: 587. Altitude: 2315 m.*
At Km 29 on Route 190 is **Ixtapaluca**, where a road heading south leads to the small town of Amecameca, the starting point for exploring Iztaccíhuatl ('the white woman'). On the way to Amecameca, see the restored 16th-century convent and church at **Chalco**, and the fine church, convent and open-air chapel of the same period at **Tlalmanalco**.

The legend of Popocatépetl and Iztaccíhuatl

The twin volcanoes Popocatépetl and Iztaccíhuatl have inspired many myths and legends during their timeless reign over the Nahua landscape, both ancient and modern. Nearly all of them concern the tragic story of two ill-fated lovers, and one popular version, passed down through generations of oral tradition, goes something like this:

Once upon a time there was a beautiful Aztec princess called Iztaccíhuatl, 'the white lady', who was cherished and admired by all her people. Iztaccíhuatl was in love with Popoca, the tribe's bravest warrior, who adored her as much as she adored him. One day, war broke out between the Aztecs and a rival tribe, and much to Izta's concern, Popoca was sent to fight. The stakes were high but so was the prize, for if Popoca could deliver the severed head of the enemy chief then Izta's father, the Aztec emperor, would grant him her hand in marriage.

The war was long and difficult but Popoca emerged victorious. However, as he trudged home from the battlefields, his enemies – eternally cruel and scheming – sent a message to the emperor telling him that Popoca was dead. When the message arrived and Izta heard this news she turned pale, fell sick from heartbreak and died. Thus Popoca returned neither to welcome parades, nor to the revelry of wedding festivities, but to the lifeless body of his one true love. He swept her away to the mountains and laid her down on a bed of flowers, where grief-stricken and hopeless, he laid beside her and gave up his life. The gods saw this and they were touched. Deciding the star-crossed lovers should never be parted, they transformed them into mountains. So to this day, Popoca smoulders with passion next to his lover, Iztaccíhuatl, the snowcapped white lady, bound for an eternity in stone.

The main attraction in **Amecameca**, 60 km from Mexico City, is the sanctuary of **El Sacromonte**ⓘ *90 m above the town, from the Zócalo take the exit under the arch and head for the first white station of the cross; the stations lead to the top where a magnificent view awaits*. This small but very beautiful church, built round a cave, was once inhabited by Fray Martín de Valencia, a conquistador who came to Mexico in 1524. It is, after the shrine of Guadalupe, the most sacred place in Mexico and has a much-venerated full-sized image of Santo Entierro weighing only 1½ kg.

Market day in Amecameca is Saturday, and there is an excellent non-touristy market on Sunday. The **tourist office**ⓘ *near the plaza, daily 0900-1500*, can provide information and guides for Iztaccíhuatl. To get to Amecameca from Mexico City, take a second-class Volcanés or Sur bus from the TAPO terminal (every 20 minutes, 1½ hrs, US$2).

Climbing Iztaccíhuatl

Before venturing out to climb Iztaccíhuatl, you must check into the offices of the **Parque Nacional Itzaccíhuatl-Popocatépetl** ⓘ *Plaza de la Constitución 9B, in Amecameca, T597-978 3829, Mon-Fri 0900-1800, Sat 0900-1500*, who need to supply any necessary permits before you can set out. They will also be able to advise you on the climb. Make sure you contact them in advance to reserve places in refuges if you plan to stay overnight. For the purposes of search and rescue, you should also notify them of your intended route. Due to the changeable, rugged and glacial nature of the terrain, it is highly recommended that you use a guide, which can be hired from various agencies in

Amecameca. Note that some rock climbing is required, so crampons and ice-picks are necessary (also available in town). If you hope to summit the volcano, you will need to spend at least one night in the park.

From Amecameca, drive (or take a taxi or *colectivo*) to the **Paso de Cortés**, a refreshing space between the two volcanoes through which Cortés once passed on his way to Aztec Tenochititlán. From here, a road goes north along a dirt road, past a TV station, for 8 km to **La Joya**, the parking nearest to the summit of Iztaccíhuatl. Near the antennae is a *refugio* called **Atzomani**, which is the safest place to park, and there is a *buzón* (box) for notifying potential rescue groups of your intended route. From there you find various routes to the summit (12-15 hours return) and three to four refuges in which to stay overnight (no furniture, bare floors, dirty). The first two huts are at 4750 m (space for 30 people), the third at 4850 m (10-15 people), and the last hut is at 5010 m (in poor condition, 10-12 people); the Luis Menéndez hut is the most salubrious. From the last hut it is 2½ to three hours to the top; set off at 0400, over two glaciers.

A more technical route starts at the *buzón* and at first descends left into the valley. Walk three to four hours from La Joya to the **Ayoloco glacier** before which is a *refugio* for eight to 10 people at 4800 m. From here it is three to four hours to the summit. You'll definitely need a guide here, as walking on glaciers without knowing the conditions is hazardous.

It's also possible to climb Iztaccíhuatl from Puebla. Take a second-class bus to Cholula from Puebla, then a *combi* from the centre to San Nicolás de los Ranchos. From here bargain with one of the few local taxis for a ride to La Joya (US$20).

Tlaxcala ⬤⬤⬤⬤ ⬤ ➤➤ pp188-194. Colour map 2, B4.

➔ *Phone code: 246. Altitude: 2240 m.*

North of Puebla the quaint old town of Tlaxcala ('red city') and capital of Mexico's smallest state, has a very pleasant centre of simple buildings washed in ochre, pink and yellow, and vast not-so-quaint suburbs. It is a place where wealthy ranchers breed fighting bulls, but the landless peasants are still poor. Tlaxcala is most famous for the treacherous alliance it struck with Cortés. Supplying him with valuable warriors and tactical information, the Tlaxcalans had hoped to undermine their eternal enemies, the Aztecs.

Tlaxcala's **tourist office** ① *Av Juárez y Landizábal, T246-465 0960, www.tlaxcala.gob. mx/turismo,* has many maps, leaflets and is very helpful. The annual **fair** is held 29 October-15 November each year.

Tlaxcala's sights are modest but diverting. In the **Palacio de Gobierno** on the main square are some extremely colourful murals depicting the indigenous story of Tlaxcala, the history of Mexico and of humankind. The church of **San Francisco**, dating from 1521, is the oldest in Mexico, from whose pulpit the first Christian sermon was preached in New Spain (Mexico). Of course, the sermon would have been for the benefit of the Spanish residents; the local indigenous people would have congregated outside at the open chapel. Almost next door is the **Museo del Estado de Tlaxcala** ① *Tue-Sun 0900-1700, US$3,* with two floors of interesting historical and artistic exhibits. The **Museo de Memoria** ① *Independencia 3, Tue-Sun 1000-1700, US$0.70,* has exhibits on indigenous culture, whilst the **Museo de Artes y Tradiciones Populares** ① *Sánchez 1, 1000-1800, Tue-Sun, US$1,* is a 'living museum' where local Otomí people demonstrate traditional arts and customs including the sweat bath, cooking, embroidery, weaving and *pulque*-making. Highly recommended.

Santuario de Ocotlán

The churrigueresque **Santuario de Ocotlán** (1541), on a hill in the outskirts of Tlaxcala, commands a view of valley and volcano. It was described by Sacheverell Sitwell as "the most delicious building in the world". Its facade of lozenge-shaped vermilion bricks, framing the white stucco portal and surmounted by two white towers with fretted cornices and solomonic pillars, is beautiful. The sumptuous golden interior, comparable with those of Taxco and Tepotztlán, was worked on for 25 years by the indigenous artist Francisco Miguel.

Tizatlán

The ruined **pyramid of Xicoténcatl** at San Esteban de Tizatlán, 5 km from Tlaxcala, has two sacrificial altars with original colour frescoes preserved under glass. The pictures tell the story of the wars with Aztecs and Chichimecs. Amid the archaeological digs at Tizatlán are a splendid 19th-century church and the 16th-century chapel of **San Esteban**. To get there from Tlaxcala, take a *colectivo* from 1 de Mayo y 20 de Noviembre; at the main square, alight when you see a yellow church dome on the left.

Cacaxtla → *Colour map 2, B4.*

① *Near San Miguel del Milagro, between Texmelucan and Tlaxcala. Tue-Sun 1000-1630. US$3.50, which also includes access to the nearby ruins of Xochitecatl. From Tlaxcala catch a colectivo from the corner of Av 20 de Noviembre and Lardizabal, US$1. From Puebla take a Flecha Azul bus marked 'Nativitas' from Calle 10 Pte y Calle 11 Norte to just beyond Nativitas where a sign on the right points to San Miguel del Milagro and Cacaxtla. Walk up the hill or take a colectivo to a large sign with its back to you, turn left here for the ruins.*

A remarkable series of pre-Columbian frescoes are to be seen at the ruins of Cacaxtla. The colours are still sharp and some of the figures are larger than life size. To protect the paintings from the sun and rain, a huge roof has been constructed. An easily accessible visitor centre has been opened but there is disappointingly little published information on the site. In theory there is a 'per picture' charge for photography, but this is not assiduously collected although flash and tripod are strictly prohibited.

Puebla south to Oaxaca ☻❼▲☻ ⇢ *pp188-194.*

Tehuacán → *Colour map 2, C5. Phone code: 238. Altitude: 1676 m.*

This charming town, southeast of Puebla, has a pleasant, sometimes cool, climate. Water from the mineral springs is bottled and sent all over Mexico by **Garci Crespo**, **San Lorenzo** and **Peñafiel**. From the small dam at Malpaso on the Río Grande, an annual race is held for craft without motors as far as the village of Quiotepec. The central plaza is pleasant and shaded. The **Museo de Minerología Romero** ① *Av Reforma, 7 Norte 356, daily 0900-1200, 1600-1800, morning only on Sat, free,* is in the ex-Convento del Carmen. It has one room with a good collection of minerals from all over the world. The *ayuntamiento* (town hall) on the Zócalo is decorated inside and out with murals and tiles. A short bus ride beyond Peñafiel Spa is the spa of **San Lorenzo** ① *US$2,* with spring-fed pools surrounded by trees.

Huautla de Jiménez

From Teotitlán it is possible to drive into the hills to the indigenous town of Huautla de Jiménez, famed for its hallucinogenic 'magic' mushrooms, see page 589.

For Sleeping and Eating price codes and other relevant information, see Essentials pages 47-51.

● Sleeping

Puebla *p177, maps p178 and p181*

Puebla has a plethora of hotels with everything from dusty old cheapies to luxury boutiques.

LL Casona de la China Poblana, Palafox y Mendoza, T222-242 5336, www.casonadela chinapoblana.com. Sumptuous and exclusive boutique hotel with stylish and individually decorated rooms. Fine restaurant and bar. Comfortable, luxurious and very expensive.

LL-L El Sueño, 9 Ote 12, T222-232 6423, www.elsueno-hotel.com. This bastion of minimalist beauty offers romantic and luxurious rooms, delectable suites, restaurant and spa facilities. Great services, comfort and impeccable taste.

LL-AL Puebla Marriott Real, Hermanos Serdán 807, near 1st Puebla interchange on Mexico City–Puebla motorway, T222-141 2000, www.marriott.com. Standards and services at the Marriott are predictably high, with a wealth of amenities including gym, pool, restaurant, bar, events room and attractive gardens. Rooms and suites are attractive, comfortable and tasteful. One of the best hotels in town, but far from the centre.

LL-A Camino Real, 7 Pte 105, T222-229 0909, www.caminoreal.com/puebla. A very elegant and atmospheric hotel in the historic and beautifully restored 16th century ex-Convento de la Concepción. There are 84 rooms and suites, all adorned with antiques and sumptuous details. Services include bar, restaurant, room service, boutiques and business centres. Quiet and luxurious.

B Colonial, 4 Sur 105, across pedestrian street from La Compañía church, T222-246 4612, www.colonial.com.mx. A superb colonial building, old-fashioned and charming, replete with big paving stones, colonial art, antique fixtures, history and character. All rooms have bath, Wi-Fi, safe, electronic locks and good double glazing. Some have high ceilings and original paintwork. Most have bath tubs and antique sinks. Helpful and recommended.

B Puebla Plaza, 5 Pte 111, near cathedral, T222-246 3175, www.hotelpueblaplaza. com.mx. Formerly Hotel Santander, the **Puebla Plaza** has an attractive, royal blue colonial facade. 48 plain but comfortable rooms with phone, TV, Wi-Fi and hot showers. Some big, bright rooms face the street. Enclosed parking.

C Imperial, 4 Ote 212, T222-242 4980, www.hotelimperialpuebla.com. Good-sized plain rooms around a central courtyard. The executive suites are a little roomier and have more character. All are clean, with TV, phones and hot shower. Services include restaurant, gym, mini-golf, parking and Wi-Fi. 30% discount for *Footprint* owners. Continental breakfast included, good value. Recommended.

C Palace, 2 Ote 13, T222-242 4030, www.hotelpalace.com.mx. A modern hotel with marble floors and a restaurant, El Ranchito, serving Mexican food. Rooms are clean and comfortable, if fairly unremarkable.

C Provincia Express, Reforma 141, close to the Zócalo, T222-246 3557, provinciaexpress_ puebla@hotmail.com. Formerly Hotel Alamada, the interior of this building is beautifully painted in Moorish style. Rooms are plain and most are windowless, but all are clean, with TV, phone and bath. Services include parking, Wi-Fi, and café.

C Royalty, Portal Hidalgo 8, T222-242 4740, www.hotelr.com. Pleasant and central with straightforward rooms and a comfortable suite. Rooms on the Zócalo have fine views, but the windows are thin.

D Granada, Blv de la Pedrera 2303, T222-232 0966. A quiet, comfortable hotel with restaurant, room service and TV in the rooms. Very close to bus terminal; the bus to the centre leaves from front door.

D Virrey de Mendoza, Reforma 538, T222-242 3903. This old colonial house has a beautiful wooden staircase and lots of plants.

Rooms are plain and fairly basic rooms with high ceilings, TV and bath.

D-E Ritz, 2 Norte 207 y 4 Ote, 2 blocks from Zócalo, T222-232 4457, www.hotelritz puebla.com. Reasonable, but drab exterior at this centrally located budget hotel. Some good rooms have balconies.

E Teresita, 3 Pte 309, T222-232 7072. Small, clean, simple rooms with hot water and bath (although the 'comedy showers' manage to get everything soaked!). Friendly.

E Victoria, near Zócalo, 3 Pte 306, T222-232 8992, www.hotelesenpuebla.com/victoria.htm. Small, basic and windowless, but clean. Reasonable budget lodgings. Friendly and recommended for thrifty travellers.

Cholula p183

LL-L Estrella de Belem, 2 Ote 410, T222-261 1925, www.estrelladebelem.com.mx. This luxurious B&B with spa facilities has an impressive roof-top terrace with views, hydro-massage pool, solarium and heated swimming pool. Lots of atmosphere, with courtyards, fountains and decorative antiques.

LL-L La Quinta Luna, 3 Sur 702, T222-247 8915, www.laquintaluna.com. Formerly a 17th-century mansion, La Quinta Luna is a sumptuous and immaculately presented high-end option with lots of character and style. A library containing 3000 books takes pride of place in this establishment and predictably, rooms and services are impeccable.

A-B Villas Arqueológicas, 2 Pte 501, T222-247 1966. Close to the pyramid and affiliated with Club Med, this hotel has 44 comfortable rooms, lush gardens, tennis court and a French restaurant. Rooms have heating, TV and phone. English and French Spoken. Prices rise at the weekends (**A**).

C Casa Calli, on Zócalo, Portal Guerrero 11, T222-261 5607, www.hotelcasa calli.com. Attractive, colonial-style lodgings with 37 rooms, Wi-Fi, cable TV, pool, restaurant and spa facilities. Chic and affordable.

E Hostal Cholollan, 2 Calle Norte 2003, Barrio de Jesús, T222-247 7038. Dorms in a lively place with great views of Popo and Izta from

the terrace. Free use of kitchen, and great meeting spot.

E Las Américas, 14 Ote 6, San Andrés, T222-247 0991. Near the pyramid, actually a motel, with modern with rooms off galleries around a paved courtyard (car park). There is a small restaurant. Clean and good value.

E Trailer Park Las Américas, 30 Ote 602. Hot showers, secure furnished apartments.

Cuetzalan and around p184

B La Casa de la Piedra, García 11, T233-331 0030, www.lacasadepiedra.com. A very beautiful and atmospheric property, formerly a coffee processing plant. Rooms are rustic yet comfortable, with attractive wooden floor boards and beams. The stonework is gorgeous. Recommended.

C Posada Cuetzalan, Zaragoza 12, T233-331 0154, www.posadacuetzalan.com. A colourful, charming hotel with lush courtyards and exuberant plant life. Rooms are comfortable and equipped with cable TV and phone. There's also a pool, laundry service, internet and bilingual guides.

D-F Taselotzin, by La Gloria waterfall, near Cuetzalan, T/F233-331 0480. Owned and operated by an association of Nahua craftswomen, this hotel has both rooms (**D**) and a set of dormitory-style *cabañas* (**F** per person), very clean with great views. Recommended.

E-F Rivello, G Victoria 3, T233-331 0139, 1 block from Zócalo. Basic, friendly and clean. Rooms have bath (cheaper without).

Amecameca p185

E San Carlos, Constitución 10, T587-978 0746. The only hotel, simple basic rooms.

Camping

Permitted at the railway station, ask at the office (leaving town, it's after the road to Tlamacas, on the right, 1-2 km away).

Tlaxcala p186

A Posada San Francisco (Club Med), Plaza de la Constitución 17, T246-462 6022, www.posadasanfrancisco.com. Lavishly decorated in colonial style, this hotel has good services including 2 restaurants, Wi-Fi, dance hall, secure parking, pool and tennis courts. Rooms are comfortable, but not astounding. Promotional deals sometimes available, check the website. Highly recommended.

C Alifer, Morelos 11, uphill from plaza, T246-462 5678, www.hotelalifer.com.mx. Central, comfortable and affordable, but slightly characterless. Rooms are spacious, carpeted and equipped with Wi-Fi. Restaurant and safe parking.

Tehuacán *p187*

C México, Reforma Norte y Independencia Pte, 1 block from Zócalo, T238-382 0019. This renovated colonial building is one of the town's better options, with attractive rooms, parking, TV, restaurant. Quiet, charming and comfortable.

D-E Iberia, Independencia Ote 217, T238-383 1500. Clean and airy, with a pleasant restaurant and nearby public parking at reduced fee with a hotel voucher. Recommended, but can be noisy Sat-Sun.

E Inter, above the restaurant of same name, close to bus station (ask there), T238-383 3620. Modern and clean with hot showers.

E Madrid, 3 Sur 105, T238-382 0272, opposite the municipal library. Cheap and comfortable with a pleasant courtyard. Rooms are cheaper without bath. Recommended.

🍴 Eating

Puebla *p177, maps p178 and p181*
Local specialities include *chiles en nogada* (*poblano* chillies stuffed with minced meat and almonds and topped with a sweet cream sauce made with ground nuts, then topped with pomegranate seeds; the green, white and red colours are supposed to represent the Mexican flag); and *mole poblano* (chicken or turkey with sauce of chillies, spices, nuts and chocolate).

🍴🍴🍴 **El Mural de los Poblanos**,
16 de Septiembre 506, T222-242 0503, www.elmuraldelospoblanos.com. Fabulous food in the fabulous setting of a 17th century courtyard. Fantastic paintings feature scenes and characters from Mexican history whilst freshly prepared regional specialities are served with impeccable grace. Pricey.

🍴🍴🍴 **Mesón Sacristía de la Compañía**, 6 Sur 304, T222-242 3554. In the old sacristy, this elegant restaurant has a marvellous patio and lots of plants. It serves regional specialities like *quesadillas de flor de calabaza* and a fiery hot *cazuelita poblana* (spicey fajitas). *Consomé de Enfermo* is a kind of chicken soup with restorative properties.

🍴🍴-🍴 **Colonial**, 4 Sur 105, across pedestrian street from La Compañía church. **Hotel Colonial**'s restaurant is the locals' favourite and best at Sun lunchtime, when it fills up. Serve international food and regional specialities. The menu changes daily and there's also a reasonable *comida corrida*. The kitchen is good and clean, and the interior is elegant.

🍴 **Fonda Santa Clara**, 3 Pte 307, with parking a couple of blocks west on 3 Pte. A good, popular place to sample local specialities and classic Puebla dishes. Excellent *mole*, *mixiote* (lamb with chilli, wrapped in paper with spicy sauce) and *chiles en nogada* (best Jul-Sep). Also serves more exotic fare like *escamoles* (ant eggs) and *gusanos de maguey* (maguey grubs). A pleasant, atmospheric interior.

🍴 **Hotel Royalty**, Portal Hidalgo 8. Pleasant busy restaurant on the plaza, under the *portales*. Sometimes serenaded by a marimba band. Serves traditional dishes including *platillos poblanos*. Packed at weekends.

🍴 **Vittorio's**, Morelos 106. Italian restaurant on the Zócalo with live music on Fri and Sat night. Good atmosphere and pizzas.

🍴-🍴 **La China Poblana**, 6 Nte 1. An open-front restaurant decorated in attractive *pubela* tiles and serving tasty, home-cooked, regional food.

🍴-🍴 **La Gardenia**, Palafox 416. A busy little locals' haunt serving good regional cuisine. Affordable and unpretentious, if a little cramped.

¶-¶ La Zanahoria, 5 Ote 206. A big, popular vegetarian place that serves juices, salads and shakes as well as other wholesome fare. Economical set meals are also available.

¶ La Princesa, Portal Juárez 101. Good variety and good prices, several other similar places nearby to choose from on Zócalo.

¶ Mercado El Alto, in the San Francisco quarter. Beautiful market covered with *azulejos*, with good local cuisine. Breakfast and lunch, 8 different menus.

Cafés, sweet shops and ice cream parlours

Nieves (drinks made of alcohol, fruit and milk) are worth trying. Calle 6 Ote has a concentration of shops that specialize in selling traditional handmade *dulces* (sweets), *camotes* (candied sweet potatoes) and *rompope* (egg nog).

Café Britannia, Reforma 528. Cheap and good coffee. Recommended.

Cafetería Tres Gallos, 4 Pte 110. Good coffee and pastries.

Super-Soya, 5 de Mayo. Good for fruit salads and juices. Several other good places for *comidas corridas* on 5 de Mayo.

Tepoznieves, 3 Pte 150, esq 3 Sur. Rustic Mexican decor, serves all varieties of tropical fruit ice cream and sherbet.

Cholula *p183*

There are many good restaurants and food stops in Cholula due to the large number of North Americans in town. Try the *licuados* at market stalls (fruit and milk and 1 or 2 raw eggs if you wish); *mixiote* is a delicious local dish of spicy lamb or goat barbecued in a bag.

¶¶ Café Enamorada, southwest corner of the Zócalo. Popular place with outdoor seating, live music most nights and a Sun breakfast buffet.

¶¶ Choloyán, Av Morelos. Good, clean and friendly. They also sell handicrafts.

¶¶ La Lunita, 6 Nte y Calzada San Andrés. An interesting joint that serves Mexican food and

cold *cerveza*. A busy bar atmosphere takes over in the evenings.

¶-¶ Los Jarrones, Portal Guerrero 7. Outdoor seating, breakfast buffet and loud music in the evenings. Popular with locals.

Cuetzalan *p184*

¶ Posada Quetzal, Zaragoza. Good, cheap restaurant.

¶ Yoloxochitl, 2 de Abril. Old juke boxes and views of the cathedral. Good for breakfasts, huge juices.

Cafés

Café-Bazar Galería, in the centre. Good sandwiches and tea, nice garden, English magazines. Recommended.

Amecameca *p185*

There are several eating places and a good food market. A good-quality *pulque* is available at the *pulquería* on the main plaza.

Tlaxcala *p186*

¶¶ Fonda del Convento, San Francisco 1. Intimate restaurant serving excellent 4-course traditional meals.

¶¶ Los Portales, main square. Popular, with regional dishes.

¶ Oscar's, Av Juárez, by corner of Zitlalpopocatl. Excellent sandwiches and juices.

Tehuacán *p187*

There are many reasonably priced eating places on the Zócalo.

¶¶ Santander. Good but pricey.

¶ Pizzería Richards, Reforma Norte 250. Good pizzas, good fresh salads.

Cafés, bars and juice stalls

Cafetería California, Independencia Ote 108. Excellent juices and *licuados*.

La Pasita, 5 Ote between 2 y 4 Sur, in front of Plaza de los Sapos. The oldest bar in Puebla, sells a drink by the same name, a local speciality. Recommended.

Bars and clubs

Puebla p177, map p178 and p181
For the latest cultural happenings, see
www.andonepuebla.com.
La Boveda, 6 Sur 503. Beery student haunt
with live rock.
La Cantina de los Remedios, Juárez 2504.
Crowded and popular. One of several
drinking holes on this stretch of Juárez.
Librería Cafetería Teorema, Reforma 540,
esq 7 Norte. Café, books and art and live
music at night. They also serve good coffee
and snacks, pastries, *platillos mexicanos*.
Recommended.

Festivals and events

Puebla p177, map p178 and p181
Mid-Apr Feria for 2 weeks.
Sep-Nov The Fiesta Palafoxiana runs from
the last Fri in Sep until mid-Nov for 9
weekends of dancing, music, theatre,
exhibitions, etc; some free performances.

Shopping

Puebla p177, map p178 and p181
5 de Mayo is a pedestrian street closed to
traffic from the Zócalo to Av 10. The entire
block containing the Capilla del Rosario/
Templo de Santo Domingo in the southeast
corner has been made into a shopping mall
(opened 1994), called the **Centro Comercial
La Victoria** after the old La Victoria market.
The old market building still exists.

Bookshops Librería Británica, Calle 25 Pte
1705-B, T222-240 8549.
Crafts The famous Puebla Talavera tiles may
be purchased from factories outside Puebla,
or from the well-known **Taller Uriarte**, Av 4
Pte 911 (spectacular building, tours at 1100,
1200 and 1300). Recommended.
Other government-sponsored shops
include **Tienda Convento Santa Rosa**,

3 Norte 1203, T222-240 8904; **Talavera de la
Reyna**, Camino a la Carcaña 2413, Recta a
Cholula. Recommended (also in **Hotel Mesón
del Angel**); **Centro de Talavera**, Calle 6 Ote 11;
D Aguilar, 40 Pte 106, opposite Convento de
Santa Mónica; and **Casa Rugerio**, 18 Pte 111.
Margarita Guevara, 20 Pte 30.

Activities and tours

Puebla south to Oaxaca p187
Language school
Escuela de Español en Tecamachalco,
Calle 29 Sur 303, Barrio de San Sebastián,
Tecamachalco, CP 75480, Apdo Postal 13,
T249-422 1121. Run by Patricia Martínez, very
good; homestays available.

Transport

Puebla p177, map p178 and p181
Air
To get to **Aeropuerto Hermanos Serdán**
(PBC) from the centre, take any form of
public transport marked 'CAPU'. The airport
has flights to **Guadalajara**, **León**, **Mexico
City**, **Monterrey** and **Tijuana**. For airline
website addresses, see page 36.
Airline offices Aero California, Blv
Atlixco 2703, Locales B y C, Col Nueva
Antequera, T222-230 4855. Aeromar, T222-
232 9633. AeroMéxico, Av Juárez 1514, Col La
Paz, T222-232 0013. Lufthansa and LanChile,
at Av Juárez 2916, Col La Paz, T222-248 4400.
Mexicana, Av Juárez 2312, between Calle 23
Sur and 25 Sur, T222-248 5600.

Bicycle
There are several bike shops in 7 Norte, north
of 4 Pte, have international spare parts.

Bus
The huge CAPU bus terminal is 4 km north of
city. From the centre take any form of transport
marked 'CAPU', many *colectivos* and buses
(route 12) on Av 9 Norte, US$3.50 per person

flat rate; or bus 37 or 21 at Av Camacho. The departure terminal has banking services (with ATM), and a good practical mix of shops including gift shops, phone booths, food shops and luggage storage.

Bus services from Puebla run to most parts of Mexico. To **Mexico City**, ADO *GL* to TAPO (eastern) terminal every 20 mins 0430-2010, 2 hrs, US$9; to Terminal del Sur every hour 0635-2135, US$6.50; to Terminal del Norte every 20-40 mins from 0520-2150, US$6.50, Estrella Roja to Mexico City airport every hour 0300-2000, 2 hrs, US$9. To Mexico City, 2nd-class every 10 mins, US$5, *plus* service US$5.50; AU, every 12 mins from 0510 to 2300. To **Acapulco**, Estrella Blanca, 10 daily, US$37.To **Chetumal**, ADO, 1145, US$66, 17 hrs. To Cuernavaca, EDO, hourly, 3 hrs, US$12. To **Mérida**, ADO, 1305, 1955, 2005, US$69-83, 17½ hrs. To **Oaxaca**, ADO, 12 daily, US$24, 4½ hrs. To **Reynosa**, ADO at 1100, US$64. To **San Cristóbal de las Casas**, Cristóbal Colón, *plus* service, 6 daily, US$66-79. To **Tapachula**, UNO, 2015, 16 hrs, US$102; Cristóbal Colón, *plus* service, 4 a day, US$68. To **Tehuacán** direct ADO every 30-45 mins 0600-2100, US$6. To **Tuxtla Gutiérrez**, ADO, 1930, 2205, 10 hrs, US$59. To **Villahermosa**, ADO *GL plus* service via *autopista*, 1835 and 2200, 8½ hrs, US$57, 1st class, 1145, 2045. 2145, 8¼ hrs, US$50; UNO at 2130, 2350, 8 hrs, US$82. To **Xalapa**, ADO *GL plus* service at 0745, 1645 and 2015, US$14, 1st class, 8 a day, 3 hrs, US$12; AU, 2nd class, 13 daily, 3½ hrs, US$11.

Bus companies Autobuses de Oriente (ADO), T01800-7028000. Mercedes Benz buses, 1st class and *'GL' plus* service. Autobuses Unidos (AU), T222-249 7366, all 2nd class without toilets. Cristóbal Colón, T222-249 7144 ext 2860, *plus* service. Estrella Blanca, T222-249 7561, 1st class, plus and élite services. Estrella Roja, T222-249 7099, 2nd class, 1st class and plus service. Oro, T222-249 7775, *gran turismo* or 1st-class service. UNO, T222-230 4014, luxury service.

Taxi
Radio Omega, T222-240 6299, radio taxi service, with new Chevrolet cars, 24-hr service, will deliver packages or pick up or medicine and deliver it to your hotel.

Train
The station is a long way from the centre, so before going there check at the tourist office to see if any passenger services are running.

Cholula *p183*
Bus Regular 2nd-class **Estrella Roja** buses to **Puebla**, 9 km on a new road, 20 mins. To **Mexico City**, Estrella Roja buses run to the capital's Terminal del Oriente every 30 mins, 2½-3 hrs, US$4.20, 2nd class every 20 mins, a scenic route through steep wooded hills. Good views of volcanoes.

Cuetzalan *p184*
Bus Direct buses to **Puebla** (Tezuitecos line only), 5 a day, 0500-1530, US$8.50; quite a few return buses, but if none direct, go to Zaragoza and change buses there. There are many buses to **Zacapoaxtla** with frequent connections for **Cuetzalan**.

Amecameca *p185*
Bus To **Mexico City** with Cristóbal Colón. Los Volcanes 2nd-class bus 1-1½ hrs, US$2.80, to the capital's Terminal del Oriente.

Tlaxcala *p186*
Bus Tlaxcala's bus station is about a 10-min walk from the centre. Frequent **Flecha Azul** buses to **Puebla**, 0600-2130, 45 mins, US$1.50. To **Cacaxtla** US$0.55.

Tehuacán *p187*
Bus ADO bus station on Av Independencia (Pte). Direct to **Mexico City**, hourly service, 5 hrs, US$15-17. To **Puebla**, every 30 mins, 2-2½ hrs, US$7-8. To **Oaxaca**, 1220, 3 hrs, US$19, Autobuses Unidos at 1430 (coming from Mexico City, may be full). To **Veracruz**, 0150, 1345 and 1645, 4½ hrs, US$14, and the Gulf: Autobuses Unidos, 2nd class on Calle 2

Ote with several buses daily to Mexico City and Oaxaca. Local bus to **Huajuapan**, 3 hrs, US$7; from there, frequent buses to Oaxaca.

❶ Directory

Puebla p177, map p178 and p181
Banks Bancomer, 3 Pte 116, changes TCs 0930-1300, good rates. On the Zócalo are Banco Santander Mexicano; Banco Inverlat at Portal Benito Juárez 109, changes money 0900-1400; and a *casa de cambio* at Portal Hidalgo 6 next to Hotel Royalty. On Av Reforma are: **Banamex**, No 135; **Bancomer**, No 113; **HSBC**, across the street. Most banks have ATMs. **Internet** Escuela Sandoval, 5 Ote. Soluciones Alternativas, Calle 4 Norte 7, 101, 1st floor, no sign. At the BUAP University, Av San Claudio esq 22 Sur, T222-244 4404, Mon-Fri 0700-2100, Sat and Sun 0800-1800, 48 PCs, but slow.
Laundry Commercial centre on Av 21 Pte and Calle 5 Sur, US$4 wash and dry, 3 hrs. Another on 9 Norte, between 2 and 4 Pte, US$2.80, good service wash. **Medical**

services Dentist: Dr A Bustos, 2 Pte 105-8, T222-232 4412, excellent, recommended. Doctors: Dr Miguel Benítez Cortázar, 11 Pte 1314, T222-242 0556, US$15 per consultation; Dr Cuauhtémoc Romero López, same address and phone. Hospitals: Beneficiencia Española, 19 Norte 1001, T222-232 0500. Betania, 11 Ote 1826, T222-235 8655. UPAEP, 5 Pte 715, T222-246 6099. The cheapest is Universitario de Puebla, 25 Pte y 13 Sur, T243-1377, where an outpatient consultation is US$5. **Post office** 5 Ote between 16 de Septiembre and 2 Sur, Mon-Fri 0800-2000.

Cholula p183
Banks There is a *casa de cambio* on the corner of the main plaza.

Tlaxcala p186
Internet Café Internet, Independencia 21, south of Av Guerrero. **Laundry** Servi-Klim, Av Juárez, 1½ blocks from plaza, dry cleaners, will launder but at dry-cleaning prices. Lavandería Acuario, Alonsa Escalona 17, between Juárez and Lira y Ortega, 3 kg US$3, self-service 4 kg US$1, daily 0830-2000.

Contents

Footprint features

Border crossings

Baja California

At a glance

⊖ **Getting around** Bus, ferry, boat and 4WD.

◉ **Time required** Two weeks for the major attractions; a month or more for a full exploration.

☼ **Weather** During winter, Oct-Apr, temperatures are generally cool and cloudy in the north; warm and sunny in the south. Summer months, May-Sep, can be blisteringly hot throughout the peninsula.

✖ **When not to go** Most activities – diving, fishing and whale-watching included – are seasonal, so plan accordingly. Do not visit the desert during the summer.

★ **Don't miss ...**

N

50 km
50 miles

Laid-back and sunny with all the airs befitting some close-knit island community, the Baja California Peninsula is a distinct and isolated region of Mexico that is simultaneously touristy and desolate. A long, narrow arm of land flanked by the Pacific Ocean on one side and the Sea of Cortés on the other, this fabled peninsula reaches southward from the US border for 1300 km. A chain of rugged and barely inhabited mountains splits its tapering length, which has an average width of just 80 km.

Baja's northern reaches are renowned for their high-spirited border culture, with the garish pleasure city of Tijuana at its epicentre – a consistent draw for revellers and day-trippers from the north. Here the old clichés ring as true as ever with strip joints, tequila bars and donkeys painted like zebras in abundance. Conversely, the south is famous for its upmarket resorts of Cabo San Lucas and San José del Cabo, home to fine beaches, bars, restaurants and all the amenities you'd expect of well established tourist centres.

But between the tourist hot spots of the far north and south, there is a vast wilderness of untapped potential. Punctuated by empty highways and weird alien landscapes of cacti, vultures and rocks, the interior is popular with free-spirited adventurers who take pleasure in exploring a rambling network of dirt roads and middle-of-nowhere locales. They come to observe whales and dolphins in their natural habitats, explore rugged national parks, discover ancient cave paintings, or merely to enjoy the awe-inspiring and ever-changing desert-scapes. For them, the peninsula, with its hundreds of kilometres of virgin coastline, is a magical place of blue skies, fresh air, solitude and refuge from the rat race north of the border.

Ins and outs

Food and accommodation tend to be more expensive than the rest of Mexico, but cheaper than the US. Tijuana, Ensenada and La Paz have a good range of duty-free shopping. Make a note of departure times of buses in Tijuana or Ensenada when travelling south: between Ensenada and Santa Rosalía it can be difficult to obtain bus information. Don't ask for menus in English if you can help it; prices are often cheaper in the Spanish version. Check change as overcharging is not uncommon. Note that hotels have widely divergent winter and summer rates; between June and November tariffs are normally lower than those given in the text (especially in expensive places). The US dollar is preferred in most places north of La Paz.

Stretching 1704 km from Tijuana to Cabo San Lucas, Highway 1 is generally in good condition, although slightly narrow and lacking hard shoulders. Roads in Baja California Norte are more potholed than those in Baja California Sur. Service stations are placed at adequate intervals along the route, but motorists should fill their tanks at every opportunity and carry spare fuel, particularly if venturing off the main roads. Stations in small towns may not have fuel, or may sell from barrels at inflated prices. The same conditions apply for Highway 5 (Mexicali–San Felipe), Highway 3 (Tecate–Ensenada–San Felipe) and Highway 2 (Tijuana 196, Mexicali–San Luis–Sonoyta). Hitchhiking is not difficult although you may have long waits, and there is very little public transport off the main highway.

Background

Cortés attempted to settle at La Paz in 1534 after one of his expeditions had brought the first Europeans to set foot in Baja, but the land's sterile beauty disguised a chronic lack of food and water; this, and sporadic hostility from local tribes, forced the abandonment of most early attempts at settlement. Jesuit missionary fathers arrived at Loreto in 1697 and founded the first of their 20 missions. The Franciscans and then Dominicans took over when the Jesuits were expelled in 1767. The fathers were devoted and untiring in their efforts to convert the peninsula's ethnic groups, but diseases introduced unknowingly by them and by ships calling along the coasts soon decimated the local population; some indigenous people remain today, but without tribal organization. Scattered about the sierras are the remains of these missions, some beautifully restored, others no more than eroded adobe foundations.

Baja California State

From the US–Mexico border as far as the 28th parallel, the sparsely populated state of Baja California comprises the northern half of the Baja peninsula. Travellers approaching from the USA can make their entrance at various of intriguing border towns, of which Tijuana is the most famous. Alive with all the commercialism and gaudy splendour of the frontier, it is rife with raucous bars, tatty souvenir shops and sleazy strip joints. It does, however, have a more sophisticated side, with a cutting-edge cultural centre. Tamer crossings further east include sedate Tecate and efficient Mexicali.

South of Tijuana, the Pacific seaport of Ensenada is a favourite stop for cruise ships, but also provides access to the burgeoning and increasingly lauded wineries scattered throughout the Valle de Guadalupe. Northeast, San Felipe is a fishing village turned low-key resort perched on the calm waters of the Sea of Cortés. South from Ensenada, the Transpeninsular highway wends through ever desolate landscapes punctuated only by dusty old roadside cafés and ramshackle ranches. It soon climbs into the rugged Sierra de San Pedro Martir, home of Baja's highest peak – Picaco Diablo – before descending into weird desert-scapes filled with rocks, exuberant cacti, sparse isolated communities and random supply centres. On the sea of Cortés, the Bahía de los Angeles, is a particularly alluring, if remote, locale. ▶▶ *For listings, see pages 208-214.*

Border towns ⚫⚫⚫⚫ ▶▶ *pp208-214. Colour map 4, A1.*

San Diego (California)

San Diego, the second largest city in California, is a world apart from its loose Mexican sister to the south, Tijuana (see page 202). This clean, wealthy city boasts excellent beaches, a famous zoo and a thriving downtown area that includes the Gaslamp district – the hub of San Diego's entertainment scene. Arriving in **San Diego International Airport**, bus No 992 stops outside all terminals and continues to the Gaslamp district and the **Greyhound station** ① *120 W Broadway, T619-239 6737, www.greyhound.com*, with many services to Los Angeles. The trolley bus service covering most of the city goes to the border at San Ysidro.

Tecate

The border town of **Tecate** is more like a Mexican city of the interior than a gaudy border town, perhaps because there is no town centre on the US side. It is also uncharacteristically clean, having been spared the heavy air pollution that has so ravaged its neighbours. Drivers heading out of Mexico may want to exit at Tecate; the crossing is calm and straightforward and the ambience decidedly civil. If arriving from the US, bus services to the interior are as frequent as any other major crossing point.

There is some disagreement about the meaning and origin of the town's name, but one popular interpretation is 'clear water' – an indigenous reference to local springs. This fits nicely with the marketers of the locally produced beer, Tecate – one of Mexico's finest brews. Aficionados can visit the world-famous brewery, **Cerveceria Cuautémoc Moctezuma** ① *Arturo Guerra 70, T665-654 9478, www.ccm.com.mx*, where fresh, locally sourced spring water is transformed into golden nectar. Call ahead for a tour.

The **Baja California Secretary of Tourism** ① *opposite the park at Libertad 1305, T665-654 5892, www.tecatebajacalifornia.com.mx*, provides a useful map of the town and other information. English spoken.

Border essentials: Baja California–USA

Note All border crossings between the USA and Mexico currently are under review (mostly due to increased drug and security concerns on the US side). For the latest information contact US Customs and Border Protection, http://apps.cbp.gov/bwt, and Crossing US Borders, http://www.dhs.gov/files/crossingborders/travelers.shtm.

At all borders Mexican authorities will issue and stamp **tourist cards** and process **car permits**. There is a buffer zone for about 120 km south of the border allows US citizens to travel without a tourist card. If you are travelling beyond Baja California, do not forget to go through immigration and customs checks or you will have serious problems at police checks later on. The same applies if you are travelling with a vehicle. In addition to those detailed below, immigration authorities are also encountered at Ensenada, Quitovac (28 km south of Sonoyta, Sonora on Highway 2), and when boarding the ferries to cross the Gulf of California, see box, page 237.

Tijuana–San Diego (California)

US freeways funnelling 12 lanes of traffic into three on the Mexican side means great congestion, particularly at weekends. It is worth considering staying in San Diego for a couple of nights, and popping over the border to orientate yourself, check out bus times and so forth without weighty baggage. A tourist office at the border gives out maps of the area explaining money-changing, buses, etc. The border is open 24 hours.

Leaving Mexico Be prepared for tough immigration procedures.

Leaving USA Due to the sheer volume of people crossing the border, it is very easy to enter Mexico without completing exit and entry formalities. Be sure to get an entry stamp on your tourist card as well as your passport. Pedestrians can get a tourist card from the immigration office just over the bridge (difficult to find; you will have to look around). After completing immigration procedures walk over another pedestrian bridge before you get to Tijuana proper where you're greeted by money changers. From there, it's a short walk to the downtown bus terminal. The main terminal is 5 km southeast of town.

Crossing with a vehicle Follow the right-hand lane marked 'Customs'. You should also be able to obtain your tourist card/vehicle permit at this office, then get a stamp from the vehicle registry office about 100 m south. Officials will ask for copies of your documents, including the vehicle permit. For insurance try **Baja Bound Insurance Services**, 750 11th Av 101, San Diego, T619-702 4292, www.bajabound.com, which also has good information on travelling requirements in Mexico.

Crossing by bicycle Note that cyclists are not allowed on Highway 1-D (the toll road), so head for Highway 1 (*libre*) to Ensenada.

Tijuana–Otay Mesa (California)

A quieter recommended alternative to Tijuana is the Otay Mesa crossing 8 km east of Tijuana, reached from the US side by SR-117. The border is open 0600-2200. Car insurance and vehicle permit facilities are no longer available here. From the Mexican side it is harder to find; continue on the bypass from Highway 1-D to near the airport and the 'Garita de Otay' sign.

Tecate–Tecate (California)

The border is open 0600-2400, but immigration and customs officers will only process vehicle papers 0800-1600; at other hours, continue to Mexicali or Sonoyta. All documents are obtainable at the border. Tourist cards may also be obtained at the bus terminal.

Leaving Mexico Immigration facilities are three blocks north, uphill, from the west side of the parque. Mexican immigration offices, Lázaro Cárdenas and Callejón Madero, T665-654 0280, are on the left.

Leaving USA US immigration facilities are opposite the Mexican offices, above.

Mexicali–Calexico (California)

The border is open 24 hours a day. Southbound flow is generally better than northbound. There is no immigration check on the Mexican side of the border.

Leaving Mexico Pedestrians travelling to Calexico should take the underpass beneath Calzada López Mateos, which passes through the Mexican immigration office before continuing to the US side.

Leaving USA Follow the diagonal Calzada López Mateos, which leads to the tourist office and train and bus stations. Highway 2 runs east from Mexicali through San Luis Río Colorado, Sonoyta and Caborca to join the Pacific Highway at Santa Ana; see page 224.

Algodones–Andrade (California)

The border is open 0600-2000, but motor vehicle documents are only processed Monday to Friday 0800-1500. Car insurance is readily available in Algodones.

Mexicali–Calexico (California) → *Phone code: 686.*

Capital of Baja California, Mexicali is not as geared to tourism as Tijuana and thus retains its busy, business-like border-town flavour. Its name is a fusion of two words 'Mexico' and 'California', hastily assigned after the city mushroomed on the banks of the Río Colorado. Once an important agricultural centre, Mexicali drew various waves of migrant workers during the 19th century, not least Chinese, whose legacy survives in a wealth of restaurants and Mexico's most thriving Chinatown. Today, the maquiladora (assembling and manufacturing) industry plays a more vital role in the city's economy. There is a **Tourism and Convention Bureau** ① *Obregón 1257, local 12 altos Col Nueva, Mon-Fri 0800-1900, www.mexicaliturismo.com*, with the usual flyers and brochures; and a **SECTUR State Tourist Office** ① *Blv Benito Juárez 1, T686-566 1277, Mon-Fri, 0800-1700, Sat-Sun 1000-1500*. The University of Baja California's **Museo Regional** ① *Av Reforma y Calle L, Tue-Fri 0900-1800, weekend 1000-1500, free*, has interesting exhibits illustrating Baja's archaeology, ethnography and missions.

Opposite Mexicali, **Calexico**, the much smaller city on the California side of the border, is so thoroughly Mexicanized that it can be difficult to find a newspaper from San Diego or Los Angeles. Mexican shoppers flock here for clothing bargains. Day visitors may prefer to park on the California side, since the extremely congested Avenida Cristóbal Colón in Mexicali, which parallels the frontier fence, is the access route to the US port of entry.

West of Mexicali, the road to Tijuana is fast and well surfaced, running across barren desert flats with organ-pipe cacti in abundance, below sea level, until reaching the eastern escarpment of the peninsula's spine. It then winds its way up the Cantú Grade to **La Rumorosa**, giving expansive, dramatic vistas of desert and mountain.

South of Mexicali, Highway 5 runs for 193 km to San Felipe, passing the **Cerro Prieto geothermal field** around Km 34. Then, after passing the Río Hardy and the **Laguna Salada** (Km 72, a vast, dry alkali flat sometimes turned into a muddy morass by rare falls of rain), the road runs straight across sandy desert. It enters **San Felipe** around a tall, white, double-arched monument. Floods can cut the road across the Laguna Salada; when it is closed, motorists have to use Highway 3 from Ensenada (see below) to get to San Felipe.
➤➤ *See Transport, page 212.*

Algodones–Andrade (California)

North of San Luis (35 km) is Baja California's last international border crossing point, the farming town of Algodones. The road north from San Luis skirts the Algodones dunes, the longest in North America. Algodones has one hotel and there are several *casas de cambio*. At Andrade, on the California side, the Quechan people from nearby Fort Yuma Reservation operate an RV park and campground.

Tijuana ⊚❺❻❶⚫▲⚫⚫ ➤➤ *pp208-214. Colour map 4, A1.*

→ *Phone code: 664.*

Sitting on the south side of the River Tijuana, 35 million people annually cross the border to Tijuana, fuelling the city's claim to be 'the world's most-visited city'. This is the frontline at which the USA and Mexico face up to each other in pleasure and politics. Often criticized as 'not being the real Mexico', it is nevertheless an historic and impassioned place. It came to prominence with Prohibition in the USA in the 1920s when Hollywood stars and thirsty Americans flocked to the sleazy bars and enterprising nightlife of Tijuana and Mexicali, both at this time little more than large villages. Today, although countless bars still vie for the visitor's dollar, it is the duty-free bargains, dog racing, cheap medicines and inexpensive English-speaking dentists that are the main draw. Modern Tijuana is Mexico's fourth largest city and one of the wealthiest. However, a walk along the *barrio* beside the border (don't go alone) to see the breached fence shows the difference between the developed and developing worlds.

Ins and outs

Getting there It is cheaper to fly south from Tijuana's airport, **Aeropuerto Rodríguez (TIJ)** ① *8 km east of downtown, 17 km (20 mins) from San Diego, CA,* than it is from any US airport. A taxi to the airport from downtown Tijuana costs US$6-7. The **bus station** is 5 km southeast of the centre at the end of Vía Oriente (at La Mesa); take any local bus marked 'Central Camionera' or 'Buena Vista' from Calle 2a. Local buses marked 'La Línea/Centro' go from the bus station to the border. ➤➤ *See Transport, page 213.*

Getting around In the centre, a selection of long-distance buses leave from Calle 2 near Revolución. When taking a taxi in Mexico (unless it is a fixed-price airport service), it is a good idea to agree on a price before travelling (some bargaining may be acceptable).

Tourist information The main **tourist office** ① *Revolución, between calles 3a and 4a, T664-685 2210, www.seetijuana.com, daily 0900-1800,* is in the heart of downtown. There are two other offices; one at the border, and one at the airport. Some of the staff speak English. For information on the state of Baja California, visit the **central tourist office** ① *Calle Juan Ruiz de Alarcón 1572, T664-682 3367, www.discoverbajacalifornia.com, Mon-Fri 0800-2000, Sat-Sun 0900-1300.* During high season, a telephone helpline operates, T078.

Sights

The main drag, **Avenida Revolución**, also known as 'La Revo', runs directly south from the tourist kiosk on the edge of the red-light district. It's home to many boisterous bars, clubs, strip joints, restaurants and souvenir shops (generally open 1000-2100), where hawkers and peddlers will try and rope you into utilising their sometimes lawful, sometimes illicit services. Just off Revolución there is a small but mildly entertaining **Wax Museum** ① *Calle 1 y Madero, daily 1000-1800, US$1.80*, with historical figures and movie stars, but nothing terribly special. East of Revolución, the **Zona Río** flanks the Tijuana river, offering a tamer, more down-to-earth experience of the city. Its bold commercialism, tree-lined boulevards, restaurants and popular night clubs are more reminiscent of North America than Mexico. If, like many visitors to Tijuana, action is indeed what you're after, you can always confess your sins – should you feel burdened – at Tijuana's principal house of worship, the **Catedral of Nuestra Señora de Guadalupe**, at Calle 2.

Centro Cultural Tijuana (CECUT) ① *Paseo de los Héroes y Av Independencia, T664-687 9600, www.cecut.gob.mx, 1000-1900, US$2*. The emblematic **Centro Cultural Tijuana** is the city's premier cultural space – a bold modern structure designed by architects Pedro

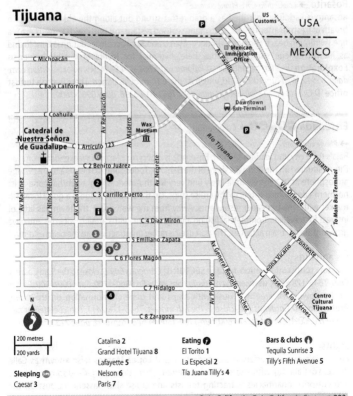

Tijuana

200 metres
200 yards

Sleeping 🛏
Caesar 3

Catalina 2
Grand Hotel Tijuana 8
Lafayette 5
Nelson 6
París 7

Eating 🍴
El Torito 1
La Especial 2
Tía Juana Tilly's 4

Bars & clubs 🍸
Tequila Sunrise 3
Tilly's Fifth Avenue 5

Ramírez Vázquez and Manuel Rosen Morrison. As well as providing a vital platform for local cultural programmes, the centre plays host to the Baja California Orchestra and the Spanish American Guitar Centre. It also contains the excellent **Museo de las Californias**, with displays on local anthropology. Elsewhere in the centre there are handicraft shops, a restaurant, concert hall, and the ultra-modern spherical **Omnimax Cinema** ① T664-684 1111, Mon-Fri 1600-2100, Sat-Sun 1100-2100, US$3.20, where three films are shown on a 180° screen; it is best to sit at the top so you don't have to lean too far back. The architecturally stunning **El Cubo** ① 1000-1900, US$3.20, is a new addition to the complex, opened in 2008. It houses visual art exhibitions.

South of Tijuana

South of Tijuana, a dramatic 106-km toll road (Highway 1-D) leads to Ensenada along Pacific cliffs; the toll is in three sections of US$2 each. There are emergency phones approximately every 2 km on the toll road. This is the safest route between the two cities and 16 exit points allow access to a number of seaside developments and villages along the coast.

Rosarito → Colour map 4, A1. Phone code: 661.

Rosarito is variously described as a drab resort strung out along the old highway, or a breath of fresh air after Tijuana, with many seafood restaurants and curio shops. There is a fine swimming beach and horse riding. In March and April accommodation is hard to find as lots of college students holiday here. Essential for lovers of the big screen is **Foxploration** ① 2 km beyond the La Paloma toll, T661-614 9444, www.foxploration.com, daily, US$12, Wed-Sun 1000-1630, which is where Titanic was filmed. There is also a **tourist office** ① Quinta Plaza Mall, Benito Juárez 96, T661-612 0396, daily 0900-1600.

Ensenada ●●●▲●● » Colour map 4, A1.

→ Phone code: 646.

Baja's third city and leading seaport, Ensenada is a popular place for weekenders from San Diego, situated on the northern shore of the Bahía de Todos Santos. There is a tourist village atmosphere at its centre with a lively and very North American nightclub/bar zone at its northern edge, which caters to the cruise ships. On the harbour fringe is a good local fish market with small, cheaper restaurants. Away from the waterfront, the town has little of interest for travellers. Commercial fishing and agriculture (with canning, wineries and olive growing) are the main activities. The port itself is rather unattractive and the beach is dirty.

Ins and outs

For state tourist information, head to **SECTUR** ① Cárdenas 609-5, close to the Baja Country Club, T646-178 8588, www.enjoyensenada.com, Mon-Fri 0800-1700, Sat 1000-1500. Closer to the downtown area is a kiosk with maps and general information on the town, **Proturismo** ① Cárdenas 540, close to the fish market, T646-178 2411, cotucoe@telnor.net, Mon-Fri 0900-1900, Sat 1000-1800, Sun 1100-1500. » See Transport, page 213.

Sights

Ensenada's principal artery is the pedestrianized **López Mateos** (also known as Calle Primera or Calle 1a), with international restaurants, bars, discos, cigar and souvenir shops and cut-price pharmacies, attracting tourists and cruise-ship passengers. Just off the northern end of the road, housed in a former 19th-century military headquarters and the town jail until 1986, is the **Museo Histórico Regional** ① *Gastelum, 0900-1700, US$2.50 suggested donation*, with an ethnographic collection on Mesoamerican people.

Boulevard Costero Cardénas runs parallel to López Mateos, skirting the seafront with a small waterside *malecón*, port, cruise-ship terminal and the **Plaza Civica** – a landscaped court containing large busts of Juárez, Hidalgo and Carranza. As it continues south, it crosses the Arroyo de Ensenada and arrives at the impressive **Riviera del Pacífico**, formerly a luxurious hotel and casino allegedly built by Al Capone. It now houses a major cultural centre and the **Museo de Historia de Ensenada** ① *0900-1730, donation*, with exhibitions on indigenous peoples and European missionaries.

Ensenada

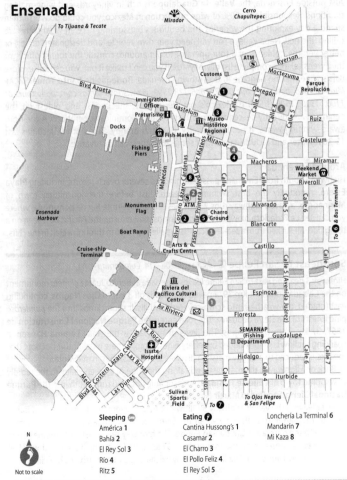

Sleeping 🛏	Eating 🍴	
América **1**	Cantina Hussong's **1**	Lonchería La Terminal **6**
Bahía **2**	Casamar **2**	Mandarín **7**
El Rey Sol **3**	El Charro **3**	Mi Kaza **8**
Río **4**	El Pollo Feliz **4**	
Ritz **5**	El Rey Sol **5**	

N — Not to scale

Ensenada has a weekend **street market** ① *Av Riverol y Calle 7, 0700-1700*, and if you're looking for cheap grub, the **fish market** at the bottom of Avenida Macheros specializes in *tacos de pescado* (fish fingers wrapped in tortilla). *Charreadas* (rodeos) are also held on summer weekends at the **charro ground** ① *Blancarte y Calle 2.*

A splendid view over the city and bay can be had from the road circling the Chapultepec Hills on the western edge of the business district. Steep but paved access is via the western extension of Calle 2a. Note that beyond the touristy downtown area, Ensenada is less Americanized and more authentically Mexican.

Wineries

Just outside Ensenada, the **Valle de Guadalupe** is rich in vineyards and wine-making traditions. Responsible for 90% of wine production in Mexico, you could do worse than spend a day exploring the wineries and boutiques blossoming here, in what some are calling 'the new Napa Valley'. You will need your own vehicle (and designated driver) or better yet, the guidance of a tour operator to get around; consult the tourist office (or their website) for a complete list of vineyards. If you can't make it out, you can still explore Baja's wine-making heritage in downtown Ensenada. **Bodegas de Santo Tomás** ① *Av Miramar 666, between Calle 6 y 7, T646-178 2509, www.santo-tomas.com, daily tours at 1100, 1300, 1500, US$2,* is Mexico's premier winery, the largest and oldest on the peninsula and directly descended from 18th-century Dominican operations. Aside from award-winning wines, it produces sherry, port and brandy. Tours of the facilities last 15-30 minutes and include a tasting of some 26 bottles; call in advance.

Around Ensenada

Highway 1 south from Ensenada passes turnings to several beach resorts, including **Playa Estero**, reportedly the best swimming beach. Just before the agricultural town of **Maneadero**, a paved highway runs 23 km west on to the Punta Banda peninsula, where you can see **La Bufadora** blowhole, one of the most powerful on the Pacific, best seen on a rising tide. Air sucked from a sea-level cave is expelled up to 16 m through a cleft in the cliffs.

Southeast to San Felipe ●❶❷❸ ▸▸ *pp208-214. Colour map 4, A1.*

Highway 3 heading east to San Felipe leaves Ensenada at Benito Juárez *glorieta* monument on the Calzada Cortés. At Km 39, a paved road leads off 3 km to **Ojos Negros**, continuing east (graded, dry weather) into scrub-covered foothills. It soon climbs into the *ponderosa* pine forests of the Sierra de Juárez. The road enters the **Parque Nacional Constitución de 1857**, 37 km from Ojos Negros. The jewel of the park is the small **Laguna Hanson**, a sparkling shallow lake surrounded by Jeffery pines; camping here is delightful, but note that the lake is reduced to a boggy marsh in dry seasons and it snows in midwinter.

Back on Highway 3, the road descends along the edge of a green valley to the rapidly developing town of **Valle de Trinidad**. A reasonable dirt road runs south into the **Parque Nacional Sierra San Pedro Mártir** (see below).

After leaving the valley, Highway 3 follows a canyon covered in dense stands of barrel cacti to the **San Matías Pass** between the Sierras Juárez and San Pedro Mártir, which leads on to the desolate **Valle de San Felipe**. The highway turns east and emerges on to open desert hemmed in by arid mountains; 201 km from Ensenada it joins Highway 5 at the La Trinidad T-junction, 142 km south of Mexicali and 51 km north of San Felipe.

San Felipe → *Colour map 4, A2. Phone code: 686.*

San Felipe is a pleasant, tranquil fishing and shrimping port on the Gulf of California, although at weekends it can become overcrowded and noisy. Long a destination for devoted sport-fishermen and a weekend retreat for North Americans, San Felipe is now experiencing a second discovery, with new trailer parks and the paving of many of the town's sandy streets. Its beaches, overlooking the Sea of Cortéz, are fine and golden. The **tourist office** ① *Mar de Cortés y Manzanillo, opposite Motel El Capitán, T686-577 1865, Mon-Fri 0900-1400 and 1600-1800, Sat 0900-1500 and Sun 1000-1300, www.visitsanfelipe bc.com*, is helpful. **Navy Day** is celebrated on 1 June with a carnival, street dancing and boat races. ▶▶ *See Transport, page 214.*

South from Ensenada: the Carretera Transpeninsular ● ▶▶ *pp208-214.*

→ *Colour map 4, A1.*

Chaparal-clad slopes begin to close in on the highway as it winds its way south, passing through the small town of **Santo Tomás**. Nearby are the ruins of the Dominican Mission of 1791 (local Santo Tomás wine is cheaper out of town). A little north of San Vicente a road heads west to **Eréndira**, a beach resort made popular and accessible by **Coyote Cal's** (see Sleeping, page 210). **San Vicente** comes next, with two Pemex stations, cafés, tyre repairs and several stores. **Colonet**, further south, is a supply centre for surrounding ranches. A dry-weather dirt road runs 12 km west to **San Antonio del Mar**, with many camping spots amid high dunes fronting a beautiful beach renowned for surf fishing and clam-digging.

A reasonable, graded road branches east, 7 km south of Colonet, to San Telmo and climbs into the mountains. At 50 km it reaches the **Meling Ranch** (also called San José), which offers resort accommodation for about 12 guests. About 15 km beyond, the road enters the **Parque Nacional Sierra San Pedro Mártir** and climbs through forests (4WD recommended) to three astronomical observatories perched on the dramatic eastern escarpment of the central range. The view is one of the most extensive in North America: east to the Gulf, west to the Pacific, and southeast to the overwhelming granite mass of the **Picacho del Diablo** (3096 m), Baja's highest peak. Turning west off the main road leads to **Campo 4 Casas** ① *small fee*, a beach resort with good services and surfing.

El Rosario → *Colour map 4, B1.*

After leaving the San Quintín valley the scenery becomes more spectacular, bypassing Santa María (fuel available), the Transpeninsular Highway (officially the Carretera Transpeninsular Benito Juárez) runs along the Pacific before darting inland at Rancho El Consuelo. It climbs over a barren spur from which there are fine views, then drops in a succession of tight curves into **El Rosario**, 58 km from San Quintín. This small, agricultural community has a Pemex station, small supermarket, a basic museum, and meals, including Espinosa's famous lobster *burritos* (expensive and not particularly good) and omelettes.

Central desert of Baja California ❼ ▶▶ *pp208-214.*

Highway 1 makes a sharp 90° turn at El Rosario and begins to climb continuously into the central plateau; gusty winds increase and astonishingly beautiful desert-scapes gradually become populated with many varieties of cacti. Prominent are the stately cardones; most intriguing are the strange, twisted cirios growing to heights of 6-10 m. They are unique to this portion of Baja California and extend as far south as the Vizcaíno Desert, and to a small area of Sonora state on the mainland. At Km 62, a 5-km track branches south to the adobe remains of **Misión San Fernando Velicatá**, the only Franciscan mission in Baja, founded by Padre Serra in 1769. About 26 km north of Cataviña (see below) is the start of a strange region of huge boulders, some as big as houses, interspersed by cacti and crouching elephant trees. This area is one of the most picturesque on the peninsula.

Cataviña → Colour map 4, A2.

Cataviña has a small grocery store/**Café La Enramada** and the only Pemex station on the 227-km stretch from El Rosario to the Bahía de Los Angeles junction (there are in fact two fuel stations, but do not rely on either having supplies). Approximately 2 km north of Cataviña there are some easily accessible **cave paintings** near Km 170 on the Transpeninsular Highway. Highway 1 continues southeast through an arid world of dry salt lakes and boulder-strewn mountains. A new graded road branches off east to Bahía San Luis Gonzaga.

Bahía de los Angeles → Colour map 4, B2.

The side road runs 68 km through cirios and datilillo cactus-landscapes and crosses the Sierra de la Asamblea to Bahía de los Angeles (no public transport but hitchhiking possible), a popular fishing town, which, despite a lack of vegetation, is one of Baja's best-known beauty spots. The bay, sheltered by the forbidding slopes of **Isla Angel de la Guarda** (Baja's largest island), is a haven for boating, although winds can be tricky for kayaks and small craft. There is good clamming and oysters. There are facilities in town and also a modest but interesting **museum**, which provides good background information on the many mines and on mining techniques used in the region around the turn of the 20th century.

There are thousands of dolphins in the bay between June and December. Some stay all year round. There are large colonies of seals and many exotic seabirds. Fishing is excellent. **La Gringa**, a beautiful beach 13 km north of town, charges a small fee for its many camping sites, pit toilets and rubbish bins. The series of tiny beaches at the foot of **Cabañas Díaz** are good for swimming, but watch out for stingrays when wading.

⦿ Baja California State listings

For Sleeping and Eating price codes and other relevant information, see Essentials pages 47-51.

⦿ Sleeping

San Diego (USA)

B-D San Diego Downtown Hostel, 521 Market St, T619-525 1531, www.sandiego hostels.org. A very clean, well-organized hostel in the heart of the San Diego's historic Gaslamp Quarter. Tidy dorms (**D**) and private rooms (**B**), breakfast included. It's a good spot and close to the **Greyhound** station. Discounts for HI members.

Tecate p199

E Frontera, Callejón Madero 131, T665-654 1342. Basic, but clean and friendly (Antonio Moller Ponce, who resides here, knows a lot about the area's history and ethno-history).
E Juárez, Juárez 230. Rooms with or without bath, hot water.

Mexicali p201

C Azteca de Oro, Industria 600, T686-557 1433, www.hotelaztecadeoro.com. A motel opposite the train station and only a few blocks from the bus terminal. Rooms have a/c, TV and phone. Services include a restaurant and bar. A bit scruffy, but convenient.

C De Anza, 233 E 4th St, Calexico, T760-357 7800. A motel on the Calexico side. Excellent value for money.

C Del Norte, Melgar y Av Madero, T686-552 8102, www.hoteldelnorte.com.mx. Big hotel across from the border. Rooms are generic, some have a/c and TV. Pleasant but a little noisy, with free parking for guests and discount coupons for breakfast and dinner. Rates are reduced when booked online.

D Rivera, near the railway station. The best of the cheaper hotels, with a/c.

Algodones p202

E Motel Olímpico. Algodones' only hotel, rather misnamed.

Camping

There is an RV park and campground, run by the Quechan people from the nearby Fort Yuma Reservation, US$12 per site with electricity, US$8 without; including hot showers and access to laundry room.

Tijuana p202, map p203

LL-AL Grand Hotel Tijuana, Blv Agua Caliente 4500, T01-800-026-6007 (toll free in Mexico), www.grandhoteltij.com.mx. A first rate high-rise hotel with 28 floors and a vast number of very comfortable rooms and suites. Amenities include business centre, golf course, pool and tennis court. Check online for discounts and packages.

C Nelson, Av Revolución 721, T664-685 4302. Clean, spacious rooms, some with views of the action below. Very noisy Fri-Sat with crooning Mariachis and discos downstairs. Coffee shop.

D Caesar, Calle 5 y Av Revolución, T664-685 1606. Lots of character, decorated with bullfight posters and at the heart of the action. Rooms have a/c and there's a restaurant. Good.

D Catalina, Calle 5 and Madero, T664-685 9748. Clean. Good standard for Tijuana.

D Lafayette, Av Revolución 325, between Calle 3 and 4, T664-685 3940. Clean, safe straightforward rooms, and right in the centre of things. Wi-Fi and drinking water in the lobby.

E París, Calle 5, No 8181, T664-685 3023. A large, adequate, value-for-money hotel.

Ensenada p204

Some of the larger hotels have different rates for summer and winter; check in advance. All hotels are filled in Ensenada at weekends, so arrive early.

LL-AL Las Rosas Hotel and Spa, 7 km west of town, Highway 1 at Km 105.5, T/F646-174 4310, www.lasrosas.com. Comfortable rooms, suites and casitas with spectacular ocean views. Amenities include pool, sauna, gym, spa and restaurant. Good rates mid-week in the low season (**A**).

L-A Quintas Papagayo, 1½ km north on Highway 1, T646-174 4575, www.hussongs. com.mx. Landscaped beach resort complex with all facilities and Hussong's Pelícano restaurant attached. Comfortable suites, rooms and cottages.

AL El Rey Sol, Av Blancarte 130, T646-178 1601, www.ensenadaexperience.com. Formerly the Ensenada Travelodge, this boutique hotel has pleasant, comfortable rooms and suites, equipped with gadgets and eco-technology. Amenities include spa, jacuzzi, gym, restaurant, pool and parking. Continental breakfast and a free all-you-can-drink 'Welcome Margarita Hour' included.

AL-A Bahía, Blv Costero y Av Alvarado, T646-178 2101, www.hotelbahia.com.mx/ing. Rooms and suites with balconies, a/c and fridges. Quiet, clean, good value and popular, with parking. Free Margarita upon registration and good promotional rates.

D América, López Mateos, T646-176 1333. Good, cosy beds, powerful showers and cable TV. Comfortable and functional.

D Ritz, Av Ruiz y Calle 4, No 379, T646-174 0501. Central location with cable TV, carpet and phone. Straightforward and economical.

E Hostal Sauzal, El Sauzal de Rodríguez, 9½ km before Ensenada, 2½ blocks from the highway up Av L (get off the bus at the traffic light in El Sauzal and walk) T646-174 6381, http://hostelsauzal. tripod.com. Price per person. 4-bed dorms, hot water, storage

lockers, kitchen and a library of books and maps on Baja. A good place to stop, chill, and pick up info before rushing south. María is very friendly and welcoming and will give you the low-down on the latest developments throughout Baja.
E-F Río, Av Miramar 231 y Calle 2. Basic facilities, but the cheapest place to stay in town. Some ultra-cheap rooms have no TV.

Southeast to San Felipe p206
C-D Mike's Sky Rancho, Parque Nacional Sierra San Pedro Mártir, T664-681 5514 (Tijuana), www.totalescape.com/lodge/ads/mikes.html. A working ranch that offers motel-style accommodation, pool, camping and guided trips into the surrounding mountains. Good meals.

San Felipe p207
A Castel, Av Misión de Loreto 148, T686-577 1282. A/c, 2 pools, tennis. Best in town.
B Cortez, Av Mar de Cortés, T686-577 1055, www.sanfelipe.com.mx/business/el_cortez. Beachside esplanade motel with a/c, pool, *palapas* on beach, launching ramp, disco, restaurant. Comfortable, if uninspiring rooms, with cable TV, a/c and ocean views.
B La Trucha Vagabunda, Mar Báltico, near Motel Cortés, T686-577 1333. Also a few RV spaces and Restaurant Alfredo (Italian), seafood, international cuisine.
D El Pescador, Mar de Cortés y Calzada Chetumal, T686-577 1044. A modest but comfortable motel with a/c.

Camping
Many trailer parks and campgrounds in town and on coast to north and south.
El Faro Beach and RV Park, on the bay, 18 km south at Km 14.
La Jolla, Playa de Laura. US$12.
Mar del Sol, Av Misión de Loreto, T686-577 1088. US$18 per site.
Playa Bonita, Golfo de California 784, T686-577 1215, playabonita@aol.com. US$15-25.
Ruben's, Golfo de California 703, T686-577 1442. Nice beach. US$12.

South from Ensenada p207
AL-A Meling Ranch (also called San José), www.melingguestranch.com. Pleasant ranch accommodation for about 12 guests. There's a pool and outdoor activities like birdwatching can be arranged.
B-E Coyote Cal's, Eréndira, T646-154 4080, www.coyotecals.com. Fun international hostel with dorms, rooms, RV and tent sites. Good range of activities available including beaches, surfing, whale watching and hiking.
D El Palomar Motel, Santo Tomás, T/F646-178 8002. Adequate but overpriced rooms, restaurant, bar, general store and gas station, RV park with full hook-ups, campsite with swimming pool, clean and refurbished.
E Campo 4 Casas, Punta San Telmo, T646-165 0010. International hostel. Beach resort with good surfing. Small entry fee.
E Motel El Cammo, Highway 1, south of San Vicente. Rooms without bath, friendly, OK restaurant.

El Rosario p207
D Sinai, Ctra Transpeninsular Km 56.6. Comfortable, very clean, small RV park, friendly owner makes good meals, but beware of overcharging.

Camping
Guillermo's Trailer Park, east of the Plaza and on the beach, T664-650 3209. Flush toilets, showers, restaurant, gift shop, boat ramp and rentals. Restaurant on the main street above the gift shop, well-prepared Mexican food, attractive. Reservations advised at weekends. US$8-12.
Sal y Mauro, 1st gravel road on left before entering town. Friendly campsite.

🍴 Eating

Tecate p199
🍴 **El Passetto**, Libertad 200 near the Parque Hidalgo. Excellent Mexican and Italian specialities.

Tijuana p202, map p203

₸₸₸-₸₸ Tía Juana Tilly's, Av Revolución at Calle 7, T664-685 6024. Excellent food, popular local open-air spot, reasonably priced.

₸₸ El Torito, Av Revolución between Calle 2 and 3. Mexican-diner style, with rock music in the evenings.

₸₸-₸ La Especial, Av Revolución 718, T664-685 6654. Surprisingly authentic Mexican food by Tijuana standards.

Ensenada p204

Plenty of places to choose from down the Blv Costero promenade, or the upper section of Av Lopéz Mateos.

₸₸₸ El Rey Sol, López Mateos 1000 y Blancarte. Award-winning cuisine including Mexican and seafood specialities.

₸₸₸ Mandarín, López Mateos 2127, between Soto and Balboa. Chinese. Elegant surroundings, good food, expensive, considered to be the best *chifa* in Ensenada.

₸₸₸-₸₸ Casamar, Lázaro Cárdenas 987. Popular place serving fine seafood and steaks, including lobster. A lively atmosphere.

₸₸ Cantina Hussong's, Av Ruiz 113. Open 1000-0100. An institution; more of a bar than a restaurant.

₸₸ El Charro, López Mateos 475. Spit-roast chicken, fish tacos, beef fajitas and other fine Mexican fare.

₸₸ El Pollo Feliz, Macheros y Calle 2. Daily 1000-2200. Grilled chicken 'Sinaloa style', fast food.

₸₸ Mi Kaza, Riveroll 87. Low-key, friendly restaurant serving breakfasts, Mexican and international food.

₸ Lonchería La Terminal, opposite bus station. Cheap and filling *comida corrida*, good but basic.

San Felipe p207

₸₸ George's, 336 Av Mar de Cortés. Steaks, seafood and live music. Pleasant, friendly and popular with US residents. Recommended.

₸₸ Green House, Av Mar de Cortés 132 y Calzada Chetumal. Daily 0730-0300. Good food, beef or chicken *fajitas* a speciality, friendly service, cheap breakfasts, 'fish fillet for a fiver'.

₸₸-₸ Las Misiones, Mar del Sol RV park. Small menu, moderately priced, seafood crêpes a speciality, popular with families, good service.

₸ Clam Man's Restaurant, Calzada Chetumal, 2 blocks west of Pemex station. Used to belong to the late, famous Pascual 'The Clam Man'. Oddly decorated, but excellent clams, steamed, fried, barbecued, at budget prices.

Bahía de los Angeles p208

₸₸-₸ Las Hamacas, on north edge of town. Budget café with bay view, slow service, popular for breakfast.

◐ Bars and clubs

Tijuana p202, map p203

Recommended nightclubs include **Flamingos**, south on the old road to Ensenada, and **Chantecler**.

Tequila Sunrise, Av Revolución, between Calle 5 and 6. Balcony bar with great opportunity to get your bearings without being hassled on the street.

Tilly's Fifth Avenue, Revolución y Calle 5, T664-685 9015. Good lively bar.

◯ Shopping

Tijuana p202, map p203

Plaza Río Tijuana Shopping Centre, Paseo de Los Héroes; opposite are the Plaza Fiesta and Plaza del Zapato malls; the latter specializes in footwear. Nearby is the colourful public market. The downtown shopping area is Av Revolución and Av Constitución. Bargaining is expected at smaller shops; and everyone is happy to accept US currency.

▲ Activities and tours

Tijuana *p202, map p203*
Breweries and wineries
Tijuana has always been a drinkers' Mecca, drawing devotees of fermented beverages for nearly 100 years.

Cerveceria Tijuana, Fundadores 2951, T664-638 8662, www.tjbeer.com. Mon-Fri 0800-1730. If you like good beer, visit this award-winning local micro-brewery, where blonde, dark and light Tijuana beers are produced. All are described as having 'a Czech twist' and can be enjoyed in the leisurely surroundings of their European-style tavern; call ahead for tours of the facilities.

LA Cetto, Cañón Johnson 2180, T664-685 3031, Mon-Fri 1000-1200 and 1500-1700. If grapes are more to your tastes, this local winery offers tastings and tours. Again, call in advance.

Bull rings and race tracks
Tijuana's love of a good party is matched only by its devotion to sporting events, especially those where gambling or bravado are involved. The city's historic bull-ring, **Plaza de Toros Monumental**, Playas de Tijuana, www.plazamonumental.com, May-Sep Sun 1600, tickets from US$11 in the *sol* (sun) to US$14 in the *sombra* (shade), is the only one in the world built on the sea shore.

Tijuana's principal race track, the **Hipódromo Agua Caliente**, Blv Agua Caliente, 18 km south of the border, has long ceased to host horse races, but greyhounds run each evening if you fancy a punt.

Charreadas (rodeos) also run at various venues between May and September; ask in the tourist office for details.

Tour operators
Honold's Travel, Av Revolución 828, T664-688 1111. Provides all the standard services and plane ticketing services.

Ensenada *p204*
Language schools
Baja California Language College, east of town towards San Quintín, PO Box 7556, San Diego, CA 92167, USA T1-877-444-2252, www.bajacal.com. Spanish immersion for business executives, teachers, travellers and students.

Sport fishing
Sport fishing is best May-Sep, when you might snag albacore, dorado, yellowtail, tuna, marlin or skipjack.

Sergio's Sport Fishing Center, El Malecón, T646-178 2185, www.sergiosfishing.com. One a few places on the *malecón*. Sergio has a fleet of 8 boats and offers local open-party trips from US$62 per person including fishing licence, reel, bait, hooks and rod. Private charters are also available, starting at US$300 for a basic *panga*. Whale-watching tours also available.

Surfing
You'll have to travel out of Ensenada to find some decent waves. The beach of **San Miguel**, 11 km north, is a very popular spot that's hosted surfing contests and festivals in the past. Otherwise, consider catching a boat to **Isla de Todos Santos**, where legendary swells can reach 5 m.

● Transport

Mexicali *p201*
Air
The airport (MXL), 25 km east, Blv Aviación, has flights to **Chihuahua**, **Ciudad Obregón**, **Guadalajara**, **Hermosillo**, **Mexico City**, **Monterrey** and **Torreón**.

Airline offices AeroMéxico, Pasaje Alamos 1008D, T686-557-2551. **Click and Mexicana**, Obregón 1170, T686-553-5920.

Bus

All buses leave from the central bus station (Camionera Central) on Av Independencia. Buses marked 'Central Camionera' run between the Civic Centre and the bus station. To **Ensenada**, 4 a day, 4 hrs, US$27. To **Guadalajara**, 1 service, 34 hrs, US$100. To **Hermosillo**, regular service, 10 hrs, US$29. To **La Paz**, daily 1630, 24 hrs, US$150. To **Mazatlán**, every 30 mins, 24 hrs, US$75. To **Mexico City**, 1 a day, 40 hrs, US$120. To **San Felipe**, 4 a day, 3 hrs, US$17. To **Tijuana** every 30 mins, 3 hrs, US$20.

To USA Golden State buses to **Los Angeles** (US$44) tickets available at trailer/kiosk across from **Hotel del Norte**, also with services within Mexico. Greyhound from **Los Angeles** to **Calexico** (901 Imperial Av), US$37, 6 hrs. **San Diego** to **Calexico** via **El Centro**, US$27, 3 hrs. Local buses are cheap, about US$0.55.

Tijuana *p202, map p203*
Air

Aeropuerto Rodríguez (TIJ), T664-607 8210, has flights to **Mexico City**, with good connections to regional airports. Also international flights to **Las Vegas**, **Los Angeles** in the USA and **Panama City**. Taxi between airport and centre US$15.

Airline offices Aero California, Plaza Río Tijuana, T664-684 2100. AeroMéxico, Plaza Río Tijuana, T664-683 8444. Click and Mexicana, Diego Rivera 1511, T664-634 6566.

Bus
Local General information is available at the bus station, T664-621 2606. It is possible to get buses to most destinations from Tijuana's **Downtown station**, Calle 2 near Av Revolución, with the office close to the pedestrian bridge. Local buses marked 'La Línea/Centro', go to the **border** from the bus station, every 30 mins until 2300, US$0.50.

Long distance There are local buses to the **Central Camionera**, the main bus station 5 km southeast of the centre at the end of Vía Oriente, from Constitución and Calle 3,

about US$0.50; in a taxi bargain for US$10. There are good facilities including a *casa de cambio*, ATM, pharmacy and a couple of fast-food outlets. Services provided by **Estrella Blanca**, T664-683 5681, **TAP**, T664-621 3903, and **Transportes del Pacífico**, T664-621 2606, for services throughout Mexico. For **Baja California** the main option is **ABC**, T664-621 2424.

All services are hourly unless otherwise stated. To **Culiacán**, 22 hrs, US$65. To **Guadalajara**, 34 hrs, US$92. To **Hermosillo**, 11 hrs, US$40. To **Los Mochis**, 19 hrs, US$55. To **Mazatlán**, 26 hrs, US$72. To **Mexicali**, 2 hrs, US$20. To **Mexico City**, 38 hrs, US$131. To **Sonoyta**, 2½ hrs, US$30.

Heading down the peninsula from north to south, with ABC departures every 30 mins, the options are: **Ensenada**, 1½ hrs, US$10; **El Rosario**, 6½ hrs, US$28; **Guerrero Negro**, 12 hrs, US$59; **Santa Rosalía**, 17 hrs, US$76; **Mulegé** 18 hrs, US$81; **La Paz**, 24 hrs, US$121.

To USA From Tijuana bus terminal Greyhound has buses every hour, US$15, 1 hr 10 mins, to **San Diego** via the Otay Mesa crossing, except after 2200, when it uses the Tijuana crossing; coming from **San Diego** stay on the bus to the main Tijuana terminal, entry stamp given at border (ask driver to get it for you), or at bus station. Long queues for immigration at lunchtime. Walk across La Línea (border) and catch a **Golden State** bus to downtown **Los Angeles**, US$13 (buy ticket inside McDonald's restaurant), 12 a day, or take trolley to downtown **San Diego** and get a **Greyhound**, US$20, or **Amtrak** train, US$25, to **Los Angeles**. Golden State is the cheapest and fastest; its terminal is about 1 km from **Greyhound** terminal in downtown LA, but stops first at **Santa Ana** and elsewhere if requested.

Ensenada *p204*
Bus
The bus terminal is located at Av Riveroll 1075, several blocks north of López Mateos. **Estrella Blanca** operates services to mainland

destinations including: **Guadalajara**, 1000, 35 hrs, US$100; and **Mexico City**, 1000, 40 hrs, US$140. ABC heads south through the peninsula with 1st-class services departing at 1420, 1815 and 2015, subject to change, including: **Guerrero Negro**, 9 hrs, US$49; and **Laz Paz**, 20 hrs, US$112. There are cheaper and more frequent 2nd-class fares also, particularly for journeys under 5 hrs. Transportes ABC and TNS buses run to **San Felipe**, direct, over the mountains, at 0800 and 1800, 3½ hrs, US$17.

Hitchhiking

Hitching is a great way to get around Baja California and is used by many budget travellers. There seems to be a slightly different approach on the peninsula to the 'mainland'. Hitching out of Tijuana would range between pointless and dangerous; Ensenada would be a good starting point if heading south.

San Felipe *p207*
Bus

The bus station is on Mar Báltico near the corner of Calzada Chetumal, in the town centre. Transportes ABC and TNS buses run to **Ensenada**, direct, over the mountains, at 0800 and 1800, 3½ hrs, US$17. To **Mexicali**, 4 a day from 0730, 2 hrs, US$12.

❻ Directory

Mexicali *p201*
Banks All major banks; currency exchange 0900-1330 only. *Casas de cambio* in Calexico give a slightly better rate. There are several

on López Mateos. **Immigration** Mexican Consulate in Calexico, T686-357 3863.

Tijuana *p202, map p203*
Banks Many banks, all dealing in foreign exchange. For Visa TCs, go to **Bancomer**. Better rate than *casas de cambio* but less convenient. Countless *casas de cambio* throughout Tijuana open day and night, most charge a commission (up to 5%), even for cash dollars; ask before changing. **Embassies and consulates** Canada, Germán Gedovius 10411-101, T664-684 0461, tijuana@ canada.org.mx. France, Av del Bosque y Calle Fresno, T664-681 3133. Spain, Av de los Olivos 3401, T664-686 5780. UK, Blv Salinas 1500, Fraccionamiento Aviación, T664-686 5320, www.britishconsulate tijuana.com. US, Tapachula 96, between Agua Caliente racetrack and the Country Club, Mon-Fri 0800-1630, T664-622 7400. **Emergencies** Fire: T135. Police: T134. **Immigration** Mexican Consulate- General, San Diego, CA, 1549 India St, T619-231 8414, portal.sre.gob.mx/sandiego, Mon-Fri 0900-1400, for visas and tourist information. **Internet** Revolución just beyond Calle 3. **Medical services** Red Cross: 132; valid for Tijuana, Rosarito, Ensenada, Tecate, Mexicali and San Luis Río Colorado. **Telephone** Computel, Calle 7 y Av Negrete, metered phones, fax, computer facilities.

Ensenada *p204*
Immigration Beside the shipyard, for tourist entry permits. **Internet** Equinoxio, Blv Lázaro Cárdenas 267 in front of Plaza Marina, T646-179 4646, US$1 per hr, with a mighty fine cappuccino served on the side.

Baja California Sur

The Transpeninsular Highway crosses the state border at the 28th Parallel – marked with a soaring, stylized eagle monument – and enters Baja California Sur. Decidedly more compelling than its northern sibling, Baja Sur offers great opportunities for adventure tourism, gregarious hospitality and stark, otherworldly landscapes. Here, ancient rock paintings lie hidden in the parched landscapes. Old Jesuit missions crumble silently in the fierce desert sun. And each year scores of whales arrive in the coastal lagoons around Guerrero Negro and San Ignacio, drawing so close you can actually touch them.

Elsewhere, at places like Loreto and Mulegé, the ocean waters teem with kaleidoscopic tropical fish, whale sharks and marlin, drawing crowds of divers and sport fishers. City-lovers should head to La Paz, near the southernmost tip of the peninsular, the most alluring – if relatively low-key – urban destination in Baja. But if you're seeking the conveniences of a well-serviced resort, try the party town of Cabo San Lucas, or its arty sister, San José del Cabo. Alternatively, bohemian Todos Santos is a world away from all such commercialism, home to artists, organic farmers and a growing community of moneyed expats. In and around all these major sights, there are an array of possible detours and excursions, from eerie deserts to tranquil bays, desolate national parks to communities dwindling on the edge of the universe. However, you will need your own high-clearance vehicle, preferably 4WD, carrying adequate equipment water and fuel. ▶▶ For listings, see pages 225-238.

◐ Clocks go forward one hour to Mountain time when entering Baja California Sur, but note that Northern Baja observes Pacific Daylight Saving Time from the first Sunday in April to the last Sunday in October; time in both states and California is thus identical during the summer.

Guerrero Negro and around ⊖❶❷❸ ▶▶ pp225-238. Colour map 4, B2.

→ Phone code: 615.

Three kilometres beyond the state line and 4 km west of the highway, Guerrero Negro is the halfway point between the US border and La Paz. For the most part it's a rather unattractive strip town with little to recommend it, but there are fuel stations, banks (**Banamex**, does not change traveller's cheques), a hospital, cafés, shops and an airport. Its name, meaning 'Black Warrior', is believed to have been taken from a US whaling ship that grounded off the coast in the 1850s. Guerrero Negro is the headquarters of **Exportadora de Sal**, the world's largest salt-producing firm, joint-owned by the Mexican government and Mitsibishi corporation. It produces more than seven million tons of salt per annum and is a cause for much concern among environmentalists.

At the far western end of town is the skeleton of a grey whale, a fitting memorial to Guerrero Negro. **Ojo de Liebre** – also known as Scammon's Lagoon, after Captain Charles Scammon, the whaler who discovered it – is a major breeding ground for grey whales. During the 19th century, crowds of bloodthirsty whalers slaughtered the beasts en masse; after driving them to near extinction, they departed to other waters in search of fresh quarry. The lagoon is now protected and the grey whale population is once again healthy and robust. At times, you can hear them breathe as you stand on shore. Now it is whale watching not whale hunting that drives the local economy, and many hotels and agencies in town thrive or die on the backs of the tourists who migrate to the region from mid-December to mid-March. The alternative base for whale-watching tours is San Ignacio 142 km to the east. See box, page 217, and page 814.

Desierto Vizcaíno → *Colour map 4, B2.*

After Guerrero Negro the highway enters the grim and desolate **Vizcaíno Desert**, protected as part of the Vizcaíno Biosphere since 1988. Coastal lagoons, mangroves, dunes and scrubland shelter surprisingly diverse species of animals including antelope, big-horn sheep and more than 200 species of birds including royal eagles, fisher eagles and peregrine falcons. The region derives its name from Sebastian Vizcaíno, a 17th-century Spanish explorer who initiated contact with the indigenous Cochimíes. Continuing south on Highway 1, a gravel road branches off due east for 42 km to El Arco and other abandoned mining areas. The road then crosses the peninsula to **San Francisquito** on its beautiful bay overlooking the Gulf of California (77 km). **Note** A gravel road from Bahía de Los Angeles (135 km) gives easier road access than from El Arco and also opens up untouched stretches of the Gulf Coast.

Vizcaíno Peninsula → *Colour map 4, B2.*

Vizcaíno Peninsula, which thrusts into the Pacific south of Guerrero Negro, is one of the most remote parts of Baja. Although part of the Vizcaíno Desert, the scenery of the peninsula is varied and interesting; isolated fish camps dot the silent coast of beautiful coves and untrodden beaches. A dry-weather road cuts west through the peninsula to **Bahía Tortugas** and the rugged headland of **Punta Eugenia**. It leaves Highway 1, 70 km beyond Guerrero Negro at the Vizcaíno Junction (also called Fundolegal). The new road is paved for 8 km to Ejido Díaz Ordaz. It passes **Rancho San José** (116 km) and the easily missed turn-off to **Malarrimo Beach** (where beach-combing is unparalleled). After a bumpy 50 km is **Bahía Tortugas**, a surprisingly large place considering its remoteness. Two roads leave the Vizcaíno–Bahía Tortuga road for Bahía Asunción, which has the peninsula's only other fuel station. From here there is a coast road south to **Punta Prieta**, **La Bocana** and **Punta Abreojos** (93 km). A lonely road runs for 85 km back to Highway 1, skirting the Sierra Santa Clara before crossing the salt marshes north of Laguna San Ignacio and reaching the main road 26 km before San Ignacio.

San Ignacio ⬤⦿⑦ ›› *pp225-238. Colour map 4, B2.*

→ *Phone code: 615.*

The highway continues southeast and, 20 km from the Vizcaíno Junction, reaches the first of 23 microwave relay towers that follow Highway 1 almost to the cape. They are closed to the public but make excellent landmarks and, in some cases, offer excellent views.

The turn-off right for the oasis town of San Ignacio, marked by a grey whale skeleton, is at San Lino, 143 km from Guerrero Negro. A road of about 3 km (US$2 in a taxi) leads to the small, attractive town of San Ignacio with pastel-coloured buildings and lush palm groves. Located close to a vital natural spring, the Cochimí called San Ignacio 'Kadacaaman' or 'Red Grass River', until Francisco Piccolo 'discovered' it in 1716. The town **mission** was founded by the Jesuit Juan Bautista Luyando in 1728 and completed by Dominican Juan Crisostomo Gómez in 1786. It is constructed of solid volcanic bricks over 1m thick. The interior contains carved wood features, a statue of the mission's founder and several religious oil paintings.

San Ignacio is one of the places along the coast where whale-watching tours (see box opposite and page 814) can be arranged and it's a far more enjoyable place to spend time than Guerrero Negro. The best season for whale watching is January to March.

Whale watching

Each autumn, thousands of California grey whales begin an astonishing 11,000 km journey from the Bering Sea off Alaska to their breeding grounds in the coastal lagoons of Baja California. The longest known migration of any mammal, the whales travel day and night at an average of 5 kph. They cover 120 km per day and complete the journey in three months.

The California grey whales, which weigh 36 tonnes when mature, are protected from hunting and now number 25,000. By contrast, their cousins in the western Pacific are now critically endangered with just 300 remaining. The Atlantic greys were hunted to extinction in the 19th century – a fate the California greys nearly suffered too, when Captain Scammon ravaged the waters around Guerrero Negro.

The first migratory whales arrive off the Baja coast in late December. These are usually pregnant mothers who have come to give birth in the sheltered, shallow waters of the lagoons where predators can't reach them. Others arrive in search of mates. Grey whale courtship is complex, often involving three or four animals. By mid-February to mid-March, most of the grey whales will have arrived in the lagoons. Filled to the capacity with nursing, calving and mating whales, this is the best time to visit. By April, the whales will start to leave, the childless and newly mated first, followed last by nursing mothers. The whales spend the summer off the coasts of Canada and Alaska before the autumn ice signals it's time to make the journey south once again. For details of whale-watching tours, see page 814

Laguna San Ignacio

A 70-km road from San Ignacio leads to Laguna San Ignacio, one of the best whale-viewing sites in Baja; mothers and calves often swim up to nuzzle the boats and allow their noses to be stroked. Whale-watching trips are US$40 per person for 2½ hours, with transport costs of US$130 shared between the number of people travelling. Try **Ecoturismo Kuyima** ⓘ *on the main plaza, T/F615-154 0070, Morelos 23, www.kuyima.com*, who can organize the trip as well as various other excursions, including to local cave paintings. The **Cooperativa Laguna de San Ignacio** ⓘ *Juárez 23, off the Zócalo in San Ignacio*, takes fishermen to the lagoon every day and can sometimes accommodate visitors.

Cave paintings

There are many cave painting sites around San Ignacio; colourful human and animal designs left by Baja's original inhabitants still defy reliable dating or full understanding, but are now believed to be 5000 years old. By law, you need a guide to visit them, as well as permission from the **Instituto de Antropología e Histótia (INAH)**, which has offices in San Ignacio and La Paz. Speak to your chosen guide or tour operator about arranging this. The paintings are now protected as a UNESCO World Heritage Site. Most of them, including those concentrated in the Cañon San Pablo, are reached by a two-day mule trek over tortuous trails. The easiest to get to is **Cueva del Ratón**, a 20-minute walk from the village of San Fransisco de la Sierra. The cave at the **Cuesta del Palmarito**, 5 km east of **Rancho Santa Marta** (50 km northwest of San Ignacio), is filled with designs of humans with uplifted arms, in brown and black, and also relatively easy to reach. Petroglyphs, iron and stone tools, and funerary relics have been found in the mysterious caves scattered throughout the Sierra de San Fransisco. Oscar Fischer, at **Motel La Posada**, arranges excursions, otherwise try **Ecoturismo Kuyima** (see above).

Santa Rosalía ⬤❶❷❸⬤ ▸▸ *pp225-238. Colour map 4, B3.*

→ *Phone code: 615.*

Some 70 km kilometres from San Ignacio is Santa Rosalía, connected to Guaymas by ferry and squeezed into a narrow bottleneck valley running off the harbour. It was built by the French El Boleo Copper Company in the 1880s, laid out in neat rows of wood-frame houses, many with broad verandas that are reminiscent of the Caribbean. There is something weird and intangible about Santa Rosalía, which is neither French nor Mexican in appearance. The Pemex station is conveniently located on the highway, unlike the one at Mulegé (see below), so larger RVs and rigs should fill up here. There is a 24-hour store a couple of hundred metres south. Note that Santa Rosalía's streets are narrow and congested; larger vehicles should park along the highway or in the ferry dock car park.

Sights

Santa Rosalía is rather grotty and shambolic, and there's no reason to hang around very long. Up the hill near the **Hotel Francés**, the dusty old street of shaded verandas is split down the middle by half a dozen rusting old engines. Subject to the fierce elements, their display is both nostalgic and pointless, but still good to see. The small **Museo Histórico Minero de Santa Rosalía** ① *off Calle Francisco next to the Impecsa warehouse, Mon-Fri 0800-1400, US$1.50*, has mining exhibits. The church of **Santa Bárbara** ① *Obregón y Calle 3, a block north of the main plaza*, is built of prefabricated galvanized iron and worth checking out. Originally showcased in the 1889 Universal Exposition of Paris, the structure was designed by Gustav Eiffel as a prototype mission intended to withstand the harsh climate of colonial Africa. After being disassembled, it was purchased by the owners of the local Boleo mines, shipped around the Horn to Baja, then reassembled in Santa Rosalía – much to the delight of resident French miners. Recently, an architectural student from the US, Angela Gardner, has suggested the construction is not by Eiffel but by the House of Duclo, but unfortunately there is no evidence to support the claim (or the original attribution to Eiffel). Also worth visiting is the *panadería* El Boleo, which has been baking and selling fresh bread for over 100 years.

Mulegé ⬤❶▲❸⬤ ▸▸ *pp225-238. Colour map 4, B3.*

→ *Phone code: 615.*

Mulegé, 61 km south of Santa Rosalía, is another oasis community, replete with lush palms and flowers that are reminiscent of the tropics. The town is a tranquil retreat outside of spring break, but also an increasingly popular hideaway for US and Canadian retirees. Ecotourism and outdoor activities are developing in Mulegé, with lovely beaches, good diving, snorkelling and boating in Bahía Concepción, and good kayaking along the teeming Río Mulegé. The old Federal territorial prison, **La Cananea**, has been converted into a museum, complete with local historical artefacts. It became known as the 'prison without doors' because the inmates were allowed out during the day to work in the town. A pleasant walk leads for 3 km out of town to the stony beach with a lighthouse with good views. The tidal lagoons are popular for collecting clams.

Just upstream from the highway bridge on the south side of the river is the **Misión de Santa Rosalía de Mulegé**, founded by the Jesuits in 1705. Above the mission there is a good lookout point over the town and its sea of palm trees. Looking the other way there is a fine view at sunset over the inland mesas. Locals swim at an excellent spot about 500 m inland from the bridge and to the right of the track to the mission. There are tours to cave painting sites, US$40 per person including drinks; a guide is necessary; recommended is Salvador Castro, ask for him at the taxi rank in the plaza.

The Pemex station is in Calle General Martínez, one block before the plaza in the centre; it's not convenient for large vehicles, which also have a one-way system to contend with. But there is another Pemex station 4½ km south of the bridge, on the road out of town towards Loreto, with restaurant and mini-market. There is good free **tourist information** in the town centre, as well as one bank and an ATM. There's nothing else for miles around, so make sure you bring enough cash just in case.

South of Mulegé

Beyond Mulegé the highway runs along the shores of Bahía Concepción for 50 km. This stretch is the most heavily used camping and boating area on the peninsula; the water is beautiful, swimming is safe, camping is excellent and there is varied marine life. **Playa Santispac**, in the cove called **Bahía Coyote**, 23 km south of Mulegé (30 minutes' drive south on the highway) is recommended. There are many small restaurants (such as **Ana's**, which sells water and bakes bread; and **Ray's**, good food, a bit pricey) and *palapas* (shelters) for hire (day or overnight, US$2.50). You can get to Santispac from Mulegé on the La Paz bus (taxi, US$12); it is also quite easy to hitch. Just south of here, in the next cove, at **Playa Concepción**, tents, *palapas* and kayaks can be hired at **Ecomundo** (see Sleeping page 227).

South from El Coyote is **Playa Buenaventura**, which has rooms at **A George's Olé**, *palapas* and three *cabañas* for rent (US$20), as well as an expensive restaurant. From the entrance to the beach at Requesón, veer to the left for **Playa La Perla**, which is secluded.

A new graded dirt road branches off Highway 1 to climb over the towering **Sierra Giganta**, whose desert vistas of flat-topped *mesas* and cardón cacti are straight out of the Wild West. The road begins to deteriorate after the junction (20 km) to San José de Comondú and limps another 37 km into San Isidro after a spectacular drop into the La Purísima Valley. The paved road leads on southwards to La Poza Grande (52 km) and Ciudad Insurgentes (85 km).

Loreto ⊜🅰🛆🅾🅶 ➤ *pp225-238. Colour map 4, C3.*

➔ *Phone code: 613.*

Some 1125 km from Tijuana, Loreto is one of the most historic places in Baja. Here, the Spanish settlement of the peninsula began with Father Juan María Salvatierra's founding of the Misión de Nuestra Señora de Loreto on 25 October 1697. Loreto was also the first capital of the Californias until a hurricane devastated it in 1829. Nestled between the slopes of the Sierra Giganta and the offshore Isla del Carmen, Loreto has recently experienced a tourist revival with fresh foreign investment, resort-style developments and private residences marketed to wealthy North American and Canadian retirees. Fortunately, most of these advances are concentrated away from the downtown area. Loreto's construction boom has also been complemented by a surge in outdoor tourism, with diving and fishing among the main pursuits. Inside the Palacio de Gobierno you'll find the **tourist office** ⓘ *Plaza Civica, T613-135 0411, www.gotoloreto.com, Mon-Fri 0800-1500*, with useful flyers and information on the town and its surroundings.

Sights

On the main plaza, the **Misión de Nuestra Señora de Loreto** is the largest structure in town and perhaps the best restored of all the Baja California mission buildings, in spite of the various natural disasters that have struck it. A sign over the door reads "Head and Mother of the Missions of Lower and Upper California". It has a gilded altar and contains the Virgen de Loreto. Next door, the **museum** ① *Tue-Sun 0900-1300, 1345-1800, US$1.80*, contains exhibitions on local history and culture and is also worth a visit. Just off Loreto's shores lies the **Parque Nacional Bahía de Loreto**, a protected marine park since 1997. It has great diving possibilities and some of best sport fishing in Baja California (see Activities and tours, page 233). Around 8 km south of town, the planned settlement of **Nopoló** is mushrooming into a resort. As a major 1970s FONATUR project that never saw fruition, this stretch of coast lay only partially developed for many years. Today, despite new foreign investment, the project is still only partly complete.

Route south of Loreto

Just south of Loreto a rough road runs 37 km through impressive canyon scenery to the village of **San Javier**, tucked in the bottom of a steep-walled valley; the settlement of some 120 people has only one store but the **Misión de San Javier** is one of the best preserved in North America; it was founded by the Jesuits in 1699 and took 59 years to complete. The thick volcanic walls, Moorish ornamentation and bell tower are most impressive in so rugged and remote a location. Taxis from Loreto can be arranged at roughly US$65 for the day, but hitching is quite possible. The trip is worth the effort.

The highway south of Loreto passes a picturesque stretch of coast. There are three lovely public beaches between Loreto and Puerto Escondido (none has drinking water): **Notrí**, **Juncalito** and **Ligüí** are palm-lined coves, which are a far cry from the bustle of the resort developments nearby. Beyond Ligüí (36 km south of Loreto) Highway 1 ascends the eastern escarpment of the Sierra Giganta (one of the most fascinating legs of Highway 1) before leaving the gulf to strike out southwest across the peninsula again to Ciudad Constitución.

Ciudad Constitución and around → *Colour map 4, C3. Phone code: 613.*

The highway runs past **Ciudad Insurgentes**, a busy agricultural town with two service stations, banks, auto repairs, shops and cafés (no hotels/motels), then runs dead straight for 26 km to **Ciudad Constitución**, which is the marketing centre for the Magdalena Plain agricultural development and has the largest population between Ensenada and La Paz (50,000). It has department stores, restaurants, banks, service stations, car repair shops, a hospital and an airport.

Whales can be seen at **Puerto López Mateos** further north (access from Ciudad Insurgentes or Ciudad Constitución); there's no hotel, but ask for the house of María del Rosario Gonzálezm, who rents rooms, or take a tent and camp at the small harbour near the fish plant. 'Mag Bay' is considered the finest natural harbour between San Francisco and Acapulco.

La Paz ⬤🅿️🅰️⬤🅾️⬤🔺⬤🅾️ » *pp225-238. Colour map 4, C3.*

→ *Phone code: 612.*

Relaxed, cosmopolitan and blessed with spectacular sunsets, La Paz is undoubtedly the finest city on peninsula. Mainlanders and gringos have long sought refuge here, to enjoy the easy pace, high standard of living and 300 days of annual sunshine. Although bursting with new construction, there are still many touches of colonial grace, arched doorways and flower-filled patios. The early afternoon siesta is still observed by many businesses, especially during summer, when the heat can be stifling and water supplies scarce.

Replete with protected islands and islets, La Paz is a growing bastion of ecotourism. You can dive with enormous whale sharks, hammerhead sharks and sea lions, before hiking out in the arid but entrancing surroundings. For more sedate travellers, there are good beaches, and the marinas at the north of town draws scores of boaters and yachtsmen. If you're looking for a challenging way to move on, hang around a while and see if you can get a crewing job with a vessel heading down the coast. La Paz is undoubtedly changing, with prices rising as more tourists arrive to enjoy its winter climate, but the free port status ensures that there are still plenty of bargains.

Ins and outs
Getting there **General Manuel Márquez de León International Airport** ① *11 km southwest of the city centre, just off Highway 1.* Fixed-price taxis run to the centre for about US$25; shared **Transporte Terrestre** *colectivos* cost around US$11 per person. The **ferry terminal** is at Pichilingue, 23 km north of the centre. Buses run to the centre of town but may take a while to fill due to lengthy security checks of passengers arriving at the terminal. Consider taking a taxi for around US$25, or a *colectivo* for US$6 – agree a price before getting in. The **bus terminal** is conveniently located on the waterfront *malecón* in the centre of town. ▶▶ *See Transport, page 236.*

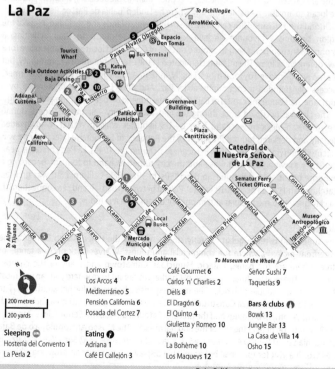

Sleeping		Eating		Café Gourmet 6	Señor Sushi 7
Hostería del Convento 1	Lorimar 3	Adriana 1	Carlos 'n' Charlies 2	Taquerías 9
La Perla 2	Los Arcos 4	Café El Callejón 3	Delís 8	
	Mediterráneo 5		El Dragón 6	**Bars & clubs**
	Pensión California 6		El Quinto 4	Bowk 13
	Posada del Cortez 7		Giulietta y Romeo 10	Jungle Bar 13
			Kiwi 5	La Casa de Villa 14
			La Bohème 10	Osho 15
			Los Maqueys 12	

200 metres
200 yards

Getting around La Paz is easily explored on foot, however, city buses and unmetered taxis are widely available. The main hub of local buses is the Mercado Municipal, Calle Degollado and Revolución.

Tourist information Head to the Palacio Municipal for the **tourist office** ① *16 de Septiembre y Domínguez, T612 125-6844, www.vivalapaz.com, Mon-Fri 0900-1700*, which has helpful staff and a profusion of flyers. In high season there is also an office at the **tourist wharf** ① *at the bottom of 16 de Septiembre, Mon-Fri 0800- 1500, Sat 0900-1300, 1400-1500, open till 1900*, which will make hotel reservations. Staff speak English and can provide tourist literature and town maps. There's a notice board for rides offered, crew wanted, etc. You could also hunt down a copy of the *Gringo Gazette*, www.gringogazette.com, an English-language newspaper with information on La Paz and other expat communities in Baja California Sur.

Background

The first Europeans to arrive in Baja California Sur were a band of mutinous sailors headed by Fortún Jiménez, but most of them met a violent end at the hands of local tribes, the Guaicura and Pericú among them. Cortés himself followed suit, establishing a short-lived colony on the peninsula in 1535. Three years later the colony was abandoned due to logistical challenges and a lack of local resources. Sebastián Vizcaíno was the next to arrive in the area, receiving a far more friendly reception than his predecessor, Jiménez. He found the locals so amiable he named the bay where he landed 'Bahía de Paz' or 'Peace Bay'.

During the 17th and 18th centuries the many caves, islands and secluded inlets of the region became a favourite enclave for pirates. In response to their activities, a reconnaissance ship was sent to explore the Sea of Cortés and locate a suitable place for a new defensive colony. The mission culminated in the establishment of a community, but this too was destroyed by local tribes. Finally, in 1810, a small group of fishers and farmers successfully founded a community at La Paz. And after Loreto was obliterated by a hurricane, it became the capital of Baja California, thriving on pearls, fishing and farming.

The city was occupied twice during the mid-19th century – first by US troops during the American-Mexican war, and later by US filibuster William Walker, who invaded illegally and declared himself President of the Republic of Sonora. He later fled and was executed for trying the same trick in Nicaragua. During the 1940s, La Paz's precious pearl industry was wiped out by disease and the city turned its hand to tourism, becoming a favourite haunt of US celebrities in the 1950s. In 1974, Baja California Sur was granted statehood and La Paz became its capital. Poised between road, air and sea connections, it quickly grew into the popular and important destination it is today.

Sights

The street grid is rectangular; westerly streets run into the Paseo Alvaro Obregón, the waterfront *malecón*, where the commercial and tourist wharves back on to a tangle of streets; here are the banks, **Palacio Municipal**, **Chinatown** and many of the cheaper *pensiones*. The local landmark is **Carlos 'n' Charlies** restaurant from where you can find most things within a couple of blocks. The more expensive hotels are further southwest. The heart of La Paz is the **Plaza Constitución**, a little east of the main tourist area, facing which are the government buildings and the graceful **Catedral de Nuestra Señora de la Paz**, built in 1861-1865 on or near the site of the original mission. The **Museo Antropológico de Baja California Sur** ① *Ignacio Altamirano y 5 de Mayo, Mon-Fri 0800- 1800, Sat 0900-1400, free*, is well worth a visit for the small but admirable display of peninsular anthropology, history and pre-history, folklore and geology. The bookshop has a wide selection on Mexico and Baja. The **Museo de la Ballena** ① *Navarro y Ignacio Altamirano, Tue-Sat 0900-1300, free*, and a carved mural depicting the history of Mexico, can be seen at the **Palacio de Gobierno** ① *Isabel La Católica, corner of Bravo*.

Beaches

There are many beaches around La Paz, the most popular are on the **Pichilingüe Peninsula**. Most have restaurants (there's a good seafood restaurant under a *palapa* at Pichilingüe). Heading north from La Paz to the ferry terminal on Highway 11 you will pass **Palmira**, **Coromuel** (popular with *Paceños* – residents of La Paz), **El Caimancito** (admission fee), and **Tesoro**. Windsurfing and catamaran trips can be arranged. Buses to **Pichilingüe** run 1000-1400 and 1600-1730, US$1.30 from the station at Paseo Alvaro Obregón and Independencia. About 100 m north of the ferry terminal is a public beach. The beaches of **Balandra** ① *palapas US$2*, and **Tecolote** ① *camping free under palapas*, are reached by the road beyond the ferry terminal (paved for some distance beyond this point; some buses on this route run beyond the ferry terminal at weekends). The road ends at a gravel pit at **Playa Cachimba** (good surf fishing), 13 km northeast of Pichilingüe; the north-facing beaches are attractive but can be windy, and there are some sandflies. **El Coyote** (no water or facilities), on the east coast, is reached by a road/track from La Paz running inland along the middle of the peninsula. Southwest of La Paz on the bay are the tranquil, no-surf beaches of **Comitán** and **El Mogote**. In October (at least) and after rain beware of stinging jellyfish in the water.

Around La Paz

There are boat tours from the tourist wharf on the *malecón* around the bay and to nearby islands like **Espíritu Santo**. Travel agencies offer a daily boat tour to **Islas de Los Lobos** (US$40-80 including lunch and snorkelling, six hours) to see pelicans, sea lions, dolphins and, with luck, whales. About 17 km west of La Paz a paved road branches northwest off Highway 1 around the bay leading to the mining village of **San Juan de la Costa**, allowing a closer look at the rugged coastal section of the Sierra de la Giganta. After San Juan (45 km), the road is passable for medium-size vehicles to **Punta Coyote** (90 km), closely following the narrow space between the mountains and the coast with wonderful untouched camping spots. There's a rewarding excursion from Coyote to **San Evaristo** (27 km), a sleepy fishing village on a delightful cove sheltered on the east by Isla San José. The track is steep and in poor condition so a rugged high-clearance vehicles is needed.

State Highway 286 leads southeast out of La Paz 45 km to San Juan de Los Planes. A fair road continues another 15 km to the beautiful **Ensenada de los Muertos**, where there is good fishing, swimming and wild camping. A further 11 km is the headland of **Punta Arena de la Ventana**, with a magnificent view of the sterile slopes of Isla Cerralvo. Six kilometres before Los Planes, a graded road leads to the **Bahía de la Ventana** and the small fishing villages of **La Ventana** and **El Sargento**, with lovely beaches facing Isla Cerralvo.

South of La Paz

South of La Paz, the central mountain spine rises again into the wooded heights of the **Sierra de la Laguna** and bulges out into the 'Cape Region', Baja's most developed tourist area.

Eight kilometres beyond **El Triunfo** is the lovely mountain town and farming centre of **San Antonio** (fuel, groceries, meals), which was founded in 1756 and served briefly as Baja's capital (1828-1830) when Loreto was destroyed. Eight kilometres south of San Antonio was the site of **Santa Ana**, where silver was first discovered in 1748. It was from this vanished village that the viceroy and Padre Junípero Serra planned the expedition to establish the chain of Franciscan missions in Alta California.

Highway 1 climbs sharply from the canyon and winds past a number of ancient mines, through the peaceful orchard-farming town of **San Bartolo** (groceries and meals) and down to the coastal flats around **Los Barriles**. A number of resort hotels are situated near here along the beautiful **Bahía de Palmas** and at nearby **Buena Vista**; none is in the budget class but all are popular.

The highway turns inland after Los Barriles (106 km from La Paz). An 'East Cape Loop' turns east off the highway through La Rivera. A new spur leads towards **Cabo Pulmo**, paralleling the coast to San José del Cabo. Off Cabo Pulmo, a beautiful headland, is the northern Pacific's only living coral reef. This is an excellent area for fishing, diving and snorkelling; enquire locally about renting equipment.

Santiago is a pleasant, historic little town 3 km off Highway 1 (bus stop at junction, two hours from La Paz, US$3.50 in a taxi from the highway). A Pemex station, café and stores are grouped around the town plaza. The Jesuits built their 10th mission in Santiago in 1723 after transferring it from Los Barriles. The town was one of the sites of the uprising of the Pericué people in 1734. There are hot springs (warm), behind a mini-dam, in a pleasant setting, 12 km away along a dirt road at the foot of the mountains. Head towards the village of **Aguascalientes** (8 km) and the hot springs are 4 km beyond this. You can walk on from the spring to a waterfall.

Some 3½ km south of the Santiago turn-off, Highway 1 crosses the **Tropic of Cancer**, marked by a large concrete sphere, and runs south down the fertile valley between the lofty **Sierra de la Laguna** (west) and the **Sierra Santa Clara** (east), to Los Cabos International Airport. San José del Cabo is 14 km further south.

Los Cabos ⊖⊘⊙▲⊙⊙ ⇒ pp225-238. Colour map 1, C1.

San José del Cabo → Phone code: 624.
The largest town south of La Paz and founded in 1730, San José del Cabo is now a modern town divided into two districts: the very Americanized resort sectors and new **Fonatur** development on the beach, and the downtown zone to the north, with the government offices and many businesses grouped near the tranquil **Parque Mijares**. The attractive church on the **Plaza Mijares** was built in 1940 on the final site of the mission of 1730; a tile mosaic over the entrance depicts the murder of Padre Tamaral by rebellious locals in 1734.

Cabo San Lucas → Colour map 1, C1. Phone code: 624.
The resort town of Cabo San Lucas has grown rapidly in recent years from the sleepy fishing village of 1500 inhabitants it was in 1970. It is now an expensive international resort with a permanent population of 8500. The place is full of North Americans who come for the world-famous fishing or to find a retirement paradise.

Ringed by pounding surf, columns of fluted rock enclose **Lover's Beach** (be careful if walking along the beach, as huge waves sweep away several visitors each year), a romantic sandy cove with views out to the seal colonies on offshore islets. At the very tip of the cape is the distinctive natural arch, **El Arco**; boats can be hired to see it close up, but care is required because of the strong currents. At the harbour entrance is a pinnacle of rock, **Pelican Rock**, which is home to vast shoals of tropical fish; it is an ideal place for snorkelling and scuba diving; glass-bottomed boats can be rented at the harbourside.

Todos Santos ☺🚫🅿️⛺🚰❶ ➤ pp225-238. Colour map 1, C1.

➔ **Phone code: 612.**

Highway 9 runs due south through a cactus-covered plain from just after San Pedro to Todos Santos. This quiet farming town just north of the Tropic of Cancer is home to a burgeoning expat community of artists, surfers, celebrities and moneyed retirees. As such, Todos Santos is rapidly changing. Some residents like to think they're a cut above the rest, exuding a quiet smugness over their corner of the world (not to mention their rapidly rising property values). But many visitors may stroll around these dusty little streets and wonder, really, what all the fuss is about. Home to a handful of trendy art galleries and overpriced restaurants, perhaps much of the town's appeal lies in its bohemian airs and sleepy village ambience. This is the place to escape the bustle and crowds at other more developed stretches of Baja's 'Cape Region'. Even if it is slightly snobby, Todos Santos makes a welcome break from all the gloss and commercialism – for now, at least.

West coast beaches

Two kilometres from Todos Santos is a stretch of the Pacific coast with some of the most beautiful beaches of the entire Baja California Peninsula. Nearest to the town is **Playa Punta Lobos,** where the local fishermen shore up (the *pangas* come in early afternoon). It is a popular picnic spot, but with too much rubbish and too many unfriendly dogs for wild camping. Next comes **Playa Las Palmas**, which is good for swimming. Cleaner for camping is the sandy cove at **Playa San Pedrito** (4 km southeast). Backed by groves of Washingtonia fan palms and coconut palms, this is one of the loveliest wild camping spots anywhere; it is also good for surfing. Opposite the access road junction is the **Campo Experimental Forestal**, a botanical garden with a well-labelled array of desert plants from all regions of Baja. Here too is the **Trailer Park San Pedrito** (see Sleeping, page 230), an open area on the beach and one of the most beautifully sited RV parks in Baja California.

Parque Nacional Sierra de la Laguna

In the rugged interior east of Todos Santos is the Parque Nacional Sierra de la Laguna. Its crowning peak is the **Picacho La Laguna** (2163 m), which is beginning to attract a trickle of hikers to its 'lost world' of pine and oak trees, doves and woodpeckers, grassy meadows and luxuriant flowers; there is nothing else like it in Baja. The trail is steep but straightforward; the panoramic view takes in La Paz and both the Gulf and Pacific coasts. It gets cold at night. The park can be reached from Todos Santos; three-day guided pack trips are also offered by the **Todos Santos Inn** (see Sleeping, page 229). Alternatively, take a taxi from Todos Santos to La Burrera, from where it is an eight-hour walk along the littered path to La Laguna.

⊙ Baja California Sur listings

For Sleeping and Eating price codes and other relevant information, see Essentials pages 47-51.

⊜ Sleeping

Guerrero Negro *p215*
A Desert Inn, off Highway 1, just west of the 28th Parallel Monument, T615-157 1304,

www.desertinns.com/GuerreroNegro. A comfortable hotel with pool, dining room, bar and trailer park attached, 60 spaces, full hook-ups, laundry and fuel at hotel.
C Malarrimo, east end of town, T615-157 0100, www.malarrimo.com. The site of a good tour operator that arranges whale-watching tours, **Malarrimo** has a mix of

comfortable family rooms, *cabañas*, standard rooms, an RV park and a good surf 'n' turf restaurant. Very clean and quiet, with TV, fan and Wi-Fi. A good deal overall.

D El Morro, Zapata 5 y División del Norte, on the road into town from the highway, T615-157 0414. Modest, clean with private bath, hot water, cable TV, parking and restaurant.

E Las Dunas, few doors from El Morro, T615-157 0650. Friendly, modest, clean. Rooms have TV and private bath.

E San José, opposite the bus terminal, T615-157 1420. This hotel has 13 clean, rooms, including singles, doubles and triples. Will help to organize whale-watching tours.

San Ignacio *p216*

A Desert Inn, on the road leading into town, T615-154 0300, www.desertinns.com/sanIgnacio. Built in colonial mission style, this comfortable hotel has a pool and all facilities. Attractive but overpriced.

D Motel La Posada, on rise 2 blocks from the Zócalo, ask in town, T615-154 0313. Well maintained, with fans and shower. Best value in town, worth bargaining.

E Chalita, south side of the plaza, T615-154 0082. Cheap and cheerful.

Santa Rosalía *p218*

B Francés, Jean Michel Cousteau 15, up the hill, T615-152 2052. This charming 2-storey French colonial building is a living piece of history; you can visit, but there is a charge. A/c, restaurant, bar, pool and excellent views overlooking the gulf.

D Real, Av Manuel Montoya near Calle 1, T615-152 0068. Rooms at the front are grubby with ancient TV sets, bath and cable. The ones at the back are nicer, and more expensive. Friendly and talkative management.

D-E Blanco y Negro, Calle 3 and Serabia, T615-152 0080. Very basic and ramshackle, but friendly, with or without bath. A few pricier rooms have a/c and TV.

E Olvera, on the plaza at entrance to town, 2nd floor, T615-152 0057. Basic and shabby, with a/c, hot water and TV.

Camping

It's possible to camp on the beach under *palapas*; access is via an unmarked road 500 m south of El Morro. Free, no facilities, a beautiful spot.

Las Palmas, 3 km south of town. Trailer park, 30 spaces, showers, laundry, good value.

San Lucas RV Park, on the beach, San Lucas. No hook-ups, flush toilets, boat ramp, ice available, restaurant, US$6 per vehicle, 75 spaces. Recommended.

Mulegé *p218*

Prices change dramatically between high and low seasons.

AL-A Serenidad, 4 km south of town near the river mouth on beachside road, T615-153 0530, www.hotelserenidad.com. Good views over the gulf and a relaxing away-from-it-all ambience. Rooms, cottages and RV hook-ups.

C Las Casitas, Callejón de los Estudiantes y Av Madero 50, T615-152 3023, www.historicolascasitas.com.mx. A pleasant, older hotel, well run, with shady garden patio, restaurant and bar. Fishing trips arranged.

D Suites Rosita, Av Madero near the main plaza, T615-153 0270. A bit run-down but good value, clean and pleasant, with a/c, kitchenettes and hot water.

D Vieja Hacienda, Madero 3, T615-153 0021, hotelhacienda_mulege@hotmail.com. Refurbished rooms around a lovely courtyard, with pool and bar. Trips to cave paintings offered. Recommended.

E Manuelita's, Moctezuma, T615-153 0175. Simple rooms around a beautiful patio.

E-F Nachita, **Canett** and **Sorpresa**. *Casas de huéspedes* on the road into town. All basic but reasonably clean.

Camping

The Orchard (Huerta Saucedo) RV Park, on river south of town, partly shaded, off Highway 1, T615-153 0300. Pool, free coffee, book exchange, boat ramp, fishing, discount with AAA/AA membership. Recommended.

Villa María Isabel RV Park, on river and highway east of Orchard, T615-153 0246.

Pool, recreation area, disposal station, American-style bakery.

South of Mulegé *p219*

D Ecomundo, Playa Escondida, Bahía Coyote, T615-153 0409, Apdo Area 60, ecomundo@ aol.com (office in Mulegé at Las Casitas hotel). Tents, *palapas* and kayaks can be hired, and there is also a bookshop, gallery, bar and restaurant. Idyllic place to hang out, run by an American couple.

Loreto *p219*

LL-L Posada de Flores, Salvatierra y Madero s/n, T613-135 1162, www.posadadelasflores. com. Very tasteful and attractive colonial-style lodgings with comfortable rooms and suites. All are equipped with a/c, satellite TV, mini-bar and a host of other amenities. Welcome cocktails and continental breakfast included.

AL El Oasis, Baja California y López Mateos s/n, T613-135 0211, www.hoteloasis.com. Comfortable rooms and suites overlooking the Sea of Cortés. Amenities include private beach, parking, Wi-Fi, pool, restaurant, spa and car rental. Pleasant tropical gardens and sports fishing offered.

A Coco Cabañas, Davis 71, T613-135 1729, www.coco-cabanas.com. Comfortable self-contained cottages with a/c and cooking facilities. Pool.

A Desert Inn, on the Sea of Cortés, 2 km north of the Zócalo, T613-135 0025, www.desertinns.com/loreto. A comfortable oceanfront hotel with pool, tennis, golf and fishing boat hire. Considered by many the best of the original 'Presidente' *paradores*. Recommended.

B Plaza Loreto, Paseo Hidalgo 2, T613-135 0280, www.loreto.com/hotelplaza. An attractive, centrally located hotel with comfortable, well-equipped rooms. It also has a travel agency and offers activities such as sports fishing and whale watching.

C Motel El Dorado, Paseo Miguel Hidalgo y Pipila, T613-135 1500, www.motelel dorado.com. Large comfortable rooms with Wi-Fi, cable TV, a/c and comfortable beds.

Services include restaurant and sports fishing charters. Friendly, helpful. Recommended.

D Salvatierra, Salvatierra, on the southern approach into town, T613-135 0021. Motel-style place near the bus station. Clean rooms have a/c, hot showers but poor water pressure, limited cable TV. Good value.

E Posada San Martín, Juárez y Calle Davis 4, 2 blocks from the beach, T613-135 0792. Clean motel with small patio and very friendly owner. The most economical rooms have fan, bath, hot water, cable TV and Wi-Fi. Laundry and parking service (extra), coffee in the morning and breakfast on request. Simple and recommended.

Camping

Ejido Loreto RV Park, on beach 1 km south of town. Full hook-ups, toilets, showers, free coffee, laundry, fishing and boat trips. Butter clams are plentiful in the sand.

Route south of Loreto *p220*
Camping

Tripui Trailer Park, 25 km south of Loreto, T613-133 0818, www.tripui.com. Claimed to be the best in Mexico. Landscaped grounds, paved roads, coin laundry, groceries, restaurant and pool, lit tennis court, playground; 31 spaces, US$15.

Ciudad Constitución and around *p220*

D Casino, Guadalupe Victoria, a block east of the Maribel, Ciudad Constitución, T613-132 0455. Quiet, 36 clean rooms, restaurant, bar.

D Maribel, Guadalupe Victoria and Highway 1, T613-132 0155, 2 blocks south of San Carlos road junction, Ciudad Constitución. Services include a/c, TV, restaurant, bar, suites available, clean, fine for overnight stop.

D-E El Arbolito, Hidalgo, Ciudad Constitución, T613-132 0431. Basic, clean and central.

E Motel Las Brisas, Bahía Magdalena, 1 block behind bus station, T613-136 0152. Clean, friendly, quiet.

E Reforma, Obregón, 2 blocks from the plaza, Ciudad Constitución, T613-132 0988. Basic, with bath. Friendly.

Camping and RV parks

Campestre La Pila, 2½ km south of Ciudad Constitución on unpaved road off Highway 1, T613-132 0562. Farmland setting, full hook-ups, toilets, showers, pool, laundry, groceries, tennis courts, ice, restaurant, bar, no hot water, US$12.

RV Park Manfred, on left of main road going north into Ciudad Constitución, T613-132 1103. Very clean, friendly and helpful, Austrian owner (serves Austrian food). US$13-18.

La Paz *p220, map p221*

AL-A Los Arcos, Alvaro Obregón 498 at Allende, T612-122 2744, www.losarcos.com. Pleasant rooms and *cabañas* with a/c. Amenities include pool, jacuzzi, bar, sauna, massage, laundry and business centre. In the throes of industrial action during the time of research, hopefully now resolved. Good value.

A La Perla, Obregón 1570, on the waterfront, T612-122 0777, www.hotelperlabaja.com. The first hotel in La Paz, founded in 1940, with a wealth of amenities including restaurant, pool, jacuzzi and car rental. Also the site of a popular night club, **La Cabaña**. Rooms are comfortable and cute.

A Mediterráneo, Allende 36, T/F612-125 1195, www.hotelmed.com. Beautiful Greek-style hotel with classic standards as you would expect. Great service, outstanding **La Pazta** restaurant with Greek and Italian dishes. Internet access, café and kayaks.

D Posada del Cortez, Av 16 de Septiembre, T612-122 8240. Clean, basic and slightly tired rooms with TV, hot fan and electric showerheads. Some have a/c, others are quite spacious, so ask to see a few. Free coffee in the morning. Not bad value for La Paz.

D-E Lorimar, Bravo 110, T612-125 3822, lorimar@prodigy.net.mx. Run by a Mexican-American couple, very clean and helpful, and a good place to meet fellow travellers. Standard rooms have good furniture, the cheaper rooms are grubby and lightly crumbling. Wi-Fi in the courtyard.

E Hostería del Convento, Madero 85, T612-122 3508. Friendly enough but pretty

basic, with fans, shower and tepid water between 0700-0900. Cheapest in town and not terribly clean.

E Pensión California, Degollado 209, near Madero, T612-122 2896, pensioncalifornia@ prodigy.net.mx. Described by the owner as a "backpacker paradise", this family-run hotel is certainly cheap. Communal kitchen with fridge, patio, Wi-Fi and hot water. Friendly, noisy and not too clean. Good budget choice.

Camping

El Cardón Trailer Park, 4 km southwest on Highway 1, T613-122 0078. Partly shaded area away from beach, full facilities.

La Paz Trailer Park, 1½ km south of town off Highway 1, access via Calle Colima, T613-122 8787. The nearest RV park to La Paz. Deluxe.

South of La Paz *p223*

C Palomar, by the hot springs, 12 km from Santiago. A/c, hot showers, restaurant, bar, on main street, modest, good meals. Camping in grounds, cold shower and toilets available.

E La Rivera RV Park, La Rivera, in palm grove next to beach. Excellent swimming in the sea, hot showers, laundry facilities, friendly. Recommended.

San José del Cabo *p224*

Several top-quality hotels along the beach front, about 1 km south of town, of varying excellence and seclusion. All are booked as part of resort holidays; some won't even allow passing trade to enter.

LL One & Only Palmilla, 8 km west at Punta Palmilla T624-146 7000, www.oneand onlyresorts.com. One of the top resorts in Baja with outstanding surf nearby. Services include a/c, showers, pool, beach, tennis, restaurant, bar, skin diving, fishing cruisers and skiffs for hire. If you can't afford to stay, come for the daily happy hour to drink margarita and appetizers and see how royalty and film stars live.

LL-AL El Encanto Inn, Calle Morales and Alvaro Obregón, T624-142 0388, www.el encanto inn.com. Easy Mediterranean feel with stylish 'upscale rustic' decor. Amenities include spa facilities, pool and leafy gardens. A good choice.

A Posada Terranova, Degollado between Doblado and Zaragoza, T624-142 0534, www.hterranova.com.mx. Pleasant rooms in a quietly professional atmosphere. There's a fine mid-price restaurant with patio dining.

B Collí, close to the centre, T624-142 0725, hotelcolli@hotmail.com. Some 30 adequate rooms at this family-run hotel, with a/c and cable TV. Parking and Wi-Fi.

C Yuca Inn, Alvaro Obregón 1, just off the main square, T/F624-142 0462, www.yuca inn.com.mx. This ramshackle hotel is home to a sweet and playful pitbull called Lulu. Several options of rooms ranging from basic to quite comfortable. None of them are fantastic, but the small pool, use of kitchen and hammock area make it a good economical choice.

D Brisa del Mar, Highway 1, 3 km southwest of town. Motel with 10 rooms, restaurant, bar, pool, modest but comfortable, behind the trailer park on an outstanding beach.

D Ceci, Zaragoza 22, 1 block west of the plaza, T624-142 0051. A basic budget place with fans, hot showers (occasionally), cable TV and parking. Clean and good value.

D Diana, Zaragoza 30, T624-142 0490. Spacious, windowless rooms with TV, bath, hot water.

D-E Nuevo San José, Alvaro Obregón. A range of economical options. The cheapest rooms have just a bed, hot water and fan. The most expensive have cable TV, bath and a/c.

Camping

Unofficial camping is possible on those few beaches not fronted by resort hotels.
Brisa del Mar Trailer Park, 100 RV sites in fenced area by great beach. Full hook-ups, flush toilets, showers, pool, laundry, restaurant, bar, fishing trips arranged, popular, good location. Recommended. US$18-25.

Cabo San Lucas p224

Cheap accommodation doesn't exist in Cabo.
LL Finisterra, perched on a promontory near Land's End, T624-143 3333, www.finisterra.com.

Upmarket hotel with comfortable rooms. Poolside bar with ocean view. Restaurant, entertainment and sport-fishing cruisers.

L-A Marina, Blv Marina y Guerrero, T624-143 0030, www.loscabosguide.com/hotels/marina1.htm. Pricey, centrally located hotel with comfortable, if slightly generic rooms. A/c, restaurant and bar. Can be noisy.

B Dos Mares, Calle Emiliano Zapata, T624-143 0330, www.loscabosguide.com/hotels/dosmares.htm. Various comfortable units with a/c, telephone and TV. Clean, with a small pool and parking space. Don't get drunk and fall down the stairs – survival unlikely. Recommended.

B Mar de Cortés, Cárdenas y Guerrero, town centre, T1-800-347 8821 (US), www.marde cortez.com. Good value suites and rooms with wooden beams, attractive furniture, a/c and showers. Pool and an outdoor bar.

C San Antonio, Av Morelos between Obregón and Carranza, 3 blocks back from the main street, T624-143 7353. Cheapest option in town, and much better than the rest.

D El Dorado, Morelos, 4 blocks from bus terminal. Clean, with fan, hot water, private bath.

Camping

El Faro Viejo Trailer Park, 1½ km northwest at Matamoros y Morales, T624-143 4211. Shade, laundry, ice, restaurant, bar, clean, out of town but good, US$15.

Todos Santos p225

LL-AL California, formerly the Misión de Todos Santos Inn, Juárez y Morelos, T612-145 0525, www.hotelcaliforniabaja.com. A historic building near the town centre, 1 block north of Highway 9. The interior is very attractive and elegant, adorned with artwork and antiques. Comfortable and popular, with a good restaurant and expensive craft shop.

LL-AL Todos Santos Inn, Calle Legaspi 33, 2 blocks north of the plaza T/F612-145 0040, www.todossantosinn.com. This elegant brick building is a refurbished 19th-century house with lots of character and stylish touches. Very tranquil and worth splashing out on.

D Miramar, south end of the village, T612-145 0341. New, with bath, hot water, fan, pool, clean, safe, parking. Recommended.
D Motel Guluarte. Calle Morelos, T612-145 0006. Spacious, if rather plain, white rooms with blinkered TV sets, hot water and fan. A laundrette is conveniently located downstairs. Comfortable enough, but nothing special.

Camping

El Molino Trailer Park, off highway at south end of town, 30 mins from beach, T612-124 0140. Full hook-ups, flush toilets, showers, laundry, American owner, very helpful, US$8 for 4. No camping here but apparently OK to use the beach (clean, but look out for dogs).

West Coast beaches *p225*
Camping

Trailer Park San Pedrito, several kilometres south of Todos Santos, T612-125 0170. This is a great location on the beach. Full hook-ups, flush toilets, showers, pool, laundry, restaurant, bar, US$13 for RVs.

🍴 Eating

Guerrero Negro *p215*
Ⅲ Malarrimo Restaurant-Bar, east end of town, T615-157 0100, www.malarrimo.com. In hotel of the same name. Good fish and steak menu, moderate prices, music, breakfast.
Ⅲ Mario's Restaurant-Bar, next to El Morro. Modest surroundings and fare, disco.
Ⅰ Taco stall, a few blocks towards town from El Morro. Excellent.

San Ignacio *p216*
Ⅲ-Ⅰ Lonchería Chalita, Zócalo. Excellent value.
Ⅰ Rice'n'Beans, Zócalo. Good, cheap.

Santa Rosalía *p218*
Ⅲ El Muelle, Constitución y Plaza. Nautically themed seafood restaurant.
Ⅲ-Ⅰ Terco's Pollito, Obregón y Playa, opposite Parque Morelos. BBQ chicken, Mexican staples and breakfasts. OK.

Ⅰ Panadería El Boleo, Av Constitución. A Santa Rosalía institution. This bakery was selling bread when the West was Wild.

Mulegé *p218*
A few bars in town offer the full range of tequila.
ⅢⅢ-Ⅲ Patio El Candil, Zaragoza. Simple outdoor dining with good breakfasts.
Ⅲ El Mezquite, Zaragoza. Good burgers and live music.
Ⅲ Equipales, Zaragoza, upstairs. Recommended for good local cooking and for breakfasts.
Ⅲ Jungle Jim, signed turn-off from highway, 2 km south. Rustic, Mexican, friendly.
Ⅲ-Ⅰ Donna Moe's Pizza, Zaragoza, on the corner of Plaza Corona. Pleasant rooftop breakfast patio and bar.

Loreto *p219*
ⅢⅢ 1697, Davis 13, on the plaza. Good Italian food, including pizzas and pastas, but not cheap. Pleasant outdoor seating.
ⅢⅢ Pachamama, Zapata 3, 1700-2200. Very good Argentine cuisine. Cosy and rustic.
ⅢⅢ-Ⅲ La Palapa, Av Hidalgo, ½ a block from the seafront. Great ambience, food and service. Delicious fresh seafood served under a giant *palapa*. Recommended.
ⅢⅢ-Ⅲ Mediteraneo, Malecón, near the corner of Hidalgo. Gourmet Mexican food, a large selection of wine and great views of the sea of Cortez. Downstairs is **Backyard Texas BBQ**.
ⅢⅢ-Ⅲ Mita Gourmet, Davis 11, on the plaza. A pleasant setting by a rock fountain where you can sometimes see hummingbirds taking a drink. A good breakfast spot, with Mexican food at other times.
Ⅲ César's, Zapata y Juárez. Good food and service, candlelit, moderate prices.
Ⅲ-Ⅰ Café Olé, Madero 14. Mexican and fast food, *palapa*-style open-air breakfasts. Order and collect from the counter.

Juice bars
El Cañaveral, just off the plaza and close to the mission. A great juice bar with baskets of fruit outside.

Ciudad Constitución p220
ⓇⓇ **Nuevo Dragón de Oro**, Av Olachea y Esgrima, 5 blocks north of plaza. Chinese.
Ⓡ **Panadería Superpan**, north of the market hall. Bakery selling excellent pastries.

La Paz p220, map p221
ⓇⓇⓇ **La Bohéme**, Esquerro y 16 de Septiembre. French-style place with great ambience, wine list and romantic garden setting. Pastas, pizzas, fish, chicken and salads.
ⓇⓇⓇ **Los Magueys**, Allende y Prieto. Excellent Mexican food and beverages, good tequila and margaritas. Popular and atmospheric.
ⓇⓇⓇ-ⓇⓇ **Carlos 'n' Charlies**, right on the seafront. A popular Mexican staple, good to know where it is, but probably not the best food.
ⓇⓇⓇ-ⓇⓇ **Kiwi**, Obregón y 5 de Mayo, on the seafront, 0800-2400. A mix of Mexican and international dishes, including meat and seafood. Good prices through the day.
ⓇⓇ **Adriana**, Obregón y Constitución, on the beachfront. Candle-lit ambience that's sort of romantic in spite of the plastic chairs. They serve mostly seafood and shrimp, but some meat and chicken too. Live music Tue-Sun, happy hour starts at 1800.
ⓇⓇ **Café El Callejon**, Callejón de la Paz. Offers good burgers, Mexican snacks and seafood. Outdoor seating, internet access and revolutionary photos. Evening music.
ⓇⓇ **El Dragón**, Esquerro 1520 y 16 de Septiembre, 2nd floor. Good, reliable Chinese fare.
ⓇⓇ **Señor Sushi**, Madero and Degollado. Good sushi, eat in or takeaway.
ⓇⓇ-Ⓡ **El Quinto**, Independencia y Belisario Domínguez. Very good vegetarian with lots of wholesome foodstuffs.
Ⓡ **Taquerías**, outside **Pensión California** and **Posada San Miguel**. Superb seafood taco stands.

Cafés and ice cream parlours
Café Gourmet, Esquerro 1520 y 16 de Septiembre, under El Dragón. Sophisticated little coffee house.
Delís, La Paz y Esquerro. Snacks, baguettes, breakfasts, coffee and cakes.

Giulietta y Romeo, Callejón de la Paz. Italian ice cream and outdoor seating on pedestrian street.

San José del Cabo p224
The town is full of tasty options, many of them courting the dollars of holidaymakers over travellers on a budget. For budget options you have to head west of the centre.
ⓇⓇⓇ **Baan Thai**, Morelos and Comonfort, opposite **Encanto Inn**, T624-142 3344. Pricey Thai restaurant with a wonderful atmosphere and quiet patio at the back.
ⓇⓇⓇ **Casa Natalia**, Blv Mijares, in the hotel of the same name. A stylish setting with a chic approach to romance.
ⓇⓇⓇ **El Vaquero**, Juárez 31 and Doblado. This restaurant is almost stately with its high-backed chairs. The menu is certainly aimed at royal wallets, with expensive meat dishes that include 20 oz steaks and slow-roasted prime-rib.
ⓇⓇⓇ-ⓇⓇ **Damiana**, Mijares 8. Gourmet Mexican food served in a converted 18th-century colonial mansion. The candle-lit patio makes for a romantic setting.
ⓇⓇⓇ-ⓇⓇ **La Dolce**, Hidalgo y Zaragoza. Italian restaurant with a pleasant ambience, nice artwork and high wood beam ceilings. Pastas include *fettucine alla romana* and *spaghetti diavola*. Good list of antipastos and pizzas too.
ⓇⓇⓇ-ⓇⓇ **Salsitas**, Obregón y Hidalgo. Closed Tue. Good Mexican food and a well-decorated interior filled with Mexican art. Open for breakfast, lunch and dinner. The *chilaquiles con pollo* are sensational.
ⓇⓇ-Ⓡ **Café La Sirena**, Doblado, behind Hotel Ceci. Pleasant arty little café serving economical breakfasts, lunches and dinners, including Mexican staples. Cute.
ⓇⓇ-Ⓡ **La Choza**, Delgallado s/n, between Zaragoza and Obregón. Open-air joint serving BBQ burgers, grilled fare, and strangely, sushi.

Cafés
Café El Armario, Imperial y Obregón. Open-air café, with plants, parasols and baguettes.

Cabo San Lucas p224

Many expensive but good eateries, particular on the promenade in front of the marina.

♥♥♥-♥♥ The Giggling Marlin, Matamoros and Blv Marina. A landmark and a fine place to experience what makes Cabo San Lucas tick. Good food, reasonable prices and the self-deprecating humour on the walls is refreshing.

♥♥ Flor de Guadalajara, Lázaro Cárdenas, on the way out of town a few blocks beyond 'Skid Row'. Good local dishes.

♥♥-♥ Paty's Garden, Niños Héroes between Zaragoza and Ocampo, T624-143 0689. Authentic atmosphere, with pool table and tasty food. A good budget choice.

Todos Santos p225

♥♥♥ Café Santa Fe, on main plaza. Gourmet Italian food, pricey but very highly rated.

♥♥♥ La Buena Vida, Centenario 40. A beautiful colonial building with wooden beams and exotic lanterns. Great ambience and great pizzas, but expensive for what it is.

♥♥♥-♥♥ Tequila Sunrise, opposite the Hotel California. A colourful spot with graffiti on the walls. Serves dishes such as peppers stuffed with lobster, as well as drinks and snacks to those venturing up from Cabo San Lucas.

♥♥ Miguel's, Degollado y Rangel. Friendly little joint that's famous for its stuffed chillies. Good, but not fine dining.

♥♥ Shut up Frank's, Degollado, opposite Miguel's. US expat hangout serving burgers and snacks. A good place to glug down some cold beers.

Cafés

Cafélix, Juárez 4. Good smoothies, cappuccinos, breakfasts and Wi-Fi, but not cheap, like everything else in Todos Santos.

🜚 Bars and clubs

La Paz p220, map p221

Bowk, Alvaro Obregón y 16 de Septiembre, next to **Jungle Bar**. White-leather lounge space with ultra-violet lighting.

Jungle Bar, Alvaro Obregón y 16 de Septiembre, on the seafront. Open-air bar with big Tvs and wildlife themes, including animal murals and zebra stripes. Popular.

La Casa de Villa, Álvaro Obregón y 16 de Septiembre. A rowdy open-air terrace with drinks specials and big-screen TVs.

Osho, 16 de Septiembre, ½ a block from the *malecón*. Cosy, dimly lit and atmospheric. Doubles up as a sushi bar.

San José del Cabo p224

There are plenty of drinking options, mostly geared towards moneyed foreign travellers. **Baja Brewing Company**, Morelos 1227, between Comonfort y Obregón, next to Baan Thai. Recommended for beer fans. Unique beers brewed on-site, including raspberry lager, cactus wheat brew and oatmeal stout. Also a good international restaurant.

Cabo San Lucas p224

Rays Tequila – The Corner Café, Los Cabos. Does what is says on the tin – a fine chap called Ray serving fine tequila.

✪ Festivals and events

La Paz p220, map p221

Feb/Mar Pre-Lenten Mardi Gras (carnival), inaugurated in 1989, is one of Mexico's finest. The *malecón* is converted into a swirling mass of dancing, games, restaurants and stalls, and the street parade is happy and colourful.

⭘ Shopping

La Paz p220, map p221

A duty-free port. Tourist shops are on the *malecón* between the wharves.

Crafts

Bazar del Sol, Obregón 1665. Quality ceramics and good Aztec art reproductions.

Casa de las Artesanías de BCS, Paseo Alvaro Obregón at Mijares, just north of **Hotel Los Arcos**. Souvenirs from all over Mexico.

Centro de Arte Regional, Chiapas y Encinas, 5 blocks east of Isabel la Católica. Pottery workshop, reasonable prices.

Fortunato Silva, Highway 1 (Abasolo) y Jalisco at south end of town. Good quality woollen and hand-woven cotton garments and articles.

Solco's, Obregón y 16 de Septiembre. Large selection of Taxco silver, leather, onyx chess sets.

General supplies

CCC Supermarket, opposite Palacio de Gobierno. Good for stocking up on food.

Ferretería, across from the main city bus terminal. Hardware store, sells white gas stove fuel (*gasolina blanca*).

La Perla de la Paz, Arreola y 21 de Agosto. Department store; general camping supplies.

Mercado Central, Revolución y Degollado, another at Bravo y Prieto. Wide range of goods (clothes, sandals, guitars, etc), plus fruit and veg.

Todos Santos *p225*

El Tecolote Libros, Calle Juárez y Hidalgo. An excellent bookshop selling good maps, books, book swap and useful local information.

▲ Activities and tours

Mulegé *p218*
Diving

Diving is off Punta Concepción or Isla Santa Inés. The best snorkelling from the shore is just past the point, opposite way up from beach by lighthouse.

Cortez Explorers, Calle Moctezuma 75A, T/F615-153 0500, www.cortez-explorer.com. Mon-Sat 1000-1300, 1600-1900. Friendly, English spoken, US$90 for 2-tank boat dive excluding equipment. US$45 snorkelling from boat with minimum of 3 people. A PADI Gold Palm centre with training up to Dive Master.

Tour operators

There is a small sports fishing fleet operating out of the harbour here. Also hires out quad bikes (must be 16 or over), mountain bikes, horse riding and fishing tours.

Day trips to nearby cave paintings at La Trinidad can be arranged from Mulegé. US$40 pp, slightly less with groups. Salvador Castro, a bilingual tour guide, runs trips to the cave paintings, T/F615-153 0232, or book through **Hotel Las Casitas**.

Loreto *p219*
Diving

Information on scuba diving and snorkelling is available from the booth on the municipal beach near the fishing pier; equipment can also be hired here. The beach stretches for 8 km, but is dusty and rocky. Beware of stingrays.

Cormorant Dive Center, Paseo Miguel Hidalgo s/n, T613-135 1146. A typical 2-tank dive costs US$95, including entrance fees for the Bahía de Loreto national maritime park, cooler, lunch, and all equipment (5-6 hrs). Most trips go to Cormorant Island, where you might see hammerhead sharks (poor visibility in winter). There's also SSI certification, including Open Water and Dive Specialist. Whale-watching tours cost US$110, including box lunch, cooler, drinks and English-speaking naturalist.

Fishing

You can catch dorado, marlin, sailfish, yellowtail, snapper and seabass in the waters around Loreto. Late Mar-early Sep is the best time.

Arturo's Sport Fishing Fleet, Calle Hidalgo s/n, 2 blocks east of the plaza, T613-135 0766, www.arturosport.com. Sports fishing and tours to the islands with a fleet of *pangas* and cruisers. Also offers whale watching, kayaking and trips to the rock paintings.

Baja Big Fish Company, Calle Juárez, T613-135 1603, www.bajabigfish.com. Specializes in fly fishing, light tackle and lure, as well as conventional bait fishing. A standard *panga* for 2 persons costs US$268 per day, including water, marine tickets, tax and fish handling. A *panga* for 4 costs US$354 per day. Additional costs including licence and bait. Fly-fishing equipment is available for hire the company makes its own flies, which are sold all over Baja. The **Baja Big Fish Company** is an International Game Fishing Association weigh station, where various fly-fishing records have been recorded.

Tour operators
Desert & Sea Expeditions, Paseo Miguel Hidalgo s/n, between Colegio and Pino Suárez. A range of 'eco-friendly' packages, including whale-watching and naturalist tours of Cormorant Island. Cultural trips to the rock art and San Javier mission also available.

La Paz p220, map p221
Biking
You can hire a bike and head out on your own, or take a tour. An all-day tour around the mountains visiting local ranches costs US$55; it's worth the effort.
Katun Tours, El Malecón, in Baja Outdoor Adventure office, next to Hotel El Moro, T612-125 5636, www.katuntours.com. Professional mountain bike tours through Baja's arid semi-desert regions.

Diving
Aug-Nov are the best months for diving. During winter, the windy weather ruins visibility. You might see moray eels, hammerhead sharks, whale sharks and sea lions.
Baja Diving and Service, Obregón 1680, T612-122 1826, www.clubcantamar.com. Dive operator that also runs a resort and marina, with accommodation and activity packages. A standard 3-tank dive is US$105. A week-long trip costs US$1600. Also offers whale watching, kayaking and sports fishing.

Sea kayaking
Baja Outdoor Activities, right on the seafront, T612-125 5636, www.kayactivities.com. Run by Ben and Alejandra Gillam. Simple half-day tours or day-trips out to Espíritu Santo Island in the gulf, also whale watching. Prices start at US$45. Excellent.

Cabo San Lucas p224
There's absolutely no shortage of sporting activities, including scuba diving (US$80 for a 2-tank dive), snorkelling (US$45), horse riding (US$65 for 2 hrs), parasailing (US$45) and so on. The latest craze is for personal submarines (US$85 for 30 mins). Plenty of tour operators.

Todos Santos p225
Surfing
Todos Santos surf shop, Rangel y Zaragoza. Board hire at US$10.50 per day, US$5.25 for a body board. Also has a kiosk at Playa Los Cerritos beyond El Pescadero. Hires tents (US$5.50 per day) and mountain bikes (US$10) at the main shop.

⊖ Transport

Guerrero Negro p215
Air The airport (GUB) is 3 km from town, just west of the Transpeninsular highway and the 28th Parallel monument. It's very handy if you want to go to **Hermosillo**; Aeroméxico Connect, Blv Zapata, operates flights. Aerocedros, also on Blv Zapata, has regular flights to **Isla Cedros** and **Ensenada**. You can also fly to **Bahía Tortugas**; information at the airport.

Bus Northbound ABC/Aguila buses depart at 0800, 1100, 1940, 2200 and 0100. Southbound buses pass at 0600, 0900, 1200, 1630, 2100 and 0100. All schedules are subject to change, so it pays to visit the bus station ahead of departure. To **La Paz**, 11 hrs, US$63. To **Mulegé**, 4½ hrs, US$22. To **Santa Rosalía**, 3 hrs, US$17. To **Tijuana**, 11 hrs, US$58.

Santa Rosalía p218
Bus ABC/Autobus Aguila station, T615-152 0150, next to the ferry terminal, is the stop for most Tijuana-La Paz buses, around 5 per day in each direction. To **La Paz**, 1100, US$45. To **Tijuana**, US$76.

Outdoor adventures in Baja California Sur

The potential for outdoor adventures in Baja Sur is vast. Off-roading in awesome desert landscapes, surfing the breaks off La Paz, scaling the sierras, hiking and biking through the hills – these are just a handful of the possibilities. As such, the activities given below are far from exhaustive, but they are the most popular.

Cave paintings The Sierra de San Francisco is home to 500 ancient cave paintings and is a UNESCO World Heritage Site. San Ignacio is a good jumping off point, as is Guerrero Negro and Mulegé. If you can't make it out there, cave tours also run from Loreto and La Paz. Note that many of the sites are remote, requiring a trek of a day or more to reach them. You will also require permission from INAH before visiting, which should be arranged in advance through a registered tour operator. Expect to pay around US$50 for a simple half-day tour.

Diving The best diving is off the shores of Mulegé, Bahía de Concepción, Loreto, Los Cabos and La Paz, where you'll encounter fine coral reefs and rich aquatic life like hammerhead sharks, sea lions and whale sharks. The best visibility is August to November. Expect to pay around US$80 for a 2-tank dive (more in the resorts); PADI certification will set you back at least US$350.

Fishing Sports fishing is spectacular in Baja Sur, particularly off the shores of Loreto, La Paz and Los Cabos. Almost everywhere else shore fishing is possible, as is chartering a boat informally – just talk to a local fishermen about your needs. Expect to pay upwards of US$150 per day for a simple *panga*. If fishing independently be aware that you will require a licence; consult a tourist office for more information.

Sea kayaking A burgeoning scene is developing in La Paz, Loreto and Mulegé, where you can make challenging trips to off-shore islands or simply explore a wealth of sheltered bays and coves. Sea kayaking is also possible in the resorts of Los Cabos, but it is reportedly less spectacular. Expect to pay around US$35 per day for equipment.

Whale watching Laguna de Ojo de Liebre, also known as Scammon's Lagoon, is Baja's most frequented whale-watching destination, accessed from the town of Guerrero Negro. Alternatively, tours to Laguna San Ignacio, another migratory site, depart from the more interesting settlement of San Ignacio. From Ciudad Constitución you can reach Puerto López Mateos and Puerto San Carlos, although these sites tend to be less popular. Whale season lasts late December to early April; expect to pay US$40-60 for a day tour.

Ferry

For ferries to **Guaymas**, see box, page 237. Fares and schedules are subject to change at all times, but particularly during winter, when the Tue sailing is sometimes cancelled. Plan ahead, and remember to check your watch when arriving in Guaymas. Get a vehicle permit from Banjercito bank, if you need one.

Mulegé p218

Air There is an airstrip for private planes beside the currently closed Hotel Vista Hermosa.

Bicycle Bike repairs near Doney's Tacos, 1 block before Casa de la Cultura, on left.

Bus Around 5 buses per day travel in each direction, although rarely to scheduled times. Ask in town as everyone knows when they come through. Allow plenty of time for your journey. The bus stop is on the highway, north of the bridge, at the entrance to town.

Loreto p219

Air The airport is 7 km south of town. Flights to **Ciudad Obregón**, **Guadalajara**, **Hermosillo**, **La Paz** and internationally to **Los Angeles**. Other destinations in high season.

Bus The bus station is at Salvatierra opposite the intersection with Zapata. Several north-bound and southbound buses throughout the day, although often to irregular schedules. To **La Paz**, 6 a day, from 0700, 5 hrs, US$24. To **Tijuana** throughout the day, US$75, 19 hrs. To **Mulegé** with Aguila, 2½ hrs, US$12.

La Paz p220, map p221

Air
General Manuel Márquez de León International Airport (LAP), 11 km southwest on paved road off Highway 1, T612-122 2959. Taxi fare US$20, *colectivo* US$14. Flights to **Chihuahua**, **Ciudad Obregón**, **Culiacán**, **Guadalajara**, **Hermosillo**, **Loreto**, **Los Mochis**, **Mazatlán**, **Mexico City**, **Monterrey**, **Tijuana**. Flights to the USA include **Los Angeles** and **Phoenix**. More charter flights in high season.

Airline offices Aero California, Alvaro Obregón 55, T612-125 4353. **AeroMéxico**, T612-124 6366.

Bicycle
Viajes Palmira, Av Obregón, opposite Hotel los Arcos, T612-122 4030. Rents bikes/mopeds.

Bus
Local Bus journeys cost about US$0.50; the depot is at Revolución de 1910 y Degollado by the Mercado Central. The **Central Camionera** (main bus station) is at Jalisco y Héroes de la Independencia, about 16 blocks from the centre (taxi US$2). However, you can get most buses you need from the promenade **Aguila** terminal on Obregón between Independencia and 5 de Mayo, 1 block up from **Carlos 'n' Charlies**.

Long distance Buses heading for the cape go clockwise or anti-clockwise. Head anti-clockwise if going to **Todo Santos** or **Cabo San Lucas**. Services at 0730, 1030, 1130, 1530 and 1930, 2½ hrs, US$10. Head clockwise if going to **San José del Cabo**. Services at 0800, 1000, 1200, 1430, 1630 and 1830, 3 hrs, US$10. Information T122-7094 ext 111.

For most long-distance journeys you'll need the main terminal. To **Guerrero Negro**, 6 per day, US$63. To **Loreto**, 3 per day, US$25. To **Tijuana**, 1300 and 2000, 22 hrs, US$121. Try to book at least 2 weeks ahead (6 weeks at Christmas, Easter and Jul-Aug).

Car
Budget, Avis, Hertz, Auto Renta Sol and **Auto Servitur** booths at the airport.

Ferry
For the schedule to **Mazatlán** and **Topolobampo**, see box opposite. The modern ferry terminal is at Pichilingüe, 21 km north on paved highway.

Tickets for the same day are sold at the terminal. Advance tickets may be bought at Baja Ferries at I La Católica y Navarro, tollfree on T01-800-337-74337, www.baja ferries.com.mx, and some local travel agents. Also has offices in Los Mochis and several other towns in the area.

In general book in advance whenever possible, especially if travelling by vehicle and your journey time is critical. **Tourist cards** must be valid. Allow 2 hrs as there are long queues when buying tickets and boarding. In the past, many motorists have had difficulty getting reservations or having them honoured. Vehicles must have **car permits**, obtainable at the ferry terminal or at **Registro Federal de Vehículos** in Tijuana; automobile clubs will provide information. Service and conditions on the ferry are improving.

Ferry schedule from Baja California

Schedules are frequently subject to change without notice. Always check locally for the latest timetable.

	La Paz–Topolobampo	Topolobampo–La Paz
Frequency	Daily	Daily
Time	1500	2300
Adult (one way)	US$76	US$76
Child (3-11 years)	US$37	US$37
Cabin (1-4 passengers)	US$54	US$54
Car	US$74	US$74

	La Paz–Mazatlán	Mazatlán–La Paz
Frequency	Mon, Wed, Fri	Tue, Thu, Sat
Time	1700	1700
Adult (one way)	US$85	US$85
Children (3-11 years)	US$42	US$42
Tourist class cabin (4 beds)	US$54	S$54
Junior Suite(2 beds, with bath)	US$64	US$64
Master Suite	US$85	US$85
Car	US$174	US$174

Baja Ferries, www.bajaferries.com, freephone T1-800-337-7437, Mazatlán T669-985 0470, Los Mochis T668-817 3752, Topolobampo, T668-862 1003, La Paz T612 125 7443, San José del Cabo T624-142 4195.

	Santa Rosalía–Guaymas	Guaymas–Santa Rosalía
Frequency	Tue, Wed, Fri, Sun	Mon, Thu, Sat
Time	Tue & Wed, 0900, Fri &Sat 2000	2000
Adult (one way)	US$52	US$52
Children (3-11 years)	US$26	US$26
Cabin	US$53	US$53
Car	US$177	US$177

Santa Rosalía Ferries, T615-152 1246, www.ferrysantarosalia.com.

The bus to **Pichilingüe** leaves from the seafront terminal in La Paz. The terminal has reasonable facilities but is crowded; large car parks, officials may permit RVs to stay overnight while awaiting ferry departures. On all ferry crossings, delays can occur from Sep if there is bad weather. Keep a flexible schedule if travelling to the mainland.

San José del Cabo *p224*

Air To Los Cabos International Airport (SJD), 14 km north of San José del Cabo , take a local bus, US$3, which drops at the entrance road to the airport, leaving a 2-km walk, otherwise take a taxi. A *colectivo* from the airport to San José del Cabo costs US$7. Good regional connections and internationally to the USA.

Airline offices Aero California, T624-146 5252. Aeromexico, T624-146 5097. American Airlines, T624-146 5300. Click and Mexicana, T624-143 5353.

Bus The bus station is on Valerio González Canseco, about 600 m south of the main road into town. To **Cabo San Lucas** with Tres Estrellas, daily from 0700, US$1.25, 30 mins. To **La Paz** daily from 0630, US$10, 3 hrs.

Cabo San Lucas p224
Bus The bus station is at 16 de Septiembre y Zaragoza; central but few facilities. Regular service to **San José del Cabo**, 30-45 mins, US$2. To **La Paz**, 6 a day from 0630, US$10.

Todos Santos p225
Bus
The bus stop is at Heróico Colegio Militar, between Zaragoza and Morelos, a few minutes from the centre. Several buses pass on the La Paz–Cabo San Lucas loop. To **La Paz**, hourly, 2 hrs, US$5.50. To **Cabo San Lucas**, 1 hr, US$4.50.

🚩 Directory

Santa Rosalía p218
Banks Banamex and Bancomer, both with ATMs. **Internet** Centcom, Obregón y Calle 9, with another place just behind the main junction entrance to the town, and at Obregón y Playa. **Laundry** Opposite **Hotel Central**, wash and dry US$2.50 per load. **Post office** Only from here and La Paz can parcels be sent abroad; customs check first, at the boat dock.

Mulegé p218
Banks There are none in town and very few places accept TCs. You can change dollars at most stores. **Laundry** Claudia, Zaragoza y Moctezuma, next to **Hotel Terrazas**, self-service and with good information boards. **Post office** and **police** in the old city hall, 1 block up from Pemex. **Telephone** Mini-supermarket Padilla, Zaragoza, 1 block from Pemex station; also from video store nearby.

Loreto p219
Bank Bancomer on southwest corner of plaza. **Internet** Gigante, estate agent above shoe shop, on Salvatierra. **Laundry** Lavanderia Casa de Lucy, Calle Zenith y Alborada 68.

La Paz p220, map p221
Banks Plenty of banks and ATMs on 16 de Septiembre: Banamex, Arreola y Esquerro. 2 *casas de cambio* on 5 de Mayo off Obregón, 0800-2000, better rates than banks. **Immigration** 2nd floor of the large building on Paseo Alvaro Obregón, opposite the pier, very helpful, able to extend visa here. **Internet** Espacio Don Tomás, Obregón between 5 de Mayo and Constitución. In an art gallery with fine snacks and coffee; and Café el Callejón, Callejón La Paz 51, with restaurant. **Laundry** Laundromat Yoli, 5 de Mayo y Rubio. Also at **Marina de La Paz**; and La Paz Lava, Ocampo y Mutualismo.

San José del Cabo p224
Banks Several *casas de cambio* around town. Bancomer on Zaragoza and BanCrecer, just off the junction of the Transpeninsular Highway and Doblado, have ATMs. **Internet** Several places, many asking silly prices. Try inside Plaza Catedral, Zaragoza, just off main plaza near Hidalgo; or Espacio Café Internet (discounts for students) on the 2nd floor opposite the hospital on Doblado. **Laundry** Lavamática San José, on Valerio Gonzaléz. **Post office** A few blocks from the centre down Blv Mijares.

Cabo San Lucas p224
Banks Plenty of branches with ATMs in town. **Internet and laundry** Kill 2 birds with one stone, log on while doing your washing at the laundromat on Leona Vicario and 20 de Noviembre, 30 mins US$2.40, 1 load wash and dry US$2.40. Cafés on the main drag are pricey. **Post office** Morelos y Niños Héroes.

Todos Santos p225
Banks BanCrecer, with ATM but doesn't change TCs, *casa de cambio* on Colegio Militar with Hidalgo does.

Contents

Footprint features

Border crossings

Pacific Northwest

At a glance

◉ **Getting around** Bus (long
distance), walking or taxis (in town).

◉ **Time required** 2 weeks is ideal,
1 week if heading for the coast only.

☼ **Weather** Temperatures are
hotter here than in most of Mexico,
and along the coast it can be humid.
Nov-Mar is the rainy season for the
north; Jun-Sep further south.
Jan-May are the best months for
a visit.

✖ **When not to go** There is no
bad time if staying on the coast,
although June-Aug inland can be
ferociously hot.

UNITED STATES

MEXICO

SONORA

SONORA

CHIHUAHUA

BAJA
CALIFORNIA
SUR

SINALOA

DURANGO

Gulf of
California

Pacific
Ocean

N

20 km
20 miles

The northwest coast of Mexico is primarily known for its surreal landscapes and vast expanses of almost primeval desert, as well as its other geographic extreme: age-old fishing villages and former missions sprinkled between famous resorts. This region includes the remote Sierra Pinta range and the El Pinacate and Gran Desierto de Altar biosphere reserves, all with awesome scenery and rare ecosystems. It also boasts the longest sand dunes in North America at Algodones, and the beaches and water sports of Puerto Peñasco. You can head south along a beautiful coastal route to explore the Jesuit Missions, enjoy sport fishing at Kino Nuevo, sample 'Old Mexico' in next door Kino Viejo, or participate in fishing tournaments at La Choya and San Carlos. Boat trips run to the islands just off the coast or you can take an overnight ferry to Santa Rosalia or La Paz in Baja California Sur.

Heading south, make a detour to the beautiful colonial town of Alamos, site of the first US-Mexico joint restoration project and home to some of the best-preserved *casonas* (old mansions) in the country. Sample the region's best seafood in Guaymas and the nearby showcase resort of San Carlos. Enjoy the music of the roaming Mariachis in Los Mochis before boarding the famous Copper Canyon train for the journey of a lifetime. The popularity of Mazatlán as a holiday resort is well established.

Travel northeast to Durango and the colonial heartland, or south-east to Tepic, Tequila (where you can visit several of the region's prime distilleries) and Guadalajara, on the way to the beaches further south or inland to Mexico City. From Tepic, take Highway 200 south to visit the mega-resorts of Puerto Vallarta and Manzanillo, or to Acapulco and all the way to the border with Guatemala.

The northernmost parts of the area are desert but fruitful wherever irrigated by water flowing from the mountains. Summers are very hot (this region is the hottest in all of Mexico), sometimes rainy; winters are mild and dry.

Northwest border to Baja California

→ *Colour map 4, A2.*

Route 2 from Tijuana runs close to the border, going through Mexicali (see page 201), San Luis Río Colorado, Sonoyta and Caborca to Santa Ana, where it joins the West Coast Highway (Route 15) by way of Hermosillo and the coast all the way to Mexico City. Route 2 continues eastward to Nogales – a major crossing – and ultimately all the way to Ciudad Juárez. The journey is seemingly endless, and precaution should be taken when crossing the desert, as beautiful as the scenery may be. You can also follow Route 3 eastward from Puerto Peñasco to Caborca, where it meets Route 2, seeing slices of an otherwise vanished Mexico along the way. Almost all smaller roads in the region at some point intersect with one of these major routes. ➜ *For listings, see pages 247-250.*

San Luis Río Colorado–San Luis (Arizona) → *Phone code: 653.*

East of Mexicali the fast four-lane highway crosses the fertile Mexicali Valley to a toll bridge over the much-diminished Colorado River (turn clocks ahead one hour when crossing), and continues to **San Luis Río Colorado**, founded in the 1920s as a military outpost but now a cheerfully tourist-oriented border town in the 'free zone' and primarily known as a regional centre for cotton and wheat. There are summer bullfights and small nightlife districts, like those of the Old West, including a so-called *zona de tolerancia*, best left to those with a taste for risk taking. The town is also the jumping-off point to visit three protected areas: the **Alto Golfo de California y Delta del Río Colorado biosphere reserve** (60 km south), the **Desierto del Altar biosphere reserve** (access by 4WD vehicle only), and the **El Pinacate biosphere reserve** (154 km east, turn after Los Vidrios). While all three are well worth a visit, infrastructure is minimal and none have nearby fuelling stations. About 50 km east of town is **Aquiles Serdán**, noted for its hot springs.

There are several border towns with *zonas de tolerancias*, each with varying degrees of permissibility. Known also as 'boys' towns' or *zona rojas*, these designated areas allow legalized prostitution (and nearly always overlook the other vices that accompany it). Along with that of San Luis Río Colorado, other *zonas* along the border exist in the towns of Tijuana, Ciudad Acuña, Agua Prieta, Piedras Negras, Ciudad Juaréz, Ojinaga, Sabinas Hidalgo, Nuevo Laredo, and Reynosa. All the *zonas*, and especially those in Tijuana and Ciudad Juárez, should be considered extremely dangerous and avoided.

Desierto de Altar

After leaving San Luis Río Colorado, Route 2 crosses the sandy wastes of the Desierto de Altar – Mexico's own mini-Sahara – for 358 km, until the tiny hamlet of **San Luisito**. The desert, home to the largest dunes in the western hemisphere, was used to train US astronauts during the lunar missions. One look at the landscape and it's easy to see why. The road is very narrow in places – watch out for overloaded Mexican trucks. For 144 km there are no facilities (fuel at Los Vidrios), only a few houses and an enveloping landscape of sand dunes, cinder cones and a dark lava flow from the **Cerro del Pinacate** (locally known as **Volcán Santa Clara**). The area around the central range is protected by the **El Pinacate biosphere reserve**. A gravel road 10 km east of Los Vidrios gives access to the northern sector of the park, which contains much wildlife, including puma, deer, antelope, wild boar, gila monster, wild sheep, quail and red-tailed eagle. The reserve's most impressive crater is **El Elegante**, 1 km wide and 120 m deep. Cerro el Pinacate (1190 m) offers amazing views but is a several-hour hike from the park's closest road.

Border essentials: northwest Mexico–USA

Note All border crossings between the USA and Mexico currently are under review (mostly due to increased drug and security concerns on the US side). For the latest information contact US Customs and Border Protection, http://apps.cbp.gov/bwt, and Crossing US Borders, http://www.dhs.gov/files/crossingborders/travelers.shtm.

San Luis Río Colorado–San Luis (Arizona)
The Puente Colorado crossing in San Luis Río Colorado is a popular 24-hour border, with most northbound traffic headed to Yuma (Arizona), 37 km northeast. A second crossing between San Luis Río Colorado and San Luis, due to be completed in 2010, will be solely for commercial vehicles in order to reduce air pollution caused by idling diesel trucks.

Sonoyta–Lukeville (Arizona)
Crossing the border at Sonoyta is not guaranteed although it is officially open 0600-2400. It closes promptly at midnight so if you are attempting a late crossing be prepared to spend the night. Queues are shortest 0600-0900 and 1600-2400. Increased weekend and holiday traffic from Rocky Point and Bahia Kino can cause major delays.

Altar–El Sásabe (Arizona)
The border is open 0800-2000 for non-commercial traffic, but there is no public transport or Mexican car insurance agency on either side. For information on road conditions, phone US customs, T602-823 4231 or see www.az511.gov/hcrsweb/sonora.jsp.

Nogales–Nogales (Arizona)
This is the most popular crossing along this stretch and the border is open 24 hours. There's no checkpoint on the Mexican side although the customs area is sometimes staffed. After you cross into Mexico, walk straight ahead for about 50 m until you get to the immigration office (on your right) where you can pick up a tourist card (FMT) and get it stamped. For transport to/from the border, see page 249.
Crossing with a vehicle Motorists are advised to use the truck crossing (0600-2000) to avoid congestion. It is reached by the Mariposa Avenida exit from Interstate 19, 4 km north of Nogales, Arizona. From Mexico to the USA, follow the sign to the 'Periférico', which avoids the downtown area. Car documents can be obtained at the Mexican customs post 21 km south of Nogales, on Highway 15 to Santa Ana, along with US insurance. There is a tourist office and *casa de cambio*. You need to have title to the car (as you can't drive someone else's car into Mexico), two photocopies of vehicle registration, driver's licence, insurance, credit card and visitor permit (approved). You can buy insurance at **Seguros Tepeyac**, www.mapfretepeyac.com.mx, in the immigration building.

Agua Prieta–Douglas (Arizona)
Winter Arizona time is the same as Agua Prieta time but during summer Agua Prieta is one hour ahead. Mexican immigration and customs are on the right as you cross the border. Pick up your FMT (tourist card) here and car documents and insurance. If you walk straight ahead you'll cross a street, with buses running to Agua Prieta bus station. Take buses east, marked '13-20', 'Ejidal' or 'P Nuevo'. Taxis cost US$3 to the bus station (10 minutes).

The not-so-impassable Sonoran Desert

The border-straddling Sonoran Desert (311,000 sq km) does not rank as one of the world's largest deserts; within Mexico itself the Chihuahuan Desert is bigger. Yet there is no spot along the US–Mexico frontier as formidable, forbidding (or as desirable for crossing) as this blazingly hot, trackless, waterless wasteland. It has just three international crossings, separated by hundreds of kilometres of relentlessly unforgiving terrain. Each year some 30,000 migrants – many from Central and South America – attempt to cross illegally somewhere along the porous border, often with horrific consequences. Death from exposure is an ever-present threat, as is abandonment by *polleros* or *coyotes* (traffickers promising safe transport to the United States). The vast majority of those who do make it are immediately sent back.

The appeal of this empty quarter has increased as the US border patrol has become more vigilant in the more populous areas. As more routes are closed, the flow of migrants has been squeezed towards the scarcely patrolled Sonoran Desert, where those hoping to cross often wait for days in isolation, awaiting a guide to take them north.

Despite the overwhelming odds against them, so many attempt the crossing each year that that an entire cottage industry has grown up around transient activity. Ranches and farms have been abandoned as their owners have turned to providing cheap housing and meals for those headed north, while once-unknown border towns like Altar and El Sásabe are experiencing heady economic growth from the trade. Human rights groups, the Mexican and US governments, and the Catholic church have come together in a joint effort to provide food and water, legal advice and medical treatment for those who attempt this notoriously dangerous crossing. Perhaps most disconcerting, however, is the rise in popularity of one-way cell phones: for those lost in the Sonoran, one call for help can spell the difference between life or death.

Sonoyta–Lukeville (Arizona) → *Colour map 4, A2.*

After a hot and monotonous 205 km from San Luis de Colorado, Route 2 reaches the sun-bleached border town of **Sonoyta**, a short distance from Lukeville (Arizona). Sonoyta has little of interest itself, but there are several American-style hotels. Arizona's picturesque **Organ Pipe Cactus National Monument**, is just across the border from Sonoyta; the **visitor centre** ① *T520-387 6849, www.nps.gov/orpi, US$12 (US$8 visitor permit valid for 7 days)*, has camping and RV hook-ups at the **Twin Peaks** campground. ►► *See border box, page 243.*

From Sonoyta, Highway 8 goes southwest through 100 km of sand dunes; outside of San Luisito at Km 80, a sign, 'Dunas – 10 km' points along a sandy road (4WD essential) that leads to dramatic, desolate inland dunes through mountain-rimmed black lava fields. Contiguous dunes in this area, devoid of all vegetation, actually form one enormous dune – technically known as an erg. This is the only erg in the Americas.

Puerto Peñasco → *Colour map 4, A2. Phone code: 638.*

Once upon a time, Puerto Peñasco was no more than a middle-of-nowhere fishing village. It has blossomed in recent years to become an overpriced resort replete with high-rise condos and luxury hotels. As with much of the Pacific coast, the pace of development has been astonishing. Visitors usually fall into two widely divergent categories: beach-starved Arizonans and young gringos out to exploit lax liquor laws (expect a healthy array of beer-drenched, North American-style bars – some tackier than others); and retirees and 'snow birds' from further north seeking to escape the US and Canadian winters. As a result, the town has an unsightly blend of resort hotels cheek and jowl with RV parks and campgrounds, many overlooking the beautiful, desert-backed beaches – the best of which are **La Choya** and **Las Conchas** to the west of town (see Sleeping, page 247).

Fishing (especially for marlin sole, and yellowtail) diving and sailing are possible popular and best arranged at the old port. Watersports, such as surfing, snorkelling, windsurfing and jet skiing, are also immensely popular.

The **Centro Intercultural de Estudios de Desiertos y Océanos (CEDO)** ① *Las Conchas residential zone (stop at guardhouse at property entrance), T638-382 0113, www.cedointer cultural.org, Mon-Sat 0900-1700*, has a wealth of information on local wildlife (rapidly diminishing thanks to unsympathetic construction projects). It runs excellent, informative tours of the region's natural highlights, including to El Pinacate biosphere reserve.

Caborca and around → *Colour map 4, A3. Phone code: 637.*
Route 2 runs from Sonoyta to Caborca (153 km), passing through a number of small towns (San Emeterio, San Luisito, Tajitos) and more mountainous but still arid land. A few kilometres south of San Emeterio there is a customs and immigration station near the gold mine centre of **Quitovac** (28 km south of Sonoyta). The paved State Highway 37 continues southeast, roughly following the rail line to Caborca (180 km) – an alternative to the inland Highway 2 route.

Caborca lies on the Mexicali–Benjamín Hill railway in the midst of a gently sloping plain. Caborca's restored church of **Nuestra Señora de la Concepción** (1693) was one of the 25 missions founded by the legendary Jesuit missionary and explorer Padre Kino in Sonora and Arizona 1687-1711. Caborca is the best base for exploring the Kino Missions (although they can also be accessed from Hermosillo to the south). Caborca also holds the distinction of being one of a handful of Mexican towns to successfully defend itself against an armed attack by US ranchers in 1857, for which it was granted the title 'Heroica' (heroic) by the Mexican government. Since then, tempers have cooled and Caborca is considered a sister city to Prescott (Arizona). On 6 April, a large celebration is held in honour of this bilateral friendship. Remarkably, this small town has an outstanding website with detailed information on just about anything happening in the area, www.vivacaborca.com.

The lovely little town of **Pitiquito** lies 12 km east of Caborca on Route 2. It has a splendid mission church, **San Diego de Pitiquito**, founded by Padre Kino in 1689, as well as a small but highly regarded leather goods *artesanía* (crafts store), **Pieles Petic** ① *2 blocks behind the church on Hidalgo 25, T637-371 0016.*

Altar–El Sásabe (Arizona) → *Colour map 4, A3.*
Highway 2 continues east through Altar (café, gas station) to join Highway 15 at Santa Ana, a small town of little note but a popular stopping point. The **Fiesta de Santa Ana** is held 17-26 July, with horse racing and fireworks. Its Franciscan mission church is worth a visit. Occasionally indigenous Yaqui can be seen in the main square selling a range of traditional handicrafts.

Keep an eye out for semi-wild longhorn cattle along the road to El Sásabe – a former ranching town turned migrant way stop. Outside the town itself (which is now almost wholly given over to illegal crossings) there is no infrastructure, and the oppressive heat and terrain of the area make it very dangerous. Make sure you take extra water and have a Mexican-enabled cellular telephone when making this trip. ›› *See border box, page 243.*

Back on Route 15, 100 km from Nogales and 17 km from Magdalena de Kino, is **Santa Ana**, where the road enters from Tijuana and Mexicali. There are three petrol stops and a pair of RV camps on the right heading out of town (see Sleeping, page 247).

Nogales → *Colour map 4, A3.*

Much like other border towns, Nogales is a scruffy, unattractive place with little to offer the casual visitor. Still, as border towns go it's not terribly unpleasant, safer than most, and makes a good place to rest before venturing further into Mexico's interior or travelling north to Tucson along US Highway 19. The town lies astride a mountain pass at 1120 m across from Nogales, Arizona, and is the largest settlement in the Pimería Alta, the area of southern Arizona and northern Sonora occupied by the Pima people at the arrival of the Spaniards. The **tourist office** ① *just past the immigration office at the border*, has friendly and helpful staff and a number of brochures. The **Pimería Alta Historical Society** ① *a block from the border in Nogales, Arizona, T(520) 287-4621, Mon-Fri 0900-1700, Sat 1000-1600, Sun 1300-1600, free*, has excellent exhibits on the history of the region, a valuable library and archives, and also organizes tours to the Sonoran missions.

Day trippers can cross the border at Deconcini Gate and take advantage of the shopping arcades, which are within walking distance from the car parks on the US side.
›› *See border box, page 243, and Transport, page 249.*

Cananea → *Colour map 4, A3. Phone code: 645.*

From Ímuris, Route 2 heads east (to Naco and Agua Prieta) through the scenic Sierra los Ajos to the historic and still important copper mining centre of Cananea, founded in 1760. This was the site of a 1906 miners' strike against the American-owned Cananea Consolidated Copper Company, one of the critical events in the last years of the Porfirio Díaz dictatorship. Hundreds of Arizona Rangers crossed the border to join the Sonora militia in putting down the strike, killing 19 Mexican workers, which is commemorated at the former city jail, now the **Museo de La Lucha Obrera** (Museum of the Workers' Struggle) ① *Av Juárez y Tercera Oeste, daily 0900-1900, T645-332 0387, US$0.20.* The Cananea Consolidated Copper Company was founded in 1899 by William Cornell Greene, a wealthy rancher and copper baron from Wisconsin who Mexicans consider the founder of the town. The nearby **Museo Mexicana de Cananea** (Museum of Cacanea) ① *Av Obregón y Octava Este, Mon-Sat 0800-1800, free*, is worth a quick visit for those interested in the area's culture.

The border town of **Naco** is adjacent to its Arizona namesake and a short distance south of the historic, picturesque copper mining town of Bisbee.

Agua Prieta–Douglas (Arizona) → *Colour map 1, A1. Phone code: 633.*

The border area of Agua Prieta–Douglas is growing rapidly with the proliferation of maquiladoras on both sides of the border. On the Douglas side, the **Chamber of Commerce** ① *1125 Pan American, T633-364 2477*, has good information on Mexico as well as Arizona, with a wealth of maps (including Agua Prieta) and brochures.

From Agua Prieta, it is 162 km east to Janos, via Route 2. The road crosses the scenic Sierra San Luis, covered by dense oak-juniper woodland, to the continental divide (elevation 1820 m) at **Puerto San Luis**, the border between the states of Sonora and Chihuahua. There are outstanding views of the sprawling rangelands. Southbound motorists from the US must present their papers to Mexican customs at **La Joya**, a lonely outpost 70 km northwest of Janos. ›› *See border box, page 243.*

For Sleeping and Eating price codes and other relevant information, see Essentials pages 47-51.

● Sleeping

Puerto Peñasco *p244*

Accommodation is no longer cheap in Puerto Peñasco and you'll be hard pressed to find a room for under US$30. Prices can double or triple on weekends, during high season, spring break, Christmas and Semana Santa.

LL-AL Viña del Mar, 1 de Junio y Blv Malecón Kino, T638-383 3600, www.vinadelmarhotel.com. Swanky, modern resort with attractive rooms, cliff-side jacuzzi, video-disco.

A Best Western Playa Inn, Sinaloa 18, T638-383 5015. Nice pool, out of town and overlooking beach.

A Motel Peñasco, Encinas, between Calle 14 and Calle 15, T638-383 3101. The best 'budget' motel in town. Rooms are large with bath, a/c and cable TV. Friendly.

B Plaza Peñasco, Sinaloa b/w Mier y Terán, T638-383 5550. Pool, friendly atmosphere, close to downtown and beaches.

B Posada La Roca, Primero de Junio 2, old port, T638-383 3199. The oldest building in the port, where Al Capone used to hang out. Rooms are slightly pokey, but it's a friendly, interesting place.

B-C Laos Mar, Paseo Balboa 90, T638-383 4700. Just a few metres behind Playa Bonita; this is the most economical option in its range, highly recommended.

C Paraíso del Desierto, Av Constitución y Simón Morua, T638-383 2175. Cheap but noisy; ask for room away from courtyard.

Camping

You'll find many more RV parks fronting the beach on Matamoros.

Playa Bonita Resort and RV Park, Av Paseo Balboa 100, T638-383 2596. 300 spaces by lovely Playa Bonita. There's a restaurant, shop and laundry. US$20-25. Nice view, but thefts are common.

Playa de Oro Trailer Resort, 2 km east, Matamoros 36, T638-383 2668, www.playa deoro-rv.com. 200 sites with laundry and boat ramp. US$21-27.

Caborca *p245*

C Casa Blanca Hotel, Blv Aviacion 280 y Ctra Internacional Mexico (Route 2), T637-372 4119, www.casablancacaborca.com. A/c, cable TV and Wi-Fi in all 28 rooms. RV hookups. Friendly staff. Rivals El Camino for top honours.

C Motel El Camino, Av Quiroz y Mora Norte 165, T637-204 6600. The best in town. Rooms have a/c, TV and private baths. Restaurant.

C-D Motel Papagos, Adalberto Sotelo y Ctra Internacional Mexico (Route 2), T637-372 0766, www.motelpapagos.com. Clean, a/c rooms with cable TV, restaurant.

C-D Plaza, Av Quiroz y Mora Sur 33, T637-372 5095. Probably the best lodgings in town, centrally located on the main square and safe, with secure parking.

D Posada del Desierto, Av Quiroz y Mora Sur, T637-372 0596. Across the street from Hotel Plaza, but inferior in everything except price. No a/c, so ask for room with fan.

Altar *p245*

Altar has become a very popular way stop for those wishing to cross the border on foot. There are now a great number of nondescript, and usually illegal, overnight lodgings along the border offering minimal security and amenities. All should be avoided.

C Motel San Francisco, off Plaza Principal in town centre, T641-324 1380. Rooms have a/c, shower and baths. Also has a restaurant.

Santa Ana

Mi Casa RV Camp, Ctra Internacional Km 165, T641-321 0090. 20 hook-ups, US$12/night.

Punta Vista RV Camp, Ctra Internacional, Km 166 (just north of Mi Casa), T641-324 0769. 7 hook-ups, tents allowed. The owners are friendly and well known throughout the RV community of Sonora. US$12/night.

Camping

Canadian-Mexican trailer park, south of town, on the right going south. A rustic spot for 9-10 trailers. A useful overnight stop.

Nogales p246

There is a wide selection of cheap hotels on Juárez, a 1-block extension of Av López Mateos between Campillo and the border, 2 blocks from the Mexican port of entry.
A-B Plaza de Nogales, Alvaro Obregon 4190, T631-314 1510, www.plazanogales.com. Restaurant, room service, outdoor pool, tennis courts, clean throughout. Nogales' top hotel.
B Hacienda del Real, Av Industrial 26, T631-314 3130. Decent restaurant with good breakfasts. All rooms have private garages. Friendly, well secured, recently remodelled.
B Miami, Campillo y Ingenieros, T631-312 5450. Friendly hotel with a good restaurant attached. Recommended.
B Olivia, Obregón 125, T631-312 4695, holivia@prodigy.net.mx. Rooms have a/c and TV. Also has a popular restaurant attached.
C Fray Marco de Niza, Campillo 91, T631-312 1651, www.hotelfraymarcosdeniza.com. Excellent restaurant, central location, otherwise nondescript building.

Cananea p246
Naco

D Motel Colonial The only formal accommodation, often full, but the manager may tolerate a night's auto camping within the motel compound.

Agua Prieta p246

A Motel La Hacienda, Calle Primera and Av 6, T633-338 0621, a few blocks from the border. The best in town.
B Motel Arizona, Av 6 between Calle 17 and 18, T633-338 2522. Pleasant place. Rooms have heating.

Douglas (Arizona) p246

A-B Gadsden, 1046 G Av, T520-364 4481, www.hotelgadsden.com. A registered historic landmark used as a location for Western films.

Fabulous lobby, completely unexpected to find such a place in a border town. Recommended.
Camping RV parks on the Arizona side charge about US$10 per night for vehicle, US$5 for tent camping: **Double Adobe Trailer Park** off Highway 80; **Copper Horse Shoe R V Park** on Highway 666.

🍴 Eating

Puerto Peñasco p244

🍴🍴 **Costa Brava**, Kino y 1 de Junio, T638-383 3130. Exotic menu, modest prices. Best in town.
🍴🍴 **La Casa del Capitán**, on top of the mountain overlooking town, follow the path for 15 mins. Great views of the bay, tasty international food and seafood. One of the best.
🍴🍴 **Lily's**, Malecón 31, T638-383 2510. Outdoor terraced restaurant, popular with gringos.
🍴 **Gamma's**, Calle Armada Nacional 28, right by the water. Popular locals' joint that serves very good seafood. Often noisy and colourful.

Nogales p246

🍴🍴🍴 **La Roca**, Elias 91. A very fine, romantic restaurant serving decent Sonoran cuisine. Probably the best place in town.
🍴🍴 **Café Olga**, Juárez 37 next to bus station. A Nogales institution, open all hours.
🍴🍴 **El Greco's**, Obregon 152 y Pierson, 4 blocks from border. Decent food; beware of vendors.
🍴 **Elvira's**, Obregón. Great food, good service, but terrible views facing border fence.
🍴 **Leo's Café**, Obregón y Campillo, T631-312 2000. Cheap and cheerful eatery serving Mexican staples.
🍴 **San San**, López y Ateos 171. Chinese (nice alternative to fast foods and taco joints), usually crowded. Recommended.

Cananea p246

🍴 **El Amigo**, Obregón 240 y 7 Este, T645-332 9025. A surprising find in the desert, health foods, light meals, yoghurt and Mexican fare.

Mariscos Los Delfines, Blv Lázaro Gutiérrez de Lara entre Calle 3 y Calle 4, T645-332 9476. Another surprise draw; offers seafood.

Agua Prieta p246
El Pollo Loco, Agua Prieta, near the plaza, for roasted chicken.
Mariscos y Carnes 'La Palapa', Calle 6 between Av 11 and 12. Seafood and meat.

⊖ Transport

Nogales p246
Bus Nogales' main bus terminal is 8 km south of the city centre, along the highway to Magdalena and Hermosillo; parking US$1 per hr. The bus station has a booth to change money. There are several other small terminals nearby, including the TBC terminal, where **Albatros** buses go to **Puerto Peñasco**.

Into Mexico Taxis at the border ask US$5 to take you to the bus station, but on the return journey the booth selling taxi vouchers charges less than US$4. A local bus, 1 peso, leaves 1 block from the border. Bus 46 from Calle Juárez goes to the terminal (US$0.25).

There are 3 bus lines that go into Mexico using the main terminal: Norte de Sonora, Transportes y Autobuses del Pacífico (TAP) and Elite. They all have high-quality buses and prices are almost always identical between carriers; TAP also runs 2nd-class buses to many destinations. To **Chihuahua**, Elite, US$50. To **Ciudad Obregón**, TAP, 9 daily, US$22.70. To **Culiacán**, TAP, 7 daily, US$44.25. To **Durango**, 1530, US$75.40. To **Guadalajara** (Tonalá, outside of city), every couple of hours, US$92.30. To **Guaymas**, hourly, US$17.70. To **Hermosillo**, hourly, US$11.15. To **Los Mochis**, hourly, US$35.40. To **Mazatlán**, hourly, US$62.70. To **Mexicali**, TAP, 1930, US$28.10. To **Tepic**, hourly, 23 hrs, US$75.80. To **Zacatecas**, direct, US$87.

Into the USA To get to the US border, as you leave the Migración building, walk to the first set of traffic lights, cross the street

and from the other side pick up a bus to the border, referred to as *La Linea*. The buses run down the same stretch of street as you'd have to walk, so you may as well take the ride, especially if crossing in the summer.

After you've crossed the border into the USA, you'll see a ramp and stairs on your left. The **Greyhound** station is at the top of the stairs; it's a small 1-room building with toilets, lockers, pay phones and a few fast food outlets. Buses leave for **Tucson** almost hourly 0630-2000. There are smaller vans that leave at 0800, 1200, and 1600. Buses leave for **Phoenix** (Arizona's largest city, about 2 hrs north of Tucson) at 0745, 1015, 1415, and 2045, US$31.75. Buses also run to **Hermosillo** and **Ciudad Obregón**.

A block from the border, **Citizen Auto Stage Company**, T520-287 5628, runs 10 buses daily from Nogales to **Tucson** (the nearest US town); the bus stops at Tucson airport en route. It's possible to stop and visit **Tumacacori Mission**, north of Nogales, along the way (no extra charge).

From Nogales, Arizona, **Autobuses Crucero** go to **Los Angeles**, 3 daily, US$84. To **Phoenix**, 5 daily, US$26.75. To **Tucson**, 4 daily, US$23.

Agua Prieta p246
Bus
The bus station in Agua Prieta is one small room with an adequate restaurant called Don Camione, and a phone service. To **Chihuahua**, every couple of hours from 0600, US$33. To **Ciudad Juárez**, 0900, 0930 and 2230, US$26. To **Durango**, 2010, US$59. To **Hermosillo**, every couple of hrs from 0600-1400, US$25. To **Mexico City**, Omnibus, 1630, US$103. To **Nogales**, every couple of hrs from 0830-1600, US$13. To **Phoenix**: every 3 hrs from 0515-1630, US$42. To **Zacatecas**, Cabellero Azteca (all 2nd class), 2130, US$56.

Douglas (Arizona) p246
Bus Has a small bus terminal, 538 14th St, between Av F and Av G, operated by

Greyhound and Autobuses Crucero. **Tucson**, US$19. **Phoenix**, US$30. **Los Angeles**: US$65. The schedules for all the buses are the same: 0545, 1145, 1515, and 1715. The terminal closes at 1600 so you'd have to wait outside for the 1715 bus.

Taxi

Armando Chávez, T633-335 2162. Recommended. If you are crossing the border, when you come to the first cross street, take a left and the office is just around the corner on the north side of the street.

ⓘ Directory

Puerto Peñasco p244

Banks There are 4 banks. Banamex, Av Campeche 97, T638-383 4380; Bancomer, Blv Juárez, T638-383 2430; Commermex, Blv Juárez 100, T638-383 2031; and Serfin Bank, Blv Juárez 87, T638-383 4288, which has an ATM. **MoneyGram** transfers are picked up at Coppel (department store) on Av Constitución (across from Super Ley Grocery store). It must say Puerto Penasco, Sonora, Mexico and the recipient must have a driver's licence or a passport and the transaction

number to retrieve funds. **Western Union** transfers may be picked up at the post office during business hours. Must show proof of ID. **Laundry** Laundromat Liz, Altamirano y Simón Morua. Also **Lavamatic Plus**, Fco León de la Barra y San Luis.

Nogales p246

Banks Casas de cambio: Money Exchange, Campillo y López Mateos. 'El Amigo', Campillo y López Mateos, local 14. Compra-venta de Dólares Serfín, Av López Mateos y Pierson 81, 1st floor. **Medical services** According to the tourist office, the best private hospital in Nogales is the **Hospital del Socorro**, Dirección Granja, T631-314 6060. Any taxi driver will know how to get there. Pharmacy: **Farmacia Benavides**, behind the immigration office. They give injections. There are other pharmacies nearby.

Agua Prieta p246

Medical services Cruz Roja, corner of Calle 17 and Av 6. From there they can take you to other hospitals. Pharmacies: open 24 hrs, 1 on the corner of Calle 3 and Av 8, and another on the corner of Av 5 and 7.

Nogales to Mazatlán: the Pacific Highway

Route 15 (the Pacific Highway) runs along the Pacific coast and provides access to several resorts, to ferry terminals for Baja California and to the Los Mochis end of the Chihuahua al Pacífico railway passing beside the Copper Canyon. From Nogales to Guaymas on the Gulf of California, the road runs along the western slopes of the Sierra Madre, with summits rising to 3000 m. From Guaymas on to Mazatlán it threads along the lowland, with the Sierra Madre Occidental's bold and commanding escarpment to the east. The Pacific Highway down the coast to Acapulco and Salina Cruz is completely paved but has intermittent military searches in the States of Nayarit, Jalisco, and Guerrero (for narcotics and arms). There are many motels along the route. ➤➤ *For listings, see pages 258-265.*

Ins and outs

Road tolls
If driving from Nogales to Mazatlán by the four-lane toll road (Route 15), there are 12 toll gates. The first is 88 km south of Nogales. No motorcycles, bicycles, pedestrians or animals are allowed on the highway, which is fenced and patrolled. The toll stations are well lit, have good public conveniences, fuel and food. The total distance from Nogales to Mazatlán is 1194 km. It is not possible to list every toll location and every deviation to avoid it. Most deviations are dirt roads and should not be taken in the rainy season. Seek advice from US motoring associations (such as the AAA, see page 42) as costs and conditions change rapidly.

Magdalena Valley ⬤🔾 ➤➤ *pp258-265.*
South of the border at Nogales, Route 15 passes through the Magdalena Valley. The Cocóspera mines are near Ímuris (64 km south). There are still a few famous gold and silver mines in operation near Magdalena de Kino as well.

Magdalena de Kino → *Colour map 4, A3. Phone code: 632.*
Eighty kilometres south of Nogales, Magdalena de Kino is an attractive city of some 40,000 inhabitants, best known abroad as the resting place of the Italian Jesuit missionary and explorer Padre Eusebio Kino. He founded numerous missions in the Pimería Alta region, what is now northern Sonora and southern Arizona, in the late 1600s and early 1700s, including the well-preserved temples at Pitquito and San Ignacio, a few miles east of Magdalena de Kino. In Mexico, the city is better known as the home town of Luis Donaldo Colosio Murrieta, a highly respected civic leader and politician who was assassinated in 1994.

There isn't a great deal to see in town, although Padre Kino's remains are displayed in a crypt built above where they were found in 1966, in what is now the park-like Plaza Monumental, constructed at great expense after the discovery. Across the plaza is the graceful **Temple of Santa María de Magdalena**, where the image of San Francisco Javier is venerated. Numerous small shops dedicated to religious mementos surround the plaza.

Magdalena de Kino comes alive during its **indigenous fiesta** (28 September-8 October), one of the best in Mexico. Apart from roaming musicians, folk artists, and all manner of regional cuisine and handicrafts (especially blankets, jewellery, and pottery) on show, members of the Tohono, O'odham, and Pascua Yaqui tribes from both sides of the border travel on foot from more than 150 km away. The last of the region's *pajareros* (indigenous tinsmiths skilled in intricate designs and noted for their cunning birdcages and knowledge

Coastal Route 15

Looking for the ultimate road trip, with sun, sand, and long stretches of coastal beauty? Try Mexico's Route 15. Granted, it starts out far from the ocean, in the border town of Nogales, to be exact. But from Guayamas to Tepic, it runs the majority of Mexico's Pacific coast, and carries on as Route 200 from there all the way to the border with Guatemala.

There aren't many places where you can drive for hours with the open expanse of the ocean on one side and everything from desert landscapes to tropical forests on the other. Route 15 is one of the best journeys anywhere and can take three days or three months, depending upon your inclination. You'll see much of what's left of 'old Mexico', with views punctuated by tiny seaside *pueblos* and colonial villages, endless fields of blue agave, prehistoric landscapes, some of the world's most famous ocean resorts, and Mayan ruins.

The road begins at Nogales and plunges southward towards the Gulf of California, taking in the wild Sonoran Desert scenery and passing through Hermosillo before reaching the coast at Guaymas. Making it this far is a journey in itself, as you cross paths with Gila monsters, roadrunners and the occasional vulture circling overhead.

From here, 100 km or so brings you to Mazatlán, the 'Pearl of the Orient', with more than 20 km of uninterrupted beaches, one of the longest stretches of sand in the world. Quaint *pueblos de pescadores* and plenty of classic Mexican scenery lie ahead before Route 15 veers inwards and heads towards Tepic. But you can continue along the coast, as most do, through the big coastal resort shrines – Puerto Vallarta, Manzanillo, Ixtapa, Acapulco, and Puerto Escondido – before reaching the border with Guatemala.

of medicinal herbs) exhibit their wares. These works are highly prized by collectors and are only available during the fiesta. The town's second festival, in May, to honour Padre Kino, is smaller but every bit as colourful.

Hermosillo ●❼❸❻ ›› pp258-265. Colour map 4, B3.

→ *Phone code: 662.*

Capital of Sonora state, Hermosillo (founded in 1700) is a thriving, hot, modern city with only few mementos of its illustrious colonial past. These can be found around the central **Plaza de Armas Ignacio Zaragoza** (invaded by noisy birds at sunset) and the nearby late 17th-century **Capilla de San Antonio**, the city's oldest building. The colonial-era **Casa Arias** and the next door **La Hoeffer house** (now the Casa de Cultura) reflect the French influence of the Porfiriato era. The imposing neoclassical **Catedral de la Asunción** (1777, rebuilt 1877), Calle Ocampo on the plaza, has a baroque dome and three naves, while the 19th-century **Palacio de Gobierno**, at the intersection of calles Dr Paliza and Comonfort, has intricately carved pillars and pediment, historical murals and grandiose statues amid landscaped gardens. The **Regional History Museum of Sonora** ⓘ *Jesús García Final, inside the old prison, Tue-Sun, 0900-1800, US$2.25*, charts the historical development of the state. It has exhibits on the Yaqui, antique arms, a mummy believed to be more than 10,000 years old and is worth a look. It's at the base of the Cerro de la Campana, a distinctive, surreally illuminated hill with great views, rising from the city centre; locals call it *El Caracol* (The Snail). Also in the centre are two picturesque chapels, **Del Carmen** and **Espíritu Santo**, worth seeing.

Just north of downtown is **University City** ① *Rosales y Transversal*, with modern buildings of Mexican architecture blended tastefully with Moorish and Mission influences. There is an active fine arts and cultural life in Hermosillo, with many events throughout the year (ask at the tourist office, see below). The excellent **La Sauceda** ① *Periférico Oeste y Blv Francisco Serna*, the most popular amusement park in northwestern Mexico, has over 90 games and exhibitions spread over two levels as well as a splendid children's museum, **La Burbuja** ① *Tue-Thu 0900-1300 and 1400-1600, Fri 0900-1300 and 1400-1800, and Sat-Sun 1000-1900, T662-212 0581, www.laburbuja.org.mx*.

Two kilometres south of Plaza Zaragoza, near the Periférico Sur, is the wonderful **Centro Ecológico de Sonora** ① *www.centroecologico.gob.mx, 0800-1700, US$2.25*, a botanical garden and zoo displaying Sonoran and other desert flora and fauna in well-cared-for surroundings. It boasts 300 different plant categories and more than 200 different animal species and should not be missed.

Hermosillo has a helpful **tourist office** ① *Paseo del Canal y Comonfort Edificio Sonora, 3rd floor, T662-217 0060, www.visitasonora.com and www.gotosonora.com*.

Bahía Kino → *Colour map 4, B3. Phone code: 662.*

A paved 107-km road runs west past the Hermosillo airport to Bahía Kino (also known as Kino del Mar), divided into the old, somnolent and somewhat down-at-heel fishing village **Kino Viejo** and, 11 km away, **Kino Nuevo**, a 'winter gringoland' of condos, trailer parks, and expensive hotels. Kino Nuevo, like Guaymas 165 km south, is set to become a major resort, with plans for several golf courses, three marinas, and a staggering 50,000 hotel rooms. Few of these exist as yet, but there is little doubt Bahía Kino will soon change.

Although the public beaches are good, most North American visitors come for the sport fishing. The indigenous Seri, who used to live across El Canal del Infiernillo (Little Hell Strait) on the mountainous Isla Tiburón, have been displaced by the Navy to the mainland. They come into Kino on Saturday and Sunday to sell their *palo fierro* (ironwood) animal sculptures and traditional basketware and can usually be found at the waterfront **Posada del Mar Hotel**. In Kino Nuevo, there is the fine **Museo Regional de Arte Seri** ① *Mar de Cortés y Progreso, Wed-Sun 0800-1700, US$0.60*.

Isla Tiburón (Shark Island) can be visited by renting a small boat and guide (around US$100 from dozens of outfitters along the waterfront in Kino or Kino Nuevo). Protected in the nearly 400 sq m biosphere reserve, the population of both the big horn sheep and mule deer has grown enormously. On the south end of the island, the water is around 50 m deep and is an excellent area for scuba-diving and fishing. **Dog Bay** provides shelter and ideal anchorage if spending the night. The bay itself is rich in wildlife: colourful tropical fish, thousands of small invertebrates, large crustaceans, devil fish, sponges and occasionally turtles are found along the coast of its islands; sea lions are known to inhabit the rocks.

Isla Patos (Duck Island), 30 minutes north of Isla Tiburón, offers the opportunity to explore the submerged Spanish vessels that once sailed the Sea of Cortés. Other islands worth visiting are **Alcatraz** (also known as Pelican Island), **Turner** and **San Esteban**.

Guaymas ●●●●● ►► *pp258-265. Colour map 4, B3.*

→ *Phone code: 622.*

Guaymas, first founded in 1703 by the Jesuits and permanently settled in 1769, was once a grotty port town set spread out over multiple bays and backed by desert mountains. Occupied 1847-1848 by US forces during the Mexican-American War, Guaymas acquired the title 'Heroic' in 1935, in memory of the valiant defence by its inhabitants during the French Invasions of 1854 and 1865. Now, along with Bahía Kino to its north, Guaymas is being touted as Mexico's next big resort, although apart from the thoroughly Americanized San Carlos section a few kilometres north, there's still little to hold a visitor here, apart from its excellent deep-sea fishing and seafood. All this is expected to change, as Guaymas gears up for resort development. On the far west of town, **Miramar Beach**, on Bocachibampo Bay with its blue sea dotted with green islets, and **Las Playitas** to the immediate south, are other up-and-coming resort sections, already home to vacation real estate and condominium agencies. The climate is ideal in winter but unpleasantly humid in summer.

In the town itself, the church and plaza of **San Fernando** ① *Av Alfonso Iberri between Calle 24 y Calle 25*, are worth a visit, as is the 17th-century church of **San José de Guaymas** ① *some 5 km northeast of town (signposted)*. The port area also boasts some worthy buildings, among which are the **Templo del Sagrado Corazón de Jesús**, the neoclassical **Banco de Sonora**, the **Palacio Municipal** (constructed in 1899), the **Ortiz Barracks** and the **Antigua Carcel Municipal** (old Municipal Prison) constructed in 1900. Other sites worth taking in are the indigenous churches of the Yaqui, the French/Arabian-inspired **Moorish Kiosk** ① *Plaza 13 de Julio*, and the monument in **Fisherman's Plaza**, the town's symbolic landmark. **Three Presidents Square**, between Calle 23 and Calle 24, was built in honour of three former presidents of Mexico, Adolfo de la Huerta, Plutarco Elías Calles, and Abelardo Rodríguez, all of them remarkably natives of this town.

Just outside of town is a pleasant mirador, **Benito Juaréz** ① *Blv García López (look for signs)*, which offers stunning views of Guaymas Bay.

Guaymas holds a popular nine-day **carnival** along its waterfront every year at the beginning of Lent; it is second only to Mazatlán as the best-known on the Pacific. On 1 June each year, the town also throws a **Navy Day** parade and fireworks.

There is a **tourist office** ① *Av Alfonso Iberri 194, 1st floor, T622-224 6459, http://guaymas.gob.mx:8086/turismo/en*.

Bahía San Carlos

Some 15 km north of Guaymas (12 km from Highway 15), Bahía San Carlos is very touristy and Americanized. Sometimes known as Nuevo Guaymas, San Carlos is a seaside haven for about 3000 residents, with the population increasing threefold in high season. *Catch 22* was filmed here and the sunsets are stunning. Above the bay a twin-peaked hill, the **Tetas de Cabra**, is a significant landmark. There is good fishing with an international tournament in July. San Carlos has several ecotourism activities such as low-impact walks and treks in protected areas, hatching and sanctuary visits and non-intrusive harbour tours, centred about **Isla San Pedro Nolasco**, home to protected sea lions and several marine birds. There's a **tourist office** ① *Av Serdán 349, T622-226 0202*, or find information online at www.sancarlosmexico.com and www.sancarlosmexicoguide.com.

Around Bahía San Carlos

Soldiers' Estuary, 20 km northwest of Guaymas, is a small (778 ha) but important coastal ecosystem soon to be a protected area. This aquatic ecosystem is a refuge for hundreds of plants and animals and the only Pacific location on the continent with three different swamp habitats co-existing in the same area. The rarely visited but spectacular **Devil's Canyon biosphere reserve** is 54 km north of town along Route 15.

Ciudad Obregón and around ⇢ *Phone code: 644.*

Head south on the highway from Guaymas for 132 km and you'll soon reach Ciudad Obregón, a rather dull agricultural centre, best avoided unless you're in the market for cowboy gear or leather goods, or have more than a passing interest in the local indigenous people, the Yaqui. If you're here on 16 July, there's the annual **Festival of the Yaqui Valley**; 24 June is another important festival, when the tribe descends upon the Río Yaqui for a communal spiritual dip. There is also a **Museum of the Yaquis** ① *centre of town, Allende y 5 de Febrero*.

In nearby **Cócorit**, 7 km north, there is a newer **Yaqui Museum** ① *T644-418 3200, centrodeculturas@hotmail.com*, home to the largest cultural display of the tribe in the country. Exhibits include art and craftwork such as masks, drums, embroidery, clothing and many other original pieces.

Alamos ⇢ *Colour map 1, B1. Phone code: 647.*

Around 50 km east of Navojoa, into the hills, is the delightfully crumbling old colonial town of Alamos, officially one of a handful of *pueblos mágicos* (enchanting towns) across the country. It is a national monument and was shortlisted as a UNESCO World Heritage Site. The town is an absolute must-see and has attracted increasing numbers of North American artists. Alamos owes much of its well-preserved ambience to gringos who started restoring the town in the 1960s. See also the useful website www.alamosmexico.com.

The town is set in a once-famous mining area, fascinating for rock enthusiasts. Although the area was explored by the Spanish in the 1530s, development did not begin for another 100 years when the Jesuits built a mission nearby. With a rich history in silver mining dating back to 1685, trips to old mine sites can easily be arranged. Fabulous old mansions also recall the town's glory days; find out more on a **house tour** ① *departing from outside the bank on the Alameda, Sat 1000, US$12*. You can hire an English-speaking guide from outside the **tourist office** on Plaza de Armas.

In addition to the mansions, a tour should include the major buildings on the plaza, the **Palacio Municipal**, the **Hacienda de los Santos**, the 18th-century church of **Purísima Concepción**, and two small but interesting museums: **Museo de María Félix** ① *Galeana*, a shrine to one of Mexico's legendary actresses; and **Museo Costumbrista de Sonora** (Museum of Sonoran Costumes) ① *Calle Guadalupe Victoria 1, T647-428 0053, Wed-Sun 0900-1800*, with a good collection of local costumes worn by indigenous peoples and settlers. A short, sharp hike up to **Los Miradores** is worth the effort, with wonderful views of the town and surrounding mountains.

Another reason for visiting Alamos is to see the famous jumping beans, a symbiotic relationship between a plant and a moth larvae. The two develop simultaneously giving the impression that the seed pod or bean is actually jumping.

La Reserva Para Protecíon de Flora y Fauna Sierra de Alamos Río Cuchujaqui

More than 400 species of birds have been recorded from the coast into the foothills at Alamos, including spectacular species such as roseate spoonbills, macaws and trogans. Alamos is also a wildlife transition zone, and many birds, mammals, plants, and reptiles find their most southern or northern limits in this region.

The La Reserva Para Protecíon de Flora y Fauna Sierra de Alamos Río Cuchujaqui consists of 81,000 ha and was declared a protected area in 1996. It takes in the Sierra de Alamos and the upper drainage of the Rio Cuchujaqui. Most of the reserve is a mix of tropical deciduous forest, and was set aside as an excellent example of this forest at its most northern limits. The Sierra de Alamos has many hiking trails and is easily accessed by foot from town. The remainder of the reserve is wilderness with access best attempted by 4WD.

Los Mochis and around ⬤🔵🔺⬤⬤ ➤➤ pp258-265. Colour map 1, B1.

→ Phone code: 668.

In spite of being 24 km from the sea, Los Mochis in Sinaloa is a fishing resort with a sizeable US colony. The name is derived either from a local word meaning 'hill like a turtle', or possibly, from *mocho*, meaning 'one-armed', perhaps after a cowboy thus mutilated. A nearby sugar cane-producing area was settled in 1886 as a utopian colony, built by the American socialist Albert Owen. The city itself was established in 1903 by another American, Benjamin Johnson, whose wife was responsible for building the Sagrado Corazón church. The family lost everything in the Revolution. Los Mochis is best known as the starting point for the uphill railway journey passing the Copper Canyon.

There isn't a great deal to see in the town but if you're bored, the **Museo Regional del Valle Fuerte** ① Obregón y Rosales, T668-812 4692, Mon-Sat 0900-1300, Sun 1000-1300, US$1.15, has mildly diverting displays on local history (in Spanish), while the **Parque Sinaloa** and next door **Botanical Garden** have mediocre botanical collections and large trees that offer some respite from the heat.

Los Mochis is also well known for its lively nightspots and bars, visited by roaming Mariachis, who play excellent music. The town retains the traditional Latin custom of promenading through downtown in the evenings (although these days it's more generally done by car than on foot), and Bulevar Gabriel Leyva becomes jammed between 2000-2230, as the street and nearby area known as the Riazo are virtually impassable.

Information for Los Mochis and the State of Sinaloa is available from the **tourist office** ① Unidad Administrativa building, Allende y Cuauhtémoc, T668-816 2015, www.vivesinaloa.com, Mon-Fri 0900-1600.

Topolobampo → Colour map 1, B1. Phone code: 668.

A side road, running southwest from Los Mochis, crosses the salt flats to Topolobampo (24 km). The town is built on several hills facing the beautiful bay indented by coastal lagoons. The bay has many outlets and contains a number of islands; sunsets here are lovely. **Punta de Copas**, a sandbar across from the bay, is locally famous for its spectacular beaches (Maviri in particular). Further out, **Isla Santa Maria** has enormous sand dunes, which are perfect for low-impact sports such as frisbee or flying kites but it's best to avoid the weekends when hordes of sand bikers arrive. There are few lodgings in Topolobampo itself, so it's best to stay in Los Mochis. Ferries from here run to La Paz in Baja California. ➤➤ See Transport, page 265.

Towards Chihuahua by train → For information on Creel and the Copper Canyon, see page 293.

The famous *Chihuahua al Pacífico* train journey is a good way to see the spectacular scenery of the Sierra Madre and the Barranca del Urique/Cobre (Urique/Copper Canyon). The *Servicio Estrella* train is scheduled to leave Los Mochis daily at 0600 (but it's often more like 0700), US$67 to Creel (10 hours), US$122 to Chihuahua (16½ hours, but expect delays). For train information and prices, check www.chepe.com.mx. Bring your own food, drinking water and toilet paper for the journey.

This is a very popular trip and tickets must be bought in advance either on the morning of departure or, in high season (July/August, Christmas/New Year, Holy Week), a day or more before. *Estrella*-class tickets can be bought from tour operators in Los Mochis to avoid long queues at the station; however they charge and 8% surcharge and they will try to persuade you to book into expensive hotels. If you are only going as far as Creel, buy a return ticket as it is impossible to reserve seats back to Los Mochis.

On the *Primera Especial* the windows do not open, so, to take photos, stand between the carriages if you can. Motorists taking the train to Creel are advised to park in front of the station at Los Mochis as it is well lit and there are always plenty of people around. There is more expensive parking downtown.

The ordinary economy-class train, *Tarahumara*, aims to leave at 0700, with prices roughly half that of the first class, but it is not possible to reserve seats. Second-class trains make many stops but are reasonably comfortable and it is possible to open the windows. On either train, sit on the right for the best views, except when approaching Temoris, when it's all jump to the left, then return to the right until the first tunnel after Temoris when the views are good on both sides.

El Fuerte → *Colour map 1, B1. Phone code: 698.*

El Fuerte is the more atmospheric gateway to the Copper Canyon – wonderfully tranquil and rich in colonial architecture, and far more enticing than Los Mochis. Founded on the verdant banks of the Río Fuerte in 1564 (1½ hours by train from Los Mochis or two hours by bus), it is a destination in its own right. The bus station is 10 km from town; taxis to the centre cost around US$6.

Aside from strolling the attractive streets, it's particularly worth visiting the **El Fuerte Mirador Museum** ① *Tue-Sun 0900-1700, US$0.50*, housed in the town's old fort that was designed to withstand attacks from local tribes. The views are commanding and more than 150 species have been spotted here, best encountered by river boat in the early morning. You can also visit local petroglyphs and the Mayo Indigenous Mission. For information, contact **El Fuerte Eco-Adventures Posada del Hidalgo**, www.hotelposadadelhidalgo.com.

For those travelling by the train, the high, long bridge over the Río Fuerte heralds the beginning of more interesting scenery (this is the first of 37 major bridges); three hours from Los Mochis the first, and longest, of the 86 tunnels is passed, then, 10 minutes later, the Chinapas Bridge (this is approximately the Sinaloa/Chihuahua state border, where clocks go forward an hour).

Culiacán ●●●● ›› *pp258-265. Colour map 1, C2.*

→ *Phone code: 667.*

From Los Mochis, it's 214 km to Sinaloa state's capital, Culiacán. There is a marked seaside feel to Culiacán in spite of it being more than 60 km from the ocean. One of Mexico's oldest cities, it was founded in 1531 by Beltrán de Guzmán. Long the centre of Mexico's drug trade, it can no longer be called a colonial city, but it is attractive and ostentatiously prosperous, and has a university, along with some noticeable displays of ill-gotten wealth in the form of casinos, flight schools, Hummer dealerships, mansions, over-the-top hotels and yacht brokers. It is also still quite dangerous; since late 2008, the city has been under the control of the Mexican Army, whose presence is markedly evident.

The centre is quite pleasant and has a number of attractive 19th-century churches, including the exceptionally beautiful **Basílica of Our Lady of Rosario** and two other nearby *templos*, those of La Lomita and Sagrado Corazón, both famed for their delicate belle epoque architecture. A stone's throw from these churches are the **Plazuela Alvaro**

Obregón, one of the finest examples of Porfiriato urban design anywhere on the west coast, and two excellent museums, the **Museum of Anthropology and Regional History** (with the world's fifth-largest meteorite) ① *C Progreso 1201, T614-412 3912, Tue-Sat 1000-1500 and 1700-2000, Sun 1100-1800*, and the **Museum of Sinaloa Arts** ① *calles Rafael Buelna y Paliza, T614-716 1750, Tue-Sat 1000-1500 and 1700-1900, Sun 1100-1700*, features works by Diego Rivera, López Saenz, and Frida Kahlo.

Culiacán is also home to a church of a different sort, the incredible **Capilla de Jesús Malverde**. This chapel commemorates a semi-legendary Robin Hood-like figure in Mexican folklore, Jesús Malverde. While not a present-day narco himself (he was hung in 1909), he is nonetheless considered the informal (no Vatican approval forthcoming) patron saint of Mexico's drug smugglers. His admirers and believers swarm the shrine erected here in his honour, papering the walls with photos of themselves (sometimes with their guns, multiple mobile phones, and snakeskin cowboy boots showing) in an effort to seek his blessing. Plaques are hung as well, entreating this 'saint' to protect them on their smuggling routes.

About 36 km east is the **Presa Sanalona**, a pleasant stopover popular for water sports. Continue south beyond Culiacán for 212 km and you'll pass the **Tropic of Cancer**. The change from temperate to tropical is marked by a shift in vegetation and atmosphere, both becoming denser and wetter. Just 30 km south of the tropical divide lies the beautiful **Bahía de Puerto Viejo** (Old Port Bay) and fabled Mazatlán itself (see page 266).

⦿ Nogales to Mazatlán: the Pacific Highway

For Sleeping and Eating price codes and other relevant information, see Essentials pages 47-51.

● Sleeping

Magdalena de Kino *p251*

B-C El Cuervo, Av 5 de Mayo 316, T632-322 3641. Various rooms, cheaper without TV.
B-C El Toro, Av Niños Héroes y Misión de Dolores, T632-322 0375. Centrally located, the largest in town and probably the best.
C Los Cisnes, Ctra Internacional Km 184, T632-322 2020. Just out of town, breakfast is included.
C San José, Ctra Internacional, Km 184, T632-322 1133. Largest and noisiest.
C-D Sahuaro Motor Hotel, Ctra Internacional Km 184, T632-322 3845. Identical location with, but on other side of highway from, Los Cisnes and San José. Can be noisy.
D Motel Kino, Dr Ernesto Rivera Magallón 100, T632-322 2212. Central and the cheapest place in town.
D Motel La Suite, Av Niños Héroes 310, T632-322 3627. Bottom of the lot but clean.

Hermosillo *p252*

Cheap hotels and *casas de huéspedes* can be found around Plaza Zaragoza and along Sonora near Matamoros (red-light activity, choose carefully).

AL Best Western Hermosillo Señorial, Blv Kino y Guillermo Carpena 203, T662-215 5155. Comfortable, top-end hotel with a/c, pool, parking, restaurant, bar.
A-B San Sebastian, Periférico Sur 96, corner with Blv Vildósola, T662-259 9550, www.hotelsansebastian.com.mx. Well on its way to becoming best hotel in town in this price range. All amenities and services.
C Colonial Hermosillo, Vado del Río 9, T662-259 0000, www.hotelescolonial.com/ hermosillo.htm. Business-oriented but with all amenities/services, relaxing atmosphere. Good location and price.
C Gándara, Blv Kino 1000, T662-214 4414. A/c, internet, TV, room service, restaurant, pool.
C Monte Carlo, Juárez y Sonora, T662-212 3354, www.discovermx.com/monte carlo.htm. Popular, inexpensive old hotel with a/c and clean rooms. Adjoining restaurant is equally popular.

C San Alberto, Serdán y Rosales, T662-213 1840. Good-value hotel with a/c, cable TV and pool. Breakfast served.

C Santiago Plaza, Blv Luis Encinas 545, T662-289 8990, www.hotelsantiago plaza.com. Downtown location, pool, restaurant, gym, all rooms have a/c and TV.

D Washington, Dr Noriega Pte 68, T662-213 1183. The best budget hotel in town. Clean, basic rooms lie off narrow courts, some have a/c. Parking for motorbikes.

E Casa de los Amigos, contact Asociación Sonorense de los Amigos, Felipe Salido 32, T/F662-217 0142. Various dorms, living room, library, garden, laundry and kitchen.

Bahía Kino *p253*

AL Posada del Mar, Av Mar de Cortés, corner with Creta s/n, southern end of Kino Nuevo, T662-242 0155. Large hotel with a pool.

A Saro, Av Mar de Cortés, north of Posada del Mar, Kino Nuevo, T662-242 0216. Sicilian-run establishment with large, cool, self-contained, apartment-style lodgings. Just over the road from the beach.

C Bungalows Caluma, Puerto Vallarta, corner of Malaga and Bilboa, T662-242 1051, www.calumabungalows.com. One block away from beach in Kino Viejo. Short- or long-term rentals. American-owned.

C Geko Apartments, Av Mar de Cortés 1120, Kino Nuevo, T662-360 1387. 6 apartments and 4 suites. Wi-Fi in the main building, great location by the water. Comfortable and quiet.

Camping

It's possible to camp on the beaches with or without a tent.

Kino Bay RV Park, Av Mar de Cortés, northernmost end of Kino Nuevo, T662-242 0216, www.kinobayrv.com. US$20.

Guaymas *p253*

B Armida, Ctra Internacional salida Norte, T622-224 3048. Recently renovated, secure parking, 2 restaurants, complimentary breakfast, clean. Suites are more expensive but no better than economy rooms.

B Santa Rita, Av Serdán y Calle 9, T622-222 8100. This comfortable hotel has clean rooms with bath and a/c. There's another more expensive motel with the same name closer to the airport.

C Flamingos, Route 2, Km 1932, T622-221 0961. With a/c, restaurant, bar, pool, cable TV.

C Playa de Cortés, Bahía de Bacochibampo 66, T622-221 1048. Great views of the ocean from this old hacienda-style hotel. Highly recommended.

D Ana, Calle 25 135, T622-222 3048. Recently remodelled but still a low-end option.

D Motel Cominse, Calle 14. Clean and simple motel, but a good choice.

F Casa de Huéspedes Martha, Calle 13, T622-222 8332. Run-down but reliable old cheapie. Rooms have bath, fan and hot water.

Camping

At Km 13 the road forks: left 1 km to 2 secluded bays with limited trailer camping, and right to the Marina Real on Sonora Bay, and beyond a beach with open camping.

Bahía San Carlos *p254*

B Fiesta San Carlos, Km 8.5 Blv Beltrones, T622-226 1318, hotelfiesta10@hotmail.com. Clean hotel with a pool. Good food. No TV or telephones in rooms, but it is on the beach.

B-C Best Western Hacienda Tetakawi, Paseo Escénico Km 8.8, T622-226 0220. Directly across from the ocean, clean, quiet.

C Dorado Condos, Almejas 148, T622-226 0307, http://doradocondos.weebly.com, after 10 km from the highway a road branches off to here. On a rocky but pleasant beach. Pool.

Camping

Totonaka RV, Blv MF Beltrones, Km 8, T622-226 0323, www.totonakarv.com. Apartments and 130 RV hook-ups. Free Wi-Fi, beginner Spanish lessons, many amenities. Highly recommended.

Ciudad Obregón *p255*

Almost all of Ciudad Obregón's hotels are located along Miguel Alemán. Those in the Zona Norte (north of the main plaza) are uniformly dreadful and should be avoided.

A Best Western Hotel San Jorge, Miguel Aleman 929 Norte, T644-410 4000, www.bestwestern.com. Colonial Spanish decor at this clean, friendly, reliable hotel. There's a restaurant, bar, pool, safe and safe parking. Rooms have a/c and TV.

A Days Inn Costa de Oro, Miguel Alemán 210 Norte, T644-414 1765. Well-kept and pleasant.

A Holiday Inn Ciudad Obregán, Miguel Alemán y Allende 200, T644-410 5090. Best hotel in town, but also the most expensive. Bilingual staff, pool, restaurant.

C Travelodge, Jalisco 350 Norte between Morelos and Naynari, T644-414 5044. Downtown, Wi-Fi, pool, restaurant, bar.

C Valle Grande Obregón, Miguel Alemán y Tebatiate, T644-410 6500, www.vallegrande obregon.com. Bilingual, friendly staff, gym, pool, restaurant. Internet available.

C Yori Inn, Miguel Alemán 770 Norte, T644-413 1111. Popular, no-nonsense and clean.

Camping

Navojoa RV and Campsite, Route 15, Km 159, T642-421 5203. Run down, shaded, US$13 for full hook-up (50 available), US$5 for car or small jeep, dollars preferred to pesos.

Alamos *p255*

LL-L Hotel Colonial, Obregón 4, T647-428 1371, www.alamoshotelcolonial.com. Beautifully decorated colonial house with 10 very different rooms and hospitable, North American management.

A Los Portales, Juárez 6, T647-428 0211. Beautiful 300-year-old hacienda on the plaza with atmospheric courtyard and wonderful murals. 9 big rooms have bath but fan only.

C Enriquez, Juárez, on the plaza, T647-428 1199. Big, crumbling rooms at this dilapidated hotel, favoured by backpackers. Only some rooms have a bath.

C La Dolisa Motel, Madero 72, T647-428 0131. This motel has 10 clean rooms, with fridge and TV, private parking, laundry, telephone.

C-D La Posada de Alamos, 2 de Abril s/n, T647-428 0045. Former historic military hospital since converted. 10 rooms, all with baths. Drab but well priced.

D Alamos Hostel, Madeo 7, jimtoeves@ yahoo.com. Write ahead for reservations. Dormitory and private rooms available, tent camping as well. Adults only.

D Motel Somar, Madero 110, T647-428 0195. One of the cheapest in town, 30 rooms with hot water, telephone service, little else.

Camping

Acosta Rancho Motel and Trailer Park, 5 de Mayo y Gpe. Posada, T647-428 0246. Bathrooms, showers, restaurant in wooded setting with swimming pool. Recommended.

El Caracol Trailer Park, Navojoa-Alamos Hwy Km 37. Rustic, good swimming pool, not always open (US$15).

Los Mochis *p256*

AL Santa Anita, Gabriel Leyva Solano e Hidalgo, T668-818 7046, www.santa anitahotel.com. Big, comfortable hotel with pleasant, modern rooms. Lots of services, including restaurant, bar, Wi-Fi and travel agency, where you can book your rail tickets and lodgings.

B Beltrán, Hidalgo 281 Pte, T668-812 0688, www.losmochishotel.com. Clean, tidy, efficient hotel with comfortable, if somewhat generic, rooms.

B Fénix, Gen Angel Flores 365 Sur, T668-815 8948, hotelfenix@email.com. Near the Riazo (so somewhat noisy) and railway station. Wi-Fi in lobby, rooms are non-smoking. Clean, if sometimes pokey quarters. Some rooms have impressive big screen cable TVs, so ask to see a few.

C El Dorado, Av Gabriel Leyva Solano 525 Norte y Av Ing Heriberto Valdez, T668-815 1111. Close to the business district in a drab setting. Restaurant, room service, lounge, swimming pool.

C Las Fuentes, Blv Adolfo López Mateos 1251-A Norte, T668-818 8871,

lasfuenteshotel@lmm.megared.net.mx.
Very friendly, a/c, TV, private parking,
close to downtown. Recommended.
C Nuevo Hotel Montecarlo, Gen Angel
Flores 322 Sur, T668-812 1818. One of
the cheapest in its range. Recently
remodelled and centrally located.
Recommended.
C-D Hidalgo, opposite Beltrán at 260 Pte,
T/F668-818 3453. The best in its range, but
low-end rooms can be dreadful. Cheap
and friendly.

Camping
RV Park Copper Canyon, Ruta 15, on the
right side of the road when entering town.
Good place to leave vehicles when visiting
the Copper Canyon.

Topolobampo *p256*
For other accommodation options go to
Los Mochis.
B Yacht, 3 km south of town. Modern, clean,
quiet hotel with a/c, good food and views,
but seems to close for the winter.
E Estilo Europeo Poama, at the ferry
terminal, 10 mins' walk from Los Mochis bus.

El Fuerte *p257*
L El Fuerte, Monteclaros 37, T698-893 0226,
www.hotelelfuerte.com.mx. A very beautiful
hotel with exquisite rooms and a jacuzzi fed
by illuminated waterfalls. The best in town
and recommended.
L Posada del Hidalgo, Hidalgo 101,
T698- 893 0242, www.mexicoscopper
canyon.com. In a historic mansion.
A very big, professional hotel with spa
facilities and a legion of staff. Rooms can
be booked through Hotel Santa Anita in
Los Mochis (see above).
A Río Vista, Cerro de las Pilas, T698-893 0413.
Housed in the old fort stables with excellent
views over the river. Lots of rusty old
antiques and a good restaurant.
E San José, Juárez 108, T698-893 0845. For
the budget explorer, small, basic rooms with
fan, some have bath. Friendly and scruffy.

Culiacán *p257*
Many hotels in Culiacán have been
implicated in money-laundering activities
and are under careful scrutiny by the Mexican
military. Be very careful and never leave your
passport or other credentials with hotel staff.
LL-L Executivo, Blv Madero, corner with
Av Alvaro Obregón s/n, T667-713 9300,
www.executivo.com.mx. The largest, most
expensive, and deluxe accommodation
in town.
L-AL San Marcos, Av Alvaro Obregón 51
Norte Pte, T667-713 7876. A slightly scaled-
down version of **Executivo**; less expensive.
AL Los 3 Ríos, Blv José Limón Norte 910,
T667-750 5280. Trailer park, US$10, pool,
resort-style, good restaurant.
A Los Caminos, Calzado Heróico Colegio
Militar y Blv Leyva Solano, T667-715 3300.
With a/c, phone, satellite TV, restaurant, pool,
nightclub, safe parking, clean rooms.
B Fiesta Inn Culiacan, J Diego Valadez Ríos
1676 Pte, T667-759-5900. Restaurant, bar,
internet, gym, pool, on Tamazula River.
Geared to business traveller but economical.
B San Francisco, Hidalgo 227, T667-713 5863.
Good, functional hotel. Rooms have a/c, bath
and cable TV. Clean, friendly, free parking.
C Microtel Inn And Suites, Blv Pedro Infante
2525 Pte, 6 km from the centre, T667-758
6300. Internet, continental breakfast,
free local calls, smoke-free rooms. Long-
or short-term stays available. Clean,
economical, and highly recommended.
C Monterreal, Colón Oeste 970, T667-715
8310. Standard accommodation, small
and quiet.
C San Luis Lindavista, Av Las Palmas 1,
T667-759-2000, www.sanluis.com.mx. Great
views, great food, great prices. If you can
make do with poor service, this may be the
best hotel in town.
C-D Palma, Blv Leyva Solano 290 Pte, T667-
712 1254, www.hotelpalmaculiacan.com.
Wake-up service, telephone/fax, private car
park, restaurant, bar. 35 rooms with
a/c and cable TV, all with panoramic view
of city. Recommended.

● Eating

Magdalena de Kino *p251*

† **Chango's**, on the plaza. Good lunches. Ask for the corn cocktail.

† **El Toro**, Av Niños Héroes s/n, T632-322 0375. Excellent beef. Highly recommended.

Hermosillo *p252*

††† **Jardín Xochimilco**, Obregón 51, T662-250 4052. A Hermosillo favourite. Good beef and top range Mexican fare.

††† **San César**, Plutarco Elías Calles 71 Pte. Excellent chop sueys, seafood and expensive gringo food.

†††-†† **Mariscos Los Arcos de Hermosillo**, Michel 43 y Ocampo, 4 blocks south of the plaza, T662-213 2220. Fresh seafood, attractive and expensive.

†† **Mariachisimo**, Pereférico Pte 325, T662/218 3555. Traditional Mexican and Guadalajara-inspired dishes. Crowded at weekends. Recommended.

†† **Sonora Steak**, Blv Kino 914 (in front of Hotel Gándara), T662-210 0313. Exactly what the name implies.

††-† **Fook Lammoon**, Rosales 91 y Morelia, T662-212 7717. Chinese.

† **El Marcos**, Av Rodríguez, T662-215 4710. International, children's menus, very popular and crowded.

† **Jaas**, Blv Gómez Farias esq. Mariscal. Tacos, heavy and light. Recommended.

Bahía Kino *p253*

†††-†† **El Pargo Rojo**, Blv Mar de Cortés, Kino Nuevo, 1426, T662-242-0205. Recommended for seafood.

†† **Jorge's Kino Bay**, Blv Mar de Cortés y Alicantes, Kino Nuevo, T662-242 0049. Typical Mexican and seafood, quiet, waterfront setting.

†† **La Palapa del Pescador**, Blv Mar de Cortés y Wellington, Kino Viejo, T662-242 0210. Reasonably priced seafood (5 types of shrimp) and burgers. Very crowded in summer.

††-† **Marlin**, Tastiota y Guaymas, Kino Viejo, T662-242 0111. Local, hard-to-find seafood

dishes. A friendly and quiet eatery. Recommended.

Guaymas *p253*

In spite of its reputation as an up-and-coming resort, outside of the major hotels, food in Guaymas still tends to be down-to-earth and unpretentious. Both Guaymas and San Carlos (see below) are dotted along the beaches with numerous seafood shacks, always unprepossessing and almost always excellent.

†† **Los Barcos**, Calle 11 y Calle 20. Excellent seafood is served here, under a giant *palapa* overlooking the bay. Atmospheric.

††-† **Los Arbolitos**, Ctra San Carlos–Guaymas. Seafood. Recommended.

† **1001 Tacos**, Av Serdán. Friendly, no-frills taco heaven, and in large servings.

† **Froggy's**, Nuevo Guaymas. Sports bar open 1100-0200 every day. Cheap eats. Live music at weekends.

† **The Dugout**, Blv García López. Unpretentious and downtown fresh seafood eatery. May be the best secret in town.

Bahía San Carlos *p254*

Restaurants in San Carlos tend to be overpriced. Unless you want the ambiance and price tag of a gringo resort, you're better off at almost any of the seaside shacks.

†† **Piccolo**, Creston 305, T622-226 0503. Good pasta, salads, original dishes, good value.

†† **San Carlos Grill**, Comercial 1, T622-226 0509. American-themed, try the gringo lingo fillet or the shrimp tequila.

††-† **Jax Snax**, Blv Beltrones s/n, T622-226 0270. Open early. Good, tasty breakfasts and filling staples, plus hamburgers and pizzas.

† **Rosa's Cantina**, Aurora 297, T622-226 1000. Open for breakfast, lunch, and dinner. Mexican food at low prices.

Alamos *p255*

†††-†† **Doña Lola Cenaduria 'Koki'**, Volantín s/n (near Palacio Municipal). Daily 1800-2400. Legendary fantastic restaurant. Famous for *antojitos mexicanos* (Mexican snacks).

₩-₩ Café del Sol, Obregón 3, www.solipaso.com. Tue-Sun 0730-1800. Breakfast, lunch, occasional dinners and speciality coffees. Relaxed and welcoming.
₩-₩ Las Palmeras, Madero 48 y Galeana. Daily 0700-2200. Family-oriented Mexican food, with superb local dishes. Very popular with locals and visitors. Full bar.
₩-₩ Papillon Restaurant and Bar, Madero 74 (on way into town near the hospital). Standard Mexican fare with emphasis on cleanliness and fresh foods, including *chiles rellenos* (cheese-stuffed poblano peppers, dipped in batter and fried), steaks and barbecued ribs. Full bar.

Los Mochis *p256*

Many *birrierías* serving *birria*, a local beef dish.
₩₩ España, Av Alvaro Obregón 525 Pte, T668-812 2221. The oldest eatery in town, upscale, very good steak and seafood, especially paella, served with style and grace.
₩₩ Mr Owen's, Av Gabriel Leyva Solano y Lázaro Cárdenas (in **Hotel Plaza**), T668-818 1042. Upscale international dining spot, the best cuisine in Los Mochis.
₩₩-₩₩ El Farallón, Angel Flores y Av Alvaro Obregón, T668-812 1428. Good seafood and service, one of the best places in town, reasonably priced.
₩₩ Cazadores, Lázaro Cárdenas 317 Pte, T668-812 8696. Hearty local beef and game.
₩₩-₩ El Taquito, Av Gabriel Leyva Solano 333 Sur, 1 block from Santa Anita T668-817 2395. Open 24 hrs. Diner-style decor. Diverse menu.
₩₩-₩ Los Arcos, Av Camarón Sábalo 1019, T668-812 6610. Seafood and steak chain. Recommended.
₩₩-₩ Sushiko, Heriberto Valdez 1300, T668-818 2043. Good Japanese, Thai food in nice location.
₩ Leñador, Rendón y Guillermo Prieto 301 Norte, T668-812 6600. Grilled meat, popular with locals.
₩ Mi Cabaña Tacos, Av Alvaro Obregón y Allende. Popular with locals, friendly atmosphere. Recommended.

Culiacán *p257*

₩₩₩-₩₩ Los Helechos, Blv Madero, corner of Alvaro Obregón (in **Hotel Executivo**), T667-713 9310. Excellent continental and Mexican dishes in quiet setting.
₩₩-₩ Mariscos Angulo, Cristobál Colón 927 Pte, T667-716 5888. Good seafood, popular with locals.
₩₩-₩ Sushi Factory, Av Sinaloa 730 Norte Local 1, T667-715 3738. Japanese, most popular restaurant in town (2 other locations).
₩ Tay-Pak, Rubi 454 sur, T667-715 2646. Japanese-Korean.

☮ Festivals and events

Alamos *p255*

Late Jan Alamos Music Festival sees pianists, symphony orchestras, choral groups, quartets, and dancers performing at venues for a week.
Early Feb Alamos Silver Festival draws the country's finest silversmiths and collectors.
Friday before Good Friday Viernes de Dolores is a southern Mexican tradition. Houses and neighbourhoods make more than 50 elaborate and beautiful *incendios* (altars) displayed in windows and doorways, commemorate the suffering of the Virgin Mary. In the evening people stroll the streets viewing altars and miracles are said to happen.
8 Dec Feast of the Immaculate Conception is a week-long celebration.

Culiacán *p257*

13 June Feast day

▲ Activities and tours

Alamos *p255*
Language school

Alamos Language and Learning, Juarez 8, T647-423 0029, www.alamoslanguage.com. Spanish or English lessons. Short- and long-term classes.

Los Mochis *p256*
Tour operators
Aracely, Av Obregón 471A Pte, T668-812
5090, lourdes@viajesaracely.com. Amex
agents, and full services with reservations
for the 1st-class train.
Viajes Flamingo, in the lobby of Hotel Santa
Anita, Av Gabriel Leyva Solano y Hidalgo,
T668-812 1613, www.mexicoscopper
canyon.com. Bookings for the trains attract
a commission of 8%.

⊖ Transport

Hermosillo *p252*
Air Gen Pesquira García Airport (HMO) is
12 km from town. Daily flights to **Mexico City**
with AeroMéxico, T662-216 8415, and
Aviacsa, T662-216 5278. Good domestic
connections. International flights to
Los Angeles, **Tucson** and **Phoenix**.

Bus The bus station is on Blv Encinas 400,
between Los Pinos and Jaffa. To **Agua Prieta**,
6 a day, 7 hrs, US$15.40. To **Guaymas**, hourly
round the clock, 2½ hrs, US$6.15. To **Kino**, 4 a
day, 1½ hrs, US$6. To **Los Mochis**, TAP, hourly,
7½ hrs through scrubland and wheat fields,
US$20.40. To **Mazatlán**, every 1-2 hrs, 10-12 hrs,
US$43.85. To **Nogales**, 9 a day, 4 hrs, US$11.15.
To **Tijuana**, every 1-2 hrs, 11 hrs, US$42.70.

Guaymas and Bahía San Carlos
p253 and p254
Air Gen José M Yáñez Airport (GYM) is 5 km
from Guaymas on the way to San Carlos.
AeroMéxico (T622-226 0123) has flights
to **La Paz**, **Mexico City** and **Phoenix**.

Boat Ferries to **Santa Rosalia** in Baja
California Sur leave from the waterfront four
times a week. Check schedules at
www.ferrysantarosalia.com.

Bus 1st-class bus to **Hermosillo**, 2½ hrs,
US$6.15. To **Mazatlán**, frequent, 12 hrs,
US$42. To **Tijuana**, 18 hrs, US$50.80. To

Culiacán, hourly, 9 hrs, US$25. To **Los
Mochis**, TAP, every 1-2 hrs, 5½ hrs, US$14.65.

Alamos *p255*
Bus Buses run to **Navojoa** every hour on the
half hour 0630-1830, 1 hr, US$1.40, good
road. If travelling from Navojoa, the bus
station to Alamos is about 8 blocks from the
main bus station; ask directions because
it is a confusing route.

Los Mochis *p256*
Air
Aeropuerto Federal (LMM) is 6½ km from
town. Flights to **Mexico City** and major
towns in northern Mexico. International
flights to **Los Angeles**, **Phoenix** and
Tucson with AeroMéxico.

Bus
Local Buses to the train station leave from
the corner of Obregón and Zaragoza; the first
leaves at 0515 in time to get tickets for the
train, US$0.30. Local buses to destinations
around Sinaloa, such as **Topolobampo**,
Guasave, **San Blas** (Sufragio) and **Culiacán**
leave from Cuauhtémoc, near the post office.
   Long distance The main bus station
is on the corner of Castro and Constitución,
about 10 mins' walk south of town. Buses
from the USA arrive here and it is the terminal
for long-distance **Futura** and **Elite** services.
   Services to the **west coast** are with **Norte
de Sonora**, T668-812 1757, 2nd-class **Estrella
Blanca** and 1st-class **Tufesa**, T668-818 2222.
The terminals are clustered together near
Degollado y Juárez, to the east of town.
   Buses to **El Fuerte** depart regularly
from inside the market on the corner of
Independencia y Degollado, US$1.40.
   To **Ciudad Obregón**, hourly or better,
3 hrs, US$9.65. All buses listed below are
considered long distance and leave from the
corner of Castro and Constitución (see
above). To **Guadalajara** (Tonalá, outside
city), hourly, 13 hrs, US$46.55. To **Guaymas**,
6 hrs, US$14.65. To **Mazatlán**, hourly or
better, 6 hrs, US$23.50. To **Mexico City**,

every couple of hrs, 24 hrs, US$87.
To **Monterrey**, 0900 and 2000, 24 hrs,
US$71.75. To **Nogales**, TAP, 8 daily, 12 hrs,
US$35.40. To **Tepic**, hourly, 10 hrs, US$40.
To **Tijuana**, hourly, 20 hrs, US$59.25.

Train

Los Mochis station is 8 km from town;
do not walk there or back in the dark. A bus
into town leaves from the corner of the
1st junction from the station from 0530.
There are toilets and local phones; the ticket
office is open 1 hr before the train leaves.

To get to the station, there is a bus service
from 0500, US$0.10 from the corner of
hotels **Hidalgo** and **Beltrán**, otherwise take
the 0500 bus from **Hotel Santa Anita**,
US$2.25 (for house guests only), or taxi.
Taxis in the centre go from Hidalgo y Leyva
(US$4.25 per car, bargaining not possible,
make sure price quoted is not per person,
rip-offs are common).

For Creel see page 293, for Chihuahua, see
page 292. If coming from Chihuahua and you
don't want to stay in Los Mochis (assuming
the train is not too delayed), you can take a
night bus to Mazatlán at 2200, arriving 0630.

Topolobampo *p256*
Ferry You can get a ferry from here to **La
Paz** in Baja California Sur. Show up early,
purchase tickets as soon as possible (space is
limited). The ferry starts boarding 3 hrs early,
and departs Sun-Fri 2300, arriving in La Paz
0600 the next day. For schedule, fares and
information, see box page 306. Enquiries in
Los Mochis, T668-817 3752; or, on day of
travel at Muelle Topolobampo office,
T668-862 0141

Culiacán *p257*
Military checks of vehicles (including buses
and taxis) are now common in Culiacán.

Air Aeropuerto Federal de Bachigualato
(CUL) is 10 km from centre. AeroMéxico,

T667-715 3772, has flights to **Mexico City**,
Acapulco, and major cities in northern
Mexico. International flights to **Los Angeles**
and **Tucson**.
Bus Buses run to all places along the west
coast, including **Guaymas**, 9 hrs, US$25.
To **Tepic**, 8½ hrs, US$28.85.

Car North of the city, the north- and
southbound carriageways are on different
levels with no divide (very dangerous).
A toll section of freeway heads nearer
to the coast, past Navolata, bypasses
Culiacán and rejoins Highway 15 a few
kilometres south.

ⓘ Directory

Bahía Kino *p253*
Banks There are no banks in the area,
only ATMs at most petrol stations and
some supermarkets in Old Kino. The
nearest bank is **Bancomer** in Miguel
Alemán, between Kino and Hermosillo,
48 km away.

Guaymas and Bahía San Carlos
p253 and p254
Bank Banamex, Mon-Fri 0830-1630).
Police/post office 7 km from the
highway, behind the shops.

Los Mochis *p256*
Banks Many banks on Leyva, with ATMs,
and a *casa de cambio* open a little later.
Internet Hugo's Internet Café, Av Gabriel
Leyva Solano 537, with printers/ scanners.
Also Cyber Más, Independencia 421.
Laundry Lavamatic, Allende 218;
Lavarama at Juárez 225. **Medical services**
Hospital Fátima, Loaizo 606 Pte, T668-815
5703, private, English spoken. **Post office**
Ordóñez Pte, between Guillermo Prieto y
Zaragoza Sur, south of centre, Mon-Fri
0900-1400, 1600-1800.

Mazatlán

→ *Colour map 1, C2. Phone code: 669.*

Mazatlán, spread along a peninsula at the foot of the Sierra Madre, is the second-largest Mexican port on the Pacific both in terms of population (Acapulco is larger) and shipping (Lazaro Cardenas is busier). Known to Mexicans as the Perla del Pacífico (Pearl of the Pacific), the idyllic setting and warm winters have inevitably turned it into a popular resort. Unfortunately with relentless expansion it has lost some of its appeal, although it is still one of the most beautiful spots along the Mexican Pacific coast.

The area of extensive development, called the Zona Dorada (Golden Zone), stretches for several kilometres north of the old town and attracts international tourists. However, in the heart of the old town you can join Mexicans taking their vacations, without the hard sell. The old town overlooks Olas Altas (High Waves) Bay, which has a very strong current. Entering Mazatlán by sea from Baja shows the city at its most impressive – two pyramid-shaped hills, one topped by a lighthouse (150 m above sea level), the other the 'rock' of Isla Piedra (which can be reached by highway or ferry), guard the harbour entrance.

Mazatlán does have other attractions besides the coast. With some 479 buildings registered as national historic monuments (the most of any Mexican town on the Pacific coast), its Carnival is one of the best in the country. The town boasts an amazing shell museum, has a remarkable 19th-century theatre in pristine condition, and its famous lighthouse – the world's second-tallest after Gibraltar's – is considered one of the world's most beautiful. ▶ *For listings, see pages 270-274.*

Ins and outs

Getting there **General Rafael Buelna International Airport** ① *20 km south of town along Route 15, T669-982 2399, www.aero/en/,* receives flights from Mexico City, destinations in northern and western Mexico and the US. Planes are met by the usual fleet of fixed-fare taxis and microbuses. The main **bus station** is 3 km north of the old town centre, with local buses and taxis providing links to the old town. First-class buses arrive from most major cities west and north of the capital, while second-class buses connect with smaller towns such as San Blas. The **ferry terminal** is at the southern end of Avenida del Puerto, quite a way from the centre; a bus runs from the street corner opposite the terminal to Avenida Ejército Méxicano near the bus station. Ferries run to La Paz, in Baja California (see box, page 237, for schedule).

For drivers, Route 15, the coastal road, heads north to the US border, and south to Tepic then inland to Guadalajara (or follow Route 200 to the border with Guatemala along the coast); Route 40, a good 20 km east of the city, is the picturesque but hair-raising road to Durango. ▶ *See Transport, page 273.*

Getting around Most local buses leave from the market. There is an express service (green and white buses), which runs from the Playa Cerritos to the city centre along the seafront to the Zona Dorada and beyond, US$0.20. Taxis are readily available and *pulmonias* (taxis that look like golf carts), will ferry you between the bus station and your hotel.

Tourist information The **tourist office** ① *Carnaval y Escobedo, T669-981 8883, www.sina loa-travel.com,* is in the old town. However, information can easily be obtained at any travel agency or hotel information desk, many of which are dotted around the Zona Dorada. Some English-language publications list local events: try *Pacific Pearl,* www.pacific pearl.com, and *Mazatlán Interactivo,* www.mazatlaninteractivo.com. See www.mazatlan.com.mx for more options. Mazatlán is the only resort with an acknowledged gay community north of Puerto Vallarta, which is served by the online magazine *Sinaloa Gay,* www.sinaloagay.net.

Sights

The old part of town is centred around **Plaza Machado**, on Carnaval. This is by far the most interesting part of the city. While Mazatlán does not give the same emphasis to its architecture and history as to its recreational side, the baroque (although constructed in the late 19th century) **Basílica de la Purísima Concepción** at the heart of the old town on the plaza is well worth a visit, with its elegant interior and two slender spires.

Half a block from the plaza, on Libertad, is the **Teatro Peralta**, the 19th-century opera house that was restored in 1987 and has been open to the public since 1922. Few interiors merit the sobriquet 'breathtaking', but this one certainly does. The history behind this building is rather interesting. In 1883, the famous opera singer Angela Peralta (known as 'The Nightingale of Mexico') arrived in Mazatlán to perform for the first time. Upon her arrival, the crowd that gathered to meet her unhitched the horses from her carriage and carried her to her hotel. She was so taken back by their enthusiasm that she performed for her fans from the balcony of the hotel that same evening. Unfortunately, the boat she arrived on carried yellow fever, and Peralta died before she could perform in the theatre (then named the Rubio). The theatre was renamed after her, and a plaque commemorates her tragic death.

Another interesting stop is the **Machado House Museum** ① *Constitución 79*, built in 1846. It originally was the home of the Canobbio family, Italian immigrants who lived on the

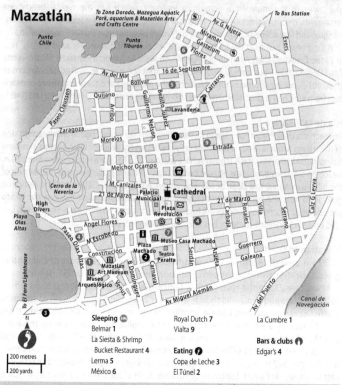

Mazatlán

To Zona Dorada, Mazagua Aquatic Park, aquarium & Mazatlán Arts and Crafts Centre

To Bus Station

Punta Chile

Punta Tiburón

Av G Nájera

Miramar

Gastelum

Flores

16 de Septiembre

Carrasco

Evers

Av del Mar

Bolívar

Quijano

Arribo

Guillermo Nelson

Benito Juárez

Lavandería

Zaragoza

Morelos

Estrada

Melchor Ocampo

J M Canizales

21 de Marzo

Palacio Municipal

Cathedral

21 de Marzo

Villa

Caliz G Leyva

Cerro de la Nevería

Plaza Revolución

Rosales

Carbaja

Serrano

High Divers

Angel Flores

Museo Casa Machado

Guerrero

Galeana

Playa Olas Altas

Paseo Olas Altas

M Escobedo

Constitución

Plaza Machado

Teatro Peralta

Serdán

Auleta

Mazatlán Art Museum

Museo Arqueológico

B Domínguez

Venus

Carnaval

Av Miguel Alemán

Av del Puerto

Canal de Navegación

To El Faro/Lighthouse

N

200 metres
200 yards

Sleeping
Belmar 1
La Siesta & Shrimp Bucket Restaurant 4
Lerma 5
México 6

Royal Dutch 7
Vialta 9

Eating
Copa de Leche 3
El Túnel 2

La Cumbre 1

Bars & clubs
Edgar's 4

upper level and used the ground level as a drugstore. Today, it has a collection of antique furniture, decoration, and Carnaval costumes. The **aquarium** ① *Av de los Deportes 111, behind Hotel Las Arenas, T669-981 7815, www.acuariomazatlan.gob.mx, just off the beach, open year-round 0900-1900, US$5*, is the largest and most interesting in the country, with a huge collection of maritime life, including sea lions, sharks and blindfish. **Mazagua Aquatic Park** ① *Av Sábalo-Cerritos, T669-988 0041, http://mazagua.com*, is a great family deal at only US$7.85 for all-day admission. The **Museo Arqueológico de Mazatlán** ① *Sixto Osuna 76, ½ a block from Hotel Freeman, US$0.65*, is small but recommended, with an interesting collection covering the State of Sinaloa. One street over is the new and very colourful **Mazatlán Art Museum** ① *Carranza y Sixto Osuna, T669-985 3502*. The **Mazatlán Arts and Crafts Centre** ① *Gaviotas y Loaiza, T669-913 5022*, has a huge selection of handicrafts from Mazatlán and all over Mexico; good quality, but not cheap.

Zona Dorada

Tourism is concentrated in the Zona Dorada, which includes the beaches of **Las Gaviotas**, **Los Sábalos**, **Los Pinos**, **Escondida**, **Delfín**, **Cerritos** (the most quiet), **Cangrejo**, and **Brujas** (a rocky area, good for snorkelling). The area is built up and accommodation is expensive. The old town, around **Olas Altas Bay**, has a distinctly more relaxed feel, but gives way to the *malecón*, a waterfront walkway, which has the typical beachfront restaurants, discos, nightclubs and hotels that you might expect. The southern end is more tranquil, and Mazatlán's boardwalk is infinitely more pleasant than that of Puerto Vallarta.

A long beach begins at the foot of the *malecón*, curves northwards around the bay, first at Paseo Claussen, then Avenida del Mar, which leads to Avenida Camarón Sábalo in the Zona Dorada (take a bus from Juárez, best from in front of the market, marked 'Sábalo Centro' US$0.40). Sunsets are superb from this side of the peninsula and there are plenty of beach bars from which to appreciate them. Buses from Arriba go to the Zona Dorada for US$0.40.

Isla de la Piedra

To reach Isla de la Piedra (which is in fact a peninsula) take a small boat from the south side of town from Armada (a naval station near Pacífico brewery, reached by 'Zaragoza' bus from Juárez outside market), it is a regular service and cost US$1.50 for a return ticket. The 30-km beach on the Mazatlán side is littered but you can walk across the peninsula either side of the hill (10 minutes) to a clean beach where there is good surfing. There is also a ferry that goes from near the lighthouse to the island (until 1700). Local *comedores* on the beach provide basic accommodation, or ask for permission to camp on the beach. Try smoked fish sold on a stick; **Victor's** *comedor* has been recommended. Beware of sandflies.

Mazatlán to Durango

At 20 km beyond Mazatlán, the Coast-to-Coast Highway heads east to Durango (a spectacular stretch of road, in good condition), turning left at Villa Unión. Heading east, after another 21 km the road reaches **Concordia**, a delightful colonial town with a well-kept plaza and a splendid church, then after 24 km climbs the foothills of the Sierra Madre Occidental, passing **Copala**, another former mining town. On this road, 40 km from Concordia, 3 km before Santa Lucía, at **La Capilla del Taxte**, 1240 m, there is a good hotel and restaurant (see Sleeping, page 271). Crossing into Durango State (add one hour) and reaching **La Ciudad** (one very basic hotel) and the plains, the road climbs to more than 567 m in less than 50 km before it goes up yet again through a spectacular section known as **Puerto Espinazo del Diablo** (Gate of the Devil's Backbone), winding

Music in western and northern Mexico

Mazatlán is the epicentre of one of Mexico's major music forms: La Banda – tuba-dominated and exuberantly-spirited music bands that include saxophones, trumpets, clarinets, several types of percussion as well as very direct voices. The polka is a preferred rhythm of 'La Banda'. An expert can tell the difference between the regional variations.

The much older, trumpet-dominated Mariachi originated outside of Guadalajara in the early 19th-century and gained popularity as the 'national' form of music in the 1930s. It is undoubtedly the best known genre of Mexican music, inside the country and around the world. Thanks to its institutionalization through films and later, television, Mariachi, with its gaudy uniforms modelled upon suits supposedly worn by *charros* (Mexican cowboys), remains the most popular style throughout the country today. Connoisseurs of the genre claim that a Mariachi ensemble always includes a full complement of nine musicians. It is de rigueur for *quinceañeras*, weddings, fairs, parties, even funerals.

A Ranchera is sung in a ballad style, and is somewhat less overtly romantic than Mariachi. It also emerged in Jalisco and dates to the Mexican Revolution. Often associated with Mariachi and largely derived from it, Ranchera is one of the most popular styles in Mexico today.

Musica Norteña (also known as Conjunto) is dominated by harmonica and a La Banda style rhythm. Originally from the State of Sinaloa but now popular throughout north and central west Mexico, it is also the most commonly heard music along the US border. Lyrically much darker than either La Banda or Mariachi, it often treats taboo topics like immigration and the drug trade (although the latter now has its own musical sub-division, Corrida). Whichever form you hear, the music permits you an insight into the spirit and character of Mexicans often not expressed in other mediums.

through many vertical-sided canyons with partly forested slopes. The road – the only paved one through the Sierra Madre Occidental for hundreds of kilometres to the north and south – is a phenomenal feat of engineering, as it is cut into the cliff side at almost 2620 m, with steep drops below. The scenery – if you can take your eyes off the serpentine road – is truly stunning.

The road crosses a narrow bridge (approximately 50 m long) with vertical drops either side and superb views to the south and north; no signs, just ask on the bus and the locals will tell you when it's coming up. If you're lucky you may be able to get the bus driver to stop. There is a plaque to the memory of the engineers' genius on the right a few kilometres after the *mirador* (viewpoint). After reaching the high plateau, the road passes through heavily logged pine forests to Durango (see page 309). Cyclists will find this road hard work in this direction, as there are many bends and steep hills. Trucks are frequent but they travel at very reduced speeds.

South of Mazatlán

Some 20 km south of Mazatlán, Route 15 continues south from Villa Unión. **Rosario**, another 36 km south, is an old mining town riddled with underground workings. There is an attractive and generally clean beach at **Playas El Caimanero**, 30 km southwest of Rosario. About 10 km km north on Route 3 is another fishing town, **La Guasima**, with superb beaches;

try the fish. Be careful of hiking around the Baluarte River Valley as there are *caimanes* (alligators), hence the name of the beach, Playa El Caimanero. There is a good seafood restaurant on the left at the entrance to Escuinapa de Hidalgo coming from Mazatlán.

Teacapán and around → *Phone code: 695.*

In Escuinapa de Hidalgo a good road (Route 1) turns off 41 km to the coast and the relatively undiscovered fishing village of **Teacapán**. A bus connects the two towns. The fishing is excellent and you can buy directly from the fishermen on Teacapán Beach. There are 30 km of fine beaches such as **Las Cabras**, **La Tambora** and **Los Angeles**, which are occasionally visited by dolphins. Buses run from Escuinapa de Hidalgo; tours from Mazatlán cost US$32 (cheaper fishing cruises are offered by locals, US$19). Teacapán has been slated for development by the Mexican government, but at the moment it remains rustic and off the beaten path, although there are several beachside RV encampments.

South of Escuinapa de Hidalgo the road passes several quaint little towns: **Acaponeta** (148 km, turn-off for El Novillero Beach, large waves and many sandflies), **Rosamorada** (197 km), **Tuxpan** (224 km) and **Santiago Ixcuintla** (248 km, several hotels), all with colonial religious buildings and archaeological museums. Nearby is the tiny island of **Mexcaltitán** and, further south (via Route 54) the beaches at **San Blas** (see page 484).

After Tepic, 55 km south of Santiago Ixcuintla, Route 15 heads inland to Guadalajara. A new motorway is being built between Escuinapa de Hidalgo and 32 km north of Tepic; when completed it will function as a *camino cuota* (toll road) and considerably shorten the distance between the two cities. It is due to be completed at the end of 2009.

⊛ Mazatlán listings

For Sleeping and Eating price codes and other relevant information, see Essentials pages 47-51.

⊜ Sleeping

Mazatlán *p266, map p267*
Old Town
AL Royal Dutch, Constitución 627, T669-981 4396, www.royaldutchcasadesantamaria. com. Pleasant and traditional Dutch-owned B&B. Rooms are very comfortable and the management is helpful, friendly and informative. Book in advance.
A La Siesta, No 11 Sur, T669-981 2640, www.lasiesta.com.mx. Good, reliable hotel with comfortable a/c rooms. Some have sea views and are more expensive. There's a decent, if noisy, restaurant downstairs.
C Belmar, Paseo Olas Altas 166 Sur, T669-985 1113, http://hotelbelmar.googlepages.com. By the beach, a block away from **La Siesta**, with spectacular views. Pool, Wi-Fi in lobby, babysitting services. Accepts US, Canadian,

and Mexican currency. Special rates for backpackers. English spoken. Reputedly haunted. Highly recommended.
D Emperador, Río Panuco s/n, right next to the bus station, T669-982 6724, www.mazatlan. com.mx/emperador. TV, a/c, restaurant. Noisy. Good price but be mindful of surroundings.
D Lerma, Simón Bolívar 622 y Aquiles Serdán, near beach, T669-982 2436. Best deal in the Old Town. Rooms are simple and quiet, with fan and hot showers. Secure parking.
D México, México 201 y Aquiles Serdán, T669-981 3806. Tidy, sometimes small rooms, basic, but a popular budget option. Ask for a quieter room facing away from the street. Rates double during Carnaval.
D Santa María, Río Panuco s/n, T669-982 2308. On the other side of the bus station to **Emperador**, same owners and very similar.
D Vialta, Azueta 2006, 3 blocks from market, T669-981 6027. Plain, simple rooms with bath and fan, all set around a pleasant central patio. Friendly and helpful.

Zona Dorada

Accommodation in Mazatlán's Zona Dorada is generally expensive and, as with other Pacific resorts, you'll be hard pressed to find a room for under US$40. Prices can double or triple on weekends, during high season, spring break, Christmas and Semana Santa. Note that many of these hotels have all-inclusive options and will automatically assume that this is what you want unless you say otherwise. Resorts are extremely crowded and noisy on weekends, so don't expect an inordinate level of peace and quiet unless you are staying in one of the top-flight hotels.

LL-L Océano Palace, Av Camarón Sábalo, T669-913 0666, www.oceanopalace.com, north end of Zona Dorada. Big all-inclusive resort with 200 rooms, pool, restaurant and abundant service.

AL Aguamarina, Av del Mar 110, T669-981 7080, www.aguamarina.com, across the road from the beach. Big comfortable, 4-star hotel with pool and all amenities. Front rooms are likely to be noisy.

A Las Arenas, Av del Mar, across the road from the beach, T669-982 0000, www.sands arenas.com. Front rooms are likely to be noisy. With pool, a/c, TV, fridge, garden, good restaurant, on beach.

A Las Palmas Suites, Camarón Sábalo 305 T669-916 5664. Good value for its range but noisy on weekends.You get what you pay for but not much more.

A-B Apartmentos Fiesta, Ibis 502, T669-913 5355, www.mazatlanapartments.com. A range of pleasant, good-value apartments surrounding a pleasant patio, some are budget (**D**). Diving and fishing tours available.
C Suites Linda Mar, Av Rodolfo Loaiza 226, T669-913 5533. Spotless, popular (so book well ahead) and straight on the ocean. The only option in this range, and a good one.

Camping

North of the city there are undeveloped beaches with free overnight camping; it is safer to camp in a group (take a bus to Sábalos and get out where it turns round). There are at least 10 trailer parks on Playa del Norte/Zona Dorada and on towards the north.

La Posta Trailer Park, Calzada R Buelna 7, T669-983 5310, A few blocks east of the beach in a tropical setting. Hot showers, coin laundry, convenience store, sundeck, *palapas*.

Las Palmas Trailer Park Camarón Sábalo, T669-983 6424. Next to Las Palmas Suites, with full hook-ups, hot showers and laundry.

Mar Rosa, on the beach next to Fiesta Americana, Zona Dorada, T669-983 6187. Apartments on premises as well.

Maravillas Trailer Park, Alfredo Tirado Apartado 1470, T669-984 0400. On Playa de Sábalo-Cerritos out of town. Quiet.

Playa Escondida Holiday Trailer Park, Playa Cerritos, T669-983 2578. Hot showers, laundry, recreation hall, and saltwater pool.

RV Park Villas al Mar, quiet place directly on the beach at the Camarón Sábalo. Good shade amongst the palms and bamboo.

San Bartolo Trailer Park, Camarón Sábalo opposite Playa Sábalo, T669-983 5755. Full services, but closed Jun-Oct.

Mazatlán to Durango p268

D Villa Blanca, La Capilla del Taxte, 3 km from Santa Lucía, T244-442 1628. A good hotel and restaurant.

South of Mazatlán p269

B Motel Virginia, Ctra Internacional Km 1107, south of Rosario and several kilometres north of Escuinapa de Hidalgo, T694-953 2755. Good clean. *Palapa* restaurant next door. Possible trailer parking.

Teacapán p270

A Rancho Los Angeles, Km 25 Ctra Escuinapa–Teacapán, 16 km north from Teacapán towards Escuinapa de Hidalgo, T/F695-953 1344. The former home of a drug baron. On the beach. Good value, luxurious swimming pool. Recommended.

D Denisse, on the square, T/F695-954 5266. 6 rooms with a/c, private baths. José Morales and Carol Snobel. Clean, next to phone office, noisy, local trips arranged.

Camping

All Teacapán RV parks are located along Teacapán Beach with direct frontage.
Isla Paraíso, on the beach. New, clean, US$12.
Oregon, on beach in town (no sign), T695-954 5308. US$10. Run down but one of better places to stay, new Mexican hotel next door.
Rancho Los Angeles RV and Camping Park, on the beach, T695-693 1609. 60 full hook-ups, pool, restaurant/bar. US$15/day, SU$100/week. Highly recommended.

❶ Eating

Mazatlán *p266, map p267*
There are many cheap street places selling fruit shakes and simple Mexican dishes at the beach end of Av Manuel G Nájera. The majority of the gringo-themed and franchise restaurants are found in the Zona Dorada. During the high season, reservations are suggested for any restaurant in the Zona.

Old Town

¶¶ Shrimp Bucket, Hotel Siesta, Olas Altas 111 y Av del Mar, T669-981 6350. Rightly famous for seafood, good environment, popular, good, live music evenings.
¶¶-¶ Copa de Leche, Av Olas Altas 1220 A Sur, T669-982 5753. Mexican food. Quaint, rustic ambiance. Sidewalk tables are perfect for enjoying your meal amid the sights and sounds of the crashing waves.
¶¶-¶ El Túnel, opposite Teatro Angela Peralta. 1200-2400. Good Mexican food in this legendary old restaurant, popular with locals and tourists. Great specialities.
¶¶-¶ La Cumbre, Benito Juárez y Hidalgo. 1100-1500. Few seats, very busy, not many tourists. Recommended.

Zona Dorada

¶¶-¶ Pedo y Lola, Constitución y Carnaval, T669-982 2589. Central. Good Mexican and continental cuisine. Casual refinement. One of the better downtown eateries.

¶ Jungle Juice, Las Garzas 101, T669-913 3315. Typical Mexican and American offerings. Breakfast and brunch only, although bar at night.
¶ Mercado. The best deal is at the market; you can get an excellent fish lunch for US$1.
¶ Pura Vida, Laguna 777, T669-916 5815. Another breakfast/brunch eatery, this one concentrating on vegetarian foods. Simple and cozy, omelets and wholewheat pancakes as well as a variety of yogurt and muffins, soy burgers and fruit plates for brunch.
¶ Señor Frog's, Av del Mar 225, T669-985 1110. Hideous but insanely popular with spring break and under-40 crowds. Service and food is better for brunch and early dinner, but far better known as a bar at night.
¶ Terraza Playa, Hotel Playa Mazatlán, Rodolfo T Loaiza 202), T669-913 4455. All-day breakfast menu, adding light meals after 1800. Highly recommended.

❶ Bars and clubs

Mazatlán *p266, map p267*
Old Town
Edgar's Bar, Aquiles Serdán y Escobedo, T669-982 7218. One of Mazatlán's oldest and most beloved drinking joints.

Zona Dorada

Bora Bora Beach Club, Av Camarón Sábado, T699-984 1777. Enormous (capacity for more than 2000 revellers) all-purpose, all-night club popular with spring break set. Rave reviews.
Joe's Oyster Bar, Av Rodolfo T Loaiza 100, T669-983 5333. Probably Mazatlán's best-known bar. Open-air, US$5 cover charge on weekends (includes 2 beers). Good music and busy in the tourist season. Dollars accepted.
Valentino's Disco, Av Camarón Sábado (next to and part of **Bora Bora Beach Club**), T699-984 1777. Daily 2100-0400. Capacity for 1200 people. Hip-hop, techno, and Spanish music. The 1st floor is mostly for dancing, and you can enjoy a drink while watching people dance from the 2nd floor.

▲ Activities and tours

Mazatlán *p266, map p267*
Mazatlán is a popular place for birdwatching (egrets, flamingos, pelicans, cranes, herons and ducks can be spotted in the mangrove swamps). Nearby at Camarones there is parasailing, drawn by motorboats. The northern beach tourist strip offers boat trips to nearby deserted islands, snorkel hire and paragliding. Bungee jumping is done at Av Camarón Sábalo y Calzado Rafael Buelna opposite McDonald's.

Boat trips
Yate Fiesta, Calzado Joel Montes Camarena 7, T668-982 3130, www.yatefiesta.com. A 3-hr harbour cruise, Tue-Sun from the ferry dock, 1100, US$13.85, 4-11 year olds US$7.70.

Bullfighting
There are bullfights at Calzado Rafael Buelna, good view from general seats in the *sombra* (shade), although you can pay much more to get seats in the first 7 rows. The event takes place on Sun at 1600, very touristy.

Fishing
Fishing is the main sport (sailfish, tarpon, marlin, etc). Mazatlán's famous fishing tournament follows Acapulco's and precedes that at Guaymas.

Swimming
Always check with the locals if swimming is safe, since strong rip currents in the Pacific run out to sea and are extremely dangerous.

Tour operators
Drive and Guide Tour Service, Laguna 400, T669-916 5714, www.mazinfo.com/tour guides. All-inclusive bilingual city tours. Expensive but very thorough.
Explora Tours, Centro Comercial Lomas, Av Camarón Sábalo 204-L-10, T669-913 9020. Very helpful. Recommended.
Hudson Tours, T669-913 1764. Good for mountain biking.

Ole Tours, Av Camarón Sábalo 7000, T669-916 6288, www.oletours.com. Regular city tours, baseball tours and sport-fishing trips.
Puesta del Sol, Av Camarón Sábalo, Plaza Valencia, T669-913 9425, www.stoneisland tour.com. Harbour and island tours
Zafari Tours, Paseo Claussen 25. Ferry bookings, helpful.

⊖ Transport

Mazatlán *p266, map p267*
Air
Aeropuerto General Rafael Buelna (MZT), 3 km from centre, has domestic flights to **Guadalajara**, **Mexico City** and major cities in northern Mexico. International connections to **San José** (Costa Rica), **Calgary** (Canada), **Denver**, **Houston**, **Los Angeles**, **Phoenix**, **Portland**, **Salt Lake City**, **San Francisco**, **Seattle** and **Spokane** (Washington).
   Airline offices AeroMéxico, T669-984 1111. **Mexicana**, T669-913 0770.

Bicycle
The Mazatlán–Tepic–Guadalajara road has been described as 'the most dangerous in the world for cyclists'. This is an over-statement (there are many in Mexico alone more dangerous) but utmost precaution should be taken as vehicles drive at excessive speeds at all times and there often is no hard shoulder.

Bus
A large central terminal, making travel a bit easier, is just off the Ctra Internacional and Ferrusquilla s/n, about 3 km north of the Old Town, 4 km south of the Zona Dorado. Take a bus marked 'Insurgentes' from the terminal to Av Ejército Mexicano for the centre, via the market at Aquiles Serdán.
   To **Chihuahua**, 1400, 1800, 16 hrs, US$44. To **Durango**, hourly 0600-1900, 7 hrs, US$27. To **Guadalajara** (at Tonalá, outside city), 8 hrs, hourly, US$30. To **Guaymas**, hourly, 11 hrs, US$42. To **Los Mochis**, hourly or better, 6 hrs, US$23.50. To **Mexicali**, TAP, 13 daily, 24 hrs,

US$70. To **Mexico City**, 17 hrs, US$70.80. To **Navojoa**, every 1½ hrs, 8 hrs, US$30.40. To **Nogales**, every 1½ hrs, 18 hrs, US$62.70. To **Puerto Vallarta**, TAP, 2300, 2430, 8 hrs, US$24.65. To **Tepic**, hourly, 5 hrs, US$14.65. To **Tijuana**, hourly, 26 hrs, US$77.75. To **Rosario**, US$1.25, you can then (with difficulty) catch bus to **Caimanero Beach**.

Buses to **Alamos** run every hour on the ½ hour from the smaller **Terminal Alamos**, Av Guerrero Ote 402, 2 blocks from market.

Bus companies Estrella Blanca, T669-982 1949; Transporte Norte de Sonora, T669-981 2335; Transportes del Pacífico, T669-981 5156.

Car

AGA, Camarón Sábalo 316, T669-914 4405. **Budget**, Camarón Sábalo 402, T669-913 2000. **National**, Camarón Sábalo 7000, T669-913 6000. US$277 per week.

Ferry

The ferry terminal is at the southern end of Av del Puerto, quite a way from the centre (take a bus marked 'Playa Sur'). Ferries run to **La Paz** in Baja California (see schedule, page 237).

La Paz ferry ticket office is only open 0830-1300 on the day of departure; arrive before 0800. Unclaimed reservations go on sale at 1100. Don't expect vehicle space for a same-day departure. Allow plenty of time for booking and customs procedure. Tickets are also sold at **Hotel Aguamarina**, Av del Mar 110, 10% commission, or from travel agents.

Taxi

Taxis charge an average US$3.50-5 between Zona Dorada and the city centre. Some may charge a higher fare in high season: avoid those that do. From Bahía del Puerto Viejo to the centre should cost US$1 (bus US$0.15).

❶ Directory

Mazatlán *p266, map p267*
Banks Many in the centre, near the plaza. Banamex, Juárez and Gen Angel Flores, also Av

Camarón Sábalo 434. Open 0900-1330, 1530-1730. *Casas de cambio* on Av Camarón Sábalo 109, 1009 and at junction with RT Loaiza; also at R T Loaiza 309. **American Express**, Av Camarón Sábalo 212, T669-913 0600, Mon-Fri 0900-1700, Sat 0900-1400. **Embassies and consulates** Canada, Hotel Playa Mazatlán, Av Playa Gaviotas 202, Local 9, T669-913 7320. Denmark, Av Ing Heriberto Frias 1509-13, T669-981 7642. France, B Domínguez 1008, T669-985 1228. Netherlands, Av Sábalo Cerritos, T669-913 5155. Germany, Av Playa Gaviotas 212, T669-914 93 10. Guatemala, Alejandro Quijano 211 Pte, T669- 981 6305. Netherlands, Av Camarón-Sábalo 6300, Apartado 575, T669- 988 0047. Norway, F Alcalde 4, T981-3237. USA, RT Loaiza, opposite Hotel Playa Mazatlán, T/F669-916 5889, Mon-Fri 0930-1300, T669-913 4455 ext 285. **Internet/ post** Mail Boxes Etc, Av Camarón Sábalo 310, T669-916 4009, mail boxes, courier service; across the street at Centro Comercial Lomas. In the Old Town, a few internet cafés on the south side of the main plaza, US$1.20 per hr. Also cheap international calls (US$1.50 per hr) and international calls and faxes, Mon-Fri 0600-2200, Sat-Sun 0900-1700. **Laundry** Lavandería, on Zúñiga and Juárez, near Hotel Lerma. **Medical services** General emergency T06; Red Cross T669-981 3690; Ambulance T669-985 1451; Police T669-982 1867. Hospitals: Hospital General, Av Ferrocarril, T669-984 0262. Cruz Roja Mexicana, Alvaro Obregón 73, T669-981 3690. There is a free Red Cross treatment station on Camarón Sábalo, opposite the Beach Man. **Post office** Juárez y 21 de Marzo, opposite the Palacio Municipal, T669-981 2121. DHL (expensive) is a couple of doors from Mail Boxes Etc on Av Camarón Sábalo, Mon-Fri 0900-1330, Sat 1500-1800, 0830-1330. **Telephone** On Av Camarón Sábalo, 1 block from American Express; also 21 de Marzo y Juárez. Computel phone and fax service, Av Aquiles Serdán 1512, T669-985 0109. Phone rental, Accetel, Av Camarón Sábalo 310-4, T669-916 5056. Public phones take international credit cards along Av Camarón Sábalo y RT Loaiza in the Zona Dorada for long-distance calls.

Contents

Footprint features

Border crossings

Northern Highlands

At a glance

◉ **Getting around** Bus, train and 4WD.

◉ **Time required** Two weeks for the major attractions; a month or more for full Copper Canyon immersion.

☼ **Weather** Winter months, Oct-Mar, can be cool or even icy at night, especially at high altitudes. The summer, Apr-Sep, can be blazingly hot, particularly inside the canyons.

✖ **When not to go** Avoid hiking in the canyons during the height of summer.

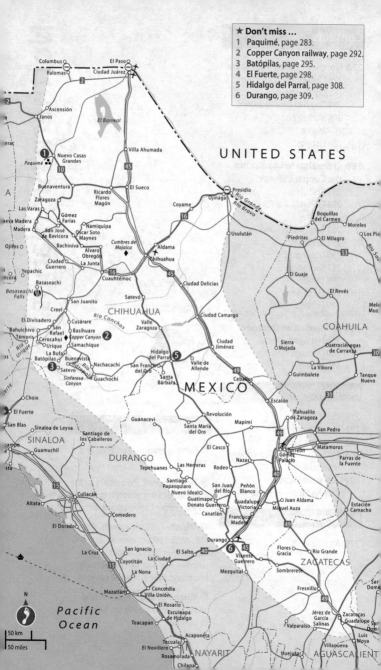

UNITED STATES

MEXICO

CHIHUAHUA

COAHUILA

DURANGO

SINALOA

ZACATECAS

NAYARIT

AGUASCALIENT

Pacific Ocean

Columbus
El Paso
Palomas
Ciudad Juárez
Ascensión
Janos
El Barreal
Villa Ahumada
Paquimé
Nuevo Casas Grandes
Buenaventura
Ricardo Flores Magón
El Sueco
Presidio
Río Grande
Ojinaga
Río Bravo
Coyame
Boquillas del Carmen
Moreles
Los Pie
Zaragoza
Las Varas
Gómez Farías
Namiquipa
Oscar Soto Maynes
San José de Bavicora
Bachiniva
Alvaro Obregón
La Junta
Cumbres de Majalca
Aldama
Usulután
Piedritas
El Milagro
eva Madera
Madera
Ojitos
Yepachic
Ciudad Guerrero
Cuauhtémoc
Chihuahua
El Guaje
El Revés
Mel Muz
Basaseachi Falls
Basaseachi
San Juanito
Satevó
Ciudad Delicias
El Divisadero
Creel
Río Conchos
Valle Zaragoza
Ciudad Camargo
Cusárare
Ciudad Jiménez
Sierra Mojada
COAHUILA
Bahuichivo
Témoris
San Rafael
Basíhuare
Copper Canyon
Samachique
Hidalgo del Parral
Cuatrociénegas de Carranza
Cerocahui
Urique
La Bufa
Nachacachi
Valle de Allende
La Vibora
Guimbalete
Tanque Nuevo
Río Urique
Batópilas
Buenavista
Satevo
Sinforosa Canyon
Guachochi
San Francisco del Oro
Santa Bárbara
Ceballos
Choix
El Fuerte
Guanacevi
Revolución
Escalón
Tlahualilo de Zaragoza
San Blas
Sinaloa de Leyva
Santa María del Oro
Mapimí
San Pedro
Santiago de los Caballeros
El Casco
Nazas
Torreón
Matamoros
Guamuchil
Tepehuanes
Las Herreras
Rodeo
Gómez Palacio
Parras de la Fuente
Culiacán
Santiago Papasquiaro
Nuevo Ideal
San Juan del Río
Peñón Blanco
Guadalupe Victoria
Juan Aldama
Estación Camacho
Comedero
Guatimape
Donato Guerrero
Canatlán
Francisco Madero
Miguel Auza
El Dorado
Durango
San Ignacio
El Salto
Vicente Guerrero
Flores Gracia
Río Grande
La Cruz
Coyotitán
La Ciudad
ZACATECAS
La Nona
Mezquital
Sombrerete
Mazatlán
Concordia
Villa Unión
Fresnillo
El Rosario
Jérez de García Salinas
Zacatecas
Guadalupe
Escuinapa de Hidalgo
Valparaíso
Teacapan
Acaponeta
Luis
Tecuala
El Novillero
Villapueva
Rosamorada
Huejuat
Chilapa

50 km
50 miles

The imposing Sierra Madre highlands of northern Mexico are rarely a destination in their own right. But these vast landscapes, at times barren and monotonous, hold some spectacular surprises.

The most important archaeological site in northern Mexico is just a couple of hours' drive south of the border at Casas Grandes (Paquimé), a maze of multi-storeyed adobe buildings, once a thriving community with over 3000 inhabitants. Don't expect to see too many dainty little dogs in Chihuahua; this, Mexico's biggest state, is the rugged land of Pancho Villa and there are museums and memorabilia dedicated to the *bandido*-turned-hero of the Revolution – even the bullet-ridden Dodge car he was finally gunned down in. It's dramatic stuff; and so is the *Chihuahua-al-Pacífico*, billed as 'the world's most scenic railroad', which wends its way across bridges, through tunnels and over the Sierra Madre down to the Pacific coast at Los Mochis – the journey of a lifetime.

Hikers will want to stop off at Creel or Divisadero to view the awe-inspiring landscapes, strange rock formations and wildlife, as well as visiting Mexico's tallest waterfall and penetrating the vertiginous depths of the Barranca del Cobre (Copper Canyon) – a vast canyon system covering an area several times larger than Arizona's Grand Canyon. This is the craggy land of the Rarámuri people, and some 60,000 live in the sierra where you can buy their hand-carved and woven crafts in any of the towns or villages. And if you're still looking for action, why not visit the Wild West and walk the streets of real Western film sets in the State of Durango.

Northern Chihuahua State

Most people hurry through northern Chihuahua State on their way to more famous sights further south. But to do so is to overlook several intriguing and off-beat destinations. The seamy industrial city of Ciudad Juárez – gritty, energetic and thoroughly uncompromising – is now at the heart of a highly publicized drugs war. Supplying teeming glimpses of urban life on the edge, this city can seem like a living testament to everything that's wrong with the life on the US–Mexico border. International TV journalists need bullet-proof vests when reporting here, but be discreet and you almost certainly won't. If such challenges don't appeal, the rugged mountains and deserts promise more sedate encounters with the pre-Hispanic past. Like the contemporary border towns of the 21st century, the ancient north was a frontier between two competing cultures; the Chichimeca hunting tribes of northern Mexico and southwestern United States; and the grand city-states of Central Mexico and Mesoamerica to the south. The superb archaeological site of Paquimé features labyrinthine complexes of undulating walls, quite unlike anything else in Mexico. Whilst the cliff-top cave city of Cuarenta Casas, is enmeshed in the landscape itself and quietly crumbling in desolation. The inhabitants of these dwellings were fine craftsmen and their artistic legacy is continued by their descendants; visiting a workshop in the village of Mata Ortiz affords the opportunity to acquire some really beautiful pottery. ›› *For listings, see pages 284-287.*

Ciudad Juárez and the border towns ⬤🚺✴🅰🅲 ›› *pp284-287.*

→ *Phone code: 656. Altitude: 1150 m.*

The sprawling border town of Ciudad Juárez has the dubious infamy of being Mexico's most violent city. In an ongoing spate of serial killings that remain largely unsolved, more than 400 women have been murdered here since 1993; a thousand more remain missing. Meanwhile, the infamous Carrillo Fuentes cartel, who manage the multi- million dollar business of trafficking cocaine to the USA, have recently stepped up their violence in a ruthless turf war, further inflamed by military crackdowns. Whether or not Juárez is truly getting to grips with its difficulties, it has a deservedly nasty reputation.

But beyond the horror stories, this town of 1.3 million inhabitants is the largest maquiladora (workshop) city in the world. Twin plant assembly and manufacturing operations now supersede tourism and agriculture in this vital centre of cross-border industry and commerce. Apart from the colourful array of drunks and day-trippers, scores of business people visit Juárez annually to negotiate trade deals or set up operations that take advantage of the cheap local labour and lax environmental protection laws.

There is, however, little here for the casual traveller, apart from sampling the gritty atmosphere, you may feel the need to leave – and quickly. Fortunately, you may also find that many of the city's inhabitants – brazen, gregarious and often endowed with a caustic wit – help soften the harshness of what is otherwise a thoroughly charmless destination. It's not all bad in Juárez. Just ugly.

Ins and outs

Getting there International flights arrive at **Aeropuerto Internacional Abraham González** ① *18 km south of the centre, T656-619 0734,* (taxi US$15-20), but you could also consider flying into El Paso International Airport (see page 287) over the border. The **Central Camionera** is 5 km southeast of the centre. If you walk from the terminal to the highway, take any bus going to the right marked 'Centro' for US$0.30. Pre-paid taxi tickets are sold from booths inside the station (to the centre or Santa Fe bridge, US$7). ›› *See Transport, page 286.*

Border essentials: northern highlands–USA

Note All border crossings between the USA and Mexico currently are under review (mostly due to increased drug and security concerns on the US side). For the latest information contact US Customs and Border Protection, http://apps.cbp.gov/bwt, and Crossing US Borders, http://www.dhs.gov/files/crossingborders/travelers.shtm.

If you cross into the USA and will be leaving by plane, you must ask for an immigration card. Make sure you have a US visa if you need one.

Ciudad Juárez–El Paso (Texas)

El Paso is on Mountain Standard Time, which is one hour behind Central Standard Time and General Mexican Time. Border formalities are minimal. From El Paso you can get on a bus outside Gate 9 of the Greyhound terminal, they depart at least every hour, 0600-2200, US$9.50; as you cross the border the driver should stop and wait for your documents to be processed. You are given 30 days entry, unless you ask for longer. Trolley buses cross the border for short trips. Alternatively, you can walk across (US$0.35 toll per person). Walking from Mexico to the USA costs US$0.55 (toll for cars leaving Mexico US$2.05).

Note there is a new border crossing at Santa Teresa (New Mexico), west of El Paso. It is good for trucks and southbound travellers avoiding the congestion of Ciudad Juárez.

Ojinaga–Presidio (Texas)

The border is open 24 hours.

Leaving USA Follow signs to Ojinaga; pass US immigration on left (if you need to, surrender US visa waiver form here). On the Mexican side, a guard will check your passport. Those with vehicles then park before doing paperwork. There are separate desks for personal and vehicle papers. Photocopying can be done for US$1. Get insurance before Presidio, no one sells it there, but you could ask **Stella McKeel Agency**, T915-229 3221/5.

Leaving Mexico The bus station is 2 km from the border. Make sure all your papers are stamped correctly.

Palomas–Columbus (New Mexico)

This modern border, 5 km south of Columbus on Highway 11, is open 24 hours. Palomas is just across the border. The Mexican immigration office is on the right as you cross the border. If driving, park just before the border and walk across to get your documents stamped. Customs is 60 m south of immigration.

Getting around The downtown area is compact and small enough to walk around. However, if you wish to venture into the Pronaf zone, it's a 40-minute walk or take a bus marked 'Plaza de las Américas' from Guerrero or Corona. Taxis charge by the zone, US$2-8. You can negotiate with the driver for hourly rates (about US$20 per hour).

Tourist information The **tourist office** ① *Av de las Américas 2551, T656-611 3174, www.visitajuarez.com, Mon-Fri 0900-1700, Sat-Sun 1000-1400*, is a good source of information, but located away from the centre in the Pronaf zone.

Safety Juárez has guns, drugs and violence, but you're unlikely to encounter any trouble as long as you stick to the main roads and don't wander off, especially at night. The usual big city rules apply and female travellers should definitely take care when choosing a hotel. The scheduled cloister of the Pronaf (Programa Nacional Fronterizo) zone is the safest place for visitors and the preferred haunt of business travellers. Despite the bad press, over a million people live and work here every day without being victims of crime.

Background

Ciudad Juárez was founded by Spanish explorers in 1659, thus establishing the long-standing Misión de Nuestra Señora de Guadalupe. Poised on an important trade route through the Rockies, the settlement was dubbed Paso del Norte (North Pass). But after the US-Mexico war, the 1848 Treaty of Guadalupe Hidalgo recognized the Río Grande as the new international border, dividing the city in two. The US half grew into the city of El Paso.

During the 19th century, Juárez stopped here before he established his Republican government in Chihuahua, fighting off the French occupation in 1856. El Paso del Norte was renamed Juárez in his honour. Then, in 1910, Pancho Villa seized the city, which would become a focus of conflict for several years. His band of rebel fighters were known as the División del Norte and are universally admired throughout northern Mexico.

In the aftermath of the Revolution, Juárez rebuilt and flourished as an entertainment centre. During the US prohibition, crowds of party-goers flocked over the border for the cheap legal booze, abundant prostitutes and exciting gambling opportunities. Little has changed. But after the signing of the North American Free Trade Agreement (NAFTA) in 1990, Juárez became much more industrial as maquiladora plants sprang up around the city. It has since grown significantly, drawing scores of migrant workers. Most find dwellings in the impoverished shanty towns skirting the city limits.

From 1993 to the present, a series of brutal serial killings, or feminicides, have been largely mishandled by the police. They remain unsolved, if diminished in frequency. Many human rights groups are

Ciudad Juárez/El Paso

N

500 metres
500 yards

Sleeping 🛏
D'Manely **8**
El Paso International Hostel **2**
Holiday Inn **7**
Impala **3**

Imperial **4**
Moran **5**
Plaza Continental **1**
Santa Fé **6**

Eating 🍴
Kentucky Club **1**
La Cueva de Chucho **2**
La Fiesta del Pueblo **3**
Martino **4**
Tacos Lucas **5**
Villa del Mar **6**

also outraged by the seeming indifference of political authorities, citing deeply embedded sexist attitudes, or worse, outright complicity, as the principal cause of their failure to halt the atrocities. In recent years, drug cartels have been battling with military forces, worsening the reputation for this big, bad border town (see box, page 282).

Sights

The main street is **Avenida Juárez**, on or near which are most of the souvenir shops, hotels, restaurants, clubs and bars. Two blocks west of Juárez on 16 de Septiembre, the **Nuestra Señora de Guadalupe de El Paso del Norte** mission was the first established in the region; the building was completed in 1668. The **cathedral** stands nearby. At the junction of Avenida Juárez and 16 de Septiembre is the Aduana, the former customs building, now the **Museo Histórico** ① *Tue-Sun 1000-1700*. In Parque Chamizal, just across the Córdova Bridge, are the **Museo de Arte Prehispánico** ① *Tue-Sun 1000-1700*, with exhibits from each Mexican state, the **Botanic Gardens** and a **memorial to Benito Juárez**. Continuing south down Avenida Lincoln, you come to the Pronaf zone with the **Museo de Arte e Historia** ① *Tue-Sun 1000-1700*. The **University Cultural Centre** and the **Fonart artisan centre**, which acts as a Mexican 'shop window', are well worth a look for the uninitiated tourist. The **Plaza Monumental de Toros** ① *López Mateos y Triunfo de la República*, holds bullfights between April and August, and *charreadas* (rodeos) are held at the **Lienzo Charro** ① *Av del Charro*.

El Paso (Texas)

Across the border from Ciudad Juárez, El Paso is similarly industrial (but slightly less nasty). There are a number of museums here, including the **Americana Museum** ① *5 Civic Plaza, T915-52 0394, Tue-Fri 1000-1700*, in the **Civic Centre** (which also houses a performing arts centre, convention centre and tourist office), the **Museum of Art** ① *1211 Montana, T915-544 0062, www.elpasoartmuseum.org, Tue-Sat 0900-1700, Thu 0900-2100, Sun 1200-1700*, and the **Fort Bliss Air Defence Museum** at the nearby air base. The **border-jumper trolley** ① *T915-544-0062, US$12.50, departs from the Convention Centre on Santa Fe street*, conducts tours of El Paso and Ciudad Juárez. For information, contact the **tourist office** ① *Civic Centre Plaza, T915-534-0601; also at the airport*.

To the east of the city, the **Ysleta Mission** is the oldest in Texas (1680), built by Franciscan monks and local Tigua tribesmen, who have a 'reservation' (more like a suburb) nearby; the **Socorro Mission** (1681) and **San Elizario Presidio** (1789, rebuilt 1877-1887) are in the same direction.

Ojinaga–Presidio (Texas) → *Phone code: 626.*

The State of Chihuahua may also be reached from the border at Ojinaga, east of El Paso/Ciudad Juárez. This route is recommended not only for the ease of crossing, but also for the spectacular scenery either side of the border.

Forty two kilometres from Ojinaga on Route 16 towards Chihuahua is **El Peguis**, over-looking an extraordinary canyon. There is also a *garita*, where vehicle papers are checked.

Palomas–Columbus (New Mexico)

Route 2 runs west from Ciudad Juárez, roughly parallel with the Mexico–US border. Between Juárez and Janos, at the northern end of lateral Mexico 24, is the dusty border town of **Palomas** (Chihuahua), opposite **Columbus** (New Mexico, USA).

Mexico's drug war

"Our insatiable demand for illegal drugs fuels the drug trade..." Hilary Clinton, US Secretary of State, March 2009.

The morgues of Juárez are busy. Execution-style murders, severed heads in ice boxes, bodies dissolved in bath tubs of acid – all signify a gruesome escalation in drug-related violence, which claimed 6000 lives in 2008 alone. Roughly a third of those victims – many of them unknown individuals – were murdered in Ciudad Juárez, the epicentre of Mexico's drug war. In a stark assessment of the troubles, the US Department of Defence issued a warning in 2009 that Mexico was in danger of becoming a failed state.

The recent surge in violence is down to rival gangs who are vying for control of the multi-billion dollar US cocaine market. Against a backdrop of splintering factions and shifting allegiances, two heavyweight cartels – the Sinaloa cartel and Carillo Fuentes cartel (also known as the Juárez cartel) – are expending a huge number of lives in an unprecedented turf war.

In response, the Mexican government has dispatched 40,000 troops to the worst affected areas. But some are fearful that if the army fails to control the problem, or becomes corrupted in the process, nothing will stand between the gangs and the government. Indeed, Economy Secretary Gerado Ruíz Mateos has already stated that Mexico runs the risk of having a drug-runner as its next president.

Generally however, the government is dismissive of such assertions. Confident that their strategy is working, they claim that recent escalations are symptoms of a desperate and increasingly failing criminal organization. Record seizures of drugs and high-profile imprisonments of gang leaders might seem to signify progress, but many interpret the worsening violence as a sign of the cartels steadying their grip on the country.

Institutional corruption is a key issue in the war, with underpaid police, bent officials and venal politicians on the cartel payrolls. But this problem, as president Felipe Calderon so astutely pointed out, necessarily affects both sides of the border. An estimated 90% of the cartel's arms are supplied by the world's greatest consumer of illegal narcotics – the United States. This fact has recently acknowledged by the Obama administration, who have pledged to tighten lax border controls and supply Mexico with high-tech helicopters.

What's more, until the age-old issue of demand is addressed, supplies will continue to flow. As such, Mexico's strategy is not to attempt the impossible by halting drug trafficking altogether, but merely to divert its course out ~ of Mexico. Meanwhile, as economic conditions in Juárez worsen, more and more young people are drawn to the wealth and promise of the drug world, which has its own music, its own language, its own codes – and its own saints. Chief among them is Santa Muerta – Saint Death – a fitting mistress for the urban poor.

Palomas itself has few attractions apart from limited duty-free shopping for liquor and pharmaceuticals, but Columbus was the site of Pancho Villa's 1916 incursion into New Mexico, which led to reprisals by the forces of American General John J Pershing. The **Columbus Historical Museum** ① *daily 1000-1600*, on the southeast corner of the highway intersection, contains many old photos of Pancho Villa, a copy of his death mask, and one of his *sombreros*; it also has exhibits on Villa's sacking and burning of Columbus.

There is a small shelf of books on the history of the town that you can browse through. The father of the museum's curator played a part in the battle.

South of Ciudad Juárez ●●● ➤ pp284-287. Colour map 1, A2.

Nuevo Casas Grandes → Phone code: 636.

Nuevo Casas Grandes is a quiet little town built around the railway. Once upon a time it was an important stop on a route that led west across the mountains, all the way from the Río Grande to the Pacific Ocean. Like most of Mexico's rail routes, it has since fallen into obscurity, and the town is now rather sleepy and unassuming. It becomes very dusty when dry, the wind blowing clouds of it down the streets and, when its wet, the main street becomes a river. There is not much to do, but there is a cinema that show US and Mexican films. The only real reason to stay is to use the town as a base for visiting the interesting ruins of **Paquimé**, by the nearby village of **Casas Grandes**. You can reach Nuevo Casas Grandes, roughly 60 km south of Janos on route 2, from Chihuahua, Ciudad Juárez or Agua Prieta.

Paquimé

ⓘ *Tue-Sun, 1000-1700, US$3.50, including museum, free Sun. From Nuevo Casas Grandes, take a yellow bus to Casas Grandes village from outside the furniture shop at 16 de Septiembre y Constitución Poniente, US$0.20, 15 mins. From the square in Casas Grandes it is possible to walk to the ruins: either take Calle Constitución south out of the square past the school, walk to the end of the road, cross a gully, then straight on for a bit, turn right and you will see the site, or take Av Juárez west out of the square and turn left at the sign to Paquimé, 1 km.*

Resembling a weird maze of adobe walls, Paquimé is quite distinct from the Mesoamerican metropolises of central and southern Mexico. Built by people more closely related to the desert cultures of the southwestern USA, it was probably a trading centre, reaching its peak between 1210 and 1261. Its commercial influence is said to have reached as far as Colorado in the north and possibly as far as southern Mexico. At its height, it had multistorey buildings; the niches that held the beams for the upper floors are still visible in some structures. A complex water system, also visible, carried hot water from thermal springs to the north, irrigated crops and acted as drainage. Whilst most of the buildings are of a type of adobe, some are faced with stone. You can see a ball court and various plazas among the buildings. The city was destroyed by fire in 1340, possibly after being sacked by a rival Apache tribe. The site is well tended and definitely worth seeing, but the areas open to the public are now quite limited.

The adjoining **Museo de las Culturas Norte** is well laid out and interesting, housing reproduction models of the site, interactive displays and captivating exhibitions on northern cultures. There is an interesting collection of ceramics, some with anthropomorphic or zoomorphic features, and often adorned in striking geometric patterns. These fascinating designs, unique to the region, have been resurrected by local potters, most notably in the town of **Mata Ortiz** (see below), 21 km southwest of Nuevo Casas Grandes.

Mata Ortiz

The sleepy of village of Mata Ortiz is an important centre of pottery production where distinctive multiform and polychrome vessels are made, continuing the vibrant artistic legacy of ancient Casas Grandes. Numerous workshops and crafts people can be visited in the village, but perhaps none are more important or influential than Juan Quezada – the man responsible for reviving the lost art of Paquimé pottery. After many years of careful experimentation, he managed to recreate the complex manufacturing techniques of his ancestors, subsequently passing his knowledge to the community who are now almost exclusively employed as artisans. Mata Ortiz pottery is all handmade without a wheel and typically decorated with intricate abstract designs. The very best can fetch thousands of dollars on the international market. Buses from Nuevo Casas Grandes to Mata Ortiz may no longer run (check locally), but a return taxi should cost around US$20-30.

Madera and the Sierra Madre 🚌🏨🍴 ▶ pp284-287. Colour map 1, A2.

Madera → Phone code: 157. Altitude: 2100 m.

Madera is in the Sierra Madre, northwest of Chihuahua, surrounded by rugged mountain scenery. It is high enough to receive snow in winter (rainy season September-March, best time to visit May-August). The region around Madera has ample scope for tourism: archaeological sites, birdwatching, fine landscapes and good infrastructure. It is also on an important waterfowl migratory route, with white-fronted, blue and snow geese, mallard, pintail, teal, widgeon and redhead duck, and sandhill crane passing through. This does mean that it has become a popular centre for shooting (mid-November to February), but birdwatching expeditions are possible.

Cuarenta Casas

ⓘ If driving from Madera, take Calle 3 in a northerly direction out of town until you come to a signed turning right to Las Varas, which leads to Casas Grandes, 1½ hrs, daily 0900-1500, free.
Cuarenta Casas is a series of cave dwellings inhabited originally by indigenous Paquimé. Some of the houses have the palette-shaped windows/doorways also seen at Casas Grandes (called here La Cueva de las Ventanas); some are two storeys high. There is a good view of the cave houses from the visitor hut at the entrance. A trail descends to the river before climbing steeply to the cave, a challenging hike that takes 45 minutes to one hour one way. Camping is possible only when personnel are staying the night; there are no facilities other than water.

Four kilometres from Cuarenta Casas towards Madera is the turn-off to **El Salto**, a 35-m waterfall, best seen after the spring thaw (March-April). The fall is along a track to the right; to see it you have to walk around the rim of a little canyon. It is possible to hike down to the river below (about one hour). Ask at the house on the track to the fall if you want to camp (no facilities).

ⓦ Northern Chihuahua State listings

For Sleeping and Eating price codes and other relevant information, see Essentials pages 47-51.

🛏 Sleeping

Ciudad Juárez p278, map p280

A-B Holiday Inn Express, Paseo Triunfo de la República 3745, T656-629 6000, www.ichotelsgroup.com/h/d/ex/1/en/hotel/juaex. Reliable **Holiday Inn** quality. Comfortable, generic rooms equipped with satellite TV, internet, coffee-makers and other gadgets. Pool and restaurant are among the amenities. Best rates online.
C Santa Fé, Lerdo 675, T656-615 1558, www.hotel-santafe-juarez.com. A large, modern hotel with 76 good comfortable rooms, all with a/c and satellite TV. Private parking, restaurant and bar are among the amenities. Recommended.
D D'Manely, Blv Oscar Flores 4431, T656-610 7330. Close to bus station: go out of

the west (taxi) entrance, walk straight across the car park to the street, cross the street, and walk left 2 blocks. Rooms have heating and private bath. Clean, but the atmosphere is slightly sketchy and depressing. Good if you need an early morning bus though.

D Impala, Lerdo 670 Nte, T656-615 0431, www.hotel-impala.com. This hotel, close to the bridge, has 56 straightforward rooms with a/c, heating, carpet, TV, phone and hot water. Enclosed parking available. Helpful.

D Imperial, Guerrero 206, T615-0323. At the bustling heart of downtown, a big hotel with straightforward rooms, all with phone, TV and a/c. Not as attractive as some other lodgings in this price bracket.

D Plaza Continental, Lerdo Sur 112, T656-615 0259. Clean and comfortable hotel with 65 rooms, all equipped with cable TV and a/c. Other services include late night restaurant, Wi-Fi, parking and bar.

E Hotel Moran, Juárez 264 Nte, T656-0862. On the main drag, close to the bars and restaurants, with basic, clean rooms for those on a budget.

El Paso (Texas) *p281, map p280*
B-E El Paso International Hostel, 311 East Franklin Av, T656-532 3661, www.elpaso hostel.com. Also known as the Gardner Hotel, this El Paso institution has been serving travellers since the 1920s. Dorms, private rooms with or without bath, common room, coffee, internet, hot water and TV.

C International, Oregon. Clean rooms with a/c and TV. Recommended.

Ojinaga *p281*
D Armendariz, Zaragoza 713, near the Zócalo, T626-453 1198. Clean rooms and safe parking.

Palomas *p281*
D Hotel Restaurant San Francisco. Reasonable accommodation.
E Motel Santa Cruz, behind seafood restaurant, opposite gas station. Fairly basic with prices to match.

Columbus (New Mexico) *p281*
A Martha's Place, Main Stand Lima St, T505-531 2467, marthas@vtc.net. Very attractive lobby and a pleasant breakfast area.
C Suncrest Inn, Highway 11, just north of Highway 9. TV and phones in rooms.

Camping Pancho Villa State Park, opposite the Columbus Historical Museum. Excellent, well-maintained sites, additional charge for electrical hook-up.

Nuevo Casas Grandes *p283*
C Paquimé, Av Benito Juárez 401, T636-694 4720, paquime_hotel@hotmail.com. Large, clean rooms with cable TV, fan or a/c.
C Piñon, Av Juárez 605, T636-694 0655, hotelpinon@prodigy.net.mx. Pleasant, friendly hotel with comfortable rooms, pool, and a selection of Paquimé pottery. Tours of the ruins occasionally offered. Recommended.
E Juárez, Obregón 110, T636-694 0233. The only budget lodgings in town. Rooms cheap and reasonably nasty. At least the management is friendly and English-speaking.

Casas Grandes (Paquimé) *p283*
B Las Guacamayas, 20 de Nov y Zona Arqueológica 1101, T636-692 4144, www.mataortizollas.com. An adobe-style B&B, located right next to the archaeological site. Interesting and comfortable, with traditional rooms, hammocks, wood beams, flowers and tiled floors. Peaceful and hospitable. Breakfast included.

Madera *p284*
C María, Calle 5 y 5 de Mayo. Clean rooms have heating, some cheap ones available. Limited parking. Restaurant open 24 hrs. Good.
F Motel Maras, Calle 5, 1 block south of Mirmay. Noisy, dusty, but otherwise clean rooms with hot water.

🍴 Eating

Ciudad Juárez *p278, map p280*

Several places offer deep fried chicken, rotisserie and other spit-roasted meats, particularly along 16 de Septiembre. That said, the smell isn't very appetizing.

♦♦♦ Martino, Juárez 643. Crystal glasses and unexpected elegance at this Juárez institution. The menu features international and Mexican food.

♦♦ Kentucky Club, Juárez 629. The Kentucky Club harks back to the prohibition era when Kentucky whisky was produced in Juárez and smuggled over the border. An atmospheric bar and grill with sports TV.

♦♦ La Fiesta del Pueblo, Juárez y González. Fun, touristy Mexican-themed restaurant serving T-bone steaks, tacos and shrimp cocktails, among other international offerings. A very well-stocked bar.

♦♦ Villa del Mar, Villa Sur 130. Clean and popular seafood joint with booth seating. They serve some meat dishes too.

♦♦-♦ La Cueva de Chucho, Villa Sur 136. Economical breakfasts and Mexican food, including *pollo con mole* and *milanesa de res*.

♦ Tacos Lucas, Mejía y Juárez. Popular fast food joint serving tacos, as the name suggests. Also *tortas*, burritos and other cheap grub.

Nuevo Casas Grandes *p283*

♦♦ Constantino, Juárez y Minerva. Open since 1954, serving wholesome Mexican fare.

♦♦-♦ Dinno's Pizza, Constitución y Minerva. Tasty pizzas and an excellent breakfast buffet.

⊛ Festivals and events

Ciudad Juárez *p278, map p280*
2-5 May Festival de la Raza, with music, dance and various cultural events.
5 May Celebrations take place on Av Juárez (Battle of Puebla).
1-4 Jun Festival Ojinaga.
Jun-Jul Feria Juárez, Parque Chamizal.
15 Sep Independence Day.

⊛ Transport

Ciudad Juárez *p278, map p280*
Air
Abraham González (CJS) airport is 18 km south of the city, T656-619 0734; taxi US$15-20. Flights to **Mexico City**, **Chihuahua**, **Ciudad Obregón**, **Culiacán**, **Durango**, **Guadalajara**, **Hermosillo**, **Ixtapa**, **León**, **Los Cabos**, **Mazatlán**, **Monterrey**, **Torreón**, **Tijuana** and **Zacatecas**.
   Airline offices Aero California, T618-3399. AeroMéxico, T656-613 8719.

Bus
The Central Camionera, Teófilo Borunda, T656-610 7083, is 5 km southeast of the centre. To get to the bus station, use route 1A or 1B from Guerrero. A shuttle bus runs to **El Paso** Greyhound Terminal, US$11, hourly.
   The bus station has good services including long-distance telephones, money-changing facilities and left-luggage. Ticket counters are on the north side of the terminal.
   The main bus lines are Estrella Blanca and its subsidiaries, Grupo Senda, Greyhound, Autobuses Americanos, ETN and Omnibus. To **Chihuahua**, every ½ hr, 4½ hrs, US$22. To **Durango**, every 2 hrs, US$50. To **Guadalajara**, 8 daily, US$80. To **León**, 8 daily, US$73. To **Mexico City**, every 1-2 hrs, 25 hrs, US$93. To **Monterrey**, 1130, 1330, 1630 and 2145, US$57. To **San Luis Potosí**, every 2 hrs, US$71. To **Zacatecas**, every 1-2 hrs, US$60.
   To USA Check Autobuses Americanos and Greyhound website, www.greyhound.com.mx, for the best fares. To **Alburquerque** (NM), 4 daily, 7½ hrs, US$45-63. To **Denver** (Colorado), 4 daily, 15 hrs, US$73-133. To **Los Angeles** (CA), 6 daily, 17hrs, US$80-144.

Taxi
Some taxis are allowed to cross the border and take you to downtown **El Paso**; US$40; or to **El Paso Airport**, US$50.

El Paso (Texas) *p281*
Air
El Paso Airport (ELP) is near Fort Bliss and Biggs Field military airbase. A *colectivo* from Ciudad Juárez airport costs US$15.50. Flights with **American**, **Delta**, **America West Airlines** and **Southwest Airlines** to all parts of the USA. There are also flights from El Paso to **Chihuahua** and **Guadalajara**.

Bus
From the **Greyhound Terminal**, corner of San Antonio and Santa Fe, you can get buses to **Laredo** and **Tucson** and other connections in the USA. A shuttle bus runs every hour on the ½ hr to **Ciudad Juárez**, US$11, 0630-2130. You can buy your ticket on the bus; it stops at the Mexican side of the border for immigration where you can pick up your FM-T (tourist card).

Car
Sanborn's, 440 Raynolds, T1-800-222-0158, www.sanborns insurance.com. Mon-Fri 0830-1700. For insurance and information.

Nuevo Casas Grandes *p283*
To **Ciudad Juárez**, several daily, 4 hrs, US$12.50. To **Chihuahua**, every 1-2 hrs, 5 hrs, US$18. To **Mexico City**, once a day via **El Sueco**, once via **Cuauhtémoc**, US$98. To **Agua Prieta** 3 times daily. Also one service a day to **Cuauhtémoc**, **Hermosillo**, **Madera**, **Monterrey**, **Nogales** and **Tijuana**.

Madera *p284*
Bus Estrella Blanca, T157-572 0431, to/from **Chihuahua** every hour, 5 hrs from the bus stop on Calle 5 y Mina in Madera. There are also 1-2 daily services to **Ciudad Juárez** and **Casas Grandes**.

⊙ Directory

Ciudad Juárez *p278, map p280*
Banks Most *cambios* are on Av Juárez and Av de las Américas; there is also a *cambio* at the bus terminal. Rates vary little. Exchange houses are better and more convenient in El Paso (see below). **Embassies and consulates** US, Victoria 3650, Ciudad Juárez, T656-227 3000. UK, Fresno 185, Campestre Juárez, T656-617 5791. **Internet** Compurent, 16 de Septiembre y Villa, US$1/hr; also at Juárez 243. **Post office** Corner of Lerdo Sur and Ignacio de la Peña.

El Paso (Texas) *p281*
Banks Banks are closed on Sat. Valuta Corp, 301 Paisano Drive, buys and sells all foreign currencies but at poor rates, wires money transfers, open 24 hrs including holidays. Melek Corp, 306 Paisano Drive, offers most of the same services as Valuta but only dollars and pesos, not open 24 hrs. **Embassies and consulates** Mexico, 910, E San Antonio, T656-533 4082.

Presidio (Texas) *p281*
Banks Bancomer on the Zócalo, changes TCs, no commission; opposite is Casa de Cambio Allende, cash only, poorer rates.

Nuevo Casas Grandes *p283*
Banks Several on 5 de Mayo and Constitución Ote; Casa de Cambio California next to hotel of that name, in Casas Grandes. **Telephone** Long-distance calls from Rivera bus office, on Alvaro Obregón, in Casas Grandes.

Madera *p284*
Banks Banamex, Bancomer and Banrural with ATMs and will change dollars (and TCs).

Chihuahua to Los Mochis: the Copper Canyon

Mexico's Copper Canyon is a land of staggering mountain-top vistas where sky, space and geological grandeur threaten to swallow you whole. A labyrinthine network of vast canyons, jagged gorges and turquoise rivers, it is simultaneously rugged and ethereal, tempered by violent elements and carved out of the land like a sublime work of art. Mining towns, lost in time, fade into gentle obscurity, dwindling on the edge of winding mule trails. Remote Rarámuri communities are punctuated by fields of golden maize and diminutive wooden houses. Old missions – painted in indigenous motifs and attended by sparsely settled villages – stand desolate in a world of weird rocks and vertical cliff faces, all mottled with moss and minerals and fierce little flowers. Outdoor enthusiasts will find much to occupy them here: hiking, biking, rock-climbing, fishing, and, as the canyon systems empty into the slow-moving Río Fuerte, kayaking. But no trip to canyon country is complete without riding the Chihuahua al Pacífico railway, a stretch of track that steers right through the mountains as far as the Pacific coast. A truly impressive engineering feat, it offers superlative views of the great chasms, waterfalls and lakes that comprise this unrelenting but entrancing land. The railway's eastern terminus, Chihuahua, is outside the copper canyon, but makes a decent place to rest up before or after forays. It is the capital of Chihuahua state and home to several interesting museums, as well as an unprecedented host of leather shops. Time to purchase some cowboy boots and get into the Wild West spirit. » For listings, see pages 299-307.

Chihuahua ⬤⬤⬤▲⬤⬤ » pp299-307. Colour map 1, B2.

→ *Phone code: 614. Altitude: 1420 m.*

The capital of Chihuahua state and centre of a mining and cattle, Chihuahua City, 375 km from the border, is mostly a modern and rather run-down industrial city, but has strong historical connections, especially with the Mexican Revolution. Pancho Villa operated in the surrounding country, and once captured the city by disguising his men as peasants going to market. There are also associations with the last days of Independence hero Padre Hidalgo. Unfortunately there's none of the handsome colonial architecture that characterizes the cities further south, but Chihuahua does have an abundance of attractive 19th century edifices. Summer temperatures often reach 40°C but be prepared for ice at night as early as November. Rain falls from July to September.

Ins and outs

Getting there **Airport Gen Fierro Villalobos (CUU)** ① *18 km from the centre on the road to Ojinaga, T614-420 5104, www.oma.aero/en/.* Airport buses run to hotels in town (US$3); taxi US$16 (the only option at night). The **bus terminal** is 8 km

Copper Canyon area

To Hermosillo ►
La Junta
Cuauhtémoc
► To Chihuahua
Yepachic
Basaseachi Falls
San Juanito
Creel
Valle de los Hongos
Laguna Arareco
Río Conchas
El Divisadero
San Rafael
Río Urique
Cusárare
Basihuare
Copper Canyon
Bahuichivo
Samachique
Cerocahui
Norogachi
To Los Mochis ►
Urique
La Bufa
Batópilas
Buenavista
Satevo
Río Fuerte
Sinforosa Canyon
Nachacachi
Río Batópilas
Guachochi

N

30 km
30 miles

southeast of the centre, 20 minutes by bus, US$0.40; taxi US$6 (fixed price). Chihuahua is the eastern terminus of the *Chihuahua al Pacífico* railway; the **train station** is a 20-25 minute walk from the downtown area, or take a 'Circunvalación 2 Sur' bus from 20 de Noviembre. Taxis to/from the station cost US$4. ▸▸ *See Transport, page 305.*

Getting around Downtown Chihuahua is reasonably compact and can be easily explored on foot. For outlying attractions, there is an extensive network of town buses (US$0.20); taxis are widespread and operate on a zone system.

Tourist information The **tourist office** ① *Palacio de Gobierno, Aldama y Guerrero, T614-429 3596, www.ah-chihuahua.com, Mon-Fri 0900-1700, Sat-Sun 1000-1500,* is small, helpful and English-speaking. They have a good selection of flyers and brochures.

Background
The first settlement at Chihuahua was founded in 1709 by Spanish explorer Antonio Deza y Ulloa. It was called El Real de Minas de San Fransisco Cuellar, but was later renamed San Felipe el Real de Chihuahua in 1718, and shortened, finally, to just Chihuahua in 1823. It developed as a ranching, agricultural and trade centre, and Catholic missionaries would converge there during their operations in the far-flung desolate mountains and deserts.

During the War of Independence, Hidalgo was held prisoner in the city jail and later executed in the Palacio de Gobierno. Today, murals inside the building commemorate the hero's struggle. Between 1864-1867, Benito Juárez ran his government-in-exile from Chihuahua, and later on in the 19th century, Chihuahua experienced a boom under the reign of Porifiro Díaz. Many regal buildings from this era can be seen today. Subsequently, during the Mexican Revolution, Pancho Villa established his base here and contributed much to the city's infrastructure and post-revolutionary identity. During the late 20th century, foreign factories moved in and the population exploded. Chihuahua is today one of the wealthiest municipalities in the who;e republic, thriving on industry and cross-border trade.

Sights
Chihuahua's streets broadly follow a grid pattern, but it is not a perfect grid or consistently logical either. The Plaza de Armas is at the centre of the city, flanked by Independencia, one of the main thoroughfares. North of the plaza, **Calle Libertad** is for pedestrians only and leads to the Palacio de Gobierno and Palacio Federal. Northwest of Juárez, Calle 4 and the streets that cross it are bustling with market stalls and economical restaurants. There are a number of old mansions around town and the **Paseo Bolívar** area is pleasant for walking. In the southeast, near Calle Zarco, are ancient **aqueducts**. Walk north along Ocampo and over the river for fine views of the city at sunset.

Plaza de Armas This square is the geographic heart of the downtown area, home to an iron bandstand and replete with pigeons, cowboys and strollers. A statue of the city's founder, Don Antonio Deza y Ulloa, flamboyantly points to the spot where work should begin. The **cathedral** was built 1725-1826 and has a baroque facade dating from 1738. Various economic setbacks hindered the cathedral's completion for more than a century. The interior is mostly unadorned, with square ochre columns, glass chandeliers and a carved altarpiece. The crypt beneath it is home to the **Museo de Arte Sacro** ① *Mon-Fri 0900-1300 and 1500-1700, US$0.70,* complete with sombre religious art.

Plaza Mayor and around The Plaza Mayor, four blocks north of the Plaza de Armas, is a large paved square that's flanked by busy traffic. This is the old political centre of the city, home to historic buildings and institutions. Here you'll find the **Angel de la Libertad**, the statue of a gold angel armed with a sword, and the **Templo de San Francisco**, the city's oldest church where Hidalgo's body was kept before its burial in Mexico City. The old Palacio Federal, now the **Museo Casa Chihuahua** ⓘ *Libertad y Guerrero, 1000-1700, US$2.80*, is the site of the old of the Capilla Real where Hidalgo awaited his exhibition. It's now home to an array of cultural exhibits, gallery and convention halls. The *calabozo* (dungeon) itself is fairly unremarkable. Nearby, the elegant 19th-century **Palacio de Gobierno** is in fine condition, with a dramatic set of murals by Aaron Piña Morales depicting Chihuahua's history that are worth checking out. There are also two museums inside: **Museo de Hidalgo** ⓘ *Tue-Sun 0900-1700, free*, with exhibits honouring the father of Independence; and **Galería de Armas** ⓘ *Tue-Sun 0900-1700, free*, with an array of Independence war weaponry.

'Quinta Luz' Museo de la Revolución Mexicana ⓘ *south of the centre, Calle 10, No 3014, Tue-Sat 0900-1900, Sun 0900-1600, US$0.70*. The former Quinta Luz mansion once belonged to Pancho Villa, the legendary 'Centaur of the North' and commander in chief of the Division del Norte. He lived and worked here whilst serving as governor of Chihuahua in 1914, subsequently leaving the property to one of his many wives, Doña Luz Corral de Villa, who remained until her death in 1981. Today the building houses the Museo de la Revolución and is certainly worth a visit. The rooms retain their early-20th-century decor and host several intriguing historic exhibits that include old weapons, uniforms, antique furniture and the car in which Villa was assassinated (looking like Swiss cheese from all the bullet holes). His death mask is displayed too, offering a slightly eerie face-to-face encounter with now the immortalized hero.

Museo Quinta Gameros ⓘ *Bolívar 401, Tue-Sun 1100-1400, 1600-1900, US$1.50*. This exquisite art noveau mansion was built by the mining magnate Don Manuel Gameros as a show of affection for his beloved fiancée, Elisa Muller, but sadly, by the time of its completion in 1910, she had already died. Soon after, the Mexican Revolution forced him to flee the country, leaving the building to revolutionary forces; both Carranza and Villa utilized it as their office. Years later, descendants of Don Manuel returned to reclaim the mansion, selling it to the government in the 1950s, who subsequently converted it into a museum. The interior is extremely fine and well worth exploring, lavishly restored and replete with sensuous wooden furniture and beautifully carved finishes. There are also displays of art and temporary cultural exhibits.

Other sights Various other museums are dotted around the city, worth checking out if you have time or a special interest. The **Museo de Arte e Industria Populares** ⓘ *Av Reforma 5, Tue-Sat 0900-1300, 1600-1900, free*, has displays of Rarámuri (Tarahumara) art and lifestyle. Sometimes known as the Museo de la Lealtad Républicana, the **Museo Casa Juárez** ⓘ *Juárez y Calle 5, Mon-Fri 0900-1500, 1600-1800*, was once the house and office of Benito Juárez himself, now housing historic displays and antiques. The charming **Museo del Mamut** ⓘ *Juárez y Calle 25a, Tue-Sun 1000-1700, US$1.50*, has some impressive fossils retrieved from the deserts of Chihuahua, once hidden beneath a vast ocean; it's fun, but ultimately low-key. More scientific exhibits can be seen at the **Museo Semilla** ⓘ *Calle 10 y Teofilo Burunda, US$3, Tue-Fri 0900-1700, Sat-Sun 1200-1900*, with hands-on exhibits suitable for kids. If you're looking for contemporary art, head to the **Casa Redonda, Escodero y Colón** ⓘ *Tue-Sun 1000-2000, US$1*. An interesting minor attraction, **Las Grutas de Nombre de Dios** ⓘ *north side of town, Tue-Fri 0900-1600, Sat-Sun 1000-1700, US$3,* *catch a 'Nombre de Dios Ojo' bus from Calle 4 y Niños Heroes,* are impressive underground caves with wonderfully surreal rock formations.

Towards the Basaseachi Falls → *Colour map 1, B2.*

Beyond the city, route 16 leads west through **Ciudad Cuauhtémoc**, which has the **Museo y Centro Cultural Menonita** ⓘ *Km 10, on the road to Alvaro Obregón, T614-428 7508, Mon-Sat 0900-1800, US$1.75,* and **La Junta** to the **Basaseachi Falls**. At 311m, this is the highest single-jump waterfall in North America and is worth the effort of getting there. The top of

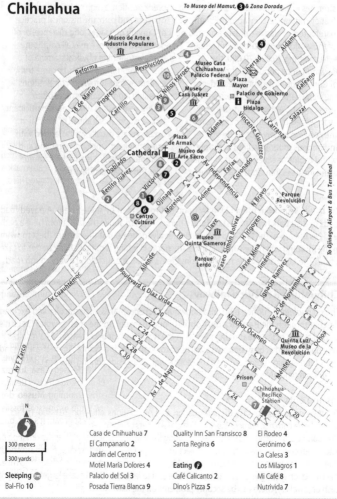

Chihuahua

	Casa de Chihuahua **7**	Quality Inn San Fransisco **8**	El Rodeo **4**
	El Campanario **2**	Santa Regina **6**	Gerónimo **6**
300 metres	Jardín del Centro **1**		La Calesa **3**
300 yards	Motel María Dolores **4**	**Eating 🍴**	Los Milagros **1**
	Palacio del Sol **3**	Café Calicanto **2**	Mi Café **8**
Sleeping 🛏	Posada Tierra Blanca **9**	Dino's Pizza **5**	Nutrivida **7**
Bal-Flo **10**			

Those who run fast

Inhabiting the remote gorges and mountains of the Copper Canyon are the indigenous Tarahumara, known in their own language as Rarámuri ('those who run fast'). Renowned for their formidable athletic skills, the average Rarámuri runner is capable of covering marathon-length stretches in just a few hours. In a stunning feat of endurance, they accomplish this barefooted, or clad in sandals, across some of the world's most unforgiving terrain.

Numbering 50,000-70,000, the Rarámuri once populated the best part of Chihuahua State but retreated into the sierras after Spanish incursions in the 16th century. Although subsequently evangelized by a handful of missions, they remain largely true to their indigenous roots. Dwelling in simple wood cabins or caves, their traditional attire includes loin cloths for the men

and brightly coloured dresses for the women. Hallucinogenic *peyote* features heavily in their religious beliefs, but tends to be the preserve of trained shamans.

Although well documented, their athletic accomplishments remain a mystery to scientists. Genetic predisposition, a high carbohydrate diet of beans and corn, the historical practice of carrying messages long-distance, or of outrunning quarry – may all contribute to the astonishing physical stamina of the Rarámuri. Their talents became truly evident in 'foot-throwing' competitions – gruelling long-distances races often lasting several days where each participant kicks a wooden ball ahead of him. Such occasions are usually well attended with much drinking, smoking, gambling and merriment – which is also the Rarámuri way, fitness fanatics take note.

the falls is 3 km from town (2 km by good dirt road, 1 km by signed trail). A paved road leads to a car park (with taco stalls) and a *mirador* 1½ km above the falls. From here a path leads to the top of the falls and continues steeply to the pool at the bottom (best to swim in the morning when the sun still strikes the pool). Hitching is difficult here; better to take a tour. The falls can also be reached from Creel via San Juanito along a very rough road.

Chihuahua al Pacífico railway

The *Chihuahua al Pacífico* train, also known as *El Chepe*, makes a spectacular and exciting descent through the **Barranca del Cobre** (Copper Canyon), to the coast beyond Creel: it's lauded as one of the great train journeys in the world and for good reason. As a result, it is very popular and at busy times you will need to book seats in advance. Sit on the left-hand side of the carriage going down to Los Mochis; right-hand side coming up from Los Mochis.
▶▶ *For train timetable, see box page 306.*

Ins and outs

For train enquiries, contact the information and reservations office on T01-800-122 4373, www.chepe.com.mx. *Primera Especial* (first class) tickets can be pre-booked at travel agents in Chihuahua, Los Mochis and some stations along the way. The schedule is an approximation of intent, but check details as they are subject to change. On average first class trains are about one hour late by the time they arrive in Los Mochis and are almost never on schedule to meet the La Paz ferry. Bring your own drinking water and toilet paper. Do not take large amounts of cash or jewellery, there can be security problems on the railway.

A *mixto* or *clase económica* (second-class) train also runs but travelling on it is much more difficult. You can only buy tickets in person; they are sold once the first train has left or passed through; the train leaves in theory about one hour after the first-class train and the timetable is quintessentially Latino – the train may be along today, or maybe tomorrow. It's really only worth taking the second-class heading west to east; if you travel east to west, it's likely to be dark by the time you reach the best sections. Prices are roughly half that of the first-class train.

The most interesting part of the journey is between Creel and Los Mochis. If wishing to see the best scenery, there is little point in taking the train Chihuahua–Creel–Chihuahua (on this stretch, the cheaper train is just as good as the *Primera Especial*). If planning to spend a few days in Creel, there are frequent buses Chihuahua–Creel. Delays are possible in the rainy season.

West of Chihuahua are high, windy and sparsely populated plains. From Chihuahua, the railway and road (Route 16, toll road but free after Km 45) cross the sierra of the Tarahumara people, who call themselves the Rarámuri (see box opposite). They were originally cave-dwellers and nomads, but now work as labourers in the logging stations and have settled around the mission churches built by the Spanish in the 17th century.

Creel and around ⬤🚻🛇🛈🛉🛂⬤🛆🛈🄲 ➤➤ pp299-307. Colour map 1, B2.

➔ *Phone code: 635. Altitude: 2356 m.*

Creel is the commercial centre of the Tarahumara region and is named after Enrique Creel (1854-1931), economist and entrepreneur, and governor of Chihuahua state in 1907. He initiated the building of the railway and planned to improve the Tarahumara's lives by establishing a colony here.

Tourism is becoming dominant in this sleepy, pine-scented mountain town, the starting point for most planned forays into the wilderness, including the Barranca del Urique and the Barranca del Cobre. It is also the place to take an unforgettable bus ride to the even sleepier village of Batópilas (see page 295). ➤➤ *See Transport, page 305.*

In lieu of an official tourist office, good maps and information are available from **Three Amigos Canyon Expeditions** ⓘ *López Mateos 46, T635-456 0179, www.amigos3.com, 0900-1900*. This is the most helpful and professional outfit in Creel, and can help arrange everything from bike tours to truck rentals. For topographical maps, head to **Artesanías Misión** on the main plaza.

There's not much to actually do in town, but it's worth checking out the **Museo de la Casa Artesanías** ⓘ *opposite the plaza, Mon-Sat 0900-1800, Sun 0900-1300, US$1*, which has interesting exhibitions on Rarámuri culture, including a fascinating collection of documentary photographs.

San Ignacio and rock formations

ⓘ *To get to the San Ignacio ejido follow Av López Mateos south and turn left before you reach the highway. Walk a short distance until you reach a dirt road running parallel. Turn right and continue heading south, passing a small cemetery before you reach an access road on the left. Follow this road up into the trees and you will arrive at the gates to the ejido, where you must pay US$1.10. Although the hikes below are simple, a map is recommended, available free from 3 Amigos in Creel, see page 304.*

The San Ignacio *ejido*, a land-owning co-operative just on the edge of town, is a great spot for easy hikes or bike rides. Dominated by open fields, vast grey cliffs, diminutive farming communities and lonely wooden houses, the landscape here offers a tentative taste of canyon country. Most interesting are the eerie rock formations, which suggest everything from human faces to brooding giants. The rocks are made from rayolite, a soft stone that easily eroded by the elements.

As you descend from the *ejido* entrance, the first site you'll reach, around 1 km away, is the **Valley of the Mushrooms**, with formations reminiscent of giant toadstools. Rarárumi women or children may be selling crafts or colourful trinkets. Continue downhill and you'll soon reach the **San Ignacio Mission**, built by Jesuits in the early 18th century.

Nearby is a school and a path heading 5 km east to the **Bisabirachi Valley** ('Valley of the Monks', also known locally as the Valley of Erect Penises), where tall, phallus-like structures rise up against a back-drop of pine trees and smooth cliffs. The Rarámuri revere this site for its associations with fertility. As you're walking towards the valley, the track rises and falls with many branch roads, so keep heading in the same rough direction. As you near the entrance, you'll arrive at a small dwelling and a signed access path. Don't forget to pay fees, US$0.70.

From Bisabirachi Valley, it is possible to make a circuit that takes in Lago Arareko (see below) before heading back to Creel. Return up the access path and head back in the direction of the San Ignacio Mission. Very soon you will reach a branch road to the left, follow this through a cattle gate (shut it behind you) and continue for 5 km through the pine trees. Keep your eye out for a distant white patch, which is the highway back to Creel. Once you reach Lago Arareko, you have the option of taking a path north to the San Ignacio Mission, or following the highway itself. Allow half a day for this circuit.

Lago Arareko
The horseshoe-shaped Lago Arareko is a tranquil expanse of water where you can simply unwind or enjoy a scenic picnic. It was created in the 1950s to serve as reservoir for Creel, but has never been used as such. There are a handful of simple lodgings dotted around the shores, managed by the **Complejo Ecoturístico Arareko** in town (see Sleeping, page 300). It's possible to rent rowing boats, US$3 per hour, and the lake is populated by large-mouth bass, mojarra and other fish; no fishing licence required. To get there from Creel, follow the highway south of town, 8 km, or hike south from the school next to the San Ignacio Mission.

Rekowata Aguas Termales
The hot springs of Rekowata are 22 km outside Creel, requiring a bike, horse or own transport to reach them. Popular with locals and tourists, the springs have been siphoned into what is essential a large public swimming pool. The waters are at body temperature, so don't expect steaming therapeutic experiences. The journey to reach the springs is certainly inspiring, but also quite demanding, so should only be attempted by the physically fit. Trucks do make the final descent, but be aware that these can be crowded and uncomfortable, and getting back up can be an issue. The springs supply Creel with the majority of its water.

Cusárare
Twenty kilometres south of Lake Arareko, is Cusárare ('place of the eagles'), with a **Jesuit church** ① *US$1.50*, dating back to 1741. Painted by indigenous craftsmen, it is one of the most beautiful and interesting missions in the area. The nearby **Museo Loyola** ① *US$1.50, Wed-Mon 1000-1700*, contains religious paintings and Rarámuri crafts. Cusárare **waterfall** is 3 km from the village entrance on the road to Creel. It is a 45-minute walk from the parking area and not very well signposted. The falls are best July to September; at other times of the year they can diminish to a sad trickle. There is very good hiking around Cusárare, but a

guide may be necessary (Señor Reyes Ramírez and his son have been recommended). The hot springs at **Basirecota** are four hours away, requiring an overnight stay in Cusárare.

You can reach Cusárare from Creel by public bus to Batópilas or Guachochi, although these run only a few times a day and you may find yourself stuck; check schedules before setting out. Cycling can be moderate to tough.

Creel to Batópilas

The road south out of Cusárare leads eventually to Batópilas. This is one of the most scenic and inspirational roads in northern Mexico, winding precariously through the mountains, trees and immense canyon systems. If you want to experience the true scale of the region, then this trip is obligatory. Ramshackle buses depart Monday to Saturday from Creel (five to six hours), requiring an overnight stay in Batópilas. It's possible to rent a 4WD vehicle from **Three Amigos Canyon Expeditions**, which also offers the option of a guided tour with a thrilling descent by bicycle into Batópilas Canyon.▶▶ *See Transport, page 305, and Activities and tours, page 304.*

Heading south from Cusárare, you will pass turn-offs to: **El Tejabán**, above the Barranca del Cobre (claimed to be the 'real' Copper Canyon); **Basíhuare** ('Sash') village, surrounded by pink and white rock formations (40 km from Creel); and the **Puente del Río Urique**, spanning the Urique Canyon. The area is ideal for camping.

At the junction Creel-Guachochi-Bufa, near Samachique, is a small restaurant/ hotel, **La Casita (F)**, which is very primitive and romantic. The road is paved as far as this junction but is bumpy from then on. Just after the junction, 3 km down into the valley is **Samachique**, where the indigenous Rarámuri start their long-distance race of kicking a wooden ball for 241 km (see box, page 292) in September. Stranded travellers can find a room and food at the bus stop (no more than a shack) in Samachique, which is 1 km off the main route to Batópilas.

If wishing to hitch to Batópilas (2½-hour drive) take the right fork as you walk back out of Samachique; it rejoins the route at a junction where you can wait for traffic both coming through and bypassing the village. Continuing south, **Quírare**, 65 km from Creel, offers views of the beautiful Batópilas Canyon. After Quírare there is an awesome 14-km descent to **La Bufa**, an overhang in the Batópilas Canyon, with a dizzying procession of turns and switch-backs. From there, you skirt the river all the way to Batópilas.

Batópilas ☺❷▲☻☺ ▶▶ *pp299-307. Colour map 1, B2.*

Batópilas, 120 km from Creel, is a delightful palm-fringed town of 1100 inhabitants hemmed in by the swirling river and cactus-studded canyon walls. Horses, pigs, goats and chickens wander freely along the cobblestone streets, while mangoes and other citrus fruits are grown in the sweltering subtropical surroundings. Batópilas was the second place in Mexico, after the capital, to receive electricity. Ironically, it now only receives it 1800-2400, although a new generator has been promised for years. Behind the main plaza is the tiny, shady **Plaza de la Constitución**. Three notable houses are the 18th-century **Casa Barfusson**, **Casa Morales** and the early-19th-century **Casa Bigleer**. The town is an excellent centre for walking and within easy reach of the Urique Canyon (see page 298). ▶▶ *See Transport, page 307.*

Batópilas was built on the back of local mineral wealth. The **Mina de Guadalupe** was constructed in 1780 by Pedro de la Cruz, but the town did not truly thrive until the 19th century, when the Shepperd family established their silver-mining operations. Their mansion (near the bridge), abandoned during Pancho Villa's campaign, must be one of the most elaborate adobe houses anywhere, but it is now overgrown and dilapidated. If Batópilas' history interests you, there is a new regional **museum** ① *Juárez s/n, the red building on the* *plaza, Mon-Sat 1100-1600, free,* with various old crucibles and equipment, historic photographs and clippings, all donated by the community. The museum sells copies of *The Silver Magnet*, by Grant Shepherd, which offers a detailed and interesting account of the town's boom years. The curator is also very helpful, knowledgeable and enthusiastic.

Around Batópilas

The **Porfirio Díaz Mine** above the bridge into town can be explored to about 3 km into the mountain (take a torch). As you enter the mine there is the sickly, sweet smell of bat droppings, and after about 1 km the air is thick with disturbed bats. There is a wonderfully remote Jesuit mission at **Satevó**, a 7-km walk from Batópilas along the river, isolated in a canyon. The walk is blistering in the daytime sun, so come prepared.

The area around Batópilas, but not the town, is inhabited by *Gentiles*. Also known as Simaroni, *Gentiles* are descendants of renegade *indígena* who refused to conform to Christian beliefs. They live in remote canyons and ranches and main pre-Columbian customs (women don't look at, or talk to men). If you go 'off road' here, beware of drug cultivation areas.

In the opposite direction to Satevó, it's possible to walk to **Cerro Colorado** (8 km, three hours each way); take the road that departs from the north side of the bridge. In this tiny village some people still mine for gold, carrying the ore down to the river by donkey where it is ground up in water-powered stone mills. Like Batópilas it has interesting architecture, drainage ditches, tunnels, canals and bridges. With luck, you can hitch to Cerro Colorado, then walk two hours to **Munérachi**, a remote village, to meet Rarámuris (best to arrange a local guide as marijuana plantations have rendered some areas unsafe, ask at your hotel). At **Cerro Yerbanis** there are amazing views of the Batópilas Canyon.

Hiking from Batópilas to Urique

A popular three-day hike goes from Batópilas to Urique (once known as the Camino Real), from where you get a ride with a truck to Bahuichivo and then a train to Creel or Los Mochis. Even if you're an experienced hiker, a guide is highly recommended because the region is a hot-bed of drug cultivation. Horse riding is possible with Librado Balderrama as a recommended guide; ask locally to find his house. He will guide to you to Urique or to surrounding attractions such as **Mesa Quimoba**, **Mesa de San José** and **Monerachi**. There are several places in town where you can hire mules (with a handler) for carrying gear.

The route is as follows: Batópilas–Cerro Colorado–Piedra Redonda–Cerro Manazno–La Estación–Los Alisos–Urique. You climb from 500 m up to 2200 m, before descending to Urique at 600 m. It can be very hot in the canyons; drink at least four litres of water a day (you can fill up at settlements en route) and take plenty of sunblock. There are many junctions and paths and so if you are without a guide it is vital to check that you are on the correct route as often as possible (try not to wander into marijuana plantations). If you are using the 'Batópilas' survery map (1:50,000 sheet G13A41, covering the entire route, available from the Artesanías Misión on the main plaza in Creel), it is recommended that you take the ridge path after Cerro El Manzano to La Estación, both for the views and directness.

Guachochi ●●●● ➡ *pp299-307. Colour map 1, B2.*

➔ Phone code: 649.

Guachochi, 156 km south of Creel, has a Wild West appearance. Founded by Jesuit missionaries in the mid-18th century, there's not much to this little backwater, although it reached infamy in 2008 when drug-related violence erupted on the streets. In every other respect, however, Guachochi is a decidedly sleepy, middle-of-nowhere place where nothing remotely racy ever happens. The local speciality is fresh trout.

Barranca de Sinforosa

From Guachochi you can walk four hours to the impressive **Barranca de Sinforosa**, widely regarded as the most beautiful of all the Chihuahua's canyons. It's not actually visible until you reach the edge. From a point several hundred metres above the Río Verde you can see an unforgettable extended system of immense gorges, grander (according to some) than the view from El Divisadero or on crossing the Barranca del Cobre. There's a path down to the river and a popular hike to **Rosalinda waterfall** takes around five hours round-trip. You will definitely need a guide if hope to explore the canyon more in-depth; the going can be rough.

Divisadero 😊😊 ►► pp299-307. Colour map 1, B2.

Beyond Creel, the *Chihuahua al Pacífico* train passes its highest point, **Los Ojitos** and, soon after, the **Lazo loop**, in which the track does a 360° turn. At Divisadero there is an all-too-brief 15-minute stop to view the quite spectacular Barranca del Cobre, grab a burrito and buy souvenirs from the Rarámuri women. If you're not taking the train, you can still admire the views by catching a local bus from Creel and exiting here. There is a luxury hotel, **Divisadero Barrancas** (see Sleeping, page 301), overlooking the canyon, but a lack of local amenities make this an inconvenient place to stay.

Around Divisadero

The **Balancing Rock** is at the edge of the canyon and it wobbles in a stomach-churning way as you stand on it. Catch a *camioneta* from the **Divisadero Barrancas** hotel, or walk 1-2 km from Divisadero (away from Creel) and on the left you will see the wooden entrance gate. From there it is 45 minutes to the rock with stops at canyon viewing points. You can also reach the canyon's floor from Divisadero or Posada Barrancas (see below). From the former it is 6-km walk (or hitch) along the dirt road that runs beside the railway to the house of Florencio Manzinas (at the first group of houses you come to). From there it's a day's hike along narrow, slippery, often steep and sometimes overgrown trails into the canyon, descending from cool pine forest into subtropical vegetation as you approach the river. Take plenty of water for the hike as, after descending the first section following a stream, you have to go over another hill before getting down to the river, which means several hours without access to water.

Posada Barrancas

Five minutes and 5 km further on from Divisadero, the train comes to Posada Barrancas, where the stunning **Hotel Posada Barrancas** claims yet more sensational views of the canyon. There is a small village, **Areponápuchi**, home to a handful of budget lodgings. Generally, however, there is a shortage of amenities.

Posada Barrancas to Bahuichivo → Colour map 1, B2.

Twenty-five minutes beyond the **Hotel Posada Barrancas** the *Chihuahua al Pacífico* reaches **San Rafael**, where there is a 10-minute stop, and then passes the **La Laja** bridge and tunnel. It is a further 20 minutes to **Cuiteco**. Next on the line comes **Bahuichivo**; if you don't want to go all the way to Los Mochis you can return from here. From Bahuichivo to Los Mochis it is five hours on the train. Bahuichivo offers access to the villages of Cerocahui and Urique, but is a rather rough-and-ready mountain town that has little attraction in itself.

Urique ⚫ ↦ *pp299-307. Colour map 1, B2.*

→ *Phone code: 635.*

From Bahuichivo, buses and pick-ups make a daily five-hour journey to Urique, in the heart of the Barranca de Urique. At the lip of the canyon is a *mirador* offering fine views. The road into the canyon is spectacular, only rivalled by the road to Batópilas. En route you'll pass the peaceful village of **Cerocahui**, increasingly popular with tourists and a pleasant place to spend time. There's a small mission and a girls' boarding school. Hiking and horseback tours can be arranged. On the canyon floor, the old silver-mining town of Urique has a hot, subtropical climate. Houses sprawl along a river punctuated by citrus groves. A walk 7 km upstream (1½ hours), leads to the mission church of **Guadalupe Coronal**. Further downstream is the village of **Guapalayna** with another small church. For hardy souls, a three-day hike connects Urique with Batópilas. There are a handful of hotels in town. The surrounding area is rife with marijuana plantations, so take care when hiking.

Bahuichivo to Témoris

Back on the train, as you approach Témoris, the track enters a tunnel in which the railway turns through 180°. **Témoris** is an attractive town, 11 km above the train station and nestled in the mining and cattle country of the lower western Sierra Madre. It is a good base for visiting working ranches, Tarahumara villages, waterfalls and swimming holes, on foot, horse or mountain bike. *Colectivos* make the trip or you may be able to hitch with local merchants. There are a few hotels in the area and several cheap restaurants.

El Fuerte ⚫🅲▲ ↦ *p299-308. Colour map 1, B1.*

The penultimate stop en route to the Pacific terminus of Los Mochis, the verdant colonial town of El Fuerte is considered the gateway to the Copper Canyon region. Wonderfully tranquil, friendly and rich in colonial architecture, you could do far worse than spend a few days exploring the town and its surroundings. Founded in 1564 by Spanish conquistador Don Fransisco de Ibarra, El Fuerte once served as an important agricultural and trading centre, where silver miners from canyon country regularly converged. The town derives its name from the large fortress built in 1610 to withstand attacks from local tribes. It now houses the **El Fuerte Mirador Museum** ① *Tue-Sun 0900-1700, US$1*, with exhibits on local history. The views from the ramparts are commanding.

Around El Fuerte

The waters from Chihuahua's major canyon systems – Sinforosa, Batópilas, Urique and Chinipas – all converge on the meandering Río Fuerte, now controlled by three dams and great for kayaking (see Activities and tours, page 304). The surrounding vegetation is a mixture of wet and dry tropical deciduous forest, home to over 150 species of bird and a riot of beautiful colour in spring. Visit at dawn, for the best show. There's good fishing too, with large populations of black bass around **Huites Dam**, one hour north of El Fuerte. At **Cerro de la Mascara**, a 1½-hour hike northeast of El Fuerte but much more easily accessed from the banks of the Río Fuerte (take a kayak tour towards Miguel Hidalgo Dam, 12 km northeast of town, and ask your guide where to exit), interesting geometric petroglyphs can be seen. Various Mayo communities offer the opportunity to encounter indigenous life firsthand.

Chihuahua to Los Mochis: the Copper Canyon listings

For Sleeping and Eating price codes and other relevant information, see Essentials pages 47-51.

Sleeping

Chihuahua *p288, map p291*
Lodgings in Chihuahua are comfortable, but not great value. The cheaper hotels are on Juárez and its cross-streets; the cheapest (and nastiest) are behind the cathedral.

AL Palacio del Sol, Independencia 116, T614-412 3456, www.hotelpalaciodelsol.com. High-rise hotel with views over the city. Rooms and suites are predictably comfortable, cable TV, telephone and gadgetry. Facilities include Wi-Fi, 2 restaurants, gym, bar and events rooms. Discounts sometimes available for groups.

A Quality Inn San Fransisco, Victoria 409, T614-415 3538, www.qualityinnchihuahua. com. A very comfortable hotel with pleasant rooms and suites. Lots of amenities including gym, café and executive centre. Good service, and centrally located close to the cathedral.

B Posada Tierra Blanca, Niños Heroes 102, T614-415 0000, www.posadatierrablanca. com.mx. Large motel-style lodgings with lots of balconies and 94 clean, carpeted rooms, all equipped with cable TV, heating and a/c. There's also a gym, pool, restaurant, Wi-Fi, bar and events room. Check out the interesting mural with esoteric themes.

C Bal-Flo, Niños Héroes y 5a, T614-201 4571, www.hotelbalflo.com. Clean, comfortable rooms with a/c, telephone, heating and satellite TV. The carpets could use a bit of a scrub, but otherwise not bad. Internet.

C El Campanario, Blv Díaz Ordaz 1405, southwest of cathedral, T614-415 4979. Good clean mid-range option. Rooms have cable TV, heating and a/c. Amenities include Wi-Fi and restaurant. Recommended.

C-E Santa Regina, Calle 3 No 102, www.hotel elsantaregina.com This hotel has 2 sections, economical and standard. Rooms are comfy enough, with cable TV, a/c and phone. Private parking and a daily buffet breakfast.

D Motel Maria Dolores, 9a No 30, T614-410 4770, motelmadol@hotmail.com. Motel-style place with small but immaculately clean rooms, quite new and tiled. Services include cable TV, hot water, coffee, drinking water, Wi-Fi and parking. Good value. Recommended.

D-E Casa de Chihuahua, www.casadechi huahua.com. A clean, pleasant hostel conveniently located opposite the train station. There's a mixture of dorms (**E**) and private rooms (**D**), all with shared bath. Facilities include giant DVD screen and tourist information. Discount for students.

D-E Jardín del Centro, Victoria 818, T614-415 1832. Clean, comfortable, modern rooms with heating and a/c, all overlooking a pleasant, plant-filled courtyard where lots of little birds are jumping around or in cages. For those on a budget, there's also slightly cheaper, less attractive quarters (**E**), many with colonial-style high ceilings. Economical restaurant attached. Recommended.

Creel *p293*
You'll need to make reservations in advance during high season. As Creel's popularity is increasing, hotel prices are inflating.

LL-A Sierra Bonita, Gran Visión s/n, T635-456 0615, www.sierrabonita.com. A way out of town with a great hill-top location, this hotel has a mixture of comfortable cabins and cosy rooms. There's a restaurant, bar and disco on site, as well as a pair of caged Bengal tigers, reportedly. Also has RV hook-ups (see Camping, below).

AL Quinta Mision, Lopez Mateos, T635-456 0021, www.quintamision.com. Newly opened luxury lodgings with 10 tastefully attired suites. All are equipped with flat screen TVs, heating, soft duvets, terraces, fridges, microwaves, elegant furniture and wooden beams. Some have a separate children's room with bunk beds. Recommended.

AL Villa Mexicana, López Mateos s/n, T635-456 0665, www.vmcoppercanyon.com. Luxury log cabins and suites with flat screen

TVs, satellite and heating. There's a good international restaurant, bar, Wi-Fi and laundry. RV hook-up for trailers. A 20-min walk out of town, although transport is provided. Also has RV hook-ups (see Camping, below).

AL-A The Lodge at Creel, Av López Mateos 61, 1 km from the plaza and railway station, T635-456 0071, www.thelodge atcreel.com. Owned by **Best Western** and one of the most luxurious places in town. Wooden, cabin-style rooms, spa facilities and an excellent restaurant.

A Parador La Montaña, Av López Mateos 44, T635-456 0023, www.hotelparadorcreel.com. A very comfortable, tasteful hotel with big rooms and fireplaces. There's also a good restaurant, bar, Wi-Fi and children's play area.

B Cascada Inn, López Mateos 49, T635-456 0253, www.motelcascadainn.com. This hotel has 30 clean, comfortable rooms with 2 beds each, TV, heating and 24-hr hot water. There's a restaurant serving international and Mexican food, an indoor pool, 2 events rooms and parking. Friendly and English-speaking, but a little over-priced.

C Margarita's Plaza Mexicana, Elfida Batista Caro, off López Mateos, T635-456 0245, www.hoteles-margaritas.com. Part of Margarita's hotel empire, which extends to Batópilas and Cerocahui. Plaza Mexicana is a comfortable hotel with pleasant, colourful rooms and lots of murals. Some rooms have been recently remodelled with big bath tubs, great for a soak after a long day hiking. There are also 2 suites with cooking facilities, large enough for 6 persons. Services include Wi-Fi, tours and information, and a simple breakfast and dinner is included in the price.

D Bertis, López Mateos 31, T635-456 0287. A bit shabby on the outside, but rooms are clean and comfortable, some with chimney, all with TV, writing desk, heating and bath. Simple and reasonable. Parking.

D Korachi, Francisco Villa 116, T635-456 0064. Right beside the station, with small, spartan, but comfortable rooms. The rustic cabins outside are much better.

D Los Valles, Elfido Batista Caro s/n, next to Margarita's Plaza Mexicana, T635-456 0092. A motel-style place with parking and restaurant; all rooms have heating, private bath and TV. Reasonable value, although rates might vary. The office is in their restaurant at the corner of Elfido Batista and López Mateos.

D-G Casa de Huéspedes Margarita, López Mateos 11, T635-456 0045. Popular backpacker joint that's packed in high season. A mix of dorms (**F**), mattresses (**G**) and more expensive double rooms (**D**). Lots of services, including bike rental, tours, laundry, Wi-Fi, hiking orientation, free maps and water refills. Breakfast and dinner included. Margarita's reps meet arriving train passengers and can be quite pushy. Book in advance in high season.

E-F Posada de Creel, Ferrocarril s/n. A low-key hostel with dorms (**F**) and cheap private rooms (**E**), tours and vouchers for food. An alternative to the long-reigning Margaritas.

RV Parks

Sierra Bonita (see above) has full hook-ups May-Oct. **Villa Mexicana** (see above), has full hook-ups for US$20.

Lago Arareko *p294*

D-E Complejo Ecoturístico Arareko, López Matoes s/n, Creel, T635-456 0126, A range of lodgings by the lake, including simple communal accommodation and more comfortable private rooms. Camping on their grounds is also an option.

Cusárare *p294*

A Sierra Lodge, visits booked through 3 Amigos Canyon Expeditions, T635-456 0179 (see Activities and tours, page 304). Rustic but romantic lodgings in an atmospheric old building. No electricity or phone, but old fashioned kerosene lamps. Rooms have cosy fireplaces and meals are included.

Creel to Batópilas *p295*

F La Casita, at the junction Creel-Guachochi-Bufa, near Samachique. A small restaurant/hotel, very primitive and romantic.

Batópilas *p295*
A Copper Canyon Riverside, T800-648 8488, www.coppercanyonlodges.com. The Copper Canyon Riverside is open irregularly and is so exclusive that it won't open its doors to passers-by. Rooms are beautifully adorned with antique furniture. Definitely book in advance.

A La Hacienda, on the road into town, T635-456 0245 (Creel), www.hoteles-margarita.com. Outside of town, 30 mins away. Very comfortable lodgings that are the jewel of Margarita's empire. This 19th-century house retains much of its Victorian character, the rooms are simple but elegant, with antique furniture and beautiful tiled bathrooms.

C Casa Real de Minas Aranasaina, just off the plaza, T649-456 9045. Beautifully decorated and colourful rooms set around a central courtyard. The best mid-range option in town.

D Juanita, Plaza Principal, T649-456 9043. Large clean rooms and lots of relaxing little enclaves. Peaceful and recommended.

E-F Batopilas, 2 blocks north of the plaza. The cheapest place in town. Simple lodgings with fan and private bath. Prices per person.

F Casa Monse, Plaza Principal, T649-456 9027. Basic rooms around a plant-filled courtyard. Lots of character, albeit it slightly off-beat.

Guachochi *p296*
C Melina, Belisario Domínguez 14, T649-543 0255. Clean and comfortable rooms with hot water. Adjoining restaurant.

D Chaparro, Francisco Villa 1, T649-543 0004. Cosy, but overpriced rooms, with cable TV and hot water. Good restaurant attached.

E Mansion, 20 de Noviembre 14, T649-543 0089. A good budget choice, with clean, straightforward rooms.

Divisadero *p297*
LL-AL Cabañas Divisadero Barrancas, close to the train station, Divisadero, T614-415 1199, www.hoteldivisadero.com. Stunning views of the canyon at this luxury hotel where the rooms are beautiful and tasteful. Prices include 3 daily meals and 2 walking tours.

Posada Barrancas *p297*
LL-AL Hotel Mirador, 3 km down the road from Divisadero Barrancas, www.hotel mirador.hotelesbalderrama.com. Another exceptional lodging. Awesome views, beautiful rooms with fire places and excellent service.

D Casa de Huéspedes Díaz, T614-578 3008. Rooms with 2 double beds, hot water on request. Prepares meals.

D-F Trail Head Inn, 2 km from town, T614-578 3007. Run by Rogelio Domínguez, who often meets the train saving the walk from town. Basic, dormitory accommodation. Great location for canyon hikes to the river and great views.

Posada Barrancas to Bahuichivo *p297*
B Cuiteco, Cuiteco. This quiet, delightful hotel has a patio with an unimpeded view of the mountains. Oil lamps and gas stove in the courtyard.

Urique *p298*
D Barrancas de Urique, Principal 201, T634-456 6076. A clean, comfortable and affordable spot by the river. However, there's a noisy *cantina* downstairs.

D-F Entre Amigos, www.among amigos.com. Laid-back American operation with a range of accommodation including camping (**F**), dorms (**F**) and private rooms in stone cabins (**D**). Pleasant, well-tended vegetable garden.

Cerocahui
AL-F Paraíso del Oso, T614-421 3372, www.mexicohorse.com. Pleasant wooden ranch-style accommodation. Private rooms (**AL**), dorms and camping (**F**) available. Run a host of tours into the surrounding countryside, including birdwatching and horse riding.

A Cabañas San Isidro, 8 km from town, T635-456 5257. Friendly, family-run lodgings on a working ranch. Rooms are rustic but comfortable and equipped with wood stoves. Meals included.

Témoris p298
D-F Campamento Adame. A good choice for backpackers, with *cabañas*, dorms and tent sites with shower and cooking facilities.

El Fuerte p298
AL Posada del Hidalgo, Hidalgo 101, T698-893 0242, www.hotelposadadelhidalgo.com. Housed by an historic mansion, **Posada del Hidalgo** is a very big, professional hotel with spa facilities and a legion of staff. Rooms can be booked through **Hotel Santa Anita** in Los Mochis (see page 260). Often visited by large tour groups, who may take priority over other guests.

B El Fuerte, Montesclaros 37, T698-893 0226, www.hotelelfuerte.com.mx. A very beautiful hotel with exquisite rooms and a jacuzzi fed by illuminated waterfalls. Tours, Wi-Fi, bar and restaurant are among the services. The best in town and recommended, even if the decor is slightly overpowering.

B La Choza, 5 de Mayo 101, T698-893 1274, www.hotellachoza.com.mx. Rooms are comfortable and spacious with attractive domed ceilings. Restaurant, pool, parking, hot water, cable TV and a/c are among the amenities. Can help arrange tours.

C Real de Carapoa, Paseo de la Juventude 102, T698-893 1796. A new place with a handful of comfortable, good-value rooms.

C Río Vista, Cerro de las Pilas, T698-893 0413, www.hotelriovista.com.mx. Housed in the old fort stables with excellent views over the river. Lots of rusty old antiques and a good restaurant. Other services include transport to the train station, Wi-Fi, birdwatching on the river and visits to indigenous communities. Recommended.

D La Herradura, Montesclaros s/n, T698-893 0512. Reasonable rooms with a/c, cable TV and Wi-Fi. Not stunning, but quite adequate and friendly.

E-G San José, Juárez 108, T698-893 0845. For the budget explorer, small, basic rooms with fan. The most expensive have bath, TV and a/c (**E**). Friendly and scruffy.

☯ Eating

Chihuahua p288, map p291
The smartest and best are in the 'zona dorada', northeast of the centre on Juárez, near Colón.

ŦŦŦ La Casona, Ocampo y Aldama. A converted 19th-century mansion with a beautiful, elegant interior. Steaks are the speciality of the house, including rib eye and New York steak. Also offers seafood, salads and soups.

ŦŦŦ Los Vitrales, Juárez 3126. A big mansion with occasional live music and Mariachi acts. Fine dining and international food.

ŦŦŦ-ŦŦ La Calesa, Juárez 3300. Elegant, upmarket restaurant serving Northern-style steaks. Smart and fancy.

ŦŦ Café Calicanto, Aldama 411. Friendly, popular establishment serving meaty Chihuahuan specialities. Live Mexican music Tue-Sun. Recommended.

ŦŦ El Rodeo, Libertad 1705. Regional cuisine with a carnivorous emphasis. Wooden booths, tables and wild west photos.

ŦŦ Gerónimo, Aldama y Calle10a. Good clean diner with a pricey but good buffet breakfast of fresh fruit, chilled juices, *huevos al gusto* and hot meat dishes, US$7. There's Wi-Fi too, so you can check your email over a coffee. Skip the lunchtime buffet, which is mediocre at best.

ŦŦ Los Milagros, Victoria 812. Meeting place set around a pleasant colonial courtyard, popular with young people. Serves light snacks and cocktails. Good atmosphere.

ŦŦ-Ŧ Dino's Pizzas, Doblado 301. Pizzas, as the name suggests, adequate but not excellent and slightly over-sweet. Also offers spaghetti and light snacks.

ŦŦ-Ŧ Mi Café, Victoria 1000. Economical diner-style place with reasonable breakfasts, Mexican staples and working class Mexicans.

Ŧ Nutrivida, Victoria 420. Health food and economical meals, for those seeking respite from the heavy Norteño cuisine.

Creel and around p293
There is not much fine dining Creel, but there are plenty of economical cafés. Try the **Best Western** hotel for a better sit-down meal.

Tío Molcas, López Mateos 35. Mexican staples and wholesome Norteño fare. One of the better ones, but not outstanding.

Pizza del Rey, López Mateos. Reasonable enough pizza.

Verónica, López Mateos 33. Good *comida corrida* and northern specialities. Lupita, a few doors down, is of a similar standard.

Mi Café, López Mateos 21. Locals' haunt serving good, cheap food. Try the apple *empanadas*, friendly.

Batópilas p295

Carolina, Plaza de la Constitución. Tasty, affordable Mexican staples. Friendly and pleasant. Recommended.

Doña Mica, Plaza de la Constitución. Opposite **Carolina**, with a similar selection of appetizing home-cooked fare. Friendly.

El Puente Colgante, off the main plaza. Cold beer, wine, steaks and seafood. Try the *plato norteño*, with excellent, full-flavoured local beef that's best washed down with a cool *tecate*, salt and lime. A raucous local atmosphere in the evening. Recommended.

Quinto Patio, inside **Hotel Mary's**, near the church. Economical fare, Mexican staples and breakfast.

El Fuerte p298

Torres, Robles 102. The restaurant inside this boutique hotel serves very good, if overpriced, food. Service should already be included in the bill. Beware overcharging.

Diligencias, 5 de Mayo 101, inside Hotel La Choza. Everything is good here, but the breakfasts are great, especially the *chilaquiles con pollo*. Full bar and seafood.

La Canastilla, Juárez 510. A reputable riverside restaurant serving tasty seafood and locally caught black bass. Recommended.

Mesón del General, Juárez 202. Reliable Mexican food that's been rated as great by some and mediocre by others.

Mi Casita, Robles y Zaragoza. Try the baked potato and taco stuffing, served with a tray of guacamole and other tasty dips.

🍸 Bars and clubs

Creel p293

Creel is lacking in decent watering holes. Most tend to be orientated to locals, who may or may not be welcoming, especially to unaccompanied women. Be discreet and you should be OK.

Tío Molcas, López Mateos 35. The one and only place geared towards foreign travellers and a great place to unwind after a long day in the canyons. It's cosy and intimate, with a roaring log fire. Recommended.

✹ Festivals and events

Creel p293

12 Dec Tarahumara festival.

◯ Shopping

Chihuahua p288, map p291

Chihuahua is a good place to pick up cowboy boots (head for Calle Libertad, between Independcia and Díaz Ordaz).

Artesanías Tarahumaras, Calle 5 y Doblado 312, T614-413 0627. Crafts, baskets, wood carvings, jewellery.

Mexican Vanilla Gallery, Victoria 424. Sells vanilla in all shapes and forms.

Creel p293

There's no shortage of *artesanía* shops in Creel. The **Artesanías Misión** on the plaza has an array of rustic crafts, as well as topographical maps of the canyons. Proceeds go to the Mission Hospital. Alternatively, buy directly from the Rarámuri.

▲ Activities and tours

Chihuahua p288, map p291
Tour operators
Conexion a la Aventura, Melgar y Miguel Schultz 3701, T614-413 7929, www.conexion

alaaventura.com. A wide range of tours and outdoor activities throughout the state of Chihuahua, including canyon excursions, kayaking, sandboarding, hiking and visits to Paquimé. Some trips further afield too.
Guillermo Bechman, T614-413 0253. Arranges stays at cabins above Bahuichivo, near the Copper Canyon.
Turismo Al Mar, T614-416 5950. Rail packages and accommodation to Copper Canyon, 5 nights and some meals, US$500 for 2 people.

Creel and around p293
Horse riding
Eco Paseos El Adventurero, next to Hotel Pueblo Viejo, T635-294 4585 (mob), www.ridemexico.com. A very professional outfit managed by Norberto, who speaks English and cares for his horses. Over 15 riding packages are available, with day tours to local rock formations, Arareco Lake and San Ignacio Mission. A 2-hr ride starts at US$15. Longer, more exciting excursions can also be arranged in advance, with 2- to 9-day adventures to Ekarine hot springs, various canyons, waterfalls and villages. Norberto also has a *cabaña* which is part of his *ranchito*, where you can stay overnight and partake in cowboy activities. Finally, his new language school lets you learn Spanish whilst getting a horsemanship experience. Recommended.

Rock climbing
Expediciones Umarike, T635-456 0632, www.umarike.com.mx. Owned by Chito Arturo, who has over 10 years experience navigating the canyons. In addition to rock climbing, Chito can organize extensive hiking and canyoning trips. For the hardcore adventure enthusiast. Reservations and queries in advance, and through the website only.

Tour operators and guides
Many people hang around the square offering tours in a variety of vehicles, or other means of transport. Most hotels also offer packages that are very similar to each other. If you don't speak Spanish, always check your guide is English-speaking before agreeing to anything. It's worth shopping around, particularly if you have a longer excursion in mind.
3 Amigos Canyon Expeditions, López Mateos 46, T635-456 0179, www.amigos3. com. The best tour operator in town and something of a Creel institution. As well as offering guided hikes, customized tours, bike rides and romantic picnic lunches with canyon views, as well as advice on best to explore the region independently. The company has good vehicles for hire, including bikes and scooters, with free maps, tools and picnic lunch if required. They also have extensive professional contacts, including experts in wildlife and geology. Anything is possible. Helpful and highly recommended.
César González Quintero, T635-456 0108, or enquire at **Margarita's Plaza Mexicana Hotel**, Elfida Batista Caro. Margarita's son, César, is a qualified English-speaking guide who offers tours of all the major canyon attractions, including Batópilas. He once guided a *Discovery Channel* expedition to Urique.
Roberto Venegas, T635-456 0049. Recommended guide, with a van.

Batópilas p295
Tour operators
Several people in Creel offer trips to Batópilas. An overnight trip for 4 (minimum) starts at around US$60 per person, plus lodging and meals, and includes a trip to Jesuit Mission at Satevo. A recommended guide is **Pedro Estrada Pérez** (limited English but patient), T649-456 0079. Also recommended is **3 Amigos Canyon Expeditions** (see above), which will drive you to the rim of Batópilas canyon and let you ride a bicycle downhill through all the turns and switch-backs. Julio, one of their guides, is particularly recommended.

El Fuerte p298
Tour operators
3 Amigos Canyon Expeditions, Reforma 100, on the waterfront, follow the signs from the plaza, T698-893 5028, www.amigos3.com.

This branch of the legendary canyon specialists, **3 Amigos**, is professionally managed by Ivan and Yolanda. It specializes in guided kayak tours, with river rides ranging from 'short and sweet' to 'rough and tumble'. Ever the champions of independent travel, it also offers stand-alone kayak and bike rentals. Recommended.

Amigo Trails, Reforma 100, same office as 3 Amigos, T698-893 5029, www.amigo trails.com. Same reputable management as 3 Amigos, organizes specialized, all-inclusive packages to canyon country, including chartered flights over the mountains.

Chal, Hotel Rio Vista (see Sleeping), T698-893 0413, www.hotelriovista.com.mx. Chal is a gregarious English-speaking guide who also owns the **Hotel Rio Vista**. He offers birdwatching, sports fishing, village tours and trips to the petroglyphs.

⊖ Transport

Chihuahua p288, map p291
Air

The airport is on Blv Juan Pablo II, 18 km from centre on the road to Ojinaga. Airport buses collect passengers from hotels, US$3; or taxi US$16.

Flights to **Ciudad Juárez**, **Ciudad Obregón**, **Culiacán**, **Guadalajara**, **Hermosillo**, **La Paz**, **Loreto**, **Los Cabos**, **Los Mochis**, **Manzanillo**, **Mazatlán**, **Mexico City**, **Monterrey**, **Tijuana** and **Torreón**.

AeroMéxico to **Los Angeles** daily, and Aerolitoral to **Dallas** and **El Paso** in the USA.

Airline offices AeroMéxico, T614-423 4715, Aerocalifornia, T614-437 1022, **American Eagle**, T614-446 8211. Interjet, T614-446 8233.

Bicycle

Bicycle spares are available from Independencia 807, 0900-2000.

Bus

The bus terminal is on Blv Juan Pablo II, 8 km southeast of town, on the way to the airport, T614-420 2286. To get there, take a bus from the centre at Niños Héroes between Ocampo and Calle 10 (20 mins, US$0.40), or a taxi (US$6 fixed price). There is an exchange office (beware short-changing), *cafetería* and left luggage. The main bus lines include **Grupo Senda**, **Omnibus**, **Estrella Blanca** and its subsidiaries.

To **Aguascalientes**, hourly, 13 hrs, US$50. To Ciudad Juárez, every 30 mins from 0530, 5 hrs, US$21. To **Creel**, 5 daily, 5 hrs, US$15. To **Durango**, hourly, US$30. To **Guadalajara**, several, US$61, including Estrella Blanca, which also goes to **Acapulco** and **Puerto Vallarta**. To **Hidalgo del Parral**, 9 daily, 2½ hrs, US$9. To **Nuevo Casas Grandes**, 13 daily, 4 hrs, US$16. To **Nuevo Laredo**, at 2030, US$35. To **Monterrey**, every 1-2 hrs, US$38. To **Mazatlán**, 2 companies, US$38, 19 hrs, heart-stopping view. To **Mexico City** (and intermediate destinations), frequent services with several companies, 20 hrs, US$75. To **Querétaro**, every 1-2 hrs, US$65. To **San Luis Potosí**, 7 daily, US$52. To **Saltillo**, 5 daily, US$37 (or go to Monterrey and backtrack). To **Torreón**, every ½ hr, US$25. To **Zacatecas**, every ½ hr, 12 hrs, US$43.

Train

The train station is a 15- to 20-min walk from downtown. To get there by bus, catch one heading southeast down Ocampo; taxi US$4.

The station for the 631-km *Chihuahua al Pacífico* railway is 1 block behind the prison (take bus marked Rosario, or walk); in the early morning you may have to take a taxi. For the train timetable, see box, page 306.

Creel and around p293
Bicycle

Bikes from several places roughly US$13 for the day; look around if you need better bikes. **3 Amigos** (see Activities and tours, page 304) has the best.

Chihuahua al Pacífico railway timetable

First class schedules and fares:

	Arrives	Departs	Fare		Arrives	Departs	Fare
Los Mochis		0600		Chihuahua		0600	
Sufragio	0810	0810	US$22	Cuauhtémoc	0815	0815	US$25
El Fuerte	0925	0925	US$22	San Juanito	1040	1040	US$49
Témoris	1220	1220	US$40	Creel	1115	1115	US$56
Bahuchivo	1315	1315	US$47	Pitorreal	1205	1205	US$63
Cuiteco	1325	1325	US$49	Divisadero	1235	1255	US$67
San Rafael	1405	1415	US$53	Posada	1300	1300	US$67
Posada	1430	1440	US$55	San Rafael	1320	1325	US$69
Divisadero	1440	1500	US$55	Cuiteco	1405	1405	US$73
Pitorreal	1525	1525	US$60	Bahuichivo	1415	1415	US$75
Creel	1610	1610	US$66	Témoris	1515	1515	US$82
San Juanito	1645	1645	US$73	El Fuerte	1810	1810	US$122
Cuauhtémoc	1855	1855	US$97	Sufragio	1920	1920	US$122
Chihuahua		2130	US$122	Los Mochis	2130		US$122

Second class schedules and fares:

	Arrives	Departs	Fare		Arrives	Departs	Fare
Los Mochis		0700		Chihuahua		0700	
Sufragio	0905	0905	US$11	Cuauhtémoc	0935	0935	US$12
El Fuerte	1035	1035	US$11	La Junta	1030	1030	US17
Loreto	1150	1150	US$11	San Juanito	1140	1140	US$24
Témoris	1335	1335	US$14	Creel	1225	1225	US$27
Bahuchivo	1430	1435	US$23	Pitorreal	1315	1315	US$31
Cuiteco	1445	1445	US$24	Divisadero	1335	1355	US$33
San Rafael	1535	1545	US$26	Posada	1400	1400	US$33
Posada	1600	1600	US$27	San Rafael	1425	1435	US$34
Divisadero	1610	1630	US$28	Cuiteco	1525	1525	US$36
Pitorreal	1655	1655	US$28	Bahuichivo	1535	1535	US$38
Creel	1745	1745	US$33	Témoris	1630	1630	US$41
San Juanito	1820	1820	US$36	Loreto	1820	1820	US$49
La Junta	1940	1940	US$43	El Fuerte	1930	1930	US$53
Cuauhtémoc	2030	2030	US$48	Sufragio	2055	2055	US$57
Chihuahua	2310		US$61	Los Mochis	2310		US$61

Bus

There are 2 bus stations in Creel, Noreste and Estrella Blanca, both located close to each other outside, across the railway track and opposite the square, near Hotel Korachi.

To **Chihuahua**, 13 daily, 5 hrs, US$15. To **Ciudad Juárez**, 0800. To **Guachochi**, 1200, 1730, US$4. To **Hidalgo del Parral**, 1210, 5 hrs. To **San Rafael** and **Divisadero**, 5 daily, US$3.

Buses to **Batópilas** depart from López Mateos, Tue, Thu and Sat at 0730, and Mon,

Wed, Fri at 0930, 5-6 hrs (paved as far as Samachique turn-off) depending on weather, US$15. Buy ticket the day before from the El Two Artesanía shop, López Mateos, as it can be very crowded.

Train

For the schedule, see box opposite. Station office Mon 0800-1000, 1100-1600, Tue-Fri 1000-1600, Sat 1000-1300. From Creel to **Los Mochis** takes about 8 hrs on the train.

Batópilas *p295*

Bus Bus to Creel Mon-Sat 0500 (have a torch handy as it is very dark).

A supply lorry leaves for **Chihuahua** Tue, Thu, Sat at 0600, takes passengers. A stunning trip.

Guachochi *p296*

Bus To **Creel** twice daily from Estrella Blanca terminal, 0730 and 1330, US$4. To **Hidalgo del Parral** several times daily with Transportes Ballezanos.

Divisadero *p297*

Bus Regular daily buses run from Divisadero to **Creel** (US$2.30) connecting with buses to **Chihuahua**.

Train

The train pauses at Divisadero for 15 mins, allowing you to snap some stunning pictures and grab a burrito.

⊙ Directory

Chihuahua *p288, map p291*

Banks Bancomer on Plaza Constitución offers better rates than Multibanco Comermex on same square. Casa de Cambio Rachasa, Independencia y Guadalupe Victoria, on the plaza, poorer rates, no commission on cash, 2% on TCs, Mon-Sat 0900-2100 (also at Aldama 711). Exchange is available in the bus terminal, but rates are slightly better downtown. **Internet** Not terribly numerous. Try the computer shop at Ocampo 1433. Or Mi Café (see Eating), which has a few terminals with bad keyboards. Most places charge around US$1/hr. **Laundry** Ocampo 1412 and Julián Carrillo 402. **Telephone** Libertad, in the Palacio Federal. Also in the central camionera. Credit card phone outside AeroMéxico office on Guadalupe Victoria, ½ a block from Plaza Constitución (towards Carranza). Main phone office on Av Universidad.

Creel and around *p293*

Banks Banca Serfín, on the square, very friendly, 0900-1300, changes dollars cash with no commission, but commission charged on TCs (US$1 per cheque), TCs must be authorized by manager, Visa and MasterCard advances, no commission. **Internet** Try Cascada.net, López Mateos 49 or Compucenter, López Mateos 33. Connections tend to be poor. **Laundry** Pink house opposite side of tracks from square, US$3 per load, 2 hrs, good, Mon-Sat 0900-2000, restricted hours on Sun. **Post office** On main square in Presidencia Municipal, no sign. **Telephone** Long-distance phone office in Hotel Nuevo.

Batópilas *p295*

Banks Tienda Grande (Casa Morales), the store on the plaza, can change TCs at a poor rate. No ATM, carry all the cash you need.

Guachochi *p296*

There is a bank in the town.

Chihuahua to Durango

From Chihuahua to Durango, highways and bus journeys lengthen inconsolably. Under the searing white hot horizons, everything is tempered by patience – harsh, uncompromising, unrelenting patience. Hours pass between settlements: nowhere towns of dust, rock and mournful scratching roosters. Gnarled posts and rusty wire fences demarcate miles of rolling territory, all flanked by wild mountains, plateaux rock towers and table-tops. Slender horses graze hopefully, flocks of black crows break the monotony, and ruined houses sprout weeds from their crumbling mud-brick walls, lost in time, lost in space. Highway 45 is particularly relentless, but rewarded with a stop at the endearing and off-beat mining town of Hidalgo del Parral, where Pancho Villa was spectacularly assassinated. Further south, the handsome city of Durango is a bastion of northern pride, hospitality and elegance, but still very much in touch with its rugged root. Hundreds of Westerns have been shot in its entrancing desert environs, alive with grandeur, energy and endless legends of bravery. ▶▶ *For listings, see pages 311-314.*

Hidalgo del Parral ●❷❸❹❺ ▶▶ *pp311-314. Colour map 1, B2.*

→ *Phone code: 627.*

Connecting to the north through Ciudad Jiménez (77 km), Hidalgo del Parral (often known just as Parral), is an old mining town with narrow streets. It's a pleasant, safe, affluent place with a compact centre with a string of shaded plazas, many bridges over the sinuous, and often dry, Río del Parral, and several churches. The city's history is split between its mining heritage and the fact that Pancho Villa was assassinated here (see box opposite). You'll find a modest **tourist office** on the main plaza, www.hdelparral.gob.mx. ▶▶ *See Transport, page 314.*

Background

In 1629, Juan Rangel de Viezma discovered La Negrita, the first mine in the area. Now known as La Prieta (see below), it overlooks the city from the top of Cerro la Prieta. Rangel founded the town in 1631 under the name of San Juan del Parral. The mine owners were generous benefactors to the city, leaving many beautiful buildings that still stand. On 8 September 1944, severe damage was caused by a flood. The decrease in population, either through drowning or flight, led to a recession.

Sights

On the Plaza Principal is the **Parroquia de San José**, with a beautiful interior. Plaza Baca has a statue to El Buscador de Ilusiones (the Dream Seeker), a naked man panning for gold. The **cathedral** is on this square and, on the opposite side, is the **Templo San Juan de Dios** with an exuberant altarpiece, painted gold. Across the road from the cathedral is the former Hotel Hidalgo (not in use), built in 1905 by mine owner Pedro Alvarado and given to Pancho Villa in the 1920s. Next door is **Casa Stallforth** (1908), the shop and house of a German family who supplied everything imaginable to the city. It is still a shop, with the original interior. Continuing along Mercaderes, before the bridge, is **Casa Griensen**, now the Colegio Angloamericano Isaac Newton. Griensen, another German, married Alvarado's sister. Behind this house is **Palacio Pedro Alvarado** ⓘ *1000-1800, US$1.45*, Alvarado's colonial mansion, recently restored and containing his personal effects. The building hides some tragic stories and sensitive souls might sense a melancholy presence in the bedroom. Crossing the bridge at the end of Mercaderes, you come to the site of Villa's death, on the corner of Plaza Juárez, where you'll find a museum

The assassination of Pancho Villa

The infamous assassination of Pancho Villa took place in the centre of Hidalgo del Parral on 20 July 1923. Villa owned a house on Calle Zaragoza (now a shop called Almacenes Real de Villa, painted pink) and was making his way from there to the Hotel Hidalgo, which he also owned, when he was ambushed on Avenida Juárez. The house chosen by the assassins is now the **Museo Pancho Villa** ⓘ *Mon-Fri 0900-2000, Sat 0900-1300*. Twelve of the 100 bullets fired hit Villa, who was taken immediately to the Hotel Hidalgo. The death mask taken there can be seen in the museum and also in the museum in Chihuahua (see page 290). His funeral took place the next day and he was buried in the Panteón Municipal; his tomb is still there even though the body has been transferred to Mexico City.

commemorating the great 'Centaur of the North', **Museo Pancho Villa** ⓘ *Juárez y Barreda, Tue-Sun 1000-1700, US$0.70*. Overlooking the town is the old mine, **La Prieta** ⓘ *Tue-Sun 1000- 1700, US$1.80*, which is part ruin, part mining museum.

Around Hidalgo del Parral

Some 26 km kilometres east of Parral on the Jiménez road, a well-signed road leads 5 km south to **Valle de Allende**. Originally called Valle de San Bartolomé, it was the site of the first Franciscan mission in Chihuahua, founded in the late 16th century by Fray Agustín Rodríguez. The original monastery building still stands on the main square, but it is unused (it has been used as a *refrigeradora* to store apples).

Cinema enthusiasts can visit the Western set of **Villa del Oeste** ⓘ *9 km from Durango, T618-112 2882, www.villadeloeste.com, Tue-Fri 1200-1900, Sat-Sun 1100-1900*, a small theme park that lays on cheesy cowboy shows.

Durango ⊖⊙⊙▲⊙⊙ ➤➤ *pp311-314. Colour map 1, C3.*

→ *Phone code 618. Altitude: 1924 m.*

Victoria de Durango, capital of Durango State, was founded in 1563 and quickly flourished thanks to the mineral rich mountains that form its backdrop. It is a modern city but retains a Wild West ambience with its wide roads, low buildings and baroque cathedral the colour of desert sand. Cowboys saunter along the pavements in jeans and Stetson hands, great silver belt buckles gleaming, whilst well-restored colonial structures hark back to a bygone era of elegance. The locals are sunny and gregarious, which some may find a welcome relief after the steely aloofness of other places further north. During the 20th century, the State of Durango served as a backdrop to not only Hollywood movies but also the Mexican film industry at its height. Classics such as *The Wild Bunch* by Sam Peckinpah (1968) or, more recently, The *Mask of Zorro* (1998) and *Bandidas* (2006) were filmed here.

Ins and outs

Getting there and around From Durango's **Guadalupe Victoria Airport (DGO)** ⓘ *12 km east of the centre*, a taxi costs US$8.50 to the centre. The bus station is a few kilometres east of the centre; buses marked 'centro' go downtown, every 5 minutes 0600-2130, US$0.25, or take a taxi, US$2-3. Downtown Durango is reasonably compact with most major attractions centrally located and within walking distance of each other. ➤➤ *See Transport, page 314.*

Tourist information The **tourist office** ① *Florida 1106, T618-811 2139, www.vistadurango. com.mx*, is helpful and friendly and has a supply of good new promotional material.

Sights

Durango's colonial architecture doesn't quite match the splendour of Mexico's heartland, but it is attractive nonetheless, and well complemented by a wealth of handsome 19th century edifices. Most areas of interest are within walking distance of the **Plaza de Armas**, Durango's lively central plaza. Skirting its northern edge is the city's main thoroughfare, Avenida 20 de Noviembre, as well as the **Catedral Basílica Menor**. Constructed between1695 and 1785, it is one of the finest baroque structures in northern Mexico, rising with elegant, if imposing, twin towers.

If you're interested in Durango's past, visit the **Museo Regional de Durango** ① *north of the plaza, Victoria 100, T618-812 5605, Tue-Sun 0900-1600, Sun 1000-1500, US$0.70*, which is devoted to the historical development of Durango. The building dates from the 19th century when the vogue was for all things European. For those who find appeal in the city's Wild West roots, there is also an **old train station** built in 1925, complete with a steam engine, 30 minutes north of the downtown area.

A block east of the plaza on 20 Noviembre stands Durango's **Palacio Municipal**, built in 1898 by businessman Pedro Escárzaga Corral and typical of the Porfirio years. Almost opposite lies the **Arzobispado** (Archbishopric) ① *20 de Noviembre y Madero*, which hosted Pop John Paul II in 1990. It is a particularly attractive 19th-century building with a simple yet elegant facade and a beautiful stone relief.

More architectural splendour lies on 5 de Febrero with the late-18th-century **Edificio de las Rosas** ① *southeast corner of the Plaza de Armas*, which boasts attractive floral carvings around its second floor windows. The baroque and extravagantly carved **Palacio del Conde del Valle de Súchil** lies a block further east. It now houses university offices.

Durango

	Florida Plaza **3**	**Eating** 🍴
	Gallo **7**	Corleone's Pizza **1**
	Hostel de la Monja **8**	El Paraíso Michoacano **4**
	Plaza Catedral **4**	El Zocabón **6**
	Posada San Jorge **5**	Gorditas Gabino **5**
	Reforma **6**	Fonda de la Tía Chonda **3**
	Rincón Real **9**	La Esquina de Café **8**
Sleeping 🛏	Roma **10**	La Fogata **9**
California **2**		La Tostada **10**
Casablanca **1**		

Los Esquipules **11**
Los Farolitos **7**
Los Quatros Vientos **12**
Pizzaly **13**
Quattros Grados **14**
Sarnadhi **2**

Bars & clubs 🍸
La Malquerida **15**

Continue east on 5 de Febrero and the environs become increasingly shabby as you pass the market. After several blocks you will arrive at the **Museo de Las Culturas Populares** ① *5 de Febrero 1107, Tue-Fri 0900-1800, Sat-Sun 1200-1800, US$0.35*, a small but compelling museum dedicated to local indigenous groups.

A block west of the Plaza de Armas on 5 Febrero lies the expansive **Plaza IV Centenario**. The **Palacio de Gobierno**, on the north side, is also known as the Palacio de Zambrano, after the wealthy miner who built it as his personal residence. It features arched portals and various interior murals depicting the history of Durango.

Just north of Plaza IV Centenario is the **Museo de Arqueología de Durango Garnot-Peschard** ① *Zaragoza 315 Sur, Tue-Fri 1000-1830, Sat-Sun 1100-1800, US$0.35*, with interesting archaeological finds belonging to Durango's northern cultures. Nearby, on 20 de Noviembre, the attractive French-style **Teatro Ricardo Castro** was constructed in 1900. After serving as a cinema, ice-skating rink and boxing ring, it has returned to its original function as a theatre with its sumptuous interior restored in 1990.

The **Instituto de Cultura del Estado de Durango (ICED)** ① *16 de Septiembre 130, T618-128 6008, www.iced.gob.mx, Tue-Fri 0900-1800, Sat-Sun 1000-1800*, is a newly opened complex of several modest cultural museums. They include the **Museo de Cine Rafael Trujillo**, with memorabilia and old film equipment commemorating Durango's golden age as a centre for cinematic productions; the rather obscure **Museo de la Revolución** 'General Domino Arrieta', with personal effects, old weapons and historical displays relating to the General; the **Museo de Arqueologíca**, with an array of archaeological finds; and the **Pinacoteca del Estado**, containing historic art works. There is a nominal charge to enter each one.

Around Durango

Cinema enthusiasts can visit the Western sets of **Villa del Oeste** ① *9 km from Durango, T618-112 2882, www.villadeloeste.com, Tue-Fri 1200-1900, Sat-Sun 1100-1900*, and Chupaderos (14 km). The former is a small theme park that lays on cheesy cowboy shows; the latter is abandoned and dilapidated but at least smells authentically of horsemanure. San Juan del Río buses pass there or take a taxi, US$14.

⊚ Chihuahua to Durango listings

For Sleeping and Eating price codes and other relevant information, see Essentials pages 47-51.

⊜ Sleeping

Hidalgo del Parral *p308*

C Adriana, Colegio 2, between Plaza Principal and Plaza Baca, T627-522 2570, www.hotel adriana.com.mx. Modern hotel with good carpeted, comfortable rooms with a/c, heating and TV. Wi-Fi, restaurant, bar, parking.

D Acosta, Agustín Barbachano 3, T627-522 0221, off Plaza Principal. Quiet, clean, centrally located hotel with an excellent rooftop terrace overlooking a plaza. Friendly, helpful

and good value. Internet and heating among the amenities. Recommended.

D Margarita, Independencia 367, near bus station, T627-523 0063. The good, clean, carpeted rooms are a decent size, with cable TV, hot water, a/c and heating. If arriving at night, a large green neon sign lights the way. 24-hr parking available in supermarket next door. Friendly, helpful and recommended.

D San José, Santiago Méndez 5, near Plaza Principal, T627-522 2453. Big, clean, carpeted rooms with a/c, heating, cable TV, writing desk, hot water and phone. Central, with safe parking.

E Chihuahua, Jesús García and Colón 1, T627-522 1513. Clean and simple with parking

and restaurant. Tiled rooms have TV, hot water, heating and phone. There's another cheapie, San Miguel, just across the street.
E Fuentes, Mercaderes 79, T627-522 0016, hotelfuentes79@hotmail.com. Clean, simple rooms with a/c, telephone cable TV and hot water. Parking and restaurant available. Cheaper without TV.

Hidalgo del Parral to Durango *p310*
D División del Norte, Madero 35, Santiago Papasquiaro, T674-862 0013. In a former convent; the owner's husband was in Pancho Villa's División del Norte.

Durango *p309, map p310*
A few cheaper places are near the market.
A Hostel de la Monja, Constitución 214 Sur, T618-837 1719, www.hostaldelamonja.com. mx. Attractive, luxurious lodgings in the typical colonial style of Durango. There are 20 rooms with high ceilings, DVD players, cable TV, a/c, crisp white sheets and wooden furniture. Very polite. Restaurant and valet parking.
B Florida Plaza, 20 de Noviembre y Independencia, T618-825 0421, www.hotelfloridaplaza.com. A large 4-star hotel with good comfortable rooms, carpets and pleasant furnishings. Services include restaurant, parking and gym.
B Posada San Jorge, Constitución 102 Sur, T618-811 3257, www.hotelposadasanjorge. com.mx. One of the best places in town. Housed in a big old colonial building, this hotel has lots of character and style, attractive courtyards and rooms. There's Wi-Fi, parking and an excellent Brazilian restaurant. Continental breakfast included. Recommended.
B-C Rincon Real, Zarco 309 Sur, T618-837 0723, www.rinconreal.com. Very spacious and comfortable apartment-style suites with kitchen, sofas, a/c, TV and alarm clock. Laundry service, restaurant and parking are among the amenities. Safe and secure, with reduced rates at the end of the week.
C Casablanca, 20 de Noviembre 811 Pte, at Zaragoza, T618-811 3599, www.hotelcasa

blancadurango.com.mx. A big old hotel with rather dubious decor. Rooms are spacious and comfortable, with cable TV, safe, carpet, a/c, Wi-Fi and hot water. Clean and friendly.
D Roma, 20 de Noviembre 705 Pte, T618-812 0122, www.hotelroma.com.mx. An old hotel, since 1918, with an interesting antiquated lift. Rooms are on the small side, but comfortable enough, with cable TV, clean bath, carpets and writing desks. Some rooms are windowless. Wi-Fi in the lobby.
D-E Plaza Catedral, Constitución 216 Sur, T618-813 2480. A big old atmospheric building that's great value for its central location. Some rooms are pokey, others are spacious, so ask to see before accepting. Services include Wi-Fi in the lobby and parking. Some TV sets are blinkered. Rooms with cathedral views are more expensive (**D**). Friendly and helpful.
E Reforma, 5 de Febrero y Madero, T618-813 1622. This hotel has an authentic 1960s lobby and clean, comfortable, straightforward rooms with cable TV and hot water. Free secure parking.
F California, Zarco 317, T618-811 4561. Ultra-cheap, basic and clean. Rooms are pokey and windowless, but equipped with TVs. For the impoverished traveller, and not bad. Also known as **Hotel Oasis**. Friendly.
F Gallo, 5 de Febrero 117 Pte, T618- 811 5920. Another cheapie with very basic quarters and limited hot water.

🍴 Eating

Hidalgo del Parral *p308*
There is little gourmet dining in Parral, but plenty of reasonable places serving whole-some, high-carb economical grub. Lots of bars and big restaurants are on Independencia, over the bridge and close to the centre.
🍴 **La Parroquia**, Hotel San José (see Sleeping). Good-value meals, including breakfast.
🍴 **Morelos**, Plazuela Morelos 22, off Plaza Principal. Sun-Thu 0700-2300, Fri-Sat 24 hrs. Serves a reasonably good, if slightly over-

priced, buffet, with fruit, eggs, lots of hot meat, stews, soups, desserts and coffee, US$6.

₩-₩ Café Corales, Flores Magón, opposite Buses Ballezano. Good beef sandwiches.

₩-₩ La Fuente, Colegio y 20 de Noviembre. Bright chequered table cloths help brighten the slightly tired interior, whilst smartly attired waiters disguise a run-of-the-mill menu of Mexican staples and breakfasts.

₩ Mercado Hidalgo, Méndez, opposite Hotel San Jose. Lots of cheap restaurants and breakfast places inside the market.

Cafés and bakeries

El Parralense, off Independencia on Calle Los Ojitos. Wide choice of bread and cakes.

Durango p309, map p310

You'll find economical restaurants along 5 de Febrero and around the market.

₩₩-₩ Fonda de la Tía Chonda, Nogal 110. An elegant Durango establishment, usually packed. Serves expensive, but tasty, traditional Mexican food. Recommended.

₩₩-₩ La Fogata, Cuauhtémoc 200 y Negrete. Long-standing Durango favourite, the place to get great cuts of meat, steaks and sizzling carnivorous fare.

₩₩-₩ Pampas, Hotel Posada San Jorge, Constitución 102 Sur. Brazilian buffet with 18 salads and 21 types of meat cuts.

₩ Corleone's Pizza, Constitución 110 Nte, at Serdán. Sweet pizzas and cocktails. Busy, popular, family place.

₩ El Zocabón, 5 de Febrero 513 Pte. Warm and cosy diner, good atmosphere at breakfast when locals and cowboys fill the tables. Spicy *huevos rancheros* and good fluffy hot cakes.

₩ La Tostada, Florida Nte 1125. Breakfast and lunch only. Pleasant, with brightly painted furniture. Home-cooked Mexican fare is rustled up before you. Good meat tacos.

₩ Los Esquipules, Florida y Negrete. A popular Mexican restaurant serving traditional dishes. Well presented.

₩ Los Quatros Vientos, Constitución 154 Nte. This seafood restaurant has a high-ceilinged colonial interior with square wooden tables and historic photos.

₩-₩ Gorditas Gabino, Constitución 112 Norte. Mexican food in a US-diner style. Cheap, good and central.

₩-₩ Pizzaly, 20 de Noviembre 1004. A fairly charmless place, but the pizza isn't bad. Quick, cheap, greasy and filling food for those in need of an unpretentious dining experience.

₩-₩ Samadhi, a couple of blocks from the cathedral on Negrete 403 Pte. Good-value vegetarian food, delicious soups and popular with locals. Small, quiet and friendly.

₩ Los Farolitos, Martínez and 20 de Noviembre. An unpretentious locals' haunt serving exquisite tacos and *burritos*.

Cafés and ice cream parlours

El Paraiso Michoacano, 20 de Noviembre, between Juárez and Victoria. For those craving a fix, ice cream and other sugary fare.

La Esquina del Café, Nogal y Florida. A cosy little coffee shop on the corner.

Quattros Grados, Negrete y Florida. Clean and modern design. Smoothies and coffees.

⊙ Bars and clubs

Durango p309, map p310

Durango has a varied nightlife, although much of it is catered towards students and young folk. Sun afternoons and early evenings often feature itinerant musicians on the main plaza, who will walk you around town and entertain you. This is a traditional form of entertainment known as a *callejoneada*.

Club Cien, Paseo del Peñon Blanco 101, Thu-Sat from 2100. Disco lounge, very popular with Durango's in-crowd. Good dance music.

La Jarra, Nogal 112. Live music on Thu, Fri, Sat, usually of the hard rock variety.

La Malquerida, Florida, opposite the tourist office. Named after a film made in Durango and adorned with pictures of actress Dolores del Río. A fun, popular bar.

▲ Activities and tours

Durango p309, map p310
Tour operators
Durango is just awakening to its potential as a centre for adventure activities. The tourist office has a list of guides and operators.
Excursiones Pantera, Pino Suárez 436 Ote, 2nd floor, T618-813 9875, www.aventura pantera.com.mx. Good selection of outdoor and adventure tours in the area, including expeditions to the Zona del Silencio, birdwatching, biking, camping and canyoning.
Durango Xtremo, Zaragoza 203, local 9, T618-185 0460, www.durangoxtremo.com. Specializes in guided excursions, wilderness training and activities like hiking and rapelling. Rents out camping equipment.

⊖ Transport

Hidalgo del Parral p308
Bus The bus station is 20 mins' walk out of town on Av Independencia, east of centre, taxi about US$2. Few bus lines start here so it is difficult to reserve seats. The main players are Estrella Blanca, Omnibus and Grupo Senda.
To **Ciudad Juárez**, several daily, 8 hrs, US$27. To **Durango**, 6 hrs, US$20. To **Zacatecas**, 9 hrs, US$37. To **Chihuahua**, frequent departures, 2½ hrs, US$9.
Ballezano buses to **Guachochi** leave from the office on Carlos Fuero y Flores Magón at 0800, 1230, 1545, US$4.

Durango p309, map p310
Air Guadalupe Victoria Airport (DGO), is 12 km from centre (taxi US$8.50). Flights to **Chihuahua, Guadalajara, Mazatlán, Mexico City, Monterrey, Tijuana** and **Torreón**.

There are also international flights to **Chicago, El Paso** and **Los Angeles**, USA.
Airline offices Aero California, T618-817 7177. AeroMéxico, next to cathedral, T618-817 8828. Mexicana, T618-813 3030.

Bus Take 'camionera' buses from 20 de Noviembere to get to the bus terminal. There are services with **Omnibus de México** and Estrella Blanca. Across the Sierra Madre Occidental to **Mazatlán** there are several buses daily, 7 hrs, US$19. The views are fantastic and recommended if you can't do the Chihuahua–Los Mochis train journey; sit on left side.
To **Chihuahua**, 5-6 daily, 8 hrs, US$30. To **Hidalgo del Parral**, 7 hrs, US$20. To **Guadalajara**, 2000 and 2200, 8 hrs, US$40. To **Mexico City**, every couple of hours, 12 hrs, US$58. To **Zacatecas**, hourly, 4½ hrs, US$15.

⊙ Directory

Hidalgo del Parral p308
Banks Banco Unión, in the Hotel Adriana complex, exchange until 1200, poor rates, similarly at Banamex opposite. Good rates at Bancomer, Plaza Principal until 1200. Opposite is Cambios de Oro, no commission, good rates, Mon-Fri 0900-1900, Sat until 1400. Also at Gasolinera Palmilla on the road to Santa Bárbara, 3 km out of town. **Internet** Ciber, Jiménez 1, US$1/hr. **Post office** Calle del Rayo, over bridge from centre, 0800-1500.

Durango p309, map p310
Banks Bancomer, and many others with ATMs neatly on the west side of the plaza by cathedral. **Internet** El Cactus, Constitución, 1 block past the cathedral heading north, open 1000-2200. Many others in town. **Post office** Av 20 de Noviembre 500 B Ote.

Contents

Northeast Mexico

At a glance

⊖ **Getting around** Bus or car rentals (distance), walking or taxis (in town).

◉ **Time required** One week is plenty for the border towns, major cities and a quick trip to the coast.

☼ **Weather** Temperatures in the northeast are surprisingly hotter than in most of Mexico, and along the coast it is humid. Nov-Mar is the rainy season except in the southernmost edge. Jan-May is the best time for a visit.

✕ **When not to go** There is no bad time to visit the northeast. Jan and Feb can be chilly, although snow is extremely rare. The further north, the hotter the summer months are (Jun-Aug).

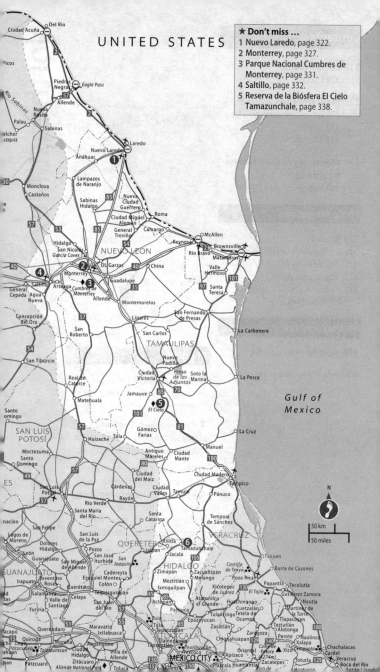

UNITED STATES

Ciudad Acuña
Del Río
Picos
Piedras Negras
Eagle Pass
Allende
Río Sabinas
Nueva Rosita
Palau
Melchor Múzquiz
Sabinas
Monclova
Castaños
Laredo
Nuevo Laredo
Anáhuac
Lampazos de Naranjo
Sabinas Hidalgo
Nueva Ciudad Guerrero
Roma
Ciudad Miguel Alemán
General Treviño
Camargo
McAllen
Reynosa
Brownsville
Río Bravo
Matamoros
Hidalgo
San Nicolás
García Caves
NUEVO LEÓN
Dr. Garzas
China
Valle Hermoso
Santa Teresa
Saltillo
Monterrey
Arteaga
Agua Nueva
General Cepeda
Cumbres de Monterrey
Guadalupe
Allende
Montemorelos
San Fernando de Presas
La Carbonera
Concepción del Oro
San Roberto
Linares
San Carlos
TAMAULIPAS
Nuevo Padilla
Real de Catorce
Ciudad Victoria
Presa de las Adjuntas
Soto la Marina
La Pesca
San Tibúrcio
Matehuala
Jamauve
El Cielo

Gulf of Mexico

Santo Domingo
SAN LUIS POTOSÍ
Huizache
Tula
Gómez Farías
Moctezuma
Santo Domingo
Antiguo Moreles
Ciudad Mante
Manuel
La Cruz
San Luis Potosí
Cárdenas
Ciudad del Maíz
Río Verde
Rayón
Ciudad Valles
Tamuín
Pánuco
Ciudad Madero
Tampico
San Felipe
Santa María del Río
Santa Catarina
Tempoal de Sánchez
Lagos de Moreno
León
Guanajuato
San Luis de la Paz
Dolores Hidalgo
Pozos
San José Iturbide
Xilitla
Jalpan
QUERÉTARO
Tamazunchale
Jacala
VERACRUZ
Tuxpan
GUANAJUATO
Irapuato
Juventino Rosas
San Miguel de Allende
Cadereyta
Colón
Zimapán
HIDALGO
Zacualtipán
Molango
Castillo de Tenyo
Barra de Cazones
Salamanca
Valle de Santiago
Yuriria
Querétaro
Celaya
San Juan del Río
Tequisquiapan
Ixmiquilpan
Meztitlán
Atotonilco el Grande
Xicotepec de Juárez
Poza Rica
El Tajín
Papantla
Tecolutla
Querédaro
Maravatío
Ixtlahuaca
Apaseo
Actopan
Pachuca
Tulancingo
Huauchinango
Cuetzalán
Tetela de Ocampo
Nautla
Martínez de la Torre
Pátzcuaro
Zitácuaro
Villa de Allende
Allende National Park
Toluca
Morelia
Quiroga
Tzintzuntzan
Angangueo
Ciudad Hidalgo
Tula
Tepotzotlán
Teotihuacan
Texcoco
MEXICO CITY
Tlalnepantla
Chignahuapan
TLAXCALA
Tlaxcala
Huamantla
Oriental
Apizaco
Cuautla
Zacapoaxtla
Zaragoza
Teziutlán
Perote
Cofre de Perote (274m)
Xico
Naolinco
Xalapa
Cempoala
Chachalacas
Cardel
Veracruz
Boca del Río

N

50 km
50 miles

Some of the most crucial battles of the 1846-1848 war between Mexico and the United States were fought in the northeast of Mexico. Brownsville (on the US side) and Matamoros (on the Mexican side) experienced the first outbreak of hostilities. Museums in the towns and cities along the way tell this and many other stories and traditions of the region, illustrating as well the fascinating culture and folklore of Old Mexico. On a more contemporary note, the galleries of Monterrey are at the cutting edge of modern Mexican art.

Outside the city you can explore Mexico's largest national park, or set out on a two-day adventure circuit involving extreme sports like river canyoning, abseiling, or swimming through tunnels. Further south you can enjoy tropical bird sanctuaries, jungles and even cloud forests and visit archaeological sites of the enigmatic Huastec and Olmec civilizations. You can even take in some deep-sea fishing before finally reaching Tampico and the Gulf Coast or heading inland to the colonial highlands.

Then there is a choice of either continuing south towards historic Veracruz or heading west to the central highlands via the old silver-mining centre of Pachuca.

Border towns

The first route to be opened between the USA and Mexico was the Gulf Route. It's the not the most inspiring introduction to the country, but its multiple access points make it the fastest way to the south.

Nowadays the old Gulf Route (named for when travellers arrived by ship at Tampico or Veracruz, two prominent ports on the Gulf of Mexico) is more commonly known as the Río Bravo (or Rio Grande if you're on the US side) Route, as most north–south traffic crosses somewhere along the length of this famous river.

Two of the crossings, at Ciudad Juárez and Nuevo Laredo, are shopping meccas and popular weekend destinations for US visitors. In recent years, these two cities have also gained a notorious (and unfortunately justified) reputation as places where anything goes, and violence is endemic.

Nearly all these crossings lead to Monterrey, from where one can head further south toward Saltillo and the venerable colonial heartland, or strike out in an easterly direction toward the coast, the northern stretches of which are almost deserted and make for good wildlife spotting.

Monterrey itself is somewhat anomalous for the region, much more akin to Mexico City or even Dallas that to the tiny settlements that otherwise make up the northeast quadrant. The only other city of any significant size (apart from the two border towns of Ciudad Juárez and Nuevo Laredo) is an hour's drive due south of Monterrey, the pleasant capital of Coahuila state, Saltillo, famous for its serapes *(rugs)*. ▶▶ *For listings, see pages 324-326.*

Ins and outs

Traffic can enter northeast Mexico through no less than 21 *puentes* (bridges) along the Río Bravo. They run from west to east: **Ciudad Juárez**, opposite El Paso (two crossings); **Nuevo Zaragoza** (also opposite El Paso); **Porvenir**, opposite Ft Hancock; **Ojinaga**, opposite Presidio; **Ciudad Acuña**, opposite Del Río; **Piedras Negras**, opposite Eagle Pass; **Colombia**, opposite Dolores; **Nuevo Laredo**, opposite Laredo (two crossings); **Nueva Ciudad Guerrero**, opposite Falcon Heights; **Ciudad Miguel Alemán**, opposite Roma; **Camargo**, opposite Rio Grande City; **Reynosa** opposite Mission; **Reynosa** opposite Hidalgo; **Reynosa** opposite Pharr; **Nuevo Progreso**, opposite Weslaco; **El Capote** opposite Los Indios; and **Matamoros**, opposite Brownsville (three crossings).

The roads from the first five crossings head toward Chihuahua in the west. The sixth leads eventually to Saltillo. The remaining routes all converge upon Monterrey (for which a toll road from Colombia or either of the two Nuevo Laredo crossings is the quickest route, US$6.50), or bypass that city and head further south to Saltillo (to the west) or Ciudad Victoria (to the east).

By car, the best way is over the Colombia Bridge, northwest of Laredo: on Interstate 35, take the exit to Milo (the first exit north of the tourist bureau, then take Farm Road 1472 west, toll US$2). This crossing has little traffic and friendly staff, but it does involve a 40-km detour (it is well signposted on the Mexican side). There is a toll on the international bridge (US$3, payable in either currency). Once in Mexico, you can continue to Monterrey either on on Route 2 to Route 85 via Nuevo Laredo, or by following the railway line (Route 1, free, but much longer) via Ciudad Anáhuac and Lampazos.

The *camino libre* (free motorway) Route 2, which after 25 km offers a sudden right turn to access the *camino cuota* (toll motorway) Route 85, should be treated with the utmost respect. So should the many federal police who are stationed at its underpasses, awaiting visitors travelling above the speed limit. Courteous to a fault, they will offer two methods of payment: a *multa inmediata* (immediate payment) of US$55.45 – payable in Mexican

Border essentials: northeast Mexico–USA

Note All border crossings between the USA and Mexico are currently under review (mostly due to increased drug and security concerns on the US side). For the latest information contact US Customs and Border Protection, http://apps.cbp.gov/bwt, and Crossing US Borders, http://www.dhs.gov/files/crossingborders/travelers.shtm.

Piedras Negras–Eagle Pass (Texas)
Piedras Negras is a small, friendly border town, often eerily quiet. Crossing the border is a quick, painless process. Many of the hotels are in decline or outright dilapidation, and there is the sense that few strangers ever stay long.

Nuevo Laredo–Laredo (Texas)
This is the most important town of the eastern border crossings and sees a lot of traffic, legal and illegal. The World Trade Bridge crosses the Rio Grande. It currently operates Monday-Friday for 24 hours and Saturday 0800-1600, Sunday 1000-1400. Formalities are straightforward if your paperwork is in order. See also Transport, page 326.

Matamoros–Brownsville (Texas)
Crossing the border by car here is quick and easy. Permission is usually granted for six months (multiple entry) for passengers and vehicle, paperwork takes only about 10 minutes if everything is in order. Visas can be obtained in Brownsville on the US side of the border from the Mexican Consulate at 940 East Washington.

pesos – or a several-hour wait until you can visit the traffic 'judge' in the next town, who, they dutifully will inform you, will be out to lunch or dinner, no matter what time you are pulled over. The former option is of course the only real one, and drivers are advised to accept it with good grace. Never suggest this is a bribe. The *federales* will offer to write you a receipt, solemnly warn you about other speed traps along the way, and point you in the direction of Route 85, before shaking hands and wishing you safe travels.

Ciudad Acuña–Del Rio (Texas) → *Colour map 1, A5. Ciudad Acuña Phone code: 877.*
Most of the time, **Ciudad Acuña** is an unassuming, if slightly ugly, middle-of-nowhere town. It comes to life at weekends when rowdy Texans pop over the border to quench their thirsts or purchase typical border trinkets. Sadly, there's little to do but join them under the neon signs, soaking up the seamy undertones. The main plaza (on the left a block or two after crossing) is surprisingly attractive, but the rest of the city ranges from nondescript at best to ugly as the norm.

Around Ciudad Acuña
About 40 km west, the **Parque Nacional Balneario de los Novillos** is a protected area accessible only by 4WD, famous for its hot springs. Much further west and over the border in Texas there's **Big Bend National Park**, www.nps.gov/bibe, well worth a visit but necessitating a return to the USA as it's really only accessible by Texas highways.

La República del Río Grande

The little-known Republic of the Río Grande was not only a Mexican Independence movement, but also managed to supremely annoy its northern neighbour, the newly proclaimed Republic of Texas. Doomed from the start, it was originally an effort by disgruntled Mexicans in the states of Tamaulipas, Nuevo León, and Coahuila to rid themselves of the autocratic rule of President Antonio Santa Ana (of Alamo fame). In January 1840, its leaders declared Independence from Mexico, and in the process claimed a huge amount of land on both sides of the Río Grande (or Río Bravo, as it is known in Mexico).

This wasn't the smartest idea, as neither Mexico nor Texas had the slightest intention of recognizing the upstart republic, much less surrendering territory to it. The Mexicans struck first. Scarcely two months after the makeshift republic's 'Independence', its tiny army was disastrously defeated by loyalist troops.

The republic's military commander, Antonio Canales, fared little better in Texas. After being given the cold shoulder by anyone who was anyone in its government, the best that the Republic of the Río Grande could manage was to scrape together a motley group of 540 ragged freebooters, all of whom Texas was happy to see the backs of in the first place. Recognizing his hopes of success were slim at best, in July Canales assigned command of his new regiment to a Texan, Samuel Jordan, who promptly left for Mexico. Incredibly, Jordan and his band of ruffians managed to capture the important town of Ciudad Victoria without firing a shot.

After nearly being led into a trap, Jordan changed direction and marched toward Saltillo. In October, he was attacked and soundly defeated by the loyalist General Vásquez, and lost most of his remaining men to desertion. (Jordan somehow managed to escape back to Texas.) The following month Canales realized the gig was up for good and surrendered his command to the Mexican army. He was promptly commissioned a general, just in case he had second thoughts about his heady days with his Río Grande gang.

And thus the Republic of the Río Grande evaporated into thin air less than nine months after its proud declaration of Independence. There is a museum dedicated to this bizarre footnote of history in Laredo, Texas.

On the Mexican side are two beautiful but remote protected areas, **Maderas del Carmen** in the state of Coahuila and, approximately 100 km west, **Cañon Santa Elena** in the state of Chihuahua. Access to either from Mexican roads – most of which are unpaved in these parts – is nearly impossible, although the crossing at Ojinaga offers entry to the western part of the Cañon Santa Elena. Entry to either park is far easier through Big Bend National Park on the Texas side.

The former crossing at **Bouquillas del Carmen**, a few kilometres west of Madera del Carmen, was closed indefinitely in 2006, after the notorious drug kingpin Pablo Escobar was shot by CIA operatives in 2004. The town is now almost non-existent but the area is still considered very dangerous due to drug smuggling. Likewise, the former crossing at **La Linda**, opposite Las Vegas Stillwell North, Texas, closed in 1997 for similar concerns, in spite of both governments now officially supporting its re-opening.

NB If crossing from Coahuila State to Chihuahua State, remember to set your clocks back one hour.

Border culture

To paraphrase George Bernard Shaw, the border culture is two cultures – *Chicano* and *Tejano* – separated by the same language. In broadest terms, *Chicano* is more urban and centred along the California-Mexico border, while *Tejano* (sometimes referred to as TexMex, more properly a style of cooking) is more rural and predominates along the Texas-Mexico boundary. While there is a great deal of difference between the two, they are linguistically very similar, share customs derived more from Mexico than its northern neighbour and, above all, show an amazing hybrid artistic vibrancy in everything from cuisine to dance to literature to music. On the US side, cities like San Antonio and Houston are hotbeds of *Tejano* expression in all forms; the same holds true with *Chicano* arts in places such as Los Angeles and Oakland. While *Tejano* culture has remained squarely in south central Texas and the Río Grande Valley, *Chicano* culture has spread to major cities across the USA, and thrives in Chicago, New York and Philadelphia.

To a higher degree than their Texas-based brethren, *Chicanos* are politically active and make a concerted effort to preserve their culture. *Tejanos* are more conservative and less likely to push their cultural autonomy. Ironically, both groups remain somewhat of a mystery to their Mexican cousins. On the south side of the border, the consensus is that they've opted for life in the fast lane on the other side. Grandparents back in Mexico worry that their grandchildren are becoming too gringo, while the kids in the States find it hard to imagine their ancestral homeland as more than a weekend visit.

It all comes together during the holidays, however. Everything else is put on hold while entire families on both sides of the border pack up and go for a week or more to exchange news, meet the newest additions to the extended family, shop till they drop, and hold what amounts to a week-long family fiesta. Gringos – apart from those who've married into one of these families –simply stand aside and let the party roll along.

Piedras Negras–Eagle Pass (Texas) → *Colour map 1, B5. Piedras Negras Phone code: 878.*
A relatively new city by Mexican standards (founded in 1849), **Piedras Negras** (meaning 'black rocks', an allusion to the region's coalfields which still operate south of town), is a hot, dusty border city whose industrial appearance does nothing to keep a visitor within its limits. On the other hand, it is far smaller in size than Ciudad Juárez or Nuevo Laredo, which makes it an easier crossing in terms of traffic. It is known to Mexicans as the birthplace of the nacho. There is little to see in the town, apart from a quick stop at the open-air **Mercado Zaragoza**, set in the midst of a small plaza near the border crossing. Popular with day-trippers from the USA, it is a handicrafts centre, selling locally made original arts and crafts, as well as candy made through traditional recipes found in the region. The **Sanctuary of Our Lady of Guadalupe**, on the main plaza, built a few years after the town was founded, has a solid white exterior and is quite pretty. At night, the **Plaza de las Culturas**, the town's newest park (2005) is attractive. A homage to Mexico's three main indigenous cultures (Aztec, Mayan, and Olmec), it features a replica of a pyramid representative of the style of each of the cultures, the biggest one relating to Teotihuacan's famous Pyramid of the Sun.

Some 10 km south of town the motorway forks. If heading to Monclova and Saltillo, stay on the main road (Route 57); if heading to Monterrey, bear left onto Route 2. From here it is another 187 km to Nuevo Laredo.

Around Piedras Negras

In the town of **Guerrero**, 53 km south from Piedras Negras on Route 2, are the ruins of **San Bernardo Mission**, which supplied many of the colonists in the region that was later to become Texas. In 1700, Franciscan missionaries from the college of Santa Cruz in Querétaro arrived in the area. Two years later, the mission of San Bernardo was erected. In 1718, the first groups of settlers to cross the Río Grande left the mission and founded what is today the city of San Antonio in Texas.

Nuevo Laredo–Laredo (Texas) → *Colour map 1, B6. Phone code: 867.*

Nuevo Laredo is a thoroughly sleazy, charmless, pit of a town – part tourist trap, part den of iniquity. Which is a shame, as for many visitors it is the first view of Mexico. If you enjoy illicit activities you can call it home, otherwise it's best to move on quickly.

While not as inherently violent as Ciudad Juárez (considered the continent's most dangerous city in 2009), Nuevo Laredo can be sketchy once you're away from the shopping area (basically, after crossing the bridge, the high street and a handful of others running parallel on either side of it). Offers to help you find your way to 'Boy's Town' or the nearest *farmacia* (apothecary or drug store) should be ignored. There have been confirmed reports of local police working in cahoots with these would-be guides to arrest tourists once they enter these locations. If you are apprehended, you will go to jail immediately unless the authorities are willing to accept a hefty bribe – often several hundred dollars.

After 120 km of grey-green semi-desert terrain, the road from Nuevo Laredo passes between the **Sierras Milpillas** and **Los Picachos**, climbing up to the **Mamulique Pass**, which it crosses at 700 m. After this it passes by Monterrey's two regional airports and then descends to Monterrey itself (see page 327). From Nuevo Laredo to Monterrey there is a toll road (Route 85) and, after La Gloria (76 km south of Nuevo Laredo), a non-toll road. The latter goes through **Sabinas Hidalgo**, after which it parallels Route 85, confusingly using the same numerical designation. There is also a lengthy and equally confusing toll bypass around Monterrey, which is not worth avoiding just to save a few pesos. The metropolitan Monterrey area is growing chaotically fast, and construction on road ways is an ongoing – and occasionally dangerous – affair. It's best to take the *cuota* road, which is Route 40 and then Route 85 if heading towards Nuevo Laredo at the border; if travelling in the

Nuevo Laredo

Sleeping
Alameda 1
Calderón García Ana 2
Camino Real 3
City Express Nuevo Laredo 4
Colon Plaza 5
Crowne Plaza 6
Diamante 7
Hilton Garden Inn 8
Holiday Inn Express 9
Motel Romanos 10
Santa María 11

The last botanicas

Until a few years ago, *botánicas* (sometimes called *herberías*) were common sights in towns throughout northern Mexico and across the border in Texas and New Mexico. No self-respecting housewife or grandmother would think of buying some new-fangled cure or medicine without first consulting the time-honoured lore and healing traditions that the owners of these shops had at the ready.

Getting married? Want a divorce? Money problems? Need to get rid of an evil spirit? You name it, you could find the answer in a *botánica*. From an earache to morning sickness to the evil eye (*mal ojo*) and any and everything else one could name, there was a remedy available at the local *botánica*. These all-purpose dispensaries were much more than mere curio shops. They stocked herbs, votive candles, amulets, statues of saints, prayer books, incense, pendants and other sure-fire answers for whatever ailment one might have. The owners would know hundreds of herbs by sight or smell alone, and were as important in their communities as the mayor or priest.

Alas, changing customs, wider availability of mainstream medicines, and the advent of the internet have all helped sound the death knell for most of the old-school *botánicas*. Others, often not Mexican in origin but from other Latin American countries, have taken their place, and there are now more north of the border than in Mexico. The University of Texas has begun interviewing the last of these medicinal men and women, whose knowledge has otherwise been lost.

But if you're lucky and passing through a small town on either side of the Río Grande, you just may find one of the last of the originals tucked away on a side street, out of view and out of sync with the 21st century and happy to stay that way.

opposite direction, the toll road is Route 85 which then becomes Route 40 a few kilometres northwest of Monterrey. Do not take the *periférico* unless you want to wander through the nondescript industrial outskirts of Monterrey.

Reynosa–McAllen (Texas) → *Colour map 1, B6. Phone code: 899.*

Opposite McAllen on the border, Reynosa has a population of just over 400,000 but there's not much to see. Invaded by the USA during the early days of the Mexican-American War, it is now a busy, industrial city, home to several maquiladores (export assembly plants located along the border with the USA); friendly enough but rather dull and unappealing. Unfortunately it has succumbed to some of the drug-related violence that plagues Ciudad Juárez and Nuevo Laredo, and daylight crossings are advised. From Reynosa, the most direct route to Monterrey (107 km southwest) is along Route 40.

Matamoros–Brownsville (Texas) → *Colour map 1, B6. Phone code: 868.*

Matamoros is the most attractive of the eastern border towns, although that's not saying much. Once you get past the industrial outskirts, the centre has a certain energy and friendliness; if you want to acclimatize, this is the best place to do it.

Founded in 1774 by families from nearby Reynosa, Matamoros nowadays is best known for its annual autumn **international festival** (www.fiomat.org), held at various cultural venues throughout the city for two weeks in October.

The pleasant historic centre holds the town's primary colonial monuments: **Plaza Hidalgo** (the main square), the **Cathedral of Our Lady of Refuge**, the **Presidencia Municipal** complex, and the former **casino**, all worth a look from an architectural perspective. The nearby **Casa Cross** (Calle 7 y Herrera), built by the Brit Milton Cross in 1885, has been beautifully restored and represents one of the finest New Orleans-style Victorian houses in Mexico. Matamoros also has a bright and well-organized museum, the **Museo Casamata** ① *Santos Degollado y Guatemala, T868-813 5929, www.museocasa mata.com, Tue-Fri 0900-1700, Sat-Sun 0900-1400*, designed to let prospective tourists know what they can expect in Mexico.

Around Matamoros

Less than 40 km to the east on Route 2 is the dubiously named **Playa Bagdad**, a still relatively undeveloped beach that provides a welcome respite from the heat (avoid during the spring university holidays, however, when it experiences spill-over from Texas' Padre Island spring break crowds). There are several small fishing villages that can be accessed from Route 180/101 heading south from Matamoros towards Ciudad Victoria. This section of Mexico is among the least visited, and while infrastructure is minimal along the coast, the area is wonderful for those looking for a coastal vacation away from the resorts.

⦿ Border towns listings

For Sleeping and Eating price codes and other relevant information, see Essentials pages 47-51.

⦿ Sleeping

Ciudad Acuña *p319*
Few hotels are good value here.
B Best Western Villa Real, Bravo 643 Sur, T877-772 7100. Formerly the **Hotel Ciudad Acuña**, modern-looking, downtown location (5 blocks from bridge). Very clean, good food, and the best by far in this price range.
B San Jorge, Hidalgo 165 Oeste, T877-772 5070. Close to the heart of the action, with comfortable rooms and ultra-clean bathrooms.
C Tarasco Motel, Blv Guerrero 150 y A Obregón, T877-772 4428. Quiet, clean and perhaps the only family-friendly hotel in town. Recommended.
C-D Daisy Inn, Lib José de las Fuentes Rodríguez 850, T877-772 8271. Best of the rest, nondescript but serviceable.

Matamoros

Sleeping ⦿
Best Western Hotel Plaza
   Matamoros **1**
Colonial **2**
Hernández **3**
Majestic **4**
México **5**
Plaza Riviera **6**

Piedras Negras *p321*

Hotels are rather neglected and overpriced.

A Best Western Autel Río, Padre de las Casas 121 Norte, T878-782 7064, autelrio@prodigy.net.mx. The best place in town, with comfortable rooms, beautiful gardens, a pool, parking space and internet.

A-B Holiday Inn Express, Av Lázaro Cardenas 2500, T878-783 6040. Overpriced and in ugly location, but 4 different types of rooms to choose from at same price. Typical Holiday Inn lodgings.

A-B Quality Inn Piedras Negras, Ctra 57 s/n, T878-783 0646. Expensive but clean, neat and quiet. Recommended.

B-C Barrokas Inn, Libramiento Perez Treviño 2810, T878-782 6670. Off the main strip, breakfast included. Clean and recommended.

Camping

The better of the 2 trailer parks is on the east side of Interstate 35, Main St exit, 10 mins from border.

Nuevo Laredo *p322, map p322*

Many new hotels, most along Av Reforma, including international chains with reduced rates at weekends. In light of escalating violence along the Mexico-US border, visitors are better off staying in one of the many franchise-operated hotels across the river in Laredo than in Nuevo Laredo itself.

L Camino Real, Av Reforma 5430, T867-711 0300. One of 2 top-end hotels in town. Glitzy, with all mod cons.

L Crown Plaza Nuevo Laredo, Av Reforma 3500, T867-711 6200. Biggest hotel in town. All amenities, business-oriented clientele.

A-B Holiday Inn Express Nuevo Laredo, Blv Luis Donaldo Colosio 5939, T867-711 9191, www.hiexpress.com/nuevolaredo. Spacious and modern with a/c, internet, coffee maker, satellite tv, and iron. Breakfast included.

B Hilton Garden Inn Nuevo Laredo, Av Reforma 5102, T867-711 4600, www.hiltongardeninn.com. Over-hyped but has everything a traveller needs, although largely geared to business crowd.

B-C Colon Plaza, Av Caésar López de Lara 3446, T867-711 9330, www.hcolonplaza.com. Clean, quiet, restaurant, bar, gym, spartan decor.

B-C Motel Romanos, Dr Mier 2420, T867-712 2391. Filled with rather cheesy mock-Romanesque decor, but the rooms are comfortable and have excellent beds.

C Alameda, González 2715, on plaza, T867-712 5050. Good spot with bright rooms.

C City Express Nuevo Laredo, Av Caésar López de Lara 3940, T867-711 0100. On the high street, breakfast included, internet in rooms.

C Santa María, Av Reforma 4446, T867-715 8870. Breakfast included, clean and neat.

C-D Diamante, Av Reforma 3760, T867-711 1596. Small, quiet, and excellent restaurant. Best in range.

E Calderón García Ana, Hermenegildo Galeana 508, T867-712 0948. In centre, run down but friendly. Rooms have bath, hot water and fan.

Reynosa *p323*

As elsewhere on the border, hotels are generally poor value in Reynosa, and an overnight stay on the other side of the border is usually a better bet. As with Nuevo Laredo, there are many new places opening up, most catering to weekend visitors.

A-B Best Western El Camino Inn & Suites, Blv Miguel Hidalgo 1480, T899-921 2770. Best hotel in town, with all mod cons. On the main strip, with gardens, pool, spa, restaurant, business centre, etc.

B Holiday Inn Reynosa Industrial Pte, Ctra Reynosa-Monterrey y Av Encino, T899-909 0170. The best in its price range. Newest hotel in city, but located in industrial park. Clean, efficient, and ideally situated on road to Monterrey and across from Reynosa's largest mall.

B Internacional, Zaragoza 1050, T899-922 2318, exportadores@aol.com. Comfortable enough rooms with bath, less than a 10-min walk from the border.

B-C City Express Reynosa, Blv Miguel Hidalgo 480, T899-921 2400. Free Wi-Fi and breakfast, fitness centre, cable TV. Some 4 km out of centre but on the main strip.

C Virrey, Blv Miguel Hidalgo y Práxedis Balboa, T899-923 1049, www.hvirrey.com.mx. Reynosa's largest and best in this range by far. Bland, but on main strip and with all amenities. Highly recommended.

Matamoros *p323, map p324*
So far Matamoros has largely escaped the violence that has plagued other Mexican border towns. While it's the easternmost crossing, it is also the safest, and probably the best in terms of security where accommodation is concerned.
A Colonial, Calle 6 y Matamoros, T868-816 6606, www.hcolonial.com. A very attractive hotel with a beautiful colonial interior and comfortable rooms. Very traditional and recommended.
A-B Best Western Plaza Matamoros, Calle 9 y Bravo 1421, T868-816 1696, www.hotelplazamatamoros.com. Business oriented and centrally located. Clean and neat.
C Hernández, Calle 6a y Laguna Madre 105, T868-812 3088, www.hotelhernandez.com. Best of the lot in this range. Central and with a touch of Old Mexico to it.
C Majestic, Abasolo 13, T868-813 3680. This is budget range for Matamoros. Large, clean rooms with hot water and friendly staff.
C México, Lauro Villar 1210 esq Marte R Gómez, T868-814 1410, www.hotelde mexico.com.mx. Pool, prívate parking, restaurant/bar. Nondescript but serviceable.
C Plaza Riviera, Morelos y Calle 10, T868-812 0768. 100 rooms (all with TV and a/c), restaurant/bar, parking, and on site shop.

❸ Transport

Nuevo Laredo *p322, map p322*
Bus The Nuevo Laredo bus station is not near the border; take a bus to the border, then walk across. You cannot get a bus from the Laredo **Greyhound** terminal to the Nuevo Laredo terminal unless you have an onward ticket. Connecting tickets from Houston via Laredo to **Monterrey** are available, 14 hrs. Some buses to Laredo connect with **Greyhound** buses in the USA. See also Border essentials, page 319.

All buses crossing into Mexico from Laredo have a mandatory 2-hr stop in Nuevo Laredo for processing.

Grupo Senda and **Estrella Blanca** manage all regional buses in and out of Nuevo Laredo. To **Guadalajara**, 13 daily, 18 hrs, US$28, executive class US$61. To **Mexico City**, 18 daily, 16 hrs, US$40-65. To **Monterrey**, every 30 mins or more, 4 hrs, US$8-11. To **San Luis Potosí**, Estrella Blanca, 13 daily, US$23. To **Tampico**, Estrella Blanca, 1445, 1745, 1915, 2045, 17 hrs, US$40.

Car hire Johnson's Mexico Insurance, Tepeyac Agent, Lafayette y Santa Ursula (59 and Interstate 35), US$2 per day, open 24 hrs, recommended. Sanborn's, 2212 Santa Ursula (Exit 16 on Interstate 35), T867-723 3657, www.sanbornsinsurance.com. Expensive, open 24 hrs.

Matamoros *p323, map p324*
Bus Several lines run 1st-class buses to **Mexico City**, 14 hrs, US$35-70. Estrella Blanca to **Ciudad Victoria** regular departures, US$15-19, 4 hrs.

❶ Directory

Nuevo Laredo *p322*
Banks UNB, Convent y Matamoros, charges 1% commission on TCs, Mon-Fri 0830-1600. IBC, no commission under US$500. **Embassies and consulates** Mexican Consulate, Farragut y Maine, 4th traffic light on the right after leaving Interstate 35, Mon-Fri 0800-1400, helpful.

Monterrey and around

→ Colour map 1, B5. Phone code: 81.

Often called 'the southernmost city in the United States' (in the same way that Texas' San Antonio is referred to by some as 'the northernmost city in Mexico'), the capital of Nuevo León state and third largest city in Mexico, Monterrey, 244 km south of the border, is dominated by the Cerro de la Silla (saddle) from the east and the Cerro de las Mitras (mitres) in the west. It is an important industrial and high technology centre in Mexico as well as the scene of a nascent cultural revival, with many fine museums to visit. All the same, it is also an unattractive city: its streets are congested, its layout seems unplanned and its architecture uninspiring, except for a few sections in the centre, which have undergone remodelling in recent years. While it is not an aesthetically pleasing spot, Monterrey is nonetheless a bold, forward-looking city, home to thriving industries and the base of much of northern Mexico's economic activity.

Few would argue that Monterrey itself is an aesthetic equal to the beautiful colonial cities of the heartland or the sunny resorts of either coast. However, the city is flanked to the west by the gorgeous Sierra El Fraile, which in turn make up the famous Parque Nacional Cumbres de Monterrey, the country's oldest national park. There are also butterfly sanctuaries in the region and several excellent trekking and off-road bicycling paths for those willing to spent a day or two finding them. There are excellent birdwatching opportunities to the east of Monterrey as well. The winding journey between this city and Saltillo to the south affords its own beautiful vistas as the peaks slowly give way to the flatlands of the interior. ▸▸ *For listings, see pages 333-337.*

Ins and outs

Getting there **Aeropuerto Internacional General Mariano Escobedo** (MTY) ① *24 km from the city centre, T81-8345 4434*, receives flights from most cities in Mexico and from the USA, Canada, Caribbean and Latin America. A taxi from the airport to the city centre costs around US$18.35. The vast, long-distance bus terminal is north of the centre on Avenida Colón (Metro Cuauhtémoc). Several major routes converge in and around Monterrey (resulting in seemingly interminable construction along the motorways that skirt the northern edges of the city), connecting the industrial city to the rest of Mexico and to Nuevo Laredo, Reynosa, and Matamoros on the US border (see box, page 319). ▸▸ *See Transport, page 336.*

Getting around The Monterrey metro system has two intersecting lines, which run north–south and east–west of the city. Buses run to all areas within the city; ask at the tourist office for a map.

Tourist information Best obtained from the **State Tourist Office** ① *Washington 648 Oeste, inside the old Palacio Federal, Mon-Fri 0900-1800, T81-8152 3333*. Many hotels have a copy of the English-language city guide *What's On Monterrey*, with details on attractions, dining, entertainment and lodgings in and around the city.

Best time to visit Monterrey's climate is fairly unattractive: it's too cold in winter (the city occasionally receives trace amounts of snow, one of the few in Mexico that does), too hot in summer (though evenings are cool), dusty at most times and has a shortage of water. That fact that Monterrey also receives much of the cement particles from the processing plants south of the city (a problem that affects Saltillo as well) only makes matters worse.

Background

With little visual evidence left to support the facts, it's hard to believe it, but Monterrey was founded in 1596. For many years, it remained little more than a way station between the then-much larger cities of Zacatecas, Querétaro and Mexico City with the far-flung Spanish settlements north of the Río Grande, territory that is now part of the US state of Texas. Cattle and goat ranching was the predominant livelihood until after the war with the USA and the arrival of the railroad, after which the city rapidly grew into Mexico's industrial powerhouse.

Sights

The centre lies just north of the Río Santa Catarina. **Plaza Zaragoza**, **Plaza 5 de Mayo**, the **Explanada Cultural** and **Parque Hundido** link with the **Gran Plaza** to the south to form the **Macro Plaza**, claimed to be the biggest civic square in the world. Its centre pieces are the **Faro de Comercio** (Commerce Beacon) and **Fuente de Neptuno** (Neptune Fountain). To the east of the *faro* is the 18th-century **cathedral**, badly damaged in the war against the USA in 1846-1847, when it was used by Mexican troops as a powder magazine. Running along the west side of the northern part of the plaza are the **Torre Latina**, **High**

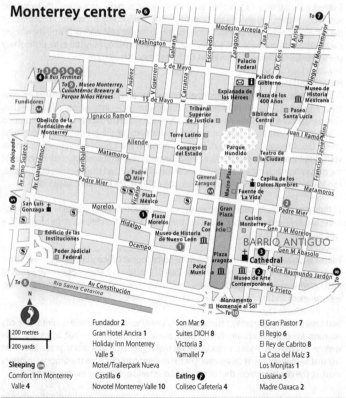

Monterrey centre

Sleeping	Fundador 2	Son Mar 9
Comfort Inn Monterrey	Gran Hotel Ancira 1	Suites DIOH 8
Valle 4	Holiday Inn Monterrey	Victoria 3
	Valle 5	Yamallel 7
	Motel/Trailerpark Nueva	
	Castilla 6	**Eating**
	Novotel Monterrey Valle 10	Coliseo Cafetería 4

El Gran Pastor 7
El Regio 6
El Rey de Cabrito 8
La Casa del Maíz 3
Los Monjitas 1
Luisiana 5
Madre Oaxaca 2

Court and **State Congress**; opposite, on the east side, are the **Biblioteca Central** and the **Teatro de La Ciudad**, both modern buildings, along with the **Capilla de los Dulces Nombres** and the **Casino Monterrey**, both considerably older. The Macro Plaza is bordered at its southern end by the **Palacio Municipal**, and at its northern limit by the **Palacio de Gobierno** (and crossing Avenida 5 de Mayo Oeste, the Palacio Federal).

East of the Macro Plaza lies the bohemian barrio **Antiguo**, the best surviving evidence of Monterrey's colonial past. An absolute must-see in this neighbourhood is the **Galería Catedral** (Cathedral Gallery) ① *Abasolo Oeste 890, T81-8345 2225, www.galeria catedral.com*, a wonderful art and antiques bazaar. The district comes alive on Friday and Saturday evenings when the city's student population takes to its bars and clubs. **Parque Fundidora** ① *east of the centre, www.parquefundidora.org*, is a surreal parkland of rolling greenery, old warehouses converted to cultural spaces, and crumbling, industrial chimneys. On the other side of the Macro Plaza is the popular **Paseo Santa Lucía** (St Lucy's Walk), a pleasant stroll that runs alongside the place where Diego de Montemayor founded Monterrey. It has an artificial lake, museum, plaza, open-air theatre, and several cafés and restaurants.

Monterrey has a number of interesting museums and galleries. The **Museo de Arte Contemporáneo (MARCO)** ① *Zuazúa y Padre Jardon, T81-8262 4500, www.marco. org.mx, Tue and Thu-Sun 1000-1800, US$1.40; Wed 1000-2000, free*, is one of the best modern art galleries in Mexico; it holds temporary shows, workshops, lectures and films, as well as live dance, music, and theatre performances and has a good bookshop. The building was designed by famed Mexican architect Ricardo Legoretta. Another highly regarded contemporary art gallery is the **Galería Arte Actual Mexicano** ① *Río Danubio 125 Pte, T81-8356 1363, www.arteactualmexicano.com, Mon-Fri 1000-1400 and 1600-1900*. Some of the best new Mexican artists are shown here before anywhere else in the country.

Other museums and art galleries with temporary exhibitions are the **Pinacoteca de Nuevo León** ① *Parque Niños Héroes, Av Alfonso Reyes y Servicio Postal, T81-8331 5462, Tue-Sun 1000-1800*, which offers visitors a look at fine art from the state of Nuevo León from the 19th century onwards; the **Museo Metropolitano** ① *corner of Zaragoza and Corregidora, T81- 8344 1971, daily 1000-2000, free*, housed in one of Monterrey's oldest (1612) buildings; the **Centro Cultural de Arte** ① *Belisario Domínguez 2140 Pte, T81-8347 1128, Mon-Fri 0900-1300, 1500-1800, free*, which has displays ranging from photography to architecture, and sculpture and painting by both local and national artists; and the mammoth **Cineteca-Foteca and Pinacoteca-Teatro complex** (known collectively as the Centro de las Artes or CONARTE) ① *Parque Fundidora, Av Fundidora y Adolfo Prieto, www.conarte.org.mx, T81-8479 0010, Tue-Sun 1000-2100, free*. The latter has a photo gallery, exhibition hall and arthouse cinema famed for its films. CONARTE manages the nearby **Casa de Cultura** ① *Av Colón 400 Oeste, T81-8374 1128, Mon-Sat 1000-1700, www.casadelaculturanl.org.mx*, and has the country's finest bookstore devoted to the arts and culture, **Cineteca de Nuevo León** ① *T81-1101 5153, Mon-Fri 1000-2100, Sat-Sun 1300-2100, www.librosarte.com.mx*. There are several other exhibitions, free spaces and galleries dotted around Parque Fundidora.

The **Instituto Tecnológico y de Estudios Superiores de Monterrey** ① *Av Garza Sada 2501*, has valuable collections of books on 16th-century Mexican history. The **Museo de la Historia Mexicana** ① *Dr Coss 445 Sur, off the north end of the plaza, T81-8342 4820, www.museohistoria mexicana.org.mx, Tue-Fri 1000-1900, Sat-Sun 1000-2000, US$1.20, Tue free*, is an excellent interactive museum, good for children, covering Mexico's history from the prehistoric era to the present. Regional history and colonial-era furnishings are the focus of the museum inside the elegant **Ex Obispado** ① *Rafael José Verger, T81-8333*

9588, www.inah.gob.mx, Tue-Sun 1000-1700, US$2.35, the wonderful old bishop's palace that overlooks the city from atop Chepe Vera hill.

The **Salón de Fama de Beisbol** ① *Av Alfonso Reyes 2202 Norte (500 m north of Metro Central), T81-8328 5746, www.salondelafama.com.mx, Tue-Sun 1100-2000, Wed 1000- 2000*, commemorates Mexico's heroes of baseball and is in the grounds of the **Cuauhtémoc Brewery** ① *visits to the brewery Mon-Fri 0930-1530, Sat 0930-1300*. The **Museo Casa de los Tieres** ① *Padre Raymundo Jardón 968 esq Minas, www.baulteatro.com, T81-8343 0604, Mon-Fri 0900-1300 and 1400-1600, US$1.20*, contains an interesting, if slightly strange, collection of marionettes. If glassware is your passion, there's a comprehensive **Museo del Vidrio** ① *Zaragoza y Magallanes 517, T81-8863 1000, www.museodevidrio.com, Tue-Sun 0900-1800, US$1.20, free Tue*.

The best popular art in Monterrey is found at **Arte Popular Carapan** ① *Hidalgo Oeste 30, T81-8345 4422, daily 0900-1900*, housed in a beautifully restored colonial building. It has one of the best collections of indigenous and folk art anywhere in Mexico, ranging from ceramics and fabrics to glass and textiles, to tin and, of course, silver. It also has a **new branch** ① *Río Mississippi Oeste 21 (Local 127) in nearby San Pedro García, T81-8989 9805, carapanartesanias@hotmail.com, daily 1000-2000*.

The **Centro Cultural Alfa** ① *Roberto Gaza Sada 1000, T81-8356 5696, Tue-Fri 1500-2100, Sat 1400-2100, Sun 1200-2100, closed Mon*, has a fine **planetarium** ① *T81-8303 0001, www.planetarioalfa.org.mx*, with an astronomy and a physics section. The centre is especially popular for its many children's exhibits. In a separate building is a Rufino Tamayo stained-glass window. The centre is reached by special bus from the west end of the Alameda, which runs hourly on the hour 1500-2000, free. Likewise, the **Centro Cultural Plaza Fátima** ① *Av San Pedro y Vasconcelos, Tue-Sun 1000-2000*, also in San Pedro García, has some excellent galleries and art shops.

Around Monterrey

In the hills around Monterrey, on the way to the beautiful Parque Nacional Cumbres de Monterrey (see box opposite), is the bathing resort of **Topo Chico** ① *6½ km northwest of Monterrey in San Nicolás de los Garza*. Water from its hot springs is bottled and sold throughout Mexico and parts of the USA.

Reached by a road heading south of Monterrey (extension of Avenida Gómez Morín), is **Chipinque** ① *municipality of San Pedro Garza García, T81-8303 2190, www.chipinque.org.mx, 0600-2000, US$1.65, cars US$2.25*, an ecological park in the foothills of the Sierra Madre, with magnificent views of the Monterrey area. It is popular for birdwatching, hiking, mountain biking and climbing, with peaks reaching 2200 m.

Northwest of Monterrey, off the Saltillo road (Route 40, as it heads southwest), are the **Grutas de García** ① *10 km from Villa de García, which is 40 km from Monterrey*. The entrance to the caves is 800 m up, by cable car, and inside are beautiful stalagmites and stalactites. A tour of the caves takes 1½ hours, and it is compulsory to go in a group with a guide. You can take a bus to Villa de García, but it is a dusty walk to the caves. On Sunday, **Transportes Saltillo-Monterrey** runs a bus to the caves at 0900, 1000 and 1100. Otherwise, it's best to book a tour with an agency such as **Osetur** (you can book at the **Hotel Ancira**).

San Nicolás Hidalgo is a small town 38 km northwest of Monterrey on the Monclova road (Route 53). Dominating the area are the massive limestone cliffs of **Potrero Chico** (4 km west of town, take the road leading on from Calle Francisco Villa). The cliffs are a

Parque Nacional Cumbres de Monterrey

Anyone approaching Monterrey, Mexico's third-largest city, by road or air has seen them: gorgeous, craggy peaks slicing through the blue skies, punctuating an otherwise flat horizon. It is as if the gods had decided to drop beautiful shards of broken terrain about the city, hiding it from view until one reaches its outskirts. These mountains are known throughout the country as the Cumbres de Monterrey. Designated a national park in 1939, for many they mark the entrance into (or passage from) the heartland, the old Mexico of vast, sweeping landscapes of cacti, tiny, centuries-old *pueblos*, and a sense of enchanted isolation impossible to find elsewhere in the country. Not for nothing are they considered Mexico's best-loved national park.

Part of the Sierra Madre Oriental range and covering 177,395 ha, it is technically administered by the federal government through two agencies that manage protected areas, but is really maintained by the municipality of Monterrey. Its best-known climbs are the quadruple-peaked Cerro de la Silla (1820 m) and Copete de las Aguilas (2200 m). Designated as a UNESCO-MAB biosphere reserve in 2008, the park contains roughly half of metropolitan Monterrey's drinking water, more than 120 species of bird (along with some rare parrots), and two dozen species of mammal, including one of the last populations of jaguars in the country. Visitors also enjoy the ideal conditions for rappelling, mountaineering and extreme sports such as hang-gliding and some of the most adrenaline-fuelled mountain biking anywhere on earth.

The park is located in the lower southwest quadrant, on the outskirts of Monterrey and very close to the State of Coahuila. There are multiple access points to the park, although many opt for entering in Garza García, a bucolic town framed by the park's forests. There the entrance is through the well-known Parque Ecológico Chipinque. Entry to the park is US$1.85; hiring a guide costs US$4.35.

---

magnet for big-wall climbers, particularly during the US winter, and have some of the hardest pitches in the world (up to 5.12d), including the 650-m-long *Sendero Luminoso* route on the central pillar of El Toro. The climbing school here is the best in Mexico. A sheet guide by Jeff Jackson describing 80 of the best climbs and places to camp is available at the store on the left before you reach the *balneario*. Accommodation is at the **Posada El Potrero Chico. Autobuses Mina** leave at hourly intervals from Monterrey bus station to Hidalgo (bus station on plaza).

Towards Parque Nacional Cumbres de Monterrey

Heading south from Monterrey, the road threads through the narrow and lovely **Huajuco Canyon**. From the village of Santiago (34 km south of Monterrey), a road runs west to within 2 km of the **Cola de Caballo** (Horsetail Falls), the largest in Mexico, in the Parque Nacional Cumbres de Monterrey (see box above). There is a first-class hotel on the way, and you can take a *colectivo*, US$1.20, from the bus stop to the falls and hire a horse to take you deeper into the park where there are other waterfalls: the 75-m **Cascada El Chipitín** and **Cascada Lagunillas**. There is a two-day circuit, *Recorrido de Matacanes*, starting at **Rancho Las Adjuntas** (off of Route 9 south of Santiago), taking in both these falls and involving river canyoning, abseiling and swimming through tunnels. Ask at **Asociación de Excursionismo y Montañismo** in Monterrey (see page 336).

Saltillo ☺🟢🟠🟣☺🟤 ↠ *pp333-337. Colour map 1, B5. Phone code: 884.*

The capital of Coahuila state is a cool, dry popular city noted for the excellence of its *sarapes* (rugs). Founded in 1577, it is the oldest colonial settlement in northern Mexico. Along with Querétaro to the south, Saltillo is considered the best city in which to live by Mexicans. Occupied by US forces during the Mexican-American War, it also saw the Battle of Buenavista to its immediate south, a decisive conflict that put the region definitively in control of the USA.

Ins and outs

Getting there and around An 89-km road (Route 40) runs west from Monterrey to Saltillo (toll and non-toll). Both the toll and non-toll sections of Route 40 are frequently under construction. The toll road (US$6.70) is always the better bet in any case.

The best way to take in Saltillo's sites is by an old-fashioned trolley tourist bus, known as a *tranvía*. These run Friday to Sunday only, and cost US$2.30. They can be hailed from several stops throughout the downtown and other important locations.

Tourist information Not far from the Ateneo Fuerte there's a **tourist office** ① *Blv Venustiano Carranza 8520, T884-432 3690*, located outside the centre.

Sights

The 18th-century **cathedral**, in the heart of the historic centre, is a mixture of Romanesque, churrigueresque, baroque and plateresque styles, and is the best in northern Mexico. Famed for its academic life, college students from the USA attend its popular **Summer School** ① *T884-416 3049, www.summerschool.com.mx.*

Saltillo is home to Mexico's most prestigious high school, the **Ateneo Fuerte** ① *Blv Venustiano Carranza s/n, daily 0900-1500, weekends only during Jul-Aug*. Many valuable murals and a gallery with an excellent collection of Mexican art are housed in the north wing of this art deco-style building. The south wing houses a natural history museum and there is also the colonial art permanent exhibit (Artemio de Valle Arizpe) with an outstanding display of colonial furniture.

In keeping with its academic and cultural prowess, Saltillo has several museums. The **Museo de las Aves de México (Bird Museum of Mexico)** ① *Hidalgo y Bolívar 151, a few blocks north of the sarape factory, www.museodelasaves.org, Tue-Sat 1000-1800, Sun 1100-1900, US$0.75, guides available*, contains hundreds of stuffed birds. Also check out the **Museo del Desierto** ① *Prolongación Pérez Treviño 3745, T844-986 9000, www.museo deldesierto.org, Tue-Sun 1000-1700, US$5*, to learn all you need to know about the Mexican desert. The house of the artist **Juan Antonio Villarreal Ríos** ① *Blv Nazario Ortiz Garza, Casa 1, Manzana 1, T884-415 2707, free*, has an exhibition in every room of Daliesque work; visitors are welcome, but phone first. Located in a 17th-century mansion, the house of the Zacatecas-born artist, **Rubén Herrera** ① *General Cepeda 105, Mon-Fri 1000-1300 and 1630-2000, Sat-Sun 1000-1300 and 1500-2000*, showcases the works of the founder of Saltillo's Academy of Painting. The nearby **Museo Manuel J García**, contains a large collection of wild animals exhibited in their natural settings. The **Centro Cultural Vito Alessio Robles (Vito Alessio Cultural Center)** ① *Hidalgo y Aldama s/n, T884-412 6180, Tue-Sun 1000-1800*, is an 18th-century repository of antiquities containing some 15,000 historical documents; it also functions as a temporary museum. The **Casa Purcell** ① *Hidalgo 231, T884-414 5536*, is a Victorian mansion built in the late 19th century by Irish merchant William Purcell and is now a cultural centre.

For a look at a neighbourhood straight out of 'Old Mexico', walk through **Barrio Santa Anita**, just off of the historic centre. Recently transformed, this traditional and historic area boasts picturesque spaces which have been restored to their original grandeur and ambiance. Two small streets in particular, Miraflores and Manuel Moreno, have been painstakingly renovated to restore their colonial look and feel.

There are good views from **El Cerro del Pueblo**, a hill 7 km northwest of the city that offers panoramic vistas of the entire region.

Matehuala → *Colour map 1, C5. Phone code: 488.*

Some 22 km south of Saltillo on Route 54, two roads run south: one (Route 54, non-toll) heads southwest to Zacatecas (see page 396) and the other (Route 57, also free) southeast to Matehuala and San Luis Potosí (see page 382). Along the Saltillo–Matehuala section the scenery is attractive, as the road winds its way through wooded valleys. The final section passes through undulating scrub country and crosses into San Luis Potosí state just 16 km northeast of Matehuala, an important road junction with a fiesta 6-20 January. There isn't much to see in town, but outside of town are a few of the last remaining *maguey* distilleries. Although its consumption now is almost non-existent, for centuries the potent drink *pulque*, distilled from *maguey*, was an essential element in everyday life throughout much of Mexico. Matehuala is also a good jumping-off point to visit the important mining town of Real de Catorce (see page 384). From Matehuala you can go via Route 57 to San Luis Potosí (190 km south) and on to Mexico City.

⊙ Monterrey and around listings

For Sleeping and Eating price codes and other relevant information, see Essentials pages 47-51.

⊜ Sleeping

Monterrey *p327, map p328*
Most accommodation aimed at tourists is notoriously expensive. There are many hotels between Colón and Reforma, but nothing below US$20. Most of the cheap hotels are around the bus station (metros Central and Cuauhtémoc).
LL Gran Hotel Ancira, Ocampo 443 Oeste, T81- 8150 7000, www.hotel-ancira.com. A sumptuous, regal hotel with a beautiful marble staircase by the entrance. Now a national historic monument. Not cheap, but a picture of elegance.
A Holiday Inn Monterrey Norte (one of 11 **Holiday Inns** in metro Monterrey), Av Universidad 101 Norte, T81-8158 0000. Out of the centre, near many maquiladoras. 195 rooms, restaurant, lobby bar, tobacconist, outdoor pool, free parking, fitness centre, tennis courts.

B Fundador, Montemayor 802, T81-8342 1694. A good location in Barrio Antiguo. Rooms are comfortable, clean and unremarkable. Lots of wood panelling.
B Novotel Monterrey Valle, Av Lázaro Cárdenas 3000 esq Dr Atl, T81-8133 8133. 238 rooms, with fitness centre, outdoor pool, restaurant, laundry facilities and bar. Wi-Fi available for a fee.
B-C Son Mar, Av Alfonso Reyes 1211 Norte, T81-8125 1300. Located directly across from Cuauhtémoc metro station. Luggage storage, restaurant, bar, parking, laundry, free breakfast and Wi-Fi.
B-C Suites DIOH, Loma Redonda 2728, T81-8122 9930, www.dioh.com/suites/ ingles/index.htm. Minutes from downtown in Colonia Lomas de San Francisco. Furnished studio suites, with internet, cable TV. Available for extended stays or long-term rentals.
C Comfort Inn Monterrey Valle, Av Lázaro Cárdenas 1009, T81-8133 5133, www.comfort innmonterrey.com. Located in the business

hotel and shopping mall area of San Pedro Garza García. Free high-speed internet in all rooms and public areas and great mountain views.

C Holiday Inn Express Monterrey Centre, Av Colon 1768 Pte, T81-8125 4600. Downtown area, 5 mins from the International Convention Center and major offices. Indoor pool, internet and health/fitness centre. Kids eat free. Best in the price range.

C Motel/Trailerpark Nueva Castilla, Ctra a Laredo Km 15.5, T81-8385 0258. Motel with spaces for RVs, pool, hot showers, clean but drab.

C Yamallel, Zaragoza 912 Norte, T81-8375 3500, www.hotelyamallel.com.mx. Centrally located, functional but boring. Restaurant, a/c, cable TV, parking.

D Victoria, Bernardo Reyes 1205 Norte, T81-8375 6919. Fading bus station 'cheapie' that's relatively economical for Monterrey. The area is noisy, so get a room that's away from the street.

Saltillo *p332*

There are several hotels a short distance from the plaza at the intersection of the main streets, Allende and Aldama. Saltillo is a conference centre with many luxury hotels (eg **Camino Real**, **Casa Mexicana**, **Quinta Real**).

A Rancho El Morillo, Prolongación Obregón Sur y Periférico L Echeverría Alvarez, T884-417 4376, www.elmorillo.com. An attractive old converted hacienda with a beautiful, sunny garden. Meals available.

B La Fuente, Blv Los Fundadores Km 3, T884-430 1599. Quiet, out of the centre and well serviced, pool, ideal for families.

B-C City Express, Periférico L Echeverría Alvarez 1630, T884-438 8250, www.city premios.com.mx/ce/ce_ing/hoteles/ micro_saltillo/saltillo.html. All mod cons, breakfast, gym, cable TV.

B-C Urdiñola, Victoria 211, T884-414 0940, jgarza@hieurotel.com. Nice rooms and centrally located. Recommended.

C Garden Express, Blv Los Fundadores 2001, T844-430 1300. Economical and best in its price range.

C Jardín, Plaza Manuel Acuña y Padre Flores 211, T884-412 5916. A good-value budget hotel with functional, spartan rooms.

C Meson de Rebeca, Victoria Pte 335, T884-412 6484. Small, family-run, on a side street, helpful to travellers.

C Saltillo, Periférico L Echeverría Alvarez 249, T844-417 2200. Small, quiet, and in an excellent central location. Breakfast included.

C-D Centenario, Periférico L. Echeverría Alvarez 1932, T844-415 4450. Best in this price range and well located.

C-D El Paso, Blv Venustiano Carranza Norte 3101, T844-415 1035. Passable but noisy, out-of-centre location towards the airport.

C-D Premier, Allende Norte 508, T844-412 1050. Functional but fading. In the centre.

D Brico, Ramos Arizpe Pte 552, T884-412 5146. Cheap, noisy and clean. Tepid water.

Camping

To find the trailer park, turn right on the road into town from Monterrey between **Hotel del Norte** and **Kentucky Fried Chicken**. Basic, with hook-ups and toilets.

Matehuala *p333*

B-C Las Palmas Midway Inn, Ctra Central (Route 57), Km 617, T488-882 0001. Clean, excellent food, best hotel for miles. Highly recommended.

C Casino del Valle, Morelos 621, T488-882 3770. Large rooms with balconies. Central location, recommended.

C Del Parque, Bocanegra 232, T488-882 5200. Best in its price range, large rooms, breakfast, secure parking, Wi-Fi. Recommended.

C El Dorado, near Las Palmas, T488-882 0174. Good value and recommended.

E Alamo, Guerrero 116, T488-882 0017. Very pleasant rooms, clean, with hot showers. Safe motorcycle parking. Friendly, recommended.

Camping

Trailerpark Las Palmas, Ctra Central (Route 57), Km 617 and adjacent to **Las Palmas Hotel**, T488-882 0001. English spoken. There's a bowling alley and miniature golf. Clean.

🍴 Eating

Monterrey *p327, map p328*

Many American chain restaurants, such as Chili's, Sirloin Stockade, Bennigan's and Applebee's have branches here, which are extremely popular. Likewise, fast food is more popular here than elsewhere in Mexico, and Burger King, Domino's, El Pollo Loco, KFC, McDonalds and Pizza Hut are all present.

🍴🍴🍴 El Regio, Gonzalitos y Vancouver, T81-8346 8650. Traditional upscale local cuisine. One of Monterrey's best restaurants.

🍴🍴🍴-🍴🍴 Luisiana, Hidalgo 530 Oeste, T81-8343 1561. Upscale continental restaurant in the centre.

🍴🍴🍴 Madre Oaxaca, Jardón 814 Oeste. A beautiful, upmarket restaurant serving fine Oaxacan cuisine.

🍴🍴-🍴 El Gran Pastor, Av Gonzalitos 702 Sur, T81-8333 3347. Serves *cabrito* (goat) and beef.

🍴🍴-🍴 El Rey de Cabrito, Constitución y Dr Coss 817 Oeste, T81-8345 3232. Exactly what the name implies: lots of goat (a Monterrey speciality) and other dishes.

🍴🍴-🍴 La Casa del Maiz, Abasolo 870B Oeste y Dr Coss, T81-8340 4332. Arty decor at this restaurant specializing in creative Mexican fare. Very pleasant.

🍴🍴-🍴 Los Monjitas, Morelos 240 Oeste. Interesting restaurant where the waitresses are dressed as nuns. Good Mexican dishes with a religious twist. Recommended.

🍴 Coliseo Cafetería, Colón 235. Cheap and cheerful 24-hr joint near the bus station. Tasty, reliable staples.

Saltillo *p332*

🍴🍴🍴 Casa Don Chuy, Allende Sur 160, T844-414 9762. Highly regarded chain of upscale Mexican restaurants.

🍴🍴🍴 El Campanario Saloon and Grill, Ocampo. Open 1200-2400. Recommended.

🍴🍴🍴 El Tapanco, Allende Sur 225, T844-414 0043. Saltillo's most popular restaurant, local dishes served with flair in beautiful surroundings. Downtown location.

🍴🍴 La Canasta, Blv Venustiano Carranza 2485, T844-415 8050. Very popular pork and steak restaurant, business crowd. Reservations recommended.

🍴 Arcasa, Victoria. Good local food.

🍴 El Mesón del Principal, Blv Venustiano Carranza y Egipto, T844-415 0015. Steaks and Mexican dishes.

🍴 Terrazza Romana, Victoria opposite Alameda, T844-414 9743. Italian. Great pastas and pizzas.

🍴 Victoria, Padre Flores 221, by Hotel Hidalgo. Reasonable *comida corriente*, good breakfasts.

✴ Festivals and events

Monterrey *p327, map p328*

Monterrey has 3 major annual festivals.

Aug The Nuevo León Theater Festival, T81-8343 8974, www.teatrodenuevo leon.com, features local, national and international theatre events.

Oct The folklore-themed Feast of St Lucy, T81-2020 2187, www.santalucia.org.mx, showcases much of Nuevo León's otherwise forgotten folklore (as well as that of other countries). Also in Oct is the acclaimed Monterrey International Book Fair, T81-8328 4282, http://fil.mty.itesm.mx. Promoting all things literary.

Nov The Old District Cultural Festival, T81-8342 2085, www.festivalbarrioantiguo. org.mx, highlights the best of the region's music, theatre, fine arts, and literature.

Saltillo *p332*

30 May and 30 Aug Indigenous dances and picturesque ceremonies

Jul The last week of Jul is given over to a celebration of the city's founding with a 9-day cultural fair, immediately followed by the city's patronal feast in honour of Santo Cristo de la Capilla, a famous 400-year-old striking sculpture of Christ crucified that hangs in the baroque chapel of the same name.

Aug A local *feria* is held during the 1st half of the month; cheap accommodation is impossible to find at this time.

Aug The best known of Saltillo's festivals is the annual **Coahuila State Fair** (last week of Aug/1st week of Sep), a *charro* (cowboy) themed extravaganza that combines many agricultural and livestock exhibits with miniature versions of Saltillo's downtown bars and stores in one giant fairground.
Oct The annual **International Festival of the Arts** is held mid-month.
Dec *Pastorelas*, telling the story of the Nativity, are performed in the neighbourhood in Christmas week.

▲ Activities and tours

Monterrey *p327, map p328*
Adventure sports
Asociación de Excursionismo y Montañismo, Washington Pte 2222-B, T81-8327 1929. Bicycle tours and low- to intermediate-level rock climbing. Paragliding and occasionally wilderness survival trips are also available.

Baseball
Estadio de Baseball Monterrey, Parque Niños Héroes, T81-8351 8022. Call ahead to see if there is a match scheduled and at what time. For the most part, matches are not posted in local papers or online.

Bullfighting
Plaza de Toros, M Barragán y Alfonso Reyes, north of bus station, T81-8374 0505. Almost all bullfights take place during the annual State Fair, although occasionally there are single-day events at other times of the year. Call to enquire; advertisements are frequently posted in barbershops and ice cream shops.

☉ Transport

Monterrey *p327, map p328*
Air
Gen Mariano Escobedo Airport (MTY), 24 km from centre. Daily flights to **Mexico City** take 1 hr 20 mins. Good links to many other Mexican cities and numerous flights to the USA, Canada and **Havana** in Cuba.
    Airline offices Aero México, T81-8343 5560. **American Airlines**, T81-8342 9717. **Aviacsa**, T81-8153 4304. **Mexicana**, T800-715 0220.

Bus
The bus terminal is on Av Colón, between Calzada B Reyes and Av Pino Suárez (Metro Cuauhtémoc), T81-318 3737. **Grupo Senda** and **Estrella Blanca** are the main companies. To **Santiago**, for **Cola de Caballo falls**, US$2. To **Mexico City**, hourly, 12 hrs, US$32-62. A more scenic trip is from Mexico City (northern bus terminal) to **Ciudad Valles**, 10 hrs, from where there are many connecting buses to Monterrey. To **Chihuahua**, 11 daily, 12 hrs, US$44-52. To **Guadalajara**, 15 daily, US$24; executive 2100, US$51. To **Matamoros**, hourly, 4 hrs, US$9-20. To **Nuevo Laredo**, hourly, 4 hrs, US$8-12. Regular buses to **Saltillo**, US$3-5. To **San Luis Potosí**, hourly, US$18-34. To **Tampico**, hourly, 7-8 hrs, US$27-38. To **Torreón**, hourly, US$17-25.

Car
If driving to **Saltillo**, there is nothing to indicate you are on the toll-road until it is too late. The toll is US$6.70. Look for the old road.
    Car hire Monterrey, Serafín Peña 740-A Sur, T81-8344 6510. **Payless**, Escobedo Sur 1011 Local 8, T81-8344 6363.

Metro
There are 2 metro lines. The blue line, the longer one, runs south from the suburb of San Bernabé and then makes a right-angle turn traversing the city eastwards passing by the bus and train stations. It connects with the green line (at Cuauhtémoc near the bus station), which runs south into the centre. Tickets bought from machines (2 pesos a ticket, less for more than one).

Saltillo *p332*
Air
The airport (SLW) is 16 km from town. There are daily flights to **Mexico City** with Mexicana. Aerolitoral flies regularly to **Guadalajara** and **Monterrey**.

Bus
The bus terminal is on Blv Echeverría, 3 km south of centre (take the yellow bus marked 'Periférico' from Allende y Lerdo de Tejada); minibuses to Pérez Treviño y Allende (for centre) will take luggage.

To **Ciudad Acuña**, Grupo Senda, 12 daily, 8 hrs, US$25-30. To **Mexico City**, Estrella Blanca and Grupo Senda, 7 daily, 11 hrs, US$30. To **San Luis Potosí**, Estrella Blanca, 1745, US$22. To **Monterrey**, almost constantly, US$3-5. To **Torreón**, 3 hrs, US$12-16, all buses originate in Monterrey and tickets are only sold when bus arrives; be prepared to stand.

Matehuala *p333*
Bus To **Mexico City**, 8 hrs, US$32. To **Monterrey**, 4 hrs, US$11.15. To **Real de Catorce**, US$3.80. To **San Luis Potosí**, with Estrella Blanca, 2½ hrs, US$5-6.

❶ Directory

Monterrey *p327, map p328*
Banks Plenty of ATMs in town. **Embassies and consulates** Canada, T81-8344 3200. Mon-Fri 0900-1330 and 1430-1730. France, T81-8336 4498. Germany, T81-8338 5223. Guatemala, T81-8372 8648. Israel, T81-8336 1325. Netherlands, T81-8342 5055. Sweden, T81-8346 3090. Switzerland, T81-8338 3675. US, T81-8345 2120. UK (Honorary), T81-8333 7598. **Medical services** Hospital General de IMSS, Pino Suárez y J Ramón, T81-8345 5355. Angeles Verdes, T81-8340 2113. Red Cross, T81-8375 1212. **Post office** Palacio Federal, Av 5 de Mayo y Zaragoza (behind Government Palace), T81-8342 4003.

Saltillo *p332*
Banks Bancomer, Allende y Victoria. Banamex, Allende y Ocampo. **Post office** Victoria 223. **Telephone** Long-distance calls from Café Victoria, Padre Flores 221, near market.

Monterrey to the Colonial Heartland

The journey south from Monterrey to the Colonial Heartland is commonly assumed to pass through Saltillo before arriving, several hundred interminably boring kilometres later, in fabled Zacatecas. This is one option, but a far more interesting one passes from Monterrey to the southeast, making for Ciudad Victoria, Tampico, Tamazunchale and Ixmiquilpan. From here one can head due south towards Mexico City or west towards Querétaro and from there to the other colonial cities.

Cities like Ciudad Victoria and Mante are still redolent of their past, while Tampico is one of the few coastal stops in the region. Tamazunchale and Ixmiquilpan will hold much interest for those interested in Mexico's flora and fauna and indigenous civilizations, respectively. ▸▸ *For listings, see pages 341-342.*

Ciudad Victoria → *Colour map 1, C6. Phone code: 834.*

The capital of Tamaulipas state and 263 km southeast of Monterrey along Route 85, Ciudad Victoria is a quiet, clean, unhurried city with a shaded plaza. The city is a centre of citrus fruit and *henequen* fabric production, made from the agave plant. At the centre and all worth a look are the **Cathedral of Our Lady of Refuge**, the **Shrine of Guadalupe**, the **Alamada Central**, the **Hidalgo Gardens**, the **Teatro Juárez** and the **Palacio Municipal**. The **Parque Siglo 21** is the same end of town as the bus station. The centrepiece is a **planetarium**, which looks like a huge red ball that landed on the banks of the Río San Marcos. The **Museo de Antropología e Historia de Tamaulipas**, also on the plaza, has a good section on the Huastec culture.

There's a **tourist office** ① *Calle 8 Anaya y Olivia Ramírez 1287, T/F834-316 1074*. The north-south streets (parellel to the Sierra) have names and numbers, the east-west streets have only names. The city holds its annual fair the week of 6 October, a huge draw for agricultural, ranching, and all things cultural in the region.

Reserva de la Biósfera El Cielo

① *The easiest access is west from Route 85 from the towns of Llera de Canales or El Guayabo, http://elcielo.tamaulipas.gob.mx, free.*

Halfway between Ciudad Victoria and Mante lies the great Reserva de la Biósfera El Cielo, a protected cloud forest covering more than 144,530 ha. The three distinct forest ecosystems are a paradise for the great quantity of species that inhabit it. There are 430 distinct species of birds, 225 local fowl, 97 amphibians and mammals, as well as white tail deer, jaguar and black bears. This density and diversity is due to El Cielo's unique climatological, biological and topographical conditions: the area is a rare transition zone between tropical, temperate and semi-desert ecosystems. The biosphere's infrastructure is first-rate, with six accommodation options, guides, and a designation from UNESCO as a biosphere reserve (MAB) of international significance.

Infrastructure in the reserve is well developed for research and guided walks, although free-form recreational activity is discouraged due to fragile ecosystems. Lodgings and meals are available at cost at several hotels near the reserve.

Mante and around → *Colour map 1, C6. Phone code: 831.*

After crossing the **Tropic of Cancer** the road enters the solid green jungle of the tropical lowlands. Mante (Route 85), 141 km south of Ciudad Victoria, is almost exactly the mid-way point between Matamoros and Mexico City and makes a convenient stopover despite being a grubby city.

Most of Mante's attractions lie outside the city itself. Amongst them are **El Nacimiento** (The Birthplace), 11 km to the south. This magnificent spring in the **Sierra de Cucharas** is a fantastic place to break the journey and picnic, swim, or take a boat ride. At the mouth of the cave the view of the light entering above the waters colours them with an emerald tint. **La Aguja** (The Needle) is another popular swimming spot, approximately 7 km from town. It was formed as a result of the construction of a nearby dam on the Mante River in 1927, then used to irrigate the large sugar cane plantations of the region. From here one can navigate upstream by kayak or small boat, arriving at El Nacimiento. The riverine beaches of **El Limón** are 12 km to the north. The crystalline Guayalejo river here is navigable as well, and two other rivers, the Sabinas and Frío, join it near the beach. The caves at **El Abra**, 10 km south of Mante, and another at **Quintero** closer to town, are popular draws as well. Neither have been fully explored. At the entrance to the Quintero cave, thousands of bats emerge every evening in search of food.

Some 45 km north of Mante is the village of **Gómez Farías**, the jumping-off point for visits to Reserva de la Biósfera El Cielo (see opposite) and an important centre for ornithological research: the highlands above the village represent the northernmost extent of several tropical vegetation formations. Many tropical bird species reach the northern limit of their range. Gómez Farías is reached by turning west off the main highway, 14 km over a paved road to the town plaza. From there, an easy 2-km walk provides excellent views of bird habitats.

Some 31 km south of Mante, at Km 548 from Mexico City, is **Antiguo Morelos** where Route 80 turns off west to San Luis Potosí (see page 382) and Guadalajara (see page 440). Continuing south as Route 85, it passes into the state of San Luis Potosí and Ciudad Valles, 53 km across the border.

Tampico → *Colour map 1, C6. Phone code: 833.*

The port of Tampico, on the Gulf of Mexico, is definitely not a tourist attraction, although fishing (both sea and river) is excellent on the nearby rivers of Tamesí and Pánuco, and on Lake Chairel. Tampico is reached by a fine road from Mante, in a rich sugar-growing area. Tampico was founded in 1522 by Gonzalo de Sandoval but was sacked by pirates in the 17th century and refounded in 1823.

While Tampico's primary attractions are nautical, its historic centre, the **Plaza de Libertad**, does have a few interesting sights. Amongst them are the **Cathedral of the Sacred Heart**, the **Vieja Aduana** (Old Customs House) from the days when Tampico was second only to Veracruz in imports, the **Museum of Huasteca Culture** and the **Palacio Municipal**. Although its beaches are vastly inferior to those found further south or on the Pacific coast, **Playa Miramar** offers waterskiing (rentals available); **Altamira**, 10 km north, is considered the best stretch.

Ciudad Valles → *Colour map 1, C6. Phone code: 481.*

Ciudad Valles, on a winding river, is a popular stopover with many hotels. **Museo Regional Huasteco Rotarios y Artes** (or **Peñaloza**) ① *Artes Rotarios 623, T481-381 1448, Mon-Fri 0900-1800, free,* is the centre of archaeological and ethnographic research for the so-called Huasteca region.

Tamazunchale → *Colour map 2, B4. Phone code: 483. Altitude: 206 m.*

With riotous tropical vegetation, Tamazunchale, 175 km and three hours south of Ciudad Valle along a phenomenally serpentine portion of Route 85, is perhaps the most popular of all the overnight stops on this route. Now heavily promoted by the Mexican government as an ideal tourist stop (see www.tamazunchale.gob.mx), the town retains a strong indigenous influence, and is a centre for birdwatching and local crafts (amongst which are its hand-crafted guitars, which take between two to four days to fashion). The Huasteca attend a weekly market in town, famed for its unique handicrafts.

Ixmiquilpan and around → *Colour map 2, B4. Phone code: 759.*

An area of 23,300 sq km north and south of Ixmiquilpan (206 km south of Tamazunchale in the state of Hidalgo, at Km 169 from Mexico City, just off the highway), is inhabited by 65,000 indigenous Otomí. The beautifully worked Otomí belts and bags may sometimes be bought at the Monday market, and also in the *artesanía* shop in the main street. Early indigenous frescoes can be seen in the old Augustinian ex-convent of **San Miguel Arcangel**, one of several 16th-century battlemented Augustinian monastery-churches; the monastery is open to the public. At sunset each day white egrets come to roost in the trees outside the church; it's worth going up on to the battlements to see them swoop down. The church of **El Carmen** has a lovely west facade and gilded altars inside. There is a 16th-century bridge over the river and a great walk along the ahuehuete tree-lined banks.

About 158 km south of Ixmiquilpan, Route 85 winds its way through the **Parque Nacional Los Marmóles** ('The Marbles'). Rarely visited, this is one of Mexico's oldest parks (created in 1936), where several different landscapes combine to provide a microclimate for trees rarely seen this far south, such as pine, fir and evergreen oak. Its name is due to the presence of rocky formations of marble, another rare sight in these parts. Camping and rock climbing are permitted, and the park is home to a wide variety of fauna, mostly felines and birds.

The **Barranca de Tolantongo** (also known as the Oasis of Mezquital) ① *37 km northeast of Ixmiquilpan, US$1.65, car parking US$1.65 at entrance to recreational area*, is about 1500 m deep with a waterfall and thermal spring; camping is permitted and at weekends there is a small eating place and horse rentals. The area is an important microclimate zone and is in stark contrast to the arid environment that surrounds this verdant spot. To get there take the road towards El Cardonal, then an unpaved (but marked) turn-off about 3 km before El Cardonal (there is a bus from Pachuca).

Actopan to Tula → *Colour map 2, B4. Phone code: 772.*

Actopan (89 km southeast of Ixmiquilpan on Route 85 at Km 119 from Mexico City), a pre-Conquest city in southern Hidalgo state, has another fine 16th-century Augustinian church, an impressive open chapel with paintings by Fray Martín de Acevedo and the astonishing **Convent of St Nicholas Tolentino** (1550-1560), considered one of the finest examples of viceregal architecture in all of Mexico. The town also has accommodation: **Hotel Rira** (**B**). The Wednesday **market** here is popular with visitors.

From Actopan, Route 17 runs west for 56 km to one of Mexico's great archaeological sites: Tula, capital of the Toltecs (see page 151). On the way to Tula there is an interesting co-operative village, **Cruz Azul**, where there are free Sunday morning concerts at 1000 in front of main market. At **Colonia** (Km 85), a road runs left for 8 km to Pachuca (see page 148).

For Sleeping and Eating price codes and other relevant information, see Essentials pages 47-51.

● Sleeping

Ciudad Victoria *p338*

There are several cheaper hotels by the bus station and in the centre.
AL Best Western Santorín, Cristóbal Colón Norte 349, T834-318 1515. Typical Best Western comfort. Rooms have a/c and TV. There's parking and a restaurant.
A Howard Johnson Hotel Everest, Cristóbal Colón Norte 126, T834-318 7070. Laundry service, airport shuttle, room service. All rooms have a/c, cable TV. Near the Best Western but cheaper.
C Las Fuentes Misión, Ctra Nacional, Km 227, T834-312 5655. On Route 85, centrally located, pool, restaurant, room service, internet. Best in this range.
C Los Monteros, Plaza Hidalgo, T834-312 0300. Downtown motel. OK for the price.

Camping
Victoria RV Trailer Park, Blv F Velazquez, T/F834-312 4824. 100 units. Good service, electricity, and hot showers. US$15.

Mante and around *p338*

A Mante, Guerrero 500 Norte, T831-232 0990. Probably the best hotel, in shaded grounds at north edge of business sector.
C Bonito Inn Mante, Luis Echeverria Oeste 204, T831-233 2842, www.bonitoinn.com. Cafeteria, room service, friendly staff.
C Monterrey, Av Juárez 503 Oeste, T831-232 2712. In the old part of town. Manager speaks English. Rooms have bath, hot water, a/c and cable TV. The restaurant isn't so good. Otherwise recommended.
C Rio, Blv Enrique Cárdenas y Azucena, T831-232-2020. Central location, a/c, tennis courts, restaurant. Excellent prices.

Tampico *p339*

Almost all hotels in Tampico are on 1 of 3 streets: Av Hidalgo, Blv Costero, or Salvador Díaz Marón.
A-B Brisas del Mar, Blv Costero 504 Pte, T833-269-0100, www.brisasdelmar.com.mx. Nice waterfront location. Restaurant, all mod cons, clean and bright. Highly recommended.
B Tampico, Capitán Emilio Carranza 513 Oeste, T833-219 0057, www.hotel tampico.com. Lots of character and an attractive tiled lobby. Rooms are slightly outdated, but clean and a good size.
B-C Colonial, Francisco I Madero 210 Oeste, T833-212 7676. Nice, quiet location. Bar, restaurant. All rooms with en suite bath, a/c, satellite/cable TV, free breakfast.
C Inglaterra, Salvador Díaz Marón 116 Oeste, T833-230 4444, www.hotelinglaterra.com.mx. Beautiful, peaceful, great restaurant, clean but dusty rooms and complaints about service.
E Hawaii, Héroes del Cañonero 609, 2 blocks east of Plaza Libertad, T833-234 1887. Dark rooms, but clean. There are other cheapies on this street.

Camping
RVs can stay in the airport car park, US$15 per vehicle, noisy from traffic.

Ciudad Valles *p339*

B San Fernando, Blv México-Laredo 17 Norte, T481-382 0184. Clean, large rooms with a/c and TV. Parking.
C Country Inn & Suites Ciudad Valles, Blv Don Antonio 151, T481-382 8300. 77 rooms, with Wi-Fi and 25-channel cable TV. Breakfast, indoor pool, fitness centre.
C Taninul, Ctra Valles-Tampico Km 15, T481-381 4616. Lovely building, with restaurant, bar, massages, sauna.
C-D Misión Ciudad Valles, Blv México-Laredo 15 Norte, T481-382 0066. Central, pool, restaurant. Good value.
D Condesa, Av Juárez 109, T481-382 0015. Clean, friendly and basic. Rooms have fan.

Camping
El Bañito, 11 km south of town. With warm sulphur pools.

Ixmiquilpan *p340*
B-C Posada Centenario, Centenario 10, T759-723 1508. Best in town. Pool, wheelchair accessible, restaurant, breakfast.
C Casa Blanca, Av Insurgentes Oeste 149, T759-723 8230. Newest in town. Fairly dull but good location.
C Diana, Av Insurgentes Pte 5, T759-723 0758. Rooms at the rear of the building are slightly more expensive. Safe parking. Recommended.
D Palacio Real, Plaza Juárez 1, T759-723 0181. Functional place, which also serves breakfast.
D Plaza Isabel, Plaza Juárez 22, T759-723 1397. On the same plaza and similar to Palacio Real.

⦿ Eating

Ciudad Victoria *p338*
¶¶ Daddy's, Cristóbal Colón 126 Norte, on the plaza, T834-318 7070. A sort of Denny's, with a Mexican touch for the homesick North American.
¶¶-¶ Mezquite, Blv Tamaulipas 1801 Norte, T834-316 5039. Very good local food. Probably the best in town.
¶ Plaza Gallo, Diez Berriozábal 1054, T834-316 4990. Serves chicken and tropical dishes.

Tampico *p339*
¶¶-¶ Jardín Corona, Av Hidalgo 1915, T833-213 9383. Good seafood and French cuisine.
¶ Centro Gastronómico, Mercado de Comida east of the market, for many cheap restaurants.
¶ El Ronco, México esq Tampico 312, T833-213 7579. Typical Mexican, dishes up large portions.
¶ Emir, Olmos, between Díaz Mirón and Madero. Good for breakfast.

▲ Activities and tours

Tampico *p339*
Fishing
Apr-Aug is the deep-sea fishing season, with several major competitions.

⊖ Transport

Ciudad Victoria *p338*
Bus The bus terminal is on the outskirts of town near the ring road northeast of the centre. Omnibuses Blancos run to **Mexico City**, 10 hrs, US$41-44.

Tampico *p339*
Air Francisco Javier Mina Airport (TAM), T833-238 0571, is 8 km from the centre. Mexicana has daily flights to **Mexico City**. Aerolitoral flies to **San Antonio** (Texas). There are good links with towns in northern Mexico and on the Gulf Coast. Continental Express flies to **Dallas** and **Houston**.
  Airline offices Aero México, T833-217 0939. Mexicana, T833-213 9600.

Bus The bus station is several kilometres from the centre on Av Ejército Mexicano on the far side of Laguna del Carpintero. *Colectivos* to the bus station leave from Olmos between the market and the plaza. To **Ciudad Valles**, US$9.50. To **Mexico City**, 8 hrs, US$34. To **Monterrey**, 7-8 hrs, US$35-38. To **San Luis Potosí**, 7 hrs, US$24.

Ciudad Valles *p339*
Bus Omnibus Oeste to **San Luis Potosí**, US$18, 4 hrs; to **Mexico City**, US$27, 10 hrs.

ⓘ Directory

Tampico *p339*
Embassies and consulates Germany, 2 de Enero, 102 Sur-A, T833-212 9784. Also deals with British affairs. **Medical services** Red Cross, T833-212 1313. **Post office** Madero 309 Oeste, T833-212 1927.

Contents

At a glance

⊖ **Getting around** Bus or car rental, walking or taxis (in towns).

◉ **Time required** Minimum of 2 weeks is required to do justice to this beautiful region; if you have less time, the 'must-sees' are Querétaro, San Miguel de Allende, Guanajuato, Zacatecas and Real de Catorce.

☀ **Weather** Most of interior Mexico is dry and hot, although not oppressively so. Aug and Sep are the rainy months. In the higher altitudes it can become quite chilly in the evenings.

✖ **When not to go** Sep, although beautiful, is rainy. Jan and Feb are cold in the higher elevations. Otherwise, just about any time is perfect.

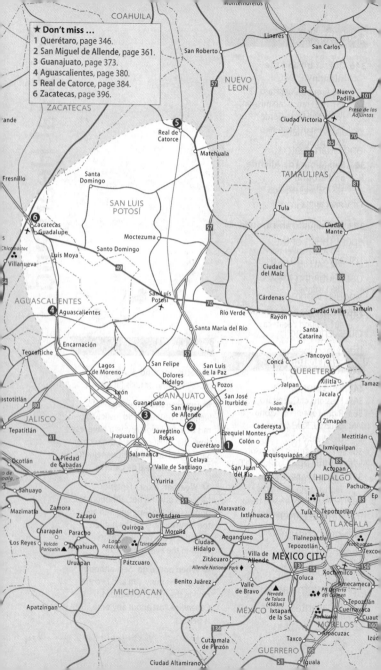

For centuries, the mines of central Mexico churned out much of the world's silver, tin, and a fair amount of gold and precious stones. Spanish-style baroque and neoclassical architecture, built with fortunes amassed from mining and cattle ranching, is at its most opulent and impressive in the magnificent towns and cities of the colonial highlands. While the mines of Zacatecas, San Luis Potosí and Guanajuato supplied the precious metal to the Spanish crown, the states of Aguascalientes and Querétaro were important supply centres and stopovers on the silver route to the capital and the port of Veracruz. Growing wealthy on the trade, the newly made nobility of these cities – many of them fantastically successful former miners – spent much of their enormous fortunes on public displays of wealth, usually with an eye toward building or endowing a convent or church, or beautifying the civic buildings of their towns. Many of these singular works survive, some still with their original form and purpose, others now as *casas de culturas* or museums. It is a testament to their cities' enduring beauty and grandeur that almost all of them have been inscribed in or are shortlisted to UNESCO's prestigious list of World Heritage Sites. The years of heavy-handed Spanish rule and obvious inequalities, especially toward the local indigenous population, led to discontent and in the early 19th century this region was the Cradle of Independence, with its epicentre in Dolores Hidalgo. Nearly every town or village played a part in the 15-year struggle to break with Spain and many museums and monuments tell the story.

Colonial rule relied heavily on the work of the missionaries and a tour of the 18th-century missions of Querétaro, well off the beaten track in the extreme northeast of that state, is well worth the hair-raising journey of '700 curves'. From Querétaro, the important centres of Celaya, San Miguel de Allende, Dolores Hidalgo, Guanajuato and Irapuato all lie within a few kilometres of each other. In the northwestern part of the region, the attractive cities of León, Aguascalientes, and the most stunning colonial jewel of all, Zacatecas, await in near-pristine condition.

Querétaro and the missions

→ *Colour map 2, B3. Phone code: 442.*

As an eastern gateway to the colonial heartland (Zacatecas being the western alternative), Querétaro hides a treasured city centre of pedestrian walkways and colonial architecture. Meaning 'Place Where the Ball is Thrown' (possibly a reference to an ancient game in which the losers were sacrificed) in Tarascan, the city was found in 1531 and has grown to be an important albeit sprawling industrial centre and state capital. Along with Aguascalientes, it is one of the fastest-growing cities in Mexico and is considered one of the five best places in the country in which to live and work. Outside of the centre (which is a World Heritage Site), its sights are somewhat limited, but the ambience makes a visit worthwhile (as well as being an excellent starting point for a trip to the Franciscan missions to the northeast) and provides time to contemplate the historical significance of the city. Hidalgo's rising in 1810 was plotted here, and it was here that Emperor Maximilian surrendered after defeat. He was tried and shot on 19 June 1867, on the Cerro de las Campanas (the Hill of Bells), outside the city. It's also a good base to plan trips to the Peñón de Bernal, local wineries, and the five rarely visited missions of Querétaro in the Sierra Gorda to the east, which are the prime attractions of this state.

The immediate environs of Querétaro are now largely suburbs of that city. However, be sure to take in the thermal baths and opal mines of Tequisquiapan and San Juan del Río en route to the famous Franciscan missions in the upper northeast quadrant of the state. This route also goes to Xilitla in neighbouring San Luis Potosí state, the jaw-dropping fantasy world created by the eccentric expatriate Edward James. ►► *See listings, pages 354-360.*

Ins and outs

Getting there The Central Camionera (bus station) is 5 km southeast of the centre on the Mexico City–León highway. There are regular services to Mexico City's Terminal del Norte and the Querétaro International Airport (QTO), at Sala D). Querétaro is at the crossroads of Route 57 (San Luis Potosí–Mexico City) and Route 45 to Celaya, León and Aguascalientes. Both are *cuota* (toll) roads. The fare from Mexico City to Querétaro is US$11.90, although from there to San Luis Potosí along Route 57 it is free. If travelling from Mexico City to León (Routes 45/110 after Querétaro) the cost is US$17.90 for the entire distance, with the Querétaro–Salamanca leg running at US$8.40. (After Salamanca there are no tolls.) ►► *See Transport, page 359.*

Getting around Querétaro centre is reasonably compact; walking tours are very popular. City buses 8 and 19 link the town centre and bus station; make sure they say 'Central Camionera' or 'Terminal de Autobuses'.

Tourist information There is a **tourist office** ① *Pasteur Norte 4 (on Plaza Independencia y Libertad), T442-238 5067, www.queretaro.travel, daily 0700-1900.*

Sights

Conspirators met secretly in the **Casa de Corregidor** ① *Av Corregidora, across from Plaza Obregón, T442-238 5000, Mon-Fri 0800-2000, Sun 0800-1800*, which was then the mayor's house and is now the **Palacio Municipal**. The austere 18th-century building was once the home of Doña Josefa 'La Corregidora' ('the mayoress') before she married and moved across the street during the early 1800s to plot a revolt against Spanish rule. Doña Josefa Ortiz de Domínguez, wife of the mayor, prominent member of a group plotting for independence, and collaborator with the revolutionaries, was eventually imprisoned in a room in this house by the Spanish. She managed to whisper a message through a keyhole, warning her fellow conspirators that their plans were in jeopardy. As a result, they were able to warn leaders in San Miguel de Allende. Later the same year (1810), again imprisoned under house arrest, she got word to Father Hidalgo that their plans for revolt had been discovered. Hidalgo thereupon immediately gave the cry (*El Grito*) for independence, in nearby Dolores Hidalgo. Nowadays, every 15 September at 2300 *El Grito* is given from the balcony of the Casa de la Corregidora and on every civic balcony throughout Mexico.)

As with most cities in the colonial heartland, the religious influence of the Spanish Catholic colonial period remains very much alive and is most visually evident in the form of its churches and former convents or monasteries. The **Santa Rosa de Viterbo church and monastery** ① *Av General Arteaga (immediately across from Plaza Mariano de las Casas)*, was remodelled by the famous colonial architect from nearby Celaya, Francisco Tresguerras. He also reconstructed the **Templo de Santa Clara** ① *Ignacio Allende Sur s/n*, one of the loveliest churches in Mexico, with fine gilded carvings. The 16th-century

Querétaro

Sleeping 🛏
El Cid 16
Hidalgo 1
Hostal Jirafa Roja 2
La Casa de la Marquesa 3
Mesón del Bosque 12
Mesón del Obispado 10
Mesón de Santa Rosa 4
Plaza 5
Posada Diamante 13
Posada Familiar 15

Quinta Lucca 11
Quinta Zoe 9
Real de Minas Inn 6
Real de Minas
   Tradicional 7
San Agustín 8
Señorial 14

Eating 🍴
1810 4
Alda Café 1

Apolonia 10
Bisquetes 2
El Arcangel 5
Expressarte Café 11
Italian Coffee Company 8
Lonergan's 12
Mesón de Chucho
   el Roto 6
Ostionería Tampico 7
San Miguelito 3
Vegetariano Natura 9

church and monastery of **Santa Cruz** ① *Av Venustiano Carranza*, served as the headquarters of Maximilian and his forces and later as the emperor's prison before he faced the firing squad in 1867. The church of **San Felipe** ① *Melchior Ocampo Sur esq Av Francisco I Madero*, recently restored, is now the cathedral.

For secular architecture, the splendid **Palacio Federal** ① *Av Francisco I Madero (immediately across from Jardín Guerrero y Pasteur)*, once an Augustinian convent with exceptionally fine cloisters, has been restored and houses an art gallery containing some beautiful works. The **Teatro de la República** ① *Juárez esq Angela Peralta (by Jardín Zenea), open to the public during the day*, is a fine mid-Victorian building influenced by French style. It twice played a major role in Mexican history: in 1867 it hosted a tribunal that decided the fate of the Emperor Maximilian; ironically, exactly 50 years later, Mexico's current constitution was drafted and signed here.

The **ex-Convento de la Cruz** is perhaps best known for having the terminus of Querétaro's famous **aqueduct** (now fully restored, the finest example of its kind in the country). The aqueduct was built with funds from one of the city's nobles, the Marqués del Villar del Aguila, who, although married, apparently was in love with one of the nuns at the convent. Learning that the convent had problems accessing water, he spent enormous sums building the aqueduct (supposedly laying some of the stones himself) and its graceful archways. The aqueduct itself has been called the greatest engineering feat in New Spain. The ex-convent is also where the ill-fated Emperor Maximilian was imprisoned before his death by firing squad. It is said that the thorn trees in the courtyard mysteriously always bear only cross-shaped thorns.

The Franciscan church of **San Francisco** and its ex-monastery, now the **Regional Museum of Querétaro** ① *Av Corregidora Sur 3 y 5 de Mayo, T442-212 2036, Tue-Sun 1000-1900, US$3.25*, was the city's first religious complex, started in 1540 but not finished until 1727. The post-Renaissance stone entrance way of the church stands out from the building's smooth white finish and the bell tower is the highest in the city. Inside, there are an amazing eleven separate altar pieces carved in stone, two chapels, several sculptures and other noteworthy pieces. The permanent exhibition galleries are dedicated to archaeology, ethnography, and three historic eras: the viceregal period, Mexican Independence, and 19th-century Querétaro. There is also an especially well-designed exhibit on the pre-Hispanic jaguar, an animal held sacred by Mexico's ancient indigenous cultures.

The **Museo Casa de la Zacatecana** ① *Independencia 59, T442-224 0758, Tue-Sun 1100-1900 (1000-1800 in winter months), www.museolazacatecana.com, US$1.50*, has a fine collection of art (much of it pure silver), from the 17th century through to the 20th century, as well as sculpture, painting and ceramics from the same eras. It is one of the better-run museums in the region and is the recipient of several awards for quality and design.

The **Casa de la Marquesa** ① *Madero 41, T442-212 0092*, is a neoclassical mansion with hand-painted murals and is by all accounts a colonial jewel with great architectural value. It is comprised in fact of two separate houses, La Casa de la Marquesa itself, which dates to the mid-18th century and La Casa Real, a much newer structure built in the early 1900s although in perfect harmony with its much older neighbour. These two buildings are separated by the smallest of streets in the heart of the Centro Histórico.

Around Querétaro ⊖❼✴⊙⊖ ➤ *pp354-360*.

➤ *pp354-360*.

There are two routes up to the Franciscan missions of Querétaro, both of which pass through the small market town of Ezequiel Montes. The first road is reached by turning

Missions of Querétaro

Querétaro boasts five 18th-century missions in the far northeast of the state, all justly named to the list of UNESCO World Heritage Sites in 2003. The missions were founded by the Franciscan friar Junípero de la Serra, who later went on to establish no less than 21 missions in what is now California (where his birthday is a state holiday), as well as in Baja California and Monterrey. The indefatigable Serra was beatified by Pope John Paul II. He is also said to have planted a miraculous tree in the convent of Santa Cruz in the city of Querétaro by thrusting his staff into the ground. The tree is apparently the only one of its kind in the world to have cruciform thorns.

The Missions of Querétaro are distinguished by a profusion of baroque carving (even by Mexican standards), their superb location and the care with which they have been conserved. Of equal interest to art and history scholars is the fact that the missions' facade stonework represents a fusion of European-native American style, common in South America but much less so in Mexico. All five missions – Jalpan, Concá, Landa de Matamoros, Tilaco and Tancoyol – have been wonderfully restored, and two of them have hotels nearby.

The journey itself to these missions requires something of a head for heights – while it is a dramatic and scenic journey climbing the massif of the Sierra Gorda, there are said to be 700 curves en route. There is a slightly shorter route, but that has more than 1000 curves! If travelling by bus, allow at least three days to really enjoy the tour of the missions. Alternatively they can be visited as day trips from Jalpan, the area's primary town. The rural settlements surrounding these missions have largely retained their bucolic, centuries-old character.

northeast from the main highway (Route 57) onto Route 4, 17 km east of Querétaro, and has two towns of interest along the way: **Colón**, 13 km off the road, which has the 17th-century Templo de Nuestra Señora de los Dolores de Soriana; and **Bernal** (see below), 35 km from the turn-off onto Route 4, which is a centre for clothing, blankets, wall hangings and carpets. The second route is a far easier trip along Route 120 – a much better road and only another 20 km south – which turns at San Juan del Río (see below) and also passes through **Tequisquiapan** (see page 350) en route to the missions.

Peñón de Bernal

Near the small town of **Bernal**, founded relatively late by local standards (1617), is the remarkable Peñón de Bernal, a massive rocky outcrop 350 m high, the geological remains of a long-extinct volcano. It is considered the third largest of its kind, after the Rock of Gibraltar and Sugarloaf Mountain in Rio de Janeiro. On the night before and the day of the spring equinox (21 March) there is a festival held here. Local indigenous people believe the mountain is an energy point, because of its distinctive shape, and come to get strength from the first sun of the year. Some also believe there is a connexion between the energy supposedly radiated from this promontory and the longevity of Bernal's inhabitants, who on average live to be 95, easily the longest lifespan of any community in the country.

San Juan del Río → *Colour map 2, B3. Phone code: 427.*

Some 47 km southeast of Querétaro on Route 57, San Juan del Río is the state's second largest city, where fighting bulls are raised. The town is a centre for handicrafts, and for polishing gemstones such as opals and amethysts. This is also wine country, and almost all local vineyards offer tours, with the obligatory stop in the tasting room afterwards, where wine can be purchased as well. San Juan del Río is also known for its many festivals (see page 359).

Tequisquiapan → *Colour map 2, B3. Phone code: 414.*

Route 120 runs northeast for 22 km from San Juan del Río to the picturesque town of Tequisquiapan, with thermal baths (the best of which are **El Rélox**, **El Oasis** and **Termas del Rey**), a fine climate, water sports, weekend residences for wealthy *querétanos* and a disproportionate number of expensive but quite good hotels. The town is deserted from Monday to Thursday so look for reductions in hotel prices. There is a geyser, at **Tecozautla**, 1¼ hours from Tequisquiapan. Just outside of town is the **Hacienda de San José**, now a winery, with a stellar local reputation (although you may think otherwise).

Cadereyta → *Colour map 2, B3. Phone code: 441.*

Cadereyta, 28 km north of Tequisquiapan (Km 75), is colonial in style with two noteworthy churches in the main square, one dedicated to **St Peter** (18th century), the other to **St Paul** (19th century). The latter houses an important collection of colonial religious art. Also in town is the little-known but fascinating **Quinta Schmoll** ① *El Pilancón 1 (Colonia de las Fuentes), T441-276 1071, www.de-paseo.com/quintaschmoll/quintaschmoll.htm*, which houses one of the world's largest cactus terrariums, including several varieties not found anywhere else and others that take between 300-500 years to flower. It also has a small restaurant attached to it. A stop here is highly recommended.

San Joaquín and the ruins of Ranas and Toluquilla → *Colour map 2, B3. Phone code: 441.*

East of Route 120, the ruins near **San Joaquín** (turn-off at Km 138 and then another 25 km), have been only partially excavated. You must register upon arriving at each site and a donation of US$0.80 is requested. The sites have been attributed to the Toltecs and the Chichimecs. **Ranas** is a 30-minute walk from the village and has stupendous views from a series of terraced platforms and pyramids; **Toluquilla** is 10 km from the village along a poorly marked road. Although it is believed there were only, at most, 200 inhabitants when the ruins were inhabited, there are six ball courts. Tarantulas abound! San Joaquín is famous for the annual **Huapango** dance festival on 15 April. A 15-minute walk from San Joaquín is the beautiful cave of **Las Grutas**.

The road to the ruins is steep and the ruins are often swathed in mist. The bends really start after Vizarrón. Much of the journey from here is through rather arid and dramatic terrain with gorges and panoramic views. The high point is called **La Puerta del Cielo** (Door to the Sky), which is apt as you can actually look down on the clouds. As the road begins to descend, the vegetation becomes more tropical and the weather gets much warmer. If driving there are plenty of petrol stations, but keep topping up just to be safe.

Amealco

Amealco is a 35-km drive on Route 120 (right turn off Route 57 approximately 37 km southeast of Querétaro). While the town itself is not of particular interest, there are often cheaper accommodation options to be had here than in the more expensive gateway towns to the missions such as San Juan del Río and Tequisquiapan. ►► *See Sleeping, page 356.*

The Franciscan missions of the Serra Gorda ⬤❶❸ ↦ *pp354-360.*

The five Franciscan missions of Querétaro's Serra Gorda were built during the last phase of the conversion to Christianity in the interior of Mexico, in the mid-18th century, and were also very important in the continuation of the evangelization of California, Arizona and Texas, as most of these efforts started from here or Zacatecas. The richly decorated church facades are of special interest as they represent an example of the joint creative efforts of the missionaries and the local indigenous peoples. All of these facades, and the churches themselves, were constructed to tell an allegorical story visually, for the benefit of the indigenous peoples who were illiterate.

The rural settlements that grew up around the missions still retain much of their colonial character. In 2003, all five towns were given UNESCO World Heritage status. Each of these Franciscan missions (although only one of their churches) was founded by Father Junípero Serra of the Franciscan Order (beatified by Pope John Paul II in 1988), who also founded important missions in Alta California, bringing the grand total to 30. No other missionary, even the Jesuit missionary Father Kino, who in Baja California and the upper reaches of Sinaloa state founded at least 24, was responsible for so many missions in North America.

In order, the five missions are **Jalpan de Serra** and **Tancoyol de Serra**, both in the municipality of Jalpan, **Landa de Matamoros** and **Tilaco**, both located in the municipality of Landa, and **Concá** in Arroyo Seco on the southern border of the state of San Luis Potosí.

Jalpan de Serra → *Colour map 2, B4. Phone code: 441.*
Jalpan, the first and the largest of the missions in the high valleys spreading out from the town, becomes visible way below in a broad, lush valley. It was founded in 1744 and has cloisters in addition to the main church. Of the five mission churches, that of Jalpan, with its pristine baroque facade, is considered the finest. The present church, built between 1751 and 1758 by Serra, is dedicated to Santiago (St James) and symbolizes 'The Triumph of the Faith'. This mission was the first to be built, and it serves as the best example of baroque art. In the first level of the facade, one can observe Santo Domingo, San Francisco, San Pedro and San Pablo, while on the second level the Virgin of Guadalupe and the Virgin of Pilar are displayed. The town itself is picturesque, without being spoilt, although there are increasing signs of external pressure here. There are also pleasant walks along tree-lined riverbanks and the town still has a classic colonial feel to it. The **Sierra Gorda Museum** ① *on the plaza, daily 1000-1500, US$0.50,* is worth a visit; utensils and diverse pre-Hispanic objects from the region are displayed, along with exhibits on Padre Serra and his work. Jalpan is very much a tourist destination these days due to its relative accessibility and more upscale accommodation and restaurants.

Jalpan makes a good base for day-trips to the other mission towns: **Landa de Matamoros**, 22 km east of Jalpan, a small town noted for its ancient Holy Week festival; **Tilaco**, 25 km beyond Landa to the east (take the Encino Solo turn-off and head east for 12 km); **Tancoyol de Serra**, 37 km to the north of Landa (take the La Vuelta turn-off and head north for 20 km); and, in a northwesterly direction, **Concá**. The roads are serpentine but good apart from the last 15 km into Tilaco.

Concá → *Phone code: 487.*
Some 38 km northwest of Jalpan is Concá. At the bridge of Concá a hot-water river flows into one with cold water. The mission is built on a ridge, creating a dramatic skyline when viewed from below. The local church is quite singular. Finished in 1754 by Serra's

associate Friar José Antonio de Murguia, the mission is dedicated to the archangel St Michael and symbolizes 'Victory in Combat'. This mission in the smallest of all, but its facade is absolutely brilliant, consisting of three tiers, with the statue of Holy Trinity at its top. The village itself is very small with two cheap restaurants; *acamaya* (freshwater crayfish) are a local speciality. There's an hourly bus to Concá from Jalpan, US$1.

Landa de Matamoros → *Phone code 441.*
From Jalpan de Serra, Route 120 runs east for 22 km before reaching Landa de Matamoros, after Jalpan de Serra itself the most popular of the five missions. Friar Serra himself had little to do with the physical construction of its church, which was built built between 1761 and 1770 by two other friars, Miguel de la Campa and Miguel de Samaniego. The church here is dedicated to the Immaculate Conception and its facade symbolizes 'Divine Knowledge'.

Tilaco → *Phone code: 441.*
Some 15 km east of Landa on Route 120 is a right-hand turn-off for Tilaco, another Franciscan mission town. (The name means 'black water' in Nahuatl.) Its beautiful church was completed in 1758 by Friar Juan Crespi; it is dedicated to Francisco de Assisi and symbolizes the 'Franciscan Dream'. Curiously, there are four mermaids adorning the facade, although no one knows why.

Tancoyol de Serra → *Phone code: 441.*
East of Landa de Matamoros on Route 120 for 22 km and then left on the turn-off (marked) a further 22 km is Tancoyol de Serra. The highlight of this tiny village is its church, which was built in 1761-1767 by the Friar Juan Ramos de Lora. This mission is dedicated to Our Lady of Light and symbolizes 'The Light of Mercy'. While Concá's interior is more stunning, this mission boasts the most elaborate facade, which depicts stone statues of San Pedro, San Pablo, San Joaquin, Santa Ana with the Virgin Mary, San Antonio and San Roque. Above the door is a niche in the shape of a cross, supported by two angels. There are another six angels surrounding the facade, each of which carries a symbolic instrument of Christ's passion, while flowers cover the rest of it.

Xilitla → *Colour map 2, B4. Phone code: 489. See www.xilitla.org for more information.*
About 87 km east of Jalpan and the first major town after crossing into San Luis Potosí state is the charming village of Xilitla, which would normally be overlooked but for the lush tropical valley and comfortable climate (although it is also the rainiest spot in the state).

Perhaps the area's most famous inhabitant was Edward James, (1907-1984), millionaire heir to the Phelps Dodge copper fortune (his family owned a 300-room mansion and 983-ha estate in England) and lifelong patron of the Surrealist movement with connections to the British royal family. He fell in love with the place and built **Las Pozas** ① *daily 0900-1800, guided tours US$15.10 (Spanish), US$18.90 (English), craft and souvenir shop (closed Wed)*, a house and gardens of architectural eccentricity that are matched only by their setting. Las Pozas is 30-minute walk from Xilitla and is fascinating with extravagant concrete structures intertwined with exuberant vegetation, waterfalls, birds and butterflies. Over a 20-year period, more than 36 surrealistic structures were built in concrete at this magnificent site. The entire estate is very well maintained and is managed by an international foundation. Highly recommended. Nearby are the ruins of an Augustinian convent built in 1557, slowly being reclaimed by vegetation.

Celaya ➔ *Colour map 2, B3. Phone code: 461.*

Celaya is 50 km west of Querétaro along Route 45 (or 55 km via the winding non-toll road that runs parallel to it) and the same distance south from San Miguel de Allende on Route 51). The town was founded in 1570 by 16 families from the Basque country. Its most famous son, Francisco Eduardo Tresguerras (1759-1833), was a great colonial architect, as well as an artist and a poet.

Celaya played a leading role in the Mexican War of Independence (1810-1821) and it was here in 1915, during the Revolution, that the bloodiest battle in Mexican history was fought, in which the future president, Alvaro Obregón, finally succeeded in defeating 'Pancho' Villa.

But Celaya's real claim to fame is the role it played in simply getting the lengthy Revolution underway. It was here, on 21 September 1810, that Hidalgo's group made its triumphal entrance, the first time it captured a city of any note. Celaya also is where the first formal organization of Mexico's insurgent army took place. This event gave Celaya its title 'Birthplace of the Mexican Army'.

Nowadays, the town is famous for its confectionery, especially a caramel spread called *cajeta* or *dulce de leche*, and its churches, many of which were built by Tresguerras himself. His best is considered to be **El Carmen**, with an elegant tower and dome. He also built a fine bridge over the Río de la Laja. The **tourist office** ⓘ *Casa del Diezmo, Benito Juárez 204, T/F461-613 7476, www.guanajuatotour.gob.mx,* is helpful.

The **Templo del Carmen**, considered Tresguerras' masterpiece, was built 1802-1807. The interior and exterior are neoclassical with a simple elegance; inside, you can see Tresguerras' own paintings. The finest of his murals are those in the Capilla del Juicio (Chapel of the Last Judgment). The **Convento de San Francisco** ⓘ *Miguel Doblado y Guadalupe Victoria,* is one of the largest in the country, with a 17th-century baroque interior; the facade of the cloisters was rebuilt by Tresguerras. The **Templo de San Francisco** was rebuilt in 1683 after the original chapel was demolished. The facade is neoclassic and was rebuilt, together with the altars, by Tresguerras in 1810-1820. **Claustro Agustino** dates from the beginning of the 17th century and was the municipal prison until 1961, but now doubles as the Casa de la Cultura. The **Templo de San Agustín** was built in 1609 in the plateresque style. **Templo de la Tercera Orden** is another of Tresguerras' neoclassic works, built in 1820 with marvellous altars. The **Columna de la Independencia** was designed by Tresguerras and was the first monument in the country to celebrate Mexico's freedom in 1828.

There are a handful of interesting sights in Celaya that are not the work of Tresguerras. **Torre Hidráulica**, also known as the *bola de agua* (ball of water), has been adopted as the symbol of the city; it was inaugurated on the centenary of Mexico's Independence from Spain and holds a million litres of water. **Casa del Diezmo**, built at the end of the 17th century, now houses the tourist office (see above). The **Presidencia Municipal** has impressive murals up the stairways in the entrance off the main square, created in 1980 by local artist Octavio Ocampo González. The **Mausoleo de Tresguerras** is a baroque chapel where the famous architect is buried, although, perhaps remarkably, he had nothing to do with its construction. The new **Mummy Museum** ⓘ *Tue-Sat 1000-1400 and 1600-1900, Sun 1000-1500, US$1.15,* in the very elaborate, high Victorian Panteón Celaya (Celaya Cemetery), is also worth taking in, if a bit gruesome (and no match for the other mummy museum in Guanajuato). A recently created museum with a permanent exhibit of 22 mummified corpses, displays include a description of the mummification process and an explanation of why the region has so many mummified remains. Tours can also be made of the monuments and tombs in the cemetery.

Irapuato → *Colour map 2, B3. Phone code: 462.*

Irapuato is the 'World Strawberry Capital' and is justly noted for the delicious fruit; asparagus is also a popular export. In the town centre, around Plaza de los Fundadores and the Jardín Hidalgo, there is a cluster of historic buildings. Dating from 1550, rebuilt in 1617 with the facade completed in 1733, the **Templo del Hospital** ① *Av Revolución y Fernando Dávila*, is said to have the country's largest chandelier. Outside, the **Cruz Monolítica** commemorates the visit of San Sebastián of Aparicio. The facade of the **Templo de San Francisco**, also known as El Convento (1799), is a mixture of baroque and neoclassical styles. The huge **Parroquia** (parish church) was rebuilt in the mid-18th century and must be seen to grasp its enormity. The 19th-century **Presidencia Municipal** incorporates a former 18th-century school, the **Colegio de Enseñanza para Niños**. The fountain, **Fuente de los Delfines**, was given to the town by Emperor Maximilian. The **Museo de la Ciudad de Irapuato** ① *Allende 276 esq 5 de Febrero, T462-626 0053*, is interesting for a cultural and historical overview of the city and region. There's a **tourist office** ① *Escuela Médico Militar 60 (Colonia Jardines), T462-6247174, www.irapuato.gob.mx*, for information.

Unfortunately, the centre of town has been invaded by unsightly and incongruous modern buildings, but just to the edge is the 16th-century church of **San José**, with fine examples of American indigenous art, and the **Templo of Nuestra Señora de Guadalupe** (1890), with a striking late neoclassical gold-leaf-decorated interior. There is a pleasant park and gardens (formerly a zoo) 15 minutes outside the centre and off of Avenida del Bosque and Carretera a la Piedad in Colonia Morelos.

⊕ Querétaro and the missions listings

For Sleeping and Eating price codes and other relevant information, see Essentials pages 47-51.

⊜ Sleeping

Querétaro *p346, map p347*

LL-L La Casa de la Marquesa, Madero 41, T442-212 0092, www.lacasadelamarquesa. com. Opulence and comfort with 3 categories of rooms, the cheapest is a steal at US$125. Mid-priced rooms are equally luxurious.

L-AL Mesón de Santa Rosa, Pasteur Sur 17, Centro, T442-224 2623, www.mesonsanta rosa.com. Small, 300-year-old inn, crammed with colonial detail. Good restaurant.

A-B Holiday Inn Querétaro Zona Diamante, Antigua Ctra al Aeropuerto, Km 1.5, T442-211 7090, www.ichotelsgroup.com. 20 luxury suites with jacuzzi and terrace, 118 rooms all with good views of city.

B Quinta Zoe, 1 block from the plaza, Santa Rosa y Vergara, T442- 130 5879, www.quinta zoe.com. Very small (4 rooms) bed and breakfast lodgings. Affordable luxury in a 17th-century villa in the heart of the Centro Histórico.

B Real De Minas Tradicional, Av Constituyentes 124 Poniente, T442-216 0444, www.travelbymexico.com/quer/realdeminas. 5 mins from the centre. Nice pool and grounds, rooms are large and excellent, all with Wi-Fi, TV and a/c.

B-C Hidalgo, Madero 11, T442-212 0081, www.travelbymexico.com/quer/hidalgo. Downtown, located near all the cultural and historic sights. The first hotel in town (1825) and in continuous operation since then. Nice interior courtyard with exquisite detail. Excellent Mexican restaurant (open to the public). Highly recommended.

B-C Mesón del Obispado, 16 de Septiembre 13, T442-224 2464, www.travelbymexico.com/ quer/mesondelobispado. On the site of the former residence of Queretaro's bishops in converted 18th-century mansion. Common areas shine, rooms are so-so.

B-C Quinta Lucca, Juárez Norte 119-A, T442-340 4444, www.travelbymexico.com/quer/

quintalucca. Just 2 blocks from Teatro de la República, free Wi-Fi, continental breakfast, parking available.

B-C Real de Minas Inn, Av Constituyentes 67 Poniente (Colonia Casablanca), T442-216 1134, www.travelbymexico.com/quer/realdeminasinn. 10 mins from bus station, 15 mins from the airport. Pool, parking, restaurant. All 116 rooms recently renovated.

B-C Turotel, Lateral Autopista México-Querétaro 2107, T442-251 8100, www.turotel.com.mx/queretaro.htm. At the entrance to town. Very modern and somewhat sterile, but with all mod cons.

C Plaza, Juárez Norte 23 (in front of Jardín Zenea and Templo de San Francisco), T442-212 1138, www.travelbymexico.com/quer/hotelplaza. 29 very comfortable rooms downtown with great views but otherwise run of the mill. Good value nonetheless.

C San Agustín, Pino Suárez 12, T442-212 3919, www.travelbymexico.com/quer/sanagustin. Small, dark rooms with Wi-Fi, handy restaurant next door..

C-D Mesón del Bosque, Allende Norte 82, T442-214 4004, www.travelbymexico.com/quer/mesondelbosque. Very basic budget hotel in the heart of the city.

C-D Posada Diamante, Ignacio Allende Sur 45, T442-212 6637, www.travelbymexico.com/quer/posadadiamante. Family-friendly atmosphere, downtown location, no-frills appearance, but rooms are comfortable and hotel is safe, clean and economical.

C-D Señorial, Guerrero Norte 10-A, T442-214 3700, www.travelbymexico.com/quer/senorial. Just north of downtown, with restaurant. Some rooms with a/c.

D El Cid, Prolongación Corregidora Sur 10, T442-214 1165. More of a motel, clean, good value, parking, but hard to find.

E Hostal Jirafa Roja, Calle 20 de Noviembre72, T442-212 4825. Reasonably close to the centre of town. Kitchen facilities. Call in advance. Good local information.

E Posada Familiar, Independencia 22, T442-212 0584. Also in the centre. Basic but OK, has a courtyard.

San Juan del Río *p350*

There are many new hotels in San Juan del Río, but almost all are in the upper range. The most inexpensive options are in centre and near the bus station.

AL Fiesta Americana Hacienda Galindo, Ctra Amealco-Galindo, Km 5.5, T427-272 0050, www.fiestamericana.com. Beautiful restored hacienda, apparently given by Cortés to his mistress, La Malinche. Recently renovated and now the best hotel in town.

AL-A Misión San Gil, Ctra Mexico-Querétaro, Km 172, T427-271 0030, www.hotelesmision.com. Family oriented. Outside of town and quiet. Restaurant, 2 bars, swimming pool, kids' pool, tennis courts, children's play area.

A San Juan Park, Ctra San Juan del Río-Tequisquiapan, Km 5.5, T427-272 7511, www.sanjuanpark.com.mx. Hotel looks as if it has been shipped over from a Pacific resort. All mod cons and a wealth of activities.

C Colonial, Av Juárez 28-30, T427-272 4022. In the centre. Very traditional. Small restaurant, some rooms with fireplaces.

C Layseca, Av Juárez 9 Oriente, T427-272 0110. Downtown in a colonial building, decent enough service, large rooms, nice furniture, car parking, no restaurant.

C Portal del Reyes, Av Juárez Poniente 9, T427-272 6239. Downtown. Shows its age, but has a good restaurant and a certain well-worn charm. Good value. Recommended.

Tequisquiapan *p350*

There is an extraordinary number of hotels in Tequisquiapan, most of them new, and almost all geared to higher-end tourism. Those in the centre tend to be less expensive than those set in the surrounding hillside, but not by much. Travellers on a budget would do better to stay in San Juan del Río or San Joaquín, or proceed directly to one of the mission towns.

LL-L Villa Florencia, Nautha 6, T414-273 3029, www.villaflorencia.com.mx. The rooms are enormous, with lots of dark wood, ornate oversized mirrors and masses of hammered silver. If you're into Caligula-like excess and

Las Vegas decor and don't mind the astronomical price, this is the place for you.

L Pozo Real, Manuel Mateus 5, T414-273 2223, www.pozareal.com.mx. Beautiful *casona* in the centre transformed into a hotel of the highest quality. Stunning exterior and interior: the courtyard is beautiful and filled with flowers, illuminated gracefully at night. Expensive but wonderful.

L-AL El Rélox, Morelos 8, T414-273 0006, www.relox.com.mx. Largest hotel in town. Attractive. Spa pool open to non-residents.

A Posada Los Arcos, Moctezuma 12, T414-273 0566. Small (8 rooms) and quiet. Pleasant spot, well maintained. Private bath, fan and TV.

A-B Del Parque, Camelinas 1, T414-273 0938, www.hoteldelparquetequis.com.mx. Near the centre. All mod cons, pool, restaurant. Nice interior, beautiful patio with pink stone. Rooms with jacuzzi, fan and hardwood floors.

A-B Villa Antigua, Ctra San del Río-Tequisquiapan, Km 11.5, T414-273 3322, www.villa-antigua.com.mx. Wonderful grounds, lots of weddings and social events held here. All rooms are large with full amenities and suites have jacuzzis.

B Posada Tequisquiapan, Moctezuma 6, T414-273 0010. Large rooms with bath and TV, some have balconies looking out onto the gardens.

B-C Sol y Fiesta, Av Heróico Colegio Militar 4, T414-273 1504, www.mexcon.net/soly fiesta.htm. In the centre, half-colonial, half-rustic style but has a certain charm. Families welcome, children's playground. Pool, solarium, restaurant. The best value in its class. Recommended.

C Neptuno, Av Juárez Oriente 5, T414-273 0224. In the centre. Run down but clean and friendly. Quiet and efficient. Probably the best bet in this price category and one of the few cheaper options.

San Joaquín p350

D Casa de Huéspedes La Rosita, Av Insurgentes 23, T441-293 5030. Nondescript, but friendly and clean and in the heart of the centre. Few single rooms.

D Mesón de Joaquín, T441-272 5315, next to the bus park. Good-value rooms for 4 and a campground with shelters and barbecue stands on the outskirts above the town.

D Posada Doña Lucy, Av Insurgentes 3, T441-293 5030. Also in the centre. Cheerful and neat; the owner will provide meals if asked. Small, basic rooms but at a good price.

Amealco p350

B-C Misión la Muralla, Ctra San Juan del Río-Amealco, Km 26, T427-101 0250. Supposedly Mexico's only theme hotel, with the road to independence as the unifying element. Nice enough, with restaurant, bar, pool, parking and disabled access.

D Posada Amealco, IV Centenario 45, T448-278 0660. Inexpensive, clean and in the centre; otherwise nondescript but will do.

Jalpan de Serra p351

A Misión Jalpan, on the main square next to the mission, T441-296 0255, www.hoteles mision.com. The best place in town, with good-sized rooms, tastefully decorated, decent restaurant and swimming pool.

B María del Carmen, Independencia 8, T441-296 0348. Recently renovated but remaining true to the original rustic theme. A nice alternative if all amenities are not needed. Pool, parking, all rooms have king-sized beds and a/c.

C Posada Fray Junípero, Ezequiel Montes 124, opposite church, T441-412 1241. Colonial style rooms have bath and TV, clean, friendly, credit cards accepted, pool, restaurant, good value but noisy because of the bus station.

C-D Mesón de Caporales, Ctra Río Verde s/n (Colonia Landa de Matamoros), T441-296 0002. Outside of town and on the way towards other missions. No surprises, inexpensive. May be crowded on weekends.

D El Aguaje del Morro, down a walkway on the north side of the main plaza, just before the bridge, T441-296 0245. Very friendly staff. Can be noisy. Excellent, cheap local food.

D El Económico, Heróico Colegio Militar, Km 179 (on the main road just downhill from

the first Pemex in town), T441-441 2960.
Clean, basic with laundry. Helpful staff.
E Posada Aurora, Hidalgo s/n, T441-296
0094. With bath, hot water, fan, clean,
friendly. Recommended.

Concá p351
AL Misión Hacienda Conca, Ctra Jalpan-Río
Verde, Km 57 (Colonia Arroyo Seco),
T01-800-029-4240 or T487-877 4252,
www.hotelesmision.com. A refuge of all-
inclusive luxury in the middle of nowhere.

Xilitla p352
AL-B El Castillo, Ocampos 105, T489-365
0038. Breakfast, pool, fine views.
B-C Hostal del Café, Av Niños Héroes 116,
T489-365 0018. In the centre, with cafeteria,
restaurant, parking, Wi-Fi, helpful
for tourist information. Recommended.
C El Lobo, El Lobo, between the northern
missions and Xilitla, T441-234-9103. Simple
but OK hotel if you need to stop.

Celaya p353
Many of the better hotels are out of the centre.
A-B Casa Inn Celaya, Av Juan José Torres
Landa 202, T461-598-6700, www.casainn.com.
mx. 5 mins from downtown. Luxurious and
comfortable rooms. Restaurant, room service,
lobby bar, gym, business centre, Wi-Fi, parking.
B City Express Celeya, Av El Sauz esq Eje
Norponiente, T461-618 5900, www.city
express.com.mx. In the heart of the shopping
district. Decent if drab rooms, all with colour
cable TV, internet and a/c. Free continental
breakfast, business centre, gym, parking.
B Euro Inn, Av Constituyentes Oriente 125,
T461-159 6001, www.euroinn.com.mx.
5 mins from downtown in a safe neighbourhood. All rooms with large-screen TV, cable
TV, Wi-Fi and a/c. Small business centre,
airport shuttle and indoor car park.
B Plaza Bajío Inn, Libertad 133, T461-613
8600. With 80 rooms, central, restaurant,
parking, medical service, laundry.
C Isabel, Hidalgo 207, T461-612 2096.
Restaurant, bar, laundry, parking.

E Guadalupe, Portal Guadalupe 108,
T461-612 1839. Very old historic hotel,
central, cheaper rooms without bath.

Irapuato p354
B-C Real de Minas, Portal Carrillo Puerto 1,
T462-627 7330. Overpriced rooms and
restaurant, quiet rooms on church side.
C Kennedy, Kennedy 830, T462-6274110.
Simple rooms with TV.

⑦ Eating

Querétaro p346, map p347
🍴🍴🍴 **Mesón de Chucho el Roto**, Plaza
Independencia. Very popular at night
with drinks, music, good food and service.
Surprisingly affordable and good value.
🍴🍴🍴 **Mesón de Santa Rosa**, Pasteur 17, in
the courtyard of the hotel of same name
(see Sleeping). Good but expensive, restored
colonial building.
🍴🍴 **Alda Café**, Río de la Loza 4, T442-224 4077.
Modern, breezy and stylish Italian café/
restaurant. Chic and popular.
🍴🍴 **Apolonia**, Andador Libertad 46, T442-212
0389. Wed-Mon 1330-2400. Inventive menu,
with unusual dishes such as a savoury
strawberry soup served hot, and green salad
with mango and cashews. Good selection
of soups and salads, other light foods.
🍴 **El Arcangel**, Plaza Jardín Guerrero. Stylish
spot with a good *menú del día*.
🍴🍴 **Lonergan's**, Plaza de Armas. Pleasant café
with small art gallery, magazines in English,
French and German.
🍴🍴🍴 **Ostionería Tampico**, Corregidora Norte 3.
Specialists in fish, and with good reason.
🍴 **San Miguelito**, Andador 5 de Mayo 39,
T442-224 2760. Tue-Sat 1300-2300, Sun
1300-1700. On the site of the partially
restored Casa de los Cinco Patios, a landmark
colonial house (closed to the public).
Serves meat and traditional Mexican dishes,
wonderfully prepared. It's beautifully lit at
night, and its quiet ambiance also makes it a
top romantic choice. Highly recommended.

♥♥-♥ Bisquetes, in arcade of old Gran Hotel on the Zócalo. Good value, popular for breakfast. Try the local Hidalgo Pinot Noir wine.

♥♥-♥ Restaurant Bar 1810, Andador Libertad 62, T442-214 3324, http://restaurante1810. com.mx. Mon-Sat 0800-2400, Sun 0800-1000. A longtime local favourite in a secluded alley just north of the centre. Predominantly Mexican food, nice ambiance. Recommended.

♥ El Patio, Ezequiel Montes Sur 196. Nicely laid out with attractive, traditional folk setting. Very clean and bright, with high-quality Mexican food (*antojos*, *quesadillas*, etc), just to the west of the centre. Recommended.

♥ Leo's, at La Cruz market. Excellent tacos and *quesadillas*, popular.

♥ Vegetariano Natura, Av Juárez 47. Good, cheap vegetarian food, with health food supplements available for sale.

Cafés

Cafetería a la Mariposa, Angela Peralta 7, T442-212 1166. Daily 0800-2130. Excellent coffee, *tortas* and fruit shakes. Home-made bread and yoghurt.

Expressarte Café, Vicente Guerrero Norte 2, T442-224 2690. Daily 0800-2400. Very arty/ hip café close to plaza. Live music, sleek decor and intimate setting. Food is mostly Mexican and some light snacks.

Italian Coffee Company, on the plaza. Pure Italian heaven in a cup.

San Juan del Río *p350*

♥ Campo Bravo, Ctra Panamericana, Km 171, T427-272 44 45. A bit outside of town, with traditional grilled chicken and meat dishes, huge portions. Recommended.

♥ El Rodeo, Pino Suárez Sur 122, T427-272 4218. Grilled meat and many types of local cheeses as sauces or side dishes.

♥ Fonda Santa María, Av Juárez Oriente 78, T427-274 69 13. Good *churrasquería*-style barbeque and grilled meat.

♥ La Troje, Av Constituyentes 10, T427-272 9010. Probably San Juan del Río's best restaurant. Downtown. Wide variety of options, including some French and Italian.

♥ Marisquería Sólo Veracruz es Bello, Av Constituyentes 10 y Av Central, Km 0.7, T427-272 9724. Pretty much exactly what the name says: seafood from Veracruz.

♥ Plaza Venecia, Ctra Panamericana 60, T427-272 4001. Also outside of town. Good Italian dishes in a pleasant atmosphere. Recommended.

♥ Portal de Reyes, Av Juárez Poniente 9, T427-272 5683. Traditional Mexican food served in a nice old restaurant. Good atmosphere; food ok.

♥ Scorpion's, Av Juárez Oriente 5, T427-272 0231. In the centre. As close to gringo food as you'll find here.

Tequisquiapan *p350*

♥♥♥ K'puchinos, north side of the main square. Excellent Mexican dishes in a stylish restaurant. The place to sit and watch the world go by.

♥♥ Maridelphi, on south side of main square. Popular local choice.

Jalpan de Serra *p351*

♥ Las Cazuelas, to right of church. Delicious tacos, very clean.

♥ Las Jacarandas, next to the bus station. Good *comida corrida*, reasonably priced, clean. Shrimp cocktails at stalls on the plaza.

Xilitla *p352*

♥ Los Cayos, Calle Alvarado. Good view. Try enchiladas *huastecas* and local coffee.

Celaya *p353*

♥♥♥ El Mezquital, Blv López Mateos 1113 Oeste. Meat and traditional barbeque.

♥♥♥ La Mansión del Marisco, Blv López Mateos 1000 esq Juárez. Fish and seafood, live music at weekends.

☺ Entertainment

Querétaro *p346, map p347*
Music

Mariachis play in the Jardín Corregidora, 16 de Septiembre y Corregidora, in the evenings. The town band plays in the Jardín Obregón on Sun evening, lovely atmosphere.

Theatre
Corral de Comedias, Venustiano Carranza 39, T442-212 0765. An original theatre company, colonial surroundings and suppers.

❀ Festivals and events

Querétaro *p346, map p347*
Dec Feria Agrícola (agricultural fair) from 2nd week of Dec until Christmas with bullfights and cockfights.
31 Dec On New Year's Eve there is a special market and performances in the main street.

San Juan del Río *p350*
17 Jan Feast of San Antonio, in which many animals, domestic and farm, are blessed.
2 Feb Candelaria, an important festival with pre-Hispanic roots, in which seeds for the coming harvest are blessed.
1 Mar Jesusito de la Portería.
3 Mar Feast of the Holy Cross, which is celebrated with particular poignancy here.
24 Jun City Fair, feast of the town's patron saint, John the Baptist, which is also the official anniversary of its foundation. Celebrations generally last a full week,
22 Nov Feast of Santa Cecilia.
11 Dec Procession of the Farolitos.

Tequisquiapan *p350*
End May/early Jun Feria del Queso y el Vino (Feast of Cheese and Wine), now more a gastronomic event than anything else, but very popular and a great opportunity to sample local cuisine and beverages.

Celaya *p353*
10-20 Jan 'Black Earth' Festival, commemorating the appearance of the Virgen de Guadalupe in the Tierrasnegras barrio, one of the oldest districts of Celaya. There is theatre, dancing, fireworks and eating a typical local *antojito: gorditas de Tierrasnegras*.

Mar/Apr Easter is marked by visiting several *balnearios* in the area and there are processions through the streets, much eating of local delicacies, and on Easter Sun, a Judas image is burned in many places in the city.
16 Jul Virgen del Carmen.

○ Shopping

Querétaro *p346, map p347*
Gems and jewels
There are local opals, amethysts and topazes for sale; mineral specimens are shaped into spheres and then polished until they look like jewels. Prices are cheaper than San Juan del Río, but more expensive than Taxco.
Joyería Villalón, Andador Libertad 24a. Recommended for fine opals at good prices.
La Cruz market, a 10-min walk from the centre. Open daily, with a street market on Sun. Very well stocked, busy and clean.

San Juan del Río *p350*
Gems and jewels
La Guadalupana, 16 de Septiembre 5. A friendly shop. Recommended.

▲ Activities and tours

Querétaro *p346, map p347*
Language schools
Centro Intercultural de Querétaro, Reforma 41, Centro, T/F442-212 2831.

⊙ Transport

Querétaro *p346, map p347*
Air The airport (QTO) has flights to **Guadalajara**, **Mexico City**, **Monterrey** and **San Luis Potosí**. Continental has international flights to **Houston**, Texas.
  Airline offices Aeromar, T442-220 6936.

Bus The bus station is 5 km southeast of the centre, near Estadio Corregidora. **Terminal A,**

modules 1 and 2, 1st class and plus; **Terminal B**, modules 3, 4 and 5, 2nd class. A new shuttle bus now runs twice daily from the airport directly to the central bus station. There are fixed-price taxis and buses; to confirm, you can pay in advance and ask for a receipt with the former; also holds true for travel from the airport. The bus station has luggage storage, restaurants (with a bar upstairs), travel agency, newsagents, telephones and toilets.

There are good connections with most towns on the US border if you are heading north. Likewise, if heading south, Querétero is a transport hub, with good connections. To **Acapulco**, 1100 and 2200, US$40. To **Aguascalientes**, 6 daily, 4 hrs, US$24. To **Chihuahua**, 1930 and 2030, US$73. To **Ciudad Juárez**, 16 a day, 20-22 hrs, US$92. To **Durango**, 1130, 1145 and 2100, 10 hrs, US$27. To **Guadalajara**, frequent services, 5-6 hrs, US$22. To **Guanajuato**, 6 a day between 0800 and 1700, 3 hrs, US$10. To **León**, every couple of hours, 2½ hrs, US$11. To **Mazatlán**, 1000, 1210 and 1830, US$48-54. To **Mexico City**, an endless stream of buses of all classes, 3 hrs, US$12-13. To **Monterrey**, 15 per day, 8 hrs, US$48. To **Morelia**, 16 per day, 4 hrs, US$10. To **Nogales**, 0015 and 1815, 25 hrs, US$102. To **Piedras Negras**, 1540, 1900 and 1955, US$60. To **San Juan del Río**, every 15 mins, 1 hr, US$4. To **San Luis Potosí**, regular throughout the day, 3 hrs, US$15. To **San Miguel de Allende**, hourly, 1 hr, US$6. To **Tula**, 2¼ hrs, US$8. To **Zacatecas**, almost hourly, 5½ hrs, US$25.

Car There is a 4-lane motorway (Route 45) from Irapuato past Querétaro to Mexico City. The Mexico City motorway (Route 57) passes close to Tula and Tepozotlán, cost is US$13.30 from Mexico City through the Querétaro caseta (toll booth), US$4.20 from there to Salamanca.

Tequisquiapan *p350*
Bus Regular service to **San Juan del Río**, 40 mins, US$0.85.

San Joaquín *p350*
Bus San Joaquín can be reached in 3 hrs by car or bus on a windy road going through desert and then misty pine forests. **Flecha Amarilla** runs 6 buses a day, earliest from **Querétaro** 0620, last 1620, US$4; **Flecha Azul** runs buses to **San Juan del Río**.

Jalpan de Serra *p351*
Bus To **Mexico City**, 3 direct, 6 hrs, US$19, beautiful trip. To **Landa de Matamoros**, hourly, US$0.70, 20 mins. To **Tilaco** and **Tancoyol**, 40-min bus journey to **La Lagunita**, hourly, then combis (on market day, Sat). To **Querétaro**, every hour, 5 hrs, US$6. To **Ciudad Valles**, frequent, via **Landa de Matamoros** and **Xilitla**, US$6.

Xilitla *p352*
Bus To **Jalpan** every hour, US$2.80, 2½ hrs.

Celaya *p353*
Bus Hourly buses to **Mexico City** with Primera Plus, US$16.50.

Irapuato *p354*
Bus The bus station is close to the centre, across from the merge of Blv San Roque y Av Primero de Mayo. Irapuato lies at the crossroads of Routes 90 and 45 and bus to all parts of Mexico make connexions here.

❶ Directory

Querétaro *p346, map p347*
Banks Banamex and Banorte ATMs on Jardín Obregón, Juárez y 16 de Septiembre, accept Visa and MasterCard. Banco Inverlat ATM (should accept Amex) at Corregidora Norte 60. *Casa de cambio* at Corregidora Norte 134. **Internet** Café Internet Asodi, Francisco Márquez 219 (Colonia Las Campanas). Café Internet Cibers Pace, Av Universidad 297 (Colonia Las Brujas). Café Internet Welo, Ezequiel Montes 67 Sur casi esq Constituyentes), T442-212 7272. Wave Internet, Venustiano Carraza, daily 0900-2200 or thereabouts, US$1 per hr. Simple set-up but good machines. **Post office** Arteaga Pte 5.

San Miguel de Allende and around

→ *Colour map 2, B3. Phone code: 415.*

This charming old town on a steep hillside facing the broad sweep of the Río Laja and the distant blue of the Guanajuato mountains is 50 km north of Querétaro by paved road. It holds the triple crown of being a monumento nacional *(national landmark),* pueblo mágico *(enchanted town) and* patrimonio mundial *(UNESCO World Heritage Site). Outside of Zacatecas, El Alamo and Taxco, probably no other place in Mexico is so redolent of its colonial past. Unfortunately, this distinction is marred by the fact that in recent years San Miguel de Allende has pretty much been taken over by North Americans seeking the combination of language schools and relaxed living with an arty edge that this pleasant colonial town still offers. The vast majority of the ex-haciendas and colonial mansions are in foreign hands, as well as most of the town's economy, although expatriates make up only about 10% of the town's permanent population. Some of this imbalance is mitigated by the fact that (as in Puerto Vallarta) the expatriate community does include the local populace in its activities, and to some extent there is an uneasy alliance between local and non-Mexican artists and cultural institutions. However, the presence of McDonald's, Starbucks, and innumerable T-shirt and trinket shops has done little to enhance San Miguel de Allende's image, although its wonderfully preserved colonial past and the natural beauty of its setting perennially keeps it high of the list of must-see locations in Mexico.*

The nearby area is pleasant if rather plain. There are no immediate environs of note. Yet in direct contrast to most Mexican cities (Zacatecas is the only exception), the landscape becomes increasingly attractive as one nears San Miguel de Allende. Fortunately, the city is ideally located almost equidistant between Dolores Hidalgo, Querétaro and Celaya and Guanajuato, so you can't go wrong from here. ▸▸ *For listings, see pages 366-373.*

Ins and outs

Getting there The long-distance bus station is west of the town centre along Canal. Any local bus marked 'Central' heading west on Canal will make a stop at the bus station. The town centre can be reached by taxi (expensive) or bus. Note that all town taxis charge a flat fee of 15 pesos (US$1.40) for the first 1½ km; it is up to the driver's discretion what to charge after this, so unless absolutely necessary, taxis are to be avoided. The nearest airport is at Silao, close to León, also called Aeropuerto del Bajío. The Querétaro airport is almost equidistant (90-minute drive) in the opposite direction. ▸▸ *See Transport, page 372.*

Getting around The city's Centro Histórico is quite compact and easily navigable, so most places of interest can be reached on foot. Probably the best way to take in the town at a leisurely pace is by a tour on foot. Sunday walking tours are popular (see Activities and tours, page 372). A magnificent view of the city can be gained from the mirador on the Querétaro road.

Tourist information The **tourist office** ① *Plaza Allende, next to the church, T415-152 6565*, is good for finding hotels, English is (usually) spoken and you can pick up a city map. There is a wealth of online resources for San Miguel de Allende, the best being the *Guide to San Miguel* (www.san miguelguide.com), the *Vamos a Guanajuato* (www.vamosaguanajuato.com, with useful information on other locations in the state), and the arts and culture-oriented *San Miguel de Allende* (www.de-paseo.com/depaseosanmiguel), which also has information on Querétaro (see page 346) and Bernal (see page 349).

Background

San Miguel de Allende was founded as a mining town by the conquistador Nicolás de San Luis Montañez as San Miguel el Grande in 1542, with 'Allende' added almost 300 years later in honour of the Independence patriot Ignacio Allende who was born there. It grew rich not so much on the strength of its mining output (which was never considerable), but on its location as a way stop for the silver trade that went from Zacatecas and Guanajuato on one side, to Mexico City and Veracruz on the other. Its twisting cobbled streets rise in terraces to the mineral spring of El Chorro, from where the blue and yellow tiled cupolas of some 20 churches can be seen.

Sights

Social life in San Miguel de Allende revolves around the market and the beautiful, tree-lined **Jardín**, or **Plaza Allende**, a sort of open-air living room with a picture-perfect gazebo, antique lampposts and wrought iron benches, all dating from the Porfiriato. Around it are the colonial **Palacio Municipal**, several hotels and, on its south side, the 17th-century **Parroquia de San Miguel church** ① *daily 0900-1900*, adorned in the late 19th century by Zeferino Gutiérrez. Remarkably, the present building was constructed without any professional expertise or models, and was based solely upon postcards of Gothic French cathedrals that Gutiérrez had sent to him. The crypt vault is said to house War of Independence heroes Felipe González and General Anastasio Bustamante.

The **Museo Histórico del Ayuntamiento de San Miguel de Allende** ① *Plaza Principal 8, T415-152 0001*. Inaugurated in 2005 and situated in a 17th-century building in the centre, the museum offers an excellent look at the city's history during the viceregal and early Independence eras, and the importance of its town council (the first in the country, dating from 1810), with nearly 100 period pieces and information on English and French as well as Spanish. The **Museo Histórico de San Miguel de Allende** ① *Cuna de Allende 1, T415-152 0171, Tue-Sun*

San Miguel de Allende

To ⑲⑳, Dolores Hidalgo & Atotonilco — To ⑰

N

100 metres
100 yards

Right continent, wrong country: San Miguel de Allende

It's hard to believe this gem of a town was founded nearly half a millennium ago as something as prosaic as a way station for wagon trains. One glance at its stunning colonial architecture (its historic centre is now a national monument and a World Heritage Site), chic boutiques and restaurants, and thriving artists' colonies will leave you wondering how on earth it ever rose from such obscure beginnings to take its place as the leading expatriate community in all of Mexico.

To say that San Miguel de Allende is popular with US and Canadian retirees, artists, entrepreneurs, teachers, and writers is a massive understatement: Better put, it is for all purposes and intents a gringo paradise in the middle of Mexico, where foreign residents outnumber Mexicans four to one. This has its advantages and disadvantages.

On the one hand, the influx of foreigners has resulted in a bilingual community blessed with many language schools, art institutes and cultural activities, not to mention chamber-music, jazz festivals, and innumerable concerts and lectures. In a cultural context, San Miguel de Allende is rivalled only by Zacatecas.

On the other hand, while locals fortunate enough to live here earn a very good living by Mexican standards, there is a clear separation between gringos and locals. With its gorgeous architecture and surroundings, it also has become a haven for tourists, and the number of tacky T-shirt shops, fast food restaurants, and fly-by-night Spanish language schools is on the rise.

There are other communities in Mexico with a disproportionate mix of locals and foreigners, but none quite like this. No matter what your feeling on the clash of cultures, San Miguel de Allende has to be seen to be believed, and should rank high on every visitor's list.

1000-1600, www.inah.gob.mx, is housed in a restored colonial building. This small museum has exhibits on the town and surrounding region from prehistoric times to the present, including a large display on Ignacio Allende, for whom the town was named.

Very close to the Plaza Allende, the **oratory of San Felipe Neri** ① *Insurgentes esq Pepe Llanos, Sat only 0800-1800*, was built by local indigenous peoples in 1712 and is made of pink stone. The interior houses 33 oil paintings, attributed to Miguel Cabrera. Off of the plaza's north side is the **Templo de Nuestra Señora de la Salud** ① *Mesones s/n, daily 0700-1900*, a pleasant 18th-century baroque church with a splayed arch portal while Its *campanario* (bell tower) has the oldest bell in the city.

Religious and cultural tourism are popular sectors in San Miguel de Allende, and other notable churches include the **San Francisco** church, which was designed by Tresguerras. Built in 1779 and financed by donations from wealthy patrons and bullfighting profits, it is one of the finest examples of churrigueresque design in Mexico. The ex-convent (now church) of **La Concepción** ① *Canal y Hernández Macías, daily 0900-1900*, built in 1734 in the neoclassical style, was inspired by the famous church of the **Disabled in Paris**. Its dome is one of the largest in Mexico. It now houses an art school, the **Centro Cultural Ignacio Ramírez Nigromonte** (locally known as Escuela de Bellas Artes). Inside there are several large murals by the celebrated Mexican painter David Alfaro Siqueiros, a former teacher. The **Capilla de la Casa de Loreto** (Chapel of the Holy House of Loreto), was constructed in 1735 to resemble the pilgrimage shrine in Loreto, Italy.

William Stirling Dickinson

The story of the life of San Miguel de Allende's best-known expatriate resident, William Stirling Dickinson, is a fascinating one. He arrived in 1937 as a teacher and art director at the now-famous art school, the Centro Cultural (see page 363). Perhaps to partially atone for what would be many future cases of cultural misunderstandings between North Americans and *sanmigueleños*, five years after arriving in San Miguel de Allende, Dickinson was named a Hijo Adoptivo Predilecto (Favorite Adopted Son) in 1942, the only American ever honoured in this way by the mayor's office. Two years later, he was honoured by the governor of the state for his work in founding a baseball team for young Mexicans. Ironically, while Dickinson was responsible for the first influx of American visitors (mostly ex-soldiers who wanted to study at the school, which holds an international accreditation), he thought the town could hold at most perhaps 100 ex-GIs. More than 6000 applied, however, and Dickinson had his hands full for the rest of his days, most of which were spent establishing important cultural and social welfare causes. He died in San Miguel de Allende in 1998 after perhaps doing more to put it on the international map than anyone else, and is buried in a simple grave.

One of the many beautiful *casonas* (old mansions) in San Miguel de Allende for many years belonged to the descendants of Manuel Tomás de la Canal, one of the city's leading citizens (although never made a member of the Spanish nobility, contrary to the house's nickname). Often referred to as the **Casa del Mayorazgo de Canal** (the Count of Canal's house) ① *northwest corner of the Plaza Allende, Tue-Sun 1000-1600*, built in 1735 and now occupied by Banamex, some of the building is open to the public. The entryway displays magnificent Ionic columns and is a rare example of high-end colonial architecture that has survived almost completely intact.

Another first-rate mansion in the centre is the summer residence of the Condes de la Canal family, the **Instituto Allende** ① *Calzada Ancha de San Antonio*. This is the town's most famous art and language school, founded in 1949 by William Stirling Dickinson.

The **Casa del Inquisidor** (House of the Inquisitor) ① *Cuadrante y Hernández Macías*, with its former gaol just across the street, was the locale office of the Inquisition. Though the Mexican Inquisition, which was created in 1571, was generally less severe than the Spanish Inquisition, it nonetheless was a force to be reckoned with and was untouchable by civil authorities. Set into the front wall of the building is a green stone cross set on blue tiles, the symbol of the Inquisitor's office. On a wall of the gaol across the street is a mural by Siqueiros. Today it serves a less dire purpose as a centre for handicapped children.

The **Casa de los Perros** (House of the Dogs) ① *Umarán 4*, was the former residence of the Independence hero Juan de Mafuele, and is now the Galeria Mafuele. The building has interesting carvings of dogs on its balconies.

There are numerous other exemplary colonial residences in town, almost all of which are within walking distance of each other. Some of the best are **La Casa del Mariscal Francisco de Lanzagorta**, **La Casa del Conde de Jaral de Berio** and **La Casa del Conde de Casa Loja**.

Around San Miguel de Allende

A good all-day hike can be made to the **Palo Huérfano mountain** on the south side of town. Take the road to just before the radio pylon then take the trails to the summit, where there are oaks and pines. **El Charco del Ingenio** ① *T415-154 4715, daily dawn-dusk (conservatory 0900-1700), US$2.30, guided tours, 2½ hrs (US$6.10),* are botanical gardens that cover an area of 64 ha, with lovely views, a deep canyon, an artificial lake and cacti garden of many species. There are great views and hikes around the canyon and lakes, and it's a good spot for watching the sunset (but don't wander too far as the gardens close at dusk). The area was formally declared an Ecological Preservation Zone in 2005.

Run by the same organization, is the protected forestry reserve (one of very few in Mexico) of 90 ha in the highlands of **Los Picachos**, to the south of the city. In 2004, the **Charco del Ingenio** was sanctified as a Peace Zone – one of five in Mexico to be free of violence and arms, and dedicated to the conservation of nature and community development – by the Dalai Lama, during his visit to Mexico. To get there, take a bus to El Gigante shopping centre, turn left and continue for 15 minutes, or go up Homobono, a more interesting and attractive route.

Dolores Hidalgo 😊🕐⊗😊😊 ≫ pp366-373. Colour map 2, B3. Phone code: 415.

This attractive small town is a good, quiet base for visiting livelier Guanajuato and more expensive San Miguel de Allende. The **tourist office** ① *main square, T/F418-182 1164,* can direct you to places making traditional Talavera tiles (called *azulejos*) and ceramics, available at very good prices.

The town is most famous as the childhood home of Father Miguel Hidalgo y Costilla, the Mexican priest and revolutionary rebel leader, whose famous *Grito de Dolores* ('Cry of Independence') in 1810 sparked the movement. His statue stands in the lovely main square, known as the **Jardín**. On one side of the square is the church of **Nuestra Señora de los Dolores** (1712-1778). Each year the traditional Cry for Independence is given from the atrium of this church (every five years by the president of the republic).

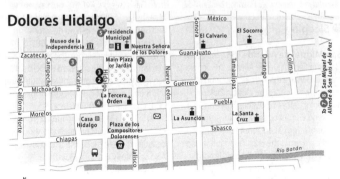

Dolores Hidalgo

100 metres
100 yards

Sleeping 😊
Casa Mia **5**
El Caudillo **1**
Hostal del Insurgente **7**
Posada Cocomacán **2**

Posada Dolores **3**
Posada Hidalgo **4**
Posada Las Campanas **6**
Relicario de la Patria **8**

Eating 😊
Fruti-Yoghurt **2**
Helado Torres **3**
Taco Pizza **1**

The **Iglesia de La Asunción** ① *Puebla y Sonora*, has a large tower at one end, a dome at the other, with extensive murals and a tiled floor inside. Two blocks away, at Puebla y Jalisco, is **Plaza de los Compositores Dolorenses**, with a bandstand. Visit Hidalgo's house, the **Casa de Diezma** (officially **Museo Casa Hidalgo**) ① *Morelos y Hidalgo, Tue-Sat 1000-1745, Sun 1000-1700, US$4*, a beautiful building with a courtyard and wells, memorabilia and one room almost a shrine. The **Museo de la Independencia** ① *Zacatecas 6, Fri-Wed 0900-1700, US$1.15*, was formerly a jail, but now has displays of striking paintings of the path to Independence.

The **Alfarería** is where Hidalgo established a school and the town's first pottery factory. What is remarkable, and very much more evident from the exhibits in this building than from the more glorified representations of Hidalgo in the museum, is just how seriously he took his commitment to the poor. He was a humanitarian to the indigenous people of his parish, teaching those with nothing how to earn a living making and selling pottery. It was, in fact, thanks to him that Dolores Hidalgo remains famous for its pottery to this day.

Hacienda de la Erre
① *5 km southeast of town on a dirt track, free entrance to the untended ruins and grounds. The walk to the ruins (1½-2 hrs) starts from the plaza. Follow Calle Guerrero to the east, then Tamaulipas to the main road. Turn left for 1 km to a gravel road on the left on a long curve. Follow this to the hacienda in a fertile area with plenty of trees.*

The history of Dolores Hidalgo is closely tied to the Hacienda de la Erre, which was founded in 1710 by Viceroy Marques de Montecarlos for cattle raising. These holdings went on to form the boundaries of the original city of Dolores Hidalgo. Padre Hidalgo's first stop on the Independence route after leaving Dolores Hidalgo proper was here. Outside is the huge mesquite tree under which Hidalgo is supposed to have said Mass for his insurgent troops.

◉ San Miguel de Allende and around listings

For Sleeping and Eating price codes and other relevant information, see Essentials pages 47-51.

● Sleeping

San Miguel de Allende *p361, map p362*
Hotels in San Miguel de Allende are generally more expensive than in neighbouring towns. If economizing, stay the night in Dolores Hidalgo or Celaya if possible. There are many weekend visitors, so book ahead. A good source of information about the few cheap rooms in town is the English-language paper published weekly by the Anglo-Mexican Library on Av Insurgentes.
LL Casa de Sierra Nevada, Hospicio 42, T01-800-701-1561, www.casadesierra nevada.com. The best hotel in town, combining colonial grace and top service.
LL Casa Misha, Chiquitos 15, T415-152 2021,

www.casamisha.com. Just down the street from Oasis (see below), the most expensive hotel by far. Still the better known of the two, and not without its die-hard devotees.
LL Oasis, Chiquitos 1A, T415-154 9850, www.oasissanmiguel.com. The finest hotel in town, and sets the standard in top-quality service. With just 4 rooms and sky-high prices, this is unquestionably the height of luxury.
LL-L Casa Luna B&B, Pila Seca 11, T/F415-152 1117, www.casaluna.com. American run, excellent breakfast included, beautiful themed rooms, no smoking inside. Also operates Casa Luna Quebrada.
LL-L Casa Schuck, Garita y Baranca esq Hospicio, T415-152 0657, www.casaschuck. com. This spacious, 18th-century colonial villa is a few blocks off of the plaza. 10 guest rooms, with every conceivable amenity. Restored in the late 1960s by American expats.

L Casa Quetzal, Hospicio 34, T415-152 0501, www.casaquetzalhotel.com. One of San Miguel's finest boutique hotels, and at an (occasionally) more affordable price than most. Centrally located but away from the din of the plaza. Highly recommended.

L-B La Mansión del Bosque, Aldama 65, T415-152 0277, www.infosma.com/mansion. Possibly the most relaxing and friendly guesthouse. Rooms are often fully booked so reserve ahead. Service is very welcoming.

A La Siesta, Salida a Celaya 82, near Jardín, T415-152 0207, www.hotellasiesta.com. Pool, fireplaces in rooms (US$35 with breakfast). Also with adjacent RV and trailer park (**C**).

A Posada de las Monjas, Canal 37, T415-152 0171, www.posadalasmonjas.com. A converted convent, clean and attractive. Rooms have shower, excellent set meals in restaurant, bar, very good value.

A Rancho El Atascadero, Prologación Santo Domingo s/n, T415-152 0206, www.hotel elatascadero.com. Hacienda-style property, located away form the centre in an oasis of peace and quiet. Pool, jacuzzi, tennis courts. Weekday discounts. Highly recommended.

A Villa Marisol, Pila Seca 35, T415-152 6685, www.villamirasolhotel.com. In the centre. A fine old house converted to a 3-storey hotel. Each room is different. Known for keeping prices reasonable. Highly recommended.

A-B Refugio de Molino, Salida Camino Real a Querétaro 1, T415-152 1818, www.hoteles refugio.com. On edge of town heading towards Querétaro. Nice pool, beautiful grounds, parking and very clean and safe.

B Mansión Villa Reyes, Canal 19, T415-152 3355, mansionvirreyes@prodigy.net.mx. Convenient location a few blocks from the Plaza de Allende and half a block from Bellas Artes. Nice courtyard and large roof terrace with view, breakfast included.

B Posada Carmina, Cuna de Allende 7, T415-152 8888, www.posadacarmina.com. 18th-century colonial building with mostly high-ceilinged rooms. Patio restaurant with orange trees. One of the first and most popular reasonably priced hotels in town.

B-C Arcada San Miguel, Calzada de la Estación 185, T415-152 8940, hotelarcada@ yahoo.com. Gym, spa, herbal steam room, room service and parking, plus continental breakfast all included in price. Excellent value.

B-C Rincón del Cielo, Hospicio 35, right next to Casa Quetzal, T415-152 1647. Rooms are large and have 2 storeys, the bedroom is upstairs with fireplace and huge bathroom with tub, living room has a bar, attractive and good value.

B-C Vista Hermosa Taboada, Cuna de Allende 11, T415-152 0078. Popular, pleasant old colonial building and centrally located.

C El Hotelito, Hidalgo 18, T415-152 7711. Newest hotel in the centre and one of the most reasonably priced. Everything is very efficient. 12 rooms, all good sizes.

C Parador San Sebastián, Mesones 7, near market, T415-152 7084. A long-time favourite. No advance reservations, so arrive early in the day in high season. With bath, charming, large rooms with fireplace, clean, car park, noisy at front, beautiful courtyard. Recommended.

C Posada El Mayorazgo, Hidalgo 8, T415-152 1309. If you stay 6 days, the 7th is free. Monthly rental available, also has 1-bed apartments.

C Posada San Miguelito, Canal 9, T415-154 8393, www.posadasanmiguelito.com. Unrivalled location (overlooks Plaza Allende) with rooftop terrace. Rooms on 3 levels open onto balconies overlooking central courtyard, a very atmospheric touch.

C Posada Santa Ana, Insurgentes 138, T415-152 0534. In centre, with typical double bed rooms and drab but functional appearance. Good price if not expecting much amenities.

C Quinta Loreto, Loreto 15 (behind Mercado de las Artesanías), T415-152 0042, hqloreto@ cybermatsa.com.mx. A perennial favourite, although can be very noisy. Motel-like rooms with 2 double beds. Small pool, restaurant, lovely gardens. Laundry service, accepts dogs.

D-E Casa de Huéspedes, Mesones 27, T415-152 1378. Looks grubby on the outside but it's clean and has hot water, popular, roof garden, nice location, good value.

E Hostal Alcatraz, Reloj 54, T415-152 8543, alcatrazhostel@yahoo.com. Clean and tidy dormitory accommodation, hot water and kitchen available. Very friendly and helpful. Recommended.

Camping
KAO campground, further out than La Siesta (see below) on the road to Guanajuato. Quiet, grassy site, all facilities, pleasant, Dutch owner.
La Siesta, Salida a Celaya 82 (on the road to Guanajuato), T418-152 0207. Trailer park with gardens. Hotel (**A**) of the same name adjacent.

Dolores Hidalgo *p365, map p365*
B Casa Mía, San Luis Potosí 9B esq Oaxaca, T418-182 2560, www.hotelcasamia.com.mx. New hotel fast gaining reputation as Dolores Hidalgo's best bet. Small, near the centre, very safe, quiet and friendly. Romantic setting is ideal for couples. Excellent value for the price.
B Posada Cocomacán, T418-182 6087, Plaza Principal 4. On the Jardín. Pleasant colonial house where Juárez once stayed, rooms are somewhat stark but very comfortable, good value, good food, parking. Recommended.
C El Caudillo, Querétaro 8, just off the plaza, opposite the church of Nuestra Señora de los Dolores, T418-182 0198. Clean, good value.
C Hostal del Insurgente, Av de los Héroes s/n (Colonia Ranchito de San Cristobal), T418-182 2407, www.dolores-hidalgo.com. mx/hoteles/ Insurgente.html. On the road to San Miguel de Allende. Drab and basic, but with nice gardens, parking, 24-hr room service. Best in its price range.
C-D El Relicario de la Patria, 12 Calzada de los Héroes, T418-120 0712. Good downtown location. Efficient and clean, with decent-sized rooms.
C-D Posada Hidalgo, Hidalgo 15, T418-182 0477. Pleasant, 20-room establishment that's close to everything. Has a gym and sauna. Friendly, safe and off-street parking available.
C-D Posada Las Campanas, Guerrero 15 y Guanajuato, T418-182 0427, www.hotel posadalascampanas.com. The largest hotel in town, minimal amenities, but in a good central location and safe. Café and internet in the lobby.

E-F Posada Dolores, Yucatán 8, T418-182 0642. With bath, clean, barely OK, small rooms, humid downstairs so ask for upper floor lodgings (which also have TV).

❼ Eating

San Miguel de Allende *p361, map p362*
As with its accommodation, the majority of San Miguel de Allende's restaurants are much more expensive than in nearby towns. Restaurants in the centre (or in hotels) are more expensive than those further out. Cheap eats can be had at several stands at the **Mercado Ignacio Ramírez** (see Shopping, page 371), and there are plenty of fast food joints in the Centro Histórico.
♈ Bella Italia, Canal 21 y Dr Hernández Macías, T415-152 4989. Daily 1300-2230. Good, perhaps even great Italian, but poor service. Chef's specials are always remarkable. Famous for its live music. Reservations essential.
♈ El Bistro Los Senderos, Los Senderos s/n, T415-155 9594. Tue, Thu, Sat-Sun 1100-sunset; Wed 1300-2100 (closed Mon and Fri). Extremely popular, in a beautiful country setting just out of town. Incredible food, live music evenings, and a *bocce* court to work off your meal.
♈-♈ Mesón de San José, Mesones 38, T415-152 3848. Open 0800-2200. Live music on Sun. Mexican and international cuisine including vegetarian dishes, excellent breakfast, in a pleasant patio.
♈ Café etc, Reloj 37, Mon-Sat 0800-2100, Sun 1000-1800. Great café atmosphere in a gallery, with internet and excellent music (some 2000 CDs).
♈ Casa Mexas, Canal 15. Good American food, clean, popular with gringos.
♈ El Buen Café, Jesús 23, T415-152 5807. Good quiche, pies, cakes and juices.
♈ El Infierno, Mesones, just below Plaza Allende. Excellent *sopa azteca*, good value.
♈ El Jardín, San Francisco, close to the plaza. Friendly service, good food including vegetarian options.

▼▼ El Tomate, Mesones. Vegetarian restaurant, attractive, spotless, excellent food, generous helpings but not cheap.

▼▼ La Fonda, Hidalgo 28, entre Insurgentes y Mesones. La Fonda is the name of the adjacent hotel and Aquí es México the restaurant, but this well-loved eatery is always known by the former. Excellent Mexican food, family run and very friendly. Impromptu music and readings. Recommended.

▼▼ Mama Mía, Umarán, west of the main square. Good meals but not cheap, free live folk music or films in the afternoon, excellent cheap breakfasts.

▼▼ Rincón Español, Correo 27 (opposite post office), T415-152 2984. Good *comida corrida* and a few authentic Spanish dishes, authentic flamenco at weekends. Recommended.

▼▼ Tío Lucas, Mesones 103, T415-152 4996, opposite Teatro Angela Peralta. Very good. Recommended.

▼▼-▼ Bugambilia, entre Insurgentes y Calzada de la Luz, T415-152 0127. Daily 1200-2300. Food is consistently average (or a little below), but a superb atmosphere and great traditional music make this a perennial favourite.

▼▼-▼ Chamonix, Díez de Sollano 12-A, T415-154 8363. Daily 1330-2200. Eclectic menu. Rustic little patio holds just a dozen tables. Usually there are a few dishes from Europe and 1 or 2 from Asia; occasionally with a Mexican twist. Slow service but still a very popular choice.

▼▼-▼ El Correo, Correo 23, across from the post office, T415-152 4951. Wed-Mon 0800-2300. Mexican standards not usually found in San Miguel de Allende: *sopes* (fried *masa* cakes topped with savoury meats and vegetables), *caldo tlalpeño* (chicken, rice, and vegetable soup), and *enchiladas del portal* (enchiladas with chile sauce).

▼▼-▼ El Pegaso, Corregidora 6 y Correo, 1 block east of the Jardín. T415-152 1351. Mon-Sat 0830-2200. Very popular with popular with expats and visitors. Good for quick eats and light meals. Crowded weekends.

▼▼-▼ Romanos, Dr Hernández Macias 93, T415-152 7454. Tue-Sat 1700-2300. Dinner-only Italian in beautiful location with indoor/outdoor dining. Great food in generous portions. Popular and recommended.

▼▼-▼ San Agustín Chocolates & Churros, San Francisco 21, T415-154 9102. Good food with fajitas, excellent *churros* and Mexican hot chocolate, lively music and quirky decor.

▼ Cha-Cha-Cha, 28 de Abril Norte 37, T415-152 6586. Tue-Sun 1300-1900. Hugely popular with travellers. *Albóndigas* (meat balls flavoured with *chipotle*), chicken in a *huazontle* sauce (similar to broccoli, but milder), and *quesadillas* with a variety of fillings, including beef in a chile *pasilla* sauce.

▼ La Piñata, Jésus 1 y Umarán, T415-152 2060. One of the few cheap, family-run Mexican restaurants left in town. No airs and graces, but great food.

▼ Olé Olé, Loreto 66 entre Insurgentes y Calzada de la Luz, T415-152 0896. Daily 1300-2100. Beef and chicken fajitas, shrimp brochettes, and lots of steaks. Some higher-end Mexican dishes, too, like *champiñones al ajillo* (mushrooms in garlic and *guajillo chile*) and *chistorra* (a Spanish-style sausage).

Dolores Hidalgo *p365, map p365*
Nearly all restaurants in Dolores Hidalgo are on or very near the Plaza. Most of the *posadas* also have small restaurants; Posada Cocomacan is easily the best.

▼ Taco Pizza, Guerrero esq Jalisco. Besides pizzas and taco (not taco pizza, however), serves hamburgers, tacos, *arrachera* (strips of marinated flank steak) and *tortas* (sandwiches). Great food, great prices.

Cafés and ice cream parlours

The legends regarding the varied flavours of home-made ice cream sold on the Jardín are largely true. If your tastes run to the exotic (or even repulsive), then this is for you. The vendors take nearly any food imaginable and turn it into ice cream. There are the typical tropical fruit flavours such as pineapple, mango, lemon, papaya and guava, as well as some occasionally encountered alcoholic drink flavours (eg piña colada, strawberry daiquiri, whiskey, tequila, rum, even *pulque* and beer).

And there are the local favourites, like mint chocolate, strawberries and cream, rice pudding, *cajeta* (caramel with goat's milk) and cheesecake. But it doesn't stop there. If you fancy fried pork rinds, corn, *mole* (a spicy-sweet chocolate sauce usually reserved for pouring over chicken or pork), avocado, shrimp or even octopus, they're all available.

Fruti-Yoghurt, Hidalgo y Guerrero (just off Jardín). Delicious yoghurt, wholefood cakes and biscuits.

Helado Torres, Hidalgo y Michoacán (south-west corner of Jardín). Excellent ice cream.

🎬 Entertainment

San Miguel de Allende *p361, map p362*
Cinema
Villa Jacaranda, hotel video bar. English-language films, US$5 including alcoholic drink and popcorn.

Theatre
Teatro Angela Peralta, Mesones 82. Theatre, musical events and dance. There's a coffee house in the front entrance hall.

🎉 Festivals and events

San Miguel de Allende *p361, map p362*
Feb Pre-Lenten carnival.
Jun Corpus Christi.
End-Jul to mid-Aug Classical Chamber Music Festival; information from Bellas Artes.
15-16 Sep Independence Day.
28 Sep-1 Oct Fiesta de San Miguel, with *conchero* dancers from many places.
2 Nov Day of the Dead.
16-24 Dec Christmas Posadas, celebrated in the traditional colonial manner. There is a Christmas season musical celebration, which attracts musicians of an international level.

Dolores Hidalgo *p365, map p365*
Mar/Apr, **Jul**, **Sep** and **Dec** (4 times a year) Handicraft Expo, highlights the vast number

of handicrafts that are available in this city, especially ceramics, *talavera* style pottery and carved wooden furniture.

Fri before Good Fri As the **Virgen de los Dolores** (Our Lady of Sorrows) is the patron saint of Dolores Hidalgo, the locals display their devotion by erecting elaborate altars in her name through the streets of the city.

Mar/Apr Semana Santa (Holy Week) This week-long celebration begins with the dedication of altars to Our Lady of Sorrows and concludes with a silent procession through the streets of the city.

15-16 Sep Independence celebrations. These traditional Mexican patriotic celebrations last the entire month of Sep and include a variety of cultural, artistic and sporting events. The most important event stakes place on the evening of 15 Sep when the 'Cry for Independence' is given from the atrium of the Parish Church. This is done by the president of Mexico every 5 years, otherwise by other dignitaries.

28 Nov-Dec 8 Immaculate Conception festival, when religious processions are held along with fireworks displays.

🛍 Shopping

San Miguel de Allende *p361, map p362*
San Miguel de Allende has a disproportionately large number of *artesanías, casas de cultura* and cultural outlets. The trick is to choose those that reflect the local and regional traditions and avoid the myriad faux Mexican establishments that generally stock low-end, mass produced merchandise. Some boutiques and shops (owned by both Mexicans and foreigners) do a remarkable job of ensuring that their employees are treated fairly, but many do not. If looking for genuine period pieces and higher-end works of art, in most cases there are better alternatives in Metepec, Mexico City, Oaxaca, Ocotlán, Puebla, Querétaro, Taxco and Zacatecas. While San Miguel de Allende contains many fine pieces of all stripes, prices here are significantly higher

and the merchandise is as often from one of these other cities as it is from in or around San Miguel itself.

Art and handicrafts

Pottery, cotton cloth and brasswork are the main local crafts. **Mercado de Artesanías** (see Markets, below), tends to sell tacky souvenirs rather than real handicrafts; prices are high and the selection poor. In spite of this, San Miguel also has an inordinate number of high-end galleries and crafts shops – more than 40 at last count. Note that almost all of these galleries and shops are in or very near the centre.

Caracol Collection, Cuadrante 30, T415-152 1617. Mon-Sat 1030-1400, 1600-1900. A rather unusual assortment of contemporary arts and crafts items from all over Mexico, specializing in *talavera* pottery, textiles from Michoacán and Oaxaca, copper and silver, and hard-to-find feather art and ebony-inlaid furniture pieces. Nice … but expensive.

Casa Vieja, Mesones 83, T415-152 1284. Mon-Fri 1000-1400, 1600-2000, Sat 1100-1500 (closed Thu). Apart from being a gallery, it also has wonderful folk art and contemporary utilitarian art housed in old *casona*. Recommended.

El Nuevo Mundo, San Francisco 17 esq Corregidora, T415-152 6180, Mon-Sat 0900-2000. Wide selection of popular and traditional art, crafts, fabrics and decorations. Good prices, very popular with tourists. Recommended.

Galería Atenea, Jesús 2, T415-152 0785, Mon-Sat 1000-1400, 1600-2000, Thu and Sun 1000-1400. Very interesting gallery that also sells jewellery, sculpture and original prints by up-and-coming Mexican artists.

Galería Azul y Plata, Cuna de Allende 15, T415-154 8192, www.azulyplata.com. Stunning contemporary design silverwork with lapis, turquoise and other hued stones.

Galería Carlos Muro, Zacateros 81 A, T415-154 8531. Tue-Sat 1000-1400, 1600-1900, Sun 1000-1400. Handcrafted copper pieces from the Bricio Pureco family of Santa Clara del Cobre, who have been making high-grade copper objects since the 18th century.

Galería Frank L. Gardner, Zacateros 75, T415-152 2926, www.unisono.net.mx/gardner. Mon-Sat 1000-1400, 1600- 1830. One of the most established and trusted galleries and good source for information on regional art. Recommended.

Galería Índigo, Mesones 76, T415-152 2749. Tue-Sat 1100-1430, 1700-2030, Sun 1100-1600. Showcases the latest Mexican artists. Highly recommended for its diverse selection.

La Casa del Vidrio, Correo 11. An excellent selection of brown-glass items at fair prices (sale prices in the summer, 40% off).

Bookshops

Libros El Colibrí, Sollano 30, T415-152 0751. Mon-Sat 1000-1400, 1600-1900. Culturally oriented books (some in English but mostly Spanish).

Libros El Tecolote, Jesús 11, T415-152 7395. Good selection of French and English books, also works on Mexican art and culture, and bilingual children's books.

Markets

Mercado Ignacio Ramírez, off Colegio, 1 block north of Mesones. Daily 0800-1900. This is a large, traditional covered emporium that supplies the town with its daily supplies (eg, fruits, vegetables, meats, flowers, clothes, toiletries and toys). In recent years, some local merchants have taken to settling up small stands here that supposedly sell colonial art and other rare finds. None of these are what they claim to be, and should be avoided. In fact, there's no reason at all to visit this market under you're looking for everyday necessities.

Mercado de Artesanías (or Artists' Market), in the *callejón* (alleyway) at Colegio y Loreto and behind the Mercado Ignacio Ramírez. Daily 0800-1900. This is where you can shop for and purchase fine works of art (although not likely at the same level of quality that a reputable gallery would offer). Artists specialize in glass, tin, metal and ceramics. It's a good place to shop for deals.

Dolores Hidalgo *p365, map p365*
Crafts
Artesanías Castillo, Ribera del Río entre Av Hidalgo y Jalisco. Beautiful ceramics at low prices. Visits to the factory can be arranged.

Markets
Tabasco, south side, between Jalisco and Av Hidalgo. There's another market, near Posada Dolores, on Yucatán.

▲ Activities and tours

San Miguel de Allende *p361, map p362*
Language and cookery schools
Many of the schools demand payment in US dollars (technically illegal) and you may prefer to arrange private tuition for US$3-5 per hr.
Academia Hispanoamericana, Mesones 4, T415-152 0349, www.ahaspeakspanish.com. Recommended for language lessons and sessions on Mexican history, folklore, literature, singing and dancing. Very helpful. Accommodation with families.
Habla Hispana Spanish School, Calzada de la Luz 25, T415-152 1535, www.mexico spanish.com. Has received good reports.
Mexican Cooking Classes, ask at El Buen Café, Jesús 23. Different menu every week.
Warren Hardy Spanish, San Rafael 6, T415-152 4728, www.warrenhardy.com. Intensive courses for beginners or intermediate level, run by Warren Hardy, the inventor of the Card Game method.

Walking tours
Walking tours are a popular way to see the town and there are several on offer, like one taking in historic houses and gardens, from Jardín Insurgentes 25, between Reloj and Hidalgo, T415-152 0293, Sun 1200, 4 hrs, US$10.

Another starts at the same time but in front of the Biblioteca Pública. Also 2 hrs, it grants access to the private residences of local millionaires, arranged through the non-profit organization Casas y Jardines, T415-152 4987, www.bibliotecasma.com.

(For those interested in rare flowers, there are some especially beautiful specimens in the garden of Los Pocitos, at Santo Domingo 38; the exquisite orchids were once tended by writer and botanist Sterling Dickinson.)

Tour operators
PMC, Hidalgo 18, T415-152 0121, www.pme xc.com. A wide range of tours and trips from walking tours of the town, workshops and language classes, through to adventure and nature tours and visits to archaeological sites.
Turísticos Rodríguez, Umarán 24B, T415-154 6168, www.sanmigueltransfers.com, excellent and knowledgeable with all local tours and trips to Dolores Hidalgo, Guanajuato, Pozos, Querétaro and more.
Viajes Vertiz, Hidalgo 1A, T415-152 1856, vvertiz@unisono.net.mx. Good travel agent, American Express agent.

☉ Transport

San Miguel de Allende *p361, map p362*
Bus
The bus station is on the outskirts, regular bus to the centre US$0.20, returns from the market or outside Posada San Francisco on the Jardín. A taxi costs about US$1.75 to the centre. Buses to the centre leave from in front of the terminal.

To **Aguascalientes**, 1235 and 1435, 2 hrs, US$11. To **Celaya**, every 15 mins, 1 hr, US$2.80. If there are no buses leaving for Guadalajara from San Miguel at the time you want to go, it's best to go to Celaya and catch a bus from there. To **Guadalajara**, 0730, 0930 and 1730, 5 hrs, US$28. To **Guanajuato**, 0745, 0945, 1245 and 1700, US$8. To **León**, 0730, 0930 and 1730, US$10. To **Mexico City** (northern terminal), 0940 and 1600, US$16.50, cheaper services every 40 mins 0520-2000, US$15. To **Querétaro**, every 40 mins 0520-2000, US$6.10. To **San Luis Potosí**, 7 a day, US$10.

International Daily buses to **Laredo**, Texas, US$42, **San Antonio** and on to **Dallas**,

US$80, at 1800. Also daily buses to **Houston** at 1800. And every Wed at 1800 to **Chicago**, US$131. All buses headed to the USA require a mandatory 2-hr wait for processing (sometimes longer) at border crossings.

Dolores Hidalgo *p365, map p365*
Bus The bus station is at Hidalgo y Chiapas, 5 mins from the main square; with restaurant, toilets, left-luggage and telephones. Frequent buses to **Guanajuato**, US$31; **Querétaro**, US$4; **León**, US$4; **Mexico City**, US$13; **San Luis Potosí**, US$5.50; **San Luis de la Paz**, US$2.20; and **San Miguel de Allende**, US$3.85. To **Aguascalientes**, US$7.25, 2nd class, via **San Felipe**.

Directory

San Miguel de Allende *p361, map p362*
Banks Casa de Cambio Deal, on Correo, opposite post office, and on Juárez.
Embassies and consulates US Consular Agent, Plaza Golondrinas arcade, Hernández

Macías, interior 111, T415-152 2357, Mon-Fri 0900-1300. **Immigration** 2nd floor Plaza Real del Conde, T415-152 2542, daily 0900-1300. For tourist card extensions, etc, take 2 copies of passport, tourist card and credit card or TCs. **Internet** Border Crossings, Correo 19, phone, fax, and email service. Café etc, Reloj 37, Mon-Sat 0800-2100, Sun 1000-1800. Good machines and so much more than an internet café with excellent music and coffee. Estación Internet, Recreo 11. La Conexión, Aldama 1, T/F415-152 1599. **Laundry** On Pasaje de Allende, same-day service; unnamed laundry at Correo 42, good. **Libraries** English-language library Biblioteca Pública on Insurgentes has an excellent selection on Mexico; very extensive bilingual library, with computer centre and English-speaking staff. Distributes the weekly Atención San Miguel, which has listings of Spanish classes, tutors and local events. **Telephone** There is a long-distance phone service at Diez de Sollano 4, just off the plaza.

Guanajuato and around

→ *Colour map 2, B3. Phone code: 461.*
The beautiful university city in the central state of Guanajuato, declared a UNESCO World Heritage Site, has been important for its silver since 1548. Its name derives from the Tarascan 'Quanax-Huato' (meaning 'place of frogs'). It stands in a narrow gorge amid wild and striking scenery. The Guanajuato River, which cuts through the city, has been covered over and several underground streets wind their way underneath the city like a human rabbit warren – an unusual and confusing system, especially if you're driving. ▸▸ *For listings, see pages 385-395.*

Ins and outs
Getting there The international **Aeropuerto del Bajío** (BJX), 40 km west of Guanajuato near the town of Silao, receives internal flights and flights from the USA. The long-distance bus terminal is on the outskirts, southwest of town. Buses leave for the centre from right outside the front of the terminal; look for 'Centro' on the front window of the bus, or the sign above the front window (20 minutes, US$0.25). A taxi to the centre costs US$2. ▸▸ *See Transport, page 393.*

Getting around Many of the interesting places are along and around Juárez and can be visited on foot in a day or two. Some streets, such as Hidalgo, are entirely enclosed so fill with traffic fumes. The Túnel Los Angeles leads from the old subterranean streets to the modern roadway that connects with the Carretera Panorámica and the monument to Pípila (see page 377). Taking traffic underground has not relieved the congestion of the surface streets, which are steep, twisted and narrow. Parking for hotels is often a fair distance away. There is a set fare of US$0.25 for city buses.

Tourist information The **tourist office** ⓘ *Plaza de la Paz 14, beside the basílica, T01-800-714-1086, www.guanajuato.gob.mx*, sells maps and has information about the area. The **Festival Cervantino** (see Festivals and events, page 392), said to be Latin America's biggest arts festival (but this is debatable), takes place in October each year.

Sights

The **cathedral**, formally known as the Basílica de Nuestra Señora de Guanajuato (1693), on Plaza de la Paz, has a beautiful yellow interior and an ornately painted vaulted ceiling. In the 18th century, the local grandee, Marquis of San Clemente, built an annex to house the niche of the Virgin of Guanajuato, which was later made into the baptistery and features a beautiful font and several paintings by Miguel Cabrera. The image itself of the Virgin was a supposedly a gift from the Spanish Emperor Charles I or Phillip II (accounts differ).

The best of the many other colonial churches include: the **Jesuit La Compañía** (1765), by the university, note the brick ceiling; the **Parroquia del Inmaculado Corazón de**

Guanajuato

200 metres
200 yards

To La Valenciana & Dolores Hidalgo
To Calle Insurgencia
To Bus Station, Museo de las Momias, Celaya & León

Museo Alfredo Dugues
University
Museo Diego Rivera
Museo del Pueblo
Pedro Lascuraín
Plaza de la Paz
Juárez
Pocitos
Juan Valle
Galarza
Alhóndiga
28 de Septiembre
Alhóndiga de Granaditas
San Roque
Mendizabal
Jardín Reforma
Plazuela San Fernando
Plazuela de los Angeles
Parroquia del Inmaculado Corazón de María
Juárez
Callejón del Beso
Juárez
Mercado Hidalgo
To Túnel Los Angeles
To Bus Station, Celaya & León

Sleeping 🛌
Casa de las Manrique **3**
Casa Kloster **1**

Central **8**
Dos Ríos **9**
El Insurgente Allende **4**
Mesón de las Poetas **2**

Mineral de Rayas **10**
Posada San Francisco **5**
Posada Santa Fe **6**
San Diego **7**

Eating 🍴
Bagel Cafetín **10**
Café Atrio **6**
Café Conquistador **3**

María, on Juárez, opposite Mercado Hidalgo, which has interesting statues on the altar; **San Cayentano on San José** with its churrigueresque adornments and three rare wooden altars covered with gold leaf; and the **Templo de San Francisco** (1671), on Sopeña, also worth visiting.

The small church of **San Roque**, (1726), on Plazuela de San Roque, a small park between Juárez and Pocitos, has a baroque facade and an attractive vaulted ceiling. The square the church sits upon has been the stage for the short comic plays known as *entremeses Cervantinos* (one-act plays by Cervantes) since 1953. These plays eventually engendered the city's famous **International Cervantino Festival** in 1972 (see Festivals and events, page 392).

Perhaps a more poignant visit is to the famous **Santuario de Cata**, outside of the centre. Built by miners between 1709-1789, construction delays were many, due to fluctuations in the production of the nearby mine at Cata. In proportion to mine production, the church was slowly erected, modified, and occasionally even abandoned when mining operations turned unprofitable and local residents, the construction workers, moved elsewhere. Nowadays the shrine is a religious centre of national importance, as worshippers from all corners of the country come to venerate the miraculous image of the Christ of Villaseca which is kept there.

The church of **San Diego** (1663), on the Jardín de la Unión, has its own fascinating story. Of the original building, nothing remains above ground, but underground it's a very different story: the many floods that have swept through Guanajuato buried the church bit by bit and led to it being rebuilt in 1694 and again 1780-1784. This last version is the one that one sees today. The work raised the floor, walls, facades and altarpieces six to eight 'rods' – a staggering 40 m above the original level.

Probably the most famous of Guanajuato's alleys and lanes is the **Callejón del Beso** ('Alley of the Kiss'), which is so narrow (69 cm) that, according to legend, two lovers kept apart by their families were able to exchange kisses from opposite balconies. And while the ritual can reach rather maudlin levels, it is said that couples who kiss while standing on the third stair are guaranteed seven years of happiness.

The **Teatro Juárez** ① *Jardín de la Unión, T473-732 0183, minimal admission fee and to take photos*, considered one of the most beautiful theatres in all of Mexico, it was inaugurated in 1903 by Porfirio Diaz, after more than three decades in the making. Its portico is in the Roman Doric style, which leads in to an astonishing art nouveau foyer.

To Presa de la Olla

Casa Valadez **7**	El Midi **2**
Chao Bella **4**	La Terraza **8**
Crepería-Café Bossanova **1**	Truco **5**
El Gallo Pitagorico **9**	

The iron legacy of Porfirio Díaz

Students of Mexican history know the name José de la Cruz Porfirio Díaz Mori (1830-1915) well. The former president of Mexico (1876-1911) ruled with an iron fist but also brought about enormous strides in the modernization of the country. In fact, probably no other figure apart from Benito Juárez or Miguel Hidalgo has left such a tangible mark upon Mexico. While historians continue to debate the long-term effects of his rule (known as the Porfiriato), its architectural legacy is beyond question. There is not a single city in Mexico that does not bear silent witness to his incessant public works campaigns, generally in the form of fin-de-siècle wrought iron work.

While it may seem odd to think of a ruthless dictator as having an obsession with metalwork, Díaz was insistent that every town of significant size have its public plaza, bandstand, fountain, and gardens. Each also had to have the usual accoutrements that adorn these spaces: fences, streetlights, lampposts, railings, hitching posts, and grille work, to name just a few. And these had to be made of iron. Not just any iron, however. They had to be wrought iron, ornately carved, usually black, and always in the height of style, which in those days meant French. Anything less was simply unacceptable, and the few functionaries who dared to skip the details or tried to save a few pesos found themselves out of a job.

Eventually Díaz was overthrown, his fall precipitating the Mexican Revolution. He escaped to exile in Europe and died in humble circumstances in Paris in 1915. However, his legacy lives on in the form of innumerable wrought iron works all over Mexico, and especially in the heartland cities of Aguascalientes, Saltillo, San Luis Potosí and Zacatecas.

Guanajuato has a series of fine museums, too. One of the most interesting is the massive **Museo Regional de Guanajuato** ① *Alhóndiga de Granaditas, Mendizábal 6, T473-732 1112, Tue-Sat 1000-1800, Sun 1000-1500, US$3.35 (extra US$3 to take photos)*. It was originally a granary, turned into a fortress and is now a museum with artefacts from the pre-Columbian and colonial periods. The collections are divided into four major areas: ethnographic, historic, archaeological and art. When Father Hidalgo took the city in 1810, the *alhóndiga* was the last place to surrender, and there was a wanton slaughter of Spanish soldiers and royalist prisoners. Later when Hidalgo was himself caught and executed, along with three other leaders, in Chihuahua, their severed heads were fixed, in revenge, at the four corners of the *alhóndiga*.

An unusual sight are the mummified bodies in the small **Museo de las Momias** ① *Panteón Municipal (above the city, off Tepetapa), daily 0900-1800, US$3.10, long queues on Sun; buses marked 'Momias' run there, and it's signposted Panteón Municipal, 10 mins, along Av Juárez, but you can walk*. The pantheon overlooks the city of Guanajuato and has wonderful panoramic views. In it, bodies of the dead were placed inside crypts above ground. Heat dried the bodies creating mummies of exceptional quality. The first mummy, a French physician, was discovered only after its removal for his family's failure to pay a burial tax in 1865. The pantheon contains the largest collection of mummies in the western hemisphere.

The **Museo Iconográfico del Quijote** ① *Manuel Doblado 1, T473-732 6721, http://museo iconografico.guanajuato.gob.mx, Tue-Sat 1000-1830, Sun 1000-1430, US$2, free Sun*, is highly recommended for its paintings, drawings and sculptures of Quijote. It houses a collection of prints, tapestries, coins and porcelain artwork dedicated to the great Spanish writer. Some of its works of art include pieces by José Luis Cuevas and Salvador Dali.

The painter Diego Rivera was born at Pocitos 47 (although he left Guanajuato at the age of six and never returned). This house is now the **Museo Casa Diego Rivera** ① *T473-732 1197, Tue-Sat 1000-1900, Sun 1000-1500, US$2, www.guanajuatocapital.com/ingles/musdiego.htm*, with a permanent collection of his work on various floors; on the ground floor are his bed and other household objects. This building is a large, staid 18th-century house, which seemingly contradicts Rivera's very bohemian lifestyle.

Also on Pocitos, just across from the university, is the **Museo del Pueblo** ① *Pocitos 47, T473-732 2990, Tue-Sat 1000-1900, Sun 1000-1500, US$2.25, www.guanajuatocapital.com/ingles/muspuebl.htm*, in a beautiful 17th-century mansion. It has one room of work by the muralist José Chávez Morado, another by the painter Olga Costa and a room of selected items of all Mexican art forms and temporary exhibitions.

The **San Gabriel de Barrera** ① *Ctra Guanajuato-Marfil, Km 2.5, T473-732 0619*, is a former hacienda dating from the 18th century, with a large colonial house where paintings, furniture and tapestries from this period are on display. Its 17 different gardens, each landscaped in a different style, are also worthy of admiration. In particular, the Queen's Garden owes its name to a visit made there by Queen Elizabeth II in 1976, while the English Garden is characterized by its 'properness' and its tall, austere trees. There is also a restoration workshop.

The **Universidad de Guanajuato** ① *Lascurain de Retana 5, T473-732 0006, www.ugto.mx*, was carefully constructed to blend in with the city's colonial architecture. The front entrance is quite remarkable and is easily the most photographed building in town. An enormous set of finely chiselled stone steps leads to an imposing *rectoría* carved of the same stone. You'd never believe this building was built (although 'carved' seems a better word) in 1945. While no tours are available, you can walk about the complex and marvel at the rooms, some of which saw earlier usage as a royal mint, a Jesuit church and a hospice. The building to the right of the entrance was constructed in 1759.

Around Guanajuato

Crowning the high hill of Hormiguera, 1 km west of the Carretera Panorámica on the southern outskirts of the city, is the **Monumento a Pípila**, the man who fired the door of the Alhóndiga so that the patriots could take it. Look for the 'Al Pípila' sign. A number of cobbled stairways through picturesque terraces go up to the monument. It's a steep but short climb (about 15 minutes) rewarded with fine panoramic views of the city. Otherwise take a local bus from **Hotel Central**, on Juárez. At its eastern end the Carretera Panorámica goes by the **Presa de la Olla**, a favourite picnic spot with good cheap food available from roadside stalls. From the dam, Paseo de la Olla runs to the city centre, passing mansions of the wealthy silver barons and the **Palacio de Gobierno** (note the use of local stone).

Over the city looms the shoulder of **La Bufa** mountain. You can hike to the summit up a trail, which takes one hour: from the Pípila monument, follow the main road for about 1 km to the hospital. Walk past the hospital to a power station where the main trail starts; if you pass the quarry, note the quality of the stone masonry on the mason's shelter.

The splendid church of **La Valenciana**, one of the most impressive in Mexico, is 5 km out of town on the Dolores Hidalgo road; it was built for the workers of the Valenciana silver mine, once the richest in the world. Built by the Conde de Valenciana, Antonio Obregón y Alcocer, owner of the famous mine, the church, built in pink cantera stone and consecrated in 1788, represents the final period of the Mexican 'ultra-baroque' (a style by then long extinct elsewhere). Particularly attractive is the side doorway into the church from the garden, with an elaborately stuccoed and decorated scallop-shell and a statue of St Joseph. The church contains three splendid churrigueresque *retablos*, partly gilded and partly polychrome. There is also very fine wood inlay with ivory and precious woods on the pulpit. Another striking feature is the doorway into the sacristy, with a carved stone lambrequin above the Mudéjar arch. The arches themselves are particularly elegant, with their bands of intricate ornamentation in local tezontle stone.

The **Valenciana mine** ① *10-min walk from the church, daily 0900-1700, US$1*, which has functioned since 1548, is surrounded by a wall with triangular projections on top, said to symbolize the crown of the King of Spain. The huge stone walls on the hillside, supported by enormous buttresses, created an artificial level surface from earth excavated higher up the slope. The mine is still working with both gold and silver being extracted. With care you can walk freely in the whole area. Guides are available to take you round on an interesting 30-minute tour.

A few kilometres east of the city (take a local bus from near the market) at the old site of **La Cata silver mine** is a church with a magnificent baroque facade and the shrine of El Señor de Villa Seca (the patron saint of adulterers) with retablos and crude drawings of miraculous escapes from harm, mostly due to poor shooting by husbands.

León ☺❼❶❻☺▲☺☻ ➤ *pp385-395. Colour map 2, B2. Phone code: 477.*

In the fertile plain of the Río Gómez, León now vies with Ciudad Juárez for the title of Mexico's fifth-largest city. Nuño de Guzmán reached the area on 2 December 1530 and subsequently local farms and estates were granted to the Spaniards. Eventually Don Martín Enríquez de Almanza decreed on 12 December 1575 that a city, called León, would be founded if 100 volunteers could be persuaded to live there for 10 years, or a town if only 50 could be found. On 20 January 1576 a town was founded by Dr Juan Bautista de Orozco, but it wasn't until 1830 that León became a city. The business centre is the delightful **Plaza de la Constitución**. León is the main shoe centre of the country and is noted for its leather work, fine silver-trimmed saddles and *rebozos* (shawls).

León is not typically regarded as a city of much interest to the tourist, and is in many ways more akin to the industrial city of Monterrey far to the north than it is to other cities of the colonial heartland. For most, it is a stop between Aguascalientes or Guadalajara on the one side, or Guanajuato or Querétaro on the other. Those passing through may want to take in a football match, as León is considered a sports-mad city. Otherwise, apart from the few shopping opportunities note above, there is little for the traveller here

Ins and outs

Getting there The international airport, **Del Bajío** (BJX) ① *18 km from León, 6 km from Silao,* has good domestic connections, as well as international flights from the USA, Guatemala and South America. Taxis are expensive from the airport to León; take one to Silao, US$13.50, and then take a bus to León or Guanajuato, or walk 1½ km to the main road and take a bus from there. The bus terminal is ideally located in the centre, at the corner of Bulevar Hilario Medina and Bulevar La Luz. ➤ *See Transport, page 394.*

Tourist information The **tourist office** ① *Edificio Cielo 501, López Mateos Poniente y Miguel Alemán, www.leon-mexico.com,* is helpful but limited. Free city maps from the Palacio Municipal.

Sights

There are many shaded plazas and gardens in León, and almost all of the sights worth seeing are in its pleasant centre. The **Palacio Municipal** ① *by the Plaza de la Constitución*, is said to have been built as a result of a winning lottery ticket bought by a local doctor. The small **cathedral** ① *Alvaro Obregón esq Av Hidalgo*, was started by Jesuits in 1744, but they were expelled from Mexico in 1767 by Carlos III and it was eventually finished in 1837 and consecrated in 1866. Adjacent to it is the **Galería de Arte Sacro** (Gallery of Sacred Art) ① *T477-717 2739, Mon-Sat 1000-1400, 1630-1830, US$0.75*. The catacombs are well worth seeing at the **Templo Expiatorio** ① *Thu-Sun 1000-1200*, which has been under construction for most of the last century and all of the current one. The exquisite **Teatro Doblado** ① *Av Hermanos Aldama esq Pedro Moreno 202, T477-716 4301*, stages events. There is also a **Casa de Cultura** ① *Plaza Fundadores, www.leonguanajuato.com/casadela cultura*, which houses exhibitions and is buzzing at night. Also worth seeing is the **Casa de Las Monas** ① *5 de Mayo 127-29*, where Pancho Villa issued the Agrarian Reform Law on 24 May 1915, and the beautiful Santuario de Guadalupe. The **Museo de León** ① *Hermanos Aldama, Tue-Sat 1000-1400 and 1630-1930, Sun 1000-1400*, has art exhibitions. On Justo Sierra, the **Museum of Anthropology and History** is housed in a beautiful building.

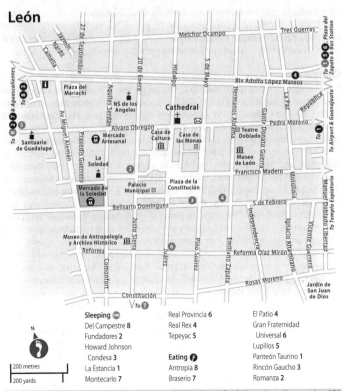

León

Sleeping	Eating
Del Campestre 8	Antropia 8
Fundadores 2	Braserio 7
Howard Johnson Condesa 3	El Patio 4
La Estancia 1	Gran Fraternidad Universal 6
Montecarlo 7	Lupillos 5
Real Provincia 6	Panteón Taurino 1
Real Rex 4	Rincón Gaucho 3
Tepeyac 5	Romanza 2

200 metres
200 yards

Founded in 1575, capital of its state, the name (hot waters) comes from its hot mineral springs. An oddity is that the city is built over a network of tunnels dug out by a forgotten local people. It has pretty parks, a pleasant climate and delicious fruits. Local specialities include drawn-linen thread work, pottery and leather goods.

Its outskirts and neighbourhoods outside of the centre may not be much to look at, but Aguascalientes' Centro Histórico does not disappoint. As with most cities in the region, its colonial foundation is where most of the activity and sights are, and in Aguascalientes' case, it's well preserved and well worth exploring. The city – now one of the fastest-growing in the country – was founded in 1575, and while little evidence remains of its earliest years, there is an abundance of art and architecture from the 17th century onwards at its epicentre.

Ins and outs

Getting there The airport (AGU) is 21 km south of town centre. The bus station about 1 km south of the centre on Avenida Circunvalación Sur, near the post office and pharmacy. ▸▸ *See Transport, page 394.*

Tourist information The **Federal Tourist Office** ① *Juan de Montoro 219, oficina 101, T449-916 7575, Mon-Fri 0800-2000, www.aguascalientes.gob.mx*, is in the Palacio de Gobierno on Plaza Patria (to the southeast of the cathedral), and a good town plan is available from the entrance booth of the Palacio Municipal on the north side of the plaza.

Sights

Aguascalientes' double-spired cathedral, technically also a basilica, **Our Lady of the Assumption** ① *daily 0700-1400 and 1700-2100*, dates from the early 18th century and anchors the **Plaza Patria** (which is confusingly also referred to as Plaza de Armas and Plaza de la Constitución) on the west side of the square. Its immaculate interior will delight even the most jaded visitor. On the south side, the baroque **Palacio de Gobierno**, started in 1664 and completed in 1700, was once the palatial home of the Marqués de Guadalupe, and has a splendid courtyard. Its interior walls form ornately decorated neoclassical arches on two levels, totalling 100 in all. The grand staircase in the centre, near a fountain (built in the 1940s), blends in magnificently. There are colourful murals by the Chilean artist Osvaldo Barra on the second floor.

The north side of Plaza Patria contains the three-storey **Palacio Municipal**, which is an early 20th-century construction (originally the sumptuous Paris Hotel) that manages to look appropriately neoclassical and complements the other buildings in the square.

Among Aguascalientes' churches, there are several that should be seen, most of which are within the centre and walking distance from each other. The 19th-century neo-baroque **Templo de San Antonio** ① *Pedro Parga 252 y Zaragoza (far north end of Plaza Patria), daily 0630-1300 and 1830-2030*, is the crowning work of José Refugio Reyes. The striking churrigueresque **Santuario de Guadalupe** ① *Guadalupe 213, daily 0700-1330 and 1700-2100*, with its massive Talavera-tiled dome, is considered one of the best representations of this style anywhere in the world. The **Templo del Encino** ① *Eliseo Trujillo 112, daily 0630-1300 and 1630-2100*, built 1773-1796, holds the statue of the Black Christ of the Oak, supposedly discovered by a wood cutter as he was cutting into an oak tree. On 13 November there is a popular local feast here to commemorate the event. It is architecturally important as one of the last great baroque churches of its era.

Teatro Morelos ① *off the Plaza Convención at Nieto 113 (a block south of the cathedral),* T449-915 1941, is a beautiful neoclassical work, built in the early years of the Porfiriato, and lovingly restored to its original grandeur. There is a small **museum** on the mezzanine level, highlighting the theatre's past. Most theatrical productions nowadays are staged at the **Teatro Antonio** ① *Leal y Romero, in the Casa de la Cultura (see below),* T449-916 4988 for performances. Also nearby, are the administrative offices of the **Universidad Autónomia de Aguascalientes**, in a fine colonial building, the ex-Convento de San Diego, just to the right of the cathedral and Exedra, by the attractive **Jardín del Estudiante,** and the **El Parián** shopping centre.

The **Casa de la Cultura** ① *Venustiano Carranza 101 y Galeana Norte,* T449-910 2010, *Mon-Fri 1000-1400*, is a fine neoclassical colonial building in the historic centre. It holds a display of *artesanía* during the April *feria*, stages theatrical events on occasion, and also has a modest gallery of early paintings of the city. **Casa Terán** ① *Rivero y Gutiérrez 110,* T449-916 9809, *daily 0930-2130*, is a fine colonial-era house, the birthplace of Aguascalientes' most distinguished politician and humanitarian, José de Jesús Rafael Terán Peredo. It's worth a look for the interesting period collections and the beautiful grounds.

Museums

The **Museo de Aguascalientes** ① *Zaragoza 507 (by the church of San Antonio),* T449-916 7142, *Tue-Sun 1100-1800, US$0.75*, with a magnificent neoclassical exterior, has a collection of contemporary art, including fine paintings by Saturnino Herrán, and works by Orozco, Angel, Montenegro and others.

The nearby **Museo Regional de Historia de Aguascalientes** ① *Venustiano Carranza 118, immediately behind the cathedral,* T449-916 5228, *Tue-Sun 0830-1730, US$2.30, free Sun*, offers exhibits on the city and state's history in a pristine Porfiriato edifice (1908), one of the finest extant examples in the county.

The newest (2007) museum in town is the already famous **Museo Nacional de la Muerte** (National Museum of Death) ① *Rivero y Gutierrez, esq Morelos, off of the Jardín del Estudiante,* T449-915 4391, *Tue-Sun 1030-1830, US$1.50, free Wed*. Not as gruesome as it sounds, this is a Mexican take on death, primarily, as reflected in its art and handicrafts. Highly recommended.

Away from the Centro Histórico, the **Museo José Guadalupe Posada** ① *Vicenta Trujillo 222 (next to the Templo del Encino on one side and the Jardín del Encino on the other),* T449-915 4556, *Tue-Sun 1100-1800, US$0.75, free Sun*, deserves a special mention. It houses a remarkable collection of prints by the great graphic artist himself, who was born in Aguascalientes in 1852 and died penniless in Mexico City in 1913. He is best known for his macabre engravings of *calaveras*, wraiths and predominantly skeletal figures illustrating and satirizing the events leading up to the Mexican Revolution. The museum is not large, but one can spend a day here poring over Posada's original signed printing plates. As one enters the city on the main highway from the south (Route 45), there is a large representation of Posada's most famous character, *la calavera catrina* (the female skeleton), greeting visitors. Ironically, Posada's drawings are now iconic associations for El Día de Muertos (the Day of the Dead), although Posada himself never intended them to be associated with this holiday.

Outside of the centre, is the beloved **Museo Ferrocarrilero de Aguascalientes** (Train Museum of Aguascalientes) ① *28 de Agosto s/n (on the Parque La Estación in the colonia by the same name),* T449-994 2761, *Tue-Sun 1100-2000, US$0.75 (double admission Wed)*. This museum is made up of two restored mid-Victorian era buildings: the old railway station itself and its former loading warehouse. The warehouse exhibits the history of the railway in Aguascalientes (which, for many years, had the largest railway depot in all of Latin America) and several related events and the railroad's role in them. The exhibits are across four vast storage rooms. In the old railway station itself, cultural exhibits predominate, with faithful recreations of a Victorian-era waiting room, ticket office and the like on the first floor. On the second floor, there is a telegraph office and another recreation, a superintendent's office. It also has a 'personalities' show room, with exhibits on many famous titans of Mexico's golden era of the railway.

Two other museums are worth a look outside of the Centro Histórico, both great for the kids. One is the **Museo de la Fauna** ① *Blv José María Chávez s/n, in the Parque Heróes Mexicanos, T449-978 5106, Tue-Sun 0900-1800, US$0.40*, which offers exhibits on the local wildlife, some in dioramas. The other is the **Descubre Museo Interactivo de Ciencias y Tecnología de Aguascalientes** (Interactive Discovery Science and Technology Museum of Aguascalientes) ① *Av San Miguel s/n, Colonia Jardines del Parque, next to Parque Rodolfo Landeros Gallegos, T449-913 7015, daily 1000-1900, www.descubre.org.mx, US$5.65, children US$4.15*. This wonderful, hands-on museum has exhibits galore on just about every aspect of science and life you can imagine, and its award-winning modules help foster creative correlation between games and learning. There's also an IMAX theatre and gift shop on the premises. Highly recommended.

Around Aguascalientes

Hacienda de San Blas, 34 km away, contains the **Museo de la Insurgencia**, with murals by Alfredo Zermeño. Some 42 km southwest of Aguascalientes, en route to Guadalajara, is the colonial town of **San Juan de los Lagos**, a major pilgrimage centre and crowded during Mexican holidays. There is also a fine view on entering this town: as the road descends you see the twin-towered church with its red, blue and yellow tiled dome. San Juan is famous for glazed fruits. There are many hotels in the town.

San Luis Potosí ⊖🅿🄵🄾🄾🄲 ➤➤ *pp385-395. Colour map 2, B3. Phone code: 444.*

San Luis Potosí, 423 km from Mexico City, is famous for its colourful glazed tiles. The main plaza is covered with them, as are the domes of many of the city's churches, and one of its shopping streets. It became an important centre after the discovery of the famous San Pedro silver mine in the 16th century. There is a festival in the second half of August.

Ins and outs

Getting there The airport (SLP) is 6 km from the centre. The bus station is on the outskirts of town 1½ km from the centre; taxi US$2. For local buses to the centre, walk out the front door of the terminal and turn right. Walk down the street to the first traffic light. Then take buses heading south on the cross street (ie to your right as you're facing it) marked 'de Mayo' or 'Los Gómez'. ➤➤ *See Transport, page 394.*

Tourist information The helpful **tourist office** ① *Obregón 520, ½ a block west of Plaza de los Fundadores, T444-812 9906, www.visitasanluispotosi.com*, in a beautiful colonial house with lovely gardens, has good brochures and maps. Parking in San Luis Potosí is very difficult. There is a car park near the police station on Eje Vial, US$1 for the first hour, US$0.85 for each subsequent hour.

Sights

The **cathedral** is on the east side of **Plaza Hidalgo**. It has a beautiful exterior of pink *cantera* (local stone), with ornately carved bell towers. The interior is beautiful with rows of stone columns, approximately 2 m in diameter, running down the length of each side. Just north of the cathedral, is the **Palacio Municipal**. Inside, above the double branching staircase, you can admire glasswork of the city's coat of arms. On the upper floor, the Cabildo Hall has a ceiling painted by Italian artist Erulo Eroli, featuring mythological Christian themes.

Four blocks south of Plaza Hidalgo, don't miss the church of **San Francisco** ① *corner of Av Ignacio Aldama y Calle Hermenegildo Galeana*, which fronts the very pleasant plaza of the same name. This church is one of the baroque jewels of the city. The construction dates back to 1686. In that year, the work of the beautiful pink limestone facade was begun but it wasn't until the next century that some of its most important features were added, such as

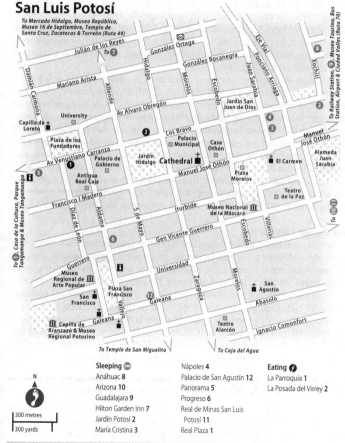

San Luis Potosí

Sleeping
Anáhuac **8**
Arizona **10**
Guadalajara **9**
Hilton Garden Inn **7**
Jardín Potosí **2**
María Cristina **3**
Nápoles **4**
Palacio de San Agustín **12**
Panorama **5**
Progreso **6**
Real de Minas San Luis Potosí **11**
Real Plaza **1**

Eating
La Parroquia **1**
La Posada del Virrey **2**

the baroque tower and the main altar. The interior is embellished with wonderful paintings, among which the works by Miguel Cabrera and Antonio Torres are the most outstanding. Worthy of admiration is the sacristy, the most magnificent in San Luis Potosí.

Next to the San Francisco church, the **Museo Regional de Arte Popular** ① *Mon 1000-1500, Tue-Sat 1000-1345, 1600-1745, Sun 1000-1400*, is housed in what used to be a private residence. Handicrafts from various parts of the state can be seen and bought, including ceramics, woodwork, *rebozos* and textiles. Nearby is the **Museo Regional Potosino** ① *Plaza de Aranzazú s/n, T444-813 0358, Tue-Fri 1000-1300, 1500-1800, Sat 1000-1200, Sun 1000-1300*, in a building that was originally a Franciscan convent. The ground floor has an exhibition of pre-Hispanic artefacts, mainly from the Huastec culture.

The baroque **Capilla de Aranzazú**, behind San Francisco, inside the regional museum (see above), should not be missed; the carved stone framework of the chapel window is one of the most beautiful pieces of baroque art in the city.

The **Palacio de Gobierno**, dating back to 1789, contains oil paintings of past governors. There is also the colonial treasury, **Antigua Caja Real** ① *some rooms may be visited Mon-Fri 0930-1330*, which was built in 1767. Of great artistic merit are the doors and windows of the chapel, carved in stone in the purist baroque style. Of special interest is the stairway leading to the first floor. It has very low steps, so that the mules, laden with precious metals, could climb easily.

There are several other interesting museums in town. The **Museo Nacional de la Máscara** ① *Plaza Carmen, daily 1000-1400, 1600-1800, US$0.50, US$0.50 for use of camera*, in what used to be the Palacio Federal, has an excellent collection of masks. The most impressive are the masks used in colonial and pre-Hispanic times in pagan religious ceremonies. In Parque Tangamanga is the **Museo Tangamanga** ① *southwest edge of the city, off Av Dr Salvador Nava Martínez and Blv Parque Chapultepec, daily 0600-1800*, in an old hacienda, and also a planetarium, observatory and open-air theatre. In Plaza España, next to Plaza de Toros, is the **Museo Taurino** ① *east of Alameda on Universidad y Triana, Tue-Sat 1100-1330, 1730-1930*, a museum about bullfighting. The newest museum in town, **Museo Francisco Cossio** ① *3 km west of the centre, Av Venustiano Carranza 1815, T444-813 2247*, has an excellent collection of modern art, much of it from relatively unknown artists or not seen elsewhere in Mexico.

Around San Luis Potosí

South of San Luis Potosí, east of the junction with Route 110, is **San Luis de la Paz**, the site of an important battle in the fight for Mexican Independence, and nowadays known for its many well-preserved neoclassical buildings. Nearby is one of Mexico's mining ghost towns, **Pozos** (altitude: 2305 m), once one of the most important mining centres of Mexico. It's very silent and a complete contrast to Real de Catorce (see below). Pozos was founded in 1576 when silver was discovered. In the 19th century the population reached 80,000 but following the Revolution most of the foreign (French and Spanish) owners left and the workforce migrated to Mexico City. Today the population is around 2000 and the whole area was decreed a historic monument in 1982. Pozos can be reached by bus from San Miguel de Allende (change at San Luis de la Paz) or San José Iturbide.

Real de Catorce ●●❶❸❸ ➤➤ *pp385-395. Colour map 2, A3. Phone code 488.*

Real de Catorce, 56 km west of Matehuala, is one of Mexico's most interesting old mining towns. This remarkable city, founded in 1772 and much larger a century ago than it is today, clustering around the sides of a valley, used to be so quiet that you could hear the river in the canyon, 1000 m below. It is becoming increasingly popular as a tourist destination and new hotels are being built.

The first church was the **Virgen del Guadalupe** (1779), a little way out of town. Beautiful ceiling paintings remain, as well as the black coffin used for the Mass of the Cuerpo Presente (a service celebrated when the body is present). Many of the images were moved to the church of **San Francisco** (1817), where miracles are believed to have occurred. The floor of the church is made of wooden panels, which can be lifted to see the catacombs below. In a room to one side of the main altar are *retablos*, touchingly simple paintings on tin, as votive offerings to the saint for his help. Next to the church is a small but worthwhile **museum** displaying mining equipment.

⊕ Guanajuato and around listings

For Sleeping and Eating price codes and other relevant information, see Essentials pages 47-51.

⊜ Sleeping

Guanajuato *p373, map p374*
Hotel rooms can be hard to find after 1400, so arrive early in the day if possible. For holidays and weekends it is advisable to book ahead, and for the Cervantino and Semana Santa, almost all hotels are booked long in advance. Hotels in the Centro Historicó can be much more expensive than elsewhere in the city.
L Hacienda del Marqués, Ctra Libre Guanajuato-Irapuato, Km 11, 3 km southwest of the city, T473-102 4367, www.elmarques hacienda.com. This marvellous ex-hacienda dates back to 1557. Tucked away amidst old trees and magnificent gardens. Facilities include a football field, tennis court, restaurant-bar, recreational activities and much more.
L-AL Howard Johnson Parador San Javier, Plaza Aldama 92, T473-732 0696. Built in the early 16th century and still redolent of the hacienda era. Very extensive grounds, some rooms have fireplaces. Sits atop a hill overlooking the Universidad de Guanajuato with beautiful vistas of the city centre.
L-AL Posada Santa Fe, Jardín de la Unión 12, T473-732 0084, www.posada-santafe.com. Plain regular rooms but the suites are very attractive with colonial-style furniture. Good restaurant on open terrace with excellent service. Tables on the plaza for dining. Recommended.

AL Casa de las Manrique, Av Juárez 116, between the mercado and the Callejón del Beso, T473-732 7678, www.mexonline. com/manrique.htm. Recently renovated and family friendly. Large, attractive suites, now with all mod cons, colonial decor, very good value for price.
AL-A Mesón de los Poetas, Pocitos 35 esq Juan Valle, T473-732 6657, www.mex online.com/poetas.htm. 30 rooms in a *casona* in the city centre. Each room pays a tribute to its poet with a hand made portrait and some verses written on a wall. Very nice courtyard. Recommended.
A El Insurgente Allende, Av Juárez 226, T473-732 3192, www.hotelinsurgente.com. Pleasant, clean, avoid rooms on 4th floor where there is a loud video bar, good breakfasts, nice rooftop terrace.
A San Diego, San Antonio 1 y de Alonso, T473-732 1300, www.hotelsandiegogto. com.mx. Good bar and restaurant but slow, colonial style, very pleasant, lovely gardens. Considered to have best location in city, but no a/c in rooms.
A-B Misión Guanajuato, Camino Antiguo a Marfil, Km 2.5, T473-732 3980, www.hoteles mision.com.mx. The exterior is beautiful, the interior less so, and rooms are very uniform. Has a restaurant, bar, pool, tennis court, and free transport to the Centro Histórico.
B Mesón de la Fragua, Juárez, T473-732 2715, at the western end and away from the tourist spots, 5 mins' walk from the centre of town. Very clean, good staff. Family run and

very traditional. Very inexpensive for what it delivers. Recommended.

B Socavón, Alhóndiga 41A, T473-732 6666, www.hotelsocavon.com.mx. Pretty restaurant/bar. Colonial decor, attractive interior courtyard, decent rooms for the price, with TV and phone.

B-C Villa de la Plata, Ctra Dolores Hidalgo 1500 (in Colonia Mineral de Valenciana), 10 mins from the centre, 20 mins from the airport, T473-732 1173, www.hotelvilla plata.com. In a tranquil neighbourhood with beautiful views of the city. Family-oriented, restaurant-bar, parking, internet in lobby. Indoor pool, gym, children's play area and lots of board games.

C Alhóndiga, Insurgentes 49, T473-732 0525. Good, clean, quiet, TV in rooms, parking, restaurant La Estancia.

C Posada San Francisco, Av Juárez 178 y Gavira, on Zócalo, T461-732 2084. Good value but outside rooms are noisy and service is slow in the afternoon. Nondescript entrance but lovely inner patio.

D Dos Ríos, Alóndiga 29, T473-732 0749. TV in rooms, cheap but not necessarily good value as it lacks most amenities, rooms on the street are noisy.

D Mineral de Rayas, Alóndiga 7, T473-732 1967. With bath, clean linen, pool, garage, restaurant, bar and Danny's Bar.

D-E Casa Kloster, Alonso 32, T473-732 0088. Book ahead, good location, very friendly, dorms for 4, a few with private bath, some without windows, clean. Not right for all (the owner lets dogs run loose and it's very noisy). Heavily oriented towards backpackers and there have been privacy complaints.

Around Guanajuato p377

D Santa Rosa Crag, Camino Real s/n, Santa Rosa, T473-729 7026. A wonderful setting in the forest. Hard to find, and deliberately has minimal amenities, but safe and very peaceful.

León p378, map p379

A-B Howard Johnson Condesa, Portal Bravo 14, on the plaza, T477-788 3929, www.hjleon. com. In the Centro Histórico with good views

of the plaza and cathedral. Good restaurant, 2 bars, room service, gym, private parking. Drab rooms. Neither the best nor the least expensive in its range but a good choice for downtown.

B La Estancia, Blv Adolfo López Mateos Oriente 1311, T477-716 3939, www.estancia. com.mx. 5 mins from downtown and Poliforo. Business oriented but an excellent choice. All suites are very clean and comfortable. Not to be confused with the more expensive Nueva Estancia, next door.

B-C Real Rex, 5 de Febrero esq Pino Suárez, T477-714 2415, www.hotelrealrex.com. One of city's longest continually operating hotels. Downtown location, recently modernized (but still has faux art deco facade). Bilingual staff, friendly, geared towards couples and small groups. Restaurant, bar, room service. Lacking in amenities, but a great value. Ask for a room on the upper floors for best views of the plaza.

C Del Campestre, Av Guanajuato 104 (Colonia Jardines de Moral), T477-718 8181, www.hoteldelcampestre.com. Out of the centre but a convenient location if driving. Gym, tanning room, restaurant, bar, room service. Wi-Fi in public areas.

C Fundadores, Joséfa Ortíz de Domínguez 218, T477-716 1727. Higher calibre of service makes it better than similarly priced hotels in the centre.

C Montecarlo, Justo Sierra 432, T477-713 1597. Clean, friendly, central.

C Real Provincia, Juárez 233, T477-716 0014, www.travelbymexico.com/guan/realprovincia. In the centre, friendly and functional, but nothing out of the ordinary.

D Tepeyac, Obregón 727, T477-716 8365. 1 star, OK, rooms are a bit dark.

Aguascalientes p380

There are several cheap hotels around the Juárez market.

LL Gran Hotel Hacienda de la Noria, Av Héroe de Nacozari Sur 1315 (Colonia La Salud), T449-918 4343, www.granhotel lanoria.com.mx. Very comfortable, jacuzzi in all rooms. Mexican, Japanese and international cuisine, gardens, swimming pool.

AL Andrea Alameda, Alameda esq Av Tecnológico, T449-970 3800, www.hotelde andreaalameda.com. Old ex-hacienda with large rooms, good restaurant, bilingual staff.
A Aguascalientes, Av Independencia 1703 (Colonia Trojes de Cristal), T449-993 3900, www.hotelaguascalientes.com. Best in its class by far, offers 3rd and 4th guests free accommodation. Very clean and quiet.
B Imperial, Moctezuma y 5 de Mayo 106, on the plaza, T449-915 1650. Large, sparse rooms.
B Las Trojes, Blv Luis Donaldo Colosio, in front of Centro Comercio Altaria, T449-194 9494, www.hotellastrojes.com.mx. At the northern edge of city in a convenient but ugly location. Rooms have all mod cons. Restaurant, bar, pool and nice grounds.
B Real del Centro, Blv María José Chávez 2100, T449-971 0845. Close to the airport on the southern edge of town. Clean, efficient, with nice bar, restaurant, pool, garage. Will store luggage. All rooms have TV, a/c, Wi-Fi. The best in its price range.
B-C Art, Eduardo J Correa esq Nieto 502, T449-917 9595. Ideal location in the centre, quiet, filled with modern art. Good for couples and individuals, but not families.
B-C La Cascada, José María Chávez 1942 (Colonia Industrial), T449-971 1010, www.hotel lacascada.com. On way to airport, very clean and quiet, nice grounds, pool. Recommended.
C Inn Galerias, Av de la Convención 125, T449-916 2669, www.inngaleriashotel.com. In the centre, with gym, covered parking, Wi-Fi. Continental breakfast included. Good value.
C Pequeño Gran Hotel, Av de la Convención 125, T449-915 8501, www.pequenogran hotelags.com. Central, with Wi-Fi, a/c, TV, cafetería. American-style breakfast included. Good value.
D Señorial, Colón 104, T449-915 1630. Rooms with phone, helpful landlady speaks English.

Around Aguascalientes *p382*

C Casa Blanca, Anguiano 107, on the plaza, Encarnación de Díaz, T475-953 2007. Hot water, secure parking nearby, reasonable restaurant. Halfway to Lagos de Moreno.

San Luis Potosí *p382, map p383*

There are many hotels between the railway station and the cathedral.
LL Palacio de San Agustín, Del Portillo esq de la Luz, T444-144 1900, www.palacio desanagustin.com. The most luxurious in the state, and one of the best in Mexico. All rooms are suites, fitted with sumptuous linens, silks, tapestries and every conceivable amenity. Service is of the highest order and the hotel and its grounds are breathtaking. No children under 12.
AL Panorama, Av Venustiano Carranza 315, T444-812 1777, www.hotelpanorama.com.mx. Price includes breakfast and a 20% discount on other meals. Large, attractive rooms. Great views of the city from the upper floors.
A Mansión Los Arcos, Av Benito Juárez 5001, a few kilometres south of San Luis Potosí, signposted, T444-824 0530. Motel with restaurant and safe parking.
A María Cristina, Juan Sarabia 110 (Colonia Altos), T444-812 9408, www.mariacristina.com.mx. Modern, clean, small rooms with phone and TV, restaurant, good value.
A Nápoles, Juan Sarabia 120, T444-812 8418. Good restaurant, TV, phones, ceiling fans. Recommended.
A-B Real de Minas San Luis Potosí, Ctra Central, Km 426, T444-499 8400, www.realde minasdesanluis.com. Conveniently located (100 m from bus station), with pool, restaurant, cafetería and parking. A bit on the expensive side, but better than most, especially as it's hard to find peace and quiet in this area of town.
B Guadalajara, Jiménez 253, near the train station, T444-812 4612. Small rooms with TV and phone, off-street parking.
B Hilton Garden Inn, Av Benito Juarez 1220, T444-834 5700, www.igougo.com. A pleasant surprise amongst the city's many business hotels. Very friendly, with attention to service and detail. Clean, bright, safe and orderly, as much for families or couples as for the business crowd. Rooms with many more amenities than most. Best in its range.
B-C Real Plaza, Av Venustiano Carranza 890, T444-814 6055, www.realplaza.com.mx.

In the centre. Friendly and helpful, bilingual staff. Gym, restaurant, bar, pool. Internet and TV in all rooms. Good value. Recommended.

C Arizona, José Guadalupe Torres 158, T444-818 1848, www.hotelarizona.com.mx. 5 mins from the bus station. Drab but efficient. Very friendly staff; restaurant, bar, parking. All rooms with TV, private bath.

C Progreso, Aldama 415, less than a block from Plaza San Francisco, T444-812 0366. Attractive colonial facade. Rooms are large but rather dark and a little run down. Not bad for the price.

C San Luis, Av Norte 315 (Colonia Americana Industrial), T444-816 0285, www.hotelsan luis.com.mx. 10 mins from both the city centre and the airport. Very clean and safe. Apart from having fans instead of a/c, rooms are top notch. The best in its price range.

D Anáhuac, Xochitl 140, T444-812 6504. Bare bones but serviceable. In the centre, off-street parking.

D-E Jardín Potosí, Los Bravo 530, T444-812 3152. Hot water, restaurant. Recommended.

Around San Luis Potosí p384

L Casa Montana, Pozos, T478-293 0032, www.casa montanahotel.com. Extreme comfort blended with great style. A wonderful place to stay in the heart of the colonial centre, but away from the crowds.

Real de Catorce p384

Accommodation is easy to find: boys greet new arrivals and will guide motorists through the peculiar one-way system (otherwise possible police fine).

A El Corral del Conde, Morelos, close to Mesón de la Abundancia, T488-887 5048. 6 rooms, fine furniture, clean, big bathrooms.

A El Real, Morelos 20. Clean, nice atmosphere, friendly, good restaurant. Recommended.

B Quinta Puesta del Sol, Calle del Cementerio 16, T488-887 5050. With bath, TV, beautiful views, poor restaurant.

E Providencia, on the main street. Hot water, clean, restaurant. Several other hotels nearby, and various restaurants.

🍴 Eating

Guanajuato *p373, map p374*

Tourists are often given the à la carte menu but ask for the *menú del día* or *comida corrida*, which will be cheaper. You can eat cheaply in the area behind Mercado Hidalgo.

♥♥♥ Galería Casa del Conde de la Valenciana, Ctra Dolores Hidalgo, Km 2, T473-732 2550. Mon-Sat 1300-2000. Located in the former administration building of the Valenciana mineworks. Beautiful furnishings and high-end Mexican food.

♥♥♥ La Lonja, on the corner of the Jardín de la Unión, opposite **Hotel San Diego**. Pleasant and lively bar, beers come with a complimentary dish of tacos and salsa.

♥♥ Las Mercedes, De Arriba 6, T473-733 9059, www.guanajuatocapital.com/ingles/Rmerced es.htm. Very high-end Mexican food and perennially popular (and crowded). Reservations needed.

♥♥ El Midi, Plaza San Fernando 41, T473-108 0892. Daily 1200-2300. Authentic French Provençal cuisine (chef is from Le Midi). Meals charged based on weight.

♥♥ Mariscos La Jaula, Blv Guanajuato 39 (Colonia Lomas de Pozuelos), T473-734 0180. Daily 1000-2000. Good seafood, the paella is formidable. Very relaxed atmosphere with Wi-Fi available for patrons. Live music on Fri.

♥♥-♥ Café de la Presa Bistró, Paseo de la Presa 109, T473-731 2598. Daily 0900-2200. Charming Parisian-style café on one of Guanajuato's nicest streets, with both local and international dishes. Highly recommended.

♥♥-♥ Casa Valadez, Jardín de la Unión 3, T473-732 9489. Very nice central location, directly on the Jardín, with excellent city views. Good Mexican and surprisingly affordable.

♥♥-♥ Chao Bella, Pocitos 25, T473-732 6764. Mon 1400-1800, Tue-Sat 1400-2200. In a charming colonial mansion, 5 mins from Jardín de la Unión. Known for good service and outstanding Italian-Mediterranean cuisine. Family atmosphere. Very reasonably priced and highly recommended.

†† -† El Gallo Pitagorico, Callejón de la
Constancia 10, behind Teatro Juárez, T473-
732 9489. Daily 1400-2400. Very romantic,
squeezed into one of the centre's quaint side
streets. Lots of chicken and traditional dishes.
†† -† La Hacienda de Marfil, Arcos de
Guadalupe 3, T473-733 1148. Good
Mexican and some international dishes.
Recommended but outside of the centre.
†† -† La Terraza, Jardín de la Unión 12,
T473-732 0084. Hard to beat for location,
ambience, service and price. Good Mexican
and French dishes. Probably Guanajuato's
best restaurant in this range.
†† -† Truco, Callejón Truco 7 (off Plaza de la
Paz), T473-732 8374. Daily 0830-2300. *Menú
del día* US$3, relaxed family atmosphere.
Theatre in back room Fri and Sat afternoon.
† Vegetariano, Callejón Calixto 20.
Inexpensive, sells wholewheat bread.

Cafés
Bagel Cafetín, Callejón de Potrero 2 Bajos,
across from Templo de San Francisco, T473-
733 9733, www.bagelcafetin.com. Mon-Fri
0830-1100, Sat 0900-1000, Sun 0900-1800.
A tiny bagel shop in the heart of the Centro
Histórico. Everything is home-made and the
staff are friendly and speak English.
Café Atrio, Agora del Baratillo s/n, ground
floor), T473-731 1213. Daily 0900-2400.
Delicious pastas, salads, bagels and
hamburgers plus finger food in popular,
centrally located café.
Café Conquistador, Pocitos 35 esq Juan Valle
(Mesón de los Poetas), T473-734 1358. Great
coffee, bread and snacks. Coffee can be
purchased to take away by the kilo, pound
or whole bean.
Corazón Parlante, Paseo de la Presa 52A,
very near La Escuela Normal, T473-731 2305,
www.corazonparlante.com.mx. Mon-Fri
0900-2200, Sat 1000-2100. Great Mexican
coffee, breakfast originals, and a wide variety
of teas, in a pleasant space. Has frequent art
exhibitions and signature jewellery on display.
Crepería-Café Bossanova, Plaza San
Fernando 53, T473-732 9930. Mon-Sat

1000-2400, Sun 1000-2000. Old World-style
terraced establishment with international
cuisine; the only crêpe restaurant in Guanajuato.
Nice al fresco setting underneath enormous
tree. Very popular on weekends and mornings.

Around Guanajuato *p377*
††† Ik-Etznab, Camino a Ojo de Agua s/n, Santa
Rosa, T473-102 5146, www.ik-etznab.com.mx.
Thu-Sat 1300-1900, Sun, Tue-Wed 1300-1800.
International haute cuisine using tasting
menus (small portions of several dishes); very
experimental, also very expensive but always
popular (reservations recommended).
††† Rancho de Enmedio, Santa Rosa. Good
dried meat specialities and beautiful scenery.

León *p378, map p379*
††† Antropia, Niebla 202 (Colonias Jardines
del Moral), T477-773 9299, www.antropia.
com.mx. Mon-Thu 1900-0130, Fri-Sat 1900-
0230. This eatery and cultural centre is home
to many café favourites as well as art shows
and cultural events.
††† Panteón Taurino, Calzada de Los Héroes
408, T477-713 4969. Mon-Sat 1300-2300, Sun
1300-1900. Expensive but worth visiting for
the incredible decor, in a former bullfighting
ring (which is also a part museum).
†† Lupillos, Blv López Mateos 2003 Oriente,
opposite the stadium, T477-771 1868.
Pasta and pizza.
†† Rincón Gaucho, Prolongación Calzada de
los Héroes 103, T477-763 0666. Argentinean
entrees of seared steaks, chops and side
dishes. Meat lovers will delight in the full
menu of cuts. Good wine selection.
†† Romanza, Blv López Mateos 1102 Oriente
(Col Los Gavilanes), T477-719 8000. Daily
1300-2300. The city's best Italian. Good wine
list. Entertainment from an Italian tenor,
whose tunes you either will appreciate or
despise, but certainly not avoid hearing.
†† -† El Braserio, Blv López Mateos 1501
Oriente, T477-763 3100. Casual eatery with
bright and colourful ambiance. Steak, chicken
and pasta entrees, traditionally prepared.
The salsa, prepared fresh at your table, is a

particular treat. Good cocktails and a selection of regional beers.

El Patio, La Paz y Libertad. This cosy eatery is named for its location – the patio of a former carriage house. Fresh soup, salads and sandwiches.

Frascati, Av Campestre 1403, T477-773 7154. Excellent pastas and noodle dishes with freshly prepared sauces. There are also good selections of hand-tossed pizzas and delectable desserts. Book ahead; gets very busy at lunchtime.

Gran Fraternidad Universal, Blv López Mateos, near IMSS building. Vegetarian snacks.

Lalo's & Charlie's, Av López Mateos esq Mérida. Near centre and very popular, noisy after 2100. Probably León's top gringo spot. Rather bizarre mod ambience features bright colours and vivid murals.

Aguascalientes p380
Try the area near 5 de Mayo for *pollo rostizado*.

De la Torre, Av Aguascalientes Sur esq Luciano Ponce 201 (Colonia Prados Sur), T449-140 5565. Excellent grilled meats. Highly recommended.

Las Glorias del Indio, Graneros 102 (Colonia Lomas del Campestre), T449-912 4461. Great food from Mazatlán in a colourful setting.

Mesón del Borrego, Av Heróe de Nacozari Sur 2500, T449-913 7011. Well known and highly regarded its meat and local dishes.

Cascadas, Av Hidalgo 402 y Jesús María, T449-963 5657. Good seafood.

La Pasta Italiana, Av Las Américas 806, T449-146 0630, www.lapastaitaliana.com. Just what the name implies. Recommended.

La Pava del Borrego, Av Heróe de Nacozari 2500 (Colonia Jardines del Parque), T449-913 7011. Authentic Mexican in traditional setting.

Sirloin Stockade, Av Heroé de Nacozari Sur 2101 (Colonia Jardines de Bugambillas), T449-917 5888. North American-style beef restaurant.

Amar, República de Brasil 111 esq Costa Rica, T449-194 4944. Lebanese.

Antigua Hacienda la Noria, Av Heró de Nacozarí Sur 1401, T449-918 2020. Good light food (and bar) in peaceful setting near an ex-hacienda.

El Fogoncito, Blv Luis Donaldo Colosio 406 casi esq Zaragoza (Colonia Las Trojes), T449-194 5740. Reputed to be city's best *taquería*.

La Jimena, Alameda 804, T449-975 3030. Popular restaurant and bar with old-fashioned *terraza*. Noisy at night.

La Palapa de Charly, Av Aguascalientes 3901 (Colonia Villa Jardín), T449-913 3000, www.lapalapadecharly. Fish and steak, and lots of it. Arrive hungry.

La Piazza, Cinco de Mayo 610, T449-915 3434. Pizza and good Italian downtown.

Las Delicias de María, José María Chávez 1122 (Colonia Linda Vista), T449-917 4344. Good Mexican food in clean, bright setting.

Los Panchos, Av Convención Sur 1014 (Colonia Linda Vista), T449-978 3408. More than 20 variations on chicken, beef and pork, served buffet style. Very popular.

Taquería Los Gallos, Av Aguascalientes Norte 709 (Colonia Bosques del Prado Sur), T449-912 7564. One of Aguascalientes' better taco and grill joints. Recommended.

San Luis Potosí p382, map p383
Many reasonably priced eating places at western end of Alameda Juan Sarabia.

Café Pacífico, Los Bravo esq Constitución, a couple of blocks from the train station. Open 24 hrs. Good hot chocolate. Nice atmosphere.

La Parroquia, Plaza de los Fundadores, Díaz de León esq Venustiano Carranza. Old building but modern inside. Good food and *comida corrida*.

La Posada del Virrey, north side of Jardín Hidalgo. Set in the beautiful covered courtyard of an old colonial building. Also has a dining room facing the plaza.

Real de Catorce p384
El Eucalyptus, on the way to the Zócalo. Italian-Swiss run. Excellent home-made pasta, vegetarian food, cakes. Pricey but recommended.

🎵 Bars and clubs

Guanajuato *p373, map p374*
El Consulado, Truco 12, T473-732 0084. Very elegant setting in the former Prussian consulate. More of a restaurant-bar with an international pub style. Suitably dark, lots of polished wood, with wide selection of beers. English spoken; popular with expats. Recommended.
La Clave Azul, Segunda de Cantaritos 31, T473-732 1561. Mon-Thu 1330-2200, Fri-Sun 1330-2400. Nowadays more of a restaurant than a bar, this little gem is tucked into a narrow walkway off Plaza de San Fernando, and is full of antiques and relics. It actually has no menu, although every day a different Mexican dish is offered. Remarkably, if you buy US$100 pesos worth of your favourite drink (not a difficult task here), a complete 4-course meal is complimentary.

Clubs
Recommended nightclubs include **Disco El Grill**, Alonso (100 m from Casa Kloster) and **Disco Los Comerciales**, Juan Valle.

León *p378, map p379*
Futbol Bar, Hidalgo 923-B, T477-717 8020. Sports oriented, beginning and ending with football.
JJ Sport, Rocío 115-A, Jardines del Moral. Pepe's Pub, Madero 120. Another football-oriented bar.

Clubs
Domus, López Mateos 2611 Oriente, T477-711 6614.
La Iguana, Centro Comercial Insurgentes, Local 4 y 5B, T477-718 1416. An all-ages club popular with the younger crowd. Weekends only.
Ossy's, Av Paseo de los Insurgentes, on exit road to Lagos de Moreno, T477-717 6880. As close to heavy metal as it gets.
Piano Bar Maya, Prolongación Calzada 112, T477-716 9734. One of León's quieter clubs, with live music (not shows).

Aguascalientes *p380*
Ajua, Blv Miguel de la Madrid, Km 1, T449-973 5111. Pure *banda*, loud and crowded; go with a local.
Cool Pool, Av Aguascalientes 402 (Colonia Bosques del Prado), T449-996 0295. Open till 0200 every night. Billiards, widescreen TVs, and finger food, too.
La Independencia, Av Independencia 1847 (Colonia Trojes de Alonso), T449-912 7717. Open for breakfast and lunch but primarily an evening spot. *Banda* music, wide selection of beers, video games.

🎭 Entertainment

Guanajuato *p373, map p374*
Music
A live band plays in Jardín de la Unión 3 times a week.

Theatre
Theatre sketches from classical authors out of doors in lovely old plazas from Apr-Aug.
Teatro Juárez, Jardín de la Unión, T473-732 0183. A magnificent French-type Second Empire building, shows art films and has symphony concerts.
Teatro Principal, Cantarranas, by Plaza Mexiamora.

Aguascalientes *p380*
Cultural centres
El Centro Cultural Los Arquitos, Narcozari y Alameda, T449-917 0023. Formerly a 19th-century bathhouse; museum, bookshop, café.

Theatre
Teatro Morelos, Nieto 113, Plaza Convención, 1 block south of the cathedral, T449-915 1941. Absolutely stunning atmosphere, but infrequent performances.
Teatro Antonio, Antonio Leal y Romero, at Venustiano Carranza 101 y Galeana in the Casa de Cultura building, T449-916 4988.

⊕ Festivals and events

Guanajuato p373, map p374
Mar/Apr Viernes de las Flores (Friday of Flowers) is held on the Fri before Good Fri, starting with the Dance of the Flowers on Thu night at about 2200 right through the night, adjourning to Jardín de la Unión to exchange flowers. Very colourful and busy.
End Oct Festival Cervantino de Guanajuato, offices at Plazuela de San Francisquito 1, T461-731 1150, www.festivalcervantino.gob.mx. An important cultural event held over the last 2 weeks of Oct. During the Cervantino, Guanajuato is transformed into a Latin Mecca of artistic expression in everything from music, opera, theatre, dance, visual arts, cinema and more, going far beyond the original one-act plays that were the basis for the festival when it started in 1953. There's a mixture of free, open-air events and paying events. Well-known artists from around the world perform. The festival, nominally in honour of Cervantes, is highly recommended and crowded; book accommodation in advance.
Dec During the Christmas period students dress up in traditional estudiantina costumes and wander the streets singing carols and playing music. Groups leave from in front of the theatre at 2030.

León p378, map p379
19-24 Jan Fiesta de San Sebastián, very crowded and good fun.
14-17 Dec Festival Internacional del Globo (International Balloon Festival), largest in the country and the 3rd largest in the western hemisphere.

Aguascalientes p380
Mid-Apr 3-week national festival, Feria de San Marcos. For almost 2 centuries this has been Mexico's most important fair and is covered by national TV networks. Its origin dates back to the year 1604 when it originally was held as a bartering session for livestock between provinces of New Spain. There are processions, cockfights (in Mexico's largest

palenque, seating 4000), bullfights (in Mexico's largest plaza de toros, seating 15,000), agricultural shows, etc. This is about as truly 'Mexican' as it gets. Plaza de Armas is lavishly decorated for the occasion. You absolutely must book accommodation in advance.

Real de Catorce p384
Mar/Apr On Good Fri, thousands of visitors gather to watch a lively Passion play, with realistic Roman soldiers and very colourful Jews and apostles.
3-4 Oct Pilgrimage for San Francisco, on foot from Matehuala. Take the local bus from Matehuala to La Paz and join the groups of pilgrims who set out from early evening onwards.

○ Shopping

Guanajuato p373, map p374
Handicrafts
Local pottery is for sale in the Mercado Hidalgo (1910), in the centre of town, and there is a casa de artesanías behind the Teatro Juárez (see Entertainment, above).
Crafts Fonart, opposite La Valenciana church (see page 377) has an excellent selection of handicrafts; high prices but superb quality.

León p378, map p379
Leatherwork
Leatherwork shops can be found along Belisario Domínguez and Plaza Piel, Hilario Medina y López Mateos.

Shopping centres
La Gran Plaza, Blv López Mateos 1902 Pte.
Plaza León, Blv López Mateos 1102 Oriente.
Plaza Mayor, Av de las Torres, corner of Prolongación Morelos.

Aguascalientes p380
Bootmakers
Zapatería Cervantes, Guerrero 101 Sur y Nieto, T449-915 1943. One of many shops selling boots made to order.

Chocolates
Xocalatl Mexica, Nieto 115, T449-171 3693, www.xocalatlmexica.com. In the centre; don't think twice, just go and get some.

Markets
The main market is at 5 de Mayo y Unión, large and clean, toilet on upper floor.

Shopping centres
Centro Galerias, Av Independencia 2351, T449'912 6612, www.centrogalerias.com.mx.
Plaza San Marcos, Av Convención Norte 2301 (Colonia San Cayetano), T449-914 7151.
Plaza Universidad, Av Universidad esq Av Aguascalientes, T449-914 4191.
Plaza Vestir, José María Chávez 1940, T449-971 0766.

San Luis Potosí *p382, map p383*
Food
Casa de Nutrición, 5 de Mayo 325. Health food store.
Chalita, Jardín San Juan de Dios entre Av Alvaro Obregón y Los Bravo. A 3-storey hypermarket.

Markets
Head north on Hidalgo and you come to Mercado Hidalgo, then Mercado República and Mercado 16 de Septiembre. Locally made *rebozos* (the best are from Santa María del Río) are for sale.

▲ Activities and tours

Guanajuato *p373, map p374*
Language schools
Academia Falcón, Paseo de la Presa 80, Guanajuato, 36000, T461-731 0745, www.academiafalcon.com. Good-quality instruction, regular recommendations.
Universidad de Guanajuato, T461-732 0006, montesa@quijote.ugto.mx. The university has many US exchange students and is regarded as one of the country's best language schools (accepts non-matriculating students).

Tour operators
Tours of the city and outskirts and south of the state are possible; if you want an English-speaking guide, prices multiply.
Transportes Turísticos de Guanajuato, underneath the Basílica on Plaza de la Paz, T461-732 2838. Tours to sites outside the city.

León *p378, map p379*
Tour operators
Viajes Sindy de León, 20 de Enero 319, T477-713 1224. Jovi de León, Madero 319 Centro, T477-714 5094.

Aguascalientes *p380*
Tour operators
Som, Adolfo López Mateos 407, T449-145 3333. Tours of city, vineyards and El Santuario del Cristo Roto, US$13.65 (children US$9.10).
Turibus Agüitas, kiosk in front of Palacio Municipal. Daily 1000-2000. Tours of the Centro Histórico daily at 1000 and 1800 (US$1.85); historic cemetery tours daily at 1800 and 2000 (US$1.85).

⊙ Transport

Guanajuato *p373, map p374*
Bus
The bus terminal is on the road to Silao, near toll gate, 20 mins from centre by bus, US$0.25 (taxi US$2). To get to the bus station from the centre, take a bus from Av Juárez in front of the Hotel Central, about a block west of the Mercado Hidalgo. The bus stop has a sign saying 'C Camionera'. The bus terminal has a place for storing luggage.

To **Ciudad Juárez**, transferring in León 1015, US$95. To **Guadalajara**, 19 buses a day 0900-2330, US$20. To **Irapuato**, 5 daily 0530-1830, US$3. To **León**, 0830, 1230 and 1730, 45 mins, US$4.20. To **Mexico City**, regular service, 4½ hrs, US$22. To **Monterrey**, 7 a day, all in the afternoon, US$41. To **Morelia**, 0700, 0820, 1210 and 1620, US$12. To **Nuevo Laredo**, 1930, US$72. To **Querétaro**, 6 daily 0710-1820, US$10.

To **San Luis Potosí**, 5 throughout the day, US$12.85. To **San Miguel de Allende**, regular service 0700-1915, 1½ hrs, US$8.10. To **Tijuana**, 1800, US$119.

For many destinations it is better to go to León and pick up the more frequent services from there (buses every 10 mins Guanajuato-León, US$1).

Around Guanajuato *p377*
Bus For **La Valenciana mine**, a local 'Valenciana' bus starts in front of Hotel Mineral de Rayas, Alhóndiga 7, leaving every 30 mins during the day, US$0.10, 10-min ride.

For **Cerro del Cubilete**, take local buses from Guanajuato, 1½ hrs, US$1, 0700, 0900, 1100, 1400, 1600 (also from Silao, US$0.60). The last bus up leaves at 1600 from Silao and Guanajuato.

León *p378, map p379*
Air
International airport, Del Bajío (BJX), 18 km southeast of León towards Guanajuato, 6 km from Silao, on the Ctra Panamericana (Route 45), known as the Blv Aeropuerto. The turn-off is well marked. Buses and taxis run from town. Good domestic connections, international flights to several US cities, also to Guatemala and South American cities.

Airline offices AeroMéxico, Madero 410, T477-716 6226. **Continental**, Blv López Mateos 2307 Pte, T477-713 5199. **Mexicana**, Blv López Mateos 401 Oeste, T477-714 9500.

Bus
The terminal, corner of Blv Hilario Medina y Blv La Luz, has a post office, long-distance phones, restaurant and shops. To **Chihuahua**, US$63. Many buses run to **Ciudad Juárez**, US$83. To **Durango**, US$127. To **Guadalajara**, every 30 mins, first at 0600, 4 hrs, US$21. To **Guanajuato**, very regular, 40 mins, US$4. To **Mexico City**, more buses than you can count, 5 hrs, US$30. To **Monterrey**, US$47. To **Poza Rica**, US$29. To **Querétaro**, hourly, 2 hrs, US$11. To **Zacatecas**, 3½ hrs, US$16.

Aguascalientes *p380*
Air
The airport (AGU) is 21 km south from the town centre. Good domestic flights and flights to **Los Angeles** with AeroMéxico. **American** flies direct to **Dallas**, and **Continental** to **Dallas** and **Houston**.

Airline offices AeroMéxico, Madero 474, T449-916 1362.

Bus
The bus station about 1 km south of centre on Av Circunvalación Sur, near post office and pharmacy; to get there take a city bus from Galeana near López Mateos.

To **Ciudad Juárez**, US$75.40. To **Chihuahua**, US$56. To **Guadalajara**, several daily, 6 hrs, US$15. To **Guanajuato**, 5 daily, 3½ hrs, US$10. To **León**, 21 a day, 2 hrs, US$8-9. To **Mexico City**, 9 a day, 7 hrs, US$33.80. To **Monterrey**, US$29-31. To **Morelia**, Primera Plus, 4 a day, US$22. To **Nuevo Laredo**, US$43-46. To **Puerto Vallarta**, at 2230, US$32. To **Querétaro**, 8 a day, 6 hrs, US$24. To **San Luis Potosí**, Futura, 16 a day 0600-2300, US$11. To **Tijuana**, 1530 and 2100, US$145. To **Zacatecas**, every 30 mins, 2½ hrs, US$7.

San Luis Potosí *p382, map p383*
Air
The airport (SLP) is 6 km from the centre. Many daily to **Mexico City**, also flights to **Aguascalientes**, **Guadalajara**, **Monterrey**, **Tampico**. There are international flights to **Chicago**, **Dallas** and **San Antonio** (Texas).

Airline offices Aeromar, Av Venustiano Carranza 1160-2, T444-911 4671. **Mexicana**, T444-917 8836. Mexicana de Aviación, T444-917 8920.

Bus
The bus station is on the outskirts of town 1½ km from the centre. Facilities at the terminal include left-luggage, telephone office and a few shops.

To **Aguascalientes**, hourly, 2½ hrs, US$10.65. To **Chihuahua**, 9 buses daily,

US$57.60. To **Ciudad Juárez**, 9 buses daily, US$80. To **Durango**, 1405, 2045 and 2330, US$16. To **Guadalajara**, hourly service, 5 hrs, US$21. To **Guanajuato**, regular service, 4 hrs, US$13. To **Nuevo Laredo**, 10 hrs, US$40. To **Mexico City**, very regular service, 5 hrs, US$16. To **Monterrey**, 14 daily, 6 hrs, US$15. To **Morelia**, regular service, US$27. To **Querétaro**, hourly from 0900, 2½ hrs, US$15. To **San Miguel de Allende**, 6 a day, 3 hrs, US$10. To **Tijuana**, 1530 and 1830, US$103. To **Zacatecas**, 7 buses daily, 2½ hrs, US$7.

International Autobuses Americanos: 2 buses daily, stopping at **Laredo**, **San Antonio**, **Dallas** and **Houston**, in Texas, and **Chicago**. All buses crossing the border into the USA are subject to a mandatory 2-hr wait for processing and drug checks.

Real de Catorce *p384*
Bus Many buses a day to **Matehuala**, from the corner of Guerrero y Mendiz, US$2 one way. A taxi can be hired for US$25-30 (depending upon time of day), economical for 4 people; local buses from office 1 block north of the Zócalo.

❶ Directory

Guanajuato *p373, map p374*
Banks Bancomer, Banca Serfín, Banamex, daily 0900-1100. **Internet** Alonso 70B, Mon-Sat 0900-1800. **Laundry** Lavandería Internacional, Alhóndiga 35A, self or service wash. La Burbuja Express, Plazuela Baratillo. Lavandería Automática Internacional, Manuel Doblado 28. **Post office** Corner of Subida San José, by La Compañía church.

Telephone International phone calls from phone booths with cards, or collect. Long-distance phone offices in **Miscelánea Unión** shop, by Teatro Principal and on Pocitos, opposite Alhóndiga de Granaditas.

León *p378, map p379*
Banks Bancomer, Belisario Domínguez 322, and **Banorte** and HSBC on the plaza. **Post office** Obregón y 5 de Mayo, Mon-Fri 0800-1900.

Aguascalientes *p380*
Banks On the plaza, Inverlat, ATM takes Amex. **Banamex**, ATM. All *centros comerciales* and *galerías* now have banks (usually Banorte) with ATMs. **Internet** Acnet, Edificio Torreplaza Bosques, 2nd floor, Av Aguascalientes (near state university), bus from Rivero Gutiérrez. Sistemas Alt 64, Vásquez del Mercado 206, T449-915 7613, Mon-Sat 1000-1400, 1600-2100. Many more in the centre. **Medical services** Red Cross, T449-915 2055. **Post office** Hospitalidad, near El Porián shopping centre.

San Luis Potosí *p382, map p383*
Internet Café Cibernético, Av Venustiano Carranza 416. **Medical services** Clínica Díaz Infante (private), Arista 730, T444-912 3737. **Hospital Central** (public), Av Venustiano Carranza 2395, T444-913 0343. **Hospital de Nuestra Señora de la Salud** (private), Madre Perla 435 (Fraccionamiento Industrias, 4 blocks behind Holiday Inn Hostal del Quixote), T444-924 5424. **Red Cross**, Av Juárez y Diez Gutiérrez, T444-9153332. **Sociedad de Beneficios Española** (private), Av Venustiano Carranza 1090, T444-913 4048. **Post office** Morelos y González Ortega.

Zacatecas and around

→ *Colour map 2, A2. Phone code: 492.*

The capital of Zacatecas state, founded in 1546, this picturesque up-and-down former mining city is built in a ravine with pink stone houses scattered over the hills. The largest silver mine in the world, processing 10,000 tonnes of ore a day or 220 tonnes of silver, is at nearby Real de Angeles. Silver has bestowed an architectural grandeur on Zacatecas that surpasses that of Guanajuato. Many travellers believe it to be the most pleasant town in this part of Mexico, if not of all of Mexico. Less oriented towards (and much less overrun by) North American retirees and backpackers than San Miguel de Allende or Guanajuato, Zacatecas' laid-back atmosphere, multitude of cultural attractions, and ideal climate make it the rival of several better-known cities. You could spend several days soaking up the atmosphere. There's also a lively nightlife with bars and discos. ▶▶ *For listings, see pages 402-406.*

Ins and outs

Getting there The international **Aeropuerto La Calera** (ZCL) is 27 km north of the city, with flights from domestic locations and several cities in the USA. Alternatively, the city can also be reached via the larger airports of Aguascalientes (see page 380) and San Luis Potosi (see page 382), which have daily bus and car rental services to Zacatecas. The bus terminal is 4 km south of town. Bus No 8 from outside the terminal leaves for the town centre every 10-15 minutes. Almost all local buses either pass through or close by the centre. ▶▶ *See Transport, page 406.*

Getting around Bulevar Adolfo López Mateos, a busy highway, runs close to the centre of town from the bus station (4 km south of town) and down the ravine. Driving in the historic centre can be a nightmare with many one-way systems.

Tourist information The **tourist office** ① *Av Hidalgo 403, 2nd floor, T492-925 1277, www.turis mozacatecas.gob.mx*, is friendly and helpful with free maps and good information on hotels and language classes as well as discounted tours and museums. Throughout the centre are yellow-, green-, and blue-shirted tourism office representatives ('Amigos de Turismo') who can provide free information, and a kiosk at the intersection of Hidalgo y Allende. Note that Zacatecas museums keep hours different from the rest of the country, generally open Fridays through to Wednesdays, and closed Mondays and Tuesdays.

Sights

For a city of fewer than 150,000 inhabitants, Zacatecas has a disproportionately large number of sights, especially for those interested in colonial architecture and history. Built between 1730 and 1752 **cathedral** ① *Av Hidalgo, T492-922 6211, daily 0700-1300 and 1630-2100*, is the centrepiece of town with a fine churrigueresque facade, considered by experts as one of the best in the world. At night its illuminated front facade is breathtaking.

To the immediate right of the cathedral and set back is the **Museo Galería Episcopal** ① *Plazuela Candelario Huízar s/n, T492-924 4307, daily 1000-1700, US$0.85*, which contains a sterling collection of Episcopal vestments and liturgical items (many of the latter of pure gold or silver) dating as far back as the 17th century and quite rare. There are also exhibits on the upper floor of 18th- and 19th-century carved saints and processional banners.

To the west, on Dr Hierro is the former ex-convento **San Agustín**, constructed in 1617 (now an occasional art gallery maintained by the Autonomous University of Zacatecas),

Semana Santa and Las Morismas in Zacatecas

If there's any doubt that Mexico's rich colonial heritage is still alive and well in some quarters, a visit to the eponymous capital of the State of Zacatecas during Holy Week (Semana Santa), or the last week of August, will quickly set the story straight. Blessed with an almost unbelievable number of colonial-era treasures, Zacatecas knows how to throw a serious, week-long party in the midst of them, whether the occasion is religious or secular.

During Semana Santa, it seems that half of Mexico finds its way to Zacatecas, and the other half arrive for Las Morismas (a series of mock battles commemorating a fight between Moors and Christians many years ago) in the final week of August, as a prelude to yet another annual extravaganza: the Zacatecas State Fair. Both traditions are well into their fourth century and have become more popular with each passing year. While visitors usually do not participate in either event,

they are welcome observers on these occasions when Zacatecas' charm and hospitality are on full display.

Semana Santa is filled with more parades, processions, and other events – mostly grouped about the impending Easter holiday – than you can count. (It often coincides with still another *zacatecano* highlight: the annual Cultural Festival.) The impressive Procesión del Silencio on Good Friday night, when local guilds (many dressed in Biblical costumes) march in silence through the historic centre of Zacatecas, is an absolute must-see. Likewise, the multi-day battle between Christians and infidels (not-so-appropriately garbed in Roman, Renaissance, and even Hindu finery, hurling slabs of red meat at each other) along the slopes of the Cerro de Bracho is a spectacle that has to be seen to be believed. These traditions may be long gone elsewhere, but to see them both in all their glory, head to Zacatecas.

with only the dome, a high wall and a few interior carvings left. The meaning of the fascinating allegory carved on its north side has been deciphered by scholars and is related to Augustine's dream which led to his conversion to Christianity. The clue to unravelling its mystery, which had intrigued experts for decades, was that the words spoken by an angel to a sleeping Augustine were carved backwards, an indication that the scene was intended to represent a dream, which in turn placed the image within the context of Augustine's autobiographical writings.

The **Palacio Municipal** and the **Plaza de las Armas** ① *Av Hidalgo (to the immediate left of the cathedral), T492-922 1211, daily 0800-2000, free*, in front of it are the former house and grounds of the counts of Santiago de Laguna, who for many years were the power brokers of Zacatecas. The building was constructed in the early 18th century, and is the best preserved baroque structure in the city. Inside are murals (unfortunately not at all aesthetically in keeping with the style or ambiance of the building) by Antonio Rodríguez, representing the struggle for Mexican Independence. The Plaza de las Armas is still where important civic announcements are made and also the venue for many cultural events.

Also worth seeing in the centre is the **Casa Moneda** ① *Dr Hierro 307, T492-922 2184, daily 0900-2000, free*, better known as the Tesorería. Founded in 1810 and used as a national mint until 1905, it has long been considered the city's most beautiful secular building apart from the theatre. It was severely damaged in the shelling by Zapata's forces in the Battle of Zacatecas. The interior is cavernous, with wonderful patios and a central fountain. By 2010, the building will house the city's new 'Citadel of Art' complex.

The **Teatro Calderón** ① *Av Hidalgo 501, 1 block down from the cathedral, T492-922 8620, daily 0930-2000, free*, built in the 1890s at the request of Zacatecas' 'leading citizens', is one of the architectural crown jewels of the city. Its enormous floor-to-ceiling mirrors were put there so the theatre's patrons could admire the figure they cut in during intermissions.

A couple of blocks to the south, east of the ex convento San Agustín, in a wing of the former *Casa de Moneda* (National Mint), is the **Museo Zacatecano** ① *Dr Ignacio Hierro 301, T492-922 6580, Wed-Mon 1000-1700, US$2.25.* Containing religious paintings, ex-

Zacatecas

Sleeping		
Argento Inn **8**	Hostal Reyna Solidad **15**	Quinta Real **9**
Casa Real **3**	Hostal San Francisco **5**	Santa Rita **12**
Casa Santa Lucía **13**	Hostal Villa Colonial **11**	
Colón **1**	Las Cuevas **7**	**Eating** 🍴
Condesa **2**	Mesón de Jobito **6**	Acrópolis **1**
Hostal del Río **4**	Mesón de la Merced **14**	Café Arlequín **15**
	Posada Tolosa **10**	Café Dalí **22**

Cazadores **5**	
El Mesón del Taco **8**	
El Paraíso **16**	
El Pueblito **6**	
Emilia Café **11**	
Florencia Pizzas **17**	
Garufa **12**	

votos, Huichol handicrafts and some colonial items, it is primarily famous for housing some of the rarest pieces of Huichol beadwork, embroidery and tapestries in the world; this collection alone is worth the visit.

A few metres before the theatre and also on Avenida Hidalgo is the **Portal de Rosales**, a former Augustinian monastery later used by the Spanish to stockpile munitions during the long fight for Mexico's Independence. In 1813, the insurgent Victor Rosales made a daring strike and captured the building and its arms. Rosales was later killed, but the action gave the rebels a moral boost (and many weapons) to continue the fight. Converted to a market soon after Independence, it is a perfect example of post-Independence architecture.

The **Palacio Legislativo** ⓘ *Fernando Villalpando s/n*, was constructed of fine local marble in only 1984-1985, but it blends in seamlessly with Zacatecas' colonial architecture and ambiance. There are murals inside by Alejandro Navas. The main hall is roofed with an amazing stained-glass window by Pedro Coronel.

The imposing Jesuit church of **Santo Domingo** ⓘ *Fernando Villalpando esq Plazuela Santo Domingo, T492-922 1083, daily 0700-1300 and 1700-2030*, built 1746-1749, features eight gorgeous baroque *retablos* (see also the frescoes in the sacristy by Francisco Martínez; ask the sacristan to turn the lights on). It is the oldest church in continual existence (apart from a brief period after the expulsion of the Jesuits) in the city.

A much newer construction, and some say the most beautiful church in town, is the **Templo de Fátima** ⓘ *behind the Francisco Goitia Museum (see below) in the Sierra de Alicia neighbourhood*, begun in 1950 and finished exactly a half-century later. This spectacular, staggered-steeple Gothic Revival jewel, constructed of orange-pink marble from nearby quarries, took so long to build because it was paid for by its parishioners. While out of the centre, the famous **Capilla de Los Remedios** or Sanctuario del Patrocinio (1728), at the very top of the Cerro de la Bufa (see below), is one of Zacatecas' most important religious monuments and a well-known shrine. In it is Zacatecas' most treasured image, a small statue of the Virgin known as El Patrocinio ('The Patron'). Every year between 3-15

Gorditas Doña Julia **7**
La Crêperie **21**
La Gaviota **13**
La Leyenda **18**
La Traviata **19**
La Unica Cabaña **9**
Locanda la Tana **20**

El Recoveco **10**
Sanborn's **14**
Trattoria Il Goloso **4**
Unagui Sushi **2**
VIPs **3**

September thousands of *zacatecanos* visit the shrine, many making there way on their knees up the steep gradient of the Bufa.

The **Mina del Edén** ① *Av Torreón y Quebradilla, western side of town, daily 1000-1800, US$2.50*, is an old mine with a short section of mine railway in operation. The tour is in Spanish and lasts one hour. In the mine there is also a disco on Thursday, Friday and Saturday 2200-0230, with varied music. You can leave the mine the way you went in or work your way through to the end and the Swiss-built **El Teleférico**, a cable car which carries you over the city, with spectacular views, to Cerro de la Bufa and the Capilla de Los Remedios.

On the Cerro de la Bufa, best visited after going through Mina El Edén and El Teleférico, is **Museo de la Toma de Zacatecas** ① *T492-922 8066, daily 1000-1700, US$2.25*. Built on the grounds of the former state asylum, the museum commemorates Pancho Villa's victory over Huerta's forces in 1914.

The hill, northeast of the centre, is recommended for views over the city. It is a pleasant walk, although crowded on Sundays. There are equestrian bronze statues of Villa and his generals Angeles and Natera, an observatory and the **Mausoleo de Los Hombres Ilustres** (US$0.15) as well as several food stands. It's a 10- or 15-minute walk back down if you follow the Stations of the Cross.

Located in the former Jesuit colegio and dating to 1646, **Museo Pedro Coronel** ① *Plaza Santo Domingo, T492-924 1663, Fri-Wed 1000-1700, US$3*, houses an excellent collection of European and modern art (including the largest collection of Goya and Miró outside of the Prado in Madrid, and several by Hogarth, Daumier and Picasso), as well as folk art from Mexico and around the world. All of these pieces – nearly 1500 in total – were gathered together by Pedro Coronel (to whose life and art a room is dedicated). There are also unique collections of coins and pre-Hispanic pipes, as well as the Elías Amador Library, which houses more than 20,000 rare texts from the 16th century through to the 19th century.

To the north of the centre is the **Museo Rafael Coronel** ① *in the Antiguo Convento de San Francisco, T492-922 8116, Thu-Tue, 1000-1630, US$3*. As if the Museo Pedro Coronel (see above) were not enough testament to one family, this mega-museum was once the collection of his brother Rafael. This wonderful old ex-monastery (dating to the 16th century) holds the world's largest collection of masks and puppets, primarily Mexican, an astonishing collection of pre-Columbian ceramics, some extremely rare Japanese scrolls, silver and tableware from the Manila Galleon trade, beautiful Porfiriato marble sculptures and wrought iron work, and has an attractive garden perfect for a small picnic. What's more, in a separate part of the building (the former sacristy) but still part of the museum, is one of the largest historical archives in the country: a priceless record of the city and country's colonial past; and the **Ruth Rivera Gallery**, containing works by Diego Rivera, José Chávez Morado and Nahuli Ollin, amongst many others. There is also a **Pre-Hispanic Art Gallery** and a **Folk Art Gallery**.

Heading south, near the fine old Acueducto El Cubo, is the **Museo Francisco Goitia** ① *Gen Enrique Estrada 102, T492-922 0211, Tue-Sun 1000-1700, www.museofranciscogoitia. com, US$3*, housed in what was once the governor's mansion, by the Parque General Enrique Estrada. The museum has modern paintings by *zacatecanos*, many of whom are acknowledged as the greatest artists of 20th-century Mexico. Its main attractions are the paintings of small-town poverty in Mexico by Goitia, who was born in nearby Patillos.

Outside of the centre, the **Centro Platero de Zacatecas** (Silver Centre of Zacatecas), ① *Guadalupe, off of Av Pedro Coronel, T492- 899 4503, daily 1000-1800*, is well worth a visit. For centuries Zacatecas led New Spain in the output of silver, and even now several of its mines still operate. While Taxco is better known outside of Mexico for silver, it pales in comparison to what Zacatecas offers. Prices are more reasonable here as well.

Around Zacatecas ⊖ ↠ *pp402-406*.

Convento de Guadalupe

ⓘ *Jardín Juárez Oriente s/n, 7 km to the east along the Blv López Portillo, T492-923 2386. Daily 1000-1630. US$2.25. To get there, take bus No 13 from López Mateos y Salazar, near the terminal, US$0.15, 20 mins.*

The Convento de Guadalupe is a national monument, with a fine church and convent, which now houses a world-class **Museum of Colonial Religious Art**, one of the largest in the western hemisphere and second only to the National Museum of San Carlos in Mexico City. The galleries of the convent are full of baroque paintings covering the life of St Francis and huge frescoes. Virtually every artist of note from viceregal Spain is represented. In addition to the unparalleled paintings and sculptures, there are also priceless collections of feather art and books dating to the 16th century. Every September the museum plays host to the famed **Baroque Festival**. The labyrinthine convent is well worth a visit and the church contains the Virgin as a child set in gold.

Museo Arqueológico La Quemada

ⓘ *56 km south on Route 54. Daily 1000-1600. US$3.85. If going by bus, take the 0800 or 1100 Línea Verde bus from the main terminal to Adjuntas (about 45 mins, US$0.60), on the Villanueva road. For the return from the junction at Adjuntas, wait for a bus back to Zacatecas.*

Also worth a visit, the Museo Arqueológico La Quemada, encompasses the Chicomostoc ruins, better known as La Quemada. It's a 30-minute walk through beautiful, silent, nopal cactus scenery to the ruins, which offer an impressive view. There is the **Palace of the Eleven Columns**, a **Pyramid of the Sun** and other remains on a rocky outcrop, in various stages of restoration. The museum itself has videos, maps, drawings and dioramas on the three main Classical period cultures (Loma de San Gabriel, Chalchihuites and Malpaso) that at one time or another inhabited the area. The museum also features an extensive collection of ceramics and stone tools. There are also workshops on site for traditional crafts, ranging from pottery to basket weaving. In themselves the ruins are not spectacular, but together with the setting they are worth the trip.

Jerez de García Salinas

Jerez de García Salinas is an old colonial town about 56 km from Zacatecas, where the wide-brimmed sombrero *charro* and *serape* are still occasionally worn. While travel is no longer as often on horseback as by car in this *pueblo magico* (the only one in the state of Zacatecas), it retains an almost tangible 'old Mexico' feel to it. There are two interesting churches in the town. **La Soledad**, begun in 1805 and completed later that century, has a baroque facade and three elaborate gateways – composites of all manner of over-the-top classical styles. **La Inmaculada** (1727), also has a baroque facade but with a neo-Romanesque interior. Also in the historic centre are the beautiful **De La Torre House** (now the town's cultural activities centre), the grand Victorian **Hinojosa Theatre** (which has a tiny and rather eclectic museum to the left; the curator will offer tours of the theatre), and the exquisite **Rafael Páez Garden**, with its architectural homage to Ramón López Velarde, one of Mexico's most beloved poets and author of its national anthem, *La Patria Suave*. Nowadays Jerez is most famous for its ice creams, which here are known as *nieves* and differ from those found elsewhere in the heartland.

Hollywood comes to town: Sierra de los Órganos

One of Hollywood's best-kept secrets lies about 1600 km southeast of its fabled studio lots and million-dollar mansions, in a remote and dusty corner of the State of Zacatecas. Here, in the state's extreme northwest and just 30 km outside of the picturesque town of Sombrerete, the quintessential Western movie set is found in the Sierra de los Órganos. Designated a national park in 2000, it is an eerie desert landscape that looks as though it might have seen the likes of John Wayne, Brad Pitt or Salma Hayek, which in fact it has (and many others as well). Long a favourite location to shoot stereotypical Westerns (*The Cisco Kid* and *The Guns of San Sebastian* were filmed here, as were the more recent releases *Bandidas* and *Dragonball Evolution*), the park is named not for pipe organ cacti – found only in Sonora State – but for its mysterious rock formations, some of which look like, well, organ pipes. These wind-carved monuments are its most arresting features.

It's also a great spot for taking in what for many is the archetypal image of interior Mexico: hot, dry, and dusty, with only the silence and blue sky for company.

The park is open all year, and there are a handful of *cabañas* for rent, but for the most part you are on your own, so bring water and food if you intend to tackle the ridges. Camping, low-impact trekking, and off-road biking are options in the Sierra de los Órganos, but for most visitors, it's a chance to break the long journey between Zacatecas and Durango in a serene if somewhat otherworldly setting. But don't be alarmed if your peaceful afternoon is suddenly interrupted by a Hollywood film crew with celebrities in tow. It wouldn't be the first time it's happened here!

Sombrerete

Sombrerete, founded in 1555 by Juan de la Tolosa (who also co-founded Zacatecas), is a beautiful little town steeped in history, some 172 km northwest of Zacatecas on Route 45 over a good road the entire way (US$0.80 toll when passing the *caseta* in Fresnillo). It is considered the second most beautiful town in the state behind only the capital, and shares many of its architectural and cultural characteristics. The **Templo de la Tercera Orden** (church of the Third Order) is unique in Mexico as the only church built in Renaissance style. For those wishing to see what Zacatecas was like a few decades ago, this is the place to go. It is also the gateway to the Sierra de Órganos, where several Hollywood 'Westerns' have been filmed, see box above.

◉ Zacatecas and around listings

For Sleeping and Eating price codes and other relevant information, see Essentials pages 47-51.

◉ Sleeping

Zacatecas *p396, map p398*
Accommodation at any level during **Semana Santa** and often during the **feria** in Sep are almost impossible to book without advance reservations. Generally the best deals are found in the **C** range *hostales* located in the Centro Histórico but not along Av Hidalgo itself.
L Hacienda del Bosque, Héroes del Chapultepec 801, T492-924 6666, http://hacienda.hotelesdelbosque.com.mx. Beautiful hotel with quiet elegance and peaceful atmosphere, pleasant grounds. Out of the city, with lovely views. Bilingual staff, nice rooms and superior furnishings. Popular for conventions, so check in advance.

L Hostal del Rio, Hidalgo 116, at epicentre of Centro Histórico, T492-924 0035. Very small (10 rooms), smart rooms and great service.

L Mesón de Jobito, Jardín Juárez 143, near Centro Histórico, T492-924 1722, www.meson dejobito.com. Small, select and very stylish hotel, attractive restaurant with international and Mexican cuisine.

L Quinta Real, Av Rayón 434, T492-922 9104, www.quintareal.com. Beautiful hotel built around the old bullring (said to be the 2nd oldest in Latin America); the aqueduct goes past the front door. Excellent.

AL Santa Rita, Av Hidalgo 507A, T492-925 1194, www.hotelsantarita.com. Zacatecas' newest hotel is one of its best, with a great location in the centre, an award-winning restaurant, an innovative floor plan (reception on the 2nd floor), spacious rooms and a Starbucks. Currently the hotel of choice for the fashionable set.

B Casa Santa Lucía, Av Hidalgo 717, T492-922 0859, www.casasantalucia.com. Boutique hotel fashioned from renovated casona. Very popular with tourists and couples. Excellent service and gaining recognition as best up-and-coming hotel in town.

B Condesa, opposite Posada de los Condes (below), Av Juárez 102, T492-922 1160, www.hotelcondesa.com.mx. OK, quiet with good views of Cerro de la Bufa, cheap restaurant.

B Posada Tolosa, Juan de Tolosa 811, also in Centro Histórico, T492-922 5105, www.hotel posadatolosa.com. Quiet, large rooms, group rates.

B-C Mesón de la Merced, Av Juárez 114, T492-922 6370, www.donmiguel.com.mx/mm. In the centre, recently renovated, attractive terrace and ample rooms. Parking can be a problem, but pleasant interior and good location make up for it.

C Argento Inn, Av Hidalgo 407, T492-925 1718. On the high street. Restaurant/bar, small business centre, smallish rooms but beautiful interior patio and fountain. Very authentic colonial period furnishings. Probably the best in its range.

C Casa Real, Blv López Portillo 12 (in next door Guadalupe), T492-923 4282. Woeful-looking exterior, but overlooks park and rooms, albeit featureless, are quite large. A/c, TV and private baths.

C Colón, Av López Velarde 508 (Colonia Barrio La Paz), near old bus station, T492-922 8925. Clean, with showers.

C Hostal San Francisco, Del Angel 415, Centro Histórico, T492-925 3974, www.hostalsanfrancisco.com.mx. Eco-friendly suites, extended-stay discounts.

C Hostal Reyna Soledad, Tacuba 170, T492-922 0790. Great little boutique hotel just behind the old Mercado Central. A bit noisy and rooms are of varying sizes (ask to see at least 2 before choosing) but has a great atmosphere. Recommended.

C-D Hostal Villa Colonial, 1 de Mayo y Callejón Mono Prieto, just south of the cathedral, right in the historic centre, T/F492-922 1980. Shared bath in a mix of dorms and private rooms. Great views from the rooftop patio. Kitchen, internet access. Good deal, recommended.

D Las Cuevas, Callejón Lancaster 109, T492-925 4135. Colonial style hotel with 12 rooms off of side street in centre. No parking, few amenities, but friendly, clean and helpful to a fault.

Camping

Morelos Trailer Park, behind the Pemex at Morelos junction, T492-931 0367, US$6, about 20 mins northwest of the city, where Route 54 Saltillo-Guadalajara crosses Route 49. Very barren and unappealing, but has 18 hook-ups, and will do for a single night.

Jerez de García Salinas p401

C Leo, Calzada Suave Patria s/n, T494-945 2001. Outside of centre a bit but with more amenities than any other lodging in town. Quiet and clean.

C Posada Santa Cecilia, Constitución y San Francisco 4, T494-945 2412. Old style, pleasant atmosphere, inexpensive.

🔴 Eating

Zacatecas p396, map p398

🍴🍴 **El Mesón del Taco**, Dr Hierro 604, T492-922 2050. Absolutely the best tacos in the city, period, many unique or Spanish (as opposed to Mexican). Expensive but well worth it.

🍴🍴 **El Paraíso**, Av Hidalgo y Plaza Goitia (at the corner of the market), T492-922 6164. Closed Sun. Bar/restaurant, good atmosphere.

🍴🍴 **La Gaviota**, Callejón de Rosales 101 upstairs, T492-925 4040. Brilliant decor, exemplary service. Best seafood restaurant in the region.

🍴🍴 **La Leyenda**, Segunda de Matamoros 216, T492-922 3853. The city's best restaurant with avant-garde ambiance and fantastic local cuisine and seafood. Beware of very spicy fish dishes: delicious but extremely hot.

🍴🍴-🍴 **Garufa**, Callejón de Cuevas, T492-924 2910. Argentine food, alfresco, charming atmosphere, popular with tourists.

🍴🍴-🍴 **La Crêperie**, Tacuba 204, T492-925 2161, www.lacreperiegourmet.com. Wonderful, tiny Parisian-style restaurant, decorated with French posters and postcards, specializing in crêpes, fondues and quiche. Can be expensive but well worth it. Highly recommended.

🍴🍴-🍴 **La Traviata**, Callejón de Cuevas 109, T492-924 2030. Wonderful Italian dishes. Outside seating, smart interior and bar.

🍴🍴-🍴 **Trattoria Il Goloso**, Dr Hierro 400, T492-125 3354. Of the city's many fine Italian restaurants, this one may be the best (frequented by Zacatecas' small expatriate Italian community), and certainly is the most authentic. Highly recommended.

🍴🍴-🍴 **Unagui Sushi**, Blv López Portillo 103C, T492-923-7900. Best Japanese food in town.

🍴🍴-🍴 **VIPS**, popular chain with 3 locations in Zacatecas, including at Av González Ortega 203, T492-924 0267. Very clean, although service can be slow. Mexican, North American and local dishes.

🍴 **Cazadores**, Callejón de la Palma 104, T492-022 0382. Good Mexican, many local specialities. Very popular with locals.

🍴 **El Pueblito**, Hidalgo 802, T492-924 3818, www.travelbymexico.com/zaca/elpueblito.

Open daily. Typical Mexican food and bar in colourful old *casona*. A bit on the touristy side, but clean and cheap.

🍴 **El Recoveco**, Torreon 413 (facing the Alameda), T492-924 2013. All-you-can eat buffets, good veggie options, good wholesome food. Cheap.

🍴 **Florencia Pizzas**, off Genaro Codina, T492-925 1241. Daily 0900-2300. Best pizza in town, in a charming little family-run establishment.

🍴 **Gorditas Doña Julia**, Av Hidalgo 409, T492-922 7109; also at Tacuba 72. Tasty and inexpensive typical Mexican. A local favourite and recommended.

🍴 **La Unica Cabaña**, Jardín de la Independencia. Cheap, excellent set meals.

🍴 **Locanda la Tana**, Genaro Codina 714, T492-925 4621. Sun-Fri 1330-1700, 1930-2200, Sat 1930-2200. Excellent Italian dishes made from scratch and good wine list.

Cafés

Acrópolis, Av Hidalgo s/n (opposite the cathedral and to the left of Mercado González Ortega), T492-922 1285. A 50-year-old café and diner, good breakfast (for which it is famous), slow service but great art inside.

Café Arlequín, Hidalgo 814, Much-loved café/lending library/mini art gallery and all-purpose gathering place for city's intellectuals (of which there are many).

Café Dali, Miguel Auza 322. Home-made sandwiches, plus great coffee in chic-funky ramshackle old building with great views of the centre. Recommended.

Emilia Café, Juan de Tolosa 902, T492-949 0611. Wonderful crêpes, flavoured coffees and teas, peaceful atmosphere, clean and pleasant all around. Highly recommended.

Healthfood store, Rayón 413. Excellent food at reasonable prices.

Sanborn's, Av Hidalgo 212 y Allende, 2nd floor, T492 922-1298. Coffees, deserts, and free internet access for patrons, with restaurant attached. There is a1950s-era shopping store on the 1st floor.

🎵 Bars and clubs

Zacatecas p396, map p398

Chinchin Camaron, Callejón de la Palma 108, T492-121 8151. Specializes in exotic, fruit-flavoured beers (lemon, coca, orange, *maracuyá*, guanabana, strawberry, etc), tacos and *ceviche*.

Cuco's, Alameda 404, T492-924 4333. Open very late. Infamous bar/dance floor popular with students, so very loud and crowded.

Huracán Superbar, Fernando Villalpando. If anything, even more over the top than Huracán Zote, below.

Huracán Zote, Genaro Codina 752. Trippy Mexican psychedelia in centre. Like something out of a 1960s movie about Carnaby Street. Completely out of place in Zacatecas, and drinks are expensive, but an absolute must-see all the same.

🎬 Entertainment

Zacatecas p396, map p398
Cultural centres
Alianza Francesa, Callejón del Santero 111, T492-924 0348. French films every Tue at 1900 (free), French lessons.

🎉 Festivals and events

Zacatecas p396, map p398
Mid-Mar Semana Santa (Holy Week) processions and events are innumerable and now world-famous as examples of customs that are extinct elsewhere in the country. The city population triples during the celebrations. Many of the events are publicized only on the doors of its churches.

The Festival Cultural, which usually runs alongside Semana Santa and spills over into the following week, is now Mexico's most popular festival, transforming the city into a 2-week-long 24-hr extravaganza with a large number of free events.

Jun Folklore Festival, very popular.

Sep The national fiesta, based at the Lienzo Charro 5 km east out of town, lasts for the entire month. There are bullfights and *charrarías* (some of the best anywhere in Mexico) on Sun, but given the growth in popularity of this very traditional fiesta you could stumble across an impromptu celebration at any time of year.

Also in Sep is an agricultural fair, held at the same fairgrounds. In nextdoor Guadalupe, the annual Baroque Music Festival is held at the Museo de Gualdalupe.

🛍 Shopping

Zacatecas p396, map p398
Bookshops
Zacatecas has innumerable bookstores scattered throughout the Centro Histórico. The best known are Universal, Zacatecas, Cristal, Andrea and Educal.

Market
Between Hidalgo y Tacuba, the elegant 19th-century market building has been converted into a pleasant shopping centre (popular café on balcony). The market is now dispersed in various locations a few blocks to the southwest. Zacatecas has 2 delicacies: the local cheese, and queso de tuna, a candy made from the fruit of the nopal cactus (don't eat too much, as it has powerful laxative properties). There are many shops along Av Hidalgo that sell excellent silver, which is still mined locally.

Silverwork
In the centre, built on the ruins of an 18th-century hacienda, there are dozens of small artisans' shops, each producing unique work and collectively ensuring that the silver-smithing traditions of Zacatecas are passed along. There are courses offered, several display rooms that form something akin to a silver museum (admission free), and of course all those shops. Some specialize in jewellery, others in functional pieces, still others in accessories or ornaments, and all do custom work.

▲ Activities and tours

Zacatecas *p396, map p398*
Language school
Fénix Language Institute, Ledezma 210, T492-922 1643, www.fenixlanguage institute.com.

Tour operators
Eme Agencias de Viajes, Av Hidalgo 411, T492-924 2447. All purpose with many city, local and countrywide tours.
Operadora Zacatecas, Hidalgo 630, T492-924 0050. The oldest in the city, offers several interesting tours.
Recepturz, Hidalgo 4, T492-925 2403. The major operator in region.
Viajes La Bufa, Félix U Gómez 609A, T492-922 1130. Certified nationally, good reputation for packaged and personalized tours at all levels. Highly regarded.
Viajes Mazzoco, Blv López Portillo 746, T492-922 0859. Tours to Chicomostoc and Jerez, US$12.50.

⊖ Transport

Zacatecas *p396, map p398*
Air
Aeropuerto La Calera (ZCL), 27 km north of the city has daily flights to **Mexico City**, **Tijuana**, **Guadalajara**, **Ciudad Juárez**, **Monterrey**, **Morelia**, **Aguascalientes** and direct flights on American to a few US cities.
    Airline offices Avolar, T1-800-712-4078, www.avolar.com.mx. Mexicana, T492-922 3248.

Bus
The bus terminal is 4 km south of town; a taxi to/from the centre costs US$2; red No 8 buses leave from Plaza Independencia (US$0.15) or white *camionetas* from Av González Ortega (old bus station on Blv López Mateos only serves local destinations). Apart from buses to Mexico City, Chihuahua and a few other

major towns, most routes do not have bookable seats. Frequent buses passing through Jerez back to **Zacatecas** with Rojo de Los Altos, US$2.40.
    To **Aguascalientes**, every 30 mins, 2½ hrs, US$6.85. To **Chihuahua**, via **Torreón**, 12 hrs, US$44. To **Durango**, 5 hrs, many throughout the day, US$14-16 (if continuing to Mazatlán, stay the night in Durango in order not to miss the views on the way to the coast). To **Guadalajara**, hourly, 4 hrs, US$21. To **Hidalgo del Parral**, 10 hrs, US$40. To **León**, 3½ hrs, US$15.60. To **Mexico City**, almost hourly, 8 hrs, US$38. To **San Luis Potosí**, 7 daily, 2½ hrs, US$7.

● Directory

Zacatecas *p396, map p398*
Banks Banamex, Av Hidalgo. Banorte, offices all over town and in next door Guadalupe as well. Bancomer, Av Hidalgo, has a Visa cash dispenser and gives cash (pesos) on Visa cards. HBSC, Av Hidalgo. Santander, Av Hidalgo. Several other banks with ATMs on Av Hidalgo. *Casa de cambio* next door to post office (see below) has excellent exchange rates. **Internet** Café@rroba, Félix U Gómez 520B, daily 0900-2200. @Internet, Hidalgo 737, daily. Cybertech, Hidalgo 771, T492-922 0870, Mon-Sat 0930-2130. Dozens of others scattered throughout centre. **Laundry** At the north end of town are Lavandería El Indio Triste, Juan de Tolosa 828 and Lavasolo, similar prices. Pressto, Av Pedro Coronel 31A (in next-door Guadalupe), T492-998 0908, outstanding laundry and dry cleaning with next-day service. **Medical services** Santa Elena Clinic, Av Guerrero, many specialists, consultation, US$12.50. **Post office** Allende entre Independencia y Hidalgo, across from Sanborn's. **Telephone** (also Western Union money transfer office, for which passport required) Telégrafos, Av Hidalgo y Juárez.

Contents

Footprint features

Michoacán

At a glance

⊖ **Getting around** Bus, combi, mule and boat.

◉ **Time required** 10 days for the main sights, 3 weeks or more for a thorough exploration.

☽ **Weather** The coast tends to hotter and more humid than inland areas, whilst the mountains can be chilly in the evening, especially Nov-Feb. Otherwise Michoacán follows a temperate pattern with cool winters and warm summers.

✖ **When not to go** Avoid visiting Apr-Oct if you want to see the butterflies. Pátzcuaro is swamped with Day of the Dead tourists from late Oct until the festival ends in early Nov.

The intensely mysterious and often overlooked state of Michoacán is steeped in the same archaic concerns that have governed its people for millennia. The health of the land, the approval of the ancestors, the cyclical motions of time, season and spirit – all remain critically important to the native Purépecha, a people directly descended from the ancient Tarascans. Against an age-old backdrop of tradition, family and wonderfully exuberant music, they produce the country's finest crafts and play host to some resplendent and evocative festivities, most notably Day of the Dead. But the cultural achievements of rural Michoacán are closely matched by its urban counterparts. The city of Morelia is a bastion of colonial beauty and power, indigenous Pátzcuaro is rich in textures and daily bustle, and off-beat Uruapan is a centre of agriculture and fine lacquer-work.

Michoacán's cultural gifts are complemented by its scintillating environmental diversity. In the east, the high-altitude Oyamel forests supply the perfect microclimate for migrating Monarch butterflies, which, in an unforgettable display of swirling colour, arrive each year in their millions. To the west, the undulating scenery offers fertile ground for untold fruits and vegetables – plantain, bananas, maize, mangos, watermelons, apples, pineapples, avocados and more – often overflowing from colourful village markets. It's no wonder Michoacán is known as the 'garden state'. Meanwhile the southern lowlands, sweltering and largely divorced from the outside world, offer a rustic retreat of empty beaches and end-of-the-world coastal communities barely touched by tourism. For those willing to break from the tourist mainstream, Michoacán's riches are many.

Eastern Michoacán

In eastern Michoacán, the urbane city of Morelia is replete with all the cultural attractions befitting a great state capital: captivating museums, historic churches, teeming grand plazas, and a seemingly insatiable array of ostentatious architecture. Here, each house relates some fragment of history and perhaps no figure has been more pivotal in this fantastic saga than Michoacán's most famous son - the Independence fighter José María Morelos, after whom Morelia is named. But beyond the state capital, rugged mountains and mist-swathed hills dominate the scenery, all punctuated by sleeping mining villages and indolent farming communities. This is the land of the Monarch butterflies, which conclude an astonishing annual migratory pilgrimage in the region's fragrant highland pines. The sight of them swirling in their thousands – like storms of ash and fire – is surely one of the world's most stunning natural phenomena, not to be missed. ➹ For listings, see pages 417-420.

Morelia ⊜⊘⊘▲⊖⊕ ➹ *pp417-420.*

Like all great university cities, Morelia boasts a wealth of grand historic architecture. An endless procession of graceful exuberant structures, al crafted from beautifully weathered pink sandstone, conspire to make this UNESCO World Heritage Site singularly aesthetic. Baroque facades, regal arches, palatial courtyards and exquisitely restored mansions are all imbued with the splendour and soaring intellectual ambitions of an age now past. Strolling through Morelia's Spanish-flavoured streets and plazas can be a refreshingly authentic and magical experience – particularly after dusk, when floodlights illuminate some of the city's most regal buildings. Undoubtedly, this is one of the finest colonial cities in Mexico, but for now, it is curiously divorced from the well-worn tourist track.

Ins and outs

Getting there The airport is about 27 km north of Morelia. Blue and white 'Aeropuerto' buses run to the centre. The new bus terminal is a long way from town. It is best to get a taxi for the 15- to 20-minute drive, around US$3; or take a local bus. Morelia is connected by Route 43 to Salamanca, Route 14 to Uruapan and Route 15 to Zamora and Mexico City. ➹ *See Transport, page 420.*

Getting around Morelia's downtown area is reasonably compact and grid-like, and therefore easily negotiable on foot. The cathedral and Plaza de Armas are its geographic centre, where the major east–west thoroughfare, Madero, changes its suffix from Oriente to Poniente (Ote to Pte). Morelos is an important north–south artery, which changes suffix (Nte to Sur) at Plaza Melchor Ocampo, just east of the Plaza de Armas.

Tourist information You'll find limited tourist information at the booths outside the cathedral. There is also an inconveniently located main **tourist office** ① *Tata Vasco 80, T443-317 8032, www.turismomichoacan.gob.mx, Mon-Fri 0800-2000, Sat and Sun 0900- 1900.* There are some good language schools in Morelia (see Activities and tours, page 419).

Safety In 2008-2009, Michoacán saw a surge in drug-related violence, including the gruesome murder of several police officers and a grenade attack on President Calderon's hometown, Morelia. The Mexican government responded by dispatching over 5000 troops to the region. At the time of research, the US State Department, www.travel.state.gov, was warning against all but essential travel to certain parts of the Michoacán. Travellers are advised to use common sense and check the safety situation before setting out.

Background

The city of Michoacán, later to become Morelia, was founded on 18 May 1541 by Antonio de Mendoza, the first viceroy of New Spain. From its outset, it was assuredly Spanish in sentiment, its first inhabitants comprising some 50 Spanish noble families and their Purépecha servants. In 1545 the city was renamed Valladolid, after its Spanish counterpart. In 1547 it was granted city status, and in 1533, a coat of arms.

However, Valladolid was not yet the capital of Michoacán, for that role had been assigned to Pátzcuaro, where Bishop Vasco de Quiroga had insisted upon taking his office. But six years after Quiroga's death in 1571, King Phillip II moved the seat of the bishopric to Valladolid, finally making it an Episcopal city. In 1580, it replaced Pátzcuaro as the capital.

During the colonial period, various religious orders set up in Valladolid, initiating a phase of growth and architectural splendour. During the War of Independence, José Maria Morelos – a poor *mestizo* son of the city – distinguished himself as a great commander and strategist. In his honour, Valladolid was renamed Morelia in 1828.

Morelia

Sleeping
Catedral 7
Colonial 5
Concordia 6
Fenix 8
Hostel Allende 9
Los Juaninos 3
Mintzicuri 10
Posada del Cortijo 11
Posada de la Soledad 4
Qualitel 2
Señorial 12

Eating
Boca del Río 1
Café Catedral 13
Café Colón 2
Café de Conservatorio 3
El Rincón de los Sentidos 4
La Flor de las Mercedes 5
Lilian's Coffee 6
Los Milagritos 7
Los Mirasoles 8
Los Pioneros 9
Mercado de Dulces 10
Michoacana 11
Viandas de San José 12

Plaza de Armas and around

At the heart of the city lies the Plaza de Armas, also known as the Plaza de los Martíres, flanked by grand historic structures, newspaper vendors, a procession of elegant *portales* and arcaded restaurants. The superb **cathedral** was built 1640-1744 and exhibits a range of styles – Herreresque, baroque and neoclassical – all blended harmoniously. Careful examination of the bell-towers reveals distinct periods of construction. The interior was heavily refurbished along neoclassical lines in the 19th century. During this time, most of the silver was removed and only a silver baroque showcase and neoclassical baptismal font remain, both dating to the 18th century. Particularly interesting is the original 16th century Lord of the Sacristy, crafted from dried maize and orchid nectar paste. The organ, boasting some 4600 pipes, is a 20th century addition.

Opposite the cathedral's northern face stands the **Palacio de Gobierno**, with a baroque facade and interior murals painted by Alfredo Zalce in 1961. Southwest of the Plaza de Armas lie a cluster of noteworthy sights, including the **Museo Michoacano** ① *Allende 305, Tue-Sat 0900-1900, Sun 0900-1600, US$2.30*, an 18th-century baroque palace where Emperor Maximilian I once stayed. The museum houses an array of archaeological artefacts from Tzintzuntzán and other Tarascan sites. Elsewhere you'll see murals and exhibitions dedicated to the colonial era. Just east of the museum, flanking the southern edge of the Plaza de Armas, stands the **Palacio de Justicia**, built in 1862 in French and baroque styles. Inside you'll find stairwell art by Agustín Cáredens and a small museum examining the state judiciary. A block south on Corregidora you'll find the **Antigua Alhóndiga**, the old public granary, now part of the Palace of Justice.

South of the cathedral

A block south of the cathedral is the **Casa Natal de Morelos** ① *Corregidora 113, 0900-1900, free*, birthplace of José Maria Morelos y Pavon, the legendary Independence hero who assumed leadership of the movement after his master and tutor, Miguel Hidalgo, was executed. The original house was shamefully demolished in 1888 and the present structure was constructed soon after. It has a baroque exterior and neoclassical interior. Next door stands the 16th-century **Templo de Agustinos** with a plateresque facade; it houses the Sacred Virgin of Socorro. A block east of Morelos' birthplace stands his house, **Casa de Morelos** ① *Morelos Sur 323, 0900-1900, US$2*, a baroque mansion built in 1758 and acquired by Morelos in 1801. It contains a modest displays of antiques, historical documents, photographs and paintings.

West on Madero

West of the Plaza de Armas on Madero are several fine buildings worth checking out. The first structure you'll pass is the modern **Centro Cultural Universitario** ① *Mon-Sat 1000-1400 and 1600-2000*, which regularly hosts cultural events. Directly opposite stands the 16th-century **Colegio de San Nicolás de Hidalgo**, the former Valladolid campus of the School of San Nicolas, founded by Bishop Vasco de Quiroga in Pátzcuaro. Hidalgo served as its rector and none other than Morelos studied here. Today it houses government and administrative offices. Nearby, at the intersection of Nigromante and Madero Pte, it's worth taking a a quick detour, one block south, to check out the handsome 18th-century **Palacio Municipal**, complete with an elegant octagonal courtyard. The structure originally served as a tobacco warehouse until becoming the municipal palace in 1859.

Continuing west on Madero, you'll pass the neoclassical **Casa de Mariano Michelena**, a one-time home of Hidalgo that was later acquired by Mariano Michelena, who later

The good bishop

After the brutal disaster of Mexico's first *audencia*, in which the peoples of Michoacán were ruthlessly tortured and killed, the Spanish crown was determined to send only the most humane and trustworthy persons to represent their colony. Bishop Vasco de Quiroga was chief among them – a humble and progressive Christian who orchestrated a legendary experiment in social Utopianism, the legacy of which survives today.

Vasco de Quiroga was born in the village of Madrigal de las Atlas Torres in 1470. The son of nobility, he went on to serve as a lawyer in Salamanca, only joining the church relatively late in life. Regardless, he progressed rapidly. In 1531 he joined Mexico's second *audencia* and assumed the bishopric of Michoacán, basing himself in Pátzcuaro.

Inspired by the ideals of Sir Thomas More, Quiroga set about fashioning his social Utopia. Empowering the lakeside villages through principles of self-government and self-sufficiency, he built untold schools, hospitals and churches. Throughout his tenure he was a champion of indigenous rights, much loved by his congregation who affectionately called him 'Tata' (father). Quiroga lived to be 90 but his legacy lives on. Having supplied the locals with tools and training, the resplendent craft traditions for which Michoacán are so famous are yet another enduring feature of his good work. God bless Tata Vasco!

---

charitably relinquished it to the state. Opposite stands the **Biblioteca Pública**, the handsome public library dating from the 17th century. It was originally the church of the **Fellowship of Jesus**. Directly behind the library stands one of the city's finest structures - the mid-17th century baroque **Palacio Clavijero**, former headquarters of the Jesuit school of San Fransisco Javier. It later served as a correctional facility for priests before becoming the home of the Congress of Michoacán in 1824. To the west, right next door, is the **Mercado de Ducles y Artesanias**, with ultra-sweet sugary treats and a range of crafts. One block further west on Madero stands the former 17th-century monastery, **Templo de la Merced**, with plateresque elements, an attractive tower and bulging *estípites* (inverted pyramidal supports).

Jardín de las Rosas

A block north of the Colegio de San Nicolas, at the end of Nigromante, the agreeable Jardín de las Rosas is a great place to sip coffee, relax and watch the world go by. Here, the elegant 18th-century baroque temple and music academy, **Templo y Conservatorio de Música de las Rosas**, sometimes hosts classical performances, as well as the famous Boys Choir of Morelia. The nearby **Museo del Estado** ① *Prieto 176, Mon-Fri 0900-2000, Sat and Sun 0900-1400 and 1400-1900, free*, is housed in an 18th-century mansion and contains displays on the archaeology, history and ethnology of Michoacán. Its mask collection is particularly interesting.

Plaza del Carmen Ruíz and around

A few blocks northeast of the Plaza de Armas stands the Plaza del Carmen Ruíz, surrounded by a handful of mildly diverting attractions. The handsome **ex-Convento del Carmen** is a baroque structure begun in 1593 with subsequent editions between the 17th and 19th centuries. It is now the **Casa de la Cultura** and Michoacán's main cultural centre, with regular events, workshops, exhibition halls and a small museum of masks. The church sacristy contains sombre works of art. On the south side of the plaza, the **Museo de Arte Colonial** ⓘ *Juárez 240, 0900-1900, free*, contains grizzly crucifixes in the usual brutal Catholic style of adoration. Just west stand two more baroque buildings: the **ex-Obispado**, the former bishops' residence, now home to the Secretary of Health; and the **Sanatorio del Sagrado Corozón**, the sacred heart hospital and one-time prison for heroes of the Independence movement.

East on Madero

East of the Plaza de Armas on Madero, a number of historic buildings have been restored and converted to commercial or governmental uses. After the Palacio de Gobierno, the first you'll see is the **Antigua Casa de Gabirel García Obeso** with a baroque interior and neoclassical facade, where much plotting took place during the Independence insurgency. It's now home to a branch of **Bancomer**. Next door, the **Banamex** is housed in the **Antigua Casa del Diezmo**, another baroque building that has variously served as a bishopric residence, offices, an inn and a hotel. Opposite you'll see the eclectic **Antiguo Hospital de los Juaninos**, built in 1785 as the Episcopal house. Continuing east, you'll next pass the **Antigua Casa del Intendent José Anzorena**, a French-style building that once housed the state legislature offices. Soon after comes the **Casa del Conde Sierra Gorda**, an 18th-century structure that now houses some administrative offices of the education secretary. Diagonally opposite, the **Templo de la Cruz** is a small, simple chapel dating to the 17th century. Further east on Madero, the **Templo de las Monjas**, built 1729-1737, belonged to an order of nuns called the Catarinas. Right next door, the **Palacio Federal** also served as a convent before government offices relocated here in 1935. The exterior boasts 18th-century French elements. If you're still hungry for historical architecture, head north a couple of blocks on Serapio Rendón, where you'll find the baroque **Templo de San José** and the 19th-century **Seminario Tridentino**, now a high school.

Plaza Valladolid and around

Several blocks east of the Plaza de Armas and one block south of Madero Ote, Plaza Valladolid is home to the handsome 16th-century **Templo de San Fransisco**. Its adjoining monastery has been converted into a superb craft market, **Casa de Artesanías** ⓘ *Mon-Sat 0900-2000, Sun 0900-1530, free*, which should not be missed. Stalls downstairs contain fine works from all over Michoacán, including pottery, lacquerwork, woodcarving, jewellery, blankets, masks, musical instruments and more. The upper floor has sections devoted to particular villages and you can often see craftspeople at work. Prices – and corresponding quality – tend to be high. Four blocks south of the Plaza Valladolid stands the **Iglesia de Capuchinas** ⓘ *Ortega y Montañez*, built 1680-1737 as a residence for the daughters of indigenous leaders. It is baroque in style and also features some churrigueresque *retablos*.

El Acueducto

Several blocks east of the Plaza de Armas, Madero Ote arrives at the **Plaza Villalongín**, named after an insurgent hero who rescued his wife from Las Animas prison. An intersection of several roads is marked by **Las Tarascas**, an exuberant fountain featuring three topless indigenous women with a large basket of tropical fruit. From here **el acueducto**, the city aqueduct, ordered by Bishop Friar Antonio de San Miguel in 1785, reaches east with some 253 arches. Formerly, it brought fresh spring water from the surrounding hills. Following its course, **Calzada Fray Antonio de San Miguel** is a pedestrian street flanked by regal 18th- and 19th-century mansions. It soon leads to **Plaza Morelos**, marked by statue of the Independence hero on horseback, the garishly adorned **Santuario de Guadalupe**, and the **Ex-Convento de San Diego**, home of the university's law faculty. South of the plaza you'll find the **Museo de Arte Contemporáneo Alfredo Zalce** ① *Acueducto 18, Tue-Sun 1000-1800, free*, a 19th-century structure with changing art exhibitions. Directly behind it stands the shady park space of **Bosque Cuauhtémoc**.

Around Morelia

Just north of Morelia there is a good road to two lakeside villages in the neighbouring state of Guanajuato. At the first, **Cuitzeo**, there is a fine Augustinian church and convent (begun in 1550), with a cloister, a huge open chapel, and good choir stalls in the sacristy. The church houses a collection of Mexican graphic art, spanning four centuries, in a gallery in the basement. **Laguna de Cuitzeo**, beside which it stands, is the second largest lake in Mexico; the road crosses it on a causeway. From here one can go through the attractive mountain scenery around **Valle de Santiago**. The second village, 33 km to the north, **Yuriria**, has a large-scale indigenous version of the splendid church and convent at Actopan. It is on **Laguna de Yuriria**, which looks like a grassy swamp.

Santuario de la Mariposa Monarca
① *The reserve is open mid-Nov to mid-Mar, 0900-1800. US$3 plus a tip for the guide.*
The high-altitude Oyamel forest of eastern Michoacán are the setting for one of the nature's most awesome spectacles. Each year, after travelling over 3000 km from their summer-time habitats in southeastern Canada, over 150 million Monarch butterflies arrive en masse. Filling the sky like clouds of orange ash, pouring over the valleys in their thousands and coating the fir trees in vast fiery bunches, the Monarchs leave burning impressions on all who witness them. Protected by the 563 km Santuario de la Mariposa Monarca, the butterflies can be visited mid-November to mid-March, but most activity in January and February when the swarms resemble dense sandstorms. There are various public sections of the reserve with El Rosario the most popular and easiest to reach (see below). Other possibilities include Sierra Chincua and Cerro Pellón. You can visit the reserve as a day trip from Mexico City or Morelia, but as this involves several hours of travel, it is not particularly recommended. Better to stay overnight in one of the nearby towns of Angangueo or Zitácuaro and visit the reserve in the early morning when tourists are sparse. As the day progresses and the air warms, the butterflies become more active. But during the hottest part of the day they settle on the forest floor in a deep, flaming, orange carpet. All visits to the habitats must be guided and require a moderate to challenging hike uphill.

Zitácuaro and around
On the eastern fringes of Michoacán lies Zitácuaro, a small, bustling town whose name means 'Place of Ropes'. It was destroyed twice during the Independence War, and again in the French intervention. The **tourist office** ① *T715-153 0675, www.zitacuaro.gob.com.mx*, is at Km 4 on the Zitácuaro-Toluca road.

There's not much to do in town, but it's warm and friendly enough, and if you're using public transport to reach the butterfly reserve at El Rosario (see below), you'll have to pass through. From the bus station, catch a local bus towards Angangueo and exit at Ocampo, 20 km away, where trucks and *combis* make the trip to the reserve (see Transport, page 420).

The incredible journey

Revered as the souls of dead warriors in transit, butterflies have always had a special place in the mythology of Michoacán's indigenous groups. It is therefore a striking coincidence that the arrival of the Monarch butterflies in early November runs parallel to the deeply felt Day of the Dead festival – a time when the spirits of the deceased travel from the underworld to spend time with their families and loved ones.

Indeed, the phenomenal 4500-km migratory journey of the Monarch butterflies runs, quite literally, from life to death and back again. They commence their odyssey in the great lakes region of southeastern Canada, and travelling south at a speed of 12 kph, arrive at the Oyamel forests of eastern Michoacán after some five weeks. These high altitude microclimates are perfectly attuned to their needs: the cool temperatures help them conserve energy and the rolling fog helps maintain their moisture levels.

They remain in the forests throughout the winter and start reproducing in spring. The females mate with many partners and the males, having served their biological purpose, die immediately afterwards. Having laid their eggs in the emergent spring milkweed (principal diet of the monarch), the females too will die. It is left to a new generation to travel north back to Canada, where they too will shortly reproduce and expire, leaving a third generation to travel south and complete the cycle. How each generation knows where to migrate is a mystery, but some believe the secret may be encoded in their DNA.

Both the age-old traditions of the Purépecha and the migratory behaviour of the Monarch butterfly seem to exalt the primacy of ancestral heritage. More than this, both phenomena are replete with powerful symbols of transformation and journey, life and death, cyclical progressions and mystery. Observing the ethereal flight of the monarch butterflies, it is easy to imbue them with transcendental characteristics. It doesn't take a great leap of poetic thought to imagine these could well be ancient Tarascan spirits in transit, just as the myths suggest.

Zitácuaro is also a good jumping-off point for the reserve at Cerro Pellón in the adjacent state of México. This is an alternative sanctuary that sees far less tourists than El Rosario, although it lacks services and is a little more complicated to reach. To get to Cerro Pellon, catch an 'Aputzio' bus to the state border, then take a taxi to either Macheros or El Capulín, both feasible entry points. Mules and guides will escort you into the mountains, US$15-30, up to two hours away, to see the butterflies.

El Rosario

El Rosario is a small village at the entrance to the most popular section of the butterfly reserve. To get there, travel first to Zitácuaro and then to Ocampo, where minibuses and taxis climb into the hills and drop you at the reserve car park. From the car park, follow the steps upwards where you will pass a procession of souvenir shops and simple eateries. Once you reach the reserve and pay the entrance fee, you will be assigned a guide to lead you to the butterfly habitats. The guides should be able to tell you about the life cycle and biology of the Monarchs, but some may speak Spanish only. If you miss anything, there's a small museum at the reserve entrance. The ascent to reach the habitats is reasonably challenging, especially if you're not acclimatized to the altitude. It takes 30-45 minutes to reach a clearing where swarms of butterflies fill the air. The sound of their wings – rippling and purring in their millions – is a truly surreal experience. The tour concludes with a visit to a forest colony where the butterflies weigh down the branches in dense clusters.

Angangueo and around

Some 30 km north of Zitacuaro and 10 km north of Ocampo lies the sleepy mountain mining town of **Angangueo**. At an elevation of 2580 m, it is significantly cooler than Zitácuaro, but also more natural and interesting, and many international travellers stop here on their way to visit the butterflies. Pack a sweater if you intend to do the same. To reach El Rosario from Angangueo, backtrack to Ocampo and catch a *combi*. In high season, minibuses also sometimes run directly from Angangueo to the reserve.

It's possible to hike to El Rosario from Angangueo through some lovely pine-forested landscapes. Ask locally for the path on the edge of town. It climbs very steeply for a kilometre or so before levelling out and winding through the mountains. You'll pass a roadside shrine, lots of ramshackle farms and the occasional itinerant local with a mule. Allow up to two hours to reach the reserve, take it easy, and be aware that you'll have another stiff climb once you actually reach El Rosario. For an easier ascent to the butterfly habitats, consider visiting the **Sierra Chincua Reserve**, 8 km from Angangueo. Catch a 'Tlalpujahua' bus, US$0.20 and ask for the 'reserva de mariposas'.

⦿ Eastern Michoacán listings

For Sleeping and Eating price codes and other relevant information, see Essentials pages 47-51.

⦿ Sleeping

Morelia *p410, map p411*
Some of the cheaper hotels may have water only in the morning; check. Prices drop by 15-20% in low season.
LL-L Los Juaninos, Morelos Sur 39, T443-312 0036, www.hoteljuaninos.com.mx.
A very luxurious and elegant hotel that was once the Episcopal Palace (1685), beautifully restored in 1998. It offers golf and spas services and has a wonderful rooftop restaurant overlooking the Zócalo.
LL Villa Montaña, Patzimba 201, T443-314 0231, www.villamontana.com.mx. On Santa María hill, south of the city, with glorious views. This gorgeous colonial-style hotel, run by French aristocrats, has 36 *casitas*. Each is unique and assuredly comfortable. Very expensive but worth it. Superb restaurant.
L Posada de la Soledad, Zaragoza 90 y Ocampo, T443-312 1888, www.hsoledad.com. Off Plaza de Armas and quiet. Luxurious rooms,

most fitted with antique furniture and fireplaces, surrounding beautiful, lightly crumbling courtyards filled with pots, palms, red flowers and colonial art. The chapel has been converted into a dining room. Services include Wi-Fi and parking. Rooms on the second patio are cheaper. Recommended.
A Catedral, Zaragoza 37, T443-313 0406, www.hotelcatedralmorelia.com. A very well-appointed, attractive colonial building with spacious rooms, bar and restaurant, although they close quite early. Some (more expensive) rooms have good cathedral views. Recommended.
C Colonial, Morelos Norte, corner with 20 de Noviembre 15, T443-312 1897. Pleasant, clean and friendly, with lots of hot water, cable TV and parking.
C Concordia, Gómez Farías 328, round corner from the old bus station, T443-312 3052, www.hotelconcordiamorelia.com.mx.
A good, clean, modern hotel with pastel shades of yellow. Rooms are clean and comfortable, if unexciting, with writing desk, complimentary water and clean bath. Services include restaurant, parking, tours and internet.

C Villa Centurión, Ctra Morelia Km 4.5, T443-313 2272. Hotel on the highway with good antiques, pool and comfortable rooms.

D Mintzicuri, Vasco de Quiroga 227 (opposite **Don Vasco**), T443-312 0664. Small, clean, carpeted rooms overlooking a courtyard, with hot water and cable TV. Parking and restaurant.

D Posada del Cortijo, E Ruiz 673, T443-312 9642, reservaciones@posadadelcortijo.com. Smallish but well cared for and comfortable enough. Rooms have hot water, cable TV and phone. Parking.

D Qualitel, E Ruiz 531, opposite the old bus station, T/F443-312 464, www.qualitel.com.mx. Formerly Hotel Matador, this clean, modern hotel has reasonable, characterless rooms with hot water and cable TV. There's a restaurant, parking, business centre and Wi-Fi. Breakfast included.

D-E Fenix, Madero Pte 537, T443-312 0512. Nice little cheapie with lots of plants, parking and clean, basic rooms. Popular with European backpackers, friendly and helpful. Cheapest rooms are without bath or TV.

D-E Hostel Allende, Allende 843, T443-312 2246, hostelallende@msn.com. Friendly hostel with 33 rooms and 2 dorms, kitchen, lockers, luggage store, tourist information and a pleasant, leafy courtyard too.

E-F Señorial, Santiago Tapía 543, 1 block south from the old bus terminal. Shabby and ultra-basic rooms around a crumbling central courtyard, but OK if you're poor and used to it. Cheapest rooms have no bath or TV.

Zitácuaro *p415*

AL-A Villa Monarca Inn, Ctra Toluca–Morelia, Km 103.5, T715-153 5346, www.villamonarca.com. Pleasant hotel on the highway with a pool, restaurant, playground and straightforward, comfortable rooms.

A Rancho San Cayetano, Ctra a Huetamo, Km 2.3, T715-153 1926, www.ranchosancayetano.com. Attractive chalets in pleasant, green grounds with views. Friendly, clean and knowledgeable

about the butterflies and the sanctuary. English spoken. Highly recommended.

D América, Revolución Sur 8, Zitácuaro, 1st block, T715-153 1116. Clean, straightforward rooms with TV and hot water. Parking.

D Lorenz, Av Hidalgo Ote 14, 9 blocks from the bus station, T715-153 8458. Very friendly, gregarious and helpful, with clean, newly furnished doubles, hot water, cable TV, parking, luggage store, restaurant and cooking facilities on request. Recommended.

D Mary, Revolución Nte 4, Zitácuaro, T715-153 0847. Clean, simple rooms with TV and hot water.

D México, Revolución Sur 22, T715-153 2811. Large, slightly grubby rooms, some overlooking the street. Services include hot water, TV, restaurant and parking.

D Posada Michoacán, 5 de Mayo Sur 26a, main square, Zitácuaro, T715-153 1246. Small, clean, carpeted rooms with hot water and drinking water. Coffee and tours available.

F Carolina, Zitácuaro, 1 block north of the plaza. Basic, grubby and friendly, with big rooms and hot water until 2100.

Angangueo *p417*

B-C Albergue Don Bruno, Morelia 92, T715-156 0026. Good, comfortable rooms but a little overpriced. Nice setting and restaurant.

C La Margarita, Morelia. Very clean and highly recommended. Owner runs tours to the butterfly sanctuary.

D-E Real Monarca, Nacional 20, Angangueo, T715-158 0187. Large comfortable rooms, hot water, friendly, meals. Highly recommended.

🍴 Eating

Morelia *p410, map p411*

†††-†† La Flor de las Mercedes, León Guzmán 47. A smart, colonial-style house with beautiful decor, well-attired waiters and a romantic ambience. The international menu includes steaks, crêpes and trout dishes.

†††-†† Los Mirasoles, Madero Pte 549. A good restaurant specializing in regional and national dishes like *sopa tarasca* and *chiles capones* – black chillies stuffed with salsa and served on a bed of fried green tomatoes and cheese. Also has a selection of international fare.

Boca del Río, Gómez Farías185. Good, clean seafood restaurant serving fish fillets, shrimps in garlic butter and octopus cocktails. Cold Coronas to wash it all down.

Café Catedral, Zaragoza 37, opposite the cathedral. One of several places on the plaza, good for a breakfast and people-watching, although you'll be approached by beggars if you sit outside. Neighbouring restaurants are similar in cost, but this one has Wi-Fi.

El Rincón de los Sentidos, Madero Pte 485. A young, hip space in a colonial building. Serves burgers, enchiladas, bar food and other snacks. Good spot for an evening beer; there's usually a drinks promotion.

La Bodega de la Iguana, Av Camelinsa 3636, T443-314 4204. Very good traditional cuisine. Highly recommended.

Viandas de San José, Alvaro Obregón 263 y Zapata. Pleasant dining around a nice, sunny colonial courtyard. Serves good cheap *comida corrida* and specializes in regional cuisine. Excellent service and recommended.

Los Milagritos, Galeana 103. Cheap and cheerful *torta* joint dishing out fast food and other economical fare. Check out the murals and *lucha libre* artwork.

Los Pioneros, Aquiles Serdán y Morelos Norte 110. Clean, pleasant and economical taco house that's popular with the locals.

Cafés, bakeries, ice cream parlours and sweet shops

Café Colón, Aquiles Serdán 265. An obscure locals' haunt with breakfast, sandwiches and a good selection of coffee.

Café de Conservatorio, on Plaza de las Rosas (opposite music academy). Not cheap but great atmosphere and tasty cakes.

Casa de la Cultura, Morelos Nte 485. Has a good café with delicious home-made cakes.

Lilian's Coffee, Madero Pte 388. Clean-cut coffee house with a corporate style, cakes and gourmet roasts.

Mercado de Dulces, Gómez Farías at the western end of the Palacio Clavijero. Famous for *ates* (fruit jellies), candies and *rompope* (an alcoholic drink similar to advocaat).

Michoacana, Madero Pte 327. For sweet ice creams.

Zitácuaro *p415*

La Trucha Alegre, Revolución Nte 2. Specializes in trout, as the name might suggest.

Angangueo *p417*

Los Arcos, Angangueo. One of several cafés and restaurants near the plaza, serving wholesome food, but not gourmet.

☻ Entertainment

Morelia *p410, map p411*

Peña Bola Suriana, Allende 355. Live traditional guitar music, open courtyard, small cover charge.

Teatro Ocampo, Ocampy y Prieto. Free weekly concerts.

▲ Activities and tours

Morelia *p410, map p411*

Language schools

Centro Mexicano de Idiomas, Calzada Fray Antonio de San Miguel 173, T443-312 4596. Intensive weekly classes; other courses include handicrafts. Homestays arranged.

Baden-Powell Institute, Antonio Alzate 565, T443-312 4070, www.baden-powell.com. Courses for all levels, plus cultural, social science and extracurricular courses. Highly recommended.

Tour operators

Tour de Leyendas de Morelia, T443-337 0350, viajescasamayavip@hotmail.com. Tours recalling Morelia's legendary past depart 2100 daily from Portal Galeana, opposite the cathedral. The same company runs trips throughout the state too. Spanish only.

Tours en Michoacán, Pino Suárez 524, T443-262 3782. Tours throughout the state, including Pátzcuaro, the Monarch butterfly sanctuary and lakeside villages. Trips further afield run to Guanajuato, Queretaro and San Miguel de Allende.

⊖ Transport

Morelia p410, map p411
Air
Francisco J Mújica Airport is 27 km north of the city; a taxi to/from downtown costs around US$18, there are no public buses.

Mexican destinations include **Cuernavaca, León, Mexico City, Tijuana, Uruapan, Veracruz** and **Zacatecas**. There are international flights to **Chicago, LA, San Francisco** and **San José** (CA).

Airline offices Aeromar, Pirindas 435, T443-324 6777. AeroMexico, Plaza Morelia Local C-18, T443-324 3604. Aviacsa, Av Camelinas 2630 Local 4, T443-324 5775. Continental, T443-317 9218. Mexicana, Enrique Ramirez 200, T443-324 5400.

Bus
The new terminal is out of town, a 15- or 20-min taxi ride, US$3. The terminal is divided into 3 sections: A, for 1st class; B, for 2nd class; and C, for 3rd class. Parkhuni, ETN, Estrella Blanca and Omnibus are among the 1st-class lines.

To **Aguascalientes**, 5 daily, 7 hrs, US$26. To **Celaya**, 18 per day, US$11. To **Colima**, 0740, 1200, US$23. To **Guadalajara**, at least hourly, 3-5 hrs, quicker on the *autopista*, US$23. To **Guanajuato**, 8 daily 0650-1525, 3½ hrs, US$11. To **León**, regular throughout the day, 4 hrs, US$14. To **Mexico City**, very regular services, some to the North terminal, some to the West terminal, 4 hrs, US$27. To **Monterrey**, 1745, 2000, 2045, US$72. To **Pátzcuaro**, hourly, 1 hr, US$4, or every 15 mins with 2nd-class autobuses Purhépecha. To **Querétaro**, very regular, 4 hrs, US$11. To **San Luis Potosí**, hourly,

US$22. To **Toluca airport**, hourly, 0500-1800. To **Uruapan**, very regular, 2 hrs, US$10. To **Zitacuaro**, hourly, US$10, 3hrs.

Zitacuaro p415
Bus The bus station is about 1 km from downtown; fixed-price taxi US$1.50, minibus US$0.40. To **Angangueo**, every ½ hr, 1½ hrs, US$1. To **Mexico City**, 1½ hrs, US$11. To **Morelia**, hourly, 3½ hrs, US$10. For the **El Rosario butterfly sanctuary**, take the Angangueo bus and exit at Ocampo. From there, *camionetas* to the reserve depart from Hidalgo y Ocampo, 45 mins, US$2.

Angangueo p417
To reach Angangueo, go to Zitacuaro and catch a bus, every ½ hr, 1½ hrs, US$1. *Colectivo* taxis also travel between the 2 towns; ask around. To reach the **El Rosario butterfly sanctuary**, catch a bus towards Zitacuaro and exit at Ocampo (see above).

⊙ Directory

Morelia p410, map p411
Banks Bancomer, Av Madero Oriente, Visa ATM. The ATM just east of **Hotel Casino** accepts Visa and MasterCard. There is a **Banco** Inverlat ATM next to the bus station that accepts AmEx. **Internet** La Central, Matamoros 72A, Mon-Sat 0900-2200. Chatroom Cybercafé, Nigromante 132A, Mon-Sat 0900-2200, Sun 1200-2100, spacious, tranquil. Shareweb Cybercafé, Av Madero Ote 573-C, Mon-Sat 0900-2200, Sun 1400-2200. **Laundry** Lavandería Chapultepec, Ceballos 881. Lavandería on Santiago Tapiá towards old bus station. **Medical services** Dentist: Dr Leopoldo Arroyo Contreras, Abraham González 35, T443-312 0751, near the cathedral. Recommended. **Post office** Madero Ote 369. Long-distance phone and fax, Gómez Farías 113, near the sweet market.

Lago de Pátzcuaro

Expansive lake Pátzcuaro is at the tranquil heart of Michoacán, upon whose shores the Tarascan empire rose and fell. One of the most populous and successful civilizations in Mesoamerica, the Tarascans were a formidable sparring partner of the Aztecs, although comparatively little is known about them. A handful of sites offer tentative glimpses of their world, most notably the capital of Tzintzuntzan, where five curious pyramids overlook the lake like a line of stationed sentries, but little else. Fortunately their living descendants, the Purépecha, maintain a vivid link to the pre-Hispanic past with dazzling festivals, dances and ceremonies that hint at a religiosity as devout as it is vibrant. More than this, the Purépecha are Mexico's most skilled artisans, continuing the vision of Bishop Vasco de Quiroga, who sought to make each community a centre of self-sufficient industry. Today, most villages specialize in a particular craft, like Santa Clara de Cobre, with its robust and internationally recognized traditions of copper-work. The lake's main urban centre is Pátzcuaro, a beautifully rendered and lightly crumbling colonial town that's great for strolling, shopping and dining on freshly caught fish. This is the best base for exploring the countryside and a superb destination in itself. ▸▸ For listings, see pages 427-430.

Pátzcuaro ⊖⊘⊘⊗⊿⊖⊕ ▸▸ *pp427-430. Phone code: 434. Altitude: 2110 m.*

Steeped in wraith-like splendour, the colonial town of Pátzcuaro is the regional centre for many Purépecha communities, who trade their vibrant crafts and produce in the market. Each morning, the piercing highland light awakens the town from its chilly, mist-swathed slumber and one by one the stalls are opened, cooking pots are filled and fires are started. Soon the streets are busy with activity. Old women sweep down the plazas with palm fronds, overseen by thick-walled adobe houses of white and terracotta, giant eucalyptus and firs, colonial arches and a sea of red clay tiles. Trucks arrive and leave, loading and unloading their parcels, boxes, crates, produce, people and livestock. Wizened old men in cowboy hats banter with the Purépecha women wrapped in indigo shawls. Replete with fascinating daily scenes, Pátzcuaro offers authentic glimpses of a provincial Mexico where time has done little to alter the style, pace or courtesy of its inhabitants. It is perhaps fitting that its original name means 'Gate to the Otherworld' in Purépecha, for this is one of the most beautiful settings in Mexico. And although home to a growing number of luxury hotels and boutique craft stores, tourism has yet to ruin to it.

Ins and outs

Getting there The nearest airports are at Morelia to the east and Uruapan to the west. The bus station is on the outskirts of town. A local bus, *colectivo* or taxi will take you to the centre. Pátzcuaro is connected by Route 14 to Morelia and Uruapan. ▸▸ *See Transport, page 429.*

Getting around It is a steep 3-km walk uphill from the lake shore to the plaza; *colectivos* run every few minutes to Plaza Chica. The downtown area itself is compact and easily explored on foot.

Tourist information The **tourist office** ⓘ *north side of Plaza Grande, next to Banca Serfín, www.turismomichoacan.gob.mx, Mon-Fri 0900-1500, variable opening hours in afternoon, usually 1700-1900, Sat and Sun 0900-1500,* is friendly and provides good information. For information on the **Day of the Dead**, see Festivals and events, page 429.

Plaza Vasco de Quiroga

Plaza Vasco de Quiroga is the heart of Pátzcuaro, also known as **Plaza Grande**, a large shady square flanked by elegant hotels, 17th-century mansions, arched *portáles* and terraced restaurants. At its centre stands a statue of Quiroga himself, proudly donning his robes and crook. In the weekend afternoons performers sometimes assemble here, stamping out the wily **danza de los viejitos**, an ancient fertility rite in which withered old men are transformed into spritely dancers (this symbolizes the transition from winter to spring). Take some time to stroll around and note the interesting antique pharmacy complete with quaint little medicine bottles. During the Day of the Dead festivities one of the country's best craft markets is held in the square, not to be missed.

Plaza Gertrudis Bocanegra

Pátzcuaro's second plaza, also known as **Plaza Chica**, is often alive with activity and colour. Named after an Independence heroine who was executed in 1818, various trimmed gardens, benches and an historic statue marks the centre. The **market** on the west side is teeming with delicious fresh fruit, vegetables and herbal medicines – the finest offerings of Michoacán state – as well as economical food stalls and limited crafts. There are also a handful of crafts stalls along Títere, on the north side, where the **library**,

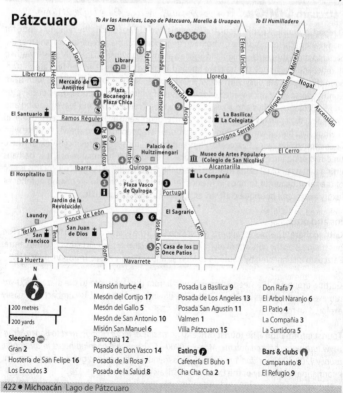

Pátzcuaro

N

200 metres
200 yards

Sleeping
Gran 2
Hostería de San Felipe 16
Los Escudos 3

Mansión Iturbe 4
Mesón del Cortijo 17
Mesón del Gallo 5
Mesón de San Antonio 10
Misión San Manuel 6
Parroquia 12
Posada de Don Vasco 14
Posada de la Rosa 7
Posada de la Salud 8

Posada La Basílica 9
Posada de Los Angeles 13
Posada San Agustín 11
Valmen 1
Villa Pátzcuaro 15

Eating
Cafetería El Buho 1
Cha Cha Cha 2

Don Rafa 7
El Arbol Naranjo 6
El Patio 4
La Compañía 3
La Surtidora 5

Bars & clubs
Campanario 8
El Refugio 9

The rise and fall of the Tarascan state

Forged in the territory of present-day Michoacán, the formidable Tarascan state was a sworn enemy of the Aztec empire. A war-like tribe renowned for their fine metal work and brutally effective weaponry, some believe that had the evolution of Mesoamerica continued without Spanish interruption, the Tarascans would ultimately have grown to dominate central Mexico entirely.

The Tarascan state, known as Iréchecua Tzintzuntzáni (lands of Tzinztuntzan) in Purépecha, was founded by the legendary first ruler or Caconzi, Tarícuari. After uniting the disparate groups on the shores of lake Pátzcuaro – Nahua, Chichimeca and Purépecha among them – Taricuari founded the first pillars of his kingdom. By the time of his death in 1350, he and his family had subjugated all major centres in the area. His sons, installed at Ihuatzio and Tzintzuntzan, went on to institutionalise a system of tributes and state bureaucracy.

As the boundaries of their empire started to swell, conflict with the Aztecs became more frequent and inevitable. By 1460, the Tarascan state reached as far as the Pacfic coast in the west, the valley of Toluca in the east, and the present-day state of Guanajuato in the north. This, the Aztecs decided, could not be tolerated. In 1470, the Aztec emperor Axayactl mounted a series of highly effective attacks that pushed back Tarascan expansion and nearly broke into their heartland. In response, the Tarascans fortified their borders with the Aztecs and installed military strongholds at strategic points.

In subsequent years, ongoing skirmishes meant the scope of the Tarascan state remained largely static. But after the Spanish conquest, radical changes were to occur. In 1522, Cristóbal de Olid arrived in Tzintzuntzan, drawn by gifts of gold that had previously been dispatched to Cortés. The Tarascan army was vast, perhaps numbering 100,000, but the Caconzi of the day, Tangáxuan II, declined to fight. Instead, he submitted to the Spanish in exchange for a degree of autonomy.

In the years after the conquest, Cortés and Tangáxuan ruled in situ, both receiving tribute from the population. But when the Spanish learned that Tangáxuan's share of tribute was significantly greater than Cortés', the brutal Nuño de Guzmán was sent to sort him – and his people – out. Guzmán tortured Tangáxuan and burned him alive before setting upon the populations of Michoacán. He was eventually recalled to Spain and imprisoned, replaced thereafter by the decidedly more peaceful Vasco de Quiroga (see box, page xx). Meanwhile the golden age of the Tarascan state – once filled with so much promise and glory – was assuredly over.

formerly the church of San Agustín, conceals a beautiful mural by Juan O'Gorman. It depicts the history of Michoacán from Pre-Hispanic times to the arrival of Bishop Vasco in busy scenes and vibrant colours; it is worth checking out.

La Basílica

Two blocks east of Plaza Chica, the unfinished **Colegiata** was commenced in 1606 and has space for some 30,000 worshippers. Known locally as La Basílica, it is home to a much-venerated patron saint and Virgin, Nuestra Señora de la Salud (Our Lady of Health), fashioned by an indigenous craftsman from a paste made with honey and *tatzingue* (cornstalk pith). Said to have been found floating in a canoe, the Virgin quickly earned a reputation as a healer and many pilgrims continue to present their ailments. Celebrations in her honour, held on 8 September, are particularly moving. Construction of the church was ordered by Don Vasco de Quiroga and built over an important ceremonial site; the great bishop's remains can be seen in a mausoleum, left of the main entrance.

Museo de Artes Populares
① *Quiroga y Lerín. Tue-Sat 0900-1900, Sun 0900-1430. English-speaking guide US$2.50.*
The very well-arranged Museo de Artes Populares is in the former Colegio de San Nicolás, founded in 1540 and possibly the first university in the Americas. The museum offers an excellent introduction to the craft traditions of Michoacán with regional ceramics, weaving, woodcarving, masks, lacquer objects, copperware and baskets. There is a mixture of ancient and modern works but all are singularly beautiful and vibrant. Like many other historic buildings in Pátzcuaro, the college was built over a pre-Hispanic structure; its ruined foundations can be seen in the grounds.

Casa de los Once Patios
① *Madrigal de las Altas Torres. Daily 1000-1900 with a lunch break.*
The 'House of the Eleven Patios' originally served as an 18th-century Dominican convent. Today it's home to several pricey but high-quality boutique stores selling regional crafts. The complex is replete with arches, fountains, and as the name might suggest, patios. Even if you don't want to shop, this is great place to stroll, admire the architecture and watch craftsmen in action, including expert weavers and painters of lacquer.

Other churches
South of the basilica is the partly restored, partly ruined 16th-century church and monastery of **La Compañía**, once part of a Jesuit training college and complete with crumbling walls and tranquil patios. Almost opposite stands the early 17th-century church of the **Sagrario** at the top of Calle Portugal. The chapel of **El Calvario** is 15 minutes' walk outside the town on Terán, on the summit of Cerro del Calvario. Nearby, a cobbled 3-km path climbs 200 m uphill to gives wide views of the lake and islands. From the *mirador*, there are another 417 steps to the summit of **Cerro del Estribo**, but the views are reportedly not much different. Around 20 minutes east of the basillica on Serato is the **El Humilladero** (place of humiliation), where the last Tarascan King, Tanganxoan II, finally submitted to the Spanish conquistador Cristóbal de Olid. This is possibly the oldest church in town and some suggest that its name is actually derived from a statue of Christ, sculpted from a single piece of stone and depicted, as ever, humiliated on the cross. The views here are also good. West of Plaza Chica at the end of Ramos is the restored **Templo del Santuario**. On Calle Terán is the church of **San Francisco**; nearby is **San Juan de Dios**, on the corner of Calle Romero.

Around Pátzcuaro ◉ ➤➤ *pp427-430.*

There are numerous towns and villages occupying the hills and lakeshores around Pátzcuaro, far more than are given here. Many specialize in particular crafts like wooden furniture, masks, leather and ceramics. Such communities have been developing their talents for centuries and browsing their workshops can be a fascinating experience. For a complete list of possibilities, consult the tourist office in Pátzcuaro. Driving is the easiest way to get around, but most villages can also be easily reached on second-class *combis*, which depart regularly from Plaza Chica. To reach the islands catch a 'lago' bus to the lakeshore, then head to the Muelle General, or the cheaper Muelle San Pedrito, 500 m further on. Tickets are available from the office dock, most last returns are at 2000, but always check in advance. Most boats leave when full.

Isla Janitzio and Isla Yunuen

The best-known lake island is **Janitzio**, which has been spoilt by souvenir shops and tourists – visit during the week if possible. Note that it is particularly inundated during **Day of the Dead**. A circular path goes around the island where there are lots of good restaurants. Crowning the hill there is an unfortunate **Monumento a Morelos** ① *US$0.50,* with a mural glorifying Independence. It nevertheless affords magnificent views from the top, but there are often long queues to climb the spiral stairs inside.

Another lake island, less touristy than Janitzio, is the Purépecha community of **Yunuen**. It is clean and quiet, although there are few *lanchas* from Pátzcuaro during the week, so be sure to arrange a return trip unless you want to spend the night. Bring provisions.

Ihuatzio

① *4 km off the Pátzcuaro-Quiroga road. Open 1000-1800. US$2.*

The ancient city of Ihuatzio is located on the lake shore some12 km north of Pátzcuaro . It is reasonably large but only partially excavated, dominated two 15-m pyramidal structures inside a large ceremonial space. Ihuatzio is believed to be the second most important city in the Tarascan empire after Tzintzuntzan. However, researchers have now revealed two distinct sections constructed by different cultures. The older section is Náhautl, built and occupied AD 900-1200; the newer section is Tarascan, dating AD 1200-1530. Buses from Plaza Bocanegra in Pátzcuaro drop you 1½ km from the site at the end of a cobblestone road. You can continue to Tzintzuntzan by catching a bus here bound for Quiroga.

Tzintzuntzan

① *On the Pátzcuaro–Quiroga road. Daily 0900-1700. US$3.*

Tzintzuntzan (pronounced rapidly *sin-soon-san*) was the pre-Conquest Tarascan capital. Its name means 'Place of Hummingbirds', although none are actually resident here – one theory suggests they were hunted out of the area centuries ago. Satellite images reveal the city once covered an area of more than 10 sq km, although only a fraction – the ceremonial centre – has been excavated. Unlike other pre-Columbian sites, Tzintzuntzan's pyramids, known as *yácatas*, are arranged in a line and not a square. They are also curiously shaped, comprising a semi-circular turret and rectangular platform. There are five of them overlooking the lake in an east–west configuration that follows the path of the sun. Be sure to check out the site's museum where you can see interesting examples of Tarascan pottery, like weird three legged vessels, similarly unique in form.

After the Conquest, the inhabitants of Tzintzuntzan were relocated to the site of the town below. The **ex-Convento de San Fransisco**, on Magdalena, was built in 1525 but closed over 250 years ago. It has been restored, but its frescoes have deteriorated badly. Inside the **Templo de San Fransisco**, built exclusively for the monks, are interesting pre-Columbian lions guarding the cross. Nearby, the **Templo de Nuestra Señora de la Salud** was constructed for the indigenous masses, home to an image of Christ that partakes in a most interesting passion play during **Semana Santa**. A much smaller chapel, built as a temporary church, is located in the grounds, complete with a baptismal pit and faded, floral murals. There are some very old olive trees too which are still bearing fruit, said to have been planted by Vasco de Quiroga. Fortuitously they were missed in a Spanish edict to destroy all Mexican olive trees when it was thought that Mexican olive oil would compete with Spain's. Also located in the grounds is the pottery studio of Manuel Morales, who produces some very fine quality ceramics, continuing the work of his forebears. Just outside the convent there are some small markets. Beautiful, hand-painted pottery, displayed everywhere, is very cheap but also brittle. (It is also available in other markets in Mexico.) Other handicrafts on sale include woodcarving, leather and basket-woven Christmas tree ornaments; good bargaining opportunities. If you're in the area for **Day of the Dead**, be sure to check out the enormous, beautifully decorated cemetery.

Quiroga

Quiroga, bustling with the second largest handicraft market in the area, lies 8 km northeast of Tzintzuntzan. Once an important pre-Hispanic site, Quiroga later developed as an important crossroads and commercial centre during the colonial era. It is quite indigenous and relatively devoid of tourists. Inside the crowded market, you may find all sorts of crafted goods including wool, ceramics, cane and wood, but the town's real speciality is leather. There is a fair and craft exhibition in December, whilst the **Fiesta de la Preciosa Sangre del Cristo** on the first Sunday in July includes an evocative candelit procession.

Santa Fe de la Laguna

A few kilometres west of Quiroga, the diminutive and somewhat idyllic village of Santa Fe de la Laguna is a bastion of revolutionary and leftist traditions. Driven by a Utopian vision, Bishop Vasco de Quiroga founded Michoacán's first mission and 'hospital' here to provide free healthcare and education to the community. He hoped to create a self-sustaining collective organized around a kind of Christian-Communist philosophy. Today, the hospital functions as a vital communal space where important public decisions are made. As a bastion of the Zapatista movement, Santa Fe continues to be resistant, progressive and self-governing. Alcohol is completely outlawed. During the 1970s, a dispute over land rights led the army to massacre many of its more outspoken inhabitants and the job of political resistance was left to the women. They are immortalized in a fascinating mural on the main plaza, upon which you'll see the words: *This community has said 'enough'.*

Santa Clara del Cobre

Santa Clara del Cobre, 25 km south of Pátzcuaro, is a sleepy highland village with red tiles and overhanging eaves. The town is famous for its hand-wrought copper vessels and there is a **Museo del Cobre** ① *Morelos 263, Tue-Sat 1000-1500, Sun 1000-1600, US$2*, where you can admire a small but well-crafted exhibition of antique productions. There are more than 200 family workshops around town where everything from minute thimbles to gigantic cauldrons can be commissioned. Check out the square too, attractively adorned with flower-filled copper pots along each arcade and a copper-roofed gazebo. There is a national **Copper Fair** in August when the town's patron saint, Santa Clara, is also honoured. Around 12 km outside of town is the pretty **Lago Zirahuén** where you can take boat trips, eat at lakeside restaurants and visit the huge adobe church.

Lago de Pátzcuaro listings

For Sleeping and Eating price codes and other relevant information, see Essentials pages 47-51.

Sleeping

Pátzcuaro *p421, map p422*
Rooms in some hotels must be reserved 4 weeks prior to Día de los Muertos; other hotels do not take reservations, so it's pot luck at this time.

AL Mansión Iturbe, Portal Morelos 59, T434-342 0368, www.mansioniturbe.com. This beautifully restored 1790s mansion on the main plaza has lots of character and 12 individually decorated rooms. There's an excellent Argentine restaurant, living room, solarium, parking, Wi-Fi and bike rental. Recommended.

AL Posada La Basílica, Arciga 4, T434-342 1108, www.posadalabasilica.com. Charming, colonial-style hotel, pleasant patios and 12 very tasteful rooms with wooden floorboards and beams. Nice restaurant with views.

A Mesón de San Antonio, Serrato 33, T434-342 2501, www.mesondesanantonio.com. An elegant 300-year-old building with a pleasant sunny garden, cacti and lemon trees. The high-ceilinged rooms are comfortable, equipped with great fire places and adorned with Mexican art and crafts. Wi-Fi available. Continental breakfast included. Friendly, helpful and recommended.

A Parroquia, Plaza Bocanegra 24, T434-342 5280, reserva_laparroquia@hotmail.com. Rooms overlook an attractive central courtyard at this pleasant colonial hotel, formerly the Fiesta Plaza. Services include cable TV, phone, hot water, business centre and Wi-Fi.

A Posada de Don Vasco, Av Lázaro Cárdenas 450, towards the lake, T434-342 0227. Attractive, colonial-style **Best Western** hotel (halfway between the lake and the town). Breakfast is good, other meals are poor. *Baile de los Viejitos* (Dance of the Old Men) is performed on Wed and Sat at 2100 at no charge, non-residents welcome but drinks very expensive. Plenty of other services, including conference hall, pool, games room and Wi-Fi.

A Villa Pátzcuaro, Av Lázaro Cárdenas 506, 1km from centre, T434-342 0767, www.villa patzcuaro.com. Very quiet and pleasant with 12 traditional rooms with fireplaces and cable TV, peaceful gardens, lots of birds and flowers. Also a camping and caravan site. Good low season reductions.

B Gran Hotel, Portal Regules 6, on Plaza Bocanegra, T434-342 0443, www.granhotel patzcuaro.com.mx. Rooms are small, clean and comfortable, but hardly a great value. The suites are nice and spacious and well-equipped. Prices include continental breakfast, parking, Wi-Fi and restaurant.

B Hostería de San Felipe, Av Lázaro Cárdenas 321, T/F434-342 1298, www.mexon line.com/hosteria-sanfelipe.htm. Friendly, clean, lodgings with attractive stonework and other interesting features. Rooms have fireplaces. A good restaurant, but closes early (2030). Highly recommended.

B Mesón del Cortijo, Obregón, off Américas, towards the lake, T434-342 1295. Often fully booked at weekends. Recommended.

B Misión San Manuel, Portal Aldama 12, on main plaza, T434-342 1050, www.misionsan manuel.com. A beautiful colonial building with spacious rooms, all decorated with rustic wooden beams, attractive tiled showers and sinks. Some have working chimneys. Hot water, internet, cable TV, restaurant, café and bar.

B-C Los Escudos, Portal Hidalgo 73, T434-342 1290. A 17th-century building with comfortable, attractive rooms, valet parking, restaurant and Wi-Fi. The suites (**A**) are very spacious with interesting furniture and wooden beams. There are cheaper rooms in the other section, very good value and comfortable, ask for one with a fireplace. *Baile de los Viejitos* (Dance of the Old Men) performed Sat at 2000. Recommended, and often full at the weekends.

C Mesón del Gallo, Dr Coss 20, T434-342 1474, hmeson@yahoo.com. 25 comfortable, pleasant rooms with tasteful furnishings. Services include bar and restaurant. Good value.

C Posada de los Angeles, Títere 16, T434-342 2440. A pleasant sunny garden and very clean, carpeted, comfortable rooms, equipped with all the usual amenities. Friendly and recommended.

D Posada de la Salud, Benigno Serrato 9, T434-342 0058, www.posadadelasalud. A clean, quiet hotel with tidy little rooms, attractive wooden furniture and a pleasant garden. 2 rooms have chimneys. Sometimes the hot water is off in the middle of the day. Recommended.

E Posada San Agustín, Portal Juárez 27 (Plaza Chica), T434-342 1108, www.mexonline.com/sanagustin.htm. Simple, basic, economical rooms, with bath, hot water and cable TV. Some rooms with windows and views. Not bad.

E Valmen, Padre Lloreda 34-A, T434-342 1161. Clean, reasonable budget lodgings with nice tiles and plants in the courtyard. Rooms have cable TV, bath and hot water.

E-F Posada de la Rosa, Portal Juárez 29 (Plaza Chica), T434-342 0811. Simple, windowless rooms, colonial-style, with bath and TV, although the doors are not very secure. Parking.

Camping

See also Villa Pátzcuaro, above.

Trailer Park El Pozo, on lakeside, opposite Chalamu, Km 20, Carretara 15, T434-342 0937. Hot showers in the morning, large, delightful, well-equipped site, owner speaks English, camping possible.

Quiroga p426

D Quiroga, Vasco de Quiroga Pte 340, Quiroga, T454-354 0035. Modern, with parking.

D Tarasco, Vasco de Quiroga Ote 9, Quiroga, T454-354 0100, eduardo_carreon_valadez@yahoo.com.mx. Colonial-style with a courtyard, hot water, clean, pleasant but front rooms noisy. Parking.

Camping

Trailer park, 3 km north of Quiroga. Old summer residence of a former Mexican president, good view over Lake Pátzcuaro.

🍴 Eating

Pátzcuaro p421, map p422

The local speciality is *pescado blanco* (white fish), and several lakeside restaurants serve fish dishes. Economical breakfasts are available from small stands in the market, usually 0600-0700 (milkshakes, rice pudding, etc). *Comida corrida* is offered at restaurants around Plaza Grande and Plaza Chica. Many places close before 2000. Most good hotels have their own restaurants.

₹₹₹-₹₹ El Gaucho Viejo, Mansión Iturbide (see Sleeping, above). Wed-Sun 1800-2400. Folk music. Argentine *churrasco* and other carnivorous fare.

₹₹₹-₹₹ La Compañia, Portal Matamoros 355. One of the better plaza options. Serves grilled meats, steaks, fish and fajitas. The wine and tequila selection is particularly healthy. Good service and a clean, pleasant colonial interior. The steak is tasty, recommended.

₹₹ Cha Cha Cha, Buenavista 7. A cheery little patio laden with plants and *artesanías*. Dishes include salmon poached in white wine sauce, lasagne, and trout in pistachio sauce. Very pleasant and highly recommended.

₹₹ El Arbol Naranjo, Plaza Vasco de Quiroga, Head upstairs for views of the plaza. A laid-back little restaurant serving fresh fish and regional specialities, all home-cooked. Pretty good.

₹₹ La Surtidora, Portal Hidalgo 71. Very good coffee, well-presented breakfasts and tables on the plaza. The shop inside sells little delicacies. Good service and a Pátzcuaro institution, but not fine dining.

₹₹-₹ Don Rafa, Mendoza 30. Small, intimate and economical dining space with *sopa Tarasca* and *pescado blanco* among the regional offerings.

₹₹-₹ El Patio, Plaza Vasco de Quiroga 19, T434-342 0484. Daily 0800-2200. Fruit and yoghurt for breakfast, also serves good meals, good service too. Recommended.

₹ Cafetería El Buho, Tejerías 8, tucked away down an alley. Service is slow but the food is very tasty and good value. Stylish and friendly. Recommended.

Mercado de Antijitos, Plaza Chica. Good chicken with vegetables and *enchiladas* over the market (budget restaurants here are usually open in the evening).

Cafés and ice cream parlours
Paletería, Codallos 24. Excellent ice cream parlour which also sells frozen yoghurt.

♪ Bars and clubs

Pátzcuaro *p421, map p422*
A handful of bars can be found on the main plaza, which fills up with people in the evening. Try:
Campanario, Plaza Grande 14. Atmospheric and cavernous drinking hole with occasional live music.
El Refugio, Portal Régules 9. Sports TV, beer and cosy corners to escape the chilly highland evenings.

⊛ Festivals and events

Pátzcuaro and around *p421, map p422*
1 Jan Los Viejitos (Old Men), in Janitzio.
2 Feb Los Sembradores (The Sowers).
4 Feb Los Apaches (at the churches).
Feb Carnaval in the Lake Pátzcuaro region; the *Danza de los Moros* (The Moors) is performed.
12 Oct Día de la Raza, when Columbus reached America, there is also a procession with the Virgin and lots of fireworks.
1-2 Nov Día de los Muertos (All Souls' Day), ceremony at midnight, at almost every village around the lake; if you are in the region at this time it is well worth experiencing. The ceremony is most touristy on Janitzio Island and at Tzintzuntzan, but at villages such as Ihuatzio, Jarácuaro and Urandén it is more intimate. The tourist office has leaflets detailing all the festivities.
6-9 Dec Virgen de la Salud, when authentic Tarascan dances are performed in front of the basillica.

12 Dec An interesting fiesta in honour of the **Virgen de Guadalupe**.

▲ Activities and tours

Pátzcuaro *p421, map p422*
Fishing
Winter is the best time for fishing in the somewhat fish-depleted lake, where locals traditionally threw nets shaped like dragonflies, now a rather rare event.

Tour operators and guides
Jorge Guzmán Orozco, T434-342 2579, Jorge_guzman_orozco@hotmail.com. Guided tours to Janitzio, Tzinzuntzan, Santa Clara del Cobre and Paricutin Volcano, among others. Spanish tours depart daily from Plaza Vasco de Quiroga; enquire about English tours. Fully licensed.
Jorge Mendez, T434-100 5783. Trips to lake-side communities, kayaking, boat trips, archaeological sites and culinary tours are among the offerings. French, English and Spanish spoken.
Miguel Angel Núñez, T434-344 0108, casadetierra@hotmail.com. Miguel, a writer and anthropologist by trade, offers truly excellent personalized tours to local communities, the butterfly sanctuary and archaeological sites. He is very knowledgeable about local cultures having spent many years immersed in them. Rates are US$12 per hr, excluding transportation costs. English-speaking and highly recommended.

⊖ Transport

Pátzcuaro *p421, map p422*
Bus The bus station (called Central) is 1½ km out of town, with a left-luggage office. Buses run between Plaza Chica and the terminal, US$0.50. Taxis cost around US$2.

To **Guadalajara**, late morning service, 6 hrs, US$17. To **Lázaro Cárdenas**, hourly from 0600, 8 hrs, long but a spectacular ride through mountains and lakes (police checks likely), US$19. To Quiroga, every ½ hr, 40 mins, US$1.50. To **Mexico City**, regular service through the day, 6 hrs, US$25. To **Morelia**, every 15 mins with 2nd-class **Purhépecha**, 1 hr, US$4. To **Santa Clara del Cobre**, every ½ hr, 30 mins, US$1. To **Toluca**, from 0915, 5 hrs, 1st class US$20. To **Tzintzuntzan**, every 15 mins, 30 mins, US$1. To **Uruapan**, every ½ hr, 1 hr, US$3.

To the lake, local buses depart from the corner of the market on Plaza Chica. *Combis* also run services between the lakeside villages.

✪ Directory

Pátzcuaro *p421, map p422*
Banks Several ATMs in the centre. Banamex, Portal Juárez 32. **Promex**, Portal Regules 9. Serfín, Portal Allende 54. Bancomer, Zaragoza 23; *casa de cambio* at Benito Mendoza 7.
Internet Several places on or around the Plaza Grande, most charge US$0.50-1.
Laundry Lavandería San Francisco, Terán 16, Mon-Sat 0900-2000. **Medical services** Dentist: Dr Antonio Molina, T434-342 3032. Doctors: Dr Jorge Asencio Medina, T434-342 4038. Dr Guadalupe Murillo, T434-342 1209. Pharmacy: Gems, Benito Mendoza 21, T434-342 0332, daily 0900-2100. **Post office** Obregón 13, 1 block from Plaza Chica, Mon-Fri 0800-1600, Sat 0900-1300.

Western Michoacán

Western Michoacán is decidedly removed from Mexico's tourist trail, with provincial Uruapan as the main centre of activity. Home to a handful of historic buildings and some very tempting park space, this easy-going market town makes a good base for exploring the surrounding countryside. As elsewhere in Michoacán, the hills are scattered with secluded villages, such as Angahuan, where you can hunt down specialist artisans or encounter indigenous life first-hand. Public announcements relayed in the local Purépecha language immerse you in the local bustle and day-to-day atmosphere of the community. Nearby, Volcán Paricutín, merely 65 years old. Nearby Volcán Paracutín, merely 65 years old, can be scaled in a day, with dead lava fields encasing the environs. Uruapan also provides highway access to the some of the most unspoilt coast-line in Mexico. For those who don't mind roughing it, there are ample opportunities to bask in the blissful isolation of empty, wave-swept beaches. However, you may need your own vehicle to get really remote.
▶▶ *For listings, see pages 434-436.*

Uruapan ●❶❸❸ ▶▶ *pp434-436. Colour map 2, B2. Phone code: 452. Altitude: 1610 m.*

From Pátzcuaro, the road continues 52 km southwest to the colonial town of Uruapan, the 'place where everything blooms'. Although suffering from traffic fumes, the town's environs are lush, subtropical, and as its name suggests, wonderfully fertile. Predictably, it owes its wealth to agriculture, especially the production of avocados, for which Uruapan is proudly known as the 'World Capital of the Avacado'. November sees a big festival in honour of this chief export. But Uruapan is also a renowned cradle of lacquer-work where pre-Columbian techniques are used to create an array of colourful and intricately adorned items including trays, boxes, masks and cups. Whilst decidedly provincial, the town is a relaxing and mostly attractive place to spend time. It also makes a good jumping-off point for surrounding attractions.

Ins and outs

Getting there Uruapan airport is 7 km southeast of the towntown area on Avenida Latinoamericana (taxi to downtown US$5-10). It's a small airport and serviced by a single terminal. You could consider flying into Guadalajara instead. The bus station is 2 km northeast of the downtown area; city buses marked 'Centro' run into town (US$0.25) until about 2100, or take a taxi to the plaza (US$3), or just walk. ▶▶ *See Transport, page 436.*

Tourist information The **tourist office** ① *Ayala 16, T452-524 7199, Mon-Sat 0900- 1400 and 1600-2000, Sun 1000-1400,* is between Independencia and Pino Suárez.

Sights

The most attractive of its three plazas is the **Zócalo**, which has the **Jardín de los Mártires** at its west end, named after five local heroes who lost their lives in the Independence struggle. Opposite the Jardín is part of the former Collegiate church of **San Francisco**, built in the17th century with some later additions, such as the interesting 1960s modern art interior. It is now home to the attractive **Casa de la Cultura** and a small museum, free, with excellent display of the history of Uruapan and the personal collections of Eduardo Ruiz. Local crafts can be bought in the *portales* or at the market. East of the Casa de la Cultura, behind the Huatapera (see below) is the **Mercado de Antojitos** where you can sample several regional dishes. Beyond it, the clothes and goods market permanently occupy several streets. On M Treviño, between A Isaac and Amado Nervo, there is a house just 1½ m wide and several storeys high – possibly Mexico's (and the world's) narrowest building. On the same street lies the old textile factory of San Pedro, established in the 19th century and still operating with antique looms and machinery.

The Huatapera

At the east end of the Zócalo is the Huatapera, a restored hospital built by Fray Juan de San Miguel in the 16th century. Like the structure in Santa Fe de la Laguna, the hospital was part of Vasco de Quiroga's grand vision for social provision. Built from wood, shingle, tile and volcanic rock, it exhibits plateresque and Mudejar styles. It now houses a good craft museum, the **Museo Regional de Arte Popular**, where you can see fine examples of locally produced lacquer objects. Adjoining it is a 16th-century chapel now converted into a craft shop.

Parque Nacional Eduardo Ruiz

① *0800-1800. US$0.85. To get there, walk 1 km from the town centre or catch a bus 1 block south of the Zócalo marked 'El Parque'.*
The Parque Nacional Eduardo Ruiz is a verdant urban park space that's considerably smaller and tamer than other national parks in Mexico, but refreshing and pleasant all the same. Replete with subtropical plants, flowers, birds, butterflies, waterfalls and boulders, this 20-ha space follows the course of the Río Cupatitzio. Its source is known as the Rodilla del Diablo (the Devil's Knee), after a myth relating how the Devil met the Virgin Mary whilst strolling in the park, knelt in submission and caused the river's water to spring forth. The park is very popular with families and there are food stalls serving economical snacks. At the entrance to the park, on the corner of Independencia and Culver City, is a **Mercado de Artesanías** selling wooden boxes and bracelets among others.

Tzararacua Falls

ⓘ *www.tzararacua.com, 1000-1800, $0.70. Catch an hourly 'Tzararacua' bus from Uruapan's Zócalo, 15-25 mins, US$1*

It is 10 km through coffee groves and orchards along Río Cupatitzio (meaning 'singing river') to the 25-m **Tzararacua Falls**, always popular with local families, especially at weekends. There are restaurants at the bus stop where you can hire a horse; otherwise you will need to hike 577 steps downhill. Once you reach the thundering crash pool, you can take a fun zipline, US$5, ensuring a more adrenalin-charged experience of the fall. You can also hike 1 km upstream to the slightly smaller **Tzararacuita waterfall**, usually less crowded than the main one.

Tinganio

ⓘ *Daily 0900-1700, US$2. To get there, take a bus towards Pátzcuaro and exit at Tingambato, where it is 1½-km walk from Calle Juárez.*

Surrounded by verdant avocado plantations, the pre-Hispanic ruins of Tinganio ('warm place') are in the town of Tingambato, 30 km from Uruapan on the Pátzcuaro highway. Inhabited between AD 450-900, the site pre-dates the Tarascan empire and although comparatively modest in size, exhibits a range of cultural influence. Most notable are the Teotihucán-style structures, including a pyramid fashioned in the distinctive talud-tablero style. Elsewhere, a ball-court recalls the Toltec civilization and a false dome (usually closed to the public) hints at Mayan architectural methods. The site is relatively low-key and although sometimes visited by Mexicans, it is quite often empty of foreign tourists.

Angahuan

If you're planning to scale Volcán Paricutín (see below), it is recommended that you spend the night in the Purépecha village of Angahuan, where a handful of rustic, dormitory-style accommodation offers an economical bed and an early start for your expedition (see Sleeping, page 434). The village has a very traditional character with interesting wooden houses constructed in the time-honoured pre-Hispanic way. Be sure to check out the church of **Santiago** on the plaza, with handsome Mudéjar features and an indigenous cross with skull and serpent motifs. It's a 10-minute walk from the bus stop to the main plaza and you are likely to be offered horses and guides from the moment you arrive.

Volcán Paricutín

The volcano of Paricutín started erupting on 20 February 1943, became fiery and violent and rose to a height of 1300 m above the 2200-m-high region. After several years of prodigious growth, it died down into a quiet grey mountain (460 m) surrounded by a sea of cold lava. The church tower of **San Juan**, a buried village, thrusting up through the lava field is a fantastic sight (although apparently, the lava flow stopped at the foot of the altar). If you are not taking an organized tour (with horses and guides included), Paricutín is best reached by taking a 'Los Reyes' bus on a paved road to **Angahuan**, US$0.85, one hour, nine a day each way (0500-2000), then hire a guide locally.

A full day's excursion with mules or horses to the area costs about US$50, with US$3-4 tip for the guide (six to seven hours); shorter journeys cost less. To go on foot with a guide costs US$25. It is 3 km from Angahuan to the San Juan ruins, an easy walk: cross the highway and walk 10 minutes into the village, turning right when you reach the main plaza. Follow the road for roughly 200 m, take the second street on the left (it is the only road that goes at an angle of 45°) and follow this cobbled street with telegraph poles for 750 m to a stone pillared gateway. At the gate turn right down a dirt path that leads to a parking area and a viewpoint of the site (overnight parking possible). Just before you enter the car park a wide dirt path with many horse tracks and footprints leads to your right and down through the forest and directly to the lava field and the church. En route you will pass the **Centro Turístico de Angahuan**, with basic accommodation. A guide on foot to the church costs US$5-10 per group.

It is a long, tough 10-km walk to the crater of the volcano (also a long day on horseback for the unaccustomed, especially if you get a wooden saddle) and a guide is necessary as it's very easy to get lost. Walk westwards round the lava field, through an avocado plantation. Wear good walking shoes with thick soles as the lava is very rough and as sharp as glass in places (some people find they cannot make the last stretch over the tennis-ball size rocks); bear in mind the altitude too, as the return is uphill. It takes seven to nine hours to the volcano and back. The cone itself is rather small and to reach it there is a stiff 30-minute climb from the base. A path goes around the tip of the crater, where activity has ceased. If going in one day, leave Uruapan by 0800 or earlier. Go even earlier in the rainy season as clouds usually build up by midday. Take a sweater for the evening and for the summit where it can be windy and cold after a hot climb. The last bus back to Uruapan leaves at 1900; but it's best not to rely on it. It is advised that you spend the night in Angahuan so you take the trip at a relaxed pace.

Paracho → *Phone code: 423.*

South east of Zamora is **Charapán** where a branch road runs 32 km south through pine woods to Paracho, a quaint, very traditional village of small wooden houses; in every other one craftworkers make guitars, violins and mandolins, worth US$15-1500. A recommended workshop is that of **Ramiro Castillo** ① *Av Independencia 259, Galeana 38*, good value, friendly. Bargaining is possible in all workshops.

Zamora → *Phone code: 351.*

Zamora (58 km east of Jiquilpan) is an agricultural centre founded in 1540. In the centre is the **Catedral Inconclusa**, a large, interesting Gothic-style church, started in 1898, but work was suspended during the Revolution. There are several other fine churches, and a **market** on Corregidora. Much of the area around the plaza is pedestrianized. Nearby is tiny **Laguna de Camécuaro**, with boats for hire, restaurants and wandering musicians; popular at holiday times. There is a **tourist office** ① *Morelo Sur 76, T351-512 4015.*

Pacific coast ⊜⊜ ›› *pp434-436. Colour map 2, B2.*

The Pacific coast of Michoacán is only just coming under development. From Uruapan, Route 37 goes to **Playa Azul**, 350 km northwest of Acapulco (bus US$12, 10½ hours minimum) and 122 km from Zihuatanejo (see page 566). Playa Azul is a coconut-and-hammock resort (reported dirty and dilapidated) frequented much more by Mexicans than foreigners, with a few large hotels. The town of **La Mira**, on the main road, is larger than Playa Azul. Forty kilometres of excellent deserted beaches stretch to the north of Playa Azul. At night there is beautiful phosphorescence at the water's edge.

Northwest up the coast, 76 km from Playa Azul, is **Caleta de Campos**. Buses run along the coast road to La Mira, then a short distance to Caleta de Campos. In this poor village perched above a beautiful bay, there is little to eat other than seafood. At the beach here, five minutes from the village, there are bars and restaurants, popular with surfers. Be careful as there are strong currents. The main **fiesta** runs from 10-13 December; at 0200 on 13 December **El Torito**, a bull mask and sculpture loaded with fireworks, makes its spectacular appearance (watch out for elaborate, if dangerous, fireworks at fiesta time).

Eighty-six kilometres further up the coast, to the northwest, is **Maruata**, unspoilt and beautiful. This is a turtle conservation area. There are floods in the rainy season and the river has washed away some of the beach. There are *cabañas* for rent and *palapas* under which you can camp. For southbound traffic seeking Maruata, road signs are inadequate.

Lázaro Cárdenas is the connecting point for buses from Uruapan, Manzanillo and Zihuatanejo. There is a **tourist office** ① *120-E Rector Hidalgo, T753-532 1547*.

⊙ Western Michoacán listings

For Sleeping and Eating price codes and other relevant information, see Essentials pages 47-51.

◉ Sleeping

Uruapan and around *p430*
L Mansión del Cupatitzio, on the road to Guadalajara, T452-523 2100, www.mansion delcupatitzio.com. A beautiful colonial-style hacienda with sumptuous rooms and grounds. Services include pool, gym, Wi-Fi, restaurant and spa. Outstanding quality.
AL El Tarasco, Independencia 2, T452-524 1500, contacto_hoteleltarasco@hotmail.com. Comfortable lodgings with pool, mountain views and a good restaurant.
A Mi Solar, Juan Delgado 10, T452-522 0912, www.hotelmisolar.com. The oldest hotel in town with 14 tastefully decorated rooms and 3 junior suites. There is a pleasant shaded patios, a fine restaurant. Services include sauna, Wi-Fi and gym.
B Pie de la Sierra, Km 4, Ctra a Charapán, on the northern outskirts, T452-524 2510, www.piedelasierra.com. Good motel with a moderately priced restaurant, comfortable rooms, pool and pleasant, well-tended grounds. There's also a trailer park.
C Concordia, Portal Carrillo 8, main plaza, T/F452-523 0400, www.hotelconcordia. com.mx. Comfortable, if unremarkable rooms with TV, phone and bath. There's a nice restaurant and a buffet breakfast for US$5. Parking and laundry service.

C Nuevo Hotel Alameda, Av 5 de Febrero, T452-523 4100, nhalameda@yahoo.com.mx. A clean, modern hotel with comfortable rooms. All have bath, a/c, TV, phone and heating. Laundry and parking.
C Villa de Flores, Emilio Carranza 15, west of the centre, T452-524 2800. The courtyard of this pleasantly furnished and quiet hotel is filled with lovely flowers. 28 rooms with cable TV and hot water. Parking. Recommended.
D Del Parque, Av Independencia 124, T452-524 3845. Quiet, simple rooms with hot water and cable TV, some cheaper ones without TV. A bit faded but perfectly adequate. Located by the entrance to national park with enclosed parking. Friendly and recommended.
D Posada Morelos, Morelos 30, T452-523 2302. A clean, adequate cheapie with a big courtyard. Rooms have cable TV and hot water. Those upstairs are slightly larger.
E Betty's, near the bus station. Basic lodgings with prices per person. Rooms have bath. Good if you need an early bus, but otherwise better to head into the centre. A few other budget lodgings in the area.
E Moderno, main plaza. A very basic place on the east side of the plaza, a lovely old building with great murals. Water is spasmodic. Just one of a few cheapies here.

Angahuan *p432*
B-E Cabañas, Angahuan. *Cabaña* sleeping 6, with a log fire, or cheaper per person in dormitory with bunk beds (dormitories

closed in low season). Both have hot showers; meals available, restaurant closes 1900 in low season, basic facilities, but clean and peaceful, warm and recommended but service poorer when few people are staying.

D Alberque Centro Turístico de Angahuan, T452-523 3934 (Uruapan). The *albergue* is signposted from the bus stop, and is about 30-min walk from there.

Zamora *p433*

L-C Fénix, Madero Sur 401, T351- 512 0266, www.hotelfenix.com. A big, clean hotel with a pool, poor ventilation and pleasant balconies. Various tariffs and standard of rooms.

C-D Posada Fénix, Morelos y Corregidora Ote 54, T351-515 1265, 1 block from Zócalo. Rooms of varying quality, nice owner (also owns Fénix, see above), good laundry service.

Pacific coast *p433*

A-B De la Curva, Nicolás Bravo 235, Lázaro Cárdenas, T753-537 3658, www.hoteldela curva.com. Good services across the board, including pool, laundry, parking, restaurant, internet and beauty salon. 76 spacious rooms, including 6 suites.

B Playa Azul, Venustiano Carranza s/n, Playa Azul, T753-536 0089. Comfortable rooms and a trailer park with 20 spaces, full hook-up, bathrooms, cold shower, 2 pools, bar and restaurant, US$13 for car and 2 people.

C Delfín, Venustiano Carranza s/n, Playa Azul, T753-536 0007. No a/c, but clean, pleasant and there's a swimming pool.

C Los Arcos, Caleta de Campos, T753-531 5038. Acceptable rooms with bath, most also have good views. Parking.

C Yuritzi, Caleta de Campos, T753- 531 5010, www.hotelyuritzi.com. Comfortable rooms with bath, a/c and TV, but cheaper without. Clean, with pool and good views from out front. Changes TCs at reasonable rates.

D Del Pacífico, Blv Francisco Villa, Playa Azul, opposite beach, T753-536 0106. Simple rooms with bath and fan. A bit run down, but clean, friendly and recommended. Hammocks on the roof.

E Cabañas, Caleta de Campos, northwest of the village, where Río Nexpa reaches the coast. Hammock space for US$1 per person.

E Costa Azul, 5 de Mayo 276, Lázaro Cárdenas, T753-532 0780. Rooms with bath.

F Cabañas, Maruata. There are *cabañas* for rent and *palapas* under which you can camp.

Eating

Uruapan *p430*

The local speciality is *cecina*, dried meat. Not much in the way of fine dining downtown, but plenty of acceptable places.

¶¶¶ La Terraza de la Trucha, Rodilla del Diablo 13, next to the national park. As the name suggests, this is the place for rainbow trout. Try it stuffed with squash flowers.

¶¶-¶ Boca del Río, Delgado 2. Since 1974, a rough-and-ready, locally flavoured seafood joint. Soups and prawn cocktail are among the offerings.

¶¶-¶ Café Tradicional, Carranza 5B. Filled with delicious coffee aromas, the interior of this restaurant is adorned with beautifully crafted wooden pillars, beams and doors. The staircase is particularly nice. Coffee by the cup or sack, breakfasts and *comida típica*.

¶¶-¶ Concordia, Portal Carrillo 8, on the main plaza, inside Hotel Concordia (see Sleeping). Good for a buffet breakfast.

¶¶-¶ Cox-Hanal, Carranza, close to the corner of Miguel Treviño. The name means 'let's go eat' in Yucatec. A clean, unpretentious restaurant serving Yucatec specialities. Photo art features the region's premier ruins and *cenotes*.

¶ Bambino's, Carranza 8. Brightly lit, busy, unpretentious eatery serving fast food like burgers, burritos, *quesadillas* and pizzas.

¶ Cocina Mary, Independencia 63. Very popular spot serving great value and diverse *comida corrida*, breakfasts, Mexican staples and economical fare. Nice mural.

¶ La Pérgola, on plaza. An interesting old place, vaguely reminiscent of a mafia den, with lots of weary characters smoking cigarettes and imbibing black coffee. Food includes mediocre Mexican staples, but the people-watching makes up for it.

Mercado de Antojitos, behind the church. Cheap meals from *comedores*. Locals eat at open-air food stalls, very picturesque.

Cafés and ice cream parlours

Several ice cream parlours on the Zócalo.
Café La Lucha, Ortiz 22. Atmospheric little coffee house with 8 decades of tradition and lots interesting old photos on the wall.

Zamora *p433*

Carnes Toluca, Madero Sur y Leonardo, and **Antigua Carnes Toluca** over the road. Not much more than meat, but plenty of it.
Café D'Gribet, on main street. Cheap and good snacks. Try the local pancakes.
El Patio, La Piedad de Cabadas, near the church. Very good, dish of the day good value.

✿ Festivals and events

Uruapan *p430*

1st week of Apr The Zócalo is filled with pottery, brought from all the surrounding indigenous villages.
Jun Las Canacuas (Crown Dance), on Corpus Christi.
15 Sep Feria in Uruapan (2 weeks either side).
16 Sep In the village of San Juan, to celebrate the saving of an image of Christ from the church at the time of the Paricutín eruption.

◷ Transport

Uruapan *p430*

Air Uruapan airport is 7 km southeast of own; taxi US$5-10. Daily flights to **Mexico City**. Also flights to **Culiacán**, **Guadalajara** and **Tijuana**.

Bus The bus station is 2 km northeast of town; to get there catch a 'central camionera' bus from the south side of the plaza; taxi US$3.

To **Colima**, 4 daily, 6 hrs, US$22. To **Guadalajara**, hourly, 4½ hrs, US$20. To

Lázaro Cárdenas, every 30 mins, 6 hrs, US$22. To **Mexico City**, more than 1 per hr, 6 hrs, US$32. To **Morelia**, every 20 mins, 2½ hrs, US$9. To **Pátzcuaro**, frequent, 1 hr, US$4.

Paracho *p433*

Bus To **Uruapan**, 45 mins, US$1. To **Morelia** via Pátzcuaro.

Zamora *p433*

Bus The bus station is at the north edge of town. To get there from the centre, take a bus from 5 de Mayo in front of Catedral Inconclusa (US0.25); taxi US$3.50.

To **Mexico City** and **Guadalajara**, US$19. To **Morelia**, US$18. To **Pátzcuaro**, 2½ hrs. To **Tamazula**, for **Ciudad Guzmán**, 3½-4 hrs, US$11.

Pacific coast *p433*

Bus Buses ply the coast road stopping at the road junction 4 km from **Plaza Azul**. *Colectivos* take you between town and the junction. If driving north it is 5 hrs to **Tecomán** (where the road from Colima comes down to the coast).

From Lázaro Cárdenas Galeana buses run to **Manzanillo** 7¾ hrs, US$18; to **Uruapan**, 6½ hrs, US$19; to **Guadalajara**, US$35 with La Línea; to **Mexico City** US$48, luxury.

❶ Directory

Uruapan *p430*

Banks Banamex, Cupatitzio y Morelos, Visa agent. Bancomer, Carranza y 20 de Noviembre. Serfín, Cupatitzio. **Internet** Logicentro Cyber Café, Av Juárez 57, Mon-Sat. Computer shop, Hotel Plaza. **Laundry** Carranza 47, Mon-Sat 0900-1400, 1600-2000. Mujer Santayo Lavandería, Michoacán 14, T452- 523 0876. **Medical services** Red Cross, T452- 524 0300. **Post office** Jalisco 81. **Telephone** Computel, Ocampo, on plaza, 0700-2200.

Zamora *p433*

Internet In the small mall on Morelos, between Colón and Ocampo.

Contents

Footprint features

At a glance

⊖ **Getting around** Local buses, walking or taxis in Guadalajara. Bus or car hire for outlying areas.

◎ **Time required** A minimum of 2 weeks is required to do justice to Jalisco and Nayarit states. If you have less time, Guadalajara, Tlaquepaque, Tonalá and the Lake Chapala region, with a quick trip to Tequila, can be managed in a week.

☽ **Weather** Pleasant all year.

✕ **When not to go** In Aug the rains can be torrential (although generally of short duration). Even then, it's perfect when it's not raining.

★ Don't miss ...
1 Guadalajara, page 440.
2 Tlaquepaque, page 448.
3 Laguna de Chapala, page 461.
4 Tapalpa, page 463.
5 Tequila, page 479.
6 Bahía de Banderas, page 494.

The state of Jalisco is the archetype of all that is 'Mexico'. This is where you'll find the town of Tequila, best known for its eponymous drink (also Mexico's best-known export); the lasso-swinging *charros* of Los Altos, the country's most cherished cultural icon; the swirling *Jarabe Tapatío* (Mexican hat dance) and the beautiful *chinas pobladas* who perform them; the Mariachis – roving musicians dressed in tight-trousered gala suits and massive sombreros of the 19th-century rural gentry; and further north, the world-famous beaches of Puerto Vallarta – the birthplace of mass tourism – and San Blas. All these originated in Jalisco and the nearby states of Colima and Nayarit.

Guadalajara is a huge, modern metropolis. But the 'pearl of the west' still has a magnificent and elegant colonial core with shady plazas, impressive colonial architecture, fine museums and the vast Mercado Libertad, to say nothing of its top-drawer modern malls, galleries, universities and parks. A short visit to the nearby famous craft centre suburbs of Tlaquepaque or Tonalá is rewarding. Take a boat ride on Mexico's largest lake, Lago de Chapala. See the majestic twin peaks of Fuego and Nevado de Colima. Cool off in the pine forests around delightful, scarcely changed colonial towns such as Tula, Tapalpa or San Sebastián del Oeste.

Jalisco is the gateway to the Pacific coast and the mega-resorts of Puerto Vallarta and its spin-off, Nuevo Vallarta, on the vast Bahía de Banderas. There are other beautiful and secluded beaches nearby. A few kilometres to the north await beautiful Bucerias and La Cruz de Huancaxtle. Further up, in neighbouring Nayarit state, sleepy San Blas is popular with surfers and birdwatchers. Away from the resorts, remote in the Sierra Madre Occidental, live the Cora and Huichol people, renowned for their stunningly beautiful *chaquira* beadwork and colourful *nierika* yarn paintings. In the western interior of Jalisco are several villages of pristine, colonial-era charm, nestled along the slopes of the Sierra Jolalpa and Sierra Tapalpa, whose legendary beauty is seldom seen by outsiders.

Guadalajara and around

→ *Colour map 2, B2. Phone code: 33. Population: 5,000,000 (metropolitan area).*
Guadalajara, Mexico's second city, was founded on 14 February 1542. For many years this 'City of Roses' was considered Mexico's most beautiful city as well as one of the most attractive in the western hemisphere. But Guadalajara suffered a fate similar to the capital in the 1970s and 1980s, when many of its finest buildings were torn down in the name of urban progress. However, in the Centro Histórico, graceful colonial portales (arcades) still flank scores of old plazas and shaded parks, and extensive, well-managed preservation efforts are underway. Guadalajara has more museums than any other city in Mexico outside of Mexico City itself. At weekends and on public holidays, the historic centre fills with people from all over the state, meandering through the streets (several of which are pedestrianized), passing the time in quaint cafés and enjoying the almost festive charm of a bygone era. ▸▸ *For listings, see pages 450-460.*

Ins and outs

Getting there **Aeropuerto Internacional Miguel Hidalgo (GDL)** ① *20 km south of the city (technically in the adjacent town of El Salto)*, receives frequent flights from Mexico City and many other domestic and international airports. Three classes of fixed-rate taxis (*especial*, *semi-especial* and *colectivo*) will take you into the city; tickets are available in the airport (no tip necessary). Two local bus routes also serve the airport.

Guadalajara is a hub for several major land routes. The vast **regional bus terminal** is 10 km southeast of the centre in next door Tonalá, near the El Alamo junction. Buses 102 and 275 run to the centre, US$0.25, frequent service; allow at least 30 minutes. There are also two luxury bus services: **Línea Azul** and **Línea Cardenal**. The **old bus station** (for local transport), a few blocks south of the city centre, serves towns within 100 km of Guadalajara, mainly with second-class buses and *colectivos* which run to the towns on Lake Chapala.

There is a **train station** at the south end of Calzada de la Independencia operating the *Tequila Express*, although nowadays there is no other passenger rail service to or from Guadalajara. (Both southern rail routes, sometimes still shown on maps, move freight only.) ▸▸ *See Transport, page 457.*

Getting around As with any large Latin American city, Guadalajara is congested on weekdays, although much less on weekends. Getting around on foot is far preferable. The most pleasant way of seeing the city is by *calandria* (horse-drawn carriage) in the late afternoon. Evening tours are romantic, but many of the sights are not as visible due to poor exterior lighting. The carriages are found outside the Museo Regional de Guadalajara at the corner of Liceo and Avenida Hidalgo and a few other places, US$20 per hour. More conventional buses and *colectivos* run to most areas of the city, although regular services can be frustratingly bad. Trolley buses and the luxury buses with guaranteed seats on a few fixed routes are a much better option. The city also has two *tren ligero* (metro) lines, one running north–south and the other west-east. Taxis tend not to use meters so agree on a price before setting off.

Best time to visit The climate is mild throughout the year, although in summer it can be thundery at night. Pollution from vehicles can be bad downtown and winter is the worst time for smog. Afternoons are usually clear and sunny and during the rainy summer season smog is less of a problem. Weekends are by far the best time to visit and most attractions are open on Saturday and Sunday. Many cultural venues are closed on Monday.

Tourist information The state and federal tourist office, **Sectur** ① *Morelos 102, Plaza Tapatía, T33-3668 1602, Mon-Fri 0800-2000, Sat-Sun 1000-1600, www.jalisco.gob.mx/srias/setur/index.html*, is helpful and has information in German and English, including a good walking tour map of the historic centre. There are tourist booths in front of the cathedral and at the eastern end of Plaza Tapatía. Another **tourist information centre** ① *Monumento Los Arcos, Av Vallarta 2641, T33-3616 9150, Mon-Fri 0800-2000, Sat-Sun 1000-1600, http://vive.guadalajara.gob.mx*, has opened in the Colonia Arcos Vallarta neighbourhood, west of the centre. The newspaper *Siglo 21* has daily music, film and arts listings, as well as a good entertainment section, *Tentaciones*, on Friday.

Guadalajara is generally safe, more so than any other large Mexican city, however the usual precautions are required against pickpockets.

Sights

Cathedral and Plaza de Armas

The heart of the city is the **Plaza de Armas**. On its north side is the **cathedral basilica** (1561-1618), which incorporates a medley of styles. In 1561 Phillip II, King of Spain, gave the order to the Franciscans to build it, although it wasn't finished until 1618; since then it has gone through many transformations. The original builder was the architect Martín Casillas, at the time New Spain's best architect. The cathedral has the second largest organ in the country. Amongst several notable pieces of art, there is a *Murillo Immaculate Conception* (painted 1650), and the famous *Virgen del Carmen*, painted by Miguel Cabrera, a Zapotec artist from Oaxaca. In the dome are frescoes of the four gospel writers and in the **Capilla del Santísimo** are more frescoes and paintings of the *Last Supper*. The entire complex is beautifully illuminated at night. The cathedral's west facade is on **Plaza de los Laureles**, on the north side of which is the **Palacio Municipal** (1952), which contains murals by Gabriel Flores depicting the city's founding.

Also on Plaza de Armas is the **Palacio de Gobierno** (1643-1770) where, in 1810, the former priest Miguel Hidalgo issued his first proclamation, abolishing slavery. This was to prove a

1 Guadalajara orientation

➡ **Guadalajara maps**
1 Guadalajara orientation, page 441
2 Guadalajara, page 442

pivotal moment in the Mexican War of Independence, and gave Guadalajara much historical prestige in the 15-year struggle. The great murals of José Clemente Orozco – arguably Guadalajara's most famous native son (although born in nearby Zapotlán) – can be seen on the central staircase; they depict Social Struggle, dominated by Hidalgo, with the Church on the left, Fascism on the right and the suffering peasants in the middle.

East of the cathedral

East of the cathedral is the **Plaza de la Liberación**, with a statue of Hidalgo, where the national flag is raised and lowered daily, with much ceremony. On the north side, the **Museo Regional de Guadalajara** ① *Liceo 60 entre Av Hidalgo y Independencia, Tue-Sat 0900-1745, Sun 0900-1630, www.inah.gob.mx, US$1.55, free on Sun, Tue and holidays, free for children and senior citizens*, is in an old seminary (1699), with a good prehistoric section including the complete skeleton of a mammoth found in the town of Jalisco. This museum has an interesting display of shaft tombs, an excellent display of Colima, Nayarit and Jalisco terracotta figures (but less extensive than those of the Museo de

Sleeping		
Aranzazú 2 C2	Castilla y León 1 B1	Quinta Real 10 B1	La Fonda de San Miguel 5 B1
Arboledas Galerías 12 B1	Francés 5 B2	Serena Centro 8 C2	La Rinconada 6 B3
Azteca 3 B3	Hostal Guadalajara	Villa Ganz 11 B1	
Best Western 15 B2	Centro 7 B3		**Bars & clubs** 🍸
	La Rotonda 18 A2	**Eating** 🍴	Femina La Latina 8 B2
	Morales 4 C2	Café D'Osio 1 C1	La Jaula 9 B2
Sleeping 🛏	Plaza los Reyes 6 C2	Café Madoka 2 B1	La Maestranza 12 B2
Aranzazú 2 C2	Posada Tapatía 17 B1	Cames Asadas El Tapatío 7 B3	La Mansión 10 B2
Arboledas Galerías 12 B1	Presidente Intercontinental	Carnes Asadas Rigo's 3 C3	La Maskara 11 B2
Azteca 3 B3	9 A3	El Mexicano 4 B3	

➡ **Guadalajara maps**
1 Guadalajara orientation, page 441
2 Guadalajara, page 442

Arqueología, see below), and one of the finest displays of 17th- to 18th-century colonial art in Mexico. Recently it has added contemporary art, with notable collections by Robert Montenegro and Dr Atl. There are also musical instruments, indigenous art and one room devoted to the history of Jalisco from the conquistadors to the reign of Emperor Agustín de Iturbide; highly recommended.

The **Palacio Legislativo Plaza de la Liberación** ① *open to the public 0900-1800*, a neo-classical building, remodelled in 1982, has a list of the names of all the Constituyentes (signers of Mexico's three main constitutions, of 1824, 1857 and 1917), from Hidalgo to Otero. At the eastern end of this plaza is the enormous and fantastically decorated **Teatro Degollado** ① *daily 1000-1400*, dating back to 1866. It has a brand-new holographic and laser art exhibit (free) projected onto the proscenium every night at hourly intervals that tells the tale of the building's fascinating history. The recently renovated (2009) interior is stunning. It's well worth seeing even if you don't go to a performance.

A pedestrian mall, **Plaza Tapatía**, has been installed between the Teatro Degollado and the former Hospicio Cabañas (1805-1810), crossing the Calzada de la Independencia, covering 16 blocks. It has plants, fountains (including a massive abstract one behind the Instituto Cultural Cabañas), statuary and a tourist office. The massive **Hospicio Cabañas**, built by one of Mexico's leading colonial architects, José Gutierrez, on a Manuel Tolsá design, is now known as **Instituto Cultural Cabañas** ① *east side of the plaza, T33-3668 1647, www.jalisco.gob.mx, Tue-Sat 1000-1800, Sun 1000-1500*. The ex-orphanage, now a World Heritage Site, is a beautiful building with 22 patios, which is floodlit at night. The contents of the former Museo Orozco in Mexico City have been transferred here. Orozco's best-known murals, *Humanity* and *The Spanish Conquest* cover the walls. See also his famous *Man of Fire* painted in the dome. While its primary purpose is to preserve the works of Orozco (of which it holds more than 50), the Instituto Cultural Cabañas also has exhibitions of Mexican and international art and other events.

Facing the Cabañas, on Morelos, is a sculpture in bronze by Rafael Zamarripa of Jalisco's royal seal: two lions supporting a tree. Immediately in front of the Cabañas are four bronze seats/sculptures by local artist Alejandro Colunga, which could be regarded as amusing or macabre, depending on your sense of humour. They include skeletons, an empty man's suit topped by a skull, and a large pair of rabbit ears. Just south of the Cabañas is the vast indoor **Mercado Libertad** (see Shopping, page 455), known locally as San Juan de Dios. The Moorish-looking entrance to this market has been called the most pristine example of Porfiriato facade anywhere in Mexico. Opposite, is the **Plaza de los Mariachis** ① *Obregón y Leonardo Vicario*.

Museo de la Ciudad de Guadalajara ① *Independencia 684, T33-3658 2537, Tue-Sun 1000-1730, Sat 1000-1430, US$0.30*, in a pretty 17th-century building (once serving as a Capuchin convent) with two columned patios, has information on the city from its founding to the present day, including maps and population statistics. It also includes collections in the cinema arts, literature, visual arts and costumes.

West of the cathedral

Immediately west of the cathedral is the **Rotonda de Los Jaliscienses Ilustres** (Mausoleum of Illustrious Men and Women of Jalisco), containing the remains of the state's most notable figures. This classically inspired work was formerly just 'Illustrious Men' until the lone female honoree, Irene Robledo García, was laid to rest here in 2000. The **Ex Convento del Carmen** ① *Av Juárez 638, T33-3614 7184, Tue-Sat 1000-2030, Sun 1500-2000*, is a 16th-century building now marvellously restored as a small museum and cultural centre. Further to the west, is the elegantly Georgian Rectoría of the **University of Guadalajara** ① *Av Juárez 975 y Tolsá, near Enrique Díaz de León*. Inside, in the *paraninfo* (main hall), are three Orozco murals portraying *Man Asleep*, *Man Meditating* and *Man Creating*; lie on your back or look in a mirror. The building also houses the **Museo de las Artes** ① *T33-3134 1664, www.museodelasartes.udg.mx, Tue-Fri 1000-1800, Sat-Sun 1000-1600*, with a good café, several contemporary art exhibits, and research and demonstration areas open to the public.

Not far from the university is the strange-looking **Templo Expiatorio** ① *López Cotilla 935, near Av Enrique Díaz de León y Madero, T33-3825 2888*, with its fine stained glass and a wonderfully intricate ceiling, built in Gothic style but still unfinished after a century. A source of much pride to historical purists, the church is mostly built in carved stone without any iron or concrete infrastructure, exactly as it would have been constructed in the Middle Ages.

Further west along Avenida Vallarta, on a pedestrian street half a block from Los Arcos (formerly the entranceway to Guadalajara proper), the **Casa Taller José Clemente Orozco** ① *Aurelio Aceves 29, T33-3616 8329, Tue-Sat 1000-1600, Sun 1000-1500*, was built in the 1940s and donated to the State of Jalisco by the family after the artist's death in 1951. Orozco never actually lived here (he died two years after buying it) and it was a source of conflict between the muralist's descendants and the state government for many years. Today, all parties seem to have agreed to use it for art classes specializing in muralism, as well an upgraded exhibition schedule.

South of the cathedral

Not far from the centre three churches are worth visiting. **San Felipe Neri** (1752-1802) ① *San Felipe 544, T33-3614 2813*, has a three-tiered altar with columns, a feature repeated on the facade. Its impressive tower is widely considered one of the most beautiful in Guadalajara. Inside are 14 Miguel Cabrera paintings of scenes of the Virgin's life, delicately worked on copper and still in their original frames. To the north is the **Jardín San Francisco**, a pleasantly shaded plaza, and the starting point for horse-drawn carriages. To the west is the church of **Nuestra Señora de Aranzazú** (1749-1752) ① *Av 16 de Septiembre 295, T33-3614 4083*, with three fantastic churrigueresque altarpieces; equally impressive are the coloured ceilings and the finely carved dado, the only light coming from high-up windows and from the open east door. Also worth a look is the **Templo de San Agustín** ① *Morelos 188, T33-3614 5365*. Originally a 16th-century convent, its facade is baroque but inside it is very plain apart from the neo-plateresque altar. Two interior sculptures, one of St Augustine and the other of his mother St Monica are also of interest. Next to the church is the **Convento de San Agustín and Santa Mónica**, now the School of Music for the University of Guadalajara.

The **Museo de Arqueología de Occidente de México** ① *Av 16 de Septiembre 889, T33-3619 0104, Tue-Sun 1000-1400, 1600-1900, US$0.30*, has a comprehensive collection of objects from Jalisco, Colima and Nayarit, including pottery, ornaments, weapons, figures and illustrations of tombs. A small booklet in English is available.

Nearby is **Parque Agua Azul** ① *Calzada Independencia Sur, Tue-Sun 0800-1900, US$0.15*, a park with a good aviary, trees, flowers and fountains (see page 447). It also contains an outdoor concert bowl, the **Teatro Experimental**, and the **Instituto de las Artesanías de Jalisco** ① *T33- 3030 9080, http://artesanias.jalisco.gob.mx/index.html, Mon-Fri 1000-1800*, (see Crafts, page 455). The park is about 15 blocks south of the centre on González Gallo 20, near the intersection of Dr R Michel y Calzada Independencia Sur; to

The birthplace of charro

Just as the USA has its ongoing love affair with cowboys, so Mexico has one with *charros*. It's hard to define precisely what a *charro* is, but one look at his colourful outfit and you'll know when you've seen him (or if it's a her, a *charra*). Partly a product of the glamourization of rural life by Mexican cinema, partly the result of Mariachi-inspired legends, and partly the wishful thinking of an increasingly urbanized populace, *charros* nowadays exist more in the imagination than in the everyday world.

However, there are a few exceptions, and meeting one of them is an experience you'll never forget. For the *charros* who still hew to the old ways, life revolves around one's horse, one's family, and one's region… often in that order. A *charro* and his horse are inseparable, and the skill, prowess, and beauty with which the two interact is astonishing. His family supports his calling – usually inherited – and his regional association is key to where and when he competes. Every Mexican state has its own *charrería* (or *charreada*) where amazing equestrian feats are performed. This is the most quintessentially Mexican event of all, and if you're lucky enough to be in town when one is held – they often coincide with annual state fairs – you're in for a treat of the first order.

The *charrería* consists of a number of scoring events staged in specific order — usually nine for men and one for women. Of course, all participants wear traditional *charro* clothing. The effect is stunning, particularly when the *charras* execute their mounted ballet, surely one of the most dangerous things that can be done on horseback. The ladies fly at each other at phenomenal speeds, only to cut back at the very last second and merge into a graceful equestrian dance. The men have several contests – throwing a bull by the tail while remaining seated, jumping off of a tame horse onto a wild one – that will have you on the edge of your seat and marvelling at their composure and skill.

All participants are judged on both style and execution, and the competition is intense (fans have no qualms letting a judge know when they think he's made a bad call). For the best experience, go with a Mexican to appreciate the pageantry and spectacle: you'll need one to explain some of the intricacies of the event. Interestingly, for all of the skill and bravery involved, *charrerías* never award money to winners, which would go against the principles of good sportsmanship and competition for love of the sport alone. (In fact, under Mexican law it is illegal to receive a monetary reward for participating.)

The *charro* lifestyle and ethic originated in a few communities (most noticeably Los Altos) in eastern Jalisco State and is still practised more or less in its original form in this region, as well as in the neighbouring state of Zacatecas. Elsewhere it is now more entertainment than anything else, but what entertainment it is!

get there take bus 52 or 54 up Avenida 16 de Septiembre or No 60 or 62 up Calzada Independencia back to centre.

North of the cathedral

North of the cathedral, is the **Museo de Periodismo y Artes Gráficas** ① *Av Alcalde 225, T33-3613 9285, Tue-Sat 1000-1800, Sun 1000-1500, US$0.65, students with ID half price, over 60s free.* The neoclassical building is known as the 'Casa de los Perros' because of two large dog statues on the roof. The first printing shop in Guadalajara was here and the first *periódico insurgente* (insurgent newspaper) in the Americas, *El Despertador Americano*, was published here in 1772. The *Gaceta de México*, dating from 1784, is still published on site. The museum contains old printing presses and newspapers as well as an extensive library dedicated to the media. When Avenida Alcalde was widened in 1950, the building's facade was moved back 9 m. **Museo López Portillo** ① *Liceo 177, T33-3613 2411, Tue-Sat 1000-1700, Sun 1000-1500*, formerly the family home of the ex-president, was restored in 1982 when he was in office. It is a colonial house with a large tiled courtyard, and surrounding rooms furnished with 18th- and 19th-century Italian and French furniture. It is also used as a recital hall and cultural centre for all ages with classes in music, dance, literature, chess, indigenous culture and languages.

Worth a visit if travelling with young children is the children's museum, **Globo** ① *5 de Febrero y Analco (just outside the centre, in the Sector Reforma neighbourhood), T33-3669 1381, www.guadalajara.gob.mx/globo, Tue-Fri 0930-1930, Sat- Sun 1000-1800*. Specifically designed for ages one to eight, this hands-on, interactive museum is one of the best on the continent in showing kids how and why things work in a fun setting. Just outside the centre, in Colonia San Carlos, is the **Museo de Paleontología de Guadalajara** ① *Dr R Michel 520, T33-3619 6546, www.guadalajara.gob.mx/dependencias/museopaleontologia, Tue-Sat 1000-1800, Sun 1100-1800*. If you're into fossils and prehistory, this is the spot for you. Another University of Guadalajara-owned building, the **Centro Cultural Casa Vallarta** ① *Av Vallarta 1668, T33-3615 4922, www.cge.udg.mx/cpdc, Tue-Fri 1000-1800, Sat-Sun 1000-1600*, a spacious circa 1830 former *casona* (old mansion), now houses a painting and photography gallery and makes for a nice break from the otherwise unremittingly modern buildings along this main street.

Churches worth seeing north of the cathedral include **Santa Mónica** (1733) ① *Reforma 423, T33-3614 6620*, which is small, but very elaborate with impressive arches full of gold under a clear atrium and a richly carved facade. Nearby, on the site of a former Dominican convent is the 19th-century church of **San José de Gracia** ① *Av Alcalde 294 y Reforma, T33-3614 2746*, with a fine gilded rococo pulpit and an interior designed to resemble a Latin cross. In the plaza outside is a statue of Núñez, defender of the Reforma (the second Mexican Constitution), who was killed in 1858. The churrigueresque **Santuario de Guadalupe** ① *Av Alcalde 527y Juan Alvarez, T33-3614 8165*, is lovely inside. The image of Our Lady of Guadalupe upon the main altar (by Alcíbar) is important for its originality and dates from 1779. Outside, in the Jardín del Santuario, are massive celebrations on 12 December, the feast day of the **Virgin of Guadalupe**, with fireworks, musicians, vendors and games. Five minute's walk away, **Nuestra Señora de Belén** ① *Hospital 290, T33-3614 6109*, is enclosed in the **Hospital Civil Viejo** and contains three fine, late 18th-century *retablos*. The main entrance has a small porch with Ionic columns and an extremely valuable sculpture of Saint Michael – one of the oldest extant in Mexico – which belonged to the hospital as far back as 1545. Behind the hospital is the **Panteón de Belén** ① *entrance at Belén 684 at the corner of Eulogio Parra, open until 1500*, a beautiful old cemetery closed to new burials for many years.

Parque Alcalde ① *Jesús García y Av de los Maestros, small entry fee*, is a pleasant enough park with a lake, rowing boats, a miniature train and a children's playground.

On the way out of the city going northeast along Calzada Independencia, near the huge **Barranca de Oblatos canyon**, there is a large and well-kept **Jardín Zoológico** ① *US$0.30 (take bus 600, 60 or 62 heading north on Independencia)*, with plenty of Central American animals and aviaries in a delightful atmosphere. Within the zoo is the **Selva**

Mágica amusement park ① *Paseo Zoológico 600, T33-3674 1418, www.selvamagica. com.mx*, which has more than 35 rides and other attractions just for the kids, including its own marine park with dolphin and seal shows. There is a planetarium nearby.

Two city parks stand out as excellent places to spend some leisure time in Guadalajara, both well maintained in every respect. **Los Colomos** ① *daily 0500-2000, US$0.65*, technically in Zapopan (see below) is located in a large, 117-ha forest, with various sculptures, gardens, pools, health courses, and other attractions within the park. There are paths that lead to other special areas, including those set aside for picnics and family outings. The **Japanese Gardens**, donated by Guadalajara's sister city of Kyoto, Japan, are a quiet, peaceful sanctuary within the park. Some of Colomos is slated to be set aside for use in the 2011 Panamerican Games, for which Guadalajara is the host city.

Parque Agua Azul, while not as bucolic as Colomos, is nonetheless a long-standing Guadalajara tradition. Located in the southern section of the city, it is divided into two parts, connected by a bridge, and is second only to Colomos in terms of size. There are large green areas, a butterfly house, bird house, orchid house and various entertainment venues, some especially for children. The large outdoor auditorium is known as **La Concha Acústica** ('The Acoustic Shell'), where different cultural shows are preformed regularly. There are usually local musicians performing along an area known as **Bulevar de los Músicos** ('Musicians' Boulevard'). All in all a great place to relax and escape the city.

Guadalajara suburbs ⊖❼⓭⓲⓪⊖ ➠ pp450-460.

Zapopan → *Colour map 2, B2. Phone code: 33.*

Zapopan, a separate city founded in 1540, shares a border with much of the western portion of the city of Guadalajara. In fact, a great deal of what many people think is Guadalajara is actually Zapopan, and many of Guadalajara's attractions are actually in Zapopan. (The city has more educational and cultural institutions per capita than any other in all of Mexico.) The centre of Zapopan is dominated by the incredible Basílica de Zapopan, visited by Pope John Paul II in 1979, and the beautiful main plaza.

Ins and outs To get to Zapopan, take bus 275 on Av Alcalde, or take Line 1 of the *tren ligero* to the Avila Camacho stop and pick up bus 175 to Zapopan (there are several different 175s, so check with driver that the bus goes all the way to Zapopan). For about US$1.15, you can also can reach Zapopan on the air-conditioned, turquoise **TUR** buses (slightly more expensive) that pass just south and west of the centre of Guadalajara. These *TUR* buses also serve the popular suburbs of Tlaquepaque and Tonalá (see below).

The **tourist office** ① *Guerrero, T33-3110 0754, Mon-Fri 0900-2100, Sat 0900-1300*, is in the Casa de la Cultura, two blocks behind the basilica.

Sights The famous **Basílica de Zapopan**, begun in 1690 and completed in 1730, is, of course, best known for its miraculous image of Nuestra Señora, known as *La Generala* ('The General'), on the main altar, given to the local people in 1541. The diminutive *La Generala* was commissioned in 1823 as 'General of the Armies of Jalisco' by the young Mexican government, a title she still carries today. Slightly less important (but a source of immense local pride) is its status as the only major church in Jalisco to have been visited by Pope John Paul II during his first tour of Latin America. The basilica houses the **Museo de la Virgen de Zapopan** ① *T33-3636-4430, Mon-Sat 0930-1330, 1530-1800, Sun 1530-1800*, which has an interesting collection of memorabilia and offerings associated with this festival. Next door is the **Museo de**

The Virgin of Zapopan

Zapopan is one of the most famous pilgrimage centres in Mexico. At the begin- ning of each rainy season (early to mid- June), thousands of people accompany the tiny (34 cm, without her ornate gold crown) image of the Virgin of Zapopan, Jalisco's patroness, to Guadalajara and as far as the shores of Lake Chapala on a tour of all 130 parishes in the metropolitan area. This is believed to protect the city against heavy rains and floods. On 12 October the image is taken back to the Basilica of Zapopan again. Her homecoming celebration is a remarkable sight. The image is carried in a car that is not driven but very slowly pulled by devout volunteers, surrounded by crowds of enthusiastic, dancing and masked followers acting as escorts. Upon her return, a stupendously large crowd (upwards of three million people have been recorded) gather to welcome her back to the basilica with a large festival.

The feast of the Virgin of Zapopan was initially a purely religious celebration of thanksgiving, but is now evolving into something more culturally transcendent. Formerly, its celebrants were exclusively the religious and the faithful laity. While these two groups still account for the majority of participants, the festival has taken on both indigenous and pop cultural overtones and has come to resemble a tamer version of Rio's Carnaval, with more than 300 *quadrilles* (dancing troupes) in flamboyant costumes and headdresses. Unlike the feasts of the two other major Virgins in western Mexico – those of San Juan de Lagos and Talpa – that of Zapopan has not only retained its original emphasis but also added to it.

Arte Huichol Wixárica ① *Eva Briseño 152, T33-3636 4430, Mon-Sat 0930-1315, 1500-1800, Sun 1000-1400, US$0.30*, with passable bilingual exhibits on Huichol culture, masks and costumes. If you're not planning to visit the smaller towns to the north and east of Guadalajara to see the Huchol in their native environment, this is a recommended stop.

Also nearby is the **Museo de Arte de Zapopan (MAZ)** ① *Andador 20 de Noviembre 166, T33-3818 2575, www.mazmuseo.com, Tue-Wed, Fri, Sun 1000-1800, Thu 1000-2200*. One of the country's best-kept museum secrets, the MAZ has exhibited several of Mexico's best artists, as well as several leading European and US artists.

A slightly bizarre if impressive little museum is the obscure **Museo de Caza Benito Albarrán** ① *Paseo de los Parques 3530, Colinas de San Javier neighbourhood, T33-3641 4511, Sat-Sun 1000-1400*. A shrine to the former owner's obsession with African and European wild game, this is the only museum in Mexico that houses such a collection, presented in dioramas depicting the animals' natural environments.

Tlaquepaque → *Colour map 2, B2. Phone code: 33*
About 7 km southeast of the city centre is the attractive suburb of Tlaquepaque, which is well worth a visit. Although the city has pre-Conquest origins, essentially it grew up as a settlement in the 1700s, clustered around its then-primary church, Nuestra Señora de la Soledad. It is now best-known for its ceramics (and many other shopping delights). In fact, from just before the Second World War until the mid 1970s, Tlaquepaque's ceramic output exceeded that of Puebla and Oaxaca. Tlaquepaque can be combined with a visit to Tonalá (see below) for an easy day-trip from central Guadalajara. However, if shopping is your motive, you need at least a full day in this charming city.

Ins and outs A taxi ride from the centre of Guadalajara should cost US$5.50-7.75. There is a helpful regional **tourist office** ① *Juárez 238, T33-3635 1220, Mon-Fri 0900-1500.*

Sights Independencia runs from Bulevar Tlaquepaque (the main avenue into Guadalajara) to the Plaza Central where you can see the restored **Parroquia de San Pedro Tlaquepaque** and the ancient **Basílica Lateranensis**. The **main plaza**, with its ornate late Victorian kiosk, is one of the most beautiful anywhere, especially in the spring and autumn. Further on is colourful and traditional **El Parián**, a very large, square building built 1883-1890 and occupying most of another plaza, with bars (pretty woodwork and tiling) and kitchens around the perimeter. The rest is an open courtyard. This is the epicentre of all that is the stereotypically Mexican 'experience', and visitors looking for the clothes, colours, fabrics, foods, handicrafts and trinkets will find them here in spades. People from all over Mexico come to shop in Tlaquepaque when building new homes or remodelling, and it should come as no surprise that Tlaquepaque is also where many interior designers come to find quintessentially Mexican arts and crafts. At night the boulevards and main square fill with diners and Mariachis (see page 454). The **Museo Regional de la Cerámica** ① *Independencia 237, T33-3635 5404, Tue-Sat 1000-1800, Sun 1000-1500*, in a beautiful colonial building, displays examples of Jalisco's ceramics and other handicrafts. There are also items for sale. ▸▸ *See Shopping, page 456.*

Somewhat surprisingly, there is more to do in Tlaquepaque than shop. It is also home to the Jesuit-run ITESO, one of Mexico's finest universities, which has the **Casa ITESO Clavigero** (1928) ① *Guadalupe Zuno 2083, T33-3615 2242, www.casaclavigero.iteso.mx, Mon-Fri 0900-1900, Sat 1000-1400*, a Luis Barragán-designed landmark of considerable importance that offers many cultural events. Also worth visiting is the **El Refugio Cultural Centre**① *Donato Guerra 160, T33-3657 6890, Mon-Fri 0900-2000, Sat 0900-1300*. This spot is a definite must-see. Originally a hospital, it is now an cultural and commercial area. The **Casa de la Cultura** itself is located in the former chapel. Temporary exhibits are shown here and much tourism information is on hand.

Tonalá → *Colour map 2, B2. Phone code: 33.*

Fifteen kilometres southeast of Guadalajara on the road to Mexico City (Routes 80/15, with the latter the eventual designation) is Tonalá, noted for its Sunday and Thursday *tianguis* (open-air markets), where you can pick up bargains in pottery, glass and especially ceramics. As with its neighbour Tlaquepaque, crafts from Tonalá for many years have been amongst the most prized in all of Mexico. Given its singular importance to the town's economy and history, there is the **Museo Nacional de Cerámica** ① *Constitución 104, T33-3683 0494, Tue-Fri 1000-1700, Sat-Sun 1000-1400*. The museum occupies a two-storey mansion and displays work from Jalisco and all over the country. There's a large gift shop in the front on the right as you enter. Admission is free, but there is a nominal fee if you wish to use a video or still camera.

The market is held on the central avenue, where all the buses from Guadalajara stop. Benito Juárez intersects this avenue and is a main shopping street. It runs to the **Zócalo** (main plaza), where it intersects with Madero, the other main shopping street in the centre, and on another block to the **Parroquia de Santiago Apostól**, a very beautiful church built in the mid-17th century. On the plaza is the cream-coloured **Iglesia del Sagrado Corazón**. The walls are lined with crucifixion paintings. Also on the plaza are the **Presidencia Municipal**, a pastel blue-green colonial-style building, and the **municipal market** (food and crafts).

There is a **regional tourist office** ① *Artesanos building, set back from the road at Atonaltecas 140 Sur y Matamoros, T33-3683 1740, Mon-Fri 0900-1500, Sat 0900-1300,* although the information kiosk diagonally across from the church in the Zócalo also has maps and information.

④ Guadalajara listings

For Sleeping and Eating price codes and other relevant information, see Essentials pages 47-51.

⑤ Sleeping

Guadalajara *p440, maps p441 and p442*
The smart business hotels are mostly in the modern western part of the city (many are technically in Zapopan but list themselves as being in Guadalajara), around the Plaza del Sol, roughly 2 km west of the Centro Histórico.

LL Presidente Intercontinental, Av López Mateos Sur y Av Moctezuma, T33-3678 1234, www.ichotelsgroup.com/h/d/icon/hd/gdlha. Some de luxe suites with private patio, high-rise tower with built-in shopping centre, cavernous lobby.

LL Quinta Real, Av México 2727 y Av López Mateos, T33-3615 0000, www.quintareal.com/eng/idt/41/quinta-real-guadalajara. Designed as a colonial manor, convenient location with 78 large, well-furnished rooms, original artwork, good restaurant.

LL Villa Ganz, López Cotilla 1739, T800-508 7923, www.mexicoboutiquehotels.com/villaganz/index.html. Converted century-old mansion with 10 rooms, each beautifully appointed. Close to Av Chapultepec, but an oasis of tranquillity. Highly recommended.

AL Aranzazú, Av Revolución 110 Pte, T33-3942 4040, www.aranzazu.com.mx. Central, very good but a bit over-priced, full business services. See the bats departing from the roof eaves at dusk.

AL Best Western Plaza Génova, Av Juárez 123, T33-3613 7500, www.hplazagenova.com. In the Centro Histórico, includes continental breakfast and welcome cocktail.

Clean, good service, good restaurant. Recommended.

A Francés, Maestranza 35, T33-3613 1190, www.hotelfrances.com. Colonial building with central patio, the oldest hotel in the city, incredibly atmospheric and much beloved by guests. Built in 1610, have a drink there at happy hour 1800-1900, to enjoy the bygone atmosphere.

A La Rotonda, Liceo 130, T/F33-3614 1017, central, near the cathedral. Remodelled 19th- century building, attractive, dining area in courtyard, cheap set lunches, nice public areas, rooms OK, with TV, phones, covered parking.

A-B Arboledas Galerias, Av Vallarta 5281 (in Zapopan), T33-3915 3275, www.arboledas galerias.com. Quiet but close to the centre. Built in 2003, with 75 rooms over 6 floors. A/c, bar, restaurant, Wi-Fi. Car park and garage.

B Azteca, Javier Mina 311, 1½ blocks east of Mercado Libertad, T33-3617 7465, www.hotel azteca.com. Clean, very friendly, some rooms with good views, parking around the corner.

B Celta, Av Mariano Otero 1570, T33-3880 0222, www.hotelcelta.com/index-en.html. Good location west of the centre. Well appointed, quiet. Best in range.

B Plaza los Reyes, Calzada Independencia Sur 164, T33-3613 0076, www.granhotellos reyes.com. Very central. Bilingual staff, 24-hr restaurant, free Wi-Fi, swimming pool. Recently remodelled, excellent value.

B-C Morales, Corona 243, T33-3658 5232, www.hotelmorales.com.mx. Wonderful old building in the Centro Histórico. Spacious rooms, bilingual staff, lovely restaurants. Excellent value and highly recommended.

C Canadá, Estadio 77, ½ block west of old bus station, T33-3619 4014. All rooms with bath, hot water, some with TV, clean, good value.

C Mesón Ejecutivo, Av México 2747, T33-3616 4591, www.mesonejecutivo.com. In the shadow of the **Quinta Real** (see above), but a good choice for the budget traveller. Primarily business-class hotel but better value than most.

C-D Castilla y León, González Ortega 77, 4 blocks west of cathedral, T33-1378 3838, www.hotelcastillayleongdl.com. Central location. Has 'lost in time' feel to it, largely bereft of mod cons but quiet and a decent price. Very friendly staff.

C-D Del Bosque, Av López Mateos Sur 265, immediately west of the centre, near Minerva, T33-3121 4700, www.hoteldelbosquegdl.com. Restaurant, gym, pool, nice gardens. Excellent value for range.

D Imperial, Allende 16, Ameca, T375-758 1415. Central, serviceable, but only if **La Hacienda**, below, is full.

D La Hacienda, Circunvalación Pte 66, Colonia Ciudad Granja, off Av Vallarta on the left before the *periférico* and head to Tepic, T33-3627 1724, ext 117. A long way from the centre of town. Motel with shaded, pool, clubhouse, hook-ups.

D Posada Tapatía, López Cotilla 619, 2-3 blocks from Federalismo, T33- 3614 9146. Colonial-style house, one of the better budget places, although traffic can be a problem.

E Estación, Independencia Sur 1297, across the main boulevard beside train station, T33-3619 0051. Quiet, clean, safe, luggage store, hot water, small, limited restaurant. Recommended.

E Hostel Guadalajara Centro, Maestranza 147, close to the centre, T33-3562 7520, www.hostelguadalajara.com. Youth Hostel-affiliated, very popular with backpackers, with good facilities including kitchen, laundry, internet and lounge area.

Tlaquepaque *p448*

Consider staying in Tlaquepaque if stocking up on gifts before heading home. A great many new B&B-style options have opened here

recently, including several very close to the main shopping district.

L-AL La Villa del Ensueño, Florida 305, T33-3635 8792, www.villadelensueno.com. 8 rooms, 2 suites, pool, breakfast, no smoking, English spoken.

A El Tapatío & Resort, Blv Aeropuerto 4275 (en route to airport), T33-3837 2929, www.hotel-tapatio.com. Fine view of city, extensive grounds, very attractive and comfortable rooms.

B Casa Campos Bed & Breakfast, Francisco de Miranda 30-A, T33-3838 5296, www.hotel casacampos.com. Right in the centre and surrounded by arts and craft stores. Charming old house with hip interior. Friendly, bilingual staff. Not particularly quiet, but has restaurant, bar, a/c, TV, Wi-Fi, free breakfast.

B La Posada de la Media Luna, Juárez 36 (1 block east of the Parián and just 15 mins south of airport), T33-3635 6054, www.hotel lamedialuna.com. Delightful rooms, with private bath, TV and telephone, includes breakfast on colourful patio. Excellent value.

B-C Casa del Retoño Bed & Breakfast, Matamoros 182, T33-3587 3989, www.lacasa delretono.com.mx. Centrally located, utterly charming patio and interior, very tranquil, free breakfast. Highly recommended.

C Festival Plaza, Ctra Guadalajara-Zapotlanejo Km 1, T33-3659 3141, http://hotelfestival.com.mx. Right off the motorway to Mexico City and just outside of city limits. Free buffet breakfast, family friendly, with pool, restaurant, parking. Good value.

Tonalá *p449*

C Casa de las Palomas, Anesagasti 125, T33-3683 5542, www.casadelaspalomas.com. Easily best hotel in town. Marvellous old building with wonderful decor in public areas. Inside parking in patio. Clean, spacious rooms. Highly recommended.

C-D Arana Hostería, Tonalá 206, T33-3683 1881, www.aranahosteria.com. Tiny B&B away from the centre, 1 block north of market and just off the motorway. Free Wi-Fi and covered parking. Very nondescript but safe and clean.

C-D Galería Tonalá, Francisco I Madero 22, T33-3683 0595, www.hoteltonala.com. Plain but in good shape, some rooms with TV. In the heart of the old town.

C-D Hacienda del Sol, Cruz Blanca 44, T33-3683 0275, www.hotelhacienda delsol.com. Great downtown location near central market, but can be noisy with bus traffic. Free Wi-Fi and covered parking.

🍴 Eating

Guadalajara *p440, maps p441 and p442*
As can be expected in a city of this size there is a wide variety of restaurants on offer, look in local tourist literature for the flavour of the month. There are also fast-food outlets, pizzerias and Mexican cafeterias and bars. The cheapest restaurants are in the streets near the old bus station, especially in **Calle de Los Angeles**, and upstairs in the large **Mercado Libertad** (San Juan de Dios) in the centre. There are also plenty of cheap *loncherías*.

₦₦₦ El Sacromonte, Pedro Moreno 1398, T33-3825 5447. Mon-Sat 1330-2400, Sun 1330-1800. Mexican haute cuisine in what many consider to be Guadalajara's most romantic (and expensive) restaurant. Highly recommended.

₦₦₦ Ochenta y Ocho, Av Vallarta 1342, T33-3826 6164. In a large French chateau with an elaborate facade, balconies and columns. Unique eatery in that fish, meat and wines are served separately. Recommended.

₦₦₦ Piaf, Marsella 126. Closed Sun. French cuisine, live music, friendly. Excellent.

₦₦₦ Suehiro, De La Paz 1701, T33-825-1880, www.suehiro.com.mx. Mon-Sat 0130-1730, 1930-1130, Sun 01330-1900. Great Japanese, considered by many as best in city – also one of the most expensive.

₦₦₦-₦₦ El Ganadero, Av Américas. Excellent beef, reasonable prices.

₦₦₦-₦₦ El Mexicano, Plaza Tapatía, Morelos 81. Rustic Mexican decor. Recommended.

₦₦₦-₦₦ La Fonda de San Miguel, Donato Guerra 25-13, T33-3613 0809, www.lafonda desanmiguel.com. Mon 0830-1800, Tue-Sat 0830-1200, Sun 0830-2100. In the historic centre, housed in a 1690 ex-convent widely reputed to be haunted. Excellent Mexican dishes served in setting that is both colourful and romantic.

₦₦₦-₦₦ La Rinconada, Morelos 86 on Plaza Tapatía. Open until 2130. A beautiful colonial building, columned courtyard, carved wood doors, separate bar.

₦₦₦-₦₦ La Trattoria, Niños Héroes 3051. Very good, reasonably priced Italian, very popular (queues form for lunch from 1400).

₦₦₦-₦₦ Nikoy, Terranova 455, T33-3640 3914, www.nikoy.com.mx. Mon-Thu 1400-2300, Fri-Sat 1400-2400, Sun 1300-1000. Gives **Suehiro** a run for its money as the best Japanese food in Guadalajara. Recommended and less expensive.

₦₦ Carnes Asadas El Tapatío, Mercado Libertad (there are 3). Strictly for carnivores, try the delicious *carne en su jugo*.

₦₦ Carnes Asadas Rigo's, Independencia 584A. Popular. Goat is a speciality, roasted each day and served with radish, onion and chilli.

₦₦ Cortijo La Venta, Federación 725, T33-3617 1675. Daily 1300-0100. Invites customers to fight young bulls (calves) after their meal (the animals are not harmed, guests might be), restaurant serves meat, soups, salads.

₦₦ Il Pomodoro, Av López Mateos Norte 145, T33-3793 1111. Fantastic Italian food (serving regular-sized portions, not Mexican ones) with outstanding wine selection. Service is top-notch. Crowded at lunch.

₦₦ Santo Coyote, Lerdo de Tejada 2379, T33-3616 8472. Wonderful, eclectic ex-hacienda-style setting. Salsa prepared at table, appetizers excellent. Higher-end Mexican.

₦₦-₦ Café Madoka, Enrique González Martínez 78, just south of Hidalgo, T33-3613 3134. Excellent very early breakfasts, well known for the men who play dominoes there. Friendly, a Guadalajara institution.

₦ Búfalo, Calderón de la Barca y Av Vallarta. Tacos and cheap *comida corrida*, very friendly.

₦ Café D'Osio, around the corner from Hotel Hamilton, on the corner of Prisciliano

Sánchez and Ocampo. Daily 0900-1800. Excellent breakfast and delicious *tortas*, especially the roast pork, not expensive.

Chai, Av Vallarta 1509, T33-3616 1299, www.chai.com.mx. Sun-Sat 0800-2400. In a beautiful restored *casona*. Hip without being pretentious. Great sandwiches and wonderful beverages. The best spot in the centre for snacks or light meals any day or night. Highly recommended.

La Bombilla, López Cotilla y Penitenciaría. Very good for *churros* and hot chocolate.

La Catedral del Antojito, Pedro Moreno 130, a pedestrian street. Colonial-style house with a restaurant upstairs above the bridal gown shop. Serves tacos, *tortas* etc, good meals for under US$2.

Zapopan *p447*

El Farallón de Tepic, Av Niño Obrero 560, T33-3121 2616. Mexican and seafood, *pescado sarandeado* (whole barbecued fish stuffed with vegetables) is the best dish. Very popular (30-min wait at times).

Asadero El Torito, Ctra a Tisistan 1027, T33-3624 1055. Very good grilled meats.

Tlaquepaque *p448*

Abajeño Campestre, Av Juárez 231, T33-3635 9097. Daily 1200-2200. One of Tlaquepaque's most atmospheric 'Old World' Mexican restaurants. In arts and crafts area.

Sin Nombre, Av Madero 80, T33-3635 4520. Mon-Thu 1100-2200, Fri-Sat 1100-2400. Tlaquepaque's most famous and beloved Mexican restaurant. Located on a beautiful terrace in the heart of the arts and crafts area; peacocks and Mariachis wander about; waiters are bilingual.

Tonalá *p449*

El Rincón del Sol, Av 16 de Septiembre 61, T33-3683 1989. An attractive restaurant serving steaks and Mexican food.

El Boquinete, Pasillo entre Juárez y Zaragoza, T33-3683 5839. Typical Mexican-style chicken and meat dishes; extensive tequila, whiskey, and beer selections. Touristy and crowded.

🍸 Bars and clubs

Guadalajara *p440, maps p441 and p442*
Just stroll down Maestranza south of Juárez from about 0830 on and listen for the noise. **La Maestranza** is very popular, and brings out the machismo with distinctive themes of the matador. **La Maskara** and **La Jaula** are on the same block, and gay friendly. **La Mansión** is round the corner, and **Femina La Latina** offers an altogether more cultured approach to the whole drinking/socializing malarkey.

Gay and lesbian

Guadalajara and Puerto Vallarta are rare examples in Mexico of cities outside of the capital that have prominent gay club scenes, although in the former the city fathers are threatening to move gay clubs out of the centre for the 2011 Pan American Games. The current favourites are:

Angels, López Cotilla 1495 B, T33-3615 2525, www.angelsclub.com.mx.

Blackcherry, Popocatepetl 40, www.blackcherry.com.mx.

Circus, Galeana 277, T33-3613 0299, www.gaygdl.com/circus.html.

Link Bar, Av La Paz 2199, T33-3331 3840, www.gaygdl.com/link.html.

Monica's Disco Bar, Alvaro Obregón 1713, T33-3643 9544, www.monicasdisco.com.

🎭 Entertainment

Guadalajara *p440, maps p441 and p442*;
Cinema
Good-quality films, some in English, are shown at the *cine-teatro* in the Instituto Cultural Cabañas (see page 443), which also has a good cafeteria.

Cultural centres
Alliance Française, López Cotilla 1199 (in Sector Juárez), T33-3825 2140.
Instituto Cultural Mexicano-Norteamericano de Jalisco, Enrique Díaz de León 300 (see Language schools, page 456).

Instituto Goethe, Morelos 2080 y Calderón de la Barca, T33-3615 6147. Library, nice garden, newspapers.

Mariachis

Mariachi music originated in the 19th century outside of Guadalajara itself (some say in Los Altos, but the actual birthplace was in Cocula to the south), during the French intervention in Mexico. The name comes from the French word for 'marriage', as these musicians were commonly used for weddings. Typical Mariachi instruments are strings (including the no-longer used harp); the omnipresent trumpet was not added until many years later. A Mariachi suit is very similar to that worn by a *charro*, although it is usually black (for men and the occasional women) and more elaborately decorated. The **San Juan de Dios** neighbourhood in Guadalajara is traditionally regarded as the best place to hear Mariachi music in town.

Music

Concerts and theatrical performances are performed in **ex-Convento del Carmen**. A band plays every Thu at 1800 in the **Plaza de Armas**, in front of the Palacio de Gobierno, free. There are organ recitals in the **cathedral**. **Peña Cuicacalli**, Av Niños Héroes esq Av Chapultepec, T33-3825 4690. Fri-Sat from 2000 (fills up fast), US$4.25 cover. Food and drink available. Local groups perform a variety of music including Latin American folk.

Theatre

Instituto Cultural Cabañas, see page 443. The Ballet Folklórico del Instituto Cultural Cabañas performs Wed 2030, US$4.25. The Instituto is also an art school, with classes in photography, sculpture, ceramics, literature, music, theatre and dance.
Teatro Degollado, Plaza de la Liberación, T33-3658 3812. The Ballet Folklórico de la Universidad de Guadalajara, performs every Sun at 1000, superb, highly recommended, pre-Hispanic and Mexican-wide dances, and other cultural shows, US$3.50-12.50 (check

before you go). The theatre is open to the public Mon-Fri 1000-1300, just to look inside. The Grupo Folklórico Ciudad de Guadalajara performs here every Thu at 2000.

Tlaquepaque *p448*
Mariachis

At night the boulevards and main square fill with diners and Mariachis, who play Fri-Sun, 1530 and 2130; roving Mariachis play for a fee. While Mariachi bands remain squarely the province of male performers, Tlaquepaque is one of the few places where you may also see a female trio or quintet.

⊛ Festivals and events

Guadalajara *p440, maps p441 and p442*
Mid Mar International Film Festival, showcasing Latin American films from 22 countries.
21 Mar Benito Juárez's birthday; everything closes.
May Festival de la Cultura.
Oct Fiestas de Octubre, throughout the month there is a great fiesta with concerts, bullfights, sports and exhibitions of handicrafts from all over Mexico. The Jalisco State Fair is the largest in the country and attracts millions of visitors. Its *charrería* is especially popular.
Late Nov/early Dec Feria Internacional del Libro, www.fil.com.mx, the 3rd largest book fair in the world, is held in Guadalajara's Gran Salón de Exposiciones. As well as the usual gathering of publishers, there are round-the-clock readings of poetry and fiction, music, dance, theatre, games, food and drink.

Zapopan *p447*
Jun-Oct In Jun, the Virgen de Zapopán, leaves her home in the basilica to spend each night in a different church where fireworks are let off. The virgin has a new car each year but the engine is not started; men pull it through the beautifully decorated streets with ropes. The climax is 12 Oct when the virgin returns from her visits to other churches and takes up her lodgings again

in the basilica, there are great crowds along the route (see box, page 448).

Tonalá *p449*
1-11 Nov Feria Nacional Artesanal (National Craft Fair), Tonala.

O Shopping

Guadalajara *p440, maps p441 and p442*
Bookshops
Hospicio Cabañas, Plaza Tapitía, T33-3617 8207, www.librosyarte.com.mx. Tue-Sat 1000-1800, Sun 1000-1500. Mexican arts and crafts books in beautiful setting; many hard-to-find titles.
Librería José Luis Martínez, Av Chapultepec Sur 198, Colonia Americana, T33-3615 1214, www.fondoculturaeconomica.com. Mon-Sat 0930-2100. Popular book seller known locally as *La Joseluisa*, has children's section and playroom, huge selection and many new titles.
Librería La Fuente, Medellín 140, near Juan Manuel in the centre, T33-3613 5238. Used books and magazines in English and Spanish, interesting to browse, some items quite old, from the 1940s and 1950s.
Librería México, Plaza del Sol, Local 14, area D, on Av López Mateos side, T33-3121 0114. US magazines and newspapers.
Sanborn's, several branches: Av Vallarta 1600 y Gen San Martín; Juárez and 16 de Septiembre; Plaza Bonita and Av López Mateos Sur 2718 (near Plaza del Sol). English books and magazines are available at a reasonable mark-up.

Crafts, furniture and textiles
The blue, green, amber and amethyst blown-glass articles are made at 2 glass factories. Many other crafts are available in Tlaquepaque (see below) and you can watch the potters at work.
Casa de Artesanías de Jalisco, González Gallo 20, Parque Agua Azul, T33-3619 4664. Mon-Sat 1000-1900, Sun 1000-1400. High-quality display (and sale) of handicrafts,

ceramics, paintings, hand-blown glass, dresses, etc (state-subsidized, reasonably priced but not cheap).
Casa de Ensueños Art Gallery, Av Libertad 1812, T33-3827 4201, www.cde-artgallery.com. Tue-Fri 1100-1400, 1600-2000; Sat 1000-1400. 6 rooms of graphic art, crafts, ceramics, sculpture, and painting from city's newest artists.
Casa de los Telares, Hidalgo 1378, some way from the main shopping area. Traditional textiles are woven on hand looms.
Galería Jesús Guerrero Santos, Av Vallarta 1222, T33-3825 9527, www.jgs.com.mx. Mon-Fri 1000-1400, 1600-1900, Sat 1000-1600. Beautiful silver and ceramic art evocative of colonial Mexico and especially Tonalá.
Galería Vértice de Luis García Jasso, Lerdo de Tejada 2418, T33-3616 0078, www.verticegaleria.com. Mon-Fri 1000-1400, 1600-1900, Sat 1000-1400. One of Mexico's most important contemporary art galleries.

Markets
Mercado Libertad (also known as San Juan de Dios), Javier Mina, has colourful items for souvenirs with lots of Michoacán crafts including Paracho guitars and Sahuayo hats, leather jackets and huaraches (sandals). Delicious food is served upstairs on the 1st level (particularly goat meat, *birria*, also very sweet coconut called *cocada*), fruit juices and other soft drinks.

Shopping malls
The best shops are no longer in the centre, although a couple of department stores have branches there. The best stores are in the shopping malls, of which there are many, small and large, mainly on the west side. The best known are: **Centro Magno**, Av Vallarta 2425, very popular; and the brand new **Palacio de Hierro**, Plaza Andares y Av Patria 2085, Zapopan. When it was built in the 1970s, **Plaza del Sol**, Av López Mateos 2375, was Mexico's largest *galleria* (shopping mall).

Tlaquepaque p448

Crafts and shopping are at the heart of any tourist experience in Tlaquepaque. The downtown alone has close to 400 different shops, and much of the area is closed to vehicles, so there is nothing to spoil a good shopping spree. Visitors will find everything from silver, glass, leather and ceramics to cowboy belts, furniture, shawls and linens.

Although you may sometimes find better bargains in Tonalá (see below), overall Tlaquepaque is the cheapest and most varied source of local crafts, with attractive shops set in old colonial villas; best buys are glass, papier-mâché goods, leather (cheapest in Mexico), and ceramics.

Crafts, furniture and textiles

Antigua de México, Independencia 255. Beautiful, expensive furniture in a lovely building, used to be a convent, the family has branches in Nogales and Tucson so furniture can be shipped to their shops there.
Galería Rodo Padilla, Independencia 139, T33-3657 3712, www.rodopadilla.com.mx. Mon-Sat 1030-1930, Sun 1100-1500. Ceramics and bronze by one of Tlaquepaque's best living craftsman.
La Casa Canela, Independencia 258 y Cruz Verde, T33-3635 3717. Sells furniture and crafts, don't miss the colonial kitchen at the back.
Museo Regional de la Cerámica, Independencia 237. See page 449.

Jewellery

Galería Sergio Bustamante, Independencia 238, T33-3639 5519. Good modern jewellery; expensive but well worth a look, a stream runs through this house with a colonial facade.

Tonalá p449

Market days are Sun and Thu.
Aldana Luna Muebles Y Decoracion, Juárez 194, T33-3683 0302. Wrought-iron furniture.
Artesanías Nuño, Juárez 59, T33-3683 0011. For brightly painted wooden animals.
Plaza Juárez, Juárez 141. A large building with several craft shops in it.

▲ Activities and tours

Guadalajara p440, maps p441 and p442
Hiking

Club Colli, bulletin board Av Juárez 460, details from Café Madrid, Juárez 264 or T33-3623 3318. Organizes day and weekend trips to the sierras west of the city; also to Colima.

Language schools

Centro de Estudios para Extranjeros de la Universidad de Guadalajara, Tomás V Gómez 125 entre Justo Sierra y Av México, T33-3616 4399, www.cepe.udg.mx. Courses arranged with or without homestay.
Instituto Cultural Mexicano-Norteamericano de Jalisco, Enrique Díaz de León 300, T33-3825 5838. 5 levels of instruction, cultural lectures on Fri, homestays possible.
Universidad Autónoma de Guadalajara (UAG), a private university, offers Spanish classes through its **Centro Internacional de Idiomas**, T33-3641 7051, ext 32251, 0800-1800, at Edificio Humanidades 1st floor, on the main campus at Av Patria 1201 (located in Colonia Lomas del Valle, 3rd section); 7 levels of instruction, each lasting 4 weeks, homestays possible.
Vancouver Language Centre, Av Libertad 1690, Colonia Americana, T33-3826 6322; T1-604-687-1600 from Vancouver), www.study-mexico.com or www.vic-guada lajara.com. 1-week intensive programmes.

Rafting

Expediciones México Verde, José María Vigil 2406 (in Colonia Italia Providencia), T/F33-3641 5598. Rafting specialists (Actopan, Jatate, Santa María, Antigua-Pescados, Filobobos and Usumacinta rivers).

Spectator sports

Baseball Apr-Sep.
Bullfights Oct-Mar. Plaza de Toros is on Calzada de la Independencia.
Charreadas (rodeos) Mid-Sep at Unión de San Antonio; lienzo charro near Parque Agua Azul at Aceves Calindo Lienzo, Sun at 1200.

Football Played all year round. The Estadio Jalisco is on Calzada de la Independencia.

⊙ Transport

Guadalajara p440, maps p441 and p442
Air
Miguel Hidalgo airport (GDL) is 20 km from town. To reach the airport, bus No 176 'San José del 15' (grey) leaves from intersection of Corona and Calzada de la Independencia every 20 mins, US$0.25. **Autotransportes Guadalajara-Chapala** from the old bus terminal stop at the airport on the way to/ from Chapala, every 15 mins, 0655-2125, US$0.30, 2nd class. A taxi to the airport costs a minimum of US$12. There are daily flights to and from virtually every city in Mexico and many around the world.

Airline offices Mexicana, reservations T33-3678 7676, arrival and departure information T33-3688 5775, ticket office: Av Mariano Otero 2353 (by Plaza del Sol), T33-3112 0011. **AeroMéxico**, reservations T33-3669 0202, airport information T33-3688 5098, ticket offices: Av Corona 196 and Plaza del Sol, Local 30, Zona A. **Air France**, Vallarta 1540-103, T33-3630 3707. **American**, Vallarta 2440, T33-3616 4090 for reservations, T33-3688 5518 at airport. **Continental**, ticket office Astral Plaza, Galerías del Hotel Presidente Intercontinental, Locales 8-9, T33-3647 4251 reservations, T33-3688 5141 airport. **Delta**, López Cotilla 1701, T33-3630 3530. **KLM**, Vallarta 1390, T33-3825 3261. **United**, Plaza Los Arcos, Av Vallarta 2440, local A13, T33-3616 9489.

Bus
Local The tourist office in Plaza Tapatía (see page 441) has a full list of local and long-distance buses. If in doubt ask the bus driver. Regular buses cost US$0.20, **Línea Azul** 'luxury' bus US$0.40. Some useful lines: **Route 275**, 16 de Septiembre y Revolución, from Zapopán-Plaza Patria-Glorieta Normal-Av Alcalde-Av 16 de Septiembre-Av Revolución-

Tlaquepaque-new bus station-Tonalá (there are different 275s, from A to F; most follow this route, check with the driver). **Route 707** also goes to Tonalá (silver-blue bus with 'Tur' on the side). **Route 60** goes along Calzada de la Independencia from zoo, passing Estadio Jalisco, Plaza de Toros, Mercado Libertad and Parque Agua Azul to the old bus terminal and the railway station (if you are going to Parque Mirador, take bus **62** northbound). There is also a trolley bus that runs along the Calzada de la Independencia to the entrance to the Mirador, better than 60 or 62. For the old bus station, take minibus **174** south along Calzada de la Independencia from Mercado Libertad, or bus **110** south along Av Alcalde. **Route 102** runs from the new bus terminal (in Tonalá) along Av Revolución, 16 de Septiembre, and Prisciliano Sánchez to Mercado Libertad. **Route 258** or **258A** from San Felipe (north of cathedral) or **258D** along Madero go to Plaza del Sol. **Route 371** runs from downtown Tonalá to Plaza del Sol. A shuttle bus runs between the 2 bus stations.

There is a luxury bus service, **Línea Azul**, running from Zapopan, along Avila Camacho, past Plaza Patria shopping centre to the Glorieta La Normal, south down Av Alcalde, through Tlaquepaque, to the new bus station and ending in downtown Tonalá. Another luxury bus service to the centre is **Línea Cardenal**. No buses after 2230.

Long distance The **old bus station**, Los Angeles y 28 de Enero, in the city centre, serves towns roughly within 100 km of Guadalajara. You have to pay 20 centavos to enter the terminal (open 0545-2215). It has 2 *salas* (wings): A and B, and is shaped like a U. The flat bottom of the U fronts Dr R Michel, where the main entrances are. There is a side entrance to Sala A from Los Angeles and to both A and B from 15 de Febrero via a tunnel. Taxi stands are on both sides of the terminal. By the entrances to the *salas* is a Computel outlet with long-distance and fax service. Shuttle buses to the **new bus station** leave from here, US$0.20.

In Sala A there are 2nd-class buses to **Tepatitlán** and **Zapotlanejo** and '**La Penal**' (the prison), with **Oriente**. 1st-class buses to the same destinations leave from the new bus terminal, which is located in Tonalá, and not in Guadalajara itself. Buses to **Chapala** (every 30 min, 0600-2140, US$1.50) and Ajijic (every 30 min, 0700-2100, US$1.65) leave from here with **Autotransportes Guadalajara-Chapala**. Round-trip package to the *balneario* at **San Juan Cosalá**, US$5 including admission to the baths.

In Sala B, **Omnibus de Rivera** sells tickets to the same *balneario* for US$1.30 and at La Alteña booth for the *balnearios* **Agua Caliente** and **Chimulco**. A **Primera Plus/Servicios Coordinados** booth sells tickets to places served by the new bus terminal. Buses to **Tequila** every 30 mins, US$3. Both rooms have several food stands serving *tortas*, etc, and there are toilets, luggage store and magazine stands.

The **new bus station** in Tonalá is 10 km east from the centre of Guadalajara, near the El Alamo junction; take buses 102 and 275 from the centre, US$0.25, frequent service (see Local transport, above), journey takes at least 30 mins; also luxury services (Línea Azul or Línea Cardenal, US0.40). A taxi from the centre to the new bus station costs US$6.50. Note that when referring to Guadalajara as a bus destination, most people will assume you know that the station itself is in Tonalá and not Guadalajara. You will need to either transfer to a local bus or take a taxi when you arrive in Tonalá.

In the centre of Guadalajara town bus information and tickets are available at 2 offices on Calzada de la Independencia underneath Plaza Tapatía (access from Independencia), daily 0900-1400, 1600-1900. Very handy because of the distance from the centre of town although it is worth getting your departure information at the bus station before you go into town. Most services sold are for the higher class travel.

The terminal itself is a nightmare if you try to understand it. Simply put, there are 7 modules at the terminal, each serving different bus companies, rather than towns or regions, within Mexico. Prices do not vary much from company to company.

The terminal is in the shape of a big U, with modules 1 to 7 evenly spaced around the outside. Buses enter the U at Module 1, following through to 7 at the other end of the U. Different companies have a presence in several modules and while they will sell you a ticket to any destination, you have to get to the correct module. So, shop around, preferably without your bag. Most terminals now have baggage storage, along with telephones, toilets, restaurants, shops and tourist information booths (not always staffed).

There are probably direct buses to every conceivable destination in Mexico. The schedules for the most commonly used are below, with modules. To **Acapulco**, 1730 and 1900, 17 hrs, US$54, Mod 7. To **Aguascalientes**, hourly 0500-2000, 4 hrs, US$15, Mods 1, 2, 6 and 7. To **Barra de Navidad**, every 2 hrs 0700-1500, and 2200 and 0100, 5 hrs, US$24, Mods 1 and 2. To **Chihuahua**, 8 between 0600 and 2000, 16 hrs, US$69, Mod 7. To **Colima**, hourly, 3 hrs, US$14, Mods 1, 2 and 6. To **Guanajuato**, hourly, 4 hrs, US$25, Mods 1, 2 and 7. To **Hermosillo**, every couple of hours, 23 hrs, US$66-77, Mods 3 and 4. To **Lagos de Moreno**, very regular, 3 hrs, US$12, best service from Mod 5. To **León**, hourly, 4 hrs, US$21, Mods 1 and 2. To **Los Mochis**, almost hourly through the day, 15 hrs, US$41-49, Mods 3 and 4. To **Manzanillo**, hourly, more regular in the afternoon, 6 hrs, US$25, Mods 1, 2 and 3. To **Mazatlán**, every hour day and night, 8 hrs, US$32, Mods 3 and 4. To **Mexicali**, every hour day and night, 34 hrs, US$85-100, Mods 3 and 4. To **Mexico City** (North Terminal), every 15 mins, 8-9 hrs, US$38, most often at Mod 1. To **Morelia**, every 2 hrs, 4 hrs, US$25, Mods 1 and 2. To **Puerto Vallarta**, every 2 hrs in the morning, 6 hrs, US$31, Mods 1, 2, 3 and 4. To **Querétaro**, every 30 mins, 5 hrs, US$22, most often at Mod 1. To **San Luis Potosí**, every 2 hrs, 5 hrs, US$22, Mod 5. To **San Miguel de Allende**, 1300 and 1500, 6 hrs, US$33, Mod 1. To **Tepic**, every ½ hr, day and night, 3½ hrs, US$16, Mods 3, 4, 6 and 7. To **Tijuana**, hourly, day and night, 33 hrs, US$88-104, Mods 3 and 4. To **Uruapan**, every 2 hrs, 4½ hrs, US$22, Mods 1 and 2. To **Zacatecas**, roughly every 3 hrs, 5 hrs, US$21, Mods 6 and 7.

Car hire

Avis, at airport, T33-3688 5656. Budget, Av Niños Héroes, esq 16 de Septiembre, T33-3613 0027. Hertz, office at Hotel Quinta Real (Av México 2727), other at airport, others scattered throughout city, T33-3614 6162. National, Niños Héroes 961, by Hotel Carlton, and other offices at the hotels Fiesta Americana, Holiday Inn Select, and the airport, T33-3614 7175. Quick, Av Niños Héroes esq Manzano, T33-3614 2247.

Metro

The metro, or *tren ligero*, has Línea 1 running under Federalismo from Periférico Sur to Periférico Norte. Línea 2 runs from Juárez station westbound and passes Mercado Libertad. Fare US$0.35, 1-peso coins needed to buy tokens.

Taxi

No meters are used. A typical ride in town costs US$2-5; evening fares are slightly higher. From the centre to the **new bus station** outside the city in Tonalá is about US$6.50; if the taxi ticket booths are open at the bus station it costs around US$3.70. A taxi to the **airport** costs a minimum of US$12.

Train

There is only freight service (no passengers allowed) to and from Guadalajara these days. The one exception is a tourist line to the northwest, the recently refurbished *Tequila Express*, see page 488.

Tonalá *p449*
Bus See page 458 for information on the new bus station.

ⓘ Directory

Guadalajara *p440, maps p441 and p442*
Banks There are numerous banks and ATMs around town representing all major Mexican banks and several foreign ones. **Embassies and consulates** Australia, López Cotilla 2018 entre Lope de Vega y Calderón de La Barca (in Colonia Arcos Vallarta), T33-36157418, 0800-1330, 1500- 1800. **Austria**, Montevideo 2695 (in Colonia Providencia), T33-3641 1834, 0900-1330. **Belgium**, Privada de la Nogalera 11 (in Colonia Las Cañadas in Zapopan), T33-3685 0402, Mon-Fri 0900-1400. **Brazil**, Av Vallarta 1222 entre Atenas y Robles Gil (in Colonia Americana), T33-3826-6444, Mon-Fri 1000-1400. **Canada**, trade officer and consul, Hotel Fiesta Americana, local 31, T33-3616 5642, 0830-1400 and 1500-1700. **Denmark**, Av López Mateos Norte 477, 6th floor (in Colonia Ladrón de Guevara), T33-3615-0706, 0900-1300, 1600-1800. **El Salvador**, Efraín González Luna 2183 (in Colonia Americana), T33-3616 4262, hours for visas 1230-1400. **France**, López Mateos Norte 484 entre Herrera y Cairo y Manuel Acuña, T33-3616 5516, 0930-1400. **Germany**, Av Madero 215, T33-3613 9623, 1130-1400. **Guatemala**, Mango 1440 (in Colonia Jardínes de la Victoria), T33-3811 1503, 1000-1400. **Honduras**, Regidores 1114 (in Colonia Chapultepec Country Club), T33-3817 4998, 1000-1400 and 1700-1900. **Israel**, Av Vallarta 2482 Altos (in Colinia Sector Juárez), T33-3616 4554, 0930-1500. **Italy**, López Mateos Norte 790, 1st floor (in Colonia Ladrón de Guevara), T33-3616 1700, Tue-Fri 1100-1400. **Netherlands**, Av Vallarta 5500, 2nd floor (in Colonia Lomas Universidad), T33-3673 2211, 0900-1400 and1630-1900. **Nicaragua**, Eje Central 1024 (in Colonia Jardínes de Guadalupe in Zapopan),

T33- 3587-2863, 1600-1800. **Norway**, Antigua Ctra a Chapala 2801 (in Colonia La Nogalera), T33-3666 0130, 0900-1400 and1600-1900. **Peru**, Bogotá 2923 entre Labrador y Av Providencia (in Colonia Providencia), T33-3641-9787, 1000-1400. **Spain**, Francisco de Quevedo 117 (in Colonia Arcos), T33-3630 0466, 0830-1330. **Sweden**, Guadalupe Monte Negro 1691 (in Colonia Moderna), T33-3825 6767, 0900-1400 and1600-1900. **Switzerland**, Av D 705 y Francisco Silva Romero (in Colonia Seattle), T33-3833 4122, 0800-1400 and1600-1900. **UK**, Jesús de Rojas 20 (in Colonia Los Pinos) T33- 3343 2296, 0900-1500 and1700-2000. **USA**, Progreso 175 (in Colonia Americana), T33-3268 2100.

Immigration Mexican tourist cards can be renewed at the **immigration office** (1st floor) in the Palacio Federal, Av Alcalde entre Juan Alvarez y Hospital (across the avenue from the Santuario de Guadalupe). There may be a long wait, so best to go early in the day. The Palacio Federal building also contains a post office and fax service. **Internet** There are hundreds of internet cafés in every section of Guadalajara. **Laundry** Aldama 125 (walk along Independencia towards train station, turn left into Aldama). **Medical services** Dentists: Dr Abraham Waxtein, Av México 2309, T33-3615 1041, speaks English. Doctors: Dr Daniel Gil Sánchez, Pablo Neruda 3265, 2nd floor, T33-3642 0213, speaks English (1st consultation, 2½ hrs, including thorough physical, US$75). Hospitals: **Hospital del Carmen**, Tarascos 3435, Fraccionamiento Monraz (behind Plaza México), T33-3813 0042, a good private hospital (take credit cards). **Hospital Angel Leaño**, off the road to Tesistán, T33-3834 3434, affiliated with UAG. **Pharmacies:** There are 3 big chains: **Farmacias Guadalajara**, Benavides and ABC. **Farmacia Guadalajara**, T33-3615 5094. **Vaccinations:** For *antirrábico* (rabies), T33- 3643 1917; to receive the vaccine you have to go to Clinic 3 of the Sector Salud, T33-3823 3262, at the corner of Circunvalación División del Norte and Federalismo, across the street from a Telmex office, near the División del Norte Station, Line 1, tren ligero; you can also get an HIV test here. Sidatel (AIDS), T33-36137546.

Post office Main post office, Venustiano Carranza, just behind Palacio de Justicia, Mon-Fri 0800-1900, Sat 0900-1300. There are also branches at the Mercado Libertad (San Juan de Dios) and at the old bus station. To send parcels abroad go to Aduana Postal in same building as main post office, Mon-Fri 0800-1300, T33-3614 9002. **FedEx** has 3 outlets: Av Américas 1395; Plaza del Sol Locales 51-55; Av Washington 1129 (next to Bolerama 2000), T33-3817 2502. **UPS**, Av Américas 981, Local 19, T01-800-902-9200.

Telephone International collect calls can be made from any coin-box phone kiosk and direct dial calls can be made from **TelMex** pay phones. You can also make long-distance calls and send faxes from **Computel** outlets: one in front of old bus station, another on Corona y Madero, opposite Hotel Fénix. Mayahuel, Paseo Degollado 55, has long-distance service, fax, sells **TelMex** cards, postcards and maps. There is a credit card phone at Ramón Corona y Av Juárez, by the cathedral. Two **USA Direct** phones, one within and another beyond the customs barrier at the airport.

Laguna de Chapala region

Laguna de Chapala, Mexico's largest lake (80 km by 50 km) is set in beautiful scenery, and is perhaps the most-photographed body of water in all of Mexico. Most of the towns in this region (often collectively known as 'Ribera') are popular resorts, particularly with retired North Americans and Mexican day-trippers. Local agencies never tire of pointing out that the Chapala region (known as 'Lakeside' to overseas residents) has the largest expat North American community (circa 45,000 inhabitants) anywhere in the world. Much of the expat population lives in and around Ajijic although many spend only winters in the area, returning north for the warmer months. Much as with Puerto Vallarta and other Pacific resort areas where Americans and Canadians predominate, the degree of integration is very much along economic lines, but there is little tension, and no discernable resentment such as is occasionally found in San Miguel de Allende or Oaxaca. ▶▶ For listings, see pages 464-468.

Chapala ⬤🏨🎡🍴🛏️ ▶▶ *pp464-468. Colour map 2, B2. Phone code: 376.*

Chapala, 38 km southeast of Guadalajara via the motorway to the airport, is on the northern shore of the lake. Founded in 1538 by the Franciscan Friar Miguel Bolonia, the town and its nearby lakefront communities, have thermal springs, virtually perfect weather year-round (along with mesmerizing sunsets), several good hotels and restaurants, four golf courses and a thriving arts scene. Several great homes of the past lie strung along the waterfront, west of the post office. Others are scattered throughout Chapala's centre (including one where DH Lawrence wrote *The Plumed Serpent* in the 1920s).

Ins and outs

Getting there There buses every 30 minutes from Guadalajara to Chapala's bus station on Avenida Madero in the centre of town. Taxi stands can be found by the bus station or by the Zócalo. ▶▶ *See Transport, page 467.*

Tourist information There is a **regional tourist office**ⓘ *Aquiles Serdán 26, T376-765 3141.* A free English-language newspaper, *El Ojo del Lago*, is available at hotels and online at www.chapala.com. See also *The Guadalajara Reporter* (http://guadalajarareporter.com) for information on the town, lake and surrounding region.

Sights

While Chapala's primary attractions are found on the shores of its lake, a trip into the town itself is equally rewarding. The 1528 church of **San Antonio** is one of Mexico's oldest, while directly south of the 18th-century church of **San Francisco**, is **Casa Braniff**ⓘ *in front of the malecón, restaurant open daily 1200-2400,* the former summer home of the Braniff family (founders of the defunct airline of the same name), now a restaurant/bar. The mansion was once a grand vacation home visited by Mexico's leading politicians, business entrepreneurs and the cream of Mexican society (as well as many European celebrities of the Edwardian era). Constructed on the former site of a Franciscan monastery, the building dates back to 1903 and the presidency of Porfirio Díaz – a time still considered Chapala's golden era. Built almost entirely from imported European materials, right down to the brick, most of the original features remain intact, with stained-glass windows, handsomely adorned ceilings, marble fireplaces and many antiques.

An extensive collection of photographic images showing the original buildings and other aspects of vanished Chapala lifestyles going back to the presidency of Porfirio Díaz may be seen in the **city archives** ① *Av Madero y Hidalgo*. There is a **market** on the east side of the Zócalo with stalls selling handicrafts, some places to eat.

There are boats for hire, some go to the **Isla de los Escorpiones** (where there is a restaurant), and others to **Isla del Presidio** or **Isla de Mezcala**, the latter of which has the ruins of a fort. Despite Chapala's ongoing ecological problems (most fish in the lake have been killed by pollution and Guadalajara's demand for fresh water has reduced the lake's levels drastically), there is waterfowl shooting in autumn and winter.

La Ribera and around ●❼❋●● » pp464-468.

San Antonio Tlayacapan → Colour map 2, B2. Phone code: 376.
San Antonio Tlayacapan is a tiny fishing village less than 4 km west of Chapala, and a good starting point for a journey along the lake's western rim. In 1521, Cortés sent men to control the area around the lake and to pacify local tribes. By 1539, the tribes had surrendered to the Spanish, who then built monasteries as refuges for the natives. The first Catholic church in the region (now in ruins) was built in this spot by the Franciscans sometime shortly after Cortés' arrival. Although its setting is straight out of a storybook with its quaint church, main plaza, and cobblestone streets, there is little to see in town. San Antonio Tlayacapan is where Dane Chandos wrote his evocative *Village in the Sun*, which subsequently attracted many foreign visitors to the area. It is also the home of the well-known **Lakeside Little Theatre**, where plays are interpreted and directed by the foreign community with some help from aspiring native dramatists and actors.

Ajijic
Seven kilometres west of Chapala, Ajijic was settled in 1522, making it one of the oldest foundations in the country. It is a small, once indigenous village and, like Chapala, now has an arty-crafty expat community (first 'colonized' in 1925) of retired North Americans.

The village is pleasant, with cobbled streets, a pretty little plaza and many single-storey villas. One block east of the plaza at the end of Parroquia is the very pretty church of **San Andrés**, started in 1749 but not finished until 1901. On Colón, in the two blocks north of the plaza, are several restaurants, boutiques and galleries. Going south from the plaza, Colón becomes Morelos, crossing Constitución and continuing some five blocks to the lake with lots more restaurants, galleries and shops.

The lakeshore has receded about 200 m from the original shoreline and is a bit smelly. The *Way of the Cross* and a passion play are performed at Easter in a chapel high above the town. Local **house and garden tours** ① *T376-766 1881, Thu 1030, 2½ hrs, US$7*, help to raise money for the Lakeside School for the Deaf.

Enormously popular with artists, the annual Ajijic **International Film Festival** is the most recent addition to the village's numerous artistic events. A number of well-known writers have worked here. During the late 1930s, Somerset Maugham finished *The Razor's Edge* here. In the 1940s, Tennessee Williams lived in town, hosting a nightly poker game that inspired a short story, *The Poker Night*, which he later expanded into *A Streetcar Named Desire*. In the last few years, four best-selling novels by Barbara Bickmore and several non-fiction books by Jim Tuck were written here. The famous **Lakeside Writers Group** serves as a venue for both established and budding writers to critique one another's efforts.

San Juan Cosalá

West of Ajijic lies the small town of San Juan Cosalá, less prosperous than Ajijic but pleasant, with cobblestone streets and fewer gringos. There are thermal springs (five pools of varied temperatures, crowded and noisy at weekends). Fish restaurants are squeezed between the *carretera* and the lake at **Barrenada**, 1 km east of town. The village is famed for the religious fervour of its native (not expatriate) inhabitants, and during **Semana Santa** (Holy Week) there is a live re-enactment of the *Passion*.

Jocotepec

Some 28 km west of Ajijic is Jocotepec, once Xuxutepeque, a small fishing village at the western end of the lake. A pre-Conquest settlement, it has been permanently inhabited by the Nahua since 1361; the Spanish arrived in 1529, formally 'founding' the settlement with a grant from Cortés himself. Jocotepec now has a population of about 18,000, with only about 5% being expats (most of whom live in private properties and gated communities). The village has limited hotels and restaurants, but those seeking authentic (as opposed to Americanized or sanitized) Mexican culture will find it here. The Sunday evening *paseo* at the plaza, where young ladies walk clockwise and young men walk in the opposite direction, is still a lively social event in Jocotepec, while it is almost extinct elsewhere in Mexico. Small restaurants under the arcades sell plates of *birria* (goat or mutton stew), and visitors come from afar to consult the town's *curanderos* (experts in the use of herbs). Jocotepec is also justly famous for its ice cream. The primary feast is in honour of **Nuestro Señor del Monte** ('Lord of the Mountain') and lasts for two weeks in late January.

Mazamitla

Some 40 km due south of Lake Chapala (but 103 km by road) is the colonial town of Mazamitla (2200 m), another of Jalisco's *pueblos mágicos* and pleasant place on the side of a range of the **Sierra del Tigre** mountains. It gets chilly at night but has a charming Zócalo and a decidedly colonial ambiance. Many artisan crafts are produced here: popular items include wooden handcrafts and chairs made of *ixtle* (a fibre from the maguey plant), little changed from centuries ago. The area around the town is ideal for day hikes and is a home to deer and mountain lion. Mountain cabins are available for longer stays, and horseback riding and beautiful waterfalls are local fixtures. A nice place to stay cool if visiting during hot weather. Most accommodation here is in the form of *cabañas*.

Tapalpa and around ●●❼ ▸▸ *pp464-468. Colour map 2, B2. Phone code: 343.*

About 140 km south of Guadalajara off Route 54 to Sayula and Ciudad Guzmán, Tapalpa is high in the Sierra Tapalpa range and a very pretty village indeed – one of Mexico's newest *pueblos* mágicos. It is a popular place for weekend homes for rich Tapatíos (inhabitants of Guadalajara). It is a three-hour drive from Guadalajara, best made by private vehicle. All buses make several detours into the hills to stop at small places such as **Zacoalco** (where there is a Sunday market) and **Amacueca**. The road up to Tapalpa is spectacular but winding, and climbs sharply and the air becomes noticeably cooler with pine trees and other conifers predominating.

The town itself, with only 11,000 inhabitants, shows ample signs of the influx of prosperity. The main street is lined with stalls, selling *sarapes* and other tourist goods on Sunday and fresh food the other days of the week. The local speciality is *ponche*, an improbable blend of tamarind and mescal, which is sold in gallon jars and recommended only for the curious or foolhardy. There is a **regional tourist office** ① *in the centre, Portal Morelos 1, T343-432 0650, www.jalisco.gob.mx.*

There are two churches, **San Antonio de Padua** and **Templo de Merced** (which features a curious atrium) and an imposing flight of stone steps between them, laid out with fountains and ornamental lamps.

Tapalpa is in cattle country and rodeo is a popular sport at weekends. Also popular is abesiling; Tapalpa holds a 'World Cup' every year.

◉ Laguna de Chapala region listings

For Sleeping and Eating price codes and other relevant information, see Essentials pages 47-51.

◉ Sleeping

Chapala *p461*

Non-budget travellers should continue on to Ajijic or further west when looking for places to stay. While Chapala has some decent lodgings in the **A-B** range, those found in Ajijic are generally better. All hotels in San Antonio Tlayacapan are commonly listed as being in Chapala. The distinction is a technical one only.

A QQ (aka **Quinta Quetzalcoatl** or **The Plumed Serpent**), Zaragoza 307, 2 blocks southeast of the plaza, T376-765 3653, www.accommodationslakechapala.com. Australian owned, friendly staff. Beautiful old house, room service, free breakfast, pool, exquisite gardens, fountains. Individually decorated rooms with fireplace and terrace. No children. Highly recommended.

A Villa Montecarlo, west edge of town on Av Hidalgo at Lourdes, T376-765 2120. Family rooms or suites, very comfortable, in beautiful grounds with palms and mangos.

B Chapala Haciendas, Ctra Chapala–Guadalajara, Km 40, T376-765 2720. Live music Wed and Sat. Unheated pool.

B Nido, Av Madero 202, close to the lake, T376-765 2116. Brick building, old photos in the reception hall, clean, cheaper without TV, accepts Visa and MasterCard, good restaurant, pool, parking for motorcycles.

B-C Lake Chapala Inn, Paseo Ramón Corona 23, T376-765 4786, www.mexonline.com/chapalainn.htm. 4 well-appointed guest rooms, with private bath, TV, Wi-Fi, parking, heated lap pool in beautiful, secluded garden.

Camping

PAL Trailer Park, Madero 232, 1 km from the lake, T376-766 0040. Trailer park, 1st-class, flush toilets and cable TV hookups. Coin laundry, recreation room and heated pool. Boat trips around Lake Chapala can be arranged.

Ajijic *p462*

Lodgings in Ajijic are by far the most expensive of any in the Lake Chapala region, but are also the most oriented to North American and European service expectations. There are also many private houses, apartments, and condominiums for rent by the week on a year-round basis, most of which are advertised online on popular sites such as **2CasaRentals**, www.2casarentals.com. For those planning a trip to the lake region for an extended period, these are almost always the best options.

AL Casa del Sol Inn, Javier Mina 7, T376-766 0050, www.casadelsolinn.com. Colourful and charming, serene and utterly romantic, gringo-oriented inn that doubles as a B&B.

AL Casa Tres Leones, Emiliano Zapata 10, T376-766 1846, www.casatresleones.com. Beautifully restored old *casona*, under new Australian management. Stunning bedrooms. Gardens, pool, and views are best in town as well. Highly recommended.

AL La Nueva Posada, Donato Guerra 9, T376-766 1444, www.hotelnuevaposada- ajijic.com. Breakfast included, vast rooms, Canadian management, horse riding, golf, tennis, theatre, gardens, pool, restaurant, attractive outdoor seating in garden overlooking lake, colonial decor, delightful. Surprisingly affordable.

AL-A Casa Flores, Zaragoza 38, T376-766 5493, www.casafloresajijic.com. Exquisite B&B-style, 2½ blocks from the main square in one of Ajijic's most beautiful *casonas*. Under new Irish-Mexican management. Gardens, grounds are immaculate, solar heated pool, gym, free Wi-Fi, guest computer, stunning rooms. Best price for its range and highly recommended.

AL-A Casa Mis Amores, Hidalgo 22-B, T376-766 4640, www.misamores.com. Right off the plaza in town. Charming and elegant, definitely for romantics. Beautiful rooms and gardens.

A-B Casa Blanca, 16 de Septiembre 29, T376-766 4440, www.casablancaajijic.com. Just 2 blocks from the centre, very private, newly redone in blazing white, with flowers everywhere. Gringo-oriented hotel with all mod cons (including Wi-Fi). Highly recommended.

B Real de Chapala, Paseo de Prado 20, T376-766 0014, www.realdechapala.com. 85 rooms (largest hotel in area) right on lake, family-friendly, outdoor activities, restaurant, free breakfast. Very clean and secure.

B-C Ajijic Suites, Hidalgo 72, T376-766 1920, www.ajijicsuites.com. Perhaps Ajijic's least expensive lodgings suitable for travellers. Close to centre; ideal for longer stays. Suites with all mod cons, tranquil, parking.

B-C Los Artistas, Constitución 105, T376-766 1027, www.losartistas.com. A long-time Ajijic top choice. 6 rooms, each with unique decor and private bath. Nice gardens, pool, fountains, fish pond. Amenities include eclectic art collection, secluded garden seating areas, purified water system, free Wi-Fi, secure off-street parking. Highly recommended.

Camping

PAL 2 Trailer Park, Allen W Lloyd 149, T376-765-3764. 1st-class, flush toilets and cable TV hookups. Coin laundry, recreation room and heated pool. Boat trips on the lake.

San Juan Cosalá *p463*

LL Monte Coxala, Rafael Osuna Oriente 100, T387-761 0111, http://montecoxala.com.

Amazing eco-health resort with new age overtones, innovative restaurant uses pre-Conquest ingredients. Only 11 suites, but all are incredible. Hidden and private, with literally everything you can think of in the way of amenities. Very expensive, but if you're going to empty your wallet anywhere in Mexico, do it here.

B-C Villas Buenaventura Cosalá, Ctra Chapala–Jocotepec Km 13.5, T387-761 0202, www.hotelvbc.com. Hotel or long-term suites. On site spas. Quiet and peaceful, very friendly bilingual staff, with jacuzzi, game room, pool, gardens.

C-D Balneario, Av La Paz 420, T387-761 0222, http://hotelspacosala.com. Name says it all. Modest accommodation but large and popular water park (daily 0900-1900), pool, spa, and grounds, with themed events; good for families with children and very friendly. Sister hotel in Jocotepec (see below).

Jocotepec *p463*

L-A Posada del Pescador, Miguel Arana 611, Jocotepec outskirts, T387-763 0028. *Cabañas* with bedroom, living room, kitchen, and bathroom, set in a lovely garden.

A-B El Chante, Ribera del Lago 170-1, Jocotepec, T367-763 2608. Lakeside hotel famous for its spa and yoga lessons. Bilingual staff, restaurant, pool, secluded and clean.

B-C Los Dos B&B, Apartado Postal 33, just outside of Jocotepec, T387-763 0657, www.mexonline.com/losdosbandb.htm. Situated at the foot of a hill and surrounded by old trees and beautiful flowers. Views of Lake Chapala, the mountains and town. B&B or bungalows. Bungalows are spacious with private entrance, patio or balcony, kitchen, and living/dining area.

C Villa Bordeaux, Ctra Chapala–Jocotepec, Km 14, T387-761 0494. Same owners as **Balneairo** in San Juan Cosalá (see above). No children.

Tapalpa *p463*

Hotel prices are increasing as the town becomes more gentrified. There are still no luxury hotels or any places available at anything lower than **C** (and nothing below **A** during pilgrimages). A better option for budget-minded visitors may be its many mid- to high-range *cabañas*.

B El Mesón del Ticuz, Privada de Pedro Loza 1, T343-432 0351. Breakfast included, self-serve bar, restaurant. Friendly ambience.

B Posada La Hacienda, Raul Quintero 120, T343-432 0193. Nice bungalows with fireplace and small kitchen.

B Villa San José, 91 Cerrada de Ignacio T López 91, T343-432 0431, www.hotelvillade sanjose.com. Locally owned, authentic regional decor and atmosphere. In centre. Bar, restaurant, excellent information about the area.

B-C Hostal La Casona de Manzano, Francisco I Madero 84, T343-432 0767, www.casonade manzano.com. A gem of a small hotel (owner's renovated birthplace). Homemade breakfast, sunsets on terrace. Superb, excellent price. Very highly recommended.

C La Casona, Capulín 54, T343-432 0552, www.hotellacasona.com. Beautifully redone old house outside of centre, 28 rooms, all colourful and clean, arranged in accordance with feng shui principles. Very friendly, breakfast included. Highly recommended.

C Mesón Luna Sacra, Luis E Bracamontes 230, T343-432 1151, www.lunasacra.com. 8 rooms (each different) in nice old central house away from plaza. Quiet and secluded, free pastries.

C Posada La Loma, Luis E Bracamontes 197, T343-432 0168, www.lalomayelvergel.com/ posada.html. In pleasant old 1933 house with interior courtyard, fountain, crafts store, local tours arranged. Friendly and affordable.

C Posada Real Tapalpa, Juaréz 229, 2 blocks west of plaza, T343- 432 0589, www.real tapalpa.com. Converted old house, bilingual staff, very friendly and helpful. Ask for room with *chimenera* (fireplace). Best in this range.

🍴 Eating

Chapala *p461*
†††-†† La Langosta Loca, Ramón Corona 1. Good seafood.

†† La Leña, Madero 236. Daily 1200-2200. Open air, serves *antojitos* and steaks from Sonora, bamboo roof.

† Beer Garden, Malecón 9. Mon-Thu 1200-2200, Fri-Sat 1200-2400. A Chapala institution, right on the lake, completely renovated and expanded in 2008.

† Café Paris, Madero 421. Daily 0900-2200. Sidewalk tables, popular, *comida corrida* US$2.50, also breakfast and sandwiches.

† El Superior, Madero 419. Mon, Wed-Sun 0800-2130, Tue 0800-1700. Mexican and North American. Patio seating in front.

Cafés and ice creams
Bing's, Madero, by the lake. Ice cream parlour. Try the *mamey* flavour.

San Antonio Tlayacapan *p462*
†††-†† Diana de Italia, Independencia 124. Tue-Sun 1200-2200. Full-course Italian meals for lunch and dinner, reasonably priced, bar, great music. Reservations needed during high season or on Thanksgiving and Christmas.

††-† Mario's, Ramón Corona 132, just off the plaza. Tue-Sun 0900-1700. Sparkling clean fonda with Mexican fare, hamburgers and french fries. Good for breakfast and lunch, popular with a younger crowd.

††-† Tony's, Ctra Chapala-Ajijic 149 (next to **Super Lake Grocery** and **Tony's Meat Market**). Daily 1100-2100. Mexican menu and salad bar, specializing in barbecue ribs. Delicious fast-fare to go or sit-down service. Highly recommended.

† Golden Fried Chicken, Ctra Chapala–Ajijic 160-B (across from **Bananas Restaurant**, near the bypass). Daily 1000-2200. Endless servings of North American-style fried chicken, mashed potatoes and coleslaw.

Ajijic *p462*
†††-†† Ajijic Grill, Morelos 5. Mon, Tue, Thu- Sun 1200-2100. International with Japanese flair, fresh fish, tempura, *tepanyaki* and sushi. Full bar.

†††-†† Bruno's Circus, Ctra Oriente 20. Mon-Fri 1230-1500, 1700-2000, Sat 1230-

2000. Newly redecorated, local favourite for grilled steaks and chicken (but healthy lunch menu). Full bar. Reservations required.

†††-†† Posada Ajijic, Morelos, opposite pier, T376-766 0744. Bar and restaurant, accepts credit cards. Pier here with fish restaurant at the end, indoor and outdoor seating and bar.

†† Ajijic, pavement café on corner of plaza. Cheap drinks, Mexican snacks, hearty *parrillada* at weekends.

†† Armandos, Ocampo 51. Wed-Mon 0800-2000, Located behind the **Danza del Sol Hotel**, this restaurant and bar has an old hacienda atmosphere. International with Mexican dishes and flambéd desserts.

†† Axixique Mesón, Ctra Chapala-Jocotepec 424, Plaza Rancho del Oro. Mon-Tue, Thu-Sun 0830-1500. Restaurant and bar with Mexican menu and specials such as paella.

†† Los Girasoles, 16 de Septiembre 18. Mexican food in walled courtyard.

† Baguettes & Company, Ctra Oriente 60-1 (across from Telmex). Tue-Sun 1000-1800. Baguettes, bagels, salads, snacks, pastries.

† Lonchería El Tapalo, Parroquía 2, on the plaza. Mon-Fri 0800-1700, Sat 0800-1800. Clean, good simple meals, cheap, grilled chicken, used by locals and Americans.

San Juan Cosalá *p463*

†† Doña Chila, Ctra Chapala-Jocotepec, Km 62. Daily 1000-1900. Beach restaurant, good for drinks and Mexican-style beach fare. Great for teens and visitors looking to unwind.

†† Ruben's, La Paz Oriente 418, T376-761 0606. Tue-Sun 0830-2100. Breakfast, lunch, and dinner in poolside setting at the *balneario* (thermal baths).

††-† Las Ollas, Ctra Chapala-Jocotepec, Km 62. Daily 1215-2000. Lakefront beach restaurant serving drinks, seafood and typical Mexican fare. Great place for lunch and great view of the lake.

† Cenaduría Lupita Taquería, Porfirio Díaz 92. Mon-Fri 1900-2200, Sat 1500-2200, Sun1600-2200. Hours for *pozóle* Sat 1500-1700. Delicious, clean Mexican food including *pozóle* on weekends, *sopas*, *flautas*, *enchiladas* and *tostadas*. Beloved by locals.

† Minera, Ctra Chapala-Jocotepec, Km 62. Daily 1100-2000. One of the beach restaurants serving Mexican and typical Mexican food and specializing in barbecue. Great place to watch the sunset over drinks.

Jocotepec *p463*

Jocotepec is famous for its ice cream.

† Cenaduría Lando, Miguel Araña 126. Daily 2000-2300. Good à la carte Mexican food.

† La Carreta, Hidalgo 75. Thu-Tue 1330-2030. Delicious Mexican grilled meat dishes with and array of accompaniments.

† Mariscol El Caracol, Hidalgo 119. Tue-Sun 1000-1830. Offers a good variety of Mexican-style seafood bar with TV.

Tapalpa *p463*

The more expensive restaurants have tables on balconies overlooking the square and all are visited by Mariachis.

†††-†† Posada Hacienda, overlooking the square (which has a US$1 cover charge). A good location.

⊛ Festivals and events

Chapala *p461*

2-3 Oct Fiesta de Francisco de Asís, with fireworks and excellent street food.

San Antonio Tlayacapan *p462*

Late Apr Mexican Salsa Competition.

5-13 Jun Patronal feast (one of the more indigenous in the area).

Christmas Its posada is considered the best along the lake, attracting many visitors.

⊝ Transport

Chapala *p461*

Bus The station is on Av Madero esq Miguel Martínez. Buses to **Guadalajara** every 30 mins, 0515-2030, 1 hr. 2 blocks south of bus station, minibuses leave every 20 mins for **Ajijic**, 2 pesos, and **San Juan Cosalá**, 3 pesos.

La Ribera and around *p462*
Bus Buses run between **Chapala** and **Ajijic** (or taxi US$2.75). **Jocotepec** can be reached from Ajijic or from the Mexico-Guadalajara highway. Bus Chapala-Jocotopec US$2, every hour in each direction.

ⓘ Directory

Chapala *p461*
Banks *Casa de cambio* at Av Madero near Beer Garden, Mon-Sat 0830-1700. **HSBC**, Madero 208, ATM taking Visa, MasterCard, and cards of Cirrus and Plus networks. Nearby is a **Banamex** with ATM. **Bancomer**, Hidalgo 212 near Madero, ATM taking Visa; across the street is a **Banca Serfín**, ATM. **Lloyds**, Madero 232, is a real estate office, *casa de cambio*, travel agency and *sociedad de inversión*; many Americans keep their money here. **Laundry** Zaragoza y Morelos. Dry cleaners at Hidalgo 235A, also repairs shoes and other leather items. **Medical services** IMSS clinic on Niños Héroes entre Zaragoza y 5 de Mayo. Centro de Salud, Flavio Romero de V y Guerrero. **Red Cross**, Parque de la Cristina.

Post office The post office is at Hidalgo 223. Nearby is a UPS office. Mail Box Etc, Ctra Chapala-Jocotepec 155, opposite PAL Trailer Park, T376-766 0747. **Shipping office** at Hidalgo 236 uses **FedEx** and **DHL**.
Telephone Computel on the plaza, long distance and fax, accepts Amex, MasterCard, AT&T. Also pay phones for long-distance calls on Zócalo and outside bus station.

Ajijic *p462*
Banks Opposite taxi stand at Colón 29 is a *casa de cambio*. On southwest corner of plaza is **Banco Promex** with 2 ATMs. **Immigration** Castellanos 4, T376-766 2042. **Laundry** About ½ blocks north at Colón 24A is a *lavandería*. **Medical services** Dentists: 2 dentists' offices on Colón, just south of plaza. Doctors: Dr Alfredo Rodríguez Quintana, T376-766 1499 (home). Hospitals and clinics: Clínica Ajijic, Ctra Oeste 33, T376-766 0662, with 24-hr ambulance service. **Post office** 1 block south of plaza, Colón esq Constitución. Ajijic Real Estate, Morelos 4, T376-766 2077, is an authorized UPS outlet. **Telephone** On the northwest corner of the plaza is a Computel booth for long-distance phone and fax, daily 0800-2100.

South to the coast

Heading southwest from Guadalajara along Route 54 brings one past increasingly green and fertile areas given over to agave and citrus fruits until, after passing by the twin volcanoes, the lovely city of Colima appears. From here, one can travel northwest along Route 200 to reach Manzanillo and eventually all the way to the Sonoran Desert (if so inclined) or strike out along the same route in a southerly direction and cross into Michoacán, home to some of Mexico's most lovely (and still largely unknown) beaches. ▶▶ *For listings, see pages 473-479.*

Colima ⊙❶❶❸❸❸ ▶▶ *pp473-479. Colour map 2, B2. Phone code: 312.*

Located 179 km southeast of Guadalajara on Route 54 (US$12.75 in tolls), the capital of the state of Colima (Mexico's smallest) was founded in 1527 and was formerly a Pacific port of great importance. It is now known to visitors primarily as the gateway to the coastal resort of Manzanillo (see below), and a most charming and hospitable town in its own right, although it lives in the shadow of an active volcano (one of two in the region, Fuego and Nevado), which can be seen smoking 30 km to the north. Ironically, while encompassed by the **Parque Nacional Volcán de Colima**, both are located in the neighbouring state of Jalisco. The city also suffers from earthquakes, the latest of which was in January 2003. It damaged many buildings and killed at least 25 people, but the city recovered quickly and has rebuilt and repaired its churches and historical buildings.

Ins and outs

The airport is 19 km from the centre and receives flights from Mexico City and Tijuana; buses run into town and a taxi costs approximately US$20. There are two bus stations on the outskirts of town. There is a **tourist office** ① *Miguel Hidalgo 96 esq 27 de Septiembre, T312-312 4360, Mon-Fri 0900-1500, www.visitacolima.com.mx.* ▸▸ *See Transport, page 478.*

Sights

The **Zócalo** is the focal point of the town, with a 19th-century Moorish-style **arcade** and a strange rebuilt Gothic ruin on the road beyond the pretty pink **cathedral** (late-19th century), which now holds the rank of minor basilica. Also on the east side of the main square are the **Palacio de Gobierno**, which contains interesting murals of the history of Mexico, the **Ayuntamiento**, and the porfiriato **Jardín de la Libertad** and its beautiful kiosk. Behind these is the **Jardín Gregorio Torres Quintero**, another pretty plaza but smaller.

The **Museo Regional de Historia** ① *on the Zócalo, Portal Morelos 1 y Reforma, T312-312 9228, www.inah.gob.mx, Tue-Sat 0900-1800, Sun 1700-2000, US$1.95 (Sun free)*, has a comprehensive collection of pre-Hispanic ceramics; look out for the figurines of dogs, which were clearly being fattened for the supper table. The ceramicists attained a high level of skill in portraying the facial expressions of people engaged in their daily tasks. **Teatro Hidalgo** ① *corner of Degollado and Morelos*, has a pink colonial facade and large carved wooden doors (only open during functions). **Parque Núñez**, five blocks east of the plaza is also attractive and twice the size of the plaza.

Colima has an abundance of museums, almost all of which are located in or near the centre. The **Museo de las Culturas de Occidente** ① *María Ahumada de Gómez, T312-306 0800, Tue-Sun 0900-1830 (US$1.10)*, in the **Casa de Cultura complex** ① *Av Calzada Pedro Galván y Ejército Nacional s/n*, deserves a visit if only for its collection of nearly 800 pre-Hispanic figurines. **La Pinacoteca Universitaria Alfonso Michel** ① *Vicente Guerrero 35, T312-312 2228, www.ucol.mx/arte/museos/pinacoteca.php, Tue-Sat 1000-1400, 1700- 2000, Sun 1000-1300*, has many works by and about the Colima-born painter Alfonso Michel and his contemporaries. The **Museo Alejandro Rangel Hidalgo** ① *in the Conjunto Cultural Nogueras, T312-315 6028, www.ucol.mx/cultura/museos/rangelhidalgo.htm, Tue-Fri 1000-1400, 1630-1900, Sat-Sun 1000-1800, US$0.75 (Sun free)*, has pre-Hispanic crafts and sculptures, as well as more modern furniture and paintings from the founder's collections in a lovely old hacienda setting. There is also the **Museo Universitario de Artes Populares** ① *María Teresa Pomar Gabino Barreda y Manuel Gallardo Zamora 99, T312-312 6869, www.ucol.mx/cultura/museos/populares.htm, Tue-Sat 1000-1400, 1700-2000, Sun 1000-1300, US$1.10 (Sun free)*, whose objective is to rescue, conserve, and promote the folklore and handicrafts of the state of Colima. It does so with its many exhibits on legends and handicrafts and has items for sale as well. Outside of the centre, there are yet more options. Of course, no visit to Colima would be complete without a stop at the **Museo de la Iguana** ① *Medellín 66, T312-330 5728, www.bios-iguana.com, US$1.10*, which is indeed just that: a museum dedicated to the iguana.

Per square metre, Colima has more parks than any other city in Mexico. One in particular, **Parque Piedra de Lisa**, bears mentioning. Located a few blocks east of the centre (any local will know where it is), the park has various stone formations, some natural, some carved, and one that for decades has been a local meeting point. The *piedra de lisa* (smooth stone) itself is a rather bland-looking large rock, but indeed smooth. Legend has it that anyone wishing to return to Colima after an initial visit need only slide down the stone to guarantee that he or she will visit the city again.

Around Colima

The archaeological site of **El Chanal** ① *2 km north of Colima's centre, Tue-Sun 0100-1700*, has a small pyramid with 36 sculptured figures, discovered in 1944. Another site, closer by, is **La Campana** ① *just off Av Tecnológico*. Both sites are open Tuesday-Sunday 1000-1700 and cost US$0.85. These largely unexcavated remains include a ball court and a few temples and platforms aligned with Colima's twin volcanoes. **El Hervidero**, 33 km southeast of Colima, is a spa in a natural lake of hot springs (25°C).

Comala, a pretty colonial town 18 km northwest of Colima with whitewashed adobe buildings (for which it is known as 'La Ciudad Blanca'), has a cooler and more comfortable climate than Colima in the summer. Comala is known as well for its excellent furniture and other crafts, including paintings and wrought iron work. The town's cobblestone streets, red-tiled roofs, whitewashed buildings, numerous restaurants, and views of the volcanos add to its attraction. There are excellent views of both volcanoes, especially the active **Volcán de Fuego** (3960 m). The surrounding vegetation is lush with coffee plantations.

Manzanillo and around ☺🏠🖈🛆🍴☺ ➤➤ pp473-479. Colour map 2, B1. Phone code: 314.

A beautiful, 157-km toll road (US$6.35, along Routes 54 and 200) now runs from Colima to Manzanillo (the *ruta libre* between the two cities still exists, but takes at least twice as long), which was once and is now once again an important port on the Pacific. The town existed long before tourists arrived, and while Manzanillo is not yet an overly touristy town it is moving inexorably in this direction.

It is the only Pacific beach resort of note between Puerto Vallarta to the north and Ixtapa-Zihuatanejo to the south. Traditional activities include deep-sea fishing (US$200-300 to hire a boat for a day, with beer, *refrescos* and *ceviche*), whale watching, water skiing, swimming and walking in the hills. There is a good snorkelling trip starting at the beach of Club Las Hadas, US$40, includes soft drinks and equipment. The water is clear and warm, with lots to see. The best beach is the lovely crescent of **Santiago**, 8 km north, but there are four others: **Playa Audiencia**, **Playa Miramar**, **Playa Azul** and **Playa Salahud**, all of which are clean, with good swimming. The first two are the best for privacy and surfing. Frequent buses serve all of these from the centre. There's a **tourist office** ① *Blv Miguel de la Madrid 4960, T314-333 2277, Mon-Fri 0900-1500*. For those done in by the sun, there is the out- standing **Museo Universitario de Arqueología** ① *Glorieta San Pedrito s/n, T314-332 2256, Tue-Sat 1000-1400, 1700-2000; Sun 1000-1300, www.ucol.mx/ arte/museos/arqueologia.php (US$0.70)*, which has excellent exhibits and programmes on the area's pre-Hispanic heritage.

Southeast of Manzanillo

Less than 50 km southeast of Manzanillo on Route 54, **Tecomán** (hailed as 'the lemon capital of the world') has a delightful atmosphere although some of its buildings still show evidence of the 2003 earthquake. It has some pleasant, uncrowded beaches, amongst them **Playa Boca Pascuales** (for surfing) and **Playa Tecuanillo** and **Playa El Real** (for surf fishing). Some 25 km west of Tecomán on Route 200, the small coastal resort of **Cuyutlán** has several pleasant, black-sand beaches, the most famous of which is **Playa**

Ola Verde, a surfer's heaven, which boasts some of the largest surf along the Pacific coast. The long **Laguna de Cuyutlán**, further to the west, has a remarkable coastal transitional ecosystem with several rare birds and intracoastal species (those that inhabit inland ponds, swamps and marshes but do not merge with the coastal species) along its shore.

In the other direction, coastal Route 200 continues southeast to the unspoilt fishing village of **Boca de Apiza** (no hotels but some seafood restaurants). There is abundant birdlife here as well, at the mouth of the river. Exactly 30 km to the southeast of Tecomán, the road crosses into the state of Michoacán, and eventually reaches **Playa Azul**, **Lázaro Cárdenas**, **Zihuatanejo** and, further still, **Acapulco**, before eventually going all the way to the border with Guatemala. For the entire length of its run in the state of Colima, the condition of Route 200 is excellent (it becomes a toll road between Manzanillo and Tecomán), although once it crosses into Michoacán, it deteriorates and for several winding stretches you cannot see the ocean. About one hour south of Tecomán (68 km), the first coastal town across the border is the village of **San Juan de Lima**, on a small beach. At 122 km south from Tecomán (or 158 km northwest of Playa Azul if approaching from the south) is another uncrowded beach, **Maruata**, where you can ask the restaurant owner if you can camp or sling a hammock.

North of Manzanillo

The entire area, called **Costa Alegre** (Happy Coast) is very much a top priority for the Mexican government's tourism initiatives. **San Patricio Melaque**, 64 km northwest of Manzanillo along Route 200, in the state of Jalisco, is in one of the most beautiful bays on the Pacific coast. While tiny, it is nonetheless very commercialized, crowded at holiday times and targets long-stay residents. The beach is long, shelving and sandy with a rocky coast at each end (**Punta Graham** to the south and **Punta El Estrecho** to the north) and pelicans diving for fish. The waves are not very big at **Playa San Patricio**, however. The week leading up to **St Patrick's Day** is fiesta time, when there are fireworks, dances, and rodeos. Ask at the **tourist office** ⓘ *Sonora 15, T314-357 0100*, for details.

Barra de Navidad, just along the beach from San Patricio de Melaque, about 1½ hours by road from Manzanillo, is commercial but pleasant. As with many of the country's Pacific resorts, there is a seaside *malecón* that offers spectacular views of the coast, especially from the pier at the end of the strip. It has a monument to the Spanish ships in the famous Legazpi expedition that set out from here in 1564 to conquer the Philippines. **El Coco Beach** is beautiful and good for swimming (surfing a bit less so except along Playa de Navidad), but crowded during holiday times. The **tourist office** ⓘ *Jalisco 67, T314-355 5100, www.barradenavidad.com, Mon-Fri 0900-1700, Sat-Sun 1000-1400*, is helpful and English is spoken.

North of Barra de Navidad

From Manzanillo to the state border the best driving option is the new toll road (US$2.90), after which there are tolls heading north until Baja California (unless taking the inland route via Tepic and Durango).

A recommended stop is **Cuestecomate**, 4 km west of Melaque off Route 200, which is blessed with a black-sand beach that is ideal for swimming, snorkelling and diving. Some 21 km north of Melaque is **La Manzanilla**, a tranquil fishing village on the **Bahía de Tenacatita** with a positively gorgeous, crescent-shaped beach. A few kilometres north is **Boca de Iguanas**, a very secluded beach town popular with campers and RVs. There are two trailer parks here: **Boca de Iguanas** and **Tenacatita** (not to be confused with the town). For both places, take the unpaved road from Highway 200 as far as the abandoned Hotel Bahía de

Tenacatita; at the T-junction, turn right, pass the hotel, and the campsites are about 500 m further on the left. **Tenacatita**, the next town up, is highly regarded by those in the know for its beach-camping opportunities. A further 20 km to the north along Route 200 is **Careyes**, the only town in the area with luxury accommodation. It is famous for the turtles that nest along its beach. **Chamela**, at 72 km from Melaque, is on the southern end of a gorgeous bay by the same name, and has several off shore islands, ideal for fishing, snorkelling, or diving. Finally, **Pérula**, an isolated hamlet at the northern tip of the bay, is a scene straight out of a 1960s surf film, with little besides a beautiful beach, even more beautiful sunsets, and an aura of lethargy over everything.

From Pérula, Route 200 continues north another 131 km to Puerto Vallarta, or, if headed back toward Manzanillo, 193 km south. There are beaches and hotels on this route and places to stay in Pérula village at the north end of Chamela Beach, about 39 km north of San Patricio de Melaque.

Many other coastal towns – some no more than seaside hamlets – lie along the coast between Barra de Navidad and Pérula (the northern terminus of the Costa Alegre). Most do not have anything more than rudimentary tourist facilities and are quiet and redolent of *México clásico*. This area is one of the least commercialized stretches of Mexico's Pacific

Manzanillo

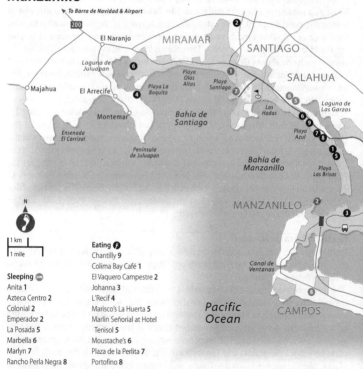

Sleeping 🛏
Anita **1**
Azteca Centro **2**
Colonial **2**
Emperador **2**
La Posada **5**
Marbella **6**
Marlyn **7**
Rancho Perla Negra **8**

Eating 🍴
Chantilly **9**
Colima Bay Café **1**
El Vaquero Campestre **2**
Johanna **3**
L'Recif **4**
Marisco's La Huerta **5**
Marlin Señorial at Hotel
  Tenisol **5**
Moustache's **6**
Plaza de la Perlita **7**
Portofino **8**

coast and well worth taking in at a leisurely pace. The 236-km drive from Barra de Navidad to Puerto Vallarta is entirely along free roads (Route 200), although there are large stretches where the road winds inland. There are only three petrol stops between the two towns, so plan accordingly. Stop off at the one in **Melaque** and you'll have enough until you reach the last Pemex outpost at **La Cumbre**, 76 km south of Puerto Vallarta.

◉ South to the coast listings

For Sleeping and Eating price codes and other relevant information, see Essentials pages 47-51.

◉ Sleeping

Colima *p468*
AL-A María Victoria Misión Colima, Blv Camino Real 999, near the financial district, T312-313 8106, www.hotelesmision.com/

A To Minatitlán

Jalipa

200

EL COLOMO

To Colima (toll-free)

Laguna de Cuyutlán

To Colima (Toll road)

mexico/colima/colima/hotels/mision-colima/description.aspx. The nicest hotel in the city. Very pleasing to the eye, with all amenities. Plenty of activities, great restaurant, and beautiful pool. By far the best in its range. Highly recommended.
A América, Morelos 162, T312-312 9596, hamerica@hotelamerica.com.mx. A/c, cable TV, phone, pretty interior gardens, travel agency, steam baths, good restaurant, central, friendly, but has suffered from a lack of upkeep.
A Best Western Ceballos, Portal Medellín 12, T312-312 4449, main square, www.hotel ceballos.com. A fine building with attractive *portales*, some huge rooms with a/c, clean, good food in its 2 restaurants (pricey), secure indoor parking, very good value. Highly recommended.
C Costeño, Blv Carlos de la Madrid Bejár 1001, T312-312 1900, www.hotelcosteno. com. 3 mins from the centre. Decent accommodation, with pool, restaurant, and parking. All rooms with a/c and TV.
C-D Gran Hotel Flamingos, Av Rey Colimán 18, near Jardín Núñez, T312-312 2525. Hardly a 'gran' hotel, but has pleasant small rooms with fan, bath, simple, clean, breakfast expensive, disco below goes on till 0300 on Sat and Sun.
C-D La Merced, Hidalgo 188 (entrance at Juárez 82), T312-312 6969. Pretty colonial house with rooms around patio filled with plants, all rooms same price, TV, bath. Highly recommended for budget travellers.
C-D Los Candiles, Blv Camino Real 399, T312- 312 3212, www.hotelloscandiles.com. In front of the university. Non-descript but functional. Can be noisy. Has restaurant and pool, parking.
E Núñez, Juárez 88 y Jardín Núñez, T312-312 7030. Basic, dark, with bath.

Manzanillo *p470, map p472*

Almost all of Manzanillo's upper-end hotels are located in the Salahua and Bahía Santiago (Playa de Olas Alas) waterfronts, with a handful also along the Las Brisas peninsula. Those located in the downtown section are invariably much less expensive and generally have more local colour to them.

A Marlyn, on Playa Santiago, T314-333 0107, www.marlyn.com.mx. Third-floor rooms with balcony overlooking the beach. Recommended.

B La Posada, Av Lázaro Cárdenas 201, near the end of Las Brisas peninsula, T314-333 1899, www.gomanzanillo.com/hotels/posada. American owned, beautifully designed rooms, some back into the rock of an outcrop.

B Rancho Perla Negra, Ctra Colima-Manzanillo (Campos exit), T314-332 0050, http://ranchoperlanegra.com. Designed with the discriminating budget traveller in mind, a great alternative lodging that has both the sea and countryside to offer. Bilingual staff, very friendly and helpful. Pool, internet, jacuzzi, many rooms with ocean views and patios. Multitude of outdoor activities available. Highly recommended.

B-C Marbella, Marbella 7, Km 9.5, T314-333 1102, www.hotelmarbella.com.mx. A rare example of a waterfront hotel that's affordably priced (although the beach is quite dangerous). All rooms with patio (60 facing ocean; the rest on boulevard), a/c, satellite TV, internet, and daily maid service. Recommended.

C Anita, on Playa Santiago, T314-333 0161. Built in 1940, has a certain funky charm, clean and on the beach.

C Azteca Centro, Allende 72, at the port, T314-332 7343, http://hotelaztecacentro.com. Fan, TV, clean, opposite the market, good value.

C Colonial, González Boncanegra 28 y Av México 100, downtown, T314-332 1080, http://hotelcolonialmanzanillo.com. The 1st hotel in Manzanillo, in a colonial building with hand-painted Mexican tiles. Good restaurant, good central location and friendly.

D Emperador, Dávalos 69, T314- 332 2374. Good value, friendly, fan, TV, cheap restaurant.

Camping

La Marmota trailer park, Ctra a Minatitlan, Km 0 (junction of Highways 200 and 98), T314-336 6248, just outside Manzanillo. Cold showers, bathrooms, pool, laundry facilities, restaurant.

Southeast of Manzanillo *p470*

C Fénix, Hidalgo 201, Cuyutlán, T313-326 4082, hotelfenixcuyutlan@yahoo.com. Family owned, the oldest hotel in town. Not beachfront but has beach views. Great food, clean rooms. Wi-Fi, money exchange, credit cards ok. Good value. Highly recommended.

C Gran Fénix, Javier Mina 460, Tecomán, T313-324 0791, www.hotelgranfenix.com.mx. Family-oriented and safe. 12-min walk from the beach. Larger rooms have a/c, smaller rooms are noisier but hotel is recommended.

C Morelos, Hidalgo 185, Cuyutlán, T313-326 4004. Short walk from the beach. Famous for its outstanding food (cheaply priced) and unique, no walls restaurant. Beautiful grounds, pool.

C Plaza, Av Insurgentes 502 y Emiliano Zapata, Tecuanillo, T313-324 3574, www.hotelplaza tecoman.com. Surely the most eclectic hotel in the state. Near the beach, run by surfing fanatics. Separate restaurant (highly regarded by locals). Pool, Wi-Fi, children's park, nice gardens and grounds, rooms a bizarre mix of kitsch and thoughtfulness.

C Real, Av Insurgentes y Manuel Gudiño s/n, Tecomán, T313-324 0100, www.realhotel.com.mx. 10 mins from the beach. Bilingual, friendly staff. Wi-Fi, restaurant/bar, pool. All rooms with TV, a/c, and double beds.

D-E Yeza, Lázaro Cárdenas 59, Tecomán. Very clean, spacious rooms in a quiet spot on the corner from the bus station, the owner's son speaks English.

North of Manzanillo *p471*

AL-A Los Artistas Bed & Breakfast, Isla Navidad, reached by ferry, T315-355 6441, www.islanavidad.com/meson. Spectacular private mansion converted into an exclusive hotel, 27 golf holes, private beaches, pools, personal service, good value.

A Club Náutico El Dorado, Valentin Gómez Farias 1, San Patrico Melaque, 2 blocks from the bus station, 4 blocks from downtown, T315-355 5770, www.hotelclubnautico.com. Very close to the beach. Excellent value, very clean and secure. Recommended.

A CocoCabanas, La Culebra s/n, Barra de Navidad, T315-100 0441, www.eco cabanas.com. Very interesting concept: a solar-powered beachside inn. Comfortable and elegant, top-quality *cabañas* off the beaten path on the 22-km-long Playa de Cocos. Recommended.

A Hacienda Melaque, Morelos 49, San Patricio Melaque, T315-355 5334, www.haciendademelaque.com. Tennis courts, kitchen, *palapas*, enormous pool, jacuzzi, children's playground, restaurant.

A-B Delfín, Morelos 23, Barra de Navidad, T315-355 5068, http://hoteldelfinmx.com. Very clean, pool, gym, hot water, friendly, family owned and family friendly. Recommended.

B Barra de Navidad, Miguel López de Legazpi 250, Barra de Navidad, T315-824 4043, www.hotelbarradenavidad.com. On the beach, rooms with balcony or bungalows where you can cook, pool.

B Casa Chips, Miguel López de Legazpi 198, Barra de Navidad, T315- 355 5555, www.casachips.com. Comfortable, clean, and quiet. 8 rooms with Wi-Fi, TV, double beds. Restaurant is well known in town. Good value for money.

B Villas Camino del Mar, Francisco Villa Obregón 6, San Patricio Melaque, T315-355 5207. Rooms or villas on beach, 2 pools, penthouse flat, patio bar, discounts for long stays.

B Vista Hermosa, Gómez Farías 23, San Patricio Melaque, T315-355 5002, www.hotel vistahermosa.com. Family owned, friendly. Can arrange fishing trips and other outings. All rooms oceanfront and clean. Great value and highly recommended.

B-C Monterrey, Valentin Gómez Farías 27, San Patricio Melaque, T315-355 5004, on beach (across from bus and taxi stations). Clean, fan, bath, parking, superb view. Can be crowded and noisy at times.

B-C San Felipe, Av Abel Salgado Velazco 335 y Alejandra, San Patricio Melaque, T315-355 6433, www.hotelsanfelipe.com. Oceanfront location 7 blocks from plaza, American hosts very knowledgeable and friendly. Buffet on Sun, can arrange fishing trips and other excursions, well-managed turtle hatchery on premises, bike rentals.

C Misión San Miguel, Prologación Galeana 52, Tomatlán, T322-298 5360. In centre, best hotel in town.

C Posada Pablo de Tarso, Valentin Gómez Farías 408, San Patricio Melaque, T315-355 5117, facing beach. Pretty, galleried building, tiled stairs, antique-style furniture.

C-D Santa María, Av Abel Salgado Velazco 85 (opposite Flamingo), San Patricio Melaque, T315-357 0338. Friendly. Pool. Rooms have TV, kitchens. Recommended.

D Caribe, Sonora 15, Barra de Navidad. Fan, friendly, kitchen facilities, family run, in heart of downtown so can be noisy.

D San Lorenzo, Av Sinaloa 7, T315-355 5139, Barra de Navidad, 1½ blocks from beach in downtown. Very clean, hot water, friendly staff, good restaurant opposite.

D San Nicolás, Valentin Gómez Farías 54, San Patricio Melaque, beside Estrella Blanca bus station and across from La Playa trailer park (see below), 1 block from beach, T315- 357 0066. Noisy but clean. Off season, very pleasant.

D Posada Pacífico, Mazatlán 136, Barra de Navidad, 1 block behind the bus station, T315-355 5359. Clean, fan, friendly, good restaurant opposite, good value.

E Posada Carmelita, Tomatlán, Km 103 south of Puerto Vallarta and 12 km inland (not to be confused with Boca de Tomatlán, on the coast), has a few modest rooms with bath, clean.

Camping

Melaque Follow the 'Melaque' signs and at the end of the main road is a free camping place on the beach at the bay, very good, easily accessible for RVs, popular for vehicles and tents.

Trailer Park La Playa, Valentin Gómez Farías 250, San Patricio Melaque, in the village, T315-

355 5065. On the beach, US$18 for car and 2 people, full hook-up, toilets, cold showers.

Tenacatita Boca Beach Camping Trailer Park, Av Tenacatita s/n, on the south side of the road on the beach itself, T317-381 0393. Hook-ups, tents, small store and hotel (**D-E**) adjacent. US$14 per car.

Chamela Villa Polinesia Trailer Park, near Chamela: Km 72 on Route 200 between Pérula and Chamela; follow signs then 2 km down a gravel road, T328-285 5247. Full hook-ups, hot showers, on a lovely beach. Recommended. Restaurant on road to trailer park, good food.

Tenacatita Trailer Park & Hotel, Av Tenacatita 32: take the unpaved road from Highway 200 north of Barra de Navidad as far as the abandoned Hotel Bahía de Tenacatita; at the T-junction, turn right, pass the hotel, and the trailer park is about 500 m further on the left, T333-115 5406. Hook-ups, cold showers, toilet, laundry facilities, restaurant. Hotel (**D-E**) adjacent to trailer park.

Eating

Colima *p468*

Colima is nationally famous for its excellent sweets, such as coconut and pineapple pastes, tamarind pulp and *pinches*, all uniformly delicious. Its best-known drinks are fresh *tuba* (made from the sweet sap of palm trees) and the refreshing *tejuino*. Typical gastronomy worth sampling includes sweet enchiladas, *sopitos, tostadas* made from scraped tortillas, white *pozole*, *atole* with meat *tamales*, and, for the stout of appetite and heart, a regional *birria* with beans and spicy sauce.

ΨΨ **El Vivero**, Constitución 61. Nice open-air plant-filled courtyard, moderately priced specialities including seafood, Mexican and Italian, live music Thu-Sun.

ΨΨ **La Troje de Ala**, Carlos de la Madrid Bejar 469, T314-312 2680. Good, Mariachis, very Mexican.

ΨΨ **Los Naranjos**, Gabino Barreda 34, ½ block north of Jardín Torres Quintero. Going since 1955, pleasant, well known.

ΨΨ-Ψ **Fonda San Miguel**, Av 27 de Septiembre 129, T312-314 4840. Regional food, popular.

ΨΨ-Ψ **La Arabica**, Gabino Barreda 4, T312- 313 7707. Arabic food, a rare find in Mexico.

ΨΨ-Ψ **La Pasta**, Genoveva Sánchez 1265. Salads, pastas, pizzas. Reasonable prices.

ΨΨ-Ψ **Livorno's**, Andando Constitución s/n, near Jardín de Libertad, T312-334 5030. Italian.

ΨΨ-Ψ **Naranas**, near Jardín Libertad. Live music nights. Good regional food, reasonable prices.

Ψ **Café de la Plaza**, at the Hotel Ceballos at Jardín de Libertad. Sidewalk café.

Ψ **El Charco de la Higuera**, Madero, 6 blocks west of Jardín de Libertad, T312-313 1092. Attractive setting, typical meat dishes, also fresh salads and pastas.

Ψ **El Trébol**, southwest corner of the Zócalo. Probably the best of several restaurants on the Zócalo serving inexpensive meals.

Cafés, bakeries and ice cream parlours

Centro de Nutrición Lakshmi, Av Madero 265. Good yoghurt and wholemeal bread run by Hari Krishnas.

Around Colima *p470*

ΨΨ-Ψ Los Portales and Comala, both in the town of Comala. Popular restaurants, with Mariachis and local specialities; open until 1800. If you sit and drink you will usually be brought complimentary food until you wilt from Mariachi overload.

Manzanillo *p470, map p472*

There are central markets with *fondas* for good cheap seafood, clean.

ΨΨΨ-ΨΨ **Chantilly**, Juárez, closed Sat. Popular café serving big traditional meals and good coffee.

ΨΨΨ-ΨΨ **L' Recif**, Cerro de Cenicero s/n, Peninsula Juluapan, T314-334 2684. Great French and seafood. Very popular and romantic location overlooking water.

ΨΨΨ-ΨΨ **Marlin Señorial**, Hotel Tenisol, Av Carrizles s/n, T314-335 0412. Excellent seafood and tropical dishes. Refined atmosphere.

ΨΨ **El Vaquero Campestre**, Av La Audencia Lote 2, T314-334 1548. Hearty Mexican meat dishes and Mariachi bands.

† **Marisco's La Huerta**, Blv Costero Miguel de la Madrid 873, T314-334 0648. Good seafood on the way to the beach.
† **Plaza de la Perlita**, next door to Portofino. Good Mexican and seafood, live music. Recommended.
† **Portofino**, Blv Costero Miguel de la Madrid 923, T314-334 1333. Italian and continental, good pizza.
† **Colima Bay Café**, Blv Costero Miguel de la Madrid 921, T314-333 1150. Nice coffee shop with views of bay.
† **Johanna**, opposite the bus station entrance. Good food, cheap.
† **Moustache's**, Puesta del Sol 3 (behind Club de Peña Colorada), T314-333 1236. Open late. Specializes in American food and light meals.

Santiago
† **Juanito's**, Blv Costero Miguel de la Madrid, Km 14.3, T314-333 1388. Burgers, breakfasts, tacos, smoothies and shakes. Very popular with backpackers and tourists. A great place to check email, send a fax, or watch TV.

Southeast of Manzanillo p470
††† **Willy's Seafood Restaurant**, Benito Rincón López s/n, Playa Azul, T314-333 1794. French owner, primarily seafood, some meat, very good, very popular.

North of Manzanillo p471
San Patricio Melaque
There are many restaurants on the beach at San Patricio Melaque but most close at 1900.
†† **Koala's at the Beach**, Alvaro Obregón 52, 2 blocks from Camino del Mar. Small, good, great food in walled garden compound off dusty street. Canadian/Australian run.
†† **Maya Melaque**, on the beach, T315-355 6881. Fine cuisine, Mediterranean style, open in high season, reservations recommended for beachside tables.

Barra de Navidad
††† **Antonio's**, Grand Bay. Award-winning restaurant, gourmet food.

†††-†† **Ambar**, Veracruz 101. Closed lunchtime. Half the menu is vegetarian, real coffee, good breakfast and crêpes. Recommended.
†††-†† **Seamaster**, on beach. Best ribs in town.
†† **Velero's**. Delicious snapper and good views.
††-† **Banana's**, on the beach, Barra de Navidad. Good breakfast and coffee.

⊕ Bars and clubs

Around Colima p470
Botanero Bucaramanga, outside the town of Comala, on the Colima road. Bar with *botanas* (snacks) and Mariachis.

⊕ Festivals and events

Colima p468
Oct-Nov The annual *feria* of the region (cattle, agriculture and industry, with much festivity) runs from the last Sat of Oct until the 1st Sun of Nov. Traditional local drinks include *jacalote* (from black maize and pumpkin seeds), *bate* (*chía* and honey), *tuba* (palm tree sap) and *tecuino* (ground, germinated maize).

⊙ Shopping

North of Manzanillo p471
There is an English- and Spanish-language book exchange improbably known as Beer Bob's, at Tampico 8 in Barra de Navidad.

▲ Activities and tours

North of Manzanillo p471
Tour operators
Dona Tours & Travel, Av Veracruz 220 (next to the bus terminal), Barra de Navidad, T315-355 5667. Travel agent.
Nautimar, Hamberto, Barra de Navidad, T315-355 5790. Snorkelling, scuba diving and waterskiing.

Sea to Sierra Outdoor Eco & Adventure, Av Veracruz 204, Barra de Navidad, T315-355 5790, www.seatosierra.com. Handles anything outdoors on the Costa Alegre. Recommended.

☺ Transport

Colima p468
Air
The airport (CLQ) is 19 km from centre, T312-314 4160. Flights to **Mexico City** and **Tijuana**. Buses and taxis (US$20) run to the airport. The best place to hail either is in the centre of town.

Airline offices Aeromar, T312-313 1340. AeroMéxico, T312-313 1340.

Bus
There are 2 bus stations on the outskirts. Suburbana is for buses within Colima state – urban buses and *combis* run to the centre, US$0.40. From Suburbana to the centre, take Routes 1 or 19, or taxi, about US$1.20. Foránea is for buses out of the state. To get there from the centre take Route 4 or 5 from Jardín Nuñez. If going to **Uruapan** it is best to go to **Zamora** (7-8 hrs, although officially 4 hrs) and change there. To **Guadalajara**, hourly service, 2½-3hrs, US$13.55. To **Manzanillo**, 3 hrs, US$8.80. To **Mexico City**, US$55. To **Comala**, regular buses, US$0.15, 20 mins.

Manzanillo p470, map p472
Air
The airport (ZLO) is 19 km from town. Taxis and buses run a direct service. The best place to hail either is in the centre of town. Taxis should cost around US$20 but are much faster than buses; agree the price beforehand.

There are frequent flights to **Mexico City** and **Guadalajara**. Other domestic destinations include **Chihuahua**, **Monterrey**, **Puerto Vallarta** and **Saltillo**, as well as to **Los Angeles** in the USA.

Airline offices Airlines Aeromar, T314-333 0151. Aerolitoral, T314-333 2424. Mexicana, T314-332 1972.

Bus
The long-distance bus terminal is on Av Hidalgo outside the centre; local buses run there from the centre, or take a taxi, US$2. Buses to **Miramar**, US$0.40, leave from J J Alcaraz, 'El Tajo' and can be picked up anywhere along Av Niños Héroes.

Several daily buses to **Guadalajara**, 6 hrs, US$24.50. To **Mexico City**, 11 hrs, US$53. To **Barra de Navidad**, 1½ hrs, US$5. To **Colima**, 3 hrs, US$11.50. Down the coast to **Lázaro Cárdenas** and crossroads for **Playa Azul** with Autobus de Occidente or Galeana, 7 hrs. To **Acapulco**, US$22.20. To **Zihuatanejo**, 2130, US$24.90. To **Puerto Vallarta**, 1st class with Trans Cihuatlán at 0800 and 1200, 4½ hrs, US$17.90.

Car hire
Budget, Blv Miguel de la Madrid, Km 10, T314-333 1445. National, Ctra Manzanillo-Santiago, Km 7, T314-333 0611.

North of Manzanillo p471
Barra de Navidad
Bus Buses from terminal on Veracruz, to **Manzanillo**, 1st class, 1215, 1615, 1815 and 2000, US$6, 2nd class; hourly from 0745, US$5.05. To **Puerto Vallarta**, 1st class, 0915 and 1315, 4 hrs, US$19; 2nd class 0900, 1000, 1200, 1400, 1600 and 1800, 5½ hrs, US$15.50.

ⓓ Directory

Colima p468
Banks Banco Inverlat, Juárez 32, on west side of Jardín Núñez, ATM takes Amex, Visa, Diner's Club. *Casa de cambio* at Morelos and Juárez on southwest corner of same park. Bacomer at Madero y Ocampo 3 blocks east of plaza, ATM takes Visa and Plus. *Casa de cambio* across the street. Banamex, 1 block south on Ocampo at Hidalgo, has an ATM. **Internet** Cyber café, Plaza Country, Av Tecnológico, 15 blocks north of centre, Mon-Fri 0900-2200, Sat and Sun 1000-2200. **Laundry** Lavandería Shell, 27 de

Septiembre 134, daily 0900-2000, inexpensive, quick. **Medical services** Hospitals and clinics: Hospital Civil, T312-312 0227. Red Cross, T312-312 1451. **Pharmacy:** Farmacia Guadalupana on northeast corner of Jardín Torres Quintero behind cathedral. Another pharmacy on northeast corner of Zócalo. **Post office** Av Francisco I Madero and General Núñez, northeast corner of Jardín Núñez. **Telephone** Computel, Morelos 234 on south side for long-distance phone and fax, and at bus station, daily 0700-2200, accepts Visa, MasterCard, Amex and AT&T cards. Fax not always in use.

Manzanillo *p470, map p472*
Medical services Hospital Civil, T314-332 4161. Red Cross, T314-336 5770.

North of Manzanillo *p471*
San Patricio Melaque
Internet Cybernet between beachfront and Gómez Farías, near Hotel Monterrey.

Barra de Navidad
Banks The Colorín liquor store, opposite Hotel Barra de Navidad, changes money and sells stamps. **Internet** Internet Ciber@net, Veracruz 212, 1 block from bus terminal, friendly and useful resource, can change money and offer friendly advice. **Medical services** Dra Herlinda Rubio, English speaking.

West to the coast: to Tepic via Tequila

Northwest of Guadalajara lie the fabled agave and tequila towns, pleasant reminders of the fact that in spite of the enormity of its capital, Jalisco remains largely an agricultural state. They also mark the entrance to the state's tourism-driven towns, none more so than the northern outpost of Puerto Vallarta and its expanding environs. But there are also several lovely villages nestled in the hills, as yet untouched by mass tourism and still redolent of their colonial past. And for those with an interest in wildlife, this relatively undisturbed region is one of the best in Mexico for birdwatching.
▶▶ *For listings, see pages 485-489.*

Tequila and around ⊖⊖⊘⊖⊕ ▶▶ *pp485-489. Colour map 2, B2. Phone code: 374.*

Tequila, Jalisco's second of four official *pueblos mágicos* (enchanted towns) can be visited as a day-trip from Guadalajara, by car, bus, or train on the revitalized *Tequila Express* (see page 488). As the bus approaches the town, the aroma of the blue agave, from which the famous Mexican drink is distilled, fills the air and the plants can be seen growing in neat rows in the pleasant, hilly countryside. Tours of the tequila distilleries – the earliest of which was founded around 1600 – are available (see box, page 481) and stores will let you sample different tequilas before you buy. Often around 20 bottles are open for tasting.

The town is attractive, a mix of colonial and more modern architecture. It is a pleasant place to stay but there is not much to do other than tour the distilleries. There is little in the way of nightlife other than imbibing the local produce (and recovering the following morning).

Ins and outs
Getting there and around Buses from Guadalajara run to Tequila every 45 minutes, US$3. Along Sixto Gorjón, where the arriving buses drop you, there are several liquor stores selling tequila, restaurants where you can eat for under US$5, pharmacies, doctors, dentists, and the Rojo de los Altos bus ticket office at 126A. The *Tequila Express* is a

comfortable way of visiting the town from Guadalajara. It's all jazzed up and smart (unlike the rest of Mexico's rail industry) and you spend the day drifting towards the town, exploring one of the plantations before returning. ▶▶ *See Transport, page 488.*

Tourist information There is a **regional tourist office** ① *Ramón Corona s/n, T374-742 0159, www.tequilajalisco.gob.mx*, which offers good information on the area. There is also a stall on the Palacio Municipal on the main square, which supposedly offers tourist information but in reality just sells tours of the distilleries including trips to the fields.

Sights
In the town centre there are two plazas next to each other. On one sits the **Templo de Santiago Apóstol**, a large, pretty, old stone building, with a 1930s municipal market next to it. About a block behind Banamex, where Sixto Gorjón ends, is the entrance to the **José Cuervo distillery** ① *T374-742 1382, tours Mon-Sat 1000, 1200, 1300 and 1400, US$1.65 (children/students US$0.65), admission goes to the José Cuervo Foundation*. At Albino Rojas 22, is the **Sauza distillery** ① *T374-742 0247, Tue-Fri 1000-1400, US$0.65*, which has its own museum with memorabilia from the Sauza family, a tequila-making dynasty second only to the Cuervos. Both distilleries offer tours, as do many others, including **Herradura**, at the picturesque San José del Refugio hacienda, www.herradura.com.

The **Museo Nacional del Tequila** ① *Ramón Corona 34, T374-742 0012, Tue-Sun 1000-1700, US$1.25 (50% discount for students)*, is full of the history of tequila, along with details of the origins, processes, cultivation and distilling processes. The brand-new **Museo de Sitio del Tequila** ① *La Cofradía s/n, T374-742 1015, daily 1000-1700, www.tequila cofradia.com*, is located inside the famous **La Cofradía Distillery**, and showcases the many different stages in the production of the drink.

Ixtlán del Río
Continuing 88 km west from tequila, Ixtlán del Río has a few souvenir shops, a **Museo Arqueológico** ① *Palacio Municipal*, and a *casa de cambio*. There is also the **Museo Regional de Ixtlán** ① *on the plaza*, with modest information on the region's history and peoples. The **harvest festival** is held in mid-September.

Two kilometres southeast of town are the ruins of **Los Toriles** ① *US$1.90*, a Toltec ceremonial centre on a warm, wind-swept plain. The main structure is the **Temple of Quetzalcoatl**, noted for its cruciform windows and circular shape. The ruins have been largely restored and some explanatory notes are posted around the site. There is a caretaker but no real facilities. Another 2 km beyond the Los Toriles site, heading north towards town, is **Motel Hacienda** (**C-D**), with a pool. The road climbs out of the valley through uncultivated land, where trees intermix with prickly pear and chaparral cactus.

If travelling by bus, the journey from Guadalajara to Tepic cannot easily be broken at Ixtlán del Río for sightseeing since buses passing through in either direction tend to be full; the bus from Guadalajara takes three hours.

Tequila to Tepic
Heading northwest from Tequila towards Tepic you can travel along the old Route 15 (*libre*) or the new Route 15 (*cuota*). The difference is significant: US$26.15. At **Ahuacatlán**, 75 km south of Tepic, the 17th-century **ex-Convento de San Juan Evangelista** stands on the Plaza Principal; handicrafts are on sale here. Nearby, the village of **Jala** has a festival mid-August. From here the distant **Ceboruco volcano** can be reached in a day. On the

"A Field of Upright Swords" – the making of Tequila

This quote from Paul Theroux's *The Old Patagonian Express* describes the swathes of blue agave grown in the dry highlands of the State of Jalisco and neighbouring states of Zacatecas and Aguascalientes. Agave is the raw material for tequila and, although there are some 400 varieties, only blue agave is suitable; the minimum content must be 51%. After eight years growing in the fields, the spiky leaves are hacked off and the central core, weighing around 45 kg, is crushed and roasted. The syrup extracted is then mixed with liquid sugar, fermented for 30-32 hours and distilled twice.

White tequila is the product of a further four months in vats. It can be drunk neat, with a pinch of salt on the back of your hand followed by a suck on a wedge of lime, or mixed into cocktails such as the margarita. Natives generally opt for sipping it neat. **Gold tequila** is a blend of white tequila and tequila aged in wooden casks. **Añejo**, aged tequila, is golden brown in colour from spending at least two years in oak casks. **Special premium** has no sugar added.

In pre-Conquest times, local people used the agave sap to brew a mildly alcoholic drink, *pulque*, still drunk today. The Spaniards, however, wanted something stronger and more refined. They developed mescal (still made in Zacatecas, where it is the official state drink) and set up distilleries to produce what later became tequila. The first of these was established in 1795 by royal decree of King Charles IV of Spain. It is still in existence today. La Rojena, the distillery of José Cuervo, known by its black crow logo, is the biggest in the country.

Tequila, like many other spirits, is blended. While the best tequila is 100% *puro de agave*, a few distilleries appear to have been blending more than they would like to admit. Some years ago the Consejo Regulador del Tequila, whose job it is to monitor standards in the industry, made a couple of surprise calls on well-established distilleries and were denied entry.

There are 129 distilleries in Jalisco State, although only 112 are certified. Around the town of Tequila there are 12 distilleries, of which 10 produce 75% of the country's tequila. Tours of the distilleries can be arranged (English tours available) and include free tastings and, of course, shopping opportunities. Tours are hourly 1000-1400, US$3.50, lasting about one hour; check locally for precise times. Well-known distilleries include: **Tequila Cuervo**, T374-742 0076 (Tequila), T33-3634 4170 (Guadalajara), the largest and oldest continuously operating distillery in the country and run by the same family since 1759. **Tequila Sauza**, T374-742 0244 (Tequila), T33-3679 0600 (Guadalajara), where you can see the famous fresco illustrating the joys of tequila. **Herradura**, 8 km from Tequila, T374-3614 9657, in an old hacienda outside Amatitlán village, with adobe walls and cobblestone streets.

Based on the Napa Valley wine tours in the USA, the *Tequila Trail* takes you through the towns of El Arenal, Amatitán, Tequila, Magdelena and Teuchitlan. There are many tours available, all heavily promoted by tour operators under the auspices of the government. For information, visit www.rutadeltequila.org.mx, or the superb www.tequilasource.com/distillerytours.htm.

When buying tequila always choose the best quality available. Apparently 100% agave tequila blends in well with the human metabolism and you don't get a hangover. If you're looking for quality, look for the stamp of CRT (the Consejo Regulador del Tequila mark), check that it is 100% agave and finally, for the very best, buy tequila that has been *reposada* (matured). If it has all three, it's a fine tequila – and you should sip it gently.

main road, a few kilometres south and heading toward Jala, is the aptly named **El Ceboruco Parador Turístico** (which has a restaurant, information, toilets and a shop); a lava flow from nearby Ceboruco is visible.

At about 40 km from Tepic is an attractive area of volcanic lagoons. Take the bus to **Santa María del Oro** for the lagoon of the same name. On the south side of the new Route 15 (*cuota*) is the **Laguna Tepeltic**. At Km 53, there is a turn-off at Chapalilla to Compostela and Puerto Vallarta. Near Chapalilla is another lake at **San Pedro Lagunillas**.

Tepic and around ◎❼▲◎❶ ➤➤ *pp485-489. Colour map 2, B1. Phone code: 311.*

Tepic, the capital of Nayarit State, was founded in 1532 near the extinct Sangagüey volcano. It is a clean but slightly scruffy town with many little squares, filled with trees and flowers. The landscape around Tepic is wild and mountainous; access is very difficult. The Huichol and Cora people live in this region; their traditional dress is very picturesque. They are well known for their craftwork – including bags (carried only by men), scarves woven into colourful designs, necklaces of tiny beads (*chaquira*) and wall-hangings of brightly coloured wool – which is available from souvenir shops. You may see them in Tepic but it is best to let them approach you when they come to town if you want to purchase any items.

The town is on the verge of becoming a major transport hub. The construction on the *cuota* (toll) Route 15 (which parallels the old *libre*, or toll-free, Route 15), just 31 km north of town, was completed in 2009. This *autopista* now links Tepic with Escuinapa de Hidalgo (and so on to Mazatlán and points north), which will open the upper Nayarit coast to further development and tourism.

Ins and outs
Getting there Amado Nervo airport (TPQ) ① *16 km south of town*, receives daily flights from Mexico City, Tampico and Tijuana, as well as connections from Los Angeles. Getting from the airport to Tepic itself can be a challenge, as the bus service is infrequent at best. Taxis run 0600-1800. The bus station is a five-minute walk from the centre. ➤➤ *See Transport, page 489.*

Tourist information The tourist office ① *Av México y Calzada del Ejército, 1 block from the cathedral, T311-213 9203, daily 0900-2000*, is helpful and English is spoken. The **municipal tourist office** ① *Puebla y Amado Nervo, T311-216 5661*, is also very helpful.

Sights
The **cathedral** (1750, rebuilt 1891) is on the Plaza Principal; it has two fine Gothic towers and is painted primrose yellow, adorned with gold. Worth seeing are the **Palacio Municipal**, painted pink; the next-door **Museo de las Artes Populares**; and the **Casa de Amado Nervo** ① *Zacatecas Norte 281, Mon-Fri 1000-1400, Sat 1000-1300*, the house of the great Mexican poet and diplomat. The **Museo Regional de Antropología e Historia** ① *Av México 91 Norte, Mon-Fri 0900-1900, Sat 0900-1500*, has a fine collection of Aztec and Toltec artefacts, exhibits on the Huichol Cora, and Tepehuán peoples, and some beautiful religious paintings from the colonial period. Right next to it is the **Casa de los Conde de Miravelle**, an 18th-century colonial residence that has been restored. **La Casa Museo de Los Cuatro Pueblos** ① *Hidalgo y Zacatecas, Mon-Fri 0900-1400, 1600-1900, Sat and Sun 0900-1400*, exhibits the work of four indigenous ethnic groups. It is worth visiting to see the colourful artwork, textiles and beadwork of the Cora,

Nahua, Huichol and Tepehuano people. **Museo de Arte Emilia Ortiz** ⓘ *Lerdo 192 Pte, Mon-Sat 0900-1400*, has works by this local artist. **Museo de Artes Visuales Aramara** ⓘ *Allende 329 Pte, Mon-Fri 0900-1400, 1600-2000, Sat 0900-1400*, is also worth a quick visit for those with an interest in modern visual arts encompassing several media. **Plaza de los Constituyentes** ⓘ *México y Juárez*, is flanked on the west side by the Palacio de Gobierno. On the summit of a hill south of the centre are the **ex-Templo** and **ex-Convento de la Cruz**. The tombs in the cemetery are worth seeing too.

La Iglesia de la Cruz de Zacate ('The Church of the Cross of Grass'), close to the centre, has a very curious history to it. It was built to commemorate a natural phenomenon first discovered by the Spanish in 1619, when a muleteer noticed a patch of grass in the shape of a cross, over which his mule refused to tread. People pray at the side chapels of this pretty neighbourhood church but even more so in front of the grass cross, which church officials say grows in that shape without receiving water or special care. Wet season or

Tepic

Sleeping 🛏
Altamirano 1
Bugamvillas 2
Camarena 3
Fray Junípero Serra 4
Ibarra 5
Real de Don Juan 6
Sierra de Alicia 8

Eating 🍴
Chante Clair 5
El Tripol 3
Fu Seng 2
Roberto's International 4
Tiki Room 1

dry, the cross can still clearly be seen (although the top portion looks more like a triangle than the separate arms of a cross). Plaques on both sides of its outdoor niche give thanks for favours granted.

There are various beaches along the coast west of Tepic. **Santa Cruz**, about 43 km from Tepic, has a rocky beach. There are no hotels but it's possible to rent an apartment or camp at **Peter's Shop**. Two buses a day run from Tepic to Santa Cruz (US$0.85, or 2½ hours by open-sided lorry, US$0.60).

Huaynamota

While the Cora villages can only be visited by air (the roads leading there are in terrible condition) it is possible to visit some of the closer Huichol villages from the small town of **Huaynamota** in the mountains northeast of Tepic. Huaynamota has become much easier to reach with the opening of the **Aguamilpas Dam**. To get to the dam from Tepic, take a *combi* from Avenida México almost where it intersects with Zaragoza, US$2.50, 1½ hours.

Despite being flooded, the area is still beautiful, particularly at the narrower parts of the dam where huge boulders hang precariously on cliff tops. Boats leave from the west end of the dam at 0900 and 1400 (US$6.50), stopping at various *embarcaderos* (jetties) for each village along the way.

The *embarcadero* for Huaynamota is at the far end of the dam, where the Río Atengo feeds in. A community truck meets the launch (US$1) and runs the 8 km up a dirt road to the town. Half the population here is Huichol and their traditional houses can be seen on the outskirts. At the edge of town, from atop the large boulder beside the road, there is a panoramic view out over the valley. In Huaynamota itself there is little of interest, except that **Semana Santa** (Easter week) is famous, and many people from surrounding communities converge here for the week-long celebration.

San Blas and around ◉❷❷◉▲◉● ▸▸ *pp485-489. Colour map 2, B1. Phone code: 328.*

This old colonial town, built as a fortress against piracy, is 66 km west of Tepic. It is usually low key, except during US and Mexican summer holidays when it suffers from over-crowding. It has become popular with teenagers and the 20-something set, and now boasts a fledgling arts and eco-tourism community. The **tourist office** ① *Mercado, 1 block from plaza, T328-255 0021, www.visitsanblas.com, Mon-Sat 0900-1300, 1800-2000, Sun 0900-1300*, has information in English on the history of San Blas as well as a town map. Note that since early 2009, merchants in San Blas no longer accept US dollars, only pesos. A number of interesting tours are available in the surrounding area. ▸▸ *See Activities and tours, page 488.*

Founded in 1768, little is left of the old Spanish fortress, **Basilio**. It was from here that the Spanish set off to colonize Baja California and North America. Above the town are **La Contaduría** ① *US$0.50*, the Spanish counting house (1773), and **La Marinera**, a ruined church. The views over the town, estuaries and mangrove swamps from beside an incredibly ugly statue on the battlements are superb.

Once famous for its extremely long surfing wave (now diminished by changes to the ocean's floor), long, wide **Playa Matanchén**, 7 km from San Blas (taxi US$2.50), is a fine beach. If you like peace and quiet, go during the week and you'll have the place to yourself. Good home-made fruitcakes and bread are sold here. Quieter than the dirty town beach is the extensive and often-deserted **Playa El Rey** on the north side of the estuary of the same name, beyond the lighthouse. Take a boat across the river from just west of the harbour, US$0.50 each way; the boatman works until 1730, but stops at lunchtime (between 1400-1600). The best beach is probably **Playa de las Islitas**, reached by bus marked 'Las Veras' from the bus station; or 'El Llano' from Paredes y Sinaloa, just off the plaza. Surfing can be done at any these beaches; check at **Tumba de Yako** for tides and times (see Activities and tours, page 488).

In addition to its many long beaches, there are many pleasant places to hike and walk around San Blas and its environs. Take a bus to **La Bajada**, a pretty village in the foothills where you'll find friendly people and good birdwatching. At one end of the town there is a hiking trail, part of the old Spanish Camino Real, which goes through coffee plantations and eventually joins the road to Tepic.

Off an unmarked road 16 km south from San Blas is the beautiful **Playa Los Cocos**, which is empty except at weekends. Here you can swim in the ocean or spend the afternoon at **Casa Mañana**, a hotel and restaurant where you can have lunch and use the pool. Ask the bus driver to let you off. The trip takes about 45 minutes due to a detour to La Palma. When you see the renovated **Hotel Delfin**, you are almost there. You can also take a taxi for about US$7.50.

La Tovara

From San Blas, it is possible to take a three-hour jungle trip in a boat to La Tovara, a small resort with a freshwater swimming hole brimming with turtles and catfish, a restaurant and not much else. Away from the swimming hole there are coatis, raccoons, iguanas, turtles, boat-billed herons, egrets and parrots. Crocodiles are kept in caves along the route. Twilight tours enable naturalists to see potoos and, if very lucky, an ocelot. Mangrove swamps can be visited on the way. The resort is crowded at midday during the summer.

Tours to La Tovara leave from the bridge 1 km west of town and cost US$25 for a canoe with six passengers. Official prices are posted but it is possible to shop around. Avoid fast motorized boats (unfortunately quite popular here) as the motor noise will scare any animals. Tours on foot are even better.

A cheaper 1½- to two-hour cruise is possible from the Embarcadero El Aguada (take the Las Islitas bus to the *embarcadero* on the road to Matenchén), US$14.80 per boat, but US$3.45 each if more than four people; it goes through a tunnel of mangroves, to the swimming hole 20 minutes away.

You can take a bus from San Blas towards Santa Cruz and get off at Matanchén Beach. From here, a boat for half-day hire includes the best part of the jungle cruise from San Blas. You can now stay overnight at the ultra-rustic **Paraje del Rey** *cabañas* (closed Tuesday, US$25), which are set in the midst of the mangroves and accessible only by boat.

◉ West to the coast: to Tepic via Tequila listings

For Sleeping and Eating price codes and other relevant information, see Essentials pages 47-51.

◉ Sleeping

Tequila *p479*
AL Casa Elisa, México 138, T33-3044 4274 (Guadalajara). Ex-hacienda outside of town, opened 2009. Rivals **La Cofradia** as the nicest accommodation in the area.

AL La Cofradia, La Cofradia 1297, T374-742 3677, www.tequilacofradia.com.mx. Owned by the well-known tequila distillery. Only 4 rooms, all exquisite. Reservations a must.
B Casa Dulce María, Abasolo 20, 1 block from main the church, T374-742 3200, www.casadulcemaria.com. Beautiful old *casona* wonderfully restored. Restaurant, parking, all rooms with Wi-Fi, private bath, and TV. Best in its range and outstanding value.

C Misión Tequillan, Abasolo 47, T374-742 3233. Nice old hotel in centre. Friendly, clean, and highly recommended.

C Plaza Jardín, José Cuervo 13, T374-742 0061, www.hotelplazajardin.com. Nice downtown location. Restaurant, bar. All rooms with balconies, private bath, a/c, TV.

C Posada del Agave, Sixto Gorjón 83, T374-742 0774. Excellent value with private bath, TV, very comfortable.

C Posada Tierra Mágica, T374-742 1414, Jésus Rodríguez de Hijar 25, www.tierra magica.com.mx. Central. Restaurant, gift shop, tequila shop, café and bar, parking. All rooms with cable TV, Wi-Fi, ceiling fans.

D Abasolo, Abasolo 80, T374-742 0195. Rather over-decorated rooms, with TV.

D Motel Delicias, Ctra Internacional 595, on the highway to Guadalajara about 1km outside Tequila, T374-742 1094. Best available in the range, TV, off-street parking.

E Colonial, Morelos 52, corner of Sixto Gorjón, T374-742 0355. Characterless, but central, clean and not run down, some rooms with private bath. A good deal.

Ixtlán del Río p480

C Plaza Hidalgo, Hidalgo 101 Pte esq. Cinco de Mayo, T324-243 2100. Best hotel in town.

D Paraíso, Hidalgo 757 Pte, T324-243 2000. Very friendly. Recommended.

Tequila to Tepic p480

C-D Bungalows and Trailer Park Koala, La Laguna, Santa María del Oro (20 km via paved road from Santa Maria del Oro turn-off on Route 15 or from Santa María del Oro caseta (toll booth) on the Guadalajara–Tepic autopista), T311-264 36 98, www.geocities.com/cfrench koala. British owner. Bungalows for up to 4 people, several trailer sites and a large campground. Good cheap meals available. Fishing and waterskiing on the nearby lagoon.

Tepic p482, map p483

AL Fray Junípero Serra, Lerdo Pte 23, on the main square, T311-212 2525, www.fray junipero.com.mx. Comfortable, big rooms,

clean, a/c, good restaurant, friendly, good service. A little noisy with the new road, but still recommended.

A Bugamvillas, Av Insurgentes 1150 y Libramiento Pte, T311-218 0225. Very comfortable rooms with a/c, TV, pool, restaurant with great food and good wine list. Recommended.

A Real de Don Juan, Av México 105 Sur (on Plaza de Los Constituyentes), T/F311-216 1888. Charming, traditional style. With parking.

B Santa Fe, Calzada de la Cruz 85, near Parque La Loma, a few mins from the centre on the main road, T311-213 1966. With TV, clean, comfortable, good restaurant, parking.

B Sierra de Alicia, Av México 180 Norte, T311-212 0322. With fan, tiled stairways, friendly.

C Ibarra, Durango Norte 297, T311-212 3870. Luxurious rooms, with bath and fan (some rooms noisy) and slightly spartan, cheaper rooms without bath, very clean.

C Tepic, Dr Martínez 438, near the bus station outside town, T311-213 1377. Recently upgraded, rooms with bath; clean, friendly but noisy. Wi-Fi in common areas, free computer use in lobby.

D Altamirano, Mina 19 Ote, T311-212 7131, near Palacio de Gobierno. Noisy, good value. Parking.

E-F Camarena, San Luis 63 Norte, 4 blocks southeast of the Zócalo. No bath, clean, friendly.

E-F Pensión Morales, Insurgentes y Sánchez, 4 blocks from bus station. Clean and friendly, family puts up backpackers in a private house.

San Blas p484

Accommodation becomes scarce and more expensive during **Semana Santa** and other holidays.

L Garza Canela, Paredes 106 Sur, T328-285 0112, www.garzacanela.com. Very clean, excellent restaurant, small pool, nice garden. Highly recommended.

AL-A Casa de Valorien, Matanchen Bay, T327-103 6876, www.casadevalorien.com. Remarkable American-owned B&B designed by architect George Szepesi. Sits directly on ocean. Wonderful food, masseuse, lovely rooms; no smoking. Hosts can arrange tours, very friendly and highly recommended.

A Hacienda Flamingos, Juárez 105, 2 blocks from the Zócalo. T328-285 0930, www.san blas.com.mx. Restored ex-hacienda universally considered the most beautiful property in San Blas. 21 charming suites, all with a/c and mod cons; a few of them are around the interior patio (ask for these). Patio, pretty garden, fountain, gym, parking. Main garden has magnificent pool. Highly recommended.

B Casa de las Cocadas, Juárez esq Comofort, T328-285 0960, www.etcbeach.com/casa-cocadas. Older building that has been tastefully renovated and decorated; huge TV screen for sports viewing. Good view of the estuary from the upstairs bar.

B Casa Mañana, Playa Los Cocos, Km 5. Austrian-run hotel and restaurant, good food. Many apartments for rent.

B Posada del Rey, Campeche 10, T328-285 0123. Very clean, swimming pool, excellent value.

C Delfín, Playa Los Cocos. With bath, balcony, good view, good value and new rooms. Longtime beloved landmark now completely renovated and upgraded. Recommended.

C Marino Inn, Heróico Batallón y Las Islitas, 2 blocks from bus the station, T328-285 0340. With a/c, friendly, pool, fair food.

C Marina San Blas, Cuauhtemoc 197, on the marina at the entrance to the bay, T328-285 0930, www.sanblas.com.mx/bocetomarina. Formerly the old Hotel Casa Morales, now completely redone and upgraded. Same owners as **Hacienda Flamingos** (see above). Everything is new and geared to outdoor types and bird/wildlife watchers.

C-D El Tesoro de San Blas, 50 m south of the dock, 5 mins from the centre. Rooms and villas, hot water, satellite TV, US owners.

D Posada Irene, Batallón 122, 4 blocks southwest of the Zócalo. Basic with a fan, few rooms with a shower and hot water. Kitchen, friendly.

D-E Posada Azul, Batallón 126, 4 blocks from the Zócalo towards the beach, T328-285 0129. 3-bedded rooms with fan and hot water, cheaper for simple 2-bedded rooms without bath, cooking facilities.

Camping

No camping or sleeping is permitted on the beaches but there are several designated campsites. All trailer parks in the town centre are plagued by mosquitoes.

Playa Amor, Los Cocos Beach, 16 km south of town in nearby Aticama. The best trailer park, good beach on a narrow strip of land between the road to Santa Cruz and the cliff. Good, popular.

❼ Eating

Tequila p479
❦❦ **El Real Marinero**, Juárez 92, T374-742 2794, www.realmarinero.com. Pleasant seafood restaurant with strolling musicians.
❦❦ **El Sauza**, Juárez 45 (beside Banamex). Restaurant/bar, Mexican atmosphere.
❦❦-❦ **El Callejón**, Sixto Gorjón 105. Rustic Mexican decor, à la carte, *antojitos* and burgers.
❦ **Manhattan**, Abasolo 74. Inexpensive, fresh seafood in this rather incongruously named eatery.

Tepic p482, map p483
The restaurant in the bus terminal is overpriced. There are lots of fish stalls by the market on Puebla Norte.
❦❦ **Chante Clair**, Insurgentes 253 Pte, T311-213 2015. Good French-Mexican food near Parque La Loma.
❦❦ **El Tripol**, Querétaro s/n, in the mall near the plaza. Excellent vegetarian food.
❦❦ **Marlin**, Calzada del Panteón 45 Oeste, T311-213 0253. Good seafood in the middle of the historic centre.
❦❦ **Tiki Room**, San Luis Norte (opposite **Hotel Camarena**). Fun restaurant with art gallery, video and bar.
❦❦-❦ **Roberto's Internacional**, Paseo de la Loma e Insurgentes, T311-213 3005. Mon-Sat 1300-2300. Typical Mexican and excellent seafood.

Fu Seng, Av Insurgentes 1199 Oeste, T311-214 5988. Good Chinese (rare in Mexico.)

San Blas *p484*
On Sun women prepare delicious pots of stew alfresco on the plaza.

El Delfin, Paredes 106 Sur, T323-285 0112. Phenomenal international cuisine and gourmet French food at reasonable prices. Head chef attended Le Cordon Bleu in Paris. Highly recommended.

La Isla (Cheff Tony), Paredes s/n esq Mercado, http://sanblasnayarit.com/laisla/laisla.html. Rumoured to be best seafood in San Blas. Friendly, no-frills atmosphere. Highly recommended.

Las Islitas, on the way to the beach. Distinctly nautical feel, good-value seafood, also sells banana bread. Recommended.

Tumba de Yako, on the way to the beach. Yoghurt and health foods, and the original version of pan de *plátano* (banana bread), advertised all over town.

Las Olas. One of many seafood restaurants on the beach. Good and cheap with good local dishes.

McDonald's, Juárez 75, 2 blocks from the plaza, T323-285 0432. Daily 0700-2200. Scottish owned. Good, simple Mexican food served in nice atmosphere and on 2 separate levels, for breakfast, lunch, or dinner. A San Blas tradition.

Wakame Gourmet, downtown, near the corner of Yucatán and Canalizó. Good Chinese and Japanese. Excellent buffet on Sun (arrive early).

O Shopping

San Blas *p484*
Crafts
Huichol Cultural Community store, Juárez 64. Claims to be non-profit making. Huichol art, including freehand beadwork with glass beads, yarn paintings, decorated masks and scented candles.

▲ Activities and tours

Tepic *p482, map p483*
Tour operators
Viajes Regina, Av México 27-3 Norte, T311-213-2638. Tours to San Blas, Playas de Ensueño, and Tepic city tour.

San Blas *p484*
Tumba de Yako (see Eating, above) rents out surf boards. Owner, Juan Bananas, former coach to the Mexican surfing team, gives lessons, speaks English. Mountain bike and kayak hire (for estuaries) also available.

● Transport

Tequila *p479*
Bus
Second class from the old terminal, Sala B, on Rojo de los Altos, Guadalajara (not new one in Tonalá), every 45 mins, up to 2 hrs, US$3.00. Return from outside Rojo de los Altos ticket office, Sixto Gorjón, 126A, every 20 mins, 0500-1400, then every 30 mins until 2030.

Taxi
To **Guadalajara**, US$20, plus US$7.05 in tolls if you take the expressway.

Train
The *Tequila Express*, T33-3880 9099 (Guadalajara), www.tequilaexpress.com.mx, is a comfortable way of visiting the town from Guadalajara. It's all jazzed up and smart-looking – not how the Mexican rail industry used to be that's for sure. You spend the day drifting towards the town and exploring one of the plantations and then return with no worries about driving. Sat and/or Sun only, leaving 1000, returning 2000, US$72.70, US$42.10 for kids. Book from tour operators in Guadalajara (or see website for options).

Ixtlán del Río *p480*
Bus Bus to **Tepic**, 84 km, 1 hr 15 mins. To **Tequila** 1 hr. To **Guadalajara**, 3 hrs.

Tepic *p482, map p483*

Air

Amado Nervo airport (TPQ), 16 km south of town, take a taxi or a local bus (infrequent). Flights to **Los Angeles**, **Mexico City**, **Tampico** and **Tijuana** daily with AeroMéxico, T311-213 9047.

Bus

The bus station is a fairly short walk from town centre, T311-213 6747, alternatively, take a bus to the terminal from Puebla Norte by the market. At the bus station there are phones, a post office, left luggage and tourist information (not always open).

To **San Blas** from main bus terminal and from the local bus station on park at Av Victoria y México, from 0615 every hour US$5.

To **Guadalajara**, frequent departures, 3½ hrs, US$16. To **Mazatlán**, 4½hrs, US$15. To **Los Mochis** on Transportes del Pacífico, US$42-44. To **Puerto Vallarta**, every 20 mins, 3 hrs, US$13-15. To **Mexico City**, 13 hrs, US$49.

San Blas *p484*

Bus The bus station is on the corner of the plaza. To **Tepic**, frequent from 0600, 1½ hrs,

US$5. To **Guadalajara** on express bus 5 hrs (local bus via **Ixlan** takes 8½ hrs), US$15-18.

❶ Directory

Tequila *p479*

Banks Banamex, Sixto Gorjón esq Juárez, 24-hr ATM accepts Visa and MasterCard. Many ATMs in town. *Casa de cambio*, Sixto Gorjón 73, daily 0900-1400, 1600-2000, change cash and TCs. **Post office** Off Plaza Principal.

Tepic *p482, map p483*

Banks *Casas de cambio* at México 91 and at 140 Norte, both open Mon-Sat 0900-1400, 1600-2000. **Telephone** Credit card phone at Veracruz Norte y Zapata Pte.

San Blas *p484*

Banks Banamex just off the Zócalo, exchange daily 0830-1000. Comercial de San Blas on the main square will change money. **Laundry** 2 blocks down toward the beach from La Familia. Will take your clothes and return them, very clean, later or the next day.

To Puerto Vallarta via the highlands

Route 70 is a little-travelled asphalt road that runs due west of Guadalajara through the highlands until the coast is reached just 10 km north of Puerta Vallarta. The gentle transition from beautiful farmlands to winding mountain roads passing through 'lost in time' villages with an Alpine look and feel and on to the colourful eastern suburbs of Puerto Vallarta makes this an unforgettable journey. This route is an excellent alternative for coastal-bound traffic during Semana Santa and Christmas, when the more popular Route 15/200 is jammed. ▸▸ *For listings, see pages 492-493.*

Ameca → *Colour map 2, B1. Phone code 375. Population: 50,000.*

Ameca is a quiet if rather nondescript city, 79 km west of Guadalajara along Route 70. It was first settled by the Nahua in 1325 and then re-settled in 1522 by the conquistador Juan de Añesta (who arrived with only a sword in his hand and was considered the son of the Sun God upon arrival). It is best known for its citrus fruits and ranching, as well as a handful of ex-haciendas built for sugar cane production in the 19th century.

Most of the noteworthy sites are located in the centre. There is an interesting shrine to the **Virgin of Guadalupe** with twin blue-tiled steeples, built in 1875. The **Palacio Municipal**, although largely re-built 1917-1924, dates from 1529. The **regional museum** ⓘ *Casa de Cultura, Mon-Sat 0900-1400, 1600-1800, free*, is the second largest in Jalisco and holds a staggering 10,000 pieces of the region's archaeological and palaeontological finds. One of the ex-haciendas outside of town, **El Cabezón** (which dates from 1844), has a chapel containing a priceless and still-intact wooden, churrigueresque *retablo* (one of only four left in the entire state) with nine carved statues.

Ameca holds fast to its folklore traditions more than most Mexican towns. Not only does each and every church in town have its own fiesta, but **Carnaval** here retains much of its medieval origins, with effigies, passion plays, and the almost-extinct custom of burning a mock 'Bad Humour' denizen all playing a prominent role.

To the north of town in the **Sierra de Ameca** are the mysterious *esferas pétreas*– rocks of volcanic origin that are almost perfectly round. For many years natives believed them to be of supernatural origin; their shape is actually due to high-pressure crystallization.

Guachinango → *Colour map 2, B1. Phone code 388.*

Follow Route 70 west for 35 km from Ameca and then take a right (signposted at turn-off), drive another 10 km and the road leads to Guachinango, hidden in the eastern foothills of the **Sierra Jolalpa**. At one time this pleasant little mining town was the state capital of Jalisco. Silver mining has taken place in this area since 1544.

None of this would be worth stopping for if it weren't for the fact that Guachinango is one of the few hillside towns in the region that is easily accessed and – in spite of its mining origins – is quite attractive. With a reputation as one of the most *'puro mexicano'* settlements in the state, it has a classical main square and an interesting 18th-century church with only one steeple. Its patronal fiesta runs from 31 January to 3 February and is highly regarded by Mexicans as an authentic example of village festivals that are otherwise long extinct. Guachinango is also well regarded for the quality of its musicians.

West of Guachinango

From Guachinango headed west, the next town of any note is **Talpa de Allende** (65 km along Route 70 before turning off), a popular pilgrimage destination during Holy Week. About 20 km after the turn-off for Talpa is **Mascota**, a tranquil town largely given over to eco-tourism, with many fine boutique hotels. The area is increasingly succumbing to the whims of North American retirees and those in search of winter residences, but for the moment still retains much of its charm and simplicity. The difficult access to most of these settlements has kept them, in the words of one writer, "seductively provincial". Yet Mascota is also the primary jumping-off point to visit the even less accessible but gorgeous hamlets of **San Sebastián del Oeste**, **Los Reyes**, **La Navidad** and **Yerbabuena**.

Mascota

Apart from those interested in church architecture or rampant land value speculation, there isn't a great deal to do in Mascota, but this will change in the next year or so. Still best known for breeding fine Arabian horses, there are several small museums being restored, including the regional **archaeological museum** (Ameca's is vastly superior), a **cultural centre**, with photography and other rotating exhibits, and the **Museo Pedregal**, the last being largely a geological showpiece. The 19th-century (but still unfinished) **Templo de la Preciosa Sangre** ('Church of the Precious Blood') is a short walk from the town's centre. Its entrance is framed in a Roman arch; its neoclassic altarpiece is one of the best in the region. It also contains a two-storey seminary in an exquisitely beautiful setting. Across from the plaza, the town's main church is in pristine condition. Outside is a large statue dedicated to the 20th-century martyr and local hero, the priest José María Roble, killed by Mexican soldiers during the Cristero Revolt and canonized by Pope John Paul II in 2000.

Talpa de Allende → *Colour map 2, B1. Phone code 388.*

Some 20 km southeast of Mascota lies the pilgrimage town of Talpa de Allende, founded in the 18th century and home to about 7000 inhabitants. It's a good bet there isn't a native Mexican anywhere in the country who hasn't heard of Talpa, and many have visited, usually on foot during Holy Week or during other major fiestas.

For centuries devout Catholics have walked to Talpa – in some cases covering hundreds of kilometres – to show their devotion to the Virgin of Talpa. The Virgin is housed in a glass case in the chapel within Talpa's basilica, which was built in her honour in 1782. The best time to be in town is for one of her three festivals: the feast of her crowning (10-12 May, when the town's population quadruples), the feast of her renovation (10 September), and most important, the feast of Our Lady of the Rosary (7 October). For online information (in Spanish) on Talpa de Allende, see http://talpadeallende.com.

San Sebastián del Oeste → *Colour map 2, B1. Phone code 322.*

Route 70 continues north from Talpa through the **Sierra Madre Occidental** (eventually winding westerly and terminating just north of Puerto Vallarta) for some 70 km, when it reaches **La Estancia**. Another 5 km north is the (poorly marked) turn-off for San Sebastián del Oeste, 15 km from the turning along some of Mexico's most serpentine roads. In spite of the increasing number of visitors, this tiny hamlet has come to epitomize the quintessential bucolic *pueblo clásico*. So much so that in 2008 it was officially designated Mexico's newest *pueblo mágico*, a select group of 34 towns that the government recognizes as having a unique charm and an outstanding history. For much the same reason, it was earlier named a UNESCO World Heritage Site in 2001.

There is plenty of good hiking in the region. A challenging climb (also accessible by car) is to the top of the nearest mountain, **La Bufa**, where there is a supposedly miraculous image of the Virgin. On a clear day the views stretch as far as the Bay of Banderas.

The town's church of **Saint Sebastian** was originally built in 1608, but rebuilt after an earthquake in 1868. There is a beautiful fresco of the martyrdom of the saint above the altar. Next to the church is the tiny local **museum** ① *US$0.60*, which has an interesting mix of exhibits on the church and town.

The town has a rapidly growing number of hotels, but two in particular also double as local landmarks. The **Hotel El Pabellón**, on the plaza, was at one time a fortress where silver shipments were stored while awaiting transport. The garrison had turrets on all corners where soldiers could thwart would-be attackers. One turret survives and is now a cozy nook in the town's most popular bar. Bandits were such a problem in the town's heyday that a tunnel had to be constructed from a mine to the fortress to transport silver so it would not be stolen en route.

At the nearby **Hacienda Jalisco**, located near a makeshift airstrip on the west side of town, mining operations reigned for many years. An expatriate artist from California came across the dilapidated 18th-century building in the late 1960s and restored it to its original state. There is no electricity (so don't expect TV, internet or telephone). The result is a fascinating look at what life might have been like in Spanish colonial Mexico. Now part museum (US$1.20), part hotel, the bottom floor has artefacts attesting to the role the hacienda played as the headquarters of a mining operation. There are also displays covering some of its more famous guests, which include John Huston, Richard Burton, Elizabeth Taylor, and Peter O'Toole.

⦿ To Puerto Vallarta via the highlands listings

For Sleeping and Eating price codes and other relevant information, see Essentials pages 47-51.

⦿ Sleeping

Ameca *p489*

While hotels in Ameca are uniformly inferior to those in Mascota, they are far less expensive. Bear in mind that the 2 towns are 189 km apart on a winding road, and it may be better to spend the night in Ameca and proceed west the following morning.
C-D Hacienda, Av Patria Oeste 7, Ameca, T375-758 2530. Central and the best hotel in town. Rooms are non-descript but functional. Can be noisy at night.

Guachinango *p490*

For lodgings in Guachinango, ask around in the main plaza. None are advertised as such, but there are several *alojamientos* available, generally in the **D** or **E** category.

Mascota *p490*

LL-AL Sierra Lago Resort and Spa, Laguna de Juanacatlán, near Mascota, www.villa grouppresorts.com/resorts/sierra-lago. Vastly over-hyped, gringo-only resort 17 km out of town on a beautiful lake. Stunning location with all amenities, peaceful and luxurious, but very expensive and hardly typical of the region.
B Mesón de Santa Elena, Hidalgo 155, T388-386 0313, www.mesondesantaelena.com. 19th-century ex-hacienda, large rooms, each with terrace, tiled baths. Cable TV, free breakfast. Romantic with gorgeous sunsets.
B Mesón del Refugio, Independencia 187, T388-386 0767, www.hotelmesondelrefugio. com. Recently restored ex-hacienda, lush gardens and very secluded. Restaurant.

Rooms on the 2nd floor are best and have wonderful views.
B-C Cabañas Rancho La Esmeralda, Salvador Chávez Magaña, T388-385 9819, www.rancholaesmeralda.com.mx. Outside of town, with a mix of suites and villas. Geared to outdoor activities. Very friendly, helpful, bilingual staff. Highly recommended.
C Hacienda La Puerta de Enmedio, Ctra Mascota–Puerto Vallarta, Km 1.5, T322-228 0879 (from Puerto Vallarta), www.lapuertade enmedio.com. Probably the cheapest hotel in town and good value for the price. Nice views of mountains, bilingual staff, spa, parking, all rooms have balconies and cable TV.

Talpa de Allende *p491*

B Haciends Jacarandas, 3 km outside of town towards the Talpa River, T388-102 7078, www.haciendajacarandas.com. Quiet location, well landscaped with lots of flowers, in harmony with the surroundings. Beautiful sunsets and views. US-owned B&B-style, individually decorated rooms, with pool and a hot tub. Delicious breakfast. Recommended.
C Condominios Cassandra, Libertad 45, T388-385 1379, www.condominios-casandra.com. Condos capable of sleeping up to 6 per unit. A 2-min walk from centre, quiet, with nice views. Long-term stays are possible at discounted rates.
C Providencia, 23 de Julio 14, T388-385 0271, hotelprovidencia@hotmail.com. The oldest and largest hotel in town, by now a local landmark and institution centrally located, recommended.
C-D Casa Grande, 23 de Julio s/n, T388-385 0709. Small colonial hotel with beautiful views of the city and its surroundings.

Restaurant, peaceful setting. Always fully booked during fiestas.

C-D María José, 23 de Julio 16, T388-385 1564. Sandwiched between the **Providencia** and the **Pedregal**. Parking, TV and Wi-Fi.
C-D Pedregal, 23 de Junio 20, 2 blocks from main plaza, T388-385 0274. Basic, comfortable rooms with own car park. Likewise impossible to book during fiestas.
D-E Los Arcos, Independencia 82, T388-385 0272. Excellent value, decent restaurant, but otherwise bare bones.

San Sebastián del Oeste *p491*
A La Galerita de San Sebastián, Hacienda la Galera 62, T322-297 3040, www.lagalerita. com.mx. Very secluded and peaceful, set amidst pines and many flowers. 3 different chalets in rustic Mexican style and outfitted with organic amenities and toiletries, fireplace, frigobar, satellite TV, Wi-Fi, outside hammock, free breakfast, parking. The best place in town and highly recommended.
B Casita Alicia, near the main plaza, http:// casita-alicia.com. Very close to the centre of town, private residence for 4 people, with maid service and fully furnished. Expensive but ideal for stays of a week or longer.
B Hacienda El Jalisco, off the main plaza, T322-222 9638, www.haciendajalisco.com. Rare, period-authentic hacienda, fully restored. No electricity, but fireplace in each room, breakfast included. No children. Pricey but good.
C Real de San Sebastián, Zaragoza 41, T322-297 3224. Nicely maintained 18th-century building on corner of the main plaza. The oldest and largest hotel in town and now a historic monument.
D El Pabellón Mexicano, López Mateos 1, T322-297 0200. A very rustic place, with a charming atmosphere.

◉ Eating

Ameca *p489*
Tucked away in Ameca, on Eucalipto, 2 blocks from main plaza, is one of the country's finest seafood restaurants. A hidden gem.

San Sebastián del Oeste *p491*
�* Italiano, 2 blocks northwest of the plaza. Quite possibly the country's finest Italian outside of Mexico City. Everything is hand-made from scratch (including the owner's selection of rare Italian grappa and other liqueurs). Enchanting setting in old farmhouse. The best restaurant for the entire stretch along Route 70 between Ameca and Puerto Vallarta.
♦ El Fortín de San Sebastián, on the plaza, T322-297 2856, www.elfortin.com.mx. Remarkable outdoor-only restaurant serving local favourites, pizzas and the like in a bucolic setting. Also has general store inside with many regional sweets, organic coffees, art, and much more. The owners are a great source of information about the town.

◉ Festivals and events

San Sebastián del Oeste *p491*
19-21 Jan The town's patronal feast day is that of St Sebastian. The church is particularly beautiful from Christmas through this time.

▲ Activities and tours

San Sebastián del Oeste *p491*
As well as hiking and horse-riding trips, ATV tours are also available from several operators grouped around the main square. There are numerous bird species in the area.

Puerto Vallarta and around

→ *Colour map 2, B1. Phone code: 322.*

Now a highly commercialized sun-and-sand holiday resort increasingly marred by congestion and widespread condominium developments, Puerto Vallarta still has its advantages. With a wonderful location on the Bahía de Banderas (Bay of Flags), one of the most striking bays in Mexico, it has wonderful beaches and dolphins frolicking in the clear waters. The resort caters to low-end mass tourism as well as high-end, member-only visitors (particularly in the northern suburbs). In the spring, Puerto Vallarta and its environs are top destinations for college students and timeshare residents, many of them North American retirees. While the weather is pleasant year-round, the high season runs from November to April. Prices drop considerably during the low season, although they remain high compared to less developed areas.

The stepped and cobbled streets of the old centre, particularly around the well-preserved Zona Romantica, are picturesque, and accommodation and restaurants, while edging towards the higher end in this more gentrified area of town, are still varied enough to suit most budgets. There is plenty of good hiking in the surrounding hills and water sports and diving are easily accessible. Increasingly it has become a base for excursions and for special-interest trips including ornithology and whale watching. And of course there are the beaches – more than 50 of them ranging from pristine, deserted shores (mostly to the north) to ultra-luxurious strands that flank the private marinas closer to the city. Development is heading inexorably north towards the still relatively untouched fishing villages that dot the bay. Travellers wishing to see what Puerto Vallarta was like 40 years ago, before the arrival of international tourism, should take a trip north to any of these villages. ▶▶ *For listings, see pages 498-504.*

Ins and outs

Getting there The **Aeropuerto Internacional Ordaz (PVR)** ① *6 km north of town centre, T322-221 1325,* has excellent national connections as well as flights from the USA and Europe (mostly package tours). To get a bus to the centre, follow the walkway to the other side of the street to the main road, US$0.30. Steer clear of timeshare touts. If you want a taxi, they're half the price if you get them from across the main road outside the airport.

Puerto Vallarta is on the Carretera Costera, Route 200, which runs south along the Pacific Coast, all the way to the Guatemalan border. The long-distance **bus station**, almost directly opposite the airport, is a 30-minute ride from town. Buses from the terminal may take the long way into the centre, so it is worth changing buses on the main road to find one that goes direct. ▶▶ *See Transport, page 503.*

Getting around Taxis are expensive in Puerto Vallarta. Local buses operate on most routes north to Nuevo Vallarta, and south to Mismaloya and Boca de Tomatlán. Buses marked 'Centro' go through town, while those marked 'Túnel' take the bypass. Taxis and buses have come under fire from local authorities for their poor driving habits. Only take official taxis, and never accept an offer from any taxi on the *malecón* (boulevard): these work in tandem with bars and clubs, charging patrons obscenely high prices for even the shortest of trips.

Orientation Greater Puerto Vallarta is drawn out along 25 km of the west-facing curve of the deeply incised Banderas Bay. It can be split into six sections. **North Central** is the oldest, with the main plaza, cathedral and seafront *malecón* as well as an uninviting strip of pebble/sand beach. **South Central**, across the Río Cuale, is newer but similarly packed with shops and bordered by the fine, deep sand of Playa de los Muertos. **South Shore** is where the mountains come to the sea, there are several cove beaches and a scattering of big hotels. The **Hotel Zone**, leading north, is a long stretch from town towards the cruise ship terminal and the airport, with mediocre beaches, many big, mass-market hotels and several commercial centres. **Marina Vallarta**, further north, has a dazzling array of

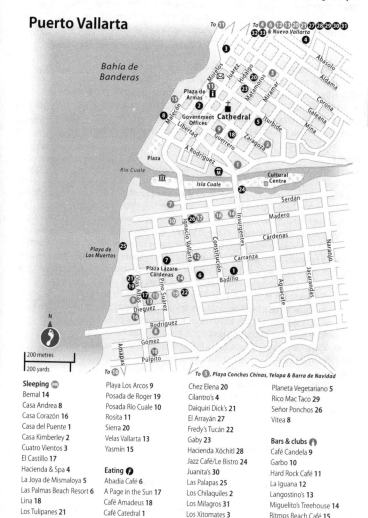

Puerto Vallarta

Bahía de Banderas

Playa de Los Muertos

200 metres
200 yards

Sleeping 🛌
Bernal **14**
Casa Andrea **8**
Casa Corazón **16**
Casa del Puente **1**
Casa Kimberley **2**
Cuatro Vientos **3**
El Castillo **17**
Hacienda & Spa **4**
La Joya de Mismaloya **5**
Las Palmas Beach Resort **6**
Lina **18**
Los Tulipanes **21**
Molina de Agua **7**
Nautilus & Marina Club **12**

Playa Los Arcos **9**
Posada de Roger **19**
Posada Río Cuale **10**
Rosita **11**
Sierra **20**
Velas Vallarta **13**
Yasmín **15**

Eating 🍴
Abadia Café **6**
A Page in the Sun **17**
Café Amadeus **18**
Café Catedral **1**
Café Olla **19**
Carlos O' Brian's **33**

Chez Elena **20**
Cilantro's **4**
Daiquiri Dick's **21**
El Arrayán **27**
Fredy's Tucán **22**
Gaby **23**
Hacienda Xóchitl **28**
Jazz Café/Le Bistro **24**
Juanita's **30**
Las Palapas **25**
Los Chilaquiles **2**
Los Milagros **31**
Los Xitomates **3**
Pepe's Tacos **32**
Pie in the Sky **7**

Planeta Vegetariano **5**
Rico Mac Taco **29**
Señor Ponchos **26**
Vitea **8**

Bars & clubs 🍸
Café Candela **9**
Garbo **10**
Hard Rock Café **11**
La Iguana **12**
Langostino's **13**
Miguelito's Treehouse **14**
Ritmos Beach Café **15**
Sama **16**

watercraft, a golf course, smart hotels and a poor quality beach (you can't walk far because of condominiums built around the marina and/or construction along the water's edge). **Nuevo Vallarta**, 15 km north of the centre, in the neighbouring state of Nayarit (one-hour time difference), which has a golf course and marina, along with dozens of modern all-inclusive hotels strung along miles of white-sand beach, but far from amenities (meaning guests pay a handsome sum to acquire them at the complexes themselves).

Most travellers will find the North or South central areas the most convenient to stay in. The accommodation in these areas is mostly attractive bed and breakfasts with some sense of style, not at all the cookie-cutter mega-complexes found further north.

Tourist information The **tourist office** ① *Independencia 123, T322-223 2500 ext 230, www.visitpuertovallarta.com,* is in the government building on the main square. A second office is located in the Hotel Canto del Sol's commercial shopping plaza, oficina 18 on the ground level, T322-224 1175. Throughout the Vallarta region, almost any hotel, and many stores and even restaurants and clubs, also provide innumerable English-language (often in French and German as well) brochures and leaflets geared to foreign tourists.

Sights

The North and South central areas are the most interesting for the majority of visitors. They are divided by the Río Cuale and a narrow island where souvenir shops, cafés, galleries, language schools, and the small **Museo Arqueológico del Cuale** ① *Isla de Rio Cuale, T322-223 2500, Tue-Sat 1000-1400, 1600-1900, Sun 1000-1400, free,* are located. The museum has exhibits on significant archaeological treasures found within the region, traditional Mexican arts and crafts, folklore displays, and some well-preserved pre-Hispanic items. The most dramatic beach in the centre is **Playa de los Muertos**, apparently named after the murderous activities of pirates in the late-16th century, although the 'dead' tag could apply equally to the fierce undertow or possibly to the pollution that affects this corner of the bay. The authorities are trying to get people to use the sunnier sobriquet of 'Playa del Sol'. **Playa Conchas Chinas** is probably the best beach close to town, being quiet and clean (at any holiday time, though, every beach is packed); it can be accessed by a short scramble around the rocky point to the south or by a cobblestone road that leads from Route 200, just after Club Alexandra.

The waterfront *malecón* is the focus for much of Vallarta's shopping, dining, drinking and dancing activities, or at least those to which the general public is welcome. There are more than 200 shops, restaurants, bars and clubs packed along the strip that extends about 16 blocks from Río Cuale to 31 de Octubre along Paseo Díaz Ordaz. Crowded, hot and noisy, it defies all attempts to modify it, and while it is probably the one spot in Vallarta where you're likely to see people at their worst (crowd behaviour here is deplorable in every sense), it is also the one place in the area where everyone seems to come together on a nightly basis to enjoy themselves, whether it's browsing through the dozens of jewellery shops and art galleries, partying until dawn in one of the many clubs, or eating and drinking in one of the restaurants that open to the ocean.

Be sure to take in an evening performance at the far end by the *Voladores de Papantla* (Flying Men of Papantla). This folkloric show features men of the Papantla region performing rivetting aerial dances. Four men at a time perch atop an 8-m pole to which their feet have been tied, while musicians on the ground below play traditional songs. At a designated point in the men above launch themselves, head first toward the ground, spinning as they descend. It's no joke and is actually quite dangerous and breathtaking.

Alternatives to Vallarta

Apart from Cancún, no other destination in Mexico – perhaps even the world – has done more to set the pace for mass tourism as Puerto Vallarta. It is the number two choice for visitors to the country, eclipsing the capital and resort luminaries such as Acapulco and Cozumel. Puerto Vallarta (which now includes Marina Vallarta and Nuevo Vallarta to the north and some smaller towns to the south) continues to expand its reach along the Pacific coast, drawing more tourists within its orbit every year. The main reason for its success? In a word, marketing.

This constant push to attract tourists to Vallarta has its downside. The mass descent upon the town has also brought the inevitable influx of less than reputable property offers (for years, tourists were forced to thread their way through high-pressure touts hawking illegal timeshares at the airport and even in taxis), shoddy knock-off merchandise, and tawdry hotels and restaurants, all catering to the hoi polloi. Combine this with the sheer number of visitors the region receives each year and if you're not crowd-friendly, you might want out before you get in.

Fortunately, the coast around Vallarta is still largely free of commercialism. Most of its tiny fishing towns are rustic, while some blend a mix of creature comforts and coastal tranquillity. One of the best is **La Cruz de Huancaxtle**, just 25 km north of the hustle and bustle. Along coastal Route 200 lie the bucolic seaside settlements of **San Francisco**, **Sayulita** and **Bucerias**. To the south, less than 30 km away on the motorway, are **El Nogalito** and **Mismaloya** (where John Huston filmed *Night of the Iguana* with Richard Burton and Elizabeth Taylor – the movie that more than anything else put Vallarta on the map).

Around Puerto Vallarta ●● » *pp498-504.*

During the rainy season (June to September) some trips are not possible. From November to April, humpback whale watching is organized. A recommended trip including snorkelling is with John Pegueros, who owns the schooner *Elías Mann* (see Puerto Vallarta Tour operators, page 503).

Playa de los Tomates, a 25-minute walk north of the marina (buses every hour from the marina), has good birdwatching, half a dozen beach restaurants and very few tourists. You can hire a boat to go to the mangroves. On the way **Las Palmas**, 25 km northeast of Puerto Vallarta and inland, is the workers' pueblo of **Ixtapa**, established by the Montgomery Fruit Co in 1925. Near here are post-Classic stone mounds scattered over a wide area. (This road if followed to the east eventually becomes Route 70, an excellent, albeit slower, alternate route from the coast to Guadalajara, see page 491.)

Exactly 10 km south of Puerto Vallarta, along the coast road is **Mismaloya**, where in 1963 John Huston made *Night of the Iguana* with Richard Burton and Ava Gardner. (Arnold Schwarzenegger's *Predator* was also filmed in nearby El Edén.) It is a lovely beach backed by a steep subtropical valley, even though the **La Jolla Mismaloya** hotel looms over the sands. The beach is clean and you can hire umbrellas and chairs for the day, US$2; beware of the undertow at low tide. The film set has been developed as **Iguana Park**. You can go horse riding in the region (as far as the Sierra Madre) with at least six different registered outfits. For a local jaunt up the valley, the trained guides of **Rancho Manolo** ① *Highway 200, Km 12 (turn beside the road bridge), in Mismaloya, T322-228 0018*, are highly recommended.

Heading north from Puerto Vallarta the coast road continues to **Las Varas** for 96 km and then veers eastwards to **Compostela** for another 34 km, where it turns north again towards Tepic, 65 km at the interchange with Route 15. From Puerto Vallarta to Las Varas the road passes some very attractive beach resorts, the first of which is **Bucerías**. Next along Route 200, **La Cruz de Huancaxtle** is slated to be the next big development and is home to the largest marina on the coast, but for now still retains much of its original charm and is highly recommended as a day trip. The beach here is not as attractive as elsewhere, but the town remains for the moment a true *pueblo pescador* (fishing village) with an ambience than is rapidly disappearing elsewhere along the bay.

Los Veneros ① *between La Cruz de Huancaxtle and Punta de Mita, T329-291 0088, daily 1000-1800, US$8.75,* is a pretty cove with fairly safe swimming. Access is through a private beach club reached down a 7-km private road through woods to the beach. The resort is beautifully designed and clean with two restaurants, bar, café and gardens terraced towards the beach. The food is excellent and there's no extra charge for sunbeds/umbrellas. You can take a shuttle bus from Los Veneros bus station.

Punta de Mita, a fishing village and beach resort at the tip of a peninsula, has fish restaurants, miles of beach and abundant birdlife. At **Playa Destiladeros** ① *daily 0700-1900, ample parking US$3.20,* there is an excellent restaurant. **Medina** or **Pacífico** buses from Puerto Vallarta pass every 15 minutes. There are boat trips to the nearby Islas Marietas, where there are caves and birds. Camping is possible on the beach. Simple accommodation is also available.

North of Punta de Mita are beaches on the coast road including **Chacala**, a pleasant free beach lined with coconut palms, good swimming, cold showers and a restaurant; it is reached by an unsurfaced road through the jungle.

◉ Puerto Vallarta and around listings

For Sleeping and Eating price codes and other relevant information, see Essentials pages 47-51.

● Sleeping

Puerto Vallarta *p494, map p495*
Be alert when making reservations at any Puerto Vallarta hotel. Almost all in the **Zona Hotelera** and **Nuevo Vallarta**, and several in the centre, operate on the all-inclusive plan. This can represent a savings for families or travellers who don't wish to stray far from the hotel, but for couples and anyone wishing to dine away from the hotel and/or take advantage of independent activities, it is generally a waste of time and money. Always check whether the hotel has mandatory all-inclusive plans, or whether rooms can be rented apart from a plan. Many hotels will not do so during the high season, but in the off season are more amenable to such requests.

LL Sierra, Nuevo Vallarta, T322-297 1300. Colourful building-block hotel, smart, modern, all inclusive.

LL Velas Vallarta, Av Costera s/n, LH2, Marina Vallarta, North Hotel Zone, T322-221 0091, www.velasvallarta.com. Rustic with Moorish touches, part timeshare hotel with verdant gardens, golf course opposite, all-inclusive options.

L Casa Kimberley, Zaragoza 445, North Central, T322-222 1336, www.casakimberley. com. Former home of Richard Burton and Elizabeth Taylor, 10 rooms full of memorabilia of the actors, breakfast included, bar, great views, pool, much cheaper in low season. Reputedly Vallarta's best B&B. Surprisingly low price for a celebrity villa.

L Hacienda and Spa, Blv Francisco Medina Ascencio 2699, North Hotel Zone, T322-224 6667, www.haciendaonline.com.mx. Modern, with colonial influence, gym, Temazcal treatments, pleasant pool. The best in the area but 100 m to the beach and on the main road. Discounts out of season.

L Las Palmas Beach Resort, Blv Medina Ascencio, North Hotel Zone, Km 2.5, T322-226 1220, www.laspalmasresort.com. Castaway-on-a-desert-island theme, all rooms with sea view, family oriented, all-inclusive plan.

L Molina de Agua, Ignacio L Vallarta 130, South Central, T322-222 1957, www.molino deagua.com. Cabins in pleasant wooded glade on bank of river, a/c, good service, 2 pools. Recommended.

L Nautilus and Marina Club, Paseo De La Marina Sur 210, Marina Vallarta, T322-221 1015, www.nautilusvallarta.mihotel.net. Olympic pool and dive tank in this resort. Most rooms have private balcony or patio.

L Playa Los Arcos Hotel Beach Resort & Spa, Olas Altas 380, South Central, T322-222 0583, www.playalosarcos.com/playalosarcos. Recently renovated, good location for restaurants, pool terrace overflows to Playa Los Muertos.

AL Casa Andrea, Rodríguez 174, South Central, T322-222 1213, www.casa-andrea. com. Small hotel suites, close to cafés and restaurants, pleasant garden with bar, pool, owner operated, good friendly service with attention to detail. Reduced rates in low season.

A Casa Corazón, Amapas 326, South Central, T/F322-222 6364, www.casacorazon vallarta.com. US-owned hideaway on steep slope above southern end of Playa Los Muertos, overpriced but 3 big rooms on top terrace with spectacular views worth the premium, including big breakfast, beach access with bar and restaurant.

A Cuatro Vientos, Matamoros 520, North Central, T322-222 0161, www.cuatro vientos.com. Up a steep cobbled street from the church, spectacular views, good restaurant perched high above city, plunge pool, breakfast included, friendly and relaxed atmosphere. Recommended.

A Los Tulipanes, Panamá 272, Zona Este, T322-223 4128, www.hotellos tulipanes.com. Quiet and with parking, swimming pool. Good value and a wise choice for those wishing to stay in Vallarta but away from the crowds.

A Posada Río Cuale, Aquiles Serdán 242, South Central, near new bridge, T/F322-222 0450. Small pool in front garden, not very private, nice, colonial-style rooms.

A-B Casa del Puente, North Central, by the bridge opposite the market, enter through the restaurant, T322-222 0749, www.casadel puente.com. Suites with kitchen in a private villa suspended above river, delightful, book months ahead, cheaper in low season, good value.

B Posada de Roger, Basilio Badillo 237, South Central, T322-222 0836, www.hotel posadaderoger.com. Communal kitchen, pool, cable TV, a/c, great breakfast restaurant Freddy's Tucan.

B-C Bernal, Francisco I Madero 423, South Central, T322-222 3605. Friendly, large rooms, fan, good showers. Recommended.

B-C Rosita, Paseo Díaz Ordaz 901, north end of the *malecón*, North Central, T322-223 2000, www.hotelrosita.com. Puerto Vallarta's original holiday hotel (1948) with pool, on the town beach. Incredibly noisy, no parking.

C-D Yasmín, Basilio Badillo 168, 1 block from the beach, South Central, T322-222 0087. Plant-filled courtyard arrangement behind Café Olla, a/c, clean, restaurant, noisy till at least 2300.

D-E El Castillo, Francisco I Madero 273, a few blocks from the beach, South Central. Fan, hot water, cable TV, cheaper without bath. Convenient for restaurants.

D-E Lina, Francisco I Madero 376, South Central, T322-222 1661. With bath, hot water, fan, run-down, rooms on the street are noisy.

Camping

Puerto Vallarta Trailer Park, north of the centre, just north of the bypass then east 2 blocks, T322-224 2828. Popular, very friendly and lush atmosphere permeates everything.

Tacho's RV and Trailer Park, 2 trailer parks, on the road to Pitillal, opposite the marina, T322-224 2163. 60 spaces but spacious, US$20 for 2 people. Pool, lush vegetation. Highly recommended.

Around Puerto Vallarta *p497*
LL Barceló La Joya de Mismaloya, Zona Hotelera Sur, Km 11.5, T322-228 0660, www.barcelolajolladdemismaloya.com. Romantic but over-developed setting on a film-set beach.

LL Majahuitas Resort, between Quimixto and Yelapa beaches, only accessible by boat, transfers included, T322-221 2277, www.mexicoboutiquehotels.com/majahuitas, run by Margot and Lirio González. All-inclusive resort, 8 guesthouses, on cove, sandy beach, rustic furniture, solar energy, horse riding and snorkelling available portion of profits go to indigenous community of Chacala, good value.

B Lagunita, Yelapa, T322-209 5055, www.hotel-lagunita.com. Cabin hotel with pool.

Camping
Beto & Felicidad, camping available 30-min walk up valley from Yelapa, US$4 per person, in beautiful setting (Felicidad's home-made tortillas are self-proclaimed 'the best in Mexico').

Camping is also possible in the fishing village of Yelapa, best reached by boat from Hotel Rosita at 1130: camp under *palapas* (shelters), about US$4 per person.

Puerto Vallarta north to Tepic *p498*
LL Villa Bella, de Monte Calvario 12, La Cruz de Huanacaxtle, T329-295 5161, www.villabella-lacruz.com. Amazing hilltop villa-turned-small B&B with 4 suites, overlooking Bahía de Banderas. Luxurious beyond belief, with every amenity imaginable and a charming hostess. Consistently ranked as one of Mexico's most outstanding. Reserve well in advance and worth every centavo.

A Estancia San Carlos, Retorno Laureles s/n, Rincón de Guayabitos, T327-274 0155, www.estanciasancarlos.com. Beautiful location

on beach. All rooms have a/c, balconies, kitchen, refrigerator, cable TV. Accessible for handicapped and family- friendly as well. Best in its class and recommended.

A-B As de Oro, Av Sol Nuevo s/n, Rincón de Guayabitos, T327-274 0337. Great prices, clean room, friendly office staff and security at night, beautiful grounds and double pool, children's activities, a few steps from beach and nightlife, souvenir shopping across the street. Highly recommended.

B Quinta Minas, Av del Coral 42, Los Ayala, T327-274 1141, www.hotelquintaminas.com. On the beach, nice pool and water activities (especially for children), friendly, bilingual staff. Standard rooms and suites available, long-term stays discounted.

B Torreblanca, Retorno Laureles s/n, Rincón de Guayabitos, T327-274 1263, www.torreblancasuites.com. Nice location on the beach, suites with all mod cons. Extended stays possible at discounted rates.

C Decameron Los Cocos, Retorno Las Palmas s/n, Rincón de Guayabitos. Among several hotels and restaurants on a rocky peninsula to the south of the beach. All-inclusive. Many complaints regarding noise and party crowds.

C Tía Adriana's bed and breakfast, Sayulita, T/F329-291 3029, www.tiaadrianas.com. Open Nov-Jun. Good, central, good value.

C Villa Serena, Lázaro Cárdenas 35, Bucerías, T329-298 1288. Nice little hideaway in the centre, quiet, very affordable, friendly. Recommended.

E Contreras, Las Varas. With fan and bath, clean, small rooms.

Camping
Hotel and Trailer Park Piedras Blancas, La Cruz de Huanacaxtle. Good, also camping, hook-ups US$15, restaurants.

Sayulita RV and Camping Park, Sayulita, 2½ km off Route 200, T329-291 3126, sayupark@prodigy.net.mx. On a beautiful beach, German owner, very friendly, well-maintained property; also has bungalows. Highly recommended.

❻ Eating

Puerto Vallarta p494, map p495
South Central

♦♦♦ Café des Artistes, Guadalupe Sánchez 740, T322-222 3228, www.cafedesartistes.com. Daily 1800-2330. Considered by many as Puerto Vallarta's best restaurant. French gourmet bistro owned by chef Thierry Blouet. Amazing (and expensive). Must reserve.

♦♦♦ Chez Elena, Matamoros 520, T322-222 0161, www.chezelena.com. In the hotel of same name; up lots of steps but worth it. Beautiful view over town from large balcony, popular well-established restaurant, award-winning food. Recommended.

♦♦♦-♦♦ A Page in the Sun, Olas Altas (opposite Los Arcos Hotel on the corner). Often cited as Vallarta's best restaurant. Coffee is excellent, cakes home-made, 2nd-hand bookshop.

♦♦♦-♦♦ Jazz Café/Le Bistro, Insurgentes, by the bridge. Garden, bamboo, beside river, pleasant for coffee and classical music (piano or harp) in morning, crowded and expensive in evening, many vegetarian dishes, clean.

♦♦♦-♦♦ Señor Ponchos, Madero 260 y Ignacio L Vallarta. Authentic Mexican, typical breakfast, seafood and lobster, moderate prices.

♦♦ Abadia Café, Basilio Badillo y Ignacio L Vallarta, T322-222 6720. Open for breakfast lunch and dinner 0800-2400. Mexican-continental cuisine. Rave reviews for years, now in a new location.

♦♦ Café Catedral, Basilio Badillo y Insurgentes. Very good breakfasts, fine coffee, good value.

♦♦ Cilantro's, Abasolo 169, T322-222 7147. Canadian-owned, unusual Mexico-meets-Pacific Northwest cuisine, with good wines.

♦♦ Daiquiri Dick's, Olas Altas 314, opposite Playa Los Muertos, T322-222 0566, www.dd pv.com. Open for breakfast, lunch and dinner. Silly, insanely popular, American-themed restaurant and bar, excellent cooking, classical harp and guitar music Sun 1300-1500.

♦♦ Las Palapas, on the beach near Playa de los Muertos. Good food, service, value, decor and atmosphere.

♦♦ Los Arbolitos, east end of Lázaro Cárdenas. 3 balconied floors above river. Mexican, good atmosphere.

♦♦ Los Xítomates, Morelos 570, T322-222 1695. Daily 1900-2330. Mexican cuisine with eclectic (pre-Columbian and colonial) items as well.

♦♦ Planeta Vegetariano, Iturbide 270, T322-222 3073. Cash-only vegetarian restaurant recently named one of world's best by Bon Appétit magazine. Remarkably low-priced. Also at Marina Del Rey L-4.

♦♦ Vitea, Libertad 2 y Malecón, T322-222 8703, www.viteapv.com. Early morning until 2400. Smart oceanfront bistro.

♦♦-♦ Café Olla, lower end of Basilio Badillo. Good-value Mexican barbecue in cramped open-fronted dining room, very popular.

♦♦-♦ El Arrayán, Allende 344, T322-222 7195, www.elarrayan.com.mx. Wed-Mon 1800-2300. Consistently voted best Mexican restaurant in Vallarta for many years running. Excellent folk music. Recommended.

♦♦-♦ Fredy's Tucán, Basilio Badillo 239. Good courtyard dining, mainly Mexican menu, good breakfast with bottomless coffee.

♦♦-♦ Hacienda Xóchitl, off the beaten path on Río Nazas 388, T322-222 3344, www. Haciendaxochitl.com. Daily 1300-2400. Huge portions of Mexican dishes, great margaritas; bilingual staff. Highly recommended.

North Central

♦♦ Café Amadeus, Miramar 271, up steps from Guerrero. Classical music, books, board games in delightful whitewashed rooms or balcony perched above old town, coffee, delectable cakes. Recommended.

♦♦ Rico Mac Taco, Av México esq Uruguay. Busy, cheap and widely popular.

♦♦-♦ Juanita's, Av México 1067. Attracts locals as well as value-seeking gringos, good.

♦♦-♦ Los Chilaquiles, Zaragosa 160, 4th floor, in Vallarta Plaza, T322-223 9482. Mon-Fri 0800-2400. Excellent new Jalisciense (from Jalisco) restaurant with upstairs water views. Reasonably priced.

♦♦-♦ Los Milagros, Juárez s/n y Pipila. Forget the queues at the popular gringo restaurants, this one is excellent, moderately priced, cosmopolitan, live music, colonial-style courtyard. Recommended.

¶ **Gaby**, Mina 252. Small, family-run, eat in the garden, excellent food, cheap and clean.

¶ **Pepe's Tacos**, Honduras, opposite Pemex at the northern end of downtown. Open all night. Cheap, ethnic and delicious in spartan pink/white dining room.

¶ **Pie in the Sky**, Lázaro Cárdenas 247, Zona Romántica, T322-223 8083. Daily 0830-2200. Also has 2nd location further north in Bucerías. Very highly recommended, especially for desserts. Also a bakery.

Nuevo Vallarta

Most restaurants in Nuevo Vallarta are not freestanding but instead are located in the many hotels that line the shore. Most are open to the public, but during high season may be reserved for hotel guests only.

Puerto Vallarta north to Tepic *p498*

¶¶-¶¶ **Mezzogiorno**, Av del Pacífico 33, Bucerías, T329-298 0350, www.mezzo giorno.com.mx. Daily 1800-2300, dinner only. Outstanding Italian and seafood at very end of street in utterly gorgeous beachfront location. Bucerías' best restaurant.

¶¶ **Black Forest German Restaurant**, Marlín 16, La Cruz de Huancaxtle, T329-2955203, Daily 1800-2400. Just what the name implies.

¶¶ **Frascati**, Av Langosta 10 y Coral, La Cruz de Huancaxtle, T329-295 6185. Daily 1700-2400. Great Italian food in delightful setting near the beach.

¶¶ **Mark's**, Lázaro Cárdenas 56, Bucerías, T329-298 0303. American-owned, highly regarded seafood and California-based cuisine.

◑ Bars and clubs

Puerto Vallarta *p494, map p495*

There are numerous bars and clubs in Puerto Vallarta (much less so in Nuevo Vallarta and the northern suburbs). Be alert especially when leaving; overcharging and theft are common. Never leave a club in an unmarked taxi. There are many clubs and late bars throughout the central area.

Puerto Vallarta's gay nightlife is commonly considered the most active in all of Mexico. There are more than 30 gay-only or predominantly gay bars and clubs, almost all of them located in the Zona Romántica. For an up-to-the-minute listing, see *Gay Guide Vallarta*, www.gayguidevallarta.com.

North Central

Cafe Candela, Guerrero 311 y Matamoros, Centro, T322-222 0743. Eclectic pizzeria and bar with unique (for Puerto Vallarta) ambiance.

Carlos O'Brian's, Malecón y Andale, Olas Altas. Attracts a motley crowd of revellers and starts hopping after 2200.

Encuentros, Lázaro Cárdenas 312, Zona Romántica, T322-222 0643. Sophisticated pizza bar and lounge; cash only. Predominantly gay clientele.

Garbo's, Púlpito 142, Zona Romántica, T322-223 5753. Quiet piano jazz bar, good drinks. Predominantly gay clientele.

Hard Rock Café, Paseo Díaz Ordaz 652 (on the *malecón*), T322-222 2230. Hugely popular with tourists. Avoid during spring break but otherwise good music late at night.

La Iguana, Lázaro Cárdenas 311, Zona Romántica, T322-222 2733. Popular with locals, many traditional Mexican Mariachi and regional bands.

Langostino's, Manuel M Diéguez 109, Zona Romántica, T322-222 0894. Popular rock club somewhat apart from the din of the *malecón*.

Miguelito's Treehouse, Basilio Badillo 287, Zona Romántica. T322-223 1263. Country and blues bar, cheap beer.

Ritmos Beach Cafe, Malecón 177, Zona Romántica, www.ritmoscafe.com. Afternoon only (1400-1700) bar on the beach with excellent music.

Sama, Olas Altas 510, Zona Romántica, T322-223 3182. Martini bar with sidewalk seating; arrive early for best seats. Predominantly gay clientele.

Nueva Vallarta

Christine, at Hotel Krystal. For spectacular light show, disco, expensive drinks, and cover. **Club Nitro**, Av de las Garzas, Zona Hotelería, T322-226 6800. One of Vallarta's more popular spots, with frequently change musical themes. Everything from *banda* to blues.

O Shopping

Puerto Vallarta *p494, map p495*
Shopping opportunities are endless, including armies of non-aggressive beach vendors. The flea market is grossly overpriced; the many shops often offer better value, but not much. Guadalajara and especially Tlaquepaque or Tonalá are cheaper for practically everything. The market, by the bridge at the end of Insurgentes, sells silver, clothes and souvenirs as well as meat and fish. There's a large, well-stocked supermarket nearby.

Bookshops
Rosas Expresso, Olas Altas 399. 2nd-hand books, English and some in German.

Jewellery
Olas de Plata, Francisco Rodríguez 132. Plaza Malecón has 28 curio shops as well a restaurant and live music.

Supermarket
GR, Constitución 136. Reasonable for basics.

▲ Activities and tours

Puerto Vallarta *p494, map p495*
Tour operators
Many agents and hotel tour desks offer boat trips, car hire and tours at big discounts if you accept a timeshare presentation.
American Express, Morelos 660, esq Abasolo, T322-223 2955. Town guide available.
John Pegueros, Lázaro Cárdenas 27, Bucerías, Nayarit, CP63732, T329-298 0060. Whale watching and snorkelling trips on the schooner *Elías Mann*. Tickets from Marina Vallarta, US$60, includes meals, starts 0800.
Open Air Expeditions, Lázaro Cárdenas 268-A y Emiliano Zapata, T322-222 7407, www.birdinginmexico.com. Oscar and Isabel run hiking trips (mountain or waterfall), whale watching (winter), kayaking, birdwatching and other trips from US$50, knowledgeable guides.
Vallarta Adventure, Av las Palmas 39, Nueva Vallarta, T/F322-297 1212, www.vallarta-adventures.com. Boat trips, whale watching (US$75-90), Sierra Madre expedition (US$90), jeep safari (US$90), dolphin encounter (US$150), Las Caletas by night or by day (US$85), also scuba-diving, PADI certification.

Cycling
Bikemex Adventures, Guerrero 361, T322-223 1834, www.bikemex.com. Offers trips for cyclists of varying grades of competence, from local environs up to 3-4 days in the old silver towns of Sierra Madre, all equipment provided including good, front-suspension bikes, from US$50, also offers hiking adventures.

Horse riding
Rancho El Charro, T322-224 0114, www.ranchoelcharro.com. Horse riding expeditions to jungle villages and Sierra Madre silver towns. Independent guides and horses congregate at lower end of Basilio Badillo; also occasionally at fishermen's wharf, by Hotel Rosita for short beach and mountain trips, agree price beforehand.

☺ Transport

Puerto Vallarta *p494, map p495*
Air
International Ordaz Airport (PVR), 6 km from centre, T322-221 1325. There is a sporadic local bus service to the airport. In high season, there is a hotel shuttle bus service for those staying at the hotel. Otherwise take a taxi. Excellent international connections to the USA, Europe, Central and South America.

Airline offices AeroMéxico, T322-2242777. Alaska Airlines, T95-800-426 033. America West, T800-235 9292, T800-533 6862. American Airlines, T91-800 90460. Continental, T91-800-90050. Delta, T91-800-90221. Mexicana, T322-224 8900. United, T911-800-00307, T800-426 5561.

Bus

Local Mismaloya–Marina, US$0.35, but complicated routing. The main southbound artery through town is México–Morelos–Vallarta; the main northbound is Juárez–Insurgentes. Plaza Lázaro Cárdenas is the main terminal in the south of town and starting point for Mismaloya–Boca buses going south. Buses marked 'Olas Altas' go to South Central, those marked 'Hoteles' or 'Aeropuerto' go to North Hotel Zone and beyond. Buses are also marked for 'Marina' and 'Mismaloya/Boca' (Boca de Tomatlán). The ones marked 'Centro' go through town, those with 'Túnel' take the bypass. Buses to outlying villages with **Medina** bus line, terminal at Brasil, between Brasilia and Guatemala, regular (15-20 mins) service to Nuevo Vallarta, San José, San Juan, Bucerías, Manzanilla, Punta de Mita and others. Fares US$1.25-3.

Long distance All buses leave from bus station almost opposite the airport (turn left when you exit from arrivals, then it's a short walk). To get to the bus station from town, the only option is by taxi.

There are frequent services to **Guadalajara**, 6 hrs, US$31. To **Tepic**, every 20 mins, 3 hrs, US$13-14.50. To **Barra de Navidad**, 4 hrs, 1st class, 0915 and 1315, 4 hrs, US$19; 2nd class 0900, 1000, 1200, 1400, 1600 and 1800, 5½ hrs, US$15.50, and **Manzanillo**, 4½ hrs, US$17.90, every couple of hours. Other regular services to **Acapulco**, **Aguascalientes**, **Ciudad Guzmán**, **Ciudad** Juárez, Colima, León, Mazatlán, San Patricio Melaque, Mexico City, Monterrey, Querétaro, Tecomán, Tijuana and Zihuatanejo.

Around Puerto Vallarta p497
Water taxi To reach **Yelapa**, take the tourist water taxi from pier (Los Muertos) US$21 return, leaves 1030, 1100. From the fisherman's quay on Malecón, by Hotel Rosita, opposite McDonald's, US$12.50 one way, leaves 1130. From **Boca de Tomatlán** (bus, US$0.35) a water taxi from the beach is US$5 one way, leaves 1030.

⊙ Directory

Puerto Vallarta p494, map p495
Banks *Casas de cambio* on nearly every street in tourist areas. Rates inferior to Guadalajara. Check **Bancomer's** *cambio* at Juárez 450, for good rates, open late. Banks offer slightly better rates (but slower service) and ATMs for Visa, MasterCard. **Embassies and consulates** Canada, Edif Vallarta Plaza, Zaragoza 160, 1st floor, T322-222 5398, daily 1000-1400. USA, Paseo de los Cocoteros Local 14, Int 17, T322-222 0069, Mon-Fri 0830-1230. **Immigration** In front of the Marina terminal, T322-224 7970. **Internet** Numerous internet cafés normally charging around US$2 per hr. **Laundry** Practically one on every block in South Central; numerous throughout the resort. **Medical services** Dra Irma Gittelson, Juárez 479, speaks French and English, very helpful. Emergency: T915- 724 7900. **Post office** Mina entre Juárez y Morelos. **Telephone** Long-distance phone (*casetas*) and fax at Lázaro Cárdenas 267, daily to 2300, also in lobby of Hotel Eloisa. Many shops bear 'Larga distancia' sign, check tariffs.

Contents

Veracruz State

At a glance

☺ **Getting around** Bus and boat.

☺ **Time required** 10 days for the main sights, a month for in-depth exploration.

☼ **Weather** Veracruz follows tropical seasons. The coast is hot and sultry year round, but especially during the summer rainy season, May-Oct. Winter months, Nov-Apr, bring cool evenings to the mountainous regions, which are generally more temperate.

✖ **When not to go** If you're heading for the coast be prepared for crowds of people and tropical storms in summer. Carnaval and Semana Santa are thronging, expensive occasions – but fun. If rafting, rapids become rougher during the wet season too.

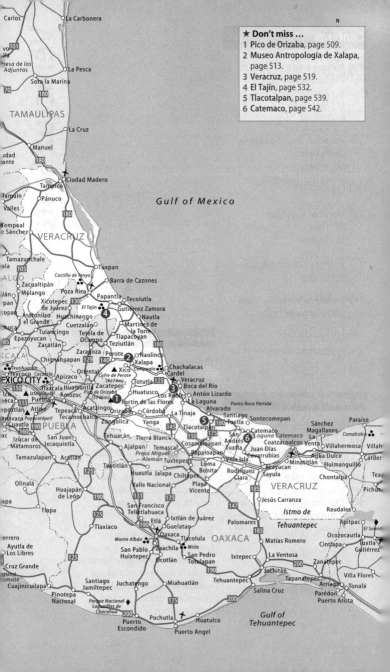

It's the cultural mix that makes Veracruz state so interesting. For 300 years, its Gulf coast port was Spain's gateway to the riches of the New World and a crucible of international flavours. The arrival of black slaves profoundly influenced the region, most notably in its music, dance and fantastic culinary traditions. Today, the famous hospitality of the Veracruzanos, also known as *jarochos*, is widely enjoyed by all. Don't miss the extraordinarily festive, tropical-port atmosphere that crescendos each spring during the liveliest carnival in Mexico.

But culture doesn't stop here. West of the port, you'll find refreshing colonial cities nestled in brooding mountain scenery. Most notable is the urbane and intellectual state capital of Xalapa, home to a world-class anthropology museum. In northern Veracruz, the Huastec people are renowned for their traditional *huapango* music and falsetto singing. In the vanilla-growing Papantla region, the spectacular *voladores* ritual, an example of surviving Totonac traditions, is performed regularly in teeming town squares. Nearby, the ancient ruin of El Tajín is one of the most magnificent archaeological sites in all the Americas, whilst southern Veracruz is the former heartland of the Olmec, a civilization shrouded in shadowy jungles and mystery.

The beaches of Veracruz – grey, windswept and occasionally murky – are only so-so. But their almost total desertion off-season makes them a wonderfully isolated retreat. More enticing are the possibilities for outdoor activities. Inland, as the fertile coastal plains give way to mountains, are Mexico's highest peak, deepest caves and fastest rapids. To the south, beyond the plains of the vast Río Papaloapan, the lush Tuxtla mountains are a birdwatcher's paradise, replete with tranquil lagoons and chattering tropical forests. There's plenty to keep you occupied in Veracruz state, a destination so often neglected by the mainstream.

Mexico City to Veracruz

Part of the dark, rolling topography of the Sierra Nevada – also known as the Trans-Mexican Volcanic belt – the central highlands of Veracruz play host to diverse geological and cultural landscapes. Somnolent farming communities and fetching colonial towns are among the settings, all surrounded by vertiginous ravines, roaring waterfalls, whitewater rapids and daunting volcanic vistas. Mexico's highest peak, Pico de Orizaba, finds its home here, drawing scores of determined adventurers out to conquer its glacial extremes. Elsewhere, the misty slopes are fertile ground for coffee fincas, tobacco plantations and a riot of tropical fruit trees. Flowers, too, are a major highland economy, bursting from teeming market stalls and colouring lively village fiestas. For those in search of more urban destinations, the colonial city of Córdoba is a relaxing provincial escape, but Xalapa, the state capital, is a formidable cultural centre that's home to verdant gardens and important universities. Don't miss the world-class anthropology museum, where you can discover the mysteries of Olmec civilization. Their monumental sculptures include giant stone heads, baby-faced figurines and curious were-jaguars that are neither human nor animal. Like the ancient landscapes that preceded it, the central highlands of Veracruz remain a bastion of strange, entrancing beauty.

Much of the area east of Mexico City constituted the eastern tribute quarter conquered by the Mexica, formerly the Aztecs, who derived great wealth from those subject nations that stretched from the Basin of Mexico to the Guatamalan border. It pays to explore the present-day tapestry of highland communities and landscapes, but if you need to reach the coast rapidly, fast toll Highway 150 runs all the way from Mexico City to Veracruz. ›› *For listings, see pages 514-518.*

Orizaba and around 🏨🍴🛍️🎯 ›› *pp514-518. Colour map 2, B5.*

→ *Phone code: 272. Altitude: 1283 m.*

The favourite resort of Emperor Maximilian, Orizaba, on the eastern edge of the mountains, lost much of its charm in the 1973 earthquake, when the bullring, many houses and other buildings were lost; the city is now heavily industrialized and not terribly attractive. The setting, however, is lovely, with Mexico's highest peak, the majestic volcanic cone of Pico de Orizaba, rising in the distance. Orizaba itself developed due to the natural springs in the valley, some of which are used by the textile and paper industries; others are dammed to form small pools for bathing beside picnic areas. Beyond the city, en route to the coast, the scenery is magnificent. The road descends to coffee and sugar-cane country and a tropical riot of flowers. It is pleasant except when a northerly wind blows, or during the wet season when it is oppressively hot and muggy.

Ins and outs
The **tourist office** ① *Palacio de Hierro, T272-728 9136, www.orizaba.gob.mx, Mon-Fri 0800-1500 and 1600-2000*, has maps and general information.

Sights
Downtown Orizaba is focussed on **Parque Castillo**, the city's central plaza or Zócalo. On the northern edge stands the market, with a wide variety of produce and local women in traditional dress, as well as the many-domed **San Miguel church** (1690-1729). There are several other interesting churches around, including the church of **Nuestra Señora del Carmen and La Concordia**. On the western flank of the Zócalo, the **ex-Palacio Municipal**, or the Palacio de Hierro (Iron Palace), is a cast-iron and steel pavilion designed by Gustave

Eiffel, brought piece by piece from France after the famous 19th-century Paris Exhibition. Over 600 tons of metal were used in its construction and it's certainly an odd sight. The **Cerro del Borrego**, west of the centre, is a hill overlooking the lush parque Alameda – a favourite early-morning climb (but best avoided in the evening for safety reasons). The **Museo de Arte del Estado** ① *4 Ote y 23 Sur, Tue-Sun 1000-1700, US$1*, in the Oratorio de San Felipe Neri, has a delightful collection of colonial and contemporary paintings, including a permanent collection by Riveras. For booze hounds, there is a big brewery in town, the **Cervecería Cuauhtémoc Moctezuma**; ask at the tourist office about tours. If you fancy a stroll, a pathway follows the river where you can admire some of the city's fine bridges.

Pico de Orizaba
① *The small town of Tlachichuca (2600 m) is the usual access point. To get there from Orizaba, take an AU bus to Ciudad Serdán, 2 hrs, US$2, then a connecting bus to Tlachichuca, 1hr, US$1. Buses also run directly from Puebla. Oct-Mar is the best time for conventional ascents.*

At 5760 m, Pico de Orizaba, also known as Citlaltépetl ('Star Mountain'), is the highest peak in Mexico and third highest mountain in North America. Views from its summit afford entrancing glimpses of other great volcanoes like Popocatépetl and Iztaccíhuatl. For experienced climbers, the ascent is not too difficult, although acclimatization to altitude is advised and there are some crevasses to be negotiated. Inexperienced climbers will require a guide. **Servimont** ① *Ortega 1A, Tlachichuca, T245-451 5082, www.servimont.com.mx*, is a recommended company run by the Reyes family, who have a long history of guiding in the mountains; contact them at least two months prior to your intended expedition. **Servimont's** base camp is located in an old soap factory, where you will spend the night before summitting early the next day. There are various routes to the summit, including one that follows the south face, therefore bypassing glaciers. If you intend to scale Pico de Orizaba independently, ensure you speak to **Servimont** about your options, as conditions are always changing. 1:50,000 maps are available from **INEGI** ① *www.inegi.org.mx, offices in Xalapa, Camacho 236, T228-8146459, Mon-Fri 0830-1630; Veracruz, Victimas de 5 y 6 Julio 1045, T229-935 4399, Mon-Fri 0830-1630; or in Mexico City (see page 71).*

South to Zongolica
A road leaves Orizaba southwards, up into the mountains of **Zongolica**, a dry, poor and isolated region, cold and inhospitable, inhabited by various indigenous groups who speak Nahuatl, the language of the Aztecs. Zongolica village is a good place to buy *sarapes* (shawls); take the early bus from Orizaba (ask for direct one) to get clear views of the mountains.

Fortín de las Flores
This small town, 15 km northeast of Orizaba, is devoted to growing and exporting flowers. Sometimes local women sell choice blossoms in small baskets made from banana tree bark. Between Orizaba and Fortín there is a viewpoint looking out over a dramatic gorge, the Barranca de Metlac, which plunges down to the river in a cascade of flame trees and luxuriant vegetation. The autopista from Oziaba to Córdoba passes over this deep valley on a concrete bridge. There isn't much to do in Fortín itself but it is a pleasant place to unwind and admire the colourful blooms. There is a flower festival in late April or May. North of Fortín, a minor road winds north towards Xalapa; en route you'll pass the town of Coscomatepec, with good cigars and leather shops.

A la Veracruzano: the culinary traditions of Veracruz

When Hernán Cortés arrived on the shores of Veracruz, he was greeted by the 'fat cacique' of Cempoala, who lavished him a sumptuous array of local culinary treasures. Tortillas forged from corn, a mouthwatering assortment of tropical fruits, untold fresh seafood, and delicious treats laced with vanilla from Papantla – all considerably whetted the conquistador's appetite.

In the years after the conquest, the indigenous cuisine fused with traditional Spanish cooking techniques. As Mexico's principle port of entry, Veracruz was a storehouse for all types of new ingredients including herbs like parsley, bay leaf, coriander, as well as vital staples like wheat, rice, olives and olive oil. A simmering *Mestizo* melting pot had been cooked up, now it only remained for African slaves to add the final, vital ingredients.

The use of peanuts, popularized in West Africa after the Portugese imported them, quickly became prevalent in Veracruzano cooking, especially when ground with onions and chiles to make sauces. Also popularized were yucca, sweet potato, and plantain – the latter is today sliced and fried to make chips, or ground into dough for *gorditas*, *tortitas* or *empanadas*. And when handfuls of slaves escaped into the mountains, they took their culinary skills with them, leaving legacies like *salsa macha*, a favourite table salsa of Orizaba.

Veracruz owe its scintillating culinary traditions to a unique tri-cultural fusion of indigenous, Spanish and African influences and should not be missed. Signature dishes you should endeavour to try include *arroz a la tumbada*, a delicious rice and seafood dish; *caldo de mariscos*, a seafood soup with medicinal properties that's said to cure hangover; and *huachinango a la veracruzana*, red snapper in a spicy tomato sauce. Buen Provecho!

Córdoba → *Colour map 2, B5. Phone code: 271. Altitude: 923 m.*
Eight kilometres beyond Fortín in the rich valley of the Río Seco, is the old colonial city of Córdoba. Founded in 1618 by 30 families who hoped to protect the area from attacks by *yangas* (escaped African slaves) the city became known as the 'city of thirty knights'. It is an agreeable, provincial place whose main claim to fine is having hosted the formal signing of Mexico's Independence declaration in 1821: the Treaty of Córdoba. Today, the city thrives on agriculture and various industries; sugar, coffee and tropical fruit among them. And although there's only a handful of sights in Córdoba, it still makes a pleasant stopover. Continuing east towards Veracruz, the road is lined, in season, with stalls selling fruit and honey, especially between Yanga and Cuitiláhuac.

Ins and outs The **tourist office** ① *Palacio Municipal, Zócalo, T271-717 1700, 0800-1900*, has maps and general information. Note the city has the highest rainfall in Mexico, falling between April and November. Rainfall is usually fierce and brief in the afternoon.

Sights Córdoba's Zócalo is spacious, leafy and elegant; at night it is lively but relaxed. Its sides are arcaded and flanked by terraced restaurants, hotels, the **Palacio Municipal** and the imposing **Catedral de la Inmaculada Concepción**, with bell towers and chiming clock. In **Portal de Zavallos**, General Iturbide and Juan O'Donojú signed the Treaty of Córdoba in 1821, setting out the terms for the Mexican nation, newly freed from the bondage of Spanish colonial rule. Look for the **Hotel Zevallos**, former home of the counts of Zevallos and built in 1687, where the actual signing took place. There's a local **museum** ⓘ *Calle 3, No 303, daily 0900-1400, 1600-2000, free,* with a small collection of archaeological and anthropological artefacts, many pertaining to Olmec and Mexica cultures. Around 1.5 km southwest of the downtown area, the **Parque Ecológico Paso Coyol** ⓘ *Calle 6 y Av 19, US$0.30,* is a new park space with pleasant winding paths.

Xalapa ⓘⓟⓞⓐⓜⓒⓖ ▶ pp514-518. Colour map 2, B5.

→ *Phone code: 228. Altitude: 1425 m.*

The capital of Veracruz state since 1885, Xalapa (also spelt Jalapa) is in the *tierra templada* ('temperate land') and is a lively, cultured town dubbed the 'City of Flowers' by German explorer Alexander Von Humboldt. It is home to several universities and throngs with a youthful, arty buzz thanks to its robust student contingent, who frequent the city's many spirited little cafés and bars. Newer sections of town are modern thriving enclaves of commercialism, replete with wide avenues and traffic. The older quarters are punctuated by cobbled, crooked streets, walled gardens and stone-built houses. Stationed beneath the peak of the mighty **Cofre de Perote**, Xalapa's surroundings are verdant and fertile, great producers of coffee, tobacco and tropical fruit. In keeping with its climate, the city is subject to refreshing drizzle and cool winter evenings. The famous *xalapeño* (*jalapeño*) chilli originally comes from the this region.

Xalapa

N Not to scale

Sleeping 🛏
Hostal de la Niebla 1
Limón 2
María Victoria 3

Mesón del Alférez 4
México 5
Misión Xalapa 6
Plaza 7
Principal 8
Salmones 9

Eating 🍴
Angelo Casa de Té Café 1

Calí Café 2
La Casona del Beaterio 3
La Fonda 4
La Parroquia 5
La Sopa 6
Le Bistrot 7
Mi Tierra 8
Tepoz Nieves Café 9

Bars & clubs 🍸
Café Lindo 10
Catedral 11
Cubanías 12

Ins and outs

Getting there The main bus station, **Central de Autobuses Xalapa (CAXA)**, 20 de Noviembre, is 2 km east of the centre with good facilities and nationwide connections. To get downtown, catch a bus or *combi* marked 'centro' on 20 de Noviembre, just downhill from the terminal. Fixed fare taxis also operate. ▶▶ *See Transport, page 518.*

Getting around Most of downtown Xalapa can be explored on foot, although you may need a bus or taxi to get to the anthropology museum, 4 km northwest; catch a bus marked 'Museo'. Some attractions outside of town, including villages, are served by local buses which depart from Mercado Los Sauces, Circuito Presidentes.

Tourist information There is a **tourist office** ① *in the Palacio Municipal, T228-842 1200, www.xalapa.gob.mx*, and a kiosk with local maps and information. The **Palacio de Gobierno** ① *south of Enriquez on Dr Lucio*, is the place for information on attractions in the wider state.

Background

The Totanacs were the first to settle at Xalapa in the 12th century, followed two centuries later by the Chichemeca, Tolteca and Teochichimeca, who all occupied separate villages. As their populations grew, the four merged into a single settlement called Xallapan ('Place of the Sandy Waters'). Later, during the 15th century, Emperor Moctezuma invaded and Xallapan became yet another subject of the mighty Aztec empire. In 1519, Cortés passed through on his way to Tenochtitlán.

After the Conquest, a Fransiscan monastery (later destroyed) was established to evangelize the local indigenous population. Little more than a village, Xalapa's population rose briefly during these early colonial years, but was subsequently stunted when the Mexico-Orizaba-Veracruz trade route opened, diverting traffic and attention away. During the 18th century, development was helped by the creation of a huge annual trading fair where merchants from New Spain congregated. As the burgeoning town gained wealth and stature, the construction of the cathedral began in 1772.

In the 19th century, Xalapa became a hot-bed of political thought, contributing ideas and plans during the Independence movement. In 1824, Xalapa was declared the state capital of Veracruz and, in 1830, attained city status. There was a passion for building and renovation in the flamboyant Gothic style during this time. During the US invasion, Santa Ana was roundly defeated in the Battle of Cerro Gordo, near Xalapa, resulting in occupation of the city. After being driven out, it was occupied by the French in 1862.

Throughout the latter half of 19th century, Governor Juan de La Luz Enríquez did much to improve the city's infrastructure, particularly its school systems. In honour, his name was incorporated into the city's name, which is Xalapa-Enríquez in full. Xalapa's profusion of educational establishments also earned it the title 'Athens of Veracruz'. Growth continued in the 20th century, with an earthquake setting back progress in 1920. Today, Xalapa retains its reputation as a urbane destination where culture and commerce sit side by side.

Sights

Parque Juárez is the geographic and spiritual heart of the city, built on the site of an ancient Fransiscan monastery. It's essentially a large paved terrace replete with monkey puzzle trees, benches and *vendedores*. There are great views of the mountains and Pico de Orizaba is visible very early in the morning, before the haze develops. On the north side of the plaza stands the **Palacio Municipal**; on the east lies the **Palacio de Gobierno**, with historic murals by José Chaves Morado. Opposite the Palacio de Gobierno stands the pink **cathedral**, begun in 1772 and exhibiting both baroque and neo-Gothic stylistic elements. There is a chapel inside dedicated to Saint Rafael Guizar (1878-1938), former Bishop of Veracruz, who was proudly canonized in 2006. Two blocks east of the cathedral on Enríquez lies Callejón Diamante, a thriving alleyway of bohemian cafés and bars that deserve at least an evening of exploration.

The excellent modern **Museo Antropología** ① *Av Xalapa s/n, Tue-Sun 0900-1700, US$3.50, audio guides available, US$1.70* , second only to the one in Mexico City, is in the northern suburbs of Xalapa. Originally founded in 1957, the museum moved to its present building, designed by New York architect Edward Durrell Stone, in 1986. Connected to the Universidad Veracruzana, new research is continually contributing to the changing exhibits. The museum is home to more than 29,000 artefacts spanning some 30 centuries of cultural development. All are beautifully presented in the building's galleries and patios, where shafts of natural light supply wonderful, atmospheric illumination. The museum concentrates on exhibits from the region's three major pre-Hispanic civilizations, showing treasures of the Olmec, Totonac and Huastec coastal cultures. It has the best collection of Olmec monumental stone sculptures in all Mexico, including several of the magnificent colossal heads from the south of Veracruz and Tabasco, and the exquisite *Señor de las Limas*. Don't miss this superb museum.

There are a handful of smaller museums that make for mild diversion. Beneath Parque Juárez, on its west side, the **Pinacoteca Diego Rivera** ① *Herrera 5, Tue-Sun 1000-1800, free*, has a small permanent collection of Rivera's paintings; more modern and contemporary art can be seen at the **Galería de Arte Contemporáneo** ① *Xalapeños Illustres 135, Tue-Sun 1000-1900, free*, with various temporary exhibitions. Fans of fire engines may want to visit the **Museo del Bombero** ① *Ortíz 5, 0900-1400 and 1600- 2000, free*, with antique engines and historical displays on the art and science of fire-fighting. The **Museo Interactivo de Xalapa** ① *Murillo Vidal, Mon-Fri 0900-1800, Sat-Sun 1000-1900, US$2.50 (US$4.50 for cinema)*, has a museum, planetarium and IMAX cinema; it's great for kids.

True to its nickname, 'City of Flowers', Xalapa has many tranquil park spaces in which you can stroll, unwind and soak up the pleasant temperate airs. Just south of Parque Juárez lies the **Parque Paseo de Los Lagos** with a cultural centre and many tidy lakeside paths. The **Parque Ecológico Macuiltépetl**, north of the city, offers panoramic views from its 1590-m-high location on a hill. Botanists should head southwest of the centre to **Jardín Botánico Clavijero** ① *Antigua Ctra a Coatepec Km 2.5*, which has a wealth of subtropical plants, ornamental flowers, reconstructed mountain habitats and a fine collection of pine trees. **Parque Tecajetes**, built over a fresh water spring and replete with trees and benches, lies 10 minutes west of Parque Juárez on Camacho.

Around Xalapa 😊❼▲ » *pp514-518.*

Ex-Hacienda El Lencero
① *12 km southeast of Xalapa, Highway Xalapa–Veracruz, Km 10, Tue-Sun 1000-1700, US$3.20. From Xalapa, take a 'Miradores' bus, US$0.70, from Plaza Cristal shopping centre.*
This hacienda was first occupied by conquistador Juan Lencero. It was subsequently sold to General Santa Ana in 1842. Today, it houses a wealth of 19th-century antiques and furniture. There is a 500-year-old fig tree in its grounds, a chapel, and a sculpture by Gabriela Mistral. The setting is very pleasant.

Coatepec

Coatepec is a sleepy coffee town just 12 km south of Xalapa and well worth a visit. The Zócalo is lined with good restaurants and open-front cafés where the aroma of fresh ground coffee permeates the air. Stock up on beans, wander the colonial streets or otherwise sample the gentle atmosphere. Northwest of the Zócalo, the **Cerro de Culebra** offers commanding views, whilst the **tourist office** ① *on the Zócalo*, has good information and maps. To get to Coatepec, catch a bus from Xalapa's Los Sauces terminal (30 minutes, $0.40) or take a taxi (20 minutes, US$10). There are plenty of lodgings, including several luxury options.

Cascada de Texcolo

The **Texolo** waterfalls are some 15 km southwest of Xalapa and 5 km from the pretty village of **Xico**, just beyond Coatepec. There is a deep ravine and a good, cheap restaurant at the falls. The old bridge is still visible but a new bridge across the ravine has been built. It is a pleasant place for a cold swim, birdwatching and walking. The film *Romancing the Stone* used Texolo as one of its locations. To get there, take a bus from Xalapa (US$0.60, every 30 minutes).

Naolinco

Naolinco is 30 minutes' ride, 40 km northeast of Xalapa up a winding hilly road. Two waterfalls, with various pools, tumble several thousand feet over steep wooded slopes. **Restaurant La Fuente** serves local food and has a nice garden. **Las Cascadas** has a mirador to admire the falls from. Both restaurants are on the way into town.

Filobobos

Two hours northwest from Xalapa is the archaeological site of **Filobobos** ① *US$2*. It includes El Cuajilote, a 400-m-wide ceremonial centre, and Vega de la Peña, an area of basalt rocks decorated with bas reliefs, a ball court and several pyramids by the river banks. Abundant wildlife here includes toucans, parrots and otters.

Perote

Route 140 towards the capital, renowned for being foggy, continues to climb to Perote, 53 km from Xalapa. The **San Carlos fort** here, now a military prison, was built 1770-1777; there is a good view of Cofre de Perote volcano (known, in Aztec times, as *Nauhtecuhtli*, 'Four Times Lord'). A road branches north to **Teziutlán**, with a Friday market, where good *sarapes* are sold. A local fair, **La Entrega de Inanacatl**, is held in the third week in June. The old convent at **Acatzingo**, 93 km beyond Perote on Route 140, is also worth seeing. Another 10 km and you join the road to Puebla and Mexico City.

⊚ Mexico City to Veracruz listings

For Sleeping and Eating price codes and other relevant information, see Essentials pages 47-51.

⊜ Sleeping

Orizaba *p508*
C-D Trueba, Ote 6 (No 485) y Sur 11, T272-724 2730, www.hoteltrueba.com. A large, modernist building with 1960s decor.

5 floors, services include business centre, bar, coffee shop and car rental. Rooms are well-equipped with cable TV, internet access and room service. Breakfast included in the price.
D De France, Ote 6 (No 186), T272-725 2311. This charming 19th-century building has clean, comfortable rooms and a reasonable restaurant. Friendly.

E América, Ote 6 (No 269). Very friendly and good value. Simple and economical.

Córdoba *p510*
B Layfer, Av 5 (No 908), between Calle 9 y 11, T271-714 0099. A 4-star hotel with swimming pool, gym, video games, restaurant, bar and secure parking. Rooms are comfortable and have a/c and cable TV. Highly recommended.

C Mansur, Av 1 (No 301) y Calle 3, on square, T271-712 6000, www.hotelmansur.com.mx. Rooms have cable TV, hot water, a/c, cable TV, room service. The restaurant serves breakfast only. Wi-Fi in the lobby and terrace.

C Virreynal, Av 1 (No 309) y Calle 1, T271-712 2377. A good central spot on the main plaza. Rooms have Wi-Fi, hot water, phone and a/c. 2 good restaurants.

D Iberia, Av 2 (No 919), T271-712 1301. The best of the budget options with good-value clean rooms around a central courtyard, with Wi-Fi and cable TV. Recommended.

E Los Reyes, Calle 3 (No 10), T271-712 2538, losreyes@prodigy.net.mx. Good, clean comfortable budget lodgings with fan, cable TV, hot water. Some bathrooms are bigger than others; some have comedy showers that soak everything. Get a quieter interior room, if possible.

Xalapa *p511, map p511*
Cheaper hotels are up the hill from the market. Town centre hotels are generally noisy, but there's plenty to choose from and they're generally good value.

AL Misión Xalapa, Victoria y Bustamante, T228-818 2222. A large, modern and comfortable hotel, 5-10 mins' walk from downtown Xalapa. Attractive grounds and a good restaurant. A mixture of rooms and suites.

A-B Mesón del Alférez, Zaragoza y Sebastián Camacho 2, T/F228-818 6351, www.pradodelrio.com. Charming colonial rooms with wooden beams and tasteful, hand-crafted furniture. 18 rooms (**B**) and 5 excellent suites (**A**). Services include cable TV, phone, safe, restaurant, parking, Wi-Fi and laundry. Recommended.

C María Victoria, Zaragoza 6, T228-818 6011, www.hotelmariavictoriaxalapa.com. A large, reasonably modern business hotel with a marbled lobby, comfortable rooms, good restaurant, bar and meeting room.

C Salmones, Zaragoza 24, T228-817 5431. The carpet on the stairs is a bit tired and shabby, but the rooms are very comfortable and spacious with lots of light, good sinks, bathrooms and kitsch details. Some have balconies and mountain views. Good little restaurant serves *comida del día*, sandwiches, breakfasts and snacks.

D Limón, Av Revolución 8, behind the cathedral, T228-817 2204, hotellimon@prodigy.net.mx. Lots of echo and noise from the hallways, but otherwise not bad for budget lodgings. Rooms are smallish but attractively tiled, with good hot showers and TV. Some have nice views.

D México, Lucio 4, T228-817 3365. Clean and simple motel-style place with parking. Rooms are straightforward and comfortable enough, some have views.

D Principal, Zaragoza 28, T228-817 6400. Although it could use a lick of paint, a lot of the rooms at this hotel aren't bad. Ask to see a few, because they're all different. Wi-Fi in the lobby.

E Plaza, Enríquez 4, T228-817 3310. Rooms are clean and bright, all have private bath and TV, although some mattresses look a bit tired. Clean, safe and friendly, with a good view of Pico de Orizaba from the roof. Recommended.

E-F Hostal de la Niebla, Calle Gutiérrez Zamora No 24, T228-817 2174, www.delaniebla.com. A good budget choice with 6-bed single sex dorms (**F**) and private rooms (**E**). Hot water, internet, kitchen, fridge and lockers. Discounts for HI members. Tourist information.

Coatepec *p514*
LL-A Posada Coatepec, Hidalgo 9, T228-816 0544, www.posadacoatepec.com.mx. A very old, beautiful colonial house with antique

furnishings and a sumptuous central courtyard complete with bubbling stone fountain and an old carriage. The lovely big rooms have double glazing and elegant details. The restaurant serves seafood. There's bikes for rent, jacuzzi, sauna, massage and a beautiful pool. Good but a little overpriced.

A El Retoño Ecolodge, Calle Tlanalapa s/n, T228-816 1428. A very decent, environmentally conscious project with birdwatching platforms, spa facilities and workshops in paper-making, ceramics and yoga. Wooden cabins are clean and cosy and surrounded by nature. Lots of tours including coffee and birding trips.

D-E Angelina Carolina, Nicolas Bravo 108, T228-816 3863. Quiet, friendly and brightly painted. Rooms are simple and good, equipped with TV and hot water.

Perote *p514*

C Central, near plaza, T228- 825 1462. Quiet and friendly, with bath and TV.

E Gran Hotel, on plaza. Basic, with only limited water.

🍴 Eating

Orizaba *p508*

In the market, try the local morning snack, *memelita picadita*.

¥ Radha's, Sur 5, between Ote 1 and 3. Indian vegetarian restaurant serving excellent *comida corrida*.

¥ Romanchú, main street. Excellent international cuisine.

¥ Crazy Foods, opposite Hotel de France. Good and cheap, nice sandwiches.

Córdoba *p510*

¥¥¥-¥¥ Cantábrico, Calle 3, No 9, 1 block from the Zócalo, T271-712 7646. Excellent meat and fish dishes, fine wines and good service, "worth a trip from Mexico City". Highly recommended.

¥¥¥-¥¥ Portal de la Jaiba, on the Zócalo. Mostly seafood with some meats, snacks and pastas. Specialities include paella and

octopus. Breakfasts are good value. The bar upstairs, La Divina Comedia, is good for an evening tipple.

¥¥¥-¥¥ Zevallos, on the Zócalo. The smartest place on the plaza with crisp table cloths, superb views and attentive staff.

¥¥-¥ Las Delicias, Av 2 No 307, between Calle 3 and Calle 5. Economical breakfast packages and Mexican staples. Clean, with bright table cloths and slack, even unhelpful service. Several city-wide branches.

Cafés and bakeries

La Colonial, Calle 5 y Av 2. A good selection of cakes, sweet rolls and breads. There are many other bakeries on the surrounding streets, most serve hot coffee too.

Xalapa *p511, map p511*

There are several good cafés on Carrillo Puerto for good-value *comida corrida*.

¥¥¥ Le Bistrot, Miguel Palacio 1. Closed Mon. Expensive French and international cuisine including fondues, peppered steak, quiche Lorraine, snails and crème brûlée.

¥¥¥-¥¥ La Casona del Beaterio, Zaragoza 20. A tastefully restored colonial-style house with patios, fountain and historic photos of Xalapa. Various seafood and meat dishes on offer, economical *comida del día* and breakfasts. The food is OK, but nothing great.

¥¥¥-¥¥ Picrecha, Illustres 144. Authentic-looking pizzeria with chequered table cloths, darkened interior and giant stone oven. Specialities include pizzas (the medium size is huge and enough for two), savoury crêpes, spaghetti and Mexican snacks. Not bad, but the pizzas are slightly oversweet.

¥¥¥-¥¥ Tango, Pánuco 7. Mon-Sat 1330-0030, Sun 1330-1800. Tasty Argentine food including meat cuts to delight any carnivore. Live music most nights and tango on Fri.

¥¥ La Fonda, Callejón Diamante 1. Atmospheric Mexican restaurant serving traditional food in vibrant surroundings. Popular.

¥¥-¥ La Parroquia, Zaragoza 18, and another on Av Camacho. A big dining hall where *café lechero* is served with typical flamboyance.

Similar menu and prices as the famous restaurant of same name in Veracruz.

¶ **La Sopa**, Callejón Diamante 3a. Economical locals' haunt serving Mexican staples.
¶ **Mi Tierra**, Enríquez 24. Greasy taco joint with giant spit-roasted meats, *tortas* and other quick, cheap, filling fare that probably tastes better after several beers.

Cafés and ice-cream parlours

Angelo Casa de Té, Primo Verdad 21A. Interesting herbal teas, cakes and snacks.
Calí Cafe, Callejón Diamante. Coffee house, always buzzing with students and arty types.
Tepoz Nieves, Enriquéz, between Revolución and Clavijero. Ice creams and fruit juices.

Coatepec p514

There are several good cafés and restaurants around the main plaza.

¶¶¶–¶¶ **Casa Bonilla**, Cuauhtémoc 20. Award-winning restaurant renowned for its delicious and varied langoustine dishes. It's worth coming to Coatepec just to eat here.
¶¶ **Arcos de Belem**, Lerdo 9. A pleasant place on the plaza with faded murals and open windows. Breakfasts, seafood and regional dishes, including trout. Years of service.
¶¶ **El Tío Yeyo**, Degollado 4. *Trucha* (trout) is the speciality of the house here, with over 2 dozen preparations. Good wine list, and an interesting interior filled with plants and *artesanías*.

♥ Bars and clubs

Xalapa *p511, map p511*
Xalapa's large student population ensures there's plenty of vibrant nightlife.
Café Lindo, Primo Verdad 21. A café by day and a bustling watering hole by night, popular with students, often has live music.
Catedral, Leandro Valle 3. This popular place fills up with students and beer-guzzlers each evening. Sells coffee during the day.
Cubanías, Callejón Gonzáles Aparicio, an alley off Primo Verdad. A busy little joint that's good

for a mojito, Cuban snacks and meeting local students. Lots of other bustling places nearby.
Kbar, Camacho 54. Popular karaoke bar, perfect for a drunken singalong.

⊛ Entertainment

Xalapa *p511, map p511*
Cultural centres
Centro de Recreación Xalapeño, Centro Recreacion Xalapeno, Ilustres 31 y Insurgentes, has exhibitions.
El Agora, underneath Parque Juárez. Live music, films and exhibitions.

▲ Activities and tours

Xalapa *p511, map p511*
Birdwatching
Club de Observadores de Aves de Xalapa, www.coaxxalapa.org. Xalapa's principal birdwatching club should be able to hook you up with fellow birders and local guides. Holds regular events.

Rafting
Amigos del Río, Chilpancingo 205, T228-815 8817, www.amigosdelrio.com.mx. Established rafting operation with offices in Xalapa and Jalcomulco. Offers a range of trips, from 1-day river descents to all-inclusive 4-day adventure packages with rappelling and other adrenaline-charged activities.
Expediciones Mexico Verde, Ctra Jalcomulco–Coatepec, Km4, 40 mins from Xalapa, just outside the town of Jalcomulco, T279-832 3734, www.mexicoverde.com. A rafting and adventure resort with charming safari-style lodgings. Aside from river expeditions, it offers climbing, walking, rappelling and corporate team building.
Viajes de Aventura, Jalcomulco, T279-832 3655, www.viajesdeaventura.com.mx. All-inclusive rafting trips including stays at the comfortable resort facilities. Based outside Xalapa in Jalcomulco.

Tour operators and guides

Roy Dudley, 812-0555, www.xalaparoy.com.
Roy Dudley, originally from Kansas, offers
historical tours of the city as well as
photography workshops and
apartment rentals.
Tranvías, Enriquez, T228-817 3425.
Trolley-bus tours of the city.

Around Xalapa *p513*
Tour operators

Finca los Tres Mundos, T044-228-164 6867,
www.finca3mundos.org. An organic farm
that offers coffee and culture tours to
Xico and Coatepec, including a Cafe-Tal
Apan coffee plantation, Texolo waterfall
and downtown Coatepec. Lunch with
panoramic views included.

⊖ Transport

Orizaba *p508*

Bus To **Córdoba**, every ½ hr, 40 mins, US$2.
To **Mexico City** (TAPO), 15 daily, 4 hrs, US$19.
To **Oaxaca**, 3 daily, 0105, 1010, 1740, 4½ hrs,
US$21. To **Puebla**, 13 daily, 2 hrs, US$11.
To **Veracruz**, every 30-60 mins, 2½ hrs,
US$9. To **Xalapa**, 10 daily, 4 hrs, US$12.

Córdoba *p510*

Bus Bus station is at the end of Av 6. To
Mexico City (TAPO), hourly, 5 hrs, US$20.
To **Oaxaca**, 4 daily, 5½ hrs, US$22. To
Orizaba, every ½ hr, 40 mins, US$2. To
Puebla, every ½ hr, 3 hrs, US$12. To
Veracruz, every ½ hr, 1½ hrs, US$8. To
Xalapa, 10 daily, 3 hrs, US$11.

Xalapa *p511, map p511*
Air

There is a small airport serving a few national
destinations, 15 km southeast of the city.

Bus

Local To reach nearby the towns of
Coatepec and **Xico** take a bus from
Mercado Los Sauces, 2 km south of the
city centre on Circuito Presidentes.
Long distance The bus station, CAXA, is
on the outskirts of town; to get there, take a
'Camacho- CAXA-SEC' bus from Camacho or
Hidalgo. To **Coatzacoalcos**, 11 daily, 6-8 hrs,
US$25. To **Mexico City** (TAPO), hourly,
5-6 hrs, US$22. To **Poza Rica**, 18 daily, 5 hrs,
US$16. To **Papantla**, 11 daily, 4 ½ hrs, US$14.
To **Puebla**, 11 daily, 2 ½ hrs, US$12. To
Veracruz, frequent, 0500-2300, 2 hrs, US$7.
To **Villahermosa**, 5 daily, 8-10 hrs, US$33.

⊙ Directory

Córdoba *p510*
Banks *Casa de cambio*, Av 3, facing Bancomer.

Xalapa *p511, map p511*
Banks Banca Serfín on Enríquez will change
TCs in major currencies. **Santander** on Carrillo
Puerto changes dollar TCs. **American Express**
at Viajes Xalapa, Carrillo Puerto 24, T228-817
6535, in centre, sells cheques against Amex
card. *Casa de cambio*, on right side of Zamora
going downhill. Rates vary a lot, so shop
around. Quick service and good rates at **Dollar
Exchange**, Gutiérrez Zamora 36. **Internet**
Serviexpress, Zaragoza 14B. Café Chat, on
Camacho opposite Parque Bicentenal, another
in shopping arcade off Enríquez. Most charge
US$2.50 per hr. **Laundry** Several on Allende
and Ursulo Galván, all charge by weight,
usually US$3 per 3 kg. **Medical services**
There are 2 dentists on Ursulo Galván. The
hospital is on Nicolás Bravo. **Post office** On
Diego Leño. **Telephone** Long-distance
phone in shop on Zaragoza with sign outside,
others behind the government palace.

Veracruz and the central Gulf coast

The steamy, seamy city of Veracruz is rich in history and spirit. Filled with lightly crumbling colonial streets, thronging plazas and hordes of ardent party-goers, this is a place where vibrant cultural heritage meets unfettered port-town hedonism. Historically significant, the region had the dubious honour of hosting Hernan Cortés and his fellow conquistadors – fathers of the Conquest and the colonial enterprise that followed – after their tentative first landing on Mexico's shores. After forging a base, they scouted the surrounding terrain, made allies at Cempoala, and learned of the complex political forces dominating the land – not to mention the great wealth of the Aztec kingdom. Soon after, the strategic port of Veracruz became New Spain's main gateway to Europe, beset by pirates, colonialists and waves of insalubrious sailors. Today, the city retains an air of decadence and pride, enlivened by non-stop music and festivities, the gregarious charms of its inhabitants, and culinary treats that include superb, fresh, spicily seasoned seafood. The expansive Plaza de Armas is the setting to enjoy all these things at once, buzzing each evening with a well attended carnival atmosphere. ▶▶ *For listings, see pages 527-530.*

Veracruz ⬛🅿🄰🄴🅾▲🄰🄲 ▶▶ *pp527-530.*

Veracruz is a city with a Caribbean soul, with feisty rhythms, feisty people, fierce sunshine, salsa and beautiful spirited madness. It is hot with music, sensuous and sensual, a city for dancers, drinkers and drunks. Part grotty industrial port, part colonial jewel, the city derives its endless energy from the melodies spilling through its streets. Guitars intoxicate the terraces, marimbas swallow the plazas, and Cuban-style bands play out their passions in bars and dimly-lit cafés across the city. And like all good port towns, it possesses style and depravity in equal abundance. The streets are awash with revellers, hawkers and peddlers: itinerant musicians seeking a commission, cigar salesmen with dubious Cuban *puros*, gypsy palm readers, whores, drunks, beggars and thieves. Everyone's out to party. But at dawn, the creatures retreat and the endless thumping of drums and headboards relents. The city takes breakfast in great dining halls with lofty, lazy ceiling fans, impeccable 1950s decor and armies of white-shirted waiters armed with kettles of hot black coffee and hot white milk. Between the bouts of savage hedonism, Veracruz is a place of impeccable character.

Ins and outs

Getting there **Aeropuerto Las Bajadas** (**VER**) is 12 km from the city centre and has a shuttle service into town. The bus terminals (first and second class) are about 3 km from the town centre, on Avenida Díaz Mirón. To get downtown, take a blue-and-white or red-and-white bus marked 'Díaz Mirón', which pass one block from the Zócalo (US$0.50); or a *colectivo* (US$0.50). Taxis cost about US$3. Highways 150 and 150D (*supercarretera*) link Mexico City to the Gulf coast at the port of Veracruz. Route 180 runs north–south along the coast. ▶▶ *See Transport, page 530.*

Getting around All places of interest are within easy walking distance of Plaza de Armas. From Zaragoza and Serdán, frequent buses run along the seafront to Mocambo or Boca del Río during the day, but at night you may have to take a taxi.

Best time to visit It is generally hot, however, if visiting between July and September, check the weather forecast because tropical storms blow themselves out in this region, bringing heavy rain. From October to January the weather is changeable, with cold, damp winds. At this time the beaches and Malecón are empty and many resorts close, except over Christmas and New Year when all road transport is booked up five days in advance.

Tourist information The helpful **tourist office** ⓘ *Palacio Municipal, T229-200 2200 or freephone on T01-800-VERATUR, or www.veratur.gob.mx, 1000-1800,,* is on the Zócalo. For up-to-date information on entertainment, browse the youthful Jarochilandia website, www.jarochilandia.com.

Background
The principal port of entry for Mexico lies on a low alluvial plain bordering the Gulf coast. Cortés landed near here at Isla de los Sacrificios on 17 April 1519 and went on to conquer the Aztecs in 1521. The first settlement was called Villa Rica de la Vera Cruz; its location was changed several times, including to La Antigua (see page 525). The present site was established in 1599. Following the Conquest, Veracruz became an important Atlantic port and a vital gateway for the soldiers, slaves, workers and missionaries who forged the great colonial project of New Spain.

The freshly plundered wealth of the New World also passed through the city en route to Europe. Treasure-laden galleons drew scores of Dutch, British and French pirates, who regularly pillaged the city, partook in its vices or otherwise harassed the Spanish forces.

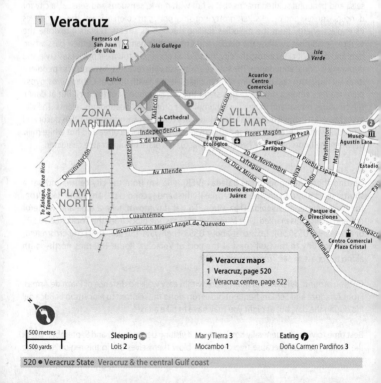

1 Veracruz

➡ **Veracruz maps**
1 Veracruz, page 520
2 Veracruz centre, page 522

500 metres
500 yards

Sleeping 😴
Lois **2**

Mar y Tierra **3**
Mocambo **1**

Eating 🍴
Doña Carmen Pardiños **3**

This led to the construction of the fortress of San Juan de Ulúa. Years later, during the war of Independence, the Spanish made a final stand there, holding out for four years after the country's liberation. The city, strategically vital, was subject to four more major bouts of hostility, which is why it is sometimes called 'Four times heroic'. In 1838, it was occupied by the French navy during the Pastry War, but General Antonio López managed to see them off. Then, in 1847, US General Winfield Scott occupied the city, killing over 1000 Mexicans in an extended siege.

In October 1861, Mexico defaulted on its foreign loan repayments, causing Spanish and British troops to occupy it. They soon departed, however, making way for eager Napoleon III, who sought nothing less than complete dominance of Mexico. He installed the poor, ill-fated Emperor Maximilian, whose troops remained for several years. They were later expelled by Juárez in 1866 and Maximilian was promptly executed. In 1872, a railway was built connecting Veracruz with the capital, bringing new wealth and investment. But then, in 1914, Major General Frederick Funston occupied the city for several months during the Tampico Affair. Today, Veracruz is an important deep-water port and party town that's popular with both Mexican and international tourists.

Sights and orientation

Downtown Veracruz is the place to be. The feisty **Plaza de Armas**, which sees a well-attended party almost every night, is at the centre of the action. Flanking its southwest

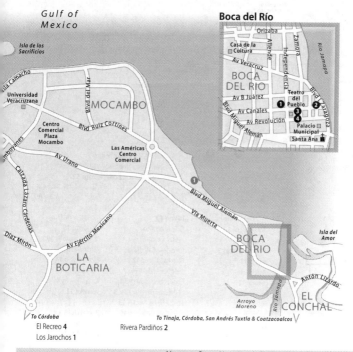

El Recreo 4
Los Jarochos 1
Rivera Pardiños 2

side is **Independencia**, the city's main thoroughfare, which changes to **20 de Noviembre** as it meets **Parque Zamora** several blocks south. Most of the city's attractions are located in the salty old streets between the plaza and **Parque Zamora**. East of the plaza, the popular waterfront **malecón** skirts the shore, passes the port and changes its name to

2 Veracruz centre

N

200 metres

200 yards

Sleeping 🛏
Amparo **1**
Baluarte **2**

Casa de Huéspedes La
  Tabasqueña **12**
Colonial **3**
Gran Diligencias **5**
Impala **13**
Mallorca **6**
Oriente **11**
Paloma **8**
Royalty **10**
Santo Domingo **9**
Santander **7**
Veracruz **4**

Eating 🍴
Café Auténtico
  Veracruzano **5**
Café de la Catedral **8**
Café La Merced **12**
Café Punta del Cielo **7**
Chanchonitas de Oro **4**
El Refugio del Pescador **3**
Fonda de las Gordas **13**
Gran Café del Portal **10**
La Nueva Parroquia **1**

Mondogo de Fruta
  Trigueros **15**
Nevería Morales **16**
Pardiñolas **6**
Pizza Angelo **14**
Tiburón **2**
Tortas Royalty **9**
Villa Rica **11**

Bars & clubs 🍸
El Rincón de la Trova **18**
Palitos **17**

➡ Veracruz maps
1 Veracruz, page 520
2 Veracruz centre, page 522

Bulevar Camacho. It then follows the coast for several kilometres more into the **Zona Hotelera**, which has beaches, but isn't as much fun (and not too clean either).

Plaza de Armas

At the heart of Veracruz lies the Plaza de Armas (Zócalo), a large paved square replete with cast-iron lamp-stands, languid palm trees, benches, hotels, restaurants and handsome colonial buildings. It comes alive in the evenings with an impressive crush of people, colour and marimba music – *danzón* or *son veracruzano*. Scores of peddlers and entertainers descend on the square in search of tourist dollars, with trinket salesmen, clowns, musicians and gypsy fortune tellers among the usual suspects. The various terraces are great places to soak up the vibe, but you will invariably be hassled if you choose to drink or dine outside.

On the plaza, the baroque **cathedral**, opened in 1721, is slightly weathered and has an unusual cross depicted with hands. The **Palacio Municipal**, built in 1621 and renovated in the 18th century, has a splendid facade and courtyard; it is one of the most beautiful buildings in the city. Also on the Zócalo is the **Fototeca** ⓘ *www.fototecadeveracruz.org, Tue-Sun 1000-1900*, with interesting temporary photographic exhibits and a good bookshop. Fine cigars can be purchased from the salesmen on the plaza, but avoid the Cuban ones, which are most likely fake (instead, purchase cigars made locally in Veracruz). From 15 July to the end of August there is jazz in the Zócalo from 1900.

Fuerte de San Juan de Ulúa

ⓘ *Tue-Sun 0900-1700, US$2.50. To get there, take the bus marked Ulúa from malecón/Av República, or catch a lancha from the malecón, US$2.50.*

The ruined **Fortress of San Juan de Ulúa** (1565), visible from the waterfront, was originally built on Isla Gallega to deter pirates and buccaneers. It is now joined by a causeway to the mainland and is the site where Cortés first arrived in Mexico. In later years, the fortress became a political prison and Mexico's 'Robin Hood', Chucho el Roto, famously managed to escape three times. Benito Juárez was also incarcerated here between 1858 and 1861. Its three main cells, utilized most notoriously during the reign of Porfirio Díaz, are known as 'purgatory', 'heaven' and 'hell'. In 1915, Venustiano Carranza converted it into a presidential palace, before it fell into the crumbling wreck it is today.

The port and around

The city's main port lies just northeast of the Zócalo, fronted by the weathered old **aduana** (customs house). Opposite lies the **Plaza de la République**, and on Morelos, the attractive and wonderfully grandiose **Registro Civil**, built in 1972, where you might witness happy wedding parties congregated outside. Continue north from the customs house and you'll pass the handsome **post office**, opened in 1910 and built in the French neoclassical style of the Porfiriato. Note the splendid gold lions guarding the structure. Further north still lies the old train station and railway line that once connected the city with the capital.

Malecón

The waterfront *malecón*, just east of the Zócalo, is a bastion of nightly entertainment, often crowded with revellers, performers and strolling tourists. There is a large *artesanía* **market** that sells mostly tat, but is still fun for a perusal. **Harbour cruises** can be sought out in this area and offshore you'll see many industrial cranes and ships. The smell can be pungent. Heading away from the Zócalo, you'll pass the **Faro Carranza**, where the 1917 Mexican Constitución was drafted. The building, completed in 1906, is flanked by a small plaza, a military cannon and a statue of Carranza. It features a lighthouse that is apparently powerful enough to be seen in Xalapa. Today, the *faro* houses naval offices. Nearby stands the modern black windowed **Edificio de Pemex**. As the *malecón* turns a corner it changes to Comodoro Manuel Azueta, and later, to Camacho.

Acuario de Veracruz
ⓘ *Inside the Plaza Acuario Shopping centre, Camacho s/n, www.acuariodeveracruz.com. Daily 1000-1900. US$6, (tiburonario, US$30).*

Designed by a Japanese architect, the modern, well-presented aquarium of Veracruz is certainly worth a visit. Salt water and fresh water organisms are amply represented, including reef fish, rays, jelly fish and sharks, all beheld through superb glass tunnels. Otters, reptiles and amphibians are kept too, but perhaps no residents are quite as disarming as the peaceful, looming manatees. If you're after excitement, head to the *tiburonario*, where you can observe the sharks at feeding time, right up close from inside a submerged underwater box.

Baluarte de Santíago
ⓘ *Francisco Canal y Gómez Farías. Tue-Sun 1000-1630. US$2.20.*

Built in 1635, the Baluarte de Santíago is the last surviving bastion that once formed part of the city defensive walls. Its basement contained gunpowder for 22 cannons and the structure now houses a small pre-Hispanic gold collection recovered from a wreck. There are bullet holes in the walls made by a firing squad in 1812.

Museo de la Ciudad
ⓘ *Zaragoza 397. Mon-Sat 1000-1800. Free.*

The Museo de la Ciudad has a good, well-displayed collection of photographs and archaeological finds. It traces the history of Veracruz from its ancient Olmec inhabitants up to the 1950s. There are also displays on the various ethnic groups that contribute to the city's sizzling mix of African, Spanish and Indigenous cultures. Opposite the museum stands the **Instituto Veracruzano de la Cultura**, once an ancient Betlemitas monastery, later a homeless hospital, and since 1973, the city's cultural institute. Two blocks towards the sea, **Las Ataranzanas** are the old colonial warehouses, built of coral and brick and worth a quick look.

Museo Histórico Naval
ⓘ *Gómez Farías and Morales. Tue-Sun 0900-1700. Free.*

The Museo Histórico Naval has an excellent and extensive collection of naval memorabilia, especially from the 1914 resistance to US invasion. Built in 1894, the building once served as the city's naval school, and later as a naval hospital, when the school was moved elsewhere in 1952. There's plenty of weaponry on display, model ships and a reproduction of the lake siege of Tenochtitlán, conducted by Cortés on small Spanish crafts. Exhibitions on ancient seafaring are interesting, as are expositions on the old Manila convoys, which brought untold wealth from Asia. Also inside the building, the **Museo Carranza** has photos of the Revolution, the life of Carranza and his battles against the Huerta regime.

Museo Agustín Lara
ⓘ *On the way to Mocambo beach, where Blv Avila Camacho meets Blv Ruiz Cortines. Tue-Sun. US$$2, free on Sun.*

The Museo Agustín Lara (La Casita Blanca) is a must for anyone interested in Mexican popular music. It was the home of the greatest 20th-century Mexican songwriter Agustín Lara, who wrote more than 700 songs (*Solamente una vez*, *Veracruz*, *Granada* and *María Bonita* among the most famous), many of which still reverberate around the streets and squares of Veracruz. A pianist plays Tuesday to Saturday 1100-1400, 1600-1900; at other times visitors are welcome to play Lara's piano.

Zona Hotelera and beaches

The high-rise and culturally sanitized Zona Hotelera skirts the shores south of the downtown area. The beaches along this stretch of waterfront, and the sea, are polluted from heavy shipping, industry and, quite possibly, sewage. As a general rule, the further you get from the city (and humanity), the cleaner it is. **Villa del Mar**, one of the closest beaches, is popular and bustling but quite scruffy too. A short bus ride from the fish market takes you to **Mocambo**, which has a superb 50-m swimming pool (with restaurant and bar), restaurants, Caribbean-style beach huts and dirty sand; the water is quite a bit cleaner but still rather uninviting. There are crabs and mosquitoes and much pestering by sellers. The beach is crowded during the summer, and at holiday time cars race up and down with music blaring. There is also a large shopping centre nearby and a handful of fairly pricey but quite famous hotels.

Boca del Río

Beyond Mocambo, some of the best beaches lie close to Boca del Río, 12 km south of downtown Veracruz. Perched on the left bank of the mouth of Río Jamapa, it offers quiet respite from the frenetic pace of the city. In 1518, the Spaniard Grijalva gave the already existing settlement here the name of Río de Banderas ('River of Flags'), as the inhabitants carried small flags in order to transmit messages. Worthy of a visit is the church of **Santa Ana** (1716). Modern buildings of interest include the **Palacio Municipal**, **Teatro del Pueblo** and the **Casa de la Cultura**, but most people come to Boca del Río to eat at one of its many fine, economical fish restaurants. Boat trips can also be arranged here, as touts may frequently remind you.

A 10-minute bus ride from Boca del Río to the other side of the river is **El Conchal**, a small residential development overlooking picturesque lagoons with a number of attractive restaurants. The bus continues along a low sandy spit to **Punta Antón Lizardo** where there is a small village with a few beach restaurants and good sand and bathing. There are also offshore islands with coral reefs; speak to a city dive shop about visiting them.

Central Gulf coast 🌐 ›› *pp527-530.*

La Antigua

La Antigua is the site of one of the earliest settlements in New Spain, 1½ km off the road to Cardel, some 25 km north of Veracruz. This languid tropical village, slung over the banks of the Río La Antigua, is home to a handful of interesting colonial ruins. The **Casa de Cortés**, strangled by roots and crumbling into almost total dereliction, is thought by some to be an old custom house and not the former home of the conquistador. The **Edificio del Cabildo**, built in 1523, was the office of the first local government in New Spain. The country's first Christian church, **Ermita del Rosario**, is also worth a look, although it has been restored several times since its initial construction. There is a giant wish-granting Ceiba tree where Cortés once moored his ships on the riverbank;

motorboats can be hired if you fancy a tour of the water. Many claim La Antigua was the first settlement in New Spain, but Villa Rica, further north, is also attributed with this importance. To get to La Antigua from Veracruz, take bus to to Cardel from the second-class part of the bus station (US$0.40) and get off at La Antigua Caseta, the first toll booth the bus comes to. It is an easy 10- or 15-minute walk from there.

Cardel

Cardel is a busy little transport hub. It connects with: Veracruz, some 35 km to the south on Highway 180; Xalapa and the highlands to the west on Highway 140; and the nearby ruins of Cempoala to the north, beyond which Highway 180 reaches into northern Veracruz state. There isn't much to do here, but there are hotels, shops and restaurants, making it a good stopover before striking out to more distant locales.

Cempoala

① *42 km north of Veracruz, 7 km north of Cardel, west of Highway 180; follow the turn-off by the Pemex stations for 4 km; or take a 2nd-class bus to Cardel, then a micro, 0900-1730, S$2.50.*
Surrounded by lush mountain scenery, the ancient Totonac city of Cempoala rose to importance in the early 13th century. Its name means 'Place of twenty waters', after the various river systems that converge here, and by the 15th century the city was home to some 30000 inhabitants. Cempoala is infamous as the first indigenous city visited by Cortés and his conquistadors, who all received a warm and rapturous welcome.

The Cempoalans were keen to forge an alliance with the Spaniards, hoping they would defeat their mortal enemies, the Aztecs, who had recently made Cempoala a subject of their empire. Cortés cordially accepted their hospitality, although acted somewhat ungraciously by destroying many of their idols and lecturing them on the virtues of Christianity. Regardless, a formidable and highly symbolic alliance was struck, and Cortés left the city in August 1519 with 200 Cempoalan porters and 50 warriors. Later, when Pánifilo Navárez was dispatched from Cuba to reign in the incipient Conquest, Cortés was forced to return. A final confrontation took place in Cempoala where Navárez was defeated and many of his troops converted to Cortés' cause. After the Conquest, in 1575, the population of Cempoala was decimated by disease. Some 20 years later, the remaining population was removed and relocated to the village under a vice-regal scheme.

Cempoala was a well developed city with defensive walls and a water system, although most of the visible structures date to the Aztec period. Particularly interesting are the round stones uniquely used in its construction. The **Templo Mayor** is an 11-m-high pyramid with staircases and shrine, grouped with others around a central plaza reminiscent of Tenochtitlán. The **Templo de Chimeneas** once served as the lodgings for Cortés and his men, whilst the **Templo de las Caritas** conceals fragments of murals. In the town, the **Templo de Ehecatl** is a circular structure dedicated to the god of wind. Sundays at the site can be very crowded, but it is usually quiet in the week. *Voladores* are often in attendance.

Chachalacas

If you're looking for beaches, head to Chachalacas, 10 km northeast of Cardel. Home to a fishing village and modest resort, its popular with Mexicans during holiday times. Out of season the grey sands are often quite blissfully empty. There's a swimming pool and changing facilities (US$1 adults) in the expensive but spotless **Chachalacas** hotel; there are various other lodgings if you want to stay. Local delicacies, including *robalito* fish, are sold from *palapas* on the beach. It is worth asking the restaurants on the beach to let you hang up your hammock. Most charge US$2 if you agree to eat at their restaurant and have showers and toilets.

⊚ Veracruz and the central Gulf coast listings

For Sleeping and Eating price codes and other relevant information, see Essentials pages 47-51.

⊚ Sleeping

Veracruz *p519, maps p520 and p522*
High season runs Jul-Oct. Prices can drop by 10-40% at other times of the year. The Zócalo is very lively at night, so rooms overlooking the square can be noisy.

Downtown
LL-L Gran Hotel Diligencias, Independencia 115, on the Zócalo, T229-933 0280, www.gran hoteldiligencias.com. A very historic and comfortable hotel that's easily the best of the plaza lodgings. Rooms are tasteful and comfortable, and there's a wide range of services including business centre, pool, gym, jacuzzi, Wi-Fi and bar. The restaurant is superb.
AL Veracruz, Independencia y Lerdo, near Zócalo, T229-989 3800, www.hotel veracruz.com.mx. This large hotel is one of the better options in the centre. Services include business centre, pool, valet parking, restaurant and bar. Predictably comfortable.
A Colonial, on Zócalo, T229-932 0193, www.hcolonial.com.mx. A long-standing Zócalo option with terrace, solarium, parking, pool, restaurant, Wi-Fi and tourist services like car rental. Good and helpful, if slightly past its prime. Significant low season discount.
B Baluarte, opposite the small fort of Baluarte, Canal 265, T229-932 5222, www.hotelbaluarte.com.mx. Good, clean, efficient rooms, all located around a central courtyard and equipped with TV, phone and a/c. Services include pool and restaurant.
C Mar y Tierra, Figueroa y Malecón, T/F229-931 3866, www.hotelmarytierra.com. Close to downtown with the best bay views in Veracruz.

Friendly and helpful, with a restaurant serving good breakfasts. Good low season discount.
C Santander, Landero y Coss 123, T229-932 4529. Recently remodelled, with good, clean rooms and pleasant bed spreads. Top floor rooms are slightly better. There are 46 rooms in total, all with a/c, bath and TV. Very clean.
D Amparo, Aquiles Serdán 482, T229-932 2738, www.hotelamparo.com.mx. Clean, economical rooms with fan, cable TV, insect screens and hot water. Friendly and good value. Parking available. Recommended.
D Casa de Huéspedes La Tabasqueña, Av Morelos 325, T229-931 9437. All rooms have fan, 2 have a/c. The upper rooms are less good, front rooms are noisy, and some have no windows. Cheap, clean, safe and helpful, if simple and slightly shabby.
D Mallorca, Aquiles Serdán 424, T229-932 7549. Basic rooms with bath, fan and radio. Very clean and highly recommended.
D Oriente, M Lerdo 20, T/F229-931 2490. Simple rooms, clean and spacious, with a/c, cable TV, phone and bath. Some have noisy street balconies, others have fan. Wi-Fi and drinking water in the lobby. OK.
D-E Impala, Orizaba 658, T229-937 1257. Straightforward rooms with bath, cold water and mosquitoes, but clean. Near bus station.
E Paloma, Av Morales y Reforma, T229-932 4260. Clean, basic and friendly. Good value, the choice of itinerant hippies.
E Santo Domingo, Serdán 481, T229- 931 6326. Good, if small, budget rooms with reliable hot water, Wi-Fi and fan. Friendly, but very noisy at night.

Zona Hotelera
Upmarket lodgings are concentrated in the Zona Hotelera. The area is quiet and sterile most hotels have access to a beach.

LL-A Mocambo, Calzada Ruiz Cortines 4000, south of the port on Playa Mocambo, T229-922 0200, www.hotelmocambo.com.mx. A 1930s palace on the beach with good service and a reputable restaurant. Rooms are large and comfortable, well-equipped, many with good ocean views. Highly recommended.
AL Lois, Ruiz Cortines 10, T229-937 8290, www.hotellois.com.mx. A slick, modern high-rise hotel perched on the coast. 107 rooms and 17 suites, all comfortable and well-equipped. Services include gym, sauna, squash court, car rental, parking and pool.

La Antigua p525
D Malinche, near the river. Quiet, laidback and peaceful.

🍴 Eating

Veracruz p519, maps p520 and 522
Downtown
In the main market, Cortés y Madero, there are cheap restaurants in the mezzanine. *Toritos* are a local drink made of egg, milk, fruit and alcohol, delicious and potent. If you eat outside, expect to be approached by hawkers.
♥♥♥ Villa Rica, on the Zócalo. The most upmarket seafood restaurant in Veracruz, with a branch in the Zona Hotelera too, where Bill Clinton once dined. The one in the plaza is very smart, with great views and atmosphere. Recommended.
♥♥♥-♥♥ Gran Café del Portal, Independencia y Zamora. Open from 0700. A historic, grand old dining hall just off the Zócalo and under the arches. Food includes breakfasts, cordon bleu chicken, *filete mignon* and an array of seafood including *filete a la Veracruzana*, prawns and whole fish.
♥♥ Café de la Catedral, Ocampo 202. An interesting and unpretentious eatery with lots of fascinating local colour and pavement seating. Try the fish stuffed with shrimps.
♥♥ La Nueva Parroquia, on the *malecón*. Famous throughout Mexico (it used to be called **Café La Parroquia**, on Plaza de Armas).

2 coffee houses the in same block, very popular, with excellent coffee, good food and lots of atmosphere. You haven't been to Veracruz until you've been here, or so they say.
♥♥ Café La Merced, Rayón 609. Another big Veracruz dining hall with lots of character. The menu has lots of meat dishes as well as Mexican snacks, seafood and *tortas*. Popular.
♥♥ Chanchonitas de Oro, Serdán y Morelos. An unpretentious seafood joint. Also breakfasts.
♥♥ Pardiñolas, Plazuela de la Campana. Locals' joint that serves oysters and other fresh seafood offerings. Outdoor seating offers great views of the evening's entertainment (see Bars and clubs, below).
♥♥ Pizza Angelo, Molina, behind the cathedral. For when you've had enough of seafood. Takeaway available.
♥♥ Tiburón, Landero y Coss 167, corner of Aquiles Serdán, 2 blocks from the Zócalo. An interesting place, run by 'Tiburón' González, the 'Rey de la Alegría', or 'Rey Feo' of carnival; the walls are covered in pictures of him and his *comparsas*, dating back to at least 1945. The food is good and inexpensive. Note the restaurant was remodelling during our last visit, but should be open to the public soon.
♥♥-♥ El Refugio del Pescador, Serdán and Landero y Cos. The gastronomic plaza occupies the old fish market and is a great place to sample good, fresh seafood with the locals. Recommended.
♥ Fonda de las Gordas, on the Zócalo. A good, clean, economical eatery that's popular with locals. Serves *gorditas*, enchiladas and other snacks.
♥ Tortas Royalty, Ocampo 215. Cheap *tortas* and fast food from this hole in the wall.

Cafés, bakeries and ice cream parlours
Café Autentico Veracruzano, off Plazuala de la Campana. A low-key coffee shop that often has chess players at its tables outside.
Café Punta del Cielo, Independencia y Arista. Modern and slightly pretentious coffee shop with a vast array of hot and cold caffeinated drinks, tasty snacks and cookies. In the vein of corporate franchises.

Mondogo de Fruta Trigueros, Morelos y Molina. Fresh fruit smoothies and snacks.
Nevería Morales, Zamora, between Zaragoza y Landero y Cos. Just one of a few ice cream parlours on this stretch of road.

Boca del Río *p525, map p521*
Boca del Río is famous for its relatively cheap and decent seafood.
††† -†† Doña Carmen Pardiños, Canales y Zamora. A large dining establishment with crisp white tablecloths and well-dressed musicians.
†† El Recreo, Revolución y Zamora. Under the arches, this seafood restaurant is good for watching the lazy activity on the plaza.
†† Rivera Pardiños, Zaragoza 127. Good value seafood including fillets stuffed with prawns and served à la Veracruzano. Generally quiet, with few hawkers approaching the outside seating.
††-† Los Jarochos, Independencia, between Juárez and Canales. Seafood, *tortas*, breakfasts and *comida del día*.

Bars and clubs

Veracruz *p519, maps p520 and 522*
Bars
Drinking in the town centre can be an interesting experience, often coloured by raucous local characters. Head for the Zócalo and the *portales* and see where the evening takes you. Every night **Plazuela de Campana** fills with locals who dance to live music – pure 1950s ambience; fantastic.
El Rincón de la Trova, Callejón de la Lagunilla, an alley off Serdán. Great live *trova* music, dancing and Cuban food.
Palitos, Tlapacoyan y Serdán. Busy, young, downtown bar with screens and jukebox, occasional drunken crooning and live music of the pop-rock variety. Ladies free Tue-Wed. Slightly sketchy.

Nightclubs
Most discos and nightclubs are located in and around the Zona Hotelera. Several

places have been recommended, including **Coralinos**, **City Bamba** and **La Comedia**.

Entertainment

Veracruz *p519, maps p520 and 522*
Culturally, Veracruz is a Caribbean city, home to the *jarocho* costume, dance and music, which features harps and guitars. The most famous dances, accompanied by the *conjunto jarocho* dressed in white, are the *bamba* and *zapateado*, with much stamping and lashing of feet related to the flamenco of Andalucía in Spain. Mexico's version of the Cuban *danzón* music and the *música tropical* add to the cultural richness. Many cultural events can be seen at the **Instituto Veracruzano de Cultura**, a few blocks from the Zócalo, which is a great place to relax with a good café and library.

Festivals and events

Veracruz *p519, maps p520 and 522*
Feb/Mar The **Shrovetide carnival** is said to be Mexico's liveliest. The carnival starts a week before **Shrove Tue** and ends on **Ash Wed**; Sat-Tue are the main days with parades. At this time of year it can be very difficult to find accommodation or transport.

Activities and tours

Veracruz *p519, maps p520 and 522*
Diving
Mundo Submarino, Camacho 3549, T229-980 6374, www.mundosubmarino.org. Day and night dives, snorkelling trips and various diving courses available, including PADI and NAUI certification.

Tour operators
Harbour tours and trips to the islands depart from the *malecón* every hour or so.

Amphibian, Lerdo 117, inside Hotel Colonial, T229-931 0997, www.amphibian veracruz.com. Adventure and eco-tours throughout the state of Veracruz, including birdwatching, hiking, rafting, diving, climbing and cycling, among others. English spoken. **Tranvías**, T229-817 3425. Musical trolley bus tours of the city, departing from the Zócalo every hour. Usually quite rowdy in the evenings.

⊖ Transport

Veracruz *p519, maps p520 and 522*
Air
Airport Las Bajadas (VER), 12 km from the centre, several flights daily to the capital and flights to coastal cities. Flights also to **Houston**, **San Antonio** and **Havana**.

Airline offices AeroMéxico, Bolívar No 952, T229-937 1765. **Mexicana**, Av 5 de Mayo y Aquiles Serdán, T229-932 2242.

Bus
Referred to as **ADO** the bus station is divided into 1st and 2nd class; the 1st-class part, mostly **ADO** company, is on the main street, Díaz Mirón y Xalapa, T229-938 2968; **Autobuses Unidos**, mostly 2nd class, is on Lafragua y Xalapa (2 blocks from ADO), T229-937 2376. Buses to the main bus station run along Av 5 de Mayo, marked **ADO**, US$0.50, or *colectivos*, also US$0.50. Taxi to **ADO** terminal from the centre, US$3.

The majority of buses are booked solid for 3 days in advance throughout summer and holiday periods; at other times queues of up to 2 hrs possible at Mexico City booking offices of bus companies (best company: ADO). Book outward journeys on arrival in Veracruz, as the bus station is some way out of town and there are often long queues.

To **Catemaco**, 9 daily, 3½ hrs, US$9. To **Córdoba**, every ½ hr, 1½ hrs, US$8. To **Mexico City**, hourly, 0600-0200, 5-6 hrs,
US$30. To **Mérida**, 4 daily, 14-18 hrs, US$59-71. To **Oaxaca**, 3 daily, 0800, 1515, 2230, 7 hrs, US$30. To **Orizaba**, every 30-60 mins, 2½ hrs, US$9. To **Papantla**, 6 daily, 4 hrs, US$13. To **Puebla**, 12 daily, 3½ hrs, US$18. To **San Andrés**, 14 daily, 3 hrs, US$8.50. To **Santiago Tuxtla**, 9 daily, 2½ hrs, US$8. To **Tampico**, every 1-2 hrs, 9½ hrs, US$30. To **Tapachula**, 2 daily, 1345 and 1830, 13-15 hrs, US$56. To **Tuxpan**, 13 daily, 6 hrs, US$17. To **Villahermosa**, 18 daily, 6-8½ hrs, US$30. To **Xalapa**, frequent, 24 hrs, 2 hrs, US$7.

❶ Directory

Veracruz *p519, maps p520 and 522*
Banks Bancomer, Independencia y Juárez, has *casa de cambio* for dollars and TCs, good rates, Mon-Fri 0930-1730, Sat-Sun 1100-1400. Banca Serfín, Díaz Mirón, 2 blocks from bus station, changes US$ cash and TCs. Banamex is at Independencia esq Juárez. **American Express** agency is Viajes Olymar, Blv Avila Camacho 2221, T229-931 3406. La Amistad, Juárez 112 (behind the hotels on the Zócalo), *casas de cambio* rates not as good as the banks but quicker; Hotel Veracruz changes money at similar rates. **Embassies and consulates** US Consular Agency, Francisco Javier Mina 506, T229-932 0227.
Internet Plenty to choose from in the downtown and tourist areas, US$0.50-1. Networld Café, Callejón Clavijero 173, near Francisco. Stationet, 5 de Mayo, between Lerdo and Zamora, Mon-Sat 0900-2100. Micro Café, Ruiz Cortines, 100 m on from Museo Agustín Lara, Mon-Sat 1000- 2300. **Laundry** Madero 616, US$4 per 3 kg, open 0730-2300. **Post office** Main post office by bridge to San Juan de Ulúa fortress, a fine building inaugurated in 1902 by Porfirio Díaz, Mon-Fri 0900-1200; also Palacio Federal, 5 de Mayo y Rayón, Mon-Fri 0800-1900.

North of Veracruz

North of Veracruz, the highway skirts a procession of windswept shores and low-key resorts, popular with Mexicans in holiday season but eerily desolate off-peak. Here, minor detours reward intrepid travellers with fascinating off-beat experiences. The ruins of the first Spanish settlement at Villa Rica, the ancient burial grounds of Quiahuitzlán, the little visited pre-Columbian city of El Pital, and a low-key turtle conservation project at Tecolutla – all are ignored by the mainstream. But continue north and you'll soon hit the Totonac heartland, marked by the colourful indigenous town of Papantla, where surviving traditions are the basis for a vivid and often teeming daily life. Perhaps no spectacle is as unforgettable as the traditional dance of the voladores, performed by four dancers who spiral down a pole on slowly twisting ropes. Resembling eagles in flight, there is no firm agreement about the symbolic meaning of the dance, although elements of its design closely correspond to the ancient Mesoamerican calendar. Nearby, at the pre-Hispanic ruins of El Tajín, the pyramid of the Niches also exhibits a reverence for time-keeping with 365 carved niches, one for each day of the year. Replete with vast ball courts and temples, El Tajín is one of Mexico's most fabulous archaeological sites, a UNESCO World Heritage Site and well worth a visit. ▸▸ *For listings, see pages 536-538.*

The coast road north ● ▸▸ *pp536-538.*

North of Chachalacas, Highway 180 skirts the often desolate coast, passing the crumbling ruins of **Villa Rica**, where Cortés is believed to have established Mexico's first Spanish settlement in 1519. It was abandoned for La Antigua some five years later. Today, there are foundations of a fortress, but little else. Nearby there is a beach, and a small church on **Cerro de la Cantera**. Around 3 km away, lies the ancient Totonac site of **Quiahuitzlán** ① *0830-1700, US$2*, largely a burial ground but also home to two pyramids. The ruins are quite isolated and offer great views of the ocean.

Nautla and around

Continuing north on Highway 180, the town of **Nautla** lies some 150 km from Veracruz; it's pleasant enough but there's little to do or see. Nearby, Route 131 branches inland to **Teziutlán** and en route passes **Tlapacoyan** on the mouth of the Río Bobos, from where you can go rafting or visit the archaeological site of **Filobobos** (see page 514).

El Pital, 15 km inland from the Gulf along the Nautla River, was identified early in 1994 as the site of an important, sprawling, pre-Columbian seaport (approximately AD 100-600), which lay hidden for centuries under thick rainforest. Now planted with bananas and oranges, the 100 or more pyramid mounds (some reaching 40 m in height) were assumed by plantation workers to be natural hills. Little excavation or clearing has yet been done, but both Teotihuacán-style and local-style ceramics and figurines have been discovered. Archaeologists believe El Pital may mark the principal end point of an ancient cultural corridor that linked the north central Gulf Coast with powerful urban centres in central Mexico. As at nearby El Tajín, ball courts have been discovered, along with stone fragments depicting what may be sacrificed ball players.

Just north of Nautla on Highway 180, the **Costa Esmeralda** is a rather desolate, windswept stretch of coast that's quite empty and abandoned off-season. You'll find good hotel deals at such times and will be able to enjoy some 20 km of rough grey sands all to yourself. During holidays, it's positively heaving.

Tecolutla

Tecolutla is a popular resort town perched on a river of the same name. Its main visitors tend to be Mexican families, although it can be refreshingly quiet off-season and during the week. The beaches here are quite good and there are various mangrove forests that can be explored by hiring a motorboat from the *embarcadero*. Turtle conservation is also blossoming with Fernando Manzano Cervantes of Vida Milenaria (T766-846 0467, http://201.116.18.153/vida), who is doing good work to protect the Kemp Ridley hatchlings. Volunteers are always needed April-May. You could also consult the **Tecolutla Turtle Preservation Project**, www.tecolutla-turtle-preservation-project.org, for more information. Tecolutla's best **fiesta** takes place two days before the carnival (February to March) in Veracruz and is recommended.

Papantla ⬤🅕🅞🅔🅒 ➤➤ *pp536-538. Colour map 2, B5.*

➤ *Phone code: 784.*

Some 40 km inland from Tecolutla is Papantla ('where banners abound'), built on the top of a hill overlooking the lush plains of northern Veracruz. It was the stronghold of a Totonac rebellion in 1836. Traditional Totonac dress is still worn: the men in baggy white trousers and sailor shirts and the women in lacy white skirts and shawls over embroidered blouses. Papantla is also the centre of one of the world's largest vanilla-producing zones, although production has decreased in recent years due to the proliferation of mass-produced synthetic vanilla. The vanilla is processed in **Gutiérrez Zamora**, a small town about 30 km east (close to Tecolutla), and a 'cream of vanilla' liqueur is also produced. The **Fiesta de la Vainilla** is held throughout the area in early June.

Ins and outs

The **tourist office** ① *Azueta 101, northwest of the Zócalo, T784-842 3837, Mon-Fri 0900- 1400, 1800- 2100,* is helpful, with good information, maps and bus schedules; English spoken.

Sights

The **Zócalo**, formally known as Plaza Téllez, is bordered by Enríquez on its downhill north edge; on the south uphill side the **Catedral de Nuestra Señora de la Asunción** (1700) has a remarkable 50-m-long mural on its northern wall called *Homenaje a la Cultura Totonaca*, by Teodoro Cano García (1979), with the plumed serpent Quetzalcoatl along its entire length. *Voladores* perform in the church courtyard each Sunday at 1100, and as many as three times daily during the colourful 10 days of **Corpus Christi** (late May or early June), along with games, fireworks, artistic exhibitions, dances and cockfights. For a sweeping view of the area, walk up Reforma to the top of the hill where the giant **Monumento al Volador** was erected in 1988. Murals and mosaic benches in the Zócalo also commemorate Totonac history and their conception of creation. Northeast of the plaza is the **Mercado Hidalgo** ① *20 de Noviembre, daily 0600-2000,* off the northwest corner of the Zócalo, where traditional handmade clothing is sold alongside fresh produce and livestock.

El Tajín ➤➤ *Colour map 2, B5.*

① *2 km from Papantla. Daily 0900-1700, except mid-Aug 0800-1900. US$3.50. There is a small modern museum, a cafetería and souvenir shops. In the wet season beware of a large, poisonous creature like a centipede. El Tajín can be visited either from Papantla (see page 532) or from Poza Rica (see page 536).*

The great city of El Tajín once covered approximately 1050 ha at the heart of which are four major groupings of structures: **Tajín proper** covers the valley floor; most of the major temples are located here. This is also the location of most of the carved and plain ball courts as well as ceremonial and market plazas. This area was the religious and commercial centre of the city. **Tajín Chico** is a huge terraced acropolis dominated by an elaborate multi-storeyed palace and administrative structures for the city's elite. The

El Tajín

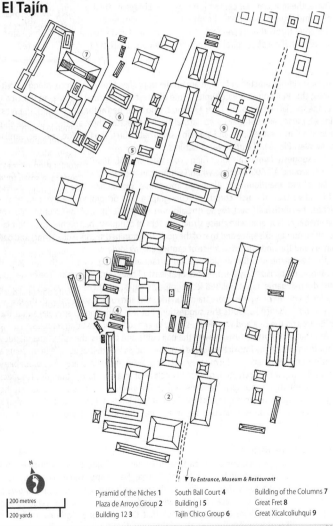

N

200 metres
200 yards

▼ **To Entrance, Museum & Restaurant**

Pyramid of the Niches **1**
Plaza de Arroyo Group **2**
Building 12 **3**

South Ball Court **4**
Building I **5**
Tajín Chico Group **6**

Building of the Columns **7**
Great Fret **8**
Great Xicalcoliuhqui **9**

The voladores of El Tajín

Traditionally, on Corpus Christi, Totonac rain dancers erect a 30-m mast with a rotating structure at El Tajín. Four *voladores* (flyers) and a musician climb to the top of the surmounting platform. There, the musician dances to his own pipe and drum music, while the roped *voladores* throw themselves into space to make a dizzy spiral descent, head first, to the ground. Each *voladore* makes 13 revolutions, symbolizing the 52-year cycle of the Aztec calendar.

Voladores are now in attendance at El Tajín every day during high season (other times just weekends), and fly if and when they think there are enough tourists (donations expected).

largest buildings erected at El Tajín are on the upper levels of Tajín Chico. Along with its Annex, the 'Building of the Columns' is the greatest architectural complex in the city. It was the special domain of the ruler 13 Rabbit, who governed at the city's zenith. The **West Ridge** is mostly an artificially tiered natural hill. The structures here are thought to be elite residences, modest temples and, perhaps, small ball courts. The **East Ridge** is very similar to the West Ridge but with fewer structures.

The suggested timescale for El Tajín's construction is AD 300-900, with a great surge of energy around AD 600, the time when Teotihuacán and Monte Albán were experiencing collapse and abandonment. Although impressive, the architecture of El Tajín is less informative than the rich corpus of iconography that decorated the Pyramid of the Niches, the North Ball Court, the South Ball Court and the Building of the Columns. Most of the imagery associated with these structures tells of conquest, ball games, the interplay between human existence and that of the gods, the dignified sacrifice of warriors and ball players and the undignified sacrifice of captive enemy lords.

The ball game was the single most important activity expressed in the imagery of El Tajín, as emphasized by the presence of at least 11 ball courts at the site. The obsession with the ball game and its related iconography suggests that the city was an immense academy where young men were trained in the skills and rules associated with the game. As yet, no evidence supports this suggestion, but it is tempting to speculate that the residences on the East and West Ridges were intended to house young trainees.

Associated almost exclusively with the ball game and players, the cult of the maguey plant (from which the intoxicant *pulque* is made) and *pulque* deities at El Tajín presents a puzzle, perplexing because the *maguey* will not grow in the general area. The probability is that the city was the creation of a small enclave of Huastecs rather than the Totonacs who then inhabited and still inhabit the region. The *maguey* proliferates throughout the Highlands, and in the mythology of the Central Highlands it was a Huastec who drank more than the stipulated four cups, became drunk, stripped naked and had to return in disgrace to his homeland.

Pyramid of the Niches

The form of the pyramid, one of the earliest structures at El Tajín, is very distinctive, and said to have 365 niches, one for each day of the year. Dated approximately AD 600, it is crowned with a sanctuary that was lined with engraved panels, one of which shows a cacao plant bearing fruit. Cacao was precious and of great commercial value to the people of the area. There is some evidence that the rulers of El Tajín controlled its

Human sacrifice at El Tajín

The ferocity of the Spanish Conquest of Mexico was due in part to the abhorrence felt by the invaders at the Aztec practice of human sacrifice. Since then, the Aztecs have received a very bad press. However, human sacrifice was practised in Mesoamerica long before the Aztecs arrived in the Valley of Mexico. Probably nowhere else in this vast area that is now Mexico are there such explicit representations of lives being offered to the gods or to glorify the omnipotence of a ruler than at El Tajín.

cultivation in the zones surrounding the site. Another trapezoidal panel depicts a priest or ruler adorned with ball game accoutrements and holding a knife ready to perform a ritual sacrifice, the scene being set within the confines of a ball court. The depiction of a skull at the foot of the executioner indicates sacrifice by decapitation.

North Ball Court

The imagery of the North Ball Court is only partially understood. Most of the problems associated with this zone derive from erosion and mutilation of the engravings. Men in bat costumes are a major theme in these panels and suggest influence from the Maya region where men dressed in this way were common images on ceramics of the Classic period. Also present in the North Ball Court is the imagery of the ball game and human sacrifice.

South Ball Court

The South Ball Court offers a fascinating glimpse into the philosophy that underpinned the whole ritual life of El Tajín. Central to the narrative is the role of the ball player who acts as an intermediary between this world and that of the gods. In the engravings, the ball player is presented to the executioner and decapitated while the gods look on. Two of the panels are bordered with the image of a laughing *pulque* deity with two bodies, and there are many Venus symbols. The death god, Mitlantecuhtli, emerges from an urn of *pulque*, and many of the known gods of the Mesoamerican pantheon are represented. In some of the painted books of the Central Highlands, the powerful gods Quetzalcoatl and Tezcatlipoca oppose each other in a ball game; at El Tajín, it is possible that the human players represented the earthly aspects of these gods. The imagery of the engravings of the South Ball Court is extremely complex, but it does imply that, through the ball game, humans can approach the realm of the gods by means of the decapitation of the principal players.

Tajín Chico

The Building of the Columns is another area with a very complex iconographical narrative. However, while the iconography of the South Ball Court expresses a communion between gods and men, the iconography of the Building of the Columns refers to themes that are much more mundane. The focus of attention is the ruler 13 Rabbit, whose glyph is repeated many times on the surface of the column drums, always with the image of a rabbit and the number 13 expressed by two bars, each counting as five, and three dots. 13 Rabbit had clearly been on a conquest campaign because a number of prisoners are lined up in preparation for the decapitation ritual. They have been divested of almost all their clothes and thus divested of their dignity. They are named by glyphs above or near their persons, which indicates that they were chiefs of opposing polities; the common warrior was rarely identified by name. Whereas the warrior/ball player of the South Ball Court approached his death with calm dignity, the prisoners of the Building of the Columns are forced toward the sacrificial block, some held by the hair. Two sacrificial sequences but two very different approaches to death. The narrative of 13 Rabbit is now in the site museum. Although seen and depicted as all-powerful, 13 Rabbit was not omnipotent enough to prevent the destruction of the city and probably the State of El Tajín, which occurred shortly after the engraving of the Building of the Columns was completed. The great centre of the ball game, like so many others, perished, but at whose hands has yet to be discovered.

Poza Rica and beyond ⊜❶❷❸❹❺ ▶ *pp536-538. Colour map 2, B5.*

→ *Phone code: 782.*

Some 21 km northwest of Papantla, **Poza Rica** is a pretty ugly oil city formed out of four old *rancherías*, which happened to lie on top of the then second largest oil strike in the world. It has an old cramped wooden market and a simple mural by O'Higgins, *From Primitive Prehispanic Agricultural Works to the Present Day Oil Industry Development* (1959) on the outside of the **Palacio Municipal**. The **tourist office** ① *T782-822 1390 ext 129*, is at the back of the Palacio Municipal on the ground floor.

From Poza Rica you can head north to visit the **Castillo de Teayo**, a pyramid with the original sanctuary and interesting carvings on top (buses run every 30 minutes and you will need to change halfway).

Tuxpan

Slung over a wide, slow-moving river, the provincial town of Tuxpan lies north of Poza Rica and is a useful supply stop en route to Tampico and Mexico's northeast. It has a languid atmosphere that is somehow reminiscent of the state's most hedonistic port town, Veracruz. Friendly and lightly decaying, but with little to actually see, Tuxpan's main attraction is the **Museo de La Amistad México-Cuba** ① *Obregón s/n, 0900-1900, free*, with displays on the long-standing friendship between Mexico and Cuba. There is a beach, 12 km east of town, and diving in offshore reefs between May and August. The **tourist office** ① *Palacio Municipal, Mon-Fri 0900-1900*, is very friendly, helpful and welcoming to visitors.

⊚ North of Veracruz listings

For Sleeping and Eating price codes and other relevant information, see Essentials pages 47-51.

⊜ Sleeping

Nautla *p531*

Camping Torre Molino trailer park, 16 km from Nautla on coastal Route 180 (towards Veracruz). Electricity, sewage disposal, hot showers, pool, on beach. Recommended.

Tecolutla *p532*
D Casa de Huéspedes Malena,
Av Carlos Prieto. Pleasant, clean rooms.

E Los Buhos, close to the beach. Very good rooms with hot shower and TV.

Papantla *p532*

C El Tajín, Nuñez y Dominguez 104, T784-842 0121, hoteltajin@hotmail.com. Clean, straightforward rooms with hot water, cable TV, a/c and writing desks. The rooms with 2 beds are better. Services include parking, 2 restaurants and a recreation centre with pool. Drinking water and room service available.
C Totonocapan, 20 de Noviembre y Olivo, T784-842 1220, www.hotelsenpapantla.com. Clean and fine, with hot water, TV, a/c and

bar/restaurant. Some rooms have interesting views. Good value.

D-E Pulido, Enriquez 205, T784-842 0036. Basic, Spartan lodgings with hot water and parking. Cheaper rooms have fan (**E**), others have cable TV and a/c (**D**). Long-term stay available, if for some strange reason you should require it.

E México, Obispo de Las Casas y Núñez (opposite **Cine Tajín**), T784-842 0086. Basic. One of the cheapest in town.

Poza Rica p536

A Poza Rica, 2 Norte, between 10 and 12 Ote, T782-822 0112. A friendly Best Western with reliable service and fairly comfortable rooms. Good restaurant.

C-D Salinas, Blv Ruiz Cortines 1905 y Cazones, T782-822 0706. Good rooms with a/c and TV. Services include restaurant, pool and secure parking.

D Nuevo León, Av Colegio Militar, T782-822 0528, opposite market. Spacious rooms, fairly clean and quiet. Recommended.

E Fénix, 6 Norte, near Av Central Ote, T782-822 3572. Basic, but one of the better cheap places.

Camping Trailer Park Quinta Alicia, Km 84, T232-321 0042. Very clean, plenty of shade in the palms. Helpful and friendly.

Tuxpan p536

B May Palace, Juárez 44, T783-834 4461. A modern hotel with 76 clean, straight-forward rooms with tiled floors, cable TV, hot water and phone. Services include internet, restaurant, parking and pool. Some rooms have good views.

B Sara, Garizuerieta 44, T783-834 0010, www.hotelsaratuxpanver.com.mx. A modern, 5-floor structure with a good rooftop pool and restaurant. Rooms are clean and comfortable.

D California, Arteaga 16, T783-834 0879. Terracotta walls and reasonable rooms with bath, simple furniture, TV and a/c (or fan). There's also a laundry service, restaurant, taxis and parking.

D Posada del Sol, Guerrero 31, T783-835 4697. Clean, comfortable rooms in pastel shades and some other pleasant, decorative touches. Quiet.

D San Ignacio, Ocampo 29, T783-834 2905. Adorned in colourful paintwork, this pleasant little hotel has an attractive garden and good rooms with cable TV, hot water and fan. Some of the beds are a bit lumpy, but otherwise a good deal.

🍴 Eating

Papantla p532

Lots of little locals' places to explore.

†††-†† Mesón del Quijote, Serdán 700. Smartish place with good wines and spirits, steaks, cuts, paella and salmon. Well staffed, tidy and clean.

††-† El Totonaco, Hotel Tajín, Nuñez y Dominguez 104. Buffet breakfasts every day for US$5 and an à la carte menu that includes spaghetti, *milanesa* and *mariscos*. A nice, clean restaurant. The hotel's other restaurant, El Parroquia, is also good, serving meat, fajitas and Mexican fare.

††-† Sorrento, Zócalo. Covered in decorative tiles and serving good, cheap seafood and *comida corrida*. Recommended.

† Taquería del Parque, Artes y Azuela. Open-front joint serving tacos and Mexican fast food.

Poza Rica p536

† Café Manolo, 10 Ote 60 y 6 Norte. Good breakfast.

† Lonchería El Petrolero, Plaza Cívica 18 de Marzo y Av Central Ote. Excellent bread baked on the premises, popular with locals.

Tuxpan p536

††-† Sabor Huasteca, Zócalo. Nice spot on the plaza serving regional cuisine such as *tamales huastecos* and *enchiladas de baile*. Since 1948.

† Las Palomas, Ocampo y Lerdo de Tejado. Friendly, economical eatery with outside seating. Serves breakfasts and Mexican staples with a smile.

⊖ Transport

Papantla p532
Bus
ADO terminal, Juárez 207, 5 blocks from the centre, T228-842 0218.

Local Many services to local destinations, including El Tajín, buses leave when full. Occasional minibus to El Tajín from south-west corner of the Zócalo, unreliable schedule about every 1-1½ hrs. Transportes Urbano- TUSPA buses for El Tajín leave from office on 16 de Septiembre near Obispo de las Casas (US$0.50).

Long distance To Mexico City (Norte), 6 daily, US$19, 6 hrs. To Poza Rica, hourly, 45 mins, US$1.70. To Tuxpan, 7 daily, 2 hrs, US$5. To Veracruz, 6 daily, 4 hrs, US$13. To Xalapa, 11 daily, 4½ hrs, US$15.

Taxi
Taxi rank on Enríquez between 5 de Mayo and the Zócalo; and on Juárez.

Poza Rica p536
Air
Airport El Tajín, 3 km south of Poza Rica, T782-822 2119; several flights daily to Mexico City.

Airline offices Aeromar, T782-824 3001. AeroMéxico, Av 6 Norte No 8, 1st floor, Local 102, Edif Anabel, T01-800-021-4010.

Bus
Local To El Tajín, buses leave every 20-30 mins, 0700-2000, from behind Monumento de la Madre statue, marked 'Chote' or 'Chote Tajín'. Ask driver for 'Las Ruinas', US$0.50, 20-25 mins, most go to the entrance. To Barra de Cazones, Transportes Papantla or Autotransportes Cazones, 1 hr, US$1.20 (often waits 30 mins in Cazones on the way back until bus fills). It is not always necessary to go to bus station to catch your bus: buses to Barra de Cazones pass through the centre along Blv Cortines.

Long distance All buses leave from the new terminal referred to as ADO, about 1½ km from centre. Take a white bus from the centre, or a

taxi (US$2-3). The terminal is divided into ADO (T782-822 0085, also office in centre, 6 Norte opposite Hotel Fénix, open daily) and all others companies. There are good facilities including a tourist office.

To Mexico City, almost hourly, 5 hrs, US$17. To Tampico, every ½ hr, 4-5 hrs, US$20. To Pachuca, 0250 and 1340, 4½ hrs, US$11. To Papantla, almost hourly, 1 hr, US$1.70, bus may be caught on Av Central Ote by Plaza Cívico 18 de Marzo. To Tecolutla, 7 daily, 1¾ hrs, US$4. To Tuxpan, hourly, 1 hr, US$1.70. To Veracruz, hourly, 4-5 hrs, US$15. To Xalapa, 15 daily, 4-5 hrs, US$16.

Tuxpan p536
Tuxpan has several bus terminals. Estrella Blanca is out of the centre at Alemán y Constitución. ADO is on Rodriguez, close to the riverbank. Omnibus de México is at Herloes y Clavijero, close to the bridge and on the riverbank.

To Mexico City (Norte), 11 daily, 6½ hrs, US$20. To Poza Rica, hourly, 1 hr, US$1.70. To Tampico, hourly, 3½ hrs, US$15. To Veracruz, 13 daily, 6 hrs, US$17. To Xalapa, 7 daily, 6 hrs, US$18

⊕ Directory

Papantla p532
Banks Bancomer and Banamex, on the Zócalo, 0900-1300, change cash and TCs till 1200. **Medical services** Hospital Civil, Madero 518, T784-842 0094. Red Cross, T842-0126. Farmacia Aparicio, Enríquez 103, daily 0700- 2200. **Post office** Azueta 198, 2nd floor, Mon-Fri 0900-1300, 1500-1800, Sat 0900-1200.

Poza Rica p536
Banks Bancomer, opposite Hotel Poza Rica. Serfín, 4 Norte y 2 Ote. **Laundry** Yee del Centro, Prolongación 20 de Noviembre. **Medical services** Cruz Roja, Blv Lázaro Cárdenas 106, T782-823 6871.

Southern Veracruz State

Several decades ago, tracts of dense, impassable rainforest consumed the southernmost stretches of Veracruz state, barely penetrated by roads or humanity. Only a few obscure settlements lay hidden in the miles of ravenous foliage, teeming canopies and bursting vegetation skirting the gulf. Today, southern Veracruz is a less dramatic land of rolling cattle pastures, remote highways and terminally poor, sluggish villages, but you can still encounter vestiges of that dark world of old: crocodile-infested lagoons, jungle shrouded rivers, isolated beaches, abundant bird life and luxuriant swimming holes all punctuate the deep green – and stiflingly humid – tropical landscape. Near Veracruz, the lesser visited Papaloapan region is replete with remote villages and brightly painted towns such as Tlacotalpan – a beautiful port that has now faded into quiet obscurity. Further south Los Tuxtlas – comprising diminutive Santiago Tuxtla and the more bustling San Andrés Tuxtla – are steeped in off-beat provincial charm, offering access to the mysterious Olmec ruins of Tres Zapotes, local waterfalls and cigar factories. At nearby Catemaco, perched on the shores of an expansive lake, the lore of traditional witchcraft is widely revered. Today, many consider the age-old art of brujería little more than superstitious ramblings, but there's no denying its fascinating cultural significance – or its strange effectiveness on those who believe in it. ►► *For listings, see pages 545-548.*

Papaloapan region ⬤🚻🏕⛰🚌🎒 ►► *pp545-548. Colour map 2, C5/C6.*

Route 180 heads southeast from the port of Veracruz along the flat, wet coastal plain through Alvarado and on the Tuxtla mountains and the Isthmus of Tehuantepec. An alternative route is to turn inland through the fertile Papaloapan region and on south into the State of Oaxaca.

Puerto Alvarado

Puerto Alvarado, a modern fishing port 1½ hours south from Veracruz by bus, is none too pleasant for women on their own as there are many bars and drunks. Crossing the Río Papaloapan ('Butterfly River') by a toll bridge along Route 180 leads to the sugar-cane area around Lerdo de Tejada and Angel R Cavada. At **El Trópico** shop a dirt road turns left to some quiet beaches such as **Salinas** and **Roca Partida**.

Tlacotalpan → *Colour map 2, C6. Phone code: 288.*

About 15 km from Alvarado, Route 175 crosses the over the Río Papaloapan at Buenavista, and heads southwards to the town of Tlacotalpan where the Papaloapan and San Juan rivers meet. This small town, once the main town in southern Veracruz, and an important international port in the steamship era, is regarded as the centre of Jarocho culture. It has many picturesque streets with one-storey houses all fronted by stuccoed columns and arches painted in bright colours. The fusion of Spanish and Caribbean traditions are preserved as a UNESCO World Heritage Site. There are two churches in the Zócalo, the **Parroquia de San Cristóbal** and the **Capilla de la Candelaria**, and a **Casa de las Artesanías** ⓘ *Chazaro, 1½ blocks from the Zócalo.* The **Museo Salvador Ferrando** ⓘ *US$1.50,* contains interesting local 19th-century paintings, furniture, artefacts and Jarocho costume. In honour of Tlacotalpan's most famous son, the **Casa Museo Agustín Lara** ⓘ *Beltrán 6, Mon-Sat 1000-1730, US$1.20,* features exhibitions on the legendary musician Agustín Lara. The **Casa de la Cultura Agustín Lara** ⓘ *Carranza 43, 0900-1700,* hosts cultural events and art exhibitions. If you fancy exploring the nearby lagoon, you

The Papaloapan dams

The river basin drained by the Papaloapan and its tributaries covers 47,000 sq km, about twice the size of the Netherlands, and is subject to a programme of regional development by the Comisión del Papaloapan. Two large dams, Miguel Alemán and Cerro de Oro, were built to control the sometimes severe flooding of the lower basin. The dams have formed a very large joint lake, which is quite scenic; the northwestern shore and islands were declared a nature reserve, Parque Natural Laguna de Temascal. A first phase of the Temascal hydroelectric plant by the Presa Alemán was completed in 1959, generating 154 megawatts, a second phase completed in 1996, generates an additional 200 megawatts.

should be able to hire a boatman from the *malecón*. The **tourist office** ① *T884-2050, Mon-Fri 0800-1400, 1500-1900, Sat and Sun 1000-1400,* is on the main plaza.

Cosamaloapan

Cosamaloapan, some 40 km beyond Tlacotalpan on Route 175, is the local market centre with a number of hotels, and the staging point for most bus lines from Veracruz, Orizaba and Oaxaca. One of the largest sugar mills in Mexico is situated just outside town – **Ingenio San Cristóbal**. From Cosamaloapan to Papaloapan the banks on either side of the river are lined with fruit trees. **Chacaltianguis**, a small town on the east bank of the river (reached by car ferry), has houses fronted by columns.

Otatitlán

Another 40 km, beyond Cosamaloapan, is a ferry to Otatitlán, also on the east bank of the river (US$0.25, leaves when enough people). The town, also known as 'El Santuario', dates back to early colonial times. Its houses have tiled roofs supported by columns, but most interesting is the church. The priest maintains that the gold-patterned dome is the largest unsupported structure of its kind in Mexico, measuring 20 m wide and 40 m high. Otatitlán has one of three black statues of Christ brought over from Spain for the son of Hernán Cortés. During the anti-clerical violence of the 1930s, attempts to burn it failed, although the original head was cut off and now stands in a glass case. The first weekend in May is the saint's day and fair, for which pilgrims flock from the sierra and from the Tuxtlas, many in local dress.

Tuxtepec

This is the natural place for a stay in the Papaloapan area. It is an important supply centre within the State of Oaxaca, a large commercial city, untouristy and tranquil; prices here are lower than in other parts of Oaxaca. The region has significant agricultural activity with local industries including a sugar mill, brewery and paper mill. The people of Tuxtepec consider themselves more *jarochos* (ie from the State of Veracruz) than *oaxaqueños*; the mixture of the music and exuberance of Veracruz with the food and handicrafts of Oaxaca is fascinating.

The city is built into a bend of the Río Santo Domingo. Avenida Independencia runs along the riverfront and has the market, shops and several *miradors* with good views. A small ferry crosses the river from below the viewpoint next to **Hotel Mirador**. **Parque Benito Juárez**, the main plaza, has a monument to the mother and child, an ample **Palacio Municipal** to the south, and a **modern cathedral** to the east. Further west is **Parque Hidalgo**, with a statue of the father of Mexico's Independence. The modern **Casa**

de la Cultura is on Daniel Soto by Bulevar Benito Juárez. The **tourist office** ① *Cámara Nacional de Comercio Serytour, Libertad esq Allende, opposite Parque Benito Juárez, T287-875 0886, Mon-Fri 0900-1400, 1700-2000, Sat 0900-1300*, has limited information.

Around Tuxtepec

The **Presa Miguel Alemán**, a lake formed by the Miguel Alemán and Cerro de Oro dams, is very scenic. There are several points of access, the most widely used being that of **Temascal**, a small town near the Alemán dam, with shops and a few places to eat.

The road west of Tuxtepec towards the State of Puebla is quite scenic; along it are a number of towns and villages that maintain an indigenous flavour, *huípiles* and crafts can be found here, especially on market day. The road is paved as far as **Jalapa de Díaz** and then continues to **San Bartolomé Ayautla** and **Huautla de Jiménez**.

San Lucas Ojitlán is a Chinantec town, 42 km from Tuxtepec, with a hilltop church dominating the surroundings. It is an important regional centre and its Sunday market gathers many people from the nearby villages; this is the best time to see Chinantec women wearing their huipiles.

Jalapa de Díaz is 70 km from Tuxtepec, near the base of Cerro Rabón, a mountain with a spectacular 500-m sheer cliff face. The town is built on several small hills, with the church on the highest. The population is mainly Mazatec, the women wear colourful *huipiles*, which may be purchased in shops and homes.

Tuxtepec to Oaxaca

The road from Tuxtepec to Oaxaca, Route 175, is a spectacular steep and winding route, cars need good brakes and it is reported to be difficult for caravans and cyclists; the latter are recommended to take a bus. It is mostly a paved road, but sections near the high passes can at times be badly potholed. The ride up from Tuxtepec to Oaxaca takes 6-7 hours, a bit less in the opposite direction. From Tuxtepec, 30 m above sea level, the road climbs gradually to Valle Nacional (see below). Just after crossing the Río Valle Nacional it climbs steeply into the **Sierra Juárez**, reaching the **El Mirador pass** (2900 m) in 2½ hours. The transition from lush lowland forest to pines is splendid, there are lovely views of the ridges and valley far below. From here the road drops in two hours to **Ixtlán de Juárez** and **San Pablo Guelatao**, the birthplace of Benito Juárez (gas station, restaurants). The route continues to drop to the dry valley of the Río Manzanillo, at 1500 m, before climbing again to **La Cumbre pass** (2700 m), from which there are fine views of Oaxaca below, one hour further.

Valle Nacional → *Colour map 2, C5. Altitude: 60 m.*

Set in the beautiful valley of the Río Valle Nacional, 48 km south of Tuxtepec, the small town of Valle Nacional sees few visitors, but offers basic services and excellent opportunities for birdwatching and walking in the surrounding hills. The town is laid out along the main road; there is a fuel station at the Tuxtepec end. Nearby are several rubber plantations (for example just across the bridge on the road to Oaxaca) and tappers may be seen at work early in the morning, especially in the dry season. The area had a horrific reputation as the 'Valle de los Miserables' in the era of Porfirio Díaz, for political imprisonment and virtual slavery.

Along the scenic Tuxtepec–Valle Nactional road are also several recreational opportunities, including **Chiltepec**, a popular bathing spot on the Río Valle Nacional, 22 km from Tuxtepec. Not far from Valle Nacional is a lovely natural spring at **Zuzul**. The setting, by the Soloyapan river and the town of **Sola de Vega**, is very pretty; although the water is chilly, it is a pleasant spot for swimming.

Los Tuxtlas ⬤🌳💧⬤ ▸▸ pp545-548. Colour map 2, C6.

Back on the coastal Route 180, southeast of Alvarado and the Papaloapan, is **Tula** where there is a spectacular waterfall, **El Salto de Tula**; a restaurant is set beside the falls. The road then climbs up into the mountainous volcanic area of Los Tuxtlas, known as 'the Switzerland of Mexico' for its mountains and perennial greenness.

Santiago Tuxtla → Colour map 2, C6. Phone code: 294.

This pleasant town of colonial origin is set on a river. In the main square is the largest known Olmec head, carved in solid stone, and the **Museo Tuxtleco** ① Mon-Sat 0900-1800, Sun 0900-1500, US$2.50, tourist information available, containing examples of local tools, photos, items used in brujería (witchcraft), the first sugar-cane press used in Mexico and another Olmec head. There is dancing to jarana bands in the Christmas fortnight. In June and July, dancers wear jaguar masks to perform the danza de los liseres.

Tres Zapotes

Travellers with plenty of time, could also consider a trip to the archaeological site of Tres Zapotes, to the west of Santiago Tuxtla. It is reached by leaving the paved road south towards Villa Isla and taking the dirt road at Tres Caminos (signposted); this route is only possible in the dry season as the road turns into a quagmire May-December. In the wet season, access can be slowly achieved by turning right at about Km 40, called Tibenal, and following the dirt road north to the **museum** ① daily 0900-1700, US$2 (if it is closed, the lady in the nearby shop has a key). The site, once the centre of the Olmec culture, is a 1-km walk (the bus cannot reach Tres Zapotes if rain has swollen the river that the road has to cross). At the museum, there is an Olmec head, also the largest carved stela ever found and stela fragments bearing the New World's oldest Long Count Date, equal to 31 BC. In this region of Mexico there are other Olmec sites at **Cerro de las Mesas**, **Laguna de los Cerros** and **San Lorenzo Tenochtitlán**.

San Andrés Tuxtla → Colour map 2, C6. Phone code: 294.

A further 15 km beyond Santiago lies San Andrés Tuxtla, the largest town of the area, with narrow winding streets, bypassed by a ring road. It has a well-stocked market with Oaxacan foods such as carne enchilada (spicy meat) and tamales de elote (cakes of maize-flour steamed in leaves). It is the centre of the cigar trade. One factory beside the main road permits visitors to watch the process and will produce special orders of puros (cigars) marked with an individual's name. The **tourist office** is at the Palacio Municipal.

Catemaco ⬤🌳⛺⬤⬤ ▸▸ pp545-548. Colour map 2, C6.

→ Phone code: 294.

Catemaco, 13 km from San Andrés, is a town famed for its traditional brujos (sorcerers) who have become a great tourist attraction. The first Friday of March sees a grand convention in their honour, but generally they are too slippery to be recommended (see box opposite). The town is pleasant enough, although not especially good-looking, and in many respects is rather isolated and economically depressed. Popular with holidaying Mexicans, it has a large colonial church and a picturesque setting on a lake. The surrounding forests and hills are lush with humidity and tropical vegetation where abundant birdlife can be spotted.

A kind of magic: sorcerers and swindlers of Catemaco

The magical traditions of Catemaco – which include pacts with the devil and a belief in mysterious animal doubles – were born out of necessity. Historically divorced from the outside world, the area's inhabitants learned to rely wholly on local remedies – the multitude of exotic plants, roots, fruits and barks supplied by the rainforest – which were far easier to acquire (and often more effective) than conventional medicines.

A culture of shamanism flourished, which many consider indistinct from brujería or witchcraft. The traditional brujo, or sorcerer, was widely revered as a 'Man of Knowledge', conversant not only with plants and medicines, but with nature's unseen spiritual forces. He was a creature of two worlds – the physical and non-physical – as well as a custodian of great secrets, an initiate in astonishing mysteries, and an emissary to weird lands.

Brujería continues to be widely practised in Catemaco today. Every year on 1 March a cavalcade of sorcerers, healers and conjurers descends upon the town in an event reminiscent of some Dark Age gathering. They perform dramatic public limpiezas (cleansings), cast spells, swap potions and engage in endless theatrics. Originally intended as a knowledge-sharing convention for the region's healers, it has now become a major tourist event with much posturing and angling.

Outside of the occasion, Catemaco's widespread fame means many of its sorcerers are now more interested in financial gain than genuine spirituality. As such, present-day brujos are pale imitations of their forebears – little more than skilled manipulators practising psychological magic on gullible believers. After all, faking your credentials is much easier than a lengthy – and potentially life-threatening – magical apprenticeship.

If you're curious about visiting a brujo, guard your wallet, don't get roped into expensive ceremonies (regardless of what they may tell you about your health) and be careful to choose one with humble lodgings – material wealth is rarely a sign of spiritual advancement. Be aware too that Catemaco's unique brand of sorcery is a hybrid creature that lacks the integrity of unbroken tradition. An eclectic mix of New Age mysticism, Mexican shamanism, Cuban Santería and many other schools of magical thought, it's hard to discern much value in the mish-mash of competing superstitions.

Some commentators have postulated that magic of this kind may act as a kind of psychotherapy for those who believe in it, healing the mind through shared unconscious symbols and rituals. But if you don't believe – or more crucially, if your unconscious lacks the same cultural elements as the magical system you're using – a trip to a brujo is likely to be a matter of theatrics. Expect an interesting performance and don't take their claims too seriously, good or bad.

Sights

There are several lakeside beaches where you can relax. At Easter, you might also be able to camp, however, for most of the year it is not recommended because of the potential for assaults and robberies. **Playa Espagoya** is the nearest, around 1 km east out of town on Avenida Hidalgo. Watch out for crocodiles if you choose to swim. Boat trips are a popular activity and you will be vociferously solicited for trade every time you walk down the waterfront malecón. Typical excursions go to the **shrine** where the Virgin 'miraculously' appeared, the spa at **Coyamé**, and the **Isla de los Monos**, which is home to a colony of macaque monkeys introduced from Thailand for the University of Veracruz. Launches to the island charge US$12.50, or you can pay US$3.20 to be rowed there by local fishermen (cheaper and more peaceful). You will also find an eco-tourism kiosk on the *malecón* with helpful information on visiting the forests. The *malecón* becomes crowded with drunks in the evening, so women should avoid it after dark.

Some of the town's most famous *brujos* belong to the **Gueixpal family** ① *Hidalgo 2, www.brujogueixpal.com, by advance appointment*, who own the big blue house and various properties in the area. Many other sorcerers can be sought out in the markets. Take care consulting any *brujo*, as prices are likely to vary according to your perceived wealth. A simple 'cleansing' might cost US$5-20, more involved ceremonies run into hundreds or thousands of dollars. Some *brujos* are also very predatory and manipulative (see box, page 543, for more advice on consulting a *brujo*).

Around Catemaco
The **Reserva Ecológica Nanciyaga** ① *7 km round the northern shore of the lake, T294-943 0808*, has rainforest with rich birdlife, including toucans. The film *Medicine Man*, with Sean Connery, was filmed using the ecological park as a 'jungle' backdrop.

Catemaco to Playa Hermosa
The Gulf coast may be reached from Catemaco along an 18-km road to **Sontecomapan**, crossing over the pass at Buena Vista and looking down to the *laguna* where, it is said, Francis Drake sought refuge. The village of Sontecomapan lies on an entry to the *laguna* and boats may be hired for the 20-minute ride out to the bar where the *laguna* meets the sea. A large part of the lagoon is surrounded by mangrove swamp, and the sandy beaches, edged by cliffs, are almost deserted except for local fishermen and groups of pelicans. Beaches, such as **Jicacal** and **Playa Hermosa**, are accessible to those who enjoy isolation.

Coatzacoalcos, Minatitlán and around ●●❼ ➤➤ *pp545-548. Colour map 2, C6.*
➔ *Phone codes: Coatzacoalcos 921, Minatitlán 922.*
The road from Catemaco heads south to **Acayucan** then east to **Minatitlán** and **Coatzacoalcos**. The latter is the Gulf coast gateway for the Yucatán Peninsula, 1½ km from the mouth of its wide river. It is hot, humid and lacking in culture. The beach is dangerous at nights, do not sleep there or loiter. **Minatitlán**, the oil and petrochemical centre, is 39 km upriver. The road between the two towns carries very heavy industrial traffic and both cities are often under a pall of smog. There is a high incidence of lung disease. Not many foreigners visit either town, but there are hotels and restaurants in both places should you choose to stay.

Acayucan, at the junction of Highway 180 and 185, makes a great place to stop if you're driving from Mexico City to points south. There's not a great deal to do, apart from wander the streets, watch the municipal game of basketball, log on in an internet café, or watch a movie, but it's a decent town.

About 40 km east of Coatzacoalcos, on a side road off Route 180 is **Agua Dulce**, where there is a campground (see Sleeping, page 546). Further east along the Gulf coast is **Sánchez Magallanes** (turn off Route 180 at Las Piedras, 70 km from Coatzacoalcos, signposted), a pleasant, friendly town where you can camp safely on the beach.

For Sleeping and Eating price codes and other relevant information, see Essentials pages 47-51.

Sleeping

Tlacotalpan *p539*

C Posada Doña Lala, Carranza 11, T288-884 2580, www.hoteldonalala.com. Centrally located on the Zócalo, this hotel has comfortable rooms with a/c and TV, cheaper with fan. A good restaurant too.

C Tlacotalpan, R Beltrán 35, T/F288-884 2063, hoteltlacoptalpan@tlaco.com.mx. Clean, good-value rooms around a central courtyard, with bath and a/c. There's also a restaurant.

E Reforma, Carranza 2 (sometimes known as Viajero), T288-884 2022. Good budget lodgings, if a little grubby. Some rooms have good views.

E-F Jarocho, Carranza 22. Seedy, but large rooms in an old house. A good view of town from the roof.

Tuxtepec *p540*

C El Rancho, Avila Camacho 435, T287-875 0722, elrancho@prodigy.net.mx. Rooms with a/c. Services include pool, restaurant, parking. Recommended.

C Hacienda, Blv Benito Juárez 409, T287-875 1500. A/c, restaurant, pool, gardens, parking.

C-D Playa Bruja, Independencia 1531, T287-875 0325. With a/c, pool, cafeteria and parking.

D María de Lourdes, 5 de Mayo 1380, T287-875 0410. A/c, cheaper with fan, hot water, good parking. Recommended.

D-E Tuxtepec, Matamoros 2 corner of Independencia, T287-875 0934. A/c or fan, hot water, restaurant, good value. Recommended.

E-F Casa de Huéspedes Ocampo, Ocampo 285 y Libertad. With bath, fan, friendly.

F Catedral, Guerrero, near the Zócalo, T287-875 0764. Very friendly, fan and shower.

Santiago Tuxtla *p542*

C Castellanos, on Plaza, T294-947 0300. Clean, comfortable rooms with hot shower. There's a pool too. Recommended.

D Estancia Olmeca, No 78 on main highway just north of ADO office, T294-947 0737. Clean and friendly, with parking.

E Morelos, Obregón 13 and Morelos, T294-947 0474. Family-run, quiet and nicely furnished.

San Andrés Tuxtla *p542*

Expect good reductions in low season.

B Del Parque, Madero 5, T294-942 0198, www.hoteldelparque.com. The best place in town. Del Parque has comfortable rooms with a/c, cable TV, phone, bath and Wi-Fi. Very clean, with a good restaurant too.

C De los Pérez, Rascón 2, T294-942 0777. A newish hotel with clean, comfortable rooms, Wi-Fi, parking and a/c.

D Posada San José, Belisario Domínguez 10, T294-942 1010, close to the plaza. Run by a lovely family and staff, this hotel has comfortable rooms with cable TV, hot water and a/c, restaurant and pick-up truck for excursions, as well as a 2nd hotel at Monte Pío. Rooms with fans are slightly cheaper.

D San Andrés, Madero 6, just off the plaza, T294-942 0604. The economical rooms here aren't bad. They're clean and equipped with a/c and cable TV, slightly cheaper with fan. The restaurant is OK and has Wi-Fi. Parking.

E Figueroa, Pino Suárez 10, T294-942 0257. In better shape than its neighbour (see below), Figueroa has straightforward rooms with hot water, fan and cable TV, just 1, a triple, has a/c (**A**). Parking and tourist information.

F Colonial, Pino Suárez, opposite Figueroa, T294-942 0552. Faded and rundown, but not without character. Rooms have bath and hot water. The lobby is filled with dozens of plants.

Catemaco *p542*

There are a number of hotels at the lakeside. High season runs Jul-Aug and Dec.

A La Finca, just outside town, T294-947 9700, www.lafinca.com.mx. A luxury resort hotel and spa with treatments like *temazcal* steam baths, massages and mineral mud baths. It has a beautiful setting on the lake, with comfortable rooms that are often full at the weekend. There's also a pool, restaurant and café, although the food and service are poor, reportedly.

B Catemaco, on main square, T294-943 0203, hcatemaco@yahoo.com.mx. This hotel on the plaza has old and new sections, Wi-Fi, a pool, cigar shop and restaurant. Rooms are comfortable, with TV, bath and phone. Low season reductions available if you ask.

B Los Arcos, Madero 7, T294-943 0003, www.arcoshotel.com.mx. A good little hotel with pleasant, clean, comfortable rooms, Wi-Fi, cafeteria, pool and parking. Significant reductions in low season.

C Del Brujo, Ocampo y Malecón, T294-943 0071. This hotel has definitely seen better days and could use a bit of remodelling. However, rooms are spacious and equipped with noiseless a/c. Some have good balconies overlooking the lake. Friendly.

C-D Juros, Playa 14, T294-943 0084. A fine, clean, motel-style place with a pool. Will allow trailers and use of parking. A good deal when staying in rooms with fan (**D**). Hot water, TV and a/c as standard.

D Acuario, corner of the plaza, T294-943 0418. Family atmosphere at this friendly hotel. Rooms have a/c, hot water and fan. Parking.

F San Francisco, Matamoros 26, T294-943 0398. Friendly little cheapie with rooms in 2 separate buildings, all with TV and hot water. Basic, but good and clean. Some have a/c (**D**).

Camping Solotepec trailer park by the lake on the road to Playa Azul. US$6.50 per vehicle, very clean. Recommended.

Coatzacoalcos, Minatitlán and around *p544*

C Kinaku, corner of Ocampo and Victoria, Acayucan, T924-245 0016. Clean, modern rooms, with a/c and TV. Restaurant and pool.

D Ritz, Acayucan. A better deal than **Kinaku**, has many new rooms, with good showers, a/c, TV, very clean, spacious and comfortable.

Camping Rancho Hermanos Graham, Agua Dulce. Nice location, full hook-up, cold showers, US$6.50 for car and 2 people.

⊙ Eating

Tlacotalpan *p539*

♈-♈ Brisas de Tlacotalpan, on the riverfront. One of several good fish restaurants with terraces by the river.

♈-♈ La Flecha. Excellent *sopa de mariscos* and *jaiba a la tlacotalpina* (crab).

Tuxtepec *p540*

♈ El Estero, Benito Juárez by Independencia. Fish dishes and local cuisine. Excellent.

♈ La Tablita, Matamoros 2. Good *comida corrida* and à la carte. Long hours.

♈ Taquería Gambrinos, 5 de Mayo 438, 1½ blocks from Parque Juárez. Excellent tacos, very popular, busy every evening.

♈ Villa de Carvajal, Muro Blv esq Nicolás Bravo, on the riverfront. Seafood and grill.

♈-♈ Los Caporales, Independencia 560. Good value *comida corrida* and à la carte.

♈ La Mascota de Oro, 20 de Noviembre 891. Cheap and very friendly.

San Andrés Tuxtla *p542*

♈ La Carreta, near the town centre, otherwise known as **Guadalajara de Noche**. It appears small from the outside but is large and pleasant inside. Well recommended. Sells *tepache*, a drink made from fermented pineapple, similar in flavour to cider, and *agua de jamaica* (hibiscus juice).

♈-♈ Caperucita, Juárez 108. Delicious home-cooked food prepared with love. Breakfast, lunch and seafood are available, but specializes in snacks such as enchiladas, tacos and *gringas*. Try the *misantleca*, a salsa-topped fried tortilla filled with ham and cheese. Drinks include coffee, hot chocolate

and amazing *licuados*. Good value and
highly recommended.

†↑-† Refugio La Casona, Madero 18.
Tasty Mexican food and lush garden.

††-† Winni's, Madero 10, on the plaza. A very
popular spot for breakfast, with a range of
good value menu del dia. Some outdoor
seating, good for people-watching.

Catemaco *p542*

Despite what some locals may tell you, *carne
de chango* is not monkey meat. It's smoked
pork. On the promenade are a number of good
restaurants. The best value are those not
directly on the lake. At the rear of the market
are some inexpensive, good restaurants
serving *comida corrida* for US$2-2.50.

†††† El Fiorentino, Malecón s/n, near the ADO
terminal. Tue-Fri from 1830. The pasta at this
slightly pricey Italian restaurant is good. Skip
the pizzas and tiramisu.

†† Café Catemaco, Carranza 8, on the
plaza. A great spot for morning coffee
and breakfast. Wi-Fi.

†† Jorge's, Malecón s/n, next to La Ola. One
of the better *malecón* restaurants, serving
breakfasts, chicken and *pescado*.

†† La Ola, Malecón s/n. Fish fillets, shrimp
cocktails, barbeque chicken and *carne de
chango*. OK, but not amazing. Nice owners
and a big deck overlooking the water.

†† Pizzeteria, Malecón s/n, under **Hotel
de Brujo**. Open Wed-Sat, evenings only.
A humble little pizza joint.

††-† La Casita, Matamoros 64. This good,
clean, open-air eatery serves decent
economical food.

††-† La Casona, Aldama 4. Home-cooked
Mexican fare including breakfasts, meat,
chicken and fish dishes. Nice interior with
Mexican art and plants. You can hear the
birds first thing in the morning.

Coatzacoalcos, Minatitlán and around *p544*

††-† Soyamar, Guerrero 23, Acayucan.
Good vegetarian snack option.

⊕ Festivals and events

Tlacotalpan *p539*

31 Jan There is a well-known **Candelmas**
fiesta here when accommodation is
impossible to find.

Tuxtepec *p540*

Jun The *fiestas patronales* in honour of
St John the Baptist are held 24 and 25 Jun.
There are fairs, fireworks and dances,
including the *flor de piña* folk dance for
which the Papaloapan region is well known.

▲ Activities and tours

Tuxtepec *p540*
Boating and fishing
The Papaloapan River and its tributaries, as
well as the Presa Miguel Alemán, offer plenty
of opportunities for watersports. Motor-
boating and rowing are popular on the rivers
and artificial lake; races are held in May.

The most common fish species found
are *robalwo* (sea bass), *mojarra* (carp),
and on the Río Tonto (Puente de Caracol)
sábalo (tarpon).

Rodeo

Tuxtepec has a *lienzo charro* with capacity for
5000 spectators, where rodeos are held; this
is an important regional tradition.

⊖ Transport

Tlacotalpan *p539*
Bus To **Santiago Tuxtla**, 7 daily, 1 hr
20 mins, US$4. To **San Andrés Tuxtla**,
7 daily, 1½ hrs, US$5.

Tuxtepec *p540*
Air The airport is in Loma Bonita, 36 km east
on the road to Sayula. Veracruz, 165 km to
the north, has the main airport in the area
(see page 530).

Car The Tuxtepec–Palomares road, Route 147, provides a shortcut to the Transístmica. The road via Sayula is 20 km longer, but much safer. AU buses covering the route from Tuxtepec to Tehuantepec, Juchitán and Salina Cruz, take only the Sayula road.

Bus There is a joint bus station for ADO, AU and Cuenca at Matamoros by Blv Avila Camacho. Other 2nd-class companies have their own stations.

To **Juchitán**, 3 daily with AU, 0200, 2205, 2335, 6 hrs, US$13. To **Tehuantepec**, 2 daily, 0200 and 2335, AU, 6½ hrs, US$14. To **Salina Cruz**, 2 daily, 0200 and 2335, AU, 7 hrs, US$15. To **Oaxaca**, 2 daily, 2225 and 2315, 7½ hrs, US$22. To **Mexico City**, 4 daily, 7½ hrs, US$28 . To **Puebla**, 2 daily, 0630 and 2315, 6 hrs, US$20. To **San Andrés Tuxtla**, 4 daily, 4 hrs, US$9. To **Valle Nacional**, every 15 mins 0500-2100, 1 hr, US$2.50. To **Veracruz**, 5 daily, 3 hrs, US$10.

Santiago Tuxtla *p542*
Bus Plenty of 2nd-class buses run to **San Andrés** and **Catemaco**. Departures below are all 1st class. To **Catemaco**, 12 daily, 1 hr, US$1.70. To **Córdoba**, 1 daily, 2335, 3½ hrs, US$14. To **Mexico City** (TAPO), 2 daily, 0005 and 2235, 8 hrs, US$32. To **Puebla**, 2 daily, 0005 and 2335, 5½ hrs, US$25. To **San Andrés**, 12 daily, ½ hr, US$1.20. To **Veracruz**, 8 daily, 2½ hrs, US$8. To **Xalapa**, 3 daily, 0710, 1410, 1925, 4½ hrs, US$14.

San Andrés Tuxtla *p542*
Bus
Plenty of 2nd-class buses run to **Santiago** and **Catemaco**. Departures below are all 1st class. To **Catemaco**, 12 daily, ½ hr, US$1. To **Córdoba**, 1 daily, 2305, 4 hrs, US$15. To **Mexico City** (TAPO), 2 daily, 2205 and 2235, 8½ hrs, US$33. To **Minatitlán**, 1845, 3 hrs,

US$7.50. To **Puebla**, 2 daily, 2205 and 2335, 6 hrs, US$26. To **Santiago**, 12 daily, ½ hr, US$1.20. To **Veracruz**, 15 daily, 3 hrs, US$9. To **Xalapa**, 3 daily, 0710, 1410, 1925, 4-5 hrs, US$15

Catemaco *p542*
Bus Plenty of 2nd-class buses run to **Santiago** and **San Andrés**. Departures below are all 1st class. To **Coatzacoalcos**, 1 daily, 1915, 3 hrs, US$8. To **Córdoba**, 1 daily, 2330, 4½ hrs, US$16. To **Mexico City** (TAPO), 2 daily, 2130 and 2300, 9 hrs, US$34. To **Minatitlán**, 1 daily, 1915, 2½ hrs, US$6.50. To **Puebla**, 2 daily, 2130 and 2300, 6½ hrs, US$27. To **San Andrés**, 12 daily, ½ hr, US$1. To **Santiago**, 12 daily, 1 hr, US$1.70. To **Veracruz**, 8 daily, 3½ hrs, US$10. To **Xalapa**, 4 daily, 0710, 1410, 1925, 4-5½ hrs, US$16

❶ Directory

Tuxtepec *p540*
Banks Bancomer, Independencia 437, cash and TCs, 0900-1400. HSBC, Independencia 895, cash and TCs. Agencia de Divisas Greco, Independencia 269, cash and TCs, poor rates. **Internet** Tuxcom, Guerrero esq Blv Muro, by riverfront. Tux-Net, Morelos 200. **Laundry** Lava Sec, Guerrero esq Independencia 1683 and Blv Muro, wash and dry US$5 per 4 kg.

Santiago Tuxtla *p542*
Banks Exchange at Banco Comermex on Plaza, TCs 0900-1330.

San Andrés Tuxtla *p542*
Internet 'Ri' Chat, Constitución Norte 106.

Catemaco *p542*
Banks Bancomer, opposite the cathedral, open Mon, Wed, Fri 0900-1400.

Contents

The Guerrero Coast

At a glance

◉ **Getting around** Bus, 4WD, boat.

◉ **Time required** 10 days to sample the best beaches, 3 weeks or more to get off the beaten track.

☀ **Weather** Guerrero's coast is hot all year, but especially during the wet season, May-Nov, when high humidity makes the temperature sweltering. Dec-Apr are dry and very slightly cooler.

✖ **When not to go** There is a danger of hurricanes Sep-Oct. High season prices run Dec-Apr, when the coast is much busier.

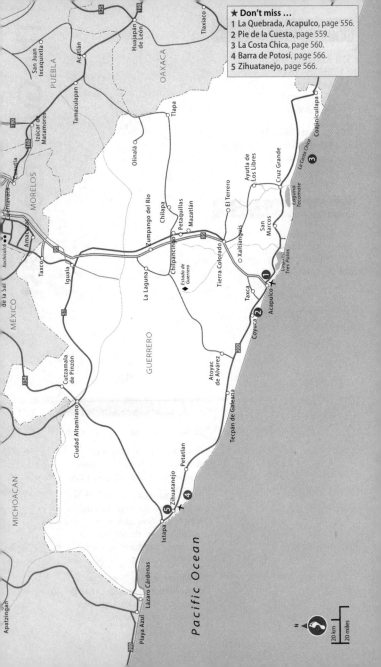

PUEBLA

San Juan
Ixcaquixtla

San Pedro

Izúcar de
Matamoros

Acatlán

Huajapán
de León

Tlaxiaco

OAXACA

Tamazulapan

MORELOS

Cuernavaca

Amacuzac

Xochicalco

MÉXICO

de la Sal

Taxco

Iguala

Tlapa

Olinalá

Zumpango del Río

Chilapa

Petaquillas

Mazatlán

El Terrero

Ayutla de
Los Libres

Cruz Grande

La Costa Chica

Coajinicuilapa

Chilpancingo

Estado de
Guerrero

Tierra Colorado

Xaltianguis

San
Marcos

Laguna
Tecomate

La Laguna

Taxca

Acapulco

Laguna
Tres Palos

Coyuca

Cutzamala
de Pinzón

GUERRERO

Atoyac
de Álvarez

Tecpán de Galeana

Ciudad Altamirano

MICHOACÁN

Petatlán

Zihuatanejo

Ixtapa

Apatzingán

Lázaro Cárdenas

Playa Azul

Pacific Ocean

N

20 km
20 miles

Punctuated by miles and miles of entrancing beaches, Guerrero's incandescent coastline is as alluring as it is legendary. But sadly, its intense natural beauty made it the focus of several resort developments – Acapulco the first and foremost among them. Immortalized by Hollywood film stars, this paragon of sun-kissed hedonism is now wanton and decayed, but its love of a great party has not abated. This is still the place to dance away the evening in some raucous nightclub or pleasure cruiser. Further west, Zihuatanejo offers a calmer, low-key alternative to Acapulco's excesses, while the planned resort of Ixtapa is a bleak example of tourist development at its most sterile. At all these places you can partake in ocean-bound activities such as sailing, sports fishing, jet-skiing and diving. And the seafood, freshly caught and prepared with all the flair and exuberance you'd expect, is delicious.

Fortunately, Guerrero's rugged topography means that it has remained, in part, relatively secluded from the world. Between the high-rise hotels and gaudy souvenir shops there are pockets of lavish natural beauty. Teeming estuaries and emerald-coloured lagoons are populated by brightly coloured birdlife, weird-looking amphibians and carnivorous reptiles. A sublime underwater world plays host to psychedelic coral reefs, whales, dolphins and schools of tropical fish. Turtles, too, lay their eggs on Guerrero's shores. From calm bays with translucent waters to isolated surf-pounded beaches backed by rugged cliffs, Guerrero promises a host of ecological attractions for those willing to depart the well-worn tourist routes. More than this, a plethora of sleepy rural villages are home to obscure local cultures, gregarious fishermen and a way of life that hasn't changed for centuries. What better place to sling a hammock and soak up the sunset?

Acapulco and around

One-time haunt of the rich and famous, the well-known resort of Acapulco is the historic and spiritual heart of Guerrero's holiday hotspot. It is a sprawling urban expanse replete with all the modern conveniences, bustle – and annoyances – of a well-developed tourist Mecca. The beaches, overlooked by concrete towers, buzzed by motorboats and scoured by pestilent touts, are not exactly beautiful or relaxing, but they are well serviced. Organized activities abound, from banana-boat rides to parasailing. And throughout the city's more commercialized stretches, scores of dizzying nightclubs draw crowds of revellers. If you enjoy gritty urban landscapes, frenetic parties and brazen, outright decadence, then make your base here. Otherwise, consider scouting the coast for more tranquil lodgings. Pie de la Cuesta, just out of town, offers the best of both worlds with peaceful shore by day and Acapulco's exuberant nightlife just a short bus ride away. For the more intrepid, Guerrero's barely developed Costa Chica is a wonderful world of adventure and untouched beauty, but really only accessible with your own vehicle. ▸▸ *For listings, see pages 560-565.*

Mexico City to Acapulco

The four-lane toll freeway from Mexico City runs west of the old highway, bypassing Chilpancingo, continuing as far as **Tierra Colorada** (where there is an exit), and on to Acapulco. The completion of the highway is the third improvement: the first motor road was pushed over the ancient mule trail in 1927, giving Acapulco its first new lease of life in 100 years; when the road was paved and widened in 1954, Acapulco began to boom.

It takes about 3½ hours to drive from the capital to Acapulco on the 406-km four-lane highway, although the toll is very high (US$20-25).

Warning You are advised not travel by car at night in Guerrero, even on the Mexico City–Acapulco highway and coastal highway, because of bandits.

South to Chilpancingo → *Colour map 2, C4. Phone code: 747. Altitude: 1250 m.*
The journey from Mexico City to Acapulco and the Pacific coast often includes a stop-off at Cuernavaca, the 'city of eternal spring' (see page 162) and a detour to the silver town of Taxco (see page 167). Further south, beyond the Mexcala River, the road passes for some 30 km through the dramatic canyon of **Zopilote** to reach the university city of **Chilpancingo**, capital of Guerrero state at Km 302. There is a small but grandly conceived plaza with solid neoclassical buildings and monumental public sculptures commemorating the workers' struggle: *El hombre hacia el futuro* and *El canto al trabajo* by Victor Manuel Contreras. In the **Palacio de Gobierno** there is a museum and murals. The colourful reed bags from the village of Chilapa (see below) are sold in the market. The **Casa de las Artesanías** for Guerrero is on the right-hand side of the old main Mexico City–Acapulco highway. It has a particularly wide selection of Olinalá lacquerware. The local fiesta starts on 16 December and lasts a fortnight.

Around Chilpancingo
Olmec cave paintings can be seen at the **Grutas de Juxtlahuaca** ① *3-hr tour US$25*, east of Chilpancingo. The limestone cavern is in pristine condition; it has an intricate network of large halls and tunnels, stalagmites and stalactites, a huge underground lake, cave drawings from about AD 500, a skeleton and artefacts. Take a torch, food and drink and a sweater if going a long way in. To reach the caves, drive to Petaquillas on the non-toll road

then take a side road (paved, but poor in parts) through several villages to **Colotlipa** (*colectivo* from Chilpancingo, see Transport, US$1.50, 1½ hours). Ask at the restaurant on the corner of the Zócalo for a guide to the caves.

Acapulco ⊖🏠🏨⛺🍴🛈 » *pp560-565. Colour map 2, C3.*

→ *Phone code: 744.*

Acapulco, the jewel of Guerrero's coast, is slung over a wide undulating bay like an ailing actress past her prime. Once upon a time, this was the place to be seen. A shimmering resort where Hollywood film stars mingled with jet-set playboys and the nouveau riche. A place to flaunt wealth and partake in starry cocktail parties, a place of glamour, elegance and style. But since then, this once great international playground has been devoured by insatiable corporate interests, grotesquely overweight fast-food franchises and flocks of drunken tourists adorned in shorts, white socks, sandles and straw sombreros. Beneath a giddying climax of sickly neon signs, something venal is festering.

Still, if you like to drink and dance, you could do worse. And beyond the soulless machinations of the high-rise hotels and exclusive timeshare complexes, there are glimpses of a more interesting, dignified age. Old Acapulco is home to a lively central plaza and a handful of diverting museums. And don't miss the iconic cliff-divers, who daily plunge from rocks as high as 45 m. The bay itself, host to a plethora of fine sandy beaches, is an assuredly seductive spectacle at nightfall. Clusters of glimmering lights illuminate the hills like some rare jewel-encrusted tiara, silhouettes of yachts dance upon the waters, and party cruisers crisscross the waves on some spirited evening adventure. In spite of its commercialism and stench, there is still great fun to be had in Acapulco.

① **Acapulco centre**

Acapulco maps
1 Acapulco centre, page 553
2 Acapulco Bay, page 554

Sleeping ⊖
Acela **5**
Asturias **6**
California **1**
Coral **8**
Misión **3**
Oliviedo **9**
Paola **2**
Sagamar **10**
Santa Lucía **4**

Eating 🍴
100% Natural **3**
El Amigo Miguel **2**
El Galeón **4**
La Flor de Acapulco **5**
La Gran Torta **6**
Mi Piacci **7**
Pipo's **1**

Ins and outs

Getting there Aeropuerto Alvarez Internacional (ACA) ⓘ *T744-435 2060, www.oma.aero,* is 23 km southeast of Acapulco. The airport shuttle, US$6 one-way, takes one hour to town; the ticket office is outside the terminal. Return trips are also available (*viaje redondo*), so keep your ticket and call 24 hours in advance for a taxi. It is possible to find a microbus for Puerto Marquez, where you can connect with buses for Costera Miguel Alemán. A private taxi from the airport to the centre should cost US$20-25. It's worth negotiating.

There are several bus stations around town. To get to the Zócalo from the main **Estrella Blanca terminal**, Central Ejido, Ejido 97, 3 km north of downtown, catch a 'Centro' or 'Caleta' bus. Estrella Blanca's other first class terminal is located next to Parque Papagayo, Central Papagayo, Cuauhtémoc 1605; it's connected to the downtown area by 'Caleta' buses or to the Zona Hotelera by 'Río-Base' buses. **Estrella de Oro**, Cuauhtémoc 1490, has its own terminal and is located two blocks east of Parque Papagayo. Taxis can be found outside all terminals, but it is much cheaper to walk half a block down the road and catch one that's passing. ▸▸ *See Transport, page 564.*

Getting around The most useful bus route runs the length of Costera Miguel Alemán, linking the older part of town to the different beaches and hotels. Bus stops are numbered, so find out which number you need to get off at.

② Acapulco Bay

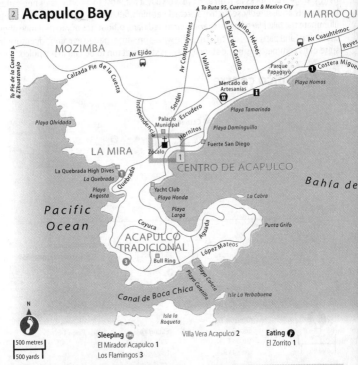

Sleeping 🛏
El Mirador Acapulco 1
Los Flamingos 3
Villa Vera Acapulco 2

Eating 🍴
El Zorrito 1

Tourist information You'll find a handy municipal tourist information kiosk on the Malecón, just opposite the Zócalo, with leaflets and simple maps. The **Acapulco Convention and Visitors Bureau** ① *Av Costera M Alemán 38-A, opposite Oceanic 2000, T744-484 8555, www.visitacapulco.com*, is larger and better equipped with glossy brochures.

Safety Acapulco has now sunk into the bloody mire of Mexico's drug war as rival cartels battle for supremacy of vital trafficking routes along the Guerrero coast. In 2006, there were several nasty execution-style murders and, to the horror of foreign holidaymakers, a decapitated head washed up on the beach. Subsequently, two Canadian tourists were caught in the cross-fire of a street battle. But since then, thanks to a heavily armed military presence that includes several thousand soldiers, you are highly unlikely to encounter any trouble first-hand. As ever, most violence is confined to the impoverished suburbs. Petty crime certainly is an issue, especially on beaches, where thieves scour the sands for unattended items. Lone women should beware sexual harassment and others be prepared for occasionally impolite hawkers, who can be dismissed with a friendly smile and a firm 'no gracias'. Hotel rooms are also sometimes looted and taxi drivers are generally untrustworthy. Don't listen to any driver who tells you your hotel is fully booked and beware of overcharging. As a foreign tourist in a commercial resort, you will be regarded as a source of revenue by scam artists and locals. You are to be milked, as much as possible, for money, money and more money.

Bars & clubs 🎵
Baby O **2**
Disco Beach **3**

Background

Acapulco derives its name from a Nahautl title 'the place where reeds were destroyed', which refers a local Yope legend concerning a tragic love affair between Prince Acatl ('reed') and Princess Quihuitl ('rain'). Belonging to rival tribes, their love could never be realised through marriage, so Prince Acatl sank into depression, died and transformed into a swamp of reeds. Upon finding him, Princess Quihuitl, who had been drifting the shores in the form of a cloud, was so heartbroken that she rained down in a storm, destroying the reeds and dying alongside her loved one.

Acapulco's colonial history began in 1521, when Fernando Chico arrived on a reconnaissance mission. He named the bay Santa Lucía and 11 years later it came under the official dominion of the Spanish crown. It was renamed 'City of Kings', and soon flourished as a major port and vital component in the Manilla trade route. Convoys of Spanish merchants would arrive to unload precious Far Eastern cargoes such as spices, ivory, silks and porcelain, then transport them overland to Veracruz, where they would be packed off for Spain. Acapulco was also the site of a giant annual trade fair, bringing yet more wealth and attention from pirates. However, after the War of Independence, the trade route collapsed and the city languished until the construction of the Mexico City highway in 1927.

Starting in the 1930s, enterprising individuals began constructing luxury hotels, restaurants and discos. Then, during the 1940s and 1950s, the city flourished as an international resort, hosting the likes of Elvis, Frank Sinatra and the Kennedys. But by the 1970s, it had become overcrowded and overdeveloped, and commercial interests moved elsewhere along the coast, settling in Ixtapa and Zihuatanejo, as well as Cancún and the Riviera Maya. Once again, Acapulco fell into decline, until the 1990s, when a government injection of one billion US dollars overhauled the city's infrastructure. Fresh waves of tourist interest ensued, North American 'spring-breakers' chief among them. But sadly, in recent years, gang-related violence has darkened the bright horizon. The global recession too, may stilt the city's plans for revitalization.

Sights and orientation

Acapulco has all the paraphernalia of a booming resort: swanky shops, nightclubs, red-light districts, golf clubs, tennis courts, touts and street vendors. And now also crime and air pollution. Flanking the crescent-shaped Bahía de Acapulco, the city is divided into two broad areas. **Old Acapulco**, sometimes known as 'Acapulco Náutico', is on the western side of the bay. This is the working heart of the city, filled with busy streets, crowded shops, people, hotels and traffic. Accommodation here tends to be cheaper than elsewhere in the city. Activity focuses on the Zócalo, Acapulco's lively central plaza, populated by shady trees, tourists and occasional musicians. It is also the site of the city cathedral, built in the 1930s and dedicated to Nuestra Señora de la Soledad. It sports a mosque-style dome and Byzantine towers. East of Old Acapulco stretches the **Zona Hotelera**, or Hotel Zone, also known as the 'Zona Dorada', replete with beaches, international restaurants and expensive hotels. This is a world away from the dirt and bustle of Old Acapulco, but the overall effect can be somewhat tacky and sterile. The two areas are joined by a single coast road that flanks the shore: Avenida Costera Miguel Alemán, also known as La Costera.

La Quebrada

ⓘ *1km southwest of the Zócalo. Daily at 1300, 1930, 2030, 2130, 2230. US$2.70.*

One sight that should not be missed is that of the iconic cliff divers at La Quebrada, who plunge up to 45 m into the water below, timing their dives to coincide with the incoming waves. The practice of cliff-diving began in the 1920s, when fishermen would jump into the sea to free up nets that had become snagged on the rocks. In 1934, it became much more of a theatrical performance, evolving into the tourist spectacle of today. Expect to see impressive somersaults and coordinated double dives, all accomplished with much bravery and bravado. Perhaps most dramatic are the night dives performed with torches. Nearby, **Hotel El Mirador Acapulco** offers a package including great views of the show, drinks and food (expensive). Don't forget to tip the divers at the end.

Diego Rivera Mural

ⓘ *Inalámbrica 6, Cerro de la Pinzona.*

Close to La Quebrada you'll find an interesting mural by Diego Rivera. It adorns the former home of Mexican businesswoman and philanthropist, Dolores Olmedo Patiño. Dolores once owned the world's largest collection of Rivera paintings, now mostly housed by a museum in Mexico City. Her deep affection for the master was certainly requited, as a host

Acapulco vice

Acapulco is a veritable den of iniquity, like all great pleasure cities, home to untold bars and strip joints and widely grinning 'amigos' who promise you everything your poor, lonely heart desires. Tread carefully, for vice is nothing new to Acapulco, most of it is illegal and the peddlers have had decades to perfect their scams.

Drugs, particularly, have always been a vital cornerstone of Acapulco's trade in illicit pleasures. Since the 1960s, hippies have sought out the local marijuana – 'Acapulco Gold' – so called for its resplendent hue, its high cost and its quality beyond compare. The weed is now world-famous, immortalized in songs by Robert Plant, Roy Harper, Catatonia and a plethora of reggae artists, as well as the dubious comic duo Cheech and Chong, and a rather forgettable 1978 film

by Burt Brinckerhoff. In recent years cocaine has superseded cannabis with tragic and violent results. As many an old hippy will tell you, drugs just aren't a nice business anymore.

But sex, too, is a historic pillar of Acapulco's vice industry. In a 1960 article by *Playboy* magazine, that bastion of good taste and sophistication, they described the city as "a favourite of New York's top call girls with their patrons in tow'" In their continuing explorations of the red light district they discovered "dozens of girls of all colours and ages, waiting for someone to buy them a drink, or ask them to dance or to retire the cubicles behind the club… for anything from forty cents up." Just as Elvis had hinted in his 1963 film, one could certainly have '*Fun in Acapulco*'.

of his flattering portraits reveal. The house was actually lived in by Rivera 1956-1957 whilst he recovered from a battle with cancer. The sculptured mural depicts Quetzalcoatl, Tlaloc and Ehécatl among other pre-Columbian gods. It is covered in bright mosaics and is entitled *Casa del Dios Ehécatl* ('House of the God of Wind').

Fuerte de San Diego

ⓘ *Calle Hornitos s/n, esq Morelos, T744-482 3828. Tue-Sun 1000-1800. Museum US$3.*
In colonial times, Acapulco was the terminal for Manila convoy, and as such, a target for marauding Dutch and British pirates. The Fuerte de San Diego was built in 1616 as the town's principal defence. It was destroyed in 1776 and rebuilt in 1783, and the last battle for Mexican Independence was also fought here. Today, the pentagonal structure has been transformed into an attractive museum of the history of Acapulco and Mexico. It has 12 permanent exhibition rooms with objects pertaining to Spanish maritime affairs, old maps and drawings, textiles and religious artefacts. There is a sound and light show during summer evenings, and the museum is well worth a visit.

La Casa de la Máscara

ⓘ *Corredor Cultrual s/n, next to the Fuerte de San Diego. Tue-Sun 1000-1400. Donation.*
This small museum houses a colourful collection of masks, some wonderfully grotesque, others wildly psychedelic, yet others strangely beautiful. There are seven rooms with expositions on death and the devil, world masks, dances of Guerrero, identity and fantasy. Particularly striking are the Huichol jaguar masks painstakingly created by pressing individual coloured beads into bees' wax. A good introduction into the exuberant world of Mexican folklore. Sadly, signs are in Spanish only.

Jardín Botánico

ⓘ *Av Heroico Colegio Military 52-52, www.acapulcobotanico.org. Daily sunrise-sunset. US$2.20.*

Inaugurated in March 2002, Acapulco's botanical garden occupies 6 ha of land in the grounds of the university. Well-marked paths snake through the boulder-strewn terrain where you will encounter several different microclimates. A range of plant life is supported, including palms, orchids, cacti, fruit trees and bromeliads. Most of the vegetation, however, is typical of lower deciduous jungle. Resident fauna includes birds, iguanas, snakes and small mammals. For those residing in Acapulco, volunteers are also welcome to help with guided tours, children's education or transplants.

Palma Sola Petroglyphs

Located around 6 km beyond downtown Acapulco is the 4-ha **El Veladero ecological zone**, home to the petroglyphs of Palma Sola. Some 400 m above sea level, it provides commanding views of the bay. Little is known of these stone carvings, dating 200 BC to AD 600, except that they occupy a sacred space where rituals took place. These were most likely connected with fertility and agriculture. There are 18 rocks in total, depicting everything from historical events to myths to aspect of daily life. Of course, these depictions are highly stylized and subject to interpretation. Bring water for the hike.

Beaches

There are some 20 beaches in and around Acapulco, all with fine golden sand. You can rent deckchairs on most stretches; the more popular ones host watersports such as banana-boating and parasailing. Under Mexican law, all beaches are free to access.

West of the Zócalo, the **Peninsula de Las Playas** arcs across the bay and is home to several good locations. The shielded, sickle-curved **Playa Caleta** and neighbouring **Playa Caletilla** are very popular with families. Flanked by various *palapa* restaurants, these beaches were a favourite haunt of the 1950s jet-set. The waters are smooth, sheltered and dirty, but the sand is clean. Just offshore is the **Mágico Mundo Marina** ⓘ *US$4.50*, on **Isla Yerbabuena**, with sharks, piranhas, eels and stingrays in an aquarium, a swimming pool with water chute and a breezy bar. Also offshore is **Isla la Roqueta**, where you can practise snorkelling or kayaking, or just languish on the busy sands. Boats to Roqueta, some of them glass-bottomed, depart from Caleta every 20 minutes, US$3 return. The hidden, sheltered beach of **Playa Angosta** offers a smaller, more secluded option a short walk from Caleta. To get to the peninsula and its beaches, walk 20 minutes from the Zócalo or catch a 'Caleta' bus from the coast road.

The majority of Acapulco's beaches, however, are slung along the shores east of the Zócalo. The straight, gentle shores of **Playa Tamarindo** soon give way to the more popular, surf-pounded beaches of **Los Hornos** and **Los Hornitos**. Note the surf is sometimes dangerous and the beaches are unsafe at night. Swimmers should also look out for motorboats close to the shore. As the bay arcs around, **Playa Condesa** is located roughly in the centre, at the heart of the hotel zone. As such, commercial ventures abound. Continuing eastwards to **Playa Icacos**, there is a marine-land amusement park **Ci-Ci** ⓘ *Costera 101, www.cici.com.mx, daily 1000-1800, US$7.50*, with a waterslide, pool with wave-machine and arena with performing dolphins and sea lions (nothing special).

Beyond Icacos lies the Naval base and a string of beaches that are increasingly tricky to reach. They include **Playa Guitarrón**, flanked by wealthy vacation homes and palm trees, and further east, around Punta Bruja and on the other side of the peninsula, the sheltered

What of the glory days?

Like some simpering misty-eyed lush slumped over a dwindling tequila sunrise, Acapulco has no shame in recalling the glory days. A visit to the older hotels – El Mirador and Villa Vera, for example – will quickly attest this city's mawkish love of nostalgia. Soft-focus black-and-white portraits exalt former guests as if they were hard won trophies – Elizabeth Taylor, Sinatra, John F Kennedy, Bridgette Bardot and many, many others.

Acapulco's meteoric rise to fame was the work of former President Miguel Alemán, who set about modernizing the city and promoting it as the 'Riviera Mexicana'. A key component in his grand post-war drive to promote Mexico – and Mexicanism – abroad, Alemán propelled a formerly humble vacation spot into a fabled international resort. As such,

Acapulco is a child of Mexico's 'golden age', when tourism, culture, consumption and media output boomed all at once.

But observing the overdeveloped, socially polarized, gaudy and somewhat polluted city it is today, perhaps Acapulco's real glory days lie further back in time, long before the developers settled en masse. In the early 20th century, before the city boasted road or air connections, a mere handful of humble *palapas* dotted the beaches. Utterly devoid of tourists, overpriced restaurants or thumping night clubs, only the most intrepid travellers made it to isolated Acapulco. After tackling miles of winding mule trails they arrived at a quiet, if lightly crumbling port town, nestled in a wide sandy bay with miles of verdant jungle flanking its shores. Now what could be more glorious than that?

waters of **Bahía Puerto Marquéz**. Fishing, sailing and other water-sports are popular here. Beyond, at **Playa Revolcadero**, upscale development has blossomed, with scores of new luxury hotels, roads and carefully sculpted landscapes. This is **Acapulco Diamante**, now the city's most exclusive – and most soulless – neighbourhood. It is possible to reach Puerto Marquéz by boat, US$3 return, or by bus from La Costera.

Around Acapulco ⬤🕐 ›› pp560-565.

Pie de la Cuesta

Twelve kilometres northwest of the city, Pie de la Cuesta is preferred by many budget travellers to Acapulco itself, but it is also commercialized. There are several bungalow-hotels and trailer parks (see Sleeping, page 561), a lagoon, and long, clean, sandy beaches. Here, you can swim and fish year round, drink delicious *coco loco* (fortified coconut milk) and watch entrancing sunsets from your gently swaying hammock. If Acapulco's hedonistic sprawl isn't to your tastes, tranquil Pie de la Cuesta is a recommended alternative.

Just beyond town, **Laguna Coyuca** (also known as 'La Barra' or 'Laguna Pie de la Cuesta'), over 10 km long, has interesting birdlife, water hyacinths and tropical flowers. These can be explored by motorboat, or by tour with a local outfit; **Coyuca 2000** is best (see Activities and tours, page 564). **Coyuca de Benítez**, near the Laguna Coyuca, is a market town selling exotic fruit, cheap hats and shoes. Pelicans fly by the lagoons, there are passing dolphins and plentiful sardines. Locals are now trying to protect the turtle eggs that young boys (and dogs) like to hunt.

Barra Vieja

A day trip south of Acapulco, 25 km east of the airport, takes you to the pleasant fishing village of **Barra Vieja**, with great beaches and sunsets. Some *cabañas* and *palapas* are available, and the good **Sol y Mar** restaurant (try the *pescador a la talla* – barbecued fish with tropical herbs and spices), which also has a good pool. Other activities include horse riding, quad bikes and visiting a bird sanctuary with flamingos. To get there take the bus from Costera Miguel Alemán to Puerto Marquéz and connect with a bus US$0.40 or *colectivo* taxi US$0.80 to Barra Vieja, or take a taxi US$20, 30 minutes.

La Costa Chica

The lesser travelled stretches of Guerrero's Costa Chica, or 'Little Coast', reach southeast from Acapulco as far as the state border with Oaxaca. The shores here are almost completely undeveloped and you will need your own vehicle – or at the very least a tent, a good map and some degree of patience – to fully explore them. If you're looking for beaches, **Playa Ventura**, close to the village of **Copala**, is possibly one of the best, home to a handful of cheap, basic lodgings. **Ometepec** is a peaceful colonial town which also has basic hotels, good for breaking a journey. If you're interested in the region's afro-*mestizo* inhabitants, who are descended from escaped African slaves, their population is concentrated in one of the region's largest settlements, **Coajinicuilapa**, where you will find a local museum dedicated to their culture and history.

◉ Acapulco and around listings

For Sleeping and Eating price codes and other relevant information, see Essentials pages 47-51.

● Sleeping

Acapulco *p553, maps p553 and p554*
Downtown

Most cheaper hotels are grouped around the Zócalo, especially on La Paz and Juárez. In the high season you should make reservations, at least for 1 night, before arriving. For the better hotels you can make reservations at the bus terminal in Mexico City. Take care with the numbering along the Costera Miguel Alemán; basically it means nothing, a better reference is to the beach names and major hotels.
C Misión, Felipe Valle 12, close to the Zócalo, T744-482 3643, hotelmision@hotmail.com. Very cool and quiet with a pleasing plant-filled patio. Rooms are comfortable, clean and tasteful, with good sinks, hot water and fan, but no TV or phone. The best ones are on the ground floor. Breakfast available.
C-D Asturias, Quebrada 45, T744-483 6548, gerardomancera@aol.com. Clean, comfortable,

friendly and decent. Rooms have a/c (cheaper without), hot water and TV. Good pool and free coffee, parking available. Recommended.
C-D Paola, Teniente Azueta 16, 2 blocks from the Zócalo, T744-482 6243. Perfectly adequate budget lodgings with a small pool and roof terrace. Rooms have hot water, the cheapest without TV and a/c. Very pink.
C-F Oliviedo, Costera Miguel Alemán 207, 1 block from the Zócalo, T744-482 1511, www.paginasprodigy.com/hotel.oviedo.acapulco. A big old 1950s building with great views from the top rooms. Economical and standard rooms, as well as dorms (**F**) for backpackers. The better rooms have a/c.
D Acela, La Paz 29, T744-482 0661. Clean, blue rooms with fan, bath, cold water and TV. Family-run and friendly, and the owner speaks English. A good little budget place.
D Coral, Quebrada 56, T744-482 0756. Fading and a bit shabby, but OK. Rooms have a/c, TV, bath and fan, get one with a balcony. Beds are slightly thin and hard. There's a pool and parking outside is not entirely secure. Reasonably quiet.

D Sagamar, Quebrada 51, T744-482 9992. Basic and a bit shabby, but helpful and friendly, with some English spoken. Rooms have fan, hot water and TV. There's a small pool.

D Santa Lucía, López Mateos 33, T744-482 0441. Family-owned and operated, slightly run-down, but helpful and clean. Rooms have fan, hot water, TV, bath. OK.

D-E California, La Paz 12, T744-482 2893, 1½ blocks west of the Zócalo. A mix of singles, double, triples, and 1 family room for 5-6 people. Rooms are good value, simple and comfortable, equipped with fan and hot water, and surrounding a patio. The owner is a good source of information for sport fishing. English and French spoken. TV is available for longer stays.

La Costa and the Zona Hotelera
The coast north and south of downtown has a concentration of upmarket high-rise hotels.

LL Villa Vera Acapulco, Lomas del Mar 35, T744-109 0570, www.clubregina.com. Formerly a private vacation home, this 'spa & racquet club' resort has been a celebrity spot since the 1950s, where Elvis once stayed. The extensive facilities include 17 swimming pools, 2 tennis courts, gym, beauty parlour and jacuzzi.

A El Mirador Acapulco, Plazoleta La Quebrada 74, at the top next to the cliff divers, T744-483 1155, www.hotelelmiradoracapulco.com. mx. Hotel with a long tradition and a great place to view the divers at La Quebrada. Private seawater pool (no beach), a/c, some rooms with jacuzzi, restaurant and bar.

A Los Flamingos, Av López Mateos s/n, T744-482 0690, www.hotellosflamingos.com. One of the finest locations in Acapulco with glorious cliff-top views. In the 1950s it was a retreat for John Wayne. Facilities include gardens, pool, restaurant and Wi-Fi. Breakfast included.

B El Tropicano, Costera Miguel Alemán 20, on Playa Icacos, T744-484 1332, www.eltropicano. com.mx. A large hotel with 137 clean, comfortable rooms, all equipped with a/c, cable TV and phone. Facilities include well-tended gardens, 2 pools, bars and restaurant. Very friendly and helpful. Recommended.

Camping
Acapulco West KDA, Barra de Coyuca. Beachfront, security patrol, pool, restaurant, hot showers, laundry, store, volleyball, basketball, Spanish classes, telephones.

Quinta Dora Pie de la Cuesta,13 km up the coast on Highway 200. *Palapas*, bathrooms, cold showers, hook-ups, US$12 for 2 plus car, US$4 just to sling hammock.

Trailer Park El Coloso, La Sabana. Small swimming pool, secure.

Trailer Park La Roca, on the road from Puerto Marquez to La Sabana. Secure.

Pie de la Cuesta *p559*
Most hotels are strung along a single road and conveniently marked by big orange signs.

A-B Casa Blanca, Playa Pie de la Cuesta 370, 744-460 0324, www.acapulcocasablanca.net. Friendly place with good management. Range of rooms and rates, from older, smaller rooms to good new rooms with sea views. All have a/c. There's also a restaurant, pool, beach access, sun loungers and hammocks.

A-C Bungalows Maria Cristina, Playa Pie de la Cuesta s/n, T744-460 0262. Filled with plants and hammocks, this friendly little hotel has 5 rooms for 2-3 persons and 3 bungalows (**A**) with kitchen, balconies, rocking chairs, fan and hot water. Some bungalows have ocean views and there is direct beach access.

B-C Villa Nirvana, Playa Pie de la Cuesta, T744-460 1631, www.lavillanirvana.com. A very friendly, hospitable hotel that works with local clinics to supply children with medicine (the owners will exchange a 30-day supply of vitamins for a drink). Wide range of rooms, all pleasant and comfortable, including family apartments equipped with kitchens (**B**). Quiet and peaceful and good for couples, families and young people. Direct beach access, pool and restaurant. Highly recommended.

B-C Villa Roxana, Playa Pie de la Cuesta 302, T744-460 3252. Good, clean, comfortable rooms with sliding doors, hot and cold water, TV, fan and hammocks. Pool and a small restaurant serving economical breakfasts (not included in rates), as well as rooms for families, some with kitchen. There's also a pleasant garden and a fridge well stocked with beer. Recommended, but no direct beach access. Rooms with king-size beds are slightly more (**B**).

B-D Quinta Karla, Playa Pie de la Cuesta 288, T744-460 1255, quintakarla@hotmail.com. 18 rooms and 1 bungalow (**B**) with fridge, fan and curtains over the bed and bathroom. There's a pool, restaurant and hammocks. No hot water. A bit shabby, but OK.

D Brisa de Oro, Playa Pie de la Cuesta, L7 Mz56, T744-460 0829, mariocg20@hotmail.com. Terraces with hammocks, a pool, good sea views and a restaurant under a *palapa* can be found at this small, friendly hotel. A handful of rooms have sofas and bed. OK.

D La Cabañita, Playa Pie de la Cuesta, L17, Mz56, T744-460 0946, aca_master@hotmail.com. A handful of basic, straightforward rooms with fan and TV, but no hot water. Parking, pool, restaurant and a talkative parrot. OK.

🍴 Eating

Acapulco *p553, maps p553 and p554*
Downtown
Fish dishes are a speciality of Acapulco. There are many cheap restaurants in the blocks surrounding the Zócalo, especially along Juárez and La Paz.

🍴🍴 Pipo's, Almirante Breton 3 (off Costera near the Zócalo). One of the first-established and best restaurants in Acapulco. Fine seafood. There are 2 other branches: Costera and Plaza Canadá; and Calle Mahahual, Puerto Marquez.

🍴🍴-🍴🍴 100% Natural, Costera Miguel Alemán s/n, on the bay. Excellent *licuados* and energy drinks, as well as very good pasta and Mexican dishes. All healthy and well prepared, with branches around town. Wi-Fi. Recommended.

🍴🍴 El Amigo Miguel, Juárez 16. Popular, buzzing seafood haunt with a 2nd branch on the opposite side of the road. Good and clean.

🍴🍴 El Galeón, Iglesias 8. Bar and seafood restaurant that's heavy on the nautical theme. Popular with tourists.

🍴🍴 La Flor de Acapulco, on the Zócalo. Good views of the square and partially obstructed views of the bay. Breakfasts, fish, meat and chicken dishes. Fans and breezes keep the dining space cool. Nothing special, but OK for a quick informal meal.

🍴🍴 Mi Piaci, on the Zócalo. Busy terrace on the plaza with average pizzas and reasonable breakfasts, including a fairly tasty fruit salad with honey, yoghurt and granola. Lots of other economical packets available. Always busy with Mexican tourists. OK, but not fantastic.

🍴 La Gran Torta, La Paz 6. Sandwiches, tacos, *tortas* and economical Mexican fare. An unpretentious locals' haunt that's often buzzing with interesting characters.

La Costa and the Zona Hotelera
The coast, and Zona Hotelera particularly, are home to an abundance of international restaurants, some good, some bland. There are a number of variously priced places along and opposite Playa Condesa, another group of restaurants along Playa Caleta walkway, and yet another group with mixed prices on the Costera opposite the Costa Club Acapulco – 250 or so to choose from. As the coast road climbs south towards Las Brisas, there are a number of restaurants with truly inspirational views (particularly after dark) over the bay.

🍴🍴🍴 Fairmont Acapulco Princess, Costera de la Palmas, T744-469 1000, A famous luxury hotel that lays on a Sun lunch buffet, including champagne and seafood – an event worth saving space for. Casual dress, but no shorts or jeans. Reservations on the day.

🍴🍴🍴 Madeira, Las Brisas. Recommended for its cuisine, atmosphere and inspirational view.

🍴🍴 El Zorrito, opposite the Costa Club Acapulco. Excellent local food with live music. There's a 2nd branch 1 block west (opposite the Howard Johnson Hotel) is open 24 hrs and very popular late after the clubs close.

Pie de la Cuesta *p559*
Most hotels have some form of restaurant.

🍴🍴 Coyuca 2000, Playa Pie de la Cuesta. Good location on the beach, with great sunsets, cocktails and peaceful hammocks. The seafood menu includes shrimp cocktail, octopus, red snapper in garlic butter and sea bass in breadcrumbs, among others.

🎵 Bars and clubs

Acapulco *p553, maps p553 and p554*
Acapulco has a superb, varied nightlife at the weekends, and every major hotel has at least one disco. Others worth trying include:
Baby O, towards the naval base on Costera Miguel Alemán.
Disco Beach, Costera Miguel Alemán, between the Diana and Hotel Fiesta Americana Condesa. Open till 0500. By the beach, informal dress. Good.
La Casa Blanca, La Paz 8. Bar popular with the locals.
Las Puertas, behind the cathedral by the stairs on Ramírez. Disco and live music.
Mangos, Costera Miguel Alemán, American sports-style bar, popular, food.

⛰ Activities and tours

Acapulco *p553, maps p553 and p554*
As you'd expect of a well-developed beach resort, a host of watersports are available. These include jet-skiing, water-skiing, banana-boating and parasailing, with operators in the upmarket hotel zone. You can also rent masks and snorkels on the beach for a simple splash around.

Bay cruises
Several operators depart from the *malecón* close to the Zócalo. Most cruises tend to be fun, boozy affairs, usually with a bilingual guide (but check).
Acarey, *malecón*, opposite the Zócalo, T744-482 3763. Low-season jaunts include the *Sunset Cruise*, departing at 1630, with live disco music, games, raffles and an open-bar; and the *Acarey Moonlight Cruise*, with similar entertainment, departing at 2230. In the high

season, *Breakfast cruises* are offered with tours of the bay, open bar and food; departs 1100. The *Puesta de Sol Cruise* leaves at 1630; *Tropical Moon* at 1930; and *Latin Moon* at 2230; all with dancing, drink and the usual colourful extravaganzas.
Fiesta & Bonanza, Costera Alemán, Gloreita Tlacopanocha, T744-482 2055, yatesfb@yahoo.com.mx. Romantic after-dinner cruises depart at 1630 with live music, dance party, open bar and views of the sunset. Other tours visit the houses of the rich and famous, and take in the cliff diving at La Quebrada. At 2230 the *Moonlight party cruise* commences with gaudy dancing, 'tropical hits' and an open bar. The views of the bay, twinkling with lights, are quite exciting.

Diving and snorkelling
Diving isn't huge in Acapulco, but there some interesting sites, including sunken ships, caves and rock formations. You might see coral, sea stars, mackerel, sea horses, turtles, rays and whale sharks. Visibility is best Nov-Feb.
Acapulco Scuba, Paseo del Pescador 13 y 14, T744-482 9474, www.acapulcoscuba.com. Daily trips include a tame snorkel excursion and 'discover scuba' course for beginners. Two tank dives cost US$70 and depart daily at 0900. PADI certification from Open Water to Instructor is also available, as are night dives and specialist dives.

Fishing
Sports fishing is quite popular in Acapulco with sailfish, tuna and dorado populating the waters. Smaller game includes bonito, roosterfish and mahi-mahi.
Fish R Us, Costera 100, T744-482 8282, www.fish-r-us.com. A well-established sport-fishing outfit managed by Captain Parker, who has 20 years experience fishing the waters off Acapulco. The company has a formidable, well-equipped fleet of yachts and arranges deep-sea fishing as well as night bottom fishing expeditions. Also on offer are diving, waterskiing and swimming lessons.

Pie de la Cuesta p559

Coyuca 2000, Playa Pie de la Cuesta, T744-460 5609, coyuca_2000@hotmail.com. Great boat tours of the surrounding ecosystems, including a visit to Bird Island, mangroves forests (where you might see iguanas, deers or boas), and Crocodile Island, where enormous 3½-m beasts languish in the waters. Tours conclude at the private island of Paraiso de Manglar, which has a beach, pool, and populations of spider monkeys. A great local outfit managed by Paulino, the 'godfather' of turtles, who can take you to the hatching site in Dec. 5-hr boat tours depart daily at 1130. Recommended.

◎ Transport

Acapulco p553, maps p553 and p554

Air

There are direct connections to many US cities and charter flights from Europe in the summer. Good domestic connections include **Mexico City**, **Ciudad Juárez**, **Cuernavaca**, **Culiacán**, **Guadalajara**, **León**, **Monterrey**, Puerto Vallarta, **Toluca** and **Tijuana**.

Airline offices Aeromar, Blv de Las Naciones s/n, Plan de Los Amates, T744-446 9394. AeroMéxico, Av Costera Miguel Alemán, No 286, T744-485 2280. American Airlines, airport, T744-446 9232. Aviacsa, Av Costera Miguel Alemán 178, T744-481 3240. Avolar, Blv de las Naciones s/n, Poblado de los Amates, T744-466 9373. Click/Mexicana de Aviacion, La Gran Plaza, Locales 8, 9 & 10, T744-486 7569. Continental, airport, T744-446 9063. Delta, airport, T800-123 4710. Interjet, Prolongación Farrallón y Av Costera Miguel Alemán, Centro Comercial Plaza Marbella 26, T744-484 5124. US Airways, airport, T800-428 4322.

Bus

Local There are several bus routes, with one running the full length of Costera Miguel Alemán and linking the older part of town to the latest hotels, marked 'Caleta-Zócalo-Base', US$0.50. Buses to **Pie de la Cuesta**, 12 km,

US$0,60. From Ejido bus terminal to the Zócalo for the 'Zócalo-Caleta' bus.

Long distance There are several bus stations. **Estrella Blanca** has two 1st-class terminals: **Terminal Ejido**, Ejido 97, for Mexico City, Taxco, Puerto Escondido, Zihuatanejo and other coastal destinations; and **Terminal Papagayo**, Cuauhtémoc 1605, with buses for Mexico City, Cuernavaca, Puebla, Guadalajara and Tijuana, among others. Nearby, the 1st-class **Estrella de Oro Terminal**, Cuauhtémoc 1490, esq Massieu, has services to Chilpancingo, Mexico City, Taxco and Zihuatanejo. The 2nd-class **Estrella Blanca Terminal**, Cuauhtémoc 97, serves mostly local destinations in Guerrero state.

To **Chilpancingo**, hourly or better, 2-3 hrs, US$7. To **Cuernavaca**, 7 daily, 5 hrs, US$22. To **Mexico City**, 6 hrs, US$30-45. To **Oaxaca**, no direct bus, so take a buses to **Puerto Escondido** (7 a day, US$24) or **Pochutla** (5 a day, US$28); also via Pinotepa Nacional (at 2100) but on a worse road. To **Puerto Escondido**, 7 a day, 9½ hrs, US$24. To **Tapachula**, take Impala 1st-class bus to **Huatulco**, arriving 1930; from there **Cristóbal Colón** at 2030 to **Salina Cruz**, arriving about 2400, then take 1st- or 2nd-class bus. To **Taxco**, 10 daily, 4 hrs, US$16. To **Zihuatanejo**, 4-5 hrs, hourly, US$12.

Taxi

Most fares around town cost US$2-5, airport shuttle to the **Zona Hotelera** costs around US$6 (private taxi US$20-25). Taxis are more expensive from outside bus terminals; catch on the street for US$3 to the Zócalo. Acapulco's *taxistas* are ruthless, so take care and beware scams, rip-offs and overcharging, especially if travelling from the bus station or airport.

Car hire

Many car hire outlets, especially in the Zona Hotelera. **Avis**, Av Costera M Alemán 139-C, T744-484 5720; **Budget**, Av Costera M Alemán 93, Local 2, T744-481 2433; **Hertz**, Av Costera M Alemán 137-A, corner of Sandoval, T744-485 8947.

Directory

Acapulco *p553, maps p553 and p554*
Banks There are numerous many banks with ATMs in the Old Town (near the Zócalo) and Zona Hotelera. **Embassies and consulates** Canada, T744-484 1306, Local 23, Centro Comercial Marbella, corner of Prolongación Farallón and Miguel Alemán, Mon-Fri 0900-1400. **France**, Av Costera M Alemán 91, T744-484 4580. **Norway**, Maralisa Hotel, T744-484 3525. **Spain**, Av Costera Miguel Alemán, T744-435 1500. **Sweden**, Av Insurgentes 2, T744-485 2935. **UK** Edificio Hemisphere, Migel Aleman 49, T744-484 3331. **USA**, Hotel Continental, Av Costera M Alemán, T744-469 0556, 0900- 1400.

Immigration Juan Sebastián el Cuno 1, Costa Azul el lado, T744-484 9021, 0800- 1400, take a 'Hornos Base' bus from Miguel Alemán, US$0.35, 30 mins, visa extensions possible. **Internet** Cafés normally charge US$1 per hr, good speeds. **Laundry** Tintorería Bik, 5 de Mayo. Lavadín, José María Iglesias 11a, T744- 482 2890, next to Hotel Colimense, recommended. Various other places on the streets around the Zócalo. **Post office** Costera 125, 2 blocks south of Zócalo. **Telephone** Public offices will not take collect calls; try from a big hotel (ask around, there will be a surcharge).

La Costa Grande

Guerrero's Costa Grande, or 'Big Coast', is a sublime stretch of Pacific shoreline punctuated by placid lagoons and drowsy villages. It reaches west of Acapulco for more than 300 km and is home to the twin resorts of Ixtapa and Zihuatanejo, now almost a single contiguous settlement with a single name. But thankfully, in spite of nearly merging, the identities of these two popular tourist towns remains distinct. Zihuatanejo has its roots as a fishing village and was a popular hippy hangout in the 1970s. It remains a relatively tranquil retreat, home to some excellent beaches and dive sites, great restaurants, and a friendly, welcoming population. Ixtapa has no such roots, owing its existence to the Mexican state, who designed its high-rise towers and complexes from scratch. It is obscenely characterless, overpriced and best avoided altogether. The Costa Grande, flanked by rolling mountains and verdant palm plantations, is traversed by Highway 200. Drivers will have access to a wealth of obscure and lesser visited attractions, including deserted beaches and luxuriant estuaries resplendent with chattering birds.
▸▸ For listings, see pages 569-572.

Acapulco to Zihuatanejo

West of Acapulco, transit along coastal Highway 200 is simple, smooth and generally quite rapid. Increasingly, however, there are military checkpoints. Beyond **Coyuca**, the road heads inland and the first place of any real size is **San Jerónimo**, roughly 100 km west of Acapulco. Here, a detour leads to a verdant lagoon and windswept beaches of **Paraíso Escondido**; turn south before crossing the bridge into town and continue through the villages of **Arenal de Alvarez** and **Hacienda de Cabañas**.

Back on Highway 200, west of San Jerónimo, the next sizeable settlement is **Técpan**, capital of the municipality with the same name. Nearby there is a beach at **Michigan**; take a southbound detour to get there. As Highway 200 continues west, it skirts the shores of **Laguna El Veinte** before passing the small towns of **San Luis Pedro** and **San Luis de la Loma**, almost a single settlement. Further on, it dips briefly towards the shore, offering access to the rugged beaches of **Piedra Tlalcoyunque**, **Ojo de Agua** and the small community of **Puerto Vicente Guerrero**.

Inland, **Papanoa** is the next sizeable settlement, followed by **Coyuquila Norte**, after which the highway dips back to the ocean. Some of the coast here is quite rugged, and there are good surf beaches around the village of **Loma Bonita**; basic accommodation is available, just ask around.

Next, the highway passes through the small town of **Juluchuca** before arriving at the more sizeable settlement of **Petatlán**. Just beyond town, a turning heads to the village of **Soledad de Maciel**, also known as La Chole, site of an important pre-Hispanic settlement. Archaeologists have uncovered some pyramids, plazas and a ball court here. Back on Highway 200, you will pass a string of small settlements before arriving at Zihuatanejo. At **Los Achotes** is the turning for popular the fishing settlement of **Barra de Potosí**, although many people like to visit as a day trip from Zihuatanejo (see below).

Barra de Potosí

Backed by peaceful green hills, the small fishing of Barra de Potosí, 40 minutes south of Zihuatanejo, makes a great contrast to the some of the more densely populated stretches of the Guerrero coast. Wonderfully rustic and utterly devoid of high-rise settlements, this beautiful sandy beach arcs around a vast curved bay. There is absolutely nothing to do here but relax in a hammock, swim in the sea and dine on a feast of freshly caught fish. Nearby is the **Laguna de Potosí**, with many species of aquatic birds. Fishermen may give you a tour in their boats, otherwise try **Zoe Kayak Tours** in Zihuatanejo (see Activities and tours, page 572) for a gentler, more intimate encounter with the wildlife. To get here from Zihuatanejo, catch a bus towards Petatlán and exit at the Barra de Potosí turning (Los Achotes), from where pick-up trucks shuttle visitors to the beach. There are some simple lodgings and a handful of pricey B&Bs, if you can't tear yourself away.

Zihuatanejo ⊖⊖⊘⊘▲⊖⊖ ➤ pp569-572. Colour map 2, C3.

Once little more than an obscure fishing village, the low-key beach resort of Zihuatanejo is an increasingly popular alternative to overdeveloped Acapulco. It owes much of its fame and prosperity to its less attractive neighbour, Ixtapa, a planned resort that brought unprecedented wealth and attention to the area. But despite being spruced up, 'Zihua', as it is called locally, still retains much of its Mexican village charm. For now, it remains reassuringly quiet, low-rise, laid-back and friendly. Perched inside a sheltered bay, the town centre is compact and easily explored on foot. There are an abundance of gaudy souvenir shops, little art galleries and, thanks to its burgeoning popularity, some very good restaurants.

The small **Museo Arqueológico** ① Av 5 de Mayo, US$0.60, in the old customs and immigration building, has exhibits on state history and anthropology, and at the town entrance, the **Plaza de Toros** has seasonal corridas. Various watersports can be pursued in Zihuatanejo, especially sports fishing, diving and snorkelling (see Activities and tours, page 571). **Tourist information** ① Zihuatanejo Pte s/n, Colonia La Deportiva, T755-554 2001, www.ixtapa-zihuatanejo.com, Mon-Fri 0800-1600, with bilingual assistance, can be obtained from the Palacio Municipal, 2 km northeast of the centre. There is a smaller office on Paseo de la Bahia, near Playa La Ropa, and a kiosk during high season, Alvarez s/n. At sunset, thousands of swallows meet in the air above the town and settle for the night on telephone poles, all in the space of a single minute.

Zihuatanejo

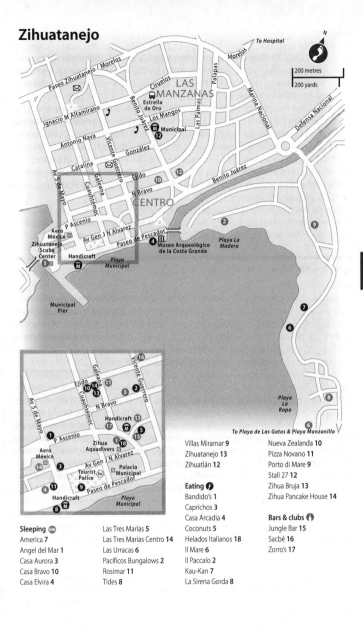

Sleeping
America **7**
Angel del Mar **1**
Casa Aurora **3**
Casa Bravo **10**
Casa Elvira **4**

Las Tres Marías **5**
Las Tres Marías Centro **14**
Las Urracas **6**
Pacíficos Bungalows **2**
Rosimar **11**
Tides **8**

Villas Miramar **9**
Zihuatanejo **13**
Zihuatlán **12**

Eating
Bandido's **1**
Caprichos **3**
Casa Arcadia **4**
Coconuts **5**
Helados Italianos **18**
Il Mare **6**
Il Paccalo **2**
Kau-Kan **7**
La Sirena Gorda **8**

Nueva Zealanda **10**
Pizza Novano **11**
Porto di Mare **9**
Stall 27 **12**
Zihua Bruja **13**
Zihua Pancake House **14**

Bars & clubs
Jungle Bar **15**
Sacbé **16**
Zorro's **17**

Beaches

There are four beaches in the bay, starting with **Playa Principal** in the centre of town. The waters here are a bit dirty and hawkers often traipse the sands, but there are bars and restaurants too, and it can be a sociable place to enjoy a few cocktails at sunset. From here, follow the walkway to reach nearby **Playa La Madera**, also a bit unclean but relatively sheltered. Much better is **Playa La Ropa**, 20 minutes' walk away. From La Madera, you will need to ascend the steps into hills and follow the road past the cliffs. Otherwise you can catch a bus from the centre of town. La Ropa ('the clothes') derives its name from the silks that washed up here when a Chinese trading ship sunk off-shore. It is a long sandy stretch flanked by various hotels and restaurants, and is possibly the bay's best beach. But also good is **Playa Las Gatas**, which is secluded, sheltered and a haven for aquatic sports. You can rent masks and snorkels from some of the restaurants; visibility is pretty good. Las Gatas can be reached by boat from the centre, US$3 return, or a 20-minute walk from La Ropa over the rocks, popular with fishermen.

Beyond the bay, feisty **Playa Larga** lies about 10 km out of town, accessible with a 'Coacoyul' *combi* (exit at the turning). Secluded **Playa Manzanillo**, with some of the best snorkelling in the area, is accessible only by boat.

Ixtapa ◉🐾🏔️▲ ›› *pp569-572. Colour map 2, C2.*

→ *Phone code: 755.*

Ixtapa (meaning 'where there are salt lakes'), 244 km northwest of Acapulco, is one of Mexico's most popular resort developments. Built in the 1980s and intended as an alternative to Cancún, its modern hotels, manicured lawns and overpriced restaurants are as unglamorous as they are devoid of soul. Unless you've got money to burn or a perverse sense of aesthetics, there's little point spending time here. That said, if you do enjoy the company of grotesquely drunken frat boys, the nightlife is far superior to anything else in the area.

Ixtapa's large luxury hotels all obtain food supplies from Mexico City, making food more expensive. There is also a wealth of overpriced amenities including a shopping complex, golf courses, parachute skiing and tennis courts. By law, all Mexican beaches are free to access, but in Ixtapa, the sly hotel owners have attempted to subvert this fact by building their structures in dense rows in front of the principal beach, **Playa del Palma**. You will need to trespass through their lobbies to reach the sand. The waters, plied by motorboats and jet skis, aren't great for swimming anyhow. At the western end of the beach is a marina and surfing spot, **Playa Escolleras**. In the next bay, on the other side of Punta Ixtapa, are two moderately better beaches: **Playa Quieta** and **Playa Linda**. Fortunately, it's not all grim in Ixtapa. Offshore lies **Isla Ixtapa**, with a few pleasant beaches, coral reefs, snorkelling spots and restaurants. Boats depart from Playa Linda, US$4 round-trip. There are also turtles, many species of shellfish, fish, and pelicans at **El Morro de los Pericos**, which can be seen by launch. **Isla Grande** has been developed as a nature park and leisure resort. Ixtapa's **tourist office** ① *T755-553 1967, 0800-2030*, is in Ixtapa Shopping Plaza.

Beyond Ixtapa

Paved Highway 134 leads directly to Toluca and Mexico City, but there are no fuel stops or supplies until **Ciudad Altamarino**. The road runs north through coconut plantations where the slightly alcoholic drink *tuba*, made from coconut milk fermented on the tree, is for sale. It also passes through remote countryside, prone to landslides, occasional bandit activity and unpredictable army checkpoints (looking for guns and drugs). Another option is to continue west on Highway 200, which heads northwest to Lázaro Cárdenas and Playa Azul in Michoacán (see page 433). The pleasant little beach town of **Troncones**, 20 km north of Ixtapa, has several restaurants and a hotel, and is worth stopping at. After passing through Barra de la Navidad, Highway 200 eventually arrives in Puerto Vallarta.

◉ La Costa Grande listings

For Sleeping and Eating price codes and other relevant information, see Essentials pages 47-51.

◔ Sleeping

Zihuatanejo *p566, map p567*
It's difficult to find accommodation during Semana Santa and around Christmas and New Year, when prices can double and the town is booked out.

Downtown
AL-A Zihuatanejo, Ramírez 2, T755-554 5330, www.ixtapa-zihuatanejo.net/zihuacenter. A large hotel with 73 good, clean, comfortable rooms, some have balconies, all have a/c, cable TV, telephone and safe. Some are larger than others, so ask to see a few. Also has apartments (**AL**), a Mexican restaurant, pool, parking and laundry service. Good low-season reductions.
A-D America, Galeana 16, T755-554 4337. Rooms here are various sizes, the cheapest without a/c. Bar and restaurant, and good little apartments with kitchens (**A**). English spoken.
B Las Tres Marías Centro, Juan Alvarez 52, T755-554 6706. An annexed and slightly pricier version of the **Las Tres Marías** on the riverside (see below). Rooms are simple, but comfortable, and the best are on the second floor. Prices double in Christmas holidays.
C-D Rosimar, Ejido 35, T755-554 2139. Starting to fade, but not bad. Standard rooms have fan, hot water and TV, some have a/c, others have kitchen facilities. Clean and reasonable. Nice plants in the courtyard.
D Casa Aurora, Nicolás Bravo 42, T755 554 3046, www.zihuatanejo.com.mx/aurora. Clean, comfortable, straightforward rooms with fan, shared fridge and access to a microwave. Some have hot water and a/c.

D Casa Bravo, Bravo 20, T755-554 2548. Clean, pleasant rooms with a/c, hot water and cable TV. Some are nice and spacious, so ask to see a few. Friendly and reasonable value. Parking.
D Casa Elvira, Alvarez 29, in the older part of town on the waterfront, T755-554 2061. A very basic hotel with lots of lovely plants draped around the inner courtyard. Rooms are simple but clean, with fan, bath and cold water only. The restaurant on the beach is a good place to watch the world go by. Good and reasonable, particularly for backpackers.
D Zihuatlán, Palapas 4, T755-554 0466. Clean and comfortable rooms with a/c, cable TV, fan. Facilities include parking and a small pool. Reasonable.
D-E Las Tres Marías, La Noria 4, across the wooden footbridge, T755-554 2191. A very pleasant place with large communal balconies overlooking the town and harbour. Rooms are clean but sparsely decorated, with tiny baths and cold water. You may get woken by the roosters and early morning activity on the river. Some rooms have a/c (**D**).
E-F Angel del Mar, Pedro Ascencio 10, T755-554 5084. Formerly Angela's, this backpacker hostel has 3 dorms with 6 beds each, and 6 private rooms with bath, hot water. Facilities include kitchen, hammocks, fridge, lockers and communal room. The restaurant opposite, **Fonda Tertulia**, serves cheap *comida corrida*. The most economical place in town. Clean.

Beaches *p568*
LL Tides, Playa La Ropa, T755-555 5500, www.tideszihuatanejo.com. A highly regarded and award-winning hotel with 2 world-class restaurants, daily events, tennis courts, fitness centre and 4 pools. The rooms and beachfront suites are luxurious and tastefully attired. If you can't afford to stay

here but want a taste of the high life, you can buy a day pass for US$25 entitling you to use the bar, restaurant, sun loungers and pool. Recommended, if you can afford it.

AL Villas Miramar, Playa La Madera, T755-554 3350, www.hotelvillasmiramar.com. A comfortable 4-star hotel with rooms spread across 4 buildings. Good amenities, including a golf course, 2 pools, massage, car rentals, tours and lovely gardens.

A-B Pacíficos Bungalows, Playa La Madera, T755-554 2112, www.bungalowspacificos. com. Advance reservation necessary. This hotel has a huge terrace with expansive ocean views, hammocks and colourful flowers, just steps from the beach. The owner, Anita, is very friendly, helpful and speaks English and German. Highly recommended.

B Las Urracas, Playa La Ropa, T755-554 2049. 17 cosy bungalows with fridge, kitchen, fan, comfortable little lounges, fully equipped ovens, utensils, hot water, cold water and pleasant verandas. Friendly and good value. No a/c.

Ixtapa p568
Accommodation in Ixtapa is high-end.
LL Barceló, Blv Ixtapa, T755-553 1858. www.barceloixtapa.com. A 5-star hotel with predictably high standards and a plethora of amenities including a panoramic lift, massage, gym, laundry, dive shop, beauty salon, tour operator, barber, tobacco shop and everything else you could possibly need. Reductions for AAA members. Recommended.
LL Las Brisas, 5-min drive south of downtown Ixtapa, T755-553 2121. A vast luxury complex with contemporary architectural design and a spectacular setting in a small jungle. Services and amenities are 1st class, from outdoor pools to tennis courts.

Camping
Playa Linda Trailer Park, at Playa Linda Hotel, Ctra Playa Linda, just north of Ixtapa. 50 spaces, full hook-ups, restaurant, recreation hall, babysitters, on beach, US$14 for 2, comfortable.

🍴 Eating

Zihuatanejo p566, map p567
There are plenty of decent restaurants in Zihuatanejo, although some of them are perched on cliffs out of town, requiring a taxi or own transport to reach them. Look out for cheaper dining nearby and in the market.

₸₸₸ Caprichos, Av 5 de Mayo 4, www.caprichos grill.com. Daily 1600-2300. This excellent restaurant has a very tasteful interior and a beautiful garden with candle-lit tables. Cuisine is international with Mexican accents, all tempered by flavours of *mesquite* charcoal, which is used a lot in the preparation of local seafood. Try the catch of the day in white wine sauce. A good wine list, with bottles from South America, France and Italy, by the glass or bottle.

₸₸₸ Coconuts, Pasaje Ramírez 1, www.restaurantcoconuts.com. Established in 1979 and housed by Zihuatanejo's oldest building, this fine restaurant serves creative offerings by Australian chef David Dawson. Seafood and meat dishes include *filet in hoja* sauce, filet mignon and chargrilled pork in mango chutney. One of the best.

₸₸₸ Il Mare, Escéncia La Ropa. Impeccable Mediterranean food and great views of the bay.

₸₸₸ Kau-Kan, Ctra Escéncia 7. Highly regarded gourmet restaurant serving creative international dishes and seafood. Up on the cliffs with views.

₸₸₸ Porto di Mare, Paseo del Pescador 56. Delicious Basque cooking with a Mexican and Mediterranean twist. Dishes include gazpacho soup, mixed paella, Italian pastas, sorbets, calamari and red bell pepper lasagne. Friendly and helpful management. Recommended.

₸₸₸-₸₸ Bandido's, Ascencio and 5 de Mayo. Touristy and open-air, but fun, with live music and satellite TV. They serve Mexican food like *chile relleno de queso*, tequila, coconut shrimps, beef fajitas and fish fillets in lobster sauce. Vaguely in the style of a colonial hacienda.

₸₸₸-₸₸ La Sirena Gorda, Paseo del Pescador 90. Thu-Tue. Popular and laid-back seafood joint that serves the usual fresh fish fare.

₹₹₹-₹₹ Pizza Novana, Bahia de Zihuatanejo Alvarez. Great pizzeria with red and white chequered table cloths and an attractive interior adorned with fairy lights.

₹₹ Casa Arcadia, Paseo del Pescador. Cheapish seafood place. The food isn't out of this world, but it's fresh and tasty and served right on the beach. One of a few similar places on this stretch. Wear mosquito repellent.

₹₹ Il Paccolo, Bravo 38. Various steak cuts, pastas, pizza and fish dishes.

₹₹-₹ Nueva Zealandia, Cuautemoc 30. Pleasant little diner with clean counter space and tables, some outside. Good coffees, breakfasts and enchiladas.

₹₹-₹ Stall 27, at the market. Very popular, cheap and good, try local lobster for about US$10; most meals cost around US$3.

₹₹-₹ Zihua Pancake House, Galeana y Ejido. A great breakfast spot that's popular with foreign tourists and expats.

₹ Las Braseros, Ejido 26. Busy little joint serving Mexican food, including a wide range of tacos.

Cafés and ice-cream parlours

Helados Italianos, Alvarez 28. Tasty, flavoursome Italian ice-cream.

Zihua Bruja, Galeana, between Ejido and Bravo. Owned and operated by a music and art teacher, Miguel Angel Quimiro, who gives free classes to the town's under-privileged kids. The space functions as an art and music school by day and a café by night, when there's often live acoustic music. They serve coffee, *refrescos*, *cervezas* and snacks.

Ixtapa *p568*

₹₹₹ Villa de la Selva, T755-553 0362. Recommended for food and views, book in advance.

₹₹-₹ Two Fat & Tropical Boys, Centro Comercial Los Arcos, T755-553 0160. A popular bar/restaurant with live music and a varied menu.

₹ Super Tacos, west of the commercial centre by the roundabout. Serves great hot sandwiches.

🍷 Bars and clubs

Zihuatanejo *p566, map p567*

Jungle Bar, Ramirez 6. Funky, popular bar with a young crowd, crazy decor, colourful murals and ice cold beers. Recommended.

Sacbé, Guerrero y Ejido. Youthful disco-lounge that's popular with Mexican students.

Zorro's, Ascenio y Galeana. Interesting bar with a slightly dingy ambience and incipient alcoholics. Their slogan: "Hey my beer's a buck, so get in here you crazy… "

Ixtapa *p568*

Every hotel without exception has at least 1 nightclub/disco and 2 bars.

⛰ Activities and tours

Zihuatanejo *p566, map p567*
Diving and snorkelling

There are some great dive sites around Zihuatanejo. Off Playa Las Gatas is an underwater wall built, according to one legend, by the Tarascan King Calzonzin, to keep the sharks away while he bathed; the wall is fairly massive and can be seen clearly.

Carlo Scuba, Playa Las Gatas, T755-554 6003, www.carloscuba.com. Dive trips include full equipment, dive master and soft drinks. A 2-tank trip costs US$85; single tank costs US$65. Also night dives, US$75, and PADI certification from Open Water to Advanced. Morning snorkel trips with the divers cost US$20. Get a 5% discount when paying cash.

Zihua Aquadivers, Alvarez 30-4, opposite the basketball court, T755-544 6666, www.divezihuatanejo.com. An established operator with 12 years of experience. Single (US$50) and 2-tank dives (US$75), to some 35 sites. Gear rentals cost extra. Naui certification, snorkelling and night dives also available. Dives depart daily at 0930 and 1130.

Zihuatanejo Dive Center, La Noria 1, over the bridge, T755-554 8554, www.zihuatanejo divecenter.com. Diving, snorkelling, sailing and fishing. 2-tank dive US$85. PADI certification available including Open Water and Advanced. English, French and Spanish spoken.

Fishing

You can commission boats from the pier, roughly US$180 for up to 4 people.
Temo Sport Fishing, Cuauhtémoc y Alvarez, T755-112 1779, temosportfishing@yahoo. com.mx. Sports fishing and salt water fly- fishing for big game and shell fish. A 7-hr expedition for 2-4 people costs around US$200, including tackle, bait and ice. Snorkel tours are also available, with trips to Manzanillo Beach where there's coral reef and clear waters.

Kayaking

Zoe Kayak Tours, T755-553 0496, www.zoekayaktours.com. Small-scale kayak tours of the mangrove reserve at Laguna de Potosi, 18 km south of Zihuatanejo. The reserve has abundant bird-life which is encountered in the early morning. Trips depart 0730 and cost US$80.

Ixtapa *p568*

Activities are numerous and much the same as for Zihuatanejo (below). **Adventours**, Hotel Villas Paraíso, T755-556 3322. Arranges walks, cycling, sea-kayaking, birdwatching and rappelling. **Ixtapa Aqua Paradise**, Hotel Barceló Ixtapa, Local 2, T755-553 1510, www.ixtapa aquaparadise.com. Scuba-diving; PADI diving courses, excursions and night dives.

☉ Transport

Zihuatanejo *p566, map p567*
Air

Ixtapa-Zihuatanejo international airport (ZIH), 20 km from town, T755-554 2070. *Colectivos* or shared taxis operate, US$8-10; a private taxi for up to four costs US$20-25. Many direct domestic flights from **Mexico City** and **Guadalajara**, with other destinations by connection. International from **Houston**, **Los Angeles**, **Phoenix**, **San Francisco** and **Seattle**.

Airline offices AeroMéxico, Centro Comercial Los Patios, T755-553 0555; Delta (airport), T755-554 3386; Click-Mexicana, Nicolas Bravo 64, T755-554 2208.

Bus

Estrella de Oro operates its own terminal on Paseo Palmar, serving **Mexico City**, with services at 0640, 2000, 2210, 2300, 9 hrs, US$45. Services to **Acapulco** (4-5 hrs) calling at **Petatlán** and **Tecpan de Galeana** at 0600, and on the hour until 1800, US$14. To **Lázaro Cárdenas** 0630, 0830, 0930, 1200 then hourly until 2000, 2 hrs, US$5.50.

The **Central de Autobuses** is on the Zihuatanejo–Acapulco highway opposite Pemex station (bus from centre US$0.40). Estrella Blanca and a range of smaller lines, including **TAP Parhikuna**, **Turistar** and **Costa**, operate from here. The terminal is clean, with several snack bars and services. Next door is the Estrella de Oro terminal.

To **Acapulco**, hourly, US$13. **Manzanillo**, 1000, 1050, 2000, 8 hrs, US$28. To **Puerto Vallarta**, 1020 and 2235. To **Mexico City**, 12 daily with various lines, US$38. To **Laredo**, 1730, 30 hrs, US$78. To **Lárazo Cárdenas**, hourly after 1230, 2 hrs, US$5. To **Puerto Escondido** and **Huatulco**, 1920, 12hrs US$25

Car hire

Hertz, Nicolás Bravo and airport, T755-554 3050; several others with offices at the airport and in Ixtapa hotels including **Avis**, **Budget**, **Dollar** and **Economy**.

❸ Directory

Zihuatanejo *p566, map p567*
Banks Several around town, including Banamex, Ejido y Guerrero; Bancomer, Juárez y Bravo; Banorte, Juárez y Ejido. **Internet** Most places charge around US$1 per hr. Try: Zihuatanejo Bar Net, Hotel Zihuatanejo, Ramírez 2; and Infinitum Internet, Bravo 12. **Laundry** Lavandería del Centro, Guerrero 17, US$2 for 1½ kg.

Contents

Footprint features

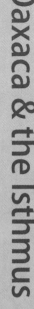

Oaxaca & the Isthmus

At a glance

Getting around Buses, domestic flights.

Time required 2-3 weeks to sample the major attractions.

Weather Temperatures stay in the mid- to high 20s most of the year, particularly on the coast, but there are often variations according to altitude. The rainy season is May-Sep.

When not to go It's good any time of the year.

★ **Don't miss ...**

1 Monte Albán and Mitla, pages 582 and 587.

2 Sierra Juárez, page 589.

3 Sample *mole*, page 593.

4 Sip mescal in one of Oaxaca's cantinas, page 594.

5 Oaxaca markets, page 596.

6 Zipolite and Mazunte, page 605.

Oaxaca is a place of brilliant colours, rich indigenous heritage and mouth-watering culinary traditions. At its heart lies the capital, Oaxaca City, a UNESCO World Heritage Site replete with gems of colonial architecture. Some of Mexico's finest historic churches can be found here – testament to Baroque at its most grandiose, but beyond mere historical appeal, Oaxaca City also has an irresistible bohemian charm. There is a thriving arts scene, as evidenced by the plethora of galleries and craft stores, often overlooked by the casual visitor.

Travel beyond the terraced cafés and plazas of the capital and an intriguing and entirely different world unfolds. The dusty Central Valleys are a land of crumbling, pre-Columbian ruins, teeming indigenous villages and otherworldly natural wonders. A visit to the hilltop ruins of Monte Albán is obligatory, but Mitla also, with its fascinating stonework, pays homage to the splendour of Oaxaca's ancient civilizations. The villages scattered throughout the valleys also conceal several interesting attractions including El Tule, one of the world's oldest trees, and countless markets. The state's finest crafts are produced in the valleys, including sleek black pottery, dazzling tapestries and psychedelic animal sculptures, *alebrijes*.

South of the capital, the Pacific Ocean pounds an exceptionally vivid shoreline, where beach communities have blossomed. Puerto Escondido is a well-established surfers' haven, where the Mexican Pipeline provides some of the world's most spectacular waves. The party town of Zipolite has long drawn an alternative crowd, while the secluded hideaways of Mazunte and San Agustinillo are only just developing their tourist potential. Puerto Angel is an old Oaxaca favourite, a former fishing village, and is popular with a slightly older crowd. The beauty of this region has not been overlooked by big business either; the resort of Huatulco further south offers a convenient, if sanitized, experience of Oaxaca's Pacific coast.

East, towards the Yucatán Peninsula and Central America, Oaxaca state narrows into the Isthmus of Tehuantepec – a region characterized by strong local culture and an absence of foreign tourists.

Mexico City to Oaxaca

The express toll road from Mexico City to Oaxaca first runs generally eastwards to Puebla (see page 177), where it turns south to wind through wooded mountains at altitudes of 1500-1800 m, emerging at last into the warm, red-earth Oaxaca valley. It has been described as a stunning bus ride along a new motorway through cactus-filled valleys and plains. The route described here, however, avoids the new motorway in favour of the less sophisticated but equally attractive Route 190, which continues from Oaxaca to Tehuantepec. The road, although paved throughout and in good condition, serpentines over the sierras and is quite beautiful. The alternative coastal route is also very attractive and of special interest to visitors who wish to engage in the many water sports available. Buses on the new express toll road now take six hours from Mexico City to Oaxaca. ▸▸ For listings, see pages 589-601.

Puebla to Oaxaca ● ▸▸ pp589-601. Colour map 2, C5.

Atlixco → Phone code: 244.
Route 190 heads south from Puebla to Izúcar de Matamoros. A side road leads to **Huaquechula** where there's a 16th-century Renaissance and plateresque chapel. The road passes through Atlixco ('the place lying on the water'), which has interesting baroque examples in the **Capilla de la Tercera Orden de San Agustín** and **San Juan de Dios**. The annual **Atlixcayotl festival** is on San Miguel hill. Nearby are the curative springs of **Axocopán**.

Izúcar de Matamoros and around → Colour map 2, C4, Phone code: 243.
After Atlixco, Route 190 continues to the town of **Izúcar de Matamoros** (from *itzocan*, meaning 'his dirty face'), famous for its clay handicrafts, the 16th-century convent of **Santo Domingo**, and two nearby spas, **Los Amatitlanes** (about 6 km away) and **Ojo de Carbón**.

A road leads southwest from Izúcar to **Axochiapan**, Morelos state, and to a paved road to the village of **Jolalpan** with the baroque church of Santa María (1553). The road continues to **Atenango del Río** in Guerrero state; the last 20-30 km are unpaved.

Acatlán to Oaxaca
From Izúcar de Matamoros, Route 190 switchbacks to **Tehuitzingo**. Then the landscape is fairly flat to **Acatlán**, a friendly village where black and red clay figures and palm and flower hats are made.

The Zapotecs

The Zapotec language is used by more than 300,000 people in the state as a first or second language (about 20% of the Oaxaca State population speaks only an indigenous language).

The Zapotec people weave fantastic toys of grass. Their dance, the Jarabe Tlacolula Zandunga, is performed by barefoot girls splendid in becoming coifs, wearing short, brightly coloured skirts, ribbons and long lace petticoats. The men, all in white with colourful hand-kerchiefs, dance opposite them with their hands behind their backs.

Only women, from Tehuantepec or Juchitán, dance the slow and stately Zandunga. Their costumes involve embroidered velvet blouses, full skirts with white pleated and starched lace ruffles and huipiles.

Carry on to Petlalcingo, then ascend to **Huajuapan de León**, an important centre for palm products. To the southeast (12 km) is the Yosocuta Dam with fish farms and recreational facilities.

After Huajuapan de León, Route 125 leads to **Pinotepa Nacional**. Next on Route 190 is **Tamazulapan** with a 17th-century church and a pink stone arch in front of the city hall.

Yanhuitlán, 72 km northwest of Oaxaca on Route 190, has a beautiful 400-year-old church, part of the Santo Domingo monastery, built on a pre-Hispanic platform – it is considered one of the best examples of 16th-century New World Hispanic architecture. Yanhuitlán is in the Sierra Mixteca, where Dominican friars began evangelising in 1526. Two other important centres in the region were San Juan Bautista at **Coixtlahuaca** and the open chapel at **Teposcolula**. The scenery and the altars, the huge convents in such a remote area are a worthwhile day trip from Oaxaca. The new highway from **Nochixtlán** to Oaxaca (103 km) has been recommended for cyclists: it has wide hard shoulders and easy gradients.

Oaxaca City ☺❸⊘∩❸❸❻▲❸❻ ▸▸ pp589-601. Colour map 2, C5.

→ *Phone code: 951. Altitude: 1546 m.*

Founded by the Spanish as Antequera in 1521 on the site of a Zapotec and Mixtec settlement, Oaxaca gracefully combines its colonial and native roots. Fine stone buildings, churches, arcades and airy patios attest to its importance during the colonial period, while its markets, crafts, dances and festive days stem from a more indigenous past. Relaxing with a coffee in one of the many street cafés and bars of Oaxaca, it's easy to while away the hours. Once you've explored the museums, cathedrals, markets and laid-back cobbled streets, you can sit down with a beer or mescal, the local firewater, to plan your days exploring the surrounding hills and valleys.

In the summer of 2006, Oaxaca City experienced the worst social unrest in its recent history as an innocuous protest over teachers' pay led to clashes resulting in deaths, violence and injuries. Today, Oaxaca is recovering from its brief foray into mayhem. The hardest hit were the poorest members of the community, whose fledgling businesses could not withstand several months without trade.

Ins and outs

Getting there **Aeropuerto Xoxocotlán** (OAX) is 9 km south of the city. **Transportación Terrestre Aeropuerto**, T951-514 4350, run *colectivos* to the centre for US$3; a private taxi

Oaxaca

200 metres
200 yards

Sleeping
Antonio's **1** C3
Casa Cid de León **3** C3
Casa Conzatti **10** A3
Casantica **11** C3
Central **2** D3
Ferri **12** D3
Hostal Pochon **18** B2
La Cabaña **13** E4
La Casona del Llano **14** A3
La Casona de Tita **29** A2
Las Rosas **4** D3
Lupita **17** D3
Marqués del Valle **20** C4

Mesón del Rey **5** D3
Mezkalito Hostel **19** D1
Monte Albán **6** D3
Palmar **21** E3
Parador San Andrés **22** D3
Parador Santo Domingo
  de Guzmán **7** A3
Paulina Youth Hostel **8** D3
Posada Catarina **24** E3
Posada del Centro **25** D3
Posada Don Matías **26** D3
Posada Las Casas **15** E3
Principal **9** C4
Rivera del Angel **27** E3
Valle de Oaxaca **28** D2

Eating
Amarantos **24** D4
Asador Vasco **18** D4
Bamby **28** C3

Café Alex **3** D2
Café Bar Tapas & Pisto **31** B3
Café Brújala **8** B3
Café Los Cuiles **30** C4
Cafetería Royalty **29** C3
Casa Grande del
  Gato Loco **14** D3
Casa Oaxaca **9** B3
Comala **7** B3
D'Florencia **17** E4
El Chef **20** D4
El Mesón **25** C4
El Naranjo **4** D3
El Shaddai **12** D2
Flor de Loto **10** C3
Flor de Oaxaca **22** D4
Gaia Organic Food **30** C4
Girasoles **11** D3
Hipocampo's **15** D3
Hostería de Alcalá **2** C3

La Abeja **33** B2
La Crepe **2** C3
La Primavera **16** D4
La Quebrada **21** D4
Los Danzantes **31** B3
Manantial Vegetariano **5** C2
Marco Polo **27** C4
Mi Tierra **13** D3
Pizza Nostrana **6** B3
Pizza Rústica **32** A3
Terranova, Taco Inn, Sushi Itto
  & Altos de Terranova **23** D4
Tito's **26** C3

Bars & clubs
Fandango **34** B2
La Cantinita **36** C4
La Divina **37** B3
La Tentación **35** C3

will cost around US$15. The first-class bus terminal is northeast of the Zócalo on Calzada Niños Héroes (some second-class buses also leave from here). The second-class terminal is west of the Zócalo on Calzada Valerio Trujano, near the Central de Abastos market. **Autobuses Unidos** (AU) has its own terminal northwest of the Zócalo at Prolongación Madero. ➤➤ *See Transport, page 599.*

Getting around Local town minibuses mostly charge US$0.30. For the first-class bus terminal, buses marked 'VW' leave from Avenida Juárez; for the second-class terminal, buses are marked 'Central'. Most major sites are in or near the centre and can be reached on foot.

Tourist information **Sectur Tourist Office**ⓘ *Av Juárez 703, T951-516 0123, daily 0800- 2000, www.aoaxaca.com*, with maps, posters, postcards and information about the city and state; ask here about the **Tourist Yú'ù** hostel programme in local communities (see Sleeping, page 591). There's a second **tourist office** ⓘ *inside the Palacio Municipal, Independencia 607, T951-516 0123*, which is very friendly and helpful. Visit the **Instituto Nacional de Estadística, Geografía e Informática (INEGI)** ⓘ *Emiliano Zapata 316, corner of Escuela Naval Militar, T951-512 4823*, for topographic maps and information about the state. Useful publications include *Oaxaca Times*, English monthly, www.oaxacatimes.com; *Oaxaca*, monthly in Spanish, English and French; *Comunicación*, in Spanish, with a few articles translated into English and French; *Guía Cultural*, published monthly by the Instituto Oaxaqueño de las Culturas, has a complete listing of musical events, exhibitions, conferences, libraries, etc.

Safety Oaxaca is a generally safe city; however, sensible precautions are advised. The **tourist police**ⓘ *Zócalo, near the cathedral*, are friendly and helpful; or you can contact the **Centro de Protección al Turista**ⓘ *T951-502 1200, extension 1595.*

Sights
The Zócalo with its arcades is the heart of town, a nicely shaded park with new paving surrounding a central bandstand. It's a pleasant place for a stroll or to sit and watch the world from one of the many street cafés. The Zócalo is always buzzing, full of activity, the surrounding cafés and restaurants busy with both Mexicans and visitors. Free music and dance events are often held in the evenings. During the day vendors sell food; in the evening they offer tourist wares. It is especially colourful on Saturday and Sunday nights when indigenous women weave and sell their goods. The colourful markets and varied crafts of Oaxaca are among the main attractions of the region, see Shopping, page 596.

Avenida Independencia is the main street running east–west, the nicer part of the old city is to the north of it; a simpler area, housing the cheaper hotels, lies to the south. Independencia is also a dividing line for the north-south streets, which change names here. Calle Macedonia Alcalá is a cobbled pedestrian walkway, which joins the Zócalo with the church of Santo Domingo, and many colonial buildings can be seen along this mall. This street and Calle Bustamante, its continuation to the south, are the dividing line for east-west streets, which change names here.

Worth visiting is the **Palacio de Gobierno**, on the south side of the Zócalo; it has beautiful murals and entry is free. There are often political meetings or protests outside, communities sometimes remaining camped outside overnight. The **Teatro Macedonio Alcalá**ⓘ *5 de Mayo y Independencia*, is an elegant theatre from Porfirio Díaz's times. It has a Louis XV-style entrance and a white marble staircase; regular performances are held here. The **Arcos de Xochimilco** on García Vigil, starting at Cosijopi, some eight blocks north of the Zócalo, is also worth a visit. In this picturesque area there are the remains of an aqueduct, cobbled passageways under the arches, flowers and shops. The house of the Maza family, for whom Benito Juárez worked and whose daughter he married, still stands at Independencia 1306 and is marked by a plaque. (A Zapotec, Benito Juárez was one of the great heroes of the nation, serving five terms as president of Mexico until his death in 1872.) Porfirio Díaz's birthplace is similarly remembered at the other end of Independencia, in a building that is now a kindergarten, near La Soledad. DH Lawrence wrote parts of *Mornings in Mexico* in Oaxaca, and revised *The Plumed Serpent* here; the house he rented is on Pino Suárez. The bar **El Favorito**, on 20 de Noviembre, a couple of blocks south of the Zócalo, supposedly inspired Malcolm Lowry's novel *Under the Volcano*, although others claim it was penned in and inspired by nearby **La Farola** (see Bars and clubs, page 594).

There is a grand view from **Cerro de Fortín**, the hill to the northwest of the centre. Here you will find the Guelaguetza amphitheatre, and a monument to Juárez stands on a hillside below. Atop the hill are an observatory and **planetarium**. Both were damaged during the social unrest of 2006 (see page 577) but the latter has since reopened to the public. It is a pleasant walk from town to the hill as far as the planetarium and antennas, but muggings have been reported on the trails that go through the woods, as well as on the dirt road that goes beyond. It's best to take a taxi.

Ciudad de las Canteras, the quarries from where the stone for the city's monumental churches and public buildings were extracted, has been converted into a beautifully landscaped park. It is located on **Calzada Niños Héroes de Chapultepec,** at the east end of Calzada Eduardo Vasconcelos; several city bus lines run there. There is a small stadium here and it is the site of the **Expo Feria Oaxaca** ① *running throughout the year, check with the tourist information*, a fair with rides, craft exhibits, food and various live performances.

Churches

Most churches now close at lunchtime between 1400-1600 after the crown of the Virgin of Soledad was stolen from an Oaxacan church when it was left unattended. The majority stay open 0700-1400 and 1600-2000.

On the Zócalo is the 17th-century **cathedral** with a fine baroque facade (watch the raising and lowering of the Mexican flag daily at 0800 and 1800 beside the cathedral), but the best sight by far, about four blocks from the square up the pedestrianized Calle Macedonio Alcalá, is the church of **Santo Domingo** ① *daily 0700-1400, 1600-2000, no flash photography allowed*, with its adjoining monastery, now the **Centro Cultural Santo Domingo**. The church is seen as one of the best examples of baroque style in Mexico. It first opened for worship in 1608 and was refurbished in the 1950s. Its gold leaf has to be seen to be believed. The ceilings and walls, sculptured and painted white and gold, are stunning.

The massive 17th-century **Basílica de La Soledad** (between Morelos and Independencia, west of Unión) has fine colonial ironwork and sculpture (including an exquisite Virgen de la Soledad). Its interior is predominantly fawn and gold; the plaques on the walls are painted like cross-sections of polished stone and the fine facade made up of stone of different colours. It is one of the best examples of carved stonework in the city. The church was built on the site of the hermitage to San Sebastián; begun in 1582, it was recommenced in 1682 because of earthquakes. It was consecrated in 1690 and the convent was finished in 1697. The **Museo Religioso de la Soledad** ① *Independencia 107, daily 0900-1400 and 1600-1900, US$0.35 donation requested*, at the back of the church, has a display of religious artefacts. In the small plaza outside the encircling wall, refreshments and offerings are sold. At **San Juan de Dios** ① *20 de Noviembre y Aldama*, there is an indigenous version in paint of the conquistadors' arrival in Oaxaca and of an anti-Catholic uprising in 1700. This was the first church in Oaxaca, originally dedicated to Santa Catalina Mártir. The church of **San Agustín** ① *Armenta y López at Guerrero*, has a fine facade, with bas relief of St Augustine holding the City of God above adoring monks (apparently modelled on that of San Agustín in Mexico City, now the National Library).

Museums

There is a cultural complex that includes a museum, exhibit halls, botanical garden, library, newspaper archives and bookshop; concerts are also performed here. It is housed in the former convent of Santo Domingo (Macedonio Alcalá y Gurrión), next to the Santo Domingo church. Construction of the convent started in 1575 and it was occupied by the Dominican friars from 1608 to 1812. After the expulsion of the church the Mexican army moved in between 1812 and 1972; later it housed the regional museum. Between 1994 and 1998, the convent was very beautifully restored, using only original materials and techniques. The **Museo de las Culturas de Oaxaca** ① *Tue-Sun1000-1900, US$4, video US$3*, housed in the Centro Cultural Santo Domingo, and sometimes referred to as 'the Louvre of Oaxaca', is a superb museum that requires at least four hours to visit; exhibits are beautifully displayed and explained in Spanish (with plans to implement a system of recorded explanations in other languages). A visit here is highly recommended. Fourteen galleries cover the history of Oaxaca from pre-Hispanic times to the contemporary period; the archaeology collection includes spectacular riches found in Tomb 7 of Monte Albán. There are also exhibits of different aspects of Oaxacan culture, such as crafts, cooking, traditional medicine etc, as well as temporary exhibits.

Also in the Centro Cultural is the interesting **Jardín Etnobotánico** ① *free guided tours in Spanish daily at 1300 and 1800, in English, Tue, Thu and Sat at 1100 and 1600 (high season only), 1 hr, sign up in advance*. This garden aims to preserve different species of plants that are native to southern Mexico. It has played, and continues to play, a role in the lives of different ethnic groups in Oaxaca. You can learn about the different species of *agaves* used to make mescal, pulque and tequila; the trees used in crafts; the *grana cochinilla*, an insect that lives in certain cacti and is used to dye cloth; the plants used in folk medicine; and many other species.

The **Museo de Arte Prehispánico Rufino Tamayo** ① *Morelos 503, Mon, Wed-Sat 1000-1400, 1600-1900, Sun 1000-1500, US$2.20*, has an outstanding display of pre-Columbian artefacts dating from 1250 BC to AD 1100, donated by the Oaxacan painter Rufino Tamayo in 1974. Information is in Spanish only and is not comprehensive. The **Museo Casa de Juárez** ① *García Vigil 609, daily 1000-1800, US$3*, is the former home of Benito Juárez (see page 767). It contains some of his possessions, historical documents and some bookbinding tools. The **Museo de Filatelia** ① *Reforma 504, Tue-Sun 1000-2000, free*, has temporary exhibits, a philatelic library and tours by appointment.

Oaxaca City is home to a flourishing arts scene, and there are dozens of galleries and workshops about town. The **Museo de Arte Contemporáneo** ① *Alcalá 202, Wed-Mon 1030-2000, US$1.50*, hosts regional exhibits in a range of media, with a library and café, housed in a late-17th-century house. The **Instituto de Artes Gráficas de Oaxaca** ① *Alcalá 507, Wed-Mon 0900-2000, donation requested*, is housed in a grand old 18th-century building. It has interesting exhibitions of national artists, a good reference library and beautiful courtyards. **Museo de los Pintores Oaxaqueños**, ① *Independencia 607 y Vigil, Tue-Sun 1000-2000, US$1.50*, is a state-run gallery that features local artists, past and present. **Colectivo Plan B** ① *2nd Privada, Av Universitaria*, is a new gallery for avant-garde

Guelaguetza (Lunes del Cerro)

This annual celebration, a well-organized large-scale folklore festival, usually takes place on the last two Mondays in July. For those interested in indigenous costumes, music and dance, it should not be missed.

The main event is a grand folkdance show held on a Monday morning at the Guelaguetza stadium on the slopes of Cerro del Fortín. The performance is lively and very colourful, with the city below serving as a spectacular backdrop.

Among the favourite presentations are *Flor de Piña*, danced by women from the Tuxtepec area with a pineapple on their shoulder, and *Danza de la Pluma*, by men from the Central Valleys wearing huge feather headdresses. The most elaborate costumes are those of the women from the Isthmus of Tehuantepec, which include the stiffly starched lace *resplandores* (halos) they wear on their heads.

The performance begins at 0900 and ends around 1300. Tickets for seats in the lower galleries (A and B) are sold in advance through **Sedetur** and cost from US\$35. Contact the **Oaxaca State Tourism Department Sectur** ① *Av Juárez 703, Centro Histórico, T951-516 0123*. Advance tickets are on sale from early May. The upper galleries (C and D) are free, line up before 0600, the gates open around 0700 and the performance begins at 1000 and finishes around 1400. Take a jumper as it is chilly in the morning, but the sun is very strong later on. A sun hat and sunscreen are essential, a pair of binoculars is also helpful in the upper galleries. Drinks and snacks are sold.

On the Saturday before Guelaguetza, at around 1800, participating groups parade down the pedestrian mall on Macedonio Alcalá, from Santo Domingo to the Zócalo. This is a good chance to see their splendid costumes close up.

On the Monday night, following Guelaguetza, the legend of Donají, a Zapotec princess who gave her life for her people, is presented in an elaborate torchlight performance at the same stadium starting around 2000.

works and cutting-edge media, while **Arte Mexicano** ① *Alcalá 407*, is a renowned workshop that specializes in high-quality prints and popular crafts. **Arte de Oaxaca** ① *Murguia 105*, was partly founded by Rudolfo Morales, a famous artist from Ocotlán. It has good exhibits of local talents. **Galería Quetzalli** ① *Calle Allende, near the Jardín del Pañuelito*, also features works by gifted locals, including Fransisco Toledo.

Monte Albán ☉ ↦ pp589-601. Colour map 2, C5.

① *Daily 0800-1800. US\$4. It is possible to stay after hours for a fee of US\$12, but you need to get a permit from the office at Monte Albán. US\$3 to use video cameras; fees for the guides who hang around the site are variable, ask several and beware of overcharging. Monte Albán receives many visitors during high season. Most people go in the morning, so it may be easier to catch the afternoon bus. To get there, see Transport, page 601.*

Monte Albán is situated about 10 km (20 minutes) west of Oaxaca, on a hilltop dominating the surrounding valley. It features pyramids, walls, terraces, tombs, staircases and sculptures of the ancient capital of the Zapotec culture, and the ruins were declared a UNESCO World Heritage Site in 1987.

Although the city of Monte Albán extended far beyond the confines of the **Main Plaza**, it is this site that archaeologists, art historians, historians and tourists have looked to, when assessing and interpreting the raison d'être of this fascinating site. Constructed 400 m up a steep mountain, without immediate access to water or cultivable land, the Main Plaza has at times been considered the site of a regional marketplace or ceremonial centre. The marketplace theory becomes less convincing when access to the site is considered: not only would the visitor have had to haul merchandise up the back-breaking hill, but entrance to the plaza was severely restricted. In ancient times the only way into the site was through three narrow passageways, which could easily have been guarded to restrict entry. The modern ramp cuts across what was the ball court to the southeast of the **North Platform**. The space at the centre of the Main Plaza would seem ideal for religious ceremonies and rituals but the absence of religious iconography contradicts this interpretation. The imagery at Monte Albán is almost exclusively militaristic, with allusions to tortured prisoners and captured settlements.

To the right, before getting to the ruins, is **Tomb 7**, where a fabulous treasure trove was found in 1932. Most items are now in the Museo de las Culturas de Oaxaca (see page 581) and the entrance is closed off by a locked gate. **Tomb 172** has been left exactly as it was found, with skeleton and urns still in place, but these are not visible. Tombs 7 and 172 are permanently closed.

There are trilingual (Spanish, English and Zapotec) signs throughout the site, as well as a good **museum** (explanations in Spanish only), exhibiting stone glyphs and sculptures as well as smaller artefacts. Note that flash photography is prohibited. Informative literature and videos in several languages are sold in the visitor centre bookshop, which also houses a small restaurant. From the ruins at Monte Albán there are paths leading to the valleys below. If you're in reasonable shape, consider hiring a bike for the day.

Main Plaza

The Main Plaza at Monte Albán is delineated north and south by the two largest structures in the city, which have been interpreted as palace and/or public building (North Platform) and temple (South Platform). Apart from these two impressive structures, the ball court and the arrow-shaped building in front of the South Platform, the Main Plaza, has 14 other structures, six along the west side of the Plaza, three in the middle and five along the east side. One structure, known as **Edificio de los Danzantes** (Dancers), has bas reliefs, glyphs and calendar signs (probably fifth century BC). During the period AD 450-600, Monte Albán had 14 districts beyond the confines of the Main Plaza: it has been proposed that each of the 14 structures located within the Main Plaza corresponded with one of the districts outside. Each pertained to a distinct ethnic group or polity, brought together to create a pan-regional confederacy or league. The arrow-shaped structure functioned as a military showcase; it also has astronomical connotations.

Confederacy

The presence of a number of structures in, or bordering, the Main Plaza that housed representatives of distinct ethnic groups supports the theory that Monte Albán came into being as the site of a confederacy or league. Its neutral position, unrelated to any single polity, lends credence to this suggestion. The absence of religious iconography, which might have favoured one group over the others, emphasizes the secular role of the area, while the presence of the Danzantes sculptures suggests a trophy-gathering group. However, although Monte Albán may have served defensive purposes, the presence of the Danzantes and the captured town glyphs argues for an offensive and expansionist role. In all, about 310 stone slabs depicting captives, some of whom are sexually mutilated

Monte Albán

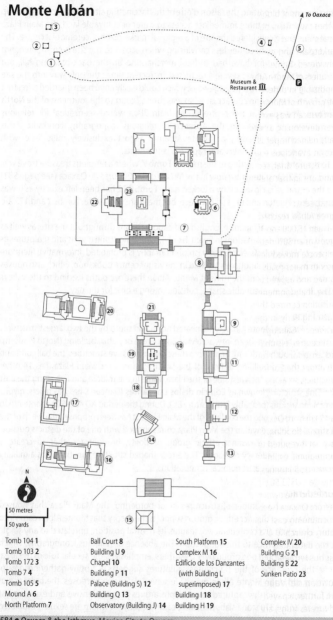

To Oaxaca

Museum & Restaurant 🏛

Tomb 104 **1**	Ball Court **8**	South Platform **15**	Complex IV **20**
Tomb 103 **2**	Building U **9**	Complex M **16**	Building G **21**
Tomb 172 **3**	Chapel **10**	Edificio de los Danzantes	Building B **22**
Tomb 7 **4**	Building P **11**	(with Building L	Sunken Patio **23**
Tomb 105 **5**	Palace (Building S) **12**	superimposed) **17**	
Mound A **6**	Building Q **13**	Building I **18**	
North Platform **7**	Observatory (Building J) **14**	Building H **19**	

with streams of blood (flowers) flowing from the mutilated parts, have been found. Some of these woeful captives are identified by name glyphs, which imply hostilities against a settlement and the capture of its warriors. The fact that most of them are nude denotes the disdain and contempt with which they were treated by their captors: nudity was considered shameful and undignified by the peoples of Mesoamerica. It is very likely that the rulers of Monte Albán were determined to bring into the confederacy as many polities as possible in order to extract tribute, which would permit the expansion of the capital. The growth of Monte Albán was a direct response to events in the Valley of Mexico, where Teotihuacán was exercising dominion over most of the area. Although Monte Albán had been developing a policy of offence and capture as early as 200 BC, the growth of the city really gained impetus with the growth of Teotihuacán, whose administrators must have cast an avaricious eye on the rich soil of the Valley of Oaxaca. From the ceramics and architecture analysed at Monte Albán, it is clear that Teotihuacán never realized its ambitions in that area; the confederacy functioned well.

Collapse

Monte Albán reached its maximum size around AD 600, with a population estimated at between 15,000 and 30,000. Shortly after, the city changed dramatically in form and function. There was an 80% decrease in population, the Main Plaza was abandoned and the majority of the people moved nearer to the valley floor, but behind protective walls. They were much closer to major roads, implying that Monte Albán was now becoming more commercially minded and aspired to be self-sufficient, which it had never been in its long history.

The abandonment of the Main Plaza was a direct result of the collapse of the political institution centred there. This collapse has been seen as a consequence of the fact that, beginning early in the seventh century AD, Teotihuacán was already showing signs of decadence. Gaining momentum, the decadence led to the massive abandonment of that great centre. It is unlikely to have been coincidental that the Main Plaza at Monte Albán was abandoned around this time. The removal of the Teotihuacán threat made redundant the Confederacy that was so costly to maintain: the collapse was complete.

Route to Mitla ●❶❷❸● ›› pp589-601.

It is 42 km from Oaxaca to Mitla, on a poor paved road (Route 190) with many potholes and occasional flooding. On the way you pass **El Tule** ① *12 km east of Oaxaca, US$0.20*, which has what is reputed to be the **world's largest tree** in the churchyard, a savino (*Taxodium mucronatum*), estimated to be 2000 years old. It is 40 m high, its base is 42 m, it weighs an estimated 550 tonnes, and is fed water by means of an elaborate pipe system. Guided tour of the tree, US$3.50 (Spanish)/US$7 (English). **Casa Breno** has unusual textiles and spindles for sale and the owners are happy to show visitors around the looms. To get here, take the bus from Oaxaca (second-class bus station), leaving every 30 minutes and costs US$1.

Continuing east along Route 190, 5 km from El Tule is **Tlacochahuaya**, with a 16th-century **church** ① *US$0.45*, and vivid indigenous murals. Visit the cloisters at the back and see the decorated organ upstairs. Again, you can catch the bus from Oaxaca's second-class bus terminal and the journey will cost US$0.70.

Teotitlán del Valle

5 km further, a paved road leads off Route 190 to Teotitlán del Valle, where wall hangings and *tapetes* (rugs) are woven, and which is now becoming touristy. There is an artisans'

market near the church, and a **Museo Comunitario** ① *daily 1000-1800, US$0.70*. The best prices for weavings can be found in the stores along the road as you come into town, but they may be even cheaper in Oaxaca where competition is stronger. Make sure you know whether you are getting all wool or a mixture and check the quality. A well-made rug will not ripple when unfolded on the floor. Buses leave every hour from 0700-2100, from second-class bus terminal (US$1); the second-class bus may provide the contacts you need to buy all the weavings you want! From the town of Teotitlán del Valle you can walk up to the nearby hills across the river or hike north to the town of Benito Juárez.

Tlacolula → *Colour map 2, C5.*

Tlacolula has a most interesting Sunday market and the renowned **Capilla del Santo Cristo** in the church. The chapel is similar in style to Santo Domingo in Oaxaca, with intricate white and gold stucco, lots of mirrors, silver altar rails and sculptures of martyrs in gruesome detail. Two beheaded saints guard the door to the main nave. There is a pleasant walled garden in front of the church. A band plays from 1930 every evening in the plaza (take a sweater as there is a cold wind most evenings). On the main street by Parque Juárez is **Casa de Cambio Guelaguetza**, which is cash only but has fair rates. The townspeople are renowned for their mescal preparation. The indoor market next to the church is very interesting. Between the church and the market you might see a local lady selling dried grasshoppers. Tlacolula can be reached by bus from Oaxaca, from the second-class bus station every 15 minutes, daily 0600-1900, US$1. Take the bus with Mitla as final destination.

Around Oaxaca

Taxis stop by the church, except on Sunday when they gather on a street behind the church; ask directions. Tlacolula's bus station is just off the main highway, several blocks from the centre; pickpockets are common here, be especially careful at the Sunday market and in the scrum to board the bus.

Santa Ana del Valle

Quality weavings can be found at Santa Ana del Valle, 3 km from Tlacolula. The village is peaceful and friendly with a small museum showing ancient textile techniques; ask any villager for the keyholder. There are two fiestas, each lasting three days. One during the second week of August, the other at the end of January. Buses leave from Tlacolula every 30 minutes.

Yagul

① *Daily 0800-1800, US$2.60. Tours in English on Tue, US$18, from Oaxaca agencies.*
Further east along Route 190 is the turn-off north for Yagul, an outstandingly picturesque archaeological site where the ball courts and priests' quarters are set in a landscape punctuated by candelabra cactus and agave. Yagul was a large Zapotec and later Mixtec religious centre. The ball court is said to be the second largest discovered in Mesoamerica; it's also one of the most perfect discovered to date. There are fine tombs (take the path from behind the ruins, the last part is steep) and temples, and a superb view from the hill behind the ruins. Take a bus to Mitla from the Oaxaca second-class terminal (see Transport, page 600) and ask to be put down at the paved turn-off to Yagul (five minutes after Tlacolula terminal). You will have to walk 1 km uphill from the bus stop to the site and you can return the same way or walk 3 km west to Tlacolula along Route 190 to catch a bus to Oaxaca.

Mitla → *Colour map 2, C5. Phone code: 951.*

① *42 km southeast of Oaxaca, Turn left off Ruta 190, 5 km after Yagul and continue for 4 km, daily 0800-1800, US$2.60, video US$3.50, literature sold at entrance.*
At Mitla (meaning 'place of the dead') there are ruins of four great palaces among minor ones. Some of the archaeology, outside the fenced-in site, can be seen within the present-day town. Magnificent bas-reliefs, the sculptured designs in the Hall of Mosaics, the Hall of the Columns and, in the depths of a palace, *La Columna de la Muerte* (Column of Death), which people embrace and then measure what they can't reach with their fingers to know how many years they have left to live (rather hard on long-armed people). After a period of closure the column can now be embraced again, but check at the entrance.

Hierve el Agua

From Mitla take a bus to San Lorenzo Albarradas (one hour, US$1). Three kilometres from there (57 km from Oaxaca) is the village of Hierve el Agua. Due to the concentration of minerals and a pre-Hispanic irrigation system, various waterfalls are now petrified over a cliff, forming an enormous stalactite. You can swim in the mineral pools in the dry season.

South of Oaxaca

Along Route 175 to Pochutla are several towns that specialize in the production of different crafts. **San Bartolo Coyotepec**, 12 km southeast of Oaxaca, is known for its black pottery. Doña Rosa de Nieto accidentally discovered the technique for the black-glazed ceramics in the 1930s, and her family continues the tradition, as do many other potters in town. **San Martín Tilcajete**, 21 km from Oaxaca, 1 km west of the main road, is the centre for the *alebrije* production - animals carved from copal wood, painted in bright colours and often having a supernatural look to them. **Santo Tomás Jalieza** is the centre for cotton and wool textiles, produced with backstrap looms and natural dyes in the surrounding villages. Market day is Friday.

Cuilapan de Guerrero

In Cuilapan, 12 km southwest of Oaxaca, there is a vast unfinished 16th-century **convent** ① *daily 0800-1800, US$2.20*, now in ruins, with a famous nave and columns, and an 'open chapel', whose roof collapsed in an earthquake. The last Zapotec princess, Donaji, daughter of the last ruler Cosijoeza, married a Mixtec prince at Tilantengo and was buried at Cuilapan. On the grave is an inscription with their Christian names, Mariana Cortez and Diego Aguilar. Reached by bus from Oaxaca from second-class bus station, on Calle Bustamante, near Arista (US$0.50).

North of Cuilapan and 6 km west of the main road is **San Antonio Arrazola**, another town where *alebrijes*, mythical animals made of copal wood are sold. **Zaachila** ① *5 km beyond Cuilapan, daily 0800-1800, US$2.20*, was the last capital of the Zapotec empire. Today this town still maintains some of its ancestral traditions in the local cooking (several restaurants). There is black pottery production, and market day is Thursday. Here are the partially excavated ruins of Zaachila, with two Mixtec tombs; the outer chamber has owls in stucco work and there are carved human figures with skulls for heads inside. Take the bus to Zaachila (US$0.60), which leaves every 30 minutes, then walk to the ruins in the valley.

Eighty kilometres south on Route 131 is **San Sebastián de las Grutas** ① *10 km northwest of El Vado, off the main road; guide obligatory, US$2*, where there is a system of caves. One 400-m-long cave, with five chambers up to 70 m high, has been explored and is open to visitors. Ask for a guide at the Agencia Municipal next to the church. Take a **Solteca** bus bound for Sola de Vega or San Pedro del Alto, from the second-class terminal, leaves 0500, 0600, 1100, 1400 and returns 0600, 0700, 0800, 1200 – you may find that this will more than likely leave you high and dry! Also note there are no hotels but camping is possible.

North of Oaxaca ❸ ⤻ *pp589-601.*

San Felipe del Agua

Oaxaca is a growing hotbed of ecotourism, with many options for tours. For good hikes, take the local bus to San Felipe del Agua, north of the city. To the left of where the buses stop at the end of the line is a car parking area; just below a dirt road starts. Follow this road and within five minutes you will reach the San Felipe Park entrance and a booth where you register with the guard. Several trails fan out from here; one follows the river valley and passes by some picnic areas and a swimming pool, continuing upstream crossing the river several times before reaching a waterfall, in about one hour. There are longer walks to the mountain to the north, crossing through several vegetation zones, from low, dry shrub to pleasant pine forest: allow five or six hours to reach the summit.

Santa María Atzompa

At Santa María Atzompa, 8 km northwest of Oaxaca, at the foot of Monte Albán, green glazed and terracotta ceramics are produced. You can see the artisans at work; their wares are sold at **La Casa del Artesano**. Buses leave from the second-class terminal.

Etla Valley

The Etla Valley, along which Route 190 runs, had a number of important settlements in pre-Hispanic times. Seventeen kilometres along this road and 2 km to the west is **San José el Mogote**, an important centre before the rise of Monte Albán; there is a small museum housing the artefacts found at this site. **San Pedro y San Pablo Etla**, 19 km from Oaxaca, has an important Wednesday market specializing in Oaxacan foods such as *quesillo* (string cheese), *tasajo* (dried meat) and different types of bread; the town has a 17th-century church and convent. At **Santiago Suchilquitongo**, 27 km from Oaxaca and atop a hill, are the ruins of **Huijazoo**, once an important centre that controlled the trade between the Central Valleys and the Cañada region; the local museum has a reproduction of a Huijazoo polychromatic mural, which has been compared to those at Bonampak. The town of **San Agustín Etla** (turn-off east from Route 190 at Guadalupe Etla) was once an important industrial centre and in the 19th century it had two large cotton mills; with the introduction of synthetic fibres came a decline to this area. Since 1998, the town has found a new use for the cotton and other natural fibres in the region, with the production of handmade paper for artists. Cotton, agave fibres, pineapple, nettle, ash, limestone and other raw materials are used in the workshop, which welcomes visitors. Further details from the Instituto de Artes Gráficas in Oaxaca city, see page 581.

Sierra Juárez

The Sierra Norte or Sierra Juárez is a region of beautiful landscapes and great biological diversity; seven of the nine types of vegetation that exist in Mexico can be found in this area. The region is starting to develop ecotourism with community participation; permits are required to camp on community land. The mountains gradually drop to the Papaloapan valley to the north. There are two access roads, Route 175 from Oaxaca to Tuxtepec, and the small roads that go north from Route 190, past Teotitlán and Santa Ana del Valle (see page 587). The Oaxaca-Tuxtepec road has been recommended as exhilarating for cyclists.

Huautla de Jiménez

The indigenous town of Huautla de Jiménez, where the local Mazatec population consume the hallucinogenic 'magic' mushrooms made famous by Dr Timothy Leary, has all four seasons of the year in each day: spring-like mornings, wet, foggy afternoons, fresh, autumn evenings and freezing nights. Hiking in the mountains here is worthwhile. There are many police and military. Drivers may be waved down by people in the road up to Huautla; do not stop for them, they may be robbers.

⓪ Mexico City to Oaxaca listings

For Sleeping and Eating price codes and other relevant information, see Essentials pages 47-51.

⓪ Sleeping

Oaxaca City *p577, map p578*
There are more than 160 hotels in Oaxaca in all price categories. Reservations are recommended during peak holiday periods (Easter, Jul-Aug, Christmas and New Year).

There are many cheap hotels in the block formed by the streets Mina, Zaragoza, Díaz Ordaz and JP García; also on Trujano (4 blocks from the Zócalo).
LL Casa Cid de León, Av Morelos 602, 2 blocks from the Zócalo, T951-514 1893, www.casaciddeleon.com. This intimate and interesting boutique hotel offers 4 different suites, all luxurious and lavishly decorated. The service is first rate and personal, overseen

by the gracious and hospitable Leticia Ricardez. The hotel organizes tours and offers massage. Low season and longer stay discounts. Highly recommended.

LL-L La Casona de Tita, Garcia Virgil 805, T951-516 1400, www.lacasonadetita.com. 6 individually decorated, spacious rooms, set around a beautiful terracotta courtyard, right next to a craft centre. One room has wheelchair access. Stylish and eco-friendly with all the mod cons. Recommended.

L Marqués del Valle, Portal de Clavería, right on the Zócalo by cathedral, T951-514 0688, www.hotelmarquesdelvalle.com.mx. An elegant lobby precedes far less interesting and over-priced rooms. However, some of them have exceptional views over the Zócalo. The staff are friendly and courteous. Also has a good restaurant, **Portal del Marqués** (see Eating).

AL Casa Conzatti, Gómez Farías 218, T951-513 8500, www.casaconzatti.com.mx. 45 rooms in refurbished colonial house, a/c, safety deposit box, exchange, restaurant.

AL Parador Santo Domingo de Guzmán, Alcalá 804, T951-514 2171, www.parador stodomingo.com.mx. An all-suite hotel with secure car parking, pool, cable TV and internet access. Suites have bedroom, sitting room and kitchen, daily maid included. Good mid-week rates. Recommended.

AL-A La Casona del Llano, Juárez 701, T951-514 7719. Clean, modern rooms in this secluded hotel, all with cable TV. There's an elegant restaurant that overlooks Paseo Juárez. Secure parking. Good low season discounts.

A Casantica, Av Morelos 601, T951-516 2673, www.hotelcasantica.com. Handsome hotel set in a beautifully restored 200-year-old colonial convent with quiet courtyards replete with palms and greenery, bubbling fountains and an inviting, if modest, pool. There's a restaurant attached, open 0730-2200, but service is reportedly slow.

A Ferri, Las Casas 405, T951-514 5290. Pretty motel-style option with clean, modern rooms, internet and parking.

A Posada Catarina, Aldama 325, T951-516 4270, www.travelbymexico.com/oaxaca/

catarina and www.hotelesde oaxaca.com. Modern colonial option, comfortable, with parking. Friendly staff, free internet for first hour and lovely views from the balcony.

B Antonio's, Independencia 601, block from Zócalo, T951-516 7227, antonios_hotel@ hotmail.com. Colonial patio, hot water, clean and spotless.

B Mesón del Rey, Trujano 212, 1 block from Zócalo, T951-516 0033, mesonrey@ prodigy.net.mx. This colonial-style hotel offers clean, modern and often cosy rooms, all quiet except for street-facing ones. Restaurant.

B Monte Albán, Alameda de León 1, T951-516 2777, www.travelbymexico.com/ oaxa/montealban. Friendly, colonial-style hotel with some elegant rooms overlooking the cathedral. Folk dance performances every night at 2030 (see Entertainment, page 594).

B Parador San Andrés, Hidalgo 405, 2 blocks from the Zócalo, T951-514 1011, www.hotel esdeoaxaca.com. Comfortable, colonial-style hotel with just 6 quiet rooms, all with lovely wood-beam ceilings. There's a tranquil and secluded terrace. Longer stay discounts.

B Rivera del Angel, Francisco Javier Mina 518, T951-516 6666, www.hotelriveradelangel.com. Large and friendly, if a bit impersonal. It takes over a whole block so you can't miss it. Lush garden, pool and volleyball court. Parking and tours available. Popular with Mexicans.

C Las Rosas, Trujano 112, T951-514 2217, hlrosasoax@hotmail.com. Plenty of charm at this friendly hotel. There's a nice patio, a good view from the roof, free internet, free tea and coffee for guests. Good family rooms.

C Posada del Centro, Independencia 403, T951-516 1874, www.mexonline.com/ posada.htm. Pretty, colourful *posada* set around courtyard, with spacious rooms. Friendly, organizes tours. Highly recommended.

C Posada Don Matías, Aldama 316, T951-501 0084, www.donmatias.net. Very pleasant, tastefully decorated hotel with a beautiful, plant-filled patio and clean, attractive rooms. Free internet.

C Posada Las Casas, Las Casas 507 y Díaz Ordaz, T951-516 2325. Clean and tidy hotel with rooms around a central courtyard. Cheaper without bath (**D**), friendly, good value.

C Principal, 5 de Mayo 208, 2 blocks from the Zócalo, T951-516 2535, hotelprincipal@gmail.com. Colonial house, slightly run-down, private shower, morning coffee and cookies included. English spoken, friendly, rooms overlooking street are a bit noisy but still heavily booked.

C Valle de Oaxaca, Díaz Ordaz 208, T951-516 3707, www.travelbymexico.com/oaxaca/hotelvalledeoaxaca. Clean, comfortable hotel with some tranquil patio space, sofas and table soccer. Friendly. Good restaurant.

C-D Lupita, Díaz Ordaz 314, T951-516 5733. Lovely, large, clean and brightly coloured rooms. Upstairs rooms have brilliant views across the city and mountains from the flat rooftop. Rooms are cheaper without bath.

D Central, 20 de Noviembre 104, 1 block from the Zócalo, T951-514 9425. This well-located cheapie has simple rooms with bath and hot water, although it isn't especially good value. Slightly scruffy and run-down. Rooms cheaper without bath.

D La Cabaña, Mina 203, T951-516 5918, F951-514 0739. This good value, economical hotel has rooms with and without bath (**E**). Clean, but can be noisy.

D Mina, Mina 304, T951-516 4966. This clean and basic hotel has rooms with shared bath only. There is hot water.

D-F Hostal Pochon, Callejón del Carmen 102, T951-516 1322, www.hostalpochon.com. Five dormitories and several private rooms, including a new junior suite in quiet part of town near Santo Domingo. Cheap long distance calls, breakfast with homemade bread, free drinking water, Wi-F, cooking lessons, excusions arranged, bike hire and bike tours. Good friendly atmosphere and multi-lingual staff. Highly recommended.

D-F Mezkalito Hostel, Xicotencatl 121, T951-514 3001, www.mezkalitohostel.com. Clean, well-managed hostel with various-sized dorms or rooms, laundry services, internet, bar and bar. Good low season and long stay discounts.

D-F Paulina Youth Hostel, Trujano 321, T951-516 2005, www.paulinahostel.com. This immaculate and professionally run youth hostel has large, clean, attractive dorms and a few private rooms. There's a pleasant garden and the interior is tastefully decorated. A simple breakfast is included.

E Palmar, JP García 504 y Mina, T951-514 9889. Family-run and slightly run-down cheapie offers comfortable rooms, even cheaper without bath. Hot water in morning, safe motorcycle parking. Longer stay discounts.

Camping

Oaxaca Trailer Park, Violeta 900, Col Reforma, north of town off the road to Mitla at a sign marked 'Infonavit' (corner of Pinos and Violetas). US$4.50 for a tent, US$12 for a camper van, secure; bus 'Carmen-Infonavit' from downtown. Slightly run down.

Route to Mitla *p585*

In 13 towns, throughout the Central Valleys around Oaxaca, including Tlacolula, there is tourist accommodation known as run by local communities (**E** per person, US$5 to camp). Each house has a room with 6 beds, equipped kitchen, bathroom with hot water. For details contact the Sectur office, see page 579.

C Mitla, Mitla town square, T951-968 0112. Private bath, simple, clean, friendly, local food.

D La Zapoteca, Mitla, before bridge on road to ruins, T951-958 0026. Private bath, hot water, parking, friendly, good food.

Eating

Oaxaca City *p577, map p578*
Around the Zócalo

Most restaurants on the main square cater for tourists, and can be pricey as a result, but generally standards are good.

ŦŦŦ-ŦŦ Asador Vasco, above Bar Jardín, Portal de Flores 10-A, www.asadorvasco.com. Live Mexican music in the evening, good regional, international and Basque food. Good service.

Ⅱ Portal del Marqués, part of Marqués del Valle (see Sleeping), on the north side of the Zócalo. Fine dining on the plaza with exciting adaptations of regional food.

Ⅱ-Ⅰ El Mesón. Good all-day buffets, good breakfasts, *comida corrida* poor value, great selection of tacos, clean, quick service.

Ⅱ-Ⅰ La Primavera, on the Zócalo. Good-value meals, international and traditional dishes, good snacks and espresso coffee, slow.

Ⅱ-Ⅰ Amarantos and Terranova Restaurant, Taco Inn, Sushi Itto and Altos de Terranova, the last 4 under one roof, Hidalgo, at east side of Zócalo. Good food and snacks, friendly, but Terranova can be pricey.

North of Independencia

ⅡⅡ Café Bar Tapas & Pisto, Macedonio Alcalá 403, upstairs. Opens 1800. Artfully renovated colonial house, excellent view from top terrace, more pricey but worth visiting just for the bathroom.

ⅡⅡ Casa Oaxaca, García Vigil 407. Where food is art, fine courtyard, excellent service and food, reservations very necessary, popular with artists and writers such as Gabriel García Márquez, excellent value. Also does accommodation.

ⅡⅡ-ⅡⅠ Hostería de Alcalá, Macedonio Alcalá 307. Excellent food and quiet atmosphere in a beautiful colonial courtyard. Mostly meat and fish dishes. Good service and expensive.

ⅡⅡⅡ-ⅡⅠ Los Danzantes, Macedonio Alcalá 403 next door to **Café Bar Tapas & Pisto**. Open 1430-2330. Mexican fusion cooking in a stylish courtyard, well-stocked bar, particularly good for mescal.

ⅡⅡⅡ-Ⅰ Marco Polo, 5 de Mayo 103. Open 0800-2100. Reputable seafood restaurant. Specialities include crab in chilli sauce, seafood shish kebab and red snapper fillet.

Ⅱ La Abeja, Porfirio Díaz 610 y Carranza. Traditional breakfasts and lunches, also good vegetarian meals, bakery, garden setting.

Ⅱ La Crêpe, Macedonio Alcalá 307. This clean, modern restaurant has a great 1st-floor location, with some tables overlooking the street. Good fresh salads, crêpes and cheap breakfast combos.

Ⅱ Pizza Rústica, Alcalá 804A y Murguía. This decent and friendly Italian restaurant dishes out fine pasta and pizza, as well as antipasto, meat and fish dishes. Friendly and authentic.

Ⅱ-Ⅰ Comala, Plaza Allende 109. Trendy cafe inspired by Juan Rulfo's novel *Pedro Páramo*. Themed cocktails and excellent Mexican dishes. Try the cucumber margarita. Good nightspot.

Ⅱ-Ⅰ Flor de Loto, Morelos 509, next to Museo Rufino Tamayo. Good value, clean, vegetarian and Mexican. Also does good breakfasts.

Ⅱ-Ⅰ Manantial Vegetariano, Matamoros with Tinoco y Palacios. Tables occupy a pleasant, fountain-filled courtyard at this renowned restaurant. There's a buffet Sat lunchtime and *comida corrida* during the week. Also serves meat dishes. Good value, recommended.

Ⅱ-Ⅰ Pizza Nostrana, corner of Allende, close to Santo Domingo church. Open 1300-2300. Delicious Italian cuisine.

Ⅱ-Ⅰ Tito's, García Vigil 116. Good, reasonably priced food including Mexican and Oaxacan staples, sandwiches and a set menu at lunch time.

Ⅰ Cafeteria Royalty, Matamoros 100B. Cheap, simple dishes. Lunch menu for US$3.

Cafés and bakeries Bamby, García Vigil 205. Big, cheap bakery where you can pick up bread and sweet rolls for a couple of pesos a piece. The place for breakfast on a budget.
Café Brújala, García Vigil 409D. The place for really excellent, carefully sourced Oaxacan coffee, as well as breakfasts, smoothies, sandwiches, salads, pizzas and other freshly prepared, homemade snacks. American-owned, friendly and popular with local artists.
Café Los Cuiles, Labastida 115. Breezy little café with Oaxacan art work on the wall. A good place to tap away on your laptop. Very friendly and popular with gringos.
Gaia Organic Food, next door, is also worth a visit for a dose of healthy food. Asking for fries will horrify the owner.

South of Independencia
The most popular place to eat *tlayudas* (oversized tortillas) and other local snacks

Mole: Oaxaca's chocolatey goodness

Mole, a rich, tasty chilli-chocolate sauce of complex flavours and colours, is integral to Mexican cooking, but no more so than in Oaxaca, where every household seems to have their own recipe. Although said to have originated in Puebla, *mole* has since made the state of Oaxaca its true culinary and spiritual home and it's here that it's been refined over the centuries, into delicious multi-ingredient combinations, from *mole verde* (green), *mole amarillo* (yellow), *mole rojo* (red) and *mole colorado* (deep red or brown), to the most famous of all, *mole negro* (black). Despite there being a lot of grinding involved in the making of mole, the word does not stem from the Spanish word *moler* (to grind), but from Nahuatl's *molli*, meaning sauce. Theories about where, how and why *mole* was invented abound, but one thing is

certain – this is a truly *mestizo* dish, combining Spanish and native Mexican ingredients to conjure up a concoction unlike any other. The average recipe will have some 20 ingredients, but more elaborate ones can contain many more. Most commonly a mole will include several types of chilli, chocolate, cinnamon, almonds, garlic, tomatoes and onion, all of which are ground together to make the sauce, traditionally served with turkey, but these days also popular with chicken and other meats, even fish. For those who would like to try making it at home, but find it too time consuming, many shops and markets in Oaxaca sell ready-ground paste, making the cooking process easier. The dish is also high on the agenda at the many places that do cooking lessons in the state.

in the evening is from stalls and restaurants along Aldama, between Cabrera and 20 de Noviembre.

††† Flor de Oaxaca, Armenta y López 311. Pricey but good Oaxacan cuisine, including tasty platters, *moles*, meat cuts and *tlayudas*. They serve chocolate and several interesting mescals too. Friendly and attentive staff. Recommended.

†† El Naranjo, Trujano 203. A pleasant restaurant set in the plant-filled courtyard of a 17th-century house. They serve tasty Oaxacan fare, and their specialities include an interesting dessert of dark chocolate torte filled with mescal crème. Also does cooking lessons, ask inside restaurant for details.

†† La Quebrada, Armenta y López 410. Open 1000-1900. A reputable and well-established seafood restaurant, open since 1964. Their menu includes various fish fillets, shrimp cocktails and a seafood curry.

††-† Café Alex, Díaz Ordaz 218 y Trujano. Over 20 different breakfasts are offered at this pleasant restaurant, including pancakes with

fruit and various Oaxacan specialities. There's also a good *comida corrida* with 4 different menus to choose from. Recommended.

††-† Casa Grande del Gato Loco, Hidalgo 410, 2 blocks from the Zócalo. Restaurant-bar with big screen TVs and mostly economical meals. Live music and karaoke in the evenings.

††-† Coronita, Díaz Ordaz 208, below **Valle de Oaxaca** (see Sleeping). Affordable Oaxacan specialities including various *mole*-based recipes, meat and fish dishes.

††-† Hipocampo's, Hidalgo 505. Mon-Sat 0800-2200, Sun 1000-1900. This rough-and-ready locals' haunt offers basic lunches.

Comedores Some of the most authentic Oaxacan food is found in the *comedores familiares*, such as **Clemente, Los Almendros, La Juchita**, but they are way out of town and could be difficult to get to, or in *comedores populares* in the market.

† D'Florencia, Zaragoza 205L. Very friendly restaurant with excellent Oaxacan specialities, run by Angel and Antonia. Good breakfasts, economical meals and lunches. Highly recommended.

El Chef, Armenta y López 422. Economical *comida corrida*, Mexican staples and simple, unpretentious meals.

El Shaddai, Av Hidalgo 121 y Galeano. Busy family-run restaurant serving tacos, other Mexican fare and set menus. Popular with locals, friendly, busy, good and cheap.

Girasoles, 20 de Noviembre 102. Popular, slightly scruffy vegetarian restaurant that offers a decent set menu at lunchtime and karaoke in the evening.

Hermanas Jiménez, Mercado de Abastos. Recommended for a local bread called *pan de yema*, made with egg yolk.

Mi Tierra, Mier y Teran 222. Closes 1830. Breakfast and lunch only, another good spot for economical home-cooking.

Route to Mitla *p585*
Teotitlán del Valle has 1 simple restaurant. Tlacolula has several simple restaurants. The market at El Tule has good food.

La Sonora, on eastern edge of El Tule. Tasty food.

María Teresa, Mitla, 100 m from site towards village. Good *comida corrida*.

🍷 Bars and clubs

Oaxaca City *p577, map p578*
Fandango, Diaz and Allende. More grungy vibes at this friendly, cavernous bar. Popular with students and rockers. Open very late.

La Candela, Murguía 413 y Pino Suárez. Salsa, merengue, live music from 2200, restaurant, popular with visitors and locals, cover US$5.

La Cantinita, Alcala 303. Large and often buzzing bar with live music and mixed clientele. Popular and loud.

La Casa de Mezcal, Flores Magón 209, in front of the market. Popular drinking hole.

La Divina, Gurrión 104. Dark, grungy bar with a gothic interior, sticky carpets and young, bohemian clientele. They play salsa, chill-out, house, trance and reggae.

La Farola, 20 de Noviembre 3C. Daily 1000-0200. Old-fashioned mescal joint of repute, selection of snacks and live music.

La Tentación, Matamoros 101, between Macedonio Alcalá y García Vigil. Live music starts 2230, open late. Salsa and merengue, friendly atmosphere. Cover US$5.

🎬 Entertainment

Oaxaca City *p577, map p578*
Cinema
Multimax, Plaza del Valle. Shopping mall with a massive multi-screen complex.

Folk dancing
Guelaguetza-style shows, when there are enough people, at:
Casa de Cantera, Murguía 102, T951-514 9522, www.casadecantera.com. Shows cost US13, with dinner US$26.
Hotel Monte Albán, Alameda de León 1, T951-516 2777, nightly at 2030, US$7, photography permitted. Book if you can. Special group prices.

🎉 Festivals and events

Oaxaca City *p577, map p578*
Jul Guelaguetza, also called Los Lunes del Cerro, is the city's most important festival. A festive atmosphere permeates the city for more than 2 weeks, particularly the last 2 Mondays of the month (see box, page 582).
Oct El Señor del Rayo, a 9-day event in the 3rd week of Oct, including excellent fireworks.
2 Nov Day of the Dead, a mixture of festivity and solemn commemoration, best appreciated at the Panteón General (main cemetery). Always ask before photographing. In recent years Oaxaca has hosted a rugby 'tournament of death' in conjunction with the festival, for information, www.planeta.com.
8-18 Dec Fiesta de la Soledad, patroness of Oaxaca, with fine processions centred around the Basílica and throughout the city.

Mescal

Mescal derives from the Nahuatl word for the agave plant, *metl*, more commonly known in Mexico as *maguey*. The drink dates from 16th-century Mexico. The natives were brewing a lightly alcoholic drink called *pulque* from agave juice, used in rituals and ceremonies. But the Spaniards were used to wine or beer with their meals, and it wasn't long before they started making mescal 'wine', using the distillation process brought over to Spain by the Moors several hundred years earlier. Despite this early start, mescal took some 400 years to develop into more than just small-scale distilling for local consumption and it wasn't until after the 1910 Mexican Revolution that production really took off. The main mescal-making territories are Oaxaca, Guerrero, Zacatecas, San Luis Potosí and Durango, with a few brands from Tamaulipas and Guanajuato. Two-thirds of mescal hails from Oaxacan soil and although up to 28 different varieties of agave can be used in the making, the espadín agave is by far the most popular, used in 90% of brands.

While tequila, from nearby Jalisco, is big business, mescal has remained low-key in comparison. Many producers, particularly in Oaxaca, are indigenous and keep production small scale and family run, making mescal the traditional way. Due to the industrialisation and production methods of tequila, quality and taste have become consistent, but with mescal this isn't always the case. Although larger scale production and regulations do exist, mescal from smaller producers – the home-made kind – is totally different.

To make mescal, traditionally, the thick stem-like leaves are chopped off, with a type of machete known as *coa*, leaving the heart of the plant, the *piña*, thus named for its resemblance to a pineapple. The *piñas* are baked or roasted in *palenques*, conical pits buried in the ground and lined with rocks. Wood is placed at the bottom of the pit, turning the rocks red hot when set alight. The *piñas* are added on top, covered with agave or palm leaves and finally a layer of earth. They are then left to cook for several days, absorbing the earthy and smoky flavours unique to mescal. After resting for up to a week, the *piñas* are mashed by a stone grinding wheel, drawn by a burro or horse. The resulting mash has pure water added to it and is left to ferment naturally, in wooden vats. At this stage sugars and other additives can be included in the mash, but by law it has to contain at least 80% agave. The alcohol content is similar to tequila, but some mescals are up to 50% proof or stronger. Once fermented, the pulp (*tepache*) yields a low-alcohol drink similar to *pulque*, which is double-, or even triple-distilled, to produce mescal. The finished product is divided into *abocado* (also known as *blanco* or *jóven*) bottled straight after distillation, *resposado* aged for up to 11 months, and finally *añejo* aged for at least 12 months.

Dec During the 9 days before Christmas, the Novenas are held. Groups of people go asking for shelter, *posada*, as Joseph and Mary did, and are invited into different homes. This is done in the centre as well as other neighbourhoods like San Felipe (5 km north) and at Xoxo, to the south. The *posadas* culminate on the night of 24 Dec with what is known as Calendas, a parade of floats representing allegories from the birth of Christ; every church in town prepares a float honouring its patron saint, the groups from all the parishes converging at the cathedral at 2300 (best seen from balcony of the restaurants around the

Zócalo; go for supper and get a window table). **23 Dec** Noche de Rábanos, outside the Palacio de Gobierno, is a unique contest of figures carved out of radishes. Stands made of flowers and corn stalks have been added in recent years to this old tradition.

Teotitlán del Valle *p585*
3 May Fiesta de las Cruces, when people climb to a cross on a beautiful summit above town (across river); good hiking at any time of year.
Jul Fiesta Antigua Zapoteca is celebrated here to coincide with the Guelaguetza in Oaxaca.
8 Sep Feast of Virgen de la Natividad.

O Shopping

Oaxaca City *p577, map p578*
Crafts
Many crafts are produced throughout the state of Oaxaca. Crafts are sold in nearby villages or may be purchased at the markets listed below. There are endless shopping temptations, such as green and black pottery, baskets and bags made from cane and rushes, embroidered shirts, skirts, painted wooden animals called *alebrijes*, hammocks, tooled leather goods, woven wall hangings and rugs. Many businesses were damaged by the 2006 social conflicts (see page 577), but trade has recovered quite well in the recent years, despite some continued unrest.
Blackbox, 5 de Mayo 412, www.la-black box.com. An interesting new store with unique and experimental creations fusing traditional techniques with modern designs. The owner, Gustavo Friedke, works closely with indigenous communities.
Casa de las Artesanías, Matamoros 105, www.casadelasartesanias.com.mx. This large, successful co-op displays the craftwork of over 60 artists. Goods include fine *alebrijes*, weavings and pottery.
Fábrica de Papel de San Agustín Etla, downhill from the university. This factory produces handmade paper. There's a small exhibit in the powerhouse nearby, as well

as an attractive range of items for sale including journals, notebooks and sketch pads. Has a small museum and school (see also Art classes, page 598).
Hecmafer, 5 de Mayo y Murguía. Good selection of jewellery, rugs and pottery, somewhat overpriced.
Instituto Oaxaqueño de las Artesanías, García Vigil 809, T951-516 9211. Government-run, cheaper and better than most, service good, with very good small market nearby on junction of García Vigil and Jesús Carranza, for beautiful coloured belts and clothes.
La Mano Mágica, Alcalá 203. The highest-quality rug collection in Oaxaca. Some of these dazzling creations fetch thousands of dollars.
Mineralia, Alcala 207. Shimmering mountains of gems, crystals and stones are on sale at this popular jewellery store. Also has branches in other parts of the country.
Mujeres Artesanas de las Regiones de Oaxaca (MARO), 5 de Mayo 204, T951-516 0670. Daily 0900-2000. Regional association of Oaxacan craftswomen.

Bookshops
Amate, Alcalá 307. A good selection of English-language books, magazines and books about Oaxaca and Mexico.
Proveedora Escolar, Independencia 1001 y Reforma. Large, excellent selection on all subjects, comparatively cheap.

Markets
The city has several main markets, all of which are worth a visit, and several smaller ones; polite bargaining is the rule everywhere.
Mercado 20 de Noviembre, Aldama on the corner of 20 de Noviembre, in the centre of town. Clean stalls selling prepared foods, cheeses and baked goods. Try the *quesadillas de flor de calabaza* – pumpkin flower quesadillas – an excellent, filling snack.
Mercado Artesanal, Zaragoza y JP García. Good selection of crafts.
Mercado Benito Juárez, next door to Mercado 20 de Noviembre. Household goods, fruits, vegetables, crafts and regional

Oaxacan cooking

The food of the state of Oaxaca is a fine representation of the complexity and variety of its cultures.

A stroll through any of Oaxaca's markets will quickly bring you into contact with vendors selling *chapulines*. These small grasshopper-like creatures, turn bright red when fried, are then served with lime and chillies. Another interesting ingredient in the diet is *gusanito*, a small red caterpillar from the agave plant, that is used to make a special sauce with pasilla chillies. This is also the worm found in some mescals.

There are local delicacies for vegetarians as well. *Flor de calabaza*, pumpkin flowers, are used in soups, *empanadas*, *quesadillas* or simply as garnish. Soup is prepared from *nopales*, young leaves of prickly-pear cactus.

The most typical regional snacks are *tlayudas*, huge crispy tortillas, covered with a variety of toppings (beef, sausage, beans or cheese) and grilled over coals. Oaxacan white string cheese, known as *quesillo*, is also famous, as is the area's excellent chocolate, best enjoyed as a hot beverage. Also popular is a slightly fermented drink made from corn flour known as *atole*.

Barbacoa is barbequed meat, often lamb or goat. Although there many veggie options with corn, cheese and mushroom dishes, Oaxacans love their meat. *Tasajo*, skirtsteak of salted beef, and *cecina*, salted pork, are popular, as is *salchicha Oaxaqueña*, beef sausages from Ejutla.

The essence of Oaxacan cooking, however, and the recipes for which the state is most famous, are its many *moles*, which come in a variety of colours. They are served as sauces accompanying turkey, chicken or even pork and fish dishes.

---

produce, such as *quesillo* (string cheese), bread and chocolate.

Mercado de Abastos, also known as the Central de Abastos, near the 2nd-class bus station, is the largest. A cacophony of sights, sounds and aromas, busiest on Sat and not to be missed. Prices here tend to be lower than in the smaller markets, and it's a good place to find cheap crafts. If all that shopping makes you hungry, why not sample the grasshopper-like creatures called *chapulines*? They're fried in huge vats of oil around the market and sold with garlic, chilli and lime juice added - crunchy. **Mercado Orgánico**, also known as 'El Pochote', García Vigil 817. Fri-Sat, 0900-1800. This new, organic market sells tasty local produce including honey, chocolate, mescal and coffee.

Photography

Centro Fotográfico Alvarez Bravo, Bravo y García Vigil. For photo exhibits and sales. Inside is the newly opened **Fonotec**, a cultural project comprising a vast music collection from around the world. A true audio feast. **Foto Rivas**, Juárez 605, opposite Parque Juárez and 20 de Noviembre 502C. Excellent collection of photographs of Oaxacan themes, also sells postcards and film.

Regional food and drink

On **Mina y 20 de Noviembre**, opposite the 20 de Noviembre market, are several mills where they grind cacao beans, almond, sugar and cinnamon into a paste for making delicious hot chocolate, the cacao smell permeates the air in this area. Brands include **Mayordomo** (very good), **Guelaguetza** and **La Soledad**. These same outlets sell Oaxacan *mole*, a thick paste used for preparing sauces. *Mole* and *quesillo*, the regional, white string cheese, are sold at the **Benito Juárez market**, where **La Oaxaqueña** stalls are recommended. Also at Mina and 20 de Noviembre is **La Casa del Dulce** sweet shop. Mescal is readily available throughout town.

⛰ Activities and tours

Oaxaca City p577, map p578
Art classes
Centro de los Artes de San Agustín,
Independencía s/n, T951-521 3043
www.centrodelasartesdesanagustin.com.
Downhill from the university, part of the
Fabrica de Papel de San Agustín Etla. Open
0900-1800. Courses in various art forms from
painting to photography to ceramics to
video. Different levels are available, including
beginner and professional. Always check
what language the classes are taught in.

Birdwatching
Almost 700 species of birds can be found in
the state of Oaxaca. Its strategic location at the
junction between North and Central America
and its geographic diversity, spanning the
Pacific and Atlantic watersheds, result in great
variety. There are birding opportunities in the
Central Valleys, in the mountain range
separating the Central Valleys from the Pacific
coast, in the coastal lagoons, in the thorn forests
along Route 190, and in the cloud forests and
lowlands of the Atlantic coast.

Cooking classes
Many language schools and restaurants
also offer cooking classes.
Susan Trilling, T951-508 0469, www.seasons
ofmyheart.com. Instruction in the sublime
art of Oaxacan cooking, culinary tours and
week-long courses. Half-day classes start at
US$50. Recommended.

Cycling
Zona Bici, García Vigil 406, T951-516 0953,
www.oaxacawebs.org/zonabici. Mon-Sat
1000-1430 and 1630-2030. New aluminium-
frame bikes, front suspension, US$12 for 24-hr
rental. They also sell bikes, along with general
cycling supplies. Tours cost US$33, make
reservations. Recommended.

Language schools
There are many schools in the city, many of
which offer homestays to enhance learning.
The following have been recommended.
Académia Vinigúlaza, Abasolo 503, T951-
513 2763, www.viniguelaza.com. Small groups,
US$105 per 20-hr week, good place to talk to
Mexican students, also cooking and salsa classes.
Amigos del Sol, Calzada San Felipe del Agua
322, T951-133 6052, www.oaxacanews.com/
amigosdelsol.htm. Small groups, US$105 per
week; cooking classes US$20, accommodation
can also be arranged.
Becari, M Bravo 210, Plaza San Cristóbal,
T951-514 6076, www.becari.com.mx, 4 blocks
north of the Zócalo. US$120 for a 15-hr week
with fully qualified teachers, courses
including culture, history, literature and
politics, with workshops on dancing, cooking
or art, flexible programmes.
Centro de Idiomas, Universidad Autónoma
Benito Juárez, Burgoa, 5 blocks south of the
Zócalo. Weekly or monthly classes (US$200
per month), or private tuition, very professional
and good value for money.
Español Interactivo, Armenta y López 311B,
T951-514 6062, www.studyspanish
inoaxaca.com. Small groups, US$105 per
week, 3 hrs per day, cooking, dancing.
Instituto Cultural Oaxaca, Av Juárez 909,
T951-515 3404, www.icomexico.com. In
addition to Spanish classes, local crafts and
culture (including dance, cooking, weaving
and pottery) are taught. 4 hrs of formal
Spanish teaching, 2 hrs spent in cultural
workshops and 1 hr of informal conversation
with a native speaker; US$115 per week.
Instituto de Comunicación y Cultura,
M Alcalá 307, 2nd floor, T951-516 3443,
www.iccoax.com. Cultural workshops and
field trips included in the programme,
US$150 per week, 3 hrs per day.
Soléxico Language and Cultural Center,
Abasolo 217 y Juárez, T951-516 5680,
www.solexico.com. Programme with options
for homestay, excursions and volunteering.
Has branches in Playa del Carmen and Puerto
Vallarta. See also Language tuition, page 59.

Public baths

Baños Reforma, Reforma 407. Daily 0700-1800. Steam bath US$4, sauna US$4.
Baños San Rafael, Tinoco y Palacios 514. Mon-Sat 0600-1800, Sun 0600-1530. Hot water.

Tour operators

There are many in town, most running the same tours, daily to Monte Albán, El Tule, Mitla and city tours; Fri to Coyotepec, Jalietza and Ocotlán; Thu to Cuilapan and Zaachila; Sun to Tlacolula, Mitla and El Tule (for local markets). Regular tours cost US$15 pp. If visiting archaeological sites, check if entry is included.
Eugenio Cruz Castaneda, T951-513 4790. Offers excellent guided trips to Monte Albán, other archaeological sites and can arrange custom itineraries throughout Oaxaca state.
Expediciones Sierra Norte, Manuel Bravo 210, T951-514 8271, www.sierranorte.org.mx. This reputable eco-tourism agency organizes expeditions to the mountains and Los Pueblos Mancomunados, 1-5 days in length. Tours depart daily; call in advance for information and reservations.
Tierraventura, Abasolo 217 y Av Juárez, T951-501 1363, www.tierraventura.com. A long-standing eco-tourism agency that runs a range of tours all over the state, from the sierras to the coast. Wildlife, indigenous medicine, birds, botany and ecology are some of their environmentally aware themes. This is a small-scale company, so best to book at least one week in advance, in case fully booked.
Viajes Xochitlán, Manuel Bravo 210 Int A, T951- 514 3628, www.xochitlan-tours.com.mx. This reputable, well-established agency runs tours to the Central Valleys, visiting all the sights including Mitla and Hierve el Agua.

⊖ Transport

Acatlán to Oaxaca *p576*

There's a 2nd-class bus from Oaxaca to **Huajuapan**, twice a day with **Sur** (1230 and 2330), which costs US$4. There are also express vans every 30 mins from **Hidalgo** (No 208), US$5.

Oaxaca City *p577, map p578*

Air

Xoxocotlán (OAX) airport is about 9 km south, direction Ocotepec. Airport taxis cost US$3.50 per person. Book at **Transportación Terrestre Aeropuerto** on Alameda de León No 1-G, opposite the cathedral in the Zócalo (T951-514 4350) for collection at your hotel to be taken to airport, office open Mon-Sat 0900-1400, 1700-2000. All prices and timetables are subject to change. The flights listed below are one-way, and the cheapest fares are web fares. To **Huatulco** with **Aerotucán**, Mon-Sat 0900, Sun 1000, 1 hr, US$156. To **Mexico City** with AeroMexico, Mon-Sat 3 flights daily, Sun 4 flights, US$84; with **Click Mexicana**, 5 daily, US$47. To **Puerto Escondido** with Aerotucán, Mon-Sat 0700, Sun 1200, 1 hr, US$156; and with **Aerovega**, 0900, daily, US$79. To **Tuxtla** with Click Mexicana, 1435, 1 hr, US$89. To most other destinations it is necessary to make a connection in Mexico City.

Airline offices For airline websites, see page 36. AeroMéxico, Av Hidalgo 513 Centro, T951-516 3765. AeroTucán, Emiliano Carranza 303, T951-502 0840. AeroVega, Hotel Monte Albán, Alameda de León 1, T951-516 4982. Aviacsa, Pino Suárez 604, T951-518 4555. Click Mexicana, Fiallo 102 y Av Independencia, T951-516 5797, Mon-Sat 0800-2000.

Bus

Local Buses mostly charge US$0.50. To the 1st-class bus station, buses marked 'VW' go from Av Juárez. Many lines marked 'Central' go by the 2nd-class bus station.
Long distance For 1st-class buses, buy tickets in advanced at the **Ticket Bus Office**, 20 de Noviembre 103, T951-514 6655, daily 0800-2000. There is a new 1st-class terminal, also referred to as **ADO** terminal, northeast of the Zócalo on Calzada Niños Héroes de Chapultepec with left luggage facilities, taxi from centre US$3. ADO, OCC, Sur and Cuenca operate from here. Note that many 2nd-class buses leave from here too. Second-class terminal is west of Zócalo on Calzada Valerio

Trujano, just west of the Periférico, across from the Central de Abastos; it is referred to as the 'Central Camionera' (has left-luggage office, open until 2100). Some 2nd-class companies also offer superior service on some runs. The **Autobuses Unidos (AU)** terminal (2nd class, 2 levels of service, 1 is very good, modern buses but without a/c) is at Santa Rosa, near the Teatro Alvaro Carillo. 1st-class terminal is the only one for **Villahermosa** and the **Yucatán**. Tickets for ADO, OCC, AU, Sur and Cuenca can also be purchased at Periférico 152, T516-3222, by the pedestrian crosswalk across from the Mercado de Abastos. To **Mexico City**, most go to TAPO (Mexico City east bus terminal) but there are also services to the North (Terminal Norte) and South (Tasqueña) terminals. Many buses throughout the day and night, prices from US$28. To **Puebla**, 1st-class buses take the *autopista*, 4½ hrs, 2nd-class buses go on the old road, 5-6 hrs, good scenery in both cases, many buses throughout the day, US$20-25. To **Veracruz**, ADO services at 0830, 2215 and 2359, 7½ hrs via the *autopista* US$28. AU service 2230 and ADO GL 22.45 on Fri and Sun (6 hrs). US$22-31.**Villahermosa**, ADO services 1700, 1900, 2130, 12hrs, US$35, book well ahead. To **Mérida**, ADO, Sun at 0900 and ADO GL 1130, 21 hrs, US$63.

The route to Chiapas from Oaxaca is via **Tehuantepec** and the first 2 hrs are on very windy roads. To **Tuxtla Gutiérrez**, OCC services at 1900, 2100 and 2230, OCC, 10 hrs, US$26; and luxury services at 2000, US$31, also luxury service with Linea 1, Thu, Fri and Sun, 2030, US$40; 2nd-class services with Oaxaca-Istmo and Fletes y Pasajes, US$18. To **San Cristóbal de las Casas**, OCC services at 1900 and 2100; 11 hrs, US$29 and a luxury service at 2000, US$33. To **Tapachula**, an OCC service at 1910, US$26, 13 hrs; and a luxury ADO service at 2100, 11½ hrs US$33. To **Tehuantepec**, frequent OCC and ADO services, US$12, 4½ hrs; 2nd class: with Oaxaca-Istmo and Fletes y Pasajes, every 30 mins 0600-2400, US$9, 5½ hrs.

First-class services to the Pacific coast go via the Isthmus of Tehuantepec, taking a long detour (best overnight). 2nd-class services are direct but unpleasant on a tortuous descent to sea level; pack Dramamine and a sick bag. It's worth considering a shuttle. To **Pochutla**, 1st-class OCC services at 0930, 2130, 2300, 2350, 10 hrs, US$18; direct 2nd-class Oaxaca Pacifico and Estrella del Valle at 2300, 6 hrs, US$9; indirect services at 0900, 1330 and 1630. To **Puerto Escondido**, 1st- class OCC services at 0930, 2130, 2300, 2350, 11 hrs, US$18.50. Direct 2nd-class Oaxaca Pacific and Estrella del Valle services (via **Pochutla**) at 0930, 2130 and 2300, 8hrs, US$19; Transol services at 0600 and 1330, US$9 and 7 daily with Estrella Roja, US$11. To **Huatulco**, 6 OCC 1st-class services, 0930, 2130 and 2300, 7 hrs, US$18; a 2nd-class service with Oaxaca Pacifico and Estrella del Valle, US$10.

To **Monte Albán**, Autobuses Turísticos depart from Hotel Rivera del Angel, Mina 518 near Díaz Ordaz (bus tickets sold in hotel), every 30 mins 0830 -1530, US$3 return, 3 hrs at the site, allowing only just enough time to visit ruins before returning (you are permitted to come back on another tour on 1 ticket for an extra US$1 but you will not, of course, have a reserved seat). Last bus at 1800, but subject to change. It's possible to walk to the site by catching a local bus marked 'Colonia Monte Albán' from in front of the Panadería México, next to Mercado de Abastos, which will drop you at the foot of the mountain. From there, it's tough uphill climb which should not be attempted alone or without water. It's more feasible to walk the 4 km downhill on the return journey. The views over Oaxaca are superb.

To **Mitla**, buses depart from the 2nd-class stations every 10 mins, 0600- 1900, 1½ hrs, US$1.50, The ruins are 10 mins walk across the village from the bus stop on the highway. Other destinations in the Central Valleys, including **Teotitlán de Valle**, **Tlacolula** and **Santa Ana del Valle**, are also served by frequent 2nd-class buses.

To **Hierve el Agua**, there is one 2nd-class bus, 0800, returning at 1430, subject to change.

Shuttles To **Pochutla** with Minibuses Atlántida, hourly. Reservations and tickets at Oficina Matriz, La Noria 101, T951-514 7077, 9 departures daily, 5½ hrs, US$12; and with **Eclipse 70**, Armenta y López 504, T951-516 1068, 12 departures daily, 5½ hrs, US$12. To **Puerto Escondido**, minibuses leave from Arista 116 several times a day, 6 hrs, US$13.

Car hire
Phone ahead to book, a week before if possible. **Alamo Rent a Car**, 5 de Mayo 203, T951-514 8534, airport, T951- 511 6220; **Hertz**, La Bastida 115, T951-514 2434; **TTN**, 5 de Mayo 217-7 y Murguía, T951-516 2577.

Monte Albán *p582*
Bus Autobuses Turísticos operate services between Monte Albán and **Oaxaca** (see under Oaxaca City long distance buses).

Route to Mitla *p585*
Bus To **Oaxaca**, 2nd-class buses depart from the highway every 10 mins, 0600-1900, 1½ hrs, US$1.50,

Hierve el Agua *p587*
Bus 2nd-class buses to **Oaxaca** depart daily at 1430, subject to change.

Huautla de Jiménez *p589*
Bus Several daily buses to/from **Mexico City** and **Oaxaca** (US$6.50); children meet buses offering lodging in their homes.

ⓘ Directory

Oaxaca City *p577, map p578*
Banks Bancomer, on García Vigil, 1 block from Zócalo, exchanges TCs in own *casa de cambio*, 0900-1700, and Visa ATM. Banco Santander Mexicano, Independencia 605, cash and TCs, good rates, TCs changed Mon-Fri 0900-1330. Amex office Viajes Micsa,

Valdivieso 2, T951-516 2700, just off Zócalo. **Escotiabank**, Periférico near Mercado de Abastos, best rates, main branch in Independencia 801. *Casa de cambio* at Armenta y López 203, near corner with Hidalgo, Mon-Sat 0900-1700, shorter hours on Sun. Change TCs at weekends at many *casas de cambio* around the Zócalo.
Embassies and consulates Canada, Pino Suárez 700-Loc 11B, T951- 513 3777. France, 3a Privada José López Alvarez 5, T951-514 2184. Italy, Alacalá 400, T951-515 3176. Spain, Porfirio Diaz 340, T951-515 5058. USA, Alacalá 207, T951-514 3054. **Immigration** Independencia 709, on the 2nd floor, Mon-Fri 0900-2000. **Internet** Many cyber cafés around town, most charge US$1 per hr.
Laundry ELA, Super Lavandería Automática, Antonio Roldán 114, Col Olímpica, washes and irons. Lavandería Azteca, Hidalgo 404 between Díaz Ordaz y J P García, Mon-Sat 0830-2000, quick service, delivers to nearby hotels, 3½ kg US$6.50. Lavandería Hidalgo, Hidalgo and J P García, Mon-Sat 0800-2000, 3½ kg US$6.50. **Libraries** Biblioteca Circulante Benedict Crowel Memorial, also known as 'The American Lending Library', Pino Suárez 519, lending library with good English books, used books and magazines for sale (Mon-Fri 1000-1300, 1600-1900, Sat 1000-1300), US$13 per year. Biblioteca Pública Central, Alcalá 200 (no sign), has a lovely courtyard and a reading room with Mexican newspapers and magazines. Next door is the library of the Museo de Arte Contemporáneo. Also libraries at the Centro Cultural Santo Domingo and the Instituto de Artes Gráficas.
Luggage storage Servicio Turístico de Guarda Equipaje y Paquetería, Av Tinoco y Palacios 312, Centro, T951-516 0432, open 24 hrs, US$15 for 30 days. **Medical services** English-speaking doctors can be found at Clínica del Carmen, Abasolo 215, T951-516 2512, close to centre; and at Hospital Molina, García Vigil 317, T951-516 3836. Pharmacies: beneath Hospital Molina and all over town. **Post office** Alameda de León, Independencia y 20 de Noviembre.

Oaxaca coast

The Oaxaca coastline is blessed with some gorgeous beach resorts, from the quiet and laid-back San Agustinillo and Mazunte to the sprawling Puerto Escondido and hedonistic Zipolite. The emphasis is firmly on the feel-good factor, with options including all-night partying, skinny dipping or being pampered with alternative treatments. Construction has been rather low-key, with the exception of Puerto Escondido, with its perfect surfers' waves, and Bahías de Huatulco, further south, a favourite stop-off point for cruise ships. Many resorts remain idyllic spots away from the bustle of Mexican cities.
▶▶ *For listings, see pages 607-622.*

Puerto Escondido ⬤🔵🔵🔵⊗⬤▲🔵🔵 ▶▶ *pp607-622. Colour map 2, C5.*

→ *Phone code: 954.*

The town and its surroundings offer some stunningly beautiful beaches with world-class surfing, good facilities for visitors, and the town is a good base for various interesting excursions. However, Puerto Escondido is at risk of becoming a case study in unsustainable tourism development, as parts of it has become downtrodden and ramshackle. It was a small and sleepy fishing village as recently as the 1980s, until the population rapidly increased, perhaps in response to grandiose plans for Acapulco-style development. These never panned out and tourism instead developed in a low-rise and haphazard manner, creating a negative environmental and social impact. The state tourist police now patrol both the main beach and tourist areas. They are English speaking and helpful.

Puerto Escondido is now a bustling and commercial seaside resort in the last decade. **El Adoquín**, the city's pedestrian tourist mall along Avenida Pérez Gasga near the beach, teems with Mexican families in season, sunburnt foreigners and hardcore surfers throughout the year; December to January are the most crowded, May to June the quietest (and hottest) months. A handful of luxury hotels are clustered above Playa Bacocho. **Playa Zicatela**, home to the Mexican Pipeline, is where surfers and their crowd hang out.

The real town, where prices are lower and there is less of a hard-sell atmosphere, is located up the hill on the other side of the highway. There is an ample selection of hotels and restaurants in all areas. Many fast-talking '*amigos*' are found at all the nearby beaches and other sites frequented by tourists offer an impressive array of goods and services for sale or hire; be polite and friendly but also wary, since there is no shortage of overpricing and trickery. **Sedetur information kiosk** ① *west end of El Adoquín, T954-582 1186, delpuerto@aoaxaca.com*, is run by Gina Machorro, who possesses in-depth knowledge of the town and region. Known and loved by locals and visitors alike, she speaks English, Spanish and French and generally takes the time to give help and advice. (See Activities and tours, page 614, for her walking tours of the area.)

Safety Even with the vast improvements in security, safety is an especially important issue in and around Puerto Escondido. A safe and pleasant stay here is possible with the appropriate precautions, but carelessness can have severe consequences. Never walk on any beach at night, alone or in groups. Although there are lifeguards now paid by the government, the ocean currents at Zicatela can be treacherous.

The **Playa Principal**, abutting El Adoquín pedestrian mall, has the calmest water but it is very close to the city and not very clean. A few fishermen still bring in the catch of the day here.

The local government began building a small pier for them and the tourist craft, but it remains unfinished, and a monument to poor planning. Immediately to the south is **Playa Marinero**, with slightly stronger surf (reportedly a good place for beginners), also built up with hotels, bars and restaurants. Further south, past a rocky outcrop called Rocas del Morro, lies the long expanse of **Playa Zicatela**, which claims to be Mexico's best surfing beach, with the Mexican Pipeline producing the world's fastest-breaking waves (they can be more than 3½ m high). It makes for breathtaking viewing. It is suitable only for experienced surfers and very dangerous for swimming. To the west of the main bay, past a lovely headland (being built up with condominiums) and a lighthouse, are a series of picturesque bays and beaches, all accessible by road or boat from town. **Playa Manzanillo** and **Puerto Angelito** share the Bahía Puerto Angelito and are the closest (an easy 15-minute walk). They are pretty with reasonably safe swimming but very commercial; every square millimetre of shade is proprietary here, so prepare to fry or fork out for a parasol. Further west is **Playa Carrizalillo**, with swimming and more gentle surfing than Zicatela, accessed by a steep path of 170 steps,

Puerto Escondido

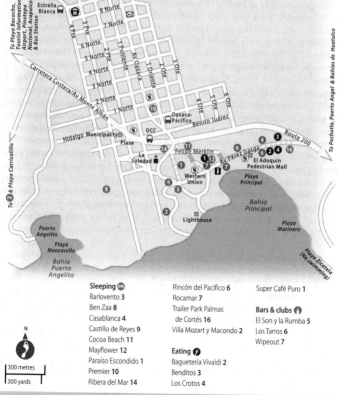

Sleeping
Barlovento 3
Ben Zaa 8
Casablanca 4
Castillo de Reyes 9
Cocoa Beach 11
Mayflower 12
Paraíso Escondido 1
Premier 10
Ribera del Mar 14

Rincón del Pacífico 6
Rocamar 7
Trailer Park Palmas
  de Cortés 16
Villa Mozart y Macondo 2

Eating
Baguetería Vivaldi 2
Benditos 3
Los Crotos 4

Super Café Puro 1

Bars & clubs
El Son y la Rumba 5
Los Tarros 6
Wipeout 7

or by boat or taxi. **Playa Bacocho** is next, a long beautiful stretch of less-developed beach, where the ocean, alas, is too dangerous for swimming but makes for great sunset viewing.

Around Puerto Escondido ●❷❸❹▲❺❻ ▸▸ *pp607-622. Colour map 2, C5.*

Seventy-four kilometres west of Puerto Escondido is the 140,000-ha **Parque Nacional Lagunas de Chacahua**, a wildlife refuge of sand dunes, interconnected lagoons, mangroves and forest. La Pastoría is the largest lagoon, connected to the sea by an estuary. It has nine islets that harbour thousands of birds, both resident and migratory. On the shores of the lagoon is the village of **Chacahua**, home to some of the area's small Afro-Mexican population. There is a crocodile hatchery nearby, aimed at preserving this native species. The easiest way to see the park and learn about its wildlife is with a **tour** ⓘ *day tour costs $44, book with* Lalo Ecotours *(see Activities and tours, page 614).* To go independently you need two days; take a minibus to Río Grande (from 2a Norte and 3a Poniente, every 20 minutes), then another one to Zapotalito from where there are boats (US$12 per person if there are enough passengers) to the village of Chacahua. It's best to leave early to avoid the tour groups and if you plan to stay the night, take a mosquito net.

Closer and easier to access than Chacahua is the **Laguna de Manialtepec**, 16 km west of Puerto Escondido, also a good place for bird-watching. This is a quiet, pretty and secluded spot, well worth a visit. There are organized tours available from **Lalo Ecotours** (see Tour operators, page 614) or it's possible to reach the lagoon off your own steam by taking a *colectivo* (US$0.70) or taxi (US$7), to the village of **Las Negras**. At restaurant **Flor del Pacífico**, right on the lagoon at the starting point for the tours run by Lalo Ecotours (see page 614) and the drop-off point for buses, it's possible to rent a kayak or canoe to explore the lagoon independently (US$4.50 per person, per hour), or alternatively rent a boat with a guide and driver (US$36 for two person, US$7 per person for larger groups). The restaurant itself is one of few women's co-operatives in the area and worth a visit for a nice meal after seeing the lagoon. Nine kilometres long, with a depth of 5-10 m, the Laguna de Manialtepec is an area of red and white mangroves, with some 320 bird species, waterlilies and other marine flora. There are salt, fresh and lagoon species of fish here and it's also the site of nesting birds, including pelicans. In rainy season (June-October) the lagoon connects with the sea at Barra Grande and nearby Río Manialtepec provides a complete contrast of flowers and vegetation. Although exploring independently is possible, taking a tour gives great insights into the bird conservation initiative, which is now in its 19th year. At Puerto Suelo at the end of the lagoon by the sea, it's possible to have a swim in the Río Manialtepec, but the sea itself is too rough. A row of shacks are also open serving refreshments December-March.

Pochutla → *Phone code: 958. Colour map 2, C5.*

Sixty-six kilometres east of Puerto Escondido and 240 km south of Oaxaca is San Pedro Pochutla, a hot and busy town with an imposing church set on a small hill. Its pleasant **Plaza de las Golondrinas**, where people stroll in the cool of the evening, is filled with many singing birds. There is a prison in Pochutla, and inmates carve crafts out of coconut husks sold by their families and local shops. The **Fiesta de San Pedro** takes place on 29-30 June.

From Oaxaca, Highway 175 to Pochutla is a very scenic but extremely winding paved road. In the Central Valleys it goes through the craft towns of **Ocotlán de Morelos** and **Ejutla de Crespo** (several places to stay), before climbing the Sierra Madre del Sur to its pine-clad ridges and the pass. Just south of the pass is **San José del Pacífico**, a hamlet with good views and a restaurant where buses make a rest stop.

Puerto Angel → *Phone code: 958. Colour map 2, C5.*

Twenty minutes south of Pochutla along a pretty road, which winds through hilly forest country before dropping to the sea, is Puerto Angel. Tourism and fishing are currently the main economic activities here. The town lies above a beautiful flask-shaped bay; unfortunately the turquoise water is polluted, but there are hopes for improvement if a planned sewage system is installed. Because of its lovely setting and chilled-out vibe it has been described as 'the ideal place to rest and do nothing'. The beach, right in town, is an ideal spot to watch the activity of the small charming dock. A short walk away, either along the road or on a concrete path built on the rocks (not safe at night), is **Playa del Panteón**, a small beach in a lovely setting, but crowded with restaurants (touts await visitors on arrival) and many bathers in season. There are cleaner and more tranquil nearby beaches east of town. **Estacahuite**, with simple *cabañas*, 1 km from town, about a 20-minute walk, has good snorkelling (gear rental from hut selling drinks and snacks) but beware of strong waves, currents and sharp coral that can cut you.

Zipolite and San Agustinillo → *Phone code: 958.*

The fabled haunt of Zipolite has long drawn an alternative crowd. Located 4 km west of Puerto Angel, it overlooks a stretch of ocean so ferocious, the waves seem to be possessed by some violent, raging spirit. If you don't break your neck trying to swim here, you'll be carried off to sea by wildly shifting rip tides. Indeed, the name 'Zipolite' is believed to be derived from a Zapotec word meaning 'beach of the dead'.

However, most people don't come here to swim, they come here to relax and enjoy themselves. Zipolite's reputation as a party town is well deserved. Hordes of young gringos, backpackers and bongo-toting hippies descend en masse during high season. A string of beach bars provide nightly entertainment and illicit drugs are readily available too, and the usual penalties for possession apply, including a long and not very comfortable stay in a Mexican prison. As a display of force the Mexican military make a point of visiting the beach, guns at the ready, every now and again – although this all seems to be just for show.

The west end of the beach is reserved for nudists (mostly older Western men). Generally, the west side of the beach is the more lively and hedonistic side, with the greatest development and the most popular places. You'll find internet cafés and paved roads here. There's a quieter, family atmosphere at the less-developed eastern side. Low season can be eerily quiet everywhere, although there is an expat community living here year round.

Another 3 km west lies **San Agustinillo**, a long, pretty beach, with an extraordinary cave in the cliffs. The western end is quite built up with private homes and the rest of this small resort is also expanding rapidly. Hotels, *cabañas* and beach bars are springing up everywhere. More facilities such as internet cafés and shops are also on the rise. The beach is smaller than in nearby Zipolite and Mazunte, but there are nice coves and cliffs to explore. The vibe is laidback and relaxing, if less alternative than hippy favourite Zipolite. Swimming is safest at the west end of the beach, surfing best near the centre. Nude bathing is prohibited. *Colectivos* ply the coast between beach resorts charging a flat fee of US$0.35, pretty much regardless of where you get on or off.

Mazunte → *Phone code: 958.*

One kilometre further west is Mazunte, a quintessential beach resort, which is a bit basic and ramshackle with buildings springing up rather haphazardly, so responsible tourism is especially important. The beach is on federal land and drug laws are strictly enforced; nude bathing is prohibited, the safest swimming is at either end of the bay. At the east end of

Mazunte is the **Centro Mexicano de la Tortuga** ① *guided tours in Spanish and English, Wed-Sat 1000-1630, Sun 1000-1430, US$15, crowded with tour buses from Huatulco 1100-1300 during high season; interested researchers may contact the director at www.centromexicanodelatortuga.org*, a government institute that studies sea turtles and works to conserve these frequently endangered species, as well as to educate visitors and the local population. There are interesting viewing tanks to observe many species of turtles underwater. A trail leads from the west end of the beach to **Punta Cometa**, a spit of land with lovely views of the thundering breakers below, a popular spot to view the sunset and well worth the 30-minute walk. With its proximity to Zipolite, Mazunte is also attracting the alternative crowd and signs for yoga, massage, vegetarian and vegan food positively abound. It's a good place to try local therapies; by the cemetery there's a spiritual healer offering to treat everything from stress to insomnia; he also does ritual cleansings.

La Ventanilla

Two kilometres west of Mazunte is a signed turn-off for La Ventanilla. It is 1½ km from here to the village and visitor centre on the shores of a lagoon. Tours are run by local residents who are working on a mangrove reforestation project (in 1997 Hurricane Pauline wiped out part of the mangroves here) and have a crocodile farm to repopulate the area. The tour combines a rowing boat ride through the mangroves for up to 10 people, a visit to the crocodile farm and a walk on the beach, US$5 per person, many birds, crocodiles and iguanas may be seen; the guides speak Spanish only. Horse riding tours along the beach are also available for US$25 per hour. Those wishing to spend the night can camp or stay with a family. Simple meals are available in the village.

Huatulco ⊕🚗🏨❀🅾🔺🌐🅲🅾 ➤➤ *pp607-622. Colour map 2, C5. Phone code: 958.*

East of Pochutla (50 km, one hour), and 112 km west of Salina Cruz on the coast road is Huatulco, a meticulously engineered and environmentally aware resort surrounded by 34,000 ha of forest reserve and nine splendid bays (where pirate ships used to shelter). It offers golf, swimming pools, international and Mexican cuisine, nightlife, beaches, water sports, excursions into the forest and exploration of archaeological sites. The final product is a safe, clean, efficient, if somewhat sanitised international vacation resort, which despite its lovely setting, hasn't entirely taken off. The bays are lined with grand schemes, that have evidently been left mid-building, adding a few eyesores to the otherwise stunning landscape. In high season, including Holy Week, July to August and November to March, Huatulco is busy, with regular charter flights from the USA and Canada. During these peak times prices can as much as double. The rest of the year, there's an altogether quieter feel, although frequent cruise ships add bursts of frenzied activity on certain days of the week.

The Sedetur tourist office ① *Blv Benito Juárez, Tangolunda, T958-581 0176, sedetur6@ oaxaca.gob.mx*, near the golf course, is helpful and informative. An **information booth** ① *Parque Central*, La Crucecita, run by the excellent, amiable and knowledgeable Señor Cipriano, is a handy source of information. A useful **website** is *www.todohuatulco.com/bahias-huatulco.html*. For boat trips and other activities, see page 614.

The Huatulco complex encompasses several interconnected towns and development areas and there are many taxis, some of which operate as *colectivos*. Prices for journeys can be found on signs at the main plaza in La Crucecita. **Tangolunda** (meaning 'beautiful woman' in Zapotec), on the bay of the same name and also known as the *Zona Hotelera*, is set aside for large luxury hotels and resorts; it also has the golf course and the most expensive restaurants, souvenir shops and nightlife. **Chahué**, on the next bay west, where development only began in 1999, has a town park with spa and beach club, a marina and a few hotels. Further west (6 km from Tangolunda) is **Santa Cruz Huatulco**, once an ancient Zapotec settlement and Mexico's most important Pacific port during the 16th century. It has the marina where tour boats leave for excursions, as well as facilities for visiting yachts and cruise ships, several upscale hotels, restaurants, shops and a few luxury homes. An attractive open-air chapel, the Capilla de la Santa Cruz, is by the beach.

La Crucecita, located 2 km inland, is the Huatulco complex, with housing for the area's employees, bus stations, banks, a small market, shops, bars, plus the more economical hotels and restaurants. It also doubles as a Mexican town, which the tourists can visit; it's more cosmetic by the manicured Plaza Principal, less so towards the highway. The old-looking but brand-new Templo de Guadalupe church stands on a small hill next to the plaza.

Huatulco's coastline extends for almost 30 km between the Río Copalita to the east and the Río Coyula to the west. Hills covered in deciduous forest – very green during the rainy season (June to September), yellow and parched in the dry – sweep down to the sea. Nine turquoise bays with 36 golden beaches line the shore, some bays have road access while others can only be reached by sea.

Around Huatulco
In the Huatulco area the **Sierra Madre del Sur** mountains drop from the highest point in the state of Oaxaca (3750 m) right down to the sea. There are ample opportunities for hiking; see Activities and tours, page 614. In the hills north of Huatulco are a number of coffee plantations that can be visited. Huatulco travel agencies arrange for full-day plantation tours, which include a meal with traditional dishes at the farm and bathing in fresh water springs or waterfalls, for US$44 per person.

Day trips to the different coastal attractions to the west, including Puerto Angel and Mazunte, are offered by travel agencies for US$20. Much ground is covered; it's a long day.

◉ Oaxaca coast listings

For Sleeping and Eating price codes and other relevant information, see Essentials pages 47-51.

◉ Sleeping

Puerto Escondido *p602, map p603*
Puerto Escondido and Playa Zicatela have more than 180 hotels in all categories.

Downtown
AL Aldea del Bazar, Benito Juárez 7, T954-582 0508, www.aldeadelbazar.mexico-hoteles.com. A veritable sultan's palace, with a garden, pool, large rooms and a good restaurant.
A Paraíso Escondido, Unión 10, Centro, T954-582 0444, www.hotelpe.com. Away from the beach, this colonial style hotel has suites and

rooms, a/c, pool and a great garden; the restaurant opens in high season and serves international cuisine.
B Barlovento, Camino al Faro, Calle 6a Sur, No 3, T954-582 0220, www.oaxaca-mio.com/hotelbarlovento.htm. Large, comfortable hotel on the way to the lighthouse, offers a/c rooms with telephone and TV. There's a pool, and cheaper rooms with fans. Great views over bay.
B-C Casablanca, Av Pérez Gasga 905 (Adoquín), T954-582 0168, www.ptohcasa blanca.com. A/c in some rooms, fan, hot water, clean, well furnished with balconies and a pool.
B-C Rincón del Pacífico, Av Pérez Gasga 900 (Adoquín), T954-582 0193, www.rincondel pacifico.com.mx. Clean and simple rooms with fan, TV and bathroom. **Danny's Beach Bar** is attached.

C Rocamar, Av Pérez Gasga 601, T954-582 0339. Decent economical rooms, most of them with a/c and cable TV.

D Ben Zaa, 3a Sur 303, T954-582 0523, www.hotelben-zaa.com, on hill climbing to the lighthouse. 30 rooms with cable TV and economical *cabañas*, complete with cooking facilities, fridges and bathrooms – daily, weekly and monthly rates available. The hospitable manager, Steve Posing, can organize sport fishing, horseback riding and bikes. There's international cuisine and daily specials. The view from the roof is sublime.

D Castillo de Reyes, Av Pérez Gasga 210, T/F954-582 0442. Clean, nice rooms, hot water, quiet, good beds, friendly, good value.

D Cocoa Beach, de los Fundadores s/n, also access from Felipe Merklin, T954-582 0428, behind the church. Ten small, clean and simple rooms with fan or a/c and mosquito nets. Also has 2 self-catering flats. Friendly and family run.

D Mayflower, Andador Libertad, on pedestrian walkway perpendicular to El Adoquín, T954-582 0367, minnemay7@ hotmail.com. This excellent hostel has dorms and rooms and offers its guests Wi-Fi, free internet, lockers, safety deposit box, kitchen facilities and pool table. There's a great terrace and upstairs sitting area with a grand piano and views over the bay. The owner, Minne Dahlberg, is a very attentive hostess. Recommended.

D Premier (formerly **Hotel Central**), Hidalgo and 1era Ote, T954- 582 0116. Another clean and basic cheapie near the bus station. Some rooms are large and offer good ocean views.

D Villa Mozart y Macondo, Av Tortugas 77, Carrizalillo, T954 104 2295, www.villa mozart.de. Hotel with rooms, apartments and bungalows close to Playa Carrizalillo. Beautiful location, German run.

D-E Ribera del Mar, Felipe Merklin 205, T954-582 0436, behind Iglesia de la Soledad. Fan, hot water, pool, clean, quiet, laundry facilities, some rooms with great views of the sea. Very good value. Recommended but beware of early morning church bells.

Camping Trailer Park Palmas de Cortés, Av Pérez Gasga y Andador Azucena, near Playa Principal, T954-582 0774. Clean bathrooms, shade, US$5 per car, US$6 per person. Recommended.

Playa Zicatela

L Santa Fe, Calle del Morro, T954-582 0170, www.hotelsantafe.com.mx. 4-star Mediterranean-style hotel concealing pleasant patios, courtyards and pool. Good seafood restaurant attached.

A-B Bungalows Zicatela, Calle del Morro s/n, T954-582 0798, www.bungalows zicatela.com.mx. Oceanfront rooms with terraces, kitchenettes and fridge. Rooms have a/c, but are cheaper with fan. There are 2 larger and 2 smaller pools and a small restaurant. Low season prices much lower.

B Bungalows Acuario, Calle del Morro, T954-582 0357, www.hotelbungalowsacuario zicatela.com.mx. Rooms and bungalows. Prices drop considerably off season, and are generally cheaper with shared bath. There's a pool, gym, good travel agent, *casa de cambio* and internet.

B-C Rockaway, Calle del Morro, T954-582 0668, www.hotelrockaway.com. Popular hang-out with hippy twist, where *cabañas* and rooms overlook a pool. *Cabañas* are completely self contained with bathroom, showers and mosquito nets. Rooms have a/c and hot water.

C Casa de las Iguanas, Av Bajada las Brisas s/n, T954-582 1995, www.casadelas iguanas.com. Friendly surfers' hotel. Comfortable rooms with a/c, jacuzzis, pool and funky bar. Clean and professionally managed. Organizes surf lessons and excursions.

C Inés, Calle del Morro, T954-582 0792, www.hotelines.com. Colourful, pleasant rooms and a chilled-out garden slung with hammocks. Also has *cabañas*, apartments and suites. There's a bar, pool and travel agency.

Pochutla *p604*

There are several hotels in Pochutla if you need to stay. But with all those miles of beautiful coast just a short ride away, why would you want to?

D Costa del Sol, Lázaro Cárdenas 47, T958-584 0318. Parking and pool at this hotel. Rooms have a/c (cheaper with fan) and cable TV.
D Izala, Lázaro Cárdenas 59, T958-584 0115. Slightly tired rooms have a/c, cheaper with fan (**C**), TV, hot water, nice patio, clean, comfortable.
E Santa Cruz, Lázaro Cárdenas 88, across from Oaxaca terminal (shuttle to Oaxaca leaves from here), T958-584 6214. Very basic and run-down, cheaper with fan.

Puerto Angel *p605*
B La Cabaña, Pedro Saenz de Baranda s/n, Playa del Panteón, T958-584 3105, www.lacabanapuertoangel.com. Clean and comfortable rooms with a/c. There's a pleasant terrace and pool.
C Puesta del Sol, on road to Playa del Panteón, T958-584 3315, www.puerto angel.net. Friendly German management has a wealth of information on the area. Comfortable rooms, movies and internet available. Rooftop terrace with hammocks, light breakfast and snacks. Recommended.
C Soraya de Puerto Angel, José Vasconcelos s/n, Playa Principal T958-584 3009. Beautiful views, clean, spacious terraces, a/c, parking.
C Villa Florencia, Calle Virgilio Uribe s/n across from town beach, T/F958-584 3044. A/c, cheaper with fan, clean, comfortable, friendly, Italian/Mexican run, restaurant, bar, library with terrace.
C-D Casa de Huéspedes Gundi y Tomás, central and up the hill opposite old military base, T958-584 3068, www.puertoangel-hotel.com. Pleasant hotel with colourful rooms and tranquil terraces. Book exchange, hammocks, communal fridge and bar. Good rates for weekly/monthly stays. Changes TCs.
D Capy's, Pedro Saenz de Baranda, on road to Playa del Panteón, T958-584 3240. Basic rooms with fan. Nice restaurant attached. Cheap for a single person.
D Posada Rincón Sabroso, Uribe s/n, near Villa Florencia, T958-584 3095. Clean rooms with hot water. Beautiful views and a terrace with hammocks. Quiet and friendly.

E Casa de Huéspedes Leal, central, T958-584 3081. Very economical and basic. Shared bath, washing facilities, friendly.

Zipolite *p605*
The shore is lined with *palapas* offering cheap meals, accommodation and informal discos. The western end of the beach is more lively and popular than the quieter eastern end.
AL-A Nude Bungalows and Sky Lounge, On the western end of beach opposite the nude beach, hence the name. This is the latest addition to Zipolite with upmarket *cabañas* boasting excellent views, an international restaurant and über-cool bar, perfect for sundowners. Most *cabañas* have TV, private bathrooms and kitchen, beach chairs and there's a nice pool.
C El Neptuno, T958-584 3219, www.hotel neptunozipolite.com, eastern end of beach. If sleeping in a hut isn't your thing, then come here. You'll find nice, bright rooms surrounded by solid walls, balconies, sea views and a restaurant serving good Mexican food.
C-D Shambhala, T958-584 3152, shambhala_ vision@excite.com, western end of beach near the rocks. "Where the 60s never end" – and they mean it. There's a strong hippy ethos at this long-standing Zipolite favourite. It has dorms (**F**) and rooms, social spaces and inspiring views over the Pacific. Café Bohemia serving good fish and Mexican dishes, attached.
D Lo Cósmico, www.locosmico.com, western end of beach. Lovely, rustic *cabañas* with excellent views. There are hammocks (**G**) if you're very impoverished (or just enjoy sleeping outdoors). Friendly owner.
D Lola's Linos, along the quieter eastern end of the beach, T958-584 3201. Colourful rooms on several floors. There's a bar and restaurant, with reasonably priced meals (ψ-ψ). Quiet setting and brightly painted pinky-purple building. Spacious rooms, friendly.
D Posada Brisa Marina, T958-584 3193, brisamarinaca@yahoo.com, western end of beach. Large, simple rooms and hammock space (**G**). Friendly owner will help with bus tickets. Free Wi-Fi. Recommended.

D Posada Mexico, T958-584 3194, www.posadamexico.com, western end of beach. Nice, spacious, comfortable *cabañas* in gorgeous colours, all kitted out with nets and hammocks. There's an attractive cactus garden and an Italian restaurant that serves authentic stone-baked pizzas in high season.

San Agustinillo p605

B Punta Placer, on main beach, www.punta placer.com. Well kept, clean and popular. Owner also runs Coco Loco surf club (www.cocolocosurfclub.com) with surf board rental, lessons in English, Spanish and French, surfing tours (also in 3 languages), mountain hikes, restaurant attached. Recommended.

D Posada San Agustín, San Agustinillo. This once-grand place has been slowly left to crumble into a ruin, but it still has the best views in San Agustinillo.

D-E Palapa Olas Altas, western end of the beach. 3 rooms with bath and several cheaper *cabañas*. Economical, but a bit basic. Restaurant attached does reasonable meals including good seafood.

Mazunte p605

Several *palapas* offer simple accommodation along the middle of the beach.

B Posada Alta Mira, on a wooded hillside overlooking the western end of the beach, T958-101 8332, www.labuenavista.com/ alta_mira. Beautiful, tidy bungalows overlooking the ocean with spectacular views. Good restaurant and low-season discounts.

C Balamjuyuc, next to Posada Alta Mira, T958-101 1808, balamjuyuc@hotmail.com. Friendly owners Emiliano and Gaby run this tranquil ecotourism venture with gorgeous views. Different types of massage and *temazcal*. The restaurant Pacha Mama does homemade veggie food with everything from the bread to the pasta made on location. Tent space or hammocks (**G**). English, German and Italian spoken. Highly recommended.

C-D Ziga, at the eastern end near Centro Mexicano de la Tortuga, www.posadaziga.com. Rooms are cheaper without bath, but not great

value. There's a good terrace with hammocks and views of the Pacific.

E Cabañas Yuri. Beach *palapa* with basic rooms, some have separate bath. There's also hammock space. Friendly and family run.

Huatulco p606

Discounts of up to 50% in the low season.

L Quinta Real, Blv Benito Juárez 2, Tangolunda, T958-581 0428, www.quinta real.com. Exclusive and secluded resort with superb views over the bay. Golf club, beach club, pool, bar and restaurant.

AL Marina Resort, Tehuantepec 112, Santa Cruz, T958-587 0963, www.hotelmarina resort.com. Various high-quality suites and a plethora of facilities including pools, restaurants, pre-Hispanic-style spa, and disco.

A Gran Hotel Huatulco, Carrizal 1406, La Crucecita, at the entrance to town, T01800-712 7355, www.granhotelhuatulco.com. 32 comfortable, if unremarkable, rooms, double beds, a/c and cable TV. Also pool, restaurant bar and parking. Good reductions in low season.

A Meigas Binniguenda, Blv Sta Cruz 201, Santa Cruz, T958-587 0077, binniguenda@ prodigy.net.mx. Colonial-style hotel with gardens, pool, restaurant and beach club.

A Plaza Huatulco, Blv Benito Juárez 23, Tangolunda, T958-581 0035, www.hotel plazahuatulco.com.mx. Small luxurious hotel with comfortable suites.

A Posada Chahué Best Western, Mixie and Mixteco, Chahué, T958-710 7889, www.bwhuatulco.com. Good, if predictable rooms with a/c and all the usual extras. Pool and terrace restaurant.

B Busanvi I, Carrizal 601, La Crucecita, T958-587 0739. A/c and fan, hot water.

B Misión de los Arcos, Gardenia 902 and Tamarindo, La Crucecita, T958-587 0165, www.misiondelosarcos.com. Elegant suites with Wi-Fi and a/c. Guests have use of Chahué beach club. Restaurant attached.

B Posada de Rambo, Guarumbo 307, La Crucecita, near main plaza, T958-587 0958. Clean and quiet with pleasant rooms. A/c, cable TV and hot water.

D Benimar, Bugambilia and Pochote, La Crucecita, T958-587 0447. Simple rooms with bath, fan and hot water.

D Casa de Huéspedes Koly, Bugambilia 301, La Crucecita, near Plaza, T958-583 1985. Very central, cheap, basic and clean rooms with fan, bath and cable TV. Fair for the price.

D Posada del Carmen, Palo Verde 307, La Crucecita, T958-587 0593. Clean, simple, straightforward rooms in this small hotel.

D San Agustín, Carrizal 1102 y Macuil, La Crucecita, T958-587 0368. Clean, basic rooms with bath and fan.

● Eating

Puerto Escondido p602, map p603
Downtown

There are more than 400 restaurants in the area, so there's plenty to choose from. Many can be found down Av Pérez Gasga, but for really cheap fare you should head to the market on 8 Norte and 3 Pte, for economical *comida corrida* and varied local food.

♥♥ **Los Crotos**, Av Pérez Gasga (Adoquín), fresh seafood and fish dishes, traditional Mexican. Access to the beach from restaurant. Friendly.

♥♥ **Super Café Puro**, off top flight of stairs of walkway that starts at the tourist information kiosk. Good for breakfast, pleasant terrace, Mexican, family-run, free Wi-Fi and an excellent spot to while away some time over a cup of fresh Oaxacan coffee. Recommended.

♥♥-♥ **Baguetería Vivaldi**, Av Pérez Gasga. Good breakfast, coffee, crêpes and sandwiches.

♥♥-♥ **Benditos**, Av Pérez Gasga. *The* place for pizza, pasta and other authentic Italian dishes. Good value.

Playa Zicatela

Restaurants front the beach all the way along.
♥♥♥ **Hotel Santa Fé**. Excellent, expensive vegetarian. Worth it for the views at sunset.

♥♥♥-♥♥ **La Galería**, Hotel Arcoiris. Specialities include lobster and jumbo prawns.

♥♥ **Cabo Blanco**, Calle del Morro. Crazy happening place with accommodation,

restaurant and bar. Big party on Monday nights, cover charge US$2 after 2200, always packed. Cajun prawns to die for and a good range of mescals from sister company Sivayaa, www.mezcalsivayaa.com.

♥♥ **El Greko**, beach restaurant and bar opposite **Cabo Blanco**. Good seafood and friendly staff, lovely for lunch by the sea. Popular with families at weekends.

♥♥ **El Tabachín**, Playa Marinero, behind **Hotel Santa Fe**. Vegetarian, café, breakfast and lunch.

♥♥ **Sabor a Mar**, Calle del Morro. Delicious seafood served under a beachfront *palapa* that overlooks the crashing waves of the Mexican pipeline. Great fillets, good service.

♥♥-♥ **El Cafecito**, Calle del Morro. This popular restaurant does excellent breakfasts and wholesome, home-cooked Mexican fare.

Carmen's Bakery, Calle del Morro. Great pastries baked on the premises, next door to El Cafecito.

Puerto Angel p605

♥♥ **Beto's** by turn-off for Playa del Panteón. Good fish (fresh tuna), lobster and chicken, cheap beer and nice views.

♥♥-♥ **Villa Florencia**, Calle Virgilio Uribe s/n across from town beach. Hotel with an excellent restaurant serving good Italian and Mexican dishes, charming place.

♥ **Cangrejo**, by Naval Base gate. Popular bar, also good breakfasts and excellent tacos.

♥ **Mar y Sol**. Cheap, good seafood.

♥ **Sirenita**. Popular for breakfast and bar.

Zipolite p605

The majority of hotels strung along the beach have a restaurant or bar attached. They mostly serve breakfasts, pizzas, seafood and good, cold beer.

♥♥♥-♥♥ **El Alquimista**, western end of beach near rocks, overlooking the nudist beach and violently crashing waves. Quality of food has gone downhill a bit, but still good for pizzas and breakfast. Also has *cabañas* for rent.

♥♥-♥ **Pacha Mama**, western end of beach at Balamjuyuc Hostel (see Sleeping, page 610). Vegetarian, home cooked, organic food.

Ψ **Café Maya**, eastern end of beach. Good sushi and cocktails. Chilled-out spot.
Ψ **El Pelicano**, western end of town, away from the beach. One set menu for US$2 serving the best barbecued chicken with rice, pasta, salad, tortillas, avocado and salsa. Very popular with locals and visitors alike.

San Agustinillo p605
ΨΨ-Ψ **El Sueño de Frida**, on main road, San Agustinillo, closed Mon and 1300-1600 daily. Frida Kahlo-themed café and ice cream parlour with outside terrace. Breakfast and dinner only.
ΨΨΨ **Un Secreto**, eastern end of main road, off beach. Salad and seafood in pleasant setting.

Mazunte p605
Some of the best food and the best views are at Posada Alta Mira, see Sleeping, page 610).
ΨΨ-Ψ **La Dolce Vita**, on main road at western end. Good Italian pizza and home-made pasta, pricey. Open Wed-Sun 1600-2300.
ΨΨ-Ψ **La Tortuguita**, opposite the turtle centre. Breakfasts, *comida corrida*, *tortas*, snacks and Oaxacan specialities.
ΨΨΨ **Brisa**, good seafood, including excellent steamed squid. Arbolito next door does good pizzas.

Huatulco p606
Restaurants on the beach, out of town, tend to be the cheapest. There are luxury restaurants at the Tangolunda hotels. In La Crucecita, prices get cheaper as you get away from the plaza; there are several restaurants along Gardenia.
ΨΨΨ **Don Porfirio**, Blv Benito Juárez s/n, Tangolunda. Lobster, shrimps, octopus, fish fillets and other fine sea fare. Specialities including shrimp fajitas with brandy.
ΨΨΨ **Il Giardio del Papa**, Flamboyán 204, La Crucecita. Italian chef was once the Pope's cook, expensive.
ΨΨΨ **Jardín del Arte**, Paseo Mitla 107 at Hotel Marlín, Santa Cruz. Menu a bit basic, popular with Mexican families.
ΨΨΨ **Las Cúpulas**, Benito Juárez 2 in Hotel Quinta Real, Tangolunda. Fine dining with

view of the harbour, also popular breakfast venue. Entertainment Fri and Sat evenings.
ΨΨΨ-ΨΨ **Oasis Café**, Flamboyán 211 and Bugambilia, by main plaza, La Crucecita. Varied menu including snacks, grilled meats, sushi, soups, seafood and regional cuisine. Japanese lunchtime specials. Recommended.
ΨΨΨ **Agave Restaurant & Bar**, Bugambilia 701 A, on main plaza, La Crucecita. Tasty Mexican fare and Italian frittatas, good breakfasts (Ψ) lunches and dinners.
ΨΨ-Ψ **El Sabor de Oaxaca**, Guamúchil 206, La Crucecita. Tasty *tlayudas*, *moles* and other Oaxacan specialities. Burgers and regular Mexican fare too.
ΨΨ-Ψ **La Crucecita**, Bugambilia and Chacah, La Crucecita. Seafood and regional cuisine, breakfast, snacks and set meals. Economical.
ΨΨ-Ψ **Los Portales**, Bugambilia 603, Plaza Principal, La Crucecita. Attached to the Iguana bar, this restaurant does beef, fish, chicken, burgers and steaks. Specialities include *nopal* cactus with melted cheese and salad. More upmarket upstairs restaurant Onix (ΨΨΨ) is also under the same management, open from 1400. Excellent seafood dishes.
Ψ **Café Huatulco**, near the marina, Santa Cruz. Regional coffee and snacks.
Ψ **La Crema**, Gardenia and Guanacastle, La Crucecita. Popular bar/restaurant, pizzas, bar food, games. Recommended.
Ψ **Mercado 3 Mayo**, Guamúchil, La Crucecita. Market stalls serving typical dishes at very cheap prices, great value.
Ψ **Toñita**, Gardenia and Chacah, La Crucecita. *Comida corrida* and à la carte menus. All home-cooked, economical fare. Very friendly.

☺ Bars and clubs

Puerto Escondido p602, map p603
Downtown
El Son y la Rumba, Av Marina Nacional. Rooftop bar with live salsa and rumba at night. Restaurant serves *comida corrida* in the day.
Los Tarros, Av Pérez Gasga 604. Lively bar with pool table, staff are nice and friendly.

Wipeout, Av Pérez Gasga. Rowdy, popular bar playing rock and techno music.

Playa Zicatela

It is not advisable to stay at bars and discos past 0300.

Art and Harry's Surf Inn, Calle del Moro. Popular surfers' bar that does 2-for-1 specials. There's a pool table and views of the ocean.

Barfly, Calle del Moro, above the popular Banana's restaurant. Plays good, lively music and regularly screens films.

Casa Babylon, Calle del Moro. Funky little bar with shelves of books and an assortment of strange, otherworldly masks.

Huatulco *p606*

Several luxury hotels have shows such as the **Barcelo's Fiesta Mexicana** with Mariachis, folk dancing and Mexican buffet. Live music in the lobby bar every night.

La Papaya, Benito Juárez, Manzana 3, Lote 1, Bahía de Chahué, T958-587 2589. Popular, US$7 cover, European-style disco, big screen, human fish tank.

Magic Tropic, Santa Cruz. With Latin dancing.

Noches Oaxaqueñas, Blv Benito Juárez, Tangolunda, reservations T958- 581 0001. US$12. Has a La Guelaguetza floric show.

⊛ Festivals and events

Puerto Escondido *p602, map p603*
Jan-Feb blues festival at various venues.
Feb Marlin fishing tournament. Bajos de Chila, 15 mins from Puerto Escondido, has an annual festival, with games and firework displays. Best to go with a local if possible, as it can get quite drunken and rowdy.
Mar Long board tournament.
Aug Master World Surf Championship.
Nov The city's festivities are held throughout the month, along with a surfing tournament and a fishing tournament. The Festival Costeño de la Danza, with colourful, lively folk dances, is held mid-month.

Dec Large-scale *posada*, visitors welcome to participate.

Puerto Angel *p605*
1 Jun Día de la Marina
1 Oct Fiesta de San Angel

Huatulco *p606*
1st week Apr Fiesta del Mar
3 May Fiesta de la Santa Cruz.
1st week May International sail-fishing tournament.
8-12 Dec Fiesta de la Virgen de Guadalupe.

O Shopping

Puerto Escondido *p602, map p603*
Crafts and souvenirs are sold in shops along El Adoquín, stalls on the main street, east of El Adoquín and on Andador Libertad, a walkway going uphill from the middle of El Adoquín. Shop around; beach vendors usually ask for higher prices and you may find better value in shops north of the highway. Surf gear and clothes are best bought from shops in Zicatela.

Ahorrará, 3a Pte y 5a Norte. Large well-stocked supermarket.

Oasis, Adoquín, opposite the tourist kiosk. Fine accessories and gifts.

Papi's. Souvenir shop with a small selection of foreign books for sale or trade.

San Agustinillo, Arte Sano Craftshop, main road away from the beach, opposite Hotel Malex. Good selection of handicraft products.

Super Che, Hidalgo and 1a Ote. A new supermarket, long anticipated by the locals.

Mazunte *p605*
Cosméticos Naturales de Mazunte, on main road out of Mazunte. Women's cosmetics collective, affiliated to the Body Shop. Good-value cosmetics and toiletries.

Huatulco *p606*
Mercado de Artesanías de Santa Cruz, Blv Santa Cruz, corner Mitla. Regional crafts.

Museo de Artesanías Oaxaqueñas, Flamboyán 216, Plaza Principal, La Crucecita, exhibits and sells Mexican crafts. Good display of regional dresses from the Guelaguetza.

▲▲ Activities and tours

Puerto Escondido *p602, map p603*
Diving
The coastline offers good opportunities for snorkelling and scuba diving; snorkelling from the beach is easiest at Puerto Angelito. There are some 70 boats available for trips, dolphin and whale watching in the area.
Aventura Submarina, Av Pérez Gasga, at western end of El Adoquín, T954-582 2353, asubmarina@hotmail.com. Tours and diving lessons with Jorge Pérez Bravo. Lessons US$75 for 1 tank; if qualified, US$43 for 1 tank.
Puerto Dive Center, T01954-102 7767, www.puertodivecenter.com. NAUI and PADI certification, equipment rental and tours. 1 tank US$45, 2 tanks US$65, 2 hr snorkel tour with gear US$25, openwater diving lessons, US$320 for a 4-day course.

Fishing
Boats can be hired for fishing at Playa Principal or through travel agencies for approximately US$40 per hr for up to 4 passengers.
Janine II T954 101 1264, josmarlin1@hotmail.com. Boat trips, fishing.
Omar Sportfishing, T954-559 4406, www.tomzap.com/omar.html. Fishing charters with Captain Omar Ramírez. He also runs dolphin-watching tours.

Horse riding
El Caballerango, T954-582 3460.

Pelota Mixteca
A modern version of an ancient Mixtec ball game is played on Sat or Sun in Bajos de Chila, 15 mins from Puerto Escondido, on the road to Acapulco. Check dates with tourist information kiosk in Bajos de Chila. In a 9 m by 35 m court, teams of 5-7 players propel a rubber ball

weighing almost 1 kg, using elaborately decorated leather mitts that weigh between 3½ kg and 6 kg. A game can take up to 4 hrs.

Surfing
Playa Zicatela is a surfer's haven, but dangerous for the novice. Board rental from US$13 a day from **Carri Surf and Oasis**. Lessons from the lifeguards on the towers, US$28.

Tour operators
Gina Machorro (speaks English and French), offers a 2-hr gastro walking tour of Puerto Escondido on Sat, US$18 pp, on coffee in the region, visiting the house of *tamales* and the house of chocolate. Sun is an archaeology tour. Both tours run in winter only. The fee goes directly to the local community. Contact via El Adoquín information, page 602.
Hidden Voyages Ecotours, Pérez Gasga 905B, T954-582 2305, www.peleewings.ca/ecco.php, inside **Turismo Dimar Travel Agency**. Tours to the lagoons with Canadian ornithologist Michael Malone; winter only. Recommended.
Lalo Ecotours, T954-588 9164, www.lalo-ecotours.com. This ecotour operator is managed by knowledgeable locals who know the region's lagoons, such as nearby Laguna de Manialtepec, intimately. Also trips to Parque Nacional Lagunas de Chacahua. Birdwatching expeditions, kayak trips and tours to bio-luminescent waters are among their services. Highly recommended.

Puerto Angel *p605*
Azul Profundo, next door to **Cordelia's** on Playa del Panteón, T958-584 3109, www.tomzap.com/azulprofundo.html. Scuba diving with experienced instructors, up-to-date equipment, PADI service available. Introduction to diving US$33. Also runs snorkelling trips to beaches along coast.

Huatulco *p606*
Boat trips
Full-day boat tours to see the different bays are offered by travel agencies for US$15 per

person, with stops for swimming, snorkelling and a meal on a catamaran, sail boat, yacht or launch. Or arrange trips at the Santa Cruz marina directly with the boatmen.

Cycling

A mountain bike is a good way to get around this area and to reach the high points with many views of the bays. You'll find rental stores in and around the hotel zones. In La Crucecita try **Erick Tours**, Flamboyán 207, T958-587 1936, just off the Plaza Principal, renting bicycles and motorcycles by the day or hour.

Diving and snorkelling

Good snorkelling areas on reefs by the beach at **La Entrega** (Bahía Santa Cruz), **Riscalillo** (Bahía Cachacual) and **San Agustín** (Bahía San Agustín). The islands of **Cacaluta** (Bahía Cacaluta) and **La Montosa** (Bahía Tangolunda) are also surrounded by reefs with several species of coral. Snorkel and fins at **Santa Cruz marina**, US$5 or through agencies who organize tours. There are good scuba-diving opportunities and the cliffs that separate the different bays continue underwater an average of 30 m.

Buceo Sotavento, Flamboyán 310, La Crucecita, T958-587 2166, www.tom zap.com/sotavento.html. Well-established dive shop. Also branch at Tangolunda, T958-581 0051.

Hurricane Divers, Playa Santa Cruz, Manzana 19, Lote 8, T958-587 1107, www.hurricanedivers.com. Package diving tours for qualified divers.

Fishing

Launches and yachts for deep-sea fishing charge US$100 per hr, minimal rental 3 hrs. **Cooperativo Tangolunda**, T958-587 0081, Bahía Santa Cruz, near beach. Cheap option.

Golf

Tangolunda golf course, T958-581 0037. An 18-hole, par-72 golf with good views.

Health spa

Baño de Temazcal de Santa Cruz, near the cruise port. Ritual herbal bath from US$8, additional treatments US$16 (aromatherapy, hydrotherapy, etc), full package US$24. Bring sandals, towel and swimsuit.

Xquenda Huatulco Spa, Vialidad Lambda s/n, Bahía Chahué, T958-583 4448, www.huatulcospa.com. Massage, beauty salon, gym, 25 m pool, *temazcal* treatments.

Hiking

There are opportunities for hiking in the forested hills to the north of Huatulco. Because part of the forest is deciduous, the experience is very different in the rainy season, when it is green, and in the dry season when the area is brown and some cacti even change from green to violet. The Río Copalita to the north and east of Huatulco is quite scenic. It has waterfalls and rapids, walking here can be combined with a visit to the Punta Celeste Zapotec archaeological site. See Tour operators below.

Rafting

Several companies run tours down the Copalita and Zimatán rivers. These can be as basic as a float down the river or as challenging as class 4-5 rapids. Half-day tours cost around US$40, full-day tours US$65-85 pp. Note that from Feb to May there may not be enough water. See also Tour operators below.

Rock climbing

Climbing at **Piedra de los Moros**, north of Route 200, on the road to Pueblo Viejo, the turn-off is west of the Bahías de Huatulco entrance road; by **Copalitilla waterfall**, on the Copalita river canyon, 65 km from Huatulco; and in **Punta Celeste**, at Botazoo Park, 8 km from Huatulco. See Tour operators below.

Sailing

Luna Azul, contact Jack Hennessey on T958-587 0945, or drop in at **Hotel Posada Chahué**, Calle Mixie L 75, Sector R Bahía de

Chahué, www.lunaazul.netfirms.com. Day and evening sailing trips and private charter.

Tour operators

Aquaterra, Plaza las Conchas 6, Tangolunda, T958-581 0012. For activities including hiking, rock climbing, canyoning and biking.

Bahías Plus, Carrizal 704, La Crucecita, T958-587 0932, and at **Hotel Binniguenda**, Santa Cruz, T958-587 0216, www.bahiasplus.com. Horse riding, airline reservations, numerous specialist tours trips. Helpful.

Explora Mexico, Sierra Juárez Edificio 13 A, Dept 202, Chahué, T958-587 2058, exploramex@prodigy.net.mx. River tours/rafting trips, 4-5 day excursions.

Jungle Tour, Blv Chahué, Lote 22, Manzana 1, T958-581 0491. Quad bike jungle tours.

Rancho Tangolunda, Blv Benito Juárez, Local 5, Tangolunda, T958-587 2126, www.ranchotangolunda.com, 10 mins from the hotel zone. Adventure sports agency organizes rafting, hiking and climbing trips. Also rents out kayaks, horses and quad bikes.

Watersports

Windsurfing, sailing, wave running and waterskiing equipment can be rented at the major hotels and beach clubs.

Zax Aventura Extrema, Av Bahía San Augustín, Lote 17, Manzana 24, Coyul, T958-587 1264. Tubing.

⊖ Transport

Puerto Escondido *p602, map p603*
Air

Airport 10 mins' drive west of town. To **Mexico City** with Click Mexicana, T954-582 2023, 1525, daily 1 hr, US$141.50; To **Oaxaca City** with Aerovega, T954-582 0151, 0730, daily, US$79. *Colectivo* from airport, US$3 pp. Most other flights via Mexico City.

Bus

Local To **Pochutla**, from corner Ctra Costera and Av Oaxaca, every 15 mins, 0530-2000, 1hr,

US$2.20. For **Puerto Angel**, **Zipolite** and other beaches: transfer in Pochutla to pick-up or *colectivo* taxi, or alternatively get off at the crossroads at San Antonio and take a *colectivo* (US$0.50, every 30 mins) or taxi (US$3-4, usually waiting at the bus stop) from there, avoiding Pochutla altogether.

Long distance To **Acapulco**, with Estrella Blanca, a/c, semi-direct service every couple of hours from 0400, 7½ hrs, US$18.50; or regular service, hourly 0500-1730, 9 hrs, US$14. To **Mexico City**, with 1st-class services at 1535, to the Southern Terminal (Tasqueña) and 1800 to TAPO and northern terminal, US$46, 18 hrs; Oaxaca-Pacífico/Estrella del Valle, 1st class, at 1800, US$33, 12 hrs via Oaxaca, arrives at **Fletes y Pasajes** terminal near TAPO (east terminal). To **Oaxaca**, with Estrella del Valle, Av Hidalgo 400 near Av Oaxaca, direct service at 0815, 1245, 2215 US$8.50, 1st class at 2230, US$10.50. OCC,3 daily, 0700, 1430 and 2045, US$18.50, 10 hrs. To **Huatulco**, via Pochutla, afternoon departures only, 2¼ hrs, US$5.80, 2nd class with SUR, frequent, 2½ hrs, US$3.50. To **Puebla**, with Oaxaca-Pacífico/Estrella del Valle, 1st class, at 1800, US$28, 10 hrs via Oaxaca, leaves you by the highway, not CAPU. First-class service 1535 and 1800, US$49, 16 hrs. To **Salina Cruz**, frequent 1st-class departures, 5 hrs 15 mins, US$11.50, Estrella Blanca, Av Oaxaca, 5 a day, 5 hrs, US$6.50. To **Tapachula**, with ADO, 1730, 15 hrs, US$33. To **Tuxtla Gutiérrez** and **San Cristóbal de las Casas**, with OCC, 1830 and 2130, Tuxtla US$26.50, 12 hrs, San Cristóbal, US$30, 13 hrs. To **Zihuatanejo**, with Estrella Blanca, 1 direct bus daily.

Shuttles To **Oaxaca** depart from Hotel Luz del Angel on Av Oaxaca, T582-0122, 6 hrs, US$13.

Car hire

Dimar Travel Agency, Av Pérez Gasga 905B, T954-582 1551.

Pochutla p604
Bus
Pochutla is a transport hub for the region, with OCC and Estrella Blanca as the main 1st-class operators. There are also several 2nd-class lines including Estrella del Valle and Transportes Rápidos de Pochutla.

Local To **Huatulco** (La Crucecita), with OCC, frequent, 1 hr, US$2.50. To **Puerto Escondido**, with small buses from side street near church, every 15 mins 0530-2000, 1½ hrs, US$2.20; also with through buses coming from Oaxaca or Salina Cruz.

Long distance To **Acapulco**, with Estrella Blanca, 0630, 0930, 1530, 1830, 2100, 9 hrs, US$28. To **Mexico City** with OCC at 1930, 16 hrs, US$46. To **Oaxaca**, with OCC, direct service 0820, 1550, 2205, 9 hrs, US$18. Second-class service, 11 daily, 9 hrs, US$7. To **San Cristóbal de las Casas**, with OCC at 2000 and 2250, US$27, 11-12 hrs. To **Salina Cruz**, with OCC, 9 daily, US$9; with Estrella Blanca, 5 daily, 4 hrs, US$10. To **Tapachula**, with OCC, 1850, 13 hrs, US$30. To **Tuxtla Gutiérrez**, with OCC, 2000 and 2250, 9½-10½ hrs, US$23.

Shuttles To **Oaxaca** include Minibuses Atlántida, from Hotel Santa Cruz, Lázaro Cárdenas 88, T958-584 0116, 9 daily, 6 hrs, US$12; and Eclipse 70 from Lazaro Cardenas 85, T958-516 0840, 12 daily, 6 hrs, US$12.

Taxi and *colectivo*
For **Puerto Angel**, **Zipolite** and other beaches, pick-up trucks with benches in the back and shared taxis (*colectivos*) do round trips on the coastal road in both directions; these taxis also offer private service (*carreras*); in Pochutla, wait at marked bus stops along the main road. To **Puerto Angel,** truck US$0.50, *colectivo* US$1 pp, taxi US$4. To **Zipolite**, truck US$0.50, *colectivo* US$1, taxi US$6. To **Mazunte**, truck US$1, *colectivo* US$1, taxi US$8. Beware of overcharging, which is especially common in this area.

Huatulco p606
Air
Aeropuerto Bahías de Huatulco is located 17 km northwest of Huatulco along Route 200, T958-581 9099; airport van service T958- 581 9014, US$27. Taxi US$12, 20 mins. To **Mexico City** with Click Mexicana, T958- 587 0223, 3 daily at 1115,1510,1905, 1½ hrs, US$74.

Bus
Local Second-class buses to **Pochutla** from Blv Chahué y Riscalillo, La Crucecita, every 15 mins 0500-2000, US$1.20, 1 hr. Second-class buses to **Salina Cruz** from Blv Chahué and Bugambilia, frequent departures, 3 hrs. *Colectivo* taxis run from Tangolunda and Crucecita (main plaza), US$0.40.

Autotransportes Istmeños, Carrizal and Blv Chahué, have frequent 2nd-class departures to Salina Cruz, Juchitán and Tehuantepec.

Long distance To **Acapulco**, with Estrella Blanca, 1st class, 4 daily, 9 hrs, US$28; 2nd class, 3 daily, 11 hrs, US18. To **Mexico City**, with OCC at 1520, 1620 and 2020, 14 hrs, US$56. TAPO with ADO GL, 1520, 14 hrs, US$55; with OCC to TAPO and Northern terminal, 1610 and 2020, US$46, 14 hrs; to Tasqueña with OCC, 1755, US$46, 14 hrs. To **Oaxaca**, 1st class with OCC, La Crucecita OCC/ ADO terminal, 0920, 1650, 2305, 8 hrs, US$17.50. To **Puerto Escondido**, with OCC, 1st class, frequent departures mornings and evenings, US$6, 2 hrs; with Estrella Blanca, Gardenia corner Palma Real, La Crucecita, 1st class, 5 daily, 2½ hrs, US$6, 2nd class, 3 daily, US$4. To Juchitán with OCC, frequent departures afternoon and evening, US$9, 3½ hrs. ADO GL, 1520, US$11. To **Salina Cruz**, with OCC, 1st class, 0920, 1610 and frequent evening departures 2½ hrs, US$7. To **Tapachula**, with OCC, 1st class, 1950, 13 hrs, US$27. To **Tuxtla Gutiérrez**, with OCC, 1st class, 2050 and 2350, 8 hrs, US$21. To **Pochutla** from Blv Chahué and Riscalillo, La Crucecita, *microbuses* every 15 mins, 0500-2000, US$2. Make connections at the crossroads at Pochutla for *colectivos*, minibuses and taxis for **Puerto Angel**, **Mazunte**, **Puerto Escondido** and **Zipolite**.

⊙ Directory

Puerto Escondido *p602, map p603*
Banks ATMs are all over town. Banamex, Av Pérez Gasga east of El Adoquín, 0900-1300. **Bancomer,** 1a Norte y 2a Pte, cash and TCs 0800-1400. **Banorte,** Oaxaca and Hildago, cash and TCs, reliable service. **HSBC,** 1a Norte y 3a Pte, cash and TCs, cash advance on Visa and MasterCard, Mon-Sat 0800-1900. 2 *Casas de cambio* on El Adoquín, open till 2000, poor rates. **Internet** Roughly 35 internet cafés about town; all charge US$1.50 per hr. **Laundry** Lavandería at east end of El Adoquín, US$1 per kg or US$3.25 per load, self-service, Mon-Sat 0900-2100. Also **Mangos** at Av Pérez Gasga by Hotel Nayar, US$2 per kg.
Medical services Doctors: Dr Max, Av Oaxaca and 5a Norte, no emergency service, Spanish only. Dr Mario Fransisco de Alba, Av Pérez Gasga 609, T954-582 3581. Hospitals and clinics: Clínica de Especialidades del Puerto, Av Oaxaca, recommended; Clínica de Loredes, 1a Pte y 1a Norte, surgery and emergency; Clínica Santa Fe, Av 5a Pte; Red Cross, T954-582 0550. Opticians: Optica Nuestra Señora de la Luz, 3a Pte, T954-582 1844. Emergency prescription glasses. Pharmacies: Farmacia San Antonio, Av Pérez Gasga 203, T954-582 0214, has in-house physician, open 24 hrs.
Post office 7a Norte by Av Oaxaca. Good for wiring money (need transfer number from sender), Western Union office next door.

Pochutla *p604*
Banks All on main street: Banamex, opposite plaza, ATM and Western Union office. Bancomer, 0830-1400, cash and TCs. Banorte, 0830-1400, cash and TCs. HSBC, 0830-1700, cash and TCs. **Internet** Email in a couple of places on Lázaro Cárdenas. **Medical services** Public hospital just south of town.

Puerto Angel *p605*
Banks Cash and TCs changed at Hotel Soraya. Banks in Pochutla. **Internet** Caseta Puerto Angel, Calle José Vasconcelos 3 (next to Hotel Soraya), T958-584 3038.

Huatulco *p606*
Banks HSBC, Bugambilia corner Sabalí, La Crucecita, cash and TCs, cash advances through ATM only. Bancomer, Blv Santa Cruz y Otitlán del Valle, Santa Cruz, cash and TCs. Escotiabank, Blv Santa Cruz, Santa Cruz, cash and TCs. American Express, Bahías Plus, Carrizal 704, La Crucecita, cash and TCs at good rates, Mon-Sat 0900-1400. *Casa de cambio,* Guamúchil near the Plaza, La Crucecita, poor rates. **Internet** Informática Mare, Guanacastle 203, 2nd floor, near market, US$3 per hr. **Laundry** Launderettes are all over La Crucecita, and upmarket hotels will do laundry for guests. **Medical services** Especialidades Médicas Santa Cruz, Flamboyán at Plaza, La Crucecita, private, English spoken. Central Médica Huatulco, Flamboyán 205, La Crucecita, T958-587 0104, private. IMSS, social security hospital, Blv Chahué, just south of La Crucecita. **Post office** Blv Chahué, at south end of La Crucecita.

Isthmus of Tehuantepec

The Isthmus provides a very different experience from the coastal resorts and the more cosmopolitan environment of Oaxaca City. This is a the traditional stronghold of Oaxaca with local culture and fiestas playing a significant part in daily life. The area has few foreign visitors, but is in no way devoid of places of interest. Salina Cruz, the main town, is a working port and mostly industrial, but there is plenty of local colour to be had in Tehuantepec and Juchitán and the markets are particularly good.

Southeast of Oaxaca ⊕🕐⊛⊕🅒 ➤➤ pp620-622. Colour map 2, C6.

From the city of Oaxaca, Route 190 heads southeast, through the towns of **San José de Gracia** and **El Camarón**, towards the Golfo de Tehuantepec and the Pacific.

Only about 210 km separate the Atlantic and the Pacific at the hot, once heavily jungled Isthmus of Tehuantepec, its highest point only 250 m. This narrowest point of Mexico is also the geographic boundary between North and Central America. There is the Trans-Isthmian Highway between Salina Cruz and Coatzacoalcos, the terminal cities on the two oceans.

The Isthmus has a strong cultural character all of its own. The people are *mestizo* and descendants of several different indigenous groups, but Zapotecs predominate. Once a matriarchal society, Zapotec women continue to play a very important role in local affairs. Their typical dress is intricate and beautiful, and they are high-pressure sales-women. The men generally work in the fields, as potters or weavers, or at the Salina Cruz oil refinery.

The climate throughout the area can be oppressive, very hot and quite humid, hence the region's cultural events usually take place late in the evening. Winds are very strong on and near the Isthmus, due to the intermingling of Pacific and Caribbean weather systems. Take extra care in the sea as the currents are very dangerous.

Salina Cruz ➤ Phone code: 971. Colour map 2, C6.
A modern, industrial city and port, with broad avenues and a large central plaza, Salina Cruz is surrounded by hills and many poor neighbourhoods. Some of the nearby beaches are quite scenic but oil pollution, high winds, dangerous surf and sharks all conspire against would-be bathers. Do not park close to the beach, as your vehicle may be sandblasted.

Ten kilometres to the southeast is a picturesque fishing village with **La Ventosa** beach, which, as the name says, is windy. In 1528 the Spanish conquerors established a shipyard here; the old lighthouse, **El Faro de Cortés**, can still be seen.

The coast west of Salina Cruz is quite scenic, with several high sand dunes and lagoons; shrimp farms have been set up in this area. Just west of the city is the village of **Salinas del Marquez**; the beach of **Las Escolleras** in Salinas is popular with locals.

Tehuantepec ➤ Phone code: 971. Colour map 2, C6. Altitude: 150 m.
Santo Domingo Tehuantepec, 257 km from Oaxaca, is a colourful town that conserves the region's indigenous flavour. Robust Zapotec matrons in bright dresses ride standing in the back of motorized tricycles known as *moto-carros*. Life moves slowly here, centred on the plaza, which has arcades on one side, and an adjacent market, the best place to admire the Zapotec dress. In the plaza is a statue of Máximo Ramón Ortiz (1816-1855) composer of the *zandunga*, the legendary music of the Isthmus, which is still very popular. The meandering Río Tehuantepec is two blocks from the plaza, by the highway. Due to the importance of Tehuantepec during the early colonial period, many churches were built here.

The **Casa de la Cultura** is housed in the run-down 16th-century Dominican ex-convent Rey Cosijopi, which has some original frescoes. There is a library and some simple exhibits of regional archaeology, history and costumes. The **Museo Casa de la Señora Juana C Romero** is a chalet built entirely with materials brought from France. Señora Romero's great-granddaughter lives there today, ask for permission to visit the house.

The two tourist offices are **SEDETUR** ① *Ctra Transístmica, next to the bridge into town*, the regional office for the Isthmus, and the **Regiduría de Turismo** ① *Palacio de Gobierno*.

Around Tehuantepec

To the northwest of town, off the road to Oaxaca, are the unrestored ruins of **Guiengola**, 'the Mexican Machu Picchu', so called because of its lonely location on a mountain. It has walls up to 3 m high, running, it is said, for 40 km; there are the remains of two pyramids and a ball court. This last fortress of the Zapotecs was never conquered (*guiengola* is the Zapotec word for fortress); Alvarado and his forces marched past it in 1522. Take the 0500 bus from Tehuantepec towards Oaxaca and get off at the Puente las Tejas bridge (8 km from Tehuantepec); this is the last place to buy water on the way to the ruins. Take the turning at the signpost 'Ruinas Guiengola 7 km'. Walk 5 km then turn left, uphill, to the car park. From here it is 1½ hours' walk to the ruins, there are no facilities or entry fees. Try to return before 0900 because it gets very hot; take plenty of water. Alternatively, take a taxi to the car park and ask the driver to return for you three hours later (US$5.50 each trip).

Juchitán and around → *Phone code: 971. Colour map 2, C6.*

Twenty-seven kilometres from Tehuantepec is the larger and more modern city of Juchitán de Zaragoza, an important commercial and cultural centre on the Isthmus. It has a nice plaza next to impressive colonial municipal buildings and many churches including that of **San Vicente Ferrer**, the city's patron saint. Many Zapotec women here still wear traditional costumes as everyday dress. The **tourist office** is at the Palacio de Gobierno. The **Mercado Central 5 de Septiembre** is the largest market on the Isthmus; traditional barter still takes place here. The crafts section on the second floor is worth a visit; this is the best place to see the elaborate embroidered Zapotec dresses, which sell for up to US$600.

⊚ Isthmus of Tehuantepec listings

For Sleeping and Eating price codes and other relevant information, see Essentials pages 47-51.

⊜ Sleeping

Salina Cruz *p619*

You'll find cheap lodgings on La Ventosa beach, where you can sling a hammock for a few dollars.

C Avistmo, Trabajo 699C, T971-714 5236, near the bus station. Motel-style place with large rooms, cable TV and secure parking. The owner speaks English and is helpful.

C Costa Real, Progreso 22, near Avila Camacho, T971-714 0293. Clean, spacious rooms with a/c. There's a restaurant attached, but it's pricey. Parking.

C María del Carmen, Manzanillo 17 and Tampico, T971-714 5625. Modern rooms with a/c. Cheaper with fan.

D Pacífico, Avila Camacho 709, T/F971-714 5552. Simple rooms with a/c, cheaper with fan. Restaurant attached.

D Posada del Jardín, Avila Camacho 108, T971-714 0162. As the name suggests, there's a lush garden. A/c, bath, cheaper with fan.

Tehuantepec *p619*

C Donají del Istmo, Juárez 10, T971-715 0064, in centre. Clean and friendly hotel with hot water in the mornings, more with a/c (**B**).

C Guiexhoba, on road to Oaxaca, T971-715 0416, guiexhoba@prodigy.net.mx. A/c, mini-fridge, pool, restaurant, parking.

E Casa de Huéspedes Istmo, Hidalgo 31, 1½ blocks from the main plaza, T971-715 0019. Very basic and quiet. Patio and hammocks.

E Oasis, Melchor Ocampo 8, 1 block from plaza, T971-715 0008, h.oasis@hotmail.com. Clean, simple rooms with bath and fan, more with a/c (**D**). Helpful owner, safe parking, internet café and restaurant attached.

Juchitán and around *p620*

The Casa de Cultura can help organize homestays with local families.

B-C Santo Domingo, Ctra Juchitán-Tehuantepec s/n 1era sección, T971-711 1959. Good rooms, a/c, restaurant, pool.

C López Lena Palace, 16 de Septiembre 70, T971-711 1388. Clean, modern, comfortable rooms, a/c. Cheaper in older wing with fan.

D Alfa, Ctra Panamericana Km 821, T971-711 0327. Basic, economical room with a/c and bath. Cheaper with fan.

E Modelo, 2 de Abril 64, T971-711 1241, Juchitán, near market. With bath, fan, basic.

⊘ Eating

Salina Cruz *p619*

† **Aloha**, Wilfrido Cruz 13-A. Seafood and regional dishes.

† **Casa Flor**, Miramar 3. Reportedly the best food in town. Breakfast specials include crêpes.

†-† **La Pasadita**, Avila Camacho 603. Large, breezy restaurant that serves shrimps, lobsters and other delicious seafood dishes.

Tehuantepec *p619*

The local *quesadillas* made of maize and cheese are delicious; sold at bus stops.

†††-† **Scaru**, Leona Vicario 4. Good food, fish and seafood specialities, courtyard and mural.

† **Mariscos Angel**, 5 de Mayo 1, by entrance from Salina Cruz. Top floor of market, serves local speciality of potato-stuffed pork or chicken.

†-† **Cafetería Almendro**, Melchor Ocampo 8, near the plaza. Cheap breakfasts, sandwiches, tacos, pizzas and burgers.

Juchitán and around *p620*

†††-† **Casa Grande**, Juárez 125, on the main square. In a beautifully restored colonial house, good food, live music.

†††-† **Deyaurihe**, 5 de Septiembre corner of Aldaman. Mexican food, *comida corrida*.

† **Los Chapulines**, 5 de Septiembre and Morelos. Regional and international food, *comida corrida* and à la carte, a/c.

† **Pizzería La Vianda**, 5 de Septiembre 54-B. Pizza, seafood, tasty, bit overpriced

✷ Festivals and events

Tehuantepec *p619*

Festivals are very important in Tehuantepec. Colourful celebrations are held all year, when women don elaborate embroidered dresses and lace halos, known as *resplandores*. Each town ward has its own patron saint. **Fiestas patronales** honour the local saint. *Velas* are formal dances in a decorated setting resembling a European palace.

19 May Vela Zandunga.

24 Jun Fiestas in honour of St John the Baptist in the San José (Saint John) neighbourhood.

1st week Aug Fiestas of Santo Domingo are held in the centre of Tehuantepec.

Mid-Aug Velas de Agosto.

26 Dec Vela Tehuantepec.

Juchitán and around *p620*

Velas (see above) are held throughout the year, the most important ones taking place during **May** in honour of San Vicente Ferrer.

◷ Transport

Salina Cruz *p619*
Bus

Regional service to **Tehuantepec** (US$1) and **Juchitán** (US$2.50) every 10 mins with Auto-transportes Istmeños, 0500-2400, from Progreso west of Tampico, by railway. To **La Ventosa** beach, buses leave every 30 mins from main square. To **Salinas del Marquez**, buses from the park every 30 mins. Frequent 2nd-class service to **Huatulco**, 3 hrs. There is a joint bus station for OCC, ADO, AU and Sur at the north end of town, by the Ctra Transístmica. The Estrella Blanca station is at Frontera 25. To **Coatzacoalcos**, 8 daily, 6 hrs, US$14.50. To **Oaxaca**, 1st class: OCC, 7 daily (1 luxury service), 5-6 hrs, US$12.50; 2nd class: Oaxaca-Istmo, 3 daily, 6 hrs, US$10. To **Pochutla**, 1st class with OCC and ADO, 7 daily, 4hrs, US$9; 2nd class; with Estrella Blanca, 5 daily, 3-4 hrs, US$10. To **Puerto Escondido**, 1st class, with OCC and ADO, 8 daily, 5 hrs, US$12. To **Tapachula**, with

OCC at 2245, 9 hrs, US$20. To **Tuxtla Gutiérrez**, with OCC and ADO, 0255, 0750, 1415, 2245, 2345, 5½ hrs, US$14.50, book in advance. To **San Cristóbal de las Casas**, with OCC at 0255 and 2345, 7-9hrs, US$18, book in advance.

Tehuantepec *p619*

Bus

Regional **Istmeños** buses leave from the highway (Ctra Cristóbal Colón), at the end of 5 de Mayo. To **Salina Cruz**, every 10 mins, 0500-2400, US$1, 45 mins. To **Juchitán**, every 10 mins, 0500-2400, US$1.50, 1 hr. There is a joint bus station for OCC, ADO, AU and Sur on the outskirts of town; taxi to Zócalo US$1, *moto-carro* US$0.50 or 15 mins' walk (walking not recommended at night).

For **Chiapas** destinations, it is not always possible to get a 1st-class reservation; you have a better chance from Salina Cruz or Juchitán, where more buses stop. To **Arriaga**, with OCC, 2355, 4 hrs, US$8. To **Cancún**, with ADO at 1330, 22 hrs, US$65. To **Coatzacoalcos**, with ADO and Sur, 10 daily, 5½-6 hrs, US$13.50. To **Oaxaca**, frequent OCC services, 4½ hrs, US$12. To **Pochutla**, with OCC, 2355, 0225, 0530, 0700, 4½ hrs, US$10. To **Puerto Escondido**, with OCC, 2355, 0225, 0530, 0700, 4½-6 hrs, US$13. To **Huatulco**, with OCC, 2355, 0225, 0530, 0700, 3½ hrs, US$8. To **Mexico City**, with ADO GL, luxury service, 1850, 2040, US$52; OCC and AU, 6 1st class daily, US$39-44. To **Tonalá** and **Tapachula**, with OCC, 2355, 4½ hrs, US$9 (Tonalá), 8½ hrs, US$19 (Tapachula). To **Tuxtepec**, with AU, 1035 and 2135, 6½ hrs, US$13. To **Veracruz**, 1st class, 1035, 2130, 2135, 7-10 hrs, US$24.50; 1 luxury service ADO GL, 2110, 6¾ hrs, US$26.50. To **Tuxtla Gutiérrez**, with OCC, 0315, 0825, 1445, 2315, 4½ hrs, US$14. To **Villahermosa**, with OCC, 0225, 1330, 1515, 1830 2230, 8-9 hrs, US$22.

Taxis

3-wheeled motorized rickshaws (*moto-carros*) take locals around town; you have to stand and hold on to the railing.

Juchitán and around *p620*

Bus

Regional bus service to **Tehuantepec** (US$1) and **Salina Cruz** (US$1.50). Every 15 mins with Istmeños, 0500-2400, from Prolongación 16 de Septiembre, by the highway to Tehuantepec. Joint bus station for OCC, ADO, Sur and AU at Prolongación 16 de Septiembre, just south of highway to Tehuantepec. To **Huatulco**, 1st class, 7 daily, 3½-4 hrs, US$9-US$11. To **Coatzacoalcos**, frequent 1st-class services, 5 hrs, US$12. To **Mexico City TAPO**, 13 1st class buses, 11-12 hrs, US$43; and a luxury service, US$75. To **Oaxaca**, frequent 1st-class services, 5 hrs, US$13; luxury service, US$16. To **Pochutla**, 1st class, 6 daily, 4½ hrs, US$12. To **Puerto Escondido**, 1st class, 6 daily, 6 hrs, US$15. To **San Cristóbal de las Casas**, with OCC, 0015, 0345, 7 hrs, US$16.50. To **Tapachula**, 1st class, 2400, 0025, 0150, 0235, 1540, 7 hrs, US$20. To **Tuxtepec**, with AU, 1110, 2210, 6 hrs, US$12. To **Tuxtla Gutiérrez**, 1st class, 6 daily, 5 hrs, US$12.50. To **Veracruz**, with AU, 1110, 2210, 9 hrs, US$22; and 1 ADO, 2200, 7 hrs, US$24; and an ADO luxury at 2145, 6 hrs, US$29

❻ Directory

Salina Cruz *p619*

Banks Bancomer, Avila Camacho. HSBC, Avila Camacho and Coatzacoalcos. Both change cash and TCs. **Internet** Cafés charge US$1 per hr. **Laundry** Laundry Carvel, Avila Camacho 503, US$1.80 per kg. **Medical services** Hospital Civil, Avila Camacho, Centre, T971-714 0110.

Tehuantepec *p619*

Banks Banorte, 5 de Mayo. All change cash and TCs. HSBC, Juana C Romero, 0800-1700. Bancomer, 5 de Mayo. **Internet** Ciber Kalipso, Melchor Ocampo s/n, near plaza, US$1 per hr.

Juchitán and around *p620*

Banks Bancomer, 16 de Septiembre by main plaza, Mon-Fri 0830-1400, cash and TCs. HSBC, 16 de Septiembre y Alvaro Obregón, Mon-Fri 0800-1900, Sat 0900-1400, cash, TCs. **Internet** Many along 16 de Septiembre, US$1 per hr.

Contents

Footprint features

Border crossings

Tabasco & Chiapas

At a glance

⊖ **Getting around** Buses, combis, taxis.

◉ **Time required** 2-3 weeks to sample the major attractions.

☼ **Weather** Temperatures vary according to altitude in Chiapas and it can get down to only a few degrees in Dec-Feb in the highlands. Tabasco on the other hand is very hot and humid with temperatures often reaching the 40s. Rainy season Jun-Sep.

✕ **When not to go** Tabasco can get unbearably hot Apr-Jun.

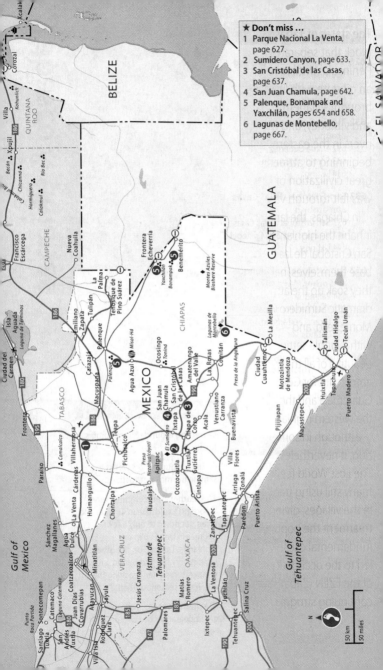

The states of Tabasco and Chiapas merge to form a geographical block that separates Mexico from Guatemala and the Yucatán Peninsula. Until recently, low-lying, jungly Tabasco was considered an oil state with little appeal for tourists, but oil wealth has brought Villahermosa, the state capital, a certain self-assurance and vibrancy, and the parks, nature reserves and huge meandering rivers in the eastern and southern regions of the state are beginning to attract visitors. Its lands once gave rise to the first great civilization of Mesoamerica, the Olmec, whose influence was felt through vast zones of Mexico and further afield.

In Chiapas, the land of the Classic Maya (whose descendants still inhabit the highland villages today), the attractions are better known: San Cristóbal de las Casas is the end of the line for many travellers who base themselves in this delightful colonial and indigenous town while they soak up the atmosphere and explore the jungle waterfalls; the dramatic Sumidero Canyon; the multi-coloured lakes of Lagunas de Montebello, and – a definite Mexico highlight – the ruins at Palenque, with a jungle setting that is arguably the most atmospheric and beautiful of all the Maya sites in the country. Chiapas is also a good entry point for Guatemala. You can head straight for northern Guatemala and the ruins of Tikal or take the popular route through the western highlands and idyllic Lake Atitlán.

Although in some ways Chiapas has fallen victim to the progress bug, it nevertheless seems impervious to the intrusion of outsiders. The Lost World feel remains, created by indigenous inhabitants, many still using traditional dress and keeping their customs alive in the villages, giving everything a timeless feel. The appalling treatment the population has suffered over centuries was the fundamental cause of the rebellion on 1 January 1994, which led to the occupation of San Cristóbal by the revolutionaries of the EZLN (Zapatista Army of National Liberation) and their continuing struggle in and beyond the boundaries of Chiapas.

Villahermosa and around

Once mostly a domestic tourist destination, Villahermosa and the surrounding area have been gaining in popularity with foreign visitors in recent years. It can be fiendishly hot during parts of the year, particularly April and May, but this verdant part of Mexico is well worth a visit for the fabulous La Venta archaeological park, featuring giant Olmec heads, in the state capital Villahermosa. New adventure and eco-tourism routes are also opening up. ➤➤ *For listings, see pages 629-632.*

Villahermosa ⬤🖈🚗⬤⊗⬤▲⬤⬤ ➤➤ *pp629-632. Colour map 3, B1.*

→ *Phone code: 933. Population: 275, 000.*

Capital of Tabasco state, hot and humid Villahermosa is a busy, prosperous and attractive city on the Río Grijalva, which is navigable to the sea. Prices here tend to be high, although it is possible to find cheaper alternatives.

Ins and outs

The **Tabasco State Tourism Office** ① *Plaza Estrada, Av Juan Estrada Torres 101, T993-310 9700, Mon-Fri 0800-1600,* has some information but is usually understaffed and the person available doesn't always speak English.

Alternatively, the **Municipal Tourism Office** ① *Prolongacion Paseo Tabasco 1401, T993-316 5201, Mon-Fri 0900-1500 and 1800-2100 and Sat 0900-1300,* is very helpful and has more information. Useful websites include www.visitetabasco.com and http://iec.tabasco.gob.mx.

Sights

The **cathedral**, away from the centre, was ruined in 1973, but has been rebuilt, its twin steeples beautifully lit at night. There is a warren of modern colonial-style pedestrian malls throughout the centre. The **Centro de Investigaciones de las Culturas Olmecas** (CICOM) is set in a new modern complex with a large public library, expensive restaurant, airline offices and souvenir shops, a few minutes' walk south, out of town along the river bank. The **Museo Regional de Antropología Carlos Pellicer** ① *Tue-Sun 0900-1700, US$1.50,* on three floors, has well laid-out displays of Maya and Olmec artefacts. Two other museums worth visiting are the **Museo de Cultura Popular** ① *Zaragoza 810, Tue-Sun 0900-1700, free,* and the **Museo de Historia de Tabasco** ① *Av 27 de Febrero corner of Juárez, Tue-Sun 0900-1700, US$1.* **Mercado Pino Suárez** ① *Pino Suárez corner of Bastar Zozaya,* offers a sensory overload as every nook and cranny is taken up with a variety of goods. It has everything from barbecued *pejelagarto* to cowboy hats, colourful handmade fabrics, spices and dangling naked chickens en route to the kettle. The local drink, *pozol,* is believed to cure a hangover. You can watch it being made here as the *pozoleros* grind the hominy into a thick dough then mix it with cold water; its grainy starchiness is somewhat of an acquired taste. When cacao is added, it's known as *chorote* and it can also have sugar, milk or vanilla mixed in. It's very popular and the *pozoleros* will serve you the drink *al gusto,* that is, with as much or as little sugar as you want.

Be sure to take insect repellent, as this state is particularly popular with mosquitoes due to the hot and humid climate, with many rivers and waterways.

Parque Nacional La Venta

ⓘ *Blv Adolfo Ruiz Cortines, T993-314 1652. Daily 0800-1700, last entry 1600. US$3.50, also includes entry to the nearby zoo; it takes up to 2 hrs to do the park justice. Excellent guides speak Spanish and English, recommended. Light and sound show Tue-Sun, check times at entrance.*

In 1925 an expedition of archaeologists discovered huge sculptured human and animal figures, urns and altars in almost impenetrable forest at **La Venta**, 120 km west of Villahermosa and once the centre of the ancient Olmec culture. In the 1950s the monuments were threatened with destruction by the discovery of oil nearby. The poet Carlos Pellicer got them hauled all the way to a woodland area near Villahermosa, now the Parque Nacional de La Venta, also called the Museo Nacional de La Venta. The 33 exhibits are dispersed in various small clearings. The huge heads, one of them weighing 20 tonnes, are Olmec; see box, page 628. The figures have suffered a certain amount of

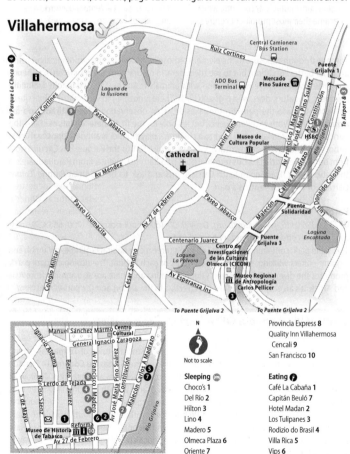

Villahermosa

Sleeping
Choco's 1
Del Río 2
Hilton 3
Lino 4
Madero 5
Olmeca Plaza 6
Oriente 7
Provincia Express 8
Quality Inn Villahermosa Cencali 9
San Francisco 10

Eating
Café La Cabaña 1
Capitán Beuló 7
Hotel Madan 2
Los Tulipanes 3
Rodizio do Brasil 4
Villa Rica 5
Vips 6

The Olmecs

The ancient Olmecs, based in what is today's Veracruz and Tabasco states, from around 1500 BC to 400 BC, paved the way for the many great civilizations to come from the Maya to the Aztecs. Most well known for their spectacular stone heads, they were first in practising ritual blood letting and playing the Mesoamerican ballgame, *juego de pelota*. The Olmecs constructed a number of temples in the region, most notably at *La Venta*, which became their most prominent centre from 900 BC until it was abandoned around 400 BC. At the time La Venta's pyramid was the largest in all of Mesoamerica and it can still be seen towering over the landscape at the site today. It is unclear what caused the sudden decline of the Olmecs between 400 and 350 BC, but their legacy of art and artefacts is some of the most astounding in the region. Much of it, including the colossal heads, can be seen at Villahermosa's La Venta museum in the state of Tabasco.

damage through exposure to the elements (those in the Xalapa anthropological museum are in far better condition) but to see them here, in natural surroundings, is an experience not to be missed. There is also a zoo with animals from the Tabasco jungle, including monkeys, alligators, deer, wild pigs and birds. There is nothing to see at the original site of La Venta. Outside the park, on the lakeside, is an observation tower, **Mirador de las Aguilas** ① *free*, with excellent views, but it's only for the fit as there are lots of stairs. The park, with scattered lakes and next to a children's playground, is almost opposite the old airport entrance (west of downtown). Taxis charge US$1 to the Parque. Bus Circuito No 1 from outside second-class bus terminal goes past Parque La Venta. From Parque Juárez in the city, take a 'Fraccionamiento Carrizal' bus and ask to be let off at Parque Tomás Garrido, of which La Venta is a part.

Parque Yumká

① *T993-356 0115, www.yumka.org. Daily 0900-1600, park closes at 1700. US$3.50, most tour agencies offer round trips for about US$14.*
This safari park, containing 108 ha of Tabasco's three major habitats – jungle, savannah and lagoon – offers walking, trolley and boat tours of each habitat. The ecological park partly promotes the diversity of the region's flora and fauna and there are also animals from Asia and Africa. It's an easy day trip; take the *colectivo* to the airport and the park is next door.

South of Villahermosa ❶❷ ➳ *pp629-632. Colour map 3, B1.*

➔ *Phone codes: Teapa 932; Bochil 932.*
South of Villahermosa on Route 195 the pleasant, clean little town of **Teapa** has several hotels and beautiful surroundings. Also in Teapa are the **Grutas de Cocona** ① *Tue-Sun 0800-1700, US$2*, which house a stunning array of stalagmites and beautiful displays of colour. The caves are approximately 500 m deep and a fresh and inviting river runs through them. There is a restaurant and campsite in the area.

Southwest of Teapa on Route 195 is **Pichucalco**, an affluent town with a lively and safe atmosphere. The Zócalo throngs in the evening with people on after-dinner *paseos*. There are hotels, restaurants and bars here. South of Pichucalco on Highway 195 on the way to Tuxtla Gutiérrez, is **Bochil**, an idyllic stopover.

In recent years, the Tabasco tourist board has taken a number of initiatives to attract visitors to the state, investing in the creation of seven different routes taking in interesting aspects of Tabasco. The routes are: the **Olmec-Zoque** route visiting the Olmec archaeological zone of La Venta and Malpasito, the only Zoque ruins open to the public, several lagoons and the waterfalls of Agua Selva; **Ríos route**, combining San Pedro river, the canyon of Usumacinta river and the Cascadas de Reforma nature reserve with activities such as sports fishing and whitewater rafting; **Villahermosa route**, taking in the highlights of the state capital and surroundings, including Yumká; **Pantanos route**, focusing on a protected area of 300,000 ha, on the borders of Campeche; **Biji Yokot'an** route, looking at the state's gastronomic traditions, including pre-Hispanic cuisine, also visiting a cigar factory; **Adventures in the mountain route**, a tour of caves, haciendas and a botanical garden, with the chance to try out abseiling and other adventure sports; finally the yummiest route of all, the **Chocolate route**, giving an insight into cacao production in the state, via cacao haciendas and the Cacao museum, with opportunities for sampling. All the above tours can be booked through **Creatur** (see Tour operators, page 631).

◉ Villahermosa and around listings

For Sleeping and Eating price codes and other relevant information, see Essentials pages 47-51.

● Sleeping

Villahermosa *p626, map p627*
Try to book hotel rooms in advance, especially during the holiday season (May onwards). Hotels tend to be full Mon-Thu; arrive before nightfall if you can. For cheaper options there are a number of hotels and guesthouses of varying standards and cleanliness along Av Constitución, in the centre, one block from the river and several near the ADO terminal.

AL-A Hilton Villahermosa, Adolfo Ruiz Cortines Ote Km 12.8, T993-313 6800, www.hilton.com. Located 1½ km from the airport and 10 mins from the centre, this is one of the city's most upmarket hotels with pool, gym, conference facilities, money exchange and multi-lingual staff. Recommended.

A Olmeca Plaza, Madero 418, T993-358 0102, www.hotelolmecaplaza.com. Large, central, professionally managed hotel with good services including restaurant, gym and pool. Some rooms have good views.

A Quality Inn Villahermosa Cencali, Juárez 105, T993-313 6611, www.qualityinn villahermosa.com. Secluded and wonderfully

a/c business hotel. It's located away from the centre, but close to commercial developments. Excellent breakfast. Recommended.

C Madero, Madero 301, T993-312 0516. Clean, if slightly damp and smelly rooms with hot water, fan and cable TV.

C Provincia Express, Lerdo 303, T993-314 5376, provincial_express@hotmail.com. Good, comfortable rooms with a/c and cable TV. Restaurant and bar, good value.

D Choco's, Lino Merino 100 y Constitución, T993-312 9444. Signposted from miles away, so not too hard to find. Clean, good value rooms with a/c and telephone. Restaurant attached.

D Oriente, Madero 425, T993-312 0121, hotel-oriente@hotmail.com. The rooms smell clean and fresh at this tidy hotel. They have hot showers and fan, pricier with a/c.

D San Francisco, Av Madero 604, T993-312 3198. Reasonable central hotel, with adequate rooms, hot water, and fan.

D-F Lino, Lino Merino 823, very close to ADO terminal. T993-148 1924. Basic rooms with good showers, quiet despite its location, more expensive with a/c.

F Del Río, Av Constitución 206 y Reforma, on plaza off Madero, T993-312 8262. Simple, slightly odd hotel with cheap rooms. You're greeted by an enormous sign telling you the management is not responsible for your belongings, so take care. The prices match the rooms.

🍴 Eating

Villahermosa p626, map p627

In high season a number of eateries, bars and discos open up along the riverfront. Good for sunset drinks and dining, but take mosquito repellent. For good tacos head to Calle Aldama, nos 611, 613 and 615, where there are 3 decent places. They are a bit cheap and cheerful, but very good value, with great selections.

There are several good *pozolerías* serving *pozol* (see page 626); try Pozolería Así es Tabasco, Av Ruiz Cortines y Av 27 de Febrero or Pozolería Lo que tiene Tabasco, Av Paseo Usumacinta 118.

₸₸₸-₸₸ Los Manglares, Madero 418, inside Hotel Olmeca Plaza (see Sleeping). Attractive restaurant serving seafood, meat, chicken and breakfast. Excellent 4-course lunch buffet.

₸₸₸-₸₸ Los Tulipanes, Malecón, south of Paseo Tabasco, 2 blocks from the bridge Puente Grijalva 2, Thu-Sun 0800-1800, Mon-Wed, 1300-1800, not open for dinner. Good location, friendly staff, good fish and seafood. Recommended.

₸₸₸-₸₸ Villa Rica, Corredor Túristico Malecón. A pleasant, modern restaurant with an enticing waterfront location. They serve tasty seafood including fish fillets and shellfish. Open 1200-2000, sometimes closed in low season.

₸₸ Capitán Beuló II, Malecón Carlos A. Madrazo, Kiosko I, T993-314 4644, ventas3@ hotelolmecaplaza.com. A novel dining experience, with gastronomic cruises along Villahermosa's waterways, accompanied by the sounds of live marimba. Gastro tour Sun, 1430, sightseeing tour Wed-Fri 1700 and Sat-Sun 1200, 1430, 1730 and 1930. Under 10s pay half price.

₸₸ El Matador, Av César Sandino 101a, www.elmatador.com.mx. Local meat dishes, *tacos al pastor*, good value. Open daily 24 hrs.

₸₸ Hotel Madan, Madero 408. Restaurant serving good breakfast, inexpensive fish dishes, a/c, newspapers, a pleasant and quiet place to escape from the heat. Also has free Wi-Fi.

₸₸ Rodizio do Brasil, Parque la Choca, Stand Grandero, T993-316 2895, informacion@ restauranterodizio.com. Speciality *espadas*, good Brazilian food.

₸₸-₸ Vips, next door to Hotel Madan. This is a well-known Mexican chain with many branches across the country. Good value breakfasts, set lunches and Mexican staples. Always popular, open early until late and free Wi-Fi.

Cafés

Café La Cabaña, Juárez 303-A, across the way from the Museo de Historia de Tabasco. Has outdoor tables where town elders congregate to debate the day's issues over piping cups of cappuccino. Very entertaining to watch. No meals.

El Café de la Calle Juárez, Juárez 513. Indoor/outdoor café, great for breakfast, good coffee, a new menu every month. The outdoor tables are great for people watching.

South of Villahermosa p628

₸₸ Restaurante Familiar El Timón, Ctra Villahermosa-Teapa Km 52, 5 s/n, Teapa.

🎭 Entertainment

Villahermosa p626, map p627

Cultural centres Centro Cultural, corner of Madero and Zaragoza, T993-312 5473. Presentations of local artists and photographers. Also, live music, workshops in literature, local handicrafts and musical interpretation. El Jaguar Despertado, Saenz 117, T993-314 1244, forum for artists and local Villahermosino intellectuals. Hosts concerts, art exhibitions and book presentations. Friendly.

⊛ Festivals and events

Villahermosa *p626, map p627*
Feb Ash Wednesday is celebrated from 1500 to dusk by the throwing of water bombs and buckets of water at anyone who happens to be on the street.

⊙ Shopping

Villahermosa *p626, map p627*
A small number of shops along Madero sell Tabasqueñan handicrafts and souvenirs of varying quality and there are also some stalls set up daily along the same street. A place to bargain for the goods.

▲ Activities and tours

Villahermosa *p626, map p627*
Tour operators
Creatur Transportadora Turística,
Paseo Tabasco 715, T993-317 7717,
www.creaturviajes.com. Tour operator organizing tours along the 7 new tourist routes, see page 629. Tours only run at weekends in low season. Recommended.

⊙ Transport

Villahermosa *p626, map p627*
Air
Airport Carlos R Pérez (VSA), 18 km from town – international flights from Havana and Houston, good national connections. VW bus to town US$5 each, taxi US$11.

Airline offices AeroMéxico, Blv Ruiz Cortines 102 local 8, T993-352 4129. **Aviacsa**, Av Vía 3, No 120, T993-316 5731. **Mexicana**, Av Vía 3, No120, locales 5 y 6, Tabasco 2000, T993-316 3132.

Taxis
City taxis charge US$1 for journeys in the centre.

Bus
Reserve your seat as soon as you can; buses to Mexico City can sometimes be booked up well in advance. 1st-class **ADO** bus terminal is on Javier Mina and Lino Merino, 12 blocks north of centre, computerized booking system. Beware of long queues at the 1st-class ticket counters. The **Central Camionera** 2nd-class bus station is on Av Ruiz Cortines, near roundabout with fisherman statue, 1 block east of Javier Mina, opposite Castillo, 4 blocks north of **ADO**.

To **Mexico City** (TAPO, Norte or Tasqueña), regular departures, 10-12 hrs, US$52-US$84; to **Cancún**, many daily, 12 hrs, US$52.50; to **Chetumal**, 7 daily, 8 ½ hrs, US$27; to **Campeche**, many daily, 6 hrs, US$18; to **Mérida**, many daily, 8 hrs, US$25-US$36; to **Palenque**, OCC 2 daily, ADO 6 daily, 2½ hrs, US$8; to **Puebla**, 4 ADO services daily, US$40; and 4 luxury services, US$49; to **San Andrés Tuxtla**, ADO services, 0255, 0930, 1100, 1925, 6 hrs, US$16; to **San Cristóbal de las Casas**, 2 OCC services at 0930 and 1230, 7 hrs, US$16; to **Tapachula**, 1 OCC at 1915, 10 hrs, US$41; and 1 ADOGL luxury at 0335, US$50; to **Veracruz**, many daily including luxury services, 8 hrs, US$26; to **Xalapa**, with ADO at 1055, 1800, 1925, 2230, 8 hrs, US$31; and 2 luxury services at 2100 and 2120, US$37 and US$48; to **Emiliano Zapata**, many daily, 2½ hrs, US$8; to **Tenosique** (for Río San Pedro crossing into Guatemala, see page 672), many daily 3½ hrs, US$10.

Car
Car hire Hertz car rental is available from the airport. **Agrisa**, Paseo Tabasco corner of El Malecón, T993-312 9184, good prices, such as US$40 per day including taxes and insurance, but it is expensive to return the car to another city.

Teapa *p628*
Bus There are buses between Teapa and **Villahermosa**, 50 km, 1 hr 20 min, US$3.50. Also to **Tuxtla Gutiérrez** at 0730, through lovely, mountainous landscape.

Pichucalco *p628*
Buses run hourly to **Villahermosa**, US$4.

Directory

Villahermosa *p626, map p627*
Banks American Express, Turismo Nieves, Sarlat 202, T01800-504 0400. **Banamex**, Madero and Reforma, Mon-Fri 0900-1700.

HSBC, Juárez and Lerdo, changes TCs at good rates. There is also a good branch on the Constitución corner of Merino, 0900-1700, Mon-Fri. **Internet** Many along the pedestrianized section of Benito Juárez, all charging about US$1.50 per hr. Others scattered around town. **Post office** On Saénz and Lerdo in the centre. DHL, parcel courier service, Paseo Tabasco and El Malecón Carlos A Madrazo.

Tuxtla Gutiérrez and around

Tuxtla Gutiérrez, the state capital, of Chiapas, is perhaps not the prettiest of cities – modern, sprawling and hectic – but it still makes for a good base, particularly for visiting nearby Chiapa de Corzo and the Sumidero Canyon, the latter a definite must-see when in the area. The centre of town is fairly compact and easy to get around. Tuxtla is also a good transport hub for buses and domestic flights, making it easy to reach other parts of Chiapas and the rest of Mexico from here. Sumidero Canyon, a spectacular 1-km-deep canyon on the Grijalva River, reached by boat from Chiapa de Corzo, is only a short bus journey away. ▸▸ *For listings, see pages 634-637.*

Tuxtla Gutiérrez ▸▸*pp634-637. Colour map 3, B1.*

→ *Phone code: 961. Altitude: 522 m.*
The capital of Chiapas, this busy, somewhat shabby city has a few worthwhile places of interest. The main sights are a long way from the centre and too far to walk.

Ins and outs
To get to the state **tourist office** ① *Belisario Domínguez 950, Plaza Instituciones, T961-602 5127, freephone T01800-280 3500 for tourist information, www.setpe-chiapas.gob.mx, daily 0800-1600,* take a *colectivo* from the junction of Avenida Central and Calle 2 Oriente. There is also a more convenient **municipal tourist office booth** ① *on the main plaza opposite the cathedral,* which provides information and can also book bus tickets, but this appears not to be open very frequently, particularly in low season. Check with main tourist office.

Orientation
The street system here is as follows: avenidas run from east to west, calles from north to south. The avenidas are named according to whether they are north (norte) or south (sur) of the Avenida Central and change their names if they are east (oriente) or west (poniente) of the Calle Central. The number before avenida or calle means the distance from the centre measured in blocks. You know whether it's an avenida or a calle by the order of the address: avenidas have their number, then sur or norte followed by east or west; calles have the east or west position first. For example, 1 Norte Oriente is the eastern part of the first avenue north of Avenida Central; 2 Oriente Norte is the north part of the second street west of Calle Central. It all sounds very complicated, but as long as you check map and road signs carefully, it is not difficult to navigate your way around the city. See Transport, page 636.

Sights

In the Parque Madero at the east end of town (Calzada de los Hombres Ilustres) is the **Museo Regional de Chiapas** ⓘ *Tue-Sun 0900-1600, US$2.50*, with a fine collection of Maya artefacts, an auditorium and a library. Nearby is the **Jardín Botánico** (botanical garden) ⓘ *Tue-Sun 0900-1800, free*.

Tuxtla is best known for its superb **zoo** ⓘ *ZOOMAT, Tue-Sun 0830-1600, US$1.40 adults, US$0.70 children; in Spanish only*, some 3 km south of town up a long hill. It was founded by Dr Miguel Alvarez del Toro, who died in 1996. His philosophy was to provide a free zoo for the children and indigenous people of the area. The zoo is very large and many of the animals are in open areas, with plenty of room to run about. Monkeys are not in cages, but in areas of trees pruned back so they cannot jump out of the enclosure. Some birds wander along the paths among the visitors. The zoo makes for a very pleasant and educational afternoon. Take mosquito repellent. *Colectivos* to 'Zoológico' and 'Cerro Hueco' from Mercado (Calle 1a Oriente Sur y 7 Sur Oriente), pass the entrance every 20 minutes; taxis charge US$2.50-3 from centre or town buses charge US$0.20. When returning, catch the bus from the same side you were dropped off as it continues up the hill to the end of the line where it fills up for the return journey.

Tuxtla Gutiérrez

N

200 metres
200 yards

Sleeping 🛏
Avenida **1**
Estrella **3**
Hostal San Míguel **5**
María Eugenia **2**
Plaza Chiapas **8**
Posada de Chiapas **4**
Regional San Marcos **10**

Eating 🍴
Antigua Fonda **1**
Bonampak **11**
Café Avenida **3**
Cherry's Liquados y Tortas **4**
El Borrego Lider **2**
El Huipil **5**
El Mesón de Quijote **7**
La Chata **6**
Las Pichanchas **13**
Los Molcajetes **12**
Mi Café **8**
Taqueria Chano y Chon **9**
Tuxtla **10**

Sumidero Canyon 🌲🏞🏠
▸▸ *pp629-676. Colour map 3, B1.*

ⓘ *www.sumidero.com. Daily 0600-1800.*
The Sumidero Canyon is a truly impressive spectacle and a trip here is a highlight of any visit to Chiapas. Native warriors, unable to endure the Spanish Conquest, hurled themselves into this hungry chasm rather than submit to foreign domination. Fortunately, you don't have to do the same to experience the awesome energy of this place. There are two ways to do it: from below, as a passenger on a high-speed boat; or from above, by visiting a series of miradors. The former method is highly recommended. The canyon is 1 km at its deepest and apart from the spectacular scenery, there is abundant birdlife and some 400 crocodiles, many of which can be seen sunning themselves along the river banks. No point putting any limbs in the water – you have been warned. Marring the beauty of the landscape somewhat is the rubbish problem of the Grijalva river and although it is reportedly cleaned regularly, with a major clean-up three years ago, large amounts of plastic and general

debris can be seen floating on the river, particularly after heavy rains. This may change as the Sumidero Canyon is attempting to reach 'New Wonder of the World' status. Ask the guides about initiatives to clean up the river.

Boats depart from the river in **Chiapa de Corzo** (see below) when full. There can be a bit of a wait in low season, when it's best to book a tour in advance to guarantee a departure without a wait of one or two hours. Tickets are available at the **Turística de Grijalva office** ① *west side of the plaza, 0800-1700, US$10 for a 2-2½ hr tour*. The **Angel Albino Corzo** agency next door also does the same tour for the same price. Both are friendly. There is a second departure point beneath Cahuaré bridge, but it is hard to get to without your own vehicle. It takes two to three hours to traverse the canyon, where you'll see prolific wildlife including crocodiles, monkeys and vultures. The trip concludes near a hydroelectric dam. Pack a sweater for the ride, as it gets chilly when you're speeding along. Remember sun block as there is no shade on the speed boats and departures are often when the sun is at its fiercest.

Alternatively, you can view the canyon from a sublime series of *miradores*. **Autobús Panorámico** leaves from outside the tourist info booth in the Parque Central on Saturday and Sunday at 0900 and 1100, throughout the year and daily in high season, visiting the main viewpoints, US$5.70. Check with Tuxtla tourist office for more details on the route and stops made. Otherwise you'll need your own vehicle or an expensive taxi. The best views are at La Coyota, especially at sunset, and there is a restaurant at the final *mirador*. Organized tours including all transport costs are widely available in San Cristóbal and Tuxtla.

Chiapa de Corzo → *Colour map 3, B1. Phone code: 961. Altitude: 456 m.*

Fifteen kilometres beyond the canyon, Chiapa de Corzo, a colonial town on a bluff overlooking the Grijalva River, is more interesting than Tuxtla. In the centre is a fine 16th-century crown-shaped **fountain**; the 16th-century church of **Santo Domingo** with an engraved altar of solid silver; and craftsmen who work with gold, jewellery and lacquer work. Chiapa de Corzo was a pre-Classic and proto-Classic Maya site and shares features with early Maya sites in Guatemala; the ruins are behind the Nestlé plant and some unrestored mounds are on private property in a field near modern houses.

The waterfall at the **Cueva de El Chorreadero** is well worth a detour of 1 km. The road to the cave is 10 km past Chiapa de Corzo, a few kilometres after you start the climb up into the mountains to get to San Cristóbal. Camping is possible but there are no facilities; take a torch.

⊙ Tuxtla Gutiérrez and around listings

For Sleeping and Eating price codes and other relevant information, see Essentials pages 47-51.

⊜ Sleeping

Tuxtla Gutiérrez *p632, map p633*
There is plenty of budget accommodation near the former 1st-class **ADO** terminal, Av 2 Norte Ote Pte 323, beyond the plaza. (Some of them have left luggage even if you're not a hotel guest. Look for signs outside.)

B María Eugenia, Av Central Oriente 507, T/F961-613 3767, www.mariaeugenia.com.mx. Pleasant rooms in the heart of town. Internet, a/c, cable TV, parking, pool and restaurant.
B Palace Inn, Blv Belisario Domínguez 1081, 4 km from centre, T961-615 0574, palaceinn@hotmail.com. Generally recommended, lovely garden, pool, video bar.
D Regional San Marcos, 1 Sur y 2 Ote Sur 176, T961-613 1940, hotelsanmarcos@

prodigy.net.mx. Comfortable rooms with bath, fan or a/c, cheaper without TV.

D-E Posada de Chiapas, 2 Pte Sur 243. Small, basic rooms with bath, fan or a/c, TV.

E Avenida, Av Central Poniente 224, T961-612 0807, mauriciog994@hotmail.com. Private bath, hot water, TV and fan. Nice and central, if a bit basic.

E Estrella, 2 Ote Norte 322, T961-612 3827. Friendly, clean hotel, slightly run down, but good value. Rooms with bath and free drinking water, recommended.

E Hostal San Miguel, 3a Av Sur Poniente 510, T961-611 4459, www.hostalsan miguel.com.mx. Nice, modern hostel with internet access, TV room, kitchen and lockers.

E Plaza Chiapas, Av 2 Norte Ote y 2 Ote Norte, T961-613 8365. Small, clean rooms with hot showers, cable TV and a/c. Cheaper with fan. Enclosed car park. Recommended.

F Posada del Sol, 3a Pte Norte and 2a Pte Nte, T961-614 6220, 1 block from former bus terminal. Rooms with hot shower and fan. Good service, good value, but quite basic. Under refurbishment, so noisy in the daytime.

Camping

F La Hacienda, Belisario Domínguez 1197 (west end of town on Route 190), T961-602 6946, www.lahaciendahotel.com. Four spaces with hook-up, hot showers, restaurant, mini-pool, a bit noisy and not easily accessible for RVs over 6 m ; owner speaks English.

🍴 Eating

Tuxtla Gutiérrez *p632, map p633*
🍴🍴 **Bonampak**, Blv Belisario Domínguez 180, T961-602 5916. Decent Mexican and North American dishes.

🍴🍴-🍴 **Antigua Fonda**, 2 Ote Sur 182, opposite La Chata. *Tortas*, *licuados*, breakfasts and general Mexican fare.

🍴🍴-🍴 **El Borrego Líder**, 2 Ote Nte 262. Breakfasts and meat dishes, popular with locals.

🍴🍴-🍴 **El Mesón de Quijote**, Central Ote 337. Clean, cheap place on the central avenue,

serves Mexican fare, including tacos for less than US$1.

🍴-🍴 **Las Pichanchas**. Av Central Ote No 857, T961-612 5351, www.laspichanchas.com.mx. Daily 1200-2400. Pretty courtyard, typical food, live marimba music 1430-1730 and 2030-2330 and folkloric ballet 2100-2200, daily. Sister restaurant at Mirador Copoya, overlooking the Sumidero Canyon.

🍴 **El Huipil**, 2 Ote Nte 250a. Clean locals' place serving *comida corrida* and *menú del día*. Also has a good breakfast selection.

🍴 **La Chata**, opposite Hotel San Marcos. Touristy; grilled meat and *menú del día*.

🍴 **Los Molcajetes**, in the arches behind the cathedral. Cheap all-day meal deals. Several other restaurants lining the arches offer similar good value.

🍴 **Taqueria Chano y Chon**, 2 Ote Nte No 120. Locals' joint serving cheap tacos.

🍴 **Tuxtla**, Av 2 Norte Pte y Central, near plaza. Good *comida corrida* and fruit salad.

Cafés and ice cream parlours
Café Avenida, Central Pte 230. Good coffee shop, does cappuccino and espresso.
Cherry's Licuados and Tortas, Central Ote 214, Local 1. Fresh fruit ice creams and *licuados*
Mi Café, 1a Pte Nte 121. Interesting locals' place serving organic coffee.

Chiapa de Corzo *p634*
There are good seafood places by the river.
🍴 **Parachic's** near main plaza, opposite the church. Does excellent breakfasts and lunches.

🎉 Festivals and events

Tuxtla Gutiérrez *p632, map p633*
Dec Feast of Virgen de Guadalupe on 12th.

Chiapa de Corzo *p634*
The fiestas here are outstanding.
Jan Daylight fiestas, Los Parachicos, to commemorate the miraculous healing of a boy ; 15, 17 and 20 Jan, and the **Chunta Fiestas**, at night, 8-23 Jan. There are parades the evenings

of the 8, 12, 17 and 19 Jan. These lead to the climax, 20-23 Jan, in honour of San Sebastián, with a pageant on the river.

25 Feb El Santo Niño de Atocha.
25 Apr Festival de San Marcos, with various *espectáculos*.

▲ Activities and tours

Tuxtla Gutiérrez *p632, map p633*
Tour operators
Carolina Tours , Av Central Pte 1138, T961-612 4281. Manager is Sr José Narváez Valencia, reliable, recommended; also coffee shop at Av Central Pte 230.
Lacandona Tours, 6a Sur Pte 1276, T961-612 9872, www.lacantours.com. Tours to all the attractions in Chiapas including the Lacandon rainforest, Bonampak and the Sumidero canyon.
Viajes Miramar, Av Central Pte 1468, T961-613 3983, www.viajesmiramar.com.mx. Good service for national flight bookings.

☉ Transport

Tuxtla Gutiérrez *p632, map p633*
Air
Aeropuerto Angel Albino Corzo is Tuxtla's new international airport, 27 km south of the city. A taxi into town costs around US$15 and from town to airport US$8. ADO buses to the airport from the OCC terminal, US$3.50.

Airline offices Aviacsa, Av Central Pte 1144, T961-612 8081; Mexicana, Belisario Domínguez 1748, T961-602 5771. All lines also have ticket offices at the airport.

Bus
There is a brand new 1st-class ADO and OCC bus terminal at 5a Norte Poniente, corner of Angel Albino Corzo, next to a new large-scale mall Plaza del Sol. There's a 2nd-class terminal at 3a Av Sur Ote and 7a Oriente Sur, about 1 km southeast of the centre.

To **Cancún**, OCC, 1055 and 1310, US$53; and ADO GL, 1430 and 1800, US$66. To **Córdoba**, 1st class (OCC and ADO), 1720, 1950, 7½ hrs, US$38. To **Chetumal**, OCC, 1310, 13 hrs, US$36.50; and ADO GL, 1430, US$43.50. To **Ciudad Cuauhtémoc**, Guatemalan border, OCC, 0630, 1015, 1615, 4½ hrs, US$13. To **Comitán**, OCC, many daily, 3 hrs, US$6. To **Mexico City**, 1st class, many daily, 12 hrs, US$56.50. To **Villahermosa**, 1st class, many daily, 4-7 hrs, US$16.50. To **Mérida**, OCC, 1500, 14 hrs, US$40; and ADO GL, 1800 US$48; or change at Villahermosa. The scenery between Tuxtla and Mérida is very fine, and the road provides the best route between Chiapas and the Yucatán. To **Oaxaca**, OCC, 1130, 1920, 2355, 10 hrs, US$25; and ADO GL, 2130, US$30. To **Palenque**, 7 OCC, 6 hrs, US$12; and ADO GL, 1430, US$14.50. To **Pochutla**, OCC, 2025 and 2310, 10 hrs, US$23. To **Puebla**, 1st class, many daily, same times as Mexico City, 10 hrs, US$49.50. To **Salina Cruz**, 1st class and luxury services, 1410, 1645, 2025, 2245, US$14.50. Take travel sickness tablets for Tuxtla-Oaxaca road if you suffer from queasiness. To **San Cristóbal de las Casas**, OCC, frequent services, 1 hr, US$3. To **Tapachula**, 1st class, many daily, 7½ hrs, US$18. To **Tonalá**, 1st and 2nd class, many daily, US$7-9. To **Tulum**, OCC, 1055, 1310, 17 hrs, US$47.50; and an ADO GL, 1430, US$56.50. To **Veracruz**, OCC, 2255, 2335, US$47; and an ADO GL, 2245, US$46.

Shuttles To **Chiapa de Corzo**, from 1 Sur Ote and 5a Ote Norte; and from the Transportes Chiapa-Tuxtla station, 2a Oriente Sur and 1a Av Sur Ote, 20 mins, US$0.70. To **San Cristóbal de las Casas**, from 2a Sur Ote 1203, between 11 and 12 Oriente Sur, 1 hr, US$2.50.

Taxis
Easy to flag down anywhere. US$3 within the centre, US$4 to the zoo, US$6 to Chiapa de Corzo (for Sumidero Canyon).

Chiapa de Corzo *p634*
Bus Frequent buses to **Tuxtla** depart from Av 21 de Octubre on the plaza. Buses to San Cristóbal now bypass Chiapa de Corzo, meaning you'll have to pick one up on the highway or go via Tuxtla.

ⓘ Directory

Tuxtla Gutiérrez *p632, map p633*
Banks Most banks open 0900-1600, HSBC stays open longer. **Bancomer**, Av Central Pte y 2 Pte Norte, for Visa and TCs, 0900-1500.

HSBC, Mon-Fri 0900-1900, Sat 0900-1500 good rates and service. For cheques and cash: 1 Sur Pte 350, near Zócalo. There are ATMs in various branches of **Farmacia del Ahorro**, all over the city. **Immigration**, 1 Ote Norte. **Internet** Free at library of **Universidad Autónoma de Chiapas**, Route 190, 6 km from centre. Various other internet cafés all over town, especially on Av Central, costing about US$1 per hr. **Post office** On main square. **Telephone** International phone calls can be made from 1 Norte, 2 Ote, directly behind post office, 0800-1500, 1700-2100 (1700-2000 Sun).

San Cristóbal de las Casas and around

The colourful colonial architecture and impressive churches of San Cristóbal de las Casas, combined with the area's indigenous culture, make this one of the most popular places to stay in Mexico. Around San Cristóbal are numerous villages, each with its own traditions and colourful weekly markets, that can easily be visited on day trips. ▸▸ *For listings, see pages 644-652.*

San Cristóbal de las Casas ⊜🅿️🏠🛍️🍴🏔️🏛️🅟 ▸▸ *pp644-652. Colour map 3, B1.*

→ *Phone code: 967. Altitude: 2110 m.*

One of Mexico's most beautiful towns, San Cristóbal de las Casas is stunningly located in the fertile Jovel valley, with the mountains of Huitepec to the west and Tzontehuitz to the east. The city is a charming blend of colonial architecture and indigenous culture, laid out in the colonial period with 21 indigenous *barrios* on the city's perimeter, which were later integrated into the totally *mestizo* city that existed by the 18th century. The indigenous population today is an important part of San Cristóbal's atmosphere, many of them earning a living by selling handicrafts in the town's two markets. The centre is rich in architectural variety, with excellent examples of baroque, neoclassical and plateresque, a Mexican style characterized by the intricate moulding of facades.

Ins and outs

Getting there The first class **OCC** and **ADO** bus terminal is at the junction of Insurgentes and Bulevar Sabines Gutiérrez, several blocks south of the centre. Other second-class lines and shuttle operators, including **AEXA** and **Rodolfo Figueroa**, also have nearby terminals on Gutiérrez, which soon becomes the Pan-American highway. The airport serving San Cristóbal is now closed to commercial traffic, Tuxtla is the nearest point of entry. Those travelling to Palenque by car will have fine views but should avoid night-time journeys because of armed robberies. ▸▸ *See Transport, page 650.*

Getting around Most places are within walking distance of each other although taxis are available in town, US$1.40 for any journey in the centre, and to the nearby villages; the cheaper *colectivos* run on fixed routes only.

San Cristóbal de las Casas

Sleeping 🛏

Barón de Las Casas **26** C2
Capri **1** E2
Casa Babylon **2** D3
Casa de Huéspedes
Chamula **29** D3
Casa de Huéspedes
Santa Lucía **4** E1
Casa Mexicana **6** B2
Casa Vieja **7** B3
El Cerrillo **9** B3
Fray Bartolomé de
las Casas **8** D2
Los Camellos **3** C4
Na Bolom **5** A4
Palacio de
Moctezuma **10** D3
Posada 5 **30** A2

Posada Diego de
Mazariegos **12** B2
Posada Doña Rosita **25** B3
Posada El Paraíso **13** B1
Posada Jovel **14** B3
Posada Los Morales **15** D1
Posada Lucella **16** E2
Posada Margarita **18** C3
Posada Media Luna **27** D2
Posada San Agustín **28** B2
Posada Vallarta **19** E2
Posadita **20** B3
Real del Valle **21** C2
Rincón del Arco **22** B4
Santa Clara **24** C2
Suites Encanto **32** B1
Tierradentro **11** C2

Eating 🍴

Adelita **1** B4
Café Museo Café **5** B3
Café San Cristóbal **7** C2
Cocodrilo Café & Bar **8** C2
Craft market **9** A2
El Fogón de Jovel **10** B2
El Gato Gordo **6** B2
El Mirador II **11** C2
El Puente **33** C3
Emiliano's Moustache **12** C1
Empanadas Loli **13** C2
Joveleño **4** C3
Juguería Ana Banana **14** D2
La Casa del Pan **33** C3
Lacteos Maya **17** C2
La Fonda Argentina **15** B3
La Margarita **24** C3

La Paloma **2** C2
La Selva Café **16** C1
Madre Tierra **18** D2
María Cartones **19** C2
Namandí **20** C1
Naturalísimo **21** B2
París-México **22** C2
Tierra y Cielo **23** C2
Tuluc **25** C2

Bars & clubs 🍸

Barfly **26** C1
Blue Bar **28** C1
El Zirko **30** B2
Makia **27** C2
Revolución **32** B2

Best time to visit Due to its altitude, San Cristóbal has a pleasantly mild climate compared to the hotter Chiapas towns such as Palenque and Tuxtla. During June, July and August, it is warm and sunny in the morning, while in the afternoon it tends to rain, with a sharp drop in temperature. Warm, waterproof clothes are needed, although the heavy rains conveniently stop in the evening, when you can enjoy San Cristóbal's many cheap restaurants and friendly bars and cafés. The winter months of December, January and February can get very chilly, particularly at night with temperatures dropping to only a few degrees above zero (celsius).

Tourist information The **tourist office** ⓘ *Hidalgo s/n, at the government offices, next to Casa de la Cultura (Centro Cultural El Carmen), T967-678 6570, Mon-Sat 0800-2100, Sun 0900-1400,* is very helpful with all types of information and it provides good maps; usually someone there speaks English. The **Municipal Office** ⓘ *on the main plaza, in the Palacio Municipal, T967-678 0665, daily, 0800-2000, English spoken,* has a good free map of the area.

Sights

The main square, **Plaza 31 de Marzo**, has a gazebo built during the era of Porfirio Díaz. In front of the plaza is the neoclassical **Palacio Municipal**, built in 1885. A few steps away is the **Catedral de San Cristóbal**, built in the 16th century, painted in ochre, brown and white, with a baroque pulpit added in the 17th century. Adjacent to the cathedral is the church of **San Nicolás**, which houses the historical archives of the diocese. The building dates from 1613, and is believed to be the only church in Mexico to preserve its original design in the architectural style of indigenous people's churches. Note that most churches here close at lunchtime, 1400-1600.

Just off the plaza, at the beginning of Insurgentes, is the former **Casa de la Sirena**, now the **Hotel Santa Clara**. Built at the end of the 16th century, this is a rare example of colonial residential architecture in the plateresque style. The interior has the four classic corridors of renaissance constructions. Heading off the plaza in the opposite direction, going north up 20 de Noviembre, you reach the **Church and Ex-Convent of Santo Domingo**. By far the most dramatic building in the city, it features an elaborate baroque facade in moulded mortar, especially beautiful when viewed in the late afternoon sun, which picks out the ornate mouldings with salmon-pink hues. The church's altarpieces are covered in gold leaf, and the pulpit is intricately carved in a style known as *churrigueresque*, even more elaborate than the baroque style of Europe. Outside the market is the main handicraft market, with dozens of stalls selling traditional textiles, handmade dolls, wooden toys and jewellery. To the west of the centre, and up a strenuous flight of steps, is the **Templo del Cerrito**, a small church with fine views of the city and the surrounding mountains. The church is called *cerrito* (small hill) because it is set on an isolated, tree-covered hill. It's not recommended for women to undertake this walk on their own, as assaults have been reported. At the other end of the city, to the east, is another little church on a hill, the **Templo de Guadalupe**. This church is used by the people of the Barrio de Guadalupe, the nearest to the centre of the 21 such indigenous neighbourhoods. Each neighbourhood is characterized by the dress of the local people, depending on which indigenous group they belong to, and by the handicrafts produced by them. Guadalupe is the *barrio* of candle makers, saddle makers, and wooden toy makers. The other *barrios*, such as Mexicanos, the oldest in the city, are further afield and not recommended for unguided visits. Although the city is generally safe, walking around alone in remoter areas isn't always recommended. The tension between Zapatistas and army has been increasing in Chiapas and assaults and robberies have also occurred. Follow local advice.

Hardship for the Chiapanecos

For the visitor to Chiapas, the state's wonders are many: lush tropical jungle, quaint colonial towns, remote Mayan villages or the modern, prosperous capital, Tuxtla Gutiérrez. However, the tranquil setting masks the troubles of the state's indigenous peoples. Their plight was splashed across the world's press with the Zapatista uprising of January 1994 and has remained a much photographed story ever since (see box, page 774).

Chiapas, the southernmost state and one of Mexico's poorest, in appearance much like its neighbour, Guatemala, shares many of the same problems. Subsistence has been a way of life for centuries, illiteracy and infant mortality are high, particularly among those who have retained their languages and traditions, shunning the Spanish culture. The Chiapas government estimates that nearly one million indigenous people live in the state, descendants of the great Maya civilization of AD 250-900. The indigenous Chiapanecos of today are spread out across the state, not speaking the same language, dressing alike, having the same customs or the same types of tribal government.

The Tzotziles and Tzeltales total about 626,000 and live mainly on the plateau and the slopes of the high altitude zones. The Choles number 119,000 and live in the towns of Tila, Tumbalá, Salto de Agua, Sabanilla and Yajalón. The 87,000 Zoques live near the volatile Chichonal volcano.

The 66,000 Tojolabales live in Margaritas, Comitán, La Independencia, La Trinitaria and part of Altamirano. On the high mountains and slopes of the Sierra Madre are the 23,000 Mames and the 11,500 Mochós and Kakchikeles. The Lacandones, named after the rainforest they occupy, number only 600 today. Along the border with Guatemala are 17,500 Chujes, Kanjobales and Jacaltecos, although that number includes some refugees still there from the Guatemalan conflict, which ended in 1996.

A minority of the indigenous population speaks Spanish, particularly in the Sierra Madre region and among the Zoques. Many have dropped their traditional clothing. Customary positions of authority along with stewardships and standard bearers have been dropped from tribal governance, but medicine men continue to practise. They still celebrate their festivals and they think about their ancestors as they have for centuries. Many now live in the large cities, but those who remain in rural areas are, for the most part, poor, subsisting on a diet of tortillas, vegetables, beans and occasional meat. Many who leave for the city end up as domestic servants, labourers or street pedlars. The scarcity of land for indigenous people has been a political issue for many decades and limited land reform merely postponed the crisis that eventually erupted in the 1990s and continues to cause the government difficulties.

Na Bolom Museum and Cultural Centre ① *Vicente Guerrero 33, T967-678 1418, www.nabolom.org, daily 1000-1900, guided tours daily, 1630 in English and Spanish, US\$3.50, US\$2.50 unguided visit; library Mon-Fri 0900-1600*, is situated in a neoclassical mansion dating from 1891. Na Bolom was founded in 1951 by the Danish archaeologist Frans Blom and his wife, the Swiss photographer Gertrudis Duby. After the death of Frans Blom in 1963, Na Bolom became a study centre for the universities of Harvard and Stanford, while Gertrudis Duby continued campaigning for the conservation of the Lacandón area (see page 659). She died in 1993, aged 92, after which the centre has continued to function as a non-profit organization dedicated to conserving the Chiapanecan environment and helping the Lacandón people. The photographic archives in the museum are fascinating and contain a detailed visual history of 50 years of daily life of the Maya people with beautifully displayed artefacts, pictures of Lacondones, and information about their present way of life. There are five galleries with collections of pre-Columbian Maya art and colonial religious paintings. There is also a good library. A shop sells products made by the indigenous people helped by the centre.

Na Bolom runs various projects, staffed by volunteers. Prospective volunteers spend a minimum of three months, maximum six, at the centre. They must have skills that can be useful to the projects, such as anthropology, organic gardening, or be multilingual. Volunteers are given help with accommodation and a daily food allowance. Na Bolom also has 17 rooms to rent (see Sleeping, page 644). They run tours (daily departures at 1000) to San Juan Chamula and San Lorenzo Zinacantán; US$15 per person, good guides, thorough explanations, respectful to indigenous locals.

The **Museo de Los Altos** ① *Calzada Lázaro Cárdenas, next to Santo Domingo church, Tue-Sun 1000-1700, US$3, free on Sun and bank holidays*, is an anthropological museum that contains a history of San Cristóbal, with an emphasis on the plight of the indigenous people, as well as a good selection of locally produced textiles.

The **Templo del Carmen** ① *Crescencio Rosas y Alvaro Obregón*, with a unique archery tower in the Moorish style, is the home of **El Carmen Cultural Centre** ① *Mon-Fri 0830-1500, 1600-1900, free*.

The **Centro de Desarrollo de la Medicina Maya** ① *Salomón González Blanco, Mon-Fri 0900-1800, Sat and Sun 1000-1600, US$1.50*, has a herb garden with detailed displays on the use of medicinal plants by the Maya for various purposes, including childbirth.

Villages near San Cristóbal

For reasons of cultural sensitivity, it is recommended that you visit Mayan villages as part of a tour. A good guide will explain the workings of a Mayan community and introduce you to villagers personally, thus making your visit welcome and enlightening. If you go independently, be prepared for culture shock and some suspicious treatment – you are an outsider after all. Travellers are strongly warned not to wander around in the hills surrounding San Cristóbal, as they could risk assault. Warnings can be seen in some places frequented by tourists. Remember that locals are particularly sensitive to proper dress (that is, no shorts or revealing clothes) and manners; persistent begging should be countered with courteous, firm replies.

You are recommended to call at Na Bolom (see above) before visiting the villages, to get information on their cultures and seek advice on the reception you are likely to get. Photography is resisted by some of the indigenous people because they believe the camera steals their souls and photographing their church is stealing the soul of God; it is also seen as invasive and sometimes profiteering. Either leave your camera behind or ask your guide to let you know when you can and cannot take pictures. Cameras have been taken by villagers when photography has been inappropriate and the locals can sometimes be vocal about inappropriate behaviour, even going as far as spitting corn kernels at offenders. Much of the population does not speak Spanish. You can visit the villages of San Juan Chamula, Zinacantán and Tenejapa. While these are popular excursions, especially when led by a guide, several visitors have felt ashamed at going to look at the villagers as if they were in a zoo; there were many children begging and offering to look after private vehicles.

Zinacantán

Zinacantán men wear pink/red jackets with embroidery and tassels, and the women wear vivid pale-blue shawls and navy skirts. Every day, at midday, the women prepare a communal meal, which the men eat in shifts. The main gathering place is around the **church** ① *US$1.40 for entering, official ticket from tourist office next door; photography inside is strictly prohibited*; the roof was destroyed by fire.

Above the municipal building on the right, creative, resourceful Antonia has opened **Antonia's House** and a craft shop, **Artesanías Tonik** ① *Calle Niño Perdido No 10*. Antonia and her family will demonstrate back-strap weaving, the making of tortillas and many other aspects of life in the village. They usually provide a simple, but very tasty meal, cooked on a hotplate over an open fire and there's the chance to sample the local tipple, *posh*. This is strong stuff, made from sugarcane and flavours include cinnamon and hibiscus flower. You are allowed to take photos of the weaving process – not always encouraged in these villages. Antonia is very easygoing and she may not charge for the meal or a sample of *posh*, but do bear in mind that she makes her living from the shop and opening her home to strangers, so buy something or leave a contribution. Only Spanish and Tzotzil spoken. Tours from San Cristóbal can be organized through Roberto Molina (see Activities and tours, page 650).

San Juan Chamula → *Colour map 3, B1.*

Signs in Chamula warn that it is dangerous to walk in the area on your own; robberies have occurred between Chamula and both San Cristóbal and Zinacantán. It's generally best to seek full advice on any travel outside San Cristóbal de las Casas.

In this Tzotzil village 10 km northwest of San Cristóbal the men wear grey, black or light pink tunics, while the women wear bright blouses with colourful braids and navy or bright blue shawls. One popular excursion is to visit the brightly painted **church** ① *a permit (US$1.50) is needed from the village tourist office and photographing inside the church is strictly forbidden*. There are no pews but family groups sit or kneel on the floor, chanting, with rows of candles lit in front of them, each representing a member of the family and certain significance is attached to the colours of the candles. The religion is centred on the 'talking

Around San Cristóbal de las Casas

stones' and three idols as well as certain Christian saints. Pagan rituals are held in small huts at the end of August. The pre-Lent festival ends with celebrants running through blazing harvest chaff. This happens just after Easter prayers are held, before the sowing season starts. Festivals in Chamula should *not* be photographed; if you wish to take other shots ask permission; people are not unpleasant, even if they refuse (although children may pester you to take their picture for a small fee). For reasons of cultural understanding and safety it is recommended that you visit Chamula on a tour.

There are many handicraft stalls on the way up the small hill southwest of the village. This has a good viewpoint of the village and valley. Take the road from the southwest corner of the square, turn left towards the ruined church then up a flight of steps on the left.

It is an interesting walk from San Cristóbal to Chamula along the main road to a point 1 km past the crossroads with the Periférico ring road (about 2½ km from town centre); turn right onto an old dirt road, it's not signposted but it is the first fork you come to between some farmhouses. Then head back via the road through the village of Milpoleta, some 8 km downhill; allow five hours for the round trip (one hour for Chamula). Best not done in hot weather. Also, you can hike from Chamula to Zinacantán in 1½ hours: when leaving Chamula, take the track straight ahead instead of turning left onto the San Cristóbal road; turn left on a small hill where the school is (after 30 minutes) and follow a smaller trail through light forest. After about an hour you reach the main road 200 m before Zinacantán (but see warning, above, about walking on your own – this is best attempted in a group or with a local guide).

Tenejapa → *Phone code: 967.*

Few tourists visit Tenejapa. The village is very friendly and many men wear local costume. Ask permission to take pictures and expect to pay. The Thursday market is traditionally for fruit and vegetables, but there are a growing number of other stalls. The market thins out by noon. Excellent woven items can be purchased from the weavers' cooperative near the church. They also have a fine collection of old textiles in their regional ethnographic **museum** adjoining the handicraft shop. The **cooperative** can also arrange weaving classes. The village is best visited with a guide who can advice on local customs and taking photographs.

Other excursions from San Cristóbal

Two other excursions can be made, by car or local bus, from San Cristóbal. The first goes south on the Pan-American Highway (30 minutes by car) to **Amatenango del Valle**, a Tzeltal village where the women make and fire pottery in their yards, and then southeast (15 minutes by car) to **Aguacatenango**, a picturesque village at the foot of a mountain. Continue one hour along this road past **Villa Las Rosas** (hotel) to **Venustiano Carranza**, where the women wear fine costumes, and there is an extremely good view of the entire valley. There is a good road from Las Rosas to Comitán as an alternative to the Pan-American highway. There are frequent buses.

Las Grutas de San Cristóbal ① *daily 0900-1700, US$0.70, plus US$0.70 if arriving by car*, are caves 10 km southeast of the town, containing huge stalagmites. They are 2445 m deep, but only lit for 750 m. Refreshments are available. Horses can be hired at Las Grutas for US$15 for a five-hour ride (guide extra) on lovely trails in the surrounding forest. Some of these are best followed on foot. Yellow diamonds on trees and stones mark the way to beautiful meadows. Stay on the trail to minimize erosion. The land next to the caves is taken up by an army football pitch, but once past this, it is possible to walk most of the way back to San Cristóbal through woods and fields. Las Grutas are reached by

Autotransportes de Pasaje '31 de Marzo' *colectivos* every 15 minutes (0600-1900, US$1) from Avenida Benito Juárez 37B, across the Pan-American Highway just south of the Cristóbal Colón bus terminal (or take a *camioneta* from the Pan-American opposite San Diego church 500 m east of Avenida Cristóbal Colón). *Colectivos* are marked 'San Cristóbal, Teopisca, Ciudad Militar, Villa Las Rosas', or ask for a minibus to 'Rancho Nuevo'. To the bus stop take 'San Diego' *colectivo* 1 block east of Zócalo to the end of Benito Juárez. When you get to Las Grutas, ask the driver to drop you at Km 94; the caves are poorly signed and 10-15 minutes' walk away from the *colectivo* drop-off point.

◉ San Cristóbal de las Casas and around listings

For Sleeping and Eating price codes and other relevant information, see Essentials pages 47-51.

🛏 Sleeping

San Cristóbal de las Casas
p637, map p638
Look on the bulletin board outside the tourist office for guesthouses advertising cheap bed and breakfast.
A Casa Mexicana, 28 de Agosto 1, T967-678 0698, www.hotelcasamexicana.com. This hotel is filled with art work and Mexican crafts. Services include sauna, Wi-Fi, parking and babysitters. The master suite has a jacuzzi, and the attractive courtyard is lush and filled with plants. There is a newer wing on the opposite side of the road with a good craft shop attached. Restaurant Los Magueys and Bar Cucaracha attached to old wing, open 0700-2200. Highly recommended.
A Casa Vieja, María A Flores 27, T967-678 6868, www.casavieja.com.mx. Elegant and relaxing converted colonial house, with TV, good restaurant, hot water, radiators in rooms if cold weather, Wi-Fi, parking and laundry service.
A Posada Diego de Mazariegos, 5 de Febrero 1, 1 block north of plaza, T967-678 0833, www.diegodemazariegos.com.mx. Comfortable and quiet, almost convent-like atmosphere. Comfy common room. Travel agency and restaurant inside and Tequila Zoo bar. Buffet on Sun at 1400. Recommended.
B Na Bolom, Vicente Guerrero 33, T967-678 1418, www.nabolom.org. Beautiful, 17-room guesthouse in a cultural centre (see

page 640). Rooms have bath and fireplace. Insightful tours available. Traditional Mexican meal every night at 1900 in the courtyard restaurant. Recommended.
B Posada El Paraíso, Av 5 de Febrero 19, T967-678 0085, www.hotelposada paraiso.com. Mexican-Swiss owned. Impeccable, light and airy rooms, many open onto pretty patio. Excellent, atmospheric restaurant, parking nearby beneath cathedral. Very friendly and highly recommended.
B Rincón del Arco, Ejército Nacional 66, 8 blocks from centre, T967-678 1313. Simply gorgeous, friendly hotel with 58 rooms and 2 junior suites, some with fireplaces. There's a pleasant garden, bar and nice restaurant. Recommended.
B Santa Clara, Insurgentes 1, on plaza, T967-678 1140, www.travelbymexico.com/chis/santaclara. Colonial-style hotel with clean rooms; some are noisy. Breakfast included. Good restaurant, Wi-Fi, travel agency, pool and pool bar. Recommended.
C El Cerrillo, Belisario Domínguez 27, T967-678 1283, www.hotelesjardines.com. Nice carpeted rooms and a lovely rooftop patio. Wi-Fi and cable TV. Recommended.
C Palacio de Moctezuma, Juárez 16, T967-678 0352, www.travelbymexico.com/chis/moctezuma. Colonial-style hotel founded in 1727. Rooms have hot water and cable TV, good Mexican food is served in the restaurant. Rooms downstairs sometimes damp, 1st floor is much better. Longer stay discounts and parking. Highly recommended.
C Posada Jovel, Flavio Paniagua 27, T967-678 1734, www.mundochiapas.com/

hotelposadajovel. Villa-style hotel with clean, comfortable rooms. Beautiful garden with fruit trees, and the roof terrace has fine views. There's a restaurant, and rooms over the road get a discount. Hotel is being expanded. Recommended.

C Posada Los Morales, Ignacio Allende 17, T967-678 1472, www.hotelhaciendalos morales.com. This brightly painted, elegant hotel can be spotted from afar, scaling Cerrito San Cristóbal. It has beautiful views over the city. The cottages here have open fires, kitchen and hot showers. The owner is a collector and exporter of rustic-style Mexican furniture and the interior richly reflects this. Substantial low-season discounts. Recommended.

C Posada Margarita, Real de Guadalupe 34, T967-678 0957, www.laposadamargarita.com. This popular, professionally managed hotel is spotless. Comfortable rooms have safes, cable TV and 24-hour hot water. There's a terrace, travel agency, free internet and an expensive restaurant serving wholefood.

C Real del Valle, Av Real de Guadalupe 14, next to plaza, T967-678 0680, hrvalle@mundo maya.com.mx. Very clean and friendly. Avoid noisy room next to the kitchen. Rooms have hot water and Wi-Fi. Well maintained and good value.

D Barón de Las Casas, Belisario Domínguez 2, T967-678 0881, www.chiapas.turista.com.mx. Clean, comfortable, good value. Recommended.

D Fray Bartolomé de las Casas, Insurgentes and Niños Héroes, T967-678 0932. Clean, comfortable quarters, set around an attractive courtyard. The better rooms have cable TV and 24-hr hot water (**B**), otherwise it runs only at set times.

D Posada Media Luna, Hermano Domínguez 5, T967-631 5590, www.hotel-lamedia luna.com. Italian run. Cheery, brightly coloured hotel with hot water, free Wi-Fi, free water, cable TV and an Italian fish restaurant, **Creuza de ma**. Also organizes tours to nearby sights and villages. Recommended.

D Suites Encanto, 1 de Marzo 42, T967-672 2679, suitesencanto5@gmail.com. This new hotel has comfortable suites with fireplaces, cookers, fridges and sofas. There are cheap dorm beds too (**F**), and the manager can organize other accommodation if full. Excellent value. Highly recommended.

E Capri, Insurgentes 54, T967-678 3018, hotelcapri81@hotelmail.com, near 1st-class bus terminal. Large, reliable hotel with plenty of rooms and differing tariffs. Quieter rooms at the back. Clean and helpful. Chinese restaurant next door, if you're fed up with Mexican grub. Recommended.

E Posada Lucella, Av Insurgentes 55, T967-678 0956, opposite Iglesia Santa Lucía (the bells can be noisy). Clean, economical rooms set around a patio, with bath, fan and hot water. Cheaper with shared bath.

E Posada San Agustín, Ejército Nacional 7, T967-678 1816. Large, clean, comfortable rooms, some with shared bath. Family run and friendly. Recommended.

E Posada Vallarta, Hermanos Pineda 10, near 1st-class bus terminal, T967-678 0465. Quiet, clean and tidy. Hot water and parking.

E-G Casa Babylon, on Josefa Ortiz Domínguez and Ramón Corona, T967- 678 0590, www.casa babylon.wordpress.com. Funky youth hostel with bargain dorm beds and private rooms (cheaper without bath). Continental breakfast included. Communal kitchen, patio space, lockers, book exchange, free Wi-Fi and laundry. Hot showers and free drinking water.

E-G Los Camellos, Real de Guadalupe 110, T967-116 0097, loscamellos@hotmail.com. Popular backpackers' hostel with dorms and private rooms. There are 24-hr hot showers, free coffee and drinking water, book exchange, shisha café and hammocks. French-Mexican run, friendly and hospitable staff.

F Casa de Huéspedes Chamula, Julio M Corzo 18, T967-678 0321. Clean, hot showers, washing facilities, friendly, parking, noisy, with shared bath, some rooms without windows.

F Casa de Huéspedes Santa Lucía, Clemente Robles 21, 1 block from the Transportes Lacondia bus terminal, T967-678 0315. Basic rooms, some with bath, some without. Hot water 24 hrs.

F Posadita, Flavio Paniagua 30. With bath, clean, laundry facilities. Recommended.

F-G Posada 5, Comitán 13, T967-674 7660, www.posada5.com. Dorms and private rooms, with or without shared bath, attractive garden, tours organized, book exchange, free internet, free coffee and tea, communal kitchen, friendly and laidback.

F-G Posada Doña Rosita, Ejército Nacional 13, T967-678 8676, posadadn_rosita@hotmail.com. Three blocks from main plaza, this economical posada is more like a friendly and caring family home, presided over by Doña Rosita, an experienced healer who knows about herbs and local affairs. She heals sick guests, offers healthy organic breakfasts, and runs courses in cooking and natural medicine. Her dorms and rooms are basic, but there's hot water 24 hrs. Highly recommended.

Camping

Rancho San Nicolás, T967-678 0057, at end of Francisco León, 1½ km east of centre. Trailer park in a beautiful, quiet location, take warm blankets or clothing as the temperature drops greatly at night, hot showers, US$7 for room in *cabaña*, US$5 to camp, US$12 for camper van with 2 people (electricity hook-up), children free, laundry facilities. Recommended.

Trailer park Bonampak, Route 190 at west end of town, T967-678 1621. There are 22 spaces with full hook-up, hot shower, heated pool in season, restaurant, US$14 per vehicle for 2 people. Also has hotel rooms.

⑥ Eating

San Cristóbal de las Casas
p637, map p638

There are several cheap, local places on Madero east of Plaza 31 de Marzo.

¶¶¶ Agapandos, Calzada Roberta 16, inside Parador San Juan de Dios. Elegant, secluded and quiet, overlooking a fragrant garden at the foot of the mountains. Sumptuous crêpes, eggs, chicken and meat dishes with a local flavour and Mediterranean twist.

¶¶¶-¶¶ La Fonda Argentina, Adelina Flores 12. Good selection of steaks, fillets and other carnivorous, Argentine cuisine.

¶¶ El Fogón de Jovel, Av 16 Septiembre 11, opposite the Jade Museum. One of the best restaurants in town and a great place to experiment and try out a variety of local dishes. Try the local liquor, *posh*. Colourful vibe with 2 themed rooms. Live music at night.

¶¶ La Casa del Pan, part of El Puente Cultural Centre, Real de Guadalupe 55. Restaurant with good food and great atmosphere. There's a lunchtime buffet.

¶¶ La Paloma, Hidalgo 3, a few doors from Zócalo. Inventive regional dishes at reasonable prices; international cuisine. Classy place, popular with tourists, best coffee, good breakfast, good pasta, art gallery next door, live music at weekends.

¶¶ Madre Tierra, Insurgentes 19 (opposite Franciscan church), T967-678 4297. Anglo-Mexican owned, European dishes, vegetarian specialities, good breakfasts, wholemeal breads from bakery (also takeaway), pies, brownies, chocolate cheesecake, Cuban and reggae music in the evenings, popular with travellers.

¶¶-¶ María Cortones, Plaza 31 de Marzo, T967-631 6002. Old-time favourite, with tables overlooking the plaza. They do breakfasts, *comida típica*, coffee and sandwiches.

¶¶ Tierra y Cielo, Juárez 1, www.tierraycielo.com.mx. International food, with a menu that changes every Sun. Modern and clean. Good breakfast buffets Thu, Sat and Sun.

¶¶ Tuluc, Insurgentes 5. Good value especially breakfasts, fresh *tamales* every morning, near plaza, popular, classical music, art for sale and toys on display.

¶¶-¶ Cocodrilo Café & Bar, Plaza 31 de Marzo. Smart café/bar on the south side of the plaza serving snacks, cocktails and cappuccinos. They host live music, salsa and merengue.

¶¶-¶ Emiliano's Moustache, Av Crescencio Rosas 7. *Taquería*, popular with Mexicans, tacos from US$0.40. Excellent value lunch menu. Recommended.

¶¶-¶ **Joveleño**, Real de Guadalupe 66, T674-6278. Pretty setting, fountain inside restaurant. Good-value Mexican dishes.

¶¶-¶ **La Margarita**, inside Posada Margarita (see above), Real de Guadalupe 34. Open from 0700. Live music in the evenings, flamenco, rumba and salsa, good tacos.

¶¶-¶ **París-México**, Madero 20. Smart, French cuisine, vegetarian dishes, excellent breakfasts, reasonably priced *comida corrida*, classical music. Tequilas for US$1 in the evenings. Highly recommended.

¶ **Adelita**, Maria Adelina Flores 49. Great selection of tacos in a traditional, *charro*-themed restaurant. 2-for-1 tacos on Tue and tacos from US$0.30 any day of the week.

¶ **Craft market**, Insurgentes. The stalls here are the cheapest places for lunch in San Cristóbal. They do set meals for US$1.20, usually beef or chicken. Numerous stalls nearby sell punch, often made with *posh*.

¶ **El Gato Gordo**, Real de Guadalupe 20, T962-678 8313. Funky place, popular with backpackers. Cheap set breakfast, crêpes, *tortas*, vegetarian.

¶ **El Mirador II**, Madero. Good local and international food, excellent *comida corrida* US$3 and pizzas US$2.50. Recommended.

¶ **Juguería Ana Banana**, Av Miguel Hidalgo 9B. Good typical Mexican food and fresh juices.

¶ **Tierradentro**, Real de Guadalupe 24. Small cultural centre serving economical breakfasts, lunch menus, baguettes, snacks and coffee.

Cafés, juice stalls and bakeries

Café Centro, Real de Guadalupe. Popular for breakfast, good *comida corrida*.

Café Museo Café, María Adelina Flores 10. Big, breezy café selling fine coffee by the bag or cup. There's an interesting museum inside charting the history of coffee in Chiapas – both café and museum are open daily.

Café San Cristóbal, Cuauhtémoc 2. Good coffee sold in bulk too, chess hangout.

Empanadas Loli, Cuauhtémoc, next door to Café San Cristóbal. Sweet and savoury, homemade empanadas.

La Casa del Pan, Dr Navarro 10 with B Domínguez. Excellent wholemeal bread, breakfasts, live music, closed Mon. Has another branch at El Puente (see above) and in Real de Guadalupe 55. Highly recommended but not cheap.

La Selva Café, Crescencio Rosas and Cuauhtémoc. Thirty types of really delicious organic coffees, owned by growers' collective, art gallery, lively in evenings. Good healthy breakfast and cakes. Recommended.

Lacteos Maya, Av J M Santiago. Excellent locally made yogurt.

Namandí, Diego de Mazariegos 16. Crêpes, baguettes, juices, coffee and cake. They have Mexican staples too, if you fancy something more substantial. Several branches in town including one in Insurgentes opposite El Templo del Carmen.

Naturalísimo, 20 de Noviembre 4. Healthy, low-fat vegetarian food, fresh (delicious) yoghurt, fruit sherbet and juices, wholewheat bread and home-baked goodies, pleasant courtyard inside. Recommended.

🔾 Bars and clubs

San Cristóbal de las Casas *p637, map p638*
Bar Makia, Hidalgo, just off plaza, above a shop. Fri and Sat from 2200 until very late.

Barfly, Crecencio Rosas 4. DJs play reggae, house and funk. Free drink on entry. Open 2000-2400.

Blue Bar, Av Crescencio Rosas 2. Live music after 2300, salsa, rock, reggae, pool table, good atmosphere.

Cocodrilo, Insurgentes 1, T967-678 0871. Cappuccinos, cocktails, beer and live music every night: reggae, *trova*, flamenco and rumba.

El Zirko, 20 de Noviembre 7. Couple of blocks north of the Zócalo. Live music.

Emiliano's Moustache, see page 646. Bar open until 0100.

Revolución, 20 de Noviembre and 1 de Marzo. Café, bar with internet upstairs, happy hour 1200-1900, 2x1 cocktails, live soul, blues and rock music at 2000, good atmosphere.

⏯ Entertainment

San Cristóbal de las Casas *p637, map p638*
Cinema and theatre
Centro Bilingüe at the Centro Cultural El Puente (see Cultural centres, page 648), Real de Guadalupe 55. Films Mon-Sat 1800, US$2, with later showings Fri and Sat, 2000. Film schedules are posted around town.
La Ventana, Real de Guadalupe 46. Cinema club showing a good range of films.
Teatro Municipal Daniel Zebadúa, 20 de Noviembre and 1 de Marzo. Film festivals each month, films at 1800 and 2100 US$2 (US$1.50 students).

Cultural centres
Casa de Cultura El Carmen, opposite El Carmen church on junction of Hermanos Domínguez and Hidalgo. Range of activities on offer: concerts, films, lectures, art exhibitions and conferences. They also do marimba music and danzón in the plaza outside the centre some evenings.
Casa/Museo de Sergio Castro, Guadalupe Victoria 47 (6 blocks from plaza), T967-678 4289. Open 1800-2000 (but best to make appointment), entry free but donations welcome. Excellent collection of indigenous garments, talks (in English, French or Spanish) and slide shows about customs and problems of the indigenous population.
El Puente, Real de Guadalupe 55, 1 block from the plaza, T/F967-678 3723, www.elpuenteweb.com. Spanish lessons with a restaurant, internet centre and a small cinema. Check their notice board for forthcoming events. A good place to meet other travellers.
Na Bolom Museum and Cultural Centre, see page 640 and Sleeping.

⏯ Festivals and events

San Cristóbal de las Casas *p637, map p*
Mar/Apr There is a popular spring festival on Easter Sun and the week after.

Jan/Feb Carnival is held during the 4 days before Lent, dates vary.
Late Nov Festival Maya-Zoque, which lasts 4 days, promoting the 12 different Maya and Zoque cultures in the Chiapas region, with dancing and celebrations in the main plaza.
12 Dec La Fiesta de Guadalupe.

Zinacantán *p642*
6 Jan, 19-22 Jan and **8-10 Aug** Annual festival days; visitors are welcome.

⏹ Shopping

San Cristóbal de las Casas *p637, map p638*
Bookshops
La Pared, Av Miguel Hidalgo 2, T967-678 6367, lapared9@yahoo.com, opposite the government tourist office. Open daily, 1000-1400 and 1600-2000. Books in English and a few in other European languages, many travel books including **Footprint** handbooks, book exchange, American owner Dana Gay very helpful.
Pasaje Mazariegos, in the block bounded by Real de Guadalupe, Av B Domínguez, Madero and Plaza 31 de Marzo. Luxury clothes and bookshops, restaurants and travel agents.
Soluna, Real de Guadalupe 13B. A few English guidebooks and a wide range of Spanish titles and postcards.

Crafts
There are many shops on Av Real de Guadalupe for amber and jade plus other *artesanías*. The market north of Santo Domingo is worth seeing as well. There are souvenir markets on Utrilla between Real de Guadalupe and Comitán.
Amber Museum Diego de Mazariegos, next La Merced.
Casa de Artesanías, Niños Héroes and Hidalgo. Top-quality handicrafts. Shop is also a museum.
Ex-Convento de Santo Domingo has been partly converted into a cooperative, Sna

Jolobil, selling handicrafts from many local villages especially textiles (best quality and expensive); also concerts by local groups. Well worth a visit.

La Casa del Jade, Av 16 de Septiembre 16. The shop, which sells top quality jade, also has a museum with replicas of jade relics and the Tomb of Pakal (Maya King of Palenque), which is now more difficult to visit at Palenque.

Taller Leñateros, Flavio A Paniagua 54, T967-678 5174, www.tallerlenateros.com. A paper-making workshop run primarily by a Maya group. Their paper and prints are made from natural materials and their profits help support around 30 Maya families.

The **craft market** at Parque Fray Bartolomé de las Casas has stands offering an assortment of local sweets such as *cocada*, balls of sweet and caramelized shredded coconut, as well as small, perfectly shaped animal figurines made, strangely enough, of sweetened hardboiled egg yolks. Different, yet tasty.

▲ Activities and tours

San Cristóbal de las Casas
p637, map p638
There are at least 25 tour operators in San Cristóbal.

Horse riding
Horse riding tours are widely available in San Cristóbal, most going to Chamula and costing US$8-12 for 4-5 hrs. Hotels, tourist offices and travel agencies can easily organize them, or look for advertising flyers in touristy cafés and restaurants. Also **Señor Ismael**, T961-678 1511, rents out horses and organizes treks. Recommended.

Language schools
Centro Cultural El Puente, Real de Guadalupe 55, T967-678 3723, www.elpuenteweb.com. Spanish programme, rates around US$10 per hr, US$145/week, one-to-one lessons, homestay

programmes available from US$230 per week, registration fee US$30. Mixed reports.
Instituto Jovel, Francisco Madero 27, T967-678 4069, www.institutojovel.com. Group or 1-to-1 classes, homestays arranged, said to be the best school in San Cristóbal as their teachers undergo an obligatory 6-week training course; very good reports from students, all teachers bilingual to some extent.
Universidad Autónoma de Chiapas, Av Hidalgo 1, Dpto de Lenguas. Offers classes in English, French and Tzotzil.

Rafting
There are several rivers in the San Cristóbal area that offer great rafting opportunities.
Explora-Ecoturismo y Aventura, 1 de Marzo 30, T/F967-674 6660, www.ecochiapas.com. Eco-sensitive company with good recommendations offer rafting, caving, sea kayaking, river trips and multi-day camping expeditions on a variety of rivers.

Tour operators and guides
There are many agencies to choose from. As a rough guide to prices: to San Juan Chamula and Zinacantán, US$12; horse riding to San Juan Chamula, US$12. Sumidero Canyon, US$20 (including the boat trip); Montebello Lakes and Amatenango del Valle, US$18; Palenque ruins, Agua Azul and Misol-Há, US$22; Toniná ruins, US$26. There's also a 3-day jungle trip option taking in Agua Azul, Misol-Há, the ruins at Bonampak, Cedro River Falls, Yaxchilán and Palenque ruins. Camping in the jungle, US$250. Day trips to Bonampak and Yaxchilán are also possible, but they are much cheaper if booked in Palenque; take care to check what is included in packages.
Kjell Kühne, T967-105 3425, kjell@ hospitalityclub.org. Kjell is a truly multilingual guide, organizing tours in and around San Cristóbal in English, Spanish, French, German, Portuguese, Chinese, Indonesian and Lingala. Topics include the Zapatistas, indigenous spirituality, law and corruption, pre-Hispanic life and Maya traditions. Recommended.

Na Bolom Museum and Cultural Centre, see page 640.

Otisa Travel agency, Real de Guadalupe 3, T967-678 1933, otisa@otisatravel.com. Daily tours to Sumidero Canyon, San Juan Chamula and Zinacantán, Lagunas de Montebello, Yaxchilán and Bonampak, among other places.

Pronatura, Pedro Moreno 1. Organizes guided bird walks with Javier Gomez, 2½ hrs starting at 0700, from US$7, and plant walks, leaving at any time of day depending on demand. These last 1½ hrs, from US$5. Recommended.

Raúl and Alejandro, T967-678 3741, alexyraultours@yahoo.com.mx or manherg@hotmail.com. Tours to San Juan Chamula, Zinacantán and other villages. They depart from in front of the cathedral at 0930 and return at 1400, in blue VW minibuses, US$15, in English, Spanish and Italian. Friendly, very good and highly recommended.

Roberto Molina, T967-672 2679. Roberto has good knowledge of medicinal plants and the ancient art of pulse-reading. He offers a spiritual interpretation of the land around San Cristóbal and can organize tours to the outlying villages, horse riding or hiking trips in the surrounding mountain areas. He also organizes visits to Antonia's House/Artesanías Tonik in Zincantán (US$15), see page 642. Find him at **Posada Doña Rosita** (see page 646). Alternatively for **Antonia's House**, contact Antonia direct, T967-100 5011 (mobile) or T967-100 9687.

Travesia Maya, 20 de Noviembre 3, T967-674 0824 or free phone T01800-397 6622, www.travesiamaya.com.mx. This friendly agency offers informative, economical tours to attractions in Chiapas, as well as private planes and direct microbuses to Guatemala.

🚌 Transport

San Cristóbal de las Casas
p637, map p638
Air
Tuxtla Gutiérrez is the nearest airport.

Bicycle hire
Los Pingüinos, Av Ecuador 4B, T967-678 0202, www.bikemexico.com/pinguinos. Open 0915-1430, 1600-1900, rents mountain bikes for US$10 for 4 hrs or US$14 per day. Guided biking tours half or full days, as well as longer guided tours, English, German spoken, beautiful countryside and knowledgeable guides, highly recommended.

Bus
Crowded microbuses to **San Juan Chamula** (every 20 mins until 1700, last one back 1900, US$1, or taxi US$4), **Zinacantán** (30 mins, sometimes with frequent stops while the conductor lights rockets at roadside shrines, US$0.75, or get a group to share a *colectivo*, US$8.50), **San Andrés Larráinzar**, **Tenejapa** and other villages depart from around the market, north of the centre on Utrilla. Don't get stranded, as there isn't any tourist infrastructure.

There is a **Ticketbus** office in the pedestrianized part of Real de Guadalupe in the centre of San Cristóbal that stays open until 2200, daily. Very convenient for booking tickets without venturing as far as the OCC terminal.

Long distance The 1st-class OCC and ADO bus terminal is at the junction of Insurgentes and Blv Sabines Gutiérrez, several blocks south of the centre. Other 2nd-class lines and shuttle operators, including **AEXA** and **Rodolfo Figueroa**, also have nearby terminals on Gutiérrez, which soon becomes the Pan-American highway. There's also a variety of smaller bus companies and shuttles services that leave from the main road near the OCC bus station, with departures as far afield as Tijuana and other parts of northern Mexico, as well as Ocosingo, Palenque and nearby villages.

From the 1st-class terminal to **Campeche**, OCC, 1820, 10 hrs, US$25. To **Cancún**, OCC, 1215, 1430, 17 hrs, US$46; and ADO GL, 1545, US$58. To **Chetumal**, 1st class (OCC and ADO), 1215, 1430, 1605, 12 hrs, US$33 ADO GL, 1545, US$40. To **Ciudad**

Cuauhtémoc, OCC, 0745, 1130, 1730, 3 hrs, US$6. To **Comitán**, OCC, frequent services, 1½ hrs, US$3. To **Mérida**, OCC, 1820, 13 hrs, US$36. To **Mexico City** OCC 1610, 1740, 1810, 2230, 13-14 hrs, US$60 and 1 ADO GL 1700, 13 hrs, US$72. To **Oaxaca**, OCC, 1805, 2245, 10 hrs, US$28; and ADO GL, 2000, US$33. To **Palenque**, 8 OCC and ADO GL daily, 5 hrs, US$9.50-11. AEXA buses to Palenque, 0630, 1150, US$6. To **Playa del Carmen**, OCC, 1215, 1430, US$47; and ADO GL, 1545, US$55.50. To **Pochutla**, OCC, 1915, 2200, 12 hrs, US$27. To **Puebla**, 4 OCC and 2 ADO GL daily, 11 hrs, US$53-64. To **Puerto Escondido**, OCC, 1915, 2200, 13 hrs, US$30. To **Tapachula**, 7 OCC daily, 8 hrs, US$16. To **Tuxtla Gutiérrez**, OCC, many daily, 1 hr, US$2. To **Tulum**, OCC, 1215, 1430, 1605, 14½ hrs, US$44; and ADO GL, 1545, 16 hrs, US$52. To **Veracruz**, OCC, 2045, 8½ hrs, US$40; and ADO GL, 2115, 9 hrs, US$47. To **Villahermosa**, OCC, 1120, 2300, 7 hrs, US$16. **Agua Azul**, 0630, 1150, US$4. **Tuxtla Gutiérrez**, combis every 10 mins from outside AEXA terminal from 0500, US$2.50. 1st-class OCC buses depart for **Ciudad Cuautémoc** and the border daily. Alternatively, there are frequent departures to **Comitán**, from where you can catch a pick-up or *colectivo*, hourly from 0700, around US$1. For details on crossing the border at **La Mesilla** see page 670.

Shuttles Shuttles to **Tuxtla** regularly depart from the terminals on Gutiérrez, near the 1st-class bus terminal, 1 hr, US$2.50. You'll find shuttles to **Ocosingo** in the same area. Several operators run direct shuttles to the Guatemalan border and beyond, including **Travesia Maya**. Destinations include **La Mesilla**, **Quetzaltenango**, **Antigua**, **Flores** and **Panajachel**, US$30-60. It's a convenient and comfortable option if you can afford it. There are also regular departures to **Guatemala** from the OCC terminal itself, all departing at 0745 daily; to **Huehuetenango**, US$14; to **Los Encuentros**, US$19; to **Cuatro Caminos**, US$17 and to **Guatemala City**, US$24.

Car hire

Optima, Diego de Mazariegos 39, T967-674 5409; and Hertz, Villas Mercedes, Paniagua 32, T967-678 1886.

Scooters

Croozy Scooters, Belisario Domínguez 7, www.prodigyweb.net.mx/croozyscooters. Open Tue-Sun 0900, closing times vary. Rents bikes and small scooters, a good way of moving around. Minimum payment US$14, minimum rental 2 hrs, US$25 per day. They provide maps and suggested routes. Deposit and ID required. Bikes US$2 per day. Friendly. Swiss-British run. Recommended.

Taxi

US$1.40 anywhere in town, *colectivo* US$0.70.

Ocosingo *p652*

Many buses and *colectivos* to **Palenque**, 2½ hrs, US$3.30 and **San Cristóbal de Las Casas**.

⊕ Directory

San Cristóbal de las Casas
p637, map p638

Banks Banamex, Insurgentes 5, changes cheques without commission, 0900-1300. Banca Serfín on the Zócalo, changes Euro, Amex, MasterCard, TCs. Bancomer, Plaza 31 de Marzo 10, charges commission, cash advance on Visa, American Express or Citicorp TCs, good rates and service. Casa de Cambio Lacantún, Real de Guadalupe 12, Mon-Fri 0900-1400, 1600-1900, Sat and Sun 0900-1300 (may close early), no commission, at least US$50 must be changed and much lower exchange than at the banks. Casa Margarita will change dollars and TCs. Banks usually open for exchange 0900-1600. HSBC, Diego de Mazariegos 6, good rates for cash and TCs (US$ only), fast, efficient, cash advance on MasterCard, open Sat afternoons. 24-hr ATM at Banorte, 5 de Febrero, adjacent to cathedral. Quetzales can be obtained for pesos or dollars in the *cambio* but better rates are paid at the border. **Immigration** On Ctra Panamericana and Diagonal Centenario, opposite Hotel Bonampak. From Zócalo take Diego de Mazariegos west, after crossing bridge take Diagonal on the left towards Highway, 30-min walk. **Internet** There are many internet cafés all over town with rates around US$0.80 per hr. Service is generally good. **Laundry** Superklin, Crescencio Rosas 48, T967-678 3275, US$1.30 per kg, for collection after 5 hrs. La Rapidita, Insurgentes 9, coin-operated machines for self-service or they will launder clothes for you 1-3 kg US$3.50. **Medical services** Doctors: Servicio Médico Bilingüe, Av

Juárez 60, T967-678 0793, Dr Renato Zarate Castañeda speaks English, is highly recommended and if necessary can be reached at home, T967-678 2998. **Hospitals and clinics: Red Cross**, Prolongación Ignacio Allende, T967-678 0772. Recommended. Pharmacies:widely available around town. **Post office** Allende and Mazariegos, Mon-Fri 0800-1600, Sat 0900-1200. **Telephone** Caseta Telefonicas can be found all over the city. There are also Ladatel phones on the plaza, but these are generally more expensive than casetas.

San Cristóbal to Palenque and other Maya sites

Not far from San Cristóbal lie the waterfalls of Agua Azul, Agua Clara and Misol-Há, (although Agua Clara is currently out of bounds due to a Zapatista-military dispute), all easily reached on a day trip. The town of Palenque does not have much to offer, but the jungle settings of its nearby Maya ruins, as well as Bonampak and Yaxchilán further afield, are a big draw, with the possibility of crossing into Guatemala by boat. ▶▶ *For listings, see pages 659-665.*

Ocosingo → *Phone code: 919. Colour map 3, B1.*
Palenque (see page 654) can be reached by paved road from San Cristóbal de las Casas, a beautiful ride via Ocosingo, which has a local airport, a colourful market and several hotels. It was one of the centres of fighting in the Ejército Zapatista de Liberación Nacional (EZLN – Zapatista Army of National Liberation) uprising in January 1994; see box, page 773.

Toniná → *Colour map 3, B1.*
ⓘ *Tue-Sun, 0800-1700. US$3. Drinks are available at the site; also toilets and parking.*
The Maya ruins at Toniná are 12 km from Ocosingo, with bus links to San Cristóbal de las Casas. A tour from San Cristóbal to Toniná costs US$15; it is possible to drive in an ordinary car or take a taxi (US$6). There are also *colectivos* (15 minutes, US$1) running from the market, or you can walk from Ocosingo
   Toniná is one of the last Classic Maya sites, with the palace high on a hill to your left. It is worth visiting the ruins, which were excavated by a French government team. The temples are in the Palenque style with internal sanctuaries in the back room, but influences from many different Maya styles of various periods have been found. The huge **pyramid complex**, seven stone platforms making a man-made hill, is 10 m higher than the Temple of the Sun at Teotihuacán and is the tallest pyramidal structure in the Maya world. Stelae are in very diverse forms, as are wall panels, and some are in styles and of subjects unknown at any other Maya site. Ask the guardian to show you the second unrestored ball court and the sculpture kept at his house. He will show you round the whole site; there is also a small **museum**.

Agua Azul

ⓘ *Entry US$1.50 (US$0.75 for the government checkpoint, and the same for the Zapatista one), US$4 for cars. Entry price is not always included in day trips from Palenque, which allow you to spend up to 3 hrs at Agua Azul. Violent robberies have been reported so don't go alone; groups of at least 4 people are best.*

The series of jungle waterfalls and rapids at Agua Azul run for 7 km and are breathtakingly beautiful. They are easily visited on a day trip from Palenque. All the travel agencies and many hotels offer a tour there for about US$8.50, including a visit to the waterfall at Misol-Há. Agua Azul's main swimming area has many restaurants and indigenous children selling fruit. Swimming is good, in clear blue water during good weather, in muddy brown water during bad (but still refreshing if very hot, which it usually is). Swimmers should stick to the roped areas where everyone else can see them; the various graves on the steep path up the hill alongside the rapids are testament to the dangers of swimming in those areas. One of the falls is called 'The Liquidizer', an area of white water in which bathing is extremely dangerous. On no account should you enter this stretch of water; many drownings have occurred. Even in the designated areas, the currents can be ferocious. Beware of hidden tree trunks in the water if it is murky. The path on the left of the rapids can be followed for 7 km, with superb views and secluded areas for picnics. There are also several *palapas* for hammocks, plenty of space for free camping and some rooms to rent.

Agua Clara and Misol-Há

Eight kilometres from Agua Azul along the river is **Agua Clara** ⓘ *entry US$1*, a nature reserve. At the time of writing this was reportedly closed due to a dispute between the Mexican army and the local Zapatistas. Check with tourist office in Palenque if it's reopened. At **Misol-Há** ⓘ *entry US$1*, there is a stunning waterfall usually visited first on day trips from Palenque. A narrow path winds around behind the falls, allowing you to stand behind the immense curtain of water. Swimming is possible in the large pool at the bottom of the tumbling cascade, but it is usually better to wait until you get to Agua Azul for a good swim. However, during the rainy season swimming is reported to be better at Misol-Há, so go by bus or check with your tour operator, as most allow only a brief half-hour stop at Misol-Há.

Palenque town → *Phone code: 916. Colour map 3, B2.*

A friendly and, at times, hot, humid and airless little town whose sole reason for being is to accommodate the large number of tourists heading for the famous archaeological site nearby. There is plenty of accommodation for every budget, with dozens of cheap *posadas* around the centre, and a new tourist *barrio*, **La Cañada**, with more expensive hotels, restaurants and bars. Souvenirs are available at lower prices than elsewhere on the Ruta Maya, making Palenque a convenient place to stop off en route to the southerly Chiapanecan towns of San Cristóbal and Tuxtla Gutiérrez. Travellers coming to Palenque from Mérida, Campeche and other cities in the Yucatán Peninsula will find it much hotter here any time of year, but particularly in June, July and August.

The **tourist office** ⓘ *Mon-Sat, 0900-2100, Sun 0900-1300*, is on Juárez, a block below the plaza and next to the craft market. They are not always helpful but provide a good free map of Palenque and the ruins. There is also a tourist information booth on the Parque Central, but opening times are erratic.

Five kilometres from Palenque town, but 3 km before the ruins, **El Panchan** ⓘ *www.palenquemx.com/elpanchan*, is host to a fascinating mix of philosophies, food and intellectual interests. Don Moisés, founder of El Panchan, first came to Palenque as an archaeologist and was one of the first guides to the ruins. He bought a plot of land, named it El Panchan – Maya for 'heaven on earth' – and started to raise a family. Now he has divided lots among his children who run various businesses. It is about 10°C cooler at El Panchan than in Palenque town due to the dense foliage cover. Although vastly different, all businesses at El Panchan have intertwined themselves into the natural jungle that surrounds them, creating an almost Robinson Crusoe setting – if you don't want to stay in town and like the idea of being based in the forest, get a bus or taxi here soon after arriving in Palenque town. ▸▸ *For listings, see pages 659-665.*

Palenque ●❷❶ ▸▸ *pp659-665. Colour map 3, B1.*

ⓘ *Daily 0800-1600 (last entry), everyone has to leave by 1645. US$3.50, entrance to national park US$1.50; guided tours possible. There are lots of souvenir stalls at the main entrance. Water at the site is expensive, so bring your own. The cheapest food are the tacos from the stalls. Colectivos back to the town leave from outside the main entrance, US$0.70, every 6-18 mins. The last bus reportedly leaves at 1800, but double check this as it's a long, hot walk of 8 km back to Palenque town if you miss it, or you would need to hitch a lift. From Palenque town, take a colectivo from the main road near the 1st-class bus station.*

Built at the height of the Classic period surrounded by jungle, Palenque is one of the most beautiful of all the Maya ruins in Mexico. From about the fourth century AD, Palenque grew from a small agricultural village to one of the most important cities in the pre-Hispanic world between AD 600 and 800. It was built for strategic purposes, with evidence of defensive apertures in some retaining walls. In the centre of the site is the Palace, a massive warren of buildings with an asymmetrical tower (probably used as an astronomical observatory and a watchtower) rising above them, and fine views to the north.

Since its discovery, choked by the encroaching jungle scaling its walls and creeping up the stairs to its temples, once climbed by rulers, priests and acolytes, the architecture of Palenque has elicited praise and admiration, while crying out for reconstruction. The corbelled vaults, the arrangement of its groupings of buildings, the impression of lightness created by walls broken by pillars and open spaces, make Palenque-style architecture unique. It was only later that archaeologists and art historians realised that the architecture of Palenque was created mainly to accommodate the extraordinary sculptures and texts that referred not only to historical individuals and the important events in their lives, but also to mythological beings who endorsed the claims of dynastic continuity or 'divine right' of the rulers of this great city. The structures most illustrative of this function are the Palace, a group of buildings arranged around four patios to which a tower was later added, the **Temple of the Inscriptions** that rises above the tomb of Lord Pacal, and the temples of the Group of the Cross, used by Chan Bahlum, Pacal's successor, who made claims, which in their audacity are awe-inspiring, in the inscriptions carved on the tablets, pillars and balustrades of these exceptional buildings.

Warning The ruins are surrounded by thick, mosquito-infested jungle so wear insect repellent and make sure you're up to date with your malaria tablets (May to November is the worst time for mosquitoes, but this is still a low-risk area). It is extremely hot and humid at the ruins, especially in the afternoon, so it is best to visit early. Unfortunately, as well as mosquitoes, there have also been reports of criminals hiding in the jungle. As ever, try and leave valuables at your hotel to minimize any loss.

The Palace

The Palace and **Temple XI** are located in the centre of the site. The Palace stands on an artificial platform over 100 m long and 9 m high. Chan Bahlum's younger brother, Kan Xul, was 57 when he became king. He devoted himself to enlarging the palace and apparently built the four-storey tower in honour of his dead father. The top of the tower is almost at the level of Pacal's mortuary temple, and on the winter solstice the sun, viewed from here, sets directly above his crypt. Large windows where Maya astronomers could observe and chart the movement of the planets, ancestors of the royal lineage of Palenque, pierce the walls of the tower. Kan-Xul reigned for 18 years before being captured and probably sacrificed by the rulers of Toniná. During his reign Palenque reached its greatest degree of expansion, although recent excavations at the site may prove differently.

Temple of the Inscriptions

The Temple of the Inscriptions, along with Temple XII and Temple XIII, lies to the south of the Palace group of buildings and is one of the rare Maya pyramids to have a burial chamber incorporated at the time of its construction. This building was erected to cover the crypt in which Lord Pacal, the founder of the first ruling dynasty of Palenque, was buried. Discovered in 1952 by Alberto Ruz-Lhuillier, the burial chamber measured at 7 m long, 7 m high and 3.75 m across, an incredible achievement considering the weight of the huge pyramid pressing down upon it. According to the inscriptions, Lord Pacal was

Palenque

➡ Palenque maps
1 Palenque, page 655
2 Palenque archaeological site, page 656

Sleeping
Avenida 1 A1
Chan Kah Centro 2 A3
Jade 7 A2
Kashlan 3 A2
La Posada Cañada 5 A1
La Selva 6 A2
Maya Tucán 21 A1
Maya Tulipanes 8 A1
Naj K'in 18 A2
Posada Aguila Real 15 A2
Posada Canek 11 A3
Posada Charito 12 B3
Posada Johanna 9 A2
Posada Kin 19 A3
Posada Nacha'n
Ka'an 20 A2
Posada San Juan 13 B2
Posada Shalom 14 A2
San Miguel 10 A2
Xibalba 16 A1

Yaxkin Hostel 4 A1
Yun-Kax 17 B2

Eating
Café de Yarra 2 A2
El Herradero 3 A2
El Tapanco Grill 4 A2
Lakan-Há 7 A3
La Mexicana 5 A2
La Oaxaceña 6 A2
La Selva 1 B1
Las Tinajas 8 A2
Mara's 9 A3
Maya 11 A3
Pizzería Palenque 10 A2

Buses
ADO/OCC, Cristóbal Colón
& Maya de Oro
Bus Terminal 1 A2
AEXA Terminal 4 B2
Auto Transportes
Rodolfo Figueroa y
Lacandonia 2 A2
Colectivo to Ruins 3 A2/B2

born in AD 603 and died in AD 684. Inside, Ruz-Lhuillier discovered his bones adorned with jade jewellery. Around the burial chamber were various figures carved in stucco, depicting the Bolontikú, the Nine Lords of the Night of Maya mythology. There was a narrow tube alongside the stairs, presumably to give Pacal spiritual access to the outside world. Pacal also left a record of his forebears in the inscriptions. These three great tablets contain one of the longest texts of any Maya monument. There are 620 glyph blocks; they tell of Pacal's ancestors, astronomical events and an astonishing projection into the distant future (AD 4772). One of the last inscriptions reveals that, 132 days after Pacal's death, his son, Chan Bahlum, ascended to power as the new ruler of Palenque.

2 Palenque archaeological site

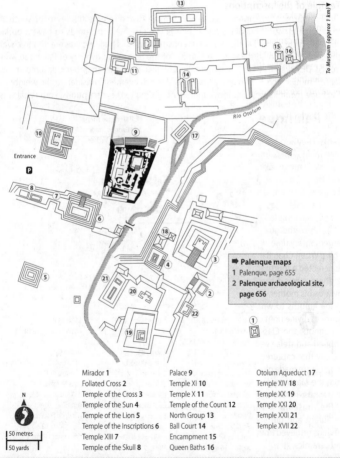

Mirador **1**	Palace **9**	Otolum Aqueduct **17**
Foliated Cross **2**	Temple XI **10**	Temple XIV **18**
Temple of the Cross **3**	Temple X **11**	Temple XX **19**
Temple of the Sun **4**	Temple of the Count **12**	Temple XXI **20**
Temple of the Lion **5**	North Group **13**	Temple XXII **21**
Temple of the Inscriptions **6**	Ball Court **14**	Temple XVII **22**
Temple XIII **7**	Encampment **15**	
Temple of the Skull **8**	Queen Baths **16**	

→ **Palenque maps**
1 Palenque, page 655
2 Palenque archaeological site, page 656

N

50 metres
50 yards

While finishing his father's funerary monument, Chan Bahlum had himself depicted as a child being presented as heir by his father. The portraits of Chan Bahlum, on the outer pillars of the Temple of the Inscriptions, display features that are both human and divine. He took and assumed attributes that rightly belong to the gods, thus ensuring that the heir to the throne was perceived as a divine human.

Group of the Cross

To the extreme southeast of the centre of the site lie Temple XIV and the buildings known as the Grupo de la Cruz. These include the Temple of the Sun, with beautiful relief carvings, which would probably have been painted in their day. The three temples in this group all have dramatic roof-combs, originally believed to have a religious significance, although traces of roof-combs have been found on buildings now known to have been purely residential. A huge stone tablet with bas relief (from whose images the name of each temple was taken) was discovered in the temples; it has now been moved to the museum.

Human and mythological time come together in the inscriptions of these temples. In each tableau carved on the tablets at the back of the temples, Chan Bahlum, the new ruler, receives the regalia of office from his father, Pacal, now in the underworld and shown much smaller than his living son. The shrines in the three temples are dedicated to the Palenque Triad, a sacred trinity linked to the ruling dynasty of the city, whose genealogy is explained in the inscriptions. They were certainly long-lived: the parents of the triad were born in 3122 or 3121 BC and the children arrived on 19 October, 23 October and 6 November, 2360 BC. It has been shown that these were dates of extraordinary astronomical phenomena: the gods were intimately related to heavenly bodies and events. They also provided a mythological origin for the dynasty, which is detailed on the three main tablets from the Group of the Cross. Rulers died and gods were born in an impressive merging of historical and mythological events. At their completion, the three temples of the Group of the Cross housed the divine sanction for the dynasty as a whole and gave the rationale for its descent through females and males.

On each set of balustrades, Chan Bahlum began his text with the birth of the patron god of each temple. On the left side of the stairs, he recorded the time elapsed between the birth of the god and the dedication of the temple. Thus, mythological time and contemporary time were fused. Each temple was named for the central image on its inner tablet. When Chan Bahlum died in 702 after ruling for 18 years, his younger brother and heir erected a fourth shrine to record the apotheosis of the departed king (Temple XIV). On these reliefs, Chan Bahlum emerges triumphantly from the underworld and dances towards his mother, Lady Ahpo-Hel.

The lengths to which the rulers of Palenque went to establish legitimacy for their claims of divine right could not guarantee the survival of Palenque after the collapse felt throughout the Classic Maya region, when the building of elite religious structures stopped and stelae were no longer engraved with the details of dynastic events. Toniná, the city that captured and probably sacrificed the Palenque ruler Kan-Xul, outlived the great centre made glorious by Pacal and Chan Bahlum. The last-known dated monument from the Maya region registers AD 909 at the lesser site; it is to be supposed that soon afterwards, Toniná went the way of the other centres of the Classic Maya world.

The **museum** ① *Tue-Sun 0900-1630, free with ticket to ruins*, with an expensive restaurant and gift shop, is on the way back towards the town. Many of the stucco carvings retrieved from the site are here, as well as jade pieces of jewellery, funerary urns and ceramics.

Ins and outs

Some tour operators in Palenque include a combination ticket for Yaxchilán and Bonampak in their packages for US$6.40. You can take a boat from Yaxchilán on the Río Usumacinta to Bethel in Guatemala. ➤➤ See Transport, page 665.

Yaxchilán → Colour map 3, B2.

ⓘ 0800-1600 (last entry), everyone has to leave site by 1645. US$3.

Yaxchilán is a major Classic Maya centre built along a terrace and hills above the Río Usumacinta, where there are more howler monkeys than people. The temples are ornately decorated with stucco and stone and the stone lintels are carved with scenes of ceremonies and conquests. The painted walls of Structure 1 at Bonampak illustrate the extravagance by the elite of this centre on the margins of the Lacandón rainforest.

Bonampak → Colour map 3, B2.

ⓘ 0800-1600. US$3.40 (free for under 13s, students and over 60s) plus US$11.50 for optional transport with the Jach Winik coop to the site; this includes toilet and locker and entry to the small museum. It's a 1-hr journey from Frontera Corozal to Bonampak.

The murals at Bonampak are very realistic with an excellent use of colour and available space. Painted on the walls, vault rises and benches of three adjoining but not interconnecting rooms, they describe the rituals surrounding the presentation at court of the future ruler. The people participating were mainly elite, including the royal family, and a strict hierarchy was observed in which eminent lords were attended by minor nobility.

In **Room 1**, the celebration opens with the presentation of the young prince, a simple act in which a porter introduces the child to an assembly of lords, dressed for the occasion in white robes. The king, dressed simply, watches from his throne. Also present are two representatives from Yaxchilán, one male and one female. It is probable that the female is the wife or consort of Chaan-Muan, the ruler of Bonampak. After this simple opening, the spectacle begins. Lords are represented dressed in sumptuous clothing and jewellery, musicians appear playing drums, turtle carapaces, rattles and trumpets and they all line up for a procession, which will bemuse the peasantry, labourers and artisans waiting outside. We never see the lower orders, but, open-mouthed, we can stand with them to observe the spectacle. The headdresses alone are enough to bedazzle us and the great diversity in the attire of the participants illustrates the wide spectrum of social functions fulfilled by those attending the ceremony.

The imagery and text of the sculptured lintels and stelae at nearby Yaxchilán proclaim the right of the heir to accede to the throne while emphasising the need to take captives to be sacrificed in honour of the king-to-be. This need is echoed in the paintings of **Room 2**, Structure 1, at Bonampak. A ferocious battle is in progress in which the ruler, Chaan-Muan, proves his right to the throne. In the midst of battle, he shines out heroically. The local warriors pull the hair of those of the opposite side, whose identity is not known. Many captives have been taken. In the ensuing scene, the full horror of the fate of those captured by the Maya is illustrated.

On a stepped structure, the ruler Chaan-Muan oversees the torture and mutilation of the captives taken in the recent battle. This event is clearly in the open air and surely witnessed by the inhabitants of Bonampak. The torture of the captives consisted of mutilation of the hands; some disconsolate individuals hold up their hands dripping blood, while one has been decapitated, his head resting on a bed of leaves. The gods demanded sacrifice, which was provided by the rulers in an extravaganza of bloodletting. It must be understood that what appears to be outright bloodthirstiness was a necessary part of Maya ritual.

The murals of the third room at Bonampak express the events that were meant to close the series of rituals designed to consolidate the claim to the throne by the son of the ruler. At first sight, the paintings that cover the walls of **Room 3** of Structure 1 appear to celebrate the sacrifices of the previous depictions in an exuberant public display of music, dance and perhaps song. The background is a pyramid and ten elegantly dressed lords dance on different levels, colourful 'dance-wings' sprouting from their hips. The dominant dancer on the uppermost level is believed to be the ruler, Chaan-Muan. In a more private corner, the royal family is portrayed preparing to engage in blood sacrifice; a servant proffers them a container that the sacred bloodletting instruments are kept in.

Lacanjá

At Lacanjá (9 km from Bonampak) there is a community of **Lacandones**. For more details ask at Na-Bolom in San Cristóbal de las Casas (see page 640). Local guides can be hired for hikes in the jungle and to the ruins of Bonampak. Lucas Chambor at the **Casa de Cultura** is a good source of advice. Lacanjá to Bonampak with locals costs US$6.50-9. The walk through the jungle is beautiful and crosses several streams. Another walk in the area is to the **Cascadas de Moctuniha** (one hour each way, US$6.50 with guide).

◉ San Cristóbal to Palenque and other Maya sites listings

For Sleeping and Eating price codes and other relevant information, see Essentials pages 47-51.

● Sleeping

Agua Azul *p653*

There are 2 places with *cabañas* for hammocks (hammock rental US$1.50 and up, US$3.50 per person in beds in dormitory); if staying, be very careful of your belongings; thefts have been reported.

Camping

Camping Casa Blanca is popular and reliable, opposite the car park; camping costs US$3.50, for a tent or hammock, and US$0.15 for use of toilets (all Agua Azul toilets charge up to US$0.50). You can also camp at the Estación Climatológica at Paso del Cayuco (**F**); it's about 15-20 mins' walk up the falls to the wire fence station.

RVs can stay overnight at Agua Azul, using the facilities, without paying extra (as long as you do not leave the park). Follow the path up the falls to a second

campsite, cheaper, less crowded. There are more *cabañas* and good places to sling a hammock further upstream, all cheaper and less touristy than lower down.

Palenque *p653, map p655*

Palenque town has a plethora of cheap lodgings, but it's generally a hot, dirty and unappealing place to stay. The only exception is La Cañada district in the northwest; a burgeoning (and more expensive) tourist zone buffeted by lush jungle foliage and trees. However, with a number of new places opening up, the jungle setting is getting a bit thinner and the area more built up. Remember that humidity and bugs can be a real scourge in Palenque – always check rooms for dampness, odours and creepy-crawlies.

A Maya Tucán, Ctra Palenque, Km 0.5 (the road from ruins into town), T916-345 0290, www.tucansihoplaya.com/palenque. Clean, pleasant hotel with pool, bar and restaurant. Rooms have a/c and lovely views.

La Cañada

A Maya Tulipanes, Cañada 6B, T916-345 0201, www.mayatulipanes.com.mx. The slightly impersonal rooms have a/c and cable TV, and vary in price, size and quality. There's a garage, pool, bar and restaurant. The restaurant does karaoke in the evenings, but luckily also has soundproof walls.

C La Posada Cañada, Nicolas Bravo, La Cañada, T916-345 0437, nochepat@hotmail.com. Cheapish, basic rooms, with hot water and fan. Brand-new kitchen facilities available to guests.

C Xibalba, Merle Green 9, T916-345 0411, www.hotelxibalba.com. A pleasant, hospitable hotel with two separate wings, one older, one newer. Clean, comfortable, bug-free rooms, with safes and a/c. There's an impressive reproduction lid of Pakal's tomb, somewhat larger than the original. The owner is friendly and knowledgeable.

E Yaxkin Hostel, Av Hidalgo corner with 5ta Pte, T916-345 0102, www.hostalyaxkin.com. This is a new, economical alternative to the more upmarket hotels in La Cañada. Dorms and bungalows include a good breakfast, popular with backpackers, free internet, movie lounge, *palapa*-style bar and restaurant area, kitchen, parking, laundry and luggage storage. Recommended.

Palenque Town

C Chan Kah Centro, corner of Juárez and Independencia, T916-345 0318, www.chan-kah.com.mx. Restaurant and terrace bar overlooking the main plaza. Sister hotel, on the road to the ruins, see page 661.

D Avenida, Juárez 173, T916-345 0116. Large rooms with fan, cable TV and hot water. Some have a/c (**A**) and balcony. Not very friendly, but convenient for bus station.

D Jade, Hidalgo 61, T916-345 0463. Family-run hotel with clean, comfortable rooms. Hot water, a/c and cable TV. Recommended. Peaceful. Will store luggage.

D Naj K'in, Hidalgo 72, T916-345 1126. Clean, comfortable, well-decorated rooms with bath, fan and 24-hr hot water. Safe parking. Some rooms with a/c.

D Posada Aguila Real, 20 de Noviembre s/n, T916-345 0004, www.posadaaguilareal.com. Very comfortable, attractive lodgings. Rooms are clean with hot water, cable TV and a/c. Helpful staff.

D Posada Kin, Abasolo s/n, 20 de Noviembre and 5 de Mayo, very near Zócalo, T916-345 1714, posada_kin@hotmail.com. Clean and large doubles with bathroom, fan, safe and luggage store. Organizes tours in the area.

D Posada Shalom, Av Juárez 156, T916-345 0944. Economic rooms with hot water, bath, fan and cable TV. Friendly and clean. Stores luggage. If full, there is also a **Posada Shalom II** a couple of blocks away with further accommodation.

D-E Posada San Juan, T916-345 0616, Emilio Robasa, corner of Allende, (from ADO go up the hill and first right, it's on the fourth block on the left). With bath, cheaper without, cold water, fan, clean, quiet, firm beds, secure locks, nice courtyard, very good for budget accommodation, safe parking available. Dorms also available (**G**).

D-E San Miguel, Hidalgo and Aldama, above Union Pharmacy, T916-345 0152. Big clean rooms with balcony, hot water and fan. Pricier with TV and a/c. There are cheap dorms too. Good value.

E Kashlan, 5 de Mayo 116, T916-345 0297, www.palenque.com.mx/kashlan. Long-standing Palenque favourite. Clean, mostly quiet rooms (except those facing the street) have bath, fan or a/c (**A**). The owners are helpful and friendly and offer a 25% discount to holders of this book.

E Posada Canek, 20 de Noviembre 43. Nice rooms and dorm beds (**G**). More expensive rooms have bath. English spoken, recently refurbished rooms have TV and a/c. Friendly, chatty and helpful owner. Restaurant set to open end of 2009.

E Posada Nacha'n Ka'an, 20 de Noviembre 25 and Allende, T916-345 4737. Rooms with hot water and fan, more expensive with a/c (**C**), but there are also cheaper dorms (**G**). Has luggage storage.

E Yun-Kax, Av Corregidora 87 (behind Santo Domingo). Quiet, clean, large rooms with hot water and fan (**C** with a/c). Recommended.

F La Selva, Av Reforma 69, T916-345 3707. Economical rooms with fan, bath and hot water. Some have TV. Good prices for groups. The owner also has a tour company organizing tours in the area.

F Posada Charito, 20 de Noviembre 15B, T916-345 0121. Clean, friendly, family-run. The rooms are basic and good value, although sometimes airless. The ground floor is best.

F Posada Johanna, 20 de Noviembre and Allende, T916-345 0687. Tidy, family-run joint with basic, good value rooms.

Road to the ruins

Exuberant rainforest flanks the road to the ruins, making accommodation here an interesting and attractive option; El Panchán, a collection of budget *cabañas*, is the most famous and popular. This area is plagued with bugs, ants and creepy-crawlies, in addition to raging humidity – this is the jungle after all. Ensure your room or *cabaña* has secure screens and a net. Bring repellent – especially in the wet season.

AL Chan Kah, T916-345 1134, www.chan-kah.com.mx. Pleasant pool and a verdant setting. Sister hotel in Palenque town (see opposite).

D-E Margarita and Ed's, El Panchán, edcabanas@yahoo.com (although the internet connection here is erratic). The plushest *cabañas* at El Panchán, all with private bath. But if you don't fancy getting too close to nature, there are modern rooms too (**B**). A friendly, restful place oozing good vibes. The mattresses are amazing.

E Chato's, El Panchán, panchan@yahoo.com.mx, inside **Don Mucho**'s restaurant. Cabins with private or shared bath.

E Elementos Naturales, on road to ruins, past El Panchán, www.elementosnaturales.org. Youth hostel, can sling hammock or camp. Includes breakfast. Pleasant outdoor feel.

E-F Jungle Palace, part of **Chato's**. Economical rooms with private or share bath.

F Betos, El Panchán. Cheap cabins and space to sling a hammock (**G**). Prepare for loud dance music at night.

F Jaguar, on the quieter side, across the road from El Panchán, but the philosophy is still the same. Shared bath only.

F-G Rakshita, El Panchán. Delightful Rakshita has seen better days – the meditation area has been dismantled, the hippies have fled and the vegetarian restaurant has closed. Still, the cabins are intact and it remains a friendly, economical place to stay. Dorm beds (**G**) and very cheap hammock spaces (**G**) are also available.

Camping

Trailer Park Mayabell, on road to ruins, 2 km before entrance, T916-341 6977, www.mayabell.com.mx. Space for tents, hammocks and caravans. There are also comfortable *cabañas* with a/c and private bath. Pool and live music in the evenings. Recommended.

E-G La Palapa, 1½ km from the ruins inside the national park. *Cabañas*, camping with or without roof cover, space for hammocks. A bit basic, but the new owners are restoring this pretty site right by a lake. They grow organic fruit and veg and run a Mexican restaurant where the food is prepared right in front of you on a grill. All-night bar with dancing, which can make it a bit noisy. All toilets are separate from the *cabañas* in order to keep the nearby lake clean. Group discounts.

Yaxchilán, Bonampak, Lacanjá and around *p658*

There is basic accommodation at Bonampak; take hammock and mosquito net. Thieving has been reported. **Camping** is restricted to the INAH site on the Usumacinta.

Camping

At Lacanjá there are 4 campsites where you can sling a hammock: **Kin Bor**, **Vicente K'in**, **Carlos Chan Bor** and **Manuel Chan Bor**.

Tenosique and Río San Pedro route *p672*

D Rome, Calle 28, 400, T934-342 2151. Clean, will change dollars for residents, bath, not bad.
E Azulejos, Calle 26, 416. With bath, fan, clean, hot water, friendly, helpful owner speaks some English, opposite church.
E Casa de Huéspedes La Valle, Calle 19. With bath, good, but a little grubby.

Río Usumacinta route *p671*

D Centro Turístico and Grutas Tsolk'in, Benemérito, www.ecoturlacandona.com. Clean, well-kept rooms with communal bathrooms. Much more friendly and helpful than the nearby **Escudo Jaguar** (which is overpriced and unfriendly). Less than 5 mins' walk from the dock. Take a right turning opposite immigration office.

ⓕ Eating

Palenque town *p653, map p655*
The classier restaurants are in the barrio of La Cañada, behind the Maya head as you enter town.

⑪⑪⑪ El Tapanco Grill, Av Juárez 65, 2 blocks below plaza above Bing ice cream shop. Good steak, balcony dining.
⑪ Pizzería Palenque, Juárez 168 and Allende, T916-345 0332. Good pizzas and prices.
⑪-⑪ La Mexicana, Juárez and 5 de Mayo. Typical Mexican fare and breakfasts.
⑪-⑪ Lakan-Há, Juárez 20. Good tacos, fast and efficient. Also serves breakfast, Mexican staples and *menú del día*.
⑪-⑪ Mara's, Juárez 1, by the Zócalo. Cheap set menus.
⑪-⑪ Maya, Hidalgo and Independencia. Popular, can get full, set-menu lunches and à-la-carte dinner. Good meat dishes, efficient service and free Wi-Fi.
⑪ Café de Yarra, Hidalgo 68. Clean, stylish café serving good value, tasty breakfasts. Occasional live music.

⑪ El Herradero, Av Juárez 120. Breakfast and reasonably priced meals, fast service, open 24 hrs. Recommended.
⑪ La Oaxaqueña, Juárez 122, opposite the ADO bus station. Serves up some economical Mexican staples and *menú del día*.
⑪ Las Tinajas, 20 de Noviembre 41 and Abasolo. Good, family run, excellent food, huge portions, recommended.
⑪ Mundo Maya, Juárez 10. Friendly, good and cheap Mexican fare.

Road to the ruins
⑪⑪⑪⑪ La Selva, Km 0.5 on Hidalgo. Excellent, smart dress preferred, live music at weekends, recommended. Open 1300-2300.
⑪⑪-⑪ Don Mucho, El Panchán. Outdoor restaurant serving excellent Italian-Mexican food and fantastic breakfast. There's good evening entertainment, including fire dancing; quite exotic given the forest backdrop. They also host 'passing through' travelling musicians.
⑪ El Mono Blanco, El Panchán. Cheaper than Don Mucho's and much lower key. They serve Mexican food, breakfasts and à la carte dishes.

ⓝ Bars and clubs

Palenque town *p653, map p655*
Numerous new bars and restaurants are springing up in La Cañada district.

Road to the ruins
La Palapa, see page 661. All-night bar with dancing.

⊛ Festivals and events

Palenque town *p653, map p655*
1st week of Aug Fiesta de Santo Domingo.

O Shopping

Palenque town *p653, map p655*
Av Juárez is lined with souvenir shops selling hammocks, blankets, Maya figurines and hats. Sales staff are less pushy than in towns in the Yucatán Peninsula; bargain for the best prices.

▲▲ Activities and tours

Palenque town *p653, map p655*
Horse riding
Tours can be booked at the **Clínica Dental Zepeda**, Juárez s/n – the dentist owns the horses. Also through **Cabañas de Safari** in Palenque archaeological zone Km 1, T916-345 0026. **Gaspar Alvaro** also rents horses. He can be located at his house on the road to the ruins, directly in front of Mayabell. Gaspar will take you on a 3-hr ride through rainforest trails in the area surrounding the ruins. Good chance of seeing monkeys and toucans. US$15 for 3 hrs. Tell him specifically that you want to go through the rainforest and not along the road.

Tour operators and guides
Alonso Méndez, El Panchán camping site, road to the ruins Km 4.5, T917-341 2218, butzchan@ gmail.com. Alonso is a well-versed guide with extensive knowledge of flora, fauna, medicinal uses of plants and an intimate knowledge of the Palenque ruins. A respected authority on Chiapanecan ethnobotany, Alonso has a gift of academic and spiritual understanding of the rainforest. He speaks English, Spanish and Tzeltzal. Full-day hiking trips US$50 for a group of 6-8 people.
Erasto Molina, T916-109 0425, erastomolina@ yahoo.com.mx. Erasto is an experienced local guide, specializing in pre-Hispanic medicine, visual arts and he is also an expert on cacao and chocolate. Try his 3-hour pre-Hispanic beverages sampling tour, one of several interesting and unusual excursions.

Fernando Mérida, T044 916-103 3649 (mob), desk set up near **Chan Kan Centro**, Av Juárez. Fernando is a Lacandón guide with some interesting views of the Maya and Mayan prophecies. He runs a range of unusual tours not offered by other companies, across Chiapas, including birdwatching expeditions on Sun lagoon. He speaks English and Italian.
José Luis Zúñiga Mendoza, T916-341 4736, tentzun@hotmail.com. Easy going, José has good knowledge of the Palenque area and in addition to guided trips around the ruins offers jungle walks and stays with local communities.
Na Chan Kan, corner of Hidalgo and Jiménez, across from Santo Domingo church, T916-345 0263, www.nachankan.com. Offers a wide selection of packages ranging from tours to Agua Azul to excursions to the Yaxchilán and Bonampak ruins, as well as transportation to Guatemala.
Shivalva (Marco A Morales), Merle Green 9, La Cañada, T916-345 0411, www.hotel xibalba.com. Tours of Guatemala, Palenque, Yaxchilán, Bonampak, and waterfalls. Friendly and well established.
Turística Maya Chiapas, Av Juárez 123, T916-345 0798, www.tmayachiapas.com.mx. Tours to the waterfalls, Lacandón jungle, Tikal and other parts of Guatemala, as well as Belize. English spoken.

Agua Azul and Misol-Há *p653*
Tour operators
All the travel agencies in Palenque do a cheap tour to both Misol-Há and Agua Azul, US$8 pp. Beware, standards vary. Since the price often doesn't include the entrance fees, a tour works out the same as doing the trip independently by bus or *colectivo* (see Transport below). Bring a swimsuit and plenty of drinking water.

Yaxchilán, Bonampak, Lacanjá and around *p658*
Tour operators
Operators from Palenque offer 1 and 2 day trips to Bonampak and Yaxchilán, all transport

and food included. To see both sites independently, it's recommended you take at least 2 days and stay overnight in Lacanjá. Otherwise, be prepared for a tough day of at least 14 hours. Local Spanish-speaking guides can be found by asking around in Lacanjá or enquiring at the entrance to Bonampak.

◉ Transport

Palenque town p653, map p655
Air
Commercial traffic through Palenque's small airport has dwindled, and it's now mainly used for specially chartered planes. Speak to a tour agent if you would like to organize flights within **Chiapas** (including Yaxchilán and Bonampak), **Yucatán** or **Guatemala**.

Bus
Local Micro buses run back and forth along the main street, passing the bus station area, to and from the ruins, every 10 mins, US$0.70 (taxi US$6). Catch one of these for **El Panchán** and other nearby accommodations.

Long distance There are 3 bus terminals. The 1st-class ADO/OCC terminal is at the western end of Juárez. The Rodolfo Figueroa y Lacandonia terminal is on the opposite side of the road, with a few 2nd-class departures to San Cristóbal. An **AEXA** terminal is almost next door to the 1st-class terminal, serving a handful of destinations in Chiapas. Also on Juárez is **Autotransportes Tuxtla**, with 2nd-class departures to **Quintana Roo**, daily at 1930. To **Cancún**, 1st class (ADO and OCC), 1720, 1935, 2110, 13 hrs, US$40; and ADO GL, 2100, US$48. To **Campeche**, 1st class, 0800, 2100, 2200, 2325, 5 hrs, US$17.50. To **Escárcega**, 1st class, 6 daily, 3 hrs, US$10. To **Mérida**, 1st class, 0800, 2100, 2200, 2325, 8 hrs, US$26. To **Mexico City**, ADO, 1830 (TAPO), 2100 (Norte), 14 hrs, US$55. To **Oaxaca**, ADO, 1730, 15 hrs, US$39. To **San Cristóbal**, 1st class, 8 daily, 5 hrs, US$9.50; and an ADO GL. Also some 2nd-class departures. To **Tulum**, 1st

class, 1720, 1935, 2000, 2110 11 hrs, US$34; and ADO GL, 2100, US$40.50. To **Tuxtla Gutiérrez**, OCC, 8 daily, 6 hrs, US$12; and an ADO GL, US$14.50. To **Villahermosa**, 1st class, 11 daily, US$2 hrs, US$7.50.

Shuttles To **Agua Azul** and **Misol-há**, Transportes Chambalú, Allende and Juárez, 0900,1000, 1200, US$8.50. They stop for 30 mins at Misol-Há and 3 hrs at Agua Azul. To **Frontera Corozal** (for **San Javier**, **Bonampak**, **Lacanjá** and **Yaxchilán**), Transportes Chamoan, Hidalgo 141, roughly hourly from 0500-1700, US$5. To **Tenosique**, Transportes Palenque, Allende and 20 de Noviembre, hourly, US$5. **Playas de Catazajá** (for Escárcega and Campeche) Transportes Pakal, Allende between 20 de Noviembre and Corregidora, every 15 mins, US$1.50.

Taxi
Taxis charge a flat rate of US$1.50 within the town, US$4 to **El Panchán** and nearby Mayabell camping areas.

Agua Azul and Misol-Há p653
Colectivos from Hidalgo and Allende, Palenque, for Agua Azul and Misol-Há, 2 a day, US$8; *colectivos* can also be organized between Misol-Há and Agua Azul, in either direction. Taxi US$40 with 2 hrs at Agua Azul, or to both falls US$55. Several buses from Palenque daily (direction San Cristóbal de las Casas or Ocosingo), to crossroads leading to the waterfall, such as Transportes Chambalu to both Misol-Ha and Agua Azul, leaving at 0900, 1000 and 1200, US$8.50, 2nd class, 1½ hrs. You can also buy bus tickets from Transportes Figueroa, 100 m from ADO bus station (in direction of the town centre) in Palenque. It's 1½ hrs from Palenque to the turn-off to the Agua Azul road. From the crossroads walk the 4 km downhill to the falls on a beautiful jungle-lined road (or hitch a ride on a minibus for US$1). Catch a ride back to Palenque on tour buses that have extra space, US$4, leaving Agua Azul car park 1500-1800. Back from the junction 1400-1600

with **Transportes Maya** buses, but some others you must change at Temo, over 20 km away, north of Ocosingo. Tour companies can also arrange bus tickets with **AEXA** from the crossroads to San Cristóbal and other places if you don't wish to return all the way to Palenque to catch an onward bus.

Yaxchilán, Bonampak, Lacanjá and around p658
Air
Flights from **Palenque** to **Bonampak** and **Yaxchilán**, in light plane for 5, about US$600 per plane, to both places, whole trip 6 hrs. Prices set, list available; **Viajes Misol-Há**, Juárez 48 at Aldama, T916-345 1614, run charter flights to Bonampak and Yaxchilán for US$150 per person return, minimum 4 passengers.

Boat
See page 671 for boat travel to Guatemala.

Bus
A few different companies run hourly *colectivo* services between **Palenque** and **Frontera Corozal**, including Transportes Chamoan (see Palenque shuttles). For **Lacanjá** or **Bonampak**, catch one of these and exit at the junction and military checkpoint at San Javier. From there, you will need to hike or take a taxi, if you can find one. Bear in mind this is a

remote destination, so pack water, travel light and plan your time accordingly. For **Yaxchilán**, take a boat from Frontera Corozal.

Car
Bonampak is over 30 km from Frontera Corozal and can be reached from the San Javier crossroads on the road to Corozal.

❶ Directory

Palenque town p653, map p655
Banks Exchange rate only comes through at 1000. **Banamex**, Juárez 28, Mon-Fri 0830-1600, Sat 0900-1500, slow. ATMs at Bancomer and Banamex, but often with long queues. **Bancomer**, in Juárez changes TCs, good rates, Mon-Fri 0830-1600, Sat 0900-1500. Many travel agencies also have *casas de cambio*, but don't usually change TCs. **Internet** Several internet cafés along Juárez with good service and prices ranging from US$1-1.50 per hr. **Laundry** Opposite Hotel Kashlan, US$2 per 3 kg, 0800-1930. At the end of Juárez is a laundry, US$3 per 3 kg. **Post office** Independencia, next to Palacio Municipal, helpful, Mon-Fri 0900-1300. **Telephone** Long-distance telephones at *casetas* along Juárez and at the bus terminals.

Routes to Guatemala

There are two main border crossings into Guatemala: at Ciudad Cuauhtémoc (La Mesilla in Guatemala), reached via Route 190 from San Cristóbal de las Casas, and the other at Tapachula along the coastal Route 200 from the neighbouring state of Oaxaca. Another option is to cross the border by boat, east of Palenque, along the rivers Usumacinta or San Pedro. Finally, you can cross at Ciudad Hidalgo, to access the Guatemalan Pacific coast. **NB** *If planning on returning to Mexico after an excursion to Guatemala, ensure you get an exit stamp at the immigration office. Pick up your tourist card and a slip of paper, take this to any bank, pay US$23 and the slip is stamped. Not doing this can lead to problems when you try to leave Mexico again.* ▸▸ *For Listings, see pages 672-676.*

San Cristóbal to Ciudad Cuauhtémoc ⊜❷❷❶ ▸▸ *pp672-676.*

Comitán → *Phone code 963.*

Ninety kilometres from San Cristóbal is Comitán de Domínguez, a small but handsome colonial city 80 km from the Guatemalan border. It's a tranquil and elevated place, offering cool respite from the stifling lowlands and a good place to relax before or after visiting Guatemala. In the centre is a large, shady Zócalo, with the state **tourist office** ① *1era Av Sur poniente 3A, T963-632 4047, Mon-Fri 0900-1400 and 1600-1900, Sat-Sun 0900-1400.* Streets (*calles*) run north to south and avenues (*avenidas*) east to west. The **municipal tourism office** ① *primera Calle Sur Poniente 26,* is confusingly where the Guatemalan consulate used

Comitán

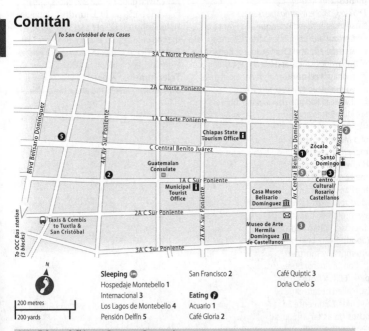

Sleeping ⊜	San Francisco **2**	Café Quiptic **3**
Hospedaje Montebello **1**		Doña Chelo **5**
Internacional **3**	Eating ❷	
Los Lagos de Montebello **4**	Acuario **1**	
Pensión Delfín **5**	Café Gloria **2**	

Rosario Castellanos

Writer, poet and feminist Rosario Castellanos, although born in Mexico City, spent her formative years in Comitán, Chiapas and much of her writing focuses on the plight of the indigenous population among whom she grew up. One of her most famous works, the semi-autobiographical *Balún-Canán* from 1957, is set near Comitán and depicts events taking place during the Lázaro Cárdenas land reforms in the 1930s, something which affected Castellanos' family personally.

Despite her premature death, aged 49, in Israel in 1974, where Castellanos was serving as Mexico's ambassador, she has managed to leave a lasting legacy as one of Mexico's most influential female writers of the 20th century. She took a strong feminist stance early on, as evidenced by books such as the 1973 *Mujer que sabe latín (Woman Schooled in Latin)*. Educated in Mexico and Europe, Castellanos was attempting to successfully bridge the gap between the Spanish, *mestizo* and indigenous cultures of Mexico, while highlighting the need for improved conditions and better understanding of the latter. Her untimely death in a freak electrical accident in Tel Aviv was a great loss, but her influence in Mexico today lives on and many places in Chiapas are dedicated to her memory.

to be. There are also helpful tourist police plying the **Zócalo** ⓘ *0800-2000, daily*. Visit the **Guatemalan Consulate** ⓘ *3rd floor, 1era Calle Sur Poinente 35 (look out for the Guatemalan flag on top of the large white building as there's no sign by the entrance), T963-632 2979. Mon-Fri 0900-1300 and 1400-1700*, if you need a visa. There's a handful of small museums including the **Museo de Arte Hermila Domínguez de Castellanos** ⓘ *Av Central Sur and 3a Sur Pte, Mon-Sat, 0900-1800, Sun 1000-1300, US$0.30*, with a collection of modern art; and **Casa Museo Belisario Domínguez** ⓘ *Av Central Sur and 2a Sur Pte, Mon-Sat 1000-1845, Sun 0900-1245, US$0.30*, filled with memorabilia and dedicated to a local doctor who was assassinated after speaking out against President Huerta.

Lagunas de Montebello and Chinkultic

Six kilometres south of Comitán take a right turn for the Maya ruins of **Tenán Puente** ⓘ *5 km, 0800-1700, US$2*, situated in a forest; there is a shortcut on foot. In 1996 the tomb of a Maya nobleman (AD 1000) was discovered here. The buildings at Tenán have been more restored than those at Chinkultic (see below). A road branches off the Pan-American Highway, 16 km further on, to a very beautiful region of multi-coloured lakes and caves, the **Lagunas de Montebello** (a national park). Off the road to **Montebello**, 30 km from the Pan-American Highway, lie the ruins of **Chinkultic** ⓘ *0800-1700, US$2.50 and US$1.50 road toll*, with temples, ball court, carved stone stelae and a *cenote* (sinkhole, good swimming) in beautiful surroundings; from the signpost the ruins are about 3 km along a dirt road. Watch and ask for the very small sign and gate where the road to the ruins starts (about 1 km back along the main road, towards Comitán from **Doña María's**, don't attempt any shortcuts); worth visiting when passing.

Combi vans or buses marked 'Tziscao' or 'Lagos' to the Lagunas de Montebello national park (60 km from Comitán, US$1.40 about one hour), via the **Lagunas de Siete Colores** (so-called because the oxides in the water give varieties of colours), leave frequently from Avenida 2 Poniente Sur and Calle 3 Sur Poniente, four blocks from the plaza in Comitán; buses go as far as Laguna Bosque Azul, a one-hour journey. For those with their own transport there are several dirt roads from Comitán to the Lagunas; a recommended route is the one via La Independencia, Buena Vista, La Patria and El Triunfo (beautiful views), eventually joining the road west of the Chinkultic ruins. There are no organized tours of the lagoons from Comitán.

Tziscao

Tziscao is 9 km along the road leading right from the park entrance, which is 3 km before Bosque Azul; hourly buses Comitán-Tziscao; the last bus and *colectivo* back connecting with the 1900 bus to San Cristóbal is at 1600. The last combi to Comitán is at 1700. A trip to the Lagunas de Siete Colores from Comitán can be done in a day (note that the less-accessible lakes are hard to get to even if staying in the vicinity). It is also possible to hire a combi, which takes 12 people, to go to the Lakes and Chinkultic for US$15 per hour. A day trip to Chinkultic and the lakes from San Cristóbal de las Casas is also possible, if exhausting (take passport and tourist card). The **Bosque Azul** area is now a reserve. The area is noted for its orchids and birdlife, including the famous *quetzal*, but it gets very busy at weekends and holidays. There are small caves nearby.

Ciudad Cuauhtémoc

South of San Cristóbal and heading for Guatemala, follow the 170-km paved road via **Teopisca** to **Comitán de Domínguez**. From Comitán the road winds down to the Guatemala border at Ciudad Cuauhtémoc via La Trinitaria (near the turn-off to Lagunas de Montebello, restaurant but no hotel).

Ciudad Cuauhtémoc, despite its name, is not a city, but just a few buildings; the OCC bus station is opposite immigration, with an overpriced restaurant and an excellent hotel. Be sure to surrender your tourist card and get your exit stamp at Mexican immigration in Ciudad Cuauhtémoc before boarding a pick-up for Guatemalan immigration; you will only have to go back if you don't. A pick-up to the Guatemalan border, 4 km, costs US$0.65 per person. Walk 100 m to immigration and customs (open until 2100). Beyond the Guatemalan post at La Mesilla, a beautiful stretch of road leads 85 km to Huehuetenango. This route is far more interesting than the one through Tapachula; the border crossing at Ciudad Cuauhtémoc is also reported to be easier than that at Talismán. See also box, page 670.

Route to Tapachula ⊛❼▲⊜❻ ⁊⁊ *pp672-676. Colour map 3, C1.*

Travelling from the neighbouring state of Oaxaca, Routes 190 and 200 merge to cross the Isthmus of Tehuantepec. Accommodation is available at **Zanatepec** and **Tapanatepec**, which is where Highway 190 heads northeast to Tuxtla Gutiérrez and Highway 200 continues southeast along the coast of Chiapas to the Guatemalan border.

Arriaga → *Phone code: 966. Colour map 2, C6.*

Arriaga is a good stopping place just across the state border that separates Oaxaca from Chiapas; many banks around Zócalo for exchange. The road from Arriaga to Tapachula is a four-lane dual carriageway.

From Arriaga, Route 200 continues to Tonalá, formerly a very quiet town but now noisy and dirty. The bus from Tonalá to Tapachula takes 3½ hours, US$11; also buses to Tuxtla. This is by far the most direct road for travellers seeking the quickest way from Mexico City to Guatemala.

Puerto Arista → *Phone code: 961. Colour map 2, C6.*

Along the coast from Tonalá to Tapachula there are several fine-looking and undeveloped beaches, although waves and currents are dangerous. Puerto Arista (17 km south of Tonalá) is now being built up, but it is still a relatively peaceful area with 32 km of clean beach to relax on with no salespeople; bus/*colectivo* from Tonalá every hour, 45 minutes, US$0.60, taxi US$2; plenty of buses to Arriaga, US$0.75. Many hotels, motels and restaurants on the beach, which is hot and, in the wet season, has sandflies.

Buses also from Tonalá to **Boca del Cielo** further down the coast, which is good for bathing and has *cabañas* with hammocks, and similarly **Cabeza del Toro**. **Paredón**, on the huge Laguna del Mar Muerto, 14 km west of Tonalá, has excellent seafood and one very basic guesthouse. You can take a local fishing boat out into the lagoon to swim; the shore stinks because fishermen clean fish on the beach among dogs and pigs. There are frequent buses.

On the way to Tapachula you pass through **Pijijiapan**. From **Huixtla**, a good, scenic road winds off into the mountains parallel to the border, towards Ciudad Cuauhtémoc and Comitán.

Tapachula → *Phone code: 962.*

Once little more than an obscure border town in a lesser-visited corner of Chiapas, over US$70 million has recently been invested in Tapachula, with a view to exploiting its strategic location on the Pacific coast. The result? **Puerto Chiapas**: a major new port large enough to receive the latest generation cruise, container and cargo ships. It is hoped that this ambitious new development will bring unprecedented visitors to Tapachula and Chiapas, and the tourist board's slick new brochures are an exercise in shameless self-promotion. Yet beyond the manicured lawns of the port, Tapachula is still the same shambling old border town it's always been, more characteristic of Central America than Mexico. For now, at least, this city has yet to blossom and instead it remains a place where no one really comes to stay – a stopping-off point before visiting Guatemala and more scenic parts of Chiapas. There is an edgy border town feel to it and the Tapachulans are not particularly used to foreign visitors. At weekends it can be hard to find anywhere to change money and tourist information on Tapachula itself is scarce.

For orientation, *avenidas* run north-south (Norte–Sur), *calles* east-west (Oriente-Poniente). Odd-numbered *calles* are north of Calle Central, odd *avenidas* are east of Avenida Central. For information, contact the **municipal tourist office** ① *8a Av Norte and 3a Pte, T962-625 0441, www.turismotapachula.gob.mx, Mon-Fri 0830-1540*; or the **state tourist office** ① *Plaza Kamico, Central Ote, T962-625 5409*, away from the centre. Tapachula has an airport and is a major crossing junction for Guatemala; see box, page 670.

There's little to see in town itself, save a small but captivating archaeological museum, **Museo Regional del Soconusco** ① *west side of the plaza, Tue-Sun 0900-1800*. But beyond the city, a flurry of new attractions have opened in anticipation of the big tourist influx.

Around Tapachula

La Ruta Café is a new agro-tourism development that includes 13 coffee *fincas*, many of German origin. Some of them are stunningly positioned, with luxury, mountain-top accommodation and spas; others have facilities for adventure sports like biking and zip-lining. Speak to the tourist office for more details.

Caicrochis ① *F962-642 6692, Tue-Sun 1000-1700, US$3*, is the oldest crocodile reserve in Mexico and home to around 1000 of the beasts. Don't dangle the kids too close! A couple of 'eco-parks' have opened that are really just touristy playgrounds with

Border essentials: Mexico–Guatemala

See also page 671 for river routes to Guatemala.

Ciudad Cuauhtémoc

Tourist cards and visas are available at the border; some reports say only 15 days are being given, but extensions are possible in Oaxaca or Mexico City. It is forbidden to bring in fruit and vegetables.

Drivers entering Mexico At the border crossing your vehicle is fumigated, US$7.25, get a receipt (if re-entering Mexico, with documents from a previous entry, papers are checked here). Proceed 4 km to Migración to obtain tourist card or visa, or have existing visa checked. Then go to **Banjército** to obtain the necessary papers and windscreen sticker or, if re-entering Mexico, to have existing papers checked. Monday to Friday 0800-1600, Saturday to Sunday 0900-1400. Mexico is one hour ahead of Guatemala.

Tapachula–Talismán

It is 8 km from Tapachula to the fairly grubby 24-hour border at Talismán, which has good onward connections to the western highlands and Quetzaltenango in Guatemala.

Immigration The Mexican Customs post is 200 m from the Guatemalan one.

Guatemalan consulate See page 676.

Crossing into Guatemala By car can take several hours. If you don't want your car sprayed inside it may cost you a couple of dollars. Do not park in the car park at the control post, as it is very expensive.

Driving into Mexico See Essentials, page 42, for information about the temporary import of vehicles. Car papers are issued at the Garita de Aduana on Route 200 out of Tapachula. There is no other road; you can't miss it. Photocopies of documents must be made in town; there are no facilities at the Garita. Reported to be a frustrating procedure – be prepared and patient.

Exchange Change money in town rather than via the aggressive moneychangers who you should avoid doing business with. They stand around Customs on the Guatemalan side; check rates before dealing with them, and haggle. There is no bank on the Guatemalan side.

Ciudad Hidalgo–Tecún Umán

There is a border crossing 37 km south of Tapachula, at the busy border town of Ciudad Hidalgo, opposite Tecún Umán in Guatemala with connections to Coatepeque, Mazatenango and Retalhuleu. A few blocks from the town plaza is Mexican immigration, at the foot of the 1-km-long bridge across the Río Suchiate; cycle taxis cross the bridge for about US$1, pedestrians pay US$0.15. You cannot change TCs here.

opportunities for activities like swimming, rock climbing and quad-biking. They include **Club Catay Maya** ① *San Agustín Jitotol, Ctra Planta Potabilizadora a Carrillo Puerto Km 6, www.cataymaya.com*; and **Parque Ecoturístico La Changa** ① *Ctra a la Presa José Cecilio del Valle s/n, T962-626 5592, www.lachanga.com.mx.*

There are several beaches near Tapachula, including Playa Linda, San Benito, Las Escolleras and Barra Cahoacán. Five kilometres from Playa Linda you'll find **Laguna de Pozuelos**, a lagoon with rich mangroves and wildlife including snakes, lizards and aquatic birds. Similarly, **La Encrucijada biosphere reserve** is home to various species of local fauna.

The ruins of **Izapa** (proto-Classic stelae, small museum) lie just off the road to Talismán; the part of the site on the north is easily visible but a larger portion is on the south side of the highway, about 1 km away, ask the caretaker for guidance. To reach Izapa take a combi from Unión Progreso bus station.

Forty-five kilometres northeast of Tapachula, beyond the turning to Talismán, is **Unión Juárez**, where you can have your papers stamped and proceed on foot via Talquián to the Guatemalan border at Sibinal.

A worthwhile hike can be made up the **Tacaná volcano** (4150 m), which takes two to three days from Unión Juárez. Ask for the road to Chiquihuete; no cars. The Tapachula tourist office can help; in Unión Juárez ask for Sr Umberto Ríos at Restaurante Montaña, he will put you in touch with guide Moisés Hernández, who charges US$15 a day. It is possible to stay overnight in Don Emilio Velásquez's barn halfway up, US$2; he offers coffee and *tortillas*. At the top are some *cabañas* in which you sleep for free; sleeping bag essential.

River routes to Guatemala

Río Usumacinta

The Río Usumacinta route takes you by road to Benemérito (southeast of Yaxchilán and Bonampak), by boat to Sayaxché, Guatemala and then by road to Flores. Autotransportes Comitán Lagos de Montebello buses (Avenida Manuel Velasco Suárez, Palenque, three blocks from food market) run eight a day starting at 0400 until 1530 to **Benemérito**, on the Mexican side of the Usumacinta, seven to 12 hours but will be quicker when the new paved road is completed. The buses are basic, crowded and the road is dreadful (it's about half the time in a *camioneta* if you can hitch a ride). You must visit immigration, about 3 km from Benemérito, to sign out of Mexico (the bus will wait).

Once in Benemérito, where there is a 2100 curfew (two basic *pensiones*), hope for a boat to Guatemala; this may take a couple of days. The boat goes to Sayaxché and should stop at Pipiles for immigration. A trading boat takes two days, US$4-5; a motorized canoe eight hours, US$5-10. You can also charter a fast boat for about US$200. From Sayaxché, buses run to Flores. For an alternative (and easier) route, take the bus from Palenque to Frontera Corozal with Transportes Chamoan, Hidalgo 141, roughly hourly from 0500-1700, US$5. About an hour down this route at Km 61 is an excellent breakfast stop, Valle Escondido. Keep an eye out for hummingbirds. In Corozal there is an immigration post (register here before crossing to Guatemala and have your documents stamped), two hotels and restaurants. It's a 30-minute *lancha* ride to Bethel, US$14 for one to two people, US$40 for three to four people; or a cheap five-minute ride to La Técnica.

Tenosique and Río San Pedro route

The Río San Pedro route starts at Tenosique, a friendly place east of Palenque (money exchange at clothing shop, Ortiz y Alvarez at Calle 28 No 404, good rates for dollars to quetzales, poor for dollars to pesos). From here, the classic route takes you by road to La Palma, by boat to El Naranjo, in Guatemala, and then by road to Flores. A newer, more convenient route begins at El Ceibo, 60 km southeast of Tenosique.

From Tenosique to **La Palma** on the Río San Pedro, *colectivos* starting at 0600 from in front of the market, one hour, US$1, two hours by bus (from Tenosique bus station, which is outside town, take taxi, US$1.70 or *colectivo* to 'Centro', or walk 20 minutes). Taxi to La Palma US$7, shared by all passengers. From La Palma boats leave to **El Naranjo** when they have enough passengers, but timings are very irregular (they wait for a minimum of five passengers), at least 4½ hours, US$22. Be at the boat one hour early, it sometimes leaves ahead of schedule; if this happens ask around for someone to chase it, US$3-4 per person for three people. If there are fewer than five passengers, the boat may be cancelled, in which case you must either wait for the next one, or hire a *rápido* (US$125, maximum four people). You may be able to arrange a slower boat for up to six people for US$100. In La Palma, one restaurant will change money at weekends at a reasonable rate.

It is a beautiful boat trip, through mangroves with herons and the occasional alligator, dropping people off at homesteads. There is a stop at the border post two hours into the journey to sign out of Mexico. Take waterproofs and torch/flashlight. There are no officials on arrival at the jetty in El Naranjo; immigration is a short way on the right (entry will cost US$5 in *quetzales*, beware extra unofficial charges at customs). Bus tickets to Flores are sold here.

For the newer, reliable route, take an hourly bus from Tenosique to El Ceibo. They depart from Calle 45 and 16, behind the market, 0600-1700, one hour. Once at the border, catch a pick-up to Río San Pedro. There are *lanchas* to El Naranjo until 1700, US$3.50, 30 minutes.

⊙ Routes to Guatemala listings

For Sleeping and Eating price codes and other relevant information, see Essentials pages 47-51.

⊜ Sleeping

Comitán *p666, map p666*

Accommodation is inferior in quality and almost twice the price of San Cristóbal de las Casas.

B Los Lagos de Montebello, Blv Belisario Domínguez 144, corner of 3era Av, T963-632 0657, www.hotellagosdemontebello.com. Noisy but good.

C Internacional, Av Central Sur Belisario Domínguez 22, T963-632 0110, near plaza. Comfortable, attractive rooms with cable TV. There's a decent restaurant attached. Rooms are cheaper in older part of hotel.

D Pensión Delfín, Av Central Sur Belisario Domínguez 21, on plaza, T963-632 0013, www.hotel-delfin-comitan.com. A pleasant colonial-style building with comfortable rooms, garden and courtyard. There's parking and cable TV. Recommended, but don't leave valuables near windows even if they appear closed.

E Hospedaje Montebello, 1a Calle Nte Pte 10, T963-632 3572, 1 block from **Delfín**. Clean, sunny courtyard, laundry, fax service, TV, internet and parking. Friendly. Recommended.

E San Fransisco, 1a Av Ote Nte 13A, T963-110 6244. The rooms are clean and economical, but still slightly pokey. There's cable TV and hot water 24 hrs.

Route to Tapachula *p668*

C Ik-Lumaal, 1era Av Nte 6, near Zócalo, Arriaga, T966-662 1164. A/c, clean, quiet, good restaurant.

C-D Posada San Rafael, Zanatepec. Very comfortable motel, safe parking.

D El Estraneo, Av Central, Pijijiapan, T918-645 0264. Very nice, parking in courtyard.

D Galilea, Av Hidalgo 111 and Callejón Ote, Tonalá, T966-663 0239. With bath, a/c, good, basic cheap rooms on 1st floor, balconies, on main square, with good restaurants.

D Motel La Misión, Tapanatepec, on Highway 190 on northern outskirts, T971-717 0140. Fan, hot water, clean, TV, hammock outside each room, affiliated restaurant, very good.

E Sabrina, Pijijiapan. Nice, clean and quiet, safe parking.

E-F Colonial, Callejón Ferrocarril 2, Arriaga, next to bus station, T966-662 0856. Clean, friendly, quiet, limited free parking.

F Iris, Callejón Ferrocarril, Arriaga, near bus station. Bath, fan, basic.

Camping

José's Camping Cabañas (ask *colectivo* from Tonalá to take you there, US$0.60 extra), at east edge of Puerto Arista, follow signs. Canadian run, well organized, clean, laundry, restaurant (including vegetarian), library.

Tapachula *p669*

A Loma Real, Ctra Costera 200, Km 244, T962-626 1440, www.hotellomareal.com.mx, 1 km north of city. Large, upmarket hotel with comfortable rooms, suites and bungalows. With pool, gym and parking.

B-C San Francisco, Av Central Sur 94, T962-620 1000, www.sucasaentapachula.com. 15 mins from centre, this large, professional hotel has clean, modern rooms with a/c and hot water. With pool, gym, bar and restaurant.

C Galerías Hotel & Arts, 4a Av Norte 21, T962-642 7596, www.galeriasartshotel.com. Modern hotel with an arty focus, 5% discount if paying by cash, a/c, cable TV, hot and cold water, Wi-Fi and parking in the centre of town.

D Plaza Guizar, 4a Av Nte 27, T962-626 1400. Clean, tidy and basic, with fan. Plenty of rooms and sitting space. Good views over the city from balcony.

D Santa Julia, next to OCC terminal, T962-626 2486. Bath, phone, TV, a/c, clean, good. Unusually does discounts in high season. Its location next to main road and bus station can make it very noisy, particularly early mornings.

F Cinco de Mayo, Calle 5 Pte y Av 12 Norte. Cheap rooms in need of a good clean. Convenient for Talismán *colectivos*, which leave half a block away.

F San Román, Calle 9 Pte between Av 10 y 12 Norte. Very cheap motel-style place. Parking for cars and bikes. Friendly.

🍴 Eating

Comitán *p666, map p666*

🍴 **Café Gloria**, 1a Calle Sur Pte 47. The place for a wholesome evening meal.

🍴-🍴 **Doña Chelo**, Calle Central Pte 67, corner 4a Av Poniente Nte. Traditional Mexican fare and seafood.

🍴 **Acuario**, Av Central Belisario Domínguez, No 9, on the plaza, opposite the church. In league with Vick's/Vicky restaurant (the sign actually has two different names) next door. Does good Mexican-standard grub, *tortas* and *comida corrida* but double check your bill before paying. Also good for cheap breakfasts.

Cafés

Café Quiptic, part of Centro Cultural Rosario Castellanos, on the plaza. Good Chiapanecan coffee and snacks.

Tapachula *p669*

There are a couple of decent and reasonably priced eateries along the south side of the main plaza, for breakfast, lunch and dinner.

🍴-🍴 **Vainilla Cous Cous**, 4a Av Sur 6, T962-118 0083. Tue-Sat 0930-2330 and Sun 0930-1700. Run by a chef and a photographer, this is a stylish new place with some of the best dining in town. International cuisine with a North African twist, fine wines and a gallery next door. Live music Fri and Sat 2100-2200, also does yoga classes Mon and Thu.

▼▼ El 7 Mares, Díaz Ordáz 11. Decent seafood, sometimes pricey.

▼ Prontos, 1era Calle Poniente 11, T962-626 5680. Meat and more meat dishes, 0600-2200.

▲ Activities and tours

Tapachula p669
Agencia de Viajes Chavez Tours, next door to Hotel Santa Julia, near the OCC bus station. Tours in the area surrounding Tapachula.
Crucero Tours, 1a Poniente 8, T962-625 2257, www.crucerotours.com.mx. Tours to ruins, mountains, beaches and *fincas*.

Tenosique and Río San Pedro route p672
Several agencies in Palenque offer tours to Flores by minibus and/or taxi, boat and public bus, via Tenosique, La Palma and El Naranjo. You probably won't meet any other travellers, so be prepared to fund the whole trip yourself, especially in low season.

⊖ Transport

Comitán p666, map p666
Bus
Buses to **San Cristóbal de las Casas**, OCC, many daily, 2 hrs, US$3, also 2 luxury services US$4. To **Mexico City** (TAPO and Norte), OCC, 1410, 1550, 1640, 2040, 15½ hrs, US$64. To **Puebla**, same timings as for Mexico City, 13 hrs, US$57. To **Palenque**, OCC, 1345, 2115, 6½ hrs, US$14.50. **Tapachula**, OCC, 6 daily, 5½ hrs, US$12. To **Tuxtla Gutiérrez**, OCC, many daily, 3 hrs, US$5.50. To **Cancún**, OCC, 1345, 20½ hrs, US$56.

Frequent combis, shuttles and taxis for nearby **Ciudad Cuauhtémoc** (US$2, every 15 mins) for **Guatemala**, **San Cristóbal** (US$2.50 combi, US$3 taxi, 1hr 10 mins),

Tuxtla and other nearby places leave from the main boulevard, Belisario Dominguez, a few blocks north from the OCC terminal. Since these are only marginally cheaper than the more comfortable buses, this is only worth it if you're very strapped for cash or time.

Ciudad Cuauhtémoc p668
Bus
Long distance OCC 1st-class buses to **Comitán**, 1215, 1240, 1855, 2200, 1½ hrs, US$3. There are also frequent *de paso* 2nd-class buses and combis. To **Mexico City**, OCC, 1240, 17 hrs, US$68. To **San Cristóbal de las Casas**, OCC, 1215, 1240, 1855, 2200, 3 hrs, US$6. To **Tuxtla Gutiérrez**, OCC, 1240, 1855, 2200, 4½ hrs, US$12. To **Tapachula** (via Arriaga), OCC, 1100, 1445, 1755, 2045, 4½ hrs, US$8. If crossing the border, there are hourly buses to **Huehuetenango** or **Quetzaltenango** departing from the Guatemalan side.

Shuttles To **Comitán**, various operators, frequently from the border, 1½ hrs, US$3. More national connections in Comitán, including services to **San Cristóbal** and **Tuxtla**.

Arriaga p668
Bus To many destinations, mostly 1st class, to **Mexico City**, 1600, 1705, 1930, 2150 12-13 hrs, US$50; **Tuxtla Gutiérrez**, with Fletes y Pasajes at 1400 and 1600, 4 hrs, US$7; **Oaxaca**, 6 hrs, US$7.

Tapachula p669
Air
Tapachula airport is 25 mins from town centre and has flights to **Mérida** and **Mexico City** daily, for other destinations connect via **Mexico City**. Combis to airport from Calle 2 Sur 40, T962-625 1287, US$1, taxis US$7. From airport to border, minibuses charge US$26 for whole vehicle, so share with others, otherwise take *colectivo* to 2nd-class bus terminal and then a bus to Ciudad Hidalgo.

Airline offices Aviacsa, Central Nte and 1a Pte, T962-625 4030. Aeroméxico, Central Ote, T962-626 7757.

Bus

OCC bus **Mexico City-Guatemala City** takes 23 hrs, with a change at the border to Rutas Lima. There is a variety of direct buses to many parts of Central America from Tapachula all leaving from the OCC Terminal. TICA Bus has some of the best connections; to **Guatemala City**, US$12; to **San Salvador**, US$24; to **Managua**, US$43; to **San José**, US$59; to **Panamá City**, US$79. Also Linea Dorada, www.tikalmayanworld.com, operates buses between **Tapachula** and **Flores**, **Guatemala City** and **Río Dulce**, **Guatemala** and **Galgos** go to **Guatemala City** and **San Salvador**. To **Mexico City**, OCC, 9 daily, 17 hrs, including 3 luxury services, from US$64. To **Oaxaca**, OCC, 1915, 12 hrs, US$25. To **Puebla**, OCC, 5 daily, 14½ hrs, US$55; and 3 luxury services, US$65-82. To **San Cristóbal de las Casas**. OCC, 0730, 0915, 1430, 1730, 2120, 7½ hrs, US$16. To **Tuxtla Gutiérrez**, OCC, 12 daily, 7 hrs, US$18; many 2nd class and 2 luxury services, 1545 and 2359, US$33. To **Salina Cruz**, OCC, 2245, 7 hrs, US$20. To **Tehuantepec**, OCC, 1915, 7½ hrs, US$19.

Border with Guatemala: Talismán
p670

Bus There are few buses between the Talismán bridge and **Oaxaca** or **Mexico City**; it is advisable therefore to travel to **Tapachula** for connection; delays can occur at peak times.

Taxi Combi vans run from near the Unión y Progreso bus station, about US$1; *colectivo* from outside **Posada de Calú** to Talismán, US$0.60, also from Calle 5 Pte between Av 12 y Av 14 Norte. Taxi **Tapachula-Talismán**, negotiate fare to about US$2. A taxi from Guatemala to Mexican Immigration will cost US$2, but it may be worth it if you are in a hurry to catch an onward bus.

Hitchhikers should note that there is little through international traffic at the Talismán bridge.

Border with Guatemala: Ciudad Hidalgo *p670*

Bus From Calle 7 Pte between Av 2 Norte and Av Central Norte, Tapachula, buses go to 'Hidalgo', US$1.

Río Usumacinta route *p671*

Shuttles From Frontera Corozal to **Palenque**, hourly, 0400-1600, 2½ hrs, US$5. Operators include Transportes Chamoan. Crossing the Río Usumacinta at **Frontera Corozal** by *lancha* costs US$3.50.

Boat

Lanchas to **Yaxchilán**, 30 mins, US$50-60. To **Bethel**, 30 mins, US$30 for 2 people, US$40 for 4. To **Técnica**, US$5 per person. To **Piedras Negras**, 2-3 days, prices negotiable (around US$100-US$150 per person) and best organized as a group. Ensure your papers are in order before crossing the border. Visit immigration offices on both sides for exit and entry stamps, and keep a photocopy of your passport handy for possible military inspection.

Tenosique and Río San Pedro route *p672*

To **Emiliano Zapata**, ADO, many daily, 1 hr, US$3. To **Mexico City**, ADO, 1700, 15 hrs, US$57. To **Villahermosa**, ADO, frequent services, 3½ hrs, US$10.

Shuttle vans To **Palenque**, hourly with Transportes Palenque, US$3.50. Or catch a Villahermosa bus to **El Crucero de la Playa** and pick up a frequent *colectivo* from there.

❶ Directory

Comitán *p666, map p666*
Banks Bancomer, on plaza will exchange Amex TCs, bring ID; 2 others on plaza, none

change dollars after 1200; also a *casa de cambio*. **Embassies and consulates** Guatemala, 1era Calle Sur Pte 35, 3rd floor (hard to spot, look for Guatemalan flag on top of building) , T963-672 0491. Mon-Fri 0800-1300, 1400-1700, visas US$25 (not needed by most nationalities), tourist card US$10 (even for those for whom it should be free), valid 1 year, multiple entry. **Internet** Several internet cafés in the streets near the main plaza, US$0.50/hr. **Post office** Av Central Sur Belisario Domínguez, 2 blocks south of main plaza.

Ciudad Cuauhtémoc *p668*

Banks Don't change money with the Guatemalan customs officials: the rates they offer are worse than those given by bus drivers or in banks (and these are below the rates inside the country). There is nowhere to change TCs at the border and bus companies will not accept cheques in payment for fares. 300 m after the border, however, you can get good rates for Tcs at the **Banco de Café**. The briefcase-and-dark-glasses brigade changes cash on the Guatemalan side only, but you must know in advance what the rates are.

Tapachula *p669*

Banks Avoid the crowds of streetwise little boys at the border; exchange is better in the town, bus station gives a good rate (cash only). **Banamex**, Blv Díaz Ordaz, 0830-1230, 1400-1600, disagreement over whether TCs are changed. **Casa de Cambio Tapachula**, Av 4 Norte y Calle 3 Pte, changes dollars, TCs, pesos, quetzales and lempiras (open late Mon-Sat), but not recommended, poor rates. Very difficult to change money or find amenities open at weekends. Try the **supermarket**. HSBC is the only bank open Sat, changes TCs. **Embassies and consulates** El Salvador, Calle 2 Ote 31 and Av 7 Sur (confusingly the old location of the Guatemalan consulate), T962-626 1252, Mon-Fri 0900-1700. Guatemalan, Av 5a Norte 5, 3rd floor, Mon-Fri 1000-1500 and 1600-1800; tourist card US$10, friendly and quick, take photocopy of passport, photocopier 2 blocks away. **Immigration** Av 14 Norte 57, T962-626 1263. **Laundry** There is a laundry, at Av Central Norte 99 between Calle 13 y 15 Ote, US$3 wash and dry, 1 hr service, about 2 blocks from **OCC** bus station, open Sun. Also on Av Central Norte between Central Ote y Calle 1, opens 0800, closed Sun. **Telephone** Several long-distance phone offices, including **Esther**, Av 5 Norte 46; **La Central**, Av Central Sur 95; **Monaco**, Calle 1 Pte 18.

Contents

Yucatán Peninsula

At a glance

◉ **Getting around** Buses, ferries, domestic flights.

◉ **Time required** 2 weeks to sample the major attractions.

☼ **Weather** Temperatures in the high 20s most of the year, particularly on the coast. Rainy season starts in June, but rains are usually short showers.

✖ **When not to go** Good at any time. Aug-Sep is hurricane season, but these are rare.

Isla
Contoy

Río
Lagartos   El Cuyo   Holbox

Chiquilá
San Felipe   San   Río   Isla Mujeres
Felipe   Lagartos   Puerto Juárez
295   Tizimín   Cancún
Telchac   Santa   Yucatán   307
Progreso   Puerto   Clara   176   Espita   Ek-Balam   Puerto
Yucalpetén   Motul   Centonillo   Xcan   180   Morelos
Sisal   Chelem   Izamal   Valladolid   Chemax   Playa del
Chicxulub   Mérida   Pisté   Carmen
Hunucmá   Hoctún   Libre   Chichén   Cobá   Paamul
Omán   Unión   Itzá   Tekom   Akumal   Cozumel
Celestún   Maxcanú   Tekax   Sotuta   Xel-Há   Tulum
Celestún   Muna   Ticul   Oxcutzcab   Ichmul   Tulum   Isla de
Bekal   YUCATÁN   295   Cozumel
Calkini   Uxmal   Tekax   Peto   Tihosuco   Punta Allen
Hecelchakán   Bolonchén   Santa Rosa   307   Bahía de la
180   de Rejón   Felipe   Ascensión
Tenabó   Chencoyi   Carrillo   Bahía del
Campeche   Hopolchén   Puerto   Espíritu Santo
Lerma   Cayal   Edzná   194   Reserva de   Punta Herrera
Seybaplaya   Dzibalchén   Polyuc   la Biosfera
Sián Ka'an
Champotón   QUINTANA ROO   Cafetal   Puerto
Bravo
Aquiles Serdán   CAMPECHE   Ursulo Galván   Majahual   Banco
Sabancuy   Bacalar   Chinchorro
Isla   261   Silvituc   Francisco   Chetumal
Aguada   Becán   Villa
Ciudad del   Calakmul Biosphere Reserve   Xpujil   186   Xcalak
Carmen   Laguna de   Francisco   Chicanná   Kohunlich   Corozal
Términos   Escárcega   Hormiguero
180   Calakmul
186   Río Bec

Gulf of
Mexico

Nueva
Coahuila   BELIZE

ABASCO   N

Emiliano   50 km
Catazajá   Zapata   Tulipán
Macuspana   La   50 miles
Palenque   Palma
Palenque   Tenosique de
Pino Suárez

Agua Azul   Misol-Há
Frontera
Echeverría

MEXICO   GUATEMALA

San Juan   Ocosingo
Chamula   Toniná
San Cristóbal de   Yaxchilán
las Casas   CHIAPAS
190   Amatenango   Bonampak
del Valle   Benemérito
Las Rosas
nustiano   Reserva de
Carranza   Comitán   la Biosfera
Montes Azules
Presa de
la
Angostura
Ciudad
Cuauhtémoc   La Mesilla

Motozintla   GUATEMALA   HONDURAS
de Mendoza
Mapastepec
200
Huixtla
Tapachula   Talismán
Ciudad Hidalgo

The Yucatán Peninsula, which includes the states of Campeche, Yucatán and Quintana Roo, is sold to tourists as the land of Maya archaeology and Caribbean beach resorts. And there's no denying it, the warm turquoise sea, fringed with fine white-sand beaches and palm groves of the 'Mayan Riviera' are second to none.

It would almost be a crime not to tread the beaten path to the sensational ruins at Chichén Itzá, Uxmal and Tulum, but it more than pays to explore beyond the main itineraries to visit some of the lesser-known Maya sites such as Cobá, Edzná or Dzibilchaltún, or the imposing Franciscan monastery and huge pyramid at Izamal.

There are flamingo feeding grounds at Celestún and Río Lagartos and more than 500 other species of bird, many of which are protected in Sian Ka'an biosphere reserve, which covers 4500 sq km of tropical forest, savannah and coastline. Ever since Jacques Cousteau filmed the Palancar Reef in the 1960s, divers have swarmed to the clear waters of Cozumel, the 'Island of the Swallows', to marvel at the many species of coral and other underwater plants and creatures, in what has become one of the most popular diving centres in the world.

Also popular, but more specialized, is diving in the many *cenotes* (sink holes), including the famous Nohooch Nah Chich, part of the world's largest underground cave system.

Background

The Maya arrived in the Yucatán about 1200 BC and built monumental stone structures during the centuries up to the end of the pre-Classic period (AD 250). Later they rebuilt their cities, but along different lines, probably due to the influence of the Toltecs, who arrived in the ninth and 10th centuries. Each city was autonomous and in rivalry with other cities.

The Spaniards found little to please them when they first arrived in the Yucatán: no gold, no concentration of natives; nevertheless Mérida was founded in 1542 and the few natives were handed over to the conquerors in *encomiendas* (see page 764). The Spaniards found them difficult to exploit: even as late as 1847 there was a major revolt, fuelled by the inhumane conditions in the *henequén* (sisal) plantations. It was the expropriation of Maya communal lands that was the main source of discontent, however. In July 1847, a conspiracy against the *Blancos*, or ruling classes from Mexico, was uncovered in Valladolid and one of its leaders, Manuel Antonio Ay, was shot. This precipitated a bloody war, known as the *Guerra de Castas* (Caste War) between the Maya and the *Blancos*. The first act was the massacre of all the non-Maya inhabitants of Tepich, south of Valladolid. The Maya took control of much of the Yucatán, laying siege to Mérida, only to abandon it to sow their crops in 1849. This allowed the governor of Yucatán to counterattack, ruthlessly driving the Maya into southern Quintana Roo. In Chan Santa Cruz (now named Felipe Carrillo Puerto), one of the Maya leaders, José María Barrera, accompanied by Manuel Nahuat, a ventriloquist, invented the 'talking cross', a cult that attracted thousands of followers. The sect, called Cruzob, established itself and renewed the resistance against the government from Mexico City. It was not until 1901 that the Mexican army retook the Cruzob's domain.

Ins and outs

A good paved road runs from Coatzacoalcos to Villahermosa, Campeche and Mérida (Route 180). An inland road from Villahermosa to Campeche gives easy access to Palenque (see page 654). If time is limited, take a bus from Villahermosa to Chetumal via Escárcega, which can be done overnight as the journey is not very interesting (unless you want to see the Maya ruins off this road). From Chetumal travel up the coast to Cancún, then across to Mérida. Route 307, from Chetumal to Cancún and Puerto Juárez, is paved and in very good condition. Find flight details from the US and Mexico City under Mérida, Cancún and Cozumel.

Quintana Roo state, on the eastern side of the Yucatán Peninsula, has become the largest tourist area in Mexico with the development of Cancún, the parallel growth of Isla Mujeres, Cozumel and the 100-km corridor south of Cancún to Tulum. There can be insufficient buses at peak times; old second-class buses may be provided for first-class tickets and second-class buses take far too many standing passengers. There is also a lack of information services. Where beaches are unspoilt they often lack all amenities. Many cheaper hotels are spartan.

Warning Many tourists speak no Spanish, so price hikes and short-changing have become common, making those places very expensive if you are not careful. In the peak (winter) season, prices increase by about 50%.

Quintana Roo (and especially Cozumel) is the main area for diving and water sports in the Yucatán Peninsula. However, water sports in Quintana Roo are expensive and touristy, although operators are generally helpful; snorkelling is often in large groups. On the more accessible reefs the coral is dying and there are no small coral fish. Further from the shore, though, there is still much reef life to enjoy. Take care not to damage these sensitive reefs further.

A useful website on the Yucatán is www.yucatantoday.com.

State of Campeche

Colonial architecture is plentiful, there are several fortified convents and Campeche city itself was fortified to protect its citizens from pirate attacks. There are many archaeological sites, most demonstrating influences of Chenes-style architecture. Relax at the resorts of Sihoplaya and Seybaplaya while watching pelicans dive and iguanas scurry. You can explore the beaches at Ciudad del Carmen, eat delicious red snapper and buy a cheap, but sturdy, Panama hat. The exhibits at several museums reflect the seafaring nature of the area and the pre-Conquest civilization that occupied these lands. The official government website is at www.campeche.gob.mx. ▶▶ *For listings, see pages 688-692.*

Tabasco to Campeche ●❶❷❸ ▶▶ *pp688-692.*

There are two routes to Campeche from the neighbouring state of Tabasco: the inland Highway 186, via Escárcega, with two toll bridges (US$5), and the slightly longer coastal route through Ciudad del Carmen, Highway 180; both converge at Champotón, 66 km south of Campeche. Highway 186 passes Villahermosa's international airport and runs fast in a sweeping curve 115 km east to the Palenque turn-off at Playas del Catazajá; beyond, off the highway, is **Emiliano Zapata**, a busy cattle centre, with a Pemex station.

Francisco Escárcega → *Colour map 3, B2. Phone code: 982.*

Escárcega is a major hub and crossroads for travellers on their way south to the states of Tabasco and Chiapas, north to Mérida in the state of Yucatán, east to Maya sites in Campeche and Quintana Roo states, and further east to the city of Chetumal and the border with Belize. The town itself is not particularly enticing, set on a busy highway with a dusty wild west atmosphere. If stuck here overnight, there are a couple of hotels, a bank and several cheap restaurants.

Coast road to Campeche ●❶❷❸❹❺ ▶▶ *pp688-692.*

Although Highway 180 via Ciudad del Carmen is narrow, crumbling into the sea in places and usually ignored by tourists intent on visiting Palenque, this journey is beautiful and more interesting than the fast toll road inland to Campeche. The road threads its way from Villahermosa 78 km north through marshland and rich cacao, banana and coconut plantations, passing turnings to tiny coastal villages with palm-lined but otherwise mediocre beaches. It finally leads to the river port of **Frontera**, where Graham Greene began the research journey back in 1938, leading to the publication of *The Lawless Roads* and later on *The Power and the Glory*.

The road briefly touches the coast at the Tabasco/Campeche state border, then runs east alongside a series of lakes (superb for birdwatching) to the fishing village of **Zacatal** (93 km), at the entrance to the tarpon-filled **Laguna de Términos**. Just before Zacatal is the lighthouse of **Xicalango**, an important pre-Columbian trading centre. A bridge crosses the lake's mouth to Ciudad del Carmen.

Ciudad del Carmen → *Colour map 3, B1. Phone code: 938.*

This is the hot, bursting-at-the-seams principal oil port of the region. Most streets in the centre are numbered; even numbers generally run west-east, and odd south-north. Calle

20 is the seafront *malecón* and the road to the airport and university is Calle 31. There is also a **tourist office** ⓘ *main plaza, near the seafront malecón, 0800-1500.*

The attractive, cream-coloured **cathedral** (Parroquia de la Virgen del Carmen), begun in 1856, is notable for its stained glass. **La Iglesia de Jesús** (1820) opposite Parque Juárez is surrounded by elegant older houses. Nearby is the Barrio del Guanal, the oldest residential quarter, with the church of the **Virgen de la Asunción** (1815) and houses with spacious balconies and tiles brought from Marseilles.

There are several good **beaches** with restaurants and water sports, the most scenic being **Playa Caracol** (southeast of the centre) and **Playa Norte**, extensive white-sand beaches with safe bathing. Fishing excursions can be arranged through the **Club de Pesca** ⓘ *Nelo Manjárrez, at Calle 40 and Calle 61, T938-382 0073.* Coastal lagoons are rich in *sábalo* (tarpon) and bonefish.

Maya ruins in south Campeche

Calakmul → *Colour map 3, B2.*
ⓘ *Daily 0800-1700, US$3, cars US$4, entrance to biosphere reserve US$4. Take Route 186 until Km 95, then turn off at Conhuás, where a paved road leads to the site, 60 km.*

Three hundred kilometres southeast from Campeche town, and a further 60 km off the main Escárcega–Chetumal road, the ruins of Calakmul are only accessible by car. It is believed to be one of the largest archaeological sites in Mesoamerica, and certainly the biggest of all the Maya cities, with somewhere in the region of 10,000 buildings in total, many of them as yet unexplored. At the centre of the site is the Gran Plaza, overlooked by a pyramid whose base covers 2 ha. One of the buildings grouped around the **Gran Plaza** is believed, due to its curious shape and location, to have been designed for astronomical observation. The **Gran Acrópolis**, the largest of all the structures, is divided into two sections: **Plaza Norte**, with the ball court, was used for ceremonies; **Plaza Sur** was used for public activities. The scale of the site is vast, and many of the buildings are still under excavation, which means that information on Calakmul's history is continually being updated.

Xpujil → *Colour map 3, B3. Phone code: 983.*
ⓘ *Daily, 0800-1700, US$2.60, US$2.60 to use a video camera.*

The architectural style is known as Río Bec, characterized by heavy masonry towers simulating pyramids and temples, usually found rising in pairs at the ends of elongated buildings. The main building at Xpujil features an unusual set of three towers, with rounded corners and steps that are so steep they are unscalable, suggesting they may have been purely decorative. The facade features the open jaws of an enormous reptile in profile on either side of the main entrance, possibly representing Itzamná, the Maya god of creation. Xpujil's main period of activity was AD 500-750; it began to decline around 1100. It can be very peaceful and quiet in the early mornings, compared with the throng of tourist activity at the more accessible sites such as Chichén Itzá and Uxmal.

The tiny village of Xpujil, on the Chetumal–Escárcega highway, is located for the three sets of ruins in this area: Xpujil, Becán and Chicanná. There are two hotels and a couple of shops. Guided tours to the more remote sites, such as Calakmul and Río Bec, can be organized through either of the two hotels, costing about US$20-30 per person for the whole day. Second-class buses from Chetumal and Escárcega stop on the highway in the centre of Xpujil, some 800 m east of the two hotels.

Becán → *Colour map 3, B3. Phone code: 996.*
ⓘ *Daily 0800-1700, US$3.*

Seven kilometres west of Xpujil, Becán is another important site in the Río Bec style. Its most outstanding feature is a moat, now dry, surrounding the entire city and believed to be one of the oldest defence systems in Mesoamerica. Seven entrance gates cross the moat to the city. The large variety of buildings on the site are a strange combination of decorative towers and fake temples, as well as structures used as shrines and palaces.

Chicanná → *Colour map 3, B2. Phone code: 981.*
ⓘ *Daily 0800-1700. US$2.60.*

Located 12 km from Xpujil, Chicanná is considered to have been a small residential centre for the rulers of the ancient regional capital of Becán. It was occupied during the late pre-Classic period (300 BC-AD 250); the final stages of activity at the site have been dated to the post-Classic era (AD 1100). Typical of the Río Bec style are numerous representations of the Maya god Itzamná, or Earth Mother. One of the temples has a dramatic entrance in the shape of a monster's mouth, with fangs jutting out over the lintel and more fangs lining the access stairway. A taxi will take you from Xpujil bus stop to Becán and Chicanná for US$10, including waiting time.

Hormiguero → *Colour map 3, B2.*
ⓘ *Daily 0800-1700, free.*

Twenty kilometres southwest of Xpujil, Hormiguero is the site of one of the most important buildings in the Río Bec region, whose elaborate carvings on the facade show a fine example of the serpent's-mouth entrance, with huge fangs and a gigantic eye.

Río Bec

Río Bec is south off the main highway, some 10 km further along the road to Chetumal. Although the site gave its name to the architectural style seen in this area, there are better examples of it at the ruins listed above. Río Bec is a cluster of several smaller sites, all of which are difficult to reach without a guide.

Champotón → *Colour map 3, A2.*

Back near the west coast of Campeche state, Route 261 runs 86 km due north from Escárcega through dense forest to the Gulf of Mexico, where it joins the coastal route at Champotón, a relaxed but run-down fishing and shrimping port spread along the banks of Río Champotón. In pre-Hispanic times it was an important trading link between the area and Guatemala, as well as the rest of Central Mexico; Toltec and Maya mingled here, followed by the Spaniards. On the south side of town can be seen the remnants of a 1719 fort built as a defence against the pirates who frequently raided this coast.

Sihoplaya and Seybaplaya → *Colour map 3, A2. Phone code: 982.*

Continuing north, Highways 180 and 261 are combined for 17 km until the latter darts off east on its way to Edzná and Hopelchen (which bypasses Campeche). A 66-km toll *autopista* is much quicker than the old Highway 180, as it bypasses Champotón and Seybaplaya. But from the old Highway 180, narrow and slow with speed bumps, you can reach the resort of Sihoplaya (regular buses from Campeche US$1). A short distance further north is the larger resort of Seybaplaya. This is an attractive place where fishermen mend nets and pelicans dry their wings along the beach. On the highway is the open-air **Restaurant Veracruz,** serving delicious red snapper (fresh fish at the seafront public market is also good value), but in general there is little to explore. Only the **Balneario Payucán** at the north end of the bay makes a special trip worthwhile; this is probably the closest decent beach to Campeche (33 km), although a little isolated. The water and sand get filthier the closer you are to the state capital, but there is still much reef life to enjoy.

Campeche 🚌🚗🚻⊛🛏️🔺🍴ℹ️ ➺ pp688-692. Colour map 3, A2.

→ *Phone code: 981.*

Campeche's charm is neatly hidden behind traffic-blocked streets, but once inside the city walls it reveals itself as a good place to break your journey out to the Yucatán. The town of Campeche has been declared a World Heritage Site by UNESCO and the clean streets of brightly painted houses give the town a relaxed Caribbean feel. The waterfront Malecón is a beautiful promenade where people stroll, cycle and walk in the evenings.

Ins and outs

Like many Yucatán peninsular towns, Campeche's streets in the Old Town are numbered rather than named. Even numbers run north-south beginning at Calle 8 (no one knows why) near the Malecón, east to Calle 18 inside the walls; odd numbers run east (inland) from Calle 51 in the north to Calle 65 in the south. Most of the points of interest are within this compact area. A full circuit of the walls is a long walk; buses marked 'Circuito Baluartes' provide a regular service around the perimeter.

The **state tourist office** ① *T01800-226 7324, www.campeche.travel, daily 0800-2100, but not always staffed until late*, is on the Malecón in front of the **Palacio de Gobierno** (walk down Calle 61 towards the sea). There is also another smaller **tourist office** ① *on the north eastern corner of the Zócalo, next to the cathedral, daily 0900-2100*. For a good orientation take the Centro Histórico tour. A regular **tourist tram** ① *runs daily on the hour from 0900, 45 mins, US$5.70, adults, children half price, English and Spanish spoken*, departs from the main plaza.

Background

Highway 180 enters the city as the Avenida Resurgimiento, passing either side of the huge **Monumento al Resurgimiento**, a stone torso holding aloft the Torch of Democracy. Originally the trading village of Ah Kim Pech, it was here that the Spaniards, under Francisco Hernández de Córdoba, first disembarked onto Mexican soil (22 March 1517) to replenish their water supply. For fear of being attacked by the native population, they quickly left, only to be attacked later by the locals further south in Champotón, where the appalling weather conditions forced them to land. It was not until 1540 that Francisco de Montejo managed to conquer Ah Kim Pech, founding the city of Campeche on 4 October 1541, after failed attempts in 1537 and earlier in 1527. The export of local dyewoods, *chicle*, timber and other valuable cargoes soon attracted the attention of buccaneers, who constantly raided the port from their bases on Isla del Carmen, then known as the Isla de Tris. Combining their fleets for one momentous swoop, they fell upon Campeche on 9 February 1663, wiping out the entire city and slaughtering its inhabitants. Five years later the Crown began fortifying the site, the first Spanish colonial settlement to be completely walled. Formidable bulwarks, 3-m thick and 'a ship's height', as well as eight *baluartes* (bastions) were built over the next 36 years. All these fortifications soon put a stop to pirate attacks and Campeche prospered as one of only two Mexican ports to have had the privilege of conducting international trade, (the other was Veracruz). After Mexican Independence from Spain, the city declined into an obscure fishing and logging town. Only with the arrival of a road from the 'mainland' in the 1950s and the oil boom of the 1970s has Campeche begun to see visitors in any numbers, attracted by its historical monuments and relaxed atmosphere (*campechano* has come to mean a pleasant, easy-going person).

Sights

Of the original walls, seven of the *baluartes* and an ancient fort (now dwarfed by two big hotels on the seafront) remain. Some of these contain museums (see below).

The heart of the city is the Zócalo, where the austere Franciscan **cathedral** (1540-1705) has an elaborately carved facade; inside is the Santo Entierro (Holy Burial), a sculpture of Christ on a mahogany sarcophagus with a silver trim. There is plenty of shade under the trees in the Zócalo, and a small bandstand with a snack bar.

Campeche

Sleeping	La Posada del Angel 4	Casa Vieja Los Arcos 9
América 7	Monkey Hostal Campeche 3	Iguana Azul 5
Baluartes 1	Reforma 12	Lafitte's 6
Colonial 9	Regis 5	La Parroquia 7
Del Mar 2	Teresita 6	La Pigua 4
Francis Drake 10		Marganzo 2
Hostal San Carlos 11	Eating	Tulum 3
La Parroquia 8	Campeche 1	Turix Café 8

Right in front of the Zócalo is the **Baluarte de Nuestra Señora de la Soledad**, the central bulwark of the city walls, from where you can do a walking tour of the **Circuito Baluartes**, the remains of the city walls, US$0.70 for the tour, US$2 including entry to the **Baluarte de San Carlos** museum. Heading east, you will come to the **Puerta del Mar**, formerly the entrance for those permitted to enter the city from the sea, which used to come up to this point. Next along the *circuito* is a pair of modern buildings, the **Palacio de Gobierno** and the **Congreso**. The latter looks like a flying saucer, and makes for a bizarre sight when viewed with the 17th-century Baluarte de San Carlos in the background. Heading west on the continuation of the *circuito*, you will come to **Templo de San José**, on Calle 10, an impressive baroque church with a beautifully tiled facade. It has been deconsecrated, and is now an educational centre. Back on the *circuito*, you will next reach the **Baluarte de Santa Rosa**, now the home of the tourist information office. Next is **Baluarte de San Juan**, from which a large chunk of the old city wall still extends, protecting you from the noisy traffic on the busy road beyond it. The wall connects with **Puerta de la Tierra** ① *a Luz y Sonido (light and sound) show takes place, US$4, Tue, Fri and Sat 2000 (for information, contact the tourist office)*. The continuation of the *circuito* will take you past the **Baluarte de San Francisco**, and then past the market, just outside the city walls. **Baluarte de San Pedro** flanks the northeast corner of the city centre, and now houses another museum. The *circuito* runs down to the northwest tip of the old city, where the **Baluarte de Santiago** houses the Botanical Gardens.

Further from the city walls is the **Batería de San Luis**, 4 km south from the centre along the coast road. This was once a lookout post to catch pirates as they approached the city from a distance. The **Fuerte de San Miguel**, 600 m inland, is now a museum. A 20-minute walk along Avenida Miguel Alemán from Baluarte de Santiago is the **San Francisco** church, 16th century. Nearby are the **Portales de San Francisco**, a beautifully restored old entrance to the city, with several good restaurants in its shadow.

The **Museo de la Arquitectura Maya** ① *Baluarte de Nuestra Señora de la Soledad, Tue-Sun, 0930-1730, US$2.20*, has three rooms of Maya stelae and sculpture. **Jardín Botánico Xmuch'Haltun** ① *Baluarte de Santiago, daily 0900-1700, free*, is a small collection of tropical plants and flowers in a peaceful setting. The **Fuerte de San Miguel** ① *Tue-Sun 0900-1730, US$2.60*, on the Malecón 4 km southwest, is the most atmospheric of the forts; it houses the **Museo Arqueológico**, with a well-documented display of pre-Columbian exhibits including jade masks and black funeral pottery from Calakmul and recent finds from Jaina.

Around Campeche

Lerma is a small industrial suburb of Campeche, with large shipyards and fish-processing plants; the afternoon return of the shrimping fleet is a colourful sight. The nearest decent beaches are at Seybaplaya (see page 683), 20 km south of Campeche. There, the beaches are clean and deserted; take your own food and drink as there are no facilities. Crowded, rickety buses marked 'Lerma' or 'Playa Bonita' run from Campeche, US$1.

Maya sites east of Campeche ⊛ ›› *pp688-692.*

A number of city remains (mostly in the Chenes architectural style) are scattered throughout the rainforest and scrub to the east of Campeche; little excavation work has been done and most receive few visitors. Getting to them by the occasional bus service is possible in many cases, but return trips can be tricky. The alternatives are one of the tours run by some luxury hotels and travel agencies in Campeche (see Tour operators, page 691) or renting a vehicle (preferably with high clearance) in Campeche or Mérida. Whichever way you travel, carry plenty of drinking water – shops and facilities are few and far between.

Edzná → *Colour map 3, A2.*
ⓘ *Daily 0800-1700, US$3, light and sound show US$8, 2000 summer, 1900 winter; guides available.*

The closest site to the state capital is Edzná, reached by the highway east to Cayal, then a right turn onto Highway 261, a distance of 61 km. A paved shortcut southeast through China and Poxyaxum (good road) cuts off 11 km; follow Avenida Nacozari out along the railway track. Situated in a tranquil valley with thick vegetation on either side, Edzná was a huge ceremonial centre, occupied from about 600 BC to AD 200, built in the simple Chenes style mixed with Puuc, Classic and other influences. The centrepiece is the magnificent, 30-m-tall, 60-sq-m **Temple of the Five Storeys**, a stepped pyramid with four levels of living quarters for the priests and a shrine and altar at the top; 65 steep steps lead up from the Central Plaza. Opposite is the **Paal U'na**, Temple of the Moon. Excavations are being carried out on the lesser temples, but most of Edzná's original sprawl remains hidden. Some of the stelae remain; others can be seen in various Campeche museums. There is also a good example of a *sacbé* (sacred road), leading to one of the smaller temples. Edzná is worth a visit in July (exact date varies), when a Maya ceremony to honour the rain god Chac is held. Beware that there are no facilities to buy food or drink here, take water. ▸▸ *See Transport, page 692.*

Hochob
ⓘ *Daily 0800-1700. US$2.20.*

Of the more remote and even less-visited sites beyond Edzná, Hochob and Dzibilnocac are the best choices for the non-specialist. Hochob is reached by turning right at **Hopelchén** on Highway 261, 85 km east of Campeche. This quiet town has an impressive fortified 16th-century church but only one hotel. From Hopelchén a narrow paved road leads 41 km south to the village of **Dzibalchén**. Don Willem Chan will guide tourists to Hochob (he also rents bikes for US$3.50 per day), is helpful, and speaks English. Directions can be obtained from the church at Dzibalchén; you need to travel 18 km southwest on a good dirt road (no public transport, hopeless quagmire in the rainy season) to the village of **Chenko**, where locals will show the rest of the way (4 km through the jungle). Bear left when the road forks; it ends at a small *palapa* and, from here, the ruins are 1 km uphill with a magnificent view over the surrounding forest. Hochob once covered a large area but, as at Edzná, only the hilltop ceremonial centre (the usual Plaza surrounded by temple buildings) has been properly excavated; although many of these are mounds of rubble. The one-room temple to the right (north) of the plaza is the most famous structure: deep-relief patterns of snakes moulded in stucco across its facade were designed to resemble a mask of the rain god Chac. A fine reconstruction of the building is on display at the **Museo de Antropología** in Mexico City. Early morning second-class buses serve Dzibalchén, but returning to Campeche later in the day is often a matter of luck.

Dzibilnocac
ⓘ *Daily 0800-1700. Free.*

Twenty kilometres northeast of Dzibalchén at **Iturbide**, this site is one of the largest in Chenes territory. Only three temples have been excavated here; the first two are in a bad state of preservation, but the third is worth the visit: a unique narrow edifice with rounded corners and remains of a stucco facade. A second-class bus leaves Campeche for the village of Dzibalchén, taking three hours, US$5, times vary, check at bus station. If driving your own vehicle, well-marked 'km' signs parallel the rocky road to Iturbide (no accommodation); bear right around the tiny Zócalo and its attendant yellow church and continue (better to walk in the wet season) for 50 m, where the right branch of a fork leads to the ruins. Other sites in the region require 4WD transport and appeal mostly to archaeologists.

Becal

Becal is the centre for weaving Panama hats, here called *jipis* (pronounced 'hippies') and ubiquitous throughout the Yucatán. Many of the town's families have workshops in cool, backyard underground caves, which are necessary for keeping moist and pliable the shredded leaves of the *jipijapa* palm from which the hats are made. Most vendors give the visitor a tour of their workshop, but are quite zealous in their sales pitches. Prices are better for *jipis* and other locally woven items in the **Centro Artesanal, Artesanías de Becaleña** ⓘ *Calle 30 No 210*, than in the shops near the plaza.

⦿ State of Campeche listings

For Sleeping and Eating price codes and other relevant information, see Essentials pages 47-51.

⦿ Sleeping

Francisco Escárcega *p681*
C Motel Akim Pech, T982-824 0240, on Villahermosa highway. A/c or fans and bath, reasonable rooms, restaurant in motel, another across the street, **Pemex** station opposite.
D Escárcega, Justo Sierra 86, T982-824 0187, around the corner from the bus terminal (turn left, then left again from the terminal). Clean, bath, parking, hot water, good restaurant, small garden.
D María Isabel, Justo Sierra 127, T982-824 0045. A/c, restaurant, comfortable, back rooms noisy from highway.

Coast road to Campeche *p681*
D San Agustín, Pino Suárez, Frontera, T913-332 0037. Very basic, fan, no mosquito net.
E Chichén Itzá, Aldama 671, Frontera, T913-332 0097. Not very clean, fan, shower, hot water.

Ciudad del Carmen *p681*
Hotel accommodation is generally poor value and can be difficult to come by Mon-Thu; book in advance and arrive early. For convenience sake, you'll find a handful of 'economical' hotels opposite the **ADO** bus station.

B Euro, Calle 22, No 208, T938-382 3044, reganem@prodigy.net.mx. Large and modern, 2 restaurants, pool, a/c, disco, built to accommodate the flow of Pemex traffic.
C Lino's, Calle 31, No 132, T938-382 0788. A/c, pool, restaurant, also has 10 RV spaces with electricity hook-ups.
E Zacarías, Calle 24, No 58B, T938-382 3506. Modern, some cheaper rooms with fans, brighter a/c rooms are better value.

Campeche *p684, map p685*
Prices are generally high. Beware of over charging and, if driving, find a secure car park.
AL-A Baluartes, Av 16 de Septiembre 128, T981-816 3911, www.baluartes.com.mx. The rooms in this large hotel are well-maintained and comfortable. There's a host of services including pool, restaurant and a disco.
AL-A Del Mar, Av Ruiz Cortines 51 near El Malecón, T981-811 9191, www.delmar hotel.com.mx. Pleasant rooms with sea views and balconies, all the mod cons and free Wi-Fi in the rooms. Pool, gym, good bar and restaurant (see Lafitte's Restaurant, page 690).
B Francis Drake, Calle 12, No 207, between Calle 63 and Calle 65, T981-811 5626, www.hotelfrancisdrake.com. Well-equipped rooms, restaurant and bar.
C América, Calle 10, No 252, T981-816 4588, www.hotelamericacampeche.com. This

centrally located hotel is clean, tidy, well staffed and has Wi-Fi. Price includes breakfast.

D La Posada Del Angel, Calle 10, No 307, T981-816 7718 (on the side entrance of the cathedral). Clean, carpeted, comfortable rooms, some without windows, some with a/c (**B**). Friendly and recommended.

D Reforma, Calle 8, No 257, between Calle 57 and Calle 59, T981-816 4464. Has a/c, hot water, TV and internet. Bit grotty, but right in the centre 1 min from the main plaza.

D Regis, Calle 12 148, between 55 and 57, T981-816 3175. Housed in a lovely old colonial building, clean, spacious rooms.

E Colonial, Calle 14, No 122, between Calle 55 and Calle 57, T981-816 2630. Rooms have fans or a/c (more expensive) and hot water. Slightly scruffy, but very friendly.

E-F Hostal San Carlos, Calle 10, No 255, Barrio Guadalupe, a few blocks out of town, T981-816 5158, info@hostelcampeche.com.mx. Private rooms and dorms, price includes continental breakfast. Well-kept hostel with hot and cold water, internet, currency exchange, laundry service and bike rental.

E-F La Parroquia, Calle 55, between 10 y 12, T981-816 2530, www.hostalparroquia.com. Offers 3 dorms and 3 private rooms; breakfast is included. Services include kitchen, internet, bike rental, TV room and terrace.

E-F Monkey Hostel Campeche, Calle 57, No 10, overlooking the Zócalo, T981-811 6605, www.hostalcampeche.com. Dorms and private rooms. There are lockers, laundry, internet, bike hire, kitchen and book exchange. Price includes breakfast and can arrange local tours. Luggage storage US$2.

F Teresita, Calle 53, No 31, 2 blocks east of plaza, T981-816 4534. Very basic rooms with fans, no hot water. Cheapest in town, but good if you're on a tight budget – ask for a room with shared bath for extra savings.

Camping

Club Náutica, 15 km south of town, on the highway out of Campeche, Km 180. T981-8167545. Big campsite with good facilities. Good spot for a few days' stay.

⦿ Eating

Francisco Escárcega *p681*

There are few places used to serving tourists, but there is a good and cheap *lonchería* opposite the bus terminal.

♥♥ Titanic, corner of the main highway and the road to the train station (turn right out of the bus terminal then right again). For a more expensive meal with a/c.

Ciudad del Carmen *p681*

♥♥ El Kiosco Calle 33 s/n, between Calle 20 and Calle 22, in **Hotel del Parque** with view of the Zócalo. Modest prices, eggs, chicken, seafood and Mexican dishes.

♥♥ Vía Veneto, in the EuroHotel (see Sleeping, page 688). Good, if quite pricey breakfasts.

♥♥-♥ El Pavo, tucked away down Calle 36A, in Colonia Guadalupe. This superb, family-run restaurant serves excellent seafood dishes at low prices. Very popular with the locals.

♥♥-♥ La Fuente, Calle 20. A 24-hr snack bar with view of the Laguna.

♥ La Mesita, outdoor stand across from the old ferry landing. Well-prepared shrimp, seafood cocktails, extremely popular all day.

Cafés

There are several tiny cafés along the pedestrian walkway (Calle 33) near the Zócalo. Inexpensive snacks are available in the thriving market.

Café Vadillo, Calle 33. The best coffee in town.

Casa Blanca, Calle 20, between Calle 29 and Calle 27. This popular and modern café-bar overlooks the seafront Malecón and serves filter coffee, cappuccinos and espressos.

Mercado Central, Calle 20 and 37, not far northwest of Zócalo.

Campeche *p684, map p685*

Campeche is known for its seafood, especially *camarones* (large shrimps), *esmedregal* (black snapper) and *pan de cazón* (baby hammerhead shark sandwiched between corn tortillas with black beans). Food stands in the market serve *tortas*, tortillas, *panuchos* and *tamales* but hygiene standards vary.

₩₩-₩₩ Casa Vieja Los Arcos, Calle 10, No 319A, on the Zócalo, T981-100 5522. Beautiful balcony dining atop the *portales* overlooking the main plaza. Specializes in local dishes, including *camarones*. Romantic setting.

₩₩-₩₩ Lafitte's, inside **Hotel del Mar** (see Sleeping). Pirate-themed restaurant with Mexican dishes and good bar. There's a terrace overlooking the sea.

₩₩ La Pigua, Av Miguel Alemán 179A, www.lapigua.com.mx. Clean, modern restaurant specializing in seafood.

₩₩ Tulum, Calle 59, No 9, between Calle 10 and Calle 12. Open from lunchtime. Friendly, modern restaurant, international menu.

₩₩-₩ Campeche, right on the Zócalo, opposite the cathedral. Extensive menu, big portions and very good value.

₩₩-₩ Iguana Azul, Calle 55, between Calle 10 and Calle 12. Bar with live music and dancing, snacks and a good selection of drinks.

₩₩-₩ La Parroquia, part of the hotel of the same name (see Sleeping, page 689). This busy locals' joint is open 24 hrs. It serves meat, fish and Mexican staples. Good breakfasts and a decent and economical *menú del día*. Free Wi-Fi. Recommended.

₩₩-₩ Marganzo, Calle 8. An elegant and widely respected fine-dining establishment. It boasts an interesting menu of seafood and *comida típica*, and regularly lays on music with a trio of musicians and regional dancing.

₩ Turix Café, Calle 57 between Calle 10 and Calle 12. This little cute café and art space a short hop from the Zócalo does a variety of salads, sandwiches and good desserts.

● Entertainment

Campeche *p684, map p685*
Cultural centres
Centro Cultural Casa 6, Calle 57, between Calle 8 and Calle 10, 0900-2100. Daily

US$0.35. Housed in a handsome old colonial building, on the main plaza and contains some fine pieces of period furniture.

Instituto Nacional de Antropología e Historia (INAH), T981-811 1314, www.inah.gob.mx. Dedicated to the restoration of Maya ruins in the state of Campeche, and supports local museums. INAH can be visited for information regarding any of the sites in the state.

● Festivals and events

Frontera *p681*
3-13 Dec Feria Guadalupana, celebrating the Virgin Guadalupe, features a host of events, including an agricultural show, bullfights, *charreadas* and regional dances.

Ciudad del Carmen *p681*
15-30 Jul Fiesta, a cheerful event honouring the town's patroness.

Campeche *p684, map p685*
6 Jan Fiesta de Polk Kekén in Lerma suburb features traditional dances.
Feb/Mar Carnival, with parades and floats and stunning Carnival Queen pageantry.
7 Aug State holiday.
Sep Feria de San Román, 2nd fortnight.
4-13 Oct Fiesta de San Francisco.

Maya sites east of Campeche *p686*
13-17 Apr A traditional Honey and Corn Festival is held in Holpechén.
3 May Día de la Santa Cruz.

Champotón
8 Dec Feast of the Immaculate Conception, celebrated with a joyous festival of a few days.

Becal
May Feria del Jipi, a 4- to 5-day festival. Dates vary.

O Shopping

Campeche *p684, map p685*
Excellent cheap **Panama** hats *(jipis)*; cheaper at the source in Becal. Handicrafts are generally cheaper than in Mérida. There are souvenir shops along Calle 8, such as **Artesanía Típica Naval**, Calle 8, No 259, with exotic bottled fruit like *nance* and *marañón*. Many high-quality craft items are available from the **Exposición** in the Baluarte San Pedro, and **Casa de Artesanías Tukulná**, Calle 10, No 333, between Calle 59 and Calle 31, open daily 0900-2000.

The **market**, from which most local buses depart, is beside Alameda Park at the south end of Calle 57. Plenty of bargains here. **Super 10** supermarket behind the post office has an excellent cheap bakery inside.

▲ Activities and tours

Campeche *p684, map p685*
Tour operators
Intermar Campeche, Av 16 de Septiembre 128, T981-816 9006, www.travel2 mexico.com. Tours, transport, flights.
Viajes Chicanná, Av Augustín Melgar, Centro Comercial Triángulo del Sol, Local 12, T981-811 3503. Flight bookings to Cuba, Miami and Central America.
Viajes del Golfo, Calle 10, No 250 D, T981-816 1745, viajesdelgolfo@hotmail.com. Domestic and international flights; tours to sites.
Viajes Xtampak Tours, Calle 57, No 14, T981-816 6473, www.xtampak.com. Daily transport to ruins including Edzná, Calakmul, Uxmal and Palenque – they collect from your hotel with 24 hrs' notice. Discount for groups; guide services at extra cost.

☉ Transport

Tabasco to Campeche *p681*
Bus Buses from Emiliano Zapata, all ADO (1st-class bus terminal): **Tenosique**, almost hourly, 1½ hrs US$3; **Villahermosa**, frequent services, 2½ hrs, US$7; **Mérida**, 0900, 1120, 1500, 2200, 7 hrs, US$23.50; **Escárcega**, 0900, 1500, 2 hrs, US$7.50; **Chetumal**, 2100, 6 hrs, US$20.

Francisco Escárcega *p681*
Bus Most buses from Chetumal or Campeche drop you off at the 2nd-class terminal on the main highway. To buy tickets, you have to wait until the outgoing bus has arrived; sit near the ticket office and wait for them to call your destination, then join scrum at the ticket office. There is a 1st-class ADO terminal west of the 2nd-class terminal; 20-min walk. From there, 1st-class buses go to **Palenque**, 0410, 0630, 1250, 2335, 3hrs, US$10; **Chetumal**, frequent services, 4 hrs, US$13; **Campeche**, frequent services, 2 hrs, US$7.50; **Mérida**, frequent, 4½ hrs, US$16.50. From the 2nd-class terminal there are buses to **Campeche**, 16 a day, 2½ hrs, US$5.60; **Chetumal**, 3 a day, 4 hrs, US$11; **Playas de Catazajá**, connecting with *colectivos* to **Palenque**, frequent, US$5; **Villahermosa**, 12 a day, 4 hrs, US$12.50. *Colectivos* to **Palenque** leave from outside the 2nd-class terminal, US$5.50.

Ciudad del Carmen *p681*
Air
Carmen's airport (CME, 5 km east of the plaza) currently only has direct flights to Mexico City, from where there are connections to the rest of the country.
Airline office Mexicana, Calle 22 y 37, T938-382 1171.

Bus
The ADO bus terminal is some distance from the centre. Take a bus or *colectivo* marked 'Renovación' or 'ADO'; they leave from around the Zócalo. There are ADO and ATS services to **Campeche**, 2½-3 hrs, US$11; **Mérida**, 6 hrs, US$21; and **Villahermosa** via the coast, 3 hrs, US$9, where connections can be made to **Palenque**. Buses travel via **Escárcega**, where you connect to **Chetumal** and **Belize**.

Car

Car hire Auto-Rentas del Carmen, Calle 33, No 121, T938-382 2376. Budget, Calle 31, No 117, T938-382 0908.

Xpujil *p682*

Bus There are 4 buses a day to **Escárcega**, between 1030 and 1500, 3 hrs, US$6. 8 buses a day run to **Chetumal**, 2 hrs, US$5. Change at Escárcega for buses to **Palenque** or **Campeche**. 1st-class buses do not stop at Xpujil.

Campeche *p684, map p685*
Air

Modern, efficient airport (CPE) on Porfirio, 3 km northeast. **Aero México** direct daily to **Mexico City**, T981-816 3109. There are no buses, but taxis charge around US$8.00. Or walk 100 m down service road (Av Aviación) to Av Nacozari, turn right (west) and wait for 'China–Campeche' bus to Zócalo.

Bus

The easiest way to reach **Edzná** is on a tourist minibus. They depart hourly and operators include **Xtampak**, Calle 57, No 14, between Calle 10 and Calle 12, T981-812 8655, xtampac_7@ hotmail.com, US$21.50 (but prices drop depending on number of passengers); and **Transportadora Turistica Jade**, Av Diaz Ordaz 67, T981-827 4885, jade_tour@ hotmail.com, US$14. To get there on public transport, catch a morning bus to **Pich** and ask to be let out at Edzná – it's a 15-min walk from the highway. Be sure to ask the driver about return schedules, as buses are quite infrequent and subject to change. There's no accommodation at Edzná and hitchhiking isn't recommended. Buses to **Seybaplaya** leave from the tiny Cristo Rey terminal opposite the market, 9 a day from 0615, 45 mins, US$1.

Long distance The main bus station is about 3 km south of the centre. Buses from outside the terminal travel the *circuito* road. A taxi costs US$2.20. The 2nd-class bus terminal is about 1 km east of the centre along Av Gobernadores, but services are steadily moving to the main terminal. To **Cancún**,

7 daily with **ADO** and **ADO GL**, 7 hrs, US$24.50-32; **Chetumal**, 1200, 6½ hrs, US$20; **Ciudad del Carmen**, frequent ADO services, 3 hrs, US$11; **Escárcega**, frequent services, 2 hrs, US$7.50; **Mérida**, frequent ADO services, 2½ hrs, US$9.50; **Mexico City**, ADO services at 1231, 2226, 2345, 18 hrs, US$68, and 2 ADO GL services at 1430, 1635, 16 hrs, US$82; **San Cristóbal de las Casas**, OCC service at 2145, 11 hrs, US$25; **Veracruz**, luxury service only, ADO GL at 2215, 11½ hrs, US$52.50; **Villahermosa**, frequent ADO services, 6-7 hrs, US$21.

Car

Car hire Mayanature, Av Ruiz Cortines 51, inside Hotel del Mar, T981-811 9191. Hertz and Autorent car rentals at airport.

ⓘ Directory

Ciudad del Carmen *p681*
Banks Banamex, Calle 24, No 63, or Banorte, Calle 30 and 33. **Post office** Calle 22, No 136.

Campeche *p684, map p685*
Banks American Express, T981-811 1010, Calle 59, Edificio Belmar, of 5, helpful for lost cheques, etc. Plenty of places to get cash on credit cards and ATMs. Banorte, Calle 8, No 237, between Calle 57 and Calle 59; Mon-Fri 0900-1700; HSBC, Calle 10, No 311, Mon-Fri 0900-1700, Sat 0900-1500; Santander Serfin, Calle 57, No 8. **Immigration** The Oficina de Migración is inside the Palacio Federal. **Internet** Many internet places including Cybercafé Campeche, Calle 61 between Calle 10 and 12, 0900-1300, US$1.50 per hr. **Laundry** Laundry Antigua Calle 57 between Calle 12 and 14, US$1 per kg. **Medical services** Red Cross, T981-815 2411. **Post office** Av 16 de Septiembre (Malecón) and Calle 53 in Edificio Federal); Mon-Fri 0800-2000, Sat 0900-1300 for *Lista de Correos*, registered mail, money orders. **Telephone** Telmex, Calle 8 between Calle 51 y 53, free; Calle 51, No 45, between Calle 12 and 14.

State of Yucatán

Chichén Itzá, Oxkintoc, Uxmal, Kabah and Labná are just a few of the archaeological sites strewn throughout the State of Yucatán. Try not to miss Dzibilchaltún; the intrusion of European architecture is nowhere more startling than here. The region's many cenotes (deep sinkholes created by the disintegration of the dry land above an underground river) were sacred to the Maya, who threw precious jewels, silverware and even humans into their depths; many are perfect for swimming. On the coast, boat trips are organized to observe pelicans, egrets and flamingos in their natural habitat. It is possible to visit some of the impressive henequén (sisal) haciendas in the more rural areas and admire the showy mansions that line the Paseo de Montejo in Mérida. ►► *For listings, see pages 704-716.*

North to Mérida

At **Maxcanú**, the road to Muná and Ticul branches east; a short way down there's the recently restored Maya site of **Oxkintoc** ① *daily 0800-1700, US$2.50.* The **Pyramid of the Labyrinth** can be entered (take a torch) and there are other ruins, some with figures. Ask for a guide at the village of **Calcehtoc**, which is 4 km from the ruins and from the Grutas de Oxkintoc (no bus service). Highway 180 continues north towards Mérida through a region of numerous *cenotes*, soon passing a turn-off to the turn-of-the-century Moorish-style *henequén* (sisal) hacienda at **San Bernardo**, one of a number in the state that can be visited; an interesting colonial **museum** chronicling the old Yucatán Peninsula tramway system is located in its lush and spacious grounds. Running beside the railway, the highway continues 47 km to its junction with the inland route at **Umán**, a *henequén* processing town with another large 17th-century **church** and convent dedicated to St Francis of Assisi; there are many *cenotes* in the flat surrounding limestone plain. If driving, Highway 180/261 is a divided four-lane motorway for the final 18-km stretch into Mérida. There is a ring road around the city.

Mérida ⊙❷❶❸❸⊙▲❸❸ ►► *pp704-716. Colour map 3, A2.*

→ *Phone code: 999.*

The capital of Yucatán state and its colonial heart, Mérida is a bustling city full of grand, Spanish-style buildings in varying states of repair. There is continual activity in the centre, with a huge influx of tourists during the high season mingling with busy Meridanos going about their daily business. Although the city has been developed over many years for tourism, there is plenty of local flavour to discover off the beaten track. Attempts to create a sophisticated Champs Elysées-style boulevard in the north of the city at Paseo Montejo have not been quite successful; the plan almost seems to go against the grain of Mérida's status as an ancient city, which has gradually evolved into a place with its own distinct identity.

Ins and outs

Getting there All buses from outside Yucatán State arrive at the CAME terminal on Calle 70 between Calle 69 y 71, a few blocks from the centre. There is another bus terminal around the corner on Calle 69, where buses from local destinations such as Uxmal arrive. The airport is 8 km from the city, bus 79 takes you to the centre. Taxis to the centre from the airport charge US$6.50. ►► *See Transport, page 713.*

Getting around You can see most of Mérida on foot. Although the city is big, there is not much to concern the visitor outside a few blocks radiating from the main plaza. The VW Beetle taxis are expensive, due to their scarcity; fares start at US$2.50 for a short journey. *Colectivo* buses are difficult to locate; they appear suddenly on the bigger roads in the city, you can flag them down anywhere. They terminate at the market; flat fare US$0.35.

Tourist information The main **tourist office** ① *Calle 60 y Calle 57 (just off Parque Hidalgo), Mon-Sat 0800-2100, Sun 0800-2000*, is very helpful. There are other tourist offices on the main plaza by the Palacio Municipio and at the airport. You'll find good information online at www.yucatan.travel and www.yucatantoday.com.

Safety Mérida is a safe city, with its own **tourist police** ① *T999-942 0060*, recognizable by their brown and white uniforms.

Best time to visit During July and August, although very hot, Mérida is subject to heavy rains during the afternoon, it gets very humid in spring, but the winter months are usually clear and pleasant.

Sights

The city revolves around the large, shady Zócalo site of the **cathedral**, which was completed in 1559 and is the oldest cathedral in Latin America. It contains the Cristo de las Ampollas (Christ of the Blisters), a statue carved from a tree that burned for a whole night after being hit by lightning, without showing any signs of damage. Placed in the church at Ichmul, it then suffered only slight charring (hence the name) when the church was burned to the ground. To the left of the cathedral on the adjacent side of the plaza is the **Palacio de Gobierno**, built in 1892. It houses a collection of enormous murals by Fernando Castro Pacheco, depicting the struggle of the Maya to integrate with the Spanish. The murals can be viewed until 2000 every day. **Casa de Montejo** is on the south side of the plaza, a 16th-century palace built by the city's founder, now a branch of the bank **Banamex**. Away from the main Plaza along Calle 60 is Parque Hidalgo, a charming tree-filled square, which borders the 17th-century **Iglesia de Jesús**. A little further along Calle 60 is the **Teatro Peón Contreras**, built at the beginning of the 20th century by an Italian architect, with a neoclassical facade, marble staircase and Italian frescoes.

There are several 16th- and 17th-century churches dotted about the city: **La Mejorada**, behind the Museum of Peninsular Culture (Calle 59 between Calle 48 and 50), **Tercera Orden**, **San Francisco** and **San Cristóbal** (beautiful, in the centre). The **Ermita**, an 18th-century chapel with beautiful grounds, is a lonely, deserted place 10 to 15 minutes from the centre.

Museo de Antropología e Historia ① *Paseo de Montejo 485, Tue-Sat 0800-1700, Sun 0800-1400, US$3*, housed in the beautiful neoclassical Palacio Cantón, has an excellent collection of original Maya artefacts from various sites in the Yucatán state. The displays are well laid out, but the explanations are all in Spanish. This museum offers a good overview of the history of the Maya.

Museo Macay ① *Calle 60, on the main plaza, www.macay.org, daily 1000-1730, free*, has a permanent exhibition of Yucatecan artists, with temporary exhibits by contemporary local artists. **Museo de Arte Popular** ① *Calle 59 corner 50, Barrio de la Mejorada, Tue-Sat 0930-1830, Sun 0900-1400, free*, has a permanent exhibition of Maya art, handicrafts and clothing, with a good souvenir shop attached. **Museo de la Canción Yucateca** ① *Calle 57 between Calle 50 and 48, Tue-Fri 0900-1700, Sat-Sun 0900-1500, free*, in the Casa de la

Mérida

Sleeping 🛏️
Casa Becil **1** *D2*
Casa Bowen **2** *D2*
Casa Mexilio **10** *B1*
Casa San Angel **18** *A3*
Casa San Juan **16** *D2*
Colonial **3** *B2*
Dolores Alba **4** *C4*
El Caminante **8** *D2*
Gobernador **5** *B2*
Gran **6** *C3*
Hostal Zócalo **17** *C2*
La Misión de
  Fray Diego **7** *C2*
Las Monjas **9** *C2*
Margarita **11** *C2*
Medio Mundo **19** *B2*
Mucuy **12** *B3*
Nómadas Youth
  Hostal **13** *B2*
Posada Toledo **14** *B3*
San José **15** *C2*
Trinidad **22** *B2*

Eating 🍴
Alberto's Continental **5** *B2*
Amaro **1** *B2*
Café Alameda **16** *B3*
Café Chocolate **23** *B3*
Café El Hoyo **15** *B2*
Café La Habana **8** *B2*
Café Petropolis **2** *D2*
El Colón Sorbetes y
  Dulces Finos **10** *C3*
El Nuevo Tucho **4** *B3*
El Trapiche **3** *C2*
El Tucho **7** *B3*
Flor de Santiago **14** *B1*
Italian Coffee
  Company **9** *C2*
Jugos California **6** *C2*
La Casa de Frida **24** *C2*

La Vía Olympo **11** *C2*
Los Almendros **7** *B4*
Marlín Azul **18** *B2*
Marys **21** *C3*
Mérida **20** *C2*
Pórtico del Peregrino **17** *B2*
Villa Maria **13** *B1*
Vito Corleone's Pizza **19** *B2*

Bars & clubs 🍸
El Cielo **25** *A4*
La Parranda **22** *C3*
Panchos **12** *B2*

Cultura, has an exhibition of objects and instruments relating to the history of music in the region. **Pinacoteca Juan Gamboa Guzmán** ① *Calle 59 between Calle 58 and 60, Tue-Sat 0900-1700, Sun 0800-1400, US$2*, is a gallery showing old and contemporary paintings and sculpture. Fans of John Lloyd Steven's seminal travelogue *Incidents of Travel in Central America, Chiapas and Yucatán* should check out **Casa Catherwood** ① *Calle 59 between Calle 72 and 74, daily 0900-1400 and 1700-2100, US$3.50*. Dedicated to Steven's companion and illustrator, Mr Catherwood, this museum contains stunning colour lithographs of Mayan ruins, as they were found in the 19th century.

Around Mérida ❶❷❸❹❺ » *pp704-716. Colour map 3, A2.*

Celestún → *Phone code: 988.*
A small, dusty fishing resort west of Mérida much frequented in summer by Mexicans, Celestún stands on the spit of land separating the Río Esperanza estuary from the ocean. The long beach is relatively clean except near the town, although rising afternoon winds usually churn up silt and there is little shade. There are beach restaurants with showers. A plain Zócalo watched over by a simple stucco church is at the centre of what little that happens in town. Even the unmarked post office ① *Mon-Fri 0900-1300*, is a private residence the rest of the week.

The immediate region is a biosphere reserve and a great area for birdwatching, created to protect the thousands of migratory waterfowl that inhabit the lagoons; fish, crabs and shrimp also spawn here, and kingfishers, black hawks, wood storks and crocodiles may sometimes be glimpsed in the quieter waterways. In the winter months Celestún plays host to the largest flamingo colony in North America, perhaps more than 20,000 birds – in the summer most of the flamingos leave Celestún for their nesting grounds in the Río Lagartos area. If visiting independently, **boat trips** to view the wildlife are best arranged just after the river bridge, 1 km back along the Mérida road, where they are cheaper (US$40 for one six people, plus US$3 per person for the reserve entrance fees, 1½ hours). If staying on the bus till the end of the road, boat owners sometimes charge as much as US$100 per boat, but there's good swimming here and a restaurant serving excellent seafood. Make sure your boatman takes you through the mangrove channel and to the Baldiosera freshwater spring in addition to visiting the flamingos. It is often possible to see flamingos from the bridge early in the morning and the road to it may be alive with egrets, herons and pelicans. January to March is the best time to see them. It's important to wear a hat and use sunscreen. Hourly buses to Mérida's terminal at Calle 50 and 65, two hours, US$3.40.

Progreso and around → *Phone code: 969.*
Thirty-six kilometres north of Mérida, Progreso has the nearest beach to the city. It is a slow-growing resort town, with the facilities improving to service the increasing number of US cruise ships that arrive every Monday and Wednesday. Progreso is famous for its industrial pier, which at 6 km is the longest in the world. It has been closed to the public since someone fell off the end on a moped and it seems unlikely to reopen any time soon. The beach is long and clean and the water is shallow and good for swimming.

Five kilometres east of Progreso is the resort of **Chicxulub**; it has a quiet beach, on which there are many boats and much seaweed. Small restaurants sell fried fish served with tortillas, mild chilli and *cebolla curtida* (pickled onion). Chicxulub is reputed to be the site of the crater made by a meteorite crash 65 million years ago, which caused the extinction of the dinosaurs. (The site is actually offshore on the ocean floor.) The beaches on this coast are often deserted and, between December and February, 'El Norte' wind blows in every 10 days or so, making the water turbid and bringing in cold, rainy weather.

Dzibilchaltún
① Daily 0800-1700. US$5.60

Halfway between Mérida and Progreso turn right for the Maya ruins of Dzibilchaltún. This unique city was founded as early as 1000 BC, according to carbon dating. The site is in two halves, connected by a *sacbé* (sacred road). The most important building is the **Templo de Las Siete Muñecas** (Temple of the Seven Dolls), at the east end, which has been partly restored. At the western end is the ceremonial centre with temples, houses and a large plaza in which one chapel, simple and austere, stands out in stark contrast. At its edge is the **Cenote Xlaca** reaching a depth of 44 m, with very clear water (you can swim in it, take mask and snorkel as it is full of fascinating fish); there's an interesting nature trail starting halfway between the temple and the *cenote*, rejoining the *sacbé* halfway along. The **museum** is at the entrance by the ticket office (site map available). Combis stop here en route to **Chablekal**, a village along the same road.

The Convent Route ●🚌🚍 ▶▶ pp704-716.

The route takes in Maya villages and ruins, colonial churches, cathedrals, convents and *cenotes*. It is best to be on the road by 0800 with a full gas tank. Get on the Periférico to Ruta 18 (signs say Kanasín, not Ruta 18). At **Kanasín**, the restaurant La Susana is known especially for local delicacies like *sopa de lima*, *salbutes* and *panuchos*. Follow the signs to **Acanceh**, which has an unusual combination of a Grand Pyramid, a colonial church and a modern church, right on the same small plaza (see Tlatelolco in Mexico City, page 112). About four blocks away is the Temple of the Stuccoes, with hieroglyphs. Eleven kilometres further south is **Tecoh**, with an ornate church and convent dedicated to the Virgin of the Assumption. There are some impressive carved stones around the altar. The church and convent both stand on the base of a large Maya pyramid. Nearby are the caverns of **Dzab-Náh**; you must take a guide as there are treacherous drops into *cenotes*. Next on the route is **Telchaquillo**, a small village with a spartan chapel, but it also has a lovely *cenote* in the plaza, with carved steps for easy access.

Mayapán and around
① Daily 0800-1700. US$2.

A few kilometres off the main road to the right you will find the Maya ruins of Mayapán, a walled city with 4000 mounds, six of which are in varying stages of restoration. Mayapán, along with Uxmal and Chichén Itzá, once formed a triple alliance, and the site is as big as Chichén Itzá, with some buildings being replicas of those at the latter site. The restoration process is ongoing. Mayapán is easily visited by bus from Mérida (every 30 minutes from from 0830 until 1600 from terminal at Calle 50 and 65 behind the municipal market, one hour, US$2.50 to Telchaquillo). It can also be reached from Oxcutzcab.

Thirty kilometres along the main road is **Tekit**, US$1.40 from same terminal, a large village containing the church of San Antonio de Padua, with many ornate statues of saints. The next village, 7 km further on, is called **Mama**, US$1.80 (all return tickets to these villages are cheaper than buying two one-ways), with what is believed to be the oldest church on the route, famous for its ornate altar, frescoes on the wall and bell-domed roof. Another 9 km is **Chumayel**, bus US$2.15, where the legendary Maya document *Chilam Balam* was found. Four kilometres ahead is **Teabo**, with a striking 17th-century church. Next comes **Tipikal**, a small village with an sombre-looking church.

Maní

Twelve kilometres further on is Maní, bus US$2.50, one of the most important stops on this route. Here you will find a large church, convent and museum with explanations in English, Spanish and one of the Maya languages. It was here that Fray Diego de Landa ordered important Maya documents and artefacts to be burned, during an intense period of Franciscan conversion of the Maya people to Christianity. When Diego realized his great error, he set about trying to write down all he could remember of the 27 scrolls and hieroglyphs he had destroyed, along with 5000 idols, 13 altars and 127 vases. The text, entitled *Relation of Things in Yucatán*, is still available today, unlike the artefacts. To return to Mérida, head for Ticul, to the west, then follow the main road via Muná.

Ticul and Oxkutzcab → *Phone code: 997. Colour map 3, A2.*

Eighty kilometres south of Mérida, Ticul (bus US$2.50) is a pleasant little village known for its *huipiles,* the embroidered white dresses worn by the older Maya women. You can buy them in the tourist shops in Mérida, but the prices and quality of the ones in Ticul will be much better. It is also a good base for visiting smaller sites in the south of Yucatán state, such as Sayil, Kabah, Xlapak and Labná (see page 699).

Sixteen kilometres southeast of Ticul is Oxkutzcab, a good centre for catching buses to Chetumal, Muná, Mayapán and Mérida (US$2.50). It's a friendly place with a market by the plaza and a church with a 'two-dimensional' facade on the other side of the square.

Grutas de Loltún and around

① *Tours daily, 0930, 1100, 1230, 1400, 1500 and 1600. Free, but it's recommended you tip the obligatory guide, 1 hr 20 mins. Recommended.*

Nearby, to the south, are the caverns and pre-Columbian vestiges at Loltún (supposedly extending for 8 km). Take a pick-up (US$0.30) or truck from the market going to Cooperativa (an agricultural town). To return, flag down a passing truck. Alternatively, take a taxi, US$10 (can be visited from Labná on a tour from Mérida). After Oxkutzcab on Route 184 is **Tekax** with **La Ermita** restaurant serving excellent Yucatacan dishes at reasonable prices. From Tekax a paved road leads to the ruins of **Chacmultún**. From the top the views are beautiful. There is a caretaker. All the towns between Muná and Peto, 14 km northeast of Oxkutzcab off Route 184, have large old churches. Beyond the Peto turn-off the scenery is scrub and swamp as far as the Belizean border.

The Puuc Route

Taking in the four sites of Kabah, Sayil, Xlapak and Labná, as well as Uxmal, this journey explores the hilly (or *puuc* in Maya) region to the south of Mérida. All five sites can be visited in a day on the **Ruta Puuc** bus ① *departs from the first-class bus station (next to CAME) in Mérida every day at 0800, US$10, entry to sites not included.* This is a good whistlestop tour, but does not give you much time at each of the ruins, but five sites in one day is normally enough for most enthusiasts; if you want to spend longer seeing these sites, stay overnight in Ticul.

Kabah

① *Daily 0800-1700. US$2.50.*

On either side of the main road, 37 km south of Uxmal and often included in tours of the latter, are the ruins of Kabah. On one side there is a fascinating **Palace of Masks** (*Codz-Poop*), whose facade bears images of Chac. The central chamber is entered via a huge Chac mask whose curling snout forms the doorstep. On the other side of this wall, beneath the figure of the ruler, Kabal, are impressive carvings on the door arches. This side of the road is mostly reconstructed; across the road the outstanding feature is a reconstructed arch marking the start of the *sacbé* (sacred road), which leads all the way to Uxmal, and several stabilized, but unscalable mounds of collapsed buildings being renovated. The style is Classic Puuc.

Sayil, Xlapak and Labná

① *Daily 0800-1700. Entrance US$5 at each site.*

Dating from AD 800-1000, Sayil has an interesting palace. The central motif on the upper part of the facade is a broad mask with huge fangs, flanked by two serpents surrounding the grotesque figure of a descending deity. From the upper level of the palace you can see a tiny ruin on the side of a mountain called the **Nine Masks**.

Thirteen kilometres from Sayil, the ruins of Xlapak have not been as extensively restored as the others in this region. It's one of the smallest ruins along the Puuc Route, with only one building in good enough condition to be of interest. In total there are 14 mounds and three partially restored pyramids. Situated close to Labná, Xlapak may have been part of that complex and dates back to approximately AD 830-1000. The main building is dedicated to the rain god Chac.

Labná has a feature that ranks it among the most outstanding sites of the Puuc region: a monumental arch connecting two groups of buildings (now in ruins), which displays an architectural concept unique to this region. Most Maya arches are purely structural, but the one at Labná has been constructed for aesthetic purposes, running right through the facade and clearly meant to be seen from afar. The two facades on either side of the arch differ greatly in their decoration; the one at the entrance is beautifully decorated with delicate latticework and stone carving imitating the wood or palm-frond roofs of Maya huts.

Uxmal ⊜❶❷❸ ↠ *pp704-716. Colour map 3, A2.*

→ *Phone code: 997.*
① *Daily 0800-1700, US$8.20, light-and-sound show US$2.80; rental of translation equipment US$2.50. Shows are at 2000 in summer and 1900 in winter. Mixed reports. Guides available with 1½ hour tours. Tours in Spanish US$32, in English, French, German and Italian US$40, for groups of up to 25 people. ↠ See transport to Uxmal, page 714.*

Built during the Classic period, Uxmal is the most famous of the ruins in the Puuc region. The characteristic features of Maya cities in this region are the quadrangular layout of the buildings, set on raised platforms, and an artificially created underground water-storage system. The 30-m-tall **Pyramid of the Sorcerer** is an unusual oval-shaped pyramid set on a large rectangular base; there is evidence that five stages of building were used in its construction. The **Nunnery** is set around a large courtyard, with some fine masks of Chac, the rain god, on the corners of the buildings. The **House of the Governor** is 100 m long, and is considered one of the most outstanding buildings in all of Mesoamerica. Two arched passages divide the building into three distinct sections. Above the central entrance is an elaborate trapezoidal motif. The **House of the Turtles** is simply adorned on the upper cornice, above a short row of tightly packed columns, which resemble the Maya palapas, made of sticks with a thatched roof, still used today. The **House of the Doves** is the oldest and most damaged of the buildings at Uxmal. It is still impressive: a long, low platform of wide columns topped by clusters of roof combs, whose similarity to dovecotes gave the building its name.

Izamal and around ⊜🕓🄾⊜🄲 ➤➤ pp704-716. Colour map 3, A3.

→ Phone code: 988.

Sixty eight kilometres east of Mérida is the friendly little town of Izamal. Once a major Classic Maya religious site founded by the priest Itzamná, Izamal became one of the centres of the Spanish attempt to Christianise the Maya.

Fray Diego de Landa, the historian of the Spanish Conquest of Mérida (of whom there is a statue in the town), founded the huge **convent** and **church**, which now face the main **Plaza de la Constitución**. This building, constructed on top of a Maya pyramid, was begun in 1549 and has the second largest atrium in the world. If you carefully examine the walls that surround the magnificent atrium, you will notice that some of the faced stones are embellished with carvings of Maya origin, confirming that, when they had toppled the pre-Columbian structures, the Spaniards re-used the material to create the imported architecture. Just 2½ blocks away, visible from the convent across a second square and signposted, are the ruins of a great mausoleum known as the **Kinich-Kakmo pyramid** ① 0800-1700, US$1, entrance next to the tortilla factory. You climb the first set of stairs to a broad, tree-covered platform, at the end of which is a further pyramid (still under reconstruction). From the top there is an excellent view of the town and surrounding henequén and citrus plantations. Kinich-Kakmo is 195-m long, 173-m wide and 36-m high, the fifth highest in Mexico. In all, 20 Maya structures have been identified in Izamal, several on Calle 27. Another startling feature about the town is that the entire colonial centre, including the convent, the arcaded government offices on Plaza de la Constitución and the arcaded second square, is painted a rich yellow ochre, giving it the apt nickname of the 'golden city'.

From Izamal you can go by bus to **Cenotillo**, where there are several fine cenotes within easy walking distance from the town (avoid the one in town itself), especially **Ucil**, which is excellent for swimming, and **La Unión**. Take the same bus as for Izamal from Mérida. Past Cenotillo is Espita and then a road forks left to Tizimín (see page 704).

The cemetery of **Hoctún**, on the Mérida-Chichén road, is also worth visiting; indeed it is impossible to miss, there is an 'Empire State Building' on the site. Take a bus from Mérida (last bus back 1700) to see extensive ruins at **Aké**, an unusual structure. Public transport in Mérida is difficult: from an unsigned stop on the corner of Calle 53 y 50, some buses to Tixkokob and Ekmul continue to Aké; ask the driver.

Chichén Itzá ⊜🕓🄾⊜🄲 ➤➤ pp704-716. Colour map 3, A3.

① Daily 0800-1700. US$8.20 light-and-sound show US$2.80, free bag storage, free for Mexicans on Sun and holidays, when it is incredibly crowded; you may leave and re-enter as often as you like on day of issue. Guided tours US$40 per group of any size; it is best to try and join one, many languages available. Best to arrive before 1030 when the mass of tourists arrives. There's a tourist centre at the entrance to the ruins with a restaurant and small museum, bookshop and souvenir shop with exchange facilities. Drinks, snacks and toilets are

Chichén Itzá

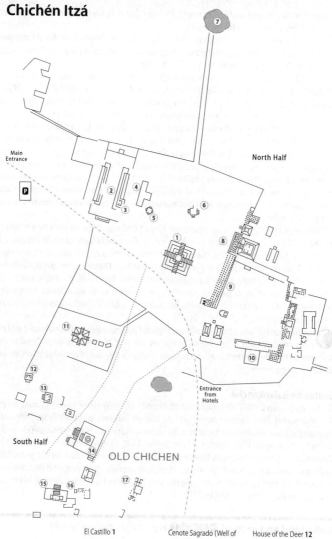

Main Entrance

North Half

South Half

OLD CHICHEN

Entrance from Hotels

N

100 metres
100 yards

El Castillo **1**
Ball Court **2**
Temple of the Jaguar **3**
Platform of the Skulls
  (Tzompantli) **4**
Platform of Eagles **5**
Platform of Venus **6**

Cenote Sagrado (Well of
  Sacrifice) **7**
Temple of the Warriors
  & Chacmool Statue **8**
Group of a Thousand
  Columns **9**
Market **10**
Tomb of the High Priest **11**

House of the Deer **12**
Red House **13**
El Caracol (Observatory) **14**
Casa de las Monjas
  (Nunnery) **15**
'Church' **16**
Akabdzilo **17**

available at the entrance and at the cenote. The site is hot, take a hat, sun cream, sunglasses, shoes with good grip and drinking water.

Chichén Itzá is one of the most spectacular of the Maya sites. The Castillo, a giant stepped pyramid dominates the site, watched over by Chacmool, a Maya fertility god. The city was built by the Maya in late Classic times (AD 600-900).

The major buildings in the north half display a Toltec influence. Dominating them is **El Castillo** ① *closed if raining*. The balustrade of the 91 stairs up each of the four sides is also decorated at its base by the head of a plumed, open-mouthed serpent. The interior ascent of 61 steep and narrow steps leading to a chamber is currently closed.

There is a **ball court** with grandstand and towering walls. El Castillo stands at the centre of the northern half of the site and almost at a right angle to its northern face runs the *sacbé* (sacred road) to the **Cenote Sagrado** (Well of Sacrifice). Into the Cenote Sagrado were thrown valuable propitiatory objects of all kinds, animal and human sacrifices. In 1962 the well was explored by an expedition, which recovered 4000 artefacts. To the east of El Castillo is the **Templo de los Guerreros** (Temple of the Warriors) with its famous reclining **Chacmool** statue. This pyramidal platform is closed off to avoid erosion.

Chichén Viejo (Old Chichén), where the Maya buildings of the earlier city are found, lies about 500 m by path from the main clearing. The famous **El Caracol**, or Observatory, is included in this group, as is the **Casa de las Monjas** (The Nunnery). A footpath to the right of the Casa de las Monjas leads to the **Templo de los Tres Dinteles** (Temple of the Three Lintels) after 30 minutes' walk. It requires at least one day to see the many pyramids, temples, ball courts and palaces, all of them adorned with astonishing sculptures. Excavation and renovation is still going on. Interesting birdlife and iguanas can also be seen around the ruins.

● *On the morning and afternoon of the spring and autumn equinoxes, the alignment of the sun's shadow casts a serpentine image on the side of the steps of El Castillo. This phenomenon can be observed, at least in part, on the days before and after the equinoxes, as well as during the equinox itself.*

Grutas de Balankanché
① *Museum open 0900-1700, closed Sat afternoons. US$6.80 (allow about 45 mins for the 300-m descent). The caretaker turns lights on and off, answers questions in Spanish, every hour on the hour, minimum 6, maximum 20 persons. Guided visits every hour 0900-1600 in Spanish, returning by 1700. Guided visits in English 1000, 1300 and 1500.*

Tours run daily to the Grutas de Balankanché caves, 3 km east of Chichén Itzá just off the highway. There are archaeological objects, including offerings of pots and *metates* in an extraordinary setting. To get there, take the Chichén Itzá or Pisté-Balankanché bus hourly at a quarter past, US$0.50, taxi US$15.

Valladolid and around ⊜❼❸❸❺❻ ►► *pp704-716. Colour map 3, A3.*

→ *Phone code: 985.*

Situated roughly halfway between Mérida and Cancún, Valladolid is a pleasant little town, until now untouched by tourism. Its proximity to the famous ruins of Chichén Itzá, however, means that Valladolid has been earmarked for extensive development by the Mexican government. A new international airport is under construction and this looks set to increase Valladolid's number of visitors from the trickle it's been receiving to a much larger influx.

Valladolid is set around a large plaza, flanked by the imposing Franciscan cathedral. Most of the hotels are clustered around the centre, as well as numerous restaurants catering for all budgets, favouring the lower end. The town's location makes it an ideal place to settle for a few days, while exploring the ruins of Chichén Itzá, the fishing village of **Río Lagartos** on the north coast, and the three beautiful *cenotes* in the area, one of which is right in the town itself, on Calle 36 y 39.

The **tourist office** ① *southeast corner of the plaza*, is not very helpful but they hand out a useful map. Much more helpful information can be obtained from **Antonio 'Negro' Aguilar** ① *Calle 44, No 195*, who runs a shop selling sports equipment, rents out bicycles and has very cheap accommodation (see Sleeping, page 708). He is glad to offer information on any of the tourist attractions in the area; if cycling around, he will personally draw you a map of the best route to take. Antonio can also help organize tours in a minivan to the ruins at Ek-Balam, minimum four people, US$3 per person.

Cenote Zací ① *Calle 36 between Calle 37 and 39, daily 0800-1800, US$1.40, half price for children or free if eating in the nearby restaurant*, is right in town, artificially lit and you can swim here, except when it is occasionally prohibited due to algae in the water. There is a thatched-roof restaurant and lighted promenades. A small town **museum** ① *Calle 41, free*, housed in Santa Ana church, shows the history of rural Yucatán and has some exhibits from recent excavations at the ruins of Ek-Balam.

Seven kilometres from Valladolid is the beautiful **Cenote X-Kekén** ① *daily 0700-1700, US$1.80*, at **Dzitnup**. It is stunningly lit with electric lights, the only natural light source being a tiny hole in the cavernous ceiling dripping with stalactites. Swimming is excellent, the water is cool and refreshing, although reported to be a little dirty, and harmless bats zip around overhead. Exploratory walks can also be made through the many tunnels leading off the *cenote*, for which you will need a torch. *Colectivos* leave when full from in front of **Hotel María Guadalupe**, US$1, they return until 1800, after which you will have to get a taxi back to Valladolid, US$4. Alternatively, hire a bicycle from Antonio Aguilar (see above) and cycle there, 25 minutes. Antonio will explain the best route before you set off. There is also the newly discovered, easily reached *cenote* close by, called **Sambulá** ① *US$1.80*.

Valladolid

Sleeping 🛏
Albergue La Candelaria **1**
Lili **2**
María de la Luz **3**
María Guadalupe **4**

Mesón del Marqués **5**
San Clemente **6**
Zací **7**

Eating 🍴
Bazar **1**
Los Campanas **2**

Ek-Balam

① Daily 0800-1700, US$2.50.

Twenty-five kilometres north of Valladolid are the recently opened Maya ruins of Ek-Balam. The ruins contain a series of temples, sacrificial altars and residential buildings grouped around a large central plaza. The main temple is an immaculate seven-tiered staircase leading up to a flattened area with the remains of a temple. The views are stunning and it's a peaceful site, well worth an exploratory tour. Well-preserved stuccoes can be seen along the main pyramid. To get there by car, take Route 295 north out of Valladolid. Just after the village of Temozón, take the turning on the right for Santa Rita. The ruins are some 5 km further on. A recommended way for those without a car is to hire a bike, take it on the roof of a *colectivo* leaving for Temozón from outside the **Hotel María Guadalupe**, and ask to be dropped off at the turning for Ek-Balam. From there, cycle the remaining 12 km to the ruins. There are also minivans to Ek-Balam run by Antonio Aguilar (see page 703).

Río Lagartos and around → *Colour map 3, A3.*

Tizimín is a scruffy little town en route to Río Lagartos, where you will have to change buses. If stuck, there are several cheap *posadas* and restaurants, but with frequent buses to Río Lagartos, there should be no need to stayovernight.

Río Lagartos is an attractive little fishing village on the north coast of Yucatán state, whose main attraction is the massive biosphere reserve containing thousands of **pink flamingos**, as well as 250 other species of bird. The only route is on the paved road from Valladolid; access from Cancún is by boat only, a journey mainly made by tradesmen ferrying fish to the resort.

Boat trips to see the flamingo reserve can be arranged by walking down to the harbour and taking your pick from the many offers you'll receive from boatmen. There are 10 different trips that can be taken by boat, out of which the two-hour flamingo trip is the most popular. As well as flamingos, there are some very rare birds, in the 47-sq-km reserve. Make sure your boatman takes you to the larger colony of flamingos near **Las Coloradas** (15 km), recognizable by a large salt mound on the horizon, rather than the smaller groups of birds along the river. Early morning boat trips can be arranged in Río Lagartos to see the flamingos (US$50, in four to six seater, 2½ to four hours, cheaper in a five-seater, fix the price before embarking; in midweek few people go so there is no chance of negotiating, but boat owners are more flexible on where they go; at weekends it is very busy, so it may be easier to get a party together and reduce costs). Check before going whether the flamingos are there; they usually nest here during May and June and stay through July and August (although salt mining is disturbing their habitat).

◉ State of Yucatán listings

For Sleeping and Eating price codes and other relevant information, see Essentials pages 47-51.

▢ Sleeping

Mérida *p693, map p695*
The prices of hotels are determined by location, with budget hotels close to the plaza and the better hotels often further away. If booking into a central hotel, always try to get a room away from the street side, as noise on the narrow streets begins as early as 0500.

LL Hacienda Xcanatun, Km 12, Ctra Mérida-Progreso, T999-941 0273, www.xcanatun.com. Carefully restored hacienda, 10 mins out of town, relaxed atmosphere, full breakfast included, restaurant **Casa de Piedra**, possibly the best in Mérida without an expensive price tag. Live music Thu, Fri and Sat.

AL Casa San Angel, Paseo de Montejo 1 with Calle 49, T999-928 1800, www.hotelcasa sanangel.com. Quiet and relaxing with a pool, restaurant and craft shop.

A Colonial, Calle 62, No 476, on the corner of Calle 57, T999-923 6444, www.hotel colonial.com.mx. Great location 2 blocks from the plaza. Small but comfortable rooms with TV and a/c, small pool. Restaurant serves good buffet meals, including breakfast. Sometimes gives good discounts in low season.

A Gobernador, Calle 59, No 535, corner of 66, T999-930 4141, www.gobernador merida.com.mx. Good clean hotel with 2 small pools. All rooms with a/c, cable TV and phone. 'Executive' rooms are better. Restaurant offers buffet breakfast. Promotional rates and free Wi-Fi. Recommended.

A La Misión de Fray Diego, Calle 61, No 524 between 64 and 66, T01800-221 0599, www.lamisiondefraydiego.com. Pleasant hotel situated around 2 courtyards. Section nearest the road is original 17th century, formerly connected to the convent behind it. Mini-bar and TV in all rooms, small pool and restaurant.

A-B Gran Hotel, Parque Hidalgo, Calle 60, No 496, with Calle 59, T999-923 6963, www.granhoteldemerida.com.mx. A great place to stay with a good atmosphere. All rooms are clean and have a/c, TV, hot water and phone, but not all have windows. Free parking.

B Casa Mexilio, Calle 68, between Calle 59 and 57, T999-928 2505, casamexilio@ earthlink.net. This old-fashioned colonial building has 3 floors complete with antique sitting room, lush courtyard and a pleasant pool. Breakfast included. Friendly hosts. Recommended.

B Medio Mundo, Calle 55, No 533 between Calle 64 and 66, T999-924 5472, www.hotel mediomundo.com. Charming hotel with 12 rooms, garden patio and swimming pool. Good handicraft shop forms part of the hotel.

C Casa San Juan, Calle 62, No 545A, between Calle 69 and 71, T999-986 2937, www.casasanjuan.com. This restored 19th-century house, close to the bus station, has a

pleasant, tranquil atmosphere. The multi-lingual owner is helpful and friendly, the rooms are large, and prices include American breakfast. Book ahead in high season.

C Dolores Alba, Calle 63, No 464, between Calle 52 and 54, T999-858 1555, www.dolores alba.com. This large, modern hotel has 2 sections and price bands. More comfortable and expensive rooms are recently remodelled and overlook the pool and courtyard. The cheaper rooms are slightly smaller and have no views. Cool, airy atmosphere and a nice pool. All rooms have a/c, and there's a sister establishment in Chichén Itzá.

C Posada Toledo, Calle 58, No 487, corner Calle 57, T999-923 1690, hptoledo@ prodigy.net.mx. Elegant, high-ceiled rooms surround a plant-filled courtyard, all adorned with antique furniture. Cheap breakfast, parking (US$4) and colour TV.

C-E Trinidad, Calle 62, No 464, corner 55, T999-923 2033, www.hotelestrinidad.com. One of Mérida's many old houses, this one is popular with budget travellers and backpackers. Relaxed, friendly vibe, pool table, DVDs, courtyard and roof-top jacuzzi. Continental breakfast included in the price.

D-E Margarita, Calle 66 (No 506) y Calle 63, T999-923 7236. With shower, clean, good, rooms a bit dark and noisy downstairs, cheaper rooms for 5 (3 beds), parking, friendly, excellent value. Some rooms have TV and a/c (pricier).

D-E San José, west of plaza on Calle 63, No 503, with Calle 62 and 64, T999-928 6657, san_jose92@latinmail.com. Bath, hot water, basic, clean, friendly, rooms on top floor are baked by the sun, one of the cheapest, popular with locals, will store luggage, good cheap meals available, local speciality *poc chuc*.

D-F Nómadas Youth Hostal, Calle 62, No 433, end of Calle 51, 5 blocks north of the plaza, T999-924 5223, www.nomadas travel.com. A clean and friendly hostel with private rooms and dorms. Hot water, kitchen, drinking water, hammocks and internet. Owner Raúl speaks English and is very helpful. Good value and a great place to meet other travellers. Free salsa classes every night. Pool opening in 2009. Live 'trova' music Mon, Wed and Fri. Recommended.

E Casa Becil, Calle 67, No 550-C, between Calle 66 and 68, T999-924 6764, hotelcasa becil@yahoo.com.mx. All rooms have fan, bath, hot water and cable TV. The owner is English speaking and hospitable. There's also a communal kitchen. Conveniently located for the bus station.

E Casa Bowen, restored colonial house, corner of Calle 66, No 521-B, and Calle 65, T999-928 6109. Open 24 hrs, if locked ring bell. Rooms have bath and hot water, cheaper with fan. It's often full at weekends. Avoid noisy rooms overlooking the street. Well located between the CAME 1st-class bus terminal and the centre.

E El Caminante, Calle 64, No 539, between Calle 65 and 67, T999-923 6730. Motel-style joint with parking, close to the bus station. Large rooms with one or two double beds, bath, colour TV, hot water 24 hrs. Clean and good value, if unexciting.

E Las Monjas, Calle 66A ,No 509, between Calle 61 and 63, T999-928 6632. Simple, family-run lodgings. Clean, quiet, friendly and good value. Can organize tours.

E Mucuy, Calle 57, No 481, between Calle 56 and 58, T999-928 5193, www.mucuy.com. Good, but 1st floor rooms are hot. There's a pool and garden, hot water and optional TV.

E-F Hostal Zócalo, on the south of the plaza, T999-930 9562, hostel_zocalo@ yahoo.com.mx. Popular hostel with economical rooms and big, clean dorms. TV, DVD, kitchen, laundry and internet. Breakfast included with private rooms.

Camping

Trailer Park Rainbow, Km 8, on the road to Progreso, T999-926 1026. US$18 for 1-2 people, hot showers, all facilities and good bus connection into town. Reports of excessive charging for use of amenities.

Celestún p696

LL-L Eco Paraíso Xixim, Km 12 off the old Sisal Highway, T988-916 2100, www.ecoparaiso.com. In coconut grove on edge of reserve, pool, tours to surrounding area including flamingos, turtle nesting, etc.

D Gutiérrez, Calle 12 (the Malecón), No 127, T988-916 2609. Fans, views, clean.

D San Julio, Calle 12, No 93A, between Calle 9 and 11, T988-916 2062. Large bright rooms and clean bathrooms.

Progreso and around p696

B-C Tropical Suites, Calle 19, No 143, T969-935 1263. Suites and rooms with cable TV, a/c, sea views.

C Progreso, Calle 29, No 142 with Calle 78 and 80, T969-935 0039. Simple rooms in the centre.

Ticul and Oxkutzcab p698

C Motel Bugambilias, Calle 23, No 291A, Ticul, T997-972 1368. Clean, basic rooms.

C Sierra Sosa, Calle 26, No 199, near Zócalo, Ticul, T997-972 0008, hospedaje_sierra@ hotmail.com. Cheap rooms that are dungeon like, but friendly, clean and helpful.

D Trujeque, Calle 48, No 102-A, Oxkutzcab, T997-975 0568. A/c, TV, clean, good value, discount for stays over a week.

E Casa de Huéspedes, near bus terminal, Oxkutzcab. Large rooms with bath, TV, fan, friendly. Recommended.

E Rosalia, Calle 54, No 101 Oxkutzcab, T997-975 0167, turn right out of bus station, right again. Double room, shower, cable TV.

Uxmal p699

There is no village at Uxmal, just the hotels. For cheap accommodation, go to Ticul, 28 km away (see above).

L Hacienda Uxmal, T997-976 2012, www.mayaland.com/HaciendaUxmal, 300-400 m from ruins. Efficient and relaxing, Yucatacan restaurant, a/c, gardens, pool.

L The Lodge at Uxmal, at entrance to ruins, T997-976 2102, www.mayaland.com/ LodgeUxmal. Same owners as **Hacienda Uxmal**. Comfortable, with a/c, bath, TV and restaurant.

A-B Misión Uxmal, 1-2 km from ruins on Mérida road, Km 78, T997-976 2022, www.hotelesmision.com.mx. Rooms a bit dark, pool.

C Rancho Uxmal, Ctra Mérida-Uxmal, Km 70, about 4 km north of ruins, T997-977 6254. Comfortable rooms, hot and cold water, camping for US$5, pool, reasonable food but not cheap (no taxis to get there).

D-F Sacbé Hostel, at Km 127 on Highway 261, T997-858 1281. A mix of private rooms (private bath), dorms and campsite, with space for hammocks, and solar-powered showers, with breakfast and dinner for a little more.

Camping

No camping allowed at the site, but there is a campsite at **Sacbé Hostel**, see above. Second-class buses from Mérida to Campeche pass by, ask to be let out at the Campo de Beisbol. Beautiful park, fastidiously clean and impeccably managed. Nine electric hook-ups (US$7-10 for motor home according to size), big area for tents (US$2.75 per person with tent), *palapas* for hammocks (US$2.65 per person), for cars pay US$1, showers, toilets, clothes-washing facilities, also 3 bungalows with ceiling fan (**E**), lunch and dinner available (US$2.65 each). Recommended. Also **Cana Nah** campsite, closer to the ruins, next door to Hotel Misión Uxmal, and at **Rancho Uxmal**, see above.

Izamal and around *p700*

B Macan-Che, Calle 22, No 305, between Calle 33 and 35, T988-954 0287, www.macanche.com. Four blocks north of plaza, pleasant bungalows, breakfast.

Chichén Itzá *p700*

LL Hacienda Chichén, T999-920 8407, www.haciendachichen.com. Luxury resort and spa, close to the ruins, with tasteful rooms, suites and bungalows. There's a garden, library and restaurant.

AL-L Villas Arqueológicas, T997-974 6020, www.villasarqueologicas.com.mx. Pool, tennis, restaurant (expensive and poor). Both are on the other side of the fenced-off ruins from the bus stop; you cannot walk through ruins, either walk all the way round, or take taxi (US$1-1.50).

A Chichén Itzá, Pisté, T999-851 0022, www.mayaland.com/BestWestern. Three types of rooms and tariffs. The best are clean, tasteful, overlook the garden and have a/c, internet, phone and fridge. The cheaper rooms (**B**) overlook the street.

B Pirámide Inn, 1½ km from ruins, at the Chichén end of Pisté, Km 117, T999-851 0115, www.chichen.com. This long-standing Pisté favourite has many clean, comfortable rooms, a pool, hammocks and *palapas*. *Temazcal* available, book 24 hrs in advance. Camping US$5, or US$15 with a car. Friendly owner, speaks English.

C Dolores Alba, Km 122, T985-858 1555, www.doloresalba.com. Small, Spanish-owned hotel, 2½ km on the road to Puerto Juárez (bus passes it), 40 clean bungalows with shower, a/c and cable TV, including breakfast. Pool, restaurant, English is spoken. Sister hotel in Mérida.

C Posada Olalde, 100 m from the main road at the end of Calle 6, between Calle 15 and 17. This lovely, family-run hotel has a handful of economical rooms and basic Yucatecan *cabañas* built the old-fashioned way.

C Stardust Posada Annex, Pisté, about 2 km before the ruins if coming from Mérida (taxi to ruins US$2.50). Simple, basic rooms and a range of tariffs to suit your budget. Slightly run down, but acceptable. There's also a pool and an average restaurant.

D Posada Maya, Calle 8, No 70, just off the main road. Small, simple rooms, desperately in need of a clean. However, there's space to sling a hammock if you're impoverished (**F**).

Valladolid and around *p702, map p703*

B María de la Luz, Calle 42, No 193-C, Plaza Principal, T985-856 1181, www.mariadelaluz hotel.com. Good, clean rooms, restaurant, tours to Chichén Itzá and Río Lagartos.

B Mesón del Marqués, Calle 39 with Calle 40 and 42, north side of Plaza Principal, T985-856 2073, www.mesondel marques.com. This hotel has 90 tasteful rooms, all with a/c and cable TV. There's a swimming pool, Wi-Fi, garden and laundry service. Recommended.

B Zací, Calle 44, No 191, T985-856 2167, hotelzaci@prodigy.net.mx. A clean, comfortable mid-range option. Rooms have a/c (cheaper with fan) and TV. There's a pool.

C María Guadalupe, Calle 44, No 198, T985-856 2068, hotelmariaguadalupe@ hotmail.com. Simple, clean rooms with fan. Good value, hot water, washing facilities.

C San Clemente, Calle 42, No 206, T985-856 2208, www.hotelsanclemente.com.mx. Many clean, comfortable rooms with a/c (cheaper with fan) and cable TV. There's a pool, restaurant, garden and free parking.

D Antonio 'Negro' Aguilar rents rooms for 2, 3 or 4 people. The best budget deal in the town for 2 or more, clean, spacious rooms on a quiet street, garden, volleyball/basketball court. The rooms are on Calle 41, No 225, before the **Maya Hotel**, but you need to book them at Aguilar's shop on Calle 44, No 195, T985-856 2125. If the shop is closed, knock on the door of the house on the right of the shop.

D Lili, Calle 44, No 192, T985-856 2163. Large, basic rooms with cable TV and fan. There's hot water and the management is friendly.

E Albergue La Candelaria, Calle 35, No 201-F, T985-856 2267, candelaria_hostel@ hotmail.com. Good cheap option, especially for solo travellers. Single-sex dorms with fan, clean, hot water, kitchen, washing facilities, hammocks out the back in the garden, TV room. Recommended.

Río Lagartos and around *p704*

E Tere and Miguel, near the harbour (ask at the bus terminal). Three rooms for rent, very nicely furnished, double and triple rooms, one with an extra hammock, sea views.

Eating

Mérida *p693, map p695*
There are a number of taco stands, pizzerías and sandwich places in Pasaje Picheta, a small plaza off the Palacio de Gobierno.

₮₮₮ Alberto's Continental, Calle 64, No 482 corner Calle 57. Yucatecan, Lebanese and international food.

₮₮₮ Casa de Piedra 'Xcanatún', Hacienda Xcanatún (see page 704), Km 12 Ctra Mérida-Progreso, T999-941 0213. Fine dining, best restaurant in the area (although a bit out of town). Reserve.

₮₮₮ Villa Maria, Calle 59, No 553, and Calle 68, T999-923 3357, www.villamariamerida.com. French, Mediterranean and Mexican cuisine at this sophisticated fine-dining establishment.

₮₮-₮ Café La Habana, Calle 59 y Calle 62. Neither the coffee nor the food is fantastic, but it's OK for a snack. Open 24 hrs. Free Wi-Fi.

₮₮ El Nuevo Tucho, Calle 60 near University. Good local dishes, mostly meat and fish, and occasional live music. Healthy and extensive drinks menu. Evening entertainment also.

₮₮ La Casa de Frida, Calle 61, between Calle 66 and 66A, www.lacasadefrida.com.mx. Mon-Sat 1800-2200. Frida Kahlo-themed restaurant in a colourful courtyard setting, traditional Mexican cuisine.

₮₮ Los Almendros, Calle 50A, No 493, corner of Calle 59. This award-winning restaurant specializes in traditional Yucatecan cuisine, serving tasty dishes like *pollo pibil* and *poc chuc*. The entrance is through the car park.

₮₮ Pórtico del Peregrino, Calle 57 between Calle 60 and 62. Dining indoors or in an attractive leafy courtyard, excellent food.

₮₮-₮ Amaro, Calle 59, No 507, between Calle 60 and 62, near the plaza. Good food, especially vegetarian; open late daily.

₮₮-₮ Café Chocolate, Calle 60, No 442, corner Calle 49, T999-928 5113, www.cafe-chocolate. com.mx. This new café and art space does good *mole*, as well as an excellent breakfast buffet, a lunchtime menu and evening meals. Free Wi-Fi and alternating art and photography exhibitions. Highly recommended.

₮₮-₮ Colonial, Hotel Colonial, Calle 62 and 57. Average coffee, but this restaurant lays on an all-you-can-eat breakfast buffet for US$6, with fruit, coffee, good juice, eggs, cereal and other offerings. Fill up on several courses and then come back for the lunch buffet – this time there are steaks, but drinks aren't included.

♯♯-♯ Flor de Santiago, Calle 70, No 478, between Calle 57 and 59. Reputedly the oldest restaurant in Mérida. There's a cafeteria and bakery in one section, serving cheap snacks and à la carte meals. Breakfast buffet is good value.

♯♯-♯ La Vía Olympo, (formerly La Valentina) on main plaza opposite cathedral. Good-value Mexican and Yucatecan dishes, brisk service and outdoor seating. Good for breakfasts, free Wi-Fi.

♯ Café Alameda, Calle 58, No 474, between Calle 57 and 55. Arabic and Mexican cuisine, breakfast and lunch only, 0730-1700.

♯ El Trapiche, Calle 62, half a block north of the plaza. Good local dishes, excellent pizzas, sandwiches, omelettes, *tortas*, tacos, burgers and freshly made juices.

♯ El Tucho, also known as El Nuevo Tucho, Calle 55 between Calle 60 and 58. A restaurant open till 2100 only, with live music, often guest performers from Cuba play. Good food.

♯ Marlín Azul, Calle 62, between Calle 57 and 59. The place for cheap seafood fare, mostly frequented by locals. Get a shrimp cocktail breakfast for a couple of dollars.

♯ Marys, Calle 63, No 486, between Calle 60 and 58. Mainly Mexican customers. Possibly the cheapest joint in town. *Comida corrida* for US\$2.50. Recommended.

♯ Mérida, Calle 62, between Calle 59 and 61. Full 3 course for US\$2.50 – a bargain, and it's tasty Yucatecan fare as well.

♯ Vito Corleone's Pizza, Calle 59, No 508, between Calle 62 and 60. Serves pop and pizza, by the slice or whole, eat in or take away. Popular with students and young Mexicans. Open from 1800.

Cafés, juices and ice cream parlours
Café El Hoyo, Calle 62, between 57 and 59. A chilled-out spot with a patio, popular with students, serving coffee, beer and snacks.
Café Petropolis, Calle 70, opposite CAME terminal. Existed long before the terminal was

built, family run, turkey a speciality, excellent quality, good *horchata* and herb teas.
El Colón Sorbetes y Dulces Finos, Calle 61 and 60. Serving ice cream since 1907, great sorbets, *meringue*, good menu with explanation of fruits in English.
Italian Coffee Company, Calle 62 between 59 and 61. Serves excellent coffee, decent toasted baguettes and tasty cakes.
Jugos California, Calle 62 and 63 good fruit salads and juices. Next door Jugos Janitzio is also good.

There's a good *panadería* at Calle 62 and 61. Parque Santa Ana, is good for cheap street fare. Closed middle of the day.

Celestún *p696*

Many beachside restaurants along Calle 12, but be careful of food in the cheaper ones; recommended is La Playita, Calle 12, No 99, T988-916 2052, for fried fish, seafood cocktails. Food stalls along Calle 11 beside the bus station should be approached with caution.
♯♯ Chivirico, Calle 12, No100, across the road from Playita, offers decent fish, shrimp and other seafood.
♯♯ El Lobo, Calle 10 and 13, on the corner of the main square. Best spot for breakfast, with fruit salads, yoghurt, pancakes, etc. Good pizza in the evenings.

Progreso and around *p696*

The Malecón at Progreso is lined with seafood restaurants, some with tables on the beach. For cheaper restaurants, head for the centre of town, near the bus terminal.
♯♯-♯ Las Palmas and El Cocalito are 2 of several reasonable fish restaurants in Chelem.
♯ Casablanca, Capitan Marisco and Le Saint Bonnet, Malecón, Progreso. Recommended.

Ticul and Oxkutzcab *p698*

♯♯ Los Almendros, Calle 23, No 207, Ticul, T997-972 0021. Nice colonial building with patio, good Yucatecan cuisine, reasonable prices. Main branch in Mérida.
♯♯ Pizzería La Góndola, Calle 23, Ticul. Good, moderately priced pizzas.

Ϋ El Colorín, near Hotel Sierra Sosa on Calle 26 No199, Ticul. Cheap local food.

Uxmal *p699*
ΫΫΫ-ΫΫ Restaurant at ruins; good but expensive.

Izamal and around *p700*
There are several restaurants on Plaza de la Constitución.

ΫΫ Kinich-Kakmó, Calle 27, No 299A, between 28 and 30, www.sabordeizamal.com. Near ruins of same name, local food.

ΫΫ Tumben-Lol, Calle 22, No 302, between 31 and 33. Yucatecan cuisine.

Ϋ El Norteño at bus station. Good and cheap.

Ϋ Wayane, near statue of Diego de Landa. Friendly, clean.

Chichén Itzá *p700*
Mostly poor and overpriced in Chichén itself (cafés inside the ruins are cheaper than the restaurant at the entrance, but are still expensive). Restaurants in Pisté close 2100-2200.

ΫΫ Fiesta Maya, Calle 15, No 59, Pisté. Reportedly the best restaurant in town. Serves Yucatecan food, tacos, meat and sandwiches. Lunch buffet every day at 1200, US$10.

Ϋ Pollo Mexicano on the main road in Pisté. One of several simple places that serves mouth-watering, barbecued chicken.

Ϋ Sayil in Pisté. Serves Yucatecan dishes like *pollo pibil*, as well as *huevos al gusto* for breakfast.

Valladolid and around *p702, map p703*
There is a well-stocked supermarket on the road between the centre and bus station.

ΫΫ El Mesón del Marqués, Calle 39, between 40 and 42. This award-winning restaurant, inside Hotel Mesón del Marqués (see Sleeping), serves seafood and Yucatecan cuisine in a tranquil colonial setting. Intimate and romantic.

ΫΫ La Sirenita, Calle 34, No 188, between 29 and 31, T985-856 1655, few blocks east of main square. Only open to 1800, closed Sun. Recommended for seafood, popular and friendly.

ΫΫ Plaza Maya, Calle 41, No 235, a few blocks east of main square. Great regional food and good *comida corrida*, a step up from the rest.

Ϋ Bazar, northeast corner of Plaza Principal, next to Mesón del Marqués. Serves up wholesome grub.

Cafés
Los Campanas, Calle 42, No 199, opposite the plaza. Serves various types of coffee.

Río Lagartos and around *p704*
For a fishing village, the seafood is not spectacular, as most of the good fish is sold to restaurants in Mérida and Cancún.

ΫΫ Isla Contoy, Calle 19, No 134, T986-862 0000. Average seafood, not cheap for the quality.

ΫΫ Los Negritos, Calle 10, No 133, off the plaza. Moderately priced seafood.

♫ Bars and clubs

Mérida *p693, map p695*
There are several good bars on the north side of the plaza, beer is moderately priced at US$1, although food can be expensive. There are a number of live music venues around Parque Santa Lucía, a couple of blocks from the main plaza.

El Cielo, Paseo de Montejo and Calle 25, www.elcielobar.com. Lounge-bar that plays house, techno and pop.

La Parranda, Calle 60, between Calle 59 and 61. This touristy *cantina* is always buzzing with atmosphere in the evenings. Live music Thu-Sat and always a steady flow of beer.

Mambo Café, Plaza Las Americanas Shopping Mall, T999-987 7533, www.mambocafe.com.mx. Big club in Mérida, mainly salsa but all kinds of music. Wed-Sat from 2100.

Panchos, Calle 59 between Calle 60 and 62. Very touristy, staff in traditional gear, but lively and busy, live music, patio.

🎭 Entertainment

Mérida p693, map p695
See the free listings magazine *Yucatán Today* for evening activities.

Cinema
There is a cinema showing subtitled films in English on Parque Hidalgo.

Cinepolis, huge Plaza de las Américas, north of the city; *colectivo* and buses take 20 mins and leave from Calle 58 between Calle 58 and 60. A 14-screen multiplex.

Hollywood Cinema, near Parque Santiago. Four screens at this cinema show international films.

Teatro Mérida, Calle 62 between Calle 59 and 61. Shows European, Mexican and independent movies as well as live theatre productions.

Cultural centres
Alliance Française, Calle 56, No 476 between Calle 55 and 57, T999-927 2403. Busy programme of events, films (Thu 1900), a library and a *cafetería* open all day.

Theatre
Teatro Peón Contreras, Calle 60 with 57. Shows start at 2100, US$4, ballet, etc. The university puts on many shows.

🎉 Festivals and events

Mérida p693, map p695
Every **Thu** there is a cultural music and dance show in Plaza Santa Lucía. Every **Sat** brings En El Corazón de Mérida, with music and dance in bars, restaurants and in the street. Every **Sun** the central streets are closed off to traffic; live music and parades abound.

6 Jan Mérida celebrates its birthday.
Feb/Mar Carnival takes place the week before Ash Wed (best on Sat). Floats, dancers in regional costume, music and dancing around the plaza.

Río Lagartos p704
17 Jul A big local *fiesta*, with music, food and dancing in the plaza.
12 Dec Virgen de Guadalupe. The whole village converges by the chapel built on the site of a vision of the Virgin Mary, where a local suddenly died after receiving a vision of the Virgin Mary.

🛍 Shopping

Mérida p693, map p695
Bookshops
Amate, Calle 60 453A, between Calle 49 and 51, T999-924 2222, www.amatebooks.com. You'll find a superb stock of literature here, covering everything from anthropology to art. Another branch in Oaxaca.

Librerías Dante, Calle 59, No 498, between Calle 58 and 60. Calle 61 between 62 and 64 (near **Lavandería La Fe**). Used books.

Cameras and film
You can get films processed at **Omega**, Calle 59 and 60; camera repairs at **Fotolandia**, Calle 62, No 479, G y 57, T999-924 8223; and also at a little shop on Calle 53 and 62.

Crafts and souvenirs
You'll find an abundance of craft shops in the streets around the plaza. The salespeople are ruthless, but they expect to receive about half their original asking price. Bargain hard. Beware of the touts around the plaza, using all sorts of ingenious ploys to get you to their shops.

There are two main craft markets in the city: the **Garcia Rejón Bazaar**, also known as Casa de la Artesanía, Calle 65 and 60, excellent for handicrafts, clothing and cheap Yucatecan fare; and the **Mercado Municipal**, Calle 56a and 67, selling everything under the sun and also good for a cheap, tasty meal.

Casa de Artesanías Ki-Huic, Calle 63, between Calle 62 and 64. Daily 0900-2100. A friendly store with a range of handicrafts. Owner Julio Chay is knowledgeable and sometimes organizes trips for visitors to his village, Tixkokob, which specializes in hammocks. Julio can also organize trips to other nearby villages.

If you're looking for a hammock, several places are recommended, but shop around for the best deal. **El Aguacate**, Calle 58, No 604, corner of Calle 73, good hammocks and no hard sell. **El Mayab**, Calle 58, No 553, and 71, is friendly, but has a limited choice. Good deals available. **La Poblana**, Calle 65 between Calle 58 and 60, will bargain, especially for sales of more than one – they also have a huge stock.

For silver, there are a handful of stores on Calle 60, just north of the plaza.

Mexican folk art, including Day of the Dead skeletons, is available from **Miniaturas**, Calle 59, No 507A; and **Yalat**, Calle 39 and 40.

If you're in the market for a *guayabera* shirt, you'll find stores all over the city, particularly on Calle 62, between Calle 57 and 61.

Supermarkets
Supermaz, Calle 56, between Calle 65 and 63.

Progreso and around *p696*
Mundo Marino, Calle 80 s/n, 1 block from the beach, T969-915 1380. Sells shark-related souvenirs.

Izamal and around *p700*
Market, Calle 31, on Plaza de la Constitución, opposite convent. Closes soon after lunch.
Hecho a mano, Calle 31, No 332, between Calle 36 and 38. Folk art, postcards, textiles, jewellery, papier-mâché masks.

▲ Activities and tours

Mérida *p693, map p695*
Language schools
Centro de Idiomas del Sureste, Calle 52, No 455, between Calle 49 and 51, T999-923 0083, www.cisyucatan.com.mx. A well-

established Spanish school offering tried and tested language and cultural programmes.
Modern Spanish Institute, Calle 15, No 500B, between Calle 16A and 18, T999-911 0790, www.modernspanish.com. Courses in Spanish and Maya culture with homestays.

Tour operators
Most tour operators can arrange trips to popular local destinations including Chichén Itzá, Uxmal, Celestún and nearby *cenotes*.
Amigo Yucatán, Av Colón, No 508-C, and offices in 3 hotels, T999-920 0104, www.amigoyucatan.com. Interesting gastronomy and tasting tours of Yucatán, as well as excursions to Maya ruins, Izamal, Puuc Route and Celestún. It's possible to book all tours online, 24 hrs in advance recommended, but also possible before 0830 on the same day (best to do this in person or on the phone). Friendly. Recommended.
Carmen Travel Services, Calle 27, No 151, between Calle 32 and 34, T999-927 2027, www.carmentravel.com. This well-established agency can organize flights, hotels and all the usual trips to the sights. Also 3 other branches. Recommended.
Ecoturismo Yucatán, Calle 3, No 235, between Calle 32A and 34, T999-920 2772, www.ecoyuc.com.mx. Specializes in educational and ecotourism tours to the natural world, including jungle trips, birding expeditions and turtle-hatching tours. Also offers adventure and archaeological packages.
Yucatan Connection, Calle 33, No 506, T044 999-163 8224, www.yucatan-connection.com. Tours to lesser visited Mayan sites like Mayapán, Tecoh and Ochil. Staff are fluent in English, Czech and Slovak.
Yucatán Trails, Calle 62, No 482, Av 57-59, T999-928 2582, www.yucatantrails.com. Canadian owner Denis Lafoy is friendly, English-speaking and helpful. He runs tours to all the popular local destinations, stores luggage cheaply, has a book exchange and throws parties on the first Fri of every month.

⊖ Transport

Mérida *p693, map p695*
Air
Aeropuerto Rejón (MID), 8 km from town. From Calle 67, 69 and 60, bus 79 goes to the airport, marked 'Aviación', US$0.35, roughly every 20 mins. Taxi-set price voucher system US$6.50; *colectivo* US$2.50. Good domestic flight connections. International flight connections with **Belize City**, **Houston**, **Miami** and **Havana**. Package tours Mérida-Havana-Mérida available (be sure to have a confirmed return flight). For return to Mexico ask for details at Secretaría de Migración, Av Colón and Calle 8.

    Airline offices AeroMéxico, Av Colón 451 and Calle 56A, T999-964 1781, www.aeromexico.com. **Aviacsa**, T999-925 6890, www.aviacsa.com.mx. **Continental**, T999-926 3100, www.continental.com. **Delta**, T01800-123 410, www.delta.com. **Mexicana** and **Click**, T01800-502 200, www.mexicana.com.mx.

Bus
There are several bus terminals in Mérida. **CAME terminal** Buses to destinations outside Yucatán State, Chichén Itzá and Valladolid operating **ADO** and **UNO** buses leave from the 1st-class CAME terminal at Calle 70, No 555, between Calle 69 and 71. The station has lockers and is open 24 hrs, left luggage charges from US$0.30 per bag, depending on size. About 20 mins' walk to centre, taxi US$2.50. The schedules change frequently.
ADO terminal Around the corner, for Yucatán destinations except Chichén Itzá, with fleets run by **Mayab**, **ATS**, **Sur** and **Oriente**. Also has left luggage open 24 hrs, bags charged by size. There are also 1st-class departures from the **Hotel Fiesta Americana**, Calle 60 and Colón, which are mostly luxury services to Cancún.

    Buses to **Progreso** depart every 20 mins, 0800-2100, US$0.85, from their own terminal at Calle 62, No 524, between 65

and 67. *Colectivos* to Progreso leave from Calle 60, between Calle 65 and 67, same timings.

    There is another 2nd-class terminal near the market at Calle 50 and 65. It deals with more obscure local destinations, including **Tizimín**, **Cenotillo**, **Izamal** and many Maya villages specializing in different crafts, including **Tixkokob**.

    To **Cancún**, hourly 1st-class ADO services, 4 hrs, US$18, and frequent 2nd-class services, US$15; **Campeche**, frequent ADO and 2nd-class services, 2 hrs, US$7-10; **Chichén Itzá** (ruins and Pisté), ADO services at 0630, 0915, 1240, 2 hrs, US$7, and cheaper, frequent 2nd-class buses stop on their way to Cancún; To **Celestún**, frequent 2nd-class Oriente services, 2 hrs, US$3.50; **Coatzacoalcos**, ADO services at 1210, 1830, 1930 and 2130; 12 hrs, US$38; **Palenque**, ADO services at 0830, 1915, 2200, 8hrs, US$26; **Ruta Puuc**, 2nd-class ATS service, 0800, US$10; **Tulum**, ADO services at 0630, 1040, 1240, 1745, 1945 6 hrs, US$9-14; **Uxmal**, 2nd-class SUR services at 0600, 0905, 1040, 1205, 1705, 1½ hrs, US$3; **Valladolid**, hourly ADO services, 1 ½ hrs, US$9, and 5 2nd-class buses, all in the afternoon and evening, US$5.50; **Villahermosa**, frequent ADO services, 9 hrs, US$30.50 and several ADO GL services, US$36; **Tuxtla Guitérrez**, an OCC service at 1915, 15 hrs, US$40, and ADO GL services at 1900 and 2315, US$55; **San Cristóbal de las Casas**, an OCC service at 1915, 13 hrs, US$36; **Tenosique**, an ADO service at 2100, US$29.

    To Guatemala Take a bus from Mérida to San Cristóbal and change there for Comitán, or to Tenosique for the route to Flores. Another alternative would be to take the bus from Mérida direct to Tuxtla Gutiérrez (times given above), then connect to Ciudad Cuauhtémoc or to Tapachula.

    To Belize Take a bus to **Chetumal**, ADO services at 0730 (except Wed and Sat), 1300, 1800, 2300, 6 hrs, US$21, and cross the Belizean border. **Premier** operate services from Chetumal to **Belize City** at 1145, 1445 and 1745, 3 hrs, US$8, schedules subject to change.

Car

Car hire Car reservations should be booked well in advance if possible. Hire firms charge around US$45-50 a day although bargains can be found in low season. All agencies allow vehicles to be returned to Cancún for an extra charge, and most have an office at the airport where they share the same counter and negotiating usually takes place. Agencies include: **Budget**, at the airport, T999-946 1323; **Easy Way Car Rental**, Calle 60, No 484, between Calle 55 and 57, T999-930 9500, www.easywayrenta car-yucatan.com; **Executive**, Calle 56A, No 451, corner of Av Colón, at the Hotel Fiesta Americana, T999-920 3732, www.executive.com.mx; **Mexico Rent a Car**, Calle 57A, No 491, between Calle 58 and 60, T999-923 3637, www.mexico-rent-acar.com.

Car service Servicios de Mérida Goodyear, Calle 59, near corner of Av 68. Very helpful, competent, owner speaks English, good coffee while you wait for your vehicle. Honest car servicing or quick oil change.

Taxi

There are 2 types: the Volkswagens, which you can flag down, prices range from US$3.50-7; cheaper are the 24-hr radio taxis, T999-928 5328, or catch one from their kiosk on Parque Hidalgo. In both types of taxi, establish fare before journey; there are set prices depending on the distance, the minimum is an expensive US$2.50 even for a few blocks.

Celestún p696

Bus Buses leave every hour from the local bus station on Calle 65 between 50 and 52, in Mérida, 2-hr journey, 1st class US$3.35, 2nd class US$3.

Progreso and around p696

Boat Boats can be hired to visit the reef of **Los Alacranes** where many ancient wrecks are visible in clear water.

Bus Buses from **Mérida** leave from terminal on Calle 62 between Calle 67 and 65, next to

Hotel La Paz, every 20 mins. US$0.85 1-way/ US$2 return. Returns every 20 mins until 2100.

Dzibilchaltún p697

Bus
6 direct buses a day on weekdays, 0720, 0930, 1135, 1332, 1540, 1830 and 4 direct on Sundays, 0800, 1100, 1400, 1700, leaving from Parque San Juan, marked 'Tour/Ruta Polígono'; returns from the site entrance on the hour, passing the junction 15 mins later, taking 45 mins from the junction to **Mérida** (US$0.50).

Colectivos leave from Calle 58 between Calle 57 and 59, in Mérida, every 30 mins.

Ticul and Oxkutzcab p698

Colectivo There are frequent VW *colectivos* to Ticul from Parque San Juan, in **Mérida**, US$2.50.

Uxmal p699

Bus 5 buses a day from **Mérida**, 0605, 0905, 1030, 1205 and 1705, leaving from 2nd-class terminal on Calle 69 between Calle 68 and 70, US$2.50. This is the Mérida-Campeche bus that takes the old road and drops you 150 m from the entrance to the ruins. There's also an 0800 bus taking in the entire Puuc Route. Return buses run every 2 hrs, or go to the entrance to the site on the main road and wait for a *colectivo*, which will take you to Muná for US$0.50. From there, many buses (US$1.70) and *colectivos* (US$1.40) go to Mérida.

Car Parking at the site costs US$1 for the whole day. Uxmal is 74 km from **Mérida**, 177 km from **Campeche**, by a good paved road. If going by car from Mérida, there is a new circular road round the city: follow the signs to Campeche, then 'Campeche via ruinas', then to 'Muná via Yaxcopoil' (long stretch of road with no signposting). Muná-Yaxcopoil is about 34 km. Parking US$1.

Izamal and around p700

Bus Bus station is on Calle 32 behind government offices, can leave bags. Second class to **Mérida**, every 45 mins, 1½ hrs, US$1.50, lovely countryside. Bus station in Mérida, Calle

67 between Calle 50 and 52. 6 a day to/from **Valladolid** (96 km), about 2 hrs, US$2.30-3.

Chichén Itzá *p700*
ADO bus office in Pisté is between Stardust and Pirámide Inn. Budget travellers going on from Mérida to Isla Mujeres or Cozumel should visit Chichén from Valladolid, although if you plan to go through in a day you can store luggage at the visitor's centre.

Bus Frequent 2nd-class buses depart from Mérida to Cancún, passing Chichen Itzá and Pisté. Likewise, there are frequent departures to/from Valladolid. The bus station in Pisté is between Stardust and Pirámide Inn. To **Mérida**, 2nd class, hourly, US$5; and 1st class, 1420, 1720 US$7. To **Cancún**, 2nd class, hourly, US$9. To **Valladolid**, 2nd class, hourly, US$2.50. To **Tulum**, 2nd class, 0810, 1420, 1615, US$11. The ruins are a 5-min ride from Pisté – the buses drop off and pick up passengers until 1700 at the top of the coach station opposite the entrance.

Valladolid and around *p702, map p703*
Bus The main bus terminal is on Calle 37 and Calle 54. To **Cancún**, ADO, frequent, 2½ hrs, US$9; and many 2nd class, 3-4 hrs, US$5.50. To **Chichén Itzá**, ADO, many daily, 30 mins; US$3; and many 2nd class, US$1.50. To **Mérida**, ADO, 16 daily, 2½ hrs, US$9. To **Playa del Carmen**, 1st and 2nd class, 11 daily, 3½ hrs, US$8.50. To **Tizimín** (for Río Lagartos), frequent 1 hr, US$1.30. To **Tulum**, frequent ADO and ATS services, 3 hrs, US$5.

Río Lagartos and around *p704*
Bus There are 2 terminals side by side in Tizimín. If coming from Valladolid en route to Río Lagartos, you will need to walk to the other terminal. Tizimín-Río Lagartos, 7 per day, 1½ hrs, US$2. To **Valladolid**, frequent, 1 hr, US$1.30. To **Mérida**, several daily, 4 hrs, US$4. There are also buses to **Cancún**, **Felipe Carrillo Puerto** and **Chetumal**.

It is possible to get to Río Lagartos and back in a day from **Valladolid**, if you leave on the 0630 or 0730 bus (taxi Tizimín-Río Lagartos US$25, driver may negotiate). Last bus back from Río Lagartos at 1730.

❶ Directory

Mérida *p693, map p695*
Banks Banamex, at Calle 56 and 59 (Mon-Fri 0900-1300, 1600-1700), ATM cash machine. Many banks on Calle 65, off the plaza. Most have ATM cash machines, open 24 hrs. The Casa de Montejo, on the main plaza is also a Banamex branch. Open 0900-1600, Mon-Fri. HSBC usually changes TCs and stays open late, 0900-1900, Mon-Fri and Sat 0900-1500. **Embassies and consulates** Austria, Av Colón, No 501, with Calle 60 and 62, T999-925 6386. Belize, Calle 58, No 498, corner of 58, T999-928 6152. Cuba, Calle 1, No 320, with Calle 42, T999-944 4216. France, Calle 60, No 385, between Calle 41 and 43, T999-930 1542. Germany, Calle 49, No 212, between Calle 30 and 32, T999-944 3252. Honduras, Instituto Monte Libano, Calle 54, No 483, between Calle 57 and 59, T999-926 1962. Netherlands, Calle 64, No 418, between Calle 47 and 49, T999-924 3122. USA, Calle 60, No 338, between Calle 29 and 31, T999-942 5700. **Internet** Many internet cafés, most charging US$1-1.50. **Laundry** Lavandería, Calle 69, No 541, 2 blocks from bus station, about US$4.50 a load, 3-hr service. La Fe, Calle 61, No 518, between Calle 62 and 64. US$4.50 for 3 kg. Highly recommended (shoe repair next door). Self service is hard to find. **Libraries** Mérida English Library at Calle 53, No 524, between Calle 66 and 68, T999-924 8401, www.meridaenglishlibrary.com. Many books on Mexico, used books for sale, bulletin board, magazines. Mon-Fri 0900-1300; Mon 1830-2100, Thu 1600-1900, Sat 1000-1300;. **Medical services** Hospitals: Centro Médico de las Américas (CEMA), Calle 54, No 365, between 33A and Av Pérez Ponce, T999- 926 2111, emergencies T999-927 3199, www.cmasureste.com, affiliated with Mercy Hospital, Miami, Florida, US. Red Cross, T999-924 9813. Dentists Dr Javier Cámara Patrón, Calle 17, No 170, between Calle 8 and 10,

T999-925 3399, www.dentistyucatan.com.
Post office Calle 53, between Calle 52 and 54. Will accept parcels for surface mail to US only, but don't seal parcels destined overseas; they have to be inspected. For surface mail to Europe try Belize, or mail package to US, Poste Restante, for collection later if you are heading that way. **Telephone** International calls are possible from caseta telefonicas. You'll find them all over town, but especially on Calle 62 and 60, north of the plaza. Calls to Europe cost around 4 pesos a minute, 2-3 pesos to the USA.

Izamal and around *p700*
Banks Bank on square with statue to Fray Diego de Landa, south side of convent. **Post office** On opposite side of square to convent.

Chichén Itzá *p700*
Banks ATMs on the main street.

Internet Available in Pisté.
Telephone International calls may be placed from Teléfonos de México, opposite Hotel Xaybe.

Valladolid and around *p702, map p703*
Banks Banamex, Calle 42, No 206; Bancomer, Calle 40, No 196; HSBC, Calle 41, No 201; Santander Serfin, Calle 39, No 229.
Internet Phonet, west side of the plaza, daily 1000-2100, internet costs US$1 per hr and there are long-distance call facilities. There are other internet cafes. **Laundry** Teresita, Calle 33 between 40 and 42, US$6 for 5½ kg.
Post office On east side of plaza, 0800-1500 (no parcels for abroad). **Telephone** Telmex phone office on Calle 42, just north of square; expensive Computel offices at bus station and next to Hotel San Clemente; Ladatel phonecards can be bought from *farmacias* for use in phone booths.

State of Quintana Roo

The burgeoning international destinations of Cancún, Playa del Carmen, Isla Mujeres and Cozumel overshadow the eastern coast of the Yucatán and the State of Quintana Roo. Resorts: either love them, hate them, but they do provide the full holiday experience, complete with beautiful beaches, luxury hotels and reliable restaurants. If Cancún is your port of entry for a trip through Mexico and Central America, it will certainly make for a good contrast to other regions. Diving in the area is popular, either off the coast of Isla Mujeres or Cozumel, or in the underwater caves or cenotes found in the region. The Maya ruins of Tulum are gloriously located, and the quieter spot of Cobá is worth a trip, as is the wilderness reserve of Sian Ka'an. To the far south, Chetumal seems a world away from the tourist hot spots, but it is the stepping-off point for travel to Belize and Guatemala. ➤➤ *For listings, see pages 733-754.*

Isla Holbox → *Phone code: 984. Colour map 3, A3.*
Also north of Valladolid, but in the neighbouring state of Quintana Roo, turn off the road to Puerto Juárez after Nuevo Xcan to Isla Holbox. Second-class buses to **Chiquilá** for boats, from Cancún, six times a day, 3½ hours, US$6; also direct from Tizimín at 1130, connecting with the ferry, US$2.20. The express ferry leaves for Holbox 0645, 1030 and 1530, 10 minutes, US$4, returning to Chiquilá at 0745, 1130 and 1630. There is also a slower ferry, 0930, 1330, 1530 and 1830, returning to Chiquilá at 0800, 1200, 1430 and 1700, 45 mins, US$2 and a car ferry at 0800 and 1330, returning 1100 and 1500, US$8.50 for one car and up to five passengers. If you miss the ferry a fisherman will probably take you (for about US$14). You can leave your car in the care of the harbour master for a small charge; his house is east of the dock. Take water with you if possible. During 'El Norte' season, the water is turbid and the beach is littered with seaweed.

There are five more uninhabited islands beyond Holbox. Beware of sharks and barracuda, although very few nasty occurrences have been reported. Off the rough and mostly unpopulated bulge of the Yucatán coastline are several islands, once notorious for contraband. Beware of mosquitoes in the area.

Cancún ➤➤ pp733-754. Colour map 3, A3.

→ *Phone code: 998.*

In 1970, when Cancún was 'discovered' by the Mexican tourist board, it was an inaccessible strip of barren land with beautiful beaches; the only road went straight past Cancún to Puerto Juárez for the ferry to Isla Mujeres, which had been a national tourist destination

1 **Cancún**

⇒ Cancún maps
1 Cancún, page 717
2 Around Cancún, page 719

200 metres
200 yards

N

Sleeping	Presidente Inter-	La Habichuela **4**
Cancún Rosa **1**	Continental **9**	Labná **8**
El Alux **3**	San Carlos **7**	La Parilla **9**
El Rey del Caribe **2**	Weary Traveller **6**	Mercado 23 **11**
Las Palmas **10**		Pastelería Italiana **5**
Le Meridien **8**	**Eating**	Pericos **6**
Margaritas **4**	El Pescador **2**	Rincón Yucateco **7**
María Isabel **11**	El Poblano **10**	
Mayan Hostel Cancún **5**	El Rincón del Vino **3**	

since the 1950s. Massive international investment and government sponsorship saw the luxury resort of Cancún completed within 25 years. The 25-km hotel zone, set on a narrow strip of land in the shape of a number seven alongside the coast, is an ultra-modern American-style boulevard, with five-star hotels, high-tech nightclubs, high-class malls and branches of US chain restaurants. Cancún's presence on the international tourism market is indisputable. From all-in-one package tours to international government conferences, it's worth a trip just to see what it's like. Despite significant damage by hurricane Wilma in 2005, Cancún has managed to recover rapidly and retains its place as Mexico's prime resort.

Ins and outs

Getting there **Cancún airport** ① www.cancun-airport.com, is 16 km south of the city. A fixed price *colectivo* taxi to the **Hotel Zone** or the centre costs US$9; pay at the kiosk outside airport. Drivers go via the Hotel Zone, but must take you to whichever part of the city centre you want. If going to the centre, make sure you know the name and address of your hotel before you get in the taxi, or the driver will offer to take you to a budget hotel of his own choice. ADO shuttle buses go to the centre via Avenida Tulum every 30 minutes from the airport. There is a tourist information kiosk in the airport, and a *casa de cambio*.
➤➤ *See Transport, page 748.*

Getting around Ruta 1 and Ruta 2 buses go from the centre to the Hotel Zone, US$0.50; Ruta 1 runs 24 hours and goes via Avenida Tulum; Ruta 2 runs 0500-0330 and goes via Avenida Cobá to the bus terminal. Buses to the Hotel Zone can be caught from many stops along Avenida Tulum. Buses to **Puerto Juárez** for the boat to Isla Mujeres leave from outside **Cinema Royal**, across Avenida Tulum from the bus terminal, US$0.70. To get around in the centre, board a bus at Plaza 2000 and ask the driver if he's going to Mercado 28; those buses go along Avenida Yaxchilán; all others go to the Hotel Zone. Taxis are cheap and abundant in Cancún. The flat rate for anywhere within the centre is US$1.50 and the Hotel Zone from the centre US$10-20. Many taxis stop at **El Crucero**, the junction of Avenida Tulum and Avenida López Portillo outside Plaza 2000, but there are often queues.

Orientation **Downtown Cancún** is a world apart from the resort area. It evolved from temporary shacks housing the thousands of builders working on the Hotel Zone, and is now a massive city with very little character. The main avenue is Tulum, formerly the highway running through the city when it was first conceived. It is now the location of the handicraft market, the main shops, banks and the municipal tourist office. There are also restaurants, but the better ones are along Avenida Yaxchilán, which is also the main centre for nightlife.

The cheaper end of the city, and a good area for budget travellers to base themselves, is around **El Crucero** (see above). The rest of the city is fairly expensive, but not as much as the Hotel Zone. The city is laid out in *supermanzanas* (SM), the blocks of streets between avenues, with smaller *manzanas* (M), or blocks, within them. Often the address you are given is, for example, SM24, M6, L3. L stands for *lote*, and is the precise number of the building within its *manzana*. This can lead to confusion when walking about, as the streets also have names, often not mentioned in the addresses. Look closely at street signs and you will see the SM and the M numbers. Taxi drivers generally respond better to addresses based on the *manzana* system. Also confusingly, there are several one-way streets with the same name, running parallel to each other, in opposite directions – this applies to all the streets with names of flowers in the centre; Margaritas, Tulipanes, etc. If you can't find a street number, chances are the place you're looking for is in the next street.

Tourist information The city's **tourist office** ① *Av Yaxchilan 6, SM17, T998-881 9000, www.qroo.gob.mx*, will furnish you with a glossy pocket guide to Cancún full of adverts for expensive restaurants. There are also **Fonatur** and **Sectur** offices ① *Av Cobá, corner of Av Nader*.

Cancún to Isla Mujeres
A strip of coastline north of **Punta Sam** is officially part of Isla Mujeres. It is being developed as a luxury resort, without the high-rise buildings.

Puerto Juárez, about 3 km north of Cancún, is the dock for the cheaper ferry services to Isla Mujeres; there is also a bus terminal, but services are more frequent from Cancún. There are many buses between Cancún and Puerto Juárez; for example, No 8 opposite the bus terminal (US$0.70). A taxi from Puerto Juárez to downtown Cancún should be no more than US$2.50, but overcharging is rife.

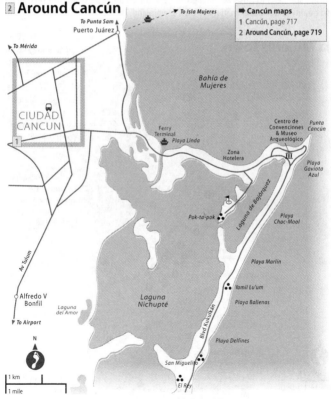

2 Around Cancún

➡ **Cancún maps**
1 Cancún, page 717
2 **Around Cancún, page 719**

→ *Phone code: 998.*

A refreshing antidote to the urban sprawl of Cancún, Isla Mujeres is a good place to relax for a few days away from the hurly-burly of package tourism. The island is especially pleasant in the evening, when all the Cancún day trippers have gone. The town is strictly low rise, with brightly coloured buildings giving it a Caribbean island feel. The island's laws prohibit the construction of any building higher than three floors and US franchises such as McDonald's and Walmart are not allowed to open branches here. Although Isla Mujeres remains laid-back and low-key compared to its mainland neighbours, there's been a lot of building on the quieter western side and by now there is only the protected area around El Garrafon and the very south that's escaped the onslaught of holidaymakers. The rougher, wilder shores of eastern Isla, where the sea is too choppy to swim in, are still quiet with only a few houses overlooking the sea.

There are several good beaches on Isla Mujeres, the best being **Playa Cocos** on the northwest coast, five minutes' walk from the town. Further south, there are several places to swim, snorkel and observe marine life. Restaurants and nightspots are plentiful, of good quality and cheaper than those on the mainland. The people are also friendlier and

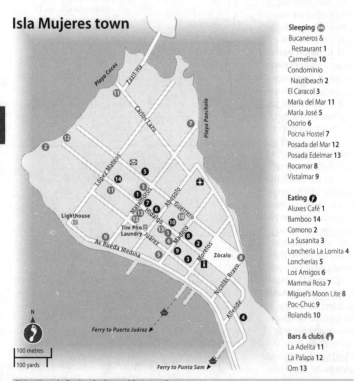

Isla Mujeres town

Sleeping 💤
Bucaneros &
  Restaurant **1**
Carmelina **10**
Condominio
  Nautibeach **2**
El Caracol **3**
María del Mar **11**
María José **5**
Osorio **6**
Pocna Hostel **7**
Posada del Mar **12**
Posada Edelmar **13**
Rocamar **8**
Vistalmar **9**

Eating 🍴
Aluxes Café **1**
Bamboo **14**
Comono **2**
La Susanita **3**
Lonchería La Lomita **4**
Loncherías **5**
Los Amigos **6**
Mamma Rosa **7**
Miguel's Moon Lite **8**
Poc-Chuc **9**
Rolandis **10**

Bars & clubs 🍸
La Adelita **11**
La Palapa **12**
Om **13**

more easygoing here. There are several ways to explore the island: you can rent a golf cart, many of which chug around the streets all day, good for families; mopeds and bicycles are cheap and easy to rent; and there's a public bus that runs all the way from the town to El Paraíso, almost at the southern tip of the island.

The name Isla Mujeres refers to the large number of clay female idols found by the Spaniards here in 1518. The island contains the only known Maya shrine to a female deity: Ixchel, goddess of the moon and fertility. The ruins of the shrine are at the southern tip of the island. The **tourist office** ① *Rueda Medina, opposite the ferry dock, Mon-Sat 0900-1800, Sun 0900-1400 (although the latter can be erratic), www.isla-mujeres.com.mx*, is very helpful. The immigration office is next door.

Sights

Most of the sights south of the town can be seen in a day. The first of these, 5 km from the town, is the **Turtle Farm** ① *daily 0900-1700, US$2*, with hundreds of sea turtles weighing from 170 g to 270 kg in a humane setting. To get there, take the bus to the final stop, Playa Paraíso, double back and walk five minutes along the main road.

At the centre of the island are the curious remains of a pirate's domain, called **Hacienda Mundaca** ① *daily 0900-1700, US$2*. A big, new arch gate marks its entrance. Paths have been laid out among the large trees, but all that remains of the estate (called Vista Alegre) are one small building and a circular garden with raised beds, a well and a gateway. To get there, get off the bus at the final stop, and turn the opposite way to the beach; the house is a short walk away.

El Garrafón national park ① *T998-193 3360, www.garrafon.com*, is a snorkelling centre 7 km from the town, being turned into an overpriced theme park à la Xcaret on the mainland (see page 726). Snorkelling is still possible, with a 12-m bronze cross submerged offshore for your exploration; by tour only. Although a national park, it can only be entered if you pay a steep US$50 for a snorkelling and meal package at the expensive restaurant. It's no longer possible to enter to have a look around and enjoy the beach without paying the full whack. Arrive after 1300 and the price drops to US$39. The snorkelling is good past the pier, along a reef with some dead coral. Large numbers of different coloured fish can be seen at very close range. If you want to walk to El Garrafón from the bus stop at Playa Paraíso (bus from town US$0.30), take the second path on the right to the beach from the main road. The first path leads through **Restaurant Playa Paraíso**, which charges US$1 for the privilege of walking through their premises to the beach. Once on the beach, you can walk all the way to El Garrafón along the coast, although it gets very rocky for the final part. It is easier to go as far as the cluster of beach villas, then cut through one of them (ask for permission) to the main road. The whole walk takes about half an hour. When you arrive at El Garrafón, turn right at the building site, go down the hill to **Hotel Garrafón del Castillo**, which is the entrance to the snorkelling centre, where you will need to pay the US$50.

A further 15 minutes' walk from El Garrafón, at the tip of the island, are the ruins of the Maya shrine **Santuario Maya a la Diosa Ixchel** ① *US$2.20*, dedicated to Ixchel the goddess of fertility. These were once free to visit, but unfortunately they have been bought and developed as part of the El Garrafón national park. A cultural centre has also been built here with large sculptures by several international artists, looking somewhat out of place. Taxis to the southernmost part of the island, Punta Sur, are US$3, cheaper than the inflated prices from El Garrafón: US$4.50 to town and US$6 to Playa Norte, even though the distance is shorter.

South of Cancún ⊕⊕⊕⊕⊕⊕⊕ ➤ pp733-754. Colour map 3, A3.

Puerto Morelos → Phone code: 998.

A quiet village 34 km south of Cancún, Puerto Morelos is one of the few places that still retains some of the charm of an unspoilt fishing village, making it a good place to stop over en route to larger towns further south, such as Playa del Carmen. The village is really just a large plaza right on the seafront with a couple of streets going off it. If on arrival at Cancún airport you don't wish to spend the night in the city, you could get a taxi directly to Puerto Morelos. This is also the place to catch the car ferry to the island of Cozumel (see below). The **Sinaltur** office on the plaza offers a range of good snorkelling, kayak and fishing trips. **Goyos**, just north of the plaza, offers jungle adventures and rooms for rent, although erratic hours are maintained.

Playa del Carmen → Phone code: 984.

What used to be a pleasant little place on the beach has lost the charms of its former existence as a fishing village. Recent development for tourism has been rapid, but Playa, as it is known locally, has not had the high-rise treatment of Cancún. The beach is a dazzling white, with crystal-clear shallow water, ideal for swimming and further out there is good scuba-diving. There is lodging for every budget, and plenty of good restaurants and bars of every type. Many travellers choose Playa as their base for trips to the ruins of Tulum in the south, and archaeological sites such as Cobá in the interior.

The town is laid out in a grid system, with the main centre of tourist activity based on Avenida 5 (pedestrianized in the central section), one block from and parallel with the beach. This is where the more expensive hotels and restaurants are, as well as being the centre for nightlife. Cheaper accommodation can be found up Avenida Juárez and further north of the beach.

Tourist information is scant, although there is a new **tourism office** ① *Av Juárez, between Av 25 and Av 30, T984-873 2804*, which has useful information and maps, and the kiosk on the main plaza (not always manned) will provide a copy of *Destination Playa del Carmen,* a useful guide with maps produced by US residents.

Cozumel ⊕⊕⊕⊕⊕⊕ ➤ pp733-754. Colour map 3, A3.

→ Phone code: 987.

The town, San Miguel de Cozumel, is a seedy, overpriced version of Playa del Carmen. Daily tour groups arrive on cruises from Miami and Cancún, and the town's services seem geared towards this type of tourist. But Cozumel is a mecca for scuba divers, with many beautiful offshore reefs to explore, as well as much interesting wildlife and birdlife. Travellers looking for a beach holiday with some nightlife will find the island disappointing compared to Playa del Carmen. There is only one good beach on the west side, and the eastern Atlantic coast is far too rugged and choppy for swimming.

Ins and outs

The airport is just north of San Miguel with a minibus shuttle service to the hotels. There are 10-minute flights to and from the airstrip near Playa del Carmen, as well as flights linking to Mexico City, Cancún, Chichén Itzá and Houston (Texas). The passenger ferry from Playa del Carmen runs every hour and the car ferry leaves twice daily from Puerto Morelos. There are no local buses, but Cozumel town is small enough to visit on foot. To get around the island, there are organized tours or taxis; otherwise hire a jeep, moped or bicycle. ►► *See Transport, page 750.*

San Miguel de Cozumel

The island's only town has very little character, mainly due to the construction of a US air base during the Second World War, whose airfield has now been converted for civilian use. There is a variety of accommodation, with a few budget hotels, but mainly focusing on the luxury end of the market.

Playa del Carmen

Sleeping 🛏
Alhambra **1** B4
Blue Parrot **2** A4
Casa Tucán **5** B3
Cielo & El Carboncito
  Restaurant **7** B3
Happy Gecko **4** A3
Hostel Playa **8** A2
Las Molcas **6** D3

Maya Bric **10** A4
Mom's **11** B2
Playacar Palace **3** D3
Posada Marinelly **13** C2
Tides Riviera Maya **9** A1
Tropical Casablanca **12** A4
Urban Hostel **14** B3

Eating 🍴
Billy the Kid **1** B2
Buenos Aires **6** B3

El Famolito **20** A4
El Fogon **8** A2
Glass Bar **12** A4
Habita Bookshop &
  Café **18** A4
Java Joe's **2** A4
Karen's **9** C3
La Parrilla **11** A4
Los Comales **10** B3
Maktub **19** A4
Pez Vela **5** C3

Rolandi **4** D3
Sushi-Tlan **21** A4
Tortas del Carmen **3** B2
Yaxche **7** A3

Bars & clubs 🍸
Beer Bucket **13** A3
Coco Maya **16** A4
El Cielo **17** A4
OM **15** A4
Tequila Barrel **14** A4

On the waterfront between Calle 4 and 6, the **Museo de la Isla** ⓘ *daily 0900-1700, US$3,* provides a history of the island. There is a bookshop, art gallery and rooftop restaurant, which has excellent food (good breakfasts) and views of the sunset.

Beaches

In the north of the island the beaches are sandy and wide, although those at the Zona Hotelera Norte were damaged in 1989 and are smaller than they used to be. At the end of the paved road, walk up the unmade road until it becomes 'dual carriageway'; turn left for the narrow beach, which is a bit dirty. Cleaner beaches are accessible only through the hotels. South of San Miguel, **San Francisco** is good, if narrow (clean, very popular, lockers at **Pancho's**, expensive restaurants), but others are generally narrower still and rockier.

1 Cozumel

➡ Cozumel maps
1 Cozumel, page 724
2 San Miguel de Cozumel, page 725

All the main hotels are on the sheltered west coast. The east Caribbean coast is rockier, but very picturesque; swimming and diving on the unprotected side is very dangerous owing to ocean undercurrents. The only safe place is at a sheltered bay at **Chen Río**. Another bay with possibilities is **Punta Morena**, which is a good surf beach. There is good accommodation (contact Matt at **Deep Blue**, page 747, for more information and transport) and seafood (try the *ceviche*). There are three good (and free) places for snorkelling. The beach in front of **Hotel Las Glorias** is 15 minutes' walk south from ferry (you can walk through the hotel's reception); **Playa Corona**, further south, is too far to walk, so hitch or take a taxi (there is a small restaurant and pier); and **Xul-Ha**, further south still, has a bar and comfortable beach chairs.

Archaeological sites
There are over 30 archaeological sites on Cozumel; those on the east coast are mostly single buildings (thought to have been lookouts and navigational aids). The easiest to see are the restored ruins of the Maya-Toltec period at *San Gervasio* ① *daily 0700-1600, US$5.50, guides are on hand, or you can buy a self-guiding booklet at the bookshop on the square in San Miguel, or at the flea market, for US$1.* Situated in the north of the island (7½ km from Cozumel town, then 6 km to the left up a paved road, toll US$1), it is an

② San Miguel de Cozumel

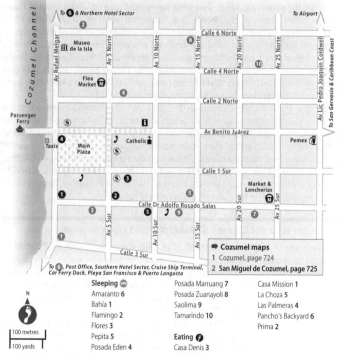

➡ **Cozumel maps**
1 Cozumel, page 724
2 San Miguel de Cozumel, page 725

N
100 metres
100 yards

To ⑥, Post Office, Southern Hotel Sector, Cruise Ship Terminal,
Car Ferry Dock, Playa San Francisco & Puerto Langosta

Sleeping
Amaranto 6
Bahía 1
Flamingo 2
Flores 3
Pepita 5
Posada Eden 4

Posada Marruang 7
Posada Zuanayoli 8
Saolima 9
Tamarindo 10

Eating
Casa Denis 3

Casa Mission 1
La Choza 5
Las Palmeras 4
Pancho's Backyard 6
Prima 2

interesting site, which is quite spread out, with *sacbés* (sacred roads) between the groups of buildings. There are no large structures, but an attractive plaza, an arch, and pigment can be seen in places. It is also a pleasant place to listen to birdsong, see butterflies, animals (if lucky), lizards, land crabs and insects. **Castillo Real** is one of many sites on the north eastern coast, but the road to this part of the island is in bad condition and the ruins themselves are very small. **El Cedral** in the southwest (3 km from the main island road) is a two-room temple, overgrown with trees, in the centre of the village of the same name. Behind the temple is a ruin, and next to it a modern church with a green and white facade. In the village are large permanent shelters for agricultural shows, rug sellers and locals who pose with *iguanas doradas* (golden iguanas). **El Caracol**, where the sun, in the form of a shell, was worshiped, is 1 km from the southernmost Punta Celarain. This is now part of the Punta Sur ecological reserve, see below. At Punta Celarain is an old lighthouse.

Around the island

A circuit of the island on paved roads can easily be done in a day. Head due east out of San Miguel (take the continuation of Avenida Juárez). Make the detour to San Gervasio before continuing to the Caribbean coast at Mescalito's restaurant. Here, turn left for the northern tip (road unsuitable for ordinary vehicles), or right for the south, passing Punta Morena, Chen Río, Punta Chiqueros (where there is good bathing and a restaurant), El Mirador (a low viewpoint with sea-worn rocks, look out for holes) and Paradise Cove. At this point, the paved road heads west while an unpaved road continues south to Punta Celarain. Here there is the **Punta Sur ecological reserve** ① *T987-872 0914, www.cozumelparks.com.mx, US$10*, an ecotourism development, with a variety of natural landscapes with lagoons and mangrove jungles. A snorkelling centre has opened here as well as a viewing platform. On the road west, opposite the turn-off to El Cedral, is a sign to **Restaurante Mac y Cía**, an excellent fish restaurant on a lovely beach, popular with dive groups for lunch. Next is Playa San Francisco (see page 724). A few more kilometres leads to the former **Holiday Inn**, the last big hotel south of San Miguel.

Just after this is **Parque Chankanab** ① *0700-1700, US$16, snorkelling mask and fins US$5, use of underwater camera US$25*, which used to be an idyllic lagoon behind the beach (9 km from San Miguel). After it became totally spoilt, it was restored as a national park, with the lagoon, crystal clear again, a botanical garden with local and imported plants, a 'Maya Area' (rather artificial), swimming (ideal for families with young children), snorkelling, dive shops, souvenirs, expensive but good restaurants and lockers (US$2). Soon the road enters the southern Hotel Zone at the Stouffer Presidente, coming to the cruise ship dock and car ferry port on the outskirts of town.

South of Playa del Carmen ●❷▲●① ›› pp733-754. Colour map 3, A3/B3.

The Maya site of **Xcaret** ① *T01800-292 2738, www.xcaret.com, US$69 adults, children US$34.50*, an ancient port called Polé, was the departure point for voyages to Cozumel. It has now been turned into an overpriced and very tacky theme park catering exclusively for day-trippers. There is a 1-km walk from the entrance to Xcaret. The alternative is to take a taxi, or a tour from Playa del Carmen or Cancún (in a multicoloured bus). You can also walk along the beach from Playa del Carmen (three hours).

A luxury resort, 102 km south of Cancún, 20 km north of Tulum, **Akumal** is reached easily by bus from there or from Playa del Carmen (30 minutes). There is a small lagoon 3 km north of Akumal, with good snorkelling. The coastline from Playa del Carmen down to just short of Tulum to the south is known as the 'Riviera Maya' – a strip of upmarket, generally all-inclusive hotels. Two ferries run daily to Cozumel. Also just south of Akumal are **Chemuyil** (*palapas* for hammocks, US$4, free shower, expensive restaurant, laundry facilities) and **Xcacel** (campsite has water, bathrooms, cold showers and restaurant, very clean, US$2 per person, vehicles free, snorkel hire US$5 a day, beautiful swimming in the bay). Ask the guards if you can go on a turtle-protection patrol at night (May to July).

Thirteen kilometres north of Tulum, 122 km from Cancún (bus from Playa del Carmen, 45 minutes), the beautiful clear lagoon of **Laguna Xel-Há** ① *daily 0830-1800, US$10*, is full of fish, but fishing is not allowed as it is a national park. Snorkelling gear can be rented at US$7 for a day, but it is often in poor repair; it's better to rent it from your hotel. Lockers cost US$1. Arrive as early as possible to see fish as the lagoon is full of tourists throughout most of the day. Snorkelling areas are limited by fencing. Bungalows, first-class hotels and fast-food restaurants are being built. The food and drink is very expensive. There is a marvellous jungle path to one of the lagoon bays. Xel-Há ruins, known also as **Los Basadres** ① *US$3.35*, are located across the road from the beach of the same name. There are few tourists here but there is not much to see. You may have to jump the fence to visit; there is a beautiful *cenote* at the end of the ruins where you can have a lovely swim.

Tulum → *Phone code: 984. Colour map 3, A3.*
① *Daily 0800-1700, last entry 1630, entry US$3.60, parking US$1.50, students with Mexican ID free. Guided tours from US$36 for 4 people, light-and-sound show US$12, 1930-2000.*
The Maya-Toltec ruins of Tulum are perched on coastal cliffs in a beautiful setting above the azure sea. The ruins are 12th century, with city walls of white stone. The temples were dedicated to the worship of the Falling God, or the Setting Sun, represented as a falling character over nearly all the west-facing doors (Cozumel was the home of the Rising Sun). The same idea is reflected in the buildings, which are wider at the top than at the bottom.

The main structure is the **Castillo**, which commands a view of both the sea and the forested Quintana Roo lowlands stretching westwards. All the Castillo's openings face west, as do most, but not all, of the doorways at Tulum. Look for the alignment of the **Falling God** on the temple of that name (to the left of the Castillo) with the pillar and the back door in the **House of the Chultún** (the nearest building in the centre group to the entrance). The majority of the main structures are roped off so that you cannot climb the Castillo, nor get close to the surviving frescoes, especially on the **Temple of the Frescoes**.

Tulum is crowded with tourists (the best time to visit is between 0800 and 0900). Take a towel and swimsuit if you wish to scramble down from the ruins to one of the two beaches for a swim (the larger of the two is less easy to get to). The reef is from 600 m to 1km from the shore, so if you wish to snorkel you must either be a strong swimmer, or take a boat trip.

There is a tourist complex at the entrance to the ruins. Guidebooks can be bought in the shops, local guides can also be hired. About two hours are needed to view at leisure. The parking area is near Highway 307 and there's a handicraft market. A small train takes you from the parking area to the ruins for US$1.40, or it is an easy 500-m walk. The paved road continues down the coast to **Boca Paila** and beyond, access by car to this road from the car park is now forbidden. To reach the road south of the ruins, access is possible 1 km from Tulum village. Public buses drop passengers at El Crucero, a crossroads 500 m north of the car park for Tulum Ruinas (an easy walk) where there is an **ADO** bus terminal that is open for a few hours from 0800; at the crossroads are some hotels, a shop (which will exchange traveller's cheques) and a little way down Highway 307 a **Pemex** station.

If you are staying in the area, the beach running south of the ruins is dotted with quiet, isolated *palapas*, *cabañas* and hotels to fit most budgets.

Alternatively the **village of Tulum** (as opposed to the ruins) is 4 km south of El Crucero. A taxi from the village to the ruins costs US$3. It is not very large but it's growing rapidly and has a bus station, post office, banks (HSBC and Scotiabank), a few grocery shops, two bakeries, hotels and restaurants. There is a **tourist information kiosk** ① *on the main road, near the bus terminal,* but on the opposite side. The information centre set up by the Weary Traveller backpacker centre had taken over as the primary source of information for this area, but at the time of writing this was currently closed. There are plans to re-open it and the hostel still has friendly and knowledgeable staff, who can give fairly impartial information on hotels, trips and restaurants. Another source of information is the **Sian Ka'an Information Centre** ① *Av Tulum between Satélite and Géminis, Tulum, T984-871 2363, siankaan_tours@ hotmail.com,* which has information about visiting the reserve (see below) and several other areas of interest.

Cobá → Phone code: 985. Colour map 3, A3.
① *Daily 0800-1700, US$4.50.*

Once an important Maya city in the eighth and ninth centuries AD, the village of Cobá lies on either side of Lago Cobá, surrounded by dense jungle, 47 km inland from Tulum. It is a quiet, friendly village, with few tourists staying overnight. However, Cobá is becoming more popular as a destination for tourist buses, which come in at 1030; arrive before that to avoid the crowds and the heat (on the 0430 bus from Valladolid, if not staying in Cobá). Take insect repellent.

The entrance to the ruins of this large but little-excavated city is at the end of the lake between the two parts of the village. A second lake, **Lago Macanxoc**, is within the site. There are turtles and many fish in the

Tulum

To Cancún (4 km)   •• Ruins

Av Tulum
Andrómeda Ote
Sol Ote

To Cobá

(4 km)

C Tulum-Boca Paila

Escorpión Sur
Libra Sur
Polar Pte
Gamma Ote
Géminis Sur
Scotia (S)
Sagitario Pte
Iguana Bike Hire
Sol Ote
Satélite Sur
Venus Ote
Centauro Sur
Mercurio Ote
Taxis
Orión Sur
Andrómeda Ote
Asteroides Ote
Neptuno Ote
Beta Sur
Casa de Cambio (S)
HSBC (S)
Osiris Sur
Alfa Sur
Polar Pte
Av Tulum

ADO

Neptuno Pte
Aurora Sur
Omega Sur
Aerolito
Jupiter Sur
Sol Pte
Saturno Pte
Luna Pte
Leo Sur
Iglesia Maya
Acuario Sur
El Mariachi

N
Not to scale

To Biosphere Reserve

Playa Condesa 6
Posada Lamar 10
Posada Margherita 9
Rancho Tranquilo 3
Weary Traveler 2
Zazil-Kin 5

Sleeping
Ana y José 12
Cabañas Diamante 7
Dos Celbas 13
Eco Tulum 8
Los Arrecifes 11
Mar Caribe 4
Maya 1

Eating
Don Cafeto 4
Doña Tinas 2
El Mariachi 1
La Zebra 5
Mezzanine 3

lakes and it's also an area good for birdwatching. Both lakes and their surrounding forest can be seen from the summit of the **Iglesia**, the tallest structure in the **Cobá Group**. There are three other groups of buildings to visit: the **Macanxoc Group**, mainly stelae, about 1½ km from the Cobá Group; **Las Pinturas**, 1 km northeast of Macanxoc, with a temple and the remains of other buildings that had columns in their construction; the **Nohoch Mul Group**, at least another kilometre from Las Pinturas. Nohoch Mul has the tallest pyramid in the northern Yucatán, a magnificent structure, from which the views of the jungle on all sides are superb. The delight of Cobá is in the architecture of the jungle, with birds, butterflies, spiders and lizards and the many uncovered structures that hint at the vastness of the city in its heyday (the urban extension of Cobá is put at some 70 sq km). An unusual feature is the network of *sacbés* (sacred roads), which connect the groups in the site and are known to have extended across the entire Maya Yucatán. Over 40 *sacbés* pass through Cobá, some local, some of great length, such as the 100-km road to Yaxuná in Yucatán state.

At the lake, toucans may be seen very early; also look out for mot-mots in the early morning. The guards at the site are very strict about opening and closing times so it is hard to get in to see the dawn or sunset from a temple.

The paved road into Cobá ends at **Lago Cobá**; to the left are the ruins, to the right **Villas Arqueológicas**, see page 738. The roads around Cobá are badly potholed. It is possible to drive into the reserve from Tulum village as far as Punta Allen (58 km; the road is opposite the turning to Cobá; it is not clearly marked, and the final section is badly potholed); beyond that you need a launch. From the south it is possible to drive to Punta Herrero (unmade road, see Mahahual, page 730).

Sian Ka'an biosphere reserve → *Colour map 3, A3.*
ⓘ *Daily 0900-1500, 1800-2000, US$2. For information, visit Los Amigos de Sian Ka'an in Cancún, T998-892 2958, www.amigosdesiankaan.org; very helpful.*
The reserve covers 4500 sq km of the Quintana Roo coast. About a third is covered in tropical forest, another third is savannah and mangrove and a third coastal and marine habitats, including 110 km of barrier reef. Mammals include jaguar, puma, ocelot and other cats, monkeys, tapir, peccaries, manatee and deer; turtles nest on the beaches; there are crocodiles and a wide variety of birds. Do not try to get there independently without a car.

Muyil
ⓘ *Daily 0800-1700, US$1.20.*
The ruins of Muyil at **Chunyaxché** comprising three partly overgrown pyramids are to be found on the left-hand side of the road towards Felipe Carrillo Puerto, 18 km south of Tulum. One of the pyramids is undergoing reconstruction; the other two are relatively untouched. They are very quiet, with interesting birdlife although they are mosquito infested. Beyond the last pyramid is Laguna Azul, which is good for swimming and snorkelling in blue, clean water (you don't have to pay for the pool if you don't visit the pyramids).

Felipe Carrillo Puerto → *Colour map 3, A3.*
The cult of the 'talking cross', see page 680, was founded here. The **Santuario de la Cruz Parlante** is five blocks west of the Pemex station on Highway 307. The beautiful main square, which has playground equipment for children, is dominated by the Catholic church, built by the Cruzob in the 19th century (see page 680). Legend has it that the unfinished bell tower will only be completed when the descendants of those who heard the talking cross reassert control of the region.

Mahahual and around → *Colour map 3, A3.*

Further south on Route 307, at Cafetal, a good road heads east to Mahahual (Majahual) on the coast (56 km from Cafetal), a peaceful, unspoilt place with clear water and beautiful beaches. The peace is occasionally interrupted by visiting cruise ships, which travel along the Mexican and Central American coast. A combi leaves from downtown at 0600, and from the bus terminal in Chetumal at 0600 and 1515, returning at 0630, 0845 and 1600. An offshore excursion is to **Banco Chinchorro**, where there is a coral bank and a white-sand beach.

About 2 km before Mahahual a paved road to the left goes to **Puerto Bravo** and on to Placer and **Punta Herrero** (in the Sian Ka'an biosphere reserve, see above).

Xcalak → *Colour map 3, B3.*

Across the bay from Chetumal, at the very tip of Quintana Roo, is this fishing village with a few shops selling basic supplies and one restaurant. A few kilometres north of Xcalak are two hotels, **Costa de Cocos** and **Villa Caracol**; the latter is good, with *cabañas*, although expensive. It also has fishing and diving. From here trips can be arranged to the islands of Banco Chinchorro or to San Pedro, Belize. In the village you may be able to rent a boat to explore Chetumal Bay and Banco Chinchorro. Do *not* try to walk from Xcalak along the coast to San Pedro, Belize; the route is virtually impassable. Xcalak can be reached from Chetumal by private launch (two hours), or by the unpaved road from Cafetal to Mahahual, then turning south for 55 km (186 km by road from Chetumal), suitable for cars but needs skilled driver). There are *colectivos* from Chetumal, daily 0700-1900, 16 de Septiembre 183 y Mahatma Ghandi, check return times. The bus runs Friday 1600 and Sunday 0600, returning Saturday morning and Sunday afternoon (details from Chetumal tourist office, see below).

Chetumal ⊜🅿🅾⏲🅰🅗🅒 ➤ *pp733-754. Colour map 3, B3.*

→ *Phone code: 983.*

Quintana Roo's state capital, 240 km south of Tulum, is a necessary stopover for travellers en route to Maya sites in the south of the peninsula, and across the frontier to Belize and Guatemala. Although attractions are thin on the ground, Chetumal does have the advantage of being a small Mexican city not devoted to tourism and thus has a more authentic feel than other towns on the Riviera Maya. The Chetumal bay has been designated as a natural protected area for manatees and includes a manatee sanctuary.

The avenues are broad and busy and the centre is lined with huge shops selling cheap imported goods. The main local activity is window shopping, and the atmosphere is more like a North American city, with an impression of affluence that can be a culture shock to the visitor arriving from the much poorer country of Guatemala. The **tourist office** ① *on the main plaza, opposite the Museo de Cultura Maya, Mon-Fri 0900-1900, Sat 0900-1300*, is mainly for trade enquiries. There is very little tourist information in Chetumal; it is usually best to go to a travel agent such as **Tu-Maya** (see page 748).

The *paseo* near the waterfront on Sunday night is worth seeing. The State Congress building has a mural showing the history of Quintana Roo. The **Museo de la Cultura Maya** ① *Av Héroes de Chapultepec by the market, Mon-Thu 0900-1900, Fri-Sun 0900-2000, US$6*, has models of sites and computers explaining the Maya calendar and glyphs. Although there are few original Maya pieces, it gives an excellent overview; some explanations in English, guided tours are available and there's a bookshop with English magazines.

Towards Bacalar

Six kilometres north of Chetumal are the stony beaches of **Calderitas** (bus every 30 minutes from Colón, between Belice and Héroes, US$1.80, or taxi US$5), with many fish restaurants and a campsite (signposted, US$2.75). Beyond are the unexcavated archaeological sites of **Ichpaatun** (13 km), **Oxtancah** (14 km) and **Nohochmul** (20 km). Sixteen kilometres north on Route 307 to Tulum is the **Laguna de los Milagros**, a beautiful lagoon for swimming. Further on, 34 km north of Chetumal, is **Cenote Azul**, more than 70 m deep, with a waterside restaurant serving inexpensive and good seafood and regional food (but awful coffee) until 1800. Both the *laguna* and the *cenote* are deserted in the week.

About 3 km north of Cenote Azul is the village of **Bacalar** (nice, but nothing special) on the **Laguna de Siete Colores**, which has swimming and skin-diving; *colectivos* from terminal (Suchaa) in Chetumal, corner of Miguel Hidalgo and Primo de Verdad, 0700-1900 every 30 minutes, US$1.60, return from plaza when full; also buses from Chetumal bus station every two hours or so, US$1.60. There is a Spanish fort, **San Felipe**, said to have been built around 1729 by the Spanish to defend the area from the English pirates and smugglers of logwood. It overlooks a beautiful shallow, clear, freshwater lagoon, which has abundant birdlife on its shores. A plaque is also here, praying for protection from the British and there is a small **museum** ⓘ *US$0.70*. British ships roamed the islands and reefs, looting Spanish galleons laden with gold, on their way from Peru to Cuba. There are many old shipwrecks on the reef and around the Banco Chinchorro, 50 km out in the Caribbean (information kindly provided by Coral Pitkin of the **Rancho Encantado**, see page 739). There is a dock for swimming from north of the plaza, with a restaurant and disco next to it. North of Bacalar a direct road (Route 293) runs to Muná, on the road between Mérida and Uxmal. Fuel is sold in a side street.

Chetumal

To Bus Station (16 blocks approx)
at Av Insurgentes
To Calderitas

Francisco Primo de Verdad

Colón

Museo de la
Cultura Maya

Colectivo
to Bacalar

Ghandi
ADO

Av Belice

Av Erain Aguilar

Héroes de
Chapultepec

Lázaro Cárdenas

Av Benito Juárez

Independencia

Av Héroes

PE Calles

16 de Septiembre

Av Miguel Hidalgo

Av Reforma

Calzada Veracruz

Zaragoza

Obregón

Othón P Blanco

5 de Mayo

H Escuela Naval

Carmen Ochoa de Merino

Sagrado
Corazón

Palacio de
Gobierno

22 de Enero

Boulevard Bahía

*Bahía de
Chetumal*

To Zoo, Bacalar, Francisco
Escárcega, Kohunlich &
Corozal (Belize)

To Guatemalan Consulate

N

200 metres
200 yards

María Dolores **7**
Palma Real **1**
Real Azteca **8**
Ucum **10**

Sleeping 🛏
Caribe Princess **2**
Cristal **3**
El Dorado **4**
Los Cocos **6**

Eating 🍴
El Emporio **2**
El Fenicio **3**
Los Milagros **4**
Pantoja **5**
Sergio Pizza **1**

Towards Francisco Villa

From Chetumal you can visit the fascinating Maya ruins that lie west on the way (Route 186) to Francisco Villa and Escárcega, if you have a car. There are few tourists in this area

Border essentials: Mexico–Belize

Chetumal

Customs and immigration Procedure can be slow, particularly at peak holiday times when Belizeans come on charter buses for cheap shopping; over the bridge is Belizean passport control. For people entering Mexico, tourist cards are available at the border. It has been reported that only 15 days are given but you can get an additional 30 days at the Servicios Migratorios in Chetumal. Note that fresh fruit cannot be imported into Belize.

Driving Leaving Mexico by car, go to the Mexican immigration office to register your exit and surrender your vehicle permit and tourist card; very straightforward, no charges. Go to the office to obtain compulsory Belizean insurance (also money-changing facilities here). Entering Belize, your car will be registered in your passport.

Exchange Money is checked on entering Belize. Excess Mexican pesos are easily changed into Belizean dollars with men waiting just beyond customs on the Belize side, but they are not there to meet the early bus. You can change US for Belizean dollar bills in the shops at the border, but this is not necessary as US$ are accepted in Belize. If you can get a good rate (dollars to pesos) in the bank, it is sometimes better to buy Belizean dollars with pesos in *casas de cambio* than to wait until you enter Belize where the US dollar/Belize dollar rate is fixed at 1:2.

and few facilities. Take plenty of drinking water. About 25 km from Chetumal at **Ucum** (where fuel is available), you can turn off 5 km south to visit **Palmara**, located along the Río Hondo, which borders Belize; there are swimming holes and restaurant.

Just before Francisco Villa (61 km from Chetumal), the ruins of **Kohunlich** ① *0800-1700, US$3*, lie 8½ km south of the main road, 1½ hours' walk along a sweltering, unshaded road; take plenty of water. Descriptions are in Spanish and English. Every hour or so the van passes for staff working at Explorer Kohunlich, a luxury resort hotel halfway to the ruins, which may give you a lift, but you'll still have 4 km to walk. There are fabulous masks (early Classic, AD 250-500) set on the side of the main pyramid, still bearing red colouring; they are unique of their kind (allow an hour for the site). About 200 m west of the turning for Kohunlich is an immigration office and a stall selling beer; wait here for buses to Chetumal or Xpujil, which have to stop, but first-class buses will not pick up passengers. *Colectivos* 'Nicolás Bravo' from Chetumal, or bus marked 'Zoh Laguna' from bus station pass the turning.

Other ruins here are **Dzibanché** and **Knichná** ① *0900-1700, US$3*. Both are recent excavations and accessible via a dirt road off the Chetumal-Morocoy road. In the 1990s the remains of a Maya king were disinterred at Dzibanché, thought to have been the largest Maya city in southern Quintana Roo, peaking between AD 300 and 1200. Its discoverer, Thomas Gann, named it in 1927 after the Maya glyphs he found engraved on the wood lintels in Temple VI: *Dzibanché* means 'writing on the wood' in Maya. Later excavations revealed a tomb in Temple I, believed to have belonged to a king. Other major structures are the **Temple of the Cormorants** and **Structure XIII**, known as 'The Captives', due to its friezes depicting prisoners. Knichná means 'House of the Sun' in Maya, christened by Thomas Gann in reference to a glyph he found there. To get here, follow the Chetumal-Escárcega road, turn off at Km 58 towards Morocoy, 9 km further on. The road to Dzibanché is 2 km down this road, crossing the turning for Knichná.

For Sleeping and Eating price codes and other relevant information, see Essentials pages 47-51.

⦿ Sleeping

Isla Holbox *p716*

AL Villa Delfines, on the beach, T984-875 2196. Twenty bungalows leading onto the beach, pool, garden and bar, expensive but nice.

AL-A Faro Viejo, Av Juárez, on the beach, T984-875 2217, www.faroviejoholbox. com.mx. Large, breezy rooms looking over the beach. Some rooms with kitchens.

A-B La Palapa, Av Morelos 231, T984-875 2121, www.hotellapalapa.com. Very clean *cabañas*, leading onto the beach.

A-B Mawimbi, T984-875 2003, www.mawimbi.com.mx. Stylishly decorated *cabañas* with kitchenette, stepping out onto the beach.

Camping

Best camping on beach east of village (north side of island).

Cancún *p717, maps p717 and p719*

Accommodation in the hotel zone starts at around US$75, rises quickly and is best arranged as part of a package holiday. The beaches are supposedly public so you don't have to stay in a hotel to hang out on the beach. The centre or downtown area has many cheaper options, but prices are still higher than other parts of the Yucatán Peninsula.

Hotel zone

Some of these hotels have special offers during Jul and Aug, listed in *Riviera Maya Hotels Guide*, available free at the airport. Discounts can be considerable. 2 good options are: **LL Le Meridien**, Retorno del Rey Km 14, T998-881 2200, and **L Presidente Inter-Continental**, Av Kukulcán Km 7.5, T998-848 8700.

Town centre

Many hotels, especially the budget ones, tend to be full during Jul. It is best to get to them as early as possible in the morning, or try to make a reservation if planning to return to Cancún after a trip to the interior or Isla Mujeres. Prices drop considerably in the low season. El Crucero, location of some of the budget hotels, is said by locals to be safe during the day, but unsafe at night.

A-B El Rey del Caribe, Av Uxmal 24, corner Náder, T998-884 2028, www.reycaribe.com. Clean, comfortable a/c rooms, some with cooker and fridge. There's a lush garden slung with hammocks and a spa.

A-B Margaritas, Yaxchilán 41, corner Jasmines, T998-881 7870, www.margaritas cancun.com. A clean and modern hotel with a range of efficient services including restaurant, bar, car rental, laundry and pool. There are more than 100 rooms, all with a/c, balcony and cable TV.

C Cancún Rosa, Margaritas 2, Local 10, T998-884 0623. Located close to the bus terminal, this hotel has tidy rooms of various sizes (including family size), all with cable TV and a/c. Management is friendly.

C-D María Isabel, Palmera 59, T998-884 9015, hotelmariaisabelCancun@yahoo.com.mx. Located near the bus station and Av Tulum, this small hotel has clean and relatively economical rooms, all with a/c and TV. Friendly and recommended, but can be noisy.

C-E Mayan Hostel Cancún, Margaritas 17 SM22, T998-892 0103, www.mayan hostel.com. Price per person. Private rooms, *palapa*-style dorms, fan or a/c, Breakfast, dinner and internet included in the price. Laundry and kitchen. Good service.

D El Alux, Av Uxmal 21, T998-884 0556, www.hotelalux.com. Turn left and first right from bus station. Clean rooms with a/c and bath. Some are cheaper and good value. Beware of the persistent tout outside, trying to take you to a cheap hovel. Recommended.

D San Carlos, Cedro 40 (5th turning onto Cedro from bus terminal), opposite Mercado 23, T998-884 0602, www.hotelsancarlos Cancún.com. Handy for the bus terminal. Mixed bag of rooms, with accordingly mixed tariffs. Some rooms are a bit noisy and smelly, the upper floor is OK and a bit cheaper. Beware of rickety stairs.

D-E Mary Tere, Calle 7 norte and Calle 10 oriente, T998- 884 0496, www.hotelmarytere. com. Lots of cheap, basic rooms. Get one upstairs, as the ones downstairs can be cramped and gloomy. There are a few other budget places in this street.

D-F Las Palmas, Palmeras 43, T998-884 2513, www.hotel-laspalmascancún.com. Clean, good value rooms with cable TV and a/c, and they'll store luggage. Breakfast is included and there's a cheap dormitory too.

F The Weary Traveler, Palmera 30, entrance in Av Uxmal, T998-887 0191, reservations@ wearytravelerhostel.com. Funky budget hostel with dorms and private rooms (**D**). There's free internet, breakfast included in the price, TV, lockers and chill-out space.

Camping

A big trailer park has been built opposite Punta Sam, 150 spaces, camping (**F** pp), shop selling basic commodities. Irregular bus service there, or hitchhike from Puerto Juárez. Check to see if restaurant is open evenings. Take mosquito repellent.

Isla Mujeres p720, map 720

L-LL Condominio Nautibeach, on Playa Los Cocos, T998-877 0606, www.nautibeach.com. Comfortable a/c apartments and condos, right on the beach, facing the sunset. **Sunset Grill**, attached, is perfect for sundowners and there's a nice pool too.

L María del Mar, Av Carlos Larzo 1, on the road down to the north beach, T998-877 0179, www.cabanasdelmar.com. Good clean rooms and *cabañas*, close to the best beach. Restaurant, pool, beach bar, hammocks and a cool, tranquil garden for chilling out. Organizes fishing excursions and cultural tours.

AL-A Rocamar, Nicolás Bravo and Zona Marítima, T998-877 0101, www.rocamar-hotel.com. A large, well-established hotel, located on the quieter, eastern side of the island, where the sea is wilder and swimming isn't recommended. There's a range of rooms; the more expensive overlook the sea and the Caribbean sunrise and also have jacuzzi.

B Bucaneros, Hidalgo 11, T998-877 1222, www.bucaneros.com. A pleasant, professionally managed hotel, right in the heart of town, with 18 modern rooms, all with calm, neutral interiors. Good restaurant attached.

C El Caracol, Av Matamoros 5, T998-877 0150, www.isla-mujeres.net/hotelelcaracol. Slightly tired, but acceptable rooms with fridge, fan and cable TV. Get one upstairs where there's more light. Low season prices almost 50% cheaper.

D Carmelina, Guerrero 4, T998-877 0006. Motel-style place with parking. The rooms are good and clean, with fridge, bath and fan. Good value.

D María José, Madero 25, T877-0130. Close to the dock. Clean, fans, friendly, reasonably quiet, scooter hire next door

D Posada Edelmar, Hidalgo, next to Bucanero hotel and restaurant. Economical alternative slap-bang in the middle of the pedestrianized section of town, seconds from the main restaurants and bars. Spacious rooms with good showers. Ask for a room at the back if you want some peace and quiet.

D Vistalmar, on promenade (Av Rueda Medina) close to the ferry dock and Pemex station, T998-877 0209. Clean, comfortable rooms with fan, bath, balcony and TV. Some have a/c (**C**). Ask for a room on the top floor.

D-F Pocna Hostel (price per person), top end of Matamoros on the northeast coast, T998-877 0090, www.pocna.com. This is now an island institution. Large, busy and warren-like, Pocna has a plethora of dorms and rooms. There's internet access, lounge and beach bar, space to sling a hammock (**F**), yoga lessons and live music in the evenings. Book in advance – as one of the few hostels on the island, it's popular.

E Osorio, Madero, 1 block from waterfront. Clean, simple rooms with fan, bath and hot water.

E-F Posada del Mar, Av Juárez s/n, between Matamoros and Juárez, T998-100 0759 (mobile), www.islahostelposadadelmar.com. This new hostel features dorms and a couple of private rooms, all with fan, hot water and safety boxes. Continental breakfast included.

Puerto Morelos p722

A Rancho Sak-Ol Libertad, next door to Caribbean Reef Club, T998-871 0181, www.rancholibertad.com. Thatched *cabañas*; the price includes breakfast, scuba diving and snorkelling gear for rent.

C Posada Amor, Av Javier Rojo Gómez, opposite the beach, T998-871 0033. Very pleasant, well-built *cabañas* with good mosquito nets, the cheaper ones have outdoor communal showers. There is also a good restaurant. Prices are reduced considerably out of season.

Playa del Carmen p722, map p723

Accommodation in Playa del Carmen is expensive and poor value, particularly around the beach and Av 5. The prices given below are for the high season, and can drop by as much as 50% at other times of the year.

LL Playacar Palace, T984-873 4960, www.palaceresorts.com. A huge luxury development just south of the ferry terminal, excellent in every respect, non-residents can use pool if they buy a day pass for US$84 – perhaps best to head for the beach.

LL Tides Riviera Maya, Rivera Maya Playa, Xcalacoco, Fracc 7, T984-877 3000, www.tidesrivieramaya.com. This boutique hotel boasts 30 villas in a jungle garden. The beach here is rocky, but they have built decking out to the sea so you can swim away from the rocks. See Activities and tours, page 745.

LL-L Alhambra, Calle 8 Norte, on corner with the beach, T984-873 0735, www.alhambra-hotel.net. Lovely, airy palatial feel at this hotel boasting spiritual inclinations. All rooms have balcony or sea view, and general services include yoga instruction, jacuzzi, massage and there is a spa. Quiet and peaceful, despite its setting near beach bars. Family run, French and English spoken. Recommended.

LL-AL Blue Parrot, at the north end of town, on a popular stretch of beach between Calle 12 and Calle 14, T01800-022 3206. A large complex of luxury studios and suites, all stylishly rendered. There are excellent services and facilities, including a popular nightclub.

AL Tropical Casablanca Hotel, Av Primera, between Calle 12 and 10, T984-873 0057, www.tropicalcasablanca.com. Clean, white, minimalist rooms. There's a garden, pool, *cenote* and impressive 6-room house for groups.

A Cielo, Calle 4, between Calle 5 and 10, T984-873 1227, www.hotelcielo.com. Right in the heart of things, rooms have a/c, cable TV, safe and also throw in beach towels and breakfast. The views from the roof terrace are superb. Restaurant Carboncito attached does great tacos.

A Maya Bric, Av 5, between Calle 8 and 10, T984-873 0011, www.mayabric.com. A friendly hotel with comfortable rooms, all with Wi-Fi and safes. There's a good garden and pool. Organizes tours and snorkelling. Good discounts in low season.

B Casa Tucán, Calle 4, between Av 10 and 15, T984-873 0283, www.casatucan.de. Simple, rustic *cabañas* and rooms. There's a lovely garden and a deep pool where diving instruction takes place. There's also a restaurant, internet café and other handy outlets attached.

B Las Molcas, T984-873 0070, www.molcas. com.mx, near ferry pier. Strange but interesting architecture at this hotel, where some of the Moorish-style corridors seem to recede into infinity. There's a pool and staff are friendly.

B Mom's Hotel, Calle 4 and Av 30, T984-873 0315, www.momshotel.com, about 5 blocks from bus station or beach. Excellent value, hotel with a pool. There are studios and apartments and good rates for long-term stays. Recommended.

C Happy Gecko, Av 10 between Calle 6 and 8, T984-147 0692, www.hostelworld.com. Canadian owned, this hotel has good rooms with kitchen, fan and bath, some with a/c. Laundry service and movies available.

D Posada Marinelly, Av Juárez between Calle 10 and 15, T984-873 0140. Centrally located with light, bright, comfortable rooms. More expensive with a/c (**A**). Handy for the ADO terminal. Friendly, bit basic.

D-F Urban Hostel, Av 10 between 4 and 6, T984-803 3378, urbanhostel@gmail.com. Funky backpackers' place with private rooms and dorms. Price includes breakfast. Internet and Wi-Fi, 2 terraces and kitchen.

E-F Hostel Playa, Av 25 with Calle 8, T984-803 3277, www.hostelplaya.com. A clean, professionally run hostel with various dorms, private rooms, kitchen and lounge space. There's a comfortable, friendly atmosphere. Prices per person, not per room.

Camping

Punta Bete, 10 km north, the right-hand one is one of 3 campsites at the end of a 5-km road, on beach. US$3 for tent, also 2 restaurants and *cabañas*.

Cozumel *p722, map p724 and p725*
Hotels are generally expensive and poor value. Expect prices to drop up to 50% during low season.

A Bahía, Av Rafael Melgar and Calle 3 Sur, T987-872 9090, www.suitesbahia.com. Comfortable, a/c rooms with cable TV, kitchenette and fridge. Some have ocean views.

A Flamingo, Calle 6 Norte 81, T954-315 9236, www.hotelflamingo.com. Tasteful, comfortable rooms with a/c, Wi-Fi, balcony and fridge. There's a penthouse on the roof, good for families. Friendly staff.

A-B Amaranto, Calle 5 Sur, between Av 15 and 20, T987-564 4262, www.cozumel.net/bb/amaranto. Lovely thatched-roof Mayan-style bungalows and

suites, complete with hammocks. There's a pool and childcare is available on request.

B Tamarindo, Calle 4 Norte 421, between Av 20 and 25, T987-872 3614, www.cozumel. net/bb/tamarind. Intimate bed and breakfast. There's a shared kitchen, hammocks, dive gear storage and rinse tank, purified drinking water, laundry, safety deposit box.

C Pepita, Av 15A Sur 120 and Calle 1 Sur, T/F987- 872 0098, www.hotelpepita cozumel.com. Modern fittings, a/c, cable TV, fridge in all rooms. Free coffee in the morning. Recommended.

C Posada Marruang, A R Salas 440, between Av 20 Sur and 25 Sur, T987-872 1678. Large rooms set back from road; barking dog ensures occasional noise and total security.

C Saolima, A R Salas 260, T987-872 0886. Clean, basic rooms with fan, showers, hot water.

D Flores, A R Salas 72, off plaza, T987-872 1429. A range of basic, acceptable rooms with cable TV, fan or a/c (**B**). Only 50 m from the sea and very cheap for the location.

D Posada Eden, Calle 2 Norte 124, T987-872 1166, gustarimo@hotmail.com. Clean, economical rooms with the usual bare necessities, including fan or a/c (**B**). There are apartments for long-term rental, 1 month minimum.

D Posada Zuanayoli, Calle 6 Norte 272, between Av 10 and Av 15 Norte, T987-872 0690. Old building in a quiet street. Clean rooms have TV, fridge, fan, some with a/c (**B**). Free coffee and drinking water for guests.

Tulum *p727*
Tulum village

Tulum village is a blossoming, but still relatively uninspiring destination. Scores of new budget hotels and restaurants are opening apace, making it a good base for backpackers and cost-conscious travellers. However, expect to offset those lower hotel rates with additional transport costs. There are no buses to the beach, only taxis and infrequent *colectivos*. For places to stay in Sian Ka'an biosphere reserve, see page 738.

C-F Rancho Tranquilo, T984-871 2784, www.ranchotranquilo.com.mx, far south end of town. Friendly backpackers' place with dorms, *cabañas* and large rooms with private bath. There's also a lounge, library, shared kitchen and verdant garden. Friendly and highly recommended.

D Maya, T984-871 2034, Av Tulum near the bus station. Large hotel with plenty of economical rooms, all with fan and bath. There's a restaurant next door serving home-cooked Mexican fare.

D-F Weary Traveler Hostel, T984-871 2390, www.wearytravelerhostel.com, 1 block south of ADO bus terminal. Tulum's premier backpackers' hostel has bunk dorms, a book exchange and internet. They run transport to the beach, regular salsa classes and you can even cook your own food on the BBQ. A good place to meet fellow travellers. Breakfast included.

E-F Mayan Hostel Tulum, Ctra Cobá–Boca Paila SN, 400 m from El Crucero, T998-112 1282, www.mayanhostel.com. Private rooms in *palapas*, dorms with a/c, breakfast and internet included in price. Bike rentals, book exchange, free short-term luggage storage.

Tulum beach

A plethora of lodgings run the length of the coast from Tulum ruins to the Sian Ka'an biosphere reserve. Development has been low key, with ramshackle *cabañas* existing alongside luxury eco-lodges. There is little infrastructure beyond these hotels, and it's best to reach them by taxi; official rates are posted on a sign at the rank in the village. Expect room costs to vary with views and proximity to the sea. Bear in mind this is a long stretch of beach and it's not always plausible to walk from hotel to hotel.

LL Ana y José, 7 km south of ruins, T984-880 5629, www.anayjose.com. Once only a collection of humble *cabañas*, Ana y José now offers elegant suites and luxurious spa accommodation. First-rate service and attention.

L Posada Lamar, 4½ km from ruins, T984-116-6386, www.posadalamar.com.

Beautiful, tranquil *cabañas*, simple yet elegant. Best to reserve in advance. Friendly management.

L Posada Margherita, T984-801 8493, www.posadamargherita.com. A decent, hospitable hotel with wheelchair access. There's 24-hr electricity and an excellent Italian restaurant attached.

L-AL Eco Tulum, T01800-514 3066, www.ecotulum.com. There are 3 beachside resorts here: **Cabañas Copal, Azulik** and **Zahra**. Each resort shares the rustic Maya Spa (www.maya-spa.com), based at Cabañas Copal, which specializes in affordable local Maya treatments. See page 747.

L-A Dos Ceibas, T984-877 6024, www.dosceibas.com, 9 km from the ruins. This verdant eco-lodge on the edge of the Sian Ka'an biosphere reserve has a handful of comfortable *cabañas*. Massage and yoga instruction available.

AL Cabañas Diamante, on the beach quite near the ruins, T984-876 2115, www.diamantek.com. Rustic and friendly. Prices for *cabañas* vary according to location and amenities, much cheaper with shared bath. There's a good bar and restaurant.

AL-C Los Arrecifes, 7 km from ruins, T984-155 2957, www.losarrecifestulum.com. *Cabañas*, trampoline, live music, restaurant.

A-B Zazil-Kin, near the ruins, T984-124 0082, www.zazilkintulum.com. Zazil-Kin is a popular, well-established Tulum favourite. A bit basic for the price, it offers a wide range of lodgings from rooms to *cabañas*, as well as restaurant, bar and gift shop. Massage available.

B Playa Condesa, next door to Diamante K. Simple, airy wooden *cabañas*, not particularly good value for the price. Electricity a few hours each evening. There's a basic, but pricey, grocery shop attached.

C-G Mar Caribe, near the ruins. Smaller complex than its neighbour, Zazil-Kin, but more peaceful. Very cheap if you bring your own hammock or tent. Organizes tours.

Know your hammock

Different materials are available for hammocks. Some you might find include sisal, which is very strong, light, hard-wearing but rather scratchy and uncomfortable; cotton, which is soft, flexible, comfortable, not as hardwearing but, with care, is good for four or five years of everyday use. It is not possible to weave cotton and sisal together. Cotton/silk mixtures are offered, but this will probably be an artificial silk. Nylon is very strong and light but it's hot in hot weather and cold when it's cold.

Never buy your hammock from a street vendor and never accept a packaged hammock without checking the size and quality. The surest way to judge a good hammock is by weight: 1½ kg is a fine item, under 1 kg is junk. Also, the finer and thinner the strands of material, the more strands there will be, and the more comfortable the hammock. The best hammocks are the three-ply, but they are difficult to find. There are three sizes: single (sometimes called *doble*), matrimonial and family (buy a matrimonial at least for comfort). If judging by end-strings, 50 would be sufficient for a child, 150 would suit a medium-sized adult, 250 a couple. Prices vary considerably so shop around and bargain hard.

Cobá p728

A-B Villas Arqueológicas (Club Méditerranée), about 2 km from site on lake shore, T985-858 1527. Open to non-members, excellent, clean and quiet, a/c, pool, good restaurant with moderate prices, but expensive beer. Don't arrive without a reservation, especially at weekends; and yet making a reservation by phone seems to be practically impossible.

F-G El Bocadito, in the village, on the street leading to the main road, T984-876 3738, www.cancunsouth.com/bocadito/. Run down, rooms with fan, intermittent water supply, poor security, good but expensive restaurant (which is popular with tour groups), books and handicrafts for sale.

Sian Ka'an biosphere reserve p729

AL Rancho Sol Caribe, Punta Allen. 4 comfortable *cabañas*, with bath, restaurant.

A Centro Ecológico Sian Ka'an, T984-871 2499, www.cesiak.org. Environmentally considerate and sensitive accommodation in the heart of the reserve. Tours, kayaking and fly fishing arranged.

Felipe Carrillo Puerto p729

C Chan Santa Cruz, Calle 68, No 782, T983-834 0021, www.hotelchansanta cruz.com, just off the plaza. Good, clean and friendly. A/c, cable TV, disabled access, fridge (**Restaurante 24 Horas** is open, as you'd imagine, 24 hrs).

C El Faisán y El Venado, Av Benito Juárez, Lote 781, 2 blocks northeast of main square. Mixed reports on cleanliness, but hot water and good-value restaurant, popular with locals.

C San Ignacio, Av Benito Juárez 761, near Pemex. Good value, a/c, bath, towels, TV, secure car park.

D María Isabel, near the plaza. Clean, friendly, laundry service, quiet, safe parking.

Mahahual and around p730

There are plenty of options for sleeping with hammocks, camping and *cabañas*.

C-F Kabah-na, T983-838 8861, kabahna@ yahoo.com. Choose from *cabañas* or a space to hang a hammock, right on the beach.

D Sol y Mar restaurant, en route to Puerto Bravo, near Mahahua. Rooms to rent, bathrooms and spaces for RVs, also coconut palms and beach.

E-F Kok Hal, Mahahual, on the beach close to the old wharf. Shared bath and hot showers.

Camping
Camidas Trailer Park, Punta Herrero road. Palm trees, *palapas*, restaurant and space for 4 RVs, US$5 per person, car free.

Chetumal *p730, map p731*
AL Los Cocos, Av Héroes 134, T983-835 0430, www.hotelloscocos.com.mx. Large hotel with clean, comfortable rooms and suites. There's a pool, bar and restaurant. Recommended.

A-B Caribe Princess, Av Obregón 168, T983-832 0520, www.caribeprincess chetumal.com. Good, clean rooms with a/c and TV. Recommended.

B Ucúm, Gandhi 167, corner 16 de Septiembre, T983-832 6186, www.hotelucum chetumal.com. Rooms with a/c, fan and bath. Pool and enclosed car park. Good value restaurant next door.

C Palma Real, Obregon 103, T983-833 0963. Friendly and helpful place with big, clean rooms. Bath, cable TV and a/c.

D Cristal, Cristóbal Colón 207, T983-832 3878. Simple rooms with fan and bath. Parking available.

D El Dorado, Av 5 de Mayo 42, T983-832 0315. Comfortable rooms with hot water and a/c. Friendly and quiet. Recommended.

D-E Real Azteca, Av Belice 186, T983-832 0720. Cheerful, friendly, but no hot shower. 2nd-floor rooms best, but still not too good.

E María Dolores, Av Alvaro Obregón 206, T983-832 0508. Bath, hot water, fan, clean, windows don't open, noisy, restaurant Solsimar downstairs good and popular. Recommended.

Towards Bacalar *p731*
LL Akal Ki, Ctra Federal 307, Km 12.5. Bacalar Lagoon, T983-106 1751, www.akalki.com. A marvellously peaceful retreat with *palapas* built right over the water. Though surrounded by jungle, this strip of the lagoon has few rocks and little vegetation, making it crystal clear and ideal for swimming. Minimum stay 3 days. See Activities and tours, page 748.

LL-L Rancho Encantado, 3 km north of Bacalar, on the west shore of the lagoon, T983-101 3358, www.encantado.com. Resort hotel, half board available, with private dock, tour boat, canoes and windsurf boards for rent, private cabins with fridge and hammock, very good. See Activities and tours, page 748.

B-C Las Lagunas, Blv Costero 479, about 2 km south of Bacalar (on left-hand side of the road going towards the village) T983-834 2206. Wonderful views, helpful, clean, comfortable, hot water, swimming pool and opposite a freshwater lake; restaurant is poor and overpriced.

Camping
Camping possible at the end of the road 100 m from the lagoon, toilets and shower, US$0.10, but lagoon perfect for swimming.

● Eating

Cancún *p717, maps p717 and p719*
The **hotel zone** is lined with expensive restaurants, with every type of international cuisine imaginable, but with a predominance of Tex-Mex and Italian. Restaurants in the centre are cheaper, and the emphasis is on local food.

The cheapest area for dinner is **SM64**, opposite **Plaza 2000**. Popular with locals, especially on Sun when it is hard to get a table; there are 4 or 5 small, family-run restaurants serving local specialities. *Comida corrida* for as little as US$2. **Mercado 28** is the best budget option for breakfast or lunch, with many cheap outdoor and indoor *loncherías* serving *comida corrida*, very popular with locals, quick service. Another good option is **Mercado 23**, 5 blocks north of the **ADO** terminal, along Calle Cedro.

♜♜♜ El Pescador, Tulipanes 28. Good seafood, well established with excellent reputation.

♜♜♜ La Habichuela, Margaritas 25. Award-winning restaurant serving delicious Caribbean seafood in a tropical garden setting. Great ambience and jazz music.

♜♜♜ La Parrilla, Yaxchilán 51. Mouth-watering grill platters, ribs and steaks. A buzzing, lively joint, always busy and popular. Try the enormous margaritas.

♜♜♜ Pericos, Av Yaxchilán 71, T998-884 3152, www.pericos.com.mx. Chicken, meat, fish fillets and seafood platters at this themed Mexican restaurant.

♜♜♜-♜♜ El Rincón del Vino, Alcatraces 29. Tapas with a seafood emphasis. A tranquil and pleasant place, with a range of international food.

♜♜♜-♜♜ Labná, Margaritas 29. The best in Yucatecan cooking, serving dishes like *poc chuc* and *pollo pibil*. Try the platter and sample a wide range of this fascinating regional cuisine. Good lunchtime buffet.

♜♜ El Poblano, Tulum and Tulipanes. Tacos, kebabs, grilled meats and steaks. A friendly, unpretentious restaurant, popular with Mexicans.

♜♜ Rincón Yucateco, Av Uxmal 24. Good grills and traditional Mexican grub from lunchtime, takeaways and delivery. Popular.

Cafés

Pastelería Italiana, Yaxchilán, just before turning of Sunyaxchén. Excellent coffee and pastries, friendly. A few other cheap eateries along Yaxchilán, tucked away between the pricey themed restaurants, some open during the day only.

Isla Mujeres *p720, map 720*

The most popular street for restaurants is Hidalgo.

♜♜♜ Mesón del Bucanero, Hidalgo, opposite Rolandis. Steaks, seafood, pasta and crêpes at this classy restaurant. There's a rich offering of cocktails too. Nice alfresco seating.

♜♜ Bamboo, Hidalgo. A sleek and trendy restaurant-bar serving sushi, Thai curries, seafood and fresh fruit juices. Live music at the weekends.

♜♜ Comono, Hidalgo. Mon-Fri 1400-2230. Israeli-run kitchen and bar that serves Mediterranean food, beer and shakes. There are nightly movies, live music on Fri, and hookah pipes. Popular with backpackers.

♜♜ Los Amigos, Hidalgo. Small, with 2 tables outside, pizzas and pasta.

♜♜ Mamma Rosa, Hidalgo and Matamoros. Formerly La Malquerida. Italian-run restaurant serving pasta and seafood with a good selection of Italian wines.

♜♜ Miguel's Moon Lite, Hidalgo 9. Expect good hospitality at this lively restaurant-bar, popular with jovial North Americans. When the booze isn't flowing, there's tacos, steaks and seafood.

♜♜ Rolandis, Hidalgo, T998-877 0700. Terrace overlooking the street. Excellent Italian food, including a good range of tasty pizzas and pastas, seafood and meat dishes.

♜ La Susanita, Juárez 5. Excellent home cooking at this cute little locals' place; when closed it is the family's living room.

♜ Lonchería La Lomita, Juárez 25B. Nice and clean and at US$3, quite possibly the best value, food in town.

♜ Loncherías, northwest end of Guerrero, surrounding the municipal market, open till 1800. Busy and bustling, good for breakfast, snacks and lunch. All serve the same local fare at similar prices.

♜ Poc-Chuc, Juárez y Madero. Rough and ready locals' joint, serving up big portions and good *tortas*.

Cafés

Aluxes Café, Av Matamoros, next to Aquí Estoy Pizza. A cheery little place serving coffee and home-made snacks.

Cafecito, Matamoros 42. Cool and tranquil. A good breakfast place, serving waffles, juice and sandwiches.

Puerto Morelos *p722*

♜♜ Johnny Cairo, with good typical food.

♜♜ Pelícano. Serves very good seafood.

Playa del Carmen *p722, map p723*

The majority of the town's restaurants line Av 5, where most tourists limit their explorations and a meal costs no less (and usually a bit more) than US$10. Popular, big name restaurants dominate the southern end of the street. Quieter, subtler settings lie north, beyond Calle 20. For budget eating, head west, away from the main drag.

ŦŦŦ Buenos Aires, Calle 6 Norte between Av 5 and Av 10, on Plaza Playa. The speciality is Argentine meats, good for a change from Mexican food.

ŦŦŦ Karen's, Av 5, between Calle 2 and 4. Always a lively, family atmosphere here. The menu includes Mexican staples, good pizzas, grilled meats and tacos. There's live music most nights. Popular.

ŦŦŦ La Parrilla, Av 5 y Calle 8. Large portions, good service, live Mariachi band every night.

ŦŦŦ The Glass Bar, Calle 10, between Av 1 and Av 5, www.theglassbar.com.mx. A sophisticated Italian restaurant serving fine wine, Mediterranean cuisine and seafood. Also has a sister restaurant, Di Vino (**ŦŦŦ**), Calle 12, corner Av 5, www.divino.com.mx, for more fine dining experiences.

ŦŦŦ Yaxche, Calle 8 between Av 5 and Av 10. Traditional Maya cuisine. Cheaper lunchtime menu (**ŦŦ**).

ŦŦŦ-ŦŦ Los Comales, Av 5 and Calle 4. Popular seafood restaurant. Dishes include Veracruz fish fillet, seafood platters, surf & turf, fajitas and Mexican fare. There's a good-value breakfast buffet for US$5.50.

ŦŦŦ-ŦŦ Maktub, Av 5, between Calle 28 and 30. Arab and Lebanese cuisine, clean and pleasant, with outdoor seating.

ŦŦŦ-ŦŦ Sushi-Tlan, Av 5, between Calle 28 and 30. Something different; a clean, fresh, sushi bar.

ŦŦ El Famolito, Busy taco joint, popular with Mexicans. Bright, clean and modern.

ŦŦ Pez Vela, Av 5 y Calle 2. Good atmosphere, food, drinks and music.

ŦŦ Rolandi, Av 5, close to the ferry dock. Superb pasta and pizza at this popular Italian place. Branches across Mexico.

Ŧ Billy the Kid, Av 15 and Calle 4. This very cheap, rough-and-ready locals' haunt does tacos and *tortas*.

Ŧ El Fogon, Av 30 and Calle 6. Locals' taco joint that serves grilled meat, wholesome *tortas* and *quesadillas*.

Ŧ Tortas del Carmen, Av 15, between Calle 4 and 2. Tasty *tortas* and *licuados*, open from 0830.

Cafés and bakeries

Java Joe's, Calle 10, between Av 5 and 10. Italian and gourmet coffees, sandwiches, pastries. Next door's café/bookshop Habita is worth a peak for its art, books and alternative cultural space.

Cozumel *p722, map p724 and p725*

There are few eating options for budget travellers. The cheapest places for breakfast, lunch or an early dinner are the *loncherías* next to the market on A R Salas, between Av 20 and 25. They serve fairly good local *comida corrida*, 0800-1930.

ŦŦŦ Lobster's Cove, Av Rafael Melgar 790. Quality seafood, live music, happy hour 1200-1400.

ŦŦŦ Pancho's Backyard, Rafael Melgar 27, in Los Cinco Soles shopping complex in big courtyard out the back. Mexican cuisine and wine elegantly served, good food.

ŦŦŦ Prima, Salas 109. Open 1600-2400. Northern Italian seafood, handmade pasta, brick-oven pizzas, non-smoking area.

ŦŦŦ-ŦŦ Casa Mission, Av 55, between Juárez and Calle 1 Sur, www.missioncoz.com. Daily 1700-2300. This restaurant survived hurricanes Wilma and Gilbert and is now a Cozumel institution. Fine Mexican, international and seafood in an elegant hacienda setting.

ŦŦŦ-ŦŦ La Choza, Salas 198 and Av 10, www.lachozarestaurant.com. Decent Mexican and regional cuisine. Popular.

ŦŦ Las Palmeras, at the pier (a people-watching spot), Av Melgar. Open 0700-1400. Very popular for breakfast, always busy.

¶¶-¶ Casa Denis, Calle 1 Sur 164, close to plaza. Open-air restaurant, very good, cheapish prices.

Tulum p727
Tulum village
Testament to Tulum's growing popularity, a plethora of new restaurants have opened in town, mostly along Av Tulum. Wander along in the evening and take your pick of everything from Argentine parrillas to seafood and pizzas.

¶¶¶-¶¶ El Pequeño Buenos Aires, Av Tulum, Argentine steak and grill house, one great meat feast, open-air setting on the main drag.

¶¶ Don Cafeto, Av Tulum 64. Popular place serving Mexican fare. Usually buzzing in the evenings. Beach branch currently shut, but set to re-open later in the year.

¶¶ La Nave, Av Tulum. Italian restaurant and pizzeria, set on 2 floors, nice rustic wooden decor. Cosy in the evenings.

¶ Doña Tinas, in a grass hut at southern end of town. Good, basic and cheap. El Mariachito next door also does good, cheap and cheerful grub.

¶ El Mariachi, cheap taco bar serving good *fajitas*.

Tulum beach
Restaurants on the beach tend to be owned by hotels. For dinner, book in advance where possible. Strolling between establishments after dark isn't really feasible.

¶¶¶-¶¶ La Zebra, Ctra Tulum-Boca Paila Km 7.5, www.lazebratulum.com. Fresh, tasty barbequed fish, shrimps, *ceviche* and Mexican fare. Lashings of margaritas at the adjacent Tequila Bar.

¶¶¶-¶¶ Margherita, Ctra Tulum-Boca Paila Km 4.5, in Posada Margherita (see Sleeping above). Excellent, freshly prepared Italian food in an intimate setting. Hospitable, attentive service. Book in advance. Closed Sundays. Recommended.

¶¶¶-¶¶ Mezzanine, Ctra Tulum-Boca Paila Km 1.5. Excellent authentic Thai cuisine and martini bar attached.

Cobá p728
There are plenty of restaurants in the village, on the road to **Villas Arqueológicas** and on the road to the ruins, all quite pricey. There's also a grocery store by **El Bocadito** and souvenir shops.

¶¶ Pirámides, on corner of track leading to **Villas Arqueológicas**. Highly recommended.

¶ Nicte-Ha, good and friendly.

Sian Ka'an biosphere reserve p729
¶¶-¶ La Cantina, Punta Allen. A good, non-touristy restaurant (US$3-4 for fish).

Felipe Carrillo Puerto p729
¶¶ Danburger Maya, next door to hotel San Ignacio. Good food, reasonable prices, helpful.

¶ Addy, on main road, south of town. Good, simple.

Chetumal p730, map p731
¶¶¶-¶¶ El Emporio, Merino 106. Delicious Uruguayan steaks served in a historic old house near the bay.

¶¶ Barracuda, about 4 blocks north of market, then 3 blocks west (another area with many restaurants). Good seafood.

¶¶ Sergio Pizza, Alvaro Obregón 182. Pizzas, fish, and expensive steak meals, a/c, good drinks, excellent service.

¶¶-¶ El Fenicio, Héroes and Zaragoza. Open 24 hrs, with mini-market at the back. Chicken, steaks, burgers and Mexican grub.

¶ Los Milagros, Zaragoza and 5 de Mayo. This locals' café serves economical Mexican fare, *comida corrida* and breakfasts.

¶ Mercado. Cheap meals in the market at the top of Av Héroes, but the service is not too good and tourists will be stared at a lot.

¶ Pantoja, Ghandi 87. Busy locals' joint serving the usual economical fare.

Towards Bacalar p731
¶¶ La Esperanza, 1 block north from plaza. Thatched barn, good seafood.

¶¶ Punta y Coma, Orizaba, 3 blocks from Zócalo. Inexpensive, large menu including vegetarian. Recommended.

♦ Bars and clubs

Cancún *p717, maps p717 and p719*
The action happens in the Zona Hotelera, around 9 km from downtown on Kukulcán Boulevard, where big clubs play to big crowds. Women can often drink for free and there's a distinctly North American flavour. Downtown has a thriving scene too, mostly focused on Yaxchilán and the surrounding streets.
Bulldog, Kukulcán Blv Km 9, www.bulldog cafe.com/cancun.html. Plays rock, hip-hop, pop and salsa. A popular, well-organized mega club with sophisticated light-and-sound rigs.
Coco Bongo, Forum by the Sea Mall, www.cocobongo.com.mx. Cancún's most famous nightclub. Expect wild theatrical displays, including dance, acrobatics, laser shows and gallons of dry ice. Loud, pumping dance music is played. Open Wed-Sat.
Dady Rock, Kukulcán Blv Km 9.5, www.dadyrock.com.mx. Two floors, 4 bars, DJs, MCs and live bands. There's frequent bikini, sexy legs and 'wet body' contests too, if that's your sort of thing.
Señor Frog's, Kukulcán Blv Km 9.5, www.senorfrogs.com. You'll get a yard glass on entry, fill it with the booze of your choice, open wide and drink. This is a long-standing Cancún favourite; and it's spawned branches in most Mexican resorts and across the Caribbean. Cover US$5.

Isla Mujeres *p720, map 720*
Most of the bars have a permanent happy hour, with 2 drinks for the price of 1. Happy Hour here also tends to favour women, who sometimes get to drink for free. There are many bars along Hidalgo and the beach – take your pick.
Chile Locos, along the beach, with live marimba music.
La Adelita, Hidalgo 12. Adelita stocks over 200 types of tequila, the bar staff really know their stuff and are happy to make recommendations.
La Palapa, on Playa Los Cocos. Serves cocktails and snacks and is busy during the

day until everyone leaves the beach, then fills up again after midnight for drinking and dancing.
Om Bar, Matamoros 15. Wed-Sat 1900 onwards. Chilled-out hippy lounge. Drink beer and cocktails under the palapa, relax to reggae or Latin Jazz. Free shots.

Playa del Carmen *p722, map p723*
Nightlife in Playa del Carmen is famously hedonistic. The best clubs are situated on Calle 12 and 14. There are also some bars in the 'gringo zone' by the ferry dock.
Beer Bucket, Calle 10, between Av 5 and 10. Popular with expats, where the grog and the conversation flow cheaply.
Blue Parrot Inn, Calle 12 y Av 1, next to beach. Dance, trance and house at this famous, sexy nightclub on the beach. Ladies night on Mon and Thu, with free drinks.
Coco Maya, Calle 12 and the beach. Beach club playing R 'n' B, hip-hop, house and dance. Lots of big TV screens, all under a *palapa*.
El Cielo, Calle 12, between Av 5 and the beach. Swanky disco playing dance and pumping tunes. Popular and well known. Cover for men US$5, women free.
Habibi and Los Aguachiles, next door to OM. A new, upmarket and trendy watering holes for the hip and happening. Worth a peak, if a bit pricey.
OM, Calle 12, between Av 5 and the beach. Suave lounge-bar with sofas, sheeshas and ethereal white drapes. Electronic music.
Tequila Barrel, Av 5 between Calles 10 and 12. Tex-Mex Bar and grill, friendly owner (Greco) and staff.

Cozumel *p722, map p724 and p725*
1.5 Tequila Lounge, Melgar and Calle 11 Sur. Boozy, sociable lunch bar, popular with visitors straight off the cruise ships.
Carlos 'n' Charlie's, Plaza Punta Langosta. Big-name chain bar, always busy with tourists.
Neptuno, Melgar and Calle 11 Sur. Long-standing Cozumel disco, playing salsa, dance and reggae.

Señor Frog's, Plaza Punta Langosta, www.senorfrogs.com. Chain bar popular with North Americans and other tourists.

⊕ Entertainment

Cancún *p717, maps p717 and p719*
Cinema
Cinepolis, Tulum 260, SM7. Large complex showing English language subtitled films.

⊕ Festivals and events

Isla Mujeres *p720, map 720*
Oct Festival of music, with Mexican and US groups performing in the main square.
1-12 Dec Fiesta for the Virgin of Guadalupe, fireworks and dances until 0400 in the plaza.

O Shopping

Cancún *p717, maps p717 and p719*
There are several US-style shopping malls in the hotel zone. The main one, **Plaza Kukulcán**, known as Luxury Avenue, www.luxuryavenue.com, has more than 200 shops, restaurants, a bowling alley and video games. It is open from 1000-2200 daily and the prices are high for most things, including souvenirs. The main **craft market** is on Av Tulum near Plaza Las Américas. It is a huge network of stalls, all selling exactly the same merchandise. Prices are hiked up to the limit, so bargain hard: most vendors expect to get half of what they originally asked for. The market called **Mercado 23** (at the end of Calle Cedro, off Av Tulum) has cheaper souvenirs and less aggressive salesmen, but it's a bit tatty and tacky, although good for cheap food; *guayabera* shirts are available on one of the stalls. Several smoking shops have appeared, cashing in on the craze for Cuban cigars; these are all located on or just off Av Tulum. Cheaper clothes shops than the hotel

zone can be found at the north end of Av Tulum, near Plaza 2000. Pricey leather goods, clothes and jewellery can be bought in the Plaza 2000 shopping mall.

Isla Mujeres *p720, map 720*
Cigars
Tobacco & Co, Hidalgo 14. Cuban cigars and smoking paraphernalia. There are several other shops in the centre selling Cuban cigars.

Souvenirs
Av Hidalgo is lined with souvenir shops, most of them selling the same things. Bargaining is obligatory – try and get the desired item for half the original asking price. There are more souvenir shops along the harbour front and Av Morelos.

Playa del Carmen *p722, map p723*
Lots of expensive souvenir shops clustered around the plaza and in Av 5; cheaper shops, for day-to-day items, are on Av Juárez. There's a cheap *panadería* at the beginning of Av Juárez. For developing photos and buying film, there are several places along Av 5.

Chetumal *p730, map p731*
Shops are open 0800-1300, 1800-2000. Av Héroes is the main shopping street. Good for foreign foodstuffs – cheaper at the covered market in the outskirts than in the centre.

▲ Activities and tours

Cancún *p717, maps p717 and p719*
Boat trips and cruises
Aquaworld, Blv Kukulcán, Km 15.2, T998-848 8327, www.aquaworld.com.mx. A range of boat trips and cruises including day trips to Isla Mujeres and Cozumel; dinner cruises on the *Cancún Queen*; and underwater explorations on their *Sub See Explorer* submarine. They also organize parasailing, jungle tours and swimming with dolphins.

Bullfighting
Plaza de Toros, Av Bonompak south. Folkloric show and bullfight every Wed at 1530, 2½ hrs. Admission US$38, tickets available at travel agents and the ring.

Dolphin encounters
Dolphin Discovery, Kukulcán km 5, T998-849 4748, www.dolphindiscovery.com. Splash around with dolphins, manatees and seals. A real winner for families.

Golf
Club de Golf Cancún, Kukulcán Km 7.5, T998-883 1230, www.cancúngolfclub.com. An 18-hole championship course, driving range and putting greens.
Hilton Cancún Beach and Golf Resort, Kukulcán Blv Km 17, T998-881 8000, www.hiltoncancún.com/golf.htm. An attractive 18-hole course on the banks of a lagoon.

Language schools
El Bosque del Caribe, Av. Náder 52 and Uxmal, T998-884 1065, www.cancún-language.com.mx.

Scuba diving and snorkelling
See also **Aquaworld**, above.
Scuba Cancún, Kukulcán Km 5, T998-849 5226, www.scubacancún.com.mx. A medium-sized dive centre run by Captain Luis Hurtado who has 54 years' diving experience. It offers a range of dives, snorkelling tours and accelerated PADI courses.

Tour operators
Many in the centre and at larger hotels. Most hotels on the hotel zone have their own travel agency.
Mayan Destinations, Cobá 31, Edificio Monaco, SM22, T998-884 4308, www.mayandestinations.com. All the usual destinations, such as Chichén Itzá, Xcaret, Tulum, as well as flights to Cuba.

Water sports
These can be organized on the beaches along the hotel zone, including parasailing, waterskiing, windsurfing and jet-skiing.

Isla Mujeres *p720, map 720*
Birdwatching
Amigos de Isla Contoy, T998-884 7483, www.amigosdeislacontoy.org and www.islacontoy.org. This environmental organization keeps lists of authorized tour boats to Isla Contoy – a protected bird sanctuary, 30 km north of Isla Mujeres. More than 10,000 birds spend the winter on this island, including cormorants, frigates, herons, boobies and pelicans.

Scuba diving and snorkelling
Carey, Av Matamoros 13-A, T998-877 0763. Small groups, bilingual staff and good range of dives, including reef dives, night dives, *cenote* dives and whale shark swimming.
El Garrafón, southern tip of the island, T998-193 3360, www.garrafon.com. This water sports centre offers a range of diving and snorkelling programmes, with a sunken cross offshore specifically placed for divers to explore. They also do dolphin encounters, kayaking and cycling.
Sea Hawk, Zazil-Ha (behind Hotel Na-Balam) T998-877 1233, seahawkdivers@hotmail.com. Certified PADI instructors, 2-tank dive US$50, introductory course including shallow dive US$85. Also snorkelling trips and fishing trips.

Tour operators
Mundaca Travel, Av Rueda Medina, inside the ferry terminal, T998-877 0845. Tours to Chichén Itzá, Tulum, Xel-Ha and Xcaret. Bus tickets and flights to Cuba. Friendly and helpful.

Playa del Carmen *p722, map p723*
Body and soul
Tides Riviera Maya, see Sleeping, page 735. Offers yoga, *temazcal*, massage, a range of other therapies, jacuzzis and steam rooms.

Cenote diving

There are more than 50 *cenotes* in this area – accessible from Ruta 307 and often well signposted – and cave diving has become very popular. However, it is a specialized sport and, unless you have a cave-diving qualification, you must be accompanied by a qualified dive master. A cave diving course involves over 12 hours of lectures and a minimum of 14 cave dives using double tanks, costing around US$700. Accompanied dives start at around US$50. Specialist dive centres offering courses are: **Aquatech**, Villas de Rosa, PO Box 25, T984-875 9020, www.cenotes.com; **Akumal Dive Adventures**, next door to La Buena Vida, on Half Moon Bay, North Akumal, T984-875 9157; **Aktun Dive Centre**, Hotel El Mesón, Tulum, T984-871 2311; Mike Madden's **CEDAM**

Dive Centres, PO Box 1, Puerto Aventuras, T/F984-873 5129; and **Cenote Dive Center**, opposite HSBC bank, Tulum, T984-871 2232, www.cenotedive.com, Norwegian owned.

Some of the best *cenotes* are Carwash, on the Cobá road, good even for beginners, with excellent visibility; Dos Ojos, just off Ruta 307 south of Aventuras, the second largest underground cave system in the world, with a possible link to the Nohoch Nah Chich, and the most famous *cenote* and part of a subterranean system recorded as the world's largest, with over 50 km of surveyed passageways connected to the sea.

A word of warning: *cenote* diving has a higher level of risk than open water diving – only dive with recognized operators.

Language schools

Playalingua, Calle 20 between Av 5 and 10, T984-873 3876, www.playalingua.com Weekend excursions, a/c, library, family stays, US$85 enrolment fee, US$220 per wk (20 hrs). **Solexico Language and Cultural Center**, Av 35 between 6 and 6 bis, T984-873 0755, www.solexico.com. Variable programme with workshops, also have schools in Oaxaca and Puerto Vallarta.

Scuba diving and snorkelling

Abyss, inside Hotel Tropical Casablanca, Av 1a, between Calle 10 and 12, T984-873 2164, www.abyssdiveshop.com. Said to be the best. Run by fully certified Canadian Instructor David Tomlinson. Services include PADI courses; reef, night and *cenote* dives. Good-value dive packages.
Tank-Ha, Calle 10, between Av 5 and 10, T984-873 0302, www.tankha.com. Experienced and well-established dive centre offering a range of packages.
Yucatek Divers, Av 15 Norte, between Calle 2 and 4, T984-803 2836,

www.yucatek-divers.com. General diving and snorkelling, including programmes for disabled people. Also a snorkelling with whale sharks option. Open 0730-1730.

Tour operators

Alltournative, Av 5, between Calle 12 and 14 and another office between Calle 2 and 4 (opposite the **ADO** terminal) T984-803 9999, www.alltournative.com. Daily 0900-1900. Culturally and ecologically sensitive tours have won this company several awards. Services include tours to archaeological sites, Mayan villages, forests, lagoons and *cenotes*.
Viajes Felgueres, Calle 6 between Av 5 and Av 10, T984-873 0142. Long-standing and reliable agency with a branch in Cancún, tours to Chichén Itzá, including transport from hotel, guide, entry, food, also bookings for national and international flights, helpful staff.

Cozumel *p722, map p724 and p725*
Scuba diving
The island is famous for the beauty of its underwater environment. The best reef for

Sweating it out – temazcal

The *temazcal* is a ritual ceremony that has been practised by the indigenous peoples of Mexico for hundreds of years. The Mexican version of the sweat lodge, it is a thanksgiving to the four elements, and a healing for the spirit as well as the body. You enter the womb of mother earth when you enter the *temazcal*, and when you exit you are born a new being. Traditionally, it was done in a square- or dome-shaped building constructed from branches and then covered with blankets, and was preceded by a day of fasting. There are *temazcal* sessions open to newcomers all over Mexico. Done properly, the experience can be intense.

Red-hot rocks are placed in the centre of the construction, and a group sits around them. The door is closed, and a medicine man leads the group in prayer and songs, all designed to connect those present to each of the four elements. During the ceremony, the door is opened four times, to allow people to leave (there is no returning), and to bring in more hot rocks. Different emotions and thoughts come up for different people, and everyone is encouraged to contribute something from their own traditions if they feel the need. After each contribution, herbal water is poured over the rocks to create more healing steam. This continues till everyone is in agreement to open the fourth and final door. Everyone then leaves, rinses off (hopefully in the sea or lagoon if you're near the coast), then shares soup and tea to break their fast.

---

scuba diving is **Palancar**, reached only by boat. Also highly recommended are **Santa Rosa** and **Colombia**. For more experienced divers the reefs at **Punta Sur**, **Maracaibo** and **Barracuda** should not to be missed. There are at least 20 major dive sites. Almost all Cozumel diving is drift diving, so if you are not used to a current, choose an operator you feel comfortable with. See also box opposite

Dive centres There are 2 different types of dive centre: the larger ones, where the divers are taken out to sea in big boats with many passengers; the smaller, more personalized dive shops, with a maximum of 8 people per small boat.

Deep Blue, A R Salas 200, corner Av 10 Sur, T987-872 5653, www.deepbluecozumel.com. The best of the smaller centres is said to be this one, run by Matt and Deborah. All PADI and NAUI certifications, eg 3-5-day dive packages US$207-325; cavern and *cenote* diving, including 2 dives, transport and lunch.

Other small dive centres are: **Black Shark**, Av 5 between A R Salas and Calle 3 Sur, T987-872 5657, www.blackshark.com.mx;

Blue Bubble Divers, Ctra Costera Sur Km 3.5, T987-872 4240, www.bluebubble.com; Diving Adventures, Calle 15 Sur, between Av 19 and 21, T987-872 3009, www.divingadventures.net.

Decompression centres Buceo Médico Mexicano, Calle 5 Sur, No 21B, T987-872 1430, immediate localization (24-hr) VHF 16 and 21. It is supported by US$1 per day donations from divers with affiliated operators. Cozumel Hyperbarics in Clínica San Miguel, Calle 6 Norte, No 135 between Av 5 and Av 10, T987-872 3070, VHF channel 65.

Tulum *p727*
Body and soul
Eco Tulum, see Sleeping, www.ecotulum.com, page 737. Offers affordable local Maya treatments including clay massage. Yoga, *temazcal* and holistic massage also available.

Diving
Several dive shops all along the Tulum corridor. See box opposite for *cenote* diving

operators and specialist courses – highly recommended if you like diving. There are many untrained snorkelling and diving outfits, take care.

Cobá p728
Tour operators
Ana y José, near Tulum (see page 737). You can also book tours to the reserve through this place.

Ecocolors, Cancún, T998-884 9580, in collaboration with **Los Amigos de Sian Ka'an**, see page 729. Tours to the reserve, US$115 for a full day, starting at 0700, hotel pick-up, everything is included. In winter the tour goes through a canal, in summer it goes birdwatching, in both cases a visit to a Maya ruin, a *cenote*, snorkelling, all equipment, breakfast and evening meal are included. Two-day camping trips can be arranged. Two-hour boat trips through the biosphere can be taken for US$75.

Chetumal p730, map p731
Tour operators
Bacalar Tours, Alvaro Obregón 167A, T987-832 3875. Tours to Mayan ruins and car rental.
Tu-Maya, Av Alvaro Obregón 312, T983-832 0555, www.casablancachetumal.com/tumaya. Day tours to Guatemala, Belize and Calakmul.

Towards Bacalar p731
Body and soul
Akal Ki, see Sleeping, page 739, www.akalki.com. A retreat offering yoga, meditation, *temazcal* (see box, page 747) and *jenzu*, a seawater massage.
Rancho Encantado, (see Sleeping, page 739), www.encantado.com. A holistic resort offering *lomi lomi*, a form of massage, *temazcal*, *qigong* and meditation.

⊙ Transport

Cancún p717, maps p717 and p719
Air
Cancún airport (CUN) has expensive shops and restaurant, exchange facilities, double check your money, especially at busy times, poor rates too, 2 hotel reservation agencies (no rooms under US$45). 2 terminals: Main and South (or 'FBO' building), white shuttle minibuses between them. From Cancún there are domestic flights and connections throughout the country. For international connections, see Getting there, page 34. For airline websites, see page 36.

Airline offices Aerocosta, Tulum 29, T998-884 0383; **Aeromar**, airport, T998-886 1100; **AeroMexico**, Cobá 80, T998-287 1868; **Aviasca**, Cobá 39, T01800-284 2272; **Click Mexicana**, Tulum 269, T998-886 0042; **Continental Airlines**, airport, T998-886 0069; **Delta airlines**, airport, T998-886 0668, **Mexicana de Aviación**, Tulum 269, T998-991 9090.

Bus
For ferries to Isla Mujeres, several buses to the terminals at Gran Puerto and Puerto Juárez run from Av Tulum – try R-13, or R-1 marked 'Pto Juárez', US$0.80. Taxi to Puerto Juárez US$2.50.

Long distance Cancún bus terminal, at the junction of Av Tulum and Uxmal, is small, well organized and handy for the cheaper hostels. The bus station is the hub for routes west to Mérida and south to Tulum and Chetumal, open 24 hrs, left luggage from US$0.30 per small bag, per hr, prices rising depending on size of bag, open 0600-2200. To **Cancún Airport**, every 30 mins, 30 mins, US$3.50. To **Chetumal**, ADO, frequent departures, 6 hrs, US$17.50. To **Chichén Itzá**; all 2nd-class buses to Mérida stop here, fewer 1st-class buses, 4 hrs, US$7.50-11.50. To **Mérida**, ADO, frequent departures, 4½ hrs, US$15. To **Palenque**, 1st class (ADO and OCC), 1415, 1545, 1930, 2030, 12½ hrs, US$40; and an

ADO GL, 1745, 13 hrs, US$48. To **Playa del Carmen** ADO shuttle, every 10 mins, 1 hr, US$3. To **Puerto Morelos**, ADO, frequent departures, 30 mins, US$1. To **San Cristóbal**, OCC, 1415, 1545, 2030 18 hrs, US$49, ADOGL, 1745, US$58. To **Tulum**, ADO, frequent departures, 2½ hrs, US$5, and many cheaper 2nd-class buses. To **Valladolid**, frequent departures, 2½ hrs, US$9. To **Villahermosa**, 1st class, many departures, 13 hrs, US$52.50-73.50. To **Xcaret**, frequent departures, 1¾ hrs, US$3. To **Xel-Há**, frequent departures, 2 hrs, US$4. Expreso de Oriente also has services to the more obscure destinations of **Tizimín** (3 hrs, US$8), **Izamal**, **Cenotillo** and **Chiquil** (for Isla Holbox ferries).

Car
Car hire There are many car hire agencies, with offices on Av Tulum, in the hotel zone and at the airport; look out for special deals, but check vehicles carefully. They include: **Budget**, Cancún airport, T998-884 6955; **Alamo**, Cancún Airport, T998-886 0179; **Mastercar Autorental**, T998-887 3929; **Top Rent a Car**, Blv Kukulcán, Km 14.5, T998-885 0094.

Car parking Do not leave cars parked in side streets; there is a high risk of theft. Use the car park on Av Uxmal.

Ferry
Ferries to **Isla Mujeres** depart from terminals at Gran Puerto and nearby Puerto Juárez, north of Av Tulum, every 30 mins between 0600-2300, 20 mins by fast ferry, US$2.50, US$5 return (doesn't need to be on the same day). The car ferry departs from Punta Sam, US$13 for the vehicle and US$2 per passenger. The ferry leaves 5 times a day from 0800, the last one leaving Isla Mujeres 1915.

Isla Mujeres *p720, map 720*
Air
The small airstrip in the middle of the island is mainly used for private planes, best arranged with a tourist office in Cancún.

Bicycle and moped
Many touts along Hidalgo offer moped rentals at similar rates: US$7 per hr, US$25 full day. **Sport Bike**, Av Juárez y Morelos, has good bikes. **Cárdenas**, Av Guerrero 105, T/F998-877 0079, for mopeds and golf carts. Bicycles are usually offered by the same places as mopeds for about US$11 per day.

Bus
A public bus runs from the ferry dock to Playa Paraíso every 30 mins, US$0.30. Timings can be erratic, especially on Sun.

Ferry
For information on ferries to and from the island, see Cancún above.

Taxi
A taxi from town to **El Garrafón** and vice versa is US$4.30. For the return journey, sharing a taxi will work out marginally more expensive than the bus for 4 people. A taxi from El Garrafón to the bus stop at Playa Paraíso is US$1. Taxis charge an additional US$1 at night. Beware that the prices are fixed, but inflated on this stretch and a taxi ride to the southernmost tip of the island, a short walk from El Garrafón, is cheaper at US$2.80. There are several places renting **golf carts**, eg Ciros, on Matamoros near Playa Cocos. Rates are generally US$32-39 per day. A credit card is usually required as a deposit.

Puerto Morelos *p722*
Bus
There are buses to **Cancún** and **Playa del Carmen** every 30 mins. Buses depart from the main road, taxi to bus stop US$3.

Ferry
Car ferries to **Cozumel** depart at 0500, 1030, 1600, the dock is 500 m south of the plaza. They return at 0800, 1330, 1900, but always check schedules in advance, US$6 per passenger, US$67 per car. Taxi from Cancún airport to Puerto Morelos cost US$25-35.

Playa del Carmen *p722, map p723*
Air
There are flights to **Cozumel** from the nearby airstrip, speak to a tourist office in Playa del Carmen about chartering a plane.

Bus
The ADO bus terminal is on Av Juárez between Av 5 and 10. All buses depart from here. The following prices and times are for ADO buses (1st class, a/c, usually showing a video on longer journeys); Premier, also 1st class; Maya de Oro, supposed to be 1st class but quality of buses can be poor; OCC, good 1st-class service. To **Cancún**, frequent departures, 1½ hrs, US$3; 2nd-class services with Mayab, less frequent, US$2. To **Cancún airport**, Riviera, frequent between 0700 and 1915, 1 hr, US$6.50. To **Chetumal**, ADO, frequent departures, 4½ hrs, US$14.50; and many 2nd-class buses. To **Chichén Itzá**, 4 departures, 0610, 0730, 0800, 1150, 4 hrs, US$8.50-15.50. To **Mérida**, frequent departures, 5 hrs, US$20.50. To **Mexico City**, ADO, 1230, 1930, 2130, 24½ hrs, US$87. To **San Cristóbal de las Casas**, OCC, 1545, 1715, 2200, 16 hrs, US$46.50; and an ADO GL, 1900, US$55.50; and 3 TRF departures, US$30. To **Tulum**, frequent departures, 1 hr, US$3.50. To **Valladolid**, frequent, 3 hrs, US$8.50 (most buses going to Mérida stop at Valladolid. 2nd-class buses to Valladolid go via Tulum). To **Xcaret**, frequent departures, 15 mins, US$0.80. To **Xel Há**, frequent departures, 1 hr, US$3.50.

Car
Car hire Avis, Av 20, between Calle 4 and 6, T984-803 0713; Budget, Hwy 307 southbound and Calle 34, T984-873 2772; Executive, Av 5a between Calle 10 and 12, T984-873 0477, Happy Rent a Car, Av 10a and Constituyentes, T984-873 1739; Hertz Rent-a-Car, Highway 307 and Calle 12, T984-873 2151; Rodar, Av 5a between Calle 2 and 4, T984-873 0088.

Ferry
Ferries to **Cozumel** depart from the main dock, just off the plaza. There are 2 competing companies, right next to each other, journeys take 30 mins with both, hourly departures on the hour from 0500 until 2200, US$20 return, more to bring a car across. Buy ticket 1 hr before journey.

Taxi
Cancún airport US$35. Beware of those who charge only US$5 as they are likely to charge an extra US$20 for luggage. Tours to **Tulum** and **Xel-Há** from kiosk by boat dock are around US$30; tours to Tulum, Xel-Há and **Xcaret**, 5-6 hrs, US$60; taxi to Xcaret US$6.65. Taxis congregate on the Av Juárez side of the square (Sindicato Lázaro Cárdenas del Río, T998-873 0032).

Cozumel *p722, map p724 and p725*
Air
To **Mexico City** direct with Mexicana, or via Cancún; Continental to **Houston**; Aerocaribe to **Cancún** and **Chichén Itzá**. Aerocaribe and Aerocozumel have almost hourly flights to **Cancún**.
Airline offices Most are based at the airport, 2 km north of the town. Aerocozumel, T987-872 0468. Continental, T987-872 0847. Mexicana, P Joaquín between Salas and Calle 3 Sur, next to Pemex, T987-872 0157.

Bicycle and moped
There is no bus service, but taxis are plentiful. The best way to get around the island is by hired moped or bicycle. Mopeds cost US$25-35 per day, credit card needed as deposit; bicycles are around US$15 per day, US$20 cash or TC deposit. El Aguila, Av Melgar, between 3 and 5 Sur, T987-872 0729; and El Dorado, Av Juárez, between 5 and 10, T987-872 2383.

Car

Car rental There are many agencies, including **Avis**, airport, T987-872 0219; **Budget**, Av 5 between 2 and 4 Nte, T987-872 0219; **Hertz**, Av Melgar, T987-872 3955; **Ejecutivo**, 1 Sur, No 19, T987-872 1308.

Tulum *p727*
Bicycle

Bikes can be hired in the village from **Iguana Bike Shop**, Calle Satélite Sur and Andrómeda, T984-119-0836 (mobile) or T984-871 2357; a good way to visit local centres (**Cristal** and **Escondido** which are recommended as much cheaper, US$2, and less commercialized than **Xcaret**).

Bus

Regular buses go up and down the coastal road travelling from **Cancún** to **Tulum** en route to **Chetumal**, stopping at most places in between. Some buses may be full when they reach Tulum; very few buses begin their journeys here. To **Chetumal**, frequent departures, 4 hrs, 2nd class, US$10, 1st class US$12. To **Cobá**, 8 departures daily, 45 mins, US$3. To **Escárcega**, ADO, 1645, 1715, 7 hrs, US$24.50. To **Felipe Carrillo Puerto**, frequent departures, 1½ hrs, US$5. To **Mérida**, ADO, 2400, 0140, 0500, 1240, 1430, 4 hrs, US$14; and several 2nd-class departures. To **Mexico City**, ADO, 1340, 23½ hrs, US$85.To **Palenque**, OCC, 1655, 1825, 10-11 hrs, US$34; and ADO GL, 2015, US$40.50. To **San Cristóbal**, OCC, 1655, 1825, 15 hrs, US$43.50; and an ADO GL, 2015, US$52. To **Villahermosa**, ADO, 1340, 2324, 11 hrs, US$38.

Taxi

Tulum town to **Tulum ruins** US$3-3.50; to the *cabañas* US$3.50; to **Cobá** about US$25 one way – bargain hard. **Tucan Kin** run shuttles to Cancún airport, T01800-702 4111 for reservations, about US$20-25 for 2 people, 1 hr 45 mins.

Cobá *p728*
Bus

Buses into the village turn round at the road end. To **Cancún**, ADO, 1330, 1530, 3 hrs, US$8. To **Playa del Carmen**, ADO, 1330, 1530, 2 hrs, US$5. To **Tulum**, ADO, 1330, 1530, 1 hr, US$2.50.

Taxi

A taxi to **Tulum** should cost you around US$25. If you miss the bus there is a taxi to be found at **El Bocadito**.

Felipe Carrillo Puerto *p729*
Bus

Bus station opposite **Pemex**. To Cancun, frequent 1st- and 2nd-class departures, 4 hrs, US$13. To **Chetumal**, frequent departures, 2½ hrs, US$8. To **Playa del Carmen**, frequent departures, 2½ hrs, US$9. To **Tulum**, frequent departures, 1½ hrs, US$5.

Chetumal *p730, map p731*
Air

Airport (CTM) 2½ km from town. Flights to **Cancún**, **Mérida**, **Belize City** (Click Mexicana), **Mexico City**, **Monterrey** and **Tijuana**.
   Airline offices Click Mexicana, Plaza Varudi, Av Héroes 125. **Aviacsa**, T983-832 7765.

Bus

Bus information T983-832 5110. The main bus terminal is 3 km out of town at the intersection of Insurgentes y Belice. Taxi into town US$1.50. There is a bus into the centre from Av Belice. **Left luggage** lockers cost US$0.20 per hr. If buying tickets in advance, go to the ADO office on Av Belice esq Ghandi, 0800-1600. There are often more buses than those marked on the display in the bus station. Always ask at the information desk. Many buses going to the border, US$0.30; taxi from Chetumal to border, 20 mins, US$6 for two. Long-distance buses are often all booked a day ahead, so avoid unbooked connections. Expect passport checks on buses leaving for Mexican destinations.

To **Bacalar**, very frequent 1st- and 2nd-class departures, 1 hr, US$2. To **Campeche**, ADO, 1200, 6 hrs, US$20. To **Cancún**, many 1st-class departures, 6 hrs, US$17.50. To **Córdoba**, ADO, 1130, 16 hrs, US$57. To **Emiliano Zapata**, 1st class (OCC and ADO), 2150, 2345, 6 ½ hrs, US$20.50. To **Escárcega**, ADO, 11 daily, 4 hrs, US$13. To **Felipe Carrillo Puerto**, many 1st- and 2nd-class departures, 2½ hrs, US$8. To **Mérida**, ADO, 0730, 1330, 1700, 2330, 5½ hrs, US$21. To **Mexico City**, ADO, 1130, 1630, 20½ hrs, US$73.50. To **Minatitlán**, ADO, 2000, 12 hrs, US$36. To **Palenque**, OCC, 0220, 2020, 2150, 7 hrs, US$23; and ADO GL, 2350, US$27. To **Playa del Carmen**, frequent 1st- and 2nd-class departures, 5 hrs, US$14.50. To **Puebla**, ADO, 2300, 17 hrs, US$66.50. To **San Cristóbal**, OCC, 0220, 2020, 2150, 12 hrs, US$33; and ADO GL 2350, US$39.50. To **Tulum**, frequent 1st- and 2nd-class departures, 4 hrs, US$12. To **Tuxtla Gutiérrez** OCC, 2030, 2150, 13 hrs, US$36.50; and ADO GL 2350, US$43.50. To **Veracruz**, 1830, 17 hrs, US$50. To **Villahermosa**, ADO, 6 daily, 8½ hrs, US$27. To **Xpujil**, 13 ADO, Sur and OCC, 2 hrs, US$6.

To Belize Premier run buses between Chetumal and **Belize City**, 1145, 1445, 1745, 3 hrs, US$8. En-route, they stop at **Orange Walk**, 2 hrs, US$4. Money changers in the bus terminal offer marginally poorer rates than those at the border. If intending to stay in Belize City, do not take a bus that arrives at night so you are advised not to look for a hotel in the dark.

To Guatemala Linea Dorada operate daily buses to **Flores** in Guatemala at 0600, US$29. Schedules are very much subject to change, so always check times in advance and be prepared to spend a night in Chetumal if necessary.

Car
There's a petrol/gas station just outside Chetumal on the road north at the beginning of the road to Escárcega, and another at Xpujil. **Garage** Talleres Barrera, helpful, on Primo de Verdad; turn east off Héroes, then past the electrical plant.

Taxi
There are no city buses; taxis run on fixed-price routes, US$1.50 on average. Cars with light-green licence plates are a form of taxi.

Colectivos To **Bacalar** and **Francisco Villa** (for Kohunlich and Xpujil) depart from the junction of Av Miguel Hidalgo and Francisco Primo de Verdad.

⦿ Directory

Cancún *p717*, maps *p717* and *p719*
Banks There are 11 Mexican banks along Av Tulum, all in SM4 and SM5. **American Express**, for changing their own TCs at better rates than anywhere else, is on Av Tulum, just south of Av Cobá. Many *casas de cambio* in the centre, mainly around the bus terminal and along Av Tulum. *Casas de cambio* in the hotel zone give slightly lower rates for TCs than those in the centre. **Cultural centres** Casa Tabasco, Av Tulum 230, displays and handicrafts for sale from the state of Tabasco, a good place to go if bored of the same old souvenirs in Cancún. **Embassies and consulates** Austria, Pecarí 37 corner Av Tulum, SM20, Centro, T998-881 5900. Canada, Plaza Caracol, 3rd floor, hotel zone, T998-883 3360. France, Pargo St Lt 24C, T998-883 9816. Germany, Punta Conoco 36, SM24, Centro, T998-884 1598; Italy, Alcatraces 39, SM22, Centro, T998-884 1261. Netherlands, International Airport, Cancún terminal 2, T998-886 0070. Spain, Blv Kukulcán corner Calle Cenzotle, hotel zone, T998-848 9989. Sweden, Nichupté Av, SM19, T998-884 9435. Switzerland, Av Cobá 12, T998-884 8446. UK, Hotel Royal Sands, hotel zone, T998-881 0100. US, Plaza Caracol 2, 3rd floor, hotel zone, T998-883 0272.
Immigration office Corner of Av Náder and Av Uxmal. There is also an office in the airport, T998-886 0492, where the staff are better trained and speak English. **Internet** Numerous cafés charging US$1-1.50 per hr. Generally good servers and open until around 2300. **Laundry** Alborada, Av Nader

5, behind tourist information building on Av Tulum. **Cox-boh**, Av Tankah 26, SM24. **Medical services** American Hospital (24-hr), Viento 15, Centro, T998-884 6133. **Total Assist** (24-hr) Claveles 5, Centro, T998-884 1058. **American Medical Centre**, Plaza Quetzal, hotel zone Km 8, T998-883 0113. **Post office** At the end of Av Sunyaxchén, near Mercado 28, Mon-Fri 0800-1900, Sat 0900-1300. **Telephone** Many public phones and call shops everywhere, phone cards available from general stores and pharmacies. Collect calls can be made without a card. Also many public phones designed for international calls, which take coins and credit cards. Fax at post office, Mon-Sat, and at San Francisco de Asís shopping mall, Mon-Sat until 2200.

Isla Mujeres *p720, map 720*
Banks HSBC, Av Reuda Medina, opposite the ferry dock. Good rates, varying daily, are offered by several *casas de cambio* on Av Hidalgo. The one opposite **Rolandis** is open daily 0900-2100. **Internet** Several internet cafés operate on the island US$1.50 per hour, but speeds can be a little slow. Many cafés and restaurants have free Wi-Fi. **Laundry** Tim Pho, Juárez y Abasolo. **Medical services** Doctors: Dr Antonio Salas, Hidalgo, next to *Farmacia*, T998-877 0477. Open 24 hrs, house calls, English spoken, air ambulance. **Post office** At the end of Guerrero towards the beach. **Telephone** Phone cards can be bought at some of the souvenir shops along Hidalgo.

Puerto Morelos *p722*
Internet There is an internet café on the corner of the plaza opposite **Posada Amor**, US$2.50 per hour, Mon-Sat 1000-1400, 1600-2100.

Playa del Carmen *p722, map p723*
Banks Banamex, Av Juárez between Calle 20 and 25. A few doors down is **Santander**. Bancomer, Av Juárez between Calle 25 and 30. **Banorte**, Av 5 between Av Juárez and the

beach. **Inverlat**, Av 5 between Av Juárez and Calle 2. HSBC, Av Juárez between Calle 10 and 15, also at Av 30 between Calle 4 and 6. There are several *casas de cambio* along Av 5, which change TCs with no commission. Count your money carefully as short changing is not uncommon and rates can be hit and miss. **Immigration office** Centro Comercial, Plaza Antigua, Av 10 Sur, T984-873 1884. **Internet** All the cybercafés in town charge between US$1.50-2 per hour. **Laundry** Av Juárez, 2 blocks from bus station; another on Av 5. Maya Laundry, Av 5 between Calle 2 and Calle 4, Mon-Sat 0800-2100. Laundry in by 1000, ready in the afternoon, many others around town. **Medical services** Dentist: Perla de Rocha Torres, Av 20 Norte between 4 and 6, T984-873 0021, speaks English. Recommended. International Medical Services: Dr Victor Macías Orosco, Av 35 between Calle 2 and 4, T984-873 0493. 24-hr emergency service, land and air ambulance, ultrasound, most major insurance accepted. Tourist Divers Medical Centre, Dr Mario Abarca, Av 10 between Av Juárez and Calle 2, T984-873 0512. Air and land ambulance service, hyperbaric and diving medicine, affiliated with South Miami Hospital, all insurance accepted. **Police** Av Juárez, T984-873 0291. **Post office** Calle 2 and Av 20, Mon-Fri 0800-1700, Sat 0900-1300.

Cozumel *p722, map p724 and p725*
Banks 4 banks on the main square, all exchange money in morning only, but not at same hours: HSBC, on Juárez (all with ATM machines), Bancomer, Banamex, Banorte. *Casas de cambio* on Av 5 Norte and around square. **Internet** Several internet cafés charging around US$1.50 per hr. **Laundry** Express, Salas between Av 5 and Av 10, T987-872 3655. Coin-op, service washes, US$9 medium load, collection service and dry cleaning. **Medical services** Dentist: Dr Hernández, T987-872 0656. Hospitals and clinics: Red Cross: A R Salas between Calle 20 and Calle

25 Sur, T987-872 1058; **Centro Médico de Cozumel**, Calle 1 Sur, No 101, corner Av 50, T987-872 3545. English spoken, international air ambulance, 24-hr emergency service. **Pharmacy**: A R Salas between Av 12 and Av 20, 0700-2400.

Post office Av Rafael Melgar y Calle 7 Sur, Mon-Fri 0900-1800, Sat 0900-1200.

Telephone Ladatel phones (if working) on main square at corner of Av Juárez and Av 5, or on A R Salas, just up from Av 5 Sur, opposite **Roberto's Black Coral Studio**. For calls to the US, go to **The Stadium**. Telmex phone offices on the main square next to Restaurant Plaza Leza, 0800-2300, and on A R Salas between Av 10 and 15. There are also expensive **Computel** offices in town, eg at the cruise ship dock. **Telephone centre** for long distance on corner of Rafael Melgar and Calle 3 Sur. Also public telephone *caseta* at Av 5 esq Calle 2, 0800-1300, 1600-2100.

Tulum *p727*
Banks HSBC, Av Tulum open 0900-1900, has an ATM, but doesn't change TCs. Scotiabank further along the same road is open Mon-Fri, 0900-1600, changes TCs and cash. Several casas de cambio in Av Tulum closer to the ADO terminal. **Telephone and internet** Long-distance phones in Av Tulum near and opposite the ADO terminal in town. Internet cafés in the same road.

Chetumal *p730, map p731*
Banks The banks all close at 1430. There are several ATMs. For exchange, **Banamex**, Obregón y Juárez, changes TCs. **Banco Mexicano**, Juárez and Cárdenas, TCs or US$ cash, quick and courteous service. Several on, or near, Av Héroes with ATMs. Banks do not change quetzales into pesos. **Embassies and consulates** Belize, Hon Consul, Lic Francisco Lechón Rosas, Rotondo Carranza 562 (behind Super San Francisco), T983-878 7728; visas can take up to 3 weeks to get, and many are only issued in Mexico City. **Guatemala**, Av Héroes de Chapultepec 356, T983-832 6565. Open for visas, Mon-Fri 0900-1700. It is best to organize your visa, if required, in your home country before travel. **Internet** Eclipse, 5 de Mayo 83 between PE Calles and Zaragoza. 0930-1500, 1800-2100, not very friendly but cheap at US$3 per hr. **Los Cebollones**, Calzada Veracruz 452, T983-832 9145, also restaurant and cocktail bar. **Laundry** Lavandería Automática 'Lava facil', corner of Héroes and Confederación Nacional Campesina. **Medical services** Malaria prophylaxis available from **Centro de Salud**, opposite hospital (request tablets for paludismo). **Post office** 16 de Septiembre y PE Calles. Mon-Fri 0800-1730, Sat 0900-1300. Packets to be sent abroad must be taken unwrapped to the bus terminal to have them checked by customs before taking them to the post office. Better to wait till another town. Parcel service not available Sat. **Western Union** office attached to post office, same hours.

Contents

Background

History, economy and government

First settlers

The first Mesoamerican peoples were nomadic hunter-gatherers possessing simple stone technologies and an appetite for mammoth. Scholars are divided over exactly when they first set foot upon American soil. It is believed that they appeared during the last ice age, also known as the Pleistocene epoch, at around 40000 BC, give or take 10,000 years.

At that time, much of the earth's water was locked up as ice and sea levels were much lower than today. What is now known as the Bering Strait – a narrow, icy body of water between northwest Canada and Russia – was then exposed land as the subcontinent of Beringea. This intercontinental bridge saw the earliest settlers migrate from Asia, wave after wave, who pursued their prey into the vast continents of the Americas.

At the end of the ice age, around 9000 BC, dramatic climatic shifts signalled profound changes in vegetation and habitat. Glaciers melted, Beringea flooded and the valleys of Mesoamerica flourished with green vegetation. A brief era of Clovis culture ensued, a culture renowned for – but not solely sustained by – its mammoth hunting. The remains of mammoths and ancient stone tools have been discovered at Santa Isabel Iztapan in the Valley of Mexico, dating to 9000 BC; and at Tepexpan, where a woman was found alongside a mammoth, dating to 8000 BC.

As the earth's melting progressed, human populations grew and environmental changes intensified, the megafauna – the giant prehistoric beasts – could no longer sustain themselves. They simply died out. The Mesoamerican peoples reverted to their traditional diet of grubs, fruits and small mammals, especially mice. Much of this humble early existence was dominated by the search for food.

No event was more critical in the emergence of Mesoamerican civilization than the domestication of plants, especially maize. This took place between 8000 and 2000 BC in an era known as the archaic or proto-agricultural. Much of our knowledge of this era is owed to the work of Richard MacNeish, who discovered beans and gourds in Tamaulipas, as well as chillies, avocado, squash and amaranth in the Tehuacán valley.

The earliest remains of maize, or sweetcorn, were also found in the Tehuacán valley, dating to 5000 BC. They indicate a crop that is far evolved from its wild ancestor, teosinte – a maize-like plant with tiny, edible fruits. The evolution from teosinte into domestic maize was not an accidental affair. The ancients were not unfamiliar with the concept of genetic engineering and relied on methods of selective breeding to produce a plant with an increasingly greater yield and larger type of fruit.

It took thousands of years to develop a maize plant productive enough to support a wholly sedentary lifestyle. But by 5000 BC, maize could be grown and stored in large quantities. It soon became the staple diet of the Mesoamerican peoples, for when served with beans in the form of tortillas, maize provides all the protein and nutrition necessary for survival. Prior to this, the early Mesoamericans lacked any sizeable domestic animals (only dogs and turkeys were on the menu) and were forced to subsist on traditional hunting and gathering. By 2000 BC agricultural villages were firmly established throughout Mesoamerica.

Formative Era

The Formative period in ancient Mesoamerican history, dating from 2000 BC to AD 200 and also known as the Pre-Classic era, sees the establishment of all the key socio-political structures, symbols, technologies and religious ideas that define the subsequent ages of the Mesoamerican tradition. In essence, Mesoamerica defines itself. Scholars have divided it into three distinct (if unimaginatively titled) phases: The Early Formative (2000 BC-1200 BC), the Middle Formative (1200 BC-400 BC) and the Late Formative (400 BC-AD 200).

Early Formative

At the dawn of the Formative era, 2000 BC, simple agricultural villages flourished in Mesoamerica's valleys and mountains, bereft of complex social structures and organized along purely egalitarian lines. No longer the tribal nomads, these early peoples were at the mercy of nature's forces. The success – or failure – of their harvests depended entirely upon environmental and climatic conditions. Shamanism flourished.

The ancient shaman was an intermediary between the worlds. Healer, counsellor and diviner, the shaman's knowledge included the use of medicinal herbs, sacred songs and healing rites. More than this, he was acquainted with the unseen otherworld of spiritual – and natural – forces. He knew the secret language of the wind, the rain and the sun and he knew how to ask favours from them. Shamanism continues to be practised across Mesoamerica. The maize plant plays a central role in the cosmic hierarchy.

The evolution of maize was accompanied by another major milestone in the evolution of Mesoamerican civilization: the use of fired ceramics. The earliest reliably dated pottery of the region belongs to a tradition called Ocos. Ocos pottery originated from the Pacific coast of Chiapas and Guatemala, but has also been found across the continent from Veracruz to Honduras. It seems that trade and communication between settlements was already widespread at this time. Clay was utilized for the production of food storage vessels, as well as the production of figurines. The hordes of 'pretty lady' dolls unearthed at Tlatilco in Mexico City indicate a preoccupation with fertility, if the accepted interpretation of their oversized thighs is correct. Other figurines have a playful aspect and depict day-to-day scenes like women nursing babies. Yet others reveal an embryonic fascination with deformity with little hunchbacks and dwarves. Clay vessels used in human burials were also uncovered at Tlatilco, indicating a ceremonial aspect to death had probably developed.

Towards the end of the Formative era, around 1200 BC, chiefdoms emerged with increasingly complex social structures including craft specialization and simple stratification. Surveys in Oaxaca have revealed large residences probably belonging to the chief, as well as public ceremonial buildings. Similar research in coastal Chiapas – the heart of Ocos culture – also reveals the emergence of such chiefdoms.

Middle Formative

The Middle Formative era of Mesoamerican development, 1200 BC to 400 BC, was dominated by the Olmec. The Olmec constructed the most advanced and powerful polities of their time, although relatively little is known of these ingenious and mysterious people. They are generally attributed with developing the first Mesoamerican calendars, as well as written glyphs. They spoke a Mixe-Zoquean language that survives only in highland Oaxaca and the Isthmus of Tehuantepec.

Olmec culture originated on Mexico's Gulf coast but came to dominate much of Mesoamerica. The site of San Lorenzo in Veracruz dates to 1500 BC, when it was settled as a simple farming village. Just 150 years later, San Lorenzo had developed a level of socio-political complexity sufficient for an elite to mobilize a sizeable labour force, evidenced by the large-scale landscape and public works projects uncovered there. Little is known about Olmec leaders, except they were believed to be imbued with divine powers.

Subsequently, by 1150 BC, San Lorenzo had acquired all the features that distinguish Olmec civilization – giant stone heads, monumental public architecture, Mesoamerica's first known ball court, a wealth of ceramic figurines, vessels and iconographic motifs. Many of these features – monumental architecture and ball courts especially – would become chief characteristics of Mesoamerican civilization as a whole.

By 900 BC, San Lorenzo was in decline and eclipsed by the polity of La Venta, where archaeological finds include elite residences, monumental architecture, tombs, offerings and mosaic masks. By the end of the Middle Formative, around 400 BC, La Venta and its contemporary Olmec polities – Laguna de los Cerros and Tres Zapotes – were in irrevocable decline. The widespread influence of Olmec culture was drawing to a close, soon to disappear.

For many years, scholars believed that Olmec culture was the colonial master of many contemporaneous cultures, as well as the originator and 'mother culture' of all subsequent Mesoamerican developments. This is no longer believed to be the case.

Many styles and symbols once thought to be classically Olmec have been discovered in great quantities at contemporaneous sites, sometimes in quantities far greater than those in the Olmec heartland. Scholars now believe that such cultures flourished alongside the dominant Olmec polities, were heavily influenced by them, but were not necessarily subordinate to them. Shared stylistic features are now often called 'X-Complex' rather then Olmec style.

Such contemporaneous cultures were not as powerful or advanced as the Olmec, but were reasonably complex nonetheless, belonging to a network of chiefdoms that traded goods and shared a common system of emblems. Their societies were stratified into elite and commoners. The elite had access to luxury trade goods, lived in larger homes and were buried in more elaborate tombs.

In the valley of Oaxaca, the polity of San José Mogote was the centre of power and economic activity for a host of secondary and tertiary centres – the former possessed public architecture, the latter were simple agricultural villages. In Chalcatzingo in Morelos, a large civic-ceremonial precinct is strongly reminiscent of Olmec monumental art. Some argue that this site traded closely with the gulf coast Olmec, emulated their style and may even have had marriage ties to it.

In the Mayan lowlands, development was rapid from the Middle Formative period, but seems to have occurred without much Olmec influence. Very few Olmec items have been identified in the earliest Mayan settlement of Petén and they did not participate in the same trade networks as the Chalcatzingo and Oaxaca chiefdoms.

Late Formative

As Chalcatzingo, La Venta and other Middle Formative polities collapsed during the last two centuries BC, the vast metropolises of Cuicuilco and Teotihuacán – both located in central Mexico - emerged as dominant centres of Mesoamerican power. Both had huge temple complexes and buildings of truly monumental proportions. In the first century AD, Cuicuilco was destroyed under a volcanic eruption, leaving its enormous circular pyramid visible under 6 m of rock. Teotihuacán became the prevailing regional force.

Further south, a confederation of Oaxaca valley chiefdoms constructed the mountain-top city of Monte Albán (Blanton). Its population grew and a successful market system developed. Soon Monte Albán became the capital of the Zapotec state and a major urban centre. It would dominate the region, often violently, for several hundred years more.

The Mayan lowlands also saw significant developments during the close of the formative era, around AD 200. In construction projects reminiscent of mighty Teotihuacán, the Maya built giant civic-ceremonial architecture, including the enormous platforms and pyramids of El Mirador in Guatemala. They practised intensive agriculture, allowing their populations to flourish, and reclaimed land from the marshes. Labour for these projects was believed to have been centrally directed, that is, under orders from a well-established elite.

From a scattering of simple agricultural settlements, Mesoamerica had evolved a burgeoning network of city-states. Village shamans were now priests, belonging to an elite social order who guarded the secrets of time. Complex and often bloody rituals were the staple diet of the gods, who dwelled among mortals as princes and kings. Slaves, artisans and warriors toiled beneath them. Giant stone pyramids, symbols of earthly and spiritual power, had risen across the continent. The stage was set for Mesoamerica's golden age ...

Classic period

This transition led to the start of the Classic period, around AD 200, which was marked by the growth of powerful urbanized empires, and the creative peak of the arts and science.

Zapotecs and Mixtecs

As Olmec influence was fading, 500 km or so to the west, in the Oaxaca Valley, the ceremonial centre of Monte Albán was being built. It was an impressive site composed of pyramids, plazas and temples, strategically placed on a levelled hilltop overlooking the valley floor. Hieroglyphs carved into the stonework here are evidence of some of the earliest texts found in the region, as well as glyphs representing the 52-year cycle, known as the Calendar Round, used as the standard system throughout the Mesoamerican world. The Zapotec people had occupied the site since its construction, and remained there throughout the Classic period, during which time architectural influence from the Teotihuacán culture was apparent. After about AD 500 however, the site fell into decline, and in its later years was occupied by the Mixtec culture, which had merged with the Zapotecs by the time of the Spanish Conquest.

Teotihuacán

The Classic period reached its crowning glory with the construction of the great planned city of Teotihuacán, near present-day Mexico City, in the Valley of Mexico, described by Michael D Coe (Professor of Anthropology at Yale University and author of many books on the pre-Columbian cultures) as the "most important site in the whole of Mexico".

Teotihuacán was also the largest city in the pre-Columbian New World, covering more than 21 sq km, with a population of up to 200,000, which, by AD 600, made it the sixth largest city in the world. The dominant constructions at Teotihuacán are the Pyramids of the Sun and the Moon, overlooking the enormous Avenue of the Dead. The site is also filled with finely constructed temples, palaces and residential compounds. Besides their superb architecture, the Teotihuacán culture were also highly skilled artists, producing many beautiful murals, ceramics, and sculptures.

How Teotihuacán grew to be such a powerful and prosperous city remains largely a mystery. Examples of Teotihuacán-style artefacts have been found as far afield as Tikal and Kaminaljuyú in Guatemala, and to the NW at Chametla near present-day Mazatlán, some 1400 km from Teotihuacán, evidence that it must have benefited from long-distance trade links.

Nevertheless, after thriving for almost 1000 years, the culture dramatically collapsed around AD 600. The centre of the city was destroyed around AD 700, after which time all evidence of their regional influence suddenly disappeared. The invaders may have been the Totonac culture from Veracruz, or possibly the Totomí, a semi-barbaric culture from the north of Mexico.

Maya

At around the same time that the Olmec and Teotihuacán civilizations were making their dramatic stage exits in the early Classic, the Maya were reaching the peak of their own magnificent dynasty. Although the heart of their culture lay outside of Mexico, the inclusion of the Mayas in this history is a reflection of the enormous influence they had throughout much of the country during and long after their days in power.

Maya-speaking people are thought to have inhabited a wide band of territory encompassing El Salvador, Guatemala, most of southeast Mexico and parts of western Honduras. As with other early Mexican cultures, the origins of the Maya is unknown, but remains of early fishing and hunting groups has been found in their westernmost territory, dating from 3000-2000 BC.

The Maya came into contact with the advanced pre-Classic cultures, particularly the Olmecs and Teotihuacán, from whom they learnt new skills and ideas. Agricultural developments allowed the growth of larger cities, especially around the Maya Lowlands of Guatemala, which became their heartland and the site of some of their greatest ceremonial centres: Tikal, Kaminaljuyú and El Mirador. The chief Maya sites in Mexico were Chichén Itzá in the Yucatán, as well as Palenque and Bonampak in Chiapas.

The architectural achievements of the Maya were exemplified in the superb temples, palaces and pyramids of their urban capitals. Again, they learnt from their predecessors, emulating Teotihuacán in the massive scale of their most important constructions. All these buildings were decorated with highly artistic sculptures, murals, and glyphs.

Mayan society became increasingly hierarchical as their cities grew larger, with power concentrated in the hands of a hereditary elite. By the end of the Classic at the peak of the Maya civilization, there may have been as many as 14 million citizens living in the Maya heartland, with powerful urban centres across Mesoamerica, from Copán in Honduras, through Guatemala, Belize and to the Yucatán Peninsula. These centres never united into an organized empire however. Each was a separate city-state which, while sharing a common cultural background with its neighbour, was also often antagonistic, competing for power.

How did the Maya become such an advanced civilization? Their interaction with other Mesoamerican cultures – and probably with seafarers from South America – could quite easily have stimulated their growth. Theories of transatlantic contacts have long been proposed, but to date not one item made in the Old World has ever been found in a Mesoamerican site. However, many fascinating cultural similarities between Asian and Mayan cultures have been pointed out, including symbols used in both cultures' calendars. This is not to suggest that Old World cultures were at the roots of the New World civilizations, but some of the New World cultures may have come into contact with peoples from the East and from whom they could have adopted selective ideas.

Around AD 900, disaster struck, causing the abandonment of all the Mayan ceremonial centres. The cause of this sudden collapse, described by Michael Coe as "one of the most profound social and demographic catastrophes of all human history", remains unknown. Theories include famine brought on by drought, internal uprising, and massacre by invading foreign tribes. Whatever the truth, the downfall of the Maya marked the end of the Classic, and with it the end of the era of great imperial urban cultures in Mexico.

Post-Classic period

The collapse of the Maya in southern Mexico was matched by the spectacular rise of new powers from the north, first among which were the Toltecs. The cultural standards reached by the Maya and the Olmecs in the Classic were never to be surpassed in this new era, from AD 900 to 1519. Instead, a phase of military aggression and authoritarianism was beginning, which would reach its own tumultuous peak with the arrival of the Spanish conquistadors.

Huastecs

The peoples of the northeast coastal fringe of Mesoamerica, to the north of Veracruz and eastern San Luis Potosí, blossomed later than neighbouring cultures to the south and west, but they left a significant impression nevertheless. Originating from the Gulf Coast region to the north of the city of Veracruz, the Huasteca people were probably closely related to the earliest Mayas during the pre-Classic period, but after about 1500 BC, their paths separated. The Huastecs produced some fine ceramics and painted murals, and built both large and small ceremonial centres (including Tamuin, near San Luis Potosí).

The most important site in the Veracruz area, however, was El Tajín, a large ceremonial centre, some 8 km southwest of Papantla, built during the early Classic period. The dominant building at El Tajín is the Pyramid of the Niches which, for its elaborate decoration and numerous niches (365 in total), ranks as one of the finest pieces of pre-Columbian architecture in all Mesoamerica. The construction of El Tajín reached its peak in the late Classic period, and included massive stone temples and at least 11 impressive ball courts (this was one of the founding regions of the cult 'sport').

The Huastecs later came into contact with the Aztecs, but despite some of their southern region falling to Aztec control, they mostly retained their own independence. Late successors to the Huastecs in the Veracruz region were the Totonacs, who arrived after the abandonment of El Tajín, in the 13th century, and who built their centres in Remojadas and El Zapotal.

Toltecs

The Toltecs were originally a mixture of tribes dominated by Nahua-speaking Toltec-Chichimecas, from western Mexico, combined with the Nonoalca people from the Puebla and Gulf Coast regions. These early descendants had peacefully farmed the fringes of western and northern Mexico since ancient times, but by the post-Classic era they had been driven south by drought and starvation.

After AD 900 the Toltecs formed their capital, Tula (aka Tollan), in the state of Hidalgo, about 80 km northwest of Mexico City, under the leadership of a king named Topiltzin. Their characteristic feature was professional warmongering, glorifying militarism in mass rituals such as bloodletting, animal and human sacrifice, and the gruesome construction of tzompantli (racks of skulls), as a public display of their victims' heads.

Tula was the centre of the Toltec culture, which rose to dominate the whole of central Mexico, in northern and western Mexico almost as far as the border with New Mexico, and south through the Yucatán Peninsula, and even into parts of the Guatemalan highlands.

Topiltzin was driven out of Tula around AD 987, following an internal conflict. He invaded and conquered Chichén Itzá, followed by the rest of the Yucatán Mayan sites, eventually creating an alternative domain to the one he had lost at Tula. Toltec-style architecture was adopted in Chichén Itzá, but there is evidence of Toltec-Maya influence in the Yucatán long before the arrival of Topiltzin.

The Toltecs plunged into decline in the second half of the 12th century. Severe droughts provoked feuds between factions of the original Toltec-Chichimeca and Nonoalca tribes. The last Toltec ruler, Huemac, moved the capital to Chapultepec (in the west of Mexico City), but failing to pacify the uprisings, he committed suicide. Some of the Toltec-Chichimecas stayed on at Tula for a few years, but others drifted south, even as far as Guatemala, where they clung to their memories of Tula's days of glory.

Independent states

Post-Classic Mexico also saw the continuation of various independent states, who had resisted overthrow by the imperial civilizations, and who subsequently managed to hold back the Aztecs. Foremost among these states were the Mixtecs, from the Oaxaca region in southwest Mexico, who united with the neighbouring Zapotecs to repel the invading Aztecs. They were a highly artistic people, renown as the finest craftsmen of gold artefacts and turquoise mosaics ever seen in Mexico, much of whose work has been uncovered in the earlier Zapotec site of Monte Albán.

The Tarascans, centred around Lake Pátzcuaro in western Mexico, were another redoubtable people who resisted the Aztecs, despite being eventually surrounded by their territory on all sides. They were highly accomplished artisans, in precious metals and stones and, with the finely cut stone pyramids of their capital, Tzintzuntzan, the Tarascans also showed their considerable skills as architects.

Aztecs

The Aztec people were Nahuatl-speakers from the northwest of Mexico, from where they migrated to the Valley of Mexico during the 12th and 13th centuries AD. Here they conquered the Chichimeca people, who were living in relative peace, following the violent collapse of the Toltec Empire.

The Aztecs were first and foremost a supremely efficient military force, rapidly expanding their territory, extracting tribute and victims for human sacrifice as they went. They were also highly adept at adopting the artistic skills and styles of their conquered foes and produced some fine works of art and architecture.

In 1344-45, they built their capital, Tenochtitlán, on an island in the middle of Lake Texcoco. The scale of this magnificent city, which at the time of the Conquest may have been occupied by as many as 300,000 inhabitants, can be appreciated by the comparison with the contemporary London of King Henry VIII, which was only one-fifth the size.

By the late 1400s the Aztecs found themselves the most powerful state in the whole country. Not only that, but their ruler, Tlacaecel, rewrote the history books to declare the Aztecs as the chosen race, who would keep the sun moving through the sky, maintaining the Toltec mythology.

Following this declaration of divine destiny, the Aztecs began a wave of military conquests that expanded their borders across most of central Mexico and south as far as Guatemala, creating an empire to equal or surpass that of the Toltecs themselves.

The Aztec leader who presided over the boom period of their empire was Ahuitzotl (1486-1502), a dynamic and resourceful man. His successor was Motecuhzoma Xocoytozin

(1502-1520). Motecuhzoma had the misfortune to come to power at the momentous time when the Spanish conquistadors arrived on Mexican soil. The dramatic ease with which these invaders overthrew the mighty Aztec Empire was partly explained by the mythical interpretations made of these bearded white-skinned foreigners. According to Toltec legends, the cult figure Quezalocoatl would return from the east and destroy the Mexicans, a theory which the Spanish were quick to propagate to help them win over their new subjects.

Spanish Conquest

Following Columbus' voyages of 1492-1504 the Spanish focused their attention on the Caribbean islands but were disappointed by the lack of gold and silver. In 1517 the demand for labour to replace the indigenous population, killed off by disease and ill treatment, led Diego Velázquez, Governor of Cuba, to send out an expedition which reached the Yucatán coast. The following year Velázquez commissioned Hernán Cortés to explore and conquer this new land. After landing on the island of Cozumel, Cortés founded the settlement of Veracruz and moved inland.

Reports reached Cortés of the powerful and wealthy Aztec Empire of Moctezuma, with its capital at Tenochtitlán, on an island on Lake Texcoco in the Valley of Mexico, nearly 400 km inland. To discourage desertion among his men Cortés destroyed his boats and marched inland making contact with the Tlaxcalans, traditional opponents of Moctezuma. Reaching Tenochtitlán Cortés was treated hospitably, but hearing rumours that the Aztecs were planning to massacre the Spaniards, he kidnapped Moctezuma. Relations between Aztecs and Spaniards worsened and Moctezuma was killed as he attempted to call off an attack by a much larger Aztec army. Under cover of night the Spanish broke out of the city, using portable bridges to cross the causeways. With support from the Tlaxcalans, Cortés led a large force, equipped with heavy cannons and boats, back to storm the Aztec capital in a battle which lasted several weeks. By the end of the battle in April 1521, the city's fine buildings had been systematically destroyed by the Spanish to prevent the Aztecs using them as cover. The Spanish victory, the result of their superior weapons and armour, their use of horses, the spread of smallpox among the Aztecs and the support of the Tlaxcalans, gave the invaders control of central Mexico and Cortés ordered the building of a new city on the site of Tenochtitlán. In the following decade expeditions were sent into the surrounding areas to conquer the other indigenous peoples throughout present-day Mexico and also further south in Central America.

Colonial period

As elsewhere in the Americas, the Spanish Conquest of New Spain was carried out by soldiers of fortune who operated with permission of the Crown but outside its control. This led to tension between the Crown and the conquerors, due to the Crown's fear of the rise of powerful rivals which wanted to secure its share of the new territories' wealth. Accused of corruption and misuse of royal funds, Cortés returned to Spain to present his case to the Spanish monarch Carlos V; though the charges were dismissed and he was granted the title of Marqués de Oaxaca, Cortés was deprived of power by the appointment of a viceroy to govern the territory on behalf of the monarch.

New Spain became one of the two great centres of the Spanish American Empire and of Spanish settlement, the other being Peru. Like Peru, it was attractive due to the discovery of precious metals and the availability of a large indigenous labour force, without which the wealth of the colonies could not be exploited by the small group of European settlers. Immediately after the Conquest the key to controlling the natives was *encomienda*: under this system native villages and their inhabitants came under the control of an *encomendero*; in return for paying tribute and providing labour, the Indians were placed in the care of the *encomendero* who was supposed to ensure order and supervise their conversion to Christianity. Although many of Cortés' supporters had been granted *encomiendas*, this practice was opposed by the Crown which feared the growth of a powerful hereditary aristocracy, similar to that which had caused Carlos V so much difficulty in Spain. Throughout this period an important role was played by the Church, which supported the Crown, providing schools and hospitals, establishing missions and working to convert the Indians. The latter role brought the missionaries into conflict with the *encomenderos* who wanted control over the Indians as a labour force. In 1542 the Crown issued the New Laws, which restricted the continuance of the *encomienda* system, but these restrictions were not enforced until the 1560s, when they provoked a revolt led by Martín Cortés, the conquistador's son, which was quickly suppressed.

By 1650 the Viceroyalty of New Spain included much of Central America, the Spanish Caribbean islands as well as northwards into California and New Mexico. Although the Viceroy possessed enormous powers, these were restricted in several ways: the Viceroyalty was subdivided into *audiencias*, administered by judges; the Crown sent *visitadores* to carry out inspections and at the end of an official's term a royal investigation occurred. At the local level each municipality was governed by the *cabildo* (town council); though initially elected, seats on it were later sold by the Crown.

The Conquest devastated the indigenous population. Disease, harsh treatment (especially in the mines), and the disruption of traditional ways of life and belief systems all contributed to the decline of the native population of Central Mexico from an estimated 25 million in 1519 to around one million in 1650, after which a slow increase began. Miscegenation was widespread and a complex hierarchy of ethnic mixtures between the white, Indian and black African populations was established.

The economy was transformed by the discovery of large deposits of silver in the 1540s, which stimulated trade within the colony. By the 1650s the Bajío, the basins of Guanajuato and Jalisco, had become major grain-producing areas. Trade with Spain was hindered by distance and the danger of pirates; the defence against the latter, the organization of an annual fleet protected by warships, restricted trade and provided opportunities for smugglers to evade Spanish commercial restrictions. By the 18th century the economy had received a further boost with new discoveries of silver and the reduction of import controls on mercury, used in silver processing.

Along with the rest of Spanish America, the colony was affected by the decline of Spain in the 17th century; unable to produce the manufactured goods required in her colonies, Spain was forced to spend the wealth from the New World on articles manufactured in northern Europe. Some improvement, however, took place in the 18th century and particularly during the reign of Carlos III (1759-1788). Attempts were made to improve colonial administration, the sale of government offices was ended and Creoles (whites born in the Americas) were replaced in the administration by Peninsulares (native-born Spaniards) since the latter were seen as being less corrupt. The administrative system was also reformed: New Spain was divided into 12 Intendencies, each headed by an Intendant appointed by the Viceroy. In 1767 the Jesuit order, considered too powerful, was expelled from Spain and the colonies, a move which led to rioting in New Spain. Restrictions on trade between the colonies were lifted and colonial defences were improved by the recruitment of regiments from the colonial population. To increase revenue, government monopolies were established over tobacco and mercury and new taxes were imposed on many goods.

While these changes benefited Spain, they alienated many Creoles. Further tensions were created by the growth of commercial agriculture in the Bajío which led to the expansion of haciendas at the expense of traditional farming communities. Despite these grievances, however, it was developments in Europe which would eventually produce the opportunity for independence.

Independence

Spanish involvement in the European wars which followed the French Revolution of 1789 affected New Spain, its wealthiest colony, in several ways: Madrid attempted to meet the expenses of war by increasing taxes and eventually, in 1804, ordered the seizure and auction of non-essential Church property. Since the Church operated as the colony's main banker and most of the wealthy owed it money, this threatened ruin. Napoleon's invasion of Spain in 1808 and replacement of King Ferdinand VII with his own brother, Joseph, provoked a crisis throughout Spanish America: did legitimate authority now lie with Joseph Bonaparte, with the Spanish resistance parliament in Cadíz or with the Viceroy?

While this situation produced wars throughout Spanish America between those supporting independence and those opposed, New Spain followed a very different route to independence. On 16 October 1810 Miguel Hidalgo, parish priest in the town of Dolores, issued a call for independence; the failure of his ally, Colonel Ignacio Allende, to rally local army units made Hidalgo dependent on the large mob of rural workers who rallied to his cause. After pillaging San Miguel and Celaya, the mob sacked the wealthy silver town of Guanajuato. The insurgents seized several other towns before finally being defeated at Puente de Calderón, near Guadalajara; most of Hidalgo's troops deserted. Hidalgo and Allende were captured and taken to Chihuahua, where they were executed; their heads were hung on public display as a warning until 1821. After Hidalgo's death the insurrection continued, initially under the leadership of José María Morelos, another priest, though he was captured and executed in 1815.

Crucial to the failure of Hidalgo's rebellion were the fears of the Creoles: though many resented aspects of Spanish rule, Hidalgo's revolt raised the spectre of an Indian revolt in which they, as well as the Peninsulares, would be the victims. The situation was, however, transformed by events in Spain, where in 1820 a military revolt forced Ferdinand VII to adopt a constitution and convene a parliament. Hostile to the more liberal government in Madrid, Creole leaders backed General Augustín de Iturbide in putting forward a manifesto, the Plan de Iguala. This proposed independence but with three guarantees to reassure the Peninsulares: a European prince was to be found for the throne; Catholicism was to be the state religion and there was to be equality of Creoles and Spaniards. With Madrid unable to send troops due to unrest in the army, independence was recognized by the Viceroy.

19th century

Independence did not, however, produce prosperity or political stability. The new government inherited large debts and an economy devastated by war. In 1822, with European princes understandably reluctant to accept the throne, Iturbide crowned himself emperor; when he was deposed a year later, Mexico became a federal republic with an elected president and congress. During the years which followed, governments

Antonio López de Santa Anna

Many tales surround Santa Anna who occupied the presidency no fewer than 11 times between 1833 and 1855. His taste for ostentation led to the furnishing of the presidential palace with European furniture. Orders were given for him to be styled 'His Most Serene Highness' instead of the usual 'His Excellency'; statues were erected and banquets were staged in his honour, and his arrival was announced by a 21-gun salute. The most bizarre incident, however, dates from 1842 when his left leg, amputated in 1838 after being smashed in a battle with a French army at Veracruz, was disinterred, paraded through the capital and placed in an urn on a huge stone pillar at a ceremony attended by high government officials.

Yet it would be wrong to see Santa Anna merely as a comic opera figure. With his lack of scruples and his use of political office for personal wealth, he set standards of political corruption which were followed by lesser officials. Moreover, his disastrous handling of the Texan issue contributed to war with the United States and the loss of over half the national territory.

succeeded one another with bewildering frequency as rival leaders backed by irregular armies competed for power.

The dominant figure during this period was Antonio López de Santa Anna, a Creole army officer who became a national hero in 1829 by leading the Mexican army which repelled a Spanish invasion at Tampico (see box above). Elected president in 1833, Santa Anna tired of everyday politics and retired to his hacienda, leaving the vice-president, Gómez Farías to run the country. When the latter introduced controls on the church and reduced the size of the army, Santa Anna overthrew him and replaced the 1824 constitution, extending the presidential term from four to eight years and increasing the power of the central government. This provoked conflict with the northern state of Texas, where settlers from the United States resisted. In 1835 Santa Anna led 6000 troops into Texas in a campaign celebrated for the Battle of the Alamo. An old Franciscan mission outside San Antonio, the Alamo was defended by Texans including Davy Crockett and Jim Bowie. The mission was stormed and all the defenders killed. A few weeks later the Mexican army was defeated by Sam Houston at San Jacinto and Santa Anna was taken prisoner. After securing his release by signing a treaty agreeing to Texan Independence, he returned to the capital where he denounced the treaty as extracted under compulsion. With Texas's independent status therefore not recognized by Mexico, the vote of the United States Congress in 1845 to annex Texas led to war in 1846. Within months US forces, their artillery proving too much for their opponents, had captured northern Mexico. In 1847 American troops seized Veracruz and occupied the capital. Peace talks resulted in the Treaty of Guadalupe Hidalgo, under which Mexico lost 55% of her territory, including the present US states of Arizona, California, Colorado, Nevada, New Mexico and Utah in addition to Texas.

Santa Anna returned to the presidency in 1853 and promptly sold another strip of territory to the US for US$10 million, before being overthrown in 1855 by a group of liberal leaders who launched a programme of reforms including the Ley Juárez, which reduced the privileges of the church and the army, and the Ley Lerdo, which ordered the sale of property held by the church and Indian communities. Opposition from the army and the Church, which threatened to excommunicate anyone swearing allegiance to the 1857 Constitution, led to a military coup and the resignation of President Comonfort. For

Benito Juárez

One of the most famous political figures of 19th-century Mexico, Benito Juárez is celebrated as a symbol of Mexican nationalism and resistance to foreign intervention. The son of Zapotec Indian parents who died before he reached the age of four, Juárez worked in the countryside until the age of 12 when he moved to Oaxaca where he was educated by the Jesuits. Rejecting the priesthood, he became a lawyer and entered politics, being elected to the Oaxaca City Council and the Mexican Congress. Exiled by Santa Anna in 1853, he moved to New Orleans where he met other opponents of Santa Anna and made a living by making cigars. With the overthrow of Santa Anna in 1855, Juárez became Minister of Justice. As President of the Supreme Court from 1857, he was constitutionally first in succession to President Comonfort who was overthrown by a military revolt in 1858. He escaped to Guanajuato and subsequently to Guadalajara where he was captured by the Conservatives and narrowly escaped execution. Released, he made his way to Veracruz where he established a Liberal government which decreed the separation of church and state, seized church property and established civil marriage and civil registration of births and deaths.

Following the defeat of the Conservatives in 1860, Juárez was elected president in his own right, but was soon forced to flee by the invading French forces. With Maximilian established as emperor in Mexico City, Juárez established a government in El Paso del Norte on the US frontier (now Ciudad Juárez). The defeat of Maximilian enabled Juárez to return to the capital. After the experience of civil war and foreign intervention he attempted to strengthen the presidency but this aroused opposition from many fellow Liberals. Re-elected president in 1867 and again in 1871, he resorted to extraordinary powers to maintain order and by the time of his death in 1872 he had become a controversial figure, seen by some as the embodiment of national independence and by others as increasingly dictatorial and arrogant in his use of presidential office.

the next three years civil war raged between the Conservatives, based in the capital, and the Liberals, led by Benito Juárez and based in Veracruz (see box, above). In December 1860 the Liberals won a decisive victory, after which Juárez was elected president. With the economy ruined, Juárez proclaimed a two-year moratorium on payments of the foreign debt. This led to a joint military occupation of Mexican ports by the creditor powers, Britain, France and Spain, which proved to be a cover for a French invasion. With the French occupying Mexico City, Juárez was forced to retreat north again in 1863, and the following year the Austrian Archduke Maximilian arrived to take the throne offered by a group of Mexican conservatives. Within three years Maximilian was dead, executed by firing squad on the orders of Juárez: abandoned by the French armies who were needed in Europe, he had alienated Mexican conservatives by refusing to return church lands or declare Catholicism the state religion. Returning once again to Mexico City, Juárez was re-elected president in 1867 and 1871, but died shortly afterwards.

From 1876 to 1911 Mexican politics were dominated by Porfirio Díaz who was president for the entire period except for 1880-1884. The Porfiriato, as it is known, was a period of rapid economic growth, much of it financed by foreign capital. Foreign companies built 15,000 miles of railroads, enabling Mexican goods to be exported and lands farmed by peasants to be seized and used for commercial crops. This was accompanied by a rapid growth in mining and manufacturing, based around the northern city of Monterrey. These changes led to the growth of a large middle class, but the fruits of economic growth were badly distributed. Peasants were hit particularly hard, often losing access to land farmed by their families for generations: by 1910 half of all peasants had become sharecroppers or wage labourers working on giant haciendas, such as those of Luis Terrazas who owned over three million hectares of land. Some estimate that by 1910 US citizens owned over 20% of the country's land. This economic and social change was accompanied by political repression as elections were carefully controlled, the press censored and the army used to maintain order.

Mexican Revolution

Modern Mexican history is dominated by the legacy of the Revolution, a bloody upheaval between 1910 and 1917 which led to the deaths of nearly two million people, one in eight of the population. In 1910 Díaz, aged 80, stood for re-election and was challenged by Francisco Madero, a northern landowner who ran under the slogan 'Effective Suffrage, No Re-election'. Defeated, Madero fled to the United States, from where he contacted other opposition groups before issuing the Plan de San Luis Potosí and calling for revolt. As rebellion spread throughout the country, Pascual Orozco seized Ciudad Juárez, which became the rebel capital and, in May 1911, Díaz resigned.

Though Madero became president in November 1911, he faced an impossible situation, between the supporters of Díaz who dominated the army, and radicals such as Orozco, Pancho Villa and Emiliano Zapata (see box opposite), who demanded land and labour reform. By February 1913, Mexico was in chaos as rival groups revolted: after 10 days of street fighting in the capital, Madero was betrayed by one of his generals, Victoriano Huerta, and murdered. Huerta took over as president but he faced three main opponents: Zapata's peasant army from Morelos, Pancho Villa's peasant and worker forces from the north, and the troops of Venustiano Carranza, a reformer and landowner from Sonora. The three formed the Constitutional coalition, but it was Villa's Division of the North which defeated Huerta's forces in a series of battles and he was forced to resign in July 1914.

At a convention held in Aguascalientes in October 1914, the Constitutionalists split and war broke out between Carranza's supporters and the radicals who backed Zapata and Villa. Villa was defeated by Carrancista general Alvaro Obregón and was forced to retreat to Chihuahua where he carried on a guerrilla struggle until 1920. Carranza called a Congress of his supporters which met at Querétaro in November 1916 and which produced the 1917 Constitution. The key features of this included a commitment to agrarian reform, social protection for workers and hostility to the Church. Carranza was then elected president but as he met opposition from supporters of Villa and Zapata he turned for allies among the pre-revolutionary elite, to some of whom he returned lands which had been seized.

Mexico since the Revolution

Although the most violent period of the Revolution came to an end in 1917, political violence persisted and political life continued to be dominated by the leading Carrancista officers. In 1920 Carranza was assassinated after attempting to engineer the presidential victory of one of his supporters. His successor was Alvaro Obregón, who survived a full four

Emiliano Zapata

A peasant guerrilla leader from Morelos, Zapata has become the most famous symbol of the Mexican revolution and a symbol of the struggle for social justice. Born in 1879 in the village of Anenecuilco in Morelos, one of the 10 children of a peasant family, Zapata received little formal schooling but he did learn to read and write. He was soon involved in the local land disputes and in 1909 was elected president of Anenecuilco village council. In March 1911, responding to Madero's call for resistance to Porfirio Díaz, he formed a guerrilla band; in May they captured Cuautla, some 80 km south of Mexico City, a move which helped overthrow Díaz. However Zapata soon clashed with Madero and the latter's allies among the landowners of Morelos and by June 1911 the Mexico City press was attacking him as the 'Atilla of the South'. Madero sent federal troops under General Huerta to Morelos, but Zapata retreated into the mountains where he issued the Plan of Ayala, which called for the return of lands stolen by hacienda owners, the expropriation of one third of all hacienda holdings and their distribution to landless villages. As the conflict spread in 1912-13 Zapata's support spread outside Morelos into neighbouring states; in November 1914 his forces occupied Mexico City. After a meeting with his ally Pancho Villa, Zapata returned to Morelos, leaving his troops in control of the capital; in Morelos he began to redistribute land. In 1915 the defeat of Villa's troops and the expulsion of Zapata's forces from the capital was followed by the invasion of Morelos by forces loyal to Carranza. Zapata retreated again to the mountains but this time his ability to conduct a guerrilla campaign was weakened by defections and internal conflict. Like so many leaders of the revolution Zapata died violently, being tricked by President Carranza into an ambush at Chinameca in April 1919.

Zapata's death removed Carranza's most implacable opponent but Zapata's name lived on as a symbol of social justice. Many believed that Zapata did not die at Chinameca; a double had been sent to the fatal meeting and Zapata went into hiding in the mountains, to return when needed by the peasantry. His symbolic importance is shown by the use of his name by the Zapatistas (see box, page 773).

years in office before handing over to Plutarco Elías Calles in 1924 but who was assassinated in 1928 after winning re-election. Calles was able to govern from behind the scenes during the three interim presidencies between 1928 and 1934. Under Calles the government came into conflict with the Church as it attempted to implement the anticlerical aspects of the Constitution; the Cristero Rebellion cost some 90,000 lives before it was ended by negotiation. The most important of Calles' initiatives was, however, the creation of a political party, the Partido Nacional Revolucionario (PNR) which, despite several name changes, has controlled the Mexican government since (see box, page 771).

Though handpicked for the presidency by Calles in 1934, Lázaro Cárdenas isolated his patron to prevent his continuing influence. Cárdenas was to become the most popular Mexican president of the 20th century, remembered in particular for two policies: agrarian reform and oil nationalization. During Cárdenas' six-year term, 20 million hectares of land were redistributed, twice as much as under all his post-Revolutionary predecessors combined. By 1940 one third of all Mexicans had received land, most of it in communal *ejidos* rather than as individual holdings. The nationalization of all foreign-owned petroleum companies in March 1938, following years of disputes between workers and management, made Cárdenas a national hero, though it temporarily soured relations with the United States.

Since the Cárdenas years, Mexican governments have focused on encouraging industrialization. Manuel Avila Camacho, who succeeded Cárdenas, was a moderate Catholic who moved away from social reform and who encouraged foreign investment to stimulate industrial growth. The succeeding administrations of Miguel Alemán (1946-1952) and Adolfo Ruiz Cortines (1952-1958) continued these policies but under Adolfo López Mateos (1958-1964) there was a move back to agrarian reform, though this time in favour of individual holdings; welfare reform and rural education were promoted. The political calm of the previous administrations was broken under the presidency of Gustavo Díaz Ordaz (1964-1970). Demands for a liberalization of the political system were rejected and several election victories by the opposition Partido Acción Nacional (PAN) were annulled. The most serious crisis came in 1968 in the run-up to the Mexico City Olympics: on 2 October security forces opened fire, killing hundreds of students at a protest in Tlatelolco in the capital.

Luis Echeverría, who succeeded Díaz Ordaz in 1970, tried to offset the political unrest caused by these events by emphasizing economic nationalism and increased state involvement in social welfare and rural development, policies which involved the most rapid expansion in the state sector since the Revolution. By the end of his presidency these policies, combined with the worldwide inflation of the early 1970s, had contributed to an economic crisis which led to a 60% devaluation of the peso in September 1976 followed by another of 40% a month later.

José López Portillo, who became president in 1976, began with the disadvantage of having been Echeverría's finance minister. Large oil discoveries mainly in the southern states of Tabasco and Chiapas and offshore in the Gulf of Mexico dated from the Echeverría administration, but under López Portillo oil production steadily increased and by 1981 Mexico was the world's fourth largest producer. This new wealth was not, however, to provide a solution to the country's problems which included a rapidly increasing urban population and rising unemployment. Increased government spending on public works, welfare schemes and subsidies on consumer goods were financed partly by international borrowing. A slump in world oil prices and an increase in global interest rates led to an economic crisis in early 1982: the peso was devalued, its rate against the dollar dropping from 26 to 100. In September 1982, in the dying months of his presidency, López Portillo nationalized the banks, a move which did little to hide his legacy of the country's worst economic crisis of the century.

Under his successor, Miguel de la Madrid (1982-1988), the depth of this crisis became apparent. Mexico was forced to renegotiate its foreign debt, accepting severe cuts in government spending, which included sacking 51,000 federal employees and reducing the salaries of others. Nevertheless the peso continued to decline, especially after another drop in oil prices from 1986, falling against the dollar to 950 in January 1987 and 2300 by December 1987. In 1987 the annual inflation rate was officially 159% and by the end of de la Madrid's presidency Mexico's foreign debts was US$105 billion. In September 1985, in the middle of these economic disasters, an earthquake destroyed parts of the centre of the capital, leaving at least 8000 people dead. However, de la Madrid's presidency had marked important changes in economic policy, with his finance minister, Carlos Salinas de Gortari, introducing cuts in state spending and selling state industries.

The Partido Revolucionario Institucional (PRI)

Until its defeat in July 2000, modern Mexican politics had been dominated by the PRI, which had governed uninterruptedly since its creation as the Partido Revolucionario Nacional by Plutarco Elías Calles in 1929. Founded to unite the victors of the Revolution and composed of military leaders, pro-government labour and peasant leaders, and regional political bosses, it became a forum for resolving disputes and settling the crucial question of the presidential succession without resorting to violence. Between 1929 and the 1980s its dominance was so complete, that it controlled the presidency, most congressional seats and all state governorships.

Until the 1960s its presidential candidates regularly received over 90% of the vote and it polled over 80% of the vote in congressional elections. From the 1960s, however, and especially after 1976, when the refusal by the right-wing Partido de Acción Nacional (PAN) to run led to the embarrassing spectacle of a presidential election without any real opposition, some attempts were made to encourage a limited role for opposition parties. In 1977 and in 1986 the electoral law was altered to guarantee opposition parties a percentage of congressional seats.

The PRI domination was not merely due to fraud and corruption, as was often claimed. Almost inseparable from the government, the party was able to use the resources of the latter to secure support by offering jobs, services and other favours. Opponents were frequently co-opted with offers of favours and the press was influenced by its reliance on government advertising.

The rise of other parties in the 1980s, however, highlighted some of the difficulties facing the PRI. As Mexican society became more urban and educated and embraced consumerism, it became more difficult to retain the old loyalties and the party was forced to rely on more blatantly fraudulent practices, such as overturning opposition victories in state governor elections. The adoption of a more liberal economic model to deal with the crisis of the 1980s also affected the party: as state industries were sold off, there were fewer jobs and contracts to offer in return for support. Since economic liberalisation was largely the work of the new type of PRI leader who emerged in the 1980s, namely gifted and highly trained specialists often educated in US business schools, opposition to economic and political change increased among the old-style PRI leaders, themselves veterans of years of party work and often labelled the dinosaurs. The potentially violent consequences of this conflict were illustrated in 1994 by the assassination in mysterious circumstances of the party's presidential candidate, Luis Donaldo Colosio.

The party's ability to come to terms with its new role in opposition may depend on the outcome of such internal conflicts. Some observers suggest that defeat may strengthen the hand of the 'dinosaurs', who will point the finger of blame for the party's defeat at the modernisers for embracing economic reform and political liberalisation. How successful they are in this may, however, depend on whether the party's traditional supporters respond to the lead provided by the 'dinosaurs' or whether, faced with the loss of the benefits of power, they desert the party and switch their support to the PAN.

Late 20th-century politics

Against this background, opposition to the PRI grew in strength in the 1980s. While the PAN drew increased support in the north, conflict within the PRI led to the defection of Cuauhtémoc Cárdenas, son of Lázaro Cardenas, whose presidential ambitions were blocked by the party leaders. In 1988 Cárdenas ran for the presidency on behalf of the Frente Democrático Nacional, a coalition of leftist parties. In a shock result the PRI candidate, Salinas de Gortari, won only just over 50% of the vote and unofficial results awarded victory to Cárdenas. Salinas continued the liberal reforms of the previous presidency and, in 1993, took Mexico into the North American Free Trade Agreement (NAFTA) with the US and Canada. Cárdenas' supporters subsequently formed the Partido Revolucionaria Democrática (PRD) and attacked the PRI for abandoning many of its traditional policies. In 1989, for the first time, the PRI accepted the loss of a state governorship, to the right wing Partido de Acción Nacional (PAN).

The PRI's dominance was further rocked by a series of crises in 1994. On New Year's Day a hitherto unknown guerrilla force, the Ejército Zapatista de Liberación Nacional (EZLN) staged an uprising in Chiapas (see box opposite). Subsequent peace talks, however, were overshadowed by the assassination, in March, of the PRI's appointed presidential candidate, Luis Donaldo Colosio. Further disquiet was caused by the murder of the Tijuana police chief and the kidnapping of several prominent businessmen in the following months. To replace Colosio, President Salinas nominated Ernesto Zedillo Ponce de León, a US-trained economist and former education minister. Further unrest in Chiapas enabled the PRI to portray its candidate as the defender of order; Zedillo won a comfortable majority in the July elections and the PRI retained control of congress. While the PRD and the PAN claimed fraud, attention centred on Chiapas where the state governorship had been won by the PRI in particularly dubious circumstances and on Tabasco where the governorship was also disputed. In September the General Secretary of the PRI, José Francisco Ruiz Massieu, was assassinated and in November his brother Mario, Deputy Attorney General and chief investigator into the murder, resigned, claiming a high level cover up of the assassinations of his brother and Colosio within the PRI.

Zedillo's inauguration on 1 December was soon upstaged by a major economic crisis and Zedillo devalued the peso. Though this move was forced on the government by a variety of economic problems, Zedillo blamed the move on capital outflows caused by political instability resulting from the situation in Chiapas. The decision, a few days after the devaluation, to allow the peso to float against the dollar caused a crisis of confidence and investors in Mexico lost billions of dollars as the peso plummeted in value. As the economic crisis worsened, the PRI was heavily defeated in a series of state elections.

The unsolved assassinations of Colosio and Ruiz Massieu caused further difficulties for the government. Zedillo appointed Antonio Lozano of PAN as attorney general; the latter uncovered PRI involvement in Colosio's murder and ordered the arrest of Raúl Salinas, brother of former president Carlos Salinas, for masterminding the murder of Ruiz Massieu. This broke the convention under which former presidents were granted immunity from criticism or prosecution in return for their silence on the activities of their successors. Carlos Salinas left Mexico acrimoniously, but this did not put an end to the scandals rocking the official party. Mario Ruiz Massieu was arrested in the US on suspicion of covering up Raúl Salinas' involvement in the murder of his brother and of receiving money from drug cartels when he had been in charge of anti-narcotics operations. Raúl Salinas was investigated for alleged money laundering and illicit enrichment after his

Subcomandante Marcos and the Zapatistas

On New Year's Day 1994, at the moment when NAFTA came into force, the Ejército Zapatista de Liberación Nacional (EZLN) briefly took control of several towns in the southern state of Chiapas. Demanding social justice, indigenous people's rights, democracy at all levels of Mexican politics, an end to government corruption and land reform for the peasantry, the EZLN attracted international attention, helped by their use of modern communications technology. The government was forced to open peace talks.

President Zedillo later suspended the controversial PRI governor, but then allowed the army to launch a brief, but unsuccessful, campaign to capture the EZLN's leader, Subcomandante Marcos. Resumed talks between the government and the EZLN led to the first peace accord being signed in February 1996. The pace of change was slow, however, and in 1997 the EZLN renewed its protests, accusing the government of trying to change the terms of the agreed legal framework for indigenous rights. Physical conflict continued with 60,000 troops heavily outnumbering the Zapatista guerrillas. In December 1997 45 civilians, mainly women and children, were massacred in Acteal near San Cristóbal de las Casas by paramilitaries linked to the PRI. Although the local mayor was implicated in the atrocity and arrested along with 39 others, there were calls for more senior government officials to be removed and in 1998 the Minister of the Interior and State Governor were forced to resign.

Nonetheless tensions remained and after Vicente Fox was elected in 2000, the constitutional reforms long promised to the EZLN once again failed to materialize. Talks broke down and in 2003 the Zapatistas turned their attention inwards, consolidating support and developing self-governing committees Juntas de Buen Gobierno (Committees of Good Government) in those villages where approval was strongest. These, however, were criticized as unaccountable and bureaucratic. In 2005, Subcommandante Marcos restyled himself Subdelegado Zero and attempted to broaden the Zapatista agenda by appealing to all groups, not just the indigenous peasantry. He toured Mexico drumming up support for his broad leftist movement, although did not gain the same momentum as the mainstream parties, who were running their 2006 presidential election campaigns at the same time. Today, the situation in Chiapas remains relatively stable, if tense.

wife was arrested in Switzerland trying to withdraw US$84 million from an account opened in a false name.

Having come to power in the aftermath of assassination and scandal, Zedillo promised political reform. Despite a boycott of talks by the PAN, the other major parties agreed to introduce direct elections for the mayor of Mexico City and to alter the constitution to permit referenda as well as measures to guarantee party political broadcasts during election campaign. Perhaps the most important reform, however, was the abolition of government control over the Federal Election Institute (IFE). Reform of the political system was taken a step further by the July 1997 mid-term congressional elections: for the first time the PRI lost overall control of Congress, gaining only 239 of the 500 seats. The PRD became the second largest party with 125 seats and its leader, Cuauhtémoc Cárdenas, won the mayoral election for Mexico City, while the PAN won 122 seats. These results gave the opposition parties more leverage to push for political reform ahead of the presidential elections of July 2000 which proved to be a landmark in the history of modern Mexico, with the PRI losing the presidency to the PAN candidate, Vicente Fox. The PRI also lost heavily in the Congressional elections to Fox's centre-right Alliance for Change, which became the largest party in Congress.

Mexico in the new millenium

Vicente Fox

In 2000, PRI hegemony was broken for the first time in 71 years with the election of PAN candidate Vicente Fox, former governor of Guanajuato and ex-president of Coca Cola's Latin America operation (see box opposite). Fox promoted himself as a down-to-earth man of the people.

An admirer of 'third way' politics and of ex-US President Bill Clinton and then UK Prime Minister Tony Blair, Fox took office on 1 December 2000 with 43% of the vote. He announced czar-led initiatives that would tackle government corruption, drug trafficking, crime and poverty, as well as the economic conditions that drive migration to the US. One critic dismissively said Fox was '90% images and 10% ideas', but nonetheless his term started on a positive note.

Fox made some notable changes to foreign policy by scrapping the long-standing Estrada Doctrine, which placed national sovereignty above all other concerns. Based on the principles of self-determination, non-intervention and mutual respect, the Estrada doctrine forbade any criticism of external regimes, thereby protecting Mexico from foreign interference. Under Fox's secretary for foreign affairs, Jorge Castañeda, the administration now opened itself to new international scrutiny and criticism, to the extent that some branded Fox 'overtly submissive' to the United States.

Another important foreign policy creation was the Puebla Panama Plan (PPP) – a neoliberal project that aims for the integration and development of the southern states of Mexico, all of Central America and Colombia. It has been criticised as providing the infrastructure for multinational corporations who exploit natural resources and act to the detriment of local communities and the environment. Some have argued that the PPP is nothing less than the apparatus of a 'colonialist' global economy that disproportionately profits the developed world.

Ultimately, Fox's administration lacked dynamism and failed to deliver the great reforms it had promised. Mid-term elections saw the pendulum swing against PAN with the old-guard PRI winning a majority of seats in the Chamber of Deputies. Suffering strained relations with congress and unable to push through PAN legislation, Fox was effectively paralyzed to make any real changes. He was, however, a force for stability. Inflation dropped significantly during his six-year term and unlike during most other presidencies, the peso did not suffer any serious devaluation. The economic outlook was generally optimistic with record highs on the Mexican stock exchange, but overall economic growth was historically low.

Felipe Calderón

Elections in July 2006 saw a new president leading Mexico. A close and ill-fought electoral result gave Felipe Calderón, the candidate of the ruling conservative National Action Party (PAN) a narrow win over Andrés Manuel López Obrador of the centre-left Party of the Democratic Revolution (PRD). Roberto Madrazo of the Institutional Revolutionary Party (PRI) was pushed into third place. The result, which was won by a margin of 0.58%, was vociferously disputed by Obrador, whose supporters camped in the Zócalo for several

Vicente Fox and the Mexican earthquake

By ending the PRI's 71-year uninterrupted control of Mexican government, the presidential elections of July 2000 mark a major turning point in the country's modern history. While opinion polls had shown the PRI candidate, Francisco Labastida, and the PAN's Vicente Fox, running neck and neck, few observers had predicted the scale of the opposition candidate's victory, winning 42.8% of the vote against Labastida's 35.7%. To some extent Fox may have benefited from the switching of votes from the third candidate, Cuauhtémoc Cárdenas of the PRD, who won 16½%. The political reforms carried out under President Zedillo played a role, the independent status granted to the Federal Election Institute not only provided fewer opportunities for electoral fraud but also helped give voters the confidence to defy pressure from local political bosses who privately warned that that welfare benefits, particularly in the rural areas, would be withdrawn from voters who deserted the governing party.

Much of the credit for Fox's victory must, however, go to the candidate himself. A former Coca Cola executive and rancher, Fox swept aside the conservative leader-ship of the PAN to seize its presidential candidacy and build an alliance with a range of smaller political parties including the little-known Green Party. Campaigning across the country on horseback, in cowboy boots, open-neck jeans and a thick belt with his name carved on the buckle, his flamboyant style contrasted with the sleek style of recent PRI presidential candidates with their educational back- grounds in the US and their careers in bureaucracy. Although PAN is usually seen as a conservative party and is close to business interests, Fox's campaign showed him to be a pragmatist; his critics accuse him of being all style and no substance, prepared to latch onto any issue to win votes.

Winning the presidency will proved easier than governing Mexico, however and Fox's skills on the campaign trail may be of limited value. Congressional elections held at the same time as the presidential poll made his Alliance for Change the largest party, but lacking a majority in either chamber. On many issues, such as privatisation of Pemex, the state oil corporation, the PRI and PRD can be expected to join forces in Congress and defeat the government. The PRI still controls 19 of the 32 state governorships, important power bases from which to resist change. Perhaps most important of all, the new government will have to work with government officials recruited on the basis of loyalty to the PRI. The new president's ability to govern at all may rest on his skill dealing with the bureaucracy and bargaining with the bosses of the PRI while fulfilling the expectations for change of his supporters.

weeks in protest. Obrador also talked about establishing an alternative government and had plans to disrupt the presidential election, but ultimately independent scrutiny of the elections found no evidence of fraud or other misdoings.

Morelia-born Calderón was the son of Luis Calderón Vega, one of the founders of PAN, and as such was involved with the party from an early age. He was president of its youth movement during his early 20s and later served as Vicente Fox's energy secretary, until disputes about his plans to run for the presidency forced him to resign. Calderón is broadly in tune with the principles of economic liberalism – flat taxes, lower taxes and free trade among them – as well as espousing a conservative religious view that opposes abortion, euthanasia and gay marriage. He has tried to spin the age-old divisions between left and right as a choice between the past and the future.

Although lacking the charisma of his predecessor, Calderón is generally regarded as an honest candidate. He came to power looking to reduce poverty, violence, tax evasion and corruption and his own salary by 10%. Plans for public infrastructure projects on roads, airports, bridges and dams are part of his scheme to stem outward migration of Mexico's workforce, a policy supported by the First Employment Program which offers cash incentives for bosses hiring first-time employees. On foreign policy, Calderón continues to adhere to the Castañeda doctrine and the Puebla Panama Plan, which he has expanded on. The Mérida initiative is a transnational security agreement aimed at stemming drug trafficking.

The drug cartels pose one of the most serious challenges to Calderón's government with some commentators suggesting that Mexico is on the verge of becoming a failed state because of them. Levels of death and violence are now comparable to those found in a war-torn country and Calderón has dispatched the army to control the situation along the US border (see box, page 282). He has also instigated several high profile arrests, including mayors, generals and gang leaders, as well as enormous seizures of drugs and arms. As such, most Mexicans approve of his tough line.

The economy is another significant issue for the administration with Mexico's economy closely tied to the USA – epicentre of the global financial crisis and recession. The value of Mexico's remaining oil reserves has been hit, as has its lucrative tourist industry. In late 2008, the peso lost a quarter of its value against the dollar, and since then unemployment has risen, exports have fallen and the costs of foreign imports spiked. In April 2009 the IMF approved a US$47 billion credit line to Mexico to help prevent any further deterioration of its economy. Mexico's robust development seems to have been stalled for now.

Economy

Mexico is the 15th largest country in the world, but it is home to the 11th largest population, now at around 100 million people, twice the number living there in the 1970s. Meeting the needs of this growing population, two-thirds of whom are under 30, is an uphill struggle for the government. The demand for new jobs is enormous. Successive economic crises since 1980 have prevented real incomes from rising as fast as the population. Tight control of the fiscal purse strings in the 1990s, with limits on spending on education and health, has also limited improvement in social indicators. Infant mortality is 17½ per 1000 live births, compared with only 7½ per 1000 across the border in the USA, while 14% of the population over 15 has no primary education. Nevertheless, Mexico has one of the strongest economies in Latin America with a GDP approximately the size of that of Australia, India or Russia. It is a founding member of the North American Free Trade Agreement (NAFTA) and is negotiating a free trade deal with the EU. Its proximity to the USA gives it a useful safety net as any financial crisis is reflected in a rise in illegal migration across the Rio Grande, a pattern Washington is keen to avoid. In the last two decades the US administration has been swift to organize financial rescue packages when required in conjunction with IMF economic programmes to enable Mexico to meet its foreign obligations and prevent a complete collapse of the peso.

Oil

Mexico has been an oil producer since the 1880s and was the world's leading producer in 1921, but by 1971 had become a net importer. This position was reversed with the discovery in 1972 of major new oil reserves and the country is now the fifth largest producer in the world. Two-thirds of its output comes from offshore wells in the Gulf of Campeche, while much of the rest is produced in the onshore fields in the Chiapas-Tabasco area in the southeast. Mexico depends on fossil fuels to generate 100% of its electricity and crude oil, oil products and natural gas account for about a third of government revenues. The international price of oil is therefore a key indicator of the likely health of the Mexican economy.

Mining

Mexico's mineral resources are legendary. Precious metals make up about a third of non-oil mineral output. The country is the world's leading producer of silver, fluorite and arsenic and is among the major producers of strontium, graphite, copper, iron ore, sulphur, mercury, lead and zinc. Mexico also produces gold, molybdenum, antimony, bismuth, cadmium, selenium, tungsten, magnesium, common salt, celestite, fullers earth and gypsum. It is estimated that although 60% of Mexico's land mass has mineral potential, only 25% is known and only 5% explored in detail.

Farming

Agriculture has lost importance since the 1970s and now contributes less than 6% to GDP, although a quarter of the workforce is still employed on the land. About 13% of the land surface is under cultivation, of which only about a quarter is irrigated. Over half of the developed cropland lies in the interior highlands. Farming fortunes are almost always related to rainfall and available water for irrigation. On average, four out of every 10 years are good, while four are drought years. In 1999 the southeast suffered floods and mudslides, while elsewhere there was drought. Maize is the staple crop throughout Mexico, but others include sorghum, wheat, barley, rice, beans, tomatoes, a variety of fruit and livestock. There are 24,000 genetic strains of maize in Mexico, but this biodiversity is under threat from contamination by genetically modified corn from the USA, which is poorly regulated and supervised. There is concern that the traditional farming practice of saving the best seed for the following year, a tradition which has continued since corn was first domesticated 9000 years ago, may be destroyed by commercialized transgenic seeds. Mexico is already growing 50,000 ha of genetically modified cotton and 6000 ha of transgenic soya, the seeds of which will be sold abroad. Genetically modified, virus-resistant potatoes are being tested.

Manufacturing

There was a huge expansion in manufacturing (including oil refining and petrochemicals) in the latter part of the 20th century and it now contributes around 20% of GDP and 90% of exports. Mexico City used to be the focal point for manufacturing activity, followed by Guadalajara and Monterrey, but the pollution caused by heavy industry led the government to offer tax incentives to get companies to relocate. Target cities are Tampico, Lázaro Cárdenas, Coatzacoalcos, and Salina Cruz, while much of the manufacturing export activity takes place in the assembly plants along the border with the USA. There are now over 3000 maquiladoras (assembly plants, usually owned by US companies that take advantage of Mexican cheap labour) in northern Mexico and they generate a considerable amount of employment, albeit at low wages with minimal labour rights and poor working conditions.

Tourism

Tourism is now the largest single employer and generates billions of dollars in foreign exchange a year. Over 20 million foreign visitors (mostly US) come annually, many to the purpose-built resorts of Cancún in the Yucatán or the beach hotels in Baja California, Acapulco and Puerto Vallarta, which help to make Mexico the eighth most popular tourist destination in the world. At the turn of the century there were 130 tourism projects in the works, worth some US$3.8 billion, aimed at attracting new visitors from South America and Europe.

Banking

Mexico has suffered several financial crises since the initial debt crisis of 1982, each of which weakened the banking sector. In 1994-95 the devaluation of the peso and dollar flight caused many businesses to face bankruptcy as they could not service their bank loans. Bank deposits fell by 18½% while non-performing loans trebled to 18% of banks total loan portfolios. Of the 18 banks privatized in 1992, seven collapsed. They and others had to be taken over by foreigners. Emergency schemes to keep banks solvent and provide interest relief for small debtors cost the government about US$70 billion by 1998. In 1999 the Institute for the Protection of Bank Savings (IPAB) was created to handle the legacy of the post-1994 crisis. The autonomous body lowered deposit insurance, raised capital and increased reserves against overdue loans to improve loan portfolios by 2003. Foreign banks were expected to increase their presence in Mexico and contribute to restoring the financial health of the banking system.

Government

Under the 1917 Constitution, Mexico is a federal republic of 31 states and a federal district containing the capital, Mexico City. The president, who appoints the ministers, is elected for six years and can never be re-elected. Congress consists of the 128-seat senate, half elected every three years on a rotational basis, and the 500-seat chamber of deputies, elected every three years. There is universal suffrage.

Local administration

The states enjoy local autonomy and can levy their own taxes, and each state has its governor, legislature and judicature. The president has traditionally appointed the chief of the federal district but direct elections were held in 1997 for the first time.

Culture

Pre-Columbian culture and society

Spanning an astonishing three millennia, pre-Columbian culture and society evolved through dynamic processes of trade, war, migration and progressive technological achievements, about which researchers always discovering something new. Each epoch and geographical region was characterized by differing social organizations and styles. Small-scale agricultural communities gave way ceremonial centres, kingships, and finally, highly organized and stratified societies.

By the advent of the Spanish Conquest, the age of empire had swept through Mesoamerica with the Aztecs playing centre stage. Pomp and splendour attended their capital, Tenochtitlán, a fully fledged imperial city fit to rival any in Europe. Grand markets, libraries, temples, schools, law courts, military academies and palaces were components in its complex and highly developed infrastructure. Social classes and strict rules governing inheritance bound all citizens beneath the emperor and state, broadly divided into land-owning nobility, a common class of traders, artisans and farmers, and slaves. It is intriguing to consider how Mexico might look today if Cortés had not interrupted its arc of evolution.

Religion

The Mesoamerican pantheon of gods, each with their own identity and purpose, played a vital role in the everyday affairs of the people. Many of these gods originated with the Olmecs and metamorphosed through various guises with subsequent cultures. By the Classic period, a complete pantheon of gods had emerged, recognized and followed throughout the whole country, albeit under a variety of names. Most corresponded to natural forces, agriculture or warfare, although in some cultures their numbers were so vast as to embrace almost every aspect of the natural universe.

Across all groups there existed a supreme god and ruler of the sky (Itzamná in Mayan tradition; Ometecuhtli among the Aztec), who together with his wife, the creation goddess, begat all other gods. Quetzalcoatl (known as Kukulcán by the Maya) was a ubiquitous and very ancient feathered-serpent deity particularly revered by the Aztecs and Toltecs. The rain god was the most important of the nature gods and had a vital role overseeing the seasonal cycles of agriculture and fertility. Known variously as Tlaloc or Chac, he was considered the centre of the universe as well as the benefactor, creator and father of agriculture. Death, a god who continues to play an important role in Mexico's spiritual life, is often depicted across cultures with a fleshless skull.

There were many lesser deities but most power was controlled by a few leading players. The gods were not generally gentle or charitable beings – they bestowed favours in return for exacting food tributes, incense and blood sacrifice. The Aztecs were extremely devout and performed religious rituals for every daily activity, each of which was undertaken only after consulting the relevant gods. From deciding when to plant the harvest, to regulating marriages, baptisms and naming ceremonies, and even over when and where to trade, hunt and fish – the gods oversaw all human activity. It was the role of the priests, and later of the secular leaders, to interpret the gods' wishes. Aztec rulers in particular exploited the control the gods exerted over peoples' lives by claiming divine descendency.

The Aztec pantheon was incredibly complex with over 200 gods, including some that had been adopted from both contemporary neighbours and ancestral cultures. Many had numerous identities and most ceremonial rituals were devoted to several deities simultaneously. The concept of duality in the gods was also common and ceramic masks found in Tlatilco in the Valley of Mexico, dating from 1400 BC, show dualistic features. This belief, therefore, ran throughout the most ancient epochs of Mexican history. Many deities seemed to have operated in pairs, sometimes embodying opposing elements. For instance, Quetzalcoatl is both the double and enemy of Tezcatlipoca (smoking mirror), and both are described as gods of creation.

Art and sculpture

As with every other aspect of their lives, the artistic output of the early Mexicans was inextricably tied to religion. Their magnificent temples and pyramids were richly decorated with murals, bas-relief scenes, sculptures, as well as beautiful treasures made of gold and precious stones. Despite the ravages of time some fine paintings have survived and can be seen today in sites such as Bonampak, Teotihuacán, Tepantitla, Atetelco, Cacaxtla and Cholula.

The earliest artists of any real accomplishment were the Olmecs. Fine murals, often depicting their cult figure – the were-jaguar – have been found throughout their region, mostly painted on stelae and temples, but also in caves. Some fascinating Olmec paintings have been found in Juxtlahuaca Cave, near Chilpancingo in Guerrero.

Despite the absence of technology and metal tools, the ancient Mexicans produced an enormous quantity of incredibly advanced stonework. Carved stelae, mostly dedicated to the gods, or to the lives and events of their rulers, were produced across Mexico from pre-Classic onwards. These reached their most elegant expression among the Classic Maya, whose rich and stunningly ornate productions were invariably embellished with complex, flowing motifs and beautifully rendered hieroglyphs. Elsewhere, temple pyramids and palaces were often sumptuously worked with bas-relief carvings such as the intriguing Dazantes of the Zapotecs in pre-Classic Monté Albán, depicting gruesome sacrificial victims and prisoners of war.

Famously, the Olmecs carved numerous giant stone heads that measured up to 2.85 m tall and weighed many tons. They have thickset, flattened faces and typically wear headgear, nicknamed football helmets, which may have been used in the traditional Mesoamerican ball game. They are thought to have been made as tributes to Olmec rulers. Elsewhere, the Olmec are renowned for their beautiful small figurines, delicate jade jewellery, stone mask pectorals and life-size figures sculpted in the round.

Trade
Much like their contemporary counterparts, ancient Mexican markets were important centres of social activity where people gathered to trade goods, gossip, news and other staples of daily life. Tenochtitlán's market at Tlatelolco saw 25,000 visitors daily – a number that doubled during a special market every fifth day. Gold, silver, jade, feathers, fowl, game, fresh produce, medicinal herbs and crafts were just some of the offerings that so dazzled the conquistadors when they first laid eyes on them. Cacao beans were used a currency. Market traders were distinguished from long-distance traders, called *pochteca* by the Aztecs, who were held in considerably higher regard. It is likely that the pochteca were an ancient class of peoples who peddled centuries of influence throughout Mesoamerica's cultural development.

One could only become *pochteca* through inheritance. Among the Aztecs they were an organized body of peoples with their own courts and laws, as well as administrative representation closely allied to the nobility. They played vital roles in important public ceremonies and travelled to far off trade centres in order to acquire rare precious stones, crafts and exotic feathers. Sometimes this would involve journeying into enemy territory, for which they would wear disguises. Although highly esteemed, *pochteca* could not rise from their social rank, nor trade outside of legally defined areas. As such, they were not capitalist in their practises.

Warfare
War is known to have been widespread between Mexican peoples from pre-Classic times onwards, and was probably a feature of life before then too. The classic era Mayan murals at Bonampak reveal a taste for bloodthirsty conflict and some scholars believe that pervasive inter-state warfare may be part of the reason for the general Mayan collapse. War was no less prominent in the post-classic era when militarism, rather than religion, became the chief engine of human activity.

The Aztecs, especially, were proponents of imperialistic aggression, and widely feared for their formidable skills on the battlefield. Their military was extensive and well-organized along a hierarchy of ranks. The Tlatoani, or emperor, was chief-in-command. Elite societies also existed where only the most exceptional could partake, but generally, warriors belonged to either eagle or jaguar cults, and wore battle costumes to reflect this. Some costumes were especially elaborate with feathers, jewellery, cloaks, headgear and shields emblazoned with emblems, such as a high-ranking soldier might possess, along with the scars of battle and ritual mutilation.

A typical long-distance campaign might have involved 200,000 Aztec warriors armed with slings and obsidian clubs. A unique class of warrior priests would accompany them, whose duty was to carry sacred idols and conduct human sacrifices on the battlefield. For militaristic expansion was not the only motivation for war. Human blood was deemed necessary for the restoration of cosmic harmony and fertility and thus in constant demand. To a certain extent, this need was fulfilled by the ritualistic 'flower wars', where rival states agreed to do battle for the purposes of acquiring fresh sacrificial victims.

The ball game

Since the earliest days of the Olmecs, Mexican peoples believed in a threshold linking life and death, the Earth and the Underworld. This threshold was symbolised by the ritual ball game. In this team event, in many ways similar to basketball, players would try to throw a solid rubber ball through large stone rings at either end of a specially constructed court. More than mere sport, however, the ball game players stood on the edge of the world, quite literally, as losers were often sacrificed as offerings to the gods.

Ball courts have been found in sites throughout Mesoamerica, but the oldest and most numerous have been found in the Olmec region of the gulf coast. At least nine courts have been found at El Tajín, the classic site in northern Veracruz. Some of these are up to 60-m long, L-shaped, with two facing stone walls, often elaborately decorated with bas-relief murals depicting the ceremonially dressed players. Due to the large number of ball courts found in this region, it is considered that the game probably originated here. The largest ball court in all Mesoamerica, however, is at Chichén Itzá. It was built after the Toltecs took over the city in the 13th century and its facing walls measuring some 82 m in length, 8.2 m in height.

Time

The basic unit of measurement was the single day. The 260-day cycle (known as Tonalpohualli to the Aztecs, and as the Tzolkin to Maya scholars) was made up of 20 consecutive day signs combined with prefix numbers from 1 to 13. Thus, for example, there would be the day 7 Ocelotl, or Jaguar, which would only come around again once 260 days had elapsed. The basis for this 260-day cycle is not known. Although unrelated to any natural patterns of event, it does roughly correspond to the period of human gestation. The cycle was sacred to the Maya and formed the basis for all their religious rituals, some of which, like the Christian Easter, shifted from one year to the next. Each day was divine, symbolised by the god that day carrying it like a load or 'burden'.

There was also another cycle, probably devised more recently from the 260-day cycle and just as common throughout Mexico during the classic era. It ran simultaneously as was very similar to our own 365-day solar year. The cycle consisted of 18 named periods of 20 days each, much like our months, plus five unlucky 'empty days', making 265 days in total. This 360-day year was called the Xihuitl by the Aztecs and the Haab by the Maya. The two calendar cycles ran concurrently but was also combined to create a further cycle of 260x365 days, or approximately 52 years.

Additionally, the Maya devised an extremely accurate system of counting centuries and millennia called the 'long count'. Some monuments feature extremely lengthy and complex dates reaching millions of years into the past using a system of representation that was far in advance of any contemporaneous old world system. Principally, the long count was used to record the movements of the stars and planets, which the Maya observed with great interest. They calculated the paths of the sun and moon, and made tables of lunar eclipses. The measuring and recording of time was such an important task to the Maya that it is often considered to be the very soul of their culture, indeed the meaning of their name is 'cycle' so they can be truly called the 'People of Time'.

Writing

The Olmecs were the first culture to use a system of writing in Mexico, although did not develop anything like the level of sophistication achieved by the Maya, whose system is recognised as the most complex of all Mesoamerican cultures. Other groups who developed their own forms of writing included Teotihuacán, Zapotec, Mixtec, Toltec and El Tajín. The earliest source of writing was in hieroglyphs, which were inscribed on upright stone monuments or stelae. The predominant theme in writing was the recording of time, particularly with regard to the seasons, upon which agricultural production depended.

By the time of the Aztecs, writing had become a large-scale professional occupation. The Tlacuilo was a highly respected and skilled craftsman, whose job it was to paint books, now called codices, on parchment or native paper. Sadly, when the Spanish conquistadors saw these folded documents they destroyed the vast majority as 'works of the devil'.

A handful of Aztec codices have survived, however, as well as several from the Mayan era, most important of which is the Codex Dresden, kept in Germany. As with the earlier Olmec glyphs, the Maya codices deal exclusively with religious and astronomical topics. Interpretations of the Codex Dresden have revealed that is an almanac, full of tables with details on which gods are to be consulted on which dates, and saying how to interpret favourable or unfavourable signs, with regard to harvests, marriages, war and hunting.

Art and architecture

Art

The pre-Hispanic civilizations of Mexican produced sculptures and mural paintings often depicting their rulers and ceremonies. Some of the best known are the giant Olmec stone sculptures of heads, whereas the Classic Maya, of an even more artistic bent, made sculptures of complex designs, showing deities and rituals. The warrior Aztecs, on the other hand, had a penchant for skulls and other depictions of war and death. After the Conquest by the Spaniards, art took on brand new forms, but a legacy of Mexico's pre-Hispanic art lingers till this day. With the Spanish came Roman Catholicism and during the era following the Conquest, much of the art was religious in nature. Skilled indigenous artisans were brought in to adorn the newly built churches and religious art blossomed, as evidenced by the many richly decorated churches that can be seen throughout Mexico today.

Independent Mexico saw the rise of a new breed of art, not afraid of satirizing society and societal problems. One of the most famous cartoonists and engravers of the time was José Guadalupe Posada (1852-1913), whose *calavera* (skull) motifs are still revered and his skulls can be seen on paper cuttings and posters around the Day of the Dead right across Mexico.

In the 1920s, following on from the Mexican Revolution, a new sense of urgency swept through the art world and Mexican society in general. There was a new emphasis on history, culture and education and the minister of education, José Vasconcelos, commissioned a number of young artists to paint a series of public murals to spread awareness to the Mexican people. Diego Rivera (1886-1957), David Alfaro Siqueiros (1896-1974) and José Clemente Orozco (1883-1949) all set to work and painted some of the greatest murals in Mexico, becoming the country's most celebrated painters as a result. Realist paintings with a message became synonymous with Mexican art for several decades to come.

Following in the footsteps of the muralists was Oaxacan painter Rufino Tamayo (1899-1991), known for his colourful watermelon motifs, stemming most probably from the fact that his father was a fruitseller. Another iconic painter in the Mexican pantheon was Rivera's wife, fellow artist Frida Kahlo (1907-1954), whose life was as interesting as her art – both of which have been the subject of numerous books and also the recent film *Frida*, from 2002 (see page 804). After suffering polio as a child and a horrific accident in her teens, Kahlo's paintings are mostly self portraits depicting her own personal agonies and traumas. Her realist and surrealist works gained international acclaim, but nothing could cure her ailing body and she died in 1954, by some believed to have committed suicide, as she was by then bedridden and crippled. See also box, page 109.

After decades dominated by the muralists, a new generation of Mexican painters led by José Luis Cuevas started what's known as *La Ruptura* (The Rupture), moving away from the previous trends and taking Mexican art in new directions.

Architecture

Historians of Mexican art and architecture agree that there are no neat chronologies or easily definable styles available that adequately describe its colonial buildings. Many obstacles disturbed the flow of ideas from Europe to the lands entitled New Spain during the time of the viceroyalty (1521-1810). Problems of communication over the ocean between Madrid and Mexico City and across the vast territories beyond, as well as between the Spanish and their subordinates, enabled other influences to take hold. This resulted in an architecture enriched by the juxtaposition of cultures which fused to create modern Mexico. Formal influences from the diverse groups of indigenous Americans (Indians), such as the Aztecs of central Mexico and the Mayans of the Yucatán, are not easy to find. The most pronounced can be seen in the 18th-century strapwork in the Santa Isabel Church, Tepetzala and the Santo Cristo Chapel, Tlacolula, the atrial crosses at Cuautitlán and Huichapan, and the folk baroque churches at Acatepec and Tonantzintla near Cholula. Differences in the ways that spaces were made and used are discernible, especially in religious buildings, and the icons and other ornamental works adorning their interiors and facades had unprecedented meanings in an alien land of 'things never heard of, seen or dreamed of before.'

The first Franciscan priests arrived in Mexico in 1523, just two years after the arrival of Cortés at the Aztec capital of Tenochtitlán, later Mexico City. Their task and that of other Mendicant Orders soon to follow was to convert the Indians to Christianity, as a way of including them within the jurisdiction of the Spanish court. Their means was through the making of places of worship: a campaign of ecclesiastical construction spread wide across Mexico. On foot they reached the principal Indian centres, dismantling or building over their temples. Dominating the landscape, the religious buildings which replaced them consisted of large gardens and walled patios or *atrios*; a solid, single-aisled vaulted church; and friary buildings (*conventos*) focused around a two-storeyed cloister and raised on a platform above the street level of the town. In a creative dynamic these buildings were improvised from memory by amateur priests and constructed by hastily trained Indian craftsmen, on site or at schools in the capital. Outstanding examples include *conventos* constructed by the Franciscans at Huejotzingo, the Augustinians at Acolman and Actopan, and the Dominicans at Teposcolula. A hybrid eclecticism characterizes these early permanent buildings, which mix elements of many styles from Europe: Isabaline Gothic (arches, canopies and carving), Romanesque (structural form), Manueline from Portugal, Spanish Plateresque (ornament around doorways and windows), early Baroque, the art of the Moors under Spanish rule – Mudéjar (elaborate timber ceilings), and Tequitqui – the art of the Indian under Spanish rule. This latter term refers to strange bi-planar carving, thought to derive from an interpretation of European prints which were used to introduce images of religious icons to the Indian imagination.

After the 16th century the exotic and pagan presence of non-European influences was suppressed. The visionary friars with their dreams of a Christian utopia were replaced by more organized and politically ambitious priests who located themselves either in the capital of Mexico City, or new outlying cities such as Puebla, Oaxaca and Guadalajara. Spanish professionals often controlled the design of buildings, which became more sophisticated in their structural and ornamental objectives, and more tightly derivative of European models. The decoration of their facades reflected trends in the metropolis, and the contributions of Indian craftsmen were made by highly trained and specialized artisans. The consensus is that Mexican Baroque began in the mid-17th century. At this time a transition was made from the single-aisled church plan of the 16th century to a cruciform vaulted church with a dome over its crossing. This was, however, the limit of influence of the spatial experimentation that characterized Italian Baroque architecture. It was in the ornamentation of church interiors, where the seeds of a hybrid Mexican sensibility had been sewn in 16th-century altarpieces, that an opulence present only in the Iberian colonies developed. Despite some resistance to Baroque ideas in Spain and Mexico due to the sobering influence of Juan de Herrera, architect of the Escorial, social aspiration made the opportunity for grandeur and excess irresistible.

The Baroque in Mexico reached its culmination in the 18th century with the onomatopoeic Churrigueresque, the architecture of the *estípite*. This innovation was introduced from Seville by Jerónimo de Balbás, who first used it in the Altar de los Reyes in Mexico Cathedral, 1718-37. The estípite is a type of pilaster tapering towards its base, a characteristic that visually releases it from any structural role. Used in the huge and overwhelming *retablos* (vault-high altarpieces), and later the facades of 18th-century buildings, it embodies the gravity-defying nature of the polychrome and gilded ornament that swarms over their surfaces, and which was constantly remodelled and enriched until the arrival of neo-classicism at the end of the century. Described as the pinnacle of Mexican religious art these assemblages were the sum of parts always individually derived from a codified European language. It is the act of synthesis, however, which is quintessentially Mexican. There is a term in Spanish, *conjunto*, which refers to the assemblage of all the visual (*plastic*) works in a space experienced as intrinsic to the building's presence.

Mexico won independence from Spain in 1821, but the spirit of its architecture by that time had been muted by an academic neoclassicism promoted by the influential Academia de San Carlos in Mexico City. Despite the tendency towards unquestioning reproduction that the fashion of neoclassicism required, explicit Indian references emerged alongside an increasing eclecticism towards the end of the 19th century. Drawn from a seemingly distant past this Indigenism was based on romantic mythologies that served nationalistic ends, rather than on contributions from contemporary Indian culture.

Ideas from Europe continued to be transformed by the Mexican imagination, including Art Nouveau at the beginning of the 20th century and a post-Revolutionary attraction to Functionalism in the 1930s. The synthetic integration of architecture with other visual arts which blossomed during colonial times was to re-emerge later, alongside another rise in Indigenism during the mid-20th century. The campus of the University City (1950-1952) in Mexico City self consciously places itself within this tradition. Some of its buildings incorporate large murals on their exterior facades which narrate Mexican histories, notably the Olympic Stadium and the Central Library, whilst others seek through their pyramidal and massive form to connect with the land and its Indian legacy.

Social issues

People

In 1900 the population was 12 million, while 100 years later it was pushing 100 million, and Mexico City is considered the most populated city on earth with 24 million inhabitants. About 9% are considered white and about 30% indigenous; about 60% are *mestizos*, a mixture in varying proportions of Spanish and Indian; a small percentage (mostly in the coastal zones of Veracruz, Guerrero and Chiapas) are a mixture of black and white or black and Indian or *mestizo*. Mexico also has infusions of other European peoples, Arab and Chinese. There is a national cultural prejudice in favour of the indigenous rather than the Spanish element, though this does not prevent indigenous from being looked down on by the more Hispanic elements. There is hardly a single statue of Cortés in the whole of Mexico, but he does figure, pejoratively, in the frescoes of Diego Rivera and his contemporaries. On the other hand, the two last Aztec emperors, Moctezuma and Cuauhtémoc, are national heroes.

Land ownership

The issue of access to the land has always been the country's fundamental problem, and it was a despairing landless peasantry that rose in the Revolution of 1910 and swept away Porfirio Díaz and the old system of huge estates. The accomplishments of successive PRI governments have been mixed. Life for the peasant is still hard. The minimum wage barely allows a simple diet of beans, rice, and tortillas. The home is still, possibly, a shack with no windows, no water, no sanitation, and the peasant may still not be able to read or write, but something was done to redistribute the land in the so-called *ejido* system, which gave either communal or personal control of the land. The peasant was freed from the landowner, and his family received some basic health and educational facilities from the state. In 1992 new legislation was approved which radically overhauled the outdated agricultural sector with far-reaching political and economic consequences. Farmers now have the right to become private property owners, if two-thirds of the ejido votes in favour; to form joint ventures with private businessmen; and to use their land as collateral for loans. Private property owners may form joint stock companies, thereby avoiding the constitutional limits on the size of farms and helping them to raise capital. The failure of any agricultural reforms to benefit the peasants of Chiapas was one of the roots of the EZLN uprising in early 1994 (see box, page 773).

Migration

There have been two major trends in migration. There has always been movement northwards to the US which fed voraciously, and continues to do so, on cheap labour, and with the crash of the peso the upper classes also moved there in greater numbers. Towns like

Tijuana and Ciudad Juárez grew rapidly as workers poured in to labour in the factories or to prepare for crossing the border. Over many years the poor have been migrating to the centre, to Estado de México, whilst parts of Mexico City have close to shantytown conditions. The states with least migration, either in or out, have been Chiapas, Yucatán, Guerrero and Oaxaca. The first three of these are often associated with past or present resistance to central government. The least stable, demographically speaking, have been Baja Norte, Baja Sur, Quintana Roo and Estado de México, either because of tourism or economic unpredictability.

Indigenous peoples

Mexicans in a mestizo land

Descended from great civilizations whose ruined pyramids still exalt the national landscape, Mexico's multicoloured tapestry of indigenous peoples is one of its most endearing features. Their cultures, which collectively predate the Conquest by tens of thousands of years, continue to fascinate anthropologists, ethnologists and travellers alike.

But the political and economic reality of Mexico's indigenous peoples is a harsh and lamentable one. Once masters of their own land, Mexico's *indigenas* now occupy the poorest and most disenfranchised sectors of society, often lorded over by powers that have changed little since colonial times. For Mexico's national identity is firmly anchored in its *mestizo* heritage. The struggles for independence and nationhood – in which Mexico was baptized with blood – were first and foremost *mestizo* struggles. Today, *mestizos* form the largest and most dominant racial group in what is a grossly unequal society. This is in stark denial of the incontrovertible facts of *mestizo* origin: *mestizos*, by definition, are born of both Spanish and indigenous blood.

The *mestizo* relationship to its indigenous mother is a curious one, for it illustrates a glaring contradiction in Mexico's psychology. Historically oppressed and humiliated, Mexico's *indigenas* have long suffered the brunt of racism, first imported and institutionalized by the Spanish *conquistadores*.

Even after Independence, the newly forged Mexican nation continued to operate along lines of racial preference. This time it was the *mestizos*, not the Spanish, who occupied the nation's institutions of economic and political power. Fortunately, this is starting to change. Once upon a time it was deemed desirable to assimilate *indigenas* into the 'ethnically superior' *mestizo* majority, but lately, subordination to *mestizo* dominance is seen as an obstacle to modernity.

Since the 1917 Constitution, rights have been extended to give many indigenous groups their own forms of social organization, land ownership, political integration and educational provision. Today, Mexico's official line is multiculturalism, not monoculturalism. But beneath this politically noble veneer the same old divisions and inequalities persist. As a nation, Mexico seems comfortable in making touristic capital out its indigenous peoples. But whether or not its *mestizo* population is truly ready to regard them as equals is a complex issue that may take many more generations to solve.

Organization and character of indigenous life

Indigenous groups are concentrated in the southern parts of Mexico; most notably, Yucatán, Oaxaca and Chiapas. Census figures put their numbers at around 10-12 million or 11-13% of the total population (some estimates are as high as 30%). There are some 62 indigenous languages in Mexico, complemented by scores of dialects. Nahuatl and Yucatec Maya are the most widely spoken indigenous idioms, but as ever, Spanish remains the lingua franca.

Life is woefully impoverished for the vast majority of indigenous communities. Their economies are largely driven by agriculture with daily activities revolving around the changing responsibilities of the maize cycle. These are often incorporated into a calendar of vibrant festivals which can be distinctly Catholic in character, but more often include elements of pre-Hispanic origin. Much depends on the individual extent of religious syncretism, as well as historic contacts with Spanish forces.

Social organization within communities is focused on the family, often extended through the patronage of godfathers. Conjugal roles are strictly delineated with men governing the public sphere and women running the domestic. Between all community members a system of cargos, or public duties, binds and directs collective life. Low-ranking cargos might include dancing at festivals; high-ranking cargos might involve guarding the village saint, or organizing the festival itself. Cargos are paid for by the bearer and deliver considerable social prestige.

Traditions remain central to indigenous life with vibrant crafts, costumes, music and dances allowing the cultural expression of ancient ideas, as well as linking contemporary *indigenas* to their ancestors. Tradition, however, is now declining. Younger generations now sport the latest clothes and haircuts they've seen on MTV, neglect to learn their native language, or travel to the US or big Mexican cities to pursue their ambitions of a better life.

Northwest cultures

Mexico's northwest is a vast and inhospitable territory where European forces struggled to penetrate. Composed of rugged sierras, arid deserts, undulating valleys and rich coastal zones, the region supplied niches for only the toughest and most tenacious groups.

As fierce nomadic and semi-nomadic hunter-gatherers – in many ways related to the Native Americans of the southwest US – they strongly resisted Hispanicisation. Today, their myths and beliefs are now interpreted in the context of Christian tradition, but remain overwhelmingly pre-Hispanic in content. Their spiritual world is one of coyotes, dwarves and giants, with the forces of nature personified and open to petition.

The Tarahumara, known as the Rarámuri in their own language, are one of the largest northwest cultures, with 121,835 persons scattered throughout the rugged Copper Canyon region of Chihuahua state. Agriculture, spiritual devotion and a social code founded on unconditional giving form the basis of their culture.

The Mayo, also known as the Yoreme, number 91,261 and are focused in southern Sonora, where farming, fishing and wage labour are the main economic activities. Their story is one of brutal suppression and rebellion, with a fervent adherence to Jesuit teachings.

The Yaqui, known to themselves as Yoeme, were particularly resistant to Spanish domination and remain one of the most organized and politicized groups in Mexico. Essentially autonomous, they self govern through a central council.

The Huichol

The Huichol are one of the most vibrant, least evangelized and culturally fascinating indigenous groups in all the Americas. Known as Wixarika in their own language, a word meaning 'seers' or 'healers', they occupy dispersed and remote communities throughout the rugged sierras of Jalisco, Nayarit, Durango and Zacatecas. The region, often called El Gran Nayar, is shared with groups of Coras, Nahuas and Tepehuanes.

Geographically isolated and historically resistant, the Huichol – now believed to number around 44,000 – answer to no one. Descended from semi-nomadic hunter-gatherer tribes, less than half of their population speak Spanish, instead employing their native Uto-Aztecan tongue.

Central to their lives is a complex pantheistic belief system which makes no distinction between the sacred and the profane – for in the Huichol universe everything is alive and imbued with soul. It is said that the Spaniards soon gave up trying to destroy Huichol sacred sites when they realized that everywhere was hallowed to them.

Their gods, who number too many for any individual to recall, are continuously honoured through prayer and ritual. The mitote, an annual ceremonial calendar, is essentially a dramatic reenactment of the creation of the world. It involves multiple pilgrimages to the edge of the Huichol universe in which the forces of nature – affectionately called Father, Mother and Grandfather – are honoured through days of non-stop ritual chanting, dancing and retelling of epic ancestral myths.

The most famous pilgrimage of all leads 300 miles from the Huichol heartland over the desolate mountains and into the Sierra de Real de Catorce. Here, the desert of Wirikuta is home to one of the most beloved of all Huichol gods: hikuli, the hallucinogenic peyote cactus, who has protected and nurtured Huicholes for centuries.

Myth recalls how the first ancestors consumed hikuli, became filled with visions and ascended to heaven. Today, male Huicholes are duty-bound to make the pilgrimage at least once in their lives. The journey is arduous, involving much fasting and purification, and if successful, concludes with their being granted 'nierika' – 'the power of seeing'. Thereafter, they have the option to train as shamans.

It is forbidden to retell the content of any peyote vision, but many Huicholes immortalize their encounters with the serpent rain god, grandfather fire and the other great spirits of their pantheon through vibrant and intricately detailed yarn paintings. Sought after by international collectors, Huichol artwork can fetch thousands of dollars and provides a much needed supplement to their often struggling economy. Poverty, high infant mortality and malnutrition remain endemic to these isolated people.

The Otomí

The Otomí number 646,875 and are Mexico's fifth largest indigenous group. Scattered over the rugged mountains and central plateau north of the capital, as well as the arid semi-desert region near the pre-Hispanic city of Tula, of which they were once a subject, the Otomí inhabit several states including México, Queretero, Hidalgo and Veracruz. Roughly half speak their native language which has multiple and often mutually unintelligible variants.

Life for the majority of Otomís remains impoverished with an economy based on small-scale agriculture, craft and wage labour. Many have now migrated to other parts of the country or the US in search of reliable employment.

Their traditional culture – largely based on the cargo system – has been significantly eroded by state-run civic organizations and Protestant missions, but remnants of pre-Hispanic practices survive. Many Otomí homes have family altars with small candles and other offerings for the saints, deceased family members and ancestors, whilst traditional herbal medicines are widely used in the treatment of day-to-day ailments.

The Otomí are most famed for their creative utilization of the maguey plant. The thorns supply nails and sewing needles, the pulp is used as soap, the hearts are roasted and eaten, fibres are extracted to make coarse textiles, and the larvae that feed off the plant are considered a supreme delicacy. The maguey is also used in the production of pulque, an ancient alcoholic drink believed to have been invented by the Otomí and still widely consumed across Mexico.

The Totonacs

The Totonacs are a fairly robust ethnic group, presently numbering 411,266 persons. Just over half retain their native language, related in unconfirmed ways to Mayan and Huastec linguistic families. Occupying territories of northern Veracruz and Puebla states since around AD 1000, the Totonacs remained relatively autonomous during the colonial era thanks to their inhospitable surroundings. However, violent *mestizo* incursions during the revolution changed all that.

The famous Dance of the Voladores, in which dancers swing through the air from a tall pole, is a vivid survivor of their pre-Columbian culture and thought to relate to the ancient calendar. But generally, traditional Totonac customs are declining.

Time-honoured indigenous and Catholic religions now compete with Pentecostal churches who dismiss their heritage as mere 'superstition'. And where once the system of cargos conferred prestige, younger Totonacs can now attain social status by becoming preachers. But beyond this, medicinal plants, sorcery and shamanism continue to play vital roles in their communities, as do the Lord of the Mountains and the God of Thunder, who preside over cycles of drought and deluge.

Since pre-Hispanic times, Totonacapan, as the territory is known, has been a voracious producer of salt and vanilla. After the Conquest, sugar, tobacco, coffee and pepper were introduced with great success. Today, agriculture is so closely tied to the essence of Totonac being that the saints are adorned in garlands of local produce during festival times.

However, such valuable crops have not been without their price. The high demand for intensive labour has disrupted traditional conjugal roles, deforestation has obliterated the ancient dwellings of spirits, and conflict over land has been an ongoing issue. Today, Totonac peasant movements continuously petition the government for fair treatment.

The Nahuas

The present-day Nahuas are descended from a vast network of pre-Hispanic polities – the Aztecs among them – who traded, warred, worshipped or otherwise interacted in complex and intensive ways. As such, the term Nahua is a generic and somewhat inadequate category applied to those peoples who today speak dialects of the ancient lingua franca, Nahuatl, which means clear or intelligible.

The Nahuas constitute Mexico's largest indigenous group with a population of 2.4 million (only 1.6 million speak Nahautl, however), mostly concentrated in the Huasteca, the Sierra Puebla, and in more dispersed settlements across Guerrero and Morelos. Other communities are widely scattered throughout the states of Hidalgo, San Luis Potosí and México, with additional pockets surviving in the capital and across the country.

Consequently, Nahuas are far from culturally or politically homogeneous. During the colonial era, Catholic authorities rigorously supplanted Nahua gods with Christian saints, but their system was similar enough to the existing one to be easily accepted. Today, Catholic festivities are intimately tied to the ancient agricultural calendar with often intriguing results.

On 3 May, the day of Santa Cruz, the Nahuas of Guerrero conduct a pilgrimage to the sacred Ameyaltepec mountain to petition the gods for rain. In the village of Totoltepec, the community annually performs the Tecuani or 'tiger dance', where a marauding 'jaguar' is symbolically sacrificed for the cosmic blessing of their crops. In the mountain town of Cuetzalan, the feast of Saint Francis is a well-attended affair marked by the sublime dance of the Quetzal, where performers adorn magnificent circular headdresses of coloured ribbon, strips and feathers. The highly choreographed dance, which continues for hours at a time, symbolizes the cyclical procession of time and the seasons.

The Nahua economy continues to be based on maize, although some highland communities now complement this with lucrative exports of coffee, flowers, avocados, citrus fruit and sugar cane. Textiles have always been a major Nahua commodity and are still woven with hand looms, although wool and silk now complement the traditional coyuchi cotton.

The Purépechas

Directly descended from the mighty Tarascans, the Purépechas occupy the highlands and valleys of the present-day state of Michoacán. Their craft traditions, institutionalized by the 16th-century humanist Bishop Vasco de Quiroga, are arguably the country's finest, with individual communities specializing in the work of copper, clay, textiles, lacquer and others.

The Purépecha number 202,884 and until 1950 retained some degree of social autonomy. Thereafter, self-governing indigenous institutions were ousted by *mestizo municipios*. They continue to practise a folk version of Catholicism with widespread devotion to the saints and virgins. However, a rich oral tradition complements European cultural forms, as does a vibrant cycle of festivities, songs and dances intended to honour the ancestors and encourage bountiful harvests. The New Year celebrations on 1 February, for example, closely echo the ancient 'New Fire' ceremonies where community hearths were lit using a single, divinely proffered flame.

Ritual healing and herbalism are also widespread. A wealth of specialist practitioners include those who help souls vacate the body during the trauma of death. Music is much loved by the Purépecha with some Pierericha (singers and composers) attaining national renown. Most recently a pan-Purépecha movement has begun and Purépecha communities now rally under their own flag and closely coordinate during festival times. There have also been moves to introduce their native language into the school system.

Peoples of Oaxaca

Jungles, forests, dunes, rivers, plains and the sweeping fertile spaces of the Valles Centrales are among the multitude of Oaxaca's ecological settings. Diverse indigenous groups have occupied and exploited these ecological niches for millennia. It is likely that maize cultivation established itself here first, making Oaxaca the cradle of Mesoamerican civilization.

Some fifteen distinct peoples now inhabit these lands where the Sierra Madre del Sur and the Sierra Madre Oriental converge, pursuing fishing, flock-tending and forestry in addition to traditional maize cultivation. Much like during the pre-Hispanic eras, two groups predominate.

The Zapotecs, builders of the mountain city of Monte Albán, now number some 777,253 and occupy the central and eastern parts of the state. Their main rival, the Mixtecs, whose name means 'people of the clouds', number 726,601 and are concentrated in western Oaxaca, Guerrero and Puebla. Together they form one of Mexico's largest indigenous populations.

The market place is a point of meeting and convergence for Oaxaca's groups with everything from squawking livestock to hand-crafted pottery traded in labyrinthine networks of stalls and alleys. Here, little has changed since pre-Columbian times.

Daily life also continues to be governed by traditional forms of organization with communally owned land, obligatory community service and ancient devotional festivities tied to maize production. Dances and processions are vital components in their cultural life with the Zapotec feather dance – where the Conquest is re-enacted with enormous headdresses of red, blue and white feathers – a particularly famous innovation. Craft traditions are another aspect of Oaxaca's culture for which its people have always been famous. Dazzling black pottery, wildly colourful wooden animals, palm textiles and tin-work are all widely produced. But it is weaving, particularly Mixtec weaving, for which the state is most renowned.

Centuries of tradition comprise this much revered art, passed between generations of mothers and daughters. Hand-woven without patterns on waist-strap looms, Mixtec textiles often feature colourful geometric shapes or stylised animals, all worked into unique productions that instantly identify their village of origin. Some articles are designed with magical purposes, effectively warding off evil spirits. So revered is this art, weavers are buried wrapped up in their finest huipils. On the international market, some rugs fetch many thousands of dollars.

The Mayans

Prior to the Conquest, the Mayans, much like the Nahua of central Mexico, were a highly developed and complex body of peoples – a patchwork of competing civilizations engaged in a process of dynamic social evolution. But unlike the Nahua, the Mayans continued to occupy the same geographical space long after the Conquest.

Grounded in the vast regions of Chiapas, Yucatán, Guatemala, Honduras and El Salvador, Mayan heritage is formidable. But whilst geographically united, the Mayans remain culturally diverse thanks to the process of colonization. Over the centuries of colonial rule, the Maya became fragmented by rugged topography and Spanish imposition, evolving into some 29 distinct ethnic groups, each with their own language. Very broadly, they can be divided into lowland and highland Mayans.

In the lowlands, the Yucatec Mayans, occupying the Yucatán peninsula of southern Mexico, are the single largest contiguous faction. Numbering some 2.45 million (with 892,723 Yucatec speakers) they are Mexico's biggest indigenous group after the Nahuas. The Yucatec Mayans speak a single language with many distinct (but mutually intelligible) regional dialects. They follow lives with differing degrees of modernity.

Life in the villages remains traditional, agricultural and family orientated. But increasingly, many Mayans now reside in the famous tourist resorts of Quintana Roo where they find employment in the service sector. Typically, they will return to their villages to partake in festivities, important life events or major agricultural activities. Shamanism is widely practised by the Yucatec Mayans. Chac, the god of rain, so vital to the parched peninsula, continues to be worshipped with fervour.

In eastern Chiapas, the Lacandón are a particularly fascinating, though sparsely numbered, lowland Mayan group. Known as Hach Winik in their own language, which means 'real people', they are believed to be descended from refugees who fled Guatemala and Yucatán during the Spanish Conquest.

Hidden in the deep rainforests, they successfully fought off Hispanicisation for centuries and thus retained many aspects of their Pre-Columbian culture. Instantly recognisable from their long black hair and white tunics, the Hach Winik traditionally forged an existence through hunting and subsistence farming, whilst dwelling in scattered family units throughout the jungle. Religion often involved pilgrimages to ancestral sites – Bonampak and Yaxchilán included – where offerings of copal incense and *balché*, a mild beer made from tree bark, were made to the gods.

Today, the Hach Winik have settled in larger communities and traded their resources for modern infrastructure, which include an air strip and an ambulance. They now hunt with guns, not bows and arrows, watch television and listen to the radio. Traditional religion has been largely abandoned, due in part to the misguided efforts of North American evangelist groups who have established missions in the area.

The last great spiritual leader of the Hach Winik was Chan Bor Kin, now immortalized as a kind of national hero. He is reported to have lived beyond 110 and fathered some 13 children by three different wives, the last when he was 99. He was a life-long smoker of cigars and highly active until his death.

The Chontal, numbering some 40,000, are another major lowland group occupying central Tabasco. Now modernized by the oil industry which mushroomed off their shores, the Chontal traditional economy was based on the bounty supplied by their lush surroundings. A closely related group, the Chol, continue to be occupied by maize and coffee production. Hardworking *milperos*, or field workers, are especially esteemed in their communities.

In the highlands of Chiapas, the rugged topography provides niches for a network of 13 distinct ethnic groups, each with their own attire. Tzeltal, Tzotzil, Tojolabal and Mam are their main languages. Community life is orientated around the family, a cargo system of civic duties, and religion – for which Alteños, as highlanders are called, are especially famous.

In the staunchly individualistic Tzotzil village of San Juan Chamula, traditions have been adhered to with an unmatched ferocity. Outsiders are generally mistrusted and barred from settling in the community. Shamans practise archaic healing ceremonies in the Catholic church, including the ritual sacrifice of chickens.

An annual round of Chamulan festivals includes some striking fusions of Christian and pre-Columbian elements. Most famous is their five-day Festival of Games, a symbolic destruction and recreation of the universe enacted on the fourth day of carnival. Whilst correlated to the Christian cycle, the event corresponds to the five-day 'lost month' of the ancient pre-Hispanic calendar. The occasion includes much feasting, exploding gunpowder and a dramatic dance on burning embers, right outside the Catholic church.

Religion

Roman Catholicism

Roman Catholicism is by far the most important religion in Mexico today, with almost 90% of the population belonging to the Catholic Church – rather surprising, given the rocky relationship between church and state over many decades. However, although the Mexican state may be secular and firmly removed from connections with the Catholic Church, the church itself has been present in the country since the arrival of the Spaniards in the 16th century and it's played an important role throughout Spanish rule and the independence struggle. Miguel Hidalgo y Costilla, the leader of the Mexican War of Independence, was himself a priest and the church has had a prominent, if sometimes reluctant, part in Mexican struggles of a political and societal kind. Relations between church and state came to a head after the 1910-16 Mexican Revolution and in the 1917 constitution the church was stripped of many of its former rights and privileges. This in turn sparked the 1926-29 Cristeros Rebellion, a three-year war fought by Catholic rebels against the liberal government. (See *The Lawless Roads* and *The Power and the Glory* by Graham Greene.) In the end the war was settled by diplomatic means, but the church-state relations were not fully restored until the 1990s when president Carlos Salinas removed most of the anti-clerical measures from the constitution and Mexico resumed diplomatic relations with the Vatican in 1992. Troubled relations between church and state notwithstanding, the Mexican people as a whole has remained remarkably loyal to the Catholic Church despite it being one of the most conservative churches in Latin America, not always known for taking sides with the poor. One of the reasons the government tried to curb the church's influence was due to the sheer fortune and large masses of land it had accumulated over the years.

Still, the Catholic Church continues to play a vital role in the lives of many Mexicans today – some 50% of the population go to mass at least once a week and many of the festivities and celebrations taking place across the nation are of a religious nature.

Instrumental in forging a bond between Catholicism and native indigenous beliefs is the story of the Virgin of Guadalupe, Mexico's patron saint. Mexico's brand of Roman Catholicism has from early on contained a strong element of syncretism, with native animist belief and other ingredients thrown into the melting pot, but with the rise of the worship of Nuestra Señora de Guadalupe religious belief took on a new fixed demeanour. The myth has it that on 12 December 1531 (the date now celebrated across Mexico as the Day of Guadalupe), a dark-skinned apparition of the Virgin Mary, known as the Virgin of Guadalupe wearing a poor peasant's cloak, appeared before the Indian Juan Diego and although the historical veracity of this claim is debatable, nonetheless the Virgin of Guadalupe is venerated by Mexicans and her shrine, the Basílica de Guadalupe in northern Mexico City, is the site of many pilgrimages. After Christmas, the Day of the Virgin of Guadalupe is Mexico's biggest religious celebration and 12 December is the date that really starts off a long period of festivities in the run-up to 24-25 December. Easter is the next large-scale religious festivity, although many parts of the country also observe Lent and celebrate Carnival, notably Veracruz. The entire Easter week (Semana Santa) is taken over by a religious fervour with processions, visits to church, special masses and family get-togethers.

Protestantism

Despite Mexico's overwhelmingly Catholic past, in recent years Protestantism, particularly Evangelical churches such as the Pentecostals, has been gaining ground. There are a large number of different Evangelical churches in operation in Mexico today of many denominations and Protestantism is growing most rapidly in the poorer southern states such as Chiapas. Catholicism isn't exactly running the risk of being phased out, but there is now a substantial minority adhering to other branches of Christianity. Much of this can be attributed to American missionaries and US influence, but it's also true that Evangelical churches are more approachable and easygoing, thus attracting more young people tired of the rigours of the Catholic faith. The Catholic Church itself, by not always taking a stance and working actively to alleviate poverty, has lost some of its appeal and the respect of the local communities, paving way for the new era of Evangelical churches springing up across the nation. There are now some five million Protestants in Mexico, including one million Jehovah's Witnesses and 500,000 Seventh-day Adventists. The actual figure of non-Catholic Christians is thought to be higher, since many Mexicans are reluctant to admit in a census that they've strayed from the traditional path. Mexico also has small Orthodox, Jewish and Muslim communities, particularly in Mexico City. Despite changes taking place in Mexican society, the vast majority of Mexicans still remain Catholic and the religious calendar is still the basis for most fiestas and celebrations throughout the nation.

Shamanism

Irrevocably tied to the land, its mysteries and an invisible order of primeval forces, shamanism is the bedrock of Mexican spirituality.

The shaman, who is often called to his role after a life-threatening bout of sickness, is above all else a healer. Carried into ecstatic trance by prayers, drum beats, sacred songs and visionary plants, he is also a vital intermediary between the earth and the otherworld. He is a traveller to strange realms.

Mexico's shamanic roots reach deep into its archaic past. The first settlers in the Americas, who arrived between 40,000 BC and 10,000 BC, are thought to have practised an elementary form of shamanism for hunting, gathering and fishing. Soon the domestication of plants (8000 BC-2000 BC) brought increasingly complex social organization and a specialization of shamanistic technique. Agricultural and ancestral cults arose with new gods devoted to the sun, wind, rain and other natural forces upon which the early settlers were dependent.

During subsequent centuries humble farming communities flourished into grand theocratic polities. Monumental architecture, elaborate ceremonies and a vast pantheon of exotic gods now embellished Mexican spiritual life. The shamans were promoted to the rank of priests and guarded secrets of astronomy, mathematics, writing and time. Simple shamanism, however, continued to be practised in the villages and ultimately would outlive the magnificent theological advances of the state. As the Spanish Conquest dismantled the grand temples, libraries and idols, indigenous shamans and priests sought the clandestine preservation of their practises in Mexico's rural backwaters. The gods were clothed as saints, ritual rounds aligned with the Christian calendar, beliefs transmitted by oral tradition, or more symbolically, in arts, crafts, songs and music. Invariably, Catholicism and pre-Hispanic spirituality fused into a hybrid religion. But this fusion was neither consistent nor complete. Today, shamanism in its purest forms continues to be practised by many indigenous groups across Mexico, including the Maya, Huichol, Nahua, Sierra Otomí, Totonac, Huastec, Tepehua, Cora and peoples of Oaxaca.

Cosmovision

Central to all forms of shamanism is the concept of animism, a philosophical notion that all things are imbued with – and 'animated' by – life force. Thus the universe of the shaman is a living, breathing phantasmagoria of spiritual entities. Trees, mountains, rocks, rivers, rain, clouds, thunder and lightning, and all features of the manifest universe – animals, vegetables and minerals – are sentient beings, and by extension, sacred. Thus animism is a profoundly ecological doctrine and some traditionally minded campesinos still beg permission before chopping down a tree, killing an animal or disturbing the natural order of the landscape.

The universe itself is delineated on three levels – the earth, sky and underworld – between which the shaman must skilfully operate. The level of earth is the stage for all human activity. Its structure correlates to the orientation points of north, south, east, west and centre, each with its own colour, spirits and associations, such as the rising sun of the east, or the sun at its zenith in the south. Directly above the earth, the sky is home to the sun and moon, stars, planets and other bodies in the celestial canopy. It is the seat of gods who preside over time, fate and all natural forces. Beneath the earth lies the underworld, where the dead reside with ancestral spirits. Honouring these ancestors remains a vital practice in many indigenous cultures. The three levels of the universe are penetrated and connected by a central axis, the axis mundi, a kind of inter-dimensional portal through which cosmic forces can pass. As an entity, the axis is symbolized by the world tree, whose branches support the sky and whose roots reach into the underworld. It is this motif that famously adorns the sarcophagus of the ancient King of Palenque, Pakal. The world tree can also be seen in the more abstract form of the Mayan cross, often found in the village squares of highland Chiapas and sometimes wrongly interpreted as a Christian crucifix.

Sacred spaces

Whilst shamans consider all spaces sacred, they do not utilize all of them for sacred practises. The shamanic altar is the quintessential microcosm of the axis mundi and the site of most magical operations. Contained either in the shaman's home or a specially appointed public temple, the altar is constructed to symbolically reflect the upper, middle and lower regions of the universe.

Upon its surface lie images of saints or tutelary gods, as well as a wealth of ritual objects like wands, feathers, crystals and candles. Offerings, too, are placed on the altar, for cures and favours are administered only when the appropriate gifts have been made. As such, reciprocity is a key element of Mexican spirituality.

But the natural landscape, too, is a classic haunt of shamans and their devotees. As a connector of earth and sky, the mountain is yet another symbolic manifestation of the axis mundi, recreated during ancient times in the form of pyramidal temples. Elsewhere, caves and *cenotes* are considered the abode of rain and earth gods, whilst lakes and springs are the dwellings of fresh water goddesses. Mountainside shrines can often be glimpsed when travelling through rural Mexico and some places hold such importance that shamans conduct arduous pilgrimages of many hundreds of miles to honour them. The annual Huichol journey to the desert of Wirikuta is one such event.

Perhaps the most vital sacred space is that of shaman himself. A successful shaman must train his body through a series of ritual trials aimed at his physical and spiritual purification. Thereafter, he is subject to stringent codes regarding his sexual and moral conduct, lest he lose his powers or even die. Once purified, trained and consumed by the fervour of ecstatic trance, he himself becomes the axis mundi and a vital conduit between the worlds. Through his body various forces and messages are communicated, sometimes directly, as in the case of spirit possession, or more commonly as visions and dreams.

Disease and medicine

Various branches of traditional medicine co-exist with Mexico's shamanic legacy. Herbalism, bone-setting, midwifery and prayer-making all complement the work of the shaman, whose exclusive preserve is supernatural communion, ritual magic and ecstatic trance. However, many shamans will also utilize these other methods in their overall treatment.

Diagnoses are typically made in visions or dreams, during which time the shaman may consult spiritual beings for guidance on a cure. Other times a different form of divination may be involved. For example, certain Nahua shamans use corn kernals to divine the appropriate assistant saint, others use pulse reading, and some Totonacs employ crystals.

Common diseases are believed to be caused by savage 'airs' which attack anyone in their vicinity. Often found lingering damp, gloomy places where someone has died, these invisible forces are dangerous and powerful, but also impersonal. Malign entities can sometimes command airs to do their bidding, and other times they dwell quietly around springs, canyons, or places where lightening has struck. Most airs can be easily treated with a simple *limpieza* (cleansing) where a ritual object – such as an egg, candle or live chicken – is passed around the body to absorb it. Other diseases are caused by foreign objects lodged inside the body. Invisible to the normal human eye, the shaman perceives these as thorns, insects, nails, coins or coffee beans. He extracts them by sucking them out through his lips or a hollow reed, often concluding his performance with a sleight of hand trick that reveals an actual physical object. However, some dangerous objects, such as those associated with sorcery, need not be lodged in the body itself, but cause sickness by being close to the victim. Soul loss is a dangerous condition that can result in death if untreated. Often caused by a sudden shock or accident, it can only be resolved by an accomplished shaman who will chant for hours or days and journey to the otherworld to retrieve it. In some cases, a malign sorcerer is responsible for stealing a patient's soul. For that, the shaman must dispatch his spirit helpers to do battle with the evil magician.

The Nagual

Among many of Mexico's indigenous groups there is a widely held and very ancient belief in spiritual counterparts or magical co-essences called naguales. Such spirit companions are a vital source of shamanic power. Also called tonalli, chanul or wayel, naguales usually take the form of animals (occasionally they are identified as natural forces like rain clouds or lightening) and are closely related to the concept of totems.

Exact beliefs concerning the nature and reality of naguales varies between ethnic groups, but most believe that all persons are inseparably tied to one, whether native or *mestizo*. One's spirit companion may be a deer, jaguar, eagle, snake, alligator, wolf, hummingbird or just about any wild creature, but rarely a domestic animal. They are born at the same moment an individual is born and live apart from humanity in the wilderness.

A person's fate and existence runs parallel to their nagual. If one gets sick, so does the other. If one goes hungry, so does the other. And if one dies, almost invariably, so does the other. If anyone should kill a nagual whilst hunting they run the risk of going insane, especially if the nagual belongs to a shaman.

Most ordinary people are incapable of perceiving their nagual, but the shaman is able to divine it through pulse-reading, dreams or mystical visions. Additionally, a shaman will know his own nagual intimately. In some traditions, he may be able to 'borrow' its form and roam the countryside as an animal, or in the case of evil sorcerers, wreak havoc on communities.

This concept is elegantly expressed by the Huichol, among whom an exclusive wolf cult exists. Only the most accomplished shamans are permitted membership, and all are able to transform themselves into wolves after a lengthy and dangerous training. As such, the wolf is held in high regard as a teacher and hunter with no less than five heavenly constellations dedicated to him.

Visionary plants

Mexico's pre-Hispanic civilizations made extensive use of a wide range of visionary plants including peyote (*Lophophora williamsii*), mushrooms (*Psilocybe cubensis*), datura (*Datura stramonium*), tobacco (*Nicotiana rustica*), diviners' sage (*Salvia divinorum)* and many others. Some ancient works of art feature teonanacatl (mushrooms) and strange stylistic motifs that can be broadly interpreted as hallucinatory.

Today, visionary plants continue to be used in Mexico, a fact widely publicized by Carlos Castaneda, author of the bestselling *The Teachings of Don Juan*. His writings concerning an apprenticeship with a Yaqui shaman have been largely discredited as works of fiction, but his essential assertion about the cultural use of hallucinogens rings true: among a handful of ethnic groups, visionary plants are still ingested as a means of mystical union, divination and shamanic journeying.

These plants, however, are regarded as gods in their own right and should be handled with utmost respect. In many cases, communities have worked with them for thousands of years. Consequently, the content of their hallucinations is firmly woven into the symbolism of their culture. This strongly contrasts with Western drug usage, where hallucinogens are consumed for fun or experimentation and often produce nothing more than intense, but ultimately disconnected, psychological experiences. Most famously, ethnologists have widely documented the cultural uses of peyote, especially among the Huicholes. Essentially a tribe of shamans, Huicholes revere the peyote cactus as a teacher capable of imparting searing mystical visions, healing sickness and guiding the aspirant to profound revelatory truths. Their artwork is emblazoned with the colours, patterns and recurring motifs of their peyote trips, and as such, the plant is a key component in their cultural life.

In the highlands of Oaxaca, hallucinogenic mushrooms continue to be used among the Mazatec, who shot to fame in the 1960s when a Time article exposed their practices. Hippies have long since visited the region to partake in the mind-altering fungi affectionately called 'saint children' by the locals.

Over a time, a divinatory practise once reserved for 'wise ones' was extended to foreigners and transformed. Drug tourism is now a robust economic sector of communities like Huautla de Jiménez, although the *ceremonia* that visitors can expect to partake in still closely resembles the Christian rite of Holy Communion. As such, magic mushrooms are nothing less than the beloved body of Christ.

The dark arts

Sorcery or *brujería* is the dark cousin of shamanism and looms disturbingly over some struggling communities where feuds and resentments run deep. Often motivated by envy and sexual jealousy, at its worst, sorcery is the art and practise of malicious magical attacks. Its ill effects include life-threatening sickness, failed crops and soul loss, all of which can only by treated by shamanic intervention.

The sorcerer, or brujo, sells his services to disgruntled individuals and acquires his power in the same way as a conventional shaman. Indeed, many sorcerers are failed shamans or novice apprentices. A sorcerer's nagual or spirit helper will frequently be a 'dark' animal such as an owl or fox, or in some cultures, an unearthly blood-sucking demon.

Some sorcerers make pacts with powerful and dangerous entities, such as the Kieri tree of Huichol tradition – a much feared plant belonging to the delirium-inducing Solanaceae family. Most acts of sorcery are confined to casting bad airs on a victim, which can be achieved in a variety of ways. For example, some Sierra Otomí sorcerers create mutilated paper figures that symbolise their intention and insult.

In reality, very few genuine acts of sorcery have been documented by ethnologists, but this does not negate the widespread belief in their existence, at least among indigenous groups. It may well be that genuine sorcery is so well hidden that researchers have failed to discover it. Some shamans have admitted to occasionally participating in sorcery, but generally, as custodians of the health of the entire community, it would be counter-productive to engage in such practices.

Beyond traditional cultures there are many who call themselves sorcerers but who are actually practitioners of a strange hybrid craft that draws on New Age, Catholic, African and other influences. Their work tends to be dominated by superstitious ritual rather than trance, but at least extends beyond malicious attacks to love potions, blessings and the divining of lost objects. Their art, however, is a less potent or interesting one.

Music

A vigorous radio, film and recording industry has helped make Mexican music highly popular throughout Latin America and there can be no more representative an image of Mexico than that of the Mariachi musician in his *charro* costume, complete with cartwheel sombrero. The Spanish *conquistadores*, and the churchmen that followed them, imposed European musical culture on the defeated natives with a heavy hand and this influence remains predominant today. Nobody knows what pre-Columbian music sounded like and even the music played today in the *indígena* communities is basically Spanish in origin although African slaves introduced another element. The music brought from Europe has over the centuries acquired a highly distinctive sound and style of which every Mexican is justly proud, even if many young people now prefer to listen to US rock and pop.

There is a basic distinction between *indígena* and *mestizo* music. The former is largely limited to festive rituals and dances, religious in nature and solemn in expression. The most common instruments are flute and drum, with harp and violin also widely used. Some of the most spectacular dances are those of the Concheros (mainly urban), the Quetzales (from the Sierra de Puebla), the Voladores (flying pole – also Sierra de Puebla and Veracruz), the Tarascan dances from around Lake Pátzcuaro and the Yaqui deer dance (Sonora).

Mestizo music clearly has more mass appeal in what is an overwhelmingly mixed population. The basic form is the *son* (also called *huapango* in eastern areas), featuring a driving rhythm overlaid with dazzling instrumentals. Each region has its own style of *son*, such as the *son huasteco* (Northeast), *son calentano* (Michoacán/Guerrero), *chilena* (Guerrero coast), *son mariachi* (Jalisco), *jarana* (Yucatán) and *son jarocho* (Veracruz). One *son jarocho* that has achieved world status is *La Bamba*. Instrumental backing is provided in almost all these areas by a combination of large and small guitars, with the violin as virtuoso lead in the *huasteca* and the harp in Veracruz. The *chilena* of Guerrero was inspired by Chilean sailors performing their national dance, the *cueca*, during a naval visit to Acapulco in 1822, while Yucatán features a version of the Colombian *bambuco*. The *son* is a dance form of flirtation between couples and often involves spectacular heel-and-toe tapping by the man. Another widespread dance rhythm is the *jarabe*, including the patriotic 'Jarabe Tapatío', better known to the English-speaking world as the 'Mexican Hat Dance'. Certain regions are known for more sedate rhythms and a quite different choice of instruments. In the north, the Conjunto Norteño leads with an accordion and favours the polka as a rhythm. In Yucatán they prefer wind and brass instruments, while the Isthmus of Tehuantepec is the home of the marimba (xylophone), which it shares with neighbouring Guatemala.

For singing, as opposed to dancing, there are three extremely popular genres. First is the *corrido*, a narrative form derived from old Spanish ballads, which swept across the country with the armies of the Revolution and has remained a potent vehicle for popular expression. A second is the *canción* (literally 'song'), which gives full rein to the romantic, sentimental aspect of the Mexican character, and is naturally slow and languid. *Las Mañanitas* is a celebrated song for serenading people on their birthdays. The third form is the Ranchera, a sort of Mexican country and western, associated originally with the cattlemen of the Bajío region, see box, page 269. Featured in a whole series of Mexican films of the 1930s and 1940s, Rancheras became known all over the Spanish-speaking world as the typical Mexican music. The film and recording industry turned a number of Mexican artists into household names throughout Latin America. The 'immortals' are Pedro Infante, Jorge Negrete, Pedro Vargas, Miguel Aceves Mejía and the Trio Los Panchos, with Agustín Lara as an equally celebrated and prolific songwriter and composer, particularly of romantic boleros. To all outsiders and many Mexicans, however, there is nothing more musically Mexican than Mariachi, a word said to be derived from the French *mariage*, introduced at the time of Maximilian and Carlota.

Originating in Jalisco, Mariachi bands arrived in Mexico City in the 1920s and have never looked back. Trumpets now take the lead, backed by violins and guitars and the players all wear *charro* (cowboy) costume, including the characteristic wide-brimmed hat. They play all the major musical forms and can be found almost every evening in Mexico City's Plaza Garibaldi, where they congregate to be seen, heard and hired. This is the very soul of Mexico.

There are also a number of distinguished 20th-century composers who have produced symphonies and other orchestral works based on indigenous and folk themes. Carlos Chávez is the giant and his *Sinfonía India* a particularly fine example. Other notable names are Silvestre Revueltas *(Sensemayá)*, Pablo Moncayo (*Huapango*), Blas Galindo (*Sones de Mariachi*) and Luis Sandi (*Yaqui Music*).

Modern artists

A number of more modern artists have been taking Mexican music to new heights, both at home and abroad, in recent decades, building on traditional styles, while adding rock, pop and other international influences to the mix. One of the most popular traditionalists on the music scene is Juan Gabriel, a singer-songwriter hailing from the state of Michoacán, who has immortalized a number of Rancheras, ballads and Mariachi songs. Apart from his own hits, Gabriel has also penned a string of songs for some of Latin America's biggest stars, produced several albums and pursued an acting career. Another famous Gabriel, although not related to Juan, is singer-songwriter Ana Gabriel, whose career is almost as long and illustrious as Juan's. Many of Ana Gabriel's albums explore traditional Mexican styles, particularly the Ranchera, but she's also famous for her Latin rock and pop songs, recording a new album every year since 1985, in addition to a number of compilations, including several with Juan Gabriel. Costa Rican-born Chavela Vargas moved to Mexico at the age of 14 to pursue a musical career not open to her in her own country and after many hard years of singing on the streets, she finally struck lucky and her first album was released in 1961. Vargas is mostly known for her strong renditions of traditional Rancheras and her butch attire; with her cigar smoking, heavy drinking, gun carrying and masculine clothing, Vargas belonged to a circle of intellectuals including Juan Rulfo, Frida Kahlo, Diego Rivera and Agustín Lara. Finally at the age of 81, Vargas openly came out as a lesbian, one of few female public figures in Mexico to do so.

The 1980s and early 90s brought about much interest in rejuvenating and exploring traditional styles, while mixing them with modern influences and several groups, although of short-lived fame, were instrumental to this shift. Between 1988 and 1994, the pop group Garibaldi, recorded some seven albums, breathing new life into Mariachi songs, *rancheras*, boleros and other traditional styles and their success in Mexico was phenomenal. The 1980s also saw the rise of Mexican mega-star Luis Miguel, one of the most prolific pop singers Mexico has ever seen. His albums have sold over 90 million copies around the world since he started his singing career aged 12 and won numerous Grammy Awards and other accolades.

In the 1990s many changes were taking place in Mexican society – the economic crisis and the rise of the Zapatista movement in Chiapas – and this was reflected in new music with a slightly rawer edge. New bands such as Mexico City-based Los de Abajo (referring to the famous novel of the Mexican Revolution with the same name) mix rock, salsa, ska, reggae, hip hop and other influences in their unique blend. They're open supporters of the Zapatistas and their music has a distinct social and political message, moving away from the crooning love songs and laments of the 80s pop and traditional Mexican music as a whole. In the same vein of protest music with a message, Lila Downs has redefined traditional Mexican songs and perhaps for the first time brought songs in indigenous Mexican languages before a wider audience. Ireland-based Mexican duo Rodrigo and Gabriela, despite remaining fairly unknown in their home country, has steadily been gaining popularity abroad since their first album in 2001, forming part of a new era of Mexican music, with artists focusing on the international market.

Literature

Most of the 16th- and 17th-century writings focusing on Mexico came from the early Spanish settlers, particularly those of a religious bent, who started chronicling their experiences of the New World. When it comes to early home-grown writers, one that stands out is 17th-century scholar, nun and Baroque writer, Sor Juana Inés de la Cruz, who is seen as a precursor to later Mexican literature. Few options for studying and getting an education were open to women in the New World at the time and Sor Juana therefore decided to take the veil in order to pursue her interests in verse drama, poetry and literature, excelling at all three. She remains one of the most influential early Mexican writers to this day, her writing commemorated and celebrated throughout Mexico.

The man credited with having written the first Spanish American novel was a Mexican, José Joaquín Fernández de Lizardi, who wrote *El periquillo sarnieto* (*The Itching Parrot*) in 1816. The novel was written in the picaresque genre, which was very popular at the time. After Independence was declared in 1810, a long period of instability followed, leading to a decline in the arts in general and it wasn't until the second half of the 19th century that Mexican literature began to be revitalized after a period of stagnation. Mexico had started to recover from its War of Independence and begun the nation-building process, but peace was short lived. Along with the 20th century, by far the most significant in terms of literary output, came the event that has shaped the nation and its writings more than any other: the Mexican Revolution. The Revolution inspired a more journalistic approach to writing, but it also spawned a new breed of realist writers, portraying the experience of war and struggle. One of the most successful Mexican novels from this time was Mariano Azuela's *Los de abajo* (*The Underdogs*) from 1915. The novel depicts the fighting against Huerta's troops, but also raises questions about the aims of the Revolution itself. The vast majority of the books dealing with the Mexican Revolution were written by male authors, but one notable exception is Nellie Campobello's *Cartucho*. Set in Chihuahua, northern Mexico, during the height of the Revolution, it portrays the events taking place through the eyes of a young girl, growing up amidst the violence and death from 1910 until 1916.

The Mexican Revolution shaped the country and influenced many of Mexico's most prominent and celebrated writers. It's a recurring theme running through the country's literature, as is the war that followed it in the 1920s, the Cristero Rebellion and many, including Juan Rulfo, Carlos Fuentes and Octavio Paz, have tried to tackle the questions the Revolution raised. Juan Rulfo is perhaps one of the best known and loved Mexican authors of all times, despite only producing two works – the novel *Pedro Páramo*, in 1955, and a volume of short stories, *El llano en llamas* (*The Burning Plain*), in 1953. These two books, now both classics, seen as some of the most popular works in all of Latin America, are set during the Revolution and the Cristero Rebellion. *Pedro Páramo* in particular can be seen as an early work of magical realism, set in the ghost town of Comala, which the main character Juan Preciado visits in search of his long lost father, the Pedro Páramo of the title.

Just as popular, and rather more prolific, are Carlos Fuentes and Octavio Paz, the latter receiving the Noble Prize for Literature in 1990. Born during the tumultuous years of the revolution, in 1914, Paz originally studied law before he took to writing and published the first of his poems, *Entre la piedra y la flor* in 1941. He worked as a Mexican diplomat alongside his writing career and among his more famous works are *El laberinto de la soledad* (*The Labyrinth of Solitude*), written in Paris in 1945, and *Las trampas de la fe* (*The Traps of Faith*) from 1982, on Sor Juana Inés de la Cruz.

Mexico and the Beatniks

Mexico came to be something of a second home for many of the US Beatnik writers. One of the foremost writers of the Beatnik generation, William Burroughs (b 1914), for example, when arrested for the possession of drugs and firearms in 1949, escaped to Mexico City with his wife, Joan, where he lay low until the case was dropped. During a wild party in 1952 Burroughs accidentally shot and killed his wife in a William Tell act, for which he spent two weeks in a Mexican prison. He later wrote about his experiences as a morphine addict in Mexico City in *Junkie: Confessions of an Unredeemed Drug Addict*, 1953.

A similar theme is relived in his autobiographical novel, *Queer* (1984). Jack Kerouac (1922-69), another of the Beatnik writers and a good friend of Burroughs, also had a Mexican connection. He spent the summer of 1950 with Burroughs at his house in Mexico City and this inspired part of his Beatnik classic, *On the Road* (1957), in which Sal Paradise (based on Kerouac) and the petty crook Dean Moriarty (based on Neal Cassady) drive across the border from the US into Nuevo Laredo, and then travel through Monterrey on their way to Mexico City. Marijuana and sex form an important part of their journey to personal illumination in Mexico.

Paz's contemporary and one of Latin America's most read authors, Carlos Fuentes, was born in Panama City to Mexican parents and spent his formative years in the Americas from Washington to Buenos Aires, before settling in Mexico. Publishing his first work at the age of 28, Fuentes soon developed into a bold writer, not afraid of trying new narrative styles when discussing Mexican history and society and *la mexicanidad* (Mexicaness) itself. This is particularly apparent in his 1962 novel *La muerte de Artemio Cruz* (*The Death of Artemio Cruz*). Other successful works include *Gringo viejo* (*Old Gringo*) from 1985, the first book by a Mexican author to become a bestseller in the US, where it was also turned into a film.

Since the 1950s there's been an upturn in Mexican women writers, several of whom have gone on to reach international acclaim, particularly in recent years. One of the pioneering feminist writers and poets was Rosario Castellanos (see box, page 667), who grew up in Chiapas in south Mexico. She was a prolific and multi-talented writer, as well as a government diplomat and up until her untimely death in an accident in Tel-Aviv, Israel, where she was serving as Mexico's ambassador, she produced poetry, three novels, a fplay and numerous essays. Her two main areas of focus in her writing were gender oppression and the plight of the indigenous population of Mexico, particularly in Chiapas, the area closest to her heart. Her most famous work, the semi-autobiographical *Balún Canán* (1957), set near Comitán, where she grew up, depicts life and struggles during the Lázaro Cárdenas land reforms and her second book *Oficio de tinieblas* (*Book of Lamentations*, 1962) is also set in Chiapas.

Castellanos' contemporary, Elena Poniatowska, born in France to a French-Mexican mother and a Polish father, settled in Mexico during the Second World War and started her career in writing as a journalist for the broadsheet *Excélsior* in the 1950s. Her first collection of short stories, *Lilus Kikus*, appeared in 1954 and since then Poniatowska has published no less than 14 books, many of which have been translated into English. No stranger to controversy, she's chosen to depict some of Mexico's best known icons, from the Revolution itself to Diego Rivera and the infamous Tlatelolco massacre of 1968 in her works.

Recent years have seen a new generation of women writers such as Angeles Mastretta and Laura Esquivel gain popularity at home and abroad, the former with her

Lawrence and Greene on Mexico

Attracted by the pantheism of the Aztecs, DH Lawrence (1885-1930) decided to go to Mexico in 1923. From March to May of that year he lodged at the Hotel Monte Carlo, at Calle de Uruguay 69 in Mexico City, and he later stayed near the shore of Lake Chapala in a house which can still be visited.

From November 1924 until February 1925 in Oaxaca, Lawrence wrote his Mexican masterpiece, *The Plumed Serpent* (1926), a tense, brooding novel inspired by the Aztecs. We follow events through the eyes of the Irish girl, Kate, middle class and aloof, as she strikes up a friendship with Ramón (who embodies Quetzalcoatl, the plumed serpent god of the Aztec pantheon) and Cipriano (who represents Huitzilopochtli, the corn god), whom she eventually marries. There are some brilliantly vivid descriptions of Mexico in *The Plumed Serpent*, particularly of the bullfight in Mexico City, and the countryside surrounding Lake Chapala (called Lake Sayula in the novel).

Graham Greene (1904-91) was sent as an unofficial envoy of the Foreign Office to Mexico from February to May 1938 in order to report on the persecution of priests in Tabasco and Chiapas. As a result, he wrote a travel book, *Lawless Roads* (1938), describing his journeys through Laredo, Monterrey, San Luis Potosí, Mexico City, Veracruz and Chiapas. Greene also published a novel based on his Mexican experience, *The Power and the Glory* (1940), seen as his masterpiece, which describes the wanderings of a whisky priest who is attempting to fulfil his priestly duties despite the constant threat of death at the hands of the revolutionary government. The arid countryside and oppressively hot climate of southern Mexico provide an appropriate backdrop to Greene's portrayal of evil as a palpable force.

breakthrough novel *Arráncame la vida* (*Tear this Heart Out*, 1985). This was turned into a film in 2008, starring Ana Claudia Talancón and Daniel Giménez Cacho (see page 805). Laura Esquivel's *Como agua para chocolate* (*Like Water for Chocolate*, 1989), was also turned into a well-received and critically acclaimed film in 1994, to coincide with the book's release in English translation (see page 803).

As well as home-grown writers, Mexico has attracted a fair share of visitors keen to pen something on a country that's fascinated travellers for centuries. Graham Greene spent time there, writing *The Lawless Roads*, as well as what is perhaps his best work, *The Power and the Glory*. Another Brit, DH Lawrence, took some time out in Mexico, which resulted in the 1927 publication of *Mornings in Mexico*, a collection of travel essays (see box, above). Perhaps one of the most famous novels ever written against the backdrop of Mexico is Malcolm Lowry's *Under the Volcano* from 1947, during Lowry's time living in Oaxaca, in southern Mexico. This semi-autobiographical work taking place on the Day of the Dead, tells the story of an alcoholic British ex-consul in the fictitious city of Quauhnahuac and this classic tale has been turned into a film on several occasions, see page 803.

The ins and outs of Mexican politics, before, during and after the 1910 Revolution, were also of keen interest to foreign visitors and John Reed, the US journalist mostly famed for his interest in the Russian Revolution, visited Mexico to cover the struggle for *Metropolitan Magazine*. He spent four months in Pancho Villa's army and this resulted in the 1914 book *Insurgent Mexico*, one of few books written by an outsider taking part in the fighting.

Film

The history of Mexican cinema goes all the way back to the very early stages of filmmaking at the beginning of the 20th century and Mexico even had a small-scale silent film industry, with movie salons opening in Mexico City as early as 1906. Early cinematic efforts were often documentaries, propagandistic in nature, particularly before and during the Mexican Revolution and it was only subsequently that the focus of filmmakers shifted towards primarily entertaining the audience, as opposed to influencing them politically or otherwise. In the aftermath of the revolution very few films were made and it was only after the instability of the Cristeros Rebellion that Mexican cinema started coming into its own. The 1940s, known as the start of the Golden Age of Mexican cinema, saw the film industry reviving after the years of war and instability and with the Second World War raging the European and US film industries offered less competition for the burgeoning Mexican cinema. This era also spawned a new generation of household names and Mexican movie stars such as Mario Moreno, also known as Cantinflas, 'the Mexican Charlie Chaplin'. Starring in a series of films in the 1940s and 1950s, Moreno's character helped usher in the golden age and his comedies were immensely popular.

It was during the 1940s and 1950s that a number of Mexican actors and actresses shot to fame at home and in Hollywood – Dolores del Río, Pedro Infante, Pedro Armendáriz and María Félix, to name a few and Mexico was also frequently used as location for foreign films, particularly Westerns, mostly shot in Durango. It was primarily US films that were responsible for portraying the entire nation as a bunch of lazy, good-for-nothing scoundrels, crooks and corrupt officials, mostly wearing large sombreros, an image that's stuck to this day. Foreign films that helped put Mexico on the big screen were *Night of the Iguana*, starring Ava Gardner and Richard Burton, Elvis Presley's *Fun in Acapulco* and the 1984 film version of Malcolm Lowry's novel *Under the Volcano* (see page 802). Spanish-born director Luis Buñuel moved to Mexico in 1946 and directed some 20 films during his long stay in the country. One of his best known films *Los olvidados* (*The Young and the Damned*) from 1950, a moving and bleak account of impoverished street children in Mexico City.

The 1960s to the 1980s saw another period of decline and stagnation in Mexican movie making and it wasn't until the early 90s that things started coming together on the Mexican film scene. Directors such as Guillermo del Toro, Alfonso Cuarón, Alejandro González Iñárritu and María Novaro were some of the names emerging after the long drought in decent films. One of the first new films to receive international acclaim and draw attention to new Mexican film talent was directed by one of few Mexican women directors, María Novaro. Her 1991 film *Danzón*, her second full-length film following *Lola* in 1989, traces the steps of one woman's journey to self discovery in the tropical port city of Veracruz. Another film exploring primarily female relationships that has turned into one of Mexico's most successful films internationally is *Como agua para chocolate*, (*Like Water for Chocolate*) from 1992, based on the novel by Laura Esquivel. A story of thwarted love set in northern Mexico during the tumultuous years of the Mexican Revolution, it beautifully depicts the relationships between the women of one landowning family, combined with the sensuality of Mexican food; see box, page 805. The year 1993 saw the release of Guillermo del Toro's *Cronos*, followed by *El callejón de los milagros* (*Midaq Alley* based on Egyptian writer Naguib Mahfouz's book) in 1994. The latter won more critical acclaim than any other Mexican film to date, with 49 international awards and nominations. It propelled Salma Hayek onto the world stage of cinema and she has pursued a Hollywood career starring in some 30 films, mostly in the US, but also in her native Mexico and in Spain.

Mexico and the Western

It was during the Mexican Revolution that Mexico first really caught the imagination of the US; Mexico was invariably depicted as a land of deserts, cacti, ruthless desperadoes (the fact the word is in Spanish tells us something), and beautiful, seductive women. In *Saved by the Flag* (1911), for example, a US army lieutenant falls in love and elopes with a sensual Mexican girl who is being pursued by a Mexican general. The films of this period overtly contrasted swarthy, uncivilized Mexicans with white, civilized Americans, and provided ideological justification for the US's military interventions south of the border, a good example being *Uncle Sam in Mexico* (1914). A number of films were made in particular about Pancho Villa, the 'greaser' revolutionary who fascinated US audiences, an example of which was Jack Conway's *Viva Villa!* (1934).

During this early period, the Mexican, whether exoticised or vilified, was always 'Other'; he represented the underbelly of the American dream. In the first major sound Western, *In Old Arizona* (1929), directed by Raoul Welsh, for example, the leading role was played by Warner Baxter as the Cisco Kid, a Mexican type on the run from a Texas ranger; Baxter won an Oscar for his performance and established in one fell swoop the South-of-the-Border Western. Other Westerns which took the theme of searching out hoodlums south of the border were Lambert Hillyer's *South of the Rio Grande* (1932), Mark Wright's *Somewhere in Sonora* (1933), starring John Wayne, George Sherman's *South of the Border* (1939), and Joseph Santley's *Down Mexico Way* (1941). In these films, Mexicans have thick moustaches, wear poncho hats, are lazy, deceitful and prone to unpremeditated, even motiveless, violence.

Salma Hayek is perhaps currently Mexico's best-known actress, and in terms of actors recent years have seen the rise and rise of Gael García Bernal. García Bernal has starred in some of the best known Mexican films in the last decade from *Amores perros* (2000) and *Y tu mamá también* (2001) to *El crimen del Padre Amaro* (*The Crime of Father Amaro*, 2002). *Amores perros*, set in Mexico City, looks at three interconnecting stories linked by a car accident. *Y tu mama también*, on the other hand, is a more light-hearted road movie and coming of age story about two teenage boys who set out on a journey towards an imaginary beach with a woman some 10 years older than them and what ensues is a tale of what it's like to grow up in contemporary Mexico, complete with sexual exploration.

Sex, religion and politics are all discussed in *El crimen del Padre Amaro* and Catholic groups in Mexico originally tried to have this controversial film banned from screening. It takes a close look at the murky dealings of a parish priest, tackling topics such as corruption and abortion, with García Bernal in the role of the young parish assistant, recently ordained and irretrievably drawn to the young Amelia, played by Ana Claudia Talancón.

The 2002 film *Frida*, starring Salma Hayek and Alfred Molina, as Frida Kahlo and Diego Rivera, depicts the tempestuous relationship between two of Mexico's best known painters and icons, see page 783. It was an international success, with a female director, American Julie Taymor. *Frida* charts the course of painter Frida Kahlo's life, depicting the traumatic accident she suffered in her late teens, her relationship with Diego Rivera, one of Mexico's foremost muralists, her own painting, her travels and her numerous affairs with both men and women, including her alleged involvement with Leo Trotsky who

Como agua para chocolate

Como agua para chocolate, directed by Alfonso Arau and based on the best-selling novel of his then wife, Laura Esquivel, was an instant international success. Set in an isolated ranch in northern Mexico near the Texas border, mainly during the Mexican Revolution (1911-19), it tells a story of star-crossed lovers. The authoritarian Mamá Elena (played by Regina Torne) offers Pedro Muzquiz (Marco Leonardi) Rosaura (Yareli Arizmendi), her eldest daughter, in marriage rather than her younger daughter, Tita (Lumi Cavazos), whom Pedro really loves, but who is destined to look after Elena until the latter dies. Pedro agrees to marry Rosaura just to be close to Tita. One of the intriguing features of the film is its use of the skeleton-in-the-cupboard motif (the father of one of the daughters, Gertrudis, is a mulatto and not Elena's husband). A stock technique of this film's varied repertoire is magical realism, such as when the house explodes into a fireworks display when Pedro and Tita finally make love, and the matter-of-fact way in which the appearance of ghosts is treated. But the most striking effect of the film is produced by the metaphor of loving and eating, the best example of which is provided by the scene in which Tita prepares a sauce from the roses Pedro gave her in order to season the quail. The effect on the participants in the meal, particularly Gertrudis, is deliciously done.

spent time with the couple in Mexico. The film also has popular Ranchera singer Chavela Vargas (see page 799) doing a version of the classic Mexican song *La Llorona*.

Recent years have seen a few Mexican gems make it overseas as well – notably Ernesto Contreras' romance, *Blue Eyelids* from 2008 and also *Arráncame la vida* (*Tear this Heart Out*) from the same year, based on the 1985 novel by Angeles Mastretta.

Mexico continues to be a popular location for international moviemakers and *Romancing the Stone* (1984), *Medicine Man* (1992), *Mask of Zorro* (1998) and the 1997 blockbuster *Titanic*, were all shot here, the latter at Rosarito, in Baja California.

Environment and ecology

In all of Latin America, Mexico is second only to Brazil in land area, at 1,972,550 sq km. This equates to roughly four times the size of France and about a quarter of the size of continental USA, with which it has 2750 km of common frontier. To the south, Mexico has 1020 km bordering Guatemala and Belize. It has 2800 km of coast along the Gulf of Mexico and the Caribbean, and 7400 km on the Pacific side, of which 40% is the long, thin peninsula of Baja California. This gives Mexico a longer shoreline than any other Latin country, including Chile and Brazil. There are several islands near coastlines and three small territories in the Pacific: Isla Guadalupe, about 350 km west of Baja California, with just 15 permanent inhabitants; the volcanic Islas Revillagigedo, 750 km west of Puerto Vallarta and with 250 permanent inhabitants, the largest of which, Socorro, is 17 km long and 16 km wide and was once colonized by Australians; and the uninhabited Rocas Alijos 300 km west of Baja California.

Mexico, the world's most populous Spanish-speaking nation, had an estimated population as of July 2009 of 111,211,789, 9% of whom live in Mexico City proper (20% within the Distrito Federal), one of the largest agglomerations of people on the planet.

Geology

Structurally, Mexico mostly belongs to North America. The central highland block is a continuation of that of the USA; indeed Cretaceous rocks stretch, virtually uninterrupted, from mid-Mexico north to the Arctic Ocean.

Northern and Central Mexico

This block is bordered by Mexico's two enormous mountain chains, to the east by the Sierra Madre Oriental, and to the west by the Sierra Madre Occidental, both rising to 3000-3500 m. Between them are the vast basins typical of the states of Chihuahua, Coahuila, Durango and Zacatecas, semi-desert because of poor soils and lack of rainfall. These regions have given rise to the image of both the hot, dusty, soporific scenery familiar as the location of many Hollywood movies (the Sierra Órganos area of northwestern Zacatecas state has been a preferred shooting location for Westerns for decades), and spectacular areas of rugged mountains and deep canyons where the intermittent rivers end in bolsones, with water-bearing strata supporting oases on the surface.

To the east, there are more recent strata and alluvial deposits bordering the Gulf of Mexico, a vast syncline which has been found to contain large reserves of oil and gas, as well as rare aquatic ecosystems. The coastline is swampy with sand bars and lagoons that have inhibited exploitation for tourism, which is virtually non-existent north of Veracruz. At the same time, these play a role as near-pristine unmanaged wildlife sanctuaries.

To the west of the central block, the geology is much more complex. It is the product of the continuing movement of the North American Plate westwards against one or more of the Pacific Plates (and most often the Cocos Plate), which has created the high mountain ranges from Alaska to Chile. (The devastating 1985 Mexico City earthquake was a result of the subduction of the Cocos Plate beneath the North American Plate.) Beyond, to the west, are the coastal plains, narrow in the south with natural harbours, coves and beaches such as Acapulco, Puerto Vallarta, Manzanillo and Mazatlán. North towards the US border, the plain grows wider, with richer soils supporting a prosperous agricultural development based on irrigation and the nearby US market. There are more bays and beaches along the coast but the very high summer temperatures and humidity limit the tourist appeal. As with the eastern coastline north of Veracruz, there are several stretches of the western coastline that play host of transitional ecosystems of great variety and importance.

Further to the west is the Gulf of California, 1000 km long. A brief look at the map will suggest a geological break here which stretches north into the US. Baja California is indeed not part of the Cocos Plate, but is on a section of the Pacific Plate moving northward relative to the mainland with which the well-known San Andreas Fault is associated. Narrow ridges rising to over 3000 m run all the way down the peninsula which for most of its length is less than 200 km wide.

Volcanoes and Southern Mexico

The two Sierra Madre ranges come together in the south, where an east-west line of some 1400 volcanic vents known as the Sierra (or Cordillera) Volcánica crosses the country from the state of Veracruz in the east, to the state of Jalisco in the west. This sierra includes the highest points in the country, Orizaba (5760 m); Popocatépetl (5426 m), see box, page 808; Iztaccíhuatl (5230 m); Nevado de Toluca (4690 m); La Malinche or Matlalcuéyetl (4461 m); and Paricutín (3170 m), the latter appearing dramatically for the first time in 1943. Some are now active, and form part of the so-called Pacific Ring of Fire which continues south

Río Bravo – Rio Grande, whose is it?

One of the most contentious international frontiers in the Americas is between Mexico and the US. Economic and cultural disparities, migration, contraband, drugs, and the expanding maquiladora industries have created many problems. Not so well known are the difficulties associated with the border itself, especially the 60% which is along the Río Bravo, known as the Rio Grande in the USA.

The border was officially settled here in 1848 as 'the middle of the river following the deepest channel'. This was fine where the river goes through gorges as at Big Bend, but a problem in flatter country where gradual silting and storm flooding move the braided channels about laterally. The semi-desert conditions most of the way from Ciudad Juárez/El Paso to the Gulf make the flow very variable. In prolonged droughts and below irrigation dams, the river can disappear altogether. One of the features of the silting process is the formation of *bancos* or elongated sand-banks between channels. Land ownership problems emerged when the larger ones were colonized and then the river changed course. In 1899, a prize fight between Maher and Fitzsimmons was prohibited by both the Mexican and the US authorities. The fight was successfully staged on a *banco* while the two governments argued about which country it belonged to.

Water rights are even more of a problem. More people in the region means more water is needed for domestic, industrial and irrigation purposes. Several dams were built which helped to meet these requirements, to control erosion and provide for recreation. Above Ciudad Juárez, all the water comes from the US. Lower down, however, the Mexican tributaries produce more volume. At one point, the US offered to trade water from the Colorado to irrigate Mexican land on the Pacific for Río Bravo concessions.

Then there are the aquifers. In several places there are significant bolsones, holding long-established underground water resources, which straddle the frontier. As more wells are sunk to draw out the water, so the level falls below the rate of replenishment from water naturally seeping in. That water may be polluted.

There has been much progress since 1848. Treaties in 1906, 1944 and 1970 have amicably resolved many problems. Nevertheless there is still plenty of scope for argument. The 1998 storms created significant floods along the course of the river with damage to crops and property. Who pays? Who is responsible? Whose water is it anyway?

---

through Central and South America, and north, after a gap, in the Pacific states of the US; for example, Mount St Helens, which most recently exploded in 1980 and recorded seismic activity through 1998.

To the east, Mexico curves round the Bay of Campeche – with more low-level shorelines with lagoons and a few beaches – to the Yucatán Peninsula, which has the best beaches and natural assets for coastal tourism.

At this point, there is a fundamental break in the geological structure. Another line of mountains, named the Sierra Madre del Sur, marks the zone where the North American Plate terminates and the Central American Bridge begins. This 'bridge' appeared about 3½ million years ago, joining the Americas together and ending a period of at least 75 million years of separation. The Sierra Madre del Sur rises to 3000 m, but is more rugged in character

Popocatépetl

On a clear day (not a very common occurrence), this shapely volcano can be seen from Mexico City. At 5452 m it is Mexico's second highest mountain after the Pico de Orizaba, about 100 km to the east. Its name in Nahuatl means smoking mountain, which it has done from time immemorial helping to add to its mystery and fables.

For many years it was considered dormant and basically harmless. This however ignores its dramatic past including violent explosions, which have left layers of pumice and ash many meters thick over hundreds of square kilometres. In historic times there were major eruptions 5000, 2150 and 1200 years ago, each time covering an area going well beyond Puebla, Tlaxcala and Mexico City. Many relics and artefacts have been found between the layers of material thrown out by the volcano evidencing settlements overwhelmed by the eruptions.

The resultant soils are some of the most productive of the country. The volcano itself, because of its height, creates a microclimate drawing moisture from the air, some of which it stores in the snow cover near the summit producing a good water supply for the slopes below. Hence it is very desirable farming land.

Recently 'El Popo' has been showing signs of greater activity, possibly as a by-product of the 1985 earthquake (which killed more than 10,000 people in the Mexico City area). Steam and gases have been produced in increasing quantities and by the end of 1994, small explosions in the crater were beginning to alarm the authorities. Now, serious attempts are being made by CENAPRED, a federal government disaster agency, to prepare for a possible major eruption which could affect the lives of about 20 million people living within the volcano's orbit. Especially vulnerable will be those who live below the snows and glaciers which, in past major eruptions, have melted, creating catastrophic flash floods and mudflows.

The mountain is now ringed with instruments to give advance warning of problems to come. When the inevitable happens, it remains to be seen if effective evacuation will be possible, given the natural reluctance of those living there to leave.

due to its more recent (late Tertiary) origin and the much greater rainfall here than further north. At the eastern end of this range is the Isthmus of Tehuantepec, about 220 km wide with a relatively low crossing point (250 m). Several times it has been considered as a possible alternative inter-ocean canal site to Panama. (James Eads, a US civil engineer, got closest in the 1880s, but his two attempts to obtain financing through the US Congress failed.) Beyond, further mountain ranges go about 300 km southeast to the border with Guatemala.

Yucatán

Most of Yucatán is structurally a limestone platform, a feature that rings the Gulf of Mexico all the way round to Florida and is recognized as a separate chunk of the North American Plate. It is comparatively flat and characterized by natural caverns, wells and sinkholes (*cenotes*) and white, sandy beaches. The northeast corner of Yucatán is the point nearest to Cuba and where the Caribbean Sea meets the Gulf of Mexico. It is the water passing north through this passage that initiates the current known as the Gulf Stream, with its dramatic effect on the climates of Europe, thousands of miles away. It is calculated that at times, driven by strong trade winds, the surface water here is moving at as much as 6 km per hour.

Perhaps the world's most dramatic geological happening ever recorded is connected to Mexico and concerned the Yucatán. It is now generally agreed that the cataclysm that almost ended life on the planet 65 million years ago was a small asteroid, weighing perhaps one billion tons, colliding with the earth at 160,000 kph. This left a hole many kilometres deep and over 150 km wide in the Yucatán, now known as the Chicxulub Crater. This event destroyed almost every living thing on the planet, from the dinosaurs to ammonites (small crustaceans), leaving only the most primitive organisms. Fortunately for us, life was able to re-establish itself. Erosion has long since removed any surface features, but scientists assure us that Mérida is unlikely to be the site of another asteroid visit.

Climate

About half of Mexico is south of the Tropic of Cancer. Whilst there are seasons, monthly average temperatures change very little near the coasts. Inland, however, variations are more pronounced where continental-style climate conditions prevail. Day and night temperature differences are much more significant the higher you go, with agreeable climates in places like Guadalajara (1650 m), Mexico City (2240 m) and Zacatecas (2496 m). Temperatures below freezing are not uncommon above 3000 m, especially in the winter months when northerly gales blow in from the US. There is permanent snow on the highest volcanoes. The highest temperatures are at the head of the Gulf of California where the July average is around 35°C. One of the highest world shade temperatures (58°C) was recorded near San Luis Potosí in central Mexico.

The deserts of southern California across to Texas continue south into Mexico. The easterly Trade winds bring a little rain to the Caribbean coast and in increasing amounts from Tampico south and round the Yucatán Peninsula. But significant regular rainfall is only found near the borders with Belize and Guatemala. Most of the rain in these wetter regions comes between June and September. The highest mean annual rainfall is around 4500 mm in Chiapas, the least less than 200 mm in Baja California.

Altitude plays an important part in the amount of precipitation. Each of the Sierra Madre mountain ranges receives more rain than the lowlands, frequently used to supply water to neighbouring cities and irrigation schemes. Much of the rain on the inside of the Sierra Madre ranges ends up in *bolsones* (reservoirs). One of the largest is the Bolsón de Mayrán which receives water from two significant rivers and supplies sufficient water for Torreón and the surrounding area. However, much of the rain comes from storms running north up the Pacific coast and especially inwards from the Caribbean during the hurricane season (June to November). Mexico rarely escapes serious annual storms – for example Hurricane César struck southern Mexico in 1996, Pauline devastated Acapulco in 1997 and there were severe floods and mudslides on the Río Bravo (Rio Grande) in Chiapas and in central Mexico August-September 1998 and again in Veracruz and the southeast in 1999. In more recent years, Mexico has been hit even harder, with the Pacific Hurricane Juliette (category four) damaging much of the country's Pacific coast in 2004, two category-five hurricanes, Emily and Wilma both occurring in 2005, and Hurricane Dean (also a category five) devastating the Yucatán Peninsula in 2007.

Flora and fauna

The diversity of Mexican flora and fauna should not be underestimated, and the space allocated here alone could never do justice to the subject. For those who wish to know more, see *Mexico: A Hiker's Guide to Mexico's Natural History* by Jim Conrad (1995); if you read Spanish, *Flora y Fauna Mexicana, Panorama Actual* by Leonardo and Jimena Manrique (1998), is a must. Those with an interest in Mexico's abundant bird life (more 1000 species) should consult the excellent Peterson guide, *A Field Guide to Mexican Birds* by Roger Tory Peterson and Edward L Chalif (1999 edition). Also recommended are the third edition of *A Field Guide to the Birds of Mexico and Adjacent Areas* by Ernest Preston Edwards (1998) and *A Bird-Finding Guide to Mexico* by Steve Howell (1999).

Especially when studying the pre-Columbian history of Mexico, a knowledge of the flora and fauna of the region is useful, as the native peoples made use of the diverse natural environment within their art and architecture, and images of plants and animals can be found not only in sculptural and painted remains, but also within the surviving books and maps, and references are rife in the Maya, Aztec, Olmec, Huichol and other local peoples' calendars and belief systems.

Central Highlands
Despite extensive deforestation, particularly in the Valley of Mexico, there are still large areas with tree cover. Pine forests cover the highlands to the northwest of the Valley of Toluca, home to the monarch butterfly, a magnificent insect which migrates from the US to winter in these woods, whilst evergreen oaks and piñón pines dominate the lower slopes, where band-tailed pigeons are hard to miss. Great horned owls and Northern pygmy owls inhabit these forests as do the brightly coloured mountain trogons, though they are rarely seen, despite their green heads and brilliant red bodies. At lower elevations look out for the fig tree, with its distinctive exposed root system, used to make amate paper.

Large areas of the highlands are dry and denuded of tree cover, such as the states of Hidalgo and Puebla, and here the maguey (agave) cactus is cultivated extensively.

Coyotes can still be seen in the mountains, though they are increasingly rare as pressure from man mounts. Amongst their prey are the local jackrabbits and long-tailed wood partridge, whilst the piñón mouse lives in the pine forests of the region. Turkey vultures, which appear everywhere in Mexico, can be easily spotted with their dark plumage and red heads, alongside their smaller cousins, the black vulture, scavenging the roadsides, squabbling with each other and anything else between them and their food. Alongside the common ground dove, little bigger than the ubiquitous sparrow, they are amongst the most frequently seen birds.

Baja California and the Sonoran Desert
The sahuaro, cardón and organ pipe cacti, long-living columnar giants (ages of up to 500 years have been recorded), are perhaps the best-known cacti species of this region; the cardón, at nearly 20 m, is the tallest cactus in the world. Other plant species include yucca, ironwood, brittlebush, paloverde and ocotillo, one form of which is the endemic boojum tree, which grows into a 12-m-high candle shape. The compact form of the ocotillo has resulted in its use as a form of hedging by desert communities. The distinctive chaparral landscape of mesquite, oak, hollyleaf buckthorn and manzanita, dominates the dry mountain slopes of the peninsula's north and the desert's east.

The coyote is still a common sight here, whilst the bighorn sheep, once found throughout northern Mexico, is confined to the interior of Baja and the El Pinacate biosphere reserve in Sonora. The metre-long chuckwalla, a type of lizard, is found on islands in the Gulf of Cones at the extreme northern end of the Gulf of California (or Sea of Cortés, as it is known in Mexico) while the horned lizard inhabits the Sonoran desert, and desert iguanas are endemic region.

Elephant seals and fur seals are on the increase after years of persecution, and can be seen on the Guadalupe Island off the west coast of Baja, but Californian sea lions can best be seen in the Sea of Cortés. The Sea of Cortés is a haven for cetaceans, with several whale and dolphin species frequenting its waters. Pacific grey whales calve in the coastal lagoons of the peninsula, and can easily be seen from the coast, as can ospreys, catching fish with a feet-first plunge.

Pacific Coast and the Sierra Madre Occidental

Juniper, pine, and cedar forests dominate the higher elevations, where common turkeys still roam wild, whilst deciduous sub-tropical acacia and mesquite woodland dominate the lower slopes, where bromeliads and orchids grow. Several species of parrot, generally green in colour, trogons, hummingbirds of many types, and screech owls inhabit the forests of this region.

It is believed the grey wolf is now extinct, though some may still live in the northern Sierra, but the mountain lion, or puma, is definitely still resident in the mountains, as is the bobcat and the lynx, but they are rarely seen during the day. Amongst the prey of the larger cats are the local pig, the collared peccary, and the common mule deer, found throughout Mexico, and the rarer white tailed deer, generally found above 1500 m. Nine-banded armadillos, racoons and skunks frequent the lower regions, and white-tailed antelope squirrels inhabit the woodlands. The coatimundi, a relative of the racoon, is common here and throughout Mexico, but you are more likely to see one as a pet than in the wild.

Chihuahua Desert

The flora of this area is dominated by typical desert scrub and cacti. With over 200 cacti species, only a few can be mentioned here, the most dominant being prickly pear. Peyote is used as an hallucinogenic by the indigenous population in various religious rites. Amongst other plant species the crucifixion thorn, creosote bush and whitethorn acacia dominate, while stands of oaks and ash abound on the desert edges, and as one moves further south, grasslands, interspersed with prickly pear, yucca and barrel cacti, dominate. In this environment crested caracaras, large long-legged birds of prey, can be seen.

The coyote is common throughout this region as well, but the pronghorn, the fastest ungulate on earth, is now a very rare sight on the grasslands. The collared peccary survives around the margins of the deserts, and the nine-banded armadillo thrives here as well, as it does throughout most of northern and central Mexico. Cottontail rabbits, adapted to desert life, are a relatively common sight, and rodents of all types abound, especially kangaroo rats, of which Mexico boasts several native species. Of course rattlesnakes (*cascabels*) are not uncommon, with 18 species living in Mexico, though most are fairly harmless and rarely encountered. Scorpions, though highly venomous, are nocturnal creatures.

In Coahuila State, one area worth visiting is the Cuatro Ciénegas Natural Protected Area, a zone of natural oases and one of only two desert spring ecosystems of its size in North America, where permission is required to enter. Here some unique species live, such as the aquatic Coahuila box turtle, and the abundance of duck and fish is truly astonishing.

Gulf Coast, Sierra Madre Oriental and Chiapas

In the north, the desert gives way to thorn scrub of mesquite, hackberry and acacia. One of Mexico's two coral snake species lives in the northeastern deserts, the other being found in Yucatán, and though venomous, its bright colour makes it fairly conspicuous. The grasslands of the coastal plains, home to the common turkey, border the forests on the lower slopes of the Sierra Madre Oriental, inhabited by several species of nightjar and the potoo, and stretch from the Texas border to Veracruz. The potoo is a large brown bird which during the day sleeps upright and motionless on branches, appearing to be part of the tree.

Cloud forests, with their distinctive Spanish moss (pachtli) formations, dominate the higher elevations further south, some of the best and easiest to see being along Route 175 from Oaxaca to the coast in Veracruz state. One of the residents of the Chiapas cloud forest is the resplendent quetzal, a type of trogon, the most spectacular of birds, with its emerald and golden green body, red belly, and tail feathers that are white from below, but, depending on the angle of vision, green or blue from above. During pre-Colombian times its tail feathers were more valued than gold, but now it is so rare that one would be privileged to see it. The lower forests are home to several parrot species, whilst hummingbirds are frequently seen, the violet sabre-wing standing apart from the usual shimmering green varieties.

The lowlands of northern Chiapas are dense jungle, where huge ceiba trees can be seen, and where a few jaguars still roam, though being nocturnal and extremely stealthy, one is most unlikely to see them. Other cat species include the spotted ocelot and its smaller (1 m-long) cousin the margay, and the dark coloured 70-cm-long juagarundi, all rare and under pressure from habitat loss. Deep in the jungle lives the rarely seen baird's tapir, while the collared peccary gives way to the larger white-lipped peccary. The forest canopy resounds to the bellow of the howler monkey, and black-headed spider monkeys can be seen swinging through the trees, but one is unlikely to see the nocturnal American opossum.

The sight of military macaws, collared and keel-billed toucans and various parrot species is not uncommon when visiting the Mayan ruins along the Usumacinta River. Glossy blue, thrush-sized lovely cotings are a common sight, as are various species of the smaller manakin birds. On the forest floor leaf-cutter ants appear to be everywhere. These small insects travel along pathways carrying sections of leaf ten times their own size back to their nest, where the leaves are used as a fertilizer for growing the fungus that the ants eat. The jungle is full of colourful insects and arachnids too numerous to mention, but one is unlikely to encounter more than the odd harmless tarantula and occasional wasp colony if only visiting ruins.

American crocodiles and alligators live along the river banks, though one is unlikely to see either, since, like many large animals, they have suffered persecution from man for many years. However, it is possible to visit nurseries devoted to breeding these animals to re-populate the area.

Harpy eagles, though quite rare, may be spotted soaring over the coastal region, but one is more likely to see hook billed kites, king vultures and black hawks. Red-throated caracaras may be seen in large groups in the humid forests of southern Veracruz and northern Chiapas, particularly when visiting the ruins of Palenque.

The tinamou, a dull-coloured tailless bird with a long down-curving beak, can be seen in the undergrowth of the lower slopes of the mountains. Rarely flying, they will take to the wing if frightened. Smaller, but more common, are quails, several species occurring in the drier parts of Mexico, the most common, the bobwhite, being found throughout the southern and eastern parts of the country. In pre-Hispanic Mexico, the quail was valued as a sacrifice to the gods. The large turkey-sized crested guan and the similar great curassow are birds well worth looking out for on the forest margins.

Coastal waters used to be home to large numbers of manatees, but now their numbers are dangerously low, and they are rarely seen, either on the Gulf Coast or around the Yucatan Peninsula.

Yucatán Peninsula

The southern part of the peninsula is dominated by tropical rainforest, where the distinctive cough of the jaguar may occasionally be heard at night, but the animal will rarely be seen. The northern half is a distinct flat savanna landscape dominated by grasslands, trees and bushes, interspersed with sisal (*henequén*) plantations, once the mainstay of the local economy. The turkey-like (but half the size) plain chachalaca may be spotted early in the morning calling from the treetops, not to be mistaken for the much larger ocellated turkey, with its blue head topped by an orange-red knob, that can be seen in the dense scrubland, especially in the east. Ovenbirds (*horneros*) and ant-birds, no larger than European blackbirds, are common in the forests and plains. The latter can sometimes be seen at the head of army ant colonies, picking off insects flushed out by the ants as they travel across the ground in wide columns in search of insect prey. One might also encounter the tropical rattlesnake, the most venomous rattler after the large western diamondback, found in northern Mexico.

Flamingos can be seen in large numbers at Celestún and on the north coast at Río Lagartos – named for the local crocodile population – where you can hire boats to the sandbars and islets to get closer to the birds. Several other bird species, such as long-legged grey-necked wood rails, and northern jacanas (easily mistaken for coots), may be seen in these coastal swamplands.

The coral reef off the east coast is part of the Belize reef, 250 km in length, and abounds in tropical fish, most easily seen by hiring snorkelling gear at Xcaret, Isla Mujeres, Chetumal and Akumal, the latter a breeding ground for green turtles. The best place to see green iguanas is along this stretch of coast, though they live in all of Mexico's humid jungles.

Whale and dolphin watching

Perhaps more than any other animal apart from the lowly *burro* (donkey), the grey whale has been associated with Mexico, and particularly with Baja California. Every year in late December, grey whales begin arriving at a series of large lagoons along the west coast of Baja California, having travelled more than 3000 km from their Arctic feeding grounds. Unlike other whale species which congregate in the open ocean to mate, calve and raise their young, the grey whales enter the protected salt-water lagoons and spend three months in sheltered waters.

In the mid-1800s, whalers led by Captain Charles Scammon discovered the entrance to the Pacific coastal lagoon that would bear his name: Scammon's Lagoon (Laguna Ojo de Liebre in Mexico). With nowhere to run, the grey whales were nearly all slaughtered in a few decades and by the early 1900s some scientists feared the species was on the brink of extinction. However, following a ban on hunting grey whales, the numbers have now returned. Today there are more than 22,000 grey whales – approximately their original numbers – in the eastern North Pacific.

The grey whale was the first whale to be watched on commercial tours, beginning in 1955 in southern California. In 1970 the first multi-day, long-range whale-watch cruises departed from San Diego to visit the grey whale lagoons on a self-contained ship. Today, the long-range trips are still offered from January to March from San Diego, as well as out of Mexican ports (such as Ensenada and La Paz), usually lasting seven to 10 days. The most popular trips go to San Ignacio Lagoon and Magdalena Bay and some visit both. Besides grey whales, it is possible to watch bottlenose dolphins mainly in the mouths of the lagoons, and often various other whale and dolphin species en route (in open waters), including common dolphins, Pacific white-sided dolphins, and even blue whales. Some trips feature camping beside the lagoons, while others utilize local Mexican boats, called pangas, which can approach fairly close to the whales.

In Baja California especially, it is important to distinguish between tours that set out to watch marine life (of which there are comparatively few) and those that seek to hunt it (of which there are very many). For more information on the former, contact: **Baja Ecotours** ① 6411 Maroon Mesa Drive, Colorado Springs, CO 80918, USA, T 619-819 2966, www.baja ecotours.com; **Baja Expeditions** ① 2625 Garnet Av, San Diego, CA 92109, USA, T858- 581 3311, www.bajaex.com; **Baja Outpost** ① Blv Adolfo López Mateos, Loreto, Baja California Sur, T613-135 1134, www.bajaoutpost.com; or **Baja Tours** ① Av Macheros y Marina, Local G-3 Plaza Marina, Ensenada, Baja California, T646-178 1045, www.bajatours.com.

If you're travelling to Mexico in the winter and want to see whales, go to Puerto Adolfo López Mateos for grey whale watching on Magdalena Bay, or to Guerrero Negro for grey whale watching in Laguna Guerrero Negro. It is usually possible to join day trips within the lagoons, using pangas.

On the other (eastern) side of Baja California, the Gulf of California, or Sea of Cortés, offers a completely different whale-watch adventure which extends throughout most of the year in one of the most diverse whale-watching areas in the world. Access is through the southern Baja ports of San José del Cabo, La Paz, Bahía de los Angeles, and Loreto, as well as Rosario. The whales include fin, humpback, sperm, short-finned pilot and minke whales as well as the difficult-to-identify Bryde's whale, the only truly tropical baleen whale (it does not migrate to cold temperate or Arctic waters). The main dolphins are common, bottlenose and Pacific white-sided dolphin. But most of all, the Gulf of California stands as one of the three or four best places in the world to see blue whales. Some of the above species are present throughout the year, others appear mainly in winter or summer.

In general, the best time for most species is January until April. Day tours are possible, but most people take one- to two-week boat excursions with a small group of participants. They live aboard the boat and are guided to a wide selection of activities and adventures throughout their trip, with whales as the centrepiece.

For multi-day cruises and tours to the above areas (some of which also offer lagoon excursions), contact: **WildWings** ① 577 Fishponds Rd, Bristol, BS16 3AF, UK, T(0)117- 9658 333, www.wildwings.co.uk; **Oceanic Society Expeditions** ① Fort Mason Quarters 35, San Francisco, CA 94123-1394 USA, T415-441 1106, www.oceansociety.org; **Natural Habitat Adventures** ① PO Box 3065, Boulder, CO 80301-9539 USA, T303-449 3711, www.nathab.com; **Ecosummer Expeditions** ① PO Box 177, Clearwater, BC V0E 1N0, Canada, T250-674 0102, www.ecosummer.com; **Discover the World** ① 29 Nork Way, Banstead, Surrey SM7 1PB, UK, T(0)1737-218800, www.discover-the-world.co.uk; **Sea Quest Expeditions** ① PO Box 2424, Friday Harbor, WA 98250 USA, T360-378 5767, www.sea-quest-kayak.com; **ACS Whale Adventures** ① PO Box 1391, San Pedro, CA 90731-0943 USA, T310-548 6279, www.acsonline.org/whalewatchtrips/index.html; and **Lindblad Expeditions** ① 1415 Western Av, Suite 700, Seattle, WA 98101, USA T206-403 1500, www.expeditions.com. In Mexico itself the Gobierno del Estado de Baja California Sur will provide whale-watching and other Baja tourism information. Contact **Coordinación Estatal de Turismo** ① Ctra al Norte, Km 5.5, Fraccionamiento Fedepaz, La Paz, Baja California Sur, México, T612-124 0103.

In recent years, whale watching for humpback whales has really taken off along the mid-Pacific Mexican coast. The tours are conducted only in winter, mainly from Punta Mita at Bahía de Banderas in the state of Nayarit. The tours visit Isabella Island. Others exist out of Mazatlán, Puerto Vallarta, San Blas and Manzanillo.

It is also possible to see bottlenose, spotted and other dolphins on the Caribbean side of the Yucatán, especially on the southeast coast near the border with Belize, as well as from the offshore resort of Isla Mujeres. Sometimes the dolphins are seen as part of diving trips. However, Belize has more developed dolphin-watching operations. Contact Oceanic Society Expeditions, listed above, for more information on their excellent programme that combines science, conservation and a wonderful holiday with dolphins.

Erich Hoyt, marine ecologist and scientific consultant to conservation groups and governments, is the author of 12 books including *Insect Lives* (1999), *The Earth Dwellers* (1998), and *Seasons of the Whale* (1998). See also www.erichhoyt.com.

National parks

Mexico is one of the world's 17 most biologically diverse countries (some reports say it is third, behind only Brazil and Colombia, although fifth is more likely, as both Indonesia and the Philippines have surpassed Mexico's tally). In 2002, Like-Minded Megadiverse Countries was formed in Mexico, consisting of countries rich in biological diversity and associated traditional knowledge. This organization does not include all the megadiverse countries as identified by the UN's World Conservation Monitoring Centre, but in either case, Mexico's surely ranks near the very top by any measurement. It boasts between 25,000 and 33,000 of the 250,000-odd known species of higher plants (including 150 conifers, and around 1000 each of ferns, orchids, and cacti), 700-717 reptiles (more than any other country), 450-460 mammals (second only to Indonesia), 289 amphibians (fourth in the world), 1023 birds, 2000-odd fish, and hundreds of thousands of insect species. Five Mexican vertebrates (all birds) become extinct in the last century, and about 35 species are now only found in other countries; 1088 of around 2370 vertebrates are listed as threatened.

This is of course an immense country, with an immense range of habitats and wildlife; the far south is in the neotropical ecozone, with a wealth of tropical forest species, while the far north is very much part of the nearctic ecozone, with typically North American species, and huge expanses of desert with unique ecosystems. The greater part of the country is a transition zone between the two ecozones, with many strange juxtapositions of species that provide invaluable information to scientists, as well as many endemic species. Many of these sites are now protected, but are often of little interest except to specialists. Rather unfortunately, most of Mexico's national parks were set up decades ago, primarily to provide green recreation areas for city dwellers. They are generally small and often now planted with imported species such as eucalyptus, and thus of no biological value. However, the country does also have a good number of biosphere reserves, special biosphere reserves (the distinction between the last two pertains to forests only), state reserves, protected areas, flora and fauna protected areas, national monuments, biological corridors and marine national parks that are both of great biological value and suitable for tourism (although in some cases also quite remote and without adequate supervision or infrastructure).

In the far south in Chiapas, the El Triunfo biosphere reserve protects Mexico's only cloud forest, on the mountains (up to 2750 m) above the Pacific coast; the main hiking route runs from Jaltenango (reached by bus from Tuxtla) to Mapastepec on the coastal highway. Groups need to book in advance through the **Dirección de la Biosfera de el Triunfo** ① *Calle Cuarta Norte Oriente 1917, 3ro Piso, Fraccionamiento Santos, Tuxtla Gutiérrez, Chiapas, T961-613 8337, www.conanp.gob.mx.*

From Jaltenango you need to hike or hitch a ride about 29 km to Finca Prusia and then follow a good muletrack for three hours to the El Triunfo *campamento* (1650 m). There are endemic species here, including the very rare azure-rumped tanager; the horned guan is found only here and across the border in the adjacent mountains of Guatemala. Other wildlife includes the quetzal, harpy eagles, jaguars, tapirs and white-lipped peccary. Turn left in the clearing for the route down to Tres de Mayo, 25 km away; this is an easy descent of five hours to a pedestrian suspension bridge on the dirt road to Loma Bonita. From here you should take a pick-up to Mapastepec, 25 km away.

Also in Chiapas is the immense Lacandón Forest, which stretches northwest into Guatemala, supposedly protected by the Montes Azules biosphere reserve but in reality being eaten away by colonization and low-level but indiscriminate logging. New plant species are still being discovered in this rainforest, best visited either from the Bonampak and Yaxchilán ruins, or by the road/boat route via Pico de Oro and Flor de Café to Montebello.

In the Yucatán, the Sian Ka'an biosphere reserve is one of the most visited in Mexico, being just south of Cancún; it's a mixture of forest, savanna and mangrove swamp, best visited on a day trip run by **Amigos de Sian Ka'an** ① *Calle Fuego 2, Colonia Benito Juárez, Cancún, Quintana Roo, T998-892 2958, www.amigosdesiankaan.org*. It is also well worth visiting the Río Lagartos and Río Celestún biosphere reserves on the north and west coasts of Yucatán, well known for their flamingos. The Calakmul biosphere reserve is important mainly for its Mayan ruins, seeming to the layman more like scrub than forest.

Across the country's centre is the transversal volcanic belt, one of the main barriers to nearctic and neotropic species; it's easiest to head for the Iztaccihuatl-Popocateptl national park (from Amecameca head east), the Zoquiapan national park (on Route 150 towards Puebla and turn north at Río Frío) or the Chichinautzin biological corridor (on Route 95 to Cuernavaca). Of course, the volcanoes themselves are well worth climbing as well.

Only small areas of the northern deserts and sierras are formally protected. The most accessible areas are in the state of Durango, including La Michilía biosphere reserve, with pine, oak and red-trunked *Arbutus* and *Arctostaphylus* trees typical of the Sierra Madre Occidental. A daily bus runs to San Juan de Michis; get off at a T-junction 2 km before the village and walk west, first getting permission from the **Jefe de Unidad Administrativo** ① *Instituto de Ecología, Ctra Durango-Mazatlán, Km 5 esquina Blv los Remedios (Route 40 if driving), T618-121 483*. The Mapimí biosphere reserve covers an area of desert matorral (scrub) which receives just 200 mm of rain a year; it lies to the east of Ceballos, on Carretera Gómez Palacio-Jiménez (Route 49), just before crossing into the state of Chihuahua. In addition to many highly specialized bushes and cacti, this is home to giant turtles, now in enclosures at the Laboratory of the Desert.

There is a great variety of protected areas in Baja California, all of considerable biological value: the highest point (Pico del Diablo, at 3000 m) is in the San Pedro Mártir national park, in the north, which receives plenty of precipitation and has largely Californian fauna and flora. A dirt road starts at San Telmo, on the main road (Route 1) down the west coast, and leads 100 km to an astronomical observatory. Desert environments are, of course, unavoidable here, with 80 endemic cacti: the Gran Desierto del Altar biosphere reserve in neighbouring Sinora is a dry lunar landscape, best seen from the main road (Route 2) along the US border, while the El Vizcaíno Desert biosphere reserve in the state of Baja California Sur protects a huge area of central Baja, characterized by agaves and drought-resistant scrub. However the main reason for stopping here is to see the migration of the grey whale to its breeding grounds. In the far south, the Sierra La Laguna biosphere reserve (now a UN-designated global biosphere reserve as well) boasts a unique type of cloud forest, with several endemic species. To get to it, you have to cross about 20 km of desert from just south of Todos Santos to San Simón, and then follow a trail for 11 km to a rangers' *campamento* at about 1750 m.

Limited information on national parks and biosphere reserves can be obtained from the **Secretaría de Medio Ambiente y Recursos Naturales (SEMARNAT)** ⓘ *Av Revolución 1425, Delegación Alvaro Obregón, México, DF (take the metro to Barranca del Muerto station), T55-5624 3532, www.semarnat.gob.mx*, where you'll also find the **National Institute of Ecology (INE)** ⓘ *www.ine.gob.mx*, for more general information on conservation; their publications are available online and are carried by the **Librería Bonilla** ⓘ *Cerro Tres Marías 354, Colonia Campestre Churubusco, DF, T55-5544 7340, www.libreriabonilla.com.mx*. They have two additional stores, one in Santa Fe and the other in Cuernavaca.

Non-governmental conservation organizations include **Naturalia** ⓘ *Apdo Postal 21541, 04021 México, DF, T55-5674 6678, www.naturalia.org.mx*; and the **Asociación Mexicano por la Conservación de la Naturaleza (PRONATURA)** ⓘ *Aspérgulas 22 (antes Pino), Colonia San Clemente, 01740 México, DF, T55-5635 5054, www.pronatura.org.mx*.

Ecotourism

Until recently, most of Mexico's protected areas and biosphere reserves, covering 12% of the country, were simply off-limits to tourism. The government tried to keep these areas free of visitors, due to the lack of qualified park guides and adequate protection for their fragile ecosystems. It didn't have to try too hard; many of the protected areas were too far from the main tourism corridors to attract many visitors anyway. Now, however, it's changing tack, and starting to open protected areas to tourism.

Given the diversity of Mexico's wildlife and natural attractions, a broad approach to tourism in the country makes sense. Since 2002's International Year of Ecotourism, development is increasingly financed by various governmental and non-governmental institutions. Recent achievements reflect a slowly but steadily maturing understanding and engagement. A revitalized national association for ecotourism and adventure tourism operators, AMTAVE, is one of the first in the world to bring together small businesses to promote their shared offerings. In 2008 the association launched a promotional campaign, México Sagaz (Astute Mexico). And in November, Mexico's Tourism Secretariat announced that it would double its budget for nature-based travel and ecotourism, committing US$38 million to the sector and more than US$7½ million to national and international promotion.

In particular, the state of Baja California is making great efforts to shift its economy away from fishing and commerce towards ecotourism. In 2000, the state made the news when a presidential decree prevented a major salt plant from expanding into breeding areas of the grey whale. And thanks to pressure from environmental groups, more than 200 islands and inlets in the Sea of Cortés are now under UNESCO protection, offering great opportunities for diving, snorkelling and kayaking whilst maintaining their pristine habitats. The governor made the state's commitment to 'environmental tourism' official a few years ago, when he ruled that it must be the main attraction in Baja California, a step since echoed by other states such as Baja California Sur, Chiapas, Zacatecas and Quintana Roo.

All the same, ecotourism remains a small part of Mexico's tourism market, and plans such as those for Yucatán's coastal zone still have to take into account the current and potential impacts of 'conventional' (ie resort) tourism. The once remote Riviera Maya in Quintana Roo now hosts colossal numbers of North American and European tourists seeking their fix of sun, sea and sand. Cruise liners ply back and forth to Cozumel, ferrying five million visitors a year, and from Cancún in the north, a strip of hotels and beach resorts now lines the coast past Playa del Carmen, Tulum and on towards the Sian Ka'an biosphere reserve in the south. Here, the classic problems of mass tourism pile up, with loss of habitats, unsustainable water use and pollution, as well as damage to the world's second largest coral reef.

Recommended books

Archaeological sites

Availability of leaflets and books at the sites in different languages is improving, but to make sure, stock up before you visit.

Bloomgarden, Richard *Panorama Guides* and *Easy Guides*. Reliable, widely available and with plans and good illustrations. (Also available are *Miniguides* to archaeological and historical sites, published in various languages by INAH, US$0.75 each.)

Coe, MD *The Maya* (Pelican Books, or large format edition, Thames and Hudson). Essential reading covering the Maya archaeological area.

Schele, L, and D Freidel *A Forest of Kings* (L William Morrow and Company, NY 1990). Iconography and writing system of the Classic Maya.

Birdwatching

Edwards, Ernest P *Finding Birds in Mexico* (Box AQ, Sweet Briar, Virginia 24595, US). Detailed and thorough.

Peterson and Chalif *A Field Guide to Mexican Birds* (Houghton Mifflin, 1973).

Mexican history

Brenner, Anita *The Wind that Swept Mexico* (University of Texas Press, 1943) Gives a good overview of the Revolution from a more conservative standpoint.

Prescott, William *History of the Conquest of Mexico* (1849) Reliable, dated, old favourite.

Reed, John *Insurgent Mexico*. Originally published in 1914 by American journalist John Reed, known for his writings on the

Russian Revolution, this is a rare account of an outsider fighting in Pancho Villa's army during the Mexican Revolution.

Thomas, Hugh *Conquest: Cortés, Montezuma, and the fall of the Old Mexico* (1995). A more up-to-date overview.

Mexican Culture

Herrera, Hayden *Frida – the Biography of Frida Kahlo* (1983). Excellent and in-depth look at the life of one of Mexico's most famous and best loved painters.

Sayer, Chloë and Carmichael, Elizabeth *The Skeleton at the Feast, the Day of the Dead in Mexico* (British Museum Press and University of Texas Press, 1997). Gives good insights into this most Mexican of traditions. Good photography.

Travel

Burlison, Bob and Riskind, David H *Back Country Mexico, A Traveller's Guide and Phrase Book* (University of Texas Press, Box 7819, Austin, Texas, 78713-7819).

Franz, Carl *The People's Guide to Mexico* (John Muir Publications, Santa Fe, NM, 1998). Highly recommended, practical, entertaining and now in its 11th edition. There is also a *People's Guide Travel Letter*.

Robins, Rudi *One-day Car Trips from Mexico City*, and *Weekend Trips to Cities near Mexico City*.

Tree, Isabella *Sliced Iguana – Travels in Mexico* (Penguin Books, 2002). Captures the real flavour of Mexico and is a great travel companion.

Contents

Footnotes

Basic Spanish

Learning Spanish is a useful part of the preparation for a trip to Latin America and no volumes of dictionaries, phrase books or word lists will provide the same enjoyment as being able to communicate directly with the people of the country you are visiting. It is a good idea to make an effort to grasp the basics before you go. As you travel you will pick up more of the language and the more you know, the more you will benefit from your stay.

General pronunciation
Whether you have been taught the 'Castilian' pronunciation (*z* and *c* followed by *i* or *e* are pronounced as the *th* in think) or the 'American' pronunciation (they are pronounced as *s*), you will encounter little difficulty in understanding either. Regional accents and usages vary, but the basic language is essentially the same everywhere.

Vowels
a	as in English *cat*
e	as in English *best*
i	as the *ee* in English *feet*
o	as in English *shop*
u	as the *oo* in English *food*
ai	as the *i* in English *ride*
ei	as *ey* in English *they*
oi	as *oy* in English *toy*

Consonants
Most consonants can be pronounced more or less as they are in English. The exceptions are:

g	before *e* or *i* is the same as *j*
h	is always silent (except in *ch* as in *chair*)
j	as the *ch* in Scottish *loch*
ll	as the *y* in *yellow*
ñ	as the *ni* in English *onion*
rr	trilled much more than in English
x	depending on its location, pronounced *x, s, sh* or *j*

Spanish words and phrases

Greetings, courtesies
hello	*hola*
good morning	*buenos días*
good afternoon/ evening/night	*buenas tardes/noches*
goodbye	*adiós/chao*
pleased to meet you	*mucho gusto*
see you later	*hasta luego*
how are you?	*¿cómo está?* *¿cómo estás?*
I'm fine, thanks	*estoy muy bien, gracias*
I'm called...	*me llamo...*
what is your name?	*¿cómo se llama?* *¿cómo te llamas?*
yes/no	*sí/no*
please	*por favor*

thank you (very much)	*(muchas) gracias*
I speak Spanish	*hablo español*
I don't speak Spanish	*no hablo español*
do you speak English?	*¿habla inglés?*
I don't understand	*no entiendo/ no comprendo*
please speak slowly	*hable despacio por favor*
I am very sorry	*lo siento mucho/ disculpe*
what do you want?	*¿qué quiere?* *¿qué quieres?*
I want	*quiero*
I don't want it	*no lo quiero*
leave me alone	*déjeme en paz/ no me moleste*
good/bad	*bueno/malo*

Questions and requests

Have you got a room for two people?
¿Tiene una habitación para dos personas?
How do I get to_?
¿Cómo llego a_?
How much does it cost?
¿Cuánto cuesta? ¿cuánto es?
I'd like to make a long-distance phone call
Quisiera hacer una llamada de larga distancia
Is service included?
¿Está incluido el servicio?

Is tax included?
¿Están incluidos los impuestos?
When does the bus leave (arrive)?
¿A qué hora sale (llega) el autobús?
When? *¿cuándo?*
Where is_? *¿dónde está_?*
Where can I buy tickets?
¿Dónde puedo comprar boletos?
Where is the nearest petrol station?
¿Dónde está la gasolinera más cercana?
Why? *¿por qué?*

Basics

bank	*el banco*	market	*el mercado*
bathroom/toilet	*el baño*	note/coin	*le billete/la moneda*
bill	*la factura/la cuenta*	police (policeman)	*la policía (el policía)*
cash	*el efectivo*	post office	*el correo*
cheap	*barato/a*	public telephone	*el teléfono público*
credit card	*la tarjeta de crédito*	supermarket	*el supermercado*
exchange house	*la casa de cambio*	ticket office	*la taquilla*
exchange rate	*el tipo de cambio*	traveller's cheques	*los cheques de viajero/*
expensive	*caro/a*		*los travelers*

Getting around

aeroplane	*el avión*	insured person	*el/la asegurado/a*
airport	*el aeropuerto*	to insure yourself against	*asegurarse contra*
arrival/departure	*la llegada/salida*	luggage	*el equipaje*
avenue	*la avenida*	motorway, freeway	*el autopista/la*
block	*la cuadra*		*carretera*
border	*la frontera*	north, south, west, east	*norte, sur, oeste*
bus station	*la terminal de*		*(occidente), este*
	autobuses/camiones		*(oriente)*
bus	*el bus/el autobús/*	oil	*el aceite*
	el camión	to park	*estacionarse*
collective/		passport	*el pasaporte*
fixed-route taxi	*el colectivo*	petrol/gasoline	*la gasolina*
corner	*la esquina*	puncture	*el pinchazo/*
customs	*la aduana*		*la ponchadura*
first/second class	*primera/segunda clase*	street	*la calle*
left/right	*izquierda/derecha*	that way	*por allí/por allá*
ticket	*el boleto*	this way	*por aquí/por acá*
empty/full	*vacío/lleno*	tourist card/visa	*la tarjeta de turista*
highway, main road	*la carretera*	tyre	*la llanta*
immigration	*la inmigración*	unleaded	*sin plomo*
insurance	*el seguro*	to walk	*caminar/andar*

Accommodation

air conditioning	*el aire acondicionado*	power cut	*el apagón/corte*
all-inclusive	*todo incluido*	restaurant	*el restaurante*
bathroom, private	*el baño privado*	room/bedroom	*el cuarto/la habitación*
bed, double/single	*la cama matrimonial/ sencilla*	sheets	*las sábanas*
		shower	*la ducha/regadera*
blankets	*las cobijas/mantas*	soap	*el jabón*
to clean	*limpiar*	toilet	*el sanitario/excusado*
dining room	*el comedor*	toilet paper	*el papel higiénico*
guesthouse	*la casa de huéspedes*	towels, clean/dirty	*las toallas limpias/ sucias*
hotel	*el hotel*		
noisy	*ruidoso*	water, hot/cold	*el agua caliente/fría*
pillows	*las almohadas*		

Health

aspirin	*la aspirina*	diarrhoea	*la diarrea*
blood	*la sangre*	doctor	*el médico*
chemist	*la farmacia*	fever/sweat	*la fiebre/el sudor*
condoms	*los preservativos, los condones*	pain	*el dolor*
		head	*la cabeza*
contact lenses	*los lentes de contacto*	period/sanitary towels	*la regla/ las toallas femeninas*
contraceptives	*los anticonceptivos*		
contraceptive pill	*la píldora anti- conceptiva*	stomach	*el estómago*
		altitude sickness	*el soroche*

Family

family	*la familia*	boyfriend/girlfriend	*el novio/la novia*
brother/sister	*el hermano/la hermana*	friend	*el amigo/la amiga*
daughter/son	*la hija/el hijo*	married	*casado/a*
father/mother	*el padre/la madre*	single/unmarried	*soltero/a*
husband/wife	*el esposo (marido)/ la esposa*		

Months, days and time

January	*enero*	Monday	*lunes*
February	*febrero*	Tuesday	*martes*
March	*marzo*	Wednesday	*miércoles*
April	*abril*	Thursday	*jueves*
May	*mayo*	Friday	*viernes*
June	*junio*	Saturday	*sábado*
July	*julio*	Sunday	*domingo*
August	*agosto*		
September	*septiembre*	at one o'clock	*a la una*
October	*octubre*	at half past two	*a las dos y media*
November	*noviembre*	at a quarter to three	*a cuarto para las tres/ a las tres menos quince*
December	*diciembre*		
		it's one o'clock	*es la una*

it's seven o'clock	son las siete	in ten minutes	en diez minutos
it's six twenty	son las seis y veinte	five hours	cinco horas
it's five to nine	son las nueve menos cinco	does it take long?	¿tarda mucho?

Numbers

one	uno/una	sixteen	dieciséis
two	dos	seventeen	diecisiete
three	tres	eighteen	dieciocho
Four	cuatro	nineteen	diecinueve
five	cinco	twenty	veinte
six	seis	twenty-one	veintiuno
seven	siete	thirty	treinta
eight	ocho	forty	cuarenta
nine	nueve	fifty	cincuenta
ten	diez	sixty	sesenta
eleven	once	seventy	setenta
twelve	doce	eighty	ochenta
thirteen	trece	ninety	noventa
fourteen	catorce	hundred	cien/ciento
fifteen	quince	thousand	mil

Food

avocado	el aguacate	goat	el chivo
baked	al horno	grapefruit	la toronja/el pomelo
bakery	la panadería	grill	la parrilla
banana	el plátano	grilled/griddled	a la plancha
beans	los frijoles/ las habichuelas	guava	la guayaba
beef	la carne de res	ham	el jamón
beef steak or pork fillet	el bistec	hamburger	la hamburguesa
boiled rice	el arroz blanco	hot, spicy	picante
bread	el pan	ice cream	el helado
breakfast	el desayuno	jam	la mermelada
butter	la mantequilla	knife	el cuchillo
cake	el pastel	lime	el limón
chewing gum	el chicle	lobster	la langosta
chicken	el pollo	lunch	el almuerzo/la comida
chilli or green pepper	el ají/pimiento	meal	la comida
clear soup, stock	el caldo	meat	la carne
cooked	cocido	minced meat	el picadillo
dining room	el comedor	onion	la cebolla
egg	el huevo	orange	la naranja
Fish	el pescado	pepper	el pimiento
fork	el tenedor	pasty, turnover	la empanada/ el pastelito
fried	frito	pork	el cerdo
garlic	el ajo	potato	la papa

prawns	*los camarones*	spoon	*la cuchara*
raw	*crudo*	squash	*la calabaza*
restaurant	*el restaurante*	squid	*los calamares*
salad	*la ensalada*	supper	*la cena*
salt	*la sal*	sweet	*dulce*
sandwich	*el bocadillo*	to eat	*comer*
sauce	*la salsa*	toasted	*tostado*
sausage	*la longaniza/el chorizo*	turkey	*el pavo*
scrambled eggs	*los huevos revueltos*	vegetables	*los legumbres/vegetales*
seafood	*los mariscos*	without meat	*sin carne*
soup	*la sopa*	yam	*el camote*

Drink

beer	*la cerveza*	ice/without ice	*el hielo/sin hielo*
boiled	*hervido/a*	juice	*el jugo*
bottled	*en botella*	lemonade	*la limonada*
camomile tea	*la manzanilla*	milk	*la leche*
canned	*en lata*	mint	*la menta*
coffee	*el café*	rum	*el ron*
coffee, white	*el café con leche*	soft drink	*el refresco*
cold	*frío*	sugar	*el azúcar*
cup	*la taza*	tea	*el té*
drink	*la bebida*	to drink	*beber/tomar*
drunk	*borracho/a*	water	*el agua*
firewater	*el aguardiente*	water, carbonated	*el agua mineral con gas*
fruit milkshake	*el batido/licuado*	water, still mineral	*el agua mineral sin gas*
glass	*el vaso*	wine, red	*el vino tinto*
hot	*caliente*	wine, white	*el vino blanco*

Key verbs

to go	**ir**	there is/are	*hay*
I go	*voy*	there isn't/aren't	*no hay*
you go (familiar)	*vas*		
he, she, it goes,			
you (formal) go	*va*	**to be**	**ser**	**estar**
we go	*vamos*	I am	*soy*	*estoy*
they, you (plural) go	*van*	you are	*eres*	*estás*

		he, she, it is,		
		you (formal) are	*es*	*está*
to have (possess)	**tener**	we are	*somos*	*estamos*
I have	*tengo*	they, you (plural) are	son	*están*
you (familiar) have	*tienes*		

This section has been assembled on the basis of glossaries compiled by André de Mendonça and David Gilmour of South American Experience, London, and the Latin American Travel Advisor, No 9, March 1996

he, she, it,
you (formal) have — *tiene*
we have — *tenemos*
they, you (plural) have — *tienen*

Index → Entries in bold refer to maps

Acknowledgements

Richard Arghiris

It was a tough but rewarding challenge bringing Footprint *Mexico* up to date. This completely revised second edition is nothing short of a brand new book, thanks to the hard work and dedication of everyone involved. In-country correspondents, readers, researchers, writers and editors all brought valuable contributions to the table.

Richard Arghiris would like to thank his co-authors Geoff Groesbeck and Anna Maria Espsäter for their hard work and enthusiasm; both were fantastic and interesting people to work with. At the office, special thanks to Nicola Gibbs for her patient and careful editing, Sarah Sorensen for her map work, Alan Murphy for putting the project on the rails, and Jo Williams for completing it. Thanks also to Peter Hutchison for his continuing good work on Footprint *Mexico and Central America*, which was integral to the creation of this book.

On the road, thanks are due to the many hoteliers, restaurant owners and tour operators who supplied useful information. Particular thanks to Julio of Three Amigos Canyon Expeditions for his skilful descent into Batopilas canyon, and Miguel Angel Nuñez for his enlightening tour of rural Michoacán. Back home, Richard is especially grateful to Jennifer Kennedy for her continued love, support and patience. Thanks also to Terri Wright, Alan Peacock Johns, Jo Arghiris, Dan and Charlie Roberts. Last but not least, thanks to Sym Gharial and Peter McCallen for their continued friendship and conversation throughout the long, challenging months of writing that this project entailed.

Anna Maria Espsäter

Anna Maria Espsäter would like to thank co-author Richard Arghiris for all his help and support during this project; also Gina Machorro and Lalo Eco tours in Puerto Escondido; Roberto Molina and Doña Rosita in San Cristóbal de las Casas; Alejandro Colinas in DF for good information on Mexican music; Paty Reyes in Oaxaca City for art advice; Lucia Samaniego in DF for good tequila; Gary G in Puerto Escondido for excellent Cajun prawns and mescal; Nick Richardson for advice on airfares; countless wonderful Mexicans who made the trip and research a joy and of course Bryony Addis-Jones for always being there for me.

Geoff Groesbeck

My sincere appreciation to the many people and institutions throughout Mexico who shared their thoughts and suggestions. If this guide offers new insight and ideas for enjoying Mexico, it is as a result of their kindness.

My thanks also to my able co-authors Anna Marie Espsäter and Richard Arghiris; the indefatigable Peter Huchinson; and Nicola Gibbs and the staff at Footprint for their unstinting help.

Most of all, I am privileged to have had the assistance and inspiration of Sofía Reyes Martínez as my companion and guide in this work. Of the many wonderful treasures I found in Mexico, the greatest of all was finding her. *Eres mi vida*.

Credits

Footprint credits

Editors: Nicola Gibbs, Davina Rungasamy, Jo Williams
Cartography: Robert Lunn, Kevin Feeney, Emma Bryers
Colour section: Kassia Gawronski
Proofreader: Jen Haddington

Managing Director: Andy Riddle
Commercial Director: Patrick Dawson
Publisher: Alan Murphy
Publishing managers: Felicity Laughton, Jo Williams
Digital Editor: Alice Jell

Cover design: Robert Lunn
Design: Mytton Williams
Marketing: Liz Harper, Hannah Bonnell
Sales: Jeremy Parr
Advertising: Renu Sibal
Finance and administration:
Elizabeth Taylor

Photography credits

Front cover: Izamal church, Alex Robinson
Back cover: Painted Xochimilco boats, Danita Delimont/Alamy

Printed in India by Aegean Offset Printers, New Delhi

Footprint feedback

We try as hard as we can to make each Footprint guide as up to date as possible but, of course, things always change. If you want to let us know about your experiences – good, bad or ugly – then don't delay, go to www.footprintbooks.com and send in your comments.

Publishing information

Footprint Mexico 2nd edition
© Footprint Handbooks Ltd
March 2010

ISBN: 978 1 906098 79 7
CIP DATA: A catalogue record for this book is available from the British Library

® Footprint Handbooks and the Footprint mark are a registered trademark of Footprint Handbooks Ltd

Published by Footprint
6 Riverside Court
Lower Bristol Road
Bath BA2 3DZ, UK
T +44 (0)1225 469141
F +44 (0)1225 469461
www.footprintbooks.com

Distributed in the USA by Globe Pequot Press, Guilford, Connecticut

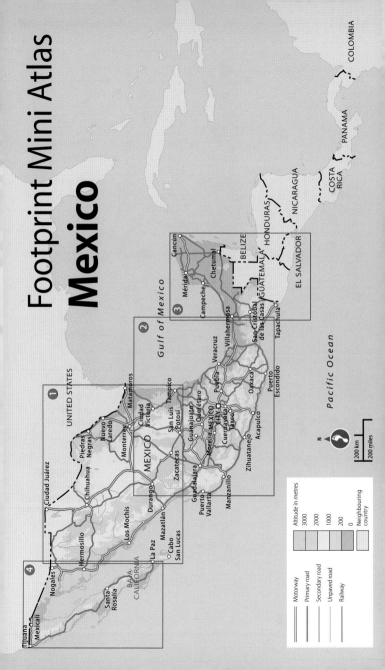

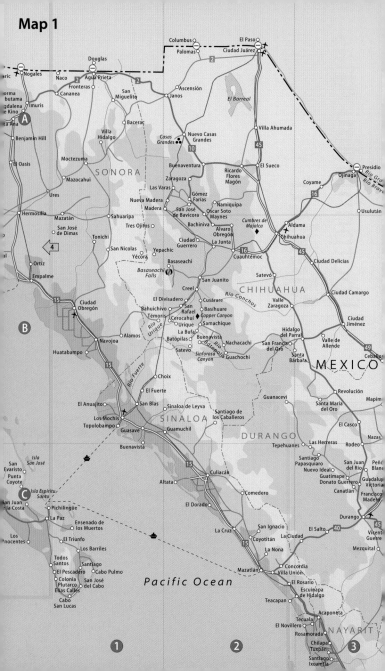

Map 1